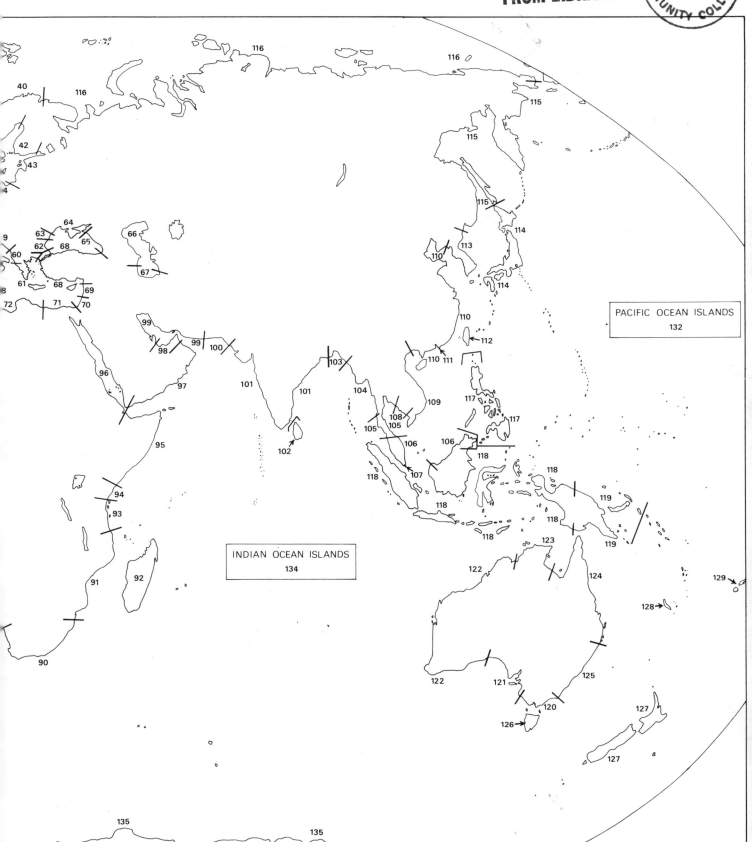

40
116
42
43
4

64
63   65
9   66
62
60   68
67
61   68   69
72   71   70

99
99
98   100
96
101   101
97
95

PACIFIC OCEAN ISLANDS
132

116
116
115
115
115
114
113
110
114
110
112
110 111
103
104
109
108
105 105
106   106
107
118   118
118
118
118
117
117
118
119
118
119
123

INDIAN OCEAN ISLANDS
134

94
93
91   92
90

122
124
129
128

122 121   125
120
126
127
127

135
135

THE WORLD'S COASTLINE

THE
WORLD'S COASTLINE

Edited by

Eric C. F. Bird

University of Melbourne, Australia

and

Maurice L. Schwartz

Western Washington University, U.S.A.

VNR VAN NOSTRAND REINHOLD COMPANY
New York

Published by Van Nostrand Reinhold Company Inc.
135 West 50th Street
New York, New York 10020

Van Nostrand Reinhold Company Limited
Molly Millars Lane
Wokingham, Berkshire RG11 2PY, England

Van Nostrand Reinhold
480 Latrobe Street
Melbourne, Victoria 3000, Australia

Macmillan of Canada
Division of Gage Publishing Limited
164 Commander Boulevard
Agincourt, Ontario MIS 3C7, Canada

15 14 13 12 11 10 9 8 7 6 5 4 3 2 1

For other books on the subject(s)
discussed in this book, look in the card
catalog, under the checked headings:

Library of Congress Cataloging in Publication Data
Main entry under title:
The World's coastline.
   Includes bibliographies and indexes.
   1. Coasts.   I. Bird, E. C. F. (Eric Charles Frederick),
1930-   . II. Schwartz, Maurice L.
GB451.2.W67   1985   551.4'57   84-17207
ISBN 0-442-21116-3

CONTENTS

PREFACE

Various estimates have been made of the length of the world's coastline, depending on the method of measurement used. Summation of 1-km linear intercepts gives a total of the order of half a million kilometers, but when all the intricacies of indented bays and promontories and offshore islands are included, the total length may be about a million kilometers. Some parts have been studied intensively, and are well documented by geologists and geomorphologists; others are less well known, and it is often difficult to find accounts of their landforms and associated features. The abundance of published data on the coastlines of North America, much of western Europe and the northern Mediterranean, and parts of Australia, New Zealand, and Japan is offset by a paucity of information from less developed sectors, especially in arctic and tropical regions. This book assembles available information on the more interesting and important coastline features on a round-the-world basis: it is a reference system to "what is where on the world's coastline," with a guide to readily available scientific literature. Our hope is that it will provide a basis for comparative studies, for the making and testing of generalizations about coastal phenomena, and that it will stimulate further research, especially on the less well-known coastlines.

The idea of compiling this book arose from our experience of working with the Commission on the Coastal Environment, set up by the International Geographical Union in 1976. This commission has been seeking worldwide data on coastline features, in particular on sectors where changes have taken place during the past century, and has built up a network of corresponding members who have sent in data from around the world's coasts. We have drawn on this network in selecting authors to provide accounts of coastline sectors.

The accounts are presented in a round-the-world sequence that begins with Alaska and proceeds counterclockwise around the Americas to Arctic Canada. Greenland and Iceland are then dealt with, and another counterclockwise sequence begins with Norway, proceeding by way of Europe and the Mediterranean, around Africa to India, Southeast Asia, China, Korea, and the Pacific and Arctic coastlines of the Soviet Union. Interruptions are made at appropriate points to include the Great Lakes and the Caspian Sea, and offshore islands such as Britain, Madagascar, and Japan. The sequence is completed by way of the Philippines, Indonesia, Papua New Guinea, Australia, New Zealand, the islands of the Pacific, Atlantic, and Indian Oceans, and finally Antarctica. The 135 sectors are indexed by way of the map that forms the end papers inside the front and rear covers of the book. A subject index provides a guide to pages where biological and geomorphological terms appear, but geographical locations have not been indexed since they occur in sequence in this round-the-world treatment. Furthermore, literature citations in the text are correlated with references listed at the end of each section, but the authors of referenced publications are also listed in a separate author index at the end of the book.

In compiling and editing such a work, we have been aware of the inherent diversity of these 135 coastline sectors, the variability of available maps and documentation, and inevitable contrasts in the ideas, perceptions, and interests of our 129 contributors. We began by circulating a sample account of a selected coastline (the state of Victoria, in southeastern Australia) as an example of the kind of data and illustration sought, acknowledging that there would be variations in the modes of treatment of coastline sectors that differ greatly in length, intricacy, diversity, and environmental (especially climatic) context. For some little-known sectors it was difficult to find a contributor, and we have had to summarize such information as we could find in the available literature: for some well-known sectors it was a question of choosing one or two from many possible contributors. Our division of the world's coastline into sectors was based largely on national boundaries, but where these were uncertain or in dispute we used arbitrary divisions, chosen for convenience and to ensure a complete coverage rather than to support any political viewpoint.

Opinions differ on the scientific significance of particular coastline features, and some may consider that important items have been omitted, or that some of the examples and illustrations used are not as significant as others that could have been included. However, the constraints imposed by endeavoring to cover the whole of the world's coastline in a single volume are severe, and as editors we have had to be selective. Our hope is that these sector-by-sector accounts do contain the essential material, and that readers will let us know of errors and omissions, as well as the results of further research that correct and extend our knowledge of the world's coastline.

ACKNOWLEDGMENTS

In the course of preparing *The World's Coastline,* we have been assisted by many people. We are grateful to the contributors, most of whom found the restrictions on length of each article frustrating as they tried to describe the complexities of their coastlines. As editors, we have often had to cut out material that we would like to have included, and we were glad of cooperation and understanding as this surgery proceeded. In Bellingham we had the assistance of Patty Combs and Joan Roley in handling correspondence and processing manuscripts, and the invaluable help of Joy Dabney with graphics. Also, at Western Washington University we had much help from the personnel of the Wilson Library. Norma Schwartz assisted with editorial work. In Melbourne, Ruth Terrell-Phillips undertook explorations of little-known coastlines by way of map and literature searches, Robert Bartlett helped with cartography, and Wendy Godber assisted with photographic work.

ERIC C. F. BIRD
MAURICE L. SCHWARTZ

CONTRIBUTORS

ENAYAT AHMAD, Dept. of Geography, Ranchi University, Ranchi, Bihar, India, *India*.

JOUKO ALESTALO, Dept. of Geography, University of Oulu, 90570, Oulu 57, Finland. *Finland*.

CHARLES S. ALEXANDER, Dept. of Geography, University of Illinois, Urbana, Illinois 61801. *Hispaniola; Tanzania*.

JOSE F. ARAYA-VERGARA, Dept. de Geografia, Universidad de Chile, Jose Pedro Alessandri 774. CAS/147, Santiago, Chile. *Chile*.

SAUL ARONOW, Dept. of Geology, Lamar University, Beaumont, Texas 77710. *Texas*.

HECTOR AYÓN, Dept. de Ingenieria Maritima y Ciencias del Mar, Escuela Superior Polytechnica del Litoral, Casilla 5863, Guayaquil, Ecuador. *Ecuador*.

RENÉ BATTISTINI, 86 rue G. Flaubert, 45100 Orléans, France. *Indian Ocean Islands; Madagascar*.

ERIC C. F. BIRD, Dept. of Geography, University of Melbourne, Parkville, Victoria 3052, Australia. *Atlantic Ocean Islands; Burma; Cuba; England and Wales; Fiji; Indonesia; Kampuchea; New Caledonia and the Loyalty Islands; Papua New Guinea; Peru; Philippines; Southern Arabia; Victoria*.

J. BRIAN BIRD, Dept. of Geography, McGill University, Montreal, Quebec, H3A 2K6, Canada. *Arctic Canada*.

JEAN-CLAUDE BODÉRÉ, Faculté des Lettres et Sciences Sociales de Brest, Université de Bretagne Occidentale, B.P. 860, 29279 Brest, France. *Iceland*.

RYSZARD K. BORÓWKA, Institute of Geography, Adam Mickiewicz University, Fredry 10, 61–701 Poznán, Poland. *Poland*.

PAUL LE BOURDIEC, U. E. R. Civilisations, Université de Nice, 117, rue de France, B. P. 255, 06007 Nice, France. *Madagascar*.

RON BOYD, Dept. of Geology, Louisiana State University, Baton Rouge, Louisiana 70803. *Louisiana*.

J. M. BREMNER, Dept. of Geology, Marine Geoscience, University of Cape Town, Rondebosch, 7700, South Africa. *Southwest Africa/Namibia*.

J. F. CAMPBELL, Hawaii Institute of Geophysics, University of Hawaii at Manoa, Honolulu, Hawaii 96822. *Hawaii*.

C. H. CARTER, Department of Geology, University of Akron, Akron, Ohio 44325. *Great Lakes*.

LIU CANGZI, Institute of the Coasts and Estuaries, Shanghai Normal University, Shanghai, China. *China*.

ROGER H. CHARLIER, Earth Sciences, Northeastern Illinois University, Chicago, Illinois 60625. *Rumania; Yugoslavia*.

JAMES M. COLEMAN, Dept. of Geology, Louisiana State University, Baton Rouge, Louisiana 70803. *Louisiana*.

P. N. COUTINHO, Av. Pedroso de Moraes, 684/602, Pinheiros-Sao Paulo, 05419, Brazil. *Brazil*.

ALAN CRAIG, Dept. of Geography, Florida Atlantic University, Boca Raton, Florida 33431. *Bahamas*.

OLGA CRUZ, Av. Pedroso de Moraes, 684/602, Pinheiros-Sao Paulo, 05419, Brazil. *Brazil.*

A. DAGORNE, Dept. de Géographie, Université de Nice, 06036 Nice, France, *Algeria.*

J. L. DAVIES, School of Earth Sciences, Macquarie University, North Ryde, New South Wales 2113, Australia. *Tasmania.*

COMPTON DEANE, 10A Saddle Rd., Maraval, Port of Spain, Trinidad. *Lesser Antilles.*

L. A. DEI, Dept. of Geography, University of Cape Coast, Cape Coast, Ghana, *Ghana.*

G. DE MOOR, Laboratorium voor Fysische Aardrijks-kundeen Bodemstudie, Geologisch Instituut, Krijgslaan 271, 9000 Ghent, Belgium. *Belgium.*

GABRIEL DENGO, Apartado 468, Guatemala City, Guatemala. *Caribbean Central America.*

E. S. DIOP, Dept. de Géographie, Faculté des Lettres et Sciences Humaines de Dakar, Senegal. *Guinea-Bissau and Republic of Guinea*

KATHLEEN S. DREW, Ecology and Environment, Inc., 108 S. Washington, Seattle, Washington 98104. *United Arab Emirates.*

G. M. DUARTE, Av. Pedroso de Moraes, 684/602, Pinheiros-Sao Paulo 05419, Brazil. *Brazil.*

ECKART EHLERS, Fachbereich Geographie der Philipps—Universitat, Deutschhausstrase 10, D-3550 Marburg/Lahn, West Germany. *Caspian Iran.*

D. EISMA, Netherlands Institute for Sea Research, Postbox 59, Den Burg, Texel, Netherlands. *North Korea and South Korea; Vietnam.*

MOHAMED T. EL-ASHRY, World Resources Institute, 1735 New York Ave., N.W., Washington, D.C. 20006. *Egypt.*

I. G. ELIOT, Dept. of Geography, University of Western Australia, Nedlands, Western Australia 6009, Australia. *Western Australia.*

LUDWIG ELLENBERG, Universidad Nacional, Escuela de Ciencias Geográficas, Apartado 86, Heredia, Costa Rica. *Venezuela.*

OGUZ EROL, Dil ve Tarik Cografya Fahultesi, Fiziki Cografya ve Jeoloji Kursusu, Ankara, Turkey. *Turkey and Cyprus.*

JOHN J. FISHER, Dept. of Geology, University of Rhode Island, Kingston, Rhode Island 02881. *Atlantic USA—North.*

B. W. FLEMMING, National Research Institute for Oceanology, P.O. Box 320, Stellenbosch, South Africa 7600. *South Africa.*

ROBERT W. GALLOWAY, Division of Water and Land Resources, C.S.I.R.O., P. O. Box 1666, Canberra City A. C. T. 2601, Australia. *Northern Territory.*

HANS GUNTER GIERLOFF-EMDEN, Geographisch Institut, University München, Luisenstrasse 37, 8000 Munchen 2, West Germany. *Baltic West Germany (Federal Republic of Germany); East Germany (German Democratic Republic); North Sea West Germany (Federal Republic of Germany).*

PIERRE GIRESSE, Centre de Récherches de Sédimentologie Marine, Université de Perpignan, 66025 Perpignan, France. *Gabon, Congo, Cabinda, and Zaïre.*

A. GOMES, Av. Pedroso de Moraes, 684/602, Pinheiros-Sao Paulo, 05419, Brazil. *Brazil.*

VYTAUTAS GUDELIS, Lietuvos TSR, Mokslu Akademija, Lenino Prosp. 3, MTP-1, Vilnius 232600, Lithuania. *Baltic USSR.*

ANDRÉ GUILCHER, Faculté des Lettres et Sciences Sociales de Brest, Université de Bretagne Occidental, B.P. 860, 29729 Brest, France. *Angola; France; Red Sea Coasts; Senegal and Gambia; Society Islands; Togo and Benin.*

MARIO GUTIÉRREZ-ESTRADA, Jefe de la Estacion "Mazatlan" del Instituto de Ciencias del Mar y Limnologia. U.N.A.M., Apdo. Postal 811, Mazatlan, Sinaloa, Mexico *Caribbean Mexico; Pacific Mexico.*

W. S. HARAS, Government of Canada, Fisheries and Oceans, Ocean Science and Surveys, Central Region, P.O. Box 5050, Burlington, Ontario L7R 4A6, Canada. *Great Lakes.*

JOHN R. HARPER, Geological Services, Dobrocky Seatech Ltd., P.O. Box 6500, Sidney, British Columbia, V8L 4M7, Canada. *British Columbia.*

MILES O. HAYES, Dept. of Geology, University of South Carolina, Columbia, South Carolina 29208. *Atlantic USA—South.*

A. E. F. HEYDORN, National Research Institute for Oceanology, P.O. Box 320, Stellenbosch, South Africa 7600. *South Africa.*

FELIX HINSCHBERGER, Dept. de Géographie, Université de Caen, Post 439, 14032 Caen Cedex, France. *Ivory Coast.*

DAVID HOPLEY, Dept. of Geography, James Cook University of North Queensland, Townsville, Queensland 4811, Australia. *Queensland.*

T. L. HSU, Geological Survey of Taiwan, P.O. Box 968, Taipei, Taiwan, Republic of China. *Taiwan.*

JACQUES ILTIS, Section de Géographie, O.R.S.T.O.M., Nouméa, New Caledonia. *New Caledonia.*

JOSE M. JACKSON, Dept. de Geografia, Facultad de H. y Ciencias, Cerrito 73, Montevideo, Uruguay. *Uruguay.*

WILMO JARA, Dept. de Ingenieria Maritima y Ciencias del Mar, Escuela Superior Politecnics del Litoral, Casilla 5863, Guayaquil, Ecuador. *Ecuador.*

SASKIA JELGERSMA, Geological Survey of the Netherlands, Spaarne 17, Postbus 157, Haarlem, Netherlands. *Netherlands.*

CHEN JIYU, Institute of the Coasts and Estuaries, Shanghai Normal University, Shanghai, China. *China.*

ELEANOR B. JONES, Dept. of Geography, University of the West Indies, Mona, Kingston 7, Jamaica. *Jamaica.*

R. JULIA, Facultad de Geologia, Dept. de Geomorfologia i Tectonica, Universitat de Barcelona, Gran Via, 585, Barcelona, Spain. *Spain.*

EMIL W. DE JULIO, Earth Sciences Dept., Northeastern Illinois University, Chicago, Illinois 60625. *Rumania.*

RAY KACZOROWSKI, G. C. O. Minerals Co., P.O. Box 4258, Houston, Texas 77210. *Texas.*

PAUL KAPLIN, Dept. of Geography, Moscow State University, Moscow 117234, U.S.S.R. *Pacific USSR.*

R. M. KIRK, Dept. of Geography, University of Canterbury, Christchurch, New Zealand. *Antarctica.*

TORMOD KLEMSDAL, Dept. of Geography, University of Oslo, Postboks 1042, Blindern, Oslo 3, Norway. *Norway.*

KAZUYUKI KOIKE, Dept. of Geography, Komazawa University, Komazawa, Setagaya-Ku, Tokyo 154, Japan. *Japan.*

PAUL D. KOMAR, School of Oceanography, Oregon State University, Corvallis, Oregon 97331. *Oregon.*

G. KOUYOUMONTZAKIS, Centre de Récherches de Sédimentologie Marine, Universite de Perpignan, 66025 Perpïgnan, France. *Gabon, Congo, Cabinda, and Zaïre.*

JOHN C. KRAFT, Dept. of Geology, University of Delaware, Newark, Delaware 19711. *Atlantic USA—Central; Greece.*

O. K. LEONTIEV, Dept. of Geography, Moscow State University, Moscow 117234, U.S.S.R. *Caspian USSR.*

M. MAHROUR, Centre National d'Etude et de Recherche pour l'Aménagement du Territoire, 33, rue Curie, El-Biar, Algeria. *Algeria.*

MONIQUE MAINGUET, Laboratoire de Geographie Physique, Université de Reims, 57 rue Taittinger, 51084 Reims, France. *Saraoui.*

M. A. MARQUÉS, Facultat de Geologia, Dept. de Geomorfologia i Tectonica, Universitat de Barcelona, Gran Via, 585, Barcelona, Spain. *Spain.*

S. B. McCANN, Dept. of Geography, McMaster University, Hamilton, Ontario LKS 4K1, Canada. *Atlantic Canada.*

ROGER F. McLEAN, University of Auckland, Private Bag, Auckland, New Zealand. *New Zealand.*

R. MOBERLY, Hawaii Institute of Geophysics, University of Hawaii at Manoa, Honolulu, Hawaii 98622. *Hawaii.*

JENS TYGE MØLLER, Laboratoriet for Fysisk Geografi, Universitat Århus, 8000 Århus C, Denmark. *Denmark.*

CARLOS MORAIS, Laboratorio Nacional de Engenharia Civil, Av. do Brasil, 1799 Lisbon Codex, Portugal. *Portugal.*

JACK MORELOCK, Dept. of Marine Sciences, University of Puerto Rico, Mayaguez, Puerto Rico 00708. *Puerto Rico.*

D. MUEHE, Ave. Pedroso de Moraus, 684/602, Pinheiros-Sao Paulo 05419, Brazil. *Brazil.*

NIELS NIELSEN, Dept. of Geography, University of Copenhagen, Haraldsgade 68, DK-2100 Copenhagen, Denmark. *Greenland.*

YAACOV NIR, Geological Survey of Israel, 30 Malkhe Israel St., Jerusalem 95-501, Israel. *Israel.*

JOHN O. NORRMAN, Dept. of Physical Geography, University of Uppsala, Sweden. *Sweden.*

DAG NUMMEDAL, Dept. of Geology, Louisiana State University, Baton Rouge, Louisiana 70803. *Louisiana; Mississippi and Alabama.*

FRANCIS F. OJANY, Dept. of Geography, University of Nairobi, P.O. Box 30197, Nairobi, Kenya. *Kenya.*

ANTONY R. ORME, Dept. of Geography, University of California, Los Angeles, California 90024. *California; Somalia.*

MARIO ARTURO ORTIZ-PEREZ, Instituto de Geografia, U. N. A. M., Ciudad Universiteria, Mexico City, 20 D. F., Mexico. *Caribbean Mexico; Pacific Mexico.*

ERVIN G. OTVOS, Geology Division, Gulf Coast Research Laboratory, Ocean Springs, Mississippi 39564. *Mississippi and Alabama.*

EDWARD H. OWENS, Woodward-Clyde Oceaneering, Abbotswell Road, Aberdeen AB1 4AD, Scotland. *British Columbia.*

A. OZER, Laboratorium voor Fysische Aardrijkskundeen Bodemstudie, Geologisch Instituut, Krijgslaan 271, 9000 Ghent, Belgium. *Belgium.*

DONG WON PARK, Dept. of Geography, Seoul National University, Seoul 151, South Korea. *North Korea and South Korea.*

ROLAND PASKOFF, 10 Square Saint-Florentin, 78150 Le Chesnay, France. *Malta; Tunisia.*

SHEA PENLAND, Dept. of Geology, Louisiana State University, Baton Rouge, Louisiana 70803. *Louisiana.*

JAMES W. PIETY, Earth Sciences Dept. Northeastern Illinois University, Chicago, Illinois 60625. *Yugoslavia.*

JOHN I. PITMAN, Dept. of Geography, King's College London, Strand, London WC2R 2LS, England. *Thailand.*

NORBERT PSUTY, Center for Coastal and Environmental Studies, Rutgers University, New Brunswick, New Jersey 08903. *Surinam.*

VIDAL TAYPE RAMOS, Instituto Panamericano de Geografia e Historia, Av. Arenales 431, OF.702, Apartado 11363, Lima 1, Peru. *Peru.*

WILLIAM RITCHIE, Dept. of Geography. University of Aberdeen, St. Mary High St., Aberdeen, Scotland AB 9 20F. *Scotland.*

TEH TIONG SA, Dept. of Geography, University of Malaya, Pantai Valley, Kuala Lumpur, Malaya. *Malaysia.*

PAUL SANLAVILLE, Maison de l'Orient Mediterranée, Université du Lyon 2, 1 rue Raulin, 69007 Lyon, France. *Arabian Gulf Coasts; Syria and Lebanon.*

ENRIQUE J. SCHNACK, Centro de Geologia de Costas, Cassilla de Correos 722, 7600 Mar del Plata, Argentina. *Argentina.*

J. C. SCHOFIELD, 43 Whakarite Rd., Ostend, Waiheke Island, New Zealand. *Pacific Ocean Islands.*

MAURICE L. SCHWARTZ, Dept. of Geology, Western Washington University, Bellingham, Washington 98225. *Cameroon and Equatorial Guinea; Caribbean Colombia; Guyana; Libya; Pacific Central America; Pacific Colombia; Washington.*

P. A. SCOTT, Dept. of Geography, Fourah Bay College, Freetown, Sierra Leone. *Sierra Leone.*

YURII D. SHUISKY, Dept. of Geography, Odessa State University, Odessa 270000, USSR. *Albania; Northern Black Sea and Sea of Azov, USSR.*

GINKA SIMEONOVA, Bulgarian Academy of Science, Laboratory of Geotechnics, II, Academic Georgi Bontchev St., Sofia 1113, Bulgaria. *Bulgaria.*

RODMAN E. SNEAD, Dept. of Geography, University of New Mexico, Albuquerque, New Mexico 87131, *Bangladesh, Pakistan.*

C. L. SO, Dept. of Geography and Geology, University of Hong Kong, Pokfulam Rd., Hong Kong. *Hong Kong.*

WILLIAM B. STANLEY, Dept. of Geography, University of South Carolina, Columbia, South Carolina 29208. *Liberia.*

NICHOLAS STEPHENS, Dept. of Geography, University College of Swansea, Singleton Park, Swansea SA2 8PP, Wales. *Ireland.*

BERNARD SWAN, Dept. of Geography, University of New England, Armidale, New South Wales 2351, Australia. *Sri Lanka.*

WILLIAM F. TANNER, Dept. of Geology, Florida State University, Tallahassee, Florida 32306. *Florida.*

THOMAS A. TERICH, Dept. of Geography, Western Washington University, Bellingham, Washington 98225. *Washington.*

BRUCE G. THOM, Dept. of Geography, University of New South Wales, Royal Military College, Duntroon, A.C.T. 2600, Australia. *New South Wales.*

K. L. TINLEY, Department of Conservation and Environment, 1 Mount Street, Perth, Western Australia 6000, Australia.

JAMES V. A. TRUMBULL, U.S. Geological Survey, Marine Division, Box 5917, Punta de Tierra Station, San Juan, Puerto Rico 00906. *Puerto Rico.*

J. F. TURENNE, O.R.S.T.O.M., Centre des Antilles, B. P. 81, Fort-de-France 97201, Martinique. *French Guiana.*

C. R. TWIDALE, Dept. of Geography, University of Adelaide, G.P.O. Box 498, Adelaide, South Australia, 5001, Australia. *South Australia.*

CHRISTOS TZIAVOS, I. O. K. A. E., Aghios Kosmas, Ellinikon, Athens, Greece. *Greece.*

E. J. USORO, Dept. of Geography, University of Calabar, P. M. B. 1115, Calabar, Nigeria. *Nigeria.*

DONALD E. VERMEER, Dept. of Geography and Anthropology, Louisiana State University, Baton Rouge, Louisiana 70803. *Mauritania.*

H. J. WALKER, Dept. of Geography and Anthropology, Louisiana State University, Baton Rouge, Louisiana 70803. *Alaska.*

M. J. WEBB, Dept. of Geography, University of Western Australia, Nedlands, Western Australia 6009, Australia. *Western Australia.*

ANDRÉ L. E. WEISROCK, Faculté des lettres et sciences humaines, Université du Maine, Route de Laval, 72000 Le Mans, France. *Morocco.*

POH POH WONG, Dept. of Geography, National University of Singapore, Kent Ridge Singapore 0511. *Singapore.*

P. J. WOODS, Dept. of Geography, University of Western Australia, Nedlands, Western Australia 6009, Australia. *Western Australia.*

V. P. ZENKOVICH, Kotelnicheskaya 1/15, kv 196, Moscow 109240, USSR. *Arctic USSR; Eastern Black Sea.*

YU ZHIYING, Institute of the Coasts and Estuaries, Shanghai Normal University, Shanghai, China. *China.*

MARCELLO ZUNICA, Instituto di Geografia, Universita di Padova, Via del Santo 26, 35100 Padova, Italy. *Italy.*

THE WORLD'S COASTLINE

1. ALASKA

Alaska, which spans 20° of latitude and 50° of longitude, has one of the world's longest, most diverse, and irregularly shaped coastlines (Figs. 1-1 and 1-2). It has a general coastline of 10,686 km and a tidal coastline of 54,564 km (National Ocean Survey 1981); both are longer than those of the rest of the United States. (The U.S. Army Corps of Engineers (1971) reported the same general length for Alaska but gave its tidal length as 76,100 km.)

Alaska occupies the northwest extension of four of North America's major physiographic divisions (Wahrhaftig 1965): the Interior Plains, the Rocky Mountain system, the Intermontane Plateaus, and the Pacific Mountain system (Fig. 1-1A, inset). All these physiographic divisions extend across Alaska's coast, and each has an important bearing on coastal geology (Fig. 1-1A) and coastline character (Fig. 1-1B).

The Alaskan portion of the Interior Plains, known as the Arctic Coastal Plain, is composed almost entirely of Quaternary sediments, most of which are unconsolidated and some of which are eolian (Fig. 1-3A). The coastal zone of the Brooks Range (Alaska's portion of the Rocky Mountain system) consists of Mesozoic and Paleozoic sedimentary and metamorphic rocks. Most of Alaska's Bering Sea coast belongs to the Intermontane Plateaus. It is composed mainly of Quaternary sediments (Fig. 1-3B and 1-3C), although Mesozoic and Paleozoic sedimentary and metamorphic rocks predominate in several sections. In addition, a few locations have Quaternary and Tertiary volcanics and intrusive igneous rocks of Tertiary age.

The geology of the Pacific Mountain system is Alaska's most diverse. Virtually all rock types are present. In the Aleutian Islands, Quaternary volcanics predominate (Fig. 1-3D); along the central Gulf of Alaska coast, sedimentary and metamorphic rocks of Quaternary, Tertiary, and Mesozoic ages are all present (Fig. 1-3E); and, along the lengthy coastline of southeastern Alaska, there is a mixture of Tertiary and Mesozoic intrusives and Mesozoic and Paleozoic sedimentary and metamorphic rocks (Fig. 1-3F).

Alaska's geological and oceanic settings combine to provide five coastal units: Arctic, Bering Sea, Aleutian Island, Gulf of Alaska, and Southeast.

The Arctic coast extends from Demarcation Point on the Canada–Alaska border west to Point Barrow and then southwest to Cape Prince of Wales (Fig. 1-2). To the east of Point Barrow is the Beaufort Sea, where the longshore current is westerly; to the west is the Chukchi Sea, where the longshore current is northeasterly.

From the Canadian border west to Point Barrow the coast is characterized by low cliffs (Hartwell 1973) except where interrupted by the numerous rivers that flow across the coastal plain. Some of these cliffs face the open sea, although most are separated from it by a series of shallow lagoons and low barrier islands (Plate 1-1A and Fig. 1-4A). Most cliffs are between 1 and 5 m high (Fig. 1-4B), although toward the east some are as much as 9 m high. The barriers, most numerous along the eastern half of the Beaufort Sea coast, are generally narrow and short and separated by wide inlets. The western half of the Beaufort Sea coast is irregular and is composed of a number of large bays. One large delta, the Colville River delta (Fig. 1-3A and Plate 1-1B), and a number of small deltas are present along the coast (Walker 1974). Ice-wedge polygons border much of the coast (Plate 1-1C).

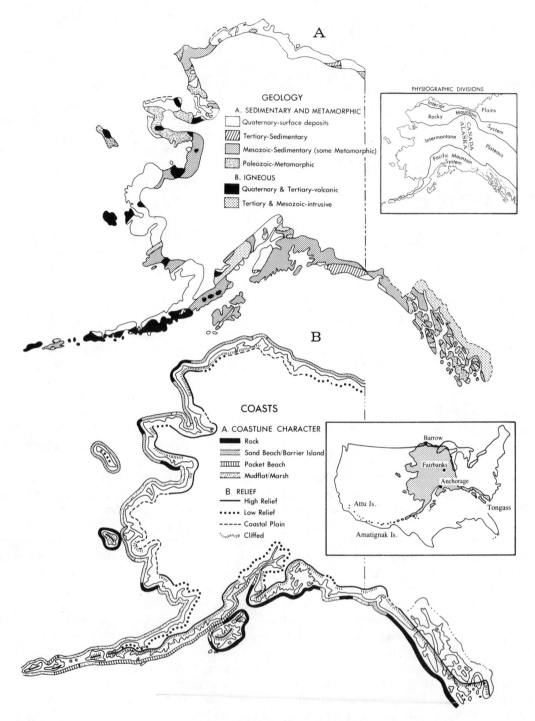

Figure 1-1. The coastline of Alaska. *A.* Coastal geology (after Joint Federal-State Land Use Planning Commission for Alaska 1973) and Physiographic Divisions (inset, after Wahrhaftig 1965); *B.* Coastline character (after Dolan et al. 1972) and coastal comparison of Alaska and conterminous United States (inset).

The Chukchi Sea coast generally has higher relief than the Beaufort Sea coast. Southwest of Point Barrow tundra cliffs (Plate 1-1*D*) are usually between 10 and 18 m high (Harper 1978), although at Cape Lisburne, where the Brooks Range extends to the shore, they are more than 300 m high (Plate 1-1*E*). Lengthy spits and barrier islands separated by narrow inlets occur along the middle section of the coast between Point Barrow and Cape Lisburne and along the

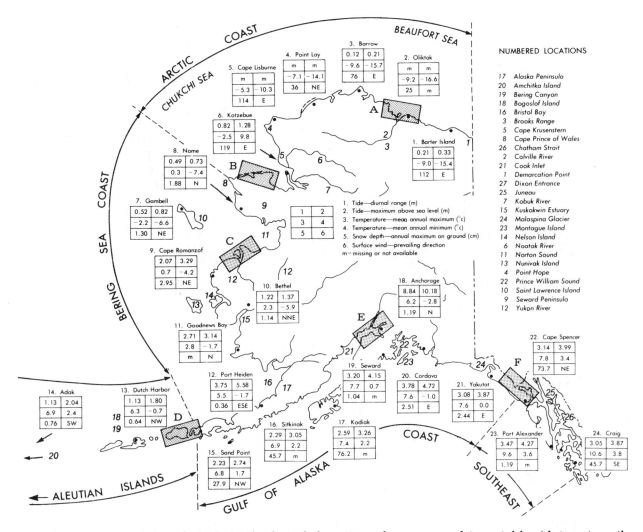

Figure 1-2. The coastline of Alaska and selected climatic and oceanographic variables (data primarily from tables in Brower et al. 1977).

northwest-facing portion of the Seward Peninsula (Fig. 1-3B). Shorter barrier islands are present along much of the rest of this coast. In some places, as at Cape Krusenstern and Point Hope, extensive beach-ridge systems have developed (Fig. 1-4C). One of the most distinctive features of the Arctic coastline is a large embayment located north of the Seward Peninsula. Sediment transported by the Noatak and Kobuk, two of Alaska's largest rivers, is rapidly filling this embayment.

Nearly all the Arctic coast is within the zone of continuous permafrost and exhibits such permafrost-related forms as ice wedges, ice-wedge polygons (Plate 1-1B), and thaw lakes and such permafrost-related processes as thermal melting and thermal erosion. Differential thaw and erosion (Fig. 1-4B) often produce an undercut, serrated, low-cliff-type coastline (Plate 1-1C). When

tapped by ocean waves, thaw lakes become part of the shallow foreshore and provide a coastline that is usually arcuate in form (Fig. 1-4A).

The Bering Sea coast, from Cape Prince of Wales to the western end of the Alaska peninsula, is dominated by two large embayments (Norton Sound to the north and Bristol Bay to the south) that are separated by the extensive Yukon-Kuskokwim deltaic complex and the southwest extension of the Kuskokwim Mountain Range.

Norton Sound, with a relatively smooth coastline, has narrow beaches backed by glaciated hills. The Yukon–Kuskokwim Delta consists of many lakes, marshes, and abandoned distributaries. Presently the Yukon River, which contributes the majority of the sediment that reaches the Bering Sea, discharges north into Norton Sound (Fig. 1-3C), where interdistributary mudflats are

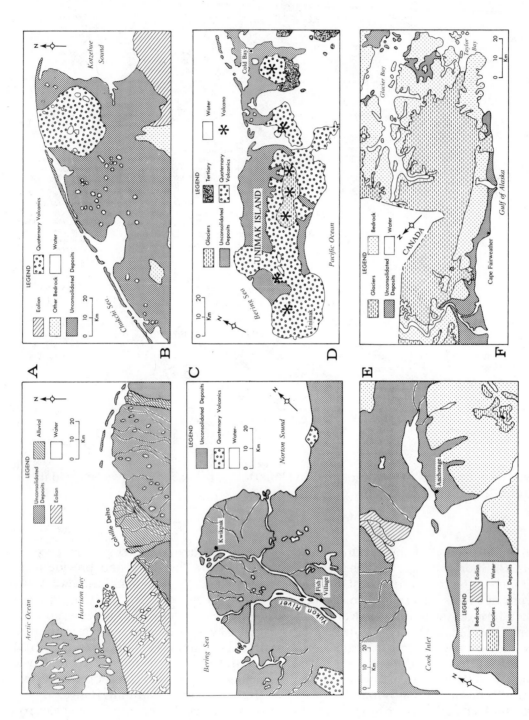

Figure 1-3. Generalized geology of six coastal zones (A–F) located on Figure 1-2 (after Selkregg 1974–1976).

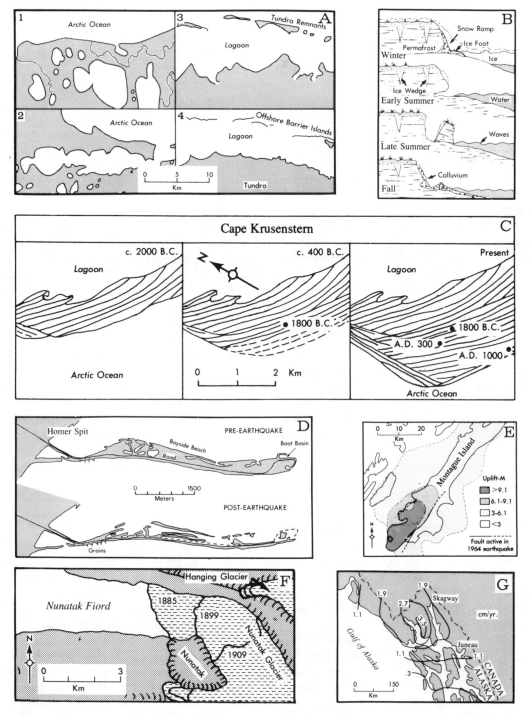

Figure 1-4. Coastal forms in Alaska. *A.* Stages in lagoon development by thaw-lake coalescence (after Wiseman et al. 1973); *B.* Seasonal changes in the retreat of a permafrost shoreline (after Walker 1982); *C.* Development of the Cape Krusenstern beach ridges (after Moore 1968); *D.* Earthquake-induced changes in Homer Spit (after Waller 1966); *E.* Uplift of Montague Island during the 1964 Alaska earthquake (after Kirkby and Kirkby 1969); *F.* Terminal positions of Nunatak Glacier (after Tarr and Martin 1914); *G.* Regional uplift, Southeast Alaska (after Hicks and Shofnos 1965).

extensive. South of today's Yukon the coast is dominated by beach ridges, many of which are undergoing rapid erosion. The Kuskokwim River, in contrast to the Yukon, flows into a 100-km-long estuary.

In the southwestern part of the deltaic complex, where Quaternary volcanic activity formed hills, gravel beaches and rocky headlands are numerous. Nelson Island near the delta and Nunivak Island, about 50 km offshore, have such coastlines. In contrast, much of the coast of Saint Lawrence Island has low sandy beaches often backed by sand dunes. South of the Kuskokwim Estuary the Kuskokwim Mountains meet the sea with high rocky cliffs and numerous stacks. Most of the Bristol Bay coast is composed of glacial and fluvial sediments and has sandy beaches, extensive mudflats, and numerous lagoons.

The Aleutian Islands extend in a gentle arc for nearly 2,000 km across the northern Pacific Ocean to Attu Island (Fig. 1-1*B*, inset), and are the sub-aerial portions of a 10–100-km-wide ridge that flanks the western half of the Aleutian Trench. This trench (over 3,000 km long and up to 7,500 m deep) is the subducting edge of the Pacific Plate. Active subduction is responsible for the occurrence of frequent earthquakes in southern Alaska and for the creation and maintenance of the 60 centers of volcanic activity that extend from near Anchorage to the western end of the Aleutian Islands. Of these 60 centers, more than 40 have been active since 1760 (Selkregg 1974–1976). Many of the coasts in the Aleutian Islands are composed of lava that flowed into the sea (Fig. 1-3*D*) or of ash that has fallen on the shore or into the water and then washed on shore; other coasts have been eliminated or altered by explosive eruptions, for example, Bogoslof Island (Shepard and Wanless 1971).

The coastlines of most of the islands are irregular. Rocky cliffs (Plate 1-2*A*) alternate with boulder beaches, but in some protected coves sandy beaches are present. Abrasion platforms are found at present-day sea level (Plate 1-2*B*) as well as at various heights below and above (up to 200 m) sea level.

The Gulf of Alaska coast, which extends in a clockwise direction from the eastern Aleutian Islands to Cape Spencer, includes a number of distinctive coastal types. The Pacific-facing portion of the Alaska peninsula is highly irregular and has numerous rocky headlands that alternate with formerly glaciated inlets. Many of the headlands are continued offshore by rugged islands and rocky stacks. One of the largest islands

in Alaska is Kodiak, which is separated from the northern part of the Alaska Peninsula by a 50-km-wide strait, and also has an irregular and rugged coastline with fjords, especially along its northwestern coast.

Cook Inlet, a deep structural basin over 300 km long, is a tidal estuary that opens into the Gulf of Alaska and has some of the world's highest tidal ranges (10–11 m). Near its head extensive tidal flats (Plate 1-2*C*) and marshlands occupy the coastal edge of a low coastal plain, which narrows gradually on the northern side of Cook Inlet and toward its mouth merges into mountains that descend directly into the sea (Plate 1-2*D*). In contrast, on the southern side of Cook Inlet pocket beaches alternate with low cliffs along most of its extent.

The coast from the mouth of Cook Inlet east around Prince William Sound is deeply indented with fjords (Plate 1-3*A*). Much sediment is transported into these fjords by the short, turbulent streams that originate in the alpine glaciers that are still present in the coastal mountains. From Prince William Sound southeast to Cape Spencer, the coastline is smooth in outline and is characterized by deltas, beach and dune ridges, outwash plains (Plate 1-3*B*), moraines, and glaciers. In some locations tidewater glaciers are present; they represent some of the most rapidly changing coastlines to be found in Alaska.

Although the entire Pacific Ocean coast of Alaska may experience earthquakes, some of the most important occur around the Gulf of Alaska and many have a direct effect on the coastline. The March 27, 1964, Alaskan Earthquake, the most intense ever recorded in North America, depressed (Fig. 1-4*D*), elevated (Fig. 1-4*E*), or otherwise modified some 16,000 km of coastline (Shepard and Wanless 1971). Earthquakes are a major (although not the only) cause of landslides (Plate 1-2*D*) in the coastal zones of Alaska. The most famous slide was triggered by an earthquake near Lituya Bay on July 9, 1958. A horizontal movement of 6.6 m and vertical movement of 10.7 m caused a rockslide that dumped over 30 million m³ of rock into the bay. It also caused 750 m of ice to calve from the terminus of Turner Glacier at the head of the Yakutat Bay, initiating a tsunami.

The Southeast Alaska coast extends from Cape Spencer south to Tongass at Dixon Entrance on the Alaska–Canada border. Although the general length of the Southeast Alaska coast, as given in the *United States Coast Pilot* (National Ocean Survey 1981) is only 460 km (4.3% of Alaska's total), its tidal shoreline is 20,530 km long, or

37.6% of the total for the state. Such a variation in its general and tidal coastline lengths is due to the large number of inlets, straits, bays, fjords, and islands that characterize this rugged region: many steep cliffs descend far below sea level. However, there are low coastal plains near the head of some of the fjords and strand flats and reefs border many islands and headlands, especially those exposed directly to the ocean (Buddington and Chapin 1929).

Many of the geomorphic details are closely related to the intensity of wave and tidal action and the regional lithology (Sharma 1979). Most of the coastline is protected from the open sea and thus not generally subjected to high-energy storm waves, but tides of at least 7 m in some of the fjords and bays are responsible for strong tidal currents and intensive scouring action.

In contrast, the gross geomorphic character of Southeast Alaska is the result of the glacial modification (Fig. 1-4*F*) of a tectonically active, complex mountainous terrain. At the maximum of the Pleistocene glaciation, ice covered most of Southeast Alaska and extended past the present coastline onto the Continental Shelf. During waxing—and, to some extent, waning—stages, the dominant trend of glacial erosion was controlled by northwest–southeast trending fault structures. Such structural control made possible the formation of exceptionally long fjords (Fig. 1-4*G*). When glacial ice dominated the landscape, however, the flow and therefore erosional trend was seaward across the structural grain.

Southeast Alaska, tectonically active since the early Paleozoic, is presently being uplifted at one of the fastest rates in the world (Selkregg 1974–1976). In some places uplift is over 3.5 cm per year (Fig. 1-4*G*), a rate that helps account for the presence of glaciomarine deposits at heights of 230 m above sea level near Juneau. Some of this uplift is considered to be the result of rebound that occurs with deglaciation. Although general rebound is still occurring, localized rebound is partially responsible for a rapid uplift that is being recorded near retreating glaciers (Hicks and Shofnos 1965).

H. JESSE WALKER

REFERENCES

Buddington, A. F., and T. Chapin, 1929, *Geology and Mineral Deposits of Southeastern Alaska*, U.S. Geol. Survey Bull. 800, Washington, D.C.

Brower, W. A., Jr., H. W. Searby, J. L. Wise, H. F. Diaz, and A. S. Prechtel, 1977, *Climatic Atlas of the Outer Continental Shelf Waters and Coastal Regions of Alaska*, 3 vols., U.S. Department of Interior, Bureau of Land Management, Anchorage.

Dolan, R., B. Hayden, G. Hornberger, J. Zieman, and N. Vincent, 1972, *Classification of the Coastal Environments of the World. Part I: The Americas*, Office of Naval Research, Washington, D.C.

Harper, J. R., 1978, Coastal erosion rates along the Chukchi Sea coast near Barrow, Alaska, *Arctic* **31:**428–433.

Hartwell, A. D., 1973, Classification and relief characteristics of northern Alaska's coastal zone, *Arctic* **26:**244–252.

Hicks, S. D., and W. Shofnos, 1965, The determination of land emergence from sea level observations in southeast Alaska, *Jour. Geophys. Research* **70:**3315–3320.

Joint Federal-State Land Use Planning Commission for Alaska, 1973, *Major Ecosystems of Alaska*, U.S. Geol. Survey Map, Washington, D.C.

Kirkby, M. J., and A. V. Kirkby, 1969, *The Alaska Earthquake: Regional effects*, U.S. Geol. Survey Prof. Paper 543-KH, Washington, D.C.

Moore, G. W., 1968, Arctic beaches, in *The Encyclopedia of Geomorphology*, R. W. Fairbridge, ed., Reinhold, New York, pp. 21–22.

National Ocean Survey, 1981, *United States Coast Pilot*, vols. 8 and 9., NOAA, U.S. Dept. of Commerce, Washington, D.C.

Selkregg, L. L., ed., 1974–1976, *Alaska Regional Profiles*, 6 vols., University of Alaska, Anchorage.

Sharma, G. D., 1979, *The Alaskan Shelf*, Springer Verlag, New York.

Shepard, F. P., and H. R. Wanless, 1971, *Our Changing Coastlines*, McGraw-Hill, New York.

Tarr, R. S., and L. Martin, 1914, *Alaskan Glacier Studies*, National Geographic Society, Washington, D.C.

U.S. Army Corps of Engineers, 1971, *National Shoreline Study, Inventory Report, Alaska region*, Alaska District, Anchorage.

Wahrhaftig, C., 1965, *Physiographic Divisions of Alaska*, U.S. Geol. Survey Prof. Paper 482, Washington, D.C.

Waller, R. M., 1966, *Effects of the Earthquake of March 27, 1964, in the Homer Area, Alaska*, U.S. Geol. Survey Prof. Paper 542-D, Washington, D.C.

Walker, H. J., 1974, The Colville River and the Beaufort Sea: some interactions, in *The Coast and Shelf of the Beaufort Sea*, J. C. Reed and J. E. Sater, eds., Arctic Institute of North America, Washington, D.C., pp. 513–540.

Walker, H. J., 1982, Arctic, Coastal Morphology, in *Encyclopedia of Beaches and Coastal Environments*, M. L. Schwartz, ed., Hutchinson Ross, Stroudsburg, Pa., pp. 57–61.

Wiseman, W. J., J. M. Coleman, A. Gregory, S. A. Hsu, A. D. Short, J. N. Suhayda, C. D. Walters, and L. D. Wright, 1973, *Alaskan Arctic Coastal Processes and Morphology*, Tech. Rept. 149, Coastal Studies Institute, Louisiana State University, Baton Rouge.

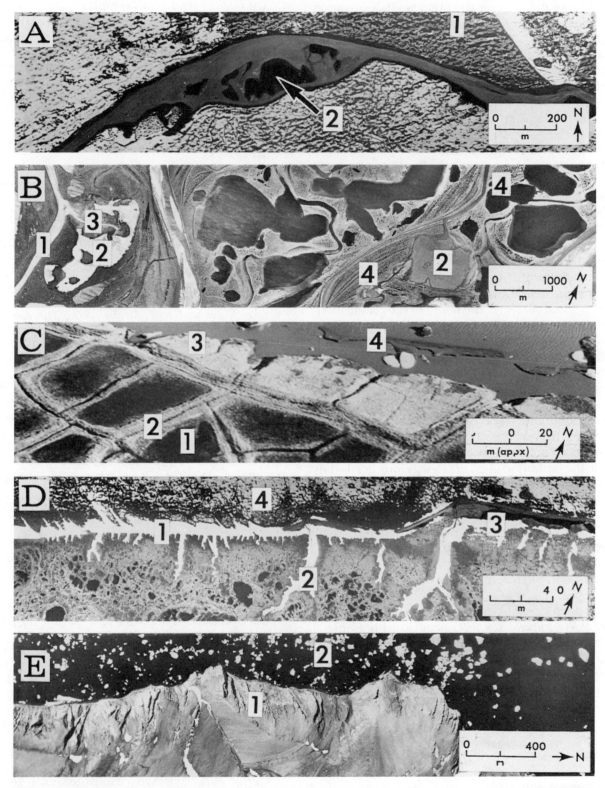

Plate 1-1. Coastal forms of Arctic Alaska. *A.* Offshore barrier bar: 1. decaying sea ice, 2. bar pond; *B.* Deltaic forms: 1. river channel, 2. tapped lake, 3. lake delta, 4. ice-wedge polygons; *C.* Polygon shoreline: 1. low-centered polygon, 2. ice-wedge crack, 3. eroding polygons, 4. stranded ice floe; *D.* Low cliffs: 1. snow ramp, 2. ravine, 3. lagoon, 4. sea ice; *E.* High cliffs: 1. nonvegetated cliffs, 2. ice floes (after Walker 1982).

Plate 1-2. Coastal forms of the Aleutian Islands and the Gulf of Alaska. *A.* Cliffs and pocket beach, Udak (photo by R. Black); *B.* Low terrace shoreline, Amchitka (photo by R. Black); *C.* Tidal flat, Cook Inlet (photo by H. J. Walker); *D.* Revegetation off coastal landslides (photo by C. O. Evans).

Plate 1-3. Glaciated coasts *A.* Glacially scoured coast on the Kenai Peninsula coast (photo by M. W. Williams); *B.* Lituya Bay (photo by R. Belous, National Park Service).

2. BRITISH COLUMBIA

The coasts of British Columbia have developed in a region of high relief associated with the North American Cordillera Mountain system. Maximum elevations up to 4,000 m occur in the coastal mountain ranges. The Coast Range, on the mainland, is separated by the Hecate Strait–Georgia Strait depression from an insular mountain range that reaches elevations of 1,200 m on the Queen Charlotte Islands and 2,200 m on Vancouver Island. Seaward of this outer island mountain range, the continental shelf is very narrow, less than 50 km in some areas. The primary structural trends of the cordillera system are northwest–southeast, and the bedrock outcrops are predominantly resistant volcanics, or intrusives, with relatively few exposures of less resistant sedimentary rocks.

Pleistocene glaciation in this region has produced a fjord coast that is characterized by a very complex shoreline of glacially eroded, U-shaped valleys in upland areas. On lowland coasts, the effect of the glaciation has been to deposit till and drift for reworking by contemporary coastal processes; however, these deposits are frequently thin and are restricted in area.

There is considerable variation in wave-energy levels at the shoreline, due to the extreme complexity of the coastline configuration. The outer shores are a high wave-energy coast, with long-period swell waves out of the western quadrant dominating the wave climate. Wave-energy levels vary seasonally as wave heights are greater during winter months than in summer, due to the greater intensity of westerly winds over the northern Pacific Ocean. Locally generated storm waves form an additional and significant component of the wave climate. Storms are more frequent during winter months, as a result of cyclonic depressions that travel from west to east across the region, so that in areas not exposed to swell waves the wave-energy maximum occurs also in winter months. Within the more sheltered regions of Hecate Strait, the Strait of Georgia, and the fjord embayments, the importance of swell waves decreases, and locally generated storm waves become the dominant component of the local wave climate. Swell waves penetrate along those straits, inlets, and fjords that parallel the direction of wave propagation, for example, the Strait of Juan de Fuca (Clague and Bornhold 1980).

The tidal range on the coasts of British Columbia increases from 2 m in southern regions to over 5 m in the north. A maximum range of 8.4 m has been recorded at Prince Rupert. The tides are predominantly mixed, semidiurnal in character, although mixed-diurnal tides occur in southern sections of the Strait of Georgia. An important aspect of the tides is that currents are restricted through narrow channels in many areas. For example, in Discovery Passage and in the Seymour Narrows, in the northwestern section of the Strait of Georgia, tidal currents up to 7 m/s are common.

Owens (1977) has described the coastal environments and shore-zone character of British Columbia in terms of six subdivisions, based on coastal geomorphology; Clague and Bornhold (1980) have described it as comprising three regions, based on regional physiography. Both approaches are similar in that they recognize the tripartite breakdown into the outer coastal range, the inter-range depression, and the mainland mountains. Clague and Bornhold present a series of maps that define the distribution of major shoreline types (Figure 2-1); the characteristics

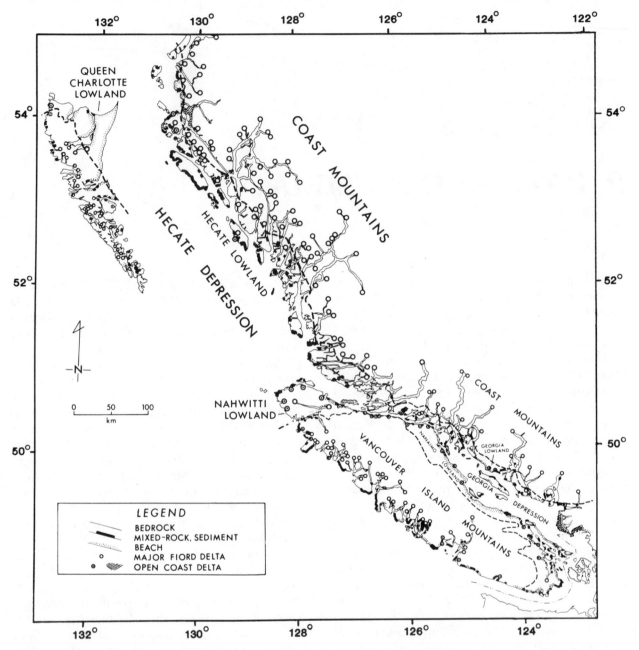

Figure 2-1. Major coastal environments of British Columbia (after Clague and Bornhold 1980).

of the major coastal environments, as defined by Owens, are presented in Table 2-1.

The character of the coast of British Columbia is controlled by structural elements, by the effects of the Pleistocene glaciations, and by wave processes that act on the shoreline. On the upland, mountainous coast, relief is generally high (Plate 2-1), sediments are scarce, and bedrock outcrops are common in the shore zone. Although the coastlines are frequently steep, there are relatively

few sections of actively retreating, wave-eroded cliffs. Small deltas occur in sheltered areas at the heads of the many fjords, but few extensive beach systems have developed. On the lowland coast, within the intermontane depressions, beach development is more common (e.g., McCann and Hale 1980), and many sections of shoreline have actively eroding, unconsolidated, and relatively unresistant bedrock cliffs. The largest depositional feature in the lowland region is the Argonaut Plain on north-

Table 2-1. Characteristics of British Columbia coastal environments (after Owens 1977).

	Geological Character	Coastal Zone		Fetch And Wave Exposure	Mean Tidal Range	Sediment Availability
		Backshore Relief	Beach Character			
Fraser River Delta	Unconsolidated fine-grained sediments; accumulation of river-borne material.	Low: marshes, usually dyked.	Flat intertidal zone of sand and mud up to 6 km wide at low tide: no beaches.	< 50 km, very sheltered.	3 m	Very abundant.
Strait of Georgia	Resistant igneous rocks on mainland: volcanics and sedimentary rocks on Vancouver Is.	Low coastal plain backed by fjords cut into mountains: cliffs in less resistant rocks or glacial deposits.	Absent or narrow, with pebble-cobble sediments: occur near glacial deposits on low-lying coasts.	Up to 200 km; outer coasts exposed, elsewhere very sheltered.	3 m	Scarce: some local concentrations.
Juan de Fuca Strait	Resistant lavas.	Low coastal plain: cliffs up to 10 m.	Pebble-cobble and narrow in east; absent or narrow in west: rock intertidal platforms.	Progressively more sheltered to the east; west shore very exposed.	2.5 m	Scarce: some local concentrations.
Outer Pacific Shore	Resistant volcanics or lavas.	Mountains or uplands incised by steep-sided fjords: narrow coastal plain on Vancouver Is.	Absent or narrow with pebble-cobble sediments: isolated wide sand beaches near eroding glacial deposits.	> 1,000 km, exposed: very high energy; sheltered inner coastal zone.	3 m	Very scarce: a few local concentrations.
Queen Charlotte Sound and Hecate Strait	Resistant igneous rocks on mainland lavas or volcanics on Q. Charlotte Islands.	Coastal lowlands give way to mountains or uplands cut by fjords.	Absent or narrow with pebble-cobble sediments: deltas at heads of fjords.	300 km– > 1,000 km, exposed outer shores, sheltered inner coastal zone.	3-5 m	Very scarce: some local concentrations.
East Graham Island	Unconsolidated glacial drift or outwash sands and gravels.	Cliffs up to 100 m high: relief < 200 m.	Wide sand or sand/gravel beaches.	Up to 300 km, exposed.	3-5 m	Abundant.

13

eastern Graham Island, where local erosion of unresistant rocks and glacial deposits has supplied a large volume of material to the littoral zone for the development of an extensive prograding beachreach plain. Two extensive deltas have formed at the mouths of the Fraser (Kellerhals and Murray 1969; Luternauer 1980) (Plate 2-2) and the Skeena rivers (Hoos 1975). These deltaic environments are in marked contrast to the remainder of the shoreline, where sediment supply is generally low.

Relative changes in sea level since the retreat of the Pleistocene glaciers have resulted in a marine transgression to approximately 200 m above present sea level, which was followed by a regressive phase, and by a slow relative rise in sea level in many areas at the present time (Clague 1975). Recent sea-level changes have been complicated by the effects of tectonic processes; portions of western Vancouver Island and the Queen Charlotte Islands are undergoing tectonic uplift and display numerous emergent landforms.

The strong seasonal variations of wave characteristics on the coast result in corresponding seasonal variations in beach sedimentation patterns. Along outer coasts, seasonal variations in wave-energy levels produce a seasonal, onshore-offshore cycling of sediments (e.g., the summer-winter beach cycle). On more protected sections of coast, seasonal variations in beach morphology are related to changes in local wind and associated wave patterns, and are more likely to result from variations in the intensity and direction of longshore transport rather than onshore-offshore transport (Harper 1980).

EDWARD H. OWENS
JOHN R. HARPER

REFERENCES

Clague, J. J., 1975, *Late Quaternary Sea Level Fluctuations, Pacific Coast of Canada and Adjacent Areas,* Canada Geol. Survey Paper 75-1C, Ottawa.

Clague, J. J., and B. D. Bornhold, 1980, Morphology and littoral processes of the Pacific coast of Canada, in *The Coastline of Canada,* S. B. McCann, ed., Canada Geol. Survey Paper 80-10, Ottawa, pp. 339–380.

Harper, J. R., 1980, Seasonal changes in beach morphology along the B.C. coast, *Canadian Coastal Conf. 1980 Proc.,* Natl. Research Council Canada, Ottawa, pp. 136–150.

Hoos, L. M., 1975, *The Skeena River Estuary: Status of Knowledge to 1975,* Canada Dept. Environment, Pacific Region, Special Estuary Series No. 3, Vancouver.

Kellerhals, P., and J. W. Murray, 1969, Tidal flats at Boundary Bay, Fraser River delta, British Columbia, *Canadian Petroleum Geology Bull.* **17:**67–91.

Luternauer, J. L., 1980, Genesis of morphologic features on the western delta front of the Fraser River, *British Columbia—status of knowledge, in The Coastline of Canada,* S. B. McCann, ed., Canada Geol. Survey Paper 80-10, Ottawa, pp. 381–396.

McMann, S. B., and P. B. Hale, 1980, Sediment dispersal patterns and shore morphology along the Georgia Strait coastline of Vancouver Island, *Canadian Coastal Conf. 1980 Proc.,* Natl. Research Council Canada, Ottawa, pp. 151–163.

Owens, E. H., 1977, *Coastal Environments of Canada: The Impact and Cleanup of Oil Spills,* Canada Dept. Fisheries and Environment, Environmental Protection Service, Econ. and Tech. Review Rept. EPS-3-EC-77-13, Vancouver.

Plate 2-2. Fraser River delta, the mouth of the Canoe Pass channel (photo by E. H. Owens).

Plate 2-1. High-energy sand beach near Tofino. Inland the beach gives way to a complex, sheltered environment of bedrock islands and channels and to the insular mountains of western Vancouver Island (photo by E. H. Owens).

3. WASHINGTON

The marine coast of the state of Washington is 4,296 km long and consists of three distinctly different regions (Fig. 3-1): the western coast, facing on the Pacific Ocean; the northern shore of the Olympic Peninsula, along the Strait of Juan de Fuca; and the inner body of water and islands, east of the peninsula, known as Puget Sound. Considering recent regional development and population growth, and its prominent location within the contiguous United States, comparatively little has been written to date about the coastal geomorphology of the area (Cooper 1958; Rau 1973, 1980; Shepard and Wanless 1971; Terich and Schwartz 1981).

The Pacific Coast region has a temperate climate, with an average annual rainfall of 287.5 cm in the rain forest area inland of LaPush. Along this coastal strip the principal trees are Western hemlock *(Tsuga heterophylla)*, western arborvitae *(Thuja plicata)*, Douglas fir *(Pseudotsuga menziesii)*, Sitka spruce *(Picea sitchensis)*, and lodgepole pine *(Pinus contorta)*. Heavy driftwood concentrations are found along the shore, where tides are mixed and range from 2 m at neap to 4 m at spring. Onshore winds in this area are highly changeable, but they may vary between north-northwest, and south-southwest. Net shore drift is predominantly to the north, as can be seen in the development in that direction of the Long Beach Peninsula (Fig. 3-2) and the northerly deflection of the mouths of such rivers as the Copalis, Moclips, Quinault, Queets, and Hoh (Figs. 3-3 and 3-4). There are occasional local reversals, as at LaPush, where wave refraction around two large stacks has caused a spit, at the mouth of the Quileute River, to develop toward the south.

The Pacific coast shore, between the Columbia River and the Strait of Juan de Fuca, can be divided into three geomorphic sectors (Fig. 3-1): Southern, Central, and Northern. The Southern Sector (Fig. 3-2) is backed by a gently rolling plain, with two large estuaries, Willapa Bay and Grays Harbor, developed by the flooding of river mouths of an older and lower sea level. Northerly migration of the main Willapa Bay inlet channel is believed to be the cause of severe erosion at Cape Shoalwater, where the shoreline has receded 3.2 km in the last 90 years; two of the three major man-made structures along the state's outer coast are jetties that help stabilize the inlet entrance to Grays Harbor.

The coast consists of broad, prograded sandy beaches fronting multiple rows of beach and dune ridges (Plate 3-1). Provenance of the accreted sand along this sector has been attributed to the Columbia River to the south. With the construction of large dams on the Columbia, during this century, it is speculated that the progradation regime may have ceased and possibly will turn to one of erosion.

The Central Sector (Fig. 3-3) consists of moderate-width sand and gravel beaches fronting cliffs of Tertiary continental and marine strata overlain by Quaternary glacial deposits (Plate 3-2). Mass wasting is a common feature along these cliffs, supplying most of the sediment that, reworked by wave action, comprises the beaches. The linearity of this sector is exceeded, in this region, only by that of the sandy beach sector to the south. Geomorphically, the Central Sector is intermediate in form between the Southern and Northern sectors.

The Northern Sector (Fig. 3-4) is one of the great scenic coasts of the world. Here, differential erosion of Tertiary continental-marine sediments

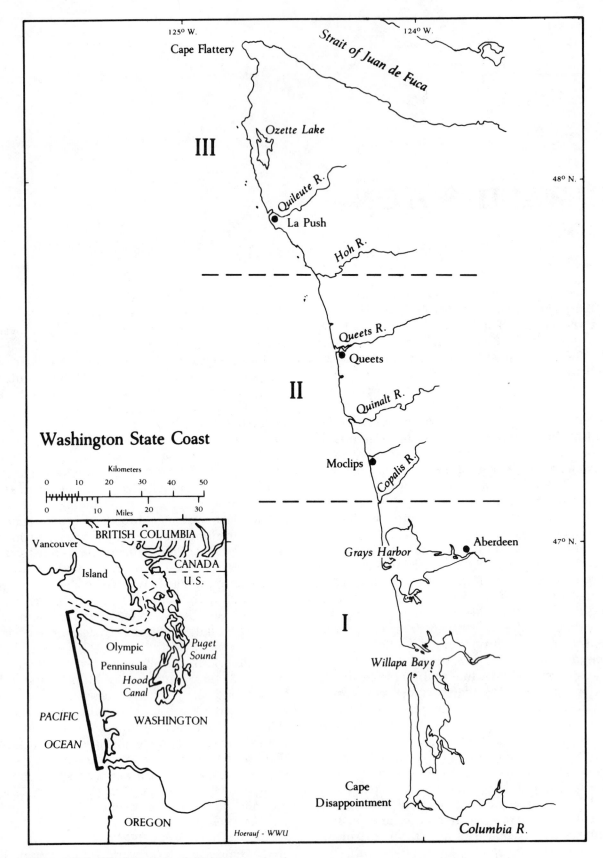

Figure 3-1. Washington state coast.

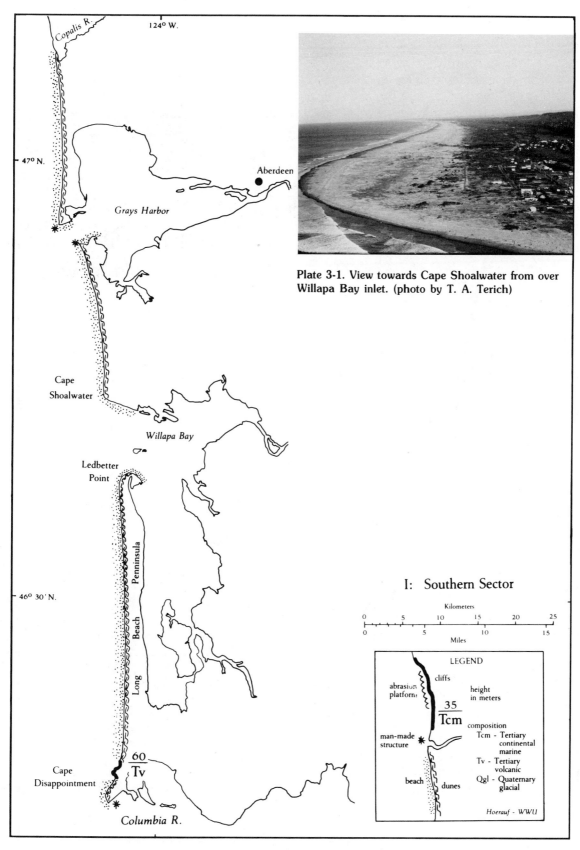

Plate 3-1. View towards Cape Shoalwater from over Willapa Bay inlet. (photo by T. A. Terich)

I: Southern Sector

Figure 3-2. Southern Sector (I).

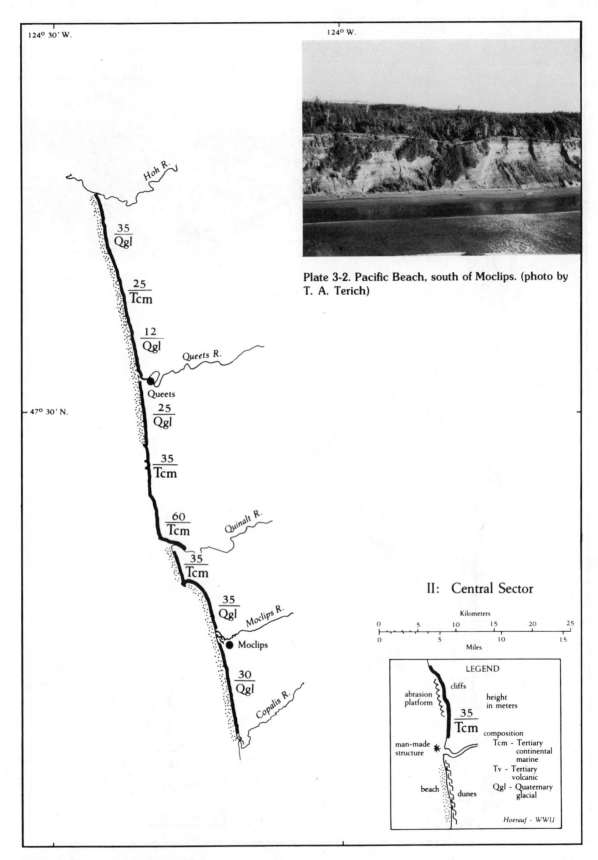

124° 30' W.

124° W.

Hoh R.

$\dfrac{35}{Qgl}$

$\dfrac{25}{Tcm}$

$\dfrac{12}{Qgl}$

Queets R.

Queets

$\dfrac{25}{Qgl}$

47° 30' N.

$\dfrac{35}{Tcm}$

$\dfrac{60}{Tcm}$

Quinalt R.

$\dfrac{35}{Tcm}$

$\dfrac{35}{Qgl}$

Moclips R.

Moclips

$\dfrac{30}{Qgl}$

Copalis R.

Plate 3-2. Pacific Beach, south of Moclips. (photo by T. A. Terich)

II: Central Sector

Kilometers

0   5   10   15   20   25

0   5   10   15

Miles

LEGEND

cliffs

abrasion
platform

height
in meters

$\dfrac{35}{Tcm}$

composition

man-made
structure

Tcm - Tertiary
        continental
        marine

Tv - Tertiary
       volcanic

beach   dunes

Qgl - Quaternary
         glacial

Hoerauf - WWU

Figure 3-3. Central Sector (II).

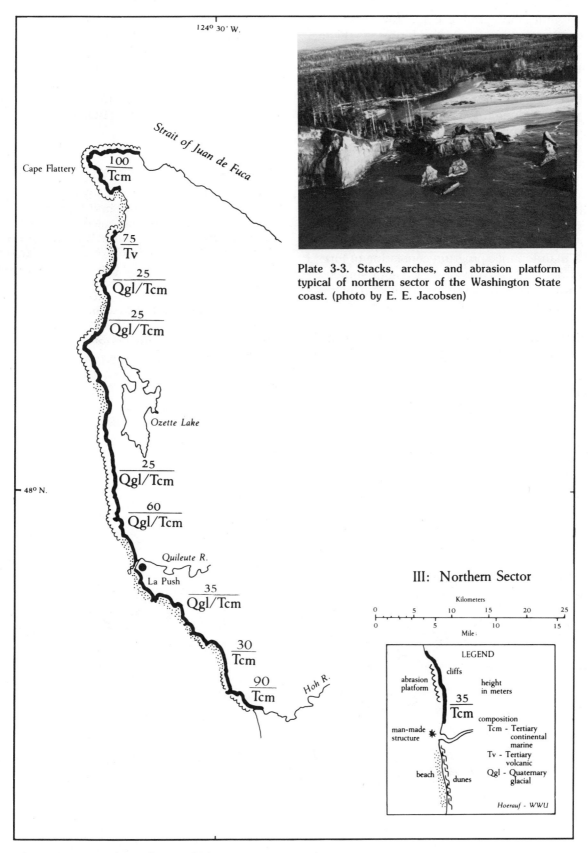

124° 30' W.

Strait of Juan de Fuca

Cape Flattery

$\frac{100}{Tcm}$

$\frac{75}{Tv}$

$\frac{25}{Qgl/Tcm}$

$\frac{25}{Qgl/Tcm}$

Ozette Lake

48° N.

$\frac{25}{Qgl/Tcm}$

$\frac{60}{Qgl/Tcm}$

Quileute R.

La Push

$\frac{35}{Qgl/Tcm}$

$\frac{30}{Tcm}$

$\frac{90}{Tcm}$

Hoh R.

Plate 3-3. Stacks, arches, and abrasion platform typical of northern sector of the Washington State coast. (photo by E. E. Jacobsen)

III: Northern Sector

Kilometers
0   5   10   15   20   25
0   5   10   15
Miles

LEGEND

abrasion platform   cliffs

$\frac{35}{Tcm}$ height in meters

composition

man-made structure ✳   Tcm - Tertiary continental marine
Tv - Tertiary volcanic
Qgl - Quaternary glacial

beach   dunes

Hoerauf - WWU

Figure 3-4. Northern Sector (III).

and volcanics has produced sea caves, stacks, arches, abrasion platforms, and high cliffs (Plate 3-3). Where sediment accumulations exist along the inner edges of the abrasion platforms, they consist mostly of coarse gravel and cobbles; sandy beaches are to be found only in the occasional embayments along this stretch.

Dungeness Spit and Ediz Hook, respectively 8 km and 5.6 km long, are the two main coastal geomorphic features along the U.S. side of the Strait of Juan de Fuca. Damming of a river and barricading the foot of a cliff, both west and updrift of Ediz Hook, has caused considerable erosion at the base of this highly industrialized spit. The U.S. Army Corps of Engineers has recently initiated a maintenance program consisting of foreshore revetment and periodic beach nourishment.

Within Puget Sound, the mainland and island shores, while rocky in places, consist mostly of beaches and bluffs developed in Pleistocene glacial drift. Spits, of many sizes and varied compass orientation, abound and there are numerous deltas where streams and rivers enter the sound. Along the eastern side of the Olympic Peninsula is the Hood Canal, a 104-km-long inundated glacial trough.

MAURICE L. SCHWARTZ
THOMAS A. TERICH

REFERENCES

Cooper, W. S., 1958, *Coastal Sand Dunes of Oregon and Washington*, Geol. Soc. America Mem. 72.

Rau, W. W., 1973, *Geology of the Washington Coast*, Washington Dept. Natl. Resources Bull. 66., Olympia.

Rau, W. W., 1980, *Washington Coastal Geology*, Washington Dept. Natl. Resources Bull. 72, Olympia.

Shepard, F. P., and H. R. Wanless, 1971, *Our Changing Coastlines*, McGraw-Hill, New York.

Terich, T. A., and M. L. Schwartz, 1981, A geomorphic classification of Washington State's Pacific Coast, *Shore and Beach* **49:**21–27.

4. OREGON

The coast of Oregon (Fig. 4-1) is part of a convergent margin where the Juan de Fuca oceanic plate to the west is subducted beneath the North American plate to the east. Such margins are characterized by abundant rocky coastal areas with inland mountains, uplifted marine terraces, and an absence of large constructional beach features such as barrier islands (Inman and Nordstrom 1971). Although the Oregon margin has been seismically quiet within historic times, it still conforms with this general setting.

Of the approximately 504-km total length of the Oregon coast, about 202 km (40%) consists of rocky sea cliffs and headlands with little or no fronting beach. Much of the southern one-third of the coast, south of Coos Bay (Fig. 4-1), consists of intensely folded and faulted sandstones, conglomerates, and volcanic rocks, Jurassic and Tertiary in ages. At Coos Bay the coast abruptly changes, with the longest beach on the Oregon coast extending northward for 80 km before reaching another headland (Heceta Head). This beach is backed by fields of both active and well-stabilized dunes (Cooper 1958; Lund 1973). The sands composing these extensive dunes were derived from the beach but are mainly old, having obtained most of their volume during previous high stands of sea level.

The northern half of the Oregon coast consists of a series of beaches of varying lengths, separated by headlands (Fig. 4-1), all but one of which are composed of resistant basalt. Sand spits are common here, some pointing northward, others southward. Many of the beaches are backed by sea cliffs cut into the uplifted marine terraces, exposing the Plio-Pleistocene terrace sands as well as indurated Tertiary marine mudstones and siltstones. Deposits from the shallow continental shelf, ancient beaches, and dunes are represented in the terrace sands (Clifton et al. 1971). Slumping of the sea cliffs is common, often endangering communities that are located on the terraces. Landsliding is particularly severe in the Newport area because of the seaward-dipping mudstones, individual slumps having removed several acres of land and destroying many homes (North and Byrne 1965; Stembridge 1975).

The stretches of beach are backed by bays and estuaries or by geological formations that have little resistance to wave attack. The pronounced rocky headlands stand in contrast, extending out into deep water. The available evidence indicates that beach sand is not able to bypass these major headlands (Komar et al. 1976a). Because of this, the stretches of beach can be viewed as self-contained pocket beaches, even though some of them extend for many kilometers. The beach sands generally have median grain diameters in the range of 0.2–0.5 mm, depending on the particular pocket beach. Sources of sand to the beaches are limited, the primary source being from sea cliff erosion into the terrace sands. The larger coastal rivers end in bays or extensive estuaries, which apparently prevent river sands from reaching the beaches. Based on analyses of heavy mineral contents of the sands, which differ in the beaches and rivers, Kulm and Byrne (1966) concluded that the Yaquina River deposits its sand within the estuary (Fig. 4-1, detail). In addition, large quantities of beach sand are carried into the estuary by tidal currents, making the estuary a deficit in the budget of beach sand. Ongoing research indicates that this is also the case for the other major bays and estuaries on the Oregon coast.

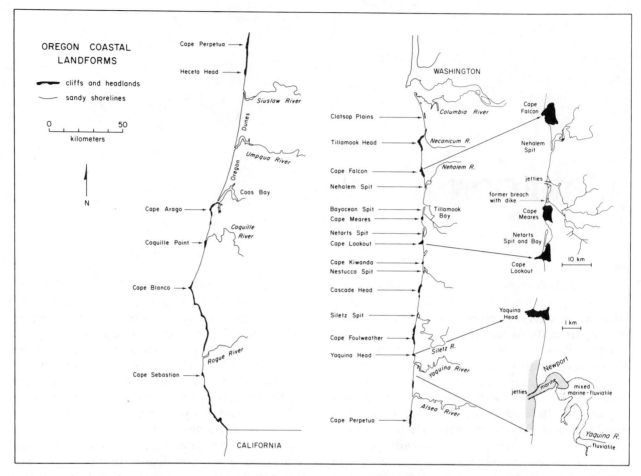

Figure 4-1. Oregon coastal landforms and details, showing a portion of the coast consisting of pocket beaches separated by pronounced rocky headlands and depositional patterns in an Oregon estuary (Yaquina Bay).

The one exception to this picture of the Oregon coast as pocket beaches with a sea cliff sand source is the Clatsop Plains area (Fig. 4-1), the beach extending southward from the Columbia River to the first headland (Tillamook Head). Although most of the sand derived from the Columbia River moves northward into Washington, this 30-km stretch of beach in Oregon represents the southern portion of the "delta" of the Columbia. Backing the modern beach is a series of old beach ridges representing the growth of the Columbia Delta (Cooper 1958).

The Oregon coast is characterized by high wave energies. This has made it difficult to maintain ordinary wave-measuring devices. Instead, wave data have been obtained on a routine basis in an unusual way, with a seismic recording system that detects microseisms produced by the waves (Quinn et al. 1974). This system has been in operation since November 1971, measuring waves

four times daily. These measurements have been analyzed and summarized by Komar et al. (1976*b*) and Creech (1977). There is an annual cycle in the wave energy level, wave breaker heights averaging about 2 m during the summer months and 3–4 m during the winter. Individual storms have been observed to generate breakers with significant wave heights up to 7 m.

Tides have a maximum spring range of about 4 m and an average range of 1.8 m. The tides are mixed, with two highs and two lows each day, the two highs usually being of markedly different levels.

Hicks (1972) has analyzed tide-gauge records from Astoria (within the Columbia River estuary), and from ports in northern California and Washington, all indicating no apparent sea-level changes over the past 30 years for this portion of coast. The present erosion of sea cliffs and headlands, and other coastal changes, must therefore be occurring more in response to a rise in sea level over the last several thousand years, for the coast has not had time to reach a new equilibrium.

Tsunamis have caused some destruction on the Oregon coast, although to a much smaller degree than on other coasts, and mainly within the bays and estuaries rather than on the marine beaches (Schatz et al. 1964; Wilson and Torum 1968). The most recent have originated in and around Alaska, including those of March 28, 1964, and May 16, 1968.

One major consequence of Oregon's beaches being pocket beaches isolated by headlands, and having only small sources and losses of sand, is that the net littoral drift is basically zero. This also results from the seasonality of the wave directions: half the year the waves dominantly arrive from the southwest, the other half from the northwest. The existence of a zero net littoral drift is best substantiated by the patterns of deposition and erosion caused by jetty construction (Komar et al. 1976a; Terich and Komar 1974). Figure 4-2A shows the shoreline changes produced by jetties on the Siuslaw River. The pattern that emerges there and at other jetty systems is one of deposition and shoreline advance to both the immediate north and the immediate south of the jetties; the amount depends on the size of the embayment created between the jetty and the pre-jetty shoreline. The sand that fills the embayments comes from erosion of the coast at greater distances from the jetties. Thus there is an approximately symmetrical pattern of deposition and erosion (Fig. 4-2B) in the case of jetties constructed on a coast with zero net drift, contrasting with coasts where a net drift produces deposition only on the updrift side and erosion in the downdrift direction.

Erosion can therefore result from jetty construction even where a zero net drift prevails, although this erosion ceases once the embayments adjacent to the jetties are filled. But this erosion can be extensive, as seen in the case of Bayocean Spit opposite Tillamook Bay (Fig. 4-1). Early in this century a vacation resort developed on the spit, but jetty construction resulted in its total destruction, eventually breaching the spit (Terich and Komar 1974; Komar and Terich 1977).

More recent episodes of erosion on the Oregon coast have resulted from extreme storms, those that produced the 7-m-high or larger breaking waves. Those erosion problems are for the most part due to natural causes, jetty construction not being a factor. In the case of the erosion of Siletz

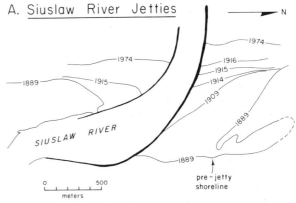

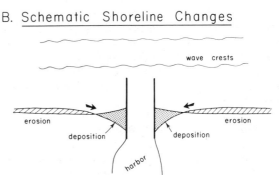

Figure 4-2. *A.* Shoreline changes produced by construction of jetties on the mouth of the Siuslaw River; *B.* A schematic of the depositional and erosional patterns produced by jetty construction on a coast with zero net littoral drift, as at the Siuslaw jetties.

Spit, beach sand mining may have enhanced the erosion (Komar and Rea 1976; Komar and McKinney 1977). Of principal importance to the erosion of Siletz Spit was the development of strong rip currents, which cut embayments into the beach, eventually reaching back to the foredunes on which homes were constructed. It was found that this zone of foredunes followed a cycle: the dunes first eroded away, then over a period of about ten years re-formed only to be eroded again. Dune re-formation resulted from sand blowing landward off the beach; drift logs helped trap the sand. The foredunes apparently had gone through many such cycles of erosion and re-formation before homes were built on them. Similar erosion has occurred on Nestucca Spit; an exceptional storm in 1978 during spring tides led to its washover and breaching, an unusual event on the emergent West Coast of the United States (Komar 1978).

PAUL D. KOMAR

REFERENCES

Clifton, H. E., R. E. Hunter, and R. L. Phillips, 1971, Depositional structures and processes in the non-barred high-energy nearshore, *Jour. Sed. Petrology* **41:**651–670.

Cooper, W. S., 1958, Coastal Sand Dunes of Oregon and Washington, *Geol. Soc. America* Mem. 72.

Creech, H. C., 1977, *Five Year Climatology (1972–1976) of Nearshore Ocean Waves off Yaquina Bay, Oregon,* Oregon State Univ. Sea Grant Program Ref. ORESU–T–27–011, Corvallis.

Hicks, S. D., 1972, On the classification and trends of long period sea level series, *Shore and Beach* **40:**20–23.

Inman, D. L. and C. E. Nordstrom, 1971, On the tectonic and morphologic classification of coasts, *Jour. Geology* **79:**1–21.

Komar, P. D., 1978, Wave conditions on the Oregon coast during the winter of 1977–78 and the resulting erosion of Nestucca Spit, *Shore and Beach* **46:**3–8.

Komar, P. D., and C. C. Rea, 1976, Erosion of Siletz Spit, Oregon, *Shore and Beach* **44:**9–15.

Komar, P. D., J. R. Lizarraga, and T. A. Terich, 1976*a*, *Oregon coast shoreline changes due to jetties*, Am. Soc. Civil Engineers Proc., *Jour. Waterways, Harbors and Coastal Engineering* **102**(WW1):13–30.

Komar, P. D., W. Quinn, H. C. Creech, C. C. Rea, and J. R. Lizarraga-Arciniega, 1976*b*, Wave conditions and beach erosion on the Oregon coast, *Ore Bin* **38:**103–112.

Komar, P. D., and B. A. McKinney, 1977, The spring 1976 erosion of Siletz Spit, Oregon, with an analysis of the causative storm conditions, *Shore and Beach* **45:**23–30.

Komar, P. D., and T. A. Terich, 1977, Changes due to jetties at Tillamook Bay, Oregon, *15th Conf. on Coastal Eng. Proc.* pp. 1791–1811.

Kulm, L. D., and J. V. Byrne, 1966, Sedimentary response to hydrology in an Oregon estuary, *Marine Geology* **4:**85–118.

Lund, E. H., 1973, Oregon coastal dunes between Coos Bay and Sea Lion Point, *Ore Bin* **35:**73–92.

North, W. B., and J. V. Byrne, 1965, Coastal landslides in northern Oregon, *Ore Bin* **27:**217–241.

Quinn, W. H., H. C. Creech, and D. E. Zopf, 1974, Coastal wave observations via seismometer, *Mariners Weather Log* **18:**367–369.

Schatz, C. E., H. Curl, and W. V. Burt, 1964, Tsunami on the Oregon coast, *Ore Bin* **26:**231–232.

Stembridge, J. E., 1975, *Shoreline Changes and Physiographic Hazards on the Oregon Coast,* Ph.D. dissertation, Dept. of Geography, Univ. of Oregon, Eugene.

Terich, T. A., and P. D. Komar, 1974, Bayocean Spit, Oregon: history of development and erosional destruction, *Shore and Beach* **42:**3–10.

Wilson, B. W., and A. Torum, 1968, *The Tsunami of the Alaskan Earthquake, 1964: Engineering evaluation,* U.S. Army Corps Engineers Coastal Eng. Research Center, Tech. Memo. 25, Washington, D.C.

5. CALIFORNIA

The California coast is about 2,900 km long, including San Francisco Bay and offshore islands. Some 70% of the coast is rocky or cliffed, although pocket and fringing beaches commonly occur below the cliffs. The rest comprises either sandy fringing beaches backed by dunes, as south of San Luis Obispo, barrier beaches fronting lagoons and wetlands, as near Eureka, or the wetlands around San Francisco Bay. About 85% of the coast is actively eroding. Although long stretches of exposed west-facing shores remain largely natural, extensive stretches around San Francisco, Los Angeles, and San Diego have been much altered by development. Of the original 80,000 ha of wetlands (excluding San Francisco Bay), 52% have been destroyed by dredging and filling, and a further 40% have been moderately or severely damaged.

The coast embraces five geomorphic provinces—the Klamath Mountains, Northern Coast Ranges, Southern Coast Ranges, Transverse Ranges, and Peninsular Ranges (Fig. 5-1). These provinces are structural units whose geology and relief reflect post-Paleozoic interaction between the westward-moving North American lithospheric plate and subducting plates farther west. California's structural framework began to emerge in late Jurassic and Cretaceous times as the Nevadan Orogeny caused the ancestral Kalmath Mountains, Sierra Nevada, and Peninsular Ranges to rise from shallow seas and an island arc along the western margins of the North American plate, accompanied by westward thrusting, volcanism, and batholith emplacement. Subduction of marine sedimentary and volcanic rocks in the deep eugeosynclinal trench along this plate margin, followed by uplift, produced the Franciscan Formation, a heterogeneous jumble of readily erodible grey-wackes, shales, and metamorphic rocks found throughout the Coast Ranges (Fig. 5-2). During late Cretaceous and Cenozoic times, great thicknesses of clastic sediments and submarine volcanics accumulated in subsiding basins along the continental margin and strike-slip faulting became significant. Orogenic activity culminated in the uplift of coastal mountains from Miocene to mid-Pleistocene times. Coastal lowlands were restricted to subsiding intermontane troughs (Ventura Basin), to pull-apart structures (Santa Maria Basin), or to the seaward ends of strike valleys (Eureka Basin). During Neogene times, the North American plate approached and then overran the East Pacific Rise, a complex spreading center in the Pacific plate. As that portion of California west of the San Andreas Fault transferred to the western limbs of this spreading center, the Peninsular Ranges mini-plate (including Baja California) accelerated northwest from 2–5 cm/yr, causing the Transverse Ranges to rotate into their present east-west alignment. Reflecting the influence of en echelon transform structures in the subducted East Pacific Rise, extensive strike-slip faulting with locally intense thrust faulting came to dominate coastal zone structures and landforms.

Tectonism has persisted throughout Quaternary times, as shown by deformed and faulted marine terraces and subsiding coastal basins. A spectacular flight of 13 marine terraces occurs on the Palos Verdes Peninsula, the highest at 380 m above sea level being equated with nearby mid-Pleistocene deposits (Woodring et al. 1946; Wehmiller et al. 1977). A similar terrace sequence occurs on San Clemente Island to the south. On San Nicolas Island farther west, a 240-m terrace

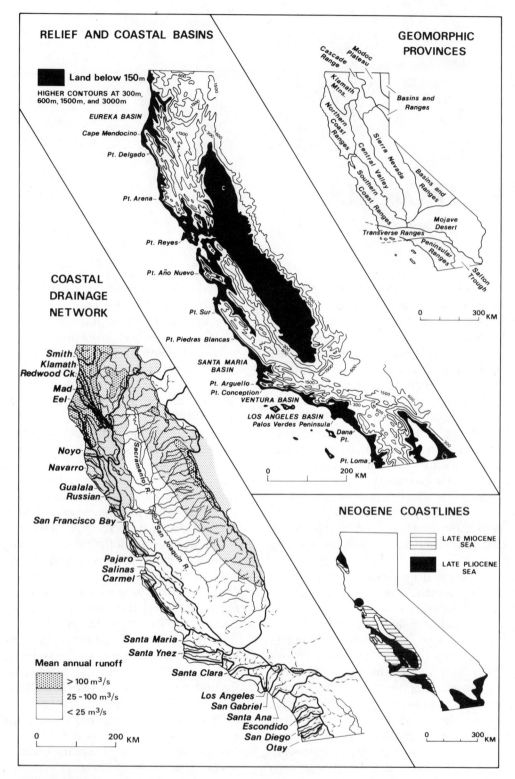

Figure 5-1. Geomorphic provinces, relief and coastal basins, coastal drainage network, and Neogene coastlines of California.

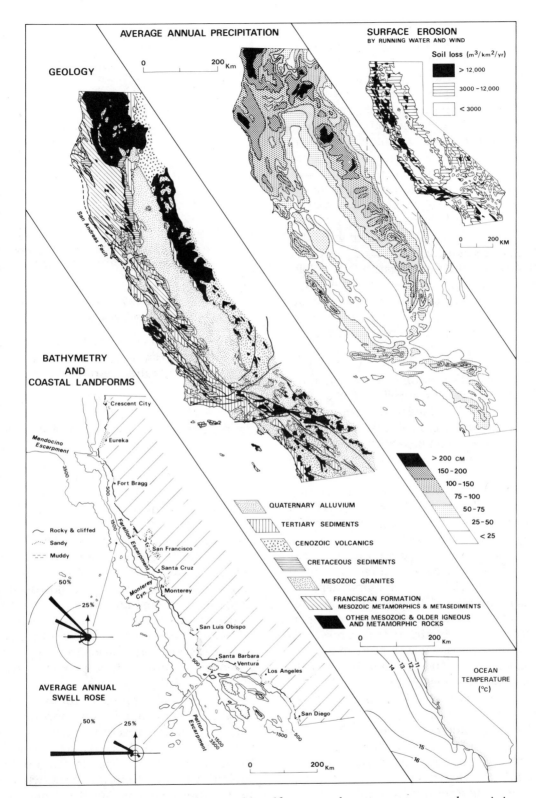

Figure 5-2. Bathymetry and coastal landforms, geology, average annual precipitation, and surface erosion of California.

is assigned a mid-Pleistocene age, while a 120-m terrace is dated at 190,000 years. Fragments of high terraces are indeed found throughout the coast — from the deformed sequence near Eureka, along the seaward slopes of the Coast Ranges, to the extensive mesas around San Diego where the 90–150-m Linda Vista terrace and its fossil barrier beaches are considered 1 million years old. However, it is the last (Sangamon) interglacial terraces that provide the most continuous record of Quaternary tectonism. Terraces at 6 m and −14 m near San Diego have been dated at 120,000 and 80,000 years B.P. (Kern 1977); a 23–45-m terrace at Palos Verdes has been dated at 85,000 years; 30-m terraces along the Malibu coast have ages of 130,000 and 105,000 years; while a Holocene terrace forms part of an impressive sequence west of Ventura, where uplift of 10 m/1,000 yr has characterized the past 0.6 million years (Yeats 1978; see Orme 1980 for comprehensive bibliography). Terrace uplift and deformation is also impressive between Santa Cruz and San Francisco.

Evidence for coastal submergence — eustatic, isostatic, tectonic — is also compelling. The Ventura Basin, for example, subsided tectonically at rates up to 9.5 m/1,000 yr from 2.0–0.6 million years ago, allowing a 7-km thickness of Plio-Pleistocene sediments to accumulate beneath the Oxnard Plain. More recently, Flandrian seas entered the Golden Gate about 10,000 years ago and, rising at a rate of 2 cm/yr, flooded laterally across San Francisco Bay as rapidly as 30 m/yr until 8,000 years ago (Atwater et al. 1977; Fig. 5-3). The rate of sea-level rise then declined and for the past 6,000 years has averaged 0.1–0.2 cm/yr. During this time, however, Holocene salt marsh deposits have undergone 5 m of tectonic and possibly isostatic subsidence, a rate of 0.8 mm/yr superimposed onto the Flandrian transgression's eustatic effects. Subsidence is even more pronounced along the San Andreas Fault zone through Bolinas Lagoon (Berquist, 1978; Fig. 5-3).

Over the past century, tide-gauge data show that sea level has been rising at an average rate of 1.5 mm/yr along much of the coast (Hicks and Crosby 1974). Thus, despite ample evidence for Quaternary uplift and deformation, recent coastal changes must be viewed against the Flandrian transgression and a continuing sea-level rise.

Tides, winds, waves, currents, tsunamis, mass wasting, sediment discharge, and human activity all influence the patterns of coastal erosion and deposition. The coast is mesotidal, spring tidal ranges average 2.5 m, and tides are mixed. Tidal currents are important, notably the swift

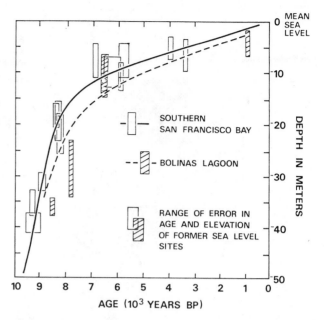

Figure 5-3. Holocene sea-level changes in southern San Francisco Bay (after Atwater et al. 1977) and Bolinas Lagoon (after Berquist 1978).

reversing currents through the Golden Gate, where the flood may reach 1.7 m/s and the ebb 2.3 m/s, augmented as it is by the head of stream discharge through San Francisco Bay. At the mouth of Tomales Bay, the ebb current clashes with incoming swells to form dangerous 3-m sneaker waves over the bar.

Prevailing winds reach the coast from the northwest as shown by sand dune orientation and predominant swell directions. This is because in summer, a strong clockwise outflow of air derives from the Hawaiian high-pressure cell to the west. In winter this cell is weaker and farther south, but counter-clockwise flow toward the Aleutian low and eastward progressions of cold fronts across California maintain these prevailing winds for much of the time. North of Point Conception, 30–50% of swells approach from the northwest and most others from the west-northwest or west (Fig. 5-2). South of Point Conception, changing coastal orientation, strong refraction, and offshore islands cause 70% of swells to pass up the Santa Barbara Channel from due west, while 80% of swells approach Los Angeles from the west-southwest. Here also, southerly swells set up by late summer hurricanes off western Mexico, by Southern Hemisphere winter storms, and by local winter depressions passing along more southerly tracks may cause erosion on south-facing beaches. Wave heights at Ventura average 1 m but range from 0.3–7.0 m (Orme 1982). The predominant northwest swells set up strong longshore currents, up to 2 m/s, and littoral drift from north to south (Plate 5-1), although northward drift may be favored by shore configuration and reversing currents. The effect of the 1,000-km-wide cold California Current (mean velocity 0.1–0.3 m/s; net discharge 11×10^6 m^3/s; Fig. 5-2) is more climatic and ecological than geomorphic, but fog affects weathering and soil moisture on coastal slopes, and the current and its inshore countercurrent can transport fines flushed out of coastal rivers. Tsunamis occasionally affect the coast, such as after the 1964 Alaska earthquake, when 7-m waves damaged Crescent City.

Stream sediment discharge, so important for nourishing California's beaches, reflects the availability of rock waste, the precipitation and runoff patterns, and the extent to which fluvial transport is blocked by dams. Along the northern California coast, erodible rocks, steep slopes, and high precipitation and runoff combine to produce frequent landslides and high erosion rates (Fig. 5-2). The Klamath, Eel, and Russian rivers alone account for 77% of all fine-grained sediment discharged to the sea north of Point Conception. Sediments yielded by the Sacramento-San Joaquin river system are mostly deposited before reaching the ocean. Farther south, Franciscan rocks and Cenozoic sediments are similarly erodible and prone to mass movement, but whether this debris reaches the coast depends on the winter precipitation regime, notably on the frequency of high-magnitude stormflows. For example, most of the 9.0×10^6 tonnes of sand delivered to the shore by the Santa Clara River between 1933 and 1938 arrived in 6 days of floods in 1938. Further, sediment discharged by this river in the 1969 floods was 47.6×10^6 tonnes, compared with 1 or 2×10^6 tonnes in relatively dry years. The coastal sediment budget of southern California thus sees years of plenty (most recently 1969, 1978, 1980, 1983) and years of famine (the 30 years preceding the 1969 floods). Mass movement from sea cliffs and coastal slopes is also an important sediment source, notably where fractured or poorly consolidated rocks occur, but this source has been both aggravated and curtailed by road and other construction, for example, along the Malibu coast west of Los Angeles and on the Big Sur coast. In many places, for one reason or another, Pleistocene landslides and slumps have been reactivated in recent times, often through changes in ground-water hydrology (Plate 5-2).

The northern California coast is underlain by pulverized eugeosynclinal Franciscan rocks whose greywackes and shales, though forest-covered, are prone to frequent mass movement and rapid erosion. These rocks strike northwest and have been eroded into narrow valleys separated by elongate ridges. The most westerly ridge, the Mendocino Range, stretches 350 km north from the Golden Gate bounded on the east by the Eel River-Russian River corridor and on the west west by the San Andreas Fault, which, except for fragments of Salinian basement to the west, defines the coast as far north as Cape Mendocino. The Russian River cuts seaward in a 1,000-m-deep gorge across the strike, reflecting recent uplift. North of Cape Mendocino, the coast turns north and several strike valleys open obliquely to the sea. On this exposed coast, 4–7-m waves are readily generated by winter storms, while waves up to 13.5 m high have been recorded at Crescent City. Prominent sea cliffs characterized by active erosion and mass movement occur north and south of the Klamath River, between Cape Mendocino and Cape Vizcaino, between the Gualala and Russian rivers, and between Drake's Bay and Bolinas and thence to the Golden Gate (Plate 5-3). Since the U.S. Coast Survey was conducted in 1859, Duxbury Point and Bolinas Point have retreated 50 and 60 m respectively, a rate of 0.5 m/yr. Marine terraces fronted by lower cliffs occur near Crescent City, Trinidad, Cape Mendocino, and between Mendocino and Fort Ross. Offshore rocks and sea stacks are common. Elsewhere abundant sediment discharge nourishes local beaches. The Smith, Klamath, Mad, Eel, Mattole, and Gualala rivers all reach the sea through wetlands fronted by unstable sand spits. The wetlands of Arcata and Humboldt bays, near Eureka, are largely separated from the ocean by a 60-km-long barrier beach topped with active and vegetated sand dunes. Barrier beaches also front lagoons south of Redwood Creek while barrier spits occur at Bodega Bay, Drake's Bay, and Bolinas Lagoon (Plates 5-1, 5-4). Sand dunes occur extensively south of the Smith River, north of Fort Bragg, Bodega Bay, and Point Arena, and for 18 km along the northwestern face of the Point Reyes peninsula—indeed, wherever coastal configuration is perpendicular to prevailing wind direction.

San Francisco Bay occupies a late Pliocene to mid-Pleistocene structural trough within the Coast Ranges. The trough has a Franciscan basement bounded by northwest-trending strike-slip faults and is largely filled with Neogene and Quaternary marine and fluvial sediments. Continuing tectonism apart, this trough has been further deepened by fluvial erosion and flooded several times by Quaternary transgressions (Atwater et al. 1977). The bay is connected to the Central Valley through the Carquinez Strait, whose bedrock channel was cut by the ancestral Sacramento River to 60 m below sea level, and to the Pacific Ocean through the Golden Gate, whose channel is scoured to -104 m. San Francisco Bay is a natural sump for an 80,000-km² drainage area comprising the Sacramento-San Joaquin system. Some 200 years ago, bay waters covered 1,800 km²; today they cover 1,100 km², and 70% of the 90-km-long bay is shallower than 4 m. This size reduction is due in part to massive fluvial sedimentation during the hydraulic gold mining period in the Sierra Nevada foothills during the latter half of the nineteenth century, in part to subsequent sedimentation, and in part to extensive shoreline reclamation. Gilbert (1917) estimated that $1,816 \times 10^6$ m³ of debris were eroded in the foothills by mining and natural processes between 1850 and 1914, of which 50% was redeposited downstream, 48% reached the bay, and only 2% reached the ocean. He also estimated that it would take 50 years (until 1964) for the upstream debris to reach the bay, after which a "normal" load of about 6×10^6 m³/yr would enter the bay—a figure that accords well with recent estimates. Present bay waters have a salinity of 27–29 parts per thousand; fetch is limited and breaker heights average 0.3 m, tidal currents rarely exceed 1 m/s within the bay, and average inflow of water from the Sacramento–San Joaquin Delta is 570 m³/s. Three environments characterize this relatively low-energy shore: tidal marshes around mean high water dominated by *Spartina leiantha*, *Distichlis spicata*, and *Salicornia ambigua* zones; upper tidal flats between mean high and mean low water; and lower tidal flats below mean low water (Pestrong 1972). About 200 km² of marshes and mudflats are exposed at mean tide level.

The Southern Coast Ranges extend 400 km southeast from the Golden Gate to Point Arguello and, as farther north, are dominated by massive deformation and faulting, strike valleys, and elongate ridges. Between the San Andreas and Nacimiento fault zones, metamorphic and granitic rocks form the 60-km-wide Salinian basement. These rocks reach the coast in rugged slide-prone cliffs south of Pacifica and again south of Monterey. Elsewhere the Salinian basement is covered with late Cretaceous and Tertiary sediments, which reach the coast north of Monterey Bay in deformed marine terraces and eroding sea cliffs (Bradley and Griggs 1976). Terrace uplift rates range from

0.16–0.26 m/1,000 yr. Long-term sea cliff erosion rates range from zero in resistant granodiorites to 0.3 m/yr or more in softer Tertiary sediments, and to 0.6 m/yr locally (Griggs and Johnson 1979). Extensive sand dunes around Monterey Bay are explained in part by the abundance of sediment formerly brought down by the Pajaro and Salinas rivers. For 150 km south from Monterey, the Santa Lucia Range dominates the coast, often reaching 1,000 m within 2 km of the shore. Where Franciscan rocks reappear west of the Nacimiento Fault, landsliding is a perennial problem (Plates 5-5, 5-6). South of Ragged Point, the mountains trend inland, marine terraces reappear, and broad structural basins are veneered with extensive dunes of late Pleistocene, early Holocene, and recent age, most notably behind 25 km of sandy beach between Pismo Beach and Point Sal (Plate 5-7). Sediment for these dunes comes mainly from the Arroyo Grande, and from the Santa Maria and Santa Ynez rivers. Cliff erosion threatens homes and roads at Cayucos, Avila Beach, and Shell Beach, despite partial shelter from northwesterly swells. The Morro Bay wetlands are largely protected by a long barrier spit.

The Transverse Ranges reach the coast in three distinct structural units: the Santa Ynez Mountains, the Oxnard Plain, and the Santa Monica Mountains. The Santa Ynez Mountains (1,430 m), extending 125 km east from Point Arguello to Ventura, are a south-dipping homocline of mostly Tertiary marine and fluvial sediments, whose Quaternary uplift is reflected in grossly deformed marine terraces along the western and southern coasts. Though protected by offshore islands, refracted westerly swells have promoted average erosion rates of 0.15 m/yr in the relatively soft Neogene sediments along the southern coast. A small barrier-lagoon system survives at Carpinteria. The Oxnard Plain is a triangular depositional lowland, created most recently by the Santa Clara River and Calleguas Creek, where the Ventura structural trough plunges westward into the Santa Barbara Channel. The coastline once comprised a sandy barrier beach, with low dunes backed by lagoons and marshes, breached by winter's flooding rivers. This natural system has been much changed by construction along the shore—a groin field at Ventura (1962–1967), Ventura Marina (1963), Channel Islands Harbor (1961, Plate 5-8), and Port Hueneme (1938–1940). With prevailing westerly swells, the predominant littoral drift is from Northwest to Southeast, moving about 750,000 m³/yr of sediment downcoast (Plate 5-9). The Santa Monica Mountains (949 m), which extend 50 km along the coast between Point Mugu and Santa Monica, and the Channel Islands (Anacapa, Santa Cruz, Santa Rosa, San Miguel) to the west are geologically similar. They are underlain by metamorphic or granitic basement rocks and mantled with thick late Cretaceous and Tertiary materials, notably by Miocene marine shales and volcanics. The Santa Monica Mountains are bounded to the south by the active Malibu thrust fault, whose impact is seen in seismic activity, deformed terraces, fractured coastal rocks, and frequent mass movement. Much of the coast is typified by unwise housing development on the backshore or beneath crumbling cliffs, creating inevitable problems during storms and southerly swells.

The Peninsular Ranges extend south-southeast for 200 km from the Malibu–Raymond Hill Fault behind Los Angeles to the Mexican border, and then a further 1,350 km to the tip of Baja California. This mini-plate, comprising basement rocks, granitic plutons, and post-batholithic sediments, has been accelerating away from the North American mainland at a mean rate of 6 cm/yr since it shifted onto the western limb of the East Pacific Rise some 4-5 million years ago. Along the coast, deformed marine terraces such as those on Palos Verdes, San Onofre Mountain, and around San Diego (Plate 5-10), and active faults, such as the Inglewood–Rose Canyon structural zone that outlines the coast between Newport Bay and San Diego, attest to continuing tectonism. Barrier-lagoon systems were once common along this coast, but most have been modified, and some obliterated, by human activity. Ballona Lagoon, once an outlet for the Los Angeles River, is now a marina; the Long Beach system is now a port-industrial-urban complex; Newport Bay, until 1915 the outlet for the Santa Ana River, is heavily developed; and San Diego Bay, formerly the San Diego River outlet, is now an important naval and commercial harbor. Even six small barrier-lagoons in northern San Diego County are controlled. Erosion is a significant problem along much of this coast. Powerful swells break through windows between the offshore islands, rocks are often poorly consolidated and, owing to flood-control dams and channelization along most local rivers, less sediment appears to be reaching the coast in recent times. Sea cliff erosion is particularly evident in front of Camp Pendleton, south of Oceanside harbor, near Encinitas and Del Mar, and at Sunset Cliffs, San Diego. Inappropriate cliff-top development has generally aggravated the problem, for example, through irrigation and lawn watering, increased impermeable surfaces, and poorly located culverts.

Offshore California is represented north of Point Conception by a shelf and slope, and southward by a continental borderland (Fig. 5-2). The relatively narrow northern shelf widens to 50 km off the Golden Gate but is dissected by several submarine canyons, notably Delgada, Noyo, and Bodega canyons off northern California and Sur, Lucia, and Arguello canyons farther south. The largest of all is the Monterey Canyon, which heads within 0.8 km of the shore but dissects the shelf and slope to a depth of over 3,500 m. A large lunate sand bar composed of terrestrial sediments lies off the Golden Gate. The continental borderland off southern California comprises a series of fault blocks and troughs, with some closed basins and rugged emergent islands. These structures trend east-west off the Transverse Ranges and northwest-southeast farther south, and their origins must be related to the Cenozoic behavior of the adjacent land areas (Emery 1960). At least 32 distinct submarine canyons dissect southern California's offshore area.

ANTONY R. ORME

REFERENCES

Atwater, B. F., C. W. Hedel, and E. J. Helley, 1977, *Late Quaternary Depositional History, Holocene Sea-Level Changes, and Vertical Crustal Movement, Southern San Francisco Bay, California*, U.S. Geol. Survey Prof. Paper 1014, Washington, D.C.

Berquist, J. R., 1978, *Depositional History and Fault-Related Studies, Bolinas Lagoon, California*, U.S. Geol. Survey Open-File Rept. 78–802, Washington, D.C.

Bradley, W. C., and G. B. Griggs, 1976, Form, genesis, and deformation of central California wave-cut platforms, *Geol. Soc. America Bull.* **87:**433–449.

Emery, K. O., 1960, *The Sea off Southern California*, Wiley, New York.

Gilbert, G. K., 1917, *Hydraulic-Mining Debris in the Sierra Nevada*, U.S. Geol. Survey Prof. Paper 105, Washington, D.C.

Griggs, G. B., and R. E. Johnson, 1979, Coastline erosion, Santa Cruz County, *California Geology* **32:**67-76.

Hicks, S. D., and J. E. Crosby, 1974, *Trends and Variability of Yearly Mean Sea Level 1893-1972*, U.S. Natl. Oceanic and Atmospheric Admin. Tech. Memo. NOS 13, Washington, D.C.

Kern, J. P., 1977, Origin and history of upper Pleistocene marine terraces, San Diego, California, *Geol. Soc. America Bull.* **88:**1553-1566.

Oakeshott, G. B., 1978, *California's Changing Landscapes*, McGraw-Hill, New York.

Orme, A. R., 1980, Marine terraces and Quaternary tectonism, northwest Baja California, Mexico, *Physical Geography* **1:**138–161.

Orme, A. R., 1982, Temporal variability of a summer shore zone, in *Space and Time in Geomorphology*, C. E. Thorn, ed., George Allen & Unwin, London.

Pestrong, R., 1972, San Francisco Bay tidelands, *California Geology* **25:**27–40.

Wehmiller, J. F., K. R. Lajoie, K. A. Kvenvolden, E. Peterson, D. F. Belknap, G. L. Kennedy, W. O. Addicott, J. G. Vedder, and R. W. Wright, 1977, *Correlation and Chronology of Pacific Coast Marine Terrace Deposits of Continental United States by Fossil Amino Acid and Stereochemistry—Technique Evaluation, Relative Ages, Kinetic Model Ages, and Geological Implications*, U.S. Geol. Survey Open-File Rept. 77–680, Washington, D.C.

Woodring, W. P., M. N. Bramlette, and W. S. W. Kew, 1946, *Geology and Paleontology of Palos Verdes Hills, California*, U.S. Geol. Survey Prof. Paper 207, Washington, D.C.

Yeats, R. S., 1978, Neogene acceleration of subsidence rates in southern California, *Geology* **6:**456–460.

Plate 5-1. Structural control is strongly evident along the northern California coast. The active San Andreas Fault zone extends 80 km northwest from Bolinas Lagoon (lower right) through Tomales Bay and Bodega Bay to beyond the Russian River (upper left), whose southward-drifting sediment plume is also seen. The Point Reyes peninsula and Bodega Head lie west of the fault zone. The epicenter of the 1906 San Francisco earthquake lay 15 km northwest of Bolinas Lagoon (photo courtesy of NASA).

Plate 5-2. Mass movement is a significant process along the California coast, as shown here on the north side of Santa Cruz Island, where a late Pleistocene slump has been reactivated in recent times and its toe is being actively cliffed. The skyline rises to 350 m (photo by A. R. Orme).

Plate 5-3. Active sea cliffs cut in gently deformed Pliocene marine sediments, Drake's Bay, Point Reyes peninsula (photo by A. R. Orme).

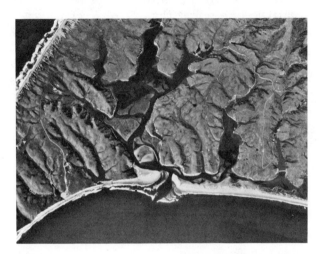

Plate 5-4. On the Point Reyes peninsula, subsidence and rising sea level have drowned Drake's Estero, which is now almost cut off from Drake's Bay by the Limantour barrier spit. Except for changes around the outlet, this barrier has been relatively stable since 1850 (photo courtesy of NASA).

Plate 5-5. Point Sur is an island of Franciscan metavolcanics tied to the mainland by a tombolo of Holocene beach and dune sand and Upper Pleistocene marine terrace deposits (photo by A. R. Orme).

Plate 5-6. For 150 km south from Monterey, pulverized Mesozoic granites, metasediments, metavolcanics, greywackes, and shales of the Santa Lucia Range descend steeply to the sea. Fragments of Pleistocene marine terraces are broken by deep canyons but long stretches of coast are dominated by active mass movement and cliff retreat (photo by A. R. Orme).

Plate 5-7. South of Pismo Beach, Santa Maria Basin, modern transverse dunes are driven inland by northwesterly winds across earlier Holocene and late Pleistocene dune complexes (photo by K. R. Mulligan).

Plate 5-8. Channel Islands Harbor, excavated in 1961 in the barrier-lagoon system fronting the Oxnard Plain, is typical of the intensive development to which portions of the California coast have been exposed. The 400-m-long entrance jetties are protected by a 700-m-long detached breakwater offset upcoast to provide a sand trap from which 750,000 m³ of sand are dredged every two years to nourish downcoast beaches (photo by L. O'Hirok).

Plate 5-10. On the west coast of Point Loma, San Diego, dipping Upper Cretaceous marine sediments are truncated by Upper Pleistocene shore platforms, backed by 100-m fossil cliffs, and overlain by raised beach and colluvial deposits. The 6-m terrace beneath these deposits is dated at 120,000 years BP (Kern 1977) (photo by A. J. Brown).

Plate 5-9. The Santa Clara River flooding seaward across the Oxnard Plain, Ventura Basin, on March 9, 1983. Consistent with the predominant littoral drift, the sediment plume is being dispersed southeast (photo by L. O'Hirok).

6. PACIFIC MEXICO

The Pacific coastline of Mexico is 6,500 km long, including the coasts of the Peninsula de California. The western edge of the Peninsula de California, and from Puerto Vallarta to Guatemala, has been classified as a continental collision coast; the eastern edge of the peninsula, and from the Colorado River delta to Puerto Vallarta, has been classified as a neo-trailing-edge coast (Inman and Nordstrom 1971, Carranza et al. 1975). The western margin of Mexico is characterized by a mountainous cordillera that is a result of tectonic activity. Ancient rocks have been folded, faulted, and metamorphosed; igneous rocks and mineralized zones have been intruded. Recently, volcanism has affected the surface. South-central Mexico contains the following cordilleras: the Sierra Madre del Sur (Late Mesozoic-Tertiary), the Sierra de Oaxaca (Mesozoic), and the Eje Neovolcánico (Late Tertiary). The Balsas River has been able to erode a channel and discharge into the ocean, across the Sierra Madre del Sur. This sierra extends parallel to the coast from Puerto Vallarta to Salina Cruz. Its core consists of hard igneous and metamorphic rocks covered by volcanics. South to Salina Cruz, the main tectonic units are the Isthmian metamorphic zone (Paleozoic-Mesozoic) and the Macizo de Chiapas (Paleozoic-Mesozoic). Northward from Puerto Vallarta is the Sierra Madre Occidental (Mesozoic-Tertiary), a large cordillera that extends from the Eje Neovolcánico to Sonora (Fig. 6-1). The Rio Grande de Santiago is located within this tectonic unit and drains the tectonic lake of Chapala. On the Peninsula de California (Fig. 6-1), the morphologic and tectonic units are the sierras de Juárez (Mesozoic) and La Giganta (Tertiary), and the basins of Victoria and Vizcaino (Cretaceous), and Purisima Iray (Tertiary). The coastal mountain flank is wide in Michoacan and Oaxaca, where it averages 70 and 90 km respectively. It can be divided physiographically into basins of coastal rivers. In addition, the mean elevation of the mountains is highest in the southeast (2,200–2,700 m), and decreases to the northwest (Tamayo 1962). Some of the largest and most influential coastal basins are those of the Tehuantepec, Ometepec, Coahuayana, Ameca, Baluarte, Huamaya, and Concepción rivers.

The shelf bordering the Sierra Madre del Sur is virtually nonexistent (Shepard 1973). The width varies from about 5 km just south of the Michoacan-Colima boundary and in western Guerrero, to 50 km in northern Sonora. At least one major submarine canyon cuts the shelf (Reimnitz and Gutiérrez-Estrada 1970). The shelf surface is irregular, consisting of areas of rocky bottom (Zihuatanejo), and flat-bottom areas of unconsolidated detrital sediments (arenaceous-argillaceous); clays are along the shelf where large rivers empty into the ocean.

On the basis of dominance of marine erosion versus terrestrial erosion, the coast can be divided into rocky eroded coasts and sediment-prograding coasts (Fig. 6-1). The former are characteristic from Puerto Vallarta to Chiapas and along the Peninsula de California coast, where the relatively high relief has caused the development of steep cliffs and coastal canyons (Plates 6-1 and 6-2); discontinuous beaches of sand with a bouldery substrate are present. Where erosive processes of the land predominate, the coast is irregular with capes and bays, pocket beaches, and esteros (Zihuatanejo). Land topography is characterized by valleys and canyons that meet the sea, as along the coast of Sinaloa, where large deltaic complexes

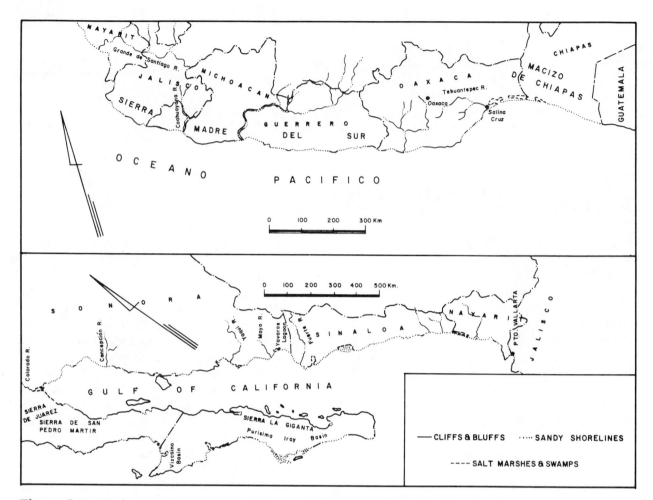

Figure 6-1. Predominant coastal landforms of the Mexico Pacific coast.

have been developed (Gutiérrez-Estrada 1972). In the latter type of coast, the relief is relatively low; the shore zone is variable in width (Plate 6-3). Beaches and adjacent coastal-deltaic plains are well developed (Tehuantepec, Nayarit, Sinaloa, Sonora) (Plate 6-4). Coastal lagoons are common (Plate 6-5) and protected from the sea by barriers formed by old beach ridges and dunes (Yavaros lagoon) (Ayala-Castañares et al. 1980). Coasts formed by active river sedimentation are arcuate to deltaic in shape. The shore zone is wide with multiple distributaries. Mangrove swamps are common (Balsas River) (Gutiérrez-Estrada 1969).

The coast is subjected to semiannual change in the direction of wave approach and littoral current. On the relatively straight shore the current is dominantly to the southeast in October to March, but it reverses during April to September. Along rocky shores (Plates 6-6, 6-7) the current has a uniform direction all the year. Tides gener-

ally are mixed-diurnal. Maximum vertical changes (80–160 cm) occur during the solstices, the minimum (20–40 cm) in the equinoxes. Tide ranges increase into the Gulf of California.

MARIO GUTIÉRREZ-ESTRADA
MARIO ARTURO ORTIZ-PEREZ

REFERENCES

Ayala-Castañares, A., V. M. Maplica-Cruz, and M. Gutiérrez-Estrada, 1980, Geología Marina de la Región de Yavaros, Sonora, México, *An. Centro Cienc. del Mar y Limnol. Univ. Nal. Autón. México* **7**(2):275–289.

Carranza-Edwards, A., M. Gutiérrez-Estrada, and R. Rodriguez-Torres, 1975, Unidades Morfo-Tectónicas Continentales de las Costas Mexicanas, *An. Centro Cienc. del Mar y Limnol. Univ. Nal. Autón. México* **2**(1):81–88.

Gutiérrez-Estrada, M., 1971, Fisiografía y Sedimentología del Delta del Río Balsas, Michoacán, México. *México Univ. Nal. Autón. Inst. Geol. Bol.* **93:**1–58.

Gutiérrez-Estrada, M., 1972, Clasificación preliminar de las costas mexicanas consideradas como bordes de placas o bordes continentales, para su análisis posterior en el proyecto de Geodinámica, *Unión Geofísica Mexicana. Reunión Anual, 1972, Programas y Resúmenes.*

Inman, D. L., and C. E. Nordstrom, 1971, On the tectonic and morphological classification of coasts, *Jour. Geology* **79**(1):1–21.

Reimnitz, E., and M. Gutiérrez-Estrada, 1970, Rapid changes in the head of the Rio Balsas submarine canyon, *Marine Geology* **8:**245–258.

Shepard, F. P., 1973, *Submarine Geology,* Harper & Row, New York.

Tamayo, L. J., 1962, *Geografía General de México,* vol. I, Inst. Mexicano de Investigaciones Económicas, Mexico City.

Plate 6-1. Rudistid reef in Cretaceous Rosario Formation at Punta Banda, Pacific coast of Peninsula de California (photo by S. R. Morgan).

Plate 6-3. Mexcaltitlan Island at Agua Brava lagoonal complex, Nayarit. Note the system of old beach ridges partially covered by water and mangrove swamps (photo courtesy of DGGTNAL).

Plate 6-2. Harbor at Santa Rosalia, Gulf of California coast of Peninsula de California (photo by S. R. Morgan)

Plate 6-4. Extensive spits that partially enclose the Matanchen Bay, Nayarit. Observe the concave system of old beach ridges (photo courtesy of DGGTNAL).

Plate 6-5. Agiabampo Lagoon, along the southern flank of the Mayo River delta, with extensive mangrove swamps nearby and at the wide tidal inlet. Curved spits indicate the prevalent longshore transport. Note the high stabilized dunes along the inner lagoonal shore (photo courtesy of CIFSA).

Plate 6-7. Sea cliffs at Bahia El Rosario, Pacific coast of Peninsula de California (photo by S. R. Morgan).

Plate 6-6. Rocky headland between Punta Eugenia and San Ignacio Bay, along the western coastline of Peninsula de California. Cliffs were cut by waves (photo courtesy of Institute of Geography, UNAM).

7. PACIFIC CENTRAL AMERICA

The Pacific Ocean coastline of Central America extends along the western to southwestern shores of six countries: Guatemala, El Salvador, Honduras, Nicaragua, Costa Rica, and Panama (Fig. 7-1). From one end to the other, approximately 2,200 km overland, there is considerable geological, tectonic, and morphologic diversity.

There are no known Precambrian rocks in Central America, the oldest rocks being the Maya Series of Paleozoic metasediments in Belize (Moody 1975). Other Paleozoics are the Guatemala Massif metamorphics. The Mesozoic is represented by Triassic and Jurassic metamorphics in the Honduras Massif and on the Santa Helena peninsula, by Triassic and Jurassic dark shale near Tegucigalpa and Todos Santos red beds in Guatemala, and by a variety of Cretaceous sediments and volcanics. Cenozoic volcanics and sediments are widespread and include Paleocene sediments in the Petén lowland; the thick Eocene clastics of the Toledo Formation in Guatemala and Eocene volcanics in Costa Rica; Oligocene and Miocene clastics, limestones, and volcanics in Costa Rica, Nicaragua, and Panama; and marine Pliocene formations in Panama. The most recent volcanics in the region are Pleistocene and Holocene in age.

There are three geotectonic provinces in Central America. As described by Moody (1975), they are: (1) the Petén lowland, a continuation of the Campeche-Yucatan basin, in Guatemala and Belize; (2) the fault-block mountainous massifs in Belize, Guatemala, and Honduras; and (3) the volcanic terrane made up of the Isthmian link, the Pacific coastal plain, the Nicaraguan volcanic upland, and the volcanic ranges of the Pacific cordillera from Mexico to Panama. The generally accepted plate tectonic theory concerning Central America holds that the region has been thrust northeastward, as part of the Caribbean-East Pacific plate, between the essentially westward-moving North and South American plates. Anderson and Schmidt (1983) have recently refined and added considerable detail to this model.

Tides on the Pacific coast of Central America are semidiurnal (Davies 1973). The tidal range is 1.5–2 m at Guatemala; 2–3 m at El Salvador and Nicaragua; 4 m in the Gulf of Fonseca; and 4.5–6 m in the Gulf of Panama (Gierloff-Emden 1982). A west coast wave environment prevails along the coast (Davies 1973), with waves in the surf zone of up to 2 m high (Gierloff-Emden 1982). Silvester has indicated a predominantly southeastward net shore-drift in the region (Davies 1973).

The coastal morphology (Fig. 7-2) and biology of the Central American Pacific coast have been outlined by Dolan and others (1972), Gierloff-Emden (1982), and Psuty and Mizobe (1982).

The coast of Guatemala consists essentially of sandy beaches and dunes, with no cliffs along the entire sector. Beach and dune biota include the creeping vines *Ipomea* and *Canavalia*; erect plants like *Uniola*, *Scaevola*, and *Distichlis*; and burrowing invertebrates such as lamellibranchs, polychaetes, and crustaceans.

The northwestern coast of El Salvador is rocky and cliffy, with red and green algae in the sublittoral

Figure 7-1. Location map of the Pacific coast of Central America.

zone. Barnacles, chitons, crabs, mussels, periwinkles, and limpets are found in the tide pools and on the rocks. Barrier islands dominate the central sector of the coast. The barriers are 1–2 m high and the lagoons behind them are 1–3 m deep, with tidal channels to a depth of about 10 m. The southeastern coast of El Salvador, outside the Gulf of Fonseca, is sandy, with dunes.

The Gulf of Fonseca is bordered by El Salvador, Honduras, and Nicaragua. The gulf extends inland about 50 km and is 70 km wide, and is backed by a largely mangrove-covered deltaic region; the largest river entering the gulf is the Goascorán, bordering El Salvador and Honduras. Three volcanic islands, 5–10 km in diameter, are in the gulf: El Tigre, Conchaquita, and Meanguera.

Southeast of the Gulf of Fonseca deltaic region, the coast of Nicaragua is first dominated by bar-

rier island and lagoon systems, then by sandy beaches and dunes. These two sectors are approximately equal in length, and have much the same biological and geomorphic features as their counterparts in Guatemala and El Salvador. At the southeastern end of the Nicaraguan coast, steep slopes with rocky shores appear.

These same steep and rocky coasts extend along most of Costa Rica, with biota as in northern El Salvador. Raised terraces are prominent along some stretches of this steep coast. The upper reach of the Gulf of Nicoya is bordered by sandy beaches.

In Panama rocky shores at steep bluffs are found at the western and eastern shores of the Gulf of Chiriqui, and the north-central and southeastern shore of the Gulf of Panama. The gulf is approximately 180 km long from east to west and 140 km

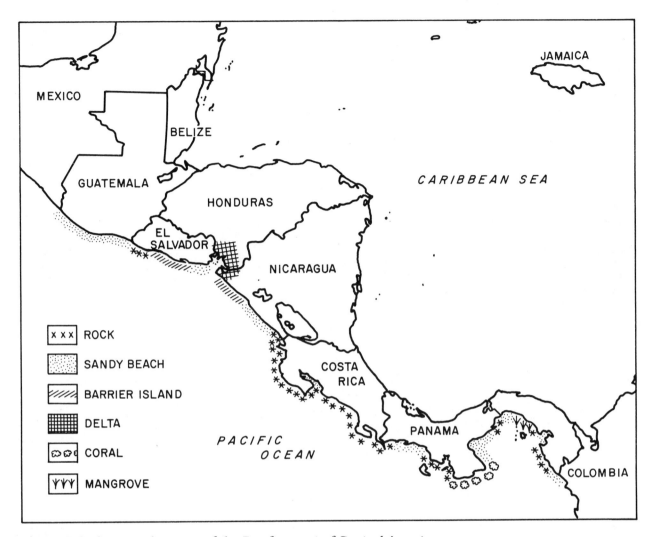

Figure 7-2. Geomorphic map of the Pacific coast of Central America.

from north to south, with depths of 50–100 m in the central region. Tidal flats are extensive along the coast west of the Panama Canal, and to the east are large areas of marsh and mangrove swamps. The main coral reefs on the Pacific coast of Central America are located in Panama off the Azuera Peninsula and Coiba Island. Coiba Island, volcanic in origin, is 24 × 40 km in size and has an elevation of 400 m.

MAURICE L. SCHWARTZ

REFERENCES

Anderson, T. H., and V. A. Schmidt, 1983, The evolution of Middle America and the Gulf of Mexico-Caribbean Sea region during Mesozoic times, *Geol. Soc. America Bull.* **94:**941–966.

Davies, J. L., 1973, *Geographical Variation in Coastal Development,* Hafner, New York.

Dolan, R., B. Hayden, G. Hornberger, J. Zieman, M. Vincent, 1972, *Classification of the Coastal Environments of the World, Part 1, The Americas,* Univ. of Virginia, Charlottesville.

Gierloff-Emden, H. G., 1982, Central America, coastal morphology, in *The Encyclopedia of Beaches and Coastal Environments,* M. L. Schwartz, ed., Hutchinson Ross, Stroudsburg, Pa., pp. 188–191.

Moody, J. D., 1975, Central America-Regional Review, in *The Encyclopedia of World Regional Geology, Part 2,* R. W. Fairbridge, ed., Dowden, Hutchinson Ross, Stroudsburg, Pa., pp. 228–237.

Psuty, N. P., and C. Mizobe, 1982, Central and South America, coastal ecology in *The Encyclopedia of Beaches and Coastal Environments,* M. L. Schwartz, ed., Hutchinson Ross, Stroudsburg, Pa., pp. 191–201.

8. PACIFIC COLOMBIA

The Pacific coast of Colombia (Fig. 8-1A), from Panama on the north to Ecuador on the south, is approximately 1,300 km long. Tides in this region are semidiurnal, with a spring range of 4–6 m (Davies 1973). A west coast swell environment prevails along the entire coast. Net shore-drift is to the north (West 1956).

Of the north-south trending Andes Mountains in Colombia, the Western Cordillera lies inland of the Pacific coast (Olsson 1956). The Coast Ranges border the shore in the north, with the coastal lowlands to the south underlain by Tertiary sediments. What southern coastal plains exist, result from fluvial systems on the mountain slopes that deposit sediment between the mountains and the sea (Psuty and Mizobe 1982).

Essentially, the Pacific coast of Colombia (Fig. 8-1B) is cliffed in the northern half and mangrove-fringed in the southern (McGill 1958, Psuty and Mizobe 1982). Sea cliffs front the coast south of the Panama border, where the Coast Ranges are close to the shore, down to Cape Corrientes. Reefs of coral bridge this sector and the entirely different one to the south. From Cape Corrientes to the San Juan Delta, a narrow coastal plain has been developed in the limited area between the mountain slopes and the sea. The coastal plain lowland then widens considerably in the region of the San Juan, Patia, and Mira deltas, that is, from Buenaventura to Tumaco. This entire coastal plain, from Cape Corrientes to a bit south of Tumaco, is fronted almost entirely by mangroves. There are along this mangrove coast three rocky sea-cliff sectors (West 1956): one 40 km in extent, west of Buenaventura Bay; a short stretch, just south of Buenaventura; and another, 24 km long, near Tumaco.

The major portion of the coast bordered by mangrove is described by West (1956, p. 100) as "four geographic belts arranged in a sequence from the sea inland: (1) a belt of shoal water and mud flats immediately off coast; (2) a series of discontinuous sand beaches, interrupted by tidal inlets, estuaries, and wide mud flats; (3) the zone of mangrove forest, usually one-half to three miles wide; (4) a belt of fresh-water tidal swamp, which lies immediately back of the brackish-water mangroves." Equatorial rain forest covers the slightly higher ground inland.

In December 1979 the Colombia-Ecuador region was jolted by a major earthquake centered southwest and offshore of Tumaco (Herd et al. 1981). The magnitude 8 shock caused extensive damage up and down the coast. Seismic shaking caused liquefaction in Holocene fluvial, lagoonal, and beach deposits, resulting in slope failures, ground cracks, sand boils, and loss of bearing strength under structures. A tsunami that hit the southern Colombia Pacific coast almost destroyed the village of San Juan, located 60 km up the coast from Tumaco, with a wave almost 2.5 m above high-tide level. Part of San Juan was flooded with more than 2 m of water. The most widespread geomorphic effect of the earthquake was subsidence of the shore zone. A sector of the Colombia coast, stretching 200 km north from the Ecuador border, subsided tectonically up to 1.6 m with a resulting effective sea-level rise along the shore. Towns and villages along the coast have been flooded or are inundated at high tide;

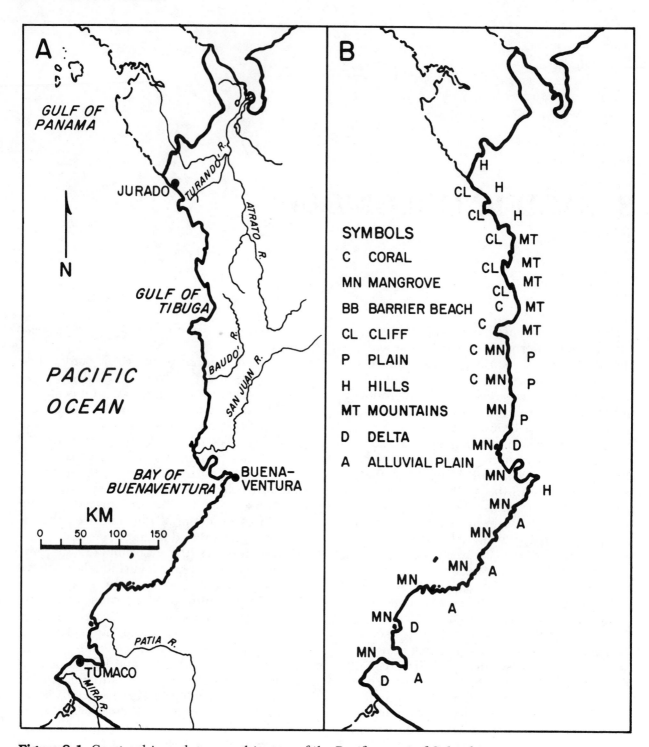

Figure 8-1. Geographic and geomorphic map of the Pacific coast of Colombia.

coastal vegetation stands, in places, in sea water; and non-halophytic plants have been killed by the intrusion of the sea. As would be expected, erosion of the coast ensued immediately after the subsidence, with accompanying reworking of the sediment and relocation of the coastline.

MAURICE L. SCHWARTZ

REFERENCES

Davies, J. L., 1973, *Geographical Variations in Coastal Development*, Hafner, New York.

Herd, D. G., T. L. Youd, C. Hansjurgen, W. J. Person, and C. Mendoza, 1981, The great Tumaco, Colombia earthquake of 12 December 1979, *Science* **211:**441–445.

McGill, J. T., 1958, Map of coastal landforms of the World, *Geog. Rev.* **48:**402–405.

Olssen, A. A., 1956, Colombia, in *Handbook of South American Geology*, W. F. Jenks, ed., Geological Society of America, New York, pp. 293–326.

Psuty, N. P., and C. Mizobe, 1982, South America coastal morphology, in *The Encyclopedia of Beaches and Coastal Environments*, M. L. Schwartz, ed., Hutchinson Ross, Stroudsburg, Pa., pp. 765–770.

West, R. C., 1956, Mangrove swamps of the Pacific Coast of Colombia, *Am. Assoc. Geographers Ann.* **46:**98–121.

9. ECUADOR

The coastline of Ecuador (Fig. 9-1), including the shores of Galapagos, Puna and Jambeli islands, is about 2,500 km long. The coastal area is divided into two well defined geological regions by the northwest-southeast Chongon-Colonche Range. The northern region is characterized by ranges with horst-like bases of pyroclastic rocks, basic lavas and dolerites underlying Cretaceous and Tertiary sediments (Faucher and Savoyat 1973). The ranges are truncated by the coastline: as a result, rocky promontories, cliffs and pocket beaches are common features along the coast

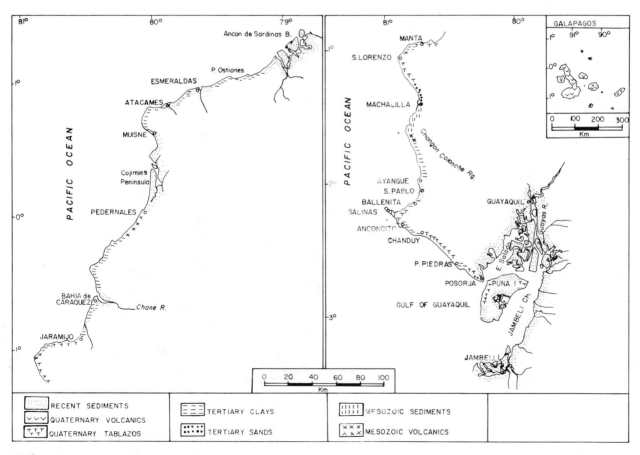

Figure 9-1. Coastal geology of Ecuador.

(Fig. 9-2). South of the Chongon-Colonche Range there is a deep basin covered by thick Tertiary and Quaternary sediments. Intensive block-faulting occurs in the region that is broadly incised by the Gulf of Guayaquil (Miro et al. 1976).

The coastal region is considered to have been unstable since Pleistocene times; the continental uplifting is evidenced mainly by the occurrence of Pleistocene beachrock (locally named *tablazos*) as high has 200m above sea level. The coast is exposed to a predominant southwesterly ocean swell. Waves are seldom higher than 3m. The semidiurnal tides range about 3m on the ocean coastline but may reach 4.6m in Guayaquil during spring tides.

Ancon de Sardinas Bay, close to the Colombian border, is a flat mangrove and salt marsh area of about 500 km². Several rivers drain into the bay. The heavy sedimentation precludes deep water navigation close to shore. Extensive offshore shoals are threaded by tidally scoured channels that run

landward into more sheltered islands fringed by mangroves.

Between Point Ostiones and Muisne, the cliffs and shore platforms cut block-faulted Miocene silty claystones. Seaward slumping is common in the cliffs. Sandy beaches develop close to the rocky cliffs (Miro et al. 1977). The Esmeraldas and Atacames rivers are estuaries close to the shore because of the high slope of the river profiles. Mud flats occur on the northeastern sides of both river mouths, evidently influenced by longshore drifting in this direction (Plate 9-1).

Cojimies Peninsula is a barrier enclosing a mangrove-fringed bay with eastern and southern fresh water supplies and sand bars developing at the mouth of the bay. Shrimp ponds are being extensively excavated in the salt marshes bounded by mangroves.

From Pedernales to Salinas, sandy beaches alternate with cliffs and shore platforms cut in Tertiary and Cretaceous sediments and Cretaceous

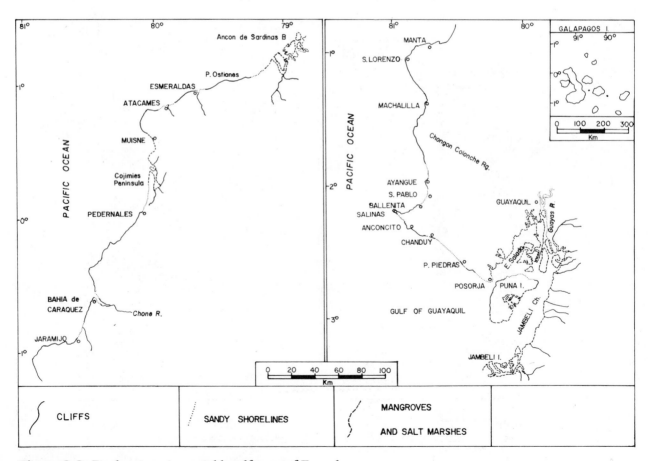

Figure 9-2. Predominant coastal landforms of Ecuador.

igneous rocks. The small rivers drain into lagoons bordered by barriers; where the river flows are high enough and their mouths are wide, mangrove fringed barriers and sandy spits develop, mainly to the north (e.g., Chone River). Coastal dunes are found in the head of broadly opened bays (Jaramijó, San Pablo). The sandy beaches are highly calcareous although quartz is the most abundant terrigenous component. Beachrock is exposed north of Ballenita (Plate 9-2) on a steep beach backed by an emerging lagoon. Tiny accumulations of coral fragments, carried by shoreward migration, can be seen in the high tide line of some pocket beaches (e.g., Ayangue, Machalilla); the coral is only associated with rocky shallow bottoms. Landslides occur in Tertiary gypsipherous claystones. The Cretaceous sediments and basalts of Salinas and San Lorenzo, respectively, show arches. Regional uplifting is testified to by the occurrence of tablazos which have been mapped as far as 27km inland. Cliffed islands close to the coast occur between San Lorenzo and Ayangue.

The Gulf of Guayaquil is a triangular-shaped area bordered landward by Puna Island separating a broad eastern and a narrow western entrance. The northeastern border is a fairly straight line of Tertiary and Quaternary sediments. Cliffs and lowlying plains alternate between Salinas and Posorja. Landslides are frequent in the hilly area between Anconcito and Chanduy (Plate 9-3). Lagoons and barriers limit the mouths of the rivers (Plates 9-4, 9-5). Some of the plains show coastal dunes (e.g., between Chanduy and Point Piedras). Black sand accumulates along the upper foreshore on most of the beaches.

The southwestern border of the gulf is an extensive fluvial plain. Fluvial sediments are fed by the Guayas River and a series of relatively short east-westerly running rivers draining the Occidental Andean Cordilerra. The shore is exposed to strong tidal currents along the broad and shallow Jambeli Channel. Small deltas outcrop during low tide at the mouths of the rivers running perpendicular to the shore fringed by mangroves. Shrimp ponds are extensively excavated along salt marshes and very often in cut mangroves. Shell rings of *Crassostrea*, outcropping up to 10m above sea level, are evidence of Holocene continental uplifting. The alluvial plain ends at the mangrove-fringed Jamebli Archipiélago which extends over an area of 260 km² (Coronel and Ayón 1981), close to the Peruvian border. The sandy beaches of these islands are prograding northward.

Between Puna Island and Guayaquil the Guayas River has built up an intricate pattern of channels and a 640km² area of mangrove-fringed salt marshes (Fig. 9-2). A narrow barrier parallel to the Guayas River, about 42km long, divides the river itself and the intricate Estero Salado. The tidal range in both navigation channels is 4.5m. Puna Island shelters the inner estuarine system of these navigation channels from the direct influence of the open ocean, although the Holocene transgression has caused estuarine sedimentation inland as far as Guayaquil (Ayón 1976).

Puna Island shows Tertiary sediments overlaid by extensive tablazos. The island is fringed by sand bars and mudflats enclosing mangrove-fringed lagoons (Plate 9-6). Occasional cliffs and platforms are present. Mangrove-fringed salt marshes fill the concave part of the curved island. The western coast is exposed to the ocean swell, and the northern coast is subject mainly to tidal currents. Recurved spits develop on the southwestern end of the island.

The coasts of the volcanic Galapagos Islands show cliffs, shore platforms, and a few pocket beaches. Some of the steeply plunging cliffs are associated with laterally eroded craters and calderas. Shore platforms are developed on seaward protruding shields and lava flows. The occurrence of submarine lavas and sedimentary rocks indicate the uplifting of some of the islands about 100m above sea level (Bristow and Hoffstetter 1977).

HECTOR AYÓN
WILMO JARA

REFERENCES

Ayón, H., 1976, *Sedimentología en El Guasmo, Guayaquil*, Instituto Oceanográfico de la Armada del Ecuador.

Bristow, C. R., and R. Hoffstetter, 1977, *Lexique Stratigraphique International*, Centre National de la Recherche Scientifique, Paris.

Coronel, V., and H. Ayón, 1980, Minerales de Arcillas en el Archipiélago de Jambelí, *Acta Oceanografica del Pacífico* 1:110–119.

Faucher, B. and E. Savoyat, 1973, Esquisse Géologique des Andes de L'Equateur, *Reu Géog. Phys. Géol. Dyn.* 15:115–142.

Miró, M., H. Ayón, and B. Benites, 1976, *Morfología y Estructura del Margen Continental del Ecuador*, Instituto Oceanográfico de la Armada del Ecuador.

Miró, M., V. Coronel, M. Franco, and J. Cuenca, 1977, *Morfolo gía y Sedimentos de la Plataforma Continental de la Provincia de Esmeraldas*, Instituto Oceanográfico de la Armada del Ecuador.

Plate 9-1. The left margin of the Esmeraldas River. The groins are built seaward and only partially preclude the heavy sedimentation from the river (photo by H. Ayón and W. Jara).

Plate 9-2. Beachrock exposed north of Ballenita. The steep beach is backed by an emerging lagoon. Note vegetated dunes over the berm (photo by H. Ayón and W. Jara).

Plate 9-3. Landslides are common features along the cliffs between Anconcito and Chanduy (photo by H. Ayón and W. Jara).

Plate 9-4. Sandy barriers between Anconcito and Chonduy obstruct the mouth of small rivers. Sea water percolates through the barrier during high tides (photo by H. Ayón and W. Jara).

Plate 9-5. The hilly hinterland of the Posorja area is bordered seaward by salt marshes, mangroves, and lagoons flanked by spits and small deltas (photo by H. Ayón and W. Jara).

Plate 9-6. The western side of Puna Island is exposed to both ocean swell and estuarine circulation. Note the development of salt marshes, lagoons, tidal flats, and mangroves (photo by H. Ayón and W. Jara).

10. PERU

The coastline of Peru (Fig. 10-1), just over 2,300 km long, is notably arid (Dresch 1961). Mean annual rainfall at coastal centers is low (Chiclayo, 15 mm; Trujillo, 28 mm; Lima, 31 mm; Mollendo, 22 mm) and variable; dessication is intense between the occasional rains. This is because coastal waters are abnormally cool for latitudes 4° to 18°S, due to the upwelling of cold water from oceanic depths as a result of trade winds blowing offshore. Sea breezes keep the coastal fringe cool, with frequent fogs but very little precipitation. Vegetation is consequently very sparse, and desert landscapes predominate.

Tectonic uplift accompanied by faulting has raised the high hinterland of the Andes Mountains, the structural grain of which is followed by the coastline. Coast ranges, extensive in Chile, are here confined to the sector between Pisco and Mollendo (Noble et al. 1978) with an outlier near Punta Aguja; intervening segments have subsided beneath the sea. Earthquakes still occur. In May 1970 a major tremor centered 50 km off Chimbote caused massive avalanches in the mountains and severe flooding down the Santa River valley to its delta region (Gajardo 1970). Many valleys are incised into the coastal slopes, but only streams fed by mountain rainfall and melting snow maintain their flow through to the coast, and even these show great variations in seasonal and annual discharge. The coastline is relatively simple in outline, with few estuarine inlets and only minor deltaic protrusions built in the face of oceanic wave action. Cliffs cut by marine erosion alternate with sandy beaches derived mainly from shoreward drifting of sea-floor sediment and some sand and shingle beaches nourished from cliff erosion and fluvial outwash. Beaches are backed

by dunes, are unvegetated, or have a sparse plant cover sustained by fog and dew. In many places, sand is drifting inland to be banked against cliffs or rising slopes, or blocking the mouths of coastal valleys and gullies.

Ocean swell arrives from the southwest; it may be accompanied by small waves generated in coastal waters by southerly breezes. Occasionally in summer there are northwesterly waves and penetration by the warm Niño current to the coast north of Negritos. Tide ranges are small, generally less than a meter, but they increase toward the Ecuador border and the Gulf of Guayaquil.

Close to the Ecuador border is the large, sandy Tumbes Delta on the southern shores of the Gulf of Guayaquil. Its estuarine distributaries are mangrove-fringed (the southern limit of mangroves on the west coast of South America is here at Punta Malpelo, 3°4′S). Parallel sandy beach, ridges, emphasized by lines of shrubs, extend southward to Caleta Le Cruz, the landing place of Fransisco Pizarro in 1527. Southwest from Zorritos the coastline is generally cliffed, cut into a fringe of uplifted Tertiary formations that dip gently seaward and are capped by a series of Quaternary marine terraces (tablazos), incised by transverse valleys (quebradas), but well preserved in this arid climate. Each terrace is a sparsely vegetated plain strewn with broken, sand-blasted pebbles, with old beach deposits to the rear, beneath bluffs that mark degraded cliffy coastlines. The oldest and highest, the Mancora terrace, stands about 360 m above sea level in the north and declines to 75 m southward. The next, the Talara terrace, falls southward from 90–40 m, while the youngest and lowest, the Lobitos terrace, declines from 40–30

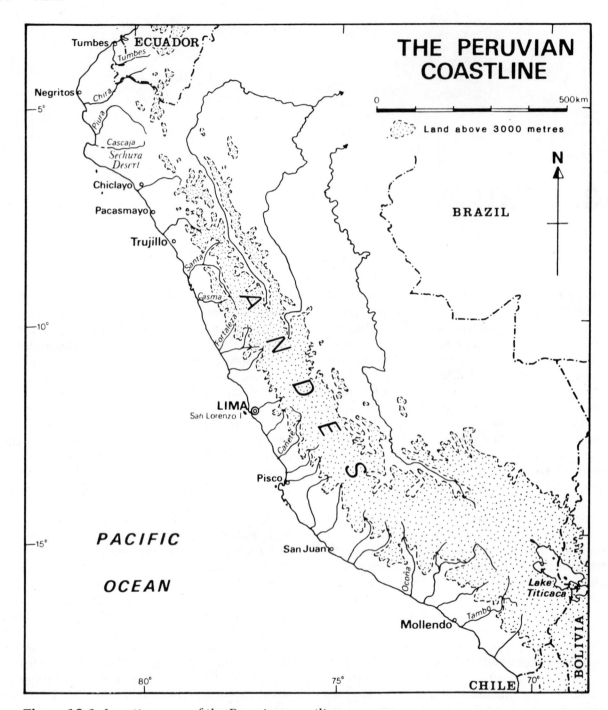

Figure 10-1. Location map of the Peruvian coastline.

m southward (Bosworth 1922). These terraces are truncated by cliffs along the present coastline: at Cabo Blanco, for example, the Mancora terrace ends in cliffs 300 m high.

An early Holocene coastline is marked by gullied bluffs behind intervening sectors of coastal plain, as at Talara. The beaches are of shelly sand with some stony material, and the coastal plains include parallel beach ridges often overlain by dunes. Near Negritos the cliffs are 80 m high, incised by valley mouths blocked by 20-m-high dunes. Southeast from Parinas Point the sandy beach, backed by dunes, is 50 km long, interrupted only by the mouth of the Chira River. Behind the dunes is a flat plain inundated by the highest tides, and covered with evaporite deposits.

Paita is on a hilly peninsula of Mesozoic rock, but the bay to the south is sandy, fronting abandoned cliffs, and paired spits border the small estuary of the Rio Piura. Punta Agula is another hilly peninsula dissected by wadis, and followed southward by a sandy coastline fringing the Sechura Desert. The extensive dunes here include barchans up to 6 m high and 15 m wide. Evaporation is intense, and the Rio Cascaja fades away before reaching the sea.

The coastal plain narrows southward from Chiclayo to Trujillo, beyond which steep coasts predominate as the Andean foothills approach and intersect the coastline. Cliffs and bluffs are cut into Mesozoic rocks and intruded granites, and there are rugged islands offshore (e.g., Isla de Macabi and Islas Guañape), many with thick guano deposits. Sectors of sandy beach (*playa*) also occur, backed by beach ridges, but south of Chimbote the coastline is hilly and embayed on Cenozoic volcanics, with shore platforms fronting cliffs and the harder elements persisting as rocky headlands, with caves and coves. The Peninsula de Ferrol is a tombolo, a high hill attached to the mainland by a sandy isthmus; its rocky seaward margin has bouldery clefts and a natural tunnel. A scalloped cliffy coastline (Fig. 10-2), notched by wadis, near Huarmey, is fringed by many white or yellow guano-mantled islands and headlands. The Rio Pativilca has built a blunt delta, while to the south Les Salinas is a small elongated barrier lagoon, and

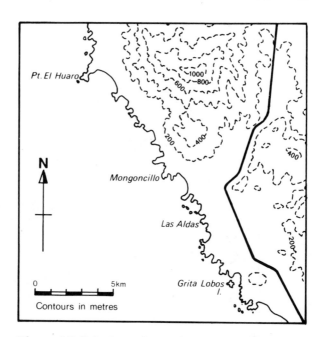

Figure 10-2. Indented coastline north of Huarmey.

Playa Grande has heavy surf breaking on a shingle beach fronting bluffs cut into the seaward margin of a gravelly pediment.

Callao, the port of Lima, has large breakwaters enclosing a harbor, with accretion of sand from Rio Rimac immediately to the north. A major spit (La Punta) protrudes in the lee of Isla San Lorenzo,

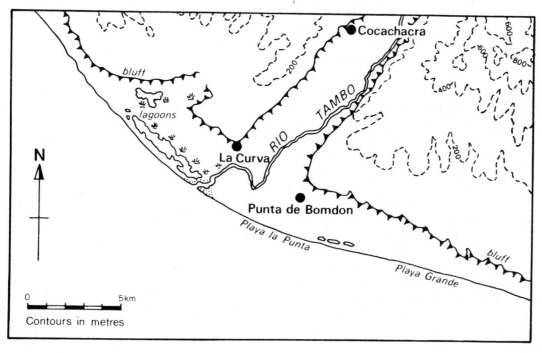

Figure 10-3. The blunt delta of the Rio Tambo, built on a coastline exposed to southwesterly ocean swell.

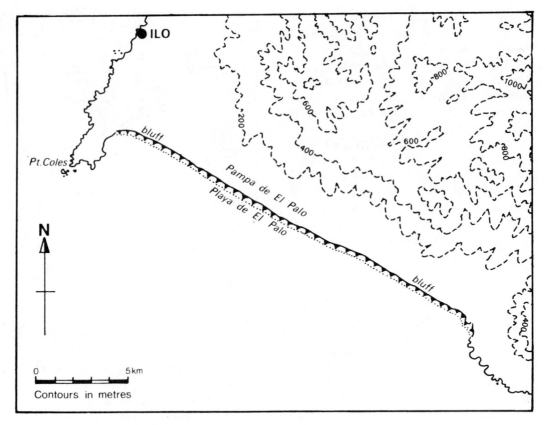

Figure 10-4. Playa de El Palo, beach-fringed cliffs cut in gravelly pediments.

a hilly offshore island on which Quaternary marine terraces are well developed. Southward the coast is undulating, with small plains at valley mouths, and the Paracas promontory at Pisco marks the beginning of a coastal mountain range. Punta Záráta is a cuspate foreland enclosing a lagoon and salt marshes, and a spit partly encloses Laguna Grande on the east coast of the Carreta Peninsula, bordering Bahia de la Independencia. Asymmetrical bays, shaped by the refraction of southwesterly swell around headlands, have developed at Bahia de Lomitas, Bahia San Nicolás, and Bahia San Juan. Locally, pebble beaches have formed from material derived from Pleistocene conglomerates deposited at old valley mouths and now exposed in cliff sections.

The coastline now faces southwest and receives strong surf produced by swell arriving through deep water inshore. Drifting sand blocks the mouth of the Ico River valley. To the south the coast is steep on granitic rocks, with many gullies, some of which reach the sea in small coves. Rio Ocona has a small estuary, but Rio Camaná has built a blunt delta with beach ridges and swale lagoons, as has the Rio Tambo southeast of Mal-

lendo (Fig. 10-3). Rio Vitor, by contrast, reaches the coast through a deep gorge. Between Mollendo and the Chilean border are several straight beaches fronting bluffs that truncate pediments: Playa de El Palo (Fig. 10-4), Playa Tacahuay, and Playa Inglesa. Perhaps because of its aridity the Peruvian coastline has received little detailed study from geomorphologists.

ERIC C. F. BIRD
VIDAL TAYPE RAMOS

REFERENCES

Bosworth, T. O., 1922, *Geology and Palaeontology of Northwest Peru,* Macmillan, London.

Dresch, J., 1961, Observations sur le désert cotier du Perou, *Annales Géographie* **70:**179–184.

Gajardo, E., 1970, *Preliminary Report on the Damages Caused by the Peru Earthquake of May 31, 1970.* Smithsonian Institute, Washington, D.C.

Noble, D. C., E. H. McKee, and F. Mégard, 1978, Eocene uplift and unroofing of the coastal batholith near Lima, Peru, *Jour. Geology* **86:**403–405.

11. CHILE

The coastline of Chile is about 34,500 km long (Figs. 11-1, 11-2 and 11-3). It runs generally parallel to the uplifted longitudinal coast ranges, but in some sectors it truncates geological units, exposing granites and slates, with volcanic and sedimentary rocks in the northern and southern parts. Despite a history of tectonic uplift, the coast has been relatively stable in late Quaternary times, as evidenced by the consistent levels of emerged coastlines, which show only minor warping locally, related to earthquakes.

Wave action is dominated by southwesterly ocean swell in central and northern Chile, with additional storm waves, especially in southern Chile, south of latitude 40°. In central Chile significant wave heights are generally 0.8–2.2 m, with occasional waves up to 4.9 m (Araya-Vergara 1971). Spring tide amplitudes are up to 2 m on the open coastline but increase to 10 m within the highly indented southern region. Occasionally earthquakes generate tsunamis, and storm surges produce cataclysmic changes along the coast.

From Arica, just south of the Peruvian border, to Punta Rincón the coastline is dominated by very high steep slopes ("mega-cliffs") cut in volcanic and sedimentary formations, along the line of a major fault (Paskoff 1978). The coastal scarp rises abruptly to about 700 m. North of Iquique its base has been cut back as a cliff with a shore platform (Plate 11-1). Emerged Holocene marine platforms are seen as discontinuous terraces backed by bluffs (abandoned cliffs). The present shore platform is narrow, and shows water-layer weathering on volcanic outcrops. North of Antofagasta the cliffs are cut in horizontally bedded Tertiary strata. Sediment supply from the hinterland is meager because of the dry climate. However, occasional

rains produce stream flows that deposit small, rounded deltas, which are subsequently reshaped into cuspate deltas by wave action (Plate 11-2). There are also dune systems, transverse and parabolic, and some Pleistocene dunes formed during low sea-level phases.

Between Punta Rincón and Curaumilla Point, there are alternations of granitic rocks with Tertiary and Quaternary sedimentary formations on a coastline with wide bays between promontories with outlying reefs. The wide bay at Coquimbo, for example, is well protected from the southwesterly ocean swell by a broad promontory of crystalline rock. Platforms at 1–2 and 4–5 m above sea level are of Holocene age (Paskoff 1970), the former being a wide peaty terrace partly overlain by modern dunes. The present beaches are on swash alignments determined by refraction of ocean swell, and many sectors have abandoned cliffs that were cut into old marine, eolian, or alluvial deposits. South from Punta Lengua de Vaca the rocky coastline is relatively straight, sectors of cliff alternating with occasional pocket beaches backed by bluffs, and south of Chigualoco it becomes more indented, with larger, slightly lobate embayments. With increasing rainfall southward, streams have supplied sand and gravel to beaches, many outlets having small barrier lagoons (Plate 11-3), and there are transverse and parabolic dunes of Holocene and Pleistocene age. Bolder, receding cliffs in Tertiary outcrops extend from Maitencilla south to Hercón (Paskoff 1970), and sandy sediment derived from these is carried northward for deposition on beaches and beach-ridge systems.

From Curaumilla to Itata River the coastline truncates granitic and metamorphic rocks and

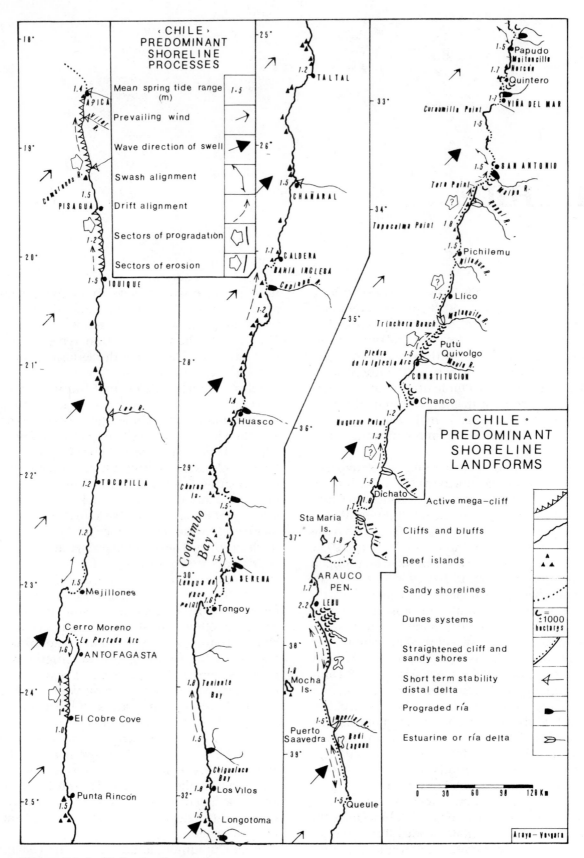

Figure 11-1. Chile, northern sector.

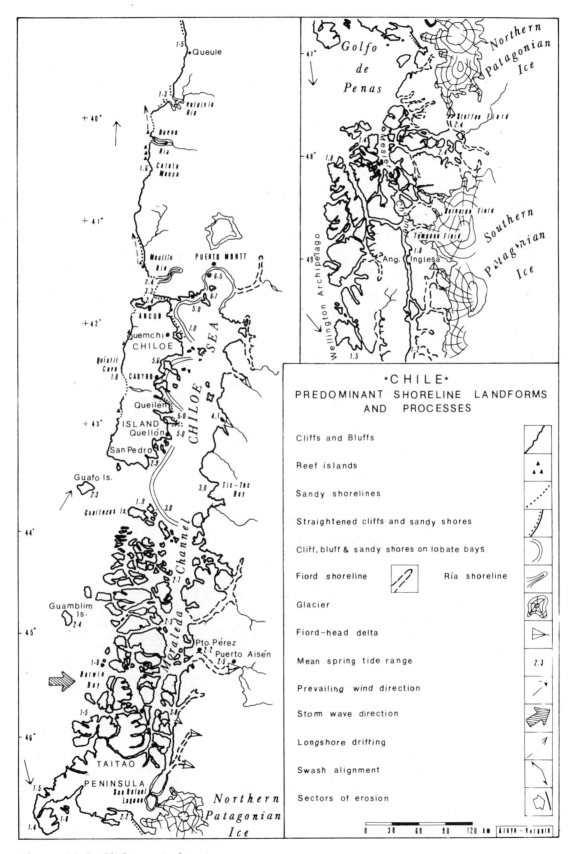

Figure 11-2. Chile, central sector.

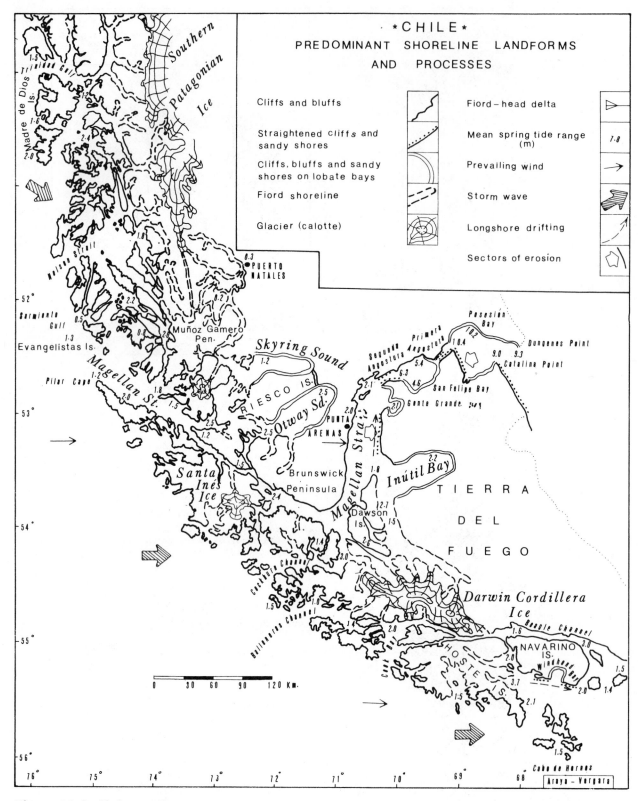

Figure 11-3. Chile, southern sector.

Tertiary sediments. Cliffs and bluffs alternate with sandy bays, and Late Quaternary emerged marine platforms occur up to 10 m above sea level; the best preserved are at 1–2 m and 4–5 m. Fluvial sands and gravels are delivered to prograding beach-ridge plains by longshore drifting north from river mouths (Plate 11-4), and dunes derived from sandy beaches are drifting inland near Constitución and Chanco. These include coalescent barchans as well as dunes parallel and transverse to the coastline. Sandy coastline progradation has been marked during the past century at Viña del Mar (96 m), San Antonio (600 m), and Trinchera-Quivolgo (also 600 m), while in San Antonio harbor and Constitución cove there has been accretion alongside breakwaters (Pomar 1962).

River outlets have complex estuarine deltas, for example that of the Itata River south of Nugurve Point. A rounded foreland with accretional beach ridges and Holocene dunes has developed north of the Maule River mouth at Constitución, while to the south spectacular arches have formed on a granitic coast during higher Late Pleistocene and Holocene sea-level episodes (Plate 11-5).

Between Itata River and Lebu two principal bays are sheltered by crystalline "horsts." Holocene lowlands are in ancient inlets or in front of abandoned cliffs. The Biobio River outlet is a present estuarine delta, incorporating—at the same time—an emerged Holocene cuspate delta (Martínez 1968). The large compound embayment of Arauco has a system of beach ridges whose sediments have been supplied both by river basins and the local soft cliffs, which appear in the external coastline of Arauco Peninsula. Tectonic deformation has resulted from earthquakes here, tilting shore platforms and raising Santa Maria Island and the Arauco Peninsula at rates of 0.08 m and 0.25 m per century, respectively (Kaizuka et al. 1973). Earthquakes caused uplift of up to 2 m between 1835 and 1960.

Between Lebu and Queule the coastline is smooth, cut in soft Tertiary and Quaternary sediments, with sectors of beach-ridge plain occupying former embayments, locally enclosing lagoons in front of abandoned cliffs. Lago Budi is a lagoon within an inlet, the mouth of which is constricted by variable barrier spits. Beach sands have been supplied partly by rivers and partly from cliff erosion (Plate 11-6), and the derived dunes south of the Arauco Peninsula are the most extensive on the Chilean coastline. During the 1960 earthquake there was up to 2 m uplift on Isla Mocha, and subsidence of a similar amount on the coast at Puerto Saavedra to the south (Plate 11-7). The earthquake produced a major tsunami, which washed over the shore platform and destroyed the town of Puerto Saavedra. Among the changes that ensued was the relocation of the mouth of the Imperial River.

Between Queule and the west coast of Chiloé Island are rocky shores on crystalline outcrops and cliffs cut in local Tertiary outcrops. A terrace that stood 1.2–1.5 m above sea level was submerged after the 1960 earthquake (Fuenzalida et al. 1965), and downwarping of the coast south from Isla Mocha led to deepening of river mouths—notably in the ria of Valdivia—and the formation of new marshes (Plate 11-7).

On the Patagonian coast, fjords and straits have been excavated in granitic and metamorphic rocks to form an intricate coastal topography related to structural lineaments and faults. In the Magellan region there are local outcrops of Mesozoic sedimentary and volcanic rocks. Some small islands are drumlins or roches moutonnées (Plate 11-8). Lobate embayments formed by glacial erosion occur behind Chiloé Island, in the almost landlocked Skyring and Otway sounds, in Magellan Strait, and on the south of Navarino Island (Araya-Vergara 1974, 1978). Beach ridges and Holocene raised beaches 3–5, 10, and 20 m above sea level (Auer 1970; Araya-Vergara 1976) are found in front of degraded cliffs that were cut in morainic and glaciolacustrine deposits (Plates 11-9 and 11-10): these features indicate glacio-isostatic Holocene uplift. Some beaches impound small lagoons. Shell middens occur on Holocene beach ridges alongside Beagle Channel, underlain and overlain by peat deposits. Beaches contain boulders and gravels derived from morainic cliffs, and have steep seaward slopes. Tide ranges of several meters occur, with much local variation. Fjord-head deltas, partly intertidal and sometimes marshy, occur in many of the steep-sided inlets.

Glaciers reach the coastline of Patagonia at several places south of latitude 46°30′. In Mesier Channel, for instance, Bernardo and Mesier Fjords are adjacent to the icecap, and valley glaciers occur behind several fjords, meltwater streams supplying morainic material to the coast. Some sectors have only recently become ice-free. The bay of Laguna de San Rafaél is one sector that was temporarily overrun by glaciers during the eighteenth-century readvance (Heusser 1960).

JOSÉ F. ARAYA-VERGARA

REFERENCES

Araya-Vergara, J. F., 1971, Determinación preliminar de las características del oleaje en Chile Central, *Mus. Nac. Hist. Nat. Not. Mens.* **15:**8–12.

Araya-Vergara, J. F., 1974, Relaciones entre los piedmonts glacigénicos y las formas marinas litorales en el Sur de Sudamérica, *Rev. Geog. Panam.* **81:**115–138.

Araya-Vergara, J. F., 1976, Reconocimiento de tipos e individuos geomorfológicos regionales en la costa de Chile, *Inform. Geog. Chile* **23:**9–30.

Araya-Vergara, J. F., 1978, La función morfogenética de las islas del Cabo de Hornos en el Würm Superior, *Inform. Geog. Chile* **25:**21–52.

Auer, V., 1970, The Pleistocene of Fuego Patagonia, *Acad. Sci. Fennicae Annales* **3:**100.

Fuenzalida, H., R. Cooke, R. Paskoff, K. Segerstrom, and W. Weischet, 1965, *High Stands of Quaternary Sea Levels Along the Chilean Coast,* Geol. Soc. America. Spec. Paper 84, pp. 473–496.

Heusser, C., 1960, Late Pleistocene environments of Laguna de San Rafael area, Chile, *Geog. Rev.* **5:**555–577.

Kaizuka, S., T. Matsuda, M. Nogami, and N. Yonekura, 1973, Quaternary tectonics and recent seismic crustal movements in the Arauco Peninsula and its environs, Central Chile, *Tokyo Metropolitan Univ. Geog. Repts.* **8:**1–38.

Martínez, R., 1968, Foraminíferos y evolución de la línea de costa Holocénica en la zona de Concepción, in *El Terciario de Chile, Zona Central,* G. Cecioni, ed., pp. 211–258.

Paskoff, R., 1970, *Recherches géomorphologiques dans le Chili semi-aride,* Biscaye Frères, Bordeaux.

Paskoff, R., 1978, Sur l'évolution géomorphologique du grand escarpement côtier du désert chilien, *Géog. Phys. Quat.* **32:**351–360.

Pomar, J., 1962, Cambios en los ríos y en la morfología de la costa de Chile, *Rev. Chilena Hist. y Geog.* **130:**318–356.

Plate 11-1. Mega-cliffs between Arica and the Camarones River, showing free faces, screes, and basal marine erosion. Tide range is small, and volcanic rocks on the shore platform undergo water-layer weathering. The modern platform is being widened at the expense of older, higher marine platforms (photo by J. F. Araya-Vergara).

Plate 11-2. Sandy coastline of Arica showing a cuspate delta derived from an originally lobate delta formed by floodwaters seven years previously as the outcome of high wave energy (photo by J. F. Araya-Vergara).

Plate 11-3. Copiapo River, toward the southern limit of the desert, is the first outlet with permanent runoff to the sea on the north–south traverse of the Chilean coastline. A small barrier built by longshore drifting encloses a lagoon, and beach ridges have been built to the north (photo by Hykon Air Survey).

Plate 11-4. Between the Maipo mouth and Toro Point, the coastline has been straightened by longshore drifting, a former embayed outline being transformed into a barrier lagoon coast. Beach ridges are overlain by dunes, which originate as barchans (photo by Hykon Air Survey).

Plate 11-5. Natural arches, pyramidal rocks, reefs, and bluffs formed by joint-guided marine dissection of granitic rocks near Constitución (photo by J. F. Araya-Vergara).

Plate 11-6. Cliffs cut in soft sandstone and shale at Budi Lagoon show notching related to stratification of the Tertiary outcrop (photo by J. F. Araya-Vergara).

Plate 11-7. Subsidence after the 1960 earthquake in Puerto Saavedra modified barriers and initiated marsh evolution. Tidal channels appeared on existing marshes (photo by J. F. Araya-Vergara).

Plate 11-8. Coastline with drumlins and roches moutonnées on Navarino Island, southern Patagonia. Spring tide range here is 3 m (photo by J. F. Araya-Vergara).

Plate 11-9. In Achao Bay, Quinchao Island, Chiloé, large tide ranges produce wide intertidal zones fronting cliffs cut in morainic, fluvioglacial, or glacio-lacustrine sediments (photo by J. F. Araya-Vergara).

Plate 11-10. Holocene beaches and beach ridges in Windhond Bay, Navarino Island. The coarse pebble and cobble beach has a seaward slope of up to 15°. Spring tide range is 3 m and storm surges occasionally attack the cliff (photo by J. F. Araya-Vergara).

12. ARGENTINA

The coastline of Argentina (Figs. 12-1 and 12-2), excluding Islas Malvinas (Falkland Islands) and the Antarctic sector, is about 5,700 km long. A very wide continental shelf extends offshore reaching in places, over 800 km in width (Fig. 12-1). Open marine and semienclosed coastal waters are associated with varying tidal regimes, from micro- to macrotides; minimum values at the northern Argentine coast and maximum ranges along the Patagonian sector (Fig. 12-3).

Main coastal landforms (Fig. 12-1) are deltas, estuaries, marshes, cliffs and wave-cut terraces, sandy and pebbly shores, and ice-fringed coastlines. Sandy coastlines are typical along the strip extending from Cabo San Antonio to Mar Chiquita lagoon. Pebbles are a common component of the Patagonian shores. Brackish and salt marshes are present along the coast, the former in the northeastern sector of Buenos Aires Province (Samborombón, Mar Chiquita), and the latter—mostly macrotidal—in Patagonia and Tierra del Fuego. The Patagonian coast is predominantly cliffy, while the Buenos Aires ("Pampas") coastline alternates between low-lying and cliffy areas.

A variety of geological settings are encountered along the coast of Argentina, from a fairly stable area in the north to an isostatically affected coastline in the extreme south. Tectonic complications may also have affected coastal development in some places. The geology of coastal Argentina is summarized in Figure 12-2.

Evidences of a higher-than-present relative sea-level stand reached during the Holocene are well-represented in the Argentine coast as shelly or pebbly beach ridges, estuarine deposits, and marine terraces (Frenguelli 1950; Feruglio 1950).

PARANÁ RIVER DELTA–BUENOS AIRES ("PAMPAS") COASTLINE

This segment comprises a set of environments developed from the Paraná River delta to the latitude of Bahía Blanca (Fig. 12-1).

The Paraná River, entering the Río de la Plata estuary, forms a large delta of 15,000 km^2 area. According to Iriondo and Scotta (1979), most of its evolution occurred during the Holocene. A variety of landforms related to fluvial and marine processes have developed (Fig. 12-4).

The Río de la Plata coast, from the delta front to the city of Buenos Aires, truncates the Pleistocene "Pampiano loess and silts" (Frenguelli 1925, 1950), and from here to Punta Rasa (at the southern end of Bahía Samborombón) an extensive low area of the Pampas Plain is occupied by Holocene marine and estuarine deposits (Frenguelli 1950; Fidalgo et al. 1973). At Samborombón Bay a brackish marsh is present and an extensive mud flat develops.

From Punta Rasa southward, the open marine coastline extends along a low-lying coastal plain. Sand dunes and beaches are typical; their development reaches the latitude of the southern tip of Mar Chiquita Lagoon. The geological substratum of this segment is also represented by estuarine and marine deposits formed during the Holocene epoch. At Mar Chiquita (Fig. 12-5) these deposits are well developed, the shelly beach ridges corresponding to the marine facies and the lagoon marginal flat built on the estuarine deposits. The evolution of these environments is associated with the transgressive-regressive phases of the last

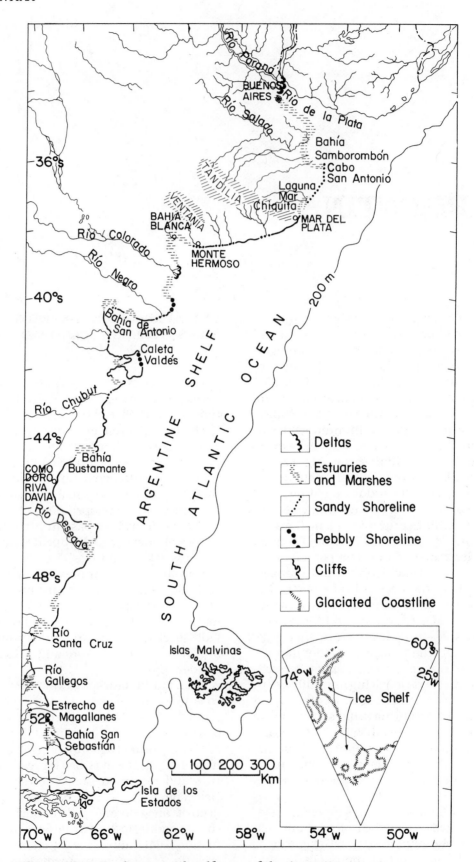

Figure 12-1. Predominant landforms of the Argentine coast.

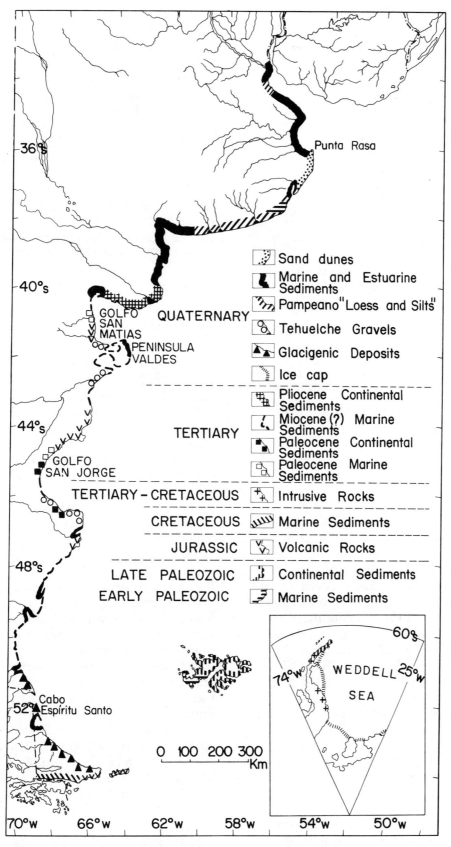

Figure 12-2. Main geological units of the Argentine coast.

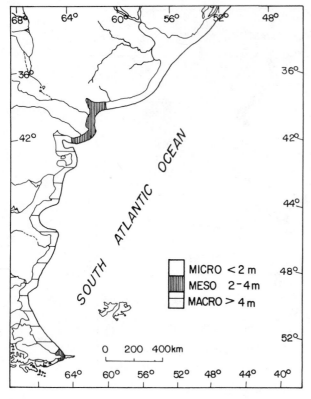

Figure 12-3. Tidal ranges along the coast of Argentina.

deglacial hemicycle. Following a maximum sea-level stand of about 2.5 m above present mean sea level, approximately 5,000 years B.P., a regressive phase coincidental with the development of a southward-prograding barrier enclosed the estuarine environment, resulting in the formation of Mar Chiquita Lagoon. Present conditions in the area suggest a transgressive character of the shoreline at least at the southern end of the lagoon (Schnack et al., in press). Here the tidal inlet (Plate 12-1) shows a historical northward migration pattern that has been interrupted several times by human intervention, resulting in environmental disturbances (Schnack 1979). Severe erosion is occurring at Mar Chiquita beach immediately south of the inlet (Fig. 12-6).

The Mar del Plata coastline is mostly cliffy. At the city itself, the Early Paleozoic quartzites of the "Tandil System" outcrop in resistant cliffs. Here concentration of wave energy normally occurs (Plate 12-2). North and south of Mar del Plata (Fig. 12-7) the Pampiano loess and silts (Pleistocene, in parts Pliocene) comprise the coastal erosion features of the area. Coastal retreat is very rapid, at times reaching rates of 2–4 m/year. The highest cliffs are exposed south of Mar del Plata (Plate 12-3).

From Mar del Plata to approximately the locality of Monte Hermoso, the Pampa Interserrana (between the Tandil and Ventana sierras) meets the coast in the form of cliffs alternating with some low segments associated with fluvial deposition. In these estuaries evidence of a former sea level is found (Frenguelli 1950). The Monte Hermoso–Bahía Blanca segment shows the presence of features related to the Holocene marine episode, the coast is lower, and a marshy area extends near Bahía Blanca (Figs. 12-1 and 12-2).

PATAGONIA

This sector comprises the southern part of the province of Buenos Aires (between Bahía Blanca and the Río Negro estuary) and from there south to the Río Gallegos estuary (Figs. 12-1 and 12-2). In this segment some common attributes are typical: climate, physiography, vegetation (related to arid conditions). The most important difference between the Buenos Aires–"Patagonian" –segment and the rest is the presence in the former of deltaic features such as the Colorado River delta and neighboring "delta like" (relict?) environments.

The main geomorphic environments adjacent to the coastline are plateaus, pediments, and hollows. The well-known "Patagonian gravels" extend over the whole region and are a common feature of the continental and marine Quaternary deposits, and of much of the modern beaches. A great part of the coast is cliffy, the materials being mainly composed of Tertiary continental and marine deposits and of Jurassic volcanic rocks (Fig. 12-2). Gulfs and embayments are also important. Evidence of a Holocene high relative sea-level stand also extends along the coast of Patagonia. Feruglio (1950) recognized six marine terraces, three of which are of Quaternary age. The most recent one, which he called "Comodoro Rivadavia Terrace," reaches an altitude of 8–12 m above mean sea level and extends from northern Patagonia to Tierra del Fuego.

Marshes are developed in some protected low-

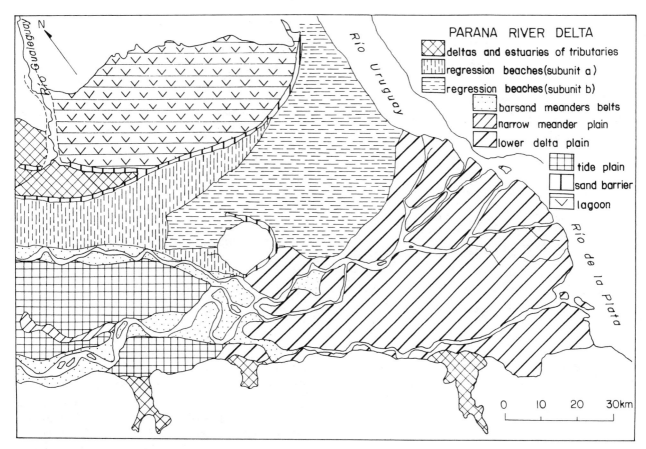

Figure 12-4. Geomorphic environments of the Paraná River delta (lower section) (after Iriondo and Scotta 1979).

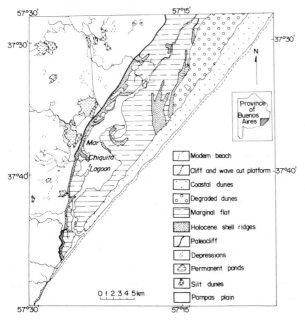

Figure 12-5. Coastal plain landforms, Mar Chiquita Lagoon area (modified after Schnack 1979).

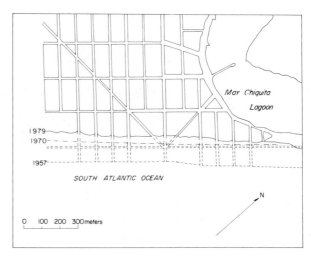

Figure 12-6. Coastal retreat at Mar Chiquita beach (based on measurements made on vertical aerial photographs; the dune break into the beach system was used as reference).

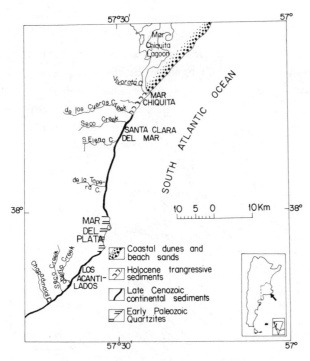

Figure 12-7. Coastline geology of Mar del Plata and adjacent area.

energy environments (Fig. 12-1). Except for the northern (Bahía Blanca–Río Negro) marshes, which are mesotidal, all the Patagonian wetlands are macrotidal (Fig. 12-3). Although not very significant in area, they are present either at estuaries (Chubut, Deseado, Santa Cruz, and Gallegos rivers) or are exposed to only low energy waves. An interesting feature of these marshes is the presence of "peaty soils" undergoing erosion. This fact was observed by R. West (pers. comm.) in several places of Patagonia and by the author at Bahía Bustamante (Fig. 12-1, Plate 12-4).

In the area of San Antonio Bay (Fig. 12-8), with a maximum spring range of 8–9 m, a set of landforms of varied origin can be recognized: flanking pediments, hollows, Holocene shelly beach ridges, and marshy deposits (Angulo et al. 1979, and in press). The modern environments consist of a tidal salt marsh without fresh-water inflow, and extensive tidal shoals composed of sandy materials are exposed at low tide at the outer part of the bay (Plate 12-5). Part of this area shows the development of a 7–8 m-high cliff and a very gently

sloping, extensive abrasion platform is also present (Fig. 12-1, Plate 12-6).

Barrier-like features are also developed at Caleta Valdés (Figs. 12-1 and 12-9), showing a predominance of pebbly materials over other constituents. Here a sequence of Quaternary beach ridges alternating with depressions (old marshes) is developed, reaching a maximum altitude of about 30 m above present mean sea level. The youngest ridge system (Plate 12-7), equivalent to Feruglio's "Terrace VI" or "Comodoro Rivadavia Terrace", is about 12 m high. This system constitutes the 30-km-long spit that separates the elongated salty bay (Caleta Valdés) from the open ocean. At the southern end, the inlet is subject to strong tidal action.

TIERRA DEL FUEGO–ISLAS MALVINAS–ANTARCTICA

The coastline situated south of Río Gallegos estuary and north of the Magellan Straits is characteristized by the presence of Quaternary glaciogenic deposits. The Quaternary marine and glaciogenic units of Tierra del Fuego have been recognized and extensively described by Feruglio (1950) and Auer (1956, 1959). The northern coast of Tierra del Fuego is a low, barrier-like environment where pebbles are a major component. A marshy environment is also developed at Bahía San Sebastián. From here southward there is a predominantly cliffy coast (Plate 12-8); the materials exposed are Quaternary glacigenic or raised marine deposits, Tertiary sediments, and Mesozoic marine and volcanic rocks. These Mesozoic units are the dominant rocks of the cliffy coast of Isla de los Estados (Caminos 1980).

The indented, cliffy coast of Malvinas is mainly composed of Lower Paleozoic marine deposits and Upper Paleozoic continental rocks. Quaternary raised shorelines have also been mentioned (Turner 1980) (see also ATLANTIC ISLANDS section).

The ice-fringed Antarctic coast shows a variety of geological units of Precambrian, Paleozoic, Mesozoic, and Cenozoic age (Craddock 1970; Caminos and Massabie 1980) (For more details see ANTARCTICA, this volume).

ENRIQUE J. SCHNACK

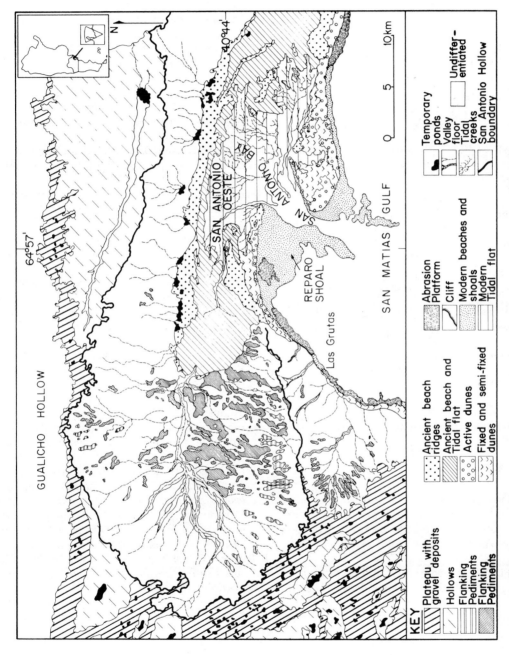

Figure 12-8. Geomorphic environments of San Antonio Bay and Hollow (after Angulo et al. 1979, 1981).

75

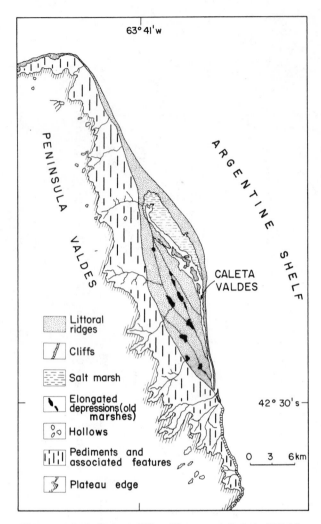

Figure 12-9. Coastal landforms at Caleta Valdés.

REFERENCES

Angulo, R., F. Fidalgo, M. Gómez Peral, and E. J. Schnack, 1979, Las ingresiones marinas cuaternarias en la Bahía de San Antonio y vecindades, Provincia de Río Negro, *Actas VII Congr. Geológico Argentino* (1978), I: 271–283.

Angulo, R., F. Fidalgo, M. Gómez Peral, and E.J. Schnack, 1981, Geología y geomorfología del Bajo de San Antonio y alrededores, Provincia de Río Negro. *Centro de Investigaciones Científicas de la Provincia de Río Negro,* Serie: Estudios y Documentos No. 8.

Auer, V., 1956, The Pleistocene of Fuego-Patagonia. Part I: the Ice and Interglacial Ages, *Acad. Sci. Fennicae Annales,* ser. A, **3:**45.

Auer, V., 1959, The Pleistocene of Fuego-Patagonia. Part III: Shoreline Displacements. *Acad. Sci. Fennicae Annales,* ser. A, **3:**60.

Caminos, R., 1980, Cordillera Fueguina, in *Geología Regional Argentina, Academia Nacional de Ciencias de Córdoba,* **2:**1463–1501.

Caminos, R., and A. Massabie, 1980, Antártida Argentina e Islas del Atlántico Sur, in *Geología Regional Argentina, Academia Nacional de Ciencias de Córdoba,* **2:**1529–1575.

Craddock, C. (comp.), 1970, Geologic map of Antarctica, *American Geographical Society,* Antarctic Map Folio Series, Plate XX, Folio 12 — Geology.

Feruglio, E., 1950, Descripción geológica de la Patagonia. *Dir. Gen. Yac. Petrol. Fisc.* 3, Buenos Aires, 431p.

Fidalgo, F., U. Colado, and F. De Francesco, 1973, Sobre ingresiones marinas cuaternarias en los Partidos de Castelli, Chascomús y Magdalena (Provincia de Buenos Aires), *Actas V Congr. Geologico Argentino,* **3:**227–240.

Frenguelli, J., 1925, Loess y limos pampianos, An. Soc. Arg. de Est. Geog. *GAEA* **1:**1–88.

Frenguelli, J., 1950, Rasgos generales de la morfología y la geología de la Provincia de Buenos Aires. *LEMIT,* Serie 2, 33, La Plata.

Iriondo, M. and E. Scotta, 1979, The evolution of the Paraná River Delta, *1978 International Symposium on Coastal Evolution in the Quaternary* Proc., Sao Paulo, Brasil, pp. 405–418.

Schnack, E. J., 1979, Estudios sobre la evolución morfológica de la zona costera del Partido de Mar Chiquita, Provincia de Buenos Aires, Resúmenes, *IIa. Reunión Informativa del Cuaternario Bonaerense* (Trenque-Lauquen), CIC, La Plata, pp. 59–69.

Schnack, E. J., J. L. Fasano, and F. I. Isla, 1982, The evolution of Mar Chiquita Lagoon coast, Buenos Aires Province, Argentina, 1981 *Int. Symp. on Sea level changes in the last 15000 years, Magnitude and Causes* Proc., Columbia, S. Carolina, pp. 143–155.

Turner, J. C., 1980, Islas Malvinas, in *Geología Regional Argentina, Academia Nacional de Ciencias de Córdoba,* pp. 1503–1527.

Plate 12-1. Mar Chiquita Lagoon inlet area and adjacent beaches. The photo was taken after an exceptionally wet period so the land drainage is unusually high. The contact between saline water and fresh water is clearly visible in the center of the photograph. The present inlet is artificial and the old channel can be seen near the right foreground. On the right is the marginal flat built on Holocene estuarine and marine sediments. The Pampas Plain can be seen in the background (photo by E. Schnack).

Plate 12-3. South of Mar del Plata (Los Acantilados, see Fig. 12-7) looking south to show vertical cliffs in continental Plio-Pleistocene pseudo-loessic silts with caliche. Note that the waves at low tide break directly onto the cliff foot on the headland, while a narrow beach is exposed at low tide in the foreground. The wave alignment indicates northerly sediment transport. (photo by E. Schnack).

Plate 12-2. Mar del Plata central beaches showing wave refraction very clearly. Beach longshore movement to the north is evident in relation to the groins. The Paleozoic quartzite outcrops in the left foreground form a headland (photo by E. Schnack).

Plate 12-4. Tidal salt marsh at Caleta Malaspina (Bahía Bustamante area) showing marsh vegetation composed of *Spartina sp.* and *Salicornia sp.* As can be seen in the photograph, the "peaty" soil is undergoing erosion (photo by J. L. Cionchi).

Plate 12-5. Looking landward from San Matías Gulf toward San Antonio Bay to show details of the morphology of the western shoal (Reparo Bank), including sand waves and channels. The fossil (Holocene) western spit is seen behind the shoal. In the distance the lighter sections are aligned hollows landward of the paleo beach ridges. Behind the spit, in the central area of the picture, the marshy environments of San Antonio Bay can be seen (for more details see Fig. 12-8) (photo by E. Schnack).

Plate 12-7. Looking seaward, Holocene pebbly beach ridges at Caleta Valdés (photo by E. Schnack).

Plate 12-6. Abrasion platform near Las Grutas (see Fig. 12-8). Two contrasting geological formations are illustrated. The Upper Pleistocene transgressive shelly conglomerate overlies the Miocene marine Patagonia Formation. The width of the abrasion platform is clearly shown in front of the sandy beach visible in the background. A vertical cliff in the Patagonia Formation is shown in the background and a dune slip is visible in the upper right. Here macrotides predominate over wave activity (photo by E. Schnack).

Plate 12-8. Cañadón Beta, approximately 10 km south of Cabo Espíritu Santo, Tierra del Fuego. Looking southward, Pleistocene drift overlies Tertiary (Pliocene) sediments (photo by J. O. Codignotto).

13. URUGUAY

The coastline of Uruguay is about 600 km long, including the shores of Rio de La Plata and the Atlantic Ocean (Figs. 13-1 and 13-2).

The coastline has been influenced by uplift of the Ballena and Animas ranges, the Southeast and Southwest highlands, and subsidence of (a) the structural trough that underlies the Santa Lucia River valley and Merin Lagoon basin, and (b) Montevideo Bay, and East Coast lagoons and river estuaries.

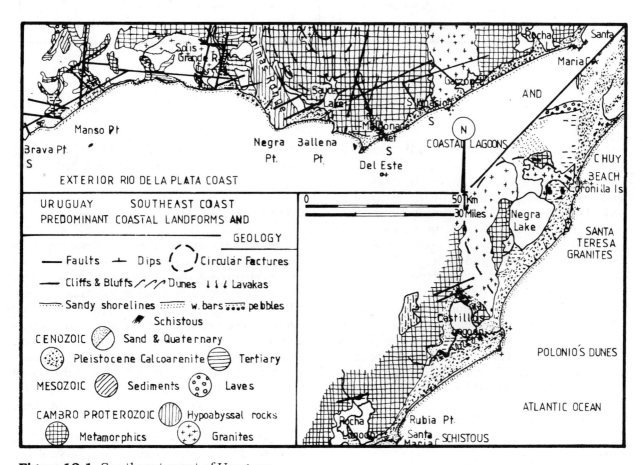

Figure 13-1. Southeast coast of Uruguay.

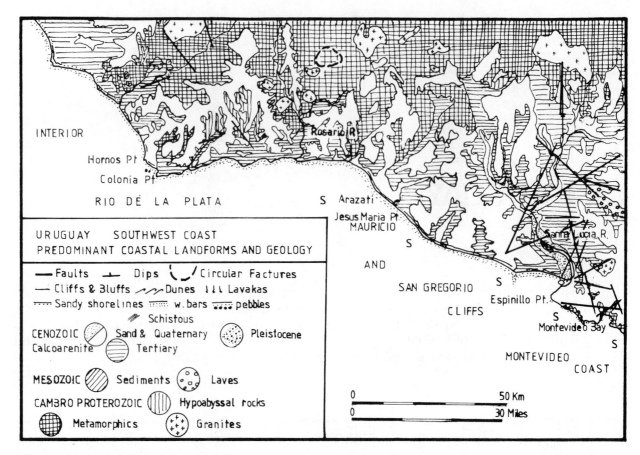

Figure 13-2. Southwest coast of Uruguay.

In the eastern part of the country the coastline truncates the geological formations of Uruguay's Eastern Highlands Shield, which here shows a north-south trend (N 10°E) in the folded and faulted rocks, and patterns of granite intrusions.

The Pre-Devonian crystalline rocks of the Brazilian craton to the west are apparent down to the south, in the Inglés and Rouen banks (Rio de La Plata), where the north slope of the Rio Salado's syncline begins (Bossi 1966).

North of the coastal region, the north-south trend of the geological formations of the Eastern Highlands is interrupted by a large complex of strike-slip faults, with a lateral displacement of 30 km, and a general direction of N 60°E between the tectonic basin of Merin Lagoon and the Arazati River mouth.

These strike faults have led to vertical uplift of local areas between alternating areas of tension and compression.

This fault zone has been filled in succession with pillow lava, rhyolitic dykes (Tertiary volcanism), and sea-floor, coastal, and continental sediments.

COASTAL STABILITY

The coast is considered to have been generally stable in late Quaternary times, indicating a higher sea level during the Holocene. Earthquakes, however, are occasionally recorded and the possibility of localized minor warping cannot be ruled out. The resultant general direction of the shoreline is northwest-southeast between Gorda Point and Colonia Point and west-northwest-east-southeast between Colonia Point and the Santa Lucia River estuary.

East of Espinillo Point to Del Este Point, there is an irregular eroded rocky coast, with many bays and beaches, and a long coastal arc tending generally in a west-east direction. East of Del Este Point to Santa Maria Cape, the general coastal direction is N 60° E, with a gradual turn to N 30° E in three sectors of the coast up to the Brazilian frontier.

The variations in coastal direction are important for local coastal dynamics (Jackson 1978).

WAVES AND CURRENTS

East of Espinillo Point the coast is exposed to a southeasterly ocean swell, modified by the shallow depths of Rio de La Plata and the epicontinental sea, and to storm waves mainly from the southeast and southwest (mouth of the Rio de La Plata).

The western sector is subject only to storm waves, mainly from the southeast and southwest, occurring in a reduced fetch zone and in shallow waters (5 m maximum depth).

Mean spring-tide ranges on the coastline are generally between 0.4 and 0.6 m, but the southeasterly winds produce storm surges between 1.9 m (Rio de La Plata mouth), 2.7 m (Montevideo), and 3.7 m (Colonia).

BEACHES

When cliffs occur, they are extensive on a variety of geological formations, and in many sections are fronted by developed beaches. Sandy beaches are the most common coastal form, fronted by sand bars and backed by beach ridges and dunes. Sand is predominantly quartzose, but sands in the east and the far west are mainly calcareous.

Longshore drifting on the ocean coast north of Santa Maria Cape is generally from southwest to northeast. Between Santa Maria Cape and Del Este Point there is no net drift, but west of Del Este Point there is some westwind drifting.

The shore between Ballena Point and Rubia Point has the coarsest sand grains (1 mm); the sand on beaches elsewhere is fine (0.1–0.2 mm) (Jackson 1979).

ESTUARIES AND LAGOONS

Most Uruguayan rivers have occasionally torrential, flow, and drain along fault-guided channels into estuarine lagoons with sea entrances blocked or encumbered by storm-in-washed sandy thresholds and flanking spits.

Swampy shores, typically with *Juncus* and *Spartina* salt marshes, occupy the more sheltered parts of the coast between Montevideo and Arazati, the margins of estuaries, and the mouths of coastal lagoons.

GEOMORPHOLOGICAL DESCRIPTION OF COASTAL SECTIONS

South East Coast (Fig. 13-1)

Chuy Beach. In the east a gently curved sandy shoreline is backed by extensive, partly mobile, quartzose-calcareous dunes, and two long Pleistocene calcarenite ridges (Plate 13-1) (PCYMP 1979).

Between the ridges are fresh-water lakes and associated swamps. These ridges are the extension to the south of the long Pleistocene spits (80 km) that enclose the lagoon systems of Merin-Patos. They are underlain by rhyolite dykes and Santa Teresa granites.

The Santa Teresa Granites. Granitic points and islands of the Santa Teresa system are apparently part of an intrusive ring pattern. The points form gently curved arcuate beaches of quartzose sand backed by dunes and bluffs of calcarenite rocks. In the lee of the Coronilla Islands, refraction has caused a major sandy breached tombolo. The southeastern Santa Teresa coast has a long sandy beach with scattered gravelly detritus. Here, the long calcarenitic ridge has been strongly dissected by lavakas. Runoff playas are transformed into mobile longitudinal fine sandy dunes by northerly and southwesterly winds.

Polonio's Dunes. South of this beach, near the granitic headlands of Polonio, Castillo Lagoon (Plate 13-2) is linked to the sea by a channel some 22 km long, which brings in brackish water occasionally. The lagoon is bordered by higher-lying Holocene beaches (2–4 m above sea level) and fresh-water swamps (Jackson 1978).

Polonio headlands are covered by mudstone and peat, and two types of fixed dunes composed of relict coarse quartzose sand; covering these systems is a recent longitudinal mobile fine dune. The layers occasionally overtop the granitic base by 60 m.

Recent dunes also occur around swale playas between the Pleistocene calcarenite ridge, which backs a long, gently curved beach (25 km).

Schistose Promontories and Coastal Lagoons. The beach is interrupted by chloritic-schist phyllites running N 25° E and dipping 80° north, which form Rubia Point promontory. Santa Maria Cape (Plate 13–3) is a complex tombolo formed in the lee of schist outcrops, and covered by mobile dunes. To the west the schists are flexured in a N 60° E direction, following the trend of the coastline between Santa Maria Cape and Del Este Point. In this section there are three littoral lagoons, a river inlet, a granite promontory, and some minor granite headlands that interrupt a 75-km-long beach backed by two bluffs cut into Pleistocene coarse-grained calcarenite. The beach has a 12% slope and consists of coarse quartzose sand. The three lagoons occupy former marine embayments in tectonic depressions, enclosed by sand barriers in Pleistocene times (Plate 13–4). The barriers were dissected during the last glacial low-sea-level phase, before the Holocene outer barrier was added to enclose the present lagoons (Jackson 1978).

All these lagoons have intermittent natural outlets. Maldonado inlet is a broad, shallow estuarine lagoon with extensive sandy shoals exposed at low tide, and shores that are fringed by salt marshes. It has a permanent natural outlet opening over a granite substratum, but this is not navigable due to a perennially recurring looped sand bar offshore.

Outer Rio de La Plata Coast. Del Este Point is a breached sandy tombolo in the lee of a granitic island. Settlers built a road connecting the island with the mainland around 1900, making this a permanent isthmus. As in the case of Santa Maria Cape, bluffs back the tombolo, which is covered by mobile dunes.

West of Del Este Point are two major peninsulas: Ballena Point, of quartz sandstone, dipping 80° west and ending in a rocky slope that plunges into deep water, and Negra Point, formed by three syenitic ridges with diabase dykes, bordered seaward by extensive rocky outcrops. The coves between the three ridges have beaches of coarse sand, but the great arc between the two peninsulas is a fine sandy beach backed by extensive dune fields. These dunes developed on a flat sedimentary basin, and have enclosed a fresh-water lake (Sauce Lake) in the bottom of a tectonic depression. Between Negra Point and Manso Point there is a large arenate beach of fine Pliocene and Plio-Pleistocene rocks overtopped by mobile quartzose sand dunes (PCYMP 1979).

The coastline has a jigsaw configuration resulting from the diagonal trend of the faults (strike-slip and oblique slip faulting) leading to movement of the coastal blocks. To the east are landslips in Tertiary formations that rise toward the Animas Range. This formation sometimes has steep coastal slopes with only limited basal cliffing behind shore platforms. The shore platforms are cut in hard Paleogene sandstones containing pebbles and cobbles, which are washed out to form beaches in the coves.

Behind the narrow Solis Grange River entrance, impeded by looped sand-and-pebble bars and a spit that has grown from west to east, there is an estuarine lagoon surrounded by salt marshes. East of this mouth the beach is backed by limestones and peaty deposits capped with dunes. The peats were formed in an estuarine environment. Seaward, these Holocene sediments have been cut back into steep cliffs (4–6m) and serrated shore platforms. The same pattern characterizes all the river mouths in this coastal sector.

Southwest Coast (Fig. 13-2)

The Rocky Coast of Montevideo. Manso Point is the easternmost of the amphibolite and pegmatite headlands characterizing the rocky coast of Montevideo. Brava Point also consists of Pre-Devonian rocks and amphibolite and pegmatite dykes dissected by marine erosion into rugged shore platforms and embayments fringed by *Spartina* and *Juncus* marshes.

On either side of Brava Point, valley mouths end in sandy coves backed by dunes.

Montevideo Bay occupies a sunkland in the amphibolic substratum between San Pedro Peninsula to the east and Lobos Peninsula to the west.

In the northeastern portion of the bay some intertidal mud flats are threatened by erosion as a consequence of dredging a navigational channel.

Sandy beaches on the eastern shore were destroyed by port construction at Montevideo. The last one, Capurro, has been completely eroded, and no more sand sources are available for its natural replenishment.

East of Montevideo Bay the coast has steep slopes (Montevideo Hill), but smaller bays are filled with sand deposits and extensive partly mobile dunes.

The sand deposited in these bays has come from the sea floor during and after the Flandrian marine transgression, but there is no longer any significant sand supply from this source.

Santa Lucia River Mouth. Structurally controlled by faults, the Santa Lucia River valley borders a scarp on its eastern margin. The Santa Lucia Delta plain is developed on a swamp area, formerly a chain of coastal lagoons, that occupied a marine embayment at the southern end of the Santa Lucia tectonic depression.

On the west coast a great complex (30 km) of sandy barriers and spits formed in Pleistocene times to close an ancient bay. Sand shoals offshore are a source of continuing beach progradation, but they have not filled the Santa Lucia River estuary. The source of this sand is the San Gregorio cliff (40 m high) cut into Plio-Pleistocene limestones and sandstones.

Landslides are typical on the Mauricio and San Gregorio cliffs (Plate 13-5). Sandy shore deposits are fringed by *Spartina*. Westward to Jesús Maria Point the shoals are cuspate, with net sand drift to the west.

The Sandy Coast of the Interior Rio de La Plata.   West to Arazati, offshore sand shoals are a source of continuing beach progradation in contrast to the prevalent erosion in the San Gregorio sector (Plate 13-6). A broad flat area with fresh-water swamps and dunes has developed here in front of a Pleistocene coastline indicated by bluffs. The mouth of Rosario River is navigable, but there are broad sand bars offshore. To the east the beach is interrupted by headlands and shore platforms of granites with diabase dykes. There are low-lying plains with dunes and bordering cliffs in Tertiary formations.

Colonia and Hornos points are two granitic

peninsulas, their westward continuation indicated by outlying islands and rocks. However, the general orientation of the coast changes to N 30° W, and the Rio de La Plata landscape becomes genuinely fluviatile, with an area of shallow fresh water some 40 km wide.

The opposing coast of the Paraná River delta, with its fringe of fine sediments, does not affect the Uruguayan coast, as the north-flowing Uruguay River, with strong currents, transports coarse sand to this area.

The gently curved beaches between peninsulas are backed by bluffs cut in Pleistocene sandstones and covered with dunes. The Miocene–Oligocene mudstone peninsulas have been eroded into steep bluffs.

JOSE M. JACKSON

REFERENCES

Bossi, J., 1966, *Geologia del Uruguay*, Departamento de publicaciones de la Universidad, Uruguay.
Jackson, J., 1978, *Etude de la zone cotière de l'Est de l'Uruguay en vue d'un etablissement portuaire*, thesis, Université de Bretagne Occidental.
Jackson, J., 1979, *Sedimentación reciente en la costa platense-atlántica del Uruguay al este de Montevideo*, Informe Ministerio de Obras Públicas, Uruguay.
(PCYMP) Proyecto de Conservación y Mefora de Playas 73/007, 1979, *Informe técnico*, Ministerio Obras Públicas, Uruguay-Programe de Naciones Unidas para el Desarrollo, UNESCO.

Plate 13-1. Chuy Beach. Gullies and lavakas eroding the Pleistocene calcarenite ridge, an ancient barrier of sand that enclosed the Merin–Patos Lagoon system (photo by J. M. Jackson).

Plate 13-2. Polonio's dunes. Extensive mobile dunes driven to the coast and into the sea by strong southwesterly winds. In the foreground can be seen the mouth of Castillo Lagoon and some fresh-water swamps (photo by J. M. Jackson).

Plate 13-3. Santa Maria Cape. The schistose strike gives the general direction of the coast. In the foreground is a major ancient tombolo (photo by J. M. Jackson).

Plate 13-5. An erosion coast. Mauricio cliffs, near Arazatí, cut into Tertiary sedimentary rocks. Note the sand banks offshore (photo by J. M. Jackson).

Plate 13-4. The mouth of the José Ignacio Lagoon is almost completely sealed off from the sea by a recent barrier of sand washed up by wave action. Generally the gaps are made through this barrier by storm surges. The ancient barrier is not affected (photo by J. M. Jackson).

Plate 13-6. A progradation coast. The Rosario River mouth, east of Mauricio cliffs, and the extensive sand shoals in the interior Rio de La Plata. Wave action is not sufficient to form a permanent sand barrier. During episodes of flooding, a gap is cut through this barrier by discharge from the river (photo by J. M. Jackson).

14. BRAZIL

The Brazilian coastline (Figs. 14-1 and 14-2), which lies between latitudes 4° N and 32° S, is about 9,200 km long (Silveira 1964). It is backed by extensive continental plateaus of igneous and metamorphic Precambrian rocks with basins of Paleozoic and younger sediments, and fronted by a continental shelf that widens northward (Martins and Coutinho 1981). There are coastal plains of Quaternary sand deposits and tidal mangrove swamps, and rocky sectors, especially in the north and northeast, where Tertiary formations reach the sea, and in the southeast, where the Precambrian basement structures of the Serra do Mar come to the coastline.

The north-facing coastline (north of Cabo de São Roque) receives waves generated by northeast trade winds, but wave energy is low in the sector of the Amazon and Para estuaries, where the continental shelf is wide and shallow. Farther south, waves generated by the southeast trade winds are effective, and they are accompanied by southerly swell arriving from the South Atlantic. Wave energy increases in the stormier environments of the far south. Tide ranges are generally small, but they increase to more than 2 m north of Cabo Frio and are augmented on the northern coastline, where ranges of up to 12 m and tidal currents of up to 250 cm/s have been recorded in the Amazon estuary (Diegues 1972).

From the Uruguay border the coast runs northeast and consists of wide, sandy barrier formations enclosing major lagoon systems, Lagoa Mirim and Lagoa dos Patos (Plate 14-1), with associated salt marshes and sedge swamps (Delaney 1965). The coastal plain of Rio Grande do Sul is up to 120 km wide, and notable for extensive dunes driven by predominantly southerly winds. North of Porto Alegre the scarped edges of sedimentary-basaltic Paraná basin develop behind a narrow coastal plain within which a chain of lagoons continues toward Cabo de Santa Marta.

In Santa Catarina Province the Precambrian basement comes to the coast with high promontories separated by valley-mouth inlets formed by Holocene marine submergence. The hilly island of Santa Catarina is noted for its beach ridge-and-dune systems (Bigarella 1979). Adjacent Cabo de Santa Marta is the southernmost limit of mangroves in Brazil.

The high indented coastline continues northward to São Francisco Island, which also has beach-ridge plains. It then becomes simpler in outline interrupted by inlets at the mouths of the steep valleys on the eastern flank of the Serra do Mar or with large bays as Paranaguá. Pleistocene and Holocene barriers enclose narrow lagoons and mangrove swamps at Cananeia, north of the hilly Ilha do Cardoso (Bigarella 1978). Ilha Comprida is an elongated sandy barrier island on which are many shell middens. Stages in the evolution of these depositional features have been traced and dated by Petri and Suguio (1973) and Suguio and Martin (1978). The tide range is less than 1.5 m, but intertidal mangroves are extensive in this lagoonal channel system of Cananéia-Tguape, including Ribeira de Iguape mouth river. Sandy beaches towards Santos are interrupted by residual coastal massifs as Tguape, Yuréia, Itatins, Itanhaem. Outlines of beaches are related to prevailing southeasterly wave action.

Santos is backed by an extensive estuarine mangrove swamp, but sandy beaches adjacent Santos continuing northeastward are interrupted by rocky promontories that become larger and more fre-

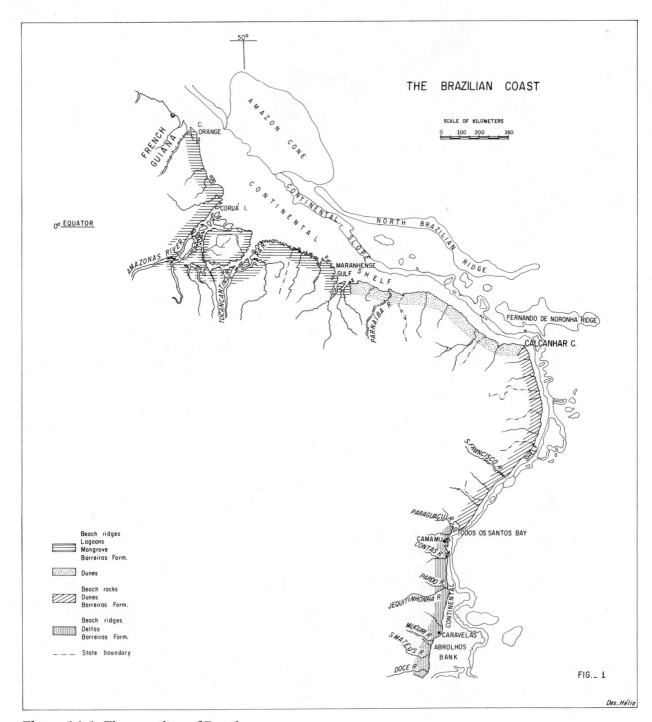

THE BRAZILIAN COAST

Figure 14-1. The coastline of Brazil.

quent as the front of the Serra do Mar approaches the coastline (Plate 14-2). A mountainous promontory runs out toward the high Ilha de São Sebastião, which stands beyond a deep, narrow strait, and the high hinterland dominates the coast between here and Rio. Embayments, some well sheltered from prevailing southeasterly wave action, have beaches and mangrove swamps. Caraguatatuba Bay is backed by a Pleistocene-Holocene beach-ridge plain, which has recently prograded following the 1967 downpour in the high hinterland, which caused catastrophic erosion and caused rivers to discharge vast quantities of sand, silt, and clay into this bay, to be

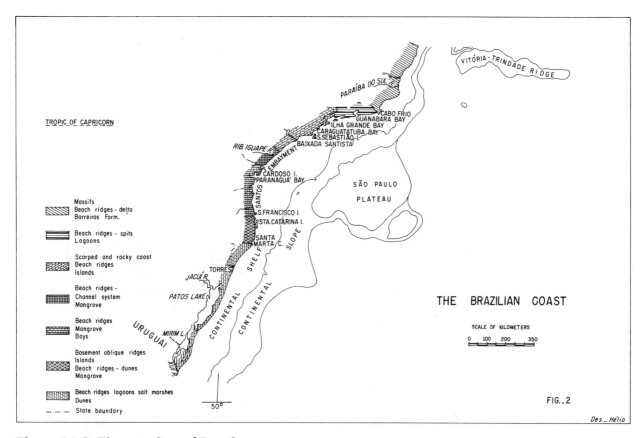

Figure 14-2. The coastline of Brazil.

reworked by wave action (Cruz 1974). Smaller bays occur as far as Ubatuba, and in the western part of the Baia de Ilha Grande very sheltered bays are backed by mangrove swamps, as at the historic town of Parati. The indented coastline of this bay is fringed by numerous high islands (Plate 14-3).

The eastern part of Baia de Ilha Grande shows a marked change in coastal features with the first of a series of large sandy barriers, the Restinga da Marambaia (Plate 14-5), running east from the high Ilha da Marambaia. Sandy beaches are interrupted by steep promontories of crystalline rock, including the sugarloafs of Rio de Janeiro, alongside a major marine inlet, the Baia de Guanabara, the inner shores of which are mangrove-fringed. Occupying a tectonic depression (Ruellan, 1944), this bay (Plate 14-4) has an area of 400 km², and has been much modified by human activities (Amador 1981).

East of Rio, former embayments have been sealed off by Holocene barrier deposition to form a series of coastal lagoons, the largest of which is the Lagoa de Araruama, close to Cabo Frio. (Plate 14-6) backed

by Barreiras Group sedimentary formations and crystalline rocks. There is generally an inner barrier, related to a higher Holocene sea-level phase, and an outer barrier developed at present sea level. Muehe (1979) has shown that the barrier sands have come from the sea floor, fluvial sediment yields having been entrapped in rias and lagoons. Evidence of a phase of higher sea level relative to the land earlier in Holocene times is abundant in the Cabo Frio area: it includes emerged beach conglomerates, shell beds, and lagoon shore features. Cabo Frio is a dry and relatively cool region, influenced by the cold Falkland Current, which here reaches its northern limit, and often subject to southeasterly winds. The high evaporation is used for extensive salt production from pans excavated in marshlands or impounded in shallow lagoon areas. The hilly Cabo Frio peninsula is attached to the mainland by a broad sandy isthmus bordered by curving beaches and surmounted by dune topography. There are partly vegetated parabolic dunes as well as barchans on drifting sand sheets: dune alignments are determined by northeasterly winds (the area is sheltered from southeasterly winds by the hilly promontory).

North from Cabo Frio the first major feature is the deltaic protrusion at the mouth of the River Paraíba do Sul, formed largely by Holocene beach-ridge progradation (Dias 1981); the southern part, near Macaé, truncates Pleistocene beach ridges. The upland margin of the Serra do Mar recedes inland and is breached by several river-valley mouths that open on to the depositional coastal plain. Locally, outlying hills reach the coast alongside deep bays, as at Vitoria. Farther north in Espirito Santo Province, the large Doce Delta is also complex, with Late Pleistocene as well as Holocene terraces and a fringe of prograded beach ridges (Suguio et al. 1981).

The coastal plain widens northward into Bahia, and includes deltaic regions at the mouths of the Doce, Jequitinhonha, Camamu rivers and the São Mateus, Mucuri, Yucuruçu, Ítanheting, Pardo Contas, Paraguaçu rivers. Beach ridges are very extensive, especially at Ponta da Baleia, a cuspate foreland south of the Itanhetinga River, in the lee of the Abrolhos archipelago, islets or banks of calcareous reef sandstone, produced by Holocene emergence. Ponta do Corumbaú is a sharper, tri-angular foreland in the lee of another group of reef islands. The Jequitinhonha delta is a Holocene formation with beach ridges built in front of the dissected remains of a similar Late Pleistocene delta (Martin et al. 1980).

It is in this sector that Tricart (1960) deduced a history of Plio-Quaternary deformation of the continental margin accompanied by climatic variations and sea-level oscillations, attributing coastal sands to shoreward movement of sediments derived from latosols produced by weathering on the emerged continental shelf during low-sea-level episodes. Transverse faulting has compli-cated coastal topography north of Itacaré, where the coastline becomes indented by rias and embayments, the largest of which is the Todos os Santos Bay, behind the hilly peninsula of Salvador. In an increasingly warm and wet climate, the sheltered shores of rias and estuaries are extensively mangrove-fringed, while the consis-tent southeast trade winds produce the waves in coastal waters that have built up beach-ridge plains. The Paraguaçu River has an estuarine mouth, opening into Todos os Santos Bay.

North from Salvador the relatively straight coast-line is bordered offshore by beach rocks in paral-lel zones and calcareous reef sandstones (Bigarella 1975), some of which are cemented dune sands (eolian calcarenites). There are coastal terraces 2–3 and 7–8 m above present sea level, and the tide range increases to between 3 and 4 m. Locally there are cliffs cut into Pliocene sedimentary for-mations, Barreiras Group (Silveira 1964). North of Aracaju the coastline curves out to the beach-ridge-fringed deltaic plains around the mouth of the São Francisco River (Plate 14-7); again, there are relics of a Pleistocene delta fronted by prograded Holocene beach ridges (Bittencourt et al. 1981).

Humid tropical conditions, with annual rain-fall between 1,000 and 2,000 mm, dominate the coastline northward Recife to Natal, but with a lengthening summer dry season. The coastal out-line remains simple, with beach-ridge plains, nearshore sandstone reefs and some cliffed sectors. Calcanhar Cape marks a major change in orienta-tion toward a north-facing equatorial sector, which runs transverse to the valleys and interfluvial ridges of Rio Grande do Norte and Ceará provinces. The coastline, however, is generally smooth and depositional, beach ridges and dunes alternating with lagoons, swampy sectors, and salts deposits. The dry season becomes pronounced, and vegeta-tion is sparse in the hinterland. Near the Parnaiba Delta are long sandy beaches backed by dunes (Plate 14-8).

The tide range increases westward along this coastline, and tidal currents are strong in the three gulfs at São Luís. The coastline in this equatorial sector is indented (Plate 14-9), with many inlets and estuaries bordered by mangrove swamps and backed by a low plateau of Tertiary Barreiras Group and early Quaternary sedimen-tary rocks, which reach the coast in several locali-ties as small cliffs (Martin and Suguio 1978). At Belém the branching funnel-shaped estuary of the Pará has strong tides with intricate and varia-ble shoal and channel topography, numerous mangrove-fringed alluvial islands, and swampy shores subject to rapid changes in configuration due to interactions of waves and of tidal-fluvial currents. It is separated from the similar Amazon estuary by the large deltaic island of Marajó, nota-ble for its extensive swamps and intersecting tidal channel systems. The vast discharge of water and sediment (sand, silt and clay) from the Amazon results in rapid accretion in and around the mouth of the river and along the adjacent coastline, espe-cially northward into French Guiana as the result of tidal movements and the longshore Guiana Current. The low-lying coast of the Amazon deltaic region consists of extensive swamps with man-groves and tropical forest, sandy beaches and cheniers (sand ridges emplaced on alluvial or swampy plains), alluvial grasslands, lagoons and numerous channels (Proj. RADAM, 1974) (Plate 14-10). The climate is perennially hot and wet, with an annual rainfall of more than 2,000 mm, and vegetation is luxuriant. Coastal waters are turbid with sediment in suspension. The low-lying swampy coastline continues north to Cabo Orange on the boundary between Brazil and French Guiana.

O. CRUZ
P. N. COUTINHO
G. M. DUARTE
A. GOMES
D. MUEHE

REFERENCES

Amador, E. S., 1981, Sedimentação de baía de Guanabara, *4th Simp. Com. Técn.-Cientif. Quaternário Pub. Esp.*, vol. 1, K. Suguio et al., eds., SBG, Brasil, pp. 24–25.

Bigarella, J. J., 1975, Reef sandstones from northeastern Brazil, *Acad. Brasiliera Ciênc. Anais* **47:**395–409.

Bigarella, J. J., 1978, *A Serra do Mar e a porção oriental do Estado do Paraná*, S.E.P.-ADEA, Curitiba, 248p.

Bigarella, J. J., 1979, Structural features at Lagoa dune field, Santa Catarina, in *A Study of Global Sand Seas*, E. D. McKee, ed., U.S. Geol. Survey Prof. Paper 1052, Washington, D.C., pp. 114–130.

Bittencourt, A. C. S. P., J. M. L. Domingues, L. Martin, and Y. A. Ferreira, 1981, Evolução do "delta" do rio São Francisco durante o Quaternário, *4th Simp. Com. Técn.-Cientif. Quaternário Pub. Esp.*, vol. 1, K. Suguio et al., eds., SBG, Brasil, pp. 10–11.

Cruz, O., 1974, *A Serra do Mar e o litoral na área de Caraguatatuba*, S. Teses e Monografias, IGEO-USP, n. 11, São Paulo.

Delaney, P. J. V., 1965, Fisiografia e geologia da superficie da planicie costeira do Rio Grande do Sul, Esc. Geol. URGS, *Pub. Esp.* 6, 105p.

Dias, G. T. M., 1981, O complexo deltáico do rio Paraíbe do Sul, Rio de Janeiro, *4th Simp. Com. Técn.-Cientif. Quaternário Pub. Esp.*, vol. 2, K. Suguio, ed., SBG, Brasil, pp. 38–88.

Diegues, F. M. F., 1972, Introdução á oceanografia do estuário Amazônico, *Anais Congr. Bras. Geol.* **2:**301–317.

Martin, L. and K. Suguio, 1978, Excursion route along the coastline between town of Cananéia (St. of São Paulo) and Guaratiba outlet (St. of Rio de Janeiro), Int. Symp. on coastal evol. in the Quaternary, IGCP-Project 61, *Special Pub.* 2, São Paulo, 97p.

Martin, L., A. C. S. P. Bittencourt, G. S. Vilas Boas, and J. M. Flexor, 1980, Mapa geológico do Quaternário costeiro do Estado da Bahia, 1:250.000, Secr. Minas Energia, CPM, Salvador.

Martins, L. R. and P. N. Coutinho, 1981, The Brazilian continental margin, *Earth Sci. Reu* **17:**87–107.

Muehe, D., 1979, Sedimentology and topography of a high energy coastal environment between Rio de Janeiro and Cabo Frio, *Acad. Brasileira Ciênc. Anais* **51:**473–481.

Petri, S. and K. Suguio, 1973, Stratigraphy of the Iguape-Cananéia lagoonal region sedimentary deposits, São Paulo, Part II, *Bol. Inst. Geosci. USP,* **4:**71-85.

Projeto RADAM, 1974, *Levantamento de recursos naturais*. Fl. Macapá 6 e Belém 5, MME-DNPM, Rio de Janeiro.

Ruellan, F., 1944, A evolução geomorfologica da baía de Guanabara e das regiões vizinhas, *Reu. Bras. Geog.* **6:**445–505.

Silveira, J. D., 1964, Morfologia do litoral, in *Brasil a Terra e o Homen,* A. Azevedo, ed., CEN, São Paulo, pp. 253–305.

Suguio, K. and L. Martin, 1978, Quaternary marine formations of the St. of São Paulo and southern Rio de Janeiro, Int. Symp. on coastal evol. in the Quaternary, IGCP-Project 61, *Special Pub. 1,* São Paulo, 55p.

Suguio, K., L. Martin, and J. M. L. Domingues, 1981, Evolução do "delta" rio Doce durante o Quaternário: influencia das variações do nível do mar, *4th Simp. Com. Técn.-Cientif. Quaternario Pub. Esp.,* vol. 1, K. Sugio et al., eds., SBG, Brasil, pp. 14–15.

Tricart, J., 1960, Problemas geomorfológicos do litoral oriental do Brasil, *Bol. Baiano Geog.* **1:**1–39.

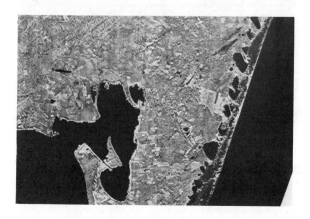

Plate 14-1. Lagoons and beach ridges on coastal plain and Patos lagoon. (Image courtesy of RADAMBRASIL).

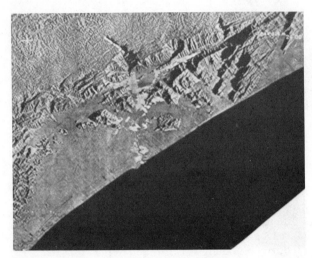

Plate 14-2. Structural influences in formation of Serra do Mar scarps behind Bairada Santista (Image courtesy of RADAMBRASIL).

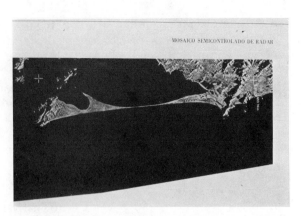

Plate 14-5. Restinga da Marambaia sandy spits and Marambaia island (Image courtesy of RADAMBRASIL).

Plate 14-3. High islands and indented coast at Baia de Ilha Grande (Image courtesy of RADAMBRASIL).

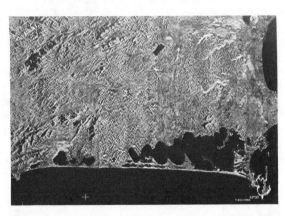

Plate 14-6. Coastal barriers at Araruama lagoon near Cabofrio (Image courtesy of RADAMBRASIL).

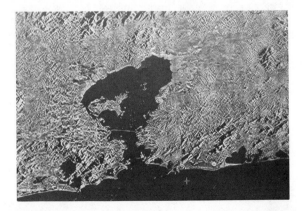

Plate 14-4. Rio de Janeiro sugarloafs alongside the Baia de Guanabara (Image courtesy of RADAMBRASIL).

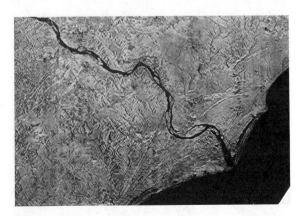

Plate 14-7. Quaternary deltaic complex at the mouth of the São Francisco River (Image courtesy of RADAMBRASIL).

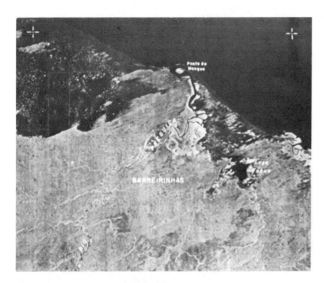

Plate 14-8. Dune fields at Lencóis Maranhenses, near the Parnaiba River delta (Image courtesy of RADAMBRASIL).

Plate 14-10. The mouth of the Amazon River with flat, swampy terrains and unstable islands (Image courtesy of RADAMBRASIL).

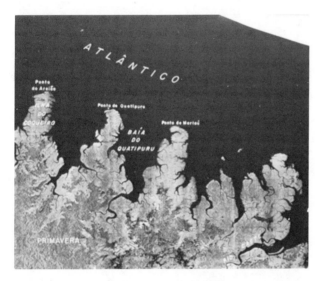

Plate 14-9. Tertiary and early Quaternary plateau fronted by mangrove-lined inlets and estuaries (Image courtesy of RADAMBRASIL).

15. FRENCH GUIANA

The coastline of French Guiana extends along the Atlantic Ocean for 370 km (Fig. 15-1). It is a landscape of mangroves and salt marshes, here and there broken by outcrops of Precambrian crystalline basement.

The outcrops of the Guianese Shield stand out from the coastline, breaking through as islands in the open sea — Le Grand and Le Petit Connetable (the High and the Low Constable, granites, 04°50′ N–51°56′W), near the coast; Le Pére (the Father, 100 m in altitude); La Mère (the Mother, 111 m); L'Enfant Perdu (the Lost Child); Le Malingre (the Sickly One, 55 m, dolerites); and Les Iles du Salut (the Salvation Islands, 66 m, gabbros-peridotites) — or as reefs that are buffeted by the waves (Malmanoury reefs).

Other outcrops are coastal relief practically filled by marine sediment of Holocene age (mainly marine clay) or Pleistocene age (fine, sorted sands of old offshore bars) — Ouanary Mountain, Montagne d'Argent (Silver Mountain, 100 m), Cayenne Mountains (234 m, migmatites and diorites), and hills of Kourou and Organabo (granitogneiss).

The coastal region of French Guiana is part of a large sedimentary area found in all three Guianas; it presents its maximum extent in the Berbice Region (Brinkman and Pons 1968). Clay deposits extend from the mouth of the Amazon to the mouth of the Orenoque. The only discontinuity occurs between Cayenne and Organabo, where the Precambrian basement protrudes, thus making a mole that continues to the sea. This tectonic partitioning, along with a slight uplift of the basement, influences the morphology of the coast, the deposit of clay, and the occurrence of sand ridges at the crystalline outcrops. The marine deposits of the Young Coastal Plain (60% clay,

mainly kaolinite and some montmorillonite; 20% fine silt) have been forming since approximately 8000 B.P. (Holocene age). Sediments from the Amazon mouth are essentially kaolinite. The clays form an unvaried plain of less than 4 m altitude, with the former shores very visible. These outlines are marked by coarse sand ridges, generally oriented southeast-northwest, often emerging from the middle of the marine clay plain.

The Old Coastal Plain, of less importance, is a landscape of old offshore bars (fine sorted sands), about 15 m high, covered with savannas and forest galleries.

Two large rivers form the boundary of the coastal plain of French Guiana: the Maroni on the west and the Oyapock on the east. Secondary rivers are the Approuague, Oyac, Cayenne, Kourou, Sinnamary, Counamama, Iracoubo, and Mana. All have their estuaries deviated to the west. Their old beds and the surface relief that they give to the landscape have considerably contributed to the penetration of the sea during the Quaternary. Anastomosed channels are typical of the estuarian environment; this is particularly true for the Cayenne Island region, so called because it is surrounded by such channels, as well as the region between the Mana and Maroni rivers. The channels are vestiges of a Quaternary fossil system, which was progressively warped by marine sediment. The channels continue to be navigable due to the movement of the tides (Choubert 1957). The remnants of an old Paleocene shoreline can be observed in this region (Boyé 1963).

The average height of the spring tide is 3 m; that of the neap tide is 2.5 m. The tide wave goes through the estuaries to the first outcrops of the basement, which causes waterfalls or rapids. The

Figure 15-1. The coast of French Guiana. Precambrian shield, ω gabbros peridotites, γ granites, δ dolerites, $\gamma\mu$ migmatites and diorites, χ schists, Young coastal plain (clays): A, salt marshes; B, mangroves; C, swamps. Old coastal plain (fine sands).

ocean current off of the Guianas, also called the Great Southern-Equatorial Current, moves southeast to northwest, at a speed varying between 2 and 3 knots. One of the coastal and subcoastal branches runs northwest, thus running into disturbances where it joins fresh water from the large rivers (Rossignol 1978).

The continental border, coastal mud, pelagic mud, and plateau sands have only a slight slope,

0.05 to 1% (Moguedet 1973); the widest point of the perpendicular bluff that is the limit of the continental plateau is found around 147 km from Isere Point (Maroni estuary), and the narrowest point is 92 km from Cap Orange (Oyapock estuary). The bottom depth drops rapidly from 100–1000 m. The mud flats (slikke) can be several kilometers long (Rossignol 1978).

The outline of the coast is subject to clay deposition and then erosion, in varying degrees depending on the moment. This alternation of mud deposition and erosion accounts for the appearance of clay marine deposits and mudbanks, which lie in a northwesterly direction. This phenomenon was analyzed by the Delft Hydraulics Laboratory (1962) in its study of the port of Demerara. They showed that mudbanks appear at any point on the Guianese coast as a result of refraction of the incidental southwesterly waves approaching the coast, with divergence or convergence of energy, inducing a macro-ripple pattern. This refraction produces calm zones (amplitude of zero vibration, minimum energy, mud deposit), and maximum agitation (amplitude of maximum vibration, maximum energy, erosion).

Under the influence of a residual current along the coast, the mudbanks shift from east to west; therefore all parts of the coast are affected by this phenomenon at one time or another. Lab studies have indicated a theoretical wave length of 40 km, moving 1.3 km per year. Thus, mud invasion would occur at 30-yr intervals for any point on the coast. The period of the vibrations shows up clearly in Figure 15-2 and Plate 15-1; the irregularities are caused by rocky obstacles on the coast (Turenne 1978). Figure 15-2 is based on a comparison of 1973 and 1976 Landsat satellite photographs.

One can see the alteration and extension of the mud flats and their shift toward the west. The balance sheet is always positive. The shoreline advances, a pioneer vegetation of *Laguncularia* establishes itself (Lescure 1975), followed by *Avicennia nitida*. Then rhyzophora begin to grow on the backside mangroves, and on the banks of the estuaries. (Villages such as Iracoubo, Tonate, and Trou Poisson are now found inside a relatively wide fringe of mangroves. The Iracoubo and Counamama rivers have a common mouth, which did not appear on the shoreline in 1956 [Misset 1968].) Lastly, this mud invasion greatly reduces the depth of the access channels to main ports. The depth is often less than 5 m. The cycles of mud deposition and erosion also affect the Cayenne Peninsula, which as recently as 1953 was bordered by mangroves. The erosion began in 1963. Landsat photographs from 1976 show that sea waters are very muddy in the Cayenne region.

Coarse sand ridges are either narrow and rectilinear ridges, 70–200 m wide, in the form of unstable coastal beaches deposited on the marine clay, or spread-out ridges with multiple crests, separated by marshy depressions. The latter are found mostly west of the rivers or near the basement outcrops (Cayenne Islands, west of Kourou [Plate 15–2], Sinnamary, Iracoubo, the Mana landscape).

From Cap Orange (04°24′ N–51°34′ W) to the Cayenne Peninsula (4°50′ N–52°22′ W) the low-lying coast is bordered by mangroves. The Silver Mountain (Montagne d'Argent) Peninsula is the only discontinuity. Cayenne Island has the only high summits; its north and northeast coasts are cut up into bays, with the points prolonged by rocks and islets. From Cayenne (Plate 15-3) to Organabo (Plate 15-4), the coast is low again, edged with mangroves. Rollers break over the mud flats. In some places, sandy ridges are found on the edge of the mangroves or salt marshes. The only irregularities are Rocky Point (Pointe des Roches, 05°09′ N–52°38′ W) and the Salvation Islands (Les Iles du Salut, 05°17′ N–52°35′ W).

The largest salt marsh landscape, with intervening tidal entrances, occurs between Organabo and Pointe Isere. In this region, the fringing sand beaches vary in size over time. They are the largest egg-laying area in the world for the luth turtle, *Dermochelys choriacea linee* (Pritchard 1971).

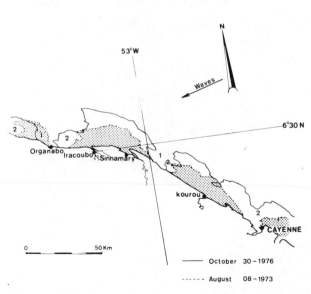

Figure 15-2. Occurrence of mudbanks and turbid waters between August 8, 1973, and October 30, 1973, from Cayenne to Organabo, French Guiana: 1. erosion; 2. occurrence of turbid waters and mudbanks.

J. F. TURENNE

REFERENCES

Boyé, M., 1963, *La Géologie des plaines basses, entre Organabo et le Maroni (Guyane Française)*. Imprimerie Nationale, Paris.

Brinkman, R., and C. J. Pons, 1968, *A Pedogeomorphological Classification and Map of the Holocene Sediments in the Coastal Plain of the Three Guianas*. Soil Survey Paper No. 4, Soil Survey Institute, Wageningen, the Netherlands.

Choubert, B., 1957, *Essai sur la morphologie de la Guyane*. BRGM, Paris.

Delft Hydraulics Laboratory, 1962, *Demerara Coastal Investigation*. Delft, the Netherlands.

Lescure, J. P., 1975, La mangrove guyanaise, architecture des jeunes stades et vie avienne, *Cahier ORSTOM, Sér. Biol.* **12**, 4:361–376.

Misset, A., 1968, *Carte pédologique IRACOUBO-ORAGANABO*. ORSTOM, Cayenne, French Guyana.

Moguedet, G., 1973, *Contribution à l'étude des sédiments superficiels du plateau continental de la Guyane Française*. Université de Nantes, France.

Pritchard, P. C. H., 1971, *Sea turtles in French Guiana*, IUCN Publications.

Rossignol, M., 1978, *Le milieu marin, La Guyane*. ORSTOM–CNRS, Paris.

Turenne, J. F., 1978, *Sédimentologie de la Plaine Côtière, Atlas des DOM, La Guyane*. ORSTOM–CNRS, Paris.

Plate 15-1. Macro-ripple pattern along the French Guiana coast (see Fig. 15-2), October 30, 1976 (Landsat photo courtesy of NASA).

Plate 15-2. Old sand ridges on the coastal plain, salt marshes, and coastal erosion of mangrove, west of Kourou (photo by J. F. Turenne).

Plate 15-4. Mudbanks at low tide, west of Organabo, with active erosion of the coast on the back side (photo by J. F. Turenne).

Plate 15-3. Outline of coastal accretion between Cayenne and Kourou (photo by J. J. de Granville).

16. SURINAM

Coastal Surinam extends for 350 km from the Marowijne River in the east to the Corantijn River at the western border (Fig. 16-1). The coastal landforms are the products of waves and currents acting on the great quantities of fine-grained sediment discharged by the Amazon River and the sand, silt, and clay discharged by the four principal rivers reaching the Surinam shore.

Coastal processes include waves that are usually out of the northeast or east, producing a westerly drift. The tides are semidiurnal with a mean range of 1.8 m and a spring tide range of 2.8–3.2 m. The westerly alongshore drift is impor-

tant in transporting silt, clay, and sand-sized particles. Vast quantities of clay are distributed northwestward by the general oceanic circulation and by waves in the nearshore zone. In a recent study, Wells and Coleman (1977) reported an unusual nearshore transportation mechanism because of high concentrations of suspended clays over mud flats. As the oceanic waves enter shallow water, their oscillatory motion changes to a solitary wave, with a unidirectional translation of sediment constantly shoreward and westward over the mud flats. There is some sand transport along the beach where the swash eventually strikes

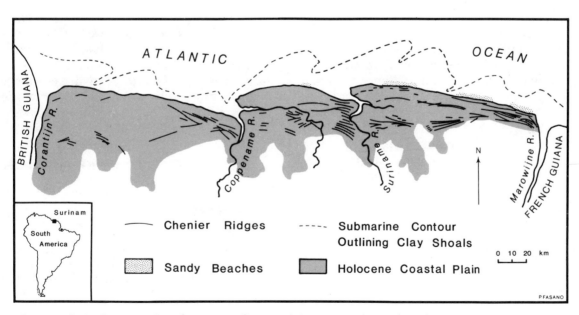

Figure 16-1. Geomorphic features of coastal Surinam (compiled from Augustinus 1978; Brinkman and Pons 1968; Vann 1959; Zonnenfeld 1954).

the shoreline. In areas where sand and shell particles accumulate, coarser sediment is transported primarily by beach drifting.

The Holocene coastal plain has been built up as a wedge thickening seaward during the latest rise of sea level. This recent accumulation has a subaerial extent of about 20 km at the eastern margin and gradually widens to a maximum of 140 km at the western boundary. The coastal deposition consists largely of clay with some lenses of sand and shell. On the surface, the general topography is one of low relief with several series of chenier ridges separated by wide mud flats. The cheniers occur in groupings that extend fan-shaped west from the major river mouths (Fig. 16-1). Each of the rivers discharges into a narrow estuary, and there is evidence (Augustinus 1978) that the cheniers are composed of sand and shell derived locally from streams and the reworking of nearby tidal flats. The chenier ridges further display evidence of episodes of cut and fill as ridges are truncated, blend into, or flare away from each other. In general, each group of ridges has a migrating fulcrum at the eastern end. Westward, these ridges show evidence of accretionary phases during periods of surplus sediment, or truncation during periods of sediment deficit. It is possible that erosion of the eastern part may have led to progradation downdrift. Some cheniers are up to 20 km inland, indicating that there has been considerable progradation of the shoreline. Further, with the exception of the western side of the Marowijne River, chenier development seems to be more characteristic of the past than of the present (Brouwer 1953; Geijskes 1952). Currently, there is a broad clay platform, 1–5 km wide, between the modern shoreline and the cheniers. Carbon-14 dates from the inner margin of this clay platform indicate that clay deposition was initiated about 1000 years ago (Brinkman and Pons 1968). The existence of this broad mud flat marks a reduction in the quantity of sand discharged from local rivers or an overwhelming receipt of fine sediment from the Amazon.

A single discontinuous chenier ridge extends along much of the present coastline, related to active beach-forming processes, the availability of sandy sediment, and the presence of wide mud shoals offshore. Several investigators (Wells et al. 1980; Vann 1980) have reported that the shoreward transport of suspended mud can accumulate large flats that protect the coastline. There are eight such flats off coastal Surinam, with dimensions of 5–10 km alongshore and 2–3 km offshore. They have a spacing of 30–60 km. At low tide the exposed banks may extend up to 1000 m. The mudbanks serve to temporarily store the mud that is transported into the region. They are shifting westward at an average rate of 1.5 km per year, although there is considerable variation.

The chenier attains its best development along the updrift margin of the mudbanks, where sand and shell are transported from the eroding edge. This material combines with the coarse sediment that is moved by beach drifting on the upper foreshore to form a chenier, perched on the clay base. In eastern Surinam cheniers are composed of medium to coarse sand, whereas in the west they consist of fine sand and extend seaward into the mud flat. The interpretation of this difference is that the western chenier is receiving finer sands produced by winnowing across the mud shoals. The cheniers are low features, 1.5–2.0 m, with an occasional small dunal cap or hummock in eastern Surinam.

In sectors between the mud shoals, the chenier form may disappear because of the paucity of available sand and shell. In these areas the clay platform is scarped, with small nips rising to 0.3–2.0 m. Frequently the platform has been eroded irregularly to produce a jagged shoreline with embayments and headlands, measured in tens of meters.

Sandy beaches are present primarily in the eastern sector, where accumulations of coarser sediments are locally available, probably from the erosion of older cheniers. The largest and best developed beach lies slightly west of the Marowijne River mouth. It is about 10 km long, and has a breadth of approximately 75 m. It has low dunal hummocks approaching 0.5 m in elevation and a wide sloping sandy washover extending into the mangroves on its inland margin. Sandy beaches are rare in central and western Surinam.

NORBERT P. PSUTY

REFERENCES

Augustinus, P., 1978, *The Changing Shoreline of Surinam.* Ph.D. thesis, University of Utrecht.

Brouwer, A., 1953, Rhythmic depositional features of the east-Surinam coastal plain, *Geologie en Mijnbouw* **15**:226–236.

Brinkman, R., and L. Pons, 1968, *A Pedogeomorphological Classification and Map of the Holocene*

Sediments in the Coastal Plain of the Three Guianas, Soil Survey Papers No. 4, Soil Survey Institute, Wageningen, the Netherlands.

Geijskes, D., 1952, On the structure and origin of the sand ridges in the coastal zone of Surinam, *Tijdschr. Kon. Ned. Aardr. Gen.* **69:**225-238.

Vann, J., 1959, The geomorphology of the Guiana coast, *Second Coastal Geography Conference,* Baton Rouge, Office of Naval Research, Washington, D.C., pp. 153-187.

Vann, J., 1980, Shoreline changes in mangrove areas, *Zeitschr. Geomorphologie,* Supplement Vol. **34:**255-261.

Wells, J., and J. Coleman, 1977, Nearshore suspended sediment variations, central Surinam coast, *Marine Geology* **24:**M47-M54.

Wells, J., D. Prior, and J. Coleman, 1980, Flowslides in muds and extremely low angle tidal flats, northeastern South America, *Geology* **8:**272-275.

Zonnenfeld, J., 1954, Waarnemingen langs de kust van Suriname, *Tijdschr. Kon. Ned. Aardr. Gen.* **71:**18-31.

17. GUYANA

The coast of Guyana (Fig. 17-1) is comprised of mangroves, mud flats, cheniers, and sandy beaches fronting a swampy coastal plain. These are developed on the Demerara Formation, which borders the entire Atlantic Ocean shore along this portion of the Guyana Shield (McConnell 1975). The coastal plain varies from 25–35 km in width and, where cleared of mangrove, is the site of extensive rice and sugar cultivation. Rivers and streams are tidal across the coastal plain. Farther inland tropical rain forest is prevalent.

There are two highly variable rainy seasons, April to August and November to January, with an annual average rainfall at the coast of 2.25 m (Brooks 1982; Smith 1962). Humidity is high, 88% in the morning and 75% in the afternoon, and the average temperature 26.9°C.

Tides are semidiurnal, with a spring range of 2–4 m. The region is in an east coast swell environment with trade monsoon influences (Davies 1980). Guyana, however, is located south of the hurricane belt (Smith 1962).

For the greater part of its length, the approximately 434-km coastline consists of mud flats, with abundant mangroves, cheniers, and occasional sandy beaches (Fig. 17-1). Both regional and local rivers and streams bring some sand and tremendous quantities of fine-grained sediments to the shore. Net sediment transport is to the west, so there is considerable deposition of this material in that direction. Sediment from the Amazon River forms migrating mud flats and associated subtidal mud banks (Wells and Coleman 1981).

Waves reworking the sediment develop cheniers, ridges of shell and sand overlying the fine-grained and mud flat deposits. Under the westward drift regime, the cheniers tend to form a prominence on the western side of river mouths and trail off in a westerly direction (Psuty and Mizobe 1982a). Accumulations of shell and sand, here and there on the seaward side of a chenier, form isolated stretches of beach over the clay and silt substrate.

Mangroves of the "Occidental Province" (Davies 1980) thrive on the open mud flats and where the flats are exposed between the cheniers. According to Psuty and Mizobe (1982b), the mangrove *Avicennia* grows seaward of *Rhizophora* here, an anomaly caused by the abundance of sand along the outer shore.

Thus the Guyana coast presents a fairly uniform front of mangrove swamp–mud flat–chenier ridge along its entire length (McGill 1958), interspersed with only a few towns developed, mainly, where a river comes down to the sea.

MAURICE L. SCHWARTZ

REFERENCES

Brooks, J. (ed.), 1982, *The 1982 South American Handbook*, Bath.

Davies, J. L., 1980, *Geomorphical Variation in Coastal Development*, Longman, New York.

McConnell, R. B., 1975, Guyana, in *The Encyclopedia of World Regional Geology, Part 1*, R. W. Fairbridge, ed., Dowden, Hutchinson & Ross, Stroudsburg, Pa., pp. 318–325.

McGill, J. T., 1958, Map of coastal landforms of the world, *Geog. Rev.* **48**:402–405.

Psuty, N. P., and C. Mizobe, 1982a, South America, coastal morphology, in *The Encyclopedia of Beaches and Coastal Environments*, M. L. Schwartz, ed., Hutchinson Ross Publishing Co., Stroudsburg, Pa., pp. 765–770.

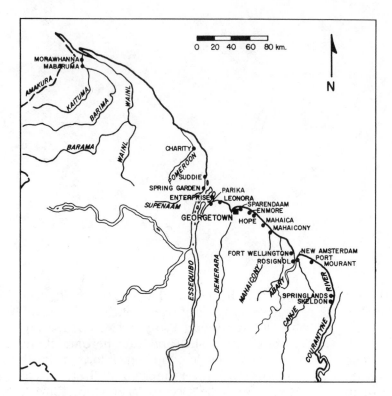

Figure 17-1. Location map and geomorphology of the Guyana coast.

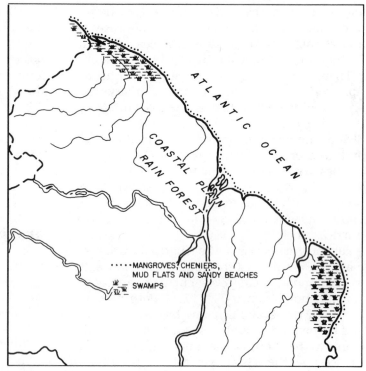

Psuty, N. P., and C. Mizobe, 1982*b*, Central and South America, coastal ecology, in *The Encyclopedia of Beaches and Coastal Environments*, M. L. Schwartz, ed., Hutchinson Ross Publishing Co., Stroudsburg, Pa., pp. 191–201.

Smith, R. T., 1962, *British Guiana*, Oxford University Press, London.

Wells, J. T., and J. M. Coleman, 1981, Periodic mudflat progradation, northeastern coast of South America: a hypothesis, *Jour. Sed. Petrology* **51:**1069–1075.

18. VENEZUELA

The coastline of Venezuela (measured on 1:100,000 maps) is about 3000 km long. Tide ranges are small, with mean spring tides only locally exceeding 50 cm. Wave action produced by the steady trade winds is from the east and northeast, with moderate energy throughout the year, and there is a strong westward longshore current. Hurricanes are very rare.

Coasts exposed to strong wave action are generally cliffed, and protected coasts are often mangrove-fringed. Biotic influences are widespread. Fringing coral reefs occur at many places, the largest being on the eastern side of the Paraguaná Peninsula, and bioerosion features are common, especially on sheltered rocky coasts.

Man's direct influence on the coast of Venezuela is still very small, less than 2% of the coastline having been altered; indirect influences are great, however, notably the destruction of vegetation and soil cover by farming and grazing in recent decades, which has increased sediment yields from rivers, especially the Orinoco, Unare, and Tocuyo.

The coast is unstable because of tectonic uplift of about 0.5 mm/yr in the Cordillera de la Costa (Schubert et al. 1977) and subsidence in the east (Fiedler 1970). Coastal outlines are influenced by the topography of the Cordillera de la Costa, the hills of Falcón and Sucre, and the mesetas of Paraguaná and Guahira. Coastal sectors (Fig. 18-1) show a variety of forms, which can be briefly characterized as follows:

1. Intensive uplift prevails on the Venezuelan coast of the Peninsula de Guajira. Cliffs of cemented gravel up to 6 m high are cut back by strong wave action, and there are interven-ing shallow bays with gravel beach ridges and dunes.

2. A low-lying coast with sandy beach ridges (Tanner 1971) is backed by swamps (Fig. 18-2). The longshore current is strong here.

3. Mangrove swamps on sheltered sectors of a shallow bay were the site of lake dwellings on piles, named "Small Venice" (i.e., Venezuela) when explorers arrived in 1499.

4. The narrow entrance to Lake Maracaibo is fault-bounded. It consists of steep coastal slopes with almost no wave action, and man-grove fringes.

5. The low-lying coast of eastern Zulia and western Falcón is backed by alluvial deposits, dunes, and Pleistocene gravel terraces. Coastal waters are shallow and wave action meager. The longshore current is weak, especially in the east, where the bird-foot delta of the Rio Mitare has grown during the past 3000 years (Fig. 18-3).

6. The tabular limestone area of Paraguaná has sheltered western shores where low-lying coasts prevail, with high fault-induced cliffs only around Punto Fijo. The more exposed eastern coast has the strongest wave action in Venezuela, with small cliffs alternating with depositional sectors behind a well-developed fringing reef.

7. A narrow low-lying isthmus, the result of recent uplift, links Paraguaná with the mainland. Its eastern shore, exposed to strong wave action, has a long beach protected by a ridge of exposed beach rock 32 km in length (Plate 18-1). On its southern tip, dune fields are crossing the isthmus (Fig. 18-4).

8. A hilly region of Oligocene to Pliocene molasse

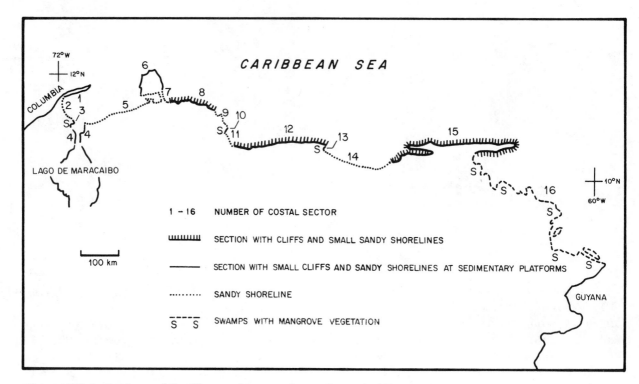

Figure 18-1. Sectors of the Venezuelan coast; see items 1–16 in text.

sediments has steep and cliffed coastal slopes and intervening bays with recent sediments.

9. Coastal beach ridges are backed by sabkhas (salt lagoons), a fringing reef protecting the San Juan peninsula (Fig. 18-5).

10. Shallow coastal water reduces wave action and mangrove swamps are extensive (Fig. 18-6). Small islands offshore (Plate 18-2) are *cayos* (similar to the Florida keys) with fringing reefs, gravel ridges, beach rock, and mangroves.

11. A sector of low-lying sandy coast was strongly eroded in recent times.

12. Here the Cordillera de la Costa (Plate 18-3) — consisting of strongly folded and faulted Mesozoic schists, metamorphic and intrusive, rocks and Tertiary-Quaternary conglomerates — borders the coastline. Cliffs occur only on rocky headlands, and in the west there are rias (Fig. 18-7).

13. Mangrove swamps occur in a bay sheltered from strong wave action, where sediments are trapped.

14. The low-lying barrier-lagoon coast shows evidence of much recent sedimentation.

15. A high hinterland of strongly folded and faulted Mesozoic limestones is dissected by deep river valleys. A subsiding coast is slowly eroding behind a very narrow shelf sector. Mangroves

are sparse in the bays, but corals are abundant (although reefs are not important).

16. Extensive mangrove swamps and sectors of barrier-lagoon coast are subject to rapid changes.

Further details are given by Picard (1974), Picard and Goddard (1975), and Ellenberg (1978).

While the variety of coastal features in Venezuela is explicable mainly in terms of geology and marine processes, climatic factors are also important. Those related to tropical conditions include the abundant coral reefs, luxuriant mangrove swamps, extensive beach rock, and such features as intensive supralittoral solution on rocky shores, rapid water-layer weathering and bioerosion, and a prevalence of fine-grained beaches and alluvial shore deposition, wave quarrying being relatively unimportant (Ellenberg 1980). The rapid transition from humid tropical conditions in the east to warm arid climate in the west is reflected in coastal geomorphology. Cliffs in soft sedimentary formations are steeper and dissected only by gully erosion in the dry sectors, gentler and subject to landsliding after heavy rain (Plate 18-4) in the wet sectors. Sabkhas (swamps in rainy seasons, saline flats in dry seasons) occur on low-lying coasts throughout Venezuela, but they are larger and more frequent in the drier parts. Dunes occur

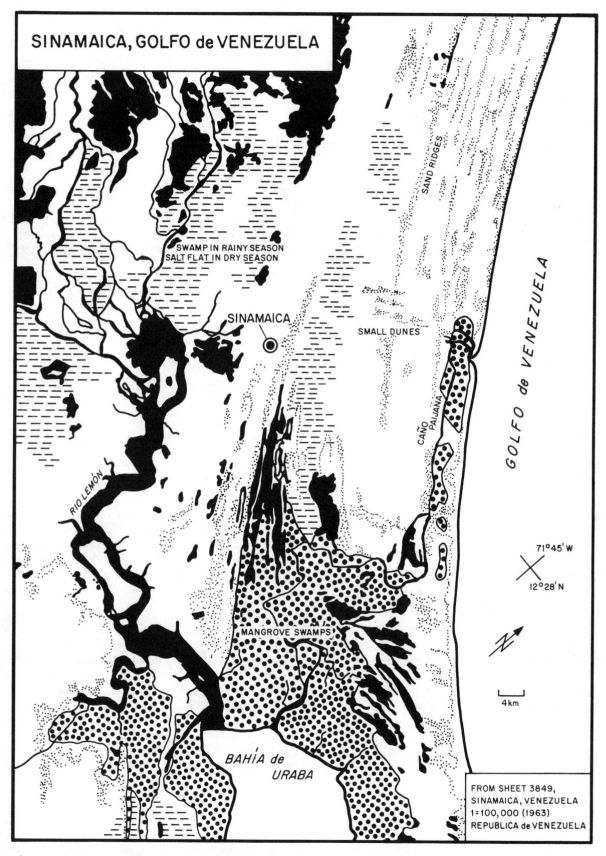

SINAMAICA, GOLFO de VENEZUELA

SWAMP IN RAINY SEASON
SALT FLAT IN DRY SEASON

SINAMAICA

SMALL DUNES

SAND RIDGES

CAÑO PAIJANA

GOLFO de VENEZUELA

71°45'W

12°28'N

N

4km

RIO LEMÓN

MANGROVE SWAMPS

BAHÍA de
URABA

FROM SHEET 3849,
SINAMAICA, VENEZUELA
1=100,000 (1963)
REPUBLICA de VENEZUELA

Figure 18-2. The complex coastal plain of Sinamaica, Gulf of Venezuela.

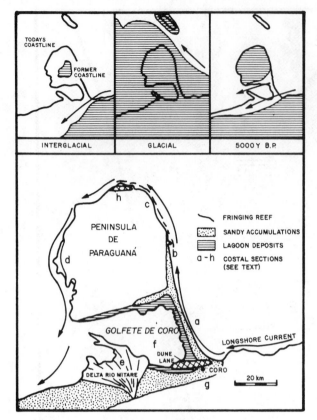

Figure 18-3. Peninsula de Paraguaná, a part of the Venezuelan coast strongly influenced by tectonic movements. About 3000 years ago the former island of Paraguaná became attached to the mainland by the uplift of the intervening sea floor (Bryan 1973). The longshore current was thus diverted around its shores, and a beach formation (a) built up along the eastern edge of the isthmus. This is now protected by a ledge of beach rock, which also extends along the southeast shore of Paraguaná (b). In northeastern Paraguaná (c) the fringing coral reef was uplifted above high tide level, and on the western shores (d) sand deposition and spit formation have ensued. West of the isthmus, in the now sheltered waters of the Golfete de Coro, the Rio Mitare (e) has built a large delta (450 km²). Sedimentation in and around this bay (f) has led to mangrove encroachment and the formation of saline clay plains, while the waters of the bay have become increasingly hypersaline. Dunes have started to cross the southern part of the isthmus (g) (see also Fig. 18-8) and in the north of Paraguaná (h) shoreline progradation has occurred as the result of dunes moving from land to sea.

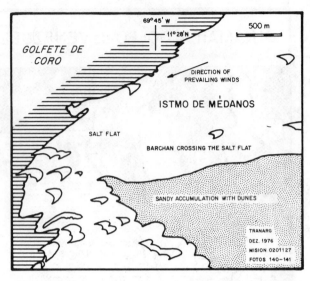

Figure 18-4. Dune field bordering the Golfete de Coro.

only in sectors where more than four months of the year are dry, and where precipitation is less than 900 mm/yr (Fig. 18-8). However, beach rock (Reuber and Ellenberg 1979), coral reefs, and mangrove swamps show no correlation with the climatic variations along the Venezuelan coast.

LUDWIG ELLENBERG

REFERENCES

Bryan, A. L., 1973, Paleoenvironments and cultural diversity in late Pleistocene of South America, *Quaternary Res.* **3,** 2:237-256.

Ellenberg, L., 1978, Coastal types of Venezuela—an application of coastal classifications, *Zeitschr. für Geomorphologie* **22:**439-456.

Ellenberg, L., 1980, Zur Klimamorphologie tropischer Küsten, *Berliner Geog. Stud.* **7:**177-191.

Fiedler, G., 1970, Die seismische Aktivität in Venezuela im Zusammenhang mit den wichtigsten tektonischen Bruchzonen, *Geol. Rundschau* **59:**1203-1215.

Picard, X., 1974, La costa de acantilados entre Puerto Cabello y Cabo Codera, Cordillera de Venezuela, *Asoc. Venezolano de Geología, Minería y Petróleo Bol. Inf.* **17,** 7-9:123-130.

Picard, X., and D. Goddard, 1975, Geomorfología y sedimentación de la costa entre Cabo Codera y Puerto Cabello, *Asoc. Venezolano de Geología, Minería y Petróleo Bol. Inf.* **18,** 1:39-106.

Reuber, I., and L. Ellenberg, 1979, Beachrock in Venezuela, *Acta Cient. Venezolana* **30:**462-447.

Schubert, C., S. Valastro, and J. B. Cowart, 1977, Evidencias de levantamiento reciente de la costa norte-central (Cordillera de la Costa), Venezuela, *Acta Cient. Venezolana* **28:**363-372.

Tanner, W. F., 1971, Growth rates of Venezuelan beach ridges, *Sed. Geology* **6:**215-220.

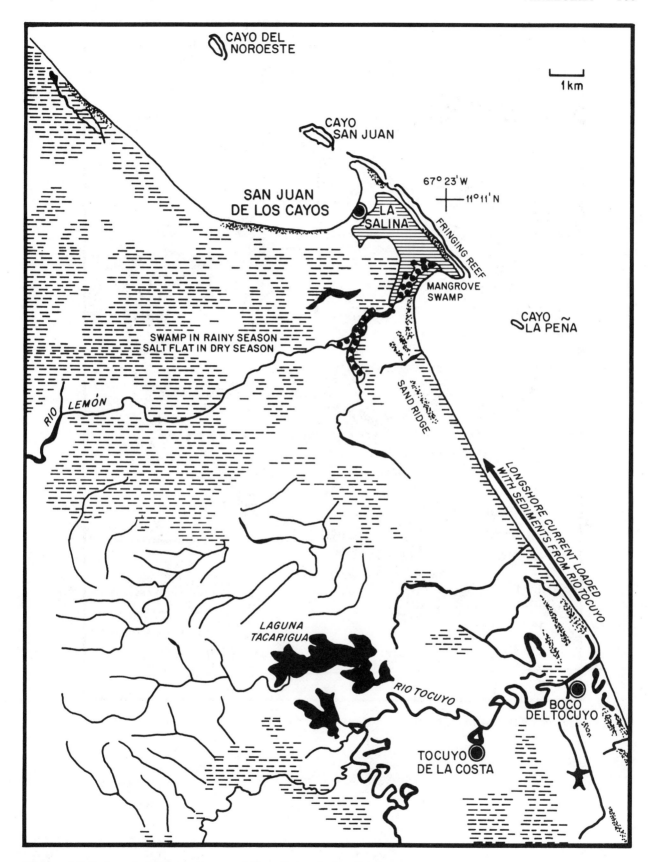

Figure 18-5. Low-lying coast around San Juan de los Cayos.

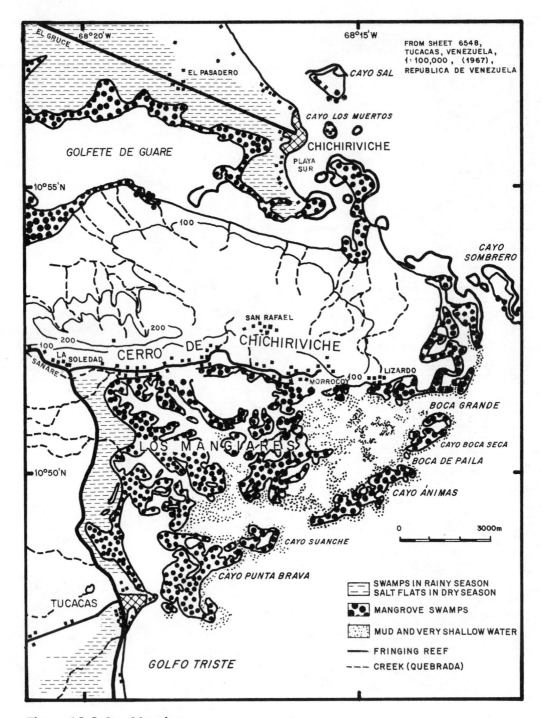

Figure 18-6. Los Manglares.

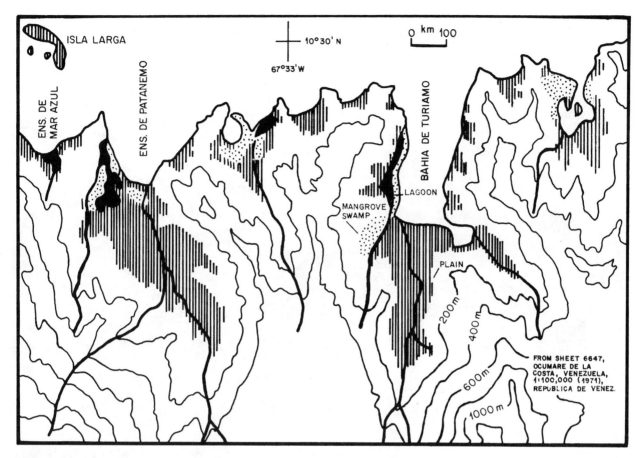

Figure 18-7. Ria coast in the western part of Cordillera de la Costa.

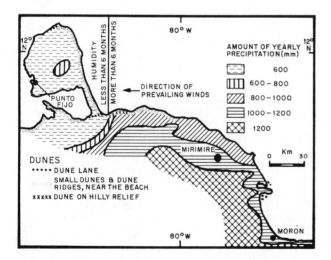

Figure 18-8. Dunes and aridity.

Plate 18-1. Ledge of beach rock, Istmo de Médanos (Fig. 18-1, sector 7) (photo by L. Ellenberg).

Plate 18-2. Cayo Sal (Fig. 18-1, sector 10) (photo by L. Ellenberg).

Plate 18-3. Macuto, Cordillera de la Costa (Fig. 18-1, sector 12) (photo by L. Ellenberg).

Plate 18-4. Slumping cliffs at Aguide (Fig. 18-1, sector 8) (photo by L. Ellenberg).

19. CARIBBEAN COLOMBIA

From the border with Panama on the west to Venezuela on the east, the Caribbean coastline of Colombia (Fig. 19-1A) is approximately 1030 km long. This coast lies in a region of tropical cyclone influence (Davies 1980). Tides are mixed and spring range is less than 2m.

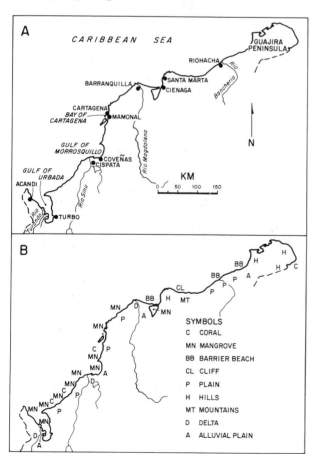

Figure 19-1. Geographic and geomorphic map of the Caribbean coast of Colombia.

In general, the north-south trending Andes Mountains in Colombia plunge toward the Caribbean to underlie the coastal plain (Olsson 1956), with the Guajira Peninsula being the northernmost pronounced extension. The coastal region is underlain by deformed (faulted and folded) marine Tertiary deposits, intruded by volcanics. In the east the extensive plains of the llanos are composed of sedimentary formations overlying the Guyana Shield.

The Caribbean coast of Colombia (Fig. 19-1B) is quite varied in its geomorphology (McGill 1958; Psuty and Mizobe 1982). From Acandi to somewhat east of Barranquilla are several large deltas where major rivers enter the sea. These include the Rio Sinu delta, where in 1942 the river breached a bordering levee during a flood and developed a new outlet eastward into the Gulf of Morrosquillo (Troll and Schmidt-Kraepelin 1965). Beach ridges and cheniers are a distinctive feature of the delta areas. Along this entire coastal sector are mud flats covered by extensive growths of mangrove. Coral reefs occur at some places along the coast. A major barrier spit, built from west to east, is located between Barranquilla and Cienaga.

East of Santa Marta, where the mountain range reaches the coast, rocky sea cliffs, with pocket beaches, are to be found. These give way along the northwestern shore of the Guajira Peninsula, toward Riohacha, to sandy beaches and dunes. Around the tip of the peninsula, on its northeastern side, there is another live coral reef.

MAURICE L. SCHWARTZ

REFERENCES

Davies, J. L., 1980, *Geographical Variations in Coastal Development,* Longman, New York.

McGill, J. T., 1958, Map of coastal landforms of the world, *Geog. Rev.* **48:**402–405.

Olssen, A. A., 1956, Colombia, in *Handbook of South American Geology,* W. F. Jenks, ed., Geological Society of America, New York, pp. 293–326.

Psuty, N. P., and C. Mizobe, 1982, South America, coastal morphology, in *The Encyclopedia of Beaches and Coastal Environments,* M. L. Schwartz, ed., Hutchinson Ross Publishing Co., Stroudsburg, Pa., pp. 765–770.

Troll, C., and E. Schmidt-Kraepelin, 1965, Das neue delta des Rio Sinu an der Karibischen Küste Kolumbiens, *Erdkunde* **19:**14–23.

20. CARIBBEAN CENTRAL AMERICA

The Central American Isthmus, between the Pacific Ocean and the Caribbean Sea, extends from Tehuantepec in Mexico to the southeast to the Atrato lowlands in northwestern Colombia. Central America proper comprises Guatemala, Belize (in the process of gaining independence from Great Britain), Honduras, El Salvador, Nicaragua, Costa Rica, and Panama. All of them, except El Salvador, border the Caribbean Sea. The total length of their Caribbean coastline, from the Mexico–Belize border to the Panama–Colombia border, is approximately 2200 km, not including the coastline of the islands.

The geology of Central America is complex. Since the early investigations (Schuchert 1935; Sapper 1937) two large areas of different tectonic history and geological structure have been recognized: namely, Nuclear Central America, from southeastern Mexico to southern Nicaragua, and the Isthmian Link from southern Nicaragua to northwestern Colombia.

Nuclear Central America has a Lower Paleozoic metamorphic and igneous basement (probably including some Precambrian rocks) that forms some of the high mountains in southeastern Mexico, central Guatemala, Honduras, and northern Nicaragua. North of the Central Cordillera of Guatemala, formed by the basement, and extending westward into Mexico, the basement is overlain by a thick sequence of upper Paleozoic (Mississippian to Middle Permian) clastic and carbonate rocks, which in turn are covered by Upper Jurassic continental red beds and by a thick Cretaceous to Eocene carbonate and evaporite sequence. Upper Tertiary marine sediments are restricted to small areas.

South of the Central Cordillera of Guatemala, the metamorphic basement is covered by Mesozoic sedimentary rocks: Upper Triassic (in Honduras), Jurassic clastics, and Cretaceous carbonates and red beds, intruded by granitic bodies. These, in turn, are overlain in extensive areas by Tertiary red beds and ignimbrite plateaus.

The geological structure north of the Central Cordillera is dominated by a Laramidian fold belt that extends from southeastern Mexico (state of Chiapas) eastward across Guatemala and southern Belize, forming an open arc concave to the north and with east-northeast trends as it reaches the Caribbean coast. North of the fold belt the structures vary from gentle to nearly horizontal in the large area of northern Guatemala and Belize and the Yucatan Peninsula in Mexico.

The Isthmian Link, also called the South Central American Orogen (Dengo 1973; Weyl 1980), has an oceanic-type basement of Late Jurassic to Late Cretaceous age, which consists mainly of basalts with associated radiolarites and clastic sedimentary rock. The basement is overlain by thick volcanoclastic rocks of Late Cretaceous to Pliocene age, with some interrelated limestones, which were formed as accretionary prisms in a complex succession of island arcs. The prevailing structures are parallel to the geographical shape of the isthmus, forming a gentle arc concave to the northeast from southern Nicaragua to Costa Rica and western Panama, and a sharp arc concave to the south in central-western Panama.

A common feature to the entire Central American Isthmus is a Quaternary volcanic mountain chain that parallels the Pacific coast in a northwest–southeast direction, and is superposed on the older structures.

The Continental Divide in Nuclear Central America is closer to the Pacific; consequently the major streams drain into the Caribbean Sea. In the Isthmian Link the Continental Divide runs essentially along its middle part, except in the area east of the Panama Canal, where it is very near the Caribbean coastline, resulting in short steep-gradient streams.

In general the rainfall is much heavier on the Caribbean side, reaching in some places as much as 5–6 m per year, and producing a larger sediment load in the streams.

The geological and physiographical features briefly described are important in understanding the following descriptions of coastal features, their origin, and the different types of beach development and sand composition.

The Caribbean coastal features may be grouped according to their similarities in morphology and origin into four main areas: (1) Chetumal Bay (Mexico–Belize) to the Sarstún River mouth (Belize–Guatemala), (2) Sarstún River to Cape Gracias a Dios (Honduras–Nicaragua), (3) Cape Gracias a Dios to Port Limón (Costa Rica), and (4) Port Limón to the Panama–Colombia border in the Urabá Gulf.

The coastal features from Chetumal Bay, or even north of it, to the Sarstún River, are characteristic of carbonate deposition and reef growth (Figs. 20-1 and 20-2). One of the largest barrier reefs in the world, second only to Australia's Great Barrier Reef, forms a prominent feature in this area. The reef is separated from the main coast by a shallow shelf filled with carbonate sediments (Bonis, Bohnenberger, and Dengo 1970; Wantland and Pusey 1975). The coastline and the distribution of the offshore coral reefs are structurally controlled by a series of subparallel normal faults trending north-northeast. Oil exploration drilling as well as marine seismic profiles have shown that the major reefs—such as Chinchorro, Turneffe, Ambergris, and Key Long—were built from the Pliocene to Holocene over basement structural highs, while the smaller linear ones are over the upthrown edges of tilted fault blocks.

The coastline in northern Belize is formed by a series of small limestone detritus sand bars and internal lagoons with mangrove growth, bordered inland by Plio-Pleistocene terraces also formed predominantly of limestone fragments derived from the older carbonate rocks (Wright et al. 1959). The area around Belize City is very low, formed by fine limestone sediments deposited by the Mopan River, which forms a small delta over which the city was built. South of this city to Stann Creek, a wider coastal plain and larger, elongated lagoons characterize the landscape. South of Stann Creek Paleozoic rocks of the Maya Mountains are close to the coast and the beach characteristics change, as well as the sand components, which contain a considerable amount of quartz. A radical change in coastal features occurs in the area around Punta Gorda, where Cretaceous limestones crop out along the coast, forming prominent cliffs separated from each other only by short, narrow beaches. These features continue to the Sarstún River flats.

The Sarstún River empties into Amatique Bay. From there to Cape Gracias a Dios, the geological features that control the shore are the east-northeast-trending mountain ranges that in some cases reach the coast, and the intervening large streams, such as the Motagua, Ulúa, Aguán, Sico, Patuca, and Coco, which provide a considerable amount of sediment (Figs. 20-1 and 20-3). Some of the predominant features (Helbig 1959) are Amatique Bay and the Caratasca Lagoon. Amatique Bay is located on a graben, along which is also Lake Izabal (Guatemala), which continues at sea as the Cayman Trough. The bay is separated from the main sea water by a large sand bar and sand spit, Manabique Point which resulted from deposition of sediment carried by the Motagua River and transported northwestward by littoral currents in that direction. The land side of the bay is a low hilly area formed by Miocene limestones and cut by the Rió Dulce gorge, the outlet of Lake Izabal. This sector has only small discontinuous beaches. The flat beach area of Manabique Point extends south to the Motagua River delta, where it forms a wide area, partly covered with mangrove growth. The beach sands are heterogeneous in composition, but they have a large component of pumice material carried by the Motagua River from the Quaternary volcanic deposits of the Guatemalan highlands.

Between Port Cortés and Cape Camarón, long and narrow beaches extend between sea cliffs of Paleozoic metamorphic rocks and Tertiary ignimbrites, except at the mouths of the Ulúa and Aguán rivers where the low valleys merge into wider coastal plains, some swampy and with mangrove. At Trujillo, near the Aguán mouth, a

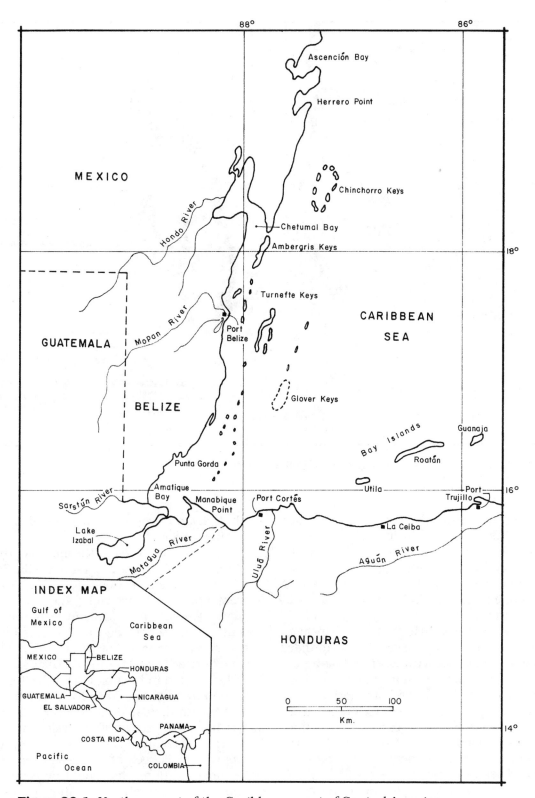

Figure 20-1. Northern part of the Caribbean coast of Central America.

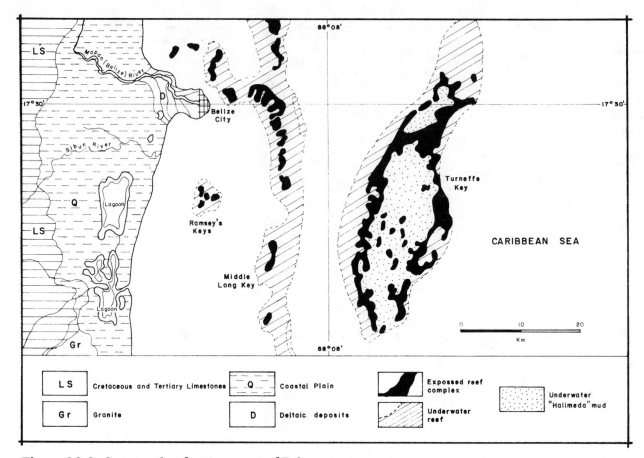

Figure 20-2. Geomorphic features, part of Belize coast.

small sand bar closes the port bay. The beach sand composition along this part is heterogeneous because the sediment source consists of metamorphic rocks, limestones, granitic intrusives, and ignimbrites. Some of the sands have a large quartz content derived from the granitic rocks and the rhyolitic ignimbrites.

The Caratasca Lagoon (Fig. 20-4), which includes several small, sand-formed islands, is surrounded by a low swampy area with extensive mangrove growth, and is separated from the sea by a long, narrow sand bar. It was probably formed as a result of changes in the low course of the Patuca River, or even by materials carried by the Coco River and transported along shore. The hinterland of the lagoon is characterized by extensive, low Plio-Pleistocene terraces.

The Bay Islands, north of the Honduras coast, are a continuation of the mountain system of Nuclear Central America. They are formed mostly by metamorphic rocks and one small volcanic cone (Utila). Their beaches are small and discontinuous, separated by low cliffs, and the whole island group is surrounded by a submarine coral reef.

Cape Gracias a Dios, at the mouth of the Coco River, is formed by the prograding delta. South of it to Port Limón in Costa Rica (Fig. 20-3) the coastal plain becomes wider and is interrupted only by low cliffs of volcanic rocks in the portion south of the Perlas Lagoon. The coastline presents several elongated lagoons bordered by long sand barriers. Outstanding for their size are the Perlas Lagoon in Nicaragua and the Tortuguero Lagoon in northern Costa Rica, which are connected with the San Juan River (Fig. 20-5).

In the northern part of this sector, near Puerto Cabezas, extensive Plio-Pleistocene low terraces occur, formed largely of quartz sand and pebbles in concentrations that could be economically important. They are a continuation of those south of the Caratasca Lagoon.

The beach sand composition is heterogeneous. South of Puerto Cabezas the coastal sediments are derived mostly from Tertiary volcanics, but they include materials from the metamorphic

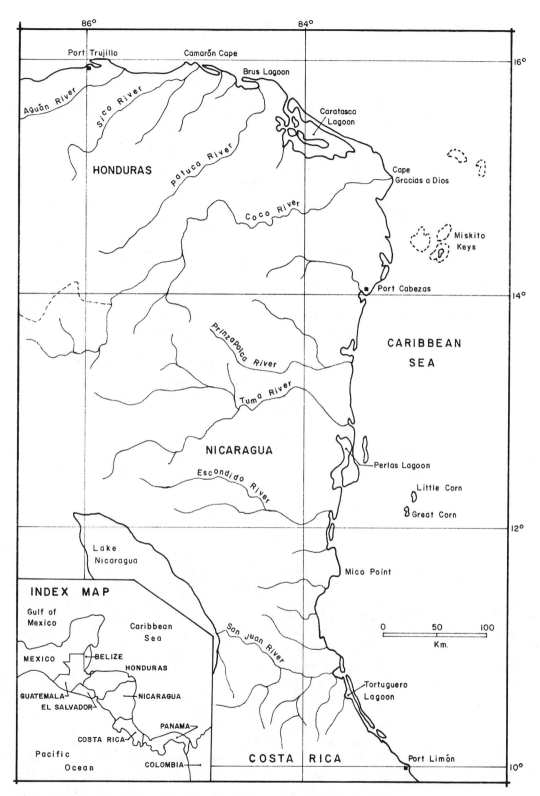

Figure 20-3. Central part of the Caribbean coast of Central America.

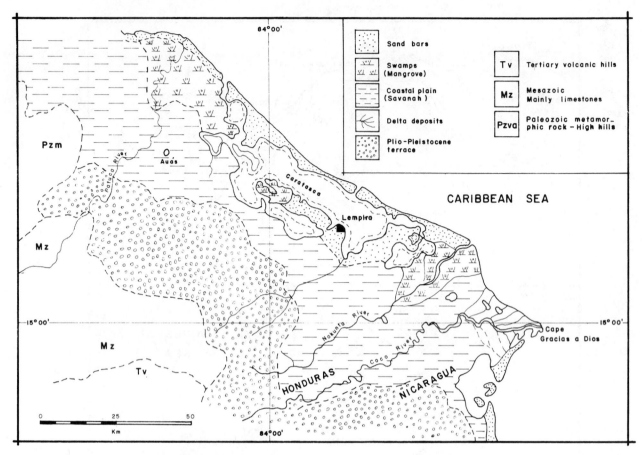

Figure 20-4. Geomorphic features, part of Honduran and Nicaraguan coast.

basement and Cretaceous limestones. South of the San Juan River, which drains the Nicaragua lake basin, the sands are derived largely from Quaternary volcanic rocks and present important concentrations of magnetite-ilmenite.

East of the coastline between Cape Gracias a Dios and Puerto Cabezas, the Miskito Keys and banks are formed by coral reefs, while the islands of Great and Little Corn to the south consist of volcanic rocks and present small beaches separated by cliffs.

The portion of the coastline between Port Limón and the Panama–Colombia border (Figs. 20-5 and 20-6) presents features quite different from those described above, due to the proximity of the mountains to the sea. Port Limón, Cahuita Point, and Mona Point are characterized by uplifted Pliocene coral reefs and by Holocene submarine reefs. The intervening beaches are long and some are fairly wide south of Port Limón and Cahuita; some of

them have economic concentrations of magnetite-ilmenite sand.

Almirante Bay is surrounded by Tertiary sedimentary and volcanic rocks, which also form the islands inside the bay. From Chiriquí Point to Manzanillo Point, the coast is formed by a succession of narrow beaches separated by low cliffs where the mountains reach the sea. In many places the tropical forest practically reaches the beach. These characteristics continue from Manzanillo to Cape Tiburón, at the Colombia border. In this sector, however, the mountains are closer to the coast and the cliffs are more abundant and more extensive. The coast is bordered by numerous small islands (San Blas Islands) made up by a drowned part of the basic igneous rock basement of southern Central America.

GABRIEL DENGO

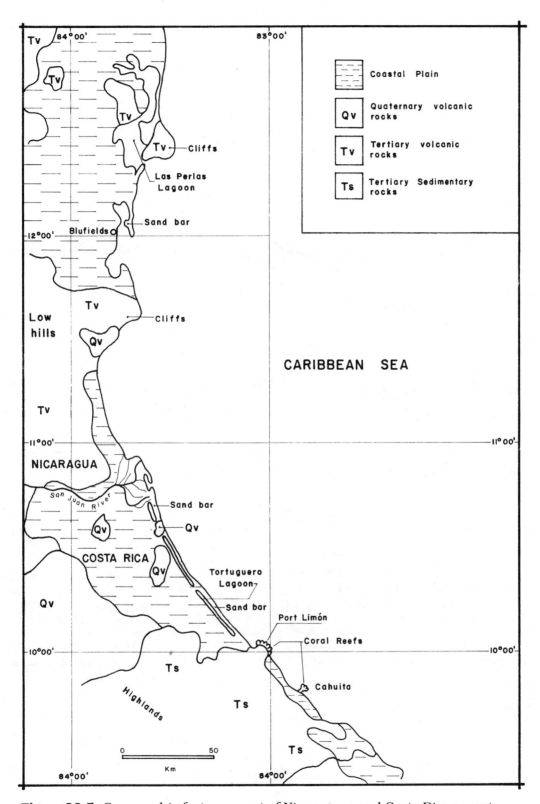

Figure 20-5. Geomorphic features, part of Nicaraguan and Costa Rican coast.

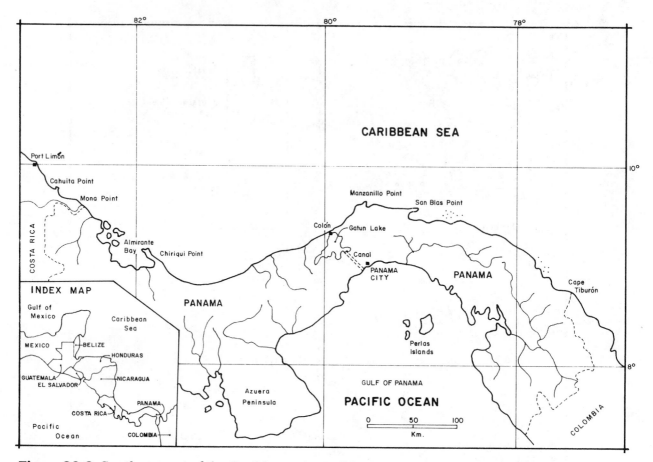

Figure 20-6. Southern part of the Caribbean coast of Central America.

REFERENCES

Bonis, S., O. Bohnenberger, and G. Dengo, 1970, Mapa Geologico de la República de Guatemala, 1:500,000, Instituto Geografico Nacional, Guatemala.

Dengo, G., 1973, *Estructura Geológica, Historia Tectónica y Morfología de América Central.* Centro Regional de Ayuda Técnica, México–Buenos Aires.

Helbig, K., 1959, *Die Landschaften von Nordost Honduras,* Geographische Kartographische Anstalt Gotha.

Sapper, K., 1937, *Mittelamerika.* Steinman und Wilckens, Heidelberg.

Schuchert, C., 1935, *Historical Geology of the Antillean Caribbean Region.* John Wiley, New York.

Wantland, K. F., and W. C.Pusey, eds., 1975, *Belize Shelf— Carbonate Sediments, Clastic Sediments and Ecology,* Studies in Geology 2, American Association of Petroleum Geologists, Tulsa, Okla.

Weyl, R., 1980, *Geology of Central America.* Gebrüder Borntraeger, Berlin.

Wright, A. C. S., D. H. Romney, R. H. Arbuckle, and V. E. Vial, 1959, *Land in British Honduras.* Colonial Research Publications, London.

21. CARIBBEAN MEXICO

The coastline between the Bravo and Hondo rivers is 2300 km long. The coast, classified as a marginal sea (Inman and Nordstrom 1971; Carranza et al. 1975), descends from the Sierra Madre foothills as a low-relief coastal plain. Near the coast, broad Quaternary alluvial terraces constitute flatland areas whose width ranges from almost nothing where the Jalapa and San Andres Tuxtla highlands reach the coast, to approximately 150 km near the major rivers. The shelf is narrow from Tampico to Veracruz and widens at Tabasco into the Campeche banks. The surface is almost flat. Modern sediments are mainly detrital (arenaceous-argillaceous); clays are present along the Tabasco and Veracruz shelf, where large rivers empty into the Gulf. The calcareous content increases into Campeche–Yucatan–Quintana Roo. The continental slope configuration is irregular; its inclination is gentle in front of Tabasco, Tamaulipas, and Veracruz, and steep along western-northwestern Yucatan. The coastal plain is characterized by the Rio Grande (Bravo), Tampico, and Isthmian embayments (Murray 1961). The Rio Grande embayment is the predominant feature of the western Gulf coastal plain. The effects of the Sierra Madre Oriental and the orogeny that formed it are apparent in the gravel deposits, in the narrowing of the coastal plain south of Rio Grande, and in the mountains of moderate relief. Belted topography is recognized in Tamaulipas, although in many areas it is masked by gravel and caliche flats. Nearshore features consist of offshore bars and islands that enclose extensive lagoons. Marshes are common.

The Tampico embayment is a physiographic unit of the coastal plain in east-central Mexico. The plain slopes gently eastward from the Sierra Madre Oriental to the Gulf. The maximum width is about 150 km. There are flat areas in its central part and along the Pánuco, Tamesi, and Tuxpan rivers, where marshes and swamps are extensive. North of the Pánuco River, the coastal plain is interrupted by the sierras de Tamaulipas, Aldama, and Madre Oriental. South of the Pánuco River, Tertiary hills have elevations of the order of 100 m just west of Laguna de Tamiahua (Fig. 21-1). The coastline consists of shallow lagoons and marshes partially enclosed by spits and barrier islands (Plate 21-1). Laguna de Tamiahua and associated cuspate bars and reefs are the principal irregularities (Ayala-Castañares et al. 1981; Murray 1961).

The Isthmian embayment, from the Jalapa highlands to the Yucatan plain, is divided into Veracruz and Tabasco segments at the Sierra de Los Tuxtlas. The northern part of the Veracruz segment is developed principally on volcanic material of late Tertiary and Quaternary ages. Maximum elevations are on the order of 200 m. The plain gradually broadens southward into the Papaloapan River basin. The coastline is fairly regular but for several cuspate bars and lagoons (Plate 21-2). There is a coastal gulfward convex arc, apparently related to volcanism and uplift. Sand dunes extend from the Jalapa highlands to the Sierra de Los Tuxtlas, and are well developed in the Veracruz–Alvarado area, where they form the barrier between the Laguna de Alvarado and the Gulf. Coral reefs are common in the vicinity of Veracruz city.

The Tabasco segment includes parts of Veracruz, Tabasco, and Campeche. The coastal plain averages 90 km in width; it is narrowest in eastern Veracruz and western Tabasco, where there are elevations of around 300 m. It widens into the

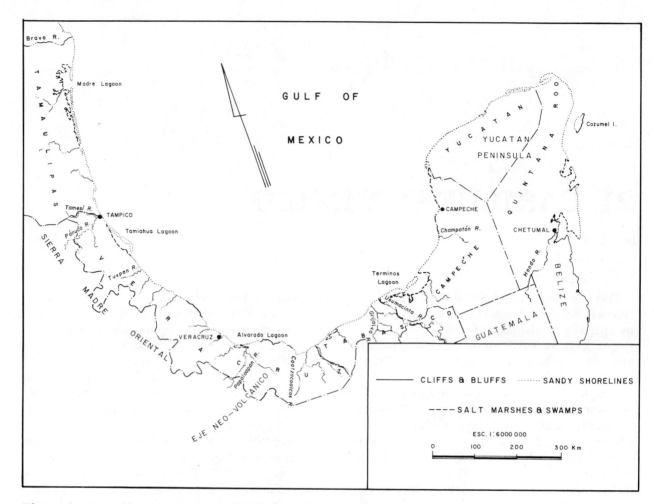

Figure 21-1. Predominant coastal landforms of the Gulf coast of Mexico.

basin of Coatzacoalcos River and the Yucatan Peninsula. The Tabasco plain is a flat lowland with coastal swamps, marshes, and lakes along the coast westward from the Laguna de Términos to the Tonalá River (Murray 1961; Psuty 1966; Thom 1967). The largest lowland area is in eastern Tabasco, where the Grijalva and Usumacinta rivers have built alluvial plains. The coast consists of lagoons and barriers with sand hills and dunes. East of the Tonalá River are coastal marshes, swamps, and shallow lagoons (Murray 1961; Gutiérrez-Estrada 1982). It is an active depositional coast. Inland there are Quaternary fluviatile and coastal alluvial terraces, deeply dissected.

East of the Laguna de Términos, the coastal plain broadens into the flat or gently rolling, karstic Yucatan Península. The western shore is rather simple with minor irregularities and narrow marshes. There are extensive lagoons and barriers across the northern, eastern and western sides of the emerged peninsula. The eastern shore is irregular and indented by bays.

MARIO ARTURO ORTIZ-PEREZ
MARIO GUTIÉRREZ-ESTRADA

REFERENCES

Ayala-Castañares, A., 1981, Foraminíferos Recientes de la Laguna de Tamiahua, Veracruz, México, *An. Centro Cienc. del Mar y Limnol. Univ. Nal. Autón. México* **8**(1):103–158.

Carranza-Edwards, A., M. Gutiérrez-Estrada, and R. Rodriguez-Torres, 1975, Unidades Morfo-Tectónicas Continentales de las Costas Mexicanas, *An. Centro Cienc. del Mar y Limnol. Univ. Nal. Autón. México* **2**(1):81–88.

Gutiérrez-Estrada, M., 1982, Geomorfología y Sedimentos Recientes del Sistema Lagunar Atasta-Pom, Campeche, México, *An. Centro Cienc. del Mar y Limnol. Univ. Nal. Autón. México* **9**(1):89–100.

Inman, D. L., and C. E. Nordstrom, 1971, On the tectonic

and morphologic classification of coasts, *Jour. Geology* **79**(1):1–21.

Murray, G. E., 1961, *Geology of the Atlantic and Gulf Coastal Province of North America,* Harper, New York.

Psuty, N. P., 1966, The geomorphology of beach ridges in Tabasco, Mexico, *Louisiana State Univ. Coastal Studies Inst. Tech. Rept.* **30**:1–51.

Thom, B. G., 1967, Mangrove ecology and deltaic geomorphology: Tabasco, Mexico, *Jour. Ecology* **55**:301–343.

Plate 21-1. Southern part of Madre Lagoon, showing prograding shoreline, extensive salt marshes, and well-developed natural levees. There is a high rate of sedimentation. The lagoon is almost filled by fine-grained sediments; mud flats are exposed at low tide (photo courtesy of Institute of Geography, UNAM).

Plate 21-2. Prograding shoreline at Alvarado Lagoon, showing barrier of sand washed up by wave action and extensive mangrove swamps in the background. Old beaches and active dunes are present. The lagoon substrate is typically of mud (photo courtesy of CIFSA).

22. TEXAS

The most comprehensive basic data sources on the Texas coastline are the seven volumes of the *Environmental Geologic Atlas of the Texas Coastal Zone* and eight studies of recent shoreline changes (Morton 1977, 1979). Several summaries of these are available, including McGowen and others (1977), and Morton and McGowen (1980). The coastline is covered by U.S. Geological Survey 1:24,000 7½-minute quadrangles with a 5-foot (~1.5-m) contour interval. Because of the dynamic and rapidly changing character of the coastline, older maps should be used with caution. Most of the geomorphic features mentioned in this article are depicted on the excellent 1:125,000 maps of the *Environmental Geologic Atlas*.

The Texas coastline is about 590 km long (Figs. 22-1, 22-2, and 22-3). Tides are diurnal to mixed diurnal with an average range of about 0.6 m and a maximum of about 0.9 m (Marmer 1954). The prevailing wind is from the southeast; it creates a seasonally shifting longshore current and drift convergence centering around 27° north latitude (central Padre Island), because the waves thus generated impinge on the curving shoreline at high angles, northeast and south, respectively, of the convergence zone (Watson 1971; Curray 1960).

The average rainfall along the coast ranges from about 140 cm at the Louisiana–Texas border to approximately 66 cm at the Rio Grande; temperatures are ~21°C to ~23°C, respectively.

The southward decrease in rainfall and increase in temperature have produced a number of regional geomorphic, pedologic, and hydrologic variations, some of which are detailed in Figure 22-2. Many of these reflect a decrease in plant cover and an increase in eolian activity. Others not specifically indicated include the southward decrease in the frequency of major stream outlets and natural tidal passes.

Hurricanes have had a major impact on the local coastal morphology and sediments. Associated storm surges over barriers may reopen previously "healed" washover (surge) channels or open new ones, add sediment to washover fans or deposit new ones, and transport beach and dune materials inland and thus cause retreats (some only temporary) of the coastline, as well as shoreline erosion within bays. In addition, sand, coarse detritus, and shells from shelf sources may be moved onshore (Hayes 1967).

Hurricane-generated storm surges along the coast can be as high as about 4.6 m, but water entering bays may be higher (on the order of 6–7 m). Storm surges are higher along the coast to the right of a hurricane's path than to the left because of the counterclockwise rotation of winds; in bays, to the left of a path, water levels may drop below mean sea level (U.S. Army Corps of Engineers 1979).

Many of the bays (lagoons) along the Texas coast have only one persistent natural tidal pass, whose location is at the southwestern end, with a roughly north–south orientation (Price 1952). Uncontrolled passes tend to migrate south in response to the longshore drift (north of the convergence zone); the southerly location and the north-south orientation result from the southward driving of bay water by winter frontal storms ("northers") from the north, northeast, and northwest. Opening of artificial passes, or increasing the tidal prism of natural ones, may cause shoaling or sealing of a nearby natural inlet. Tidal

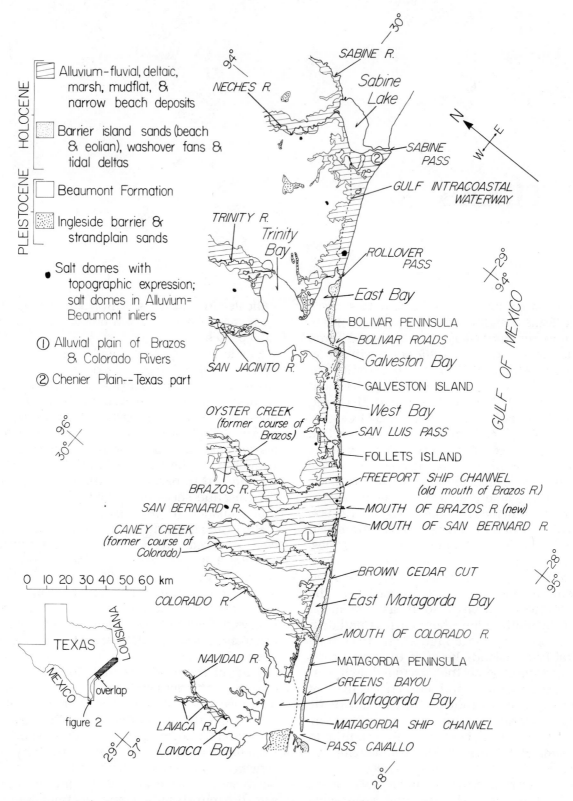

Figure 22-1. Map of northern Texas coast from Sabine Pass to Pass Cavallo showing coastal features and geology. Base map from 1962 USGS 1:500,000 map of Texas.

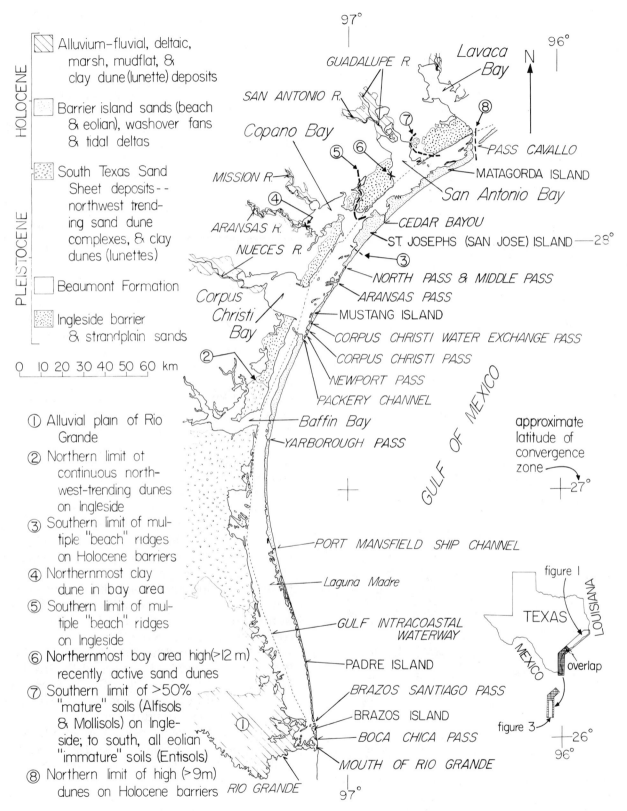

HOLOCENE

- Alluvium–fluvial, deltaic, marsh, mudflat, & clay dune (lunette) deposits
- Barrier island sands (beach & eolian), washover fans & tidal deltas

PLEISTOCENE

- South Texas Sand Sheet deposits–– northwest trending sand dune complexes, & clay dunes (lunettes)
- Beaumont Formation
- Ingleside barrier & strandplain sands

0 10 20 30 40 50 60 km

① Alluvial plain of Rio Grande
② Northern limit of continuous north-west-trending dunes on Ingleside
③ Southern limit of multiple "beach" ridges on Holocene barriers
④ Northernmost clay dune in bay area
⑤ Southern limit of multiple "beach" ridges on Ingleside
⑥ Northernmost bay area high (>12 m) recently active sand dunes
⑦ Southern limit of >50% "mature" soils (Alfisols & Mollisols) on Ingleside; to south, all eolian "immature" soils (Entisols)
⑧ Northern limit of high (>9m) dunes on Holocene barriers

97°
96°

Lavaca Bay

N

GUADALUPE R.

SAN ANTONIO R.

Copano Bay

⑦
⑧

PASS CAVALLO

MISSION R.

⑤ ⑥

MATAGORDA ISLAND

④

San Antonio Bay

ARANSAS R.

CEDAR BAYOU

ST. JOSEPHS (SAN JOSE) ISLAND —28°

NUECES R.

③

NORTH PASS & MIDDLE PASS

ARANSAS PASS

Corpus Christi Bay

MUSTANG ISLAND

CORPUS CHRISTI WATER EXCHANGE PASS

CORPUS CHRISTI PASS

②

NEWPORT PASS

PACKERY CHANNEL

Baffin Bay

YARBOROUGH PASS

GULF OF MEXICO

approximate latitude of convergence zone
27°

PORT MANSFIELD SHIP CHANNEL

Laguna Madre

GULF INTRACOASTAL WATERWAY

PADRE ISLAND

BRAZOS SANTIAGO PASS

BRAZOS ISLAND

①

BOCA CHICA PASS

MOUTH OF RIO GRANDE

RIO GRANDE

97°

figure 1

TEXAS

LOUISIANA

MEXICO

overlap

figure 3

26°

96°

Figure 22-2. Map of southern Texas coast from Pass Cavallo to the mouth of the Rio Grande showing coastal features and geology. Base map from 1962 USGS 1:500,000 map of Texas.

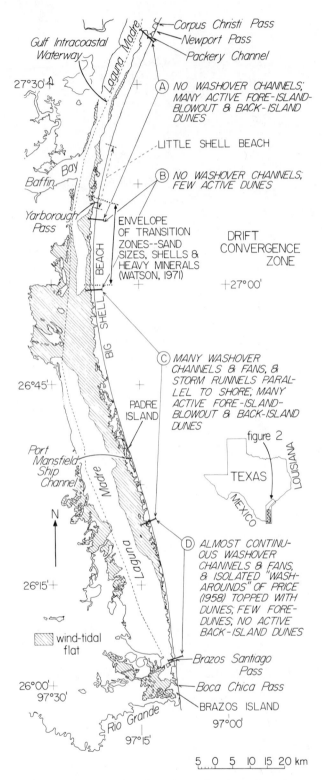

Figure 22-3. Map of Padre Island and vicinity showing wind-tidal flats of Laguna Madre, drift convergence zone, and geomorphic zones of Padre Island. Base map from USGS 1:250,000 maps in part compiled from photography taken in the 1950s.

currents through passes are on the order of 0.9–1.2 m/s. Most persistently open passes have at least subaqueous ebb and flood tidal deltas.

Of the 15 largest Texas streams (Figs. 22-1 and 22-2) only four discharge directly into the Gulf: the Brazos, San Bernard, Colorado, and the Rio Grande; of these, only the Brazos has an active delta. The others, discharging into bays, have poorly developed estuarine deltas, or digitate or birdsfoot deltas, for example, the Trinity (McEwen 1959) and the Guadalupe-San Antonio (Donaldson et al. 1970).

The northern streams in general have higher discharges of fresh water, and the higher discharges per area of drainage basin (see Table 22-1). This is a reflection of the southward and westward decrease in rainfall and increase in evaporation, and the building of dams for agricultural, industrial, and municipal purposes. The discharges of the Rio Grande and the Lavaca-Navidad are similar although the drainage basin of the Rio Grande is 76 times as large.

The Gulf Intracoastal Waterway runs from Florida to the Brazos Santiago Pass. In Texas it is about 681 km long, about 3.7 m deep, and has a bottom width of about 38 m (U.S. Army Corps of Engineers 1979). It traverses all major bays and, passing inland, cuts through alluvial plains and coastal marshes to connect Sabine Pass with Brazos Santiago Pass. The waterway is paralleled by spoil piles and hummocky ridges up to 4.5 m high 0.5 km wide. It requires periodic maintenance by dredging. Because spoil disposal and the erosion of spoil contribute to bay filling and turbidity, and to the reduction of coastal marshes, careful disposal of spoil is a major consideration in any dredging operation. Similar considerations apply to the dozen or so deep draft navigation channels (most about 9–14 m deep) that connect major ports to the Gulf.

All the maintained navigation passes (Sabine Pass, Bolivar Roads, Freeport Ship Channel, Matagorda Ship Channel, Aransas Pass, Port Mansfield Ship Channel, and Brazos Santiago Pass) have jetties extending into the Gulf. These have caused nearby deposition on an otherwise eroding coast, with locally increased shore erosion, downdrift. In addition several water exchange passes (Rollover Pass, Corpus Christi Water Exchange Pass, and Yarborough Pass) have been cut to allow mixing of bay and Gulf waters with the intent of changing bay salinity, allowing movement of organisms in and out of bays, and promoting sport fishing.

Table 1. Fresh-water discharge of major Texas coastal rivers*

River (S)	Average Annual Discharge (Q) m³/year × 10⁹	Drainage Basin Area (A) km² × 10³	Q/A Ratio m³ × 10⁵ km²
Sabine	7.3	25.3	2.9
Neches	6.2	25.9	2.4
Trinity	7.3	46.5	1.6
San Jacinto	2.3	10.3	2.2
Brazos	7.2	115.6	0.6
San Bernard	0.6	2.6	2.3
Colorado	2.2	108.2	0.2
Lavaca–Navidad	1.0	6.2	1.6
Guadalupe–San Antonio	2.3	26.5	0.9
Mission–Aransas	0.4	4.8	0.8
Nueces	0.7	43.9	0.2
Rio Grande	1.0	471.9	0.02

* Q and A data adapted from U.S. Army Corps of Engineers (1979) where given in English units.

The Texas coast shows a contrast between the outer smooth, mainly barrier island coastline and the inner embayed, ragged coastline (LeBlanc and Hodgson 1959). The outer coastline of barriers, peninsulas, beaches, eroded deltas, and alluvial plains, although dynamic and changing, has achieved its present configuration since sea level stabilized approximately 3000 years B.P. Beaches are present along virtually the entire Texas coastline; they are generally composed of very fine to fine well-sorted sand, mostly quartz with small admixtures of feldspars and heavy minerals. Shell material, volcanic rock fragments, calcareous concretions, and calcite-cemented rock fragments are locally abundant.

Apart from temporary reductions during hurricanes, beaches vary in width from about 15–120 m. The narrower beaches tend to be steeper, around 4°, the wider ones, 1.5°–2.5°. Beaches with a shell content of over 50% may be as steep as 6°. The narrower beaches are found along eroding sectors.

The major features of the inner coastline were formed during the Last Glacial phase of low sea level, when streams, graded to a lower, more distant Gulf of Mexico, deepened their channels and flowed across the exposed continental shelf. These paleochannels incise the concealed Pleistocene surfaces, and underlie the several bays, barrier islands, and alluvial plains at depths of greater than 30 m. The succeeding marine transgression drowned these channels and filled them with landward-advancing estuarine deposits while the

areas between them were the sites of now-drowned and eroded barriers, beaches, and other littoral features. Detailed studies (e.g., Wilkinson and Byrne 1977; Wilkinson and Basse 1978) have shown that stream channel deposits just upstream from deltas, alluvial plains along the coast, and estuaries are underlain by sediments laid down during this transgression. The scalloped—in some places, cliffed—edges of bays, and the segmentation of some bays, are the result of shoreline changes since the sea reached its present level. In a few places, as around the deltas of the Trinity and San Jacinto rivers, shoreline concavities are actually large meander scars. Streams like the Rio Grande, Brazos, and Colorado have long since filled their bays, while others, like Trinity and Nueces, have yet to fill them with fluvial and deltaic deposits. Bay filling has also been promoted by the deposition of the products of bay shoreline erosion and by the growth of flood tidal deltas. The bays are seldom more than 4 m deep, except in the vicinity of passes and navigation channels. Subsidence is slowly increasing the depth of some bays, for example, Galveston Bay.

The inner coastline is carved out of the Beaumont Formation, a unit that extends from the western margin of the Holocene flood plain of the Mississippi in Louisiana (where it is known principally as the Prairie Formation) to the Holocene alluvial plain of the Rio Grande. Most of the formation consists of clays and silts of deltaic, flood basin, estuarine, mudflat, coastal marsh, and lagoonal origin in which many linear sand bodies of mainly fluvial or delta-distributory origin are set at depths of 3–6 m. The surface is flat (slopes < 0.6 m/km) and undissected. Estimates on the age of the Beaumont Formation range from Sangamon ($\approx$126,000 years B.P.) to mid-Wisconsin ($\approx$25,000–30,000 years B.P.).

The Ingleside part of the inner coastline (see Figs. 22-1 and 22-2) was first identified as a barrier island system by Price (1933). Wilkinson, McGowen, and Lewis (1975) have suggested its origin as a strand plain resting on the Beaumont Formation, at least south of Matagorda Bay. In southern Texas the Ingleside is up to 10 km wide, displays many parallel beach ridges and tends to be immediately landward of Holocene lagoons; to the north, it is much narrower and ridge development is poor to absent. As shown in Figure 22-2, the degree of soil development and ridge preservation may in part be a function of climate. Between Corpus Christi and Baffin bays the Ingleside surface is taken over by the northwest-trending longitudinal dune pattern of the South Texas Sand Sheet; south of Baffin Bay on the surface it becomes indistinguishable from the Sand Sheet.

The northernmost part of the Texas coast is separated from Louisiana by a navigable, maintained natural pass, Sabine Pass. The bulge flanking the channel to the southwest is an extension of the chenier plain of southeastern Louisiana, an accretionary area of marshes separated by shelly beaches ridges (Nummedal 1982). The shoreline here is mainly low, mud flat or sandy beaches (Plate 22-1). The development of the chenier plain around the pass enclosed Sabine Lake in Holocene time.

Between the chenier plain bulge and Rollover Pass (a water exchange pass completed in 1955), the coastline is mostly erosional (transgressive) and bordered by a narrow beach (< 25 m wide), which is progressively moving inland and overriding marsh deposits (Plate 22-2). The Beaumont Formation here is at depths shallower than 3 m and is periodically exposed after storms, especially in the vicinity of High Island, a salt dome-elevated Beaumont inlier (3.5 km in diameter; 7.5 m high). The beach surface is often littered with calcareous concretions derived from erosion of the Beaumont Formation.

Bolivar Peninsula, located between Rollover Pass and Bolivar Roads (a natural, but maintained pass) encloses East Bay. The peninsula is about 32 km long and up to 5 km wide; the beach is about 50 m wide. A series of accretionary "beach" ridges (relief > 2 m) follow its axis and record its growth in a seaward and southwesterly direction. Accretionary "beach" ridges here and elsewhere along the Texas coast probably originate as foredunes and high storm berms. Divergence of ridges at the southwestern end causes a slight bend. The bulges on the lagoonal side of the peninsula are inactive washover fans deposited during hurricane storm surges when surge channels sliced through.

Bolivar Roads, a major Gulf navigation channel, has only subaqueous ebb and flood tidal deltas; the large island (Pelican Island) north of Galveston Island and the Intracoastal Waterway is largely comprised of dredged spoil.

Galveston Island, southwest of Bolivar Roads, is about 46 km long and up to 5 km wide. The island, deposited in the past 5300 years, has a sand thickness of about 15 m and a volume of about 1.4 km^3. The beach at the eastern end of the island, East Beach (about 5 km long), is accreting; most of the remainder, West Beach, is eroding despite the building of groins and jetties. The easternmost 16 km of the island—where most of the city of Galveston lies—is protected by a massive concrete seawall 4.5–5.0 m high, the largest such structure in the Texas Gulf coast (see Nummedal, 1982). Like Bolivar Peninsula, Galveston Island is marked by many parallel to subparallel "beach" ridges, generally less than 4 m high with swales occupied by lakes, and cat-eye ponds.

San Luis Pass (2–8 m deep), between Galveston and Follets Island, is natural and unmaintained, it is crossed by a highway bridge (see Plate 22-3). A large, very active, subaerial flood tidal delta lies northwest of the pass; a subaqueous ebb tidal delta extends about 6 km southeast of the pass.

Folletts Island (Nummedal 1982) is a small, eroding, transgressive, and now land-tied barrier about 15 km long and less than 2 km wide; the beach is 1 km wide. Dunes are poorly developed and less than 2 m high. Bulges on the landward side are old washover fans.

Southwest of Follets Island is the broad (50 km) transgressive face of the Brazos–Colorado Holocene alluvial plain, which is roughly bracketed between Oyster Creek (a recently abandoned—about 1000 years B.P.—course of the Brazos) and Caney Creek (a recently beheaded and abandoned—a few hundred years ago—course of the Colorado). Both are sealed from the Gulf by transgressive beach deposits (Plate 22-4). Other than in the area of the new mouth and delta of the Brazos River, the beach is less than 1 km wide; dunes are less than 4 m high. Immediately inland are mainly marshes and lakes on subsided clayey fluvial sediment. The truncation of both Oyster and Caney creeks in a meandering pattern (versus a possible deltaic one) suggests considerable Holocene erosion of the alluvial plain from an original seaward extent of at least 14 km offshore (Morton 1979; Wilkinson and Basse 1978).

The Brazos River until 1929 discharged through the present Freeport Ship Channel. Because of maintainance problems a new channel was cut past the Bryan Mound salt dome (5 m high, 1.3 km in diameter) to the southwest. The old channel is sealed from the Brazos and serves the city of Freeport. The new mouth has the only active delta building into the Gulf along the Texas coast. The subaerial portion extends into the Gulf about 2 km; the subaqueous portion, about 8 km, and about 24 km parallel to the coast. Since its formation it has migrated southwestward, paralleling the longshore drift (cf. Seelig and Sorenson 1973; Nummedal 1982). The delta is cuspate and "high-destructive wave dominated" (Morton and McGowen 1980), with many concave Gulfward-facing beach ridges and intervening ponds and marshes. Prior to 1929 a similar cuspate delta existed at the old mouth of the Brazos, but it has since been eroded away.

Matagorda Peninsula, about 80 km long and up to 2 km wide, extends from the southwest edge of the alluvial plain to Pass Cavallo and is pierced by Brown Cedar Cut, the Colorado River, Greens Bayou, and the Matagorda Ship Channel. The peninsula displays no regressive accretionary ridge pattern and, like Follets Island, is a transgressive feature. Both Follets Island and Matagorda Peninsula apparently retreated as flanking features synchronously with the transgressive margin of the alluvial plain. Sealed washover channels (rarely more than 2 km apart) and washover fans are numerous except between Greens Bayou and Cavallo Pass where dunes less than 2 m high are fairly continuous and in places rise to more than 6 m. Beaches are 30–90 m wide. Mainly between Brown Cedar Cut and Colorado, on the back beach (berm) are many, probably shelf-derived, calcareous gravel-to-boulder-sized rock fragments, calcite cemented Pleistocene fluvial sands, lacustrine clays, and "beach rock" (Wilkinson 1975).

Brown Cedar Cut, a tidal pass (< 3 m deep), may have been artificially cut about 1905, and was enlarged by hurricanes in 1916 and 1919. It has small subaqueous tidal deltas (Seelig and Sorenson 1973).

The Colorado River discharged into Matagorda Bay prior to 1936, when a channel was cut across the peninsula to the Gulf. For part of the nineteenth century and up to 1925, the Colorado was blocked by a log jam or raft, causing flooding and navigation problems. The last of the jam was removed by floods and in 1929 and 1935, and a delta, previously very small, by 1935 extended completely across Matagorda Bay. Since the 1936 channel cutting, no subaerial delta has accumulated on the Gulf coastline (Wadsworth 1966).

Greens Bayou, a washover channel, usually closed by littoral drift, was first opened by a storm in 1934 and has been open intermittently since the cutting of the artificial Matagorda Ship Channel was completed in 1967 following the unsuccessful maintainance of Pass Cavallo for navigation. Pass Cavallo, a natural pass (2.7–9 m deep) was abandoned for major shipping after over 100 years of control attempts. Shoaling has increased since the opening of the Matagorda Ship Channel and the prolonging of Colorado to the Gulf.

Matagorda Island (54 km long, up to 6 km wide) is the barrier between Pass Cavallo and Cedar Bayou. The beach is 60–90 m wide. Most of the island has an accretionary ridge pattern (relief about 2 m) with ponds in some swales (Plate 22-5). Dunes are frequent and reach heights of greater than 9 m. Most of the shoreline is stable at present and may have reached its maximum Gulfward regression (Wilkinson 1975). The northwestern part of the island is being eroded as Pass Cavallo migrates southwestward. The irregular pattern southwest of Pass Cavallo is in part due to the truncation of a washover fan by pass migration, and in part to active tidal delta growth. The bulges on the lagoonward side of the island (the southern and central parts) may be in origin part flood tidal deltas deposited earlier in the island history through passes now sealed by regressive deposition (Wilkinson 1975) or washover fans.

Cedar Bayou, a natural, northward-striking pass, has been periodically opened by dredging and storm surges. To the northeast it borders St. Joseph's Island (37 km long and up to 7 km wide), which has the largest recently active, and best studied (Andrews 1970) washover fan on the Texas Gulf Coast. The beaches are 30–90 m wide. The bulk of the island is of washover fan origin; beach and dune sediments predominate to the southwest. The northern two-thirds of the island display a narrow zone (< 1 km wide) of partly dune-obliterated accretionary ridges, which end abruptly about 13 km northwest of Aransas Pass (Fig. 22-2). Dunes on the island may be higher than 9 m (near Aransas Pass). The shoreline is fairly stable; over half of it is undergoing accretion.

North Pass and nearby Middle Pass were opened by a hurricane in 1919 and closed by 1924.

Aransas Pass (Nummedal 1982), natural but maintained, bounds Mustang Island on the northeast. Harbor Island and smaller islands just inside the pass comprise an active subaerial flood tidal delta enhanced by dredged spoil.

Mustang Island (26 km long, at widest about 2 km) is bounded by Aransas Pass on the north and Corpus Christi Pass (only intermittently open) on the south. Like the southern part of St. Josephs Island, it exhibits no accretionary ridge pattern, and except for the area near Aransas Pass, the coastline is eroding. Beaches are 60–90 m wide, backed by almost continuous foredunes. The highest dunes (> 10 m) are near Aransas Pass. The most active sector of washover activity is that which includes Packery, Newport, and Corpus Christi passes, all of which are open only intermittently during and after hurricane storm surges. The high efficiency of Aransas Pass may contribute to this. The nearby Corpus Christi Water Exchange Pass was cut in 1975 as a response to the failure of these three passes (Nummedal 1982).

From Aransas Pass to Brazos Santiago Pass is about 210 km, the combined Mustang Island–Padre Island having no permanently open natural passes, and thus being among the world's longest barrier islands, more than one-third of the Texas coastline (Fig. 22-3).

Laguna Madre, landward of Padre Island, is shown in Figure 22-3. Most of the lagoon is less than 1 m deep; the deepest point is about 2.4 m. Major portions of the lagoon and Padre Island are bordered by "wind tidal flats." The astronomical tidal range in the lagoon is less than 0.15 m; in the adjacent Gulf, it is about 0.4 m. The major water-level changes in the lagoon are caused by wind or "meterological" effects, which may cause variations up to 0.6 m. The wind tidal flats are those areas intermittently flooded by wind-driven water, for example, during a winter "norther." Flooding also occurs during hurricanes when rainfall is heavy, washover channels are open, and wind velocities are at their greatest (Weise and White 1980). The irregularity of the western margins of the lagoon and the area between the lagoon and the Rio Grande is principally the result of the accumulation of clay dunes (lunettes) (Stelting and Van de Werken 1981) promoted by

the intermittent wetting and drying of the wind tidal flats. The lagoon is diminishing in area and depth through infilling by washover sediments and eolian sands from Padre Island. These changes have given rise to continuing litigation among landowners, oil companies, and the state of Texas.

The convergence of littoral currents from north and south respectively at around 27°N along central Padre Island yield variations of heavy minerals, sand sizes, and shell species (Fig. 22-3). Sands from the Rio Grande have an abundance of basaltic hornblende and pyroxene; from rivers to the north, hornblende, tourmaline, zircon, staurolite, and kyanite. The provenance picture is rendered complex, however, by additions to Padre Island from Pleistocene shelf sources of fluvial, deltaic, and littoral origin whose distribution is at variance with present-day sources (Curray 1960). The sands of Padre Island are mainly fine, those in the southern part of the island, of Rio Grande origin, being slightly coarser than those in the northern part of the island, which are of northern origin. These sands mix and are less well sorted in the transition zone. Two beaches, Big Shell Beach and Little Shell Beach (Fig. 22-3), have shell contents of over 50 percent, with different species and genera. Big Shell Beach has species of the pelecypods *Eontia, Mercenaria, Echinochama;* Little Shell Beach has a species of *Donax.* These mix in the transition zone where the larger shells mask the smaller *Donax;* hence most of the transition zone is coincident with Big Shell Beach. The bigger shells are from southern sources, the smaller *Donax* from northern (Watson 1971). Toward the south, the shell content drops to 20% and less; toward the north, it drops abruptly at the northern limit of Little Shell Beach. The high shell content of the beaches is attributed to the lagoonward deflation of sand, which leaves the shells as a coarse lag deposit. Where the shell content of the beaches is over 50 percent the beach slopes are steepest: on the order of 6°. As the shell content decreases, so does the beach slope—to around 1.5–4°.

The eolian, beach, washover, and wind-tidal flat landforms of Padre Island are numerous and varied (Price 1958; Weise and White, 1980). Only a small number, sufficient to characterize Padre Island geomorphically, will be discussed. The island can be divided into four zones based essentially on the presence or absence of washover effects and on dune activity (Fig. 22-3). In zones A, B, and C the beaches are about

60–100 m wide; in zone D, they narrow to about 45 m. All are wider in the vicinity of washover channels.

The northernmost zone, A, is about 52 km long and contains the widest part of the island. It has no recently active washover channels, but many stabilized vegetated foredunes (up to 12 m high), which when eroded (fore-island blow-out dunes) yield sand to produce the active back-island dunes. A little more than half of the shoreline is currently accreting. Yarborough Pass, near the southern end of this zone, was cut in 1941 as a water exchange pass but closed within five months due to littoral drift; it has since been almost obliterated by dunes.

Zone B, about 20 km long, is approximately coextensive with the drift transition zone. It likewise has no recently active washover channels, but it has very stable high (up to 12 m) vegetated foredunes, which contribute very little to active back-island dunes; hence the narrowing of the island in this zone. The extensive foredune development here is related to the trapping of the sand in the convergence zone (Watson 1971). Most of this zone is currently stable or accreting. Port Mansfield Ship Channel was cut in 1957 for navigation, and last jettied in 1962. It is the shallowest (~4 m deep) of the navigation channels maintained along the Texas coast.

In zone C washover fans, channels, and storm runnels (or runways) parallel to the coast are abundant (about 21 channels in the 67-km length of the zone, or about one every 3.2 km) and, all of which upon deflation, may contribute to back-island dunes. As in zone A, blowouts from foredunes also add to the back-island dunes. The active back-island dunes provide the ragged intrusion of this unit into the tidal flats (Fig. 22-3 and Plate 22-6). The northern 17 km of this zone is accreting or stable, the rest eroding. The main-land South Texas Sand Sheet (Fig. 22-2) displays an overall longitudinal northwest-trending grain of complex banner dunes (Price 1958). In contrast, many of the active back-island dunes of zones A and C show linear patterns that are "oblique," neither parallel to nor transverse to the principal southwest wind direction. Their trend is mainly east–west. A recent study of the internal structure of one group in zone C suggests that they are reversing dunes, their orientation the result of the prevailing southeast wind and the northern winds of winter "northers."

Zone D, about 30 km long, terminates at Brazos Santiago Pass. It is the narrowest and most rapidly eroding (greater than 2 m/yr) part of the island. This rapid erosion is probably related, among other factors, to the construction of jetties at the pass (1936) and to the closing of the Falcon Dam on the Rio Grande, both of which have diminished the northward movement of sand from the Rio Grande. The major relief features are the elliptical to irregular vegetated "washarounds" of Price (1958) (Plate 22-7). Their hummocky surfaces may rise to over 7 m. They may be wind-modified washover-fan deposits. They are surrounded by poorly vegetated or unvegetated washover channels and fans, sand flats, and dunes. Back-island dunes are largely absent from this zone. Foredunes are rare but were abundant before 1930. After 1930 the sand-trapping vegetation may have been in part destroyed by overgrazing, hurricane washovers, and droughts.

The surface of the alluvial plain north of the Rio Grande (Fig. 22-2) has many avulsed and abandoned meandering courses (locally known as *resacas*) extending to the southern limits of the Sand Sheet. Differential compaction and subsidence of the clayey delta plain sediments have provided the wind tidal flats and basins, the source areas of clay dunes, along the southwestern margins of Laguna Madre (Fig. 22-3). In a manner similar to the alluvial plain of the Brazos-Colorado, this part of the Rio Grande alluvial plain probably extended considerably Gulfward, and was abandoned about 2000 years B.P. (Morton and McGowen 1980). As subsidence continues, southern Padre Island retreats—hence the slightly bowed pattern of this part of the island.

Brazos Santiago Pass, the only natural inlet south of Aransas Pass, has been maintained for navigation for over 100 years. Brazos Island, between this pass and the mouth of the Rio Grande, is about 10 km long. During the period from 1854 to 1937 the coastline was accreting; between 1937 and 1975 it was eroding. The presence of volcanic rock fragments imparts a reddish color to the predominantly quartz sands of Brazos Island and southern Padre Island. The landforms (including beaches) are similar to those of zone D of Padre Island except for the occurrence of "stepped-back ridged eolian plains" or "gavilian mesas" mentioned by Price (1958), landward of the washover fan and channel deposits (Plate 22-8). They are accretionary dune forms of clay, silt, and sand. Boca Chica Pass was opened briefly by a hurricane in 1937 and has been closed since.

The mouth of the Rio Grande has shifted north and south through 2000 m during the past 120 years (1854–1975), but it has returned to its 1854 position.

SAUL ARONOW
RAYMOND T. KACZOROWSKI

REFERENCES

Andrews, P. B., 1970, *Facies and genesis of a hurricane-washover fan, St. Joseph Island, Central Texas coast,* Texas Univ. Bur. Econ. Geology Rept. Inv. 67, Austin.

Curray, J. R., 1960, Sediments and history of the Holocene transgression, continental shelf, northwest Gulf of Mexico, in *Recent Sediments, Northwest Gulf of Mexico,* F. P. Shepard, F. B. Phleger, and T. H. van Andel, eds., American Association of Petroleum Geologists, Tulsa, Okla., pp. 221–266.

Donaldson, A. C., R. H. Martin, and W. H. Kanes, 1970, Holocene Guadalupe delta of Texas Gulf coast, in *Deltaic Sedimentation, Modern and Ancient,* J. P. Morgan, ed., Soc. Econ. Paleontologists and Mineralogists Spec. Pub. 15, pp. 107–137.

Hayes, M. O., 1967, *Hurricanes as Geological Agents: Case Studies of Hurricanes Carla, 1961 and Cindy, 1963,* Texas Univ. Bur. Econ. Geology Rept. Inv. 61.

LeBlanc, R. J., and W. D. Hodgson, 1959, Origin and development of the Texas shoreline, *Gulf Coast Assoc. Geol. Socs. Trans.* **9:**197–220.

McEwen, M. C., 1969, Sedimentary facies of the modern Trinity delta, *Holocene Geology of the Galveston Bay Area,* R. R. Lankford and J. J. W. Rogers, eds., Houston Geological Society, Houston, pp. 53–77.

McGowen, J. H., L. E. Garner, and B. H. Wilkinson, 1977, *The Gulf Shoreline of Texas: Processes, Characteristics, and Factors in Use,* Texas Univ. Bur. Econ. Geology Geol. Circ. 77-3.

Marmer, H. A., 1954, Tides and sea level in the Gulf of Mexico, in *Gulf of Mexico, Its Origin, Water and Marine Life,* P. S. Galtsoff, ed., Fish and Wildlife Service Fishery Bull. 89, pp. 101–118.

Morton, R. A., 1977, Historical shoreline changes and their causes, Texas Gulf Coast, *Gulf Coast Assoc. Geol. Socs. Trans.* **27:**352–364.

Morton, R. A., 1979, Temporal and spatial variations in shoreline changes and their implications, examples from the Texas Gulf Coast, *Jour. Sed. Petrology* **49:**1101–1112.

Morton, R. A., and J. H. McGowen, 1980, *Modern Depositional Environments of the Texas Coast,* Texas Univ. Bur. Econ. Geology Guidebook 20.

Nummedal, D., ed., 1982, *Sedimentary Processes and Environments along the Louisiana-Texas coast;* Field Trip Guidebook: 1982 Annual Meeting, Geological Society of America, New Orleans, Lousiana, Earth Enterprises, Austin, Tex.

Price, W. A., 1933, Role of diastrophism in topography of Corpus Christi area, South Texas, *Am. Assoc. Petroleum Geologists Bull.* **17:**907–962.

Price, W. A., 1952, Reduction of maintainance by proper orientation of ship channels through tidal inlets, *2nd Conf. on Coastal Engineering Proc.* J. W. Johnson, ed., Council on Wave Research pp. 243–255.

Price, W. A., 1958, Sedimentology and Quaternary geomorphology of South Texas, *Gulf Coast Assoc. Geol. Socs. Trans.* **8:**41–75.

Seelig, W. N., and R. M. Sorenson, 1973, *Investigation of Shoreline Changes at Sargent Beach, Texas,* Texas A&M Univ. SG-73-212.

Stelting, C. E., and M. C. Van de Werken, 1981, Clay dunes—unique eolian deposits of the semi-arid region of south Texas, in *Modern Depositional Environments of Sands in South Texas: 1981 Gulf Coast Association of Geological Societies Field Trip Guidebook,* C. E. Stelting and J. L. Russell, eds., Gulf Coast Association of Geological Societies Austin pp. 47–52.

U.S. Army Corps of Engineers, 1979, *Texas Coast Hurricane Study:* Feasibility Report, 2 vols. U.S. Army Engineer District, Galveston.

Wadsworth, A. H., 1966, Historical deltation of the Colorado River, Texas, in *Deltas in their Geologic Framework,* M. L. Shirley and J. A. Ragsdale, eds., Houston Geol. Soc., pp. 99–105.

Watson, R. L., 1971, Origin of shell beaches, Padre Island, Texas, *Jour. Sed. Petrology* **41:**1105–1111.

Weise, B. R., and W. A. White, 1980, *Padre Island National Seashore—A Guide to the Geology, Natural Environments, and History of a Texas Barrier Island,* Texas Univ. Bur. Econ. Geology Guidebook 17.

Wilkinson, B. H., 1975, Matagorda Island, Texas: the evolution of a Gulf Coast barrier complex, *Geol. Soc. America Bull.* **86:**959–967.

Wilkinson, B. H., and J. R. Byrne, 1977, Lavaca Bay—transgressive deltaic sedimentation in central Texas estuary, *Am. Assoc. Petroleum Geologists Bull.* **61:**527–545.

Wilkinson, B. H., and R. A. Basse, 1978, Late Holocene history of the central Texas coast from Galveston Island to Pass Cavallo, *Geol. Soc. America Bull.* **89:**1592–1600.

Wilkinson, B. H., J. H. McGowen, and C. R. Lewis, 1975, Ingleside strandplain sand of central Texas coast, *Am. Assoc. Petroleum Geologists Bull.* **59:**347–352.

Plate 22-1. Oblique photo, taken October 29, 1970, of Sabine Pass area, looking north. Sabine Pass is in upper right; Louisiana is in upper right corner. The accretionary beach and marsh pattern of Texas is part of the chenier plain. In the fore-ground and to the right is mostly mud flat, bordered by discontinuous and poorly developed beach (photo courtesy of Galveston District, Corps of Engineers).

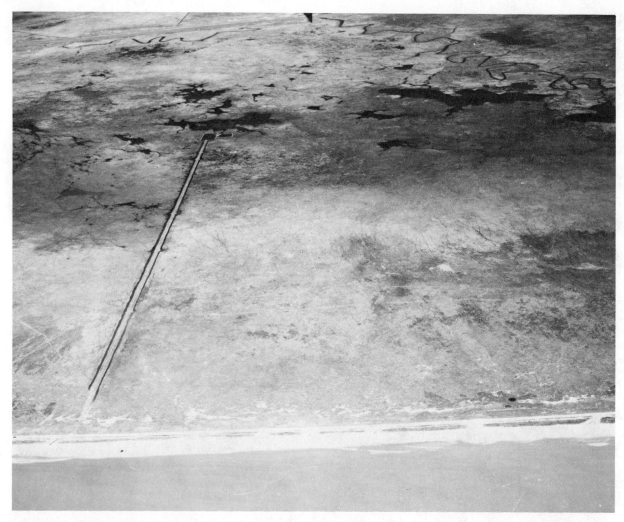

Plate 22-2. Oblique photo, 10-9-70, looking north toward narrow beach and coastal marsh area between Rollover Pass and Sabine Pass, about 15 km northeast of Rollover Pass. The meandering stream is tidal and connects shallow lakes in marsh. The lighter areas in the marsh are very thin washover and eolian sands. The shoreline is transgressive. The linear feature perpendicular to shoreline is road to oil well site (photo courtesy of Galveston District, Corps of Engineers).

Plate 22-3. Oblique photo, 2-9-74, looking northwest through San Luis Pass. Galveston Island is to the right, and accreting. The diagonal line is the state highway across pass. Water-surrounded features, vegetated and otherwise, are parts of the flood tidal delta of the pass. At the top of photo are subsided portions of alluvial plain of Brazos (photo courtesy of Galveston District, Corps of Engineers).

Plate 22-4. Oblique photo, 10-9-70, looking northwest to seaward edge of alluvial plain of Brazos and Colorado Rivers, with transgressing (eroding) beach. The Gulf Intracoastal Waterway crosses the photo from left to right. Note houses near the shore. Arcuate lakes and marshes are meanders of Caney Creek, a former course of the Brazos sealed off from the Gulf by littoral drift (photo courtesy of Galveston District, Corps of Engineers).

Plate 22-6 *(at right).* Oblique photo, 10-28-70. Hurricane Celia made its landfall on 8-3-70, with its eye in the vicinity of Corpus Christi Channel. The photo looks southwest toward central Padre Island (zone C of text), about 14 km south of Port Mansfield Ship Channel. The washover channel is in the center flanked by foredunes with blowouts and coppice dunes. Note the oblique, almost east–west trending, active back-island dunes. The vegetated area on the wind-tidal flat (upper left) is Deer Island, "a flying spit made oval by a beach plain growth and now captured by eolian plain of Padre Island" (Price 1958) (photo courtesy of Galveston District, Corps of Engineers).

TEXAS   143

Plate 22-5. Oblique photo, 10-29-70, of Matagorda Island, looking north, about 18 km northeast of Cedar Bayou. Photo shows the accretionary "beach" ridge pattern with marshy and lacustrine swales. Foredune blowout can be seen to the right. A subsided marshy area is to the upper left, at the edge of a washover fan. San Antonio Bay is in the upper part of photo. Note that the wave pattern conforms to that needed for southwestward littoral drift (photo courtesy of Galveston District, Corps of Engineers).

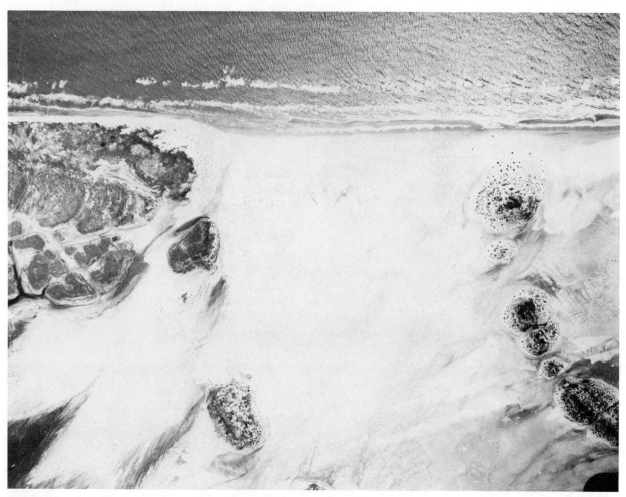

Plate 22-7. Vertical photo, 9-24-77, showing South Padre Island, about 24 km south of Port Mansfield Ship Channel (zone D of text). Note wind-modified, vegetated washover fan deposits ("washarounds"), and washover fan and channel deposits (photo courtesy of Galveston district, Corps of Engineers).

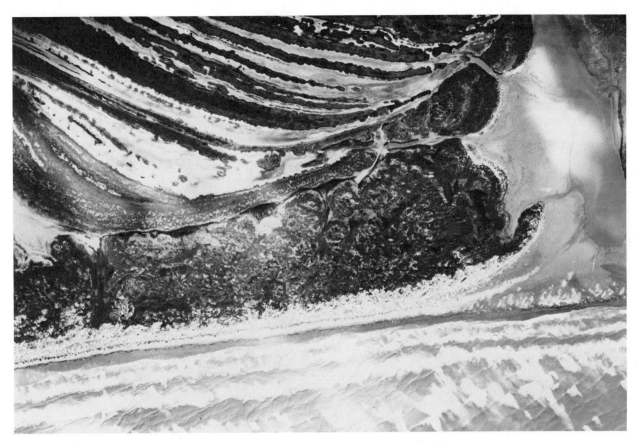

Plate 22-8. Vertical air photo, 1-28-70, showing part of Brazos Island. A washover channel is at right. From bottom to top: beach deposits along Gulf; vegetated, wind-modified washover fan deposits ("washarounds"); ridged area, a clay dune complex or a "stepped-back eolian plain" of Price (1958) (photo courtesy of Galveston District, Corps of Engineers).

23. LOUISIANA

The Louisiana coast consists entirely of Holocene components of the Mississippi River delta system. This delta is the area where sediment enters and infills the Gulf Coast sedimentary basin. Once introduced to the marine current field, some of the clastic sediments move along the shore and across the adjacent continental shelf. Coarse-grained barrier–forming sand of Mississippi River origin is limited to the Louisiana coast, whereas the mud fraction is a major sediment source for both the Louisiana and Texas shelves. Prevailing westward currents prevent the river sediments from having any significant influence on the Alabama-Mississippi coast to the east.

Three major subdivisions of the Louisiana coastal plain are recognized: the active deltas, the abandoned deltas, and the delta margin chenier plain. The juxtaposition of these environments reflects the process of periodic switching of the major river channel and the attendant cycles of sedimentation within the delta complex (Scruton 1960; Coleman and Gagliano 1964). The constructional phase of active delta growth is characterized by rapid progradation of the local shoreline and the formation of a thick wedge of terrigenous clastics. At present there are two active deltas: the modern Mississippi Delta (birdfoot delta) and the Atchafalaya Delta (Fig. 23-1). After about a thousand years of active delta growth, a major channel switch occurs in response to hydraulic gradient advantages. The old delta lobe then changes into its destructional phase characterized by shoreline retreat, development of flanking barriers, and deposition of thin units of laterally continuous organic-rich sediments. Concurrent subsidence will gradually lower the old delta lobe sufficiently to make it a potential site

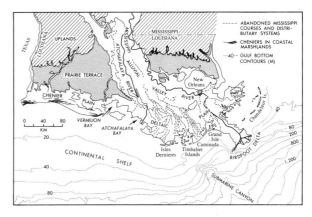

Figure 23-1. Major geological provinces of the Louisiana coastal plain.

for a new episode of active delta growth, that is, the start of a new cycle. As a consequence, the deltaic fill consists of a series of stacked imbricate sedimentary bodies, each body representing one deltaic cycle.

THE ACTIVE DELTAS

Rapid deposition of sediment is the most fundamental attribute that distinguishes delta building from other types of marine regression. At the modern Mississipi Delta this is accomplished by the daily average discharge of 1–1.5 million tons of sediment; of this about 2% is fine sand, and 98% is silt and clay (Scruton 1960). There is a rapid seaward decrease in grain size away from the river mouth as a result of settling fractionation of particles through the water column. Sands and coarse silts are deposited on the river mouth bars. As these advance seaward, elongate bar finger sands develop (Fisk 1961). Compaction of underlying muds permits the bar fingers to attain a thickness in excess of 70 m.

The development of this pattern of extensional "birdfoot" bar fingers (Plate 23-1) is possible because the Mississippi Delta is perhaps the most strongly fluvially dominated of all major deltas in the world. Fluvial dominance is a consequence of both the moderate wave energy in the semi-enclosed Gulf of Mexico and the very gentle nearshore profile off the Mississippi Delta built by a rapid influx of large quantities of fine sediments. The shallow delta front provides very effective attenuation of the waves before they reach the shoreline (Wright and Coleman 1973).

Concurrent with the development of extensional bar finger distributaries, interdistributary bays are being infilled with fine-grained organic-rich sediments and coarser, broadly lenticular sandy silt units, the crevasse splays (Plate 23-2). The crevasse splays, formed by flood breaching of the channel levees, represent scaled-down versions of the major deltaic lobes, both in space and time. Typically, major crevasse splays remain active for about a century. Crevasse splays forming over the last 200 years account for most of the subaerial extent of the modern Mississippi Delta (Coleman and Gagliano 1964).

Seaward of the distributary mouths, the loading of dense bar finger sand and silt upon less dense prodelta clays causes a sedimentary instability with consequent folding, diapiric intrusion, and thrust faulting of the clay into and through the accumulating sands of the river mouth bar. The resulting "mud lump" islands may rise to elevations of 10 m above sea level, and expose prodelta and shelf clays thrust to the surface from depths in excess of 100 m (Morgan et al 1968).

Submarine landslides play an important role on the delta front slope. Collapse depressions, elongate flow slides, mudflow gullies, and overlapping mudflow lobes cover virtually the entire submarine delta (Plate 23-3). Many instabilities are continually active. Sea-floor mapping with side-scan sonar demonstrates that many mudflow lobes move downslope at rates up to 1 km per year. Moreover, it is probable that large-scale surges are part of the dynamics of this submarine mud transport. Triggering of the initial instability results from the action of external stress from cyclic loading by storm waves or localized rapid sediment influx, combined with a reduction in sediment strength through the internal generation of biogenic methane gas (Prior and

Coleman 1978). Once inititated, the instabilities may expand through upslope and lateral retrogressive flow sliding, and downslope loading-induced substrate failures. In an area as heavily covered with offshore pertroleum production facilities as the Louisiana shelf and slope, these submarine landslides constitute one of the major natural hazards.

A second active delta is currently building at the mouth of the Atchafalaya River (Fig. 23-1). The Atchafalaya Delta emerged as a subaerial feature after the large 1973 flood and continues to grow (van Heerden and Roberts 1980). The submarine delta front presently extends to the shell reefs at the entrance to Atchafalaya Bay. Prodelta muds of Atchafalaya origin extend into the Gulf and migrate westward as mudbanks along the chenier plain shoreline. Were it not for the Army Corps of Engineers' flood control structure at the Old River site, the Mississippi River would by now probably have switched its entire discharge to the Atchafalaya course.

THE ABANDONED DELTAS

The history of the Mississippi River has been one of frequent channel switching and delta abandonment. Stratigraphic studies and carbon-14 dating across the Louisiana coastal plain has led to the recognition of six major delta complexes (Fig. 23-2) dating back some 7000 years (Kolb and Van Lopik 1966; Frazier 1967). Within these complexes 18 distinct episodes of distributary

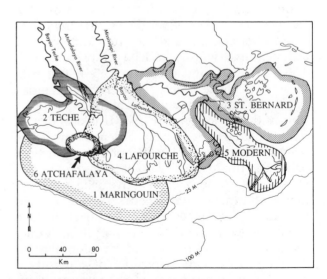

Figure 23-2. Location of the six major Holocene delta complexes constituting the Mississippi Delta plain.

flow can be identified. As illustrated in Figure 23-3, concurrent occupancy of multiple distributaries has been common.

After delta complex abandonment, marine processes dominate in sediment dispersal. Deltaic sand bodies supply coarse sediment to the nearshore current field. The abandoned lobe rapidly becomes an eroding headland with barrier spits and islands extending downdrift The complex has reached stage 1 in a sequence of barrier evolution (Fig. 23–4; Penland et al. 1981). On the

present Louisiana coast the Caminada-Moreau headland, with the flanking barriers of Caminada Spit and Grand Isle to the east and the Timbalier Islands to the west, represents a stage 1 barrier complex. The barriers occupy the former margin of the Late Lafourche lobe of the Mississippi Delta (Fig. 23-2). Erosion is rapid at the headland, up to 10 m per year on the Caminada coast.

With increasing age of the abandoned lobe, two further changes enter the coastal sediment transport regime as a consequence of subsidence. Marine incursion of the back-barrier marshes causes a lagoon (or bay) to develop and sinking or erosion of the old distributary mouth bars removes the active coarse-grained sediment source. As a consequence, at this barrier stage (stage 2, Fig. 23-4) the waves rework a finite sediment volume. The subaerial islands decrease in size as the sand moves seaward onto an inner shelf sand sheet and coastwise or landward into a gradually deepening lagoon. The Isles Dernieres on the flanks of a delta complex of Early Lafourche age, and the Chandeleur Islands, on the margin of the St. Bernard delta (Fig. 23-5 and Plate 23-4), represent two examples of stage 2 barriers. The change in morphology of Lake Pelto behind the Isles Dernieres over the last century illustrates well the subsidence-induced mainland beach detachment that characterizes the change from a stage 1 to a stage 2 barrier complex (Fig. 23-5).

Because of subsidence of the sand source, the

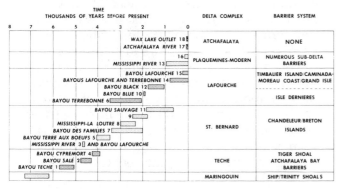

Figure 23-3. Chronology of development of the Mississippi Delta plain. Note the common situation of simultaneous occupancy of multiple distributaries, some even within different delta complexes (after Frazier 1967).

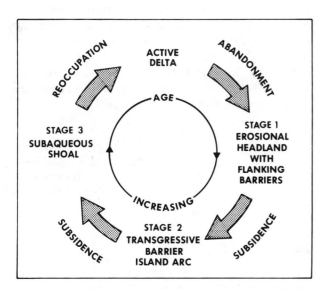

Figure 23-4. Schematic representations of the cyclic development of a delta complex from an active, regressive stage through three different stages of transgressive barrier development and ultimate reoccupation by an active delta. (after Penland et al. 1981).

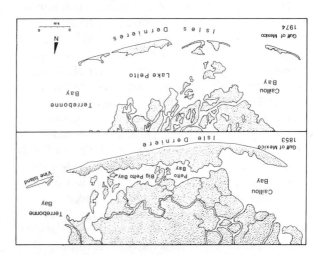

Figure 23-5. The evolution of Lake Pelto behind the Isles Dernieres during the last century provides an excellent example of the mainland beach detachment that is characteristic of the transition from a stage 1 to a stage 2 barrier system (after Penland et al. 1981).

subaerial delta flank barrier is ultimately destroyed. The remaining vestige of the barrier will be a submarine sand shoal. Such shoals, of Teche and Maringouin delta origin, include Tiger, Trinity, and Ship shoals on the western Louisiana continental shelf. These are excellent examples of barrier-derived inner shelf sand bodies during a phase of shoreline transgression. Tiger and Trinity shoals are now being encroached upon by the prodelta muds of the new Atchafalaya Delta. This is the beginning of a new cycle of active delta sedimentation in this region.

Louisiana examples indicate that models for barrier genesis should include the regional geological history. As here described, stage 1 is dominated by a Gilbert (1885) mode of recurved spit growth, and perhaps a DeBeaumont (1845) mode of vertical bar accretion. The transition from stage 1 to stage 2, on the other hand, is a clear example of Hoyt's (1967) concept of mainland beach-ridge detachment. Multiple causality (Schwartz 1971) is a truly valid concept for these barriers.

THE CHENIER PLAIN

The chenier plain (French *chêne,* "oak," describing the chenier's characteristic vegetation) extends from the western end of Vermillion Bay to the east flank of the Pleistocene Trinity Delta in Texas, a distance of about 200 km (Fig. 23-1; Plate 23-5).

The plain consists of a seaward-thickening Holocene wedge of largely muddy sediments with essentially shore-parallel ridges of sand and shell-hash. Stratigraphically, one can clearly recognize a basal onlapping sequence of inner-shelf muds associated with Holocene sea-level rise, overlain by an offlap sequence of alternating chenier ridges and inter-ridge mud flat and marsh deposits. The entire Holocene sequence is about 7–8 m thick at the present shoreline (Gould and McFarlan 1959).

It has been generally accepted that this sequence of ridges and marsh reflects changes in the main discharge point of the Mississippi River (Russell 1940; Byrne et al. 1959; Gould and McFarlan 1959). The classical chenier plain model associates the building of extensive coastal mud flats with a westerly Mississippi discharge. During periods of easterly river *debouchment,* the mud flat deposits were supposed to have been reworked into chenier ridges. This concept appears to be of general validity, but it does not explain the multiplicity of ridges nor the fact that most ridges do not correlate with known Mississippi River channel avulsions.

The dictum that "the present is the key to geological processes, and processes are the key to the past" appears to be particularly well supported by the chenier plain problem. As already mentioned, the Atchafalaya River supplies large amounts of mud to the transport system of the western Louisiana coast. As a consequence, many segments of the chenier plain coastline are presently prograding. The pattern of progradation, however, is not a simple, uniform mud flat development in front of the beach. The pattern of progradation is, in part, controlled by wave refraction across the shoals on the inner shelf (stage 3 barriers), but it also appears to be controlled by the dynamics of coastwise mud transport. The existence of multiple accretionary zones may reflect the formation of extensive coastal mudbanks of a type similar to those on the Surinam coast (Wells and Coleman 1981). In Surinam, the chenier ridges form as a result of local transgressions during passage of the embayments between adjacent mudbanks.

The concept that mud flats prograde during periods of abundant sediment supply, while ridges are associated with local shoreline retreat, is still valid. The pulses of sedimentation, however, may reflect the passage of individual mudbanks rather than large-scale fluctuations in position of the original sediment source (the Amazon River for Surinam; the Mississippi River for the Louisiana chenier plain). Further development of the Atchafalaya Delta is likely to increase the supply of mud to the western Louisiana coast. The attendant evolution of the chenier plain will remain an interesting study.

DAG NUMMEDAL
JAMES M. COLEMAN
RON BOYD
SHEA PENLAND

REFERENCES

Byrne, J. V., D. O. LeRoy, and C. M. Riley, 1959, The chenier plain and its stratigraphy, southwestern Louisiana, *Gulf Coast Assoc. Geol. Socs. Trans.* **9:**237–260.

Coleman, J. M., and S. M. Gagliano, 1964, Cyclic sedimentation in the Mississippi River deltaic plain, *Gulf Coast Assoc. Geol. Socs. Trans.* **14:**67–80.

DeBeaumont, E., 1845, *Leçons de geologie practique.* P. Bertrand, Paris, pp. 223–252.

Fisk, H. N., 1961, Bar-finger sands of the Mississippi delta, in *Geometry of Sandstone Bodies,* J. A. Peterson and J. C. Osmond, eds., Am. Assoc. Petroleum Geologists Spec. Pub., pp. 29–52.

Fisk, H. N., and E. McFarlan, Jr., 1955, Late Quaternary deltaic deposits of the Mississippi River, in *Crust of the Earth,* A. Poldervaart, ed., Geol. Soc. America Spec. Paper 62, pp. 279–302.

Frazier, D. E., 1967, Recent deltaic deposits of the Mississippi River, their development and chronology, *Gulf Coast Assoc. Geol. Socs. Trans.* **17:**287–315.

Gilbert, G. K., 1885, The topographic features of lake shores, *U.S. Geol. Survey 5th Ann. Rept.,* pp. 69–123.

Gould, H. R., 1970, The Mississippi delta complex, in *Deltaic Sedimentation, Modern and Ancient,* J. P. Morgan and R. H. Shaver, eds., Soc. Econ. Paleontologists and Mineralogists Spec. Pub. 15, pp. 3–30.

Gould, H. R., and E. McFarlan, 1959, Geologic history of the Chenier Plain, southwestern Louisiana, *Gulf Coast Assoc. Geol. Socs. Trans.* **9:**261–270.

Hoyt, J. H., 1967, Barrier island formation, *Geol. Soc. America Bull.* **78:**1125–1136.

Kolb, C. R., and J. R. Van Lopik, 1966, Depositional environments of the Mississippi River deltaic plain, southeastern Louisiana, in *Deltas in Their Geologic Framework,* M. L. Shirley, ed., Houston Geol. Soc., pp. 17–61.

Morgan, J. P., J. M. Coleman, and S. M. Gagliano, 1968, Mudlumps, diapiric structures in Mississippi delta sediments, in *Diapirism and Diapirs,* J. Braunstein and G. D. O'Brien, eds., Am. Assoc. Petroleum Geologists Mem. 8, pp. 145–161.

Murray, G. E., 1961, *Geology of the Atlantic and Gulf Coastal Province of North America,* Harper, New York.

Penland, P. S., R. Boyd, D. Nummedal, and H. Roberts, 1981, Deltaic barrier development on the Louisiana coast, *Gulf Coast Assoc. Geol. Socs. Trans.* **31:**471–476.

Prior, D. B., and J. M. Coleman, 1978, Disintegrating retrogressive landslides on very-low-angle subaqueous slopes, Mississippi Delta, *Marine Geotechnology* **3:**37–60.

Russell, R. J., 1940, Quaternary history of Louisiana, *Geol. Soc. America Bull.* **51:**1199–1233.

Schwartz, M. L., 1971, The multiple causality of barrier islands, *Jour. Geology* **79:**91–94.

Scruton, P. C., 1960, Delta building and the deltaic sequence, in *Recent Sedimentation, Northwest Gulf of Mexico,* F. P. Shepard, F. B. Phleger, and T. H. van Andel, eds., Am. Assoc. Petroleum Geologists Spec. Pub., pp. 82–102.

van Heerden, I. L., and H. H. Roberts, 1980, The Atchafalaya delta—Louisiana's new prograding coast, *Gulf Coast Assoc. Geol. Socs. Trans.* **30:**497–506.

Wells, J. T., and J. M. Coleman, 1981, Physical processes and fine-grained sediment dynamics, coast of Surinam, South America, *Jour. Sed. Petrology,* **51:**1053–1068.

Wright, L. D., and J. M. Coleman, 1973, Variations in morphology of major river deltas as functions of ocean wave and river discharge regimes, *Am. Assoc. Petroleum Geologists Bull.* **57:**370–398.

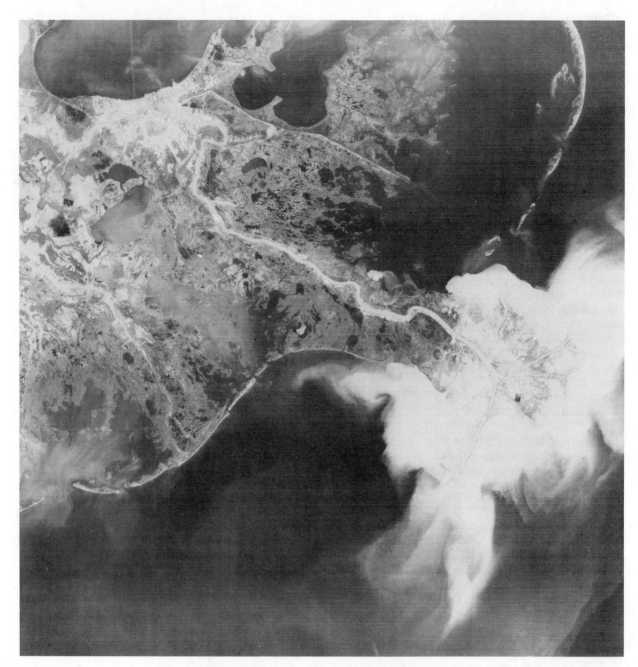

Plate 23-1. Landsat image of the Mississippi Delta region. The image was obtained on January 16, 1973, in band MSS 5. New Orleans is located between the Mississippi River and Lake Pontchartrain in the upper left corner of the image; the Chandeleur Islands are visible in the upper right. The birdfoot delta, issuing large quantities of suspended sediment, dominates the right part of the image. The Grand Isle–Timbalier Island system is visible in the lower left (Landsat photo courtesy of NASA).

Plate 23-2. Low-altitude oblique airphoto of a small crevasse splay in West Bay on the modern delta (photo by D. Nummedal).

Plate 23-4. Oblique view to the north of a segment of the Chandeleur Islands (photo by S. Penland).

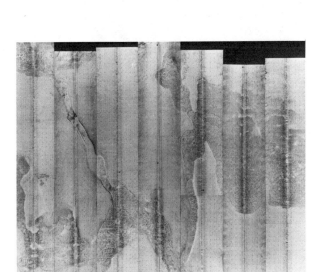

Plate 23-3. Mosaic of side-scan sonar records of the Mississippi Delta front. Extensive areas of collapsed sea floor are connected by debris channels. Material flowed toward the bottom of the mosaic. The tick marks are 25 m apart; the relief on the channel walls is on the order of a few meters (photo by J. Coleman).

Plate 23-5. Oblique aerial view to the north of the mud flats, the recent coastal marsh and the chenier ridges in the Chenier au Tigre area. (photo by P. Kemp).

24. MISSISSIPPI AND ALABAMA

Transport of both fine and coarse sediment along the northern coast of the Gulf of Mexico is toward the west in response to prevailing southeasterly winds. The Mississippi Delta, therefore, which controls sedimentation along the entire Louisiana coast, has negligible direct influence farther east. As a consequence of limited Holocene sedimentation, pre-Holocene deposits outcrop extensively along the Mississippi–Alabama coast. The major morphological components of this coastal region include mainland beaches, the Holocene marshes and swamps along rivers and bay margins, and the (mostly) Holocene barrier island chain (Fig. 24-1).

The entire coastal plain is Cenozoic in age. Late Pleistocene beach-ridge plains (Gulfport Formation) form the mainland Mississippi shore. Holocene barrier spits and beach-ridge plains

form the Alabama shore east of the entrance to Mobile Bay. Marshes fringe the distributaries of the Pearl, Jourdan, Wolf, Biloxi, Pascagoula, Mobile-Tensaw, and relict Escatawpa rivers. The lower parts of the eastern bluffs of Mobile Bay are composed of the sandy-clayey Upper Miocene Ecor Rouge Formation (Isphording 1977). This is believed to correlate with the Pascagoula Formation, which is widespread in southern Mississippi. Alluvial deposits of the Late Pliocene Citronelle Formation cap these Miocene units. Among deposits of Late Pleistocene age (Sangamon) along the northeastern Gulf Coast, the alluvial Prairie Formation and the barrier beach-ridge Gulfport Formation are widespread (Otvos 1981a).

The coastal plain rivers incised deep valleys during the Late Pleistocene low stand of sea level. The subsequent rate of sea-level rise generally

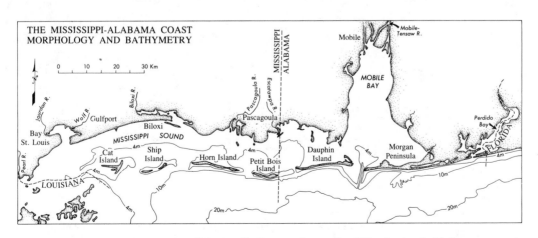

Figure 24-1. Location map of major features along the Mississippi–Alabama coast.

exceeded the rate of fluvial aggradation, thus forming estuaries at St. Louis, Biloxi, Mobile, and Perdido bays. Mobile Bay may be structurally controlled by the seaward extension of the Mobile graben system (Ryan 1969).

The rate of Holocene sea-level rise was greatly reduced about 4000 years B.P., permitting the initiation of regressive beach-ridge plain development along the southeastern Alabama shoreline (Shepard and Wanless 1971) and the building of a barrier island chain along the seaward margin of Mississippi Sound. Development of the St. Bernard lobe of the Mississippi Delta (see *Louisiana*) interrupted island evolution west of Ship Island and initiated growth of a protected large marshland along the southwestern shores of Mississippi Sound (Otvos 1978, 1979).

Tectonic evolution of the region has influenced coastal morphology. Position of Late Pleistocene and Holocene shorelines, river courses, and Pliocene and Pleistocene escarpments on the coastal plain are clear indications of this (Otvos 1981a). Most lineaments are coast-parallel or oblique (Fig. 24-2; Plate 24-1), but the trends of the Pearl, Pascagoula, and Mobile-Tensaw rivers and Mobile Bay are perpendicular to the coast. In sharp contrast with southern Louisiana, uplift or relative stability has characterized the Mississippi–Alabama coast since the end of the Miocene.

MAINLAND COAST

The late Pleistocene Gulfport Formation forms a 7.5–10-m-high strand plain surface immediately behind the mainland shores of Harrison and western Jackson counties, Mississippi. Fur-

ther landward, one finds progressively older units outcropping at the surface. Several formation boundaries form distinctive topographic scarps (Fig. 24-2). Waves impinging on the Gulfport Formation sand have produced extensive beaches and a wide, subtidal platform with complex bar morphology. The bars appear to be of two distinctly different types: multiple longshore bars (Plate 24-2) caused by waves being reflected from the steep beach face, and transverse bars (Plate 24-3), which are probably related to nearshore circulation cells.

In eastern Jackson County, Mississippi, and Mobile County, Alabama, the Gulfport strand plain is absent. Here a fringe of Holocene marsh separates Mississippi Sound from the Prairie Formation of the Pleistocene upland, except where the abandoned Escatawpa River delta (Fig. 24-1) has been reworked into an erosional sand-fringed headland (Grand Batture) with adjacent subaqueous shoals and eroding islets. In essence this is equivalent to stage 1 in the temporal sequence of Louisiana barrier island formation (see *Louisiana*). All the major rivers of the region have built bay-head deltas, of which the Mobile and Pascagoula deltas are the largest. In spite of a progradational recent history, the Mobile delta is today receding (Hardin et al. 1976), probably because of sediment impoundment by dams in the drainage basin.

Mobile Bay illustrates the difference between upwind and downwind bay coastline development. The western, downwind, coast is characterized by an eroding margin of the upland Prairie Formation, and a straight beach fronted by multiple parallel longshore bars. The eastern shore, on

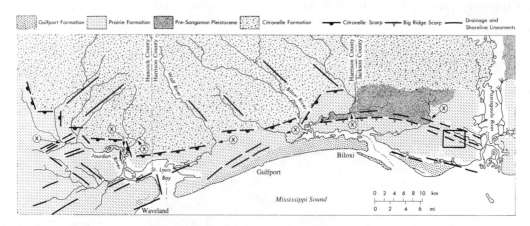

Figure 24-2. Lineaments and escarpments between the Pearl and Pascagoula rivers, Mississippi. Many lineaments correspond to formation boundaries (see legend). The open square locates the area shown in Plate 24-1 (after Otvos 1981a).

the contrary, has remained stable or progradational (Hardin et al. 1976). A wide slope separates the agricultural fields of the Pleistocene surface from the bay coast (Plate 24-4).

Only in the easternmost segment of the two-state region do spits attached to the mainland face the open Gulf of Mexico (Fig. 24-1). Here, in Baldwin County, Alabama, a series of curving Holocene beach ridges with distinct topographic relief separate the more subdued Pleistocene Gulfport beach-ridge plain from the sea (Plate 24-4). The complex patterns of beach-ridge truncations demonstrate multiple episodes of coastal erosion and accretion in Holocene time. Along most of the coastline, erosion has clearly been the norm in the recent past, except at the tip of the Morgan Peninsula, which has prograded westward 344 m between 1917 and 1974.

BARRIER ISLANDS

The barrier island chain begins with Dauphin Island, across the entrance to Mobile Bay from the Morgan Peninsula (Fig. 24-3). At its eastern end, Dauphin Island consists of a Pleistocene core. Sediment moving westward across the ebb-tidal delta at the Mobile Bay entrance accreted on this core and formed a long, low-profile Holocene spit. Much of this sediment was probably supplied from the Baldwin County coast and sources farther east. Five additional islands extend west from Dauphin Island to the eastern edge of the St. Bernard lobe of the Mississippi Delta. These

are Petit Bois, Horn, East and West Ship, and Cat islands. There are no reliable dates from the upper parts of the barrier island sequence itself, but wood samples and dispersed plant debris underlying the island sands have been dated at about 8000–4000 years B.P. (Otvos 1979).

The Holocene deposits along the Mississippi-Alabama coast reach a maximum thickness of about 15–20 m beneath the barriers and thin rapidly landward underneath Mississippi Sound. Stratigraphic sections across the sound from Pascagoula to Horn Island (Fig. 24-4) show a facies pattern typical for the area. The subaerial barrier island occupies the top of a relatively broad sand platform. Sets of parallel beach ridges, particularly well developed on Cat, Horn and Petit Bois islands, reflect intervals of regressive island development (Plates 24-5 and 24-6). The timing of most of these intervals for the Mississippi islands is unknown.

Local erosion and accretion occur to some extent on all Gulf and sound shores of the islands. Erosion is intense at the eastern island tips, whereas the western ends are rapidly prograding (Waller and Malbrough 1976). In recent years the westward spit extension has been dramatically slowed by maintenance dredging of navigation channels through some of the tidal passes.

Cat Island has a unique shape for a barrier (Fig. 24-1). After formation of the St. Bernard Delta, waves arriving at Cat Island were restricted to a narrow window from the east-southeast. This led to truncation of the former beach ridges and

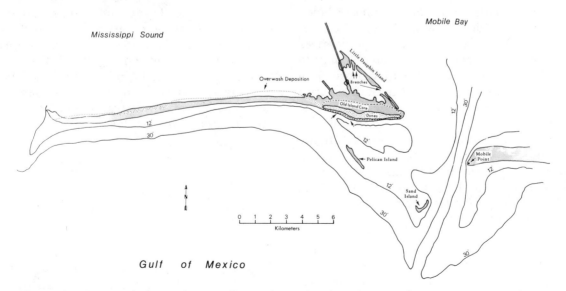

Figure 24-3. Morphological map of Dauphin Island, Alabama, after Hurricane Frederic.

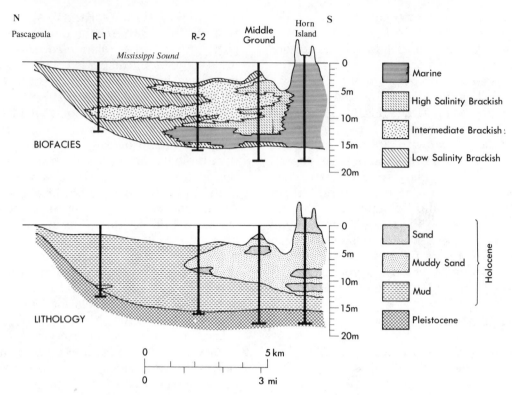

Figure 24-4. Cross-sections of Mississippi Sound from the Pascagoula River delta to Horn Island. Note the broad sand platform underlying the subaerial island (right end of cross-section) (after Otvos 1981b).

the development of two transverse spits nearly perpendicular to the old trend. This probably accounts for the T-shape of the present island.

Hurricanes and tropical storms play a major role in the temporal changes of the barrier islands. The historical patterns of change for most islands are well known (Waller and Malbrough 1976; Otvos 1979), and the record shows that major changes have been brought about as sudden response to hurricane impacts (Otvos 1981b). Central Ship Island was temporarily cut at least five times during the last 130 years. Hurricane Camille (the most intense hurricane in recent U.S. history) formed a 3-km-wide cut in 1969, separating the island into the present eastern and western parts.

The last major storm to have an impact on the region was Hurricane Frederic, in September 1979. The impact was most severely felt on Dauphin Island, where multiple hurricane channels and a continuous washover terrace were formed across the entire Holocene spit. Individual depositional lobes extended far into Mississippi Sound (Plate 24-7). The most severe beach erosion and intense overwash occurred immediately west of the

Pleistocene core, an area that coincides with the western flank of the ebb-tidal delta platform off the entrance to Mobile Bay. Wave refraction studies indicate that this was the location of maximum wave energy during the hurricane because of the focusing effect of the nearshore bathymetry on incident storm waves (Nummedal et al. 1980). It is interesting to note that two earlier hurricanes in this century, in 1916 and 1947, both breached the island at the same location. This is a dramatic example of the strong control that nearshore bathymetry exerts on barrier island processes and morphology.

DAG NUMMEDAL
ERVIN G. OTVOS

REFERENCES

Hardin, J. D., C. D. Sapp, J. L. Emplaincourt, and K. E. Richter, 1976, *Shoreline and Bathymetric Changes in the Coastal Area of Alabama*, Alabama Geol. Survey Inf. Ser. No. 50.

Isphording, W. C., 1977, Petrology and stratigraphy of the Alabama Miocene, *Gulf Coast Assoc. Geol. Socs. Trans.* **27:**304–313.

Nummedal, D., S. Penland, R. Gerdes, W. Schramm, J. Kahn, and H. H. Roberts, 1980, Geologic response to hurricane impact on low-profile Gulf Coast barriers, *Gulf Coast Assoc. Geol. Socs. Trans.* **30:**183–195.

Otvos, E. G., 1978, New Orleans–South Hancock Holocene barrier trends and origins of Lake Pontchartrain, *Gulf Coast Assoc. Geol. Socs. Trans.* **28:**337–355.

Otvos, E. G., 1979, Barrier island evolution and history of migration, north central Gulf Coast, in *Barrier Islands,* S. P. Leatherman, ed., Academic Press, New York, pp. 291–319.

Otvos, E. G., 1981a, Tectonic lineaments or Pliocene and Quaternary shorelines, northeast Gulf Coast, *Geology* **9:**398–404.

Otvos, E. G., 1981b, Barrier island formation through nearshore aggradation—stratigraphic and field evidence, *Marine Geology* **43:**195–243.

Ryan, J. J., 1969, *A Sedimentological Study of Mobile Bay, Alabama,* Florida State Univ. Sedimentol. Research Lab. Contr. 32.

Shepard, F. P., and H. R. Wanless, 1971, *Our Changing Coastlines,* McGraw-Hill, New York.

Waller, T. H., and L. P. Malbrough, 1976, *Temporal Changes in the Offshore Islands of Mississippi,* Mississippi State Univ. Water Resource Inst. Bull.

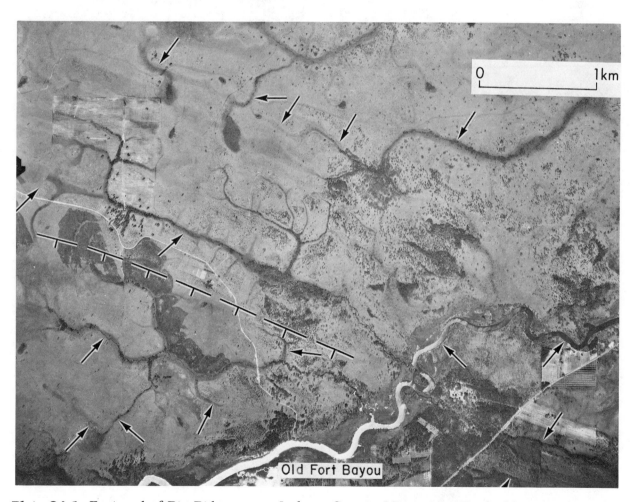

Plate 24-1. East end of Big Ridge scarp, Jackson County, Mississippi. Dashed lines with teeth indicate toe of escarpment. Arrows point to rectangular, fine-textured drainage lineaments (photo from Otvos 1981a, with permission from the Geological Society of America).

Plate 24-2. Oblique aerial view toward the east of multiple parallel longshore bars off Bay St. Louis, Mississippi (photo by D. Nummedal).

Plate 24-3. Oblique aerial view toward the east of the nearshore platform off central Harrison County, Mississippi. Note the complex interference of transverse and longshore bars. Both this photo and that in Plate 24-2 were taken on a day of exceptionally low water caused by strong offshore winds (photo by D. Nummedal).

Plate 24-4. Southeastern corner of Mobile Bay, Alabama (photo courtesy of NASA).

Plate 24-5. Oblique aerial view of Horn Island, Mississippi (photo by D. Nummedal).

Plate 24-6. Oblique aerial view of Petit Bois Island, Mississippi (photo by D. Nummedal).

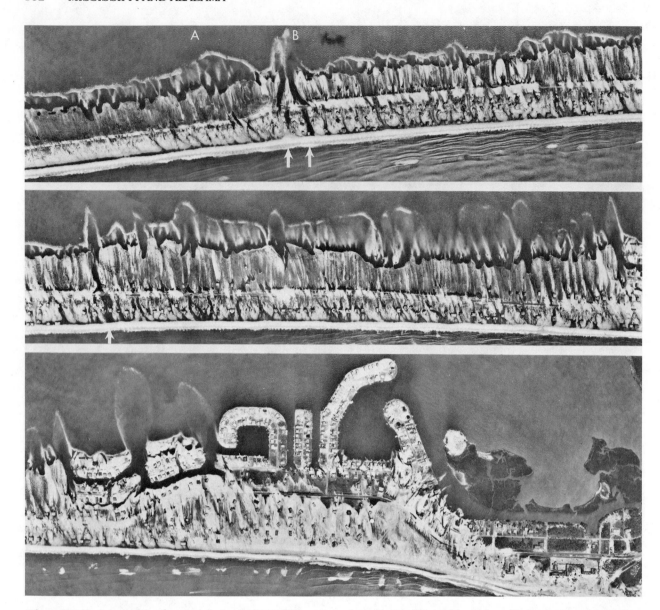

Plate 24-7. A mosaic of vertical airphotos of the central portion of Dauphin Island taken nine days after the landfall of Hurricane Frederic in September 1979, (Photo courtesy of the U.S. Army Engineers, Mobile District. Reproduced from Nummedal et al 1980, with permission from the Gulf Coast Association of Geological Societies.)

25. FLORIDA

Florida has low relief, the maximum for the state being only a little more than 100 m. The tidal range is moderate (typically a meter or less), and surf zone wave-energy levels—on the open coast—range from "zero" (average breaker height less than about 4 cm) to "high" (average close to 1 m).

The "zero" or "very low" energy coasts include protected strips (in lagoons, sounds, and estuaries, and behind reefs) and exposed strips. The biggest example of the latter is the "Big Bend" coast (between Tallahassee and Tampa); its "zero" energy condition derives from several facts: (a) prevailing winds blow from land to sea; (b) the concavity of the coastline provides for divergence of wave orthogonals and hence energy reduction; (c) the offshore bottom is unusually shallow and wide (slope about 0° 1'), so that essentially all deepwater wave energy is dissipated by frictional processes in the passage across the shelf; and (d) the Gulf of Mexico does not produce the upper parts of the typical ocean spectrum of periods and heights.

Sandy barrier islands occur along all the moderate- to high-energy coasts except where the shelf is extremely narrow and steep (1.5°) (e.g., lower east coast, east and southeast of Lake Okeechobee). These sandy barrier islands are generally undergoing erosion (Tanner 1975), and the narrow segments tend to migrate landward.

There is no integrated littoral drift system along the coasts of Florida; instead, there are many littoral drift cells (Stapor 1974), each typically only a few kilometers or a few tens of kilometers long. Where barrier islands are short, cells are particularly small; where barrier islands are long, cells are nevertheless not long, because either (a) the primary transport direction is transverse to the shoreline, rather than parallel to it, or (b) offshore bathymetry controls wave refraction in such a way that littoral-power gradients along the coast control cell structure, without the necessity of having rocky capes or other obvious interruptions (Stapor 1980).

The map in Figure 25-1 presents the cell structure along part of the coast, with cell boundaries shown by horizontal lines. The arrows indicate littoral drift at only a few places; each cell has a dominant direction of littoral drift, which may or may not be opposite from the sense of drift in adjacent cells. The arabic numerals show the computed littoral power, in joules per meter-second, at selected points along the beach (littoral power, rather than wave height or energy, is the key to coastal erosion and deposition). Erosion can be expected to occur where littoral power is either high or increasing, and deposition can be expected where it is decreasing. North of the mapped area is the "zero-energy" coast of Florida, and south of the mapped area is the entrance to Tampa Bay; therefore the many cells shown here constitute an isolated system. Erosion is, in fact, severe, at the indicated places.

There are no alluvial streams draining the peninsula and emptying into either the Atlantic Ocean or the Gulf of Mexico. The Suwannee River and the St. Johns River, in the northern part of the peninsula, carry no alluvial load, and have no deltas, even though they flow into the Gulf and the Atlantic, respectively. Fisheating Creek, which has built a small delta into Lake Okeechobee (southern part of peninsula), does not flow to the sea. The overland flow that drains the Everglades (extreme south), even where channeled by canal cutting, is not alluvial and hence makes no deltas.

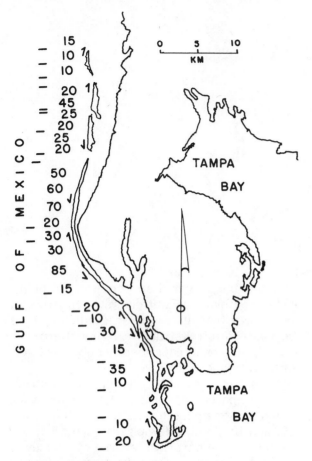

Figure 25-1. Map of the Gulf of Mexico coast of much of Pinellas County, immediately west of Tampa Bay. The city of Tampa is across the bay to the east. For explanation, see text.

Only in the Panhandle can river deltas be found, and they occur only in estuaries; the largest example is that of the Apalachicola River, west of Tallahassee.

Throughout much of the state, the sand is roughly medium-grained (approximately 0.25-mm-diameter) quartz, typically having less than 1% of other detrital minerals. In and immediately north of the Florida Keys (the coral reef tract), beach sands are almost exclusively $CaCO_3$ (calcite or aragonite), and there are patches of carbonate sand in other parts of the state. In the Keys this sand is mostly reef detritus; elsewhere it is pelecypod and gastropod shell fragments, with a small admixture of other materials. The quartz sand was derived originally from the southern Appalachian Mountains, in Georgia and Alabama (to the north), but at present sea level the delivery system has been interrupted

in various ways (including the complicated cell structure in the littoral system). Clay minerals are rare along the Florida coast, except in river delta settings in the estuaries of the Florida Panhandle (west of Tallahassee) (triangles in Fig. 25-2).

There are three reef types in the coastal waters of the state, the best known being the so-called coral reef (dominantly coral) in the Florida Keys, at the southern tip. Living coral reefs line the Keys to the south and southeast, and many of the islands themselves (large individual keys) are high parts (now above sea level) of the Sangamon reef tract (dated at about 120,000 years ago; Osmond et al. 1965). Roughly equal in area is the reef system built by sabellariid worms (Kirtley and Tanner 1968) in the surf and subtidal zones along the east coast. Whereas corals require warm, clean water and considerable wave agitation, the sabellariid worms require sand-size particles in wave transport; these grains are used in tube construction. Sabellariid reefs look like ordinary firm sand, except where built on pilings and seawalls. Sabellariid reefs extend in discontinuous fashion along the east coast of the state, where wave-energy levels are high and sand is in adequate supply. They are best examined at extremely low tide. Vermetid gastropod reefs occur in small patches, very difficult to locate, in the low-wave-energy strip in the southwest part of the peninsula. These organisms develop best in clear, warm water having very little wave energy and no sediment in transport.

Beach ridges occur along many parts of the coast, but they are particularly well developed in five Holocene beach-ridge plains: (1) and (2) St. Vincent Island (Fig. 25-3) and Dog Island, on the rim of the Apalachicola River delta, quartz sand; (3) Sanibel Island, south of Tampa Bay, mostly shell-hash; (4) Marco Island, near the south end of the quartz sand beach chain on the lower west coast, quartz sand; and (5) Cape Canaveral, on the east coast, quartz sand. All these beach-ridge plains were built primarily by swash action, as sediment was driven shoreward. Narrower beach-ridge plains, and single beach ridges, occur elsewhere. Where datable, they are less than 5000 years old, and mostly less than 4000 years old (Stapor and Mathews 1980).

A well-developed Holocene beach-ridge field appears on St. Vincent Island, in the Florida Panhandle, near the Apalachicola River delta, showing beach-ridge sets (note capital letters) rather than individual beach ridges, which exceed 150 in number (Fig. 25-3). Dashed lines represent the

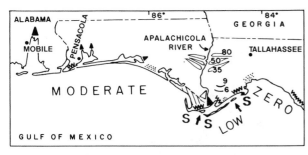

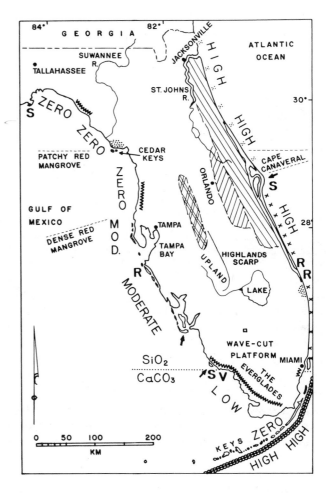

R	rocky coasts (wave-cut cliff, wave-cut platform)
S	large offshore shoal, measured in kilometers
V	scattered reefs and patches of vermetid gastropods
▓▓▓▓▓	living coral reef
x x x x	spectacular exposures of sabellariid worm reefs in the intertidal zone
x x x	scattered sabellariid worm reefs
→	well-developed beach ridge plains of late Holocene age—from west to east: St. Vincent Island, Dog Island, Sanibel Island, Marco Island (in good part destroyed by urbanization), and Cape Canaveral.
⁙	dune fields
∿∿∿∿∿	the +1.5-m mid-Holocene high-sea-level shoreline
▲	growing deltas
Δ	Pre-Holocene delta, perhaps Sangamon in age
□	point from which the wave-cut platform radiates outward in three directions (E, S, W).
NW-SE shading	beach-ridge plains, pre-Holocene in age, probably Sangamon
NE-SW shading	beach ridge plains, perhaps Sangamon but perhaps older Pleistocene
Cross hatching	old coalesced sets of beach ridges, poorly preserved, perhaps Pliocene in age

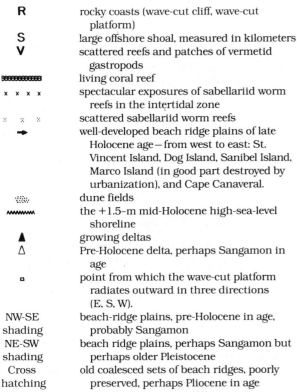

Figure 25-2. (Map of Florida, in two parts). The breaker-zone energy levels are given in terms of "high" (average breaker height > 50 cm), "moderate" (10–50 cm), "low" (< 10 cm), and "zero" (< 4 or 5 cm).

80, 50, 35: marine terraces, Mio-Pliocene in age (numbers refer to height, in meters); each terrace includes a barrier island and a lagoon basin. 9, 6: immature barrier islands at 9 and 6 m altitudes, respectively, perhaps of Yarmouth age (roughly 500,000 years old). The Highlands Scarp, in the south-central part of the state, is a dune-topped wave-cut scarp, with associated wave-cut platform, perhaps of Pliocene age (Tanner and Hajishafie 1978).

typical orientation within each set; from these lines, one can deduce truncation and other events between sets (observe, for example, that set F truncates sets C, D, and E). Small lakes and ponds, near the eastern ends of the individual ridges, show that, as a general rule, these ridges did not continue any farther eastward than their present ends (with the exception of set E). This fact, along with other data, supports the inference that the ridges were built largely from offshore, rather than by a littoral drift mechanism. A detailed plane-table traverse shows that set D stands lower, in general, than the other sets, and hence the notations "MSL Down" (Mean Sea Level down) and "MSL Up" are warranted. The northernmost ridges in set A are also lower than the remaining ridges, hence indicate "MSL Up." Sets H, I, J, and L appear to have been the product of develop-

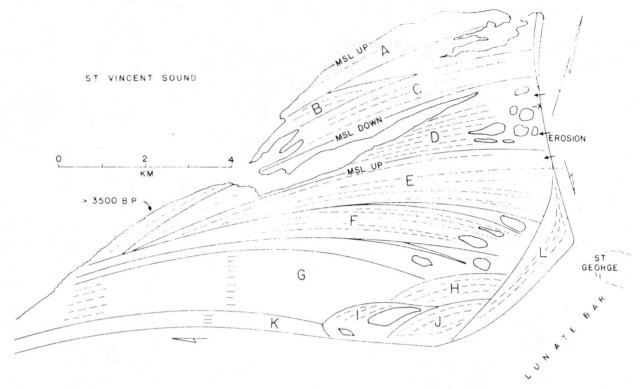

Figure 25-3. Diagrammatic map of the beach-ridge field on St. Vincent Island, in the Florida Panhandle, near the Apalachicola River delta, showing beach-ridge sets (note capital letters) rather than individual beach ridges, which exceed 150 in number. For discussion, see text.

ment and destruction, on an oscillating schedule, of the lunate bar and its associated shoal; the latter was fed by littoral drift from St. George Island, and hence sets H, I, J, and L have a history quite different from that of the remaining sets. The entire island was constructed in approximately 3000–4000 years, continuing up to about 1960. Whether that construction is now over, or merely has been interrupted prior to deposition of a new beach ridge set, cannot be answered beyond any argument, but it is highly probable that island growth has been completed. Modest erosion has been taking place on the island front (south edge) since about 1965.

All the Holocene beach-ridge plains are presently undergoing erosion; construction appears to have been terminated one or more decades ago (Tanner and Stapor 1972; May and Tanner 1973; Silberman 1980).

Sangamon beach-ridge plains occur primarily along the Atlantic coast (but also in the Panhandle); individual ridges are still faintly discernible. The few radiometric dates are in the range of 100,000–120,000 years ago (Osmond et al. 1970). Pre-Sangamon coalesced beach-ridge sets, including

some of probable Pliocene age, occur in the state at higher elevations; individual ridges no longer can be recognized.

Dune decoration of beach ridges has been converted into dune-ridge construction, where (a) the coastline has been stable in position, but sand has been moving in the littoral drift system, or (b) the youngest beach ridge has been undergoing modest erosion. In a few places a single massive beach ridge has been built by storm swash, instead of the series that make up a beach-ridge plain. Internal bedding in typical beach ridges and in the massive variety is commonly 80% (or more) of the swash type.

Outside of beach-ridge areas, sand dunes occur here and there in the coastal strip, locally reaching heights of about 15 m. Cedar Key is a drowned example. Many of these dunes show wind directions not aligned with either the modern sea breeze or the modern prevailing wind; they presumably reflect Wisconsin-age glacial air flow (20,000 to perhaps 60,000 or more years ago).

The plus-1.5-m shoreline is well preserved in various parts of the state. It can be seen clearly at several locations in Coral Gables (southern part of Greater Miami), where it appears as a wave-cut cliff, wave-cut notch, and wave-cut platform in Sangamon-age limestone, and therefore cannot be as old as 120,000 years. It also appears here and there in the Panhandle, where it was cut in loose, clean sand and still shows the angle of repose, and hence cannot be nearly as old as Sangamon. Because the Panhandle localities are generally located landward of barrier islands having ages of 3000-4000 years, the scarp is taken to be about 5000 years old (Tanner and Hockett 1973). This represents the first return of sea level, recorded in the southeastern states, to or above its present position, in post-Sangamon time.

Humate can be found at several locations in the state (Swanson and Palacas 1965), occurring as beds, lenses, and false dikes. In the latter example, the exposure appears, from a distance, to be a more-or-less vertical basalt dike, but closer inspection shows that it is humate, with sand bedding and cross-bedding continuing through it. In some locations humate is clearly post-Sangamon in age, but it is unlikely that it developed in the last half of Holocene time.

The extent of red mangrove is shown on the map; the black variety extends farther than shown into the cooler northern part of the state, but does not make up well-developed mangrove swamps. The red variety grows along the exposed coast in areas of zero to low wave energy; where surf activity is greater, mangroves are restricted to lagoons, sounds, and estuaries.

WILLIAM F. TANNER

REFERENCES

Kirtley, D., and W. F. Tanner, 1968, Sabellariid worms: builders of a major reef type, *Jour. Sed. Petrology* **38**:73–78.

May, J. P., and W. F. Tanner, 1973, The littoral power gradient and shoreline changes, in *Coastal Geomorphology,* D. R. Coates, ed., State University of New York, Binghamton, N.Y., pp. 43–60.

Osmond, J. K., J. R. Carpenter, and H. L. Windom, 1965, Th^{230}/U^{234} age of the Pleistocene corals and oolites of Florida, *Jour. Geophys. Research* **70**:1843–1847.

Osmond, J. K., J. P. May, and W. F. Tanner, 1970, Age of the Cape Kennedy barrier-and-lagoon complex, *Jour. Geophys. Research* **75**:469–479.

Silberman, L., 1980, Beach sediments on Sanibel and Captiva Islands, Florida, in *Shorelines Past and Present,* W. F. Tanner, ed., Florida State University, Tallahassee, Fla., pp. 427–490.

Stapor, F. W., 1974, The "cell" concept in coastal geology, in *Sediment Transport in the Near-Shore Zone,* W. F. Tanner, ed., pp. 1–11.

Stapor, F. W., 1980, The nature of long-term littoral transport along the northeast Florida coast as deduced from beach and dune sand characteristics, in *Shorelines Past and Present,* W. F. Tanner, ed., Florida State University, Tallahassee, Fla., pp. 343ff.

Stapor, F. W., and T. D. Mathews, 1980, C-14 chronology of Holocene barrier islands, Lee County, Florida: a preliminary report, in *Shorelines Past and Present,* W. F. Tanner, ed., Florida State University, Tallahassee, Fla., pp. 47–67.

Swanson, V. E., and J. G. Palacas, 1965, Humate in coastal sands of northwest Florida, *U.S. Geol. Survey Bull.,* **1214-B:** 1–29.

Tanner, W. F., 1973, Advances in near-shore physical sedimentology: a selective review, *Shore and Beach* **41**:22–27.

Tanner, W. F., 1975, Symposium on beach erosion in Middle America: Introduction, *Gulf Coast Assoc. Geol. Socs. Trans.* **25**:365–368.

Tanner, W. F., and M. Hajishafie, 1978, High-level Plio-Pleistocene shoreline in South Florida, *Gulf Coast Assoc. Geol. Socs. Trans.* **28**:647–650.

Tanner, W. F., and J. C. Hockett, 1973, Beach ridge slope angles vs. age, *Southeastern Geology* **15**:45–51.

Tanner, W. F., and F. W. Stapor, 1972, Accelerating crisis in beach erosion, *Internat. Geography* **2**:1020–1021.

U.S. Geological Survey, 1973, *NASA-ERTS-1 Satellite Image Mosaic, Florida;* 1:500,000; false color; one sheet.

26. CUBA

The island of Cuba (Fig. 26-1) has a much-indented coastline about 3200 km long. It is generally hilly, with more mountainous ranges in the western peninsula (Pinar del Rio) and in the southeast (Sierra Maestra). Geologically complex, Cuba forms part of the Greater Antilles island arc (Khudoley 1967; Fairbridge 1975). Sectors of steep, sometimes cliffed coastline alternate with sandy beaches, and mangroves are extensive on low-energy shores behind broad, shallow coralline seas that are bordered by reefs and island chains. There are numerous rias formed by Holocene marine submergence of river valleys. Much of the coastal region is fringed by marine Quaternary deposits, including emerged coral limestone and associated calcarenites, and there is widespread terracing indicative of higher relative sea levels

and tectonic movements in the Pleistocene (Bermudez 1963).

Lying immediately south of the Tropic of Cancer, Cuba has a humid to subhumid tropical climate. The north coast is exposed to northeast trade winds that bring heavy rainfall in the summer months: Havana has a mean annual rainfall of 1270 mm. The south coast is somewhat drier, but the whole island is subject to hurricanes, especially from August through October. Tide ranges are small.

Although the marine provinces bordering Cuba are rich in biogenic sediments, beaches on the more exposed parts have been eroding in recent decades (Plate 26-1). On the other hand, some river sediment yields are being augmented by the effects of open-cast nickel mining in their

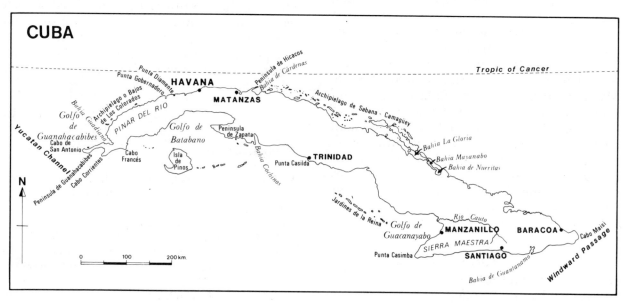

Figure 26-1. Cuba—location map.

catchments, and this is likely to accelerate accretion at river mouths.

NORTH COAST

From Cabo de San Antonio, the westernmost point, the coastline is low-lying and mangrove-fringed behind the lagoonal Golfo de Guanahacabibes and the outlying barrier chain of reefs and islands known as the Archipielago o Bajos de Los Colorados, but north of the large ria of Bahia Guadiana the lagoon narrows and the coast steepens along the northern flank of the Pinar del Rio mountains. Numerous short, steep rivers flow down to the coast, which is slightly indented at their mouths. Off Punta Gobernadoro the reefs are close inshore, and beyond Punta Diamante they fade out, leaving the steep coast more exposed to northeasterly waves arriving through deep inshore waters. Valley-mouth inlets become larger, as at Havana and Matanzas, as the hinterland declines to hilly topography. Terraces in this region stand 8, 16, between 15 and 33, and from 25–51 m above sea level, respectively, indicating tilting as well as sea-level oscillations (Ducloz 1963). There are occasional fringing reefs.

East of Havana the nearshore waters become shallower, beaches and cliffs line the coast, and a major recurved spit, the Peninsula de Hicacos, shelters the wide Bahia de Cardenas at the beginning of another major reef and island fringed coast, the Archipielago de Sabana-Camagüey. The outer cordon of reefs, cays, and coral limestone islands is backed by shallow lagoonal waters and an extremely intricate mainland coastline, much of which is mangrove-fringed. To the southeast the islands become larger and the lagoon breaks up into a series of landlocked bays (Bahia La Gloria, Bahia Mayanabo, Bahia de Nuevitas) separated by swampy corridors. Eventually the islands of limestone become linked to the mainland as a coastal plain, possibly the outcome of transverse tilting of the coastal region. This plain narrows as spurs from the hilly hinterland encroach on it, and to the southeast a steep reef-fringed coast extends to Baracoa, where it declines to the low-lying eastern extremity of Cuba at Cabo Maisi.

SOUTH COAST

West from Cabo Maisi the hinterland again becomes hilly, and sectors of steep coast are interrupted by marine inlets such as Bahia de Guantanamo and estuaries as at Santiago de Cuba. Farther west is the almost straight bold coast rising to the mountains of Sierra Maestra, with many short, steep rivers between interfluves with terraces uplifted to various levels. At the western end these mountains decline to low hills on the peninsula of Punta Casimba.

Here the coastline swings northeast along the relatively shallow Golfo de Guacanayaba, and becomes low-lying and swampy, with extensive mangroves. North of Manzanillo the large Rio Cauto has built a delta, the shores of which are partly sandy and partly muddy and mangrove-fringed. The mangroves continue westward along low-energy shores behind a wide, shallow sea area in the lee of the reefs and cays of the Jardine de la Reina. Some of the cays are low wooded islands with associated mangroves. As on the north coast, the reef and island chain runs inshore, the low energy coastline ending at a recurved spit, Punta Casilda, southwest of the town of Trinidad. A steep coast bordering the Sierra de Trinidad then gives way to coastal lowlands with extensive swamps, and west of the wide inlet of Bahia Cochinos these continue in the wide, low mangrove-fringed Peninsula de Zapata. The nearshore shelf then widens offshore again, with an outlying chain of reefs and cays seaward of the Golfo de Batabano, backed by a mangrove-fringed mainland coast. Offshore, Isla de Pinos is a large, sandy island with a core of metamorphic rocks forming internal hill country: its shores are partly cliffed and partly beach-lined. To the west, Cabo Francés marks the end of the shallow nearshore seas and the beginning of hilly country, which extends to the limestone Peninsula de Guanahacabibes. Cliffs and bluffs here form a coastline bordered by deep water close inshore on either side of Cabo Corrientes. To the west the nearshore shelf reappears off Cabo de San Antonio, beside the Yucatan Channel, beyond which lies the Mexican mainland.

ERIC C. F. BIRD

REFERENCES

Bermudez, P. J., 1963, *Las Formaciones Geológicas do Cuba*. Instituto Cubano de Recursos Minerales, Havana.

Ducloz, C., 1963, Étude géomorphologique de la Région de Matanzas, Cuba, *Archives Sci.* **16,** 2: 351–402.

Fairbridge, R. W., 1975, Cuba, in *Encyclopedia of World Regional Geology*, Vol. I, Dowden, Hutchinson & Ross, Stroudsburg, Pa., pp. 252–255.

Khudoley, K. M., 1967, Principal features of Cuban geology, *Am. Assoc. petroleum Geologists Bull.* **51,** 5:668–677.

Plate 26-1. Erosion of the sandy beach at Santa María del Mar, near Havana, during the stormy winter of 1976–1977, resulted in the undercutting of *Casuarina equisetifolia* trees (photo by C. Buría).

27. JAMAICA

Jamaica lies at the northwestern end of the Caribbean Archipelago, 145 km south of Cuba, from which it is separated by the Cayman Trench. This trench, which reaches a depth of approximately 7000 m, represents the northern limit of the Caribbean plate. Jamaica lies on the northern margin of this plate, and at the eastern end of the Nicaraguan Rise.

Jamaica is located in the trade wind belt and the northeast trades are the prevailing winds. Winds and waves approach the north coast mainly from a northeasterly direction and the south coast from the southeast. The tidal range along the entire shore is generally small — being less than 0.30 m in most areas.

The coastline is extremely varied, but there are important distinctions between the north and south coasts. A narrow coastal plain rings the shoreline for most of its length, the important exception being sections of the south coast. There the coastal plain reaches its maximum width in the contiguous Liguanea, St. Catherine, and Clarendon plains (Fig. 27-1). Farther west, along the coast, the Black River morass, an extensive wetland, extends irregularly inland for 10 km, whereas Georges Plain in the southwest stretches for 6 km inland.

Sections of the coast are cliffed. The south-central area just east of the Black River morass, and the stretch of coast between Yallahs and Bull Bay, are fault-bounded, both areas exhibiting virtually straight scarps.

The extensive coastal plains of the south coast are alluvial and are drained by the largest rivers of the island, almost all of which empty onto the south coast. These rivers are sediment-laden and carry a heavy load to the shore.

Jamaica's main watershed produces north- and south-flowing streams, and whereas the larger streams empty onto the south coast, the north coastal plain, with a few exceptions, is crossed by short, seasonal streams. These streams originate at the foot of the limestone hills, against which the coastal plain abuts.

The difference in drainage characteristics has also contributed to a significant variation in the composition of beach material. The north coast exhibits buff-colored coralline sand derived largely from the fringing reefs. The section of coast drained by rivers from the Blue Mountains is the exception, dark sand there being derived mainly from river load. Material on the south coast is predominantly dark-colored; it ranges in texture from shingle to very find sand. Black magnetite sand occurs between Cuckold Point and Alligator Pond, and is derived from deposits offshore. These sands occur nowhere else on the shore. The Alligator Pond area also exhibits well-developed sand dunes.

It is significant also that prograding and accretionary beaches predominate on the south coast and are associated with the river systems that empty there. Beaches around Savanna-La-Mar, Milk River Bay (Plate 27-1), Portland Ridge, Palisadoes, and Yallahs are the major examples (Fig. 27-1). Beach material is composed of varying combinations of clastic and carbonate material; the carbonates are derived mainly from the marine shelf (Wood 1976).

Deltas, spits, and bars characterize many sections of the south coast (Plates 27-1 and 27-2). The Palisadoes (Fig. 27-2), which marks the southern boundary of Kingston Harbor, is a distinctive tombolo that derives its material largely from the Hope River immediately to the east. The Palisadoes

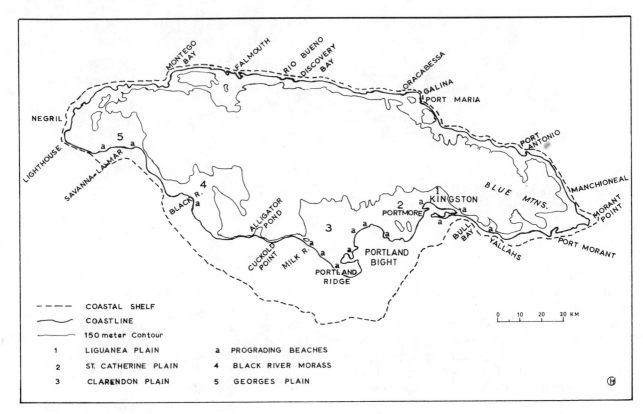

Figure 27-1. Coastal features of Jamaica.

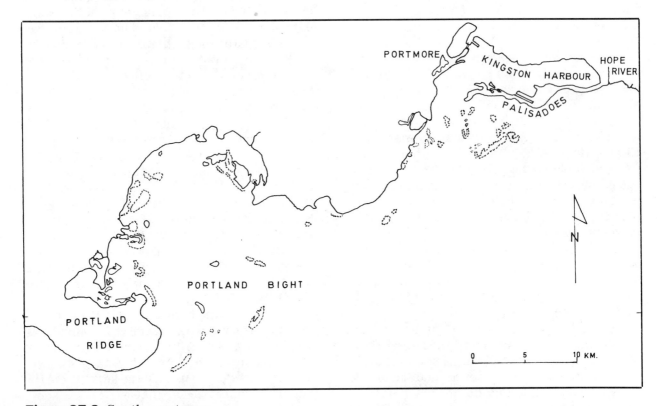

Figure 27-2. South coast cays.

in its development incorporated cays as well as an island at the western end, thereby acquiring the classification of tombolo. There is evidence of drowned spits, one seaward of the present Palisadoes and two within Kingston Harbor, now represented by shoals (Goreau and Burke 1966). The orientation of spits and bars, and the general movement of coastal sediment, reflects the westward drift of longshore currents and the predominantly westerly direction of wave approach.

The south coast also exhibits maximum development of cays, although there are several groups around the island. The Morant Cays, 37 km southeast of Kingston, and the cays of the Portland Bight are the major groups of the south coast, whereas on the north coast the cays of Montego Bay (Plate 27-3) were an important group until the mid-1960s. Some of the Montego Bay cays have since been incorporated into a major reclamation project. The Portland Bight cays are superimposed on the island shelf, and vary in their surface characteristics through bare sand, shingle, beach rock, mangrove, and shrubs.

Raised reef terraces are yet another significant aspect of Jamaica's coastal morphology. Although characteristic of the entire shoreline, these terraces are more numerous and more extensively developed along the south coast. Exposures are particularly well developed in the Port Maria–Oracabessa, Discovery Bay–Falmouth, and Negril areas (Fig. 27-1; Plates 27-4 and 27-5). The terraces reach their maximum development in the Port Maria–Oracabessa area, where up to seven levels have been identified and the highest altitude (180 m) recorded. The Negril area, particularly along the southwest coast in the vicinity of Lighthouse (Fig. 27-1), records a maximum terrace height of 95 m, and four levels have been identified.

Caves and notches are etched into the terraces and these are particularly distinctive in the Discovery Bay–Falmouth area (Fig. 27-5), where double and triple sea-level notches have been identified. Horsfield (1972) has suggested that block faulting has influenced the discontinuity in terrace height; the fact that fault scarps face northwest, anomalous to the topographic grain of the island, affords additional evidence.

Modern coral reefs are also more dominant along the north coast, where they form a discontinuous fringe at the edge of the coastal shelf. On the south coast these reefs exist only as patches, and they are located inshore of the shelf edge (Woodley and Robinson 1977).

Goreau (1969) has suggested that modern reefs started developing 5000 years ago when sea level achieved its present height. Eighteen thousand years ago sea level was 130 m below the present position, and it rose with intermittent halts, at which times reefs developed. Reef profiles vary from place to place along the coast; these variations are largely a function of differences in the profile of the basement on which the reefs are located (Woodley and Robinson 1977).

Many aspects of the aforementioned differences between the north and south coasts have been attributed to a slow tilting of the island to the south during the Quaternary (Horsfield 1972, 1973). It is this tilting that contributed to uplift on the north coast and submergence on the south coast. As a result, the northern coastal shelf is narrow, extending only about 1 km offshore, whereas the shelf extends about 20 km offshore on the south (Fig. 27-1).

Man has also played an important role in shaping the present coastal outline. Land has been reclaimed along many stretches of the coast to facilitate housing and the development of amenities for tourism. Many of these reclamation projects have involved wetlands (Montego Bay, Falmouth, Portmore), and the effects on ecology and coastal circulation systems have manifested themselves. Dredge and fill is the predominant method, and hundreds of hectares of land have been created.

In Montego Bay (Plates 27-3 and 27-6) 140 ha were reclaimed to create Montego Freeport. Shoals and cays (Bogue Islands) were incorporated. Twenty additional hectares have been reclaimed to upgrade and expand the waterfront area, a project that includes the creation of new beaches (Plate 27-6). Ochos Rios has had a similar fate, in that resort facilities have been developed on man-made land.

Kingston Harbor and the adjacent Portmore areas have also been subject to extensive reclamation schemes. Kingston Harbor was developed largely for port and commercial use, and Portmore for housing (Plates 27-7 and 27-8). Mangrove swamps have been destroyed in the Portmore–Kingston area, as they were in Falmouth. The natural phosphorescence of Falmouth Bay disappeared as the microscopic dinoflagellates were destroyed.

ELEANOR B. JONES

REFERENCES

Burke, K., 1967, The Yallahs Basin: A sedimentary basin southeast of Kingston, *Marine Geology* **5:**45–60.

Goreau, T., 1969, Post-Pleistocene urban renewal in coral reefs, *Micronesia* **2:**323–326.

Goreau, T., and K. Burke, 1966, Pleistocene-Holocene geology of the island shelf near Kingston, *Marine Geology* **4:**207–225.

Horsfield, W., 1972, A Late Pleistocene sea level notch, and its relation to block faulting on the north coast of Jamaica, *Jour. Geol. Soc. Jamaica* **12:**18–22.

Horsfield, W., 1973, Late Tertiary and Quaternary crustal movements in Jamaica, *Jour. Geol. Soc. Jamaica* **13:**6–13.

Wood, P., 1976, Beaches of accretion and progradation in Jamaica, *Jour. Geol. Soc. Jamaica* **15:**24–31.

Woodley, J., and E. Robinson, 1977, *Field Guide Book to the Ancient and Modern Reefs of Jamaica*, 3rd Int'l Symposium on Coral Reefs, Atlantic Reef Committee, University of Miami, Miami, Fla.

Plate 27-1. Milk River mouth on the south coast. This river carries a heavy silt load during the rainy season. The bar has developed over a 10-year period. Note abandoned meander loops. The western edge of Clarendon Plain is in the background (photo by J. Tyndale-Biscoe).

Plate 27-2. Yallahs River delta on the south coast. The river carries a heavy load as it drains a highly erodible basin. East of the delta are the salt ponds and saline lagoons (photo by J. Tyndale-Biscoe).

Plate 27-3. Montego Bay before reclamation scheme, showing Bogue Islands (cays) in the background (photo by J. Tyndale-Biscoe).

Plate 27-4. Oracabessa, an extensive manifestation of reef terraces. Seven levels have been identified; the maximum elevation is 180 m. In the foreground is reclaimed land for the development of a deep-water pier; Santa Maria Island (cay) has been retained. Development has ceased temporarily (photo by J. Tyndale-Biscoe).

Plate 27-5. Exposure of reef terrace on Discovery Bay to Falmouth stretch. Sea-level notches and caves are evident (photo by J. Tyndale-Biscoe).

Plate 27-6. Montego Bay after reclamation; new beaches and Montego Freeport are shown (photo by J. Tyndale-Biscoe).

Plate 27-7. Rio Cobre Delta, marshes, and mangrove islands west of Kingston in Portmore area before reclamation (photo by J. Tyndale-Biscoe).

Plate 27-8. Rio Cobre area after reclamation, showing reclaimed land for port facilities in the foreground and housing in Portmore. The delta now has a straight channel (photo by J. Tyndale-Biscoe).

28. HISPANIOLA

Hispaniola, a mountainous island, is about 660 km long and up to 260 km wide. Four nearly parallel west-northwest–trending mountain ranges are separated by relatively narrow, alluvial-filled, longitudinal structural depressions (Fig. 28-1). Coastal plains also occur, but they are most extensive on the southeast coast of the Dominican Republic. In Haiti, where the mountains frequently come close to the shore, the area of coastal plain is relatively small.

As a consequence of the island's location on the northern boundary of the Caribbean plate, it has been subjected to folding, faulting, uplift, and depression since the early Cretaceous (Bowen 1975). Raised coral reef terraces, all of Quaternary age, occur at a number of places along the coast, indicating that local uplift continued at least well into the Pleistocene.

Although geological studies of Hispaniola are relatively numerous (Nagle et al. 1979), coastal geomorphologic studies are rare. Most of the subsequent information is derived from the work of Woodring et al. (1924), Barrett (1954, 1962), and Butterlin (1954, 1956, 1960). Of these, only Barrett's work dealt specifically with the study of coastal geomorphology.

This discussion of the island's coastal features will start at the international boundary on the south coast and work clockwise around the island.

From the international boundary to Tiburon, the coast is mostly bordered by steep cliffs. Between the boundary and Jacmel, the cliffs are occasionally 200 m high and the mountains meet the sea (Butterlin 1960). Coral reefs are relatively rare and mangrove growth is confined to a few protected bays. West of Aquin are a number of small bays with islands and detached coral reefs at the

entrances of some. (U.S. Naval Oceanographic Service 1958).

Between Jacmel and Aquin and northwest of Pointe l'Abacou, there are at least two marine terraces, one of which shows evidence of differential uplift (Butterlin 1954; Woodring et al. 1924). There is also evidence at Jacmel of a third high sea-level stand (Butterlin 1960). At Grante Pointe there is a 10-km-long gravel beach 3–5 m high, behind which is a low gravel terrace (Butterlin 1954; Woodring et al. 1924).

From Tiburon to Pointe-Dame Marie (approximately) are a number of small bays separated by cliffed headlands. The cliffs are occasionally more than 100 m high (Butterlin 1960).

The north coast of the Jacmel peninsula is cliffed for long sections, the cliffs ranging from 10–18 m in height. Coral reefs are relatively rare and, along with mangroves, are mainly confined to sheltered locations (Woodring et al. 1924; U.S. Naval Oceanographic Service 1958). A single, slightly arched terrace occurs from slightly west of Jérémie to Miragoâne (Butterlin 1954; Woodring et al. 1924). Near Grand-Goave the cliffs give way to a zone where rapid alluviation dominates the coast and much of the shore is lined by mangroves and mud flats (Woodring et al. 1924).

Gonâve Island is about 57 km long and 15 km wide at its maximum. Its shores are almost entirely bounded by coral reefs except for the high cliffed section along the northwest end (U.S. Naval Oceanographic Service 1958). Steep cliffs also occur on the southeastern end of the island and low mangrove shores lie between the cliffed sections. Ten or more well-preserved limestone terraces occur on the north coast (Butterlin 1954).

The alluvial lowlands along the west coast of

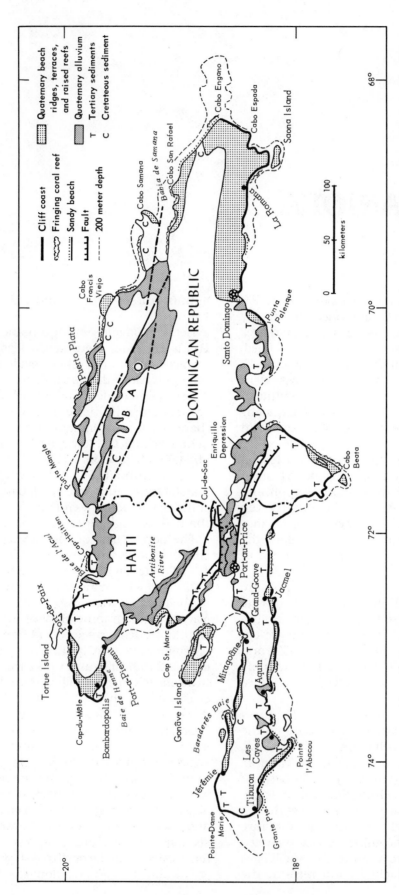

Figure 28-1. The coastal features of Hispaniola. Because of the small map scale, certain features have been exaggerated, for example, the Quaternary marine features at Cabo Francis Viejo.

Hispaniola have flat, marshy shores with fringing mangrove. One of these lowlands, the Cul-de-Sac, has several coral limestone terraces along its inland margins, deposited when a Quaternary sea extended deeply into the lowland. Subsequently, the terraces appear to have been tilted (Butterlin 1954, 1960; Woodring et al. 1924).

Four prominent limestone terraces on the southeastern side of Cap St. Marc also show evidence of crustal tilting. On the northern side of the promontory, two terraces skirt the shore of St. Marc Bay (Butterlin 1960). Except at the head of the bay, the shore is bordered by an almost continuous cliff 20–30 m high (Woodring et al. 1924).

A remarkable set of well-preserved Quaternary terraces occurs around the western end of the northwest peninsula. They increase in number and size westward along both coasts of the peninsula from Port-de-Paix and Port-a-Piement respectively, eventually extending to a limestone plateau 640 m high (Butterlin 1954, 1960; Woodring et al. 1924). Successively higher terraces are veneered with progressively older limestones. At least 20 terraces were counted along the road from Baie de Henne to Bombardopolis. There are at least eight higher, prominent terraces leading up to the top of the plateau (Woodring et al. 1924). Uranium series dating of corals from the crests of the three lowest terraces of this series yielded mean dates of $81,000 \pm 3000$ years B.P. (Mole, 16m), $108,000 \pm 5000$ years B.P. (Saint, 28m), and $130,000 \pm 6000$ years B.P. (Nicolas, 52m). Assuming sea level was 6 m higher than at present during the formation of the Nicholas reef, the local uplift rate is calculated to be 0.35 m/1000 yr (Dodge et al. 1983).

Tortue Island is 37 km long and up to 7 km wide. The entire north coast is dominated by high sea cliffs and is inaccessible. There are two terraces, best preserved at the ends of the island, where the slope is relatively gentle. On the southern side the terraces have been virtually destroyed by marine erosion (Woodring et al. 1924).

From Port-de-Paix to the Dominican Republic, the coast is approximately equally divided into sections bounded by cliffs and by lowlands. Coral reefs are generally abundant in sheltered bays and bay mouths. West of Baie de l'Acul is a 10 km section of tombolo coast with long, curving beaches (Woodring et al. 1924; U.S. Naval Oceanographic Service 1958). Between the Baie de l'Acul to Cap-Haitien, the coast is again steeply cliffed (U.S. Naval Oceanographic Service 1958).

From Cap-Haitien to the Dominican border,

the coast is backed by a broad alluvial plain, the landward limit of which is a beveled rock platform possibly formed by marine erosion. The platform ranges in elevation from 150 m in the east to 75 m in the west (Woodring et al. 1924).

The low, mangrove-fringed coast continues, more or less uninterrupted, into the Dominican Republic as far east as Punta Mangle. Sandy and pebble beaches occur at places along the coast from Punta Mangle to Cabo Francis Viejo but are backed by mountainous terrain. Coral reef formations are common and, in the case of the broad bight between Puerto Plata and Cabo Francis Viejo, the reef may extend as much as 12 km offshore (U.S. Naval Oceanographic Service 1958). Barrett (1954) has reported a number of marine terraces at Puerto Plata and in the vicinity of Cabo Francis Viejo.

South from Cabo Francis Viejo, the coast is low and bounded by a fringing reef. The north shore of the Samana peninsula is steep and rocky with coral reefs. Marine terraces have been mentioned as occurring near Cabo Samana and at places along the south coast of the Bahia de Semana (Butterlin 1956). Coral reefs are abundant in the bahia. From Cabo San Rafael to Cabo Engano, the coast is low and is surrounded by an intermittent reef (U.S. Naval Oceanographic Service 1958). Much of the shore consists of a calcareous sand beach backed by a low dune ridge, both of which rest on coastal limestone (Barrett 1962).

Between Cabo Engano and the international border, most of the shore is bounded by marine cliffs of varied height, and in places mountains come close to the sea (U.S. Naval Oceanographic Service 1958). From Cabo Engano to Punta Palenque, the coast is almost continuously cliffed, the cliff height varying from less than a meter to about 18 m (Barrett 1962) (Plate 28-1). Nearly everywhere the cliff is topped by a low ridge of calcareous debris that may obscure the cliff where it is low. Where prominent, the cliff can be divided into two general levels, a submerged level at about 2 fm and an emerged level or secondary cliff at about 3–4 m (Barrett 1962).

Barrett (1954, 1962) studied the marine terraces between Cabo Engano and Punta Palenque. The inner edge of the coastal plain lies at an elevation of about 120 m, but clearly defined shore features are absent above 78–82 m. Below 78–82 m are numerous marine-eroded scarps and benches but none are continuous for long distances (Plate 28-2). However, the scarps and benches can be grouped into a number of composite terraces. Of these, eight are described in some detail. The most important is the composite terrace at 29–32 m, which can be traced from east of La Romana to Punta Palenque. The terrace surfaces do not appear to have been warped or tilted and are thought to be eustatic in origin. A variety of evidence from overdeepened river valleys, sand dune remnants, and submerged marine terraces suggests a lowering of sea level by at least 50 fm (Barrett 1962). Uranium series dating of corals from Barrett's 3–6-m and 8–9-m terraces indicate the age of the lower to range between 95,000–120,000 years B.P., whereas one sample from the upper (probably) gave an age of 190,000–210,000 years B.P. (Schubert and Cowart 1978).

Weyl (1953) mentions three terraces occurring in the vicinity of Cabo Beata. The lowest has an elevation of about 40 m. The second lies between 90 and 250 m, whereas the third has an elevation of about 400 m. Weyl believes the terraces indicate the amount of Pleistocene uplift in the area.

CHARLES S. ALEXANDER

REFERENCES

Barrett, W., 1954, *Marine and Stream Terraces of the Southeastern Coastal Plain of the Dominican Republic*, U.S. Office of Naval Research Prelim. Rept. NONR222 (11) 388067.

Barrett, W., 1962, Emerged and submerged shorelines of the Dominican Republic, Inst. Pan. Am. de Geog. e Hist. *Reu. Geog.* **30:**51–77.

Bowen, C., 1975, The geology of Hispaniola, in *The Ocean Basins and Margin, Vol. 3: The Gulf of Mexico and the Caribbean*, A. E. M. Nairn and F. G. Stehli, eds., Plenum, New York, pp. 501–522.

Butterlin, J., 1954, *La Géologie de la Republique d'Haiti*, Mémoires de l'Inst. Français d'Haiti Mem.

Butterlin, J., 1956, *La Constitution Géologique et la Structure des Antilles*, Centre National de la Recherche Scientifique, pp. 89–138.

Butterlin, J., 1960, *Géologie Générale et Régionale de la Republique d'Haiti*, Inst. Hautes Etudes Amérique Latine Trav. et Mem. 6.

Dodge, R. E., R. G. Fairbanks, L. K. Benninger, and F. Maurrasse, 1983, Pleistocene sea levels from raised coral reefs of Haiti, *Science* **219:**1423–1425.

Nagle, F., H. C. Palmer, and G. A. Antonini, 1979, Hispaniola, tectonic focal point of the northern Caribbean, in *Three Geological Studies in the Dominican Republic*, B. Lidz and F. Nagle, eds., Miami Geological Society, Miami, Fla., p. 96

Schubert, C., and J. B. Cowart, 1978, Uranium series ages of Pleistocene marine terraces, southeastern Dominican Republic, in *Tenth International Congress on Sedimentology*, G. M. Friedman, ed., *Abstracts*, vol. II, p. 590.

U.S. Naval Oceanographic Service, 1958, *Sailing Directions for the West Indies*, Pub 21.

Weyl, R., 1953, Die Sierra de Bahoruco von Santo Domingo und ihre Stellung in Antillenbogen, *Neues. Jahrb. für Geologie u. Paläeontologie Abh. B* **98:**1–27.

Woodring, W. P., J. S. Brown, and W. S. Burbank, 1924, *Geology of the Republic of Haiti*, Lord Baltimore Press, Port-au-Prince.

Plate 28-1. The sea cliffs at Boca de Yuma on the southeast coast of the Dominican Republic near Cabo Espada (photo by W. Barrett).

Plate 28-2. Raised sea cliff near Boca de Yuma (photo by W. Barrett).

29. PUERTO RICO

The coastline of Puerto Rico is composed of rocks that range from unconsolidated sediments to limestone and igneous outcrops, thus it varies greatly in resistance to erosion. Subaerial and marine processes have acted on the 740 km of coastline to produce a variety of shore types. More than 150 beaches cover 208 km (28%) of the coast (Liegel 1972). The beaches are relatively short, and they are divided into separate, distinct systems that have little interaction. Analyses of the mineral composition of the beach sands have been useful in identifying individual beach systems. These systems differ markedly in composition and reflect a combination of input from offshore biogenic and relict sand bodies, rivers, and coastal erosion.

The tectonic setting is dominated by an east-trending central mountain range of volcanic and plutonic igneous rocks that is flanked on the north and south by shallow-water limestone beds (Kaye 1959). River discharge, rainfall, and vegetation cover are greater on the north coast, which has most of the major rivers. The offshore sediments of the narrow (2–4 km wide) north and northwest insular shelf are dominantly terrigenous. The major protection from wave action is provided by remnants of former eolianite lines. The south coast is semiarid. It varies in width from 1–10km and is the site of numerous coral reefs. The southwest and east areas of the shelf are relatively wide and are dominantly coral and carbonate sediment areas (Morelock 1978).

From Cabo San Juan, on the northwest corner of Puerto Rico, to San Juan, the coast is dominantly beach plain with a barrier coast at the mouth of the Rio de Loiza and eolianite coasts at Puerto Vacia Talega and Punta Maldonado (Fig. 29-1). The coastal area is low and sandy except for occasional bluffs. The lowland extends inward for 5–7 km. Here the several large mangrove areas do not form the coast, but lie several hundred meters inland behind sand beaches. The beach sediments are dominantly carbonate except between Punta Uvero and Punta Vacia Talega, where the beach receives a significant input of river sediments. Quartz content is especially high because the upper drainage basin of the Rio Loiza is a plutonic rock area (Gillou and Glass 1957). Although quartz content decreases and carbonate increases west of Punta Vacia Talega, there is enough quartz to indicate bypassing of sediments. At San Juan, the beaches are thin coverings of sand over a rocky shore.

Westward from San Juan to Arecibo, the coast is sand beach, eolianite, and beach-rock in front of a low coastal plain. The sand spit at the mouth of the Rio de la Plata forms a barrier coast (Plate 29-1). West of this is rocky eolianite shore, which has been breached in many places to form small lunate bays bordered with sand and beachrock. Except for the locally terrigenous sediments supplied by the Bayamon and La Plata rivers, the beach sands are dominantly carbonate from San Juan to the Rio Manati. West of the mouth of the Rio Manati, the beach sands are igneous rock fragments, dark minerals, quartz, and some feldspar (Plate 29-2). There is a slow decrease in terrigenous material westward until, near Arecibo, the sediments are again carbonate. Part of the beach sands is being incorporated into dunes behind the beaches by wind action.

The northwest coast from Arecibo to Aguadilla is a series of rocky, karst-eroded limestone cliffs that form a secondary shore type as a result of

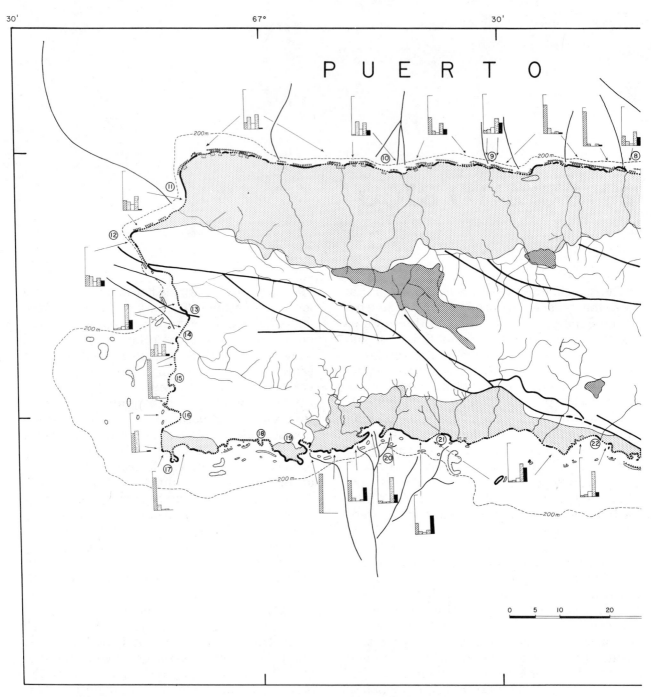

P U E R T O

1. Cabo San Juan
2. Punta Uvero
3. Rio de Loiza
4. Punta Vacia Talega
5. Punta Maldonado
6. San Juan
7. Rio Bayamon

8. Rio de la Plata
9. Rio Manati
10. Arecibo
11. Aguadilla
12. Punta Higuero
13. Mayaguez
14. Punta Guanajibo

Figure 29-1. Puerto Rico coastal landforms and beach sand composition.

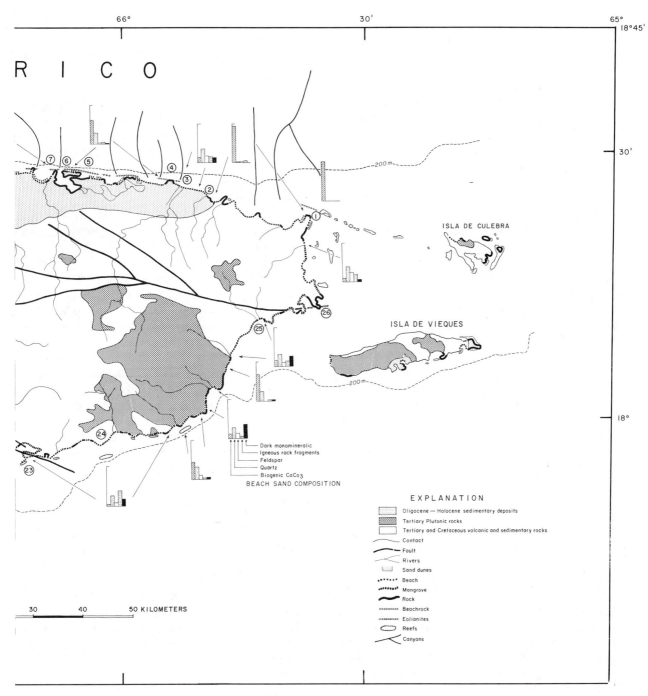

BEACH SAND COMPOSITION

- Dark monomineralic
- Igneous rock fragments
- Feldspar
- Quartz
- Biogenic CaCo₃

EXPLANATION

Oligocene — Holocene sedimentary deposits
Tertiary Plutonic rocks
Tertiary and Cretaceous volcanic and sedimentary rocks
Contact
Fault
Rivers
Sand dunes
Beach
Mangrove
Rock
Beachrock
Eolianites
Reefs
Canyons

ISLA DE CULEBRA

ISLA DE VIEQUES

R I C O

30   40   50 KILOMETERS

15. Punta Ostiones
16. Boqueron
17. Cabo Rojo
18. Punta Montalvo
19. Guanica
20. Punta Verraco

21. Ponce
22. Salinas
23. Punta Las Marias
24. Arroyo
25. Naguabo
26. Punta Lima

wave erosion. Where there is a narrow coastal plain in front of the limestones, sand from the beach is being incorporated into backing dunes.

From Aguadilla to Punta Cabo Rojo, the western coast is dominated by the termination of structural mountain ridges separated by broad alluvial valleys (Kaye 1959). The ridges form a rocky coast, and the coastline bordering the alluvial valleys is occupied by sand beaches or mangrove. Between Aguadilla and Punta Higuero, the beach has sands with almost equal parts of carbonate shelf material, quartz and feldspar, dark minerals, and dark volcanic rock fragments. The sand composition is similar south of Punta Higuero to Mayaguez, although there is an increase in dark minerals and rock fragments southward.

At Mayaguez the submarine canyon of the Rio de Yaguez separates the beaches to the south and north; the composition changes drastically. The south beach is composed of igneous rock fragments and dark minerals, mainly serpentine. The absence of carbonate shell material indicates almost no onshore transport of sediments.

South of Mayaguez, the insular shelf is relatively broad and covered with reef shoals over a platform of less than 20 m depth. There is an increase of mangrove coastline behind the protection from wave action offered by the shelf. The beaches south of Punta Guanajibo are carbonate with quartz and some igneous rock fragments. Some of the terrigenous materials in the beaches north of Punta Guanajibo bypass the rocky point and return to the beach system. From Punta Ostiones south, the sands are carbonate. The sands of Boqueron Beach and to the south are carbonate with quartz derived from the alluvial plains east of Boqueron.

East of the Punta Cabo Rojo beaches the coastline is a narrow fringe of mangroves to Punta Montalva, with low tidal flats and salinas to the rear (Plate 29-3). The coast east of Punta Montalva is formed by wave erosion of limestone. There are small pockets of sand and gravel at the base of limestone cliffs. All the beaches are composed of carbonate shell material.

Coastal development on the south is related to whether the adjacent land area is limestone bedrock, igneous rock, or sediment fans and alluvial plains of unconsolidated material. The limestones form a rocky irregular coast with small sand and gravel beaches. In many places this coast has been altered by the growth of mangroves. The alluvial plains are either beach or unconsolidated cliffs that are retreating to form a wave erosion coastline straightened by wave action.

From Punta Verraco eastward, the coast is a low-lying alluvial plain with a coastline either of beach plain or of mangrove, and wave erosion where alluvial cliffs form the coast. East of Ponce, there is almost continuous beach plain, interrupted by short spans of mangrove, eroding alluvial plain, and man-made rock riprap. More than 50% of this coast is suffering severe erosion. The beach sediments are primarily igneous rock fragments and dark igneous minerals. Many of these beaches have gravel-sized material in the surf zone of the beach.

From Punta Las Marias eastward, the coastline is dominantly the result of wave erosion of the unconsolidated alluvial plain that lies south of the central mountains. There is extensive development of narrow beaches of sand and gravel at the base of wave-cut cliffs. East of Arroyo there is again beach plain and rock coastline (Plate 29-4). The sands are dominated by fragments of igneous rock material, with magnetite, dark minerals, and some quartz and feldspar. There is an increase in the amount of quartz and feldspar derived from the large southeast batholith.

From Arroyo to Naguabo rocky headlands alternate with a few small beach plains and pocket beaches. The eastern end of the island is bordered by a shallow shelf with abundant coral and marine organisms forming carbonate shelf sands. As a consequence, the beaches are a mixture of carbonate grains from the offshore and of quartz and feldspar with igneous rock material from the hinterland. All the beaches have a relatively high quartz content, reflecting drainage from the batholiths of the eastern part of Puerto Rico. There is local variation in the amount of shell material, but the beaches are similar in composition. The physical boundaries formed by the rocky headlands divide this coast into a series of separate and distinct beach systems, but there is limited transfer of sand from one to another across the shelf. The coast between Fajardo and Cabo San Juan is a fringing reef (Plate 29-5).

JACK MORELOCK
JAMES V. A. TRUMBULL

REFERENCES

Gillou, R. B., and J. J. Glass, 1957, A reconnaissance study of beach sands of Puerto Rico, *U. S. Geol. Survey Bull. 1052-I*, pp. 273-303.

Kaye, C. A., 1959, *Shoreline Features and Quaternary*

Shoreline Changes, Puerto Rico, U. S. Geol. Survey Prof. Paper 317-B.

Liegel, L. H., 1972, *NCERI Beach—Offshore Study of Mainland Puerto Rico*, Puerto Rico Area of Natural Resources, Department of Public Works.

Morelock, J., 1978, *Shoreline of Puerto Rico*. Puerto Rico Coastal Zone Program, Department of Natural Resources.

Plate 29-1. Rio de la Plata. Barrier spit coastline, beach plain east (left) and eolianite west (photo by J. Morelock).

Plate 29-4. Punta Tuna. Beach plain coastline and rocky headlands (photo by J. Morelock).

Plate 29-2. Rio Manati. Eolianite coastline with beach plain and beachrock types (photo by J. Morelock).

Plate 29-5. Cabo San Juan. Fringing coral reef coastline and rocky headland (photo by J. Morelock).

Plate 29-3. La Parguera. Mangrove coastline (photo by J. Morelock).

30. LESSER ANTILLES: VIRGIN ISLANDS TO TRINIDAD

The Lesser Antilles encloses the eastern part of the Caribbean Sea, which it separates from the Atlantic Ocean, and extends from the Virgin Islands (latitude 18°30'N) to Trinidad (latitude 10° N) in the south. Physiographically, the Virgin Islands, with the exception of St. Croix, are an extension of the Greater Antilles, while Trinidad is the northeasternmost extension of the South American continent.

The Lesser Antillean chain consists of two main arcs. The outer arc, which has been in existence from the early Tertiary, stretches from Sombrero past Anguilla to Grenada in the south. The islands of this arc are much lower than those of the inner arc of young unfolded volcanics and actual volcanics that came into existence in the later Miocene and Pliocene (Martin-Kaye 1969). The island of Barbados is the highest point on the Barbados Ridge, which lies east of the main Antillean chain (Senn 1947).

Coral reefs occur in the seas surrounding all the islands. These reefs are most extensive around the islands of the outer arc.

Sea conditions are dominated by the easterlies; the major disturbances to the wave climate are occasioned by the passage of tropical cyclones in the summer and by swell traveling from North Atlantic tropical cyclones during winter. The tides have little effect on coastal features, as mean spring tide ranges from 0.4 m in the north to 0.7 m in the south.

The coastal landforms displayed in this island chain are affected by the orientation of the island and the protection afforded by coral reefs. Nevertheless, the coasts can be broadly classified as windward, littoral drift, or leeward coasts.

St. Vincent is one of the youngest of the islands of the inner volcanic arc. The northern end of the island is formed by the active volcano, the Soufrière, while the southern end is composed of the remains of several extinct volcanoes. The Soufrière attained its present size in the Pleistocene and was active as recently as 1977. All rocks are of Pleistocene to recent origin, with the most common type being andesitic and basaltic agglomerates. The offshore profile is quite steep on the younger northern part of the island and broadens out on the older portion to the south (Fig. 30-1).

The Colonaire River, draining the newer volcanics, has formed a large delta. The coastline between the resistant headlands at Black Rock and Sans Souci is being reshaped by southward littoral drift (Fig. 30-2).

The discharges of several small rivers draining the older volcanics to the south have formed beaches separated from each other by headlands of more resistant rocks. Seven different terrace levels are observable on these headlands, with the highest at 210 m (Plate 30-1). The east coast of St. Vincent terminates in the massive sand dunes at Brighton, which extend for 1 km with maximum elevations above 60 m (Fig. 30-2). These dunes were formed when sediments—which could not be transported to the south coast because of

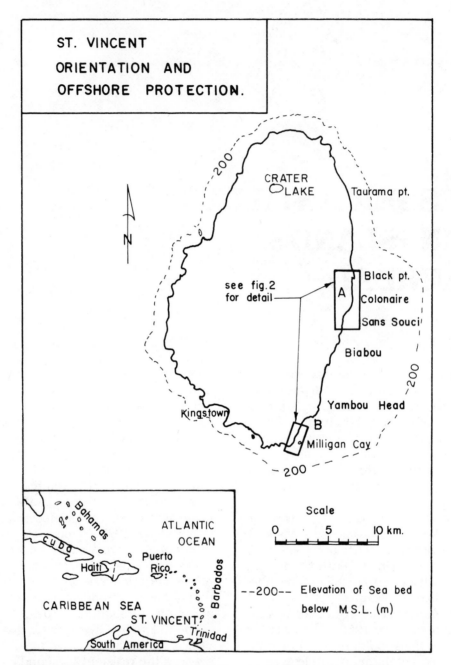

Figure 30-1. St. Vincent orientation and offshore protection.

the formation of a tombolo opposite Milligan Cay— were blown landward by the trade winds.

All the beach and offshore sediments along the windward coast of St. Vincent are dominated by volcanic ash fragments and heavy minerals (Adams 1968).

Along the windward northeast coast of Barbados, the Pleistocene coral limestone that covers the rest of the island has disappeared because of breakup and erosion, exposing the less resistant underlying strata. A long, wide beach backed by low sand dunes of quartzose sands occupies most of this coast. A characteristic feature is the exposure of blocks of limestone from the eroded cap in the offshore area.

The major characteristic of the east coast of Trinidad is the presence of three long, sandy bays oriented toward the direction of the nearshore waves (Saunders 1968). Matura and Mayaro bays, at the north and south respectively, have been

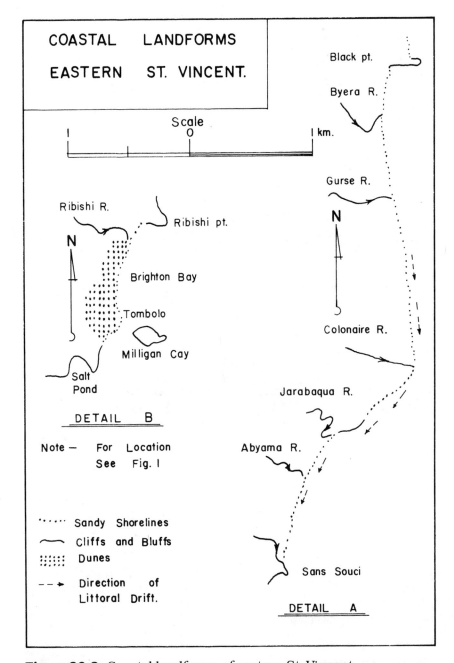

Figure 30-2. Coastal landforms of eastern St. Vincent.

formed by cliff erosion of Miocene and Pliocene deposits and by river transport.

Between those two bays lies the long, straight Cacos Bay. A 20 km-long barrier beach has been developed by the sea, and behind it three rivers have been ponded to make the large freshwater Nariva Swamp, 70 km² in extent. The barrier beach is broken only once, at the center, where the Nariva River reaches the sea. The river flows parallel to the barrier beach for 5 km, indicating that the opening to the sea was farther north in earlier times. The present opening has been stabilized by the construction of a revetment forcing the high velocity jet to discharge perpendicular to the coast (Plate 30-2).

The north and south coasts of western Anguilla and the south coasts of Trinidad and Barbados are most representative of littoral drift coastlines.

Anguilla, one of the most northerly of the outer arc islands, lies on the extensive Anguilla bank (Fig. 30-3). The island is low-lying and is composed of a Lower Miocene limestone and marl

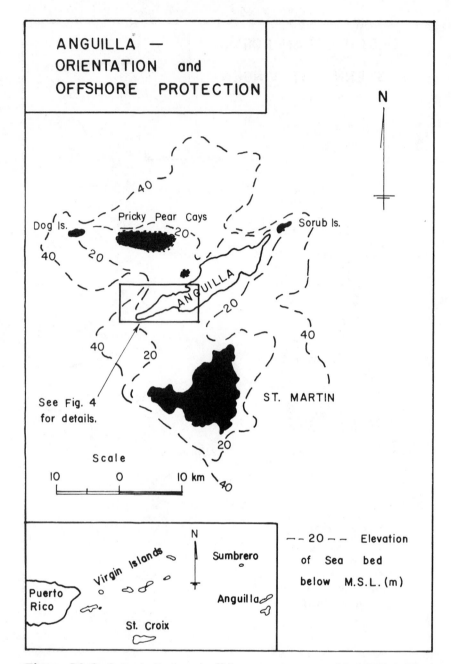

Figure 30-3. Orientation and offshore protection of Anguilla.

series overlying volcanic rocks (Christman 1953). Products of the breakdown of the coral reef are transported westward by littoral drift along the north and south coasts.

Along the north coast, west of Road Point, beaches have formed between limestone outcrops at Road, Long, Mead's, and Barnes bays. The barrier beaches at Road and Mead's bays have enclosed salt marshes (Fig. 30-4).

Along the south coast west of Shaddick Point, the littoral transport from the reefs of the Anguilla bank has formed beaches at Rendezvous, Cove, and Maunday's bays. Shoal Bay appears to have been formed from products of the breakdown of a very active fringing reef, located west of Maunday's Bay. Rendezvous Bay once extended farther west, but is now separated from Cove Bay by a tombolo that has reached the fringing reef (Fig. 30-4).

Sand dunes with elevations rising to 10 m have formed on all the barrier beaches and have completely sealed the salt marshes behind them. The widest sand dunes are found at Maunday's

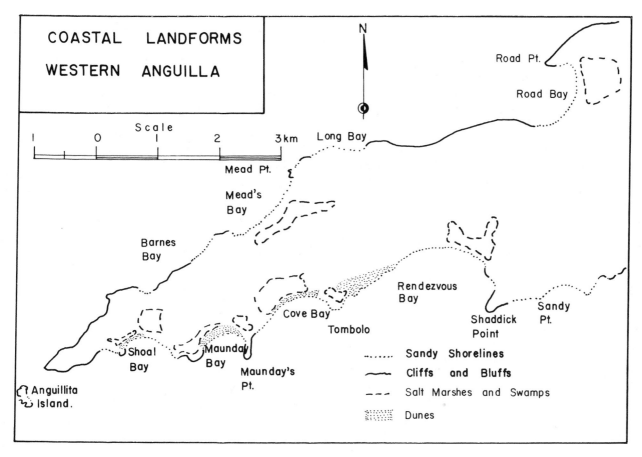

Figure 30-4. Coastal landforms of western Anguilla.

Bay, the terminal point for the major littoral transport along the coast.

The water in all the salt marshes, locally called salt ponds, is hypersaline. Road Bay Salt Pond is still used for the commercial production of salt, the major export of Anguilla.

Along the south coast of Barbados, coral, shell, and algal fragments are transported westward from a very active reef to the south of the island. Beaches have been formed between outcrops of limestone. The only dunes are at Long Bay, and the littoral transport terminates in a spit at Needham Point.

Littoral transport along the south coast of Trinidad terminates in the massive Icacos spit located at the southwestern tip of the island. The major contributor to sediment arises from erosion of the western section of the south coast, where cliffs composed of sands, clays, and weakly cemented sandstones of Miocene, Pliocene, and Pleistocene ages are interspersed with low areas of recent deposits.

The coastal landforms on the leeward coasts of the volcanic islands are governed by the haphaz-ard manner in which the volcanic sediments were deposited. The older leeward coasts of Barbados and Trinidad are representative of conditions to be expected along protected coasts.

The contemporary west coast of Barbados consists of a narrow terrace that has moved forward with time, leaving a narrow coral sand beach between the shore and the earlier coastline. Nineteen beach cells separated by coral fringed headlands have been identified (Bird et al. 1979). These beach cells show seasonal changes in beach planform and profile, intensified by extensive construction of tourist facilities close to the shoreline (Plate 30-3).

The southwestern coastline of Trinidad, where outcrops of Miocene sands and clays are exposed, is slowly being transformed into three large bays. Annual rates of erosion of the unconsolidated deposits range from 0.5–2.0 m (Deane 1974). This stretch of coast terminates at Los Gallos in stacks of slightly more resistant Pleistocene sandstones (Plate 30-4).

COMPTON A. W. DEANE

REFERENCES

Adams, R. D., 1968, Distribution of littoral sediment on the Windward Coast St. Vincent, W.I., *5th Carib. Geol. Conf., St. Thomas, V.I., Trans.* Queen's College Press, Flushing, N.Y., pp. 55–59.

Bird, J. B., A. Richards, and P. P. Wong, 1979, Coastal subsystems of western Barbados, West Indies, *Geog. Annaler,* **61A**(3-4):221–236.

Christman, R. A., 1953, Geology of St. Bartholomew, St. Martin and Anguilla, Lesser Antilles, *Geol. Soc. America Bull.* **64**(1):65–96.

Deane, C., 1974, Coastal processes point Fortin to Icacos, Trinidad, *Jour. Geogr. Assn., Trinidad and Tobago,* **3:**1–16.

Martin-Kaye, P. H. A., 1969, A summary of the geology of the Lesser Antilles, *Overseas Geol. and Min. Resources* **10**(2):173–206.

Saunders, J. B., 1968, The relationship between land and sea around the islands of Trinidad and Tobago, *Documenta Geigy Nautilus* **4:**6–8.

Senn, A., 1947, Die Geologie der Insel Barbados, B.W.I. (Kleine Antillen) und die Morphogenese der umlilgenden marinen Grossformen, *Eclogae Geol. Helvetia* **40:**200–222.

Plate 30-1. The east coast of St. Vincent between Biabau and Yambou Head. Along this stretch of coast the older volcanics are exposed, and small, sandy bays have formed between headlands of more resistant rocks. One old terrace level can be observed on the headland in the foreground (Biabau), while two levels are seen on the center headland, and three are visible on Yambou Head in the background (photo by C. Deane).

Plate 30-2. The mouth of the Nariva River on the east coast of Trinidad. The Nariva River, which runs parallel to the barrier beach in the foreground, is seen discharging to sea past a revetment that diverts the high velocity jet. Coconuts are cultivated on the barrier beach, a small fringe of mangrove grows west of the river, and a large freshwater swamp is visible in the background (photo by D. Key).

Plate 30-3. A beach cell on the west coast of Barbados a few months after hurricane attack in August 1980. The northern reef-fringed headland is at extreme left of the photograph, while accelerated erosion caused by construction of buildings too close to the shore is evident in the background (photo by C. Deane).

Plate 30-4. Stacks at Los Gallos, Trinidad. The stacks are of late Miocene sandstones and mark the extreme southwestern outcrop of that period. In the foreground is part of the Icacos spit formed south of the Miocene deposits by littoral transport along the south coast (photo by C. Deane).

31. BAHAMAS

Great contrasts exist between the relatively subdued coastal morphology of some 1400 Bahama islands (approximately 11,300 km²) and the much larger submerged sedimentary platforms upon which they have been formed. Beneath the surface, the world's deepest canyons are created by the steep-walled topography that winds down past abrupt platform dropoffs to abyssal plains that may be more than 6000 m deep (Andrews et al. 1970). Subaerially, Pleistocene eolianites (Plate 31-1) reach a height of 67 m at Mt. Alverina (Cat Island), the highest point in the Bahamas (Fig. 31-1). The four principal Bahamian banks (Little Bahama, Great Bahama, Cay Sal, and Acklins Island) constitute a trend that extends a considerable distance to the southeast. Although not politically a part of the Bahamas, the Turks and Caicos islands and three more shallow banks (Mouchoir, Silver, and Navidad) are all apparently geologically similar, thus extending this entire coastline province to a total distance of slightly more than 1000 km.

Genesis of the major elements of the Bahamian banks is still unclear, but it is known that more than 5000 m of Cretaceous-Tertiary carbonates underlie the Cay Sal platform (Newell 1955). Hess (1933, 1960) has postulated a much older tectonic and erosional origin for the banks and intervening trenches, but most workers (Busby 1962; Newell 1955; Newell and Rigby 1957) suspect isostatic down-warping from accumulated biogenic sediments as the principal factor involved. Curiously, the Bahamas have not been readily integrated into our rapidly expanding knowledge of plate tectonics associated with adjacent parts of the Caribbean.

Depositional analogues of great interest to petrographers, paleoecologists, and geomorphologists occur on the shallow, microtidal Bahamas banks, which are typically no deeper than 4 m (Newell et al. 1951; Illing 1954; Newell et al. 1959; Cloud 1961; Purdy 1963; Purdy and Imbrie 1964; Shinn et al. 1965; Hoffmeister et al. 1967; Ball 1967; Taft et al. 1968). The definitive ecologic study of Bahamian coral reefs remains that of Storr (1964), who first related differences in shelf topography to wave energy conditions. Most of these workers conducted their investigations in the more accessible parts of Great Bahama Bank south of the Biminis and along Andros Island. Very little scientific work has been done in the southern "Out Islands" such as Great Inagua and Mayaguana. Even less has been done in the Turks and Caicos (Plate 31-2).

Lind (1968) has made a major contribution to coastal geomorphology of the Bahamas, especially Cat Island, and Doran (1955) described some of the lesser-known southeastern islands. According to Lind, the typical Bahamian island has distinct windward and leeward shorelines with analogous features on both sides. Coastlines facing open waters of the Atlantic are subjected to large swell and occasional "rages" (storm surf) that sweep in over the narrow coral-covered shelf slope and break on the barrier reef rim. Between the barrier rim and beach there is usually a comparatively broad, shallow backreef shelf with varying amounts of biogenic sand in the process of being transported toward the shoreline. Many coastlines show evidence of contemporary erosion in the form of beach nips and low cliffs (Plate 31-1). Outcrops of beachrock are rather uncommon and unevenly distributed throughout the islands. Inland on Cat Island, Holocene sand

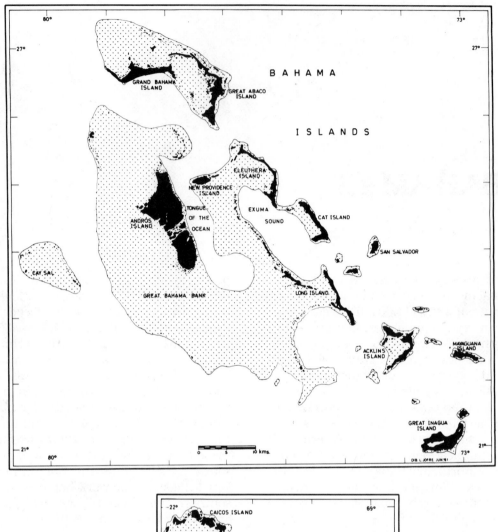

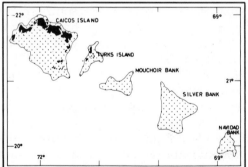

Figure 31-1. Location map of Bahama, Turks, and Caicos islands.

ridges (<5m) occur in truncated sets forming successively higher terraces that are occasionally capped with stabilized dunes. Pleistocene calcarenites, generally well indurated and having conspicuous karst solution features, are common outcrops in the interior and underlie high (>20m) dune ridges.

Leeward coastlines may have very wide barrier rim shelves (e.g., Great Abaco, Andros, Eleuthera,

Aklins, and Caicos islands), where "fish muds," "sand bores," and other forms of highly mobile, fine-grained calcareous sediments occur as shoals. Under favorable conditions oölitic sands (Illing 1954, Newell et al. 1960) and grapestone (Winland and Matthews 1974) are formed. Large shoal-water sand waves are often dissected by tidal channels (Plate 31-3) in patterns that have been described as "a river delta turned inside-out"

(Shinn et al. 1969). Surf reaching leeward beaches is seldom more than 1 m in height, so that both depositional and erosional features tend to be subdued. Fossil beaches and hypersaline lagoons with abandoned tidal channels are common. Sets of parallel and truncated beach ridges occupy positions equivalent to the more extensive series found on the windward shore.

Lind (1968) concludes there is much geomorphologic evidence on Cat Island to support theories invoking Holocene eustatic sea level fluctuations, and he minimizes the role of hurricanes in the formation of beach ridge terraces. Other workers (Perkins and Enos 1968, Shinn et al. 1969) have found evidence to the contrary, particularly on Andros Island. The effects of severe storms on the Great Bahama Bank and shore of the Bahamas in general appear to depend in large measure on the unique combinations of local conditions associated with each event. Some hurricanes have crossed the Bahamas leaving little trace, but ordinarily, substantial changes of a localized nature are to be expected. Deep, subparallel channels cutting through low-lying islands are known as bogues (east end of Grand Bahama and central sector of Andros) and are believed to be storm-related features (Plate 31-4).

Throughout the Bahamas vegetation has been disturbed by cultural activity. Nearshore species are uniformly halophytic and the Australian "pine" (*Casuarina equisetifolia*) is ubiquitous (Plate 31-5). The interior of Andros supports native pine stands, but a complex, dense coppice is typical of other islands. Red mangroves (*Rhizophora mangle*) are often found along leeward shores.

In general, the coastal morphology of the Bahamas has such low relief that it does not lend itself well to ground-level photography. However, a series of accurate sketches of landfalls and color air photographs of important harbors appears in yachtmen's guides and contains much useful information on coastal morphology.

ALAN K. CRAIG

REFERENCES

Andrews, J. E., F. P. Shepard, and R. J. Hurley, 1970, Great Bahama Canyon, *Geol. Soc. Amer. Bull.* **81:**1061–1108.

Ball, M. M., 1967, Carbonate sands of Florida and the Bahamas, *Jour. Sed. Petrology,* **37**(2):556–591.

Busby, R. F., 1962, *Submarine Geology of the Tongue of the Ocean, Bahamas,* U.S. Naval Oceanog. Off. Tech. Rept., TR-108.

Cloud, P. E., 1961, *Environment of Calcium Carbonate Deposition West of Andros Island, Bahamas.* U.S. Geol. Survey Prof. Paper 350.

Doran, E., Jr., 1955, *Landforms of the Southeast Bahamas,* University of Texas Publication 5509.

Hess, H. H., 1933, Interpretation of geological and geophysical observations in Navy – Princeton Gravity Expedition to the West Indies in 1932, U.S. Hydrographic Office, *Annual Report* pp. 26–38.

Hess, H. H., 1960, The origin of the Tongue of the Ocean and other great valleys of the Bahama banks, *2d. Caribbean Geol. Conf. Trans.* pp. 160–161.

Hoffmeister, J. E., K. W. Stockman, and H. G. Multer, 1967, Miami limestone of Florida and its recent Bahamian counterpart, *Geol. Soc. Amer. Bull.* **78:**175–190.

Illing, L. V., 1954, Bahamian calcareous sands, *Am. Assoc. Petroleum Geologists Bull.* **38:**1–95.

Lind, A. O., 1968, *Coastal Landforms of Cat Island, Bahamas: A Study of Holocene Accretionary Topography and Sea-Level Change,* Ph.D. thesis, University of Wisconsin.

Newell, N. D., 1955, *Bahamian platforms,* Geol. Soc. of Amer. Spec. Paper 62, pp. 303–315.

Newell, N. D., J. K. Rigby, A. J. Whiteman, and J. S. Bradley, 1951, Shoal-water geology and environs, Eastern Andros Island, Bahamas, *Amer. Mus. Nat. Hist. Bull.* **97:**1–30.

Newell, N. D., and J. K. Rigby, 1957, *Geological Studies on the Great Bahama Bank,* Soc. Econ. Paleontologists and Mineralogists Spec. Pub. No. 5, pp. 15–72.

Newell, N. D., J. Imbrie, E. G. Purdy, and D. L. Thurber, 1959, Organism communities and bottom facies, Great Bahama Bank, *Am. Mus. Nat. History Bull.* **117:**183–228.

Newell, N. D., E. G. Purdy, and J. Imbrie, 1960, Bahamian oölitic sand, *Jour. Geology* **68:**481–497.

Perkins, R. D., and P. Enos, 1968, Hurricane Betsy in the Florida-Bahama Area – geologic effects and comparison with Hurricane Donna, *Jour. Geology* **76:**710–717.

Purdy, E. G., 1963, Recent calcium carbonate facies of the Great Bahama Bank, *Jour. Geology* **71:**334–355, 472–497.

Purdy, E. G., and J. Imbrie, 1964, *Carbonate Sediments, Great Bahama Bank,* Geol. Soc. of Amer. Guide Book for Field Trip No. 2.

Shinn, E. A., R. N. Ginsburg, and R. M. Lloyd, 1965, Recent supratidal dolomite from Andros Island, Bahamas, in *Dolomitization and Limestone Diagenesis – A Symposium,* L. C. Pray and R. C. Murray, eds., Society of Economic Paleontologists and Mineralogists, Tulsa, Okla. pp. 112–123.

Shinn, E. A., R. M. Lloyd, and R. N. Ginsburg, 1969, Anatomy of a modern carbonate tidal-flat, Andros Island, Bahamas, *Jour. Sed. Petrology* **39**(3):1202–1228.

Storr, J. F., 1964, *Ecology and Oceanography of the Coral-Reef Tract, Abaco Island, Bahamas,* Geol. Soc. America Spec. Paper No. 79.

Taft, W. H., F. Arrington, A. Haimovitz, C. MacDonald, and C. Woolheater, 1968, Lithification of modern marine carbonate sediments at Yellow Bank, Bahamas, *Bull. Marine Sci.* **18:**762–828.

Winland, H. D., and R. K. Matthews, 1974, Origin and significance of grapestone, Bahama Islands, *Jour. Sed. Petrology* **44**(3):921–927.

Plate 31-1. Strong tropical lapies solution surface on Pleistocene eolianites (foreground) and fossil dunes (background) along windward shoreline of New Providence (photo by Bahamas Tourist Bureau).

Plate 31-2. Northern shore of Grand Turk with hypersaline lagoons (right center). Strongly breaking surf marks the barrier rim with refracted waves sweeping in over the backreef platform (photo by R. Menzies).

Plate 31-4. A bogue shore developed between Providenciales and Mangrove Cay in the Caicos Cays. At left center background a prominent visor and deep notch are evident (photo by R. Menzies).

Plate 31-3. A typical tidal scour channel with delta (background) established between naturally vegetated islets in the Berry Islands (photo by Bahamas Tourist Bureau).

Plate 31-5. Condominium development on Paradise Island (leeward shore of New Providence). Shallow water calcarenite ledges and patch reefs occupy the foreground and left center opposite Hartford Beach. Coastlines and vegetation have been severely affected by development (photo by Bahamas Tourist Bureau).

32. ATLANTIC USA—SOUTH

The coastline of Georgia, South Carolina, and North Carolina flanks a wide plain on the trailing edge of the North American plate, which is generally tectonically stable to slightly downwarping (Inman and Nordstrom 1971). The coastline is, for the most part, depositional with Holocene barrier island, bay/lagoonal, and estuarine deposits blanketing an irregular topography eroded during the low stands of the sea in the Pleistocene epoch. The three states border the northwest flank of the Georgia Embayment, a large indentation in the coastline that shows a remarkable range in tidal and wave regime around its margin (Fig. 32-1). Waves range from a high mean value of approximately 1.5 m at Cape Hatteras, North Carolina, to a low of less than 80 cm at the Georgia/South Carolina border; spring tides range from 0.9 m at Cape Hatteras to 2.8 m at St. Helena Sound, South Carolina. This changing ratio of tides to waves along the perimeter of the embayment is a major factor influencing the coastal morphology of the area, in that the North Carolina coast tends to be wave dominated and the South Carolina and Georgia coasts tend to be tide dominated.

The climate in the area is humid subtropical with abundant rainfall throughout the year. Hurricanes frequent the area in later summer and early fall; on average, about three storms cross the North Carolina coastline each decade. Extratropical cyclones are common during the winter months. Except during the passage of these cyclonic storms, the winds blow prevailingly offshore, making the area a leeward shore.

North Carolina's Holocene coastline is primarily a wave-dominated barrier island/lagoonal complex. Major sounds (e.g., Pamlico) occupy large

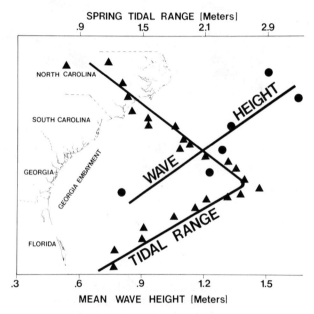

Figure 32-1. The coastlines of Georgia, South Carolina, and North Carolina relative to the Georgia Embayment. Tide data from NOAA tide tables and wave data from Nummedal et al. (1977).

river valleys carved during Pleistocene low stands of the sea. The barrier islands are long and continuous, with few tidal inlets (Plate 32-1) as a result of their microtidal, wave-dominated setting. For the most part, the barrier islands are eroding at dramatic rates and are migrating landward. Studies of the Holocene stratigraphy by graduate students at Duke University (e.g., Moslow and Heron 1978; Susman and Heron 1979) show these barriers to be primarily transgressive (i.e., eroding), as illustrated in Figure 32-2. Although these barrier islands contain few inlets at present, the

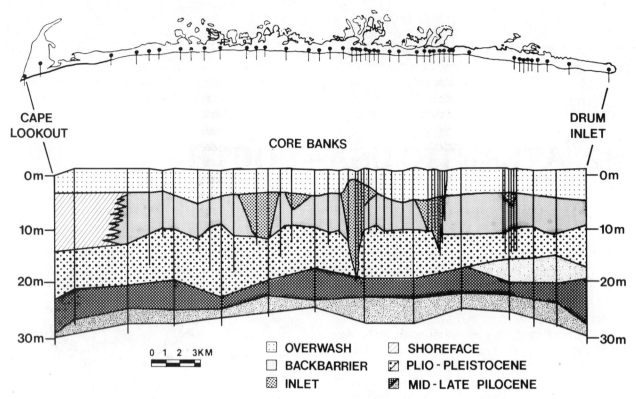

Figure 32-2. Stratigraphy of Core Banks, North Carolina. The bulk of the island is transgressive in nature, as evidenced by the juxtaposition of barrier island sands over back-barrier (lagoonal) sediments. Inlets were activated by major hurricanes. (Courtesy of Thomas F. Moslow after Moslow and Heron 1978).

cores reveal numerous buried tidal inlet sediments (Fig. 32-2) deposited in inlets opened during major hurricanes. Regressive (i.e., prograding) barrier islands occur in the lee of the prominent capes, such as Cape Lookout.

Inasmuch as most of the barrier islands are retreating landward, many structures built on the islands by man have washed away or are seriously endangered (Pilkey et al. 1978; Dolan and Godfrey 1973). It is generally thought, however, that the transgressive barriers have moved landward without diminishing greatly in subaerial extent.

South Carolina's Holocene coastline changes from a wave-dominated strand plain abutting a Pleistocene mainland to the north (arcuate strand of Fig. 32-3) to large tide-dominated estuaries to the south. The Santee Delta, the largest river delta on the east coast of the United States, occurs just south of the arcuate strand. The dominant morphology of the central shoreline is a mesotidal

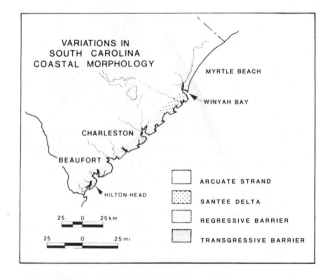

Figure 32-3. Map of South Carolina coast showing the four major morphological zones (after Brown 1977).

barrier island complex intersected by numerous tidal inlets and backed by extensive salt marshes and tidal flats. The barrier islands have drumstick-shaped configurations, as illustrated by the map of Kiawah Island in Figure 32-4A. Detailed studies of the tidal inlets in South Carolina by Hubbard et al. (1979) and FitzGerald (1976) show the character of the inlets to change from complex and sand choked (wave dominated) toward the north to deep and seaward extended (tide dominated) toward the south. Two examples of South Carolina tidal inlets are shown in Plate 32-2. The southern inlets contain huge ebb-tidal deltas of the type illustrated in Figure 32-4B. The ebb-tidal deltas are giant sediment traps, which markedly influence erosional and depositional patterns on the adjacent barrier islands.

Stratigraphic studies by graduate students at the University of South Carolina show South Carolina barriers to be both transgressive and regressive in nature, with regressive barriers being the more common type. Inlet fill is an important component of most of the barrier sand bodies.

Erosion problems have arisen for coastal developers who have built structures too close to the unstable and shifting tidal inlets. Captain Sam's Inlet, located between Kiawah and Seabrook Islands, is migrating to the south at the rate of 60-70 m/yr (Sexton and Hayes 1983).

Georgia's Holocene coastline is in morphological continuum with South Carolina's coast; however, the width of the Holocene component of the barrier islands diminishes significantly into Georgia. With the largest tides in the southeastern United States and the flattest coastal plain, the coast of Georgia is essentially inundated twice daily by the tides. It is dominated by large estuarine embayments flanked by extensive salt marshes. Research by University of Georgia scien-

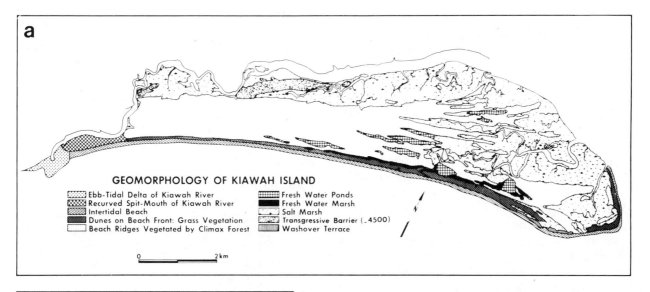

GEOMORPHOLOGY OF KIAWAH ISLAND

- Ebb-Tidal Delta of Kiawah River
- Recurved Spit-Mouth of Kiawah River
- Intertidal Beach
- Dunes on Beach Front: Grass Vegetation
- Beach Ridges Vegetated by Climax Forest
- Fresh Water Ponds
- Fresh Water Marsh
- Salt Marsh
- Transgressive Barrier (-4500)
- Washover Terrace

0   2 km

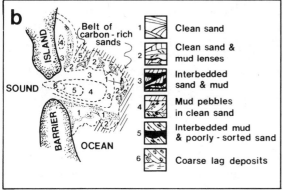

Belt of (carbon-rich sands)

ISLAND

SOUND

BARRIER

OCEAN

1	Clean sand
2	Clean sand & mud lenses
3	Interbedded sand & mud
4	Mud pebbles in clean sand
5	Interbedded mud & poorly-sorted sand
6	Coarse lag deposits

Figure 32-4. *a.* Geomorphology of Kiawah Island, South Carolina, a drumstick-shaped barrier in a mesotidal setting (after Hayes and Kana 1976). *b.* Diagrammatic representation of ebb-tidal delta sediments of a typical tidal inlet in Georgia (modified from Oertel 1973). Ebb-tidal deltas dominate the inner shelf on the Georgia and South Carolina coasts.

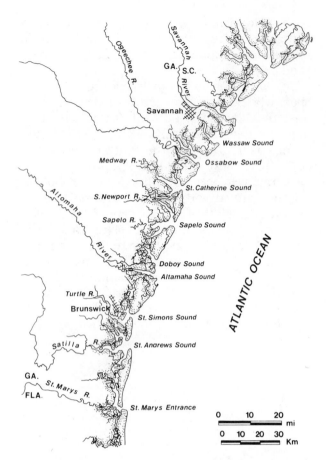

Figure 32-5. Distribution of major estuaries on the Georgia coast (after Howard and Frey 1980).

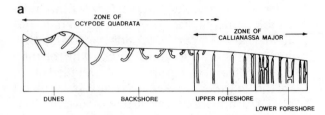

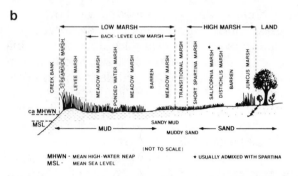

Figure 32-6. *a.* Zonation of decapod burrows in Georgia beaches and dunes (after Edwards and Frey 1977). *b.* Diagrammatic cross-section of the salt marsh at Sapelo Island, Georgia (after Edwards and Frey 1977). These diagrams give results typical of the numerous organism/sediment relationships that have been studied on the Georgia coast.

tists has focused on the marshes and other biological components of the estuarine systems (Fig. 32-5). Howard and Frey (1980), in a summary article on the entire Holocene system of Georgia, classified the estuaries into two main categories: riverine and salt marsh. Salt marsh estuaries, the more abundant type, are dominated by marine waters. They contain sandy point bars, which are distinguished from fluvial point bars by their more abundant biogenic structures and mud content. Riverine estuaries are fed by piedmont or coastal plain rivers. Sediments carried by the piedmont rivers are more immature mineralogically than those of coastal plain rivers, which have passed through more than one cycle of erosion and deposition.

The biogenic structures of the Holocene sediments of coastal Georgia have been studied extensively by Frey, Howard, and associates (Howard and Frey 1980, Frey and Mayou 1971). The typical sequence of decapod structures on beaches (Fig. 32-6A) and a model for the salt

marsh behind Sapelo Island (Fig. 32-6B) are examples of their work.

MILES O. HAYES

REFERENCES

Brown, P. J., 1977, Variations in South Carolina coastal morphology, *Southeastern Geology* **18**(4):249–264.

Dolan, R., and P. J. Godfrey, 1973, Effects of hurricane Ginger on the barrier islands of North Carolina, *Geol. Soc. America Bull.* **84:**1329–1334.

Edwards, J. M., and R. W. Frey, 1977, Substrate characteristics within a Holocene marsh, Sapelo Island, Georgia, *Senckenberg. Marit.* **9:**215–259.

FitzGerald, D. M., 1976, Ebb-tidal delta of Price Inlet, South Carolina, in *Terrigenous Clastic Depositional Environments; Some Modern Examples,* M. O. Hayes and T. W. Kana, eds., Coastal Res. Div., Univ. South Carolina, Tech. Rept. 11-CRD, pp. II-143–II-157.

Frey, R. W., and T. V. Mayou, 1971, Decapod burrows in Holocene barrier island beaches and washover fans, Georgia, *Senckenberg. Marit.* **3:**53–77.

Hayes, M. O., and T. W. Kana, 1976, *Terrigenous Clastic Depositional Environments; Some Modern Examples,* Coastal Res. Div., Univ. South Carolina, Tech. Rept. 11-CRD.

Howard, J. D., and R. W. Frey, 1980, Holocene depositional environments of the Georgia coast and continental shelf, *Guidebook 20: Excursions in Southeastern Geology; The Archaeology-Geology of the Georgia Coast,* 1980 Ann. Mtg., Geol. Soc. America, pp. 66–134.

Hubbard, D. K., G. Oertel, and D. Nummedal, 1979, The role of wave and tidal currents in the development of tidal-inlet sedimentary structures and sand body geometry: examples from North Carolina, South Carolina, and Georgia, *Jour. Sed. Petrology* **49:**1073–1092.

Inman, D. L., and C. E. Nordstrom, 1971, On the tectonic and morphologic classification of coasts, *Jour. Geology* **79**(1):1–21.

Moslow, T. F., and S. D. Heron, 1978, Relict inlets: preservation and occurrence in the Holocene stratigraphy of southern Core Banks, North Carolina, *Jour. Sed. Petrology* **48:**1275–1286.

Nummedal, D., G. F. Oertel, D. K. Hubbard, and A. C. Hine, 1977, Tidal inlet variability—Cape Hatteras to Cape Canaveral, *Coastal Sediments '77,* American Society of Civil Engineers, Charleston, S.C., pp. 543–562.

Oertel, G. F., 1973, Examination of textures and structures of mud in layered sediments at the entrance of a Georgia tidal inlet, *Jour. Sed. Petrology* **43:**33–41.

Pilkey, O. H., Jr., W. J. Neal, and O. H. Pilkey, Sr., 1978, *From Currituck to Calabash,* N.C. Science and Tech. Res. Center, Research Triangle Park.

Sexton, W. J., and M. O. Hayes, 1983, Natural bar-bypassing of sand at a tidal inlet, *18th Intl. Conf. on Coastal Eng. Proc.,* Cape Town, South Africa, in press.

Susman, K. R., and S. D. Heron, 1979, Evolution of a barrier island, Shackleford Banks, North Carolina, *Geol. Soc. America Bull.* **90:**205–215.

Plate 32-1. The North Carolina coast: Cape Hatteras, upper left; Cape Lookout, lower left. Note extensive barrier islands with few tidal inlets (photo courtesy of NASA).

Plate 32-2. Examples of tidal inlets in South Carolina. (a) Price Inlet. (b) Fripp Inlet (photos by M. O. Hayes).

33. ATLANTIC USA—CENTRAL

The coastlines of the Mid-Atlantic Bight of the eastern United States lie on the coastal plain/continental shelf—which is, structurally, a major continental margin geosyncline (the Baltimore Canyon Trough geosyncline), which extends to depths of greater than 35,000 feet of sediments, as early as Triassic in age. The actual position of the shore from northern New Jersey, Delaware and Maryland through Virginia varies widely in terms of position on the continental shelf/coastal plain. For instance, at the northern edge of New Jersey (Sandy Hook) the Atlantic Ocean coast approaches the older hard-rock core of the North American continent, whereas at the southerly end of this coastal system (Cape Hatteras, North Carolina) the coastline is near the outer edge of the continental shelf.

The reasons for these extreme coastal positions lying across the geosyncline are probably glaciotectonic. The northern end of this coastal system is very close to the southernmost extension of the North American continental glacial ice sheet of the Quaternary period. Many believe that a continental bulge formed, upwarping the area peripheral to the ice sheet at its maximum extent. With the waning of the ice sheet and its disappearance to its present core in the subcontinent Greenland, the peripheral bulge subsided rapidly. At the same time sea level rose approximately 130 m. Therefore, at the more stable southerly end of this coastal system, sea level did not transgress very far inland in Holocene time, whereas in the area of the collapsed peripheral glacial bulge in the vicinity of the Hudson River valley and submerged Hudson River canyon, sea level rose rapidly and transgressed inland to the inner edge of the coastal plain.

The entire shore of the Mid-Atlantic Bight is transgressing rapidly landward from its early position in the late Wisconsin (Riss-Würm) glacial low at the outer edge of the continental shelf. Several scarps occur along the continental shelf, possibly indicating temporary stable shoreline positions during the transgression. At first, sea level rose very rapidly at rates of tens of meters per millenium. About 6000 years ago the rate of sea level rise began to slow, with a further retardation approximately 3000 years ago (Kraft 1976; Belknap and Kraft 1977). In addition, the shore is one of major storm tracks from south to north. Very intense hurricanes move along this coastal system, in addition to common "northeasterly storms" (cyclonic) with a major wind-wave component from the northeast. The northeasters occur at random, sometimes as many as five or six a year; whereas hurricanes are statistically projected to occur once in 16 years along this shore. The transgression of the shore is sometimes very rapid or cataclysmic during hurricanes and northeasters, but the southeasterly waves flowing across the great fetch of the Atlantic Ocean form a continuum of coastal erosion, littoral transport of sediment into the major estuaries of the Hudson River, the Delaware Bay, and the Chesapeake Bay, with some sediment permanently removed by erosion in the shore face (0 to 10 m) and deposited on the inner shelf.

Fisher (1973) recognized that the coastal system from New Jersey to the Carolinas could be divided into compartments (Fig. 33-1). He noted a northerly littoral transport forming northerly projecting spits or capes at Sandy Hook in New Jersey, Cape Henlopen in Delaware, and Cape Henry in Virginia. South of the spits he defined a

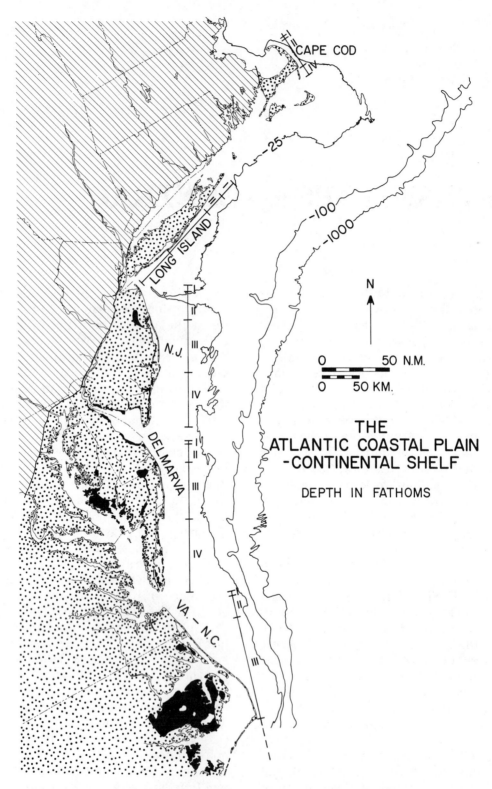

Figure 33-1. A map of the east coast of North America along the Mid-Atlantic Bight, showing the relationship of the coastal plain to the continental shelf in the area of the Baltimore Canyon Trough geosyncline.

zone of eroding highlands, which provide sediment into the littoral transport stream but also onto the inner shelf during times of storm wave activity and erosion of the shore face. The composition of the highlands varies considerably in the study area. For instance, in New Jersey the highlands are composed of a Quaternary veneer of sediments overlying Cretaceous and Tertiary sediments. In the Delaware compartments Quarternary marine sediments are undergoing erosion. Similarly in the Virginia highland compartment, Quaternary sediments are undergoing erosion. In both the Delaware-Maryland and Virginia areas, the Pleistocene-age sediments form a thin veneer of approximately 30-50 m overlying late Tertiary or Neogene sediments. A third set of compartments identified by Fisher included a lagoon-barrier coastal system with strong littoral transport supplying wide sandy barriers between the coastal lagoons and the Atlantic Ocean. The southerly compartment of Fisher's system included a series of barrier islands set offshore, sometimes backed by marshes and sometimes by lagoons, and formed of southerly littoral transport of sediments. For instance, in the area of Delaware-Maryland, this compartment starts at the southerly end of the eroding highlands and continues to Cape Charles at the mouth of Chesapeake Bay in Virginia.

The coastal systems are dominated by the large estuaries of the Chesapeake Bay and the Delaware Bay, which were originally drowned river valleys at the time of the peak latest Wisconsin glaciation. Similarly, the Hudson River estuary, although not a bay, fits this system. The northerly trending spits are of particular interest. Holmes (1964) developed a model for a spit evolving into a deeper body of water from a highland. This is very similar to Gilbert's concept of barrier spit formation by littoral transport from highlands across embayments (Kraft 1980). Figure 33-2A is a schematic illustration of Holmes's (really Gilbert's) concept. Figure 2B, Sandy Hook, New Jersey, is a simple recurved spit evolving from a highland in its earliest stage of evolution. Figure 2C is Cape Henry, Virginia, a mature cuspate foreland spit with many recurves enclosing a lagoon and marsh area, at the southerly entrance to Chesapeake Bay. Figure 2D is the Cape Henlopen spit complex in Delaware, which, before the arrival of European man, was very similar to Cape Henry, Virginia: a cuspate foreland surrounding a marsh lagoon area with recurved spits dating back 2000 years ago. With human intrusion building a breakwa-

ter in the offshore area of the cuspate foreland Cape Henlopen, the flow of littoral sand transport was sharply changed, and a simple spit began to build northward as at Sandy Hook. This simple spit is tending to recurve to the northwest, and it is predicted to reform into a cuspate foreland spit in the next 300-500 years (Kraft et al. 1976).

The transgressive spit-highland-lagoon barrier coastline of Atlantic coastal Delaware and the transgressive estuarine shoreline of Delaware Bay are probably among the most intensively studied transgressive barrier systems of the world. Over 85 papers have been written on the geology of the coastal systems, their environments, processes, and so forth. Kraft et al. (1980), Kraft et al. (1976), and Kraft (1971) document in detail the geology of the coastal environments and the ongoing transgression.

Figure 3A is a geologic cross-section from the highlands across the lagoon, Rehoboth Bay, and then across the coastal barrier into the shallow marine inner shelf. The geographic distribution of the coastal sedimentary environments is in precise sequence in the vertically drilled section. Thus a proof of Walther's Law is presented. Figure 3B is a simplified model of a lagoon barrier transgressive coast of the type typical of the eastern North American shoreline.

A dominant control on the format of the coastal environments and the transgressive sedimentary environmental lithosomes formed is the pre-Holocene topography being transgressed. Figure 33-4 presents a number of small schematic geological interpretations of the many variants of estuarine and Atlantic coastal transgressive elements. These vary from a shore of marsh along the upper Delaware Bay, with no barrier present because of lack of sediment supplied to the littoral transport stream, to continuous sandy barriers along the southern end of Delaware Bay, with broad marshes extending to the highlands landward. Drill studies clearly show that extensive lagoonal systems occurred in this area over the past several thousand years, but some have now been filled in by lagoonal sediment and salt marshes.

The elements of the outer coast or the Atlantic coast are much larger because of the greater wave regime both in storms and under normal conditions of waves from the southeast. Accordingly, the sedimentary environmental lithosomes are all larger than those of the estuarine barrier shoreline (Fig. 33-4). The southerly ends of the models presented are deprived of coarse clastic sediment;

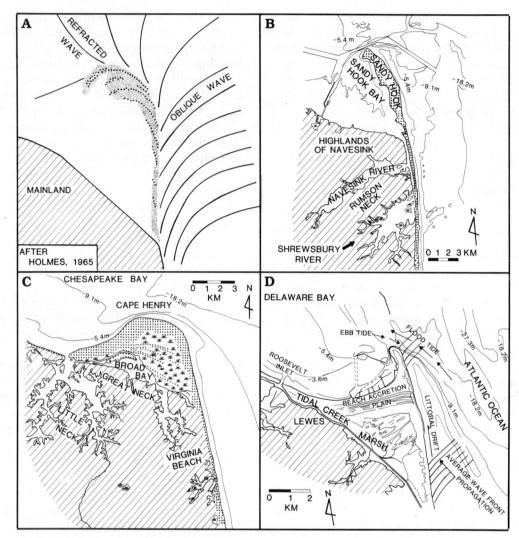

Figure 33-2*A*. A schematic diagram of the formation of a spit. *B*. The simple spit, Sandy Hook, extending northward from the North Jersey highlands. *C*. Cape Henry, Virginia, a cuspate foreland with older recurves and a lagoon-marsh system. *D*. The Cape Henlopen spit complex, Delaware, showing geomorphic elements of the spit complex related to average wave and tidal processes.

accordingly marsh and lagoons dominate the system. A notable feature is the scarp lying inland along the southern end of the Delmarva Peninsula. A similar scarp occurs in southern New Jersey. It is believed that this scarp represents an earlier Holocene shoreline (circa 3000-4000 years B.P.) now bypassed by sediment transported in the littoral transport stream from north to south.

Human instrusion is one of the major problems in this particular coastal setting. Humans have heavily occupied highlands by building cities such as Rehoboth Beach, Delaware. In New Jersey a great majority of the barriers are occu-

pied by small coastal cities, mainly for recreational purposes. Ocean City, Maryland, which is built on a low-lying barrier, is a very large city that includes an extensive chain of condominiums. Poor planning and building practices have led to development and building over the dune fields on to the berm in many of the coastal areas of the Mid-Atlantic Bight. As a result, northeaster storms and hurricanes have wreaked havoc on this shore for the past few hundred years. Building in this coastal zone is currently accelerating rapidly. Planners are attempting to legislate setback lines to limit the cost of storm destruction, which in the

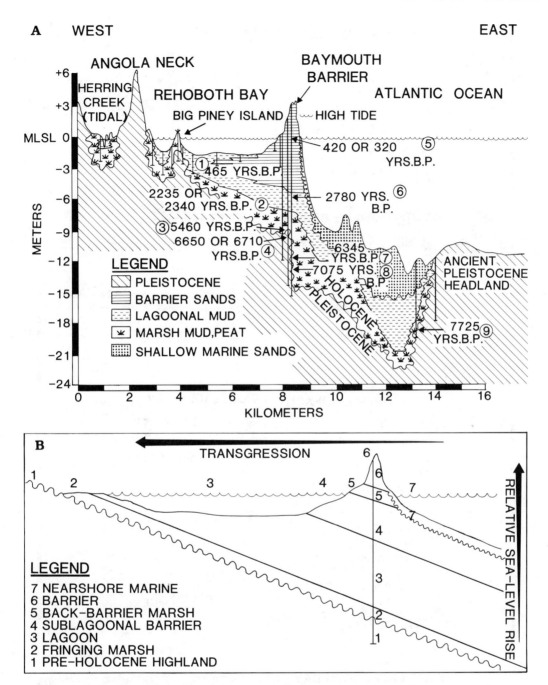

Figure 33-3*A*. A geological cross-section of the transgressive Holocene coastal environments in the vicinity of Rehoboth Bay, Delaware. *B*. A schematic transgressive model illustrating Walther's Law, based on Figure 2A.

past has come to many billions of dollars. Although the nature of the transgression and the coastal sedimentary environments and their lithosomes are well understood, there have been few links between planners, engineers, and geologists. This is mainly because the development has been conducted by the private sector, and only in the last decade have many people recognized that a serious problem may be developing. Plates 33-3*A, B, C,* and *D* illustrate the problem.

The Atlantic coastline from northern New Jersey to southern Virginia probably illustrates all the transgressive elements that might be typical of any coastal plain in the world. Much of

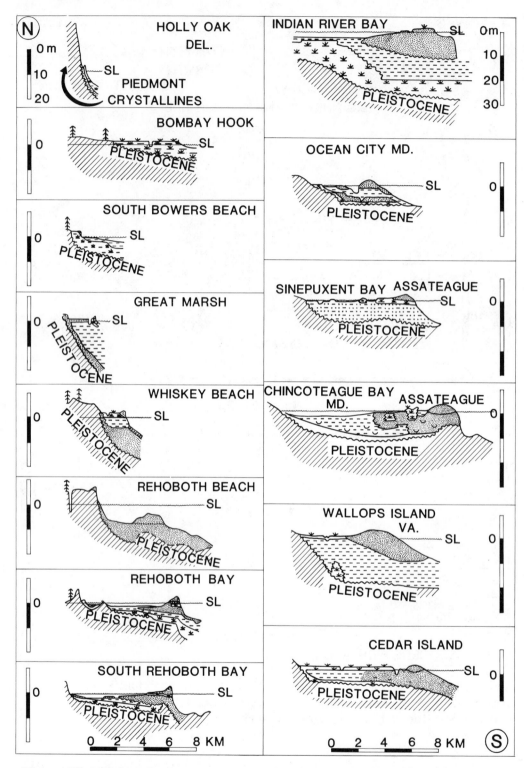

Figure 33-4. Schematic cross-sections of the transgressive shorelines of Delaware Bay and the Atlantic coast of Delaware, Maryland, and Virginia.

the work done in this area thus can serve as a model for studies elsewhere or can be used by planners forming rational developmental plans for undeveloped coasts in North America and elsewhere in the world. In North America, unless federal and state legislatures act promptly, the future promises continuing coastal destruction of human structures, with damages in the hundreds of billions of dollars.

JOHN C. KRAFT

REFERENCES

Belknap, D. F., and J. C. Kraft, 1977, Holocene relative sea level changes and coastal stratigraphic units on the northwest flank of the Baltimore Canyon Trough geosyncline, *Jour. Sed. Petrology* **47:**610–629.

Dolan, R., B. Hayden, C. Rea, and J. Heywood, 1979, Shoreline erosion rates along the middle Atlantic coast of the United States, *Geology* **7:**602–606.

Fischer, A. G., 1961, Stratigraphic record of transgressing seas in light of sedimentation on Atlantic coast of New Jersey, *Amer. Assoc. Petroleum Geologists Bull.* **45:**1656–1666.

Fisher, J. J., 1973, Origin of barrier island chain shorelines, Middle Atlantic states (abs.), *Geol. Soc. America Spec. Paper 115*, pp. 66–67.

Holmes, A., 1964, *Principles of Physical Geology*, Ronald Press, New York.

Kraft, J. C., 1971, Sedimentary facies patterns and geologic history of a Holocene marine transgression, *Geol. Soc. America Bull.* **82:**2131–2158.

Kraft, J. C., 1976, *Radiocarbon Dates in the Delaware Coastal Zone (Eastern Atlantic coast of North America)*, College of Marine Studies, University of Delaware.

Kraft, J. C., 1979, Lateral and vertical facies relation of transgressive barrier, *Am. Assoc. Petroleum Geologists Bull.* **63:**2128–2144.

Kraft, J. C., 1980, Grove Karl Gilbert and the origin of barrier shorelines, in *The Scientific Ideas of G. K. Gilbert*, E. Yochelson, ed., Geol. Soc. America Spec. Paper 183, pp. 105–113.

Kraft, J. C., R. B. Biggs, and S. D. Halsey, 1973, Morphology and vertical sedimentary sequence models in Holocene transgressive barrier systems, in *Coastal Geomorphology*, D. R. Coates, ed., State University of New York, Binghamton, New York, pp. 321–354.

Kraft, J. C., and C. J. John, 1976, *The Geological Structure of the Shorelines of Delaware*, College of Marine Studies, University of Delaware.

Kraft, J. C., and C. J. John, 1979, Lateral and vertical facies relations of transgressive barrier, *Am. Assoc. Petroleum Geologists Bull.* **63**(12):2145–2163.

Kraft, J. C., E. A. Allen, D. F. Belknap, C. J. John, and E. M. Maurmeyer, 1976, *Delaware's Changing Shoreline*, Tech. Rept. No. 1, Delaware Coastal Management Program, Delaware State Planning Office.

Kraft, J. C., E. A. Allen, D. F. Belknap, C. J. John, and E. M. Maurmeyer, 1980, Processes and morphologic evolution of an estuarine and coastal barrier system, in *Barrier Islands, from the Gulf of St. Lawrence to the Gulf of Mexico*, S. P. Leatherman, ed., Academic Press, New York, pp. 149–183.

Plate 33-1. A landsat photograph of the Delmarva Peninsula with the Chesapeake Bay on the left, Delaware Bay in the upper right, and the Atlantic Ocean to the right. The lagoon-barrier shoreline and linear strand of southern New Jersey (upper right) and the Delmarva Peninsula (center) are well shown. The compartmentalization units shown in Figure 1 can be well seen in the Delmarva Peninsula component (photo by NASA).

A

B

C

D

Plate 33-2. *A.* Cape Henlopen recurved spit complex, first recurve 2000 Y.B.P. (photo by J. C. Kraft). *B.* The Atlantic coastal barrier between the Atlantic Ocean on the left and Rehoboth and Indian River Bays (lagoons) to the right (photo by J. C. Kraft). *C.* The same barrier area as shown in Plate 2B, showing major storm washover sand lobes formed during a northeaster storm in 1962. Sand removed to the shore face eventually migrates back onto the beach and berm, whereas the sand on the inner shelf is permanently lost in the system (photo by Delaware State Highway Department). *D.* The Atlantic coastline at low tide after a northeaster storm. A berm 2 m thick has been removed, exposing the remanents of a back-barrier pine forest 350 Y.B.P. (photo by J. C. Kraft).

A

B

C

D

Plate 33-3. *A.* A very low-lying sandy barrier at Ocean City, Maryland, with a line of condominiums subject to storm erosion. In 1962, a condominium rolled over on its side in a northeaster (photo by J. C. Kraft). *B.* A house constructed on the northerly highland compartment, destroyed by a storm in 1962. Destruction was by wave erosion of the landward edge of the berm (photo by J. C. Kraft). *C.* An air photograph of a small coastal barrier village. Houses are being built on the berm in front of the wave-cut scarp. Older houses fall into the sea while new houses are being built (photo by J. C. Kraft). *D.* A photograph of houses as shown in Plate 3C. Major storms of hurricane force would be expected to destroy the houses totally (photo by J. C. Kraft).

34. ATLANTIC USA—NORTH

The New England-New York 1150 km long coast (Figs. 34-1 and 34-2) is unique in being the only marine United States coast influenced by continental glaciation (Shepard and Wanless 1971). New England's embayed coastline consists of Maine (365 km), New Hampshire (21 km), Massachusetts (310 km), Rhode Island (64 km), and Connecticut (193 km). New York's embayed and barrier island (Long Island) coastline is 200 km. Unconsolidated Pleistocene glacial deposits, primarily Wisconsin, influence southern coastlines, while resistant igneous and metamorphic rocks of Precambrian and Paleozoic age dominate northern coastlines (Johnson 1925). During the Paleozoic, drifting North American and European tectonic plates collided, and then separated in the Mesozoic leaving behind parts of Europe and Africa as the bedrock geology of the New England and Canadian coasts, now recognized as the Avalon subcontinent.

Holocene sea level has been rising eustatically since about 7500 B.P., first rapidly, then decreasing since 3000 B.P. at rates of 2 (south) to 6 (north) cm per century. Maine alone experienced glacial downwarping about 13,000 B.P., with marine clays deposited 70 km inland to 60 m elevation. Wave energy is greater during the winter months, with cyclonic lows called northeasters producing dominant northeasterly winds driving a southward longshore drift. During summer months, prevailing lesser winds are from the southwest. Hurricanes are common along the southern coast during August and September. Mean tidal range increases from 1 m along Long Island and Rhode Island, 2 m along Connecticut and Cape Cod, to 3 m from Boston north to a maximum of 6 m at Eastport, Maine.

Mainland cliffs range from consolidated bedrock in Maine (60–100 m) to unconsolidated glacial sediments (30–60 m) from Cape Cod south. Beach sediments range from cobble and shingle in the north to sand in the south. Dunes are minor (7–10 m) except on northern Cape Cod (60 m). Major bays are drowned river valleys in less resistant rocks, although major rivers empty into smaller estuaries. Tidal marshes are minor. Submerged glacial deposits offshore form the Georges Banks fishing grounds.

New York City proper, Manhattan Island, is underlain by resistant igneous and metamorphic bedrock. Surrounding it, the Hudson River on the west is a drowned river valley, tidal 230 km inland while the tidal East River, not a true river, connects to Long Island Sound. South of Manhattan, the Wisconsian terminal moraine extending from Staten Island on the west to Long Island on the east is breached at the Narrows, separating the upper and lower New York harbors.

Long Island is the longest island (190 km) in the United States. Its shape and coastline are the result of continental glacial deposits (Fuller 1914). Extending east from the Narrows, Harbor Hill terminal moraine divides the island, with the ground moraine to the north and the outwash plain to the south. At the 40 km point, this moraine separates into a recessional moraine extending to Orient Point and the Ronkonkoma terminal moraine extending to the Montauk Point sea cliffs. Prominent barrier islands, from Coney Island to Fire Island's National Seashore, make up Long Island's south shore, backed by large bays with tidal marsh islands (Plate 34-1). Outwash plain sands submerged by a rising sea are the source material for these barrier islands, although ero-

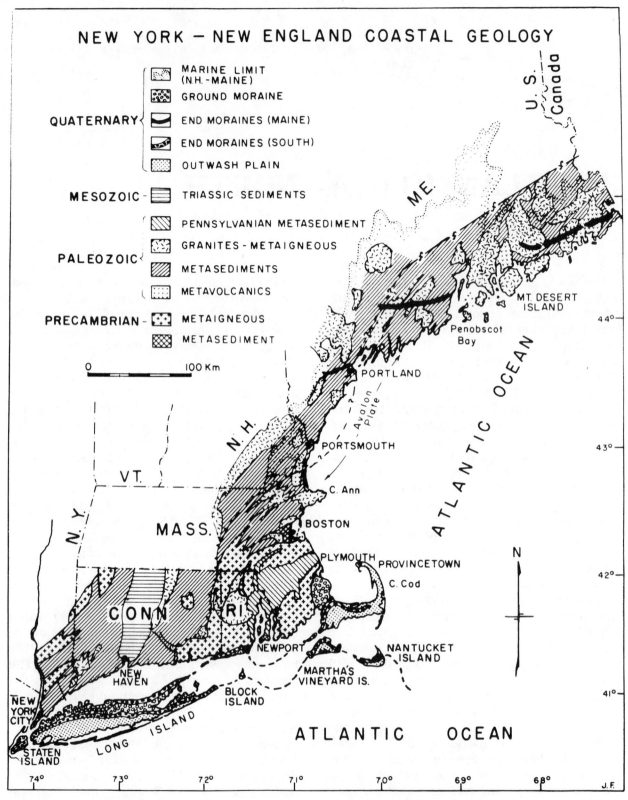

Figure 34-1. Coastal geology of New England and New York (Long Island). Resistant igneous and metamorphic rocks make up most of the New England coast, with basins of less resistant sedimentary rocks making up the bays. Long Island and the southern New England coast are dominated by glacial deposits.

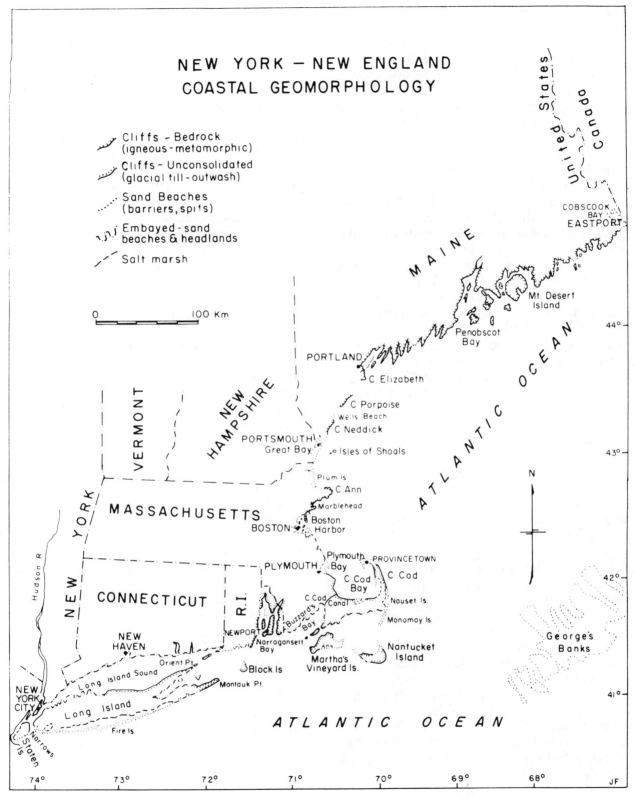

Figure 34-2. Coastal geomorphology of New England and New York (Long Island). Embayed headlands, both consolidated and unconsolidated, make up much of the New England coast, with baymouth barrier beaches and spits forming where sand is available from glacial deposits. Extensive barrier islands exist along the south coast of Long Island.

sion of the Montauk Point sea cliffs may assist in maintaining present-day barriers (Plate 34-2). Earlier barriers may have existed offshore before drowning by the same rising sea (Sanders and Kumar 1975). Reflecting a submerged ground moraine, the western half of Long Island's north shore is highly embayed, but wave action across Long Island Sound has eroded the recessional moraine into sea cliffs along the eastern half.

The Connecticut coast is slightly embayed, with several rivers draining southward and emptying into Long Island Sound through moderate-sized estuaries (Plate 34-3). Bedrock geology consists primarily of schists, gneisses, and granites with Triassic sediments in the New Haven area. Glacial deposits are ground moraine till, with localized areas of sandy outwash sediments and ice-contact-stratified drift of sand and gravel. Postglacial sea level rise submerged the irregular ground moraine surface with south-trending proglacial stream valleys producing the embayed coast. Some headlands are composed of glacial deposits, primarily till, while many have a bedrock core exposed by wave erosion. The presence of Long Island to the south allows limited fetch in Long Island Sound, and wave action is not intense. Recent wave erosion and longshore transport have modified the initial submerged shoreline. Pocket beaches are common between bedrock or till headlands. Spits and baymouth barriers develop where sufficient glacial sands are present. Bays or estuaries behind these barriers, once open water, are now filling with tidal marsh vegetation as sea level rises (Bloom and Stuiver 1963).

Rhode Island's coastline is deeply embayed by Narragansett Bay in the east, and the west is composed of baymouth barrier beaches. Narragansett Bay, the most prominent bay in southern New England, is a structural basin of less resistant Carboniferous metasediments, primarily slates and schists. Within this structural basin Narragansett Bay developed from preglacial drainage patterns. Large islands of bedrock mantled with glacial till within the bay are actually former valley divides of this drowned river valley system. Small, sandy pocket beaches are located between rocky headlands along the Newport shore. Most of the bay lacks sandy beaches except for cuspate forelands. In contrast, the western shore is an unbroken line of sandy barrier beaches (Plate 34-4). These beaches developed from wave action reworking glacial outwash sands south of a recessional moraine extending across the state (Fisher and Simpson 1979). Longshore transport from the west deposited them across the mouth of

wide, shallow former proglacial outwash stream valleys to produce baymouth barrier beaches (Dillon 1970). Offshore is Block Island, part of the terminal moraine that extends from Montauk Point. Wave action has eroded this moraine and its adjacent ground moraine into extensive unconsolidated sea cliffs (Plate 34-5). Sand beaches along the east and west shore develop by longshore transport from sediments eroded from these cliffs. The coastal geology of Massachusetts' is strongly influenced by its glacial geology (Woodsworth and Wigglesworth 1934). The Buzzards Bay coastline, west of Cape Cod, is moderately embayed, not cliffed, since it has developed on ground moraine. Few beaches occur, because of limited wave fetch across Buzzards Bay to the south. On Cape Cod (Plate 34-6) the same recessional moraine that extends across southern Rhode Island first appears offshore as the Elizabeth Islands. It continues north to Woods Hole and the Cape Cod Canal, where it trends east to the Cape Cod National Seashore (Strahler 1966). South of this moraine, sandy outwash plains with proglacial valleys submerged during recent sea level rise produced an embayed, baymouth barrier coastline. Dramatic unconsolidated cliffs (60 m) along the Atlantic coast of the Cape Cod National Seashore result from wave erosion of glacial outwash. This interlobate outwash plain developed between the Cape Cod Bay and Atlantic Ocean ice lobes. Longshore transport along these eroding cliffs formed extensive spits, the Provincetown spit and dune field to the north, the Nauset and Monomoy Islands barrier spit complex to the south (Plate 34-7).

South of Cape Cod, two of the largest islands in southern New England, Martha's Vineyard and Nantucket Island, developed from the same terminal moraine forming Long Island and Block Island. Cliffed coastlines of Martha's Vineyard result from wave erosion of interlobate morainic deposits, while baymouth barrier beaches of its southern shore developed from proglacial outwash plain valleys submerged by a rising sea level with longshore transport forming the barriers (Plate 34-8). Nantucket Island is similar to Martha's Vineyard, but the lobate moraine and cliffs are less prominent. Rhythmic cuspate spits form a unique north shore beach.

Cape Cod Bay shores are slightly cliffed, embayed coastlines, notably Barnstable Harbor on Cape Cod and Plymouth Bay on the mainland. Sand eroded by wave action from ground moraine, together with longshore transport has produced notable spits at these bays and harbors. Boston

Harbor developed in a Precambrian basin of metasediments and contains a submerged drumlin field. Wave erosion and longshore transport have produced striking spit and tombolo islands. North from Boston Harbor the coastline changes markedly as plutonic granites outcrop to form rocky headlands just below Marblehead to Cape Ann. North of Cape Ann, the coast again changes markedly with a prominent barrier island, Plum Island, which has migrated upward and landward first under a rising, then a stable sea level (Jones and Cameron 1977).

New Hampshire's coastline is dominated by the influence of the bedrock headlands, which control the longshore transport, producing crescent-shaped beaches oriented generally parallel to the overall coast trend and perpendicular to the headland areas that separate them (Tuttle 1960). The entire coastal area is one of low relief, and no prominent cliffed coastline exists. Upland, postglacial uplifted emergent marine sediments extend 25 km inland from the coastal area, mantling the underlying glacial ground moraine. Also present are several estuaries having quite restricted outlets to the sea. The largest, on the northern boundary between New Hampshire and Maine, is Great Bay on the Piscataqua River. Great Bay is some 15 km inland from the coast and is connected to Portsmouth Harbor, directly on the ocean, by a narrow section of the river. Offshore, a series of small granitic islands, the Isles of Shoals are divided between the states of New Hampshire and Maine.

Maine's highly embayed coastline, unlike those of the other New England states, was modified only slightly by glacial deposits. Sandy pocket beaches and boulder-cobble pavements result from longshore transport and wave action acting on glacial outwash and ground moraines (Nelson and Fink 1980). Postglacial marine deposits mantle the ground moraine along the coast to elevations of 60 m (south) to 90 m (north). Possible localized glacial erosion may have modified the narrow, long bays along the central Maine coast, but although they resemble glacial fjords, extensive glacial erosion is questionable. Along the southern coast, two prominent headlands at Cape Neddick and Cape Porpoise developed around granitic plutons; between them, baymouth barrier beaches (e.g., Wells Beach, Kennebunk Beach) formed at the mouths of smaller submerged river valleys. North of Cape Elizabeth, long, narrow bays with equally narrow intervening headlands have developed on tightly folded metasedimentary rocks, trending first northeast and then north.

North from Penobscot Bay to the Canadian border, granitic plutonic masses dominate the coastal zone and produce most of the prominent broad headlands (Chapman 1962). One of the larger of these granitic plutons forms the core of Mount Desert Island National Park (Plate 34-9). The deepwater bays are wider along this section of the coast as a result of the more equidimensional shape of the granitic plutons. The bays in this northernmost section of the coastline are less fjord-like than those in the central section. Consolidated bedrock cliffs exist along the entire Maine coast at the headlands (Plate 34-10). End moraines are common inland along this northern coast.

JOHN J. FISHER

REFERENCES

Bloom, A. L., and M. Stuiver, 1963, Submergence of the Connecticut coast, *Science* **131:**332–334.

Chapman, C. A., 1962, Bays-of-Maine igneous complex, *Geol. Soc. America Bull.* **73:**883–888.

Dillon, W. P., 1970, Submergence effects on a Rhode Island barrier and lagoon and inference on migration of barriers, *Jour. Geology* **78:**94–106.

Fisher, J. J., and Simpson, E. J., 1979, Washover and tidal sedimentation rates as factors in development of a transgressive barrier shoreline, in *Barrier Islands,* S. P. Leatherman, ed., Academic Press, New York, pp. 127–148.

Fuller, M. L., 1914, *The Geology of Long Island, New York,* U.S. Geol. Survey Prof. Paper 82, Washington, D.C.

Johnson, D. W., 1925, *The New England–Acadian Shoreline,* John Wiley.

Jones, J. R., and B. Cameron, 1977, Landward migration of barrier island sands under stable sea-level conditions, *Jour. Sed. Petrology* **47:**1475–1483.

Nelson, B. W., and L. K. Fink, 1980, *Geological and Botanical Features of Sand Beach Systems in Maine,* Maine Sea Grant Public., Bulletin 14.

Sanders, J. E., and N. Kumar, 1975, Evidence of shoreface retreat and in place "drowning" during Holocene submergence of barriers, *Geol. Soc. America Bull.* **86:**65–76.

Shepard, F. P., and H. R. Wanless, 1971, *Our Changing Coastlines,* McGraw-Hill.

Strahler, A. N., 1966, *A Geologist's View of Cape Cod,* Natural History Press, Garden City, N.Y.

Tuttle, S. D., 1960, Evolution of the New Hampshire shoreline, *Geol. Soc. America Bull.* **71:**1211–1222.

Woodworth, J. B., and E. Wigglesworth, 1934, *Geography and Geology of the region including Cape Cod, Elizabeth Is., Nantucket, Martha's Vineyard, No Mans Land and Block Is.,* Museum of Comparative Zoology, Harvard University, Memoir 52.

Plate 34-1. Barrier island, along western Long Island, Rockaway Beach, bridge over Rockaway Inlet, which has migrated to west (right) as tip of Rockaway Beach has extended by accretion. Tidal marsh island (left), former airfield, now part of Gateway National Recreation Area with Jamaica Bay far left (photo by J. Fisher).

Plate 34-2. Barrier spit, along eastern Long Island, Southampton to east (right) on outwash plain, terminal moraine across top of photo. Shinnecock Inlet on Shinnecock Bay reopened by hurricane of 1938. Inlet maintained by jetties and dredging. Longshore transport from east to west with updrift jetty deposition (photo by J. Fisher).

Plate 34-3. Embayed coast, eastern Connecticut, Niantic with crescentric Niantic baymouth barrier beach separating Niantic Bay from Niantic River (drowned river valley). Submergence of ground moraine by rising sea level produced embayed coast (photo by J. Fisher).

Plate 34-4. Barrier beach coast, western Rhode Island, view southwest along Charlestown recessional moraine. Barrier beaches and bays to south (left) formed on outwash plain. Watch Hill on coast (top of photo) sea cliff eroded from recessional moraine by wave action (photo by J. Fisher).

Plate 34-5. Sea cliff coast, Block Island, south of Rhode Island, Mohegan Bluffs, wave erosion of unconsolidated terminal moraine deposits at annual rate 1 m. Landslide slump block promi-nent on east (right) side of cliff below lighthouse. Similar sea cliffs on Cape Cod, Martha's Vineyard, and Nantucket (photo by J. Fisher).

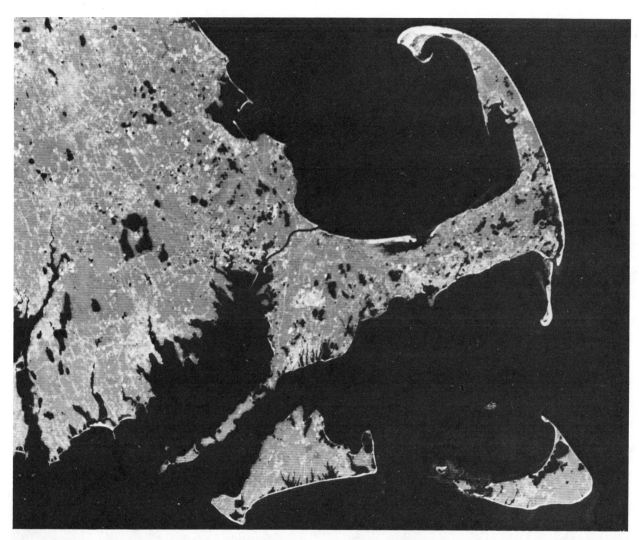

Plate 34-6. Southeastern New England (primarily Massachusetts) Landsat satellite image extending from Narragansett Bay (drowned river valley) in west (left) to Cape (recessional moraine and outwash plains) in east (right). Martha's Vineyard (center bottom) and Nantucket Island (right bottom) developed from terminal moraine of Wisconsian glaciation. Cape Cod Bay, ice lobe area (center top), with Plymouth Harbor (spit enclosed) to west. Kettle-hole lakes (black circles) on glacial deposits (gray tone) with postglacial baymouth barrier beaches and spits (white tone) along exposed coasts (photo by NASA).

Plate 34-7. Spit growth, southern end Monomoy Island, south of Cape Cod, Massachusetts. Relict spit beach ridges have grown southward (left) by longshore transport under dominant northeast winds as island, updrift, erodes. First prominent recurved ridge (center photo) is mid-1800s coastline, 1 km from present shore (photo by J. Fisher).

Plate 34-8. Baymouth barrier beaches, southern shore, Martha's Vineyard, Massachusetts. Glacial outwash stream valleys running north-south (left-right) submerged by rising sea level. Wave action eroded outwash plain headlands and longshore transport closed bays with barrier beaches. Process common throughout New England (photo by J. Fisher).

Plate 34-9. Central embayed Maine consolidated bedrock coast, Landsat satellite image with Mt. Desert Island (Acadia National Park) in center of photo. Roughly circular island resulting from submergence of eroded granitic pluton. Northwest-southeast (top-bottom photo) trending valleys and bays (Frenchman Bay in east, Blue Hill Bay in west) due to continental glacial erosion (photo by NASA).

Plate 34-10. Sea cave, Mt. Desert Island, Maine. Cave formed by wave action eroding highly fractured granitic rock. Mountain in background, Cadillac Mountain, on Mt. Desert Island, considered highest point (466 m) on the Atlantic seaboard. Glacial erosion has smoothed and removed all overburden from mountain top (photo by J. Fisher).

35. ATLANTIC CANADA

Much of the eastern coastline of Canada within the provinces of Quebec, New Brunswick, Nova Scotia, Prince Edward Island, and Newfoundland (including Labrador) is rocky, barren, and subarctic in character. Many hundreds of kilometers of coastline are difficult to reach and remain unexplored in terms of coastal geomorphology, though inventory-style descriptions based on reconnaissance observations of the more remote areas are now in progress. Two distinctive, and quite different, coastal environments in the south have been intensively studied in the last ten years: the macrotidal, tide-dominated headward embayments of the Bay of Fundy and the microtidal, wave-dominated barrier island shorelines of the southern Gulf of St. Lawrence. These two environments are probably the best documented in Canada in terms of coastal morphology, sediments, and processes. The characteristics of the wide Atlantic continental shelf are also well known. A third distinctive coastal setting in eastern Canada, dominated by a different set of coastal processes—the action of drift ice—is typified in the boulder-strewn salt marshes of the St. Lawrence estuary and the bouldery tidal flats of Labrador, Northern Quebec, and James Bay. The characteristics of these three environments will be considered below, following an introductory statement about coastal conditions in the area as a whole and its division into coastal regions (Fig. 35-1).

Geologically, eastern Canada south of the St. Lawrence forms the northern section of the Appalachian system and consists predominantly of deformed Paleozoic sedimentary rocks trending NE-SW. North of the St. Lawrence most of the remainder of Quebec and Labrador consists of

Figure 35-1. Coastal regions of eastern Canada. 1. Bay of Fundy; 2. S. Gulf of St. Lawrence; 3. N. Gulf of St. Lawrence; 4. St. Lawrence Estuary; 5. Atlantic Nova Scotia-S. Newfoundland; 6. E. Newfoundland and Labrador; 7. Hudson Strait; 8. Hudson Bay; 9. James Bay. Provinces: A. Quebec; B. New Brunswick; C. Nova Scotia; D. Prince Edward Island; E. Newfoundland.

Precambrian rocks of the Canadian Shield. Easily eroded rocks, largely Carboniferous, Permian, and Triassic sandstones, occur only around the southern Gulf of St. Lawrence and the head of the Bay of Fundy, where they provide an abundant supply of new sediment for the shore zone. Elsewhere, beach sediments are often scarce and largely derived from the erosion of glacial deposits. The effects of glaciation are evident throughout

235

the region, most of which was glaciated as recently as the late Wisconsin. Glacial erosion produced the fjords of northern Labrador, glacial deposits cover much of the shallow continental shelf, and changes in relative sea level due to deglaciation and isostatic rebound are important everywhere. Raised shoreline deposits occur most notably in James Bay and along the St. Lawrence estuary.

Sea ice is present along much of the eastern Canadian seaboard in winter; only the outer coast of Nova Scotia and southern Newfoundland can be considered ice-free coasts, and even there ice may develop in sheltered bays. The ice season is three to four months in the estuary and Gulf of St. Lawrence, six months in Labrador and James Bay, and seven to nine months in Hudson Bay and Hudson Strait. An ice foot forms along all these coasts in winter and persists into the breakup season. The offshore ice cover in the south is usually dense, slowly moving pack ice, but in the north there is commonly a broad zone of fast ice extending seaward for many kilometers between the shore ice and the mobile pack. The presence of sea ice for many months each year reduces the period when wave processes can be effective, but it also introduces other effects into the shore zone, particularly at breakup when erosion, transport, and deposition by drift ice are key processes.

Local storm-generated waves, rather than ocean swell, dominate the wave climate of the region. The outer coast of Nova Scotia, southern and eastern Newfoundland, and the coast of Labrador experience the severest wave conditions. These coastlines are influenced by waves generated during the west-east passage of cyclonic storms across the northern Atlantic and Labrador Sea. In contrast the Gulf of St. Lawrence is a protected sea environment. Hudson Bay and Hudson Strait can experience severe storm wave conditions during the open water season.

Tidal conditions vary considerably throughout the region, with very high tidal ranges prevailing in the Bay of Fundy and in Ungava Bay on Hudson Strait in northern Quebec. Very low ranges prevail in the southern Gulf of St. Lawrence and in parts of Hudson Bay. Around most of Nova Scotia (excluding the Fundy shore) and Newfoundland, mean ranges are commonly less than 2 m, but they are somewhat higher along much of the Labrador coast. In the funnel-shaped St. Lawrence estuary, mean tidal range increases headward to more than 4 m near Quebec City.

Nine major coastal regions can be defined in eastern Canada (see also Owens and Bowen 1977).

The important features of each are listed below in the following order: a = mean tidal ranges, b = relative wave energy, c = coastal character.

Bay of Fundy: a. 5–15 m; b. low; c. easily eroded cliffs, large intertidal zone, tide-dominated sand bars.

S. Gulf of St. Lawrence: a. 1–2 m; b. moderate; c. low unresistant cliffs, abundant beach sediment, barrier islands, and spits.

N. Gulf of St. Lawrence: a. 1–2 m; b. moderate; c. resistant upland coasts with large deltas.

St. Lawrence estuary: a. 3–5 m; b. low; c. resistant upland coast with tidal flats and salt marshes.

Atlantic Nova Scotia and S. Newfoundland: a. 1–4 m; b. high; c. resistant rock shores of varying elevation, pocket beaches.

Eastern Newfoundland and Labrador: a. 1–3 m; b. high; c. resistant upland coast, fjords, pocket beaches.

Hudson Strait: a. 3–9 m; b. low; c. juxtaposition of high cliffs and wide tidal flats.

Hudson Bay: a. 1–4 m; b. moderate; c. mostly resistant upland coast.

James Bay: a. 1–2 m; b. low; c. flat, highly indented lowland coast with myriads of rock islands (Dionne 1980).

A unique, very dynamic coastal environment, not large enough to be considered in the list above, is Sable Island, a small arcuate deposit of unconsolidated sand, situated 200 km southeast of mainland Nova Scotia on the outer margin of the continental shelf. It is only 35 km long, with a maximum width of about 2 km. Vegetated dunes occur in the central section. Cameron (1965) documented considerable changes in the morphology and size of the end points of the island.

BAY OF FUNDY

The tides of the Bay of Fundy are reputed to have the largest ranges in the world. Mean tidal range increases from 4 m at the entrance to almost 12 m in the Minas Basin (Fig. 35-2A), where a maximum fair weather range of 16.3 m has been recorded at Burnt Coat Head. The tide is semidiurnal, with only a small diurnal inequality, and tidal range has increased over the last 6000 years as the dimensions of the bay have changed because of eustatic sea level rise and isostatic recovery. Much of the recent inter-

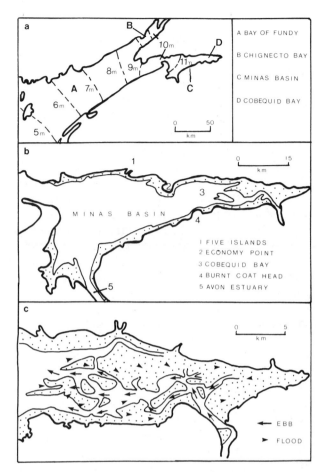

Figure 35-2. A. Mean tidal range in the Bay of Fundy. B. Intertidal zone in the Minas Basin. C. Sand bars and tidal current transport in Cobequid Bay.

est in the tides and their influence on sediment dynamics is related to the possibilities for tidal power generation.

Sedimentary conditions are better known in the Minas Basin (Fig. 35-2*B*) than in the other headward arm of the Bay of Fundy System, Chignecto Bay. The basin is bounded by rapidly eroding cliffs, largely of sandstone and glacial deposits, which contribute an abundant supply of new sediment each year. Amos and Long (1980) estimated that there is a net annual sediment input into the Basin of 4.8×10^6 m³, of which 3.09×10^6 m³ is derived from cliffline recession. There is a very wide intertidal zone around most of the basin. A narrow gravel beach commonly occurs at high water level and is succeeded seaward by a gravel lag with a thin mud veneer. This in turn gives way to wide sand flats and large sand bars. The sand bars, which are generally

composed of medium to coarse sands, are elongate in shape and may be several kilometers in length, with an amplitude of 10–15 m. Their surfaces are covered with large bedforms generated by tidal currents, which reach velocities in excess of 1.5 m/s^{-1} (Plate 35-1). Much attention has focused on the genesis of these features.

The very large tidal range results in a highly dynamic, current-dominated regime, and it is possible, because of the extensive exposure of the intertidal sand bodies, to examine directly the array of bedforms, sedimentary structures, and sandbar geometries. On the basis of observations near Five Islands and Economy Point, Klein (1970) suggested that the large sand bars are equilibrium forms subjected to a dispersal system of alternating flood and ebb transport. Knight (1980) defined the tidal current regime and sediment transport pathways that maintain the pattern of sand bars and channels in Cobequid Bay at the head of the Minas Basin (Fig. 35-2*C*). An analysis of a basinwide compendium of bedform and hydraulic data by Dalrymple et al. (1978) indicates that there are four basic lower-flow-regime bedforms present on the sand bars: current ripples (height < 0.05 m; wavelength < 0.3 m), two types of mega-ripples (0.05 m/ 1.0 m; 0.5 m/ 15 m) and sandwaves (0.2–3 m; 15–200 m). The flow conditions (current speed and water depth) and grain size characteristics that control their formation were also considered. Most sand waves have mega-ripples superimposed on them, and ripples are superimposed on all larger bedforms. As a result of these and similar studies, the Minas Basin is a key reference area for models of sedimentation in this type of coastal situation.

The combination of coarse grain size and mobile sediments means that the intertidal fauna of the sand bars are sparse, but muddier tidal flats in other locations support a wide variety of organisms. Resuspension of biodeposits contributes significantly to the turbidity of the Minas Basin waters. Large areas of salt marsh occur in protected embayments and estuaries, and early Acadian settlers established an extensive series of dikes and reclamation schemes.

SOUTHERN GULF OF ST. LAWRENCE

The Gulf of St. Lawrence is a microtidal protected sea environment with a maximum SW-NE extent of 800 km. Barrier shorelines occur mainly in the southwest, where coastal relief is low and developed in soft sandstones. The barrier islands, barrier beaches, and spits that have developed across embayments and estuaries are basically transgressive in character, though some progradational, dune ridge sequences occur in downdrift situations. There are four distinct barrier systems (Fig. 35-3A), incorporating 350 km of shoreline and 30 tidal inlets, and exhibiting a wide variety of shoreline conditions (McCann 1979). The most remarkable shoreline configuration occurs in the Magdalen Islands in the center of the southern Gulf (Fig. 35-3B) where two long tombolo systems of barrier beaches and dunes join a series of rock islands and enclose central lagoons (Owens and McCann 1980). Together with complex terminal spits they make a continuous narrow land area 70 km long.

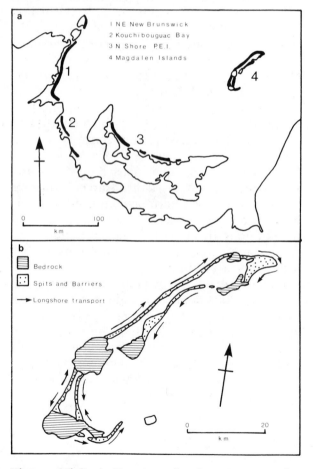

Figure 35-3. A. Barrier island systems in the Southern Gulf of St. Lawrence. B. Barriers of the Magdalen Islands.

Most of the barrier shorelines experience tidal ranges during spring tides smaller than 1.6 m, and tidal currents are only important near inlets. The wave climate is dominated by short-period waves generated within the Gulf. Three of the barrier systems occur on lee shores with respect to the prevailing westerly winds, and the important waves are generated in occasional storms with winds from the northeast. As a result, net longshore transport is directed to the south in these three barriers. Westerly winds and waves are only important in the Magdalen Islands, and the most dynamic beaches in the southern Gulf occur along the west-facing barriers of the islands.

The tidal inlets that breach the barriers vary in size from small, temporary inlets, only tens of m wide and 2–3 m deep, to large permanent inlets 1 km wide and 15 m deep at the throat. The largest, such as Portage Gully at the southern end of the northeast New Brunswick system (Reinson 1977), occur opposite the largest estuaries and have extensive ebb- and flood-tidal deltas. They have remained in the similar positions throughout the period of historical record (i.e., about 200 years), though there have been changes in the pattern of channels and shoals. Tidal inlets, both past and present, have been the most important sites for the landward transfer of sediment in these transgressive barriers. Overwash at the sites of former inlets is an important process in this respect. General overwash, away from tidal inlets, occurs along the low narrow barriers of northeast New Brunswick, but it is not a feature of Prince Edward Island, where more substantial barriers, with higher dunes, occur. At the Malpeque barriers at the western end of the Prince Edward Island system, a high dune shoreline is maintaining its dimensions during slow barrier retreat (Plate 35-2). Longshore transport rates are high at this location, and subtidal erosion of the shore face appears to contribute a continuing supply of new sediment (Armon and McCann 1977).

Nearshore bar topography is a ubiquitous and permanent feature of the shore zone, though there are differences in bar characteristics between barrier system. Kouchibouguac Bay, where there are two bars—the outermost 200-300 m offshore in about 2 m water depth—has become a type locality for the study of these features (Davidson-Arnott and Greenwood 1976). On the more dynamic west coast of the Magdalen Islands there are three bars, the outermost 700-1000 m offshore in a water depth of 4-6 m.

DRIFT ICE ACTION

Reference to three areas will illustrate the variety of drift ice effects that occur along many kilometers of the coastline of eastern Canada. Along the southern shore of the St. Lawrence estuary mean tidal range varies from 3–5 m; the ice foot persists for four months when there is a thick cover of mobile pack ice offshore. The salt marshes (schorre) are characterized by a high proportion of coarse material and the presence of erratic boulders due to ice rafting, and the vegetation cover is torn up by ice block erosion. Dionne (1972) distinguishes two types of cold region salt marsh: pitted schorre and boulder-strewn schorre. He indicates that many of the boulders have been transported across the estuary from the north shore by drifting ice. Ice effects dominate the tidal flats in Labrador and Ungava Bay, notably in the development of boulder barricades, elongate rows of boulders usually along the seaward margin of the intertidal zone. The ice season is longer than in the St. Lawrence, and the offshore ice forms a more solid cover, which remains in place during the earlier breakup of the ice in the intertidal zone. In Labrador, where the mean tidal range is 1.4 m, Rosen (1979) invokes ice rafting as the agent of boulder transport, but in Ungava Bay, where the mean tidal range is 9.3 m, Lauriol and Gray (1980) suggest that pushing (bulldozing) of boulders by ice floes is important. They indicate that the great concentration of boulders in the tidal flats is a result of slow downslope movement of boulders during the progressive displacement of the intertidal zone over the past 7000 years of isostatic emergence.

S. B. McCANN

REFERENCES

Amos, C. L., and B. F. N. Long, 1980, The sedimentary character of the Minas Basin, Bay of Fundy, in *The Coastline of Canada*, S. B. McCann, ed., Canada Geol. Survey Paper 80-10, pp. 153–180.

Armon, J. W., and S. B. McCann, 1977, Longshore sediment transport and a sediment budget for the Malpeque barrier system, Southern Gulf of St. Lawrence, *Canadian Jour. Earth Sci.* **14:**2429–2439.

Cameron, H. L., 1965, The shifting sands of Sable Island, *Geog. Rev.* **44:**363–376.

Dalrymple, R. W., R. J. Knight, and J. T. Lambiase, 1978, Bedforms and their hydraulic stability in a tidal environment, Bay of Fundy, Canada, *Nature* **275:**100–104.

Davidson-Arnott, R. G. D., and B. Greenwood, 1976, Facies relationships on a barred coast, Kouchibouguac Bay, New Brunswick, in *Beach and Nearshore Sedimentation*, R. A. Davies and R. L. Ethington, eds., Soc. Econ. Paleontologists and Mineralogists Spec. Pub. 24, pp. 149–168.

Dionne, J. C., 1972, Caractéristiques des schorres des regions froides, en particulier de l'estuaire du Saint-Laurent, *Zeitschr. Geomorphologie* **15:**137–180.

Dionne, J. C., 1980, An outline of the eastern James Bay coastal environments, in *The Coastline of Canada*, S. B. McCann, ed., Canada Geol. Survey Paper 80-10, pp. 311–338.

Klein, G. deV., 1970, Depositional and dispersal dynamics of intertidal sand bars, *Jour. Sed. Petrology* **40:**1095–1127.

Knight, R. J., 1980, Linear sand bar development and tidal current flow in Cobequid Bay, Bay of Fundy, Nova Scotia, in *The Coastline of Canada*, S. B. McCann, ed., Canada Geol. Survey Paper 80-10, pp. 123–152.

Lauriol, B., and J. T. Gray, 1980, Processes responsible for the concentration of boulders in the intertidal zone in Leaf Basin, Ungava, in *The Coastline of Canada*, S. B. McCann, ed., Canada Geol. Survey Paper 80-10, pp. 281–292.

McCann, S. B., 1979, Barrier islands in the southern Gulf of St. Lawrence, in *Barrier Islands from the Gulf of St. Lawrence to the Gulf of Mexico*, S. P. Leatherman, ed., Academic Press, New York, pp. 29–63.

Owens, E. H., and A. J. Bowen, 1977, Coastal environments of the Maritime Provinces, *Maritime Sediments* **13:**.1–13.

Owens, E. H., and S. B. McCann, 1980, The coastal geomorphology of the Magdalen Islands, Quebec, in *The Coastline of Canada*, S. B. McCann, ed., Canada Geol. Survey Paper 80-10, pp. 51–72.

Reinson, G. E., 1977, Tidal current control of submarine morphology at the mouth of the Maramichi estuary, New Brunswick, *Canadian Jour. Earth Sci.* **14:**2524–2532.

Rosen, P., 1979, Boulder barricades in central Labrador, *Jour. Sed. Petrology* **49:**1113–1123.

Plate 35-1. Tidal current generated bedforms (ripples and mega-ripples) on the sand bars of Cobequid Bay, at the head of the Minas Basin in the Bay of Fundy (photo by S. B. McCann).

Plate 35-2. High dune, barrier island shoreline in the Malpeque barrier system at the eastern end of the Prince Edward Island barrier shorelines. The dune is maintaining its dimensions during slow landward retreat of the barrier (photo by S. B. McCann).

36. ARCTIC CANADA

North of the American continent is a major archipelago; roughly triangular in shape, it extends for nearly 3000 km from east to west and 1500 km from south to north. The apex of the triangle, at Cape Columbia on Ellesmere Island, is in 83°N, and the southern edge is close to the Arctic Circle. The archipelago is environmentally wholly within the Arctic. Its many hundreds of islands include Baffin, Victoria, and Ellesmere islands, which are among the largest in the world. Provisional estimates indicate that the total length of coastline exceeds 90,000 km.

Although the archipelago is in a particularly hostile environmental zone, from the sixteenth century onward it was visited by Europeans in search of a route around continental North America between the Atlantic and the Pacific oceans. The first discoveries had been made earlier, about 1000 A.D., when the Vikings sailing west from their colonies in Greenland reached the rocky shores of Baffin Island. It was evident from early explorations that a broad range of coastal types existed, and by the mid-nineteenth century all the major varieties had been visited except those in the Sverdrup group of islands in the far northwest. However, not until the last two decades, with the completion of medium-scale mapping of the archipelago, have the main coastal characteristics' origins been identified.

The main configuration of the archipelago (and adjacent areas) results from events beginning in the late Precambrian and culminating in the disruption of a tectonic, lithospheric plate in the Cenozoic. Subsequently, considerable modification of the coasts occurred during the Pleistocene and detailed changes have followed in postglacial times.

COASTAL CONFIGURATION OF THE SOUTHERN ARCHIPELAGO: STRUCTURAL CONTROL

The core of the North American continent is the Precambrian Canadian Shield, which occupies nearly half of Canada and when the buried sections of the craton are included, more than half of North America. In the archipelago, the coasts of the eastern margin are developed on Shield rocks and much of the remaining coasts south of Parry Channel on younger sedimentary rocks resting on a Shield basement. The surface of the Shield in the north has an arch and trough (or basin) form that was initiated in late Precambrian times and has a wavelength of several hundred kilometers. The northern perimeter of the Shield is consequently not a simple boundary close to the mainland, but rather a series of projections, corresponding to the arches, that extend north into the archipelago and are separated by sedimentary basins containing carbonate rocks deposited during a major Paleozoic transgression. The highest arch, of which only the western side survives in Canada, may be considered a northward extension from Labrador with breaks to Baffin, east Devon, and southeastern Ellesmere islands. Other arches, separated by troughs, are a dominant physiographic element elsewhere in the southern archipelago (Fig. 36-1).

Parts of the North American craton experienced sedimentation in the late Precambrian, but only remnants of these events survive in the archipelago, notably in northern Baffin and Bylot islands. Marine transgressions across the Shield followed in the Paleozoic; in particular, a transgression of Ordovician age left limestones and dolomites of

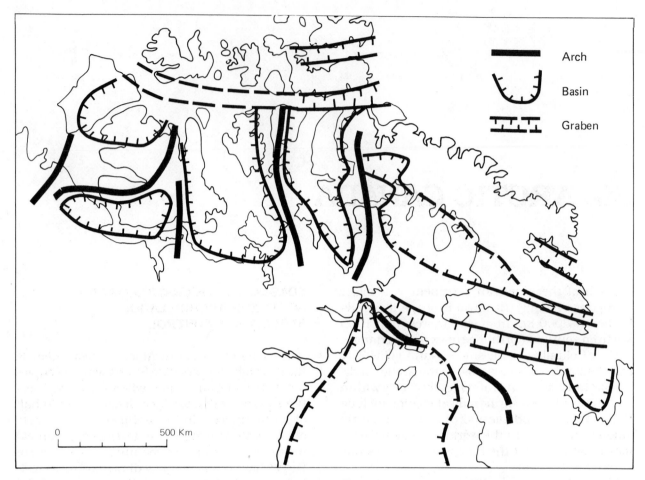

Figure 36-1. Structural elements on the surface of the northern Canadian Shield.

great thickness in the southern archipelago, where they survive to the present. They are more than 500 m thick in some exposures and remain predominantly flat-lying; they have, however, been eroded from the crests of the basement arches. Today the basement and Paleozoic platform rocks determine the two major physiographic regions and the associated coasts of the southern archipelago. A third, narrow region is found along the northwest margin of the archipelago, where a coastal plain has evolved on Tertiary clastic sediments of the Beaufort Formation.

Although the character of much of the coasts and shores of the southern archipelago is derived from the lithology of the basement and Paleozoic rocks, and from the warping of the surface of the Shield, later tectonic events have intervened in the eastern Arctic. During the Jurassic, the North American (including Greenland) and Eurasian tectonic plates began to separate with the breakup of Pangaea. Initial separation in the north between

Baffin Island and Greenland formed the Labrador Sea and, extending northwestward, Baffin Bay opened up the early Tertiary. Before separation came to a halt and was replaced by plate spreading between Greenland and Europe, graben arms developed on the west side of the Baffin Bay–Smith Sound rift. These smaller tectonic features are now occupied by Hudson Strait, Frobisher Bay, Cumberland Sound, Lancaster Sound, and Jones Sound. Additional faulting associated with these events controls the configuration of the coasts of Prince Regent Inlet, Peel Sound, and Barrow Strait, and it has been speculated that the westward extensions of Lancaster Sound (known as Parry Channel) for 1400 km to the Arctic Ocean has a similar origin. It is evident, therefore, that the principal coasts of the eastern margin of the archipelago were defined by faulting, although in the last 50 million years, other events, mainly denudational, have produced considerable modification. However, some coasts, of which the south side of Frobisher Bay is a particularly striking example, remain identifiably fault-line scarps.

South of Parry Channel the coasts have evolved either on Shield or platform sedimentary rocks; this twofold division provides a simple classification for description of the coasts. A third, smaller region, the Arctic Coastal Plain, is found along the shores of the Beaufort Sea and Arctic Ocean. It extends from the Bering Strait (Alaska) to Meighen Island and is essentially the landward edge of a continental shelf that has experienced repeated transgressions and withdrawals of the sea; today unconsolidated sands, gravel, and silts, several hundred feet thick of late Tertiary age, form the coastal zone.

GEOLOGICAL EVENTS NORTH OF PARRY CHANNEL

Along the eastern margin of the Queen Elizabeth Islands, Shield and platform rocks, similar to those found south of Parry Channel, are exposed. Between this sector and the Arctic Coastal Plain, adjacent to the Arctic Ocean, is a complex zone of folded sediments. For discussion of the coastline, three regions may be recognized: a southern region of Paleozoic sedimentary beds that was folded in the Ellesmerian orogeny and is today exposed in the Parry Islands and central Ellesmere Island. In the west of this region, folding is Appalachian in type and has provided strong structural control for the coasts, especially in Melville, Bathurst, and northwest Devon islands, where plateaus dominate the topography; in the north, wide lowlands and upland topography are characteristic. Rocks of similar age are preserved in northern Ellesmere Island, but they experienced some metamorphism and greater deformation than the Parry Island belt. Between these two geosynclinal areas is the Sverdrup Basin, which contains a succession of Paleozoic to Cenozoic sediments more than 10 km deep that has been intruded by evaporites. The rocks in the west are gently folded, whereas on Axel Heiberg Island they are intensely deformed.

MODIFICATION OF THE ARCHIPELAGO DURING THE LATE CENOZOIC

The evolution of the coasts of the archipelago has been described so far in terms of sedimentation and tectonic activity. Although faulting had a key role in the fragmentation of the archipelago land mass, fluvial activity appears to have played a part in the evolution of many channels, and particularly in vigorous incision of the eastern edge of the Shield and northern Ellesmere Island by streams (Bird 1967).

As the Tertiary period drew to a close, glacierization that had already appeared in Greenland spread to the highest parts of the archipelago. For the final 2–3 million years of their history, the islands underwent repeated glaciations, interrupted by periglacial phases during which sea level fluctuated widely.

The number of glaciations, their extent, and their duration in the archipelago are not known. Some of their characteristics may be inferred from reconstruction of events during the Wisconsin, but even these are frequently speculative. During the maximum of the last glaciation, Laurentide ice covered the islands south of Parry Channel except for much of Banks Island and small upland areas in western Victoria Island, which remained unglaciated. The Queen Elizabeth Islands (north of Parry Channel) were covered by the Franklin (Innuitian) Ice Complex, consisting of inactive ice domes over the present islands and ice streams in many of the channels associated with Laurentide ice: a pattern that was also found south of Parry Channel, on Prince of Wales, Somerset, and northern Baffin islands (Fig. 36-2).

The direct effect of the glaciations on the properties of the present coastlines varied greatly. In the unglaciated zones and around the lowland Queen Elizabeth Islands, modifications throughout the era were slight. In the south-central islands (eastern Victoria, western Prince of Wales, King William), glacial sediments, frequently in the form of drumlinized till, dominate much of the coastal zone, and many of the small islands in this sector of the archipelago are partly drowned drumlins.

The most conspicuous modification by glaciers was concentrated in the east and extreme north of the archipelago with the evolution of fjord coasts. It has already been shown that the eastern margin of the archipelago experienced crustal uplift and widespread faulting, associated with the separation of northern Canada from Greenland in the Cretaceous and early Cenozoic. Valleys formed by stream incision in the resulting uplands were occupied repeatedly in the Quaternary by active glaciers. Virtually the entire 1200 km east coast of Baffin Island is cut by fjords that closely resemble the Norwegian type. Steep, often vertical sides

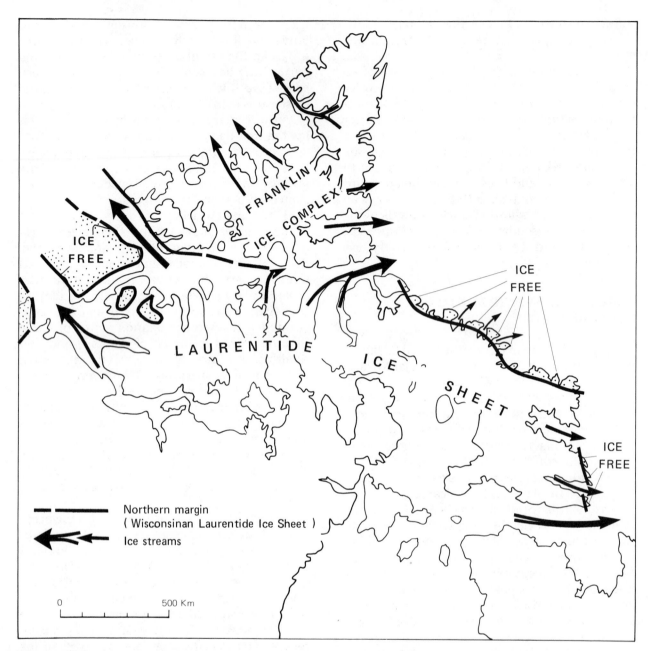

Figure 36-2. The glacierization of the Archipelago during the Wisconsin.

rise 1000–1500 m out of the sea and penetrate up to 100 km into the interior of the island. Similar fjords are widely distributed along the east and northwest coasts of Ellesmere Island (Fig. 36-3).

Other varieties of fjord with more restricted distribution are found in the archipelago. These include drowned valleys—morphologically transitional between cirques and short, glaciated valleys—that are found on the south side of

Frobisher Bay and in eastern Southampton Island. Several islands underlain by Paleozoic sedimentary rocks, which support plateau surfaces 250–1000 m above the sea, are dissected by Finnmark-type fjords that are shorter, straighter, wider, and shallower than the Baffin Island type; they are located on south Devon Island around Jones Sound and on Melville Island (Bird 1967).

The fjords described so far appear to have been modified predominantly by glaciers of local origin.

Figure 36-3. Fjords in the Canadian Arctic Archipelago.

The large ice streams that discharged from the continental ice sheets also modified existing valleys through overdeepening, leaving steep coasts and characteristic underwater fjord profiles. This type of fjord reaches its finest development between Axel Heiberg and Ellesmere islands, where Nansen Sound and its extensions, Greely and Tanqueray fjords, penetrate 400 km into the center of these northern islands. Several other inlets including Admiralty, Prince Regent, and Navy Board inlets, resemble this type in one or more of their features.

QUATERNARY CHANGES OF SEA LEVEL

Quaternary glaciations changed sea levels significantly in coastal areas throughout the world. In the Canadian arctic islands three sets of sea-level changes have been identified. Regional modifications of sea level in the Cenozoic in conjunction with crustal uplift along the eastern margin of the archipelago have already been described; in the west, crustal/sea-level changes were associated with the deposition of the Beaufort Formation. It is not clear whether these are continuing, although some coastal submergence in the postglacial period is indicated (Forbes 1980).

In the late Quaternary all the arctic islands, including those in ice-free areas of the northwest, were depressed by the weight of the ice sheets. As the ice withdrew the land recovered, accompanied by a regression of the sea. The total amount of recovery in postglacial times, in general, increases from the perimeter toward the geographical center of the Laurentide ice cap in the Hudson Bay area, but the detailed picture is complex because of the survival of remnant ice caps that locally delayed the entry of the sea, and because sea level, on a global basis, was unusually low at the time of the withdrawal of the ice around the margins (Andrews 1978).

Three patterns of postglacial land/sea movement may be recognized in the Canadian arctic islands. First, in the northwest around the Beaufort Sea and particularly on Banks and Prince Patrick islands, sea level appears to have risen throughout postglacial times because of a combination of a global rise of sea level (the Flandrian transgression) and crustal sinking. Second, in an interior zone including the coasts of Prince of

Wales, Somerset, northwest Baffin, and western Devon islands, as well as adjacent smaller islands, the crust appears to have emerged continuously (but not constantly) during postglacial time, although at all periods more rapidly than the Flandrian rise of sea level (Fig. 36-4,b). Today these are emergent coasts and contain vast numbers of raised strandlines. Between the two sectors, many coasts reveal signs of both postglacial emergence and submergence. In some localities the rates of crustal rebound and Flandrian submergence coincided for a period, and the coastal processes were concentrated for a time at a particular plane. Subsequent elevation raised the resulting beaches; they are conspicuous features and may be traced for long distances on the east coast of Baffin Island (Fig. 36-4,a).

It must be assumed that similar fluctuations of sea level occurred during interglacial periods (and possibly Wisconsinan interstadials), but their influence on the coastline has been largely obliterated by subsequent events. A possible exception is at localities on the east coast of Baffin Island, where a rock platform about 5 m above high tide is preserved. The presence of till on the platform near Broughton Island indicates an age older than the last glaciation; it may be tenta-

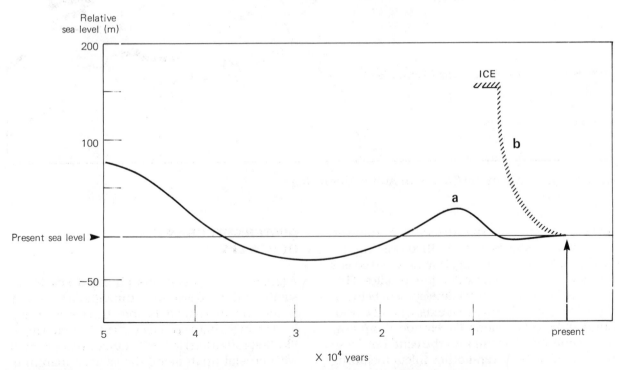

Figure 36-4. Sea level fluctuations in the past 50,000 years: a. along the eastern coasts of the Archipelago (Baffin Island); b. around the interior coasts of the southern Archipelago.

tively assigned to an interglacial high sea level. Its survival at the base of marine cliffs suggests that there has been little retreat of cliffs in crystalline Shield rocks in postglacial times.

CONTEMPORARY BEACH DEVELOPMENT

The effectiveness of littoral processes in beach development has been examined at a number of sites in the archipelago. Summaries of work on periglacial marine littoral processes are found in Bird (1967) and John and Sugden (1975). Recent studies include: Bird (1977), Kovacs and Sodhi (1980), Lauriol and Gray (1980), McCann et al. (1981), Taylor (1978, 1980), Taylor and McCann (1976), and Sadler and Serson (1981). Most processes are the same as in other parts of the world, but the presence of ice on the sea for part of the year (and in the channels of the northwestern islands frequently for several years at a time) clearly reduces the annual period in which waves are active. In many of the channels in the north or west of the archipelago, onshore high-energy sea waves are rare or nonexistent as the onset of onshore wind blows pack ice onto the shore, effectively protecting the coastline. In the late summer and early fall, strong wave action may be found around the shores of the Beaufort Sea, but the principal high-energy wave activity in the archipelago is found on the west side of Baffin Bay and Davis Strait. Swell waves from the open ocean are damped down in a few hundred meters by drift ice, but when ice is absent from the Bay and Strait in the late summer and early fall, strong wave action on the coasts follows the passage of disturbances in the Labrador Sea.

Processes associated with pack ice forced into beaches by onshore winds have attracted attention, for if oil and gas pipelines are laid between islands in the future, they will be subject to interference where they come ashore. The most conspicuous result of periglacial littoral processes is the redistribution of beach sediments, particularly large boulders that are pushed inland or concentrated off low headlands, and the formation of ridges and hummocks at the rear of beaches. These are pronounced on the beaches of the northwestern islands, where small tidal range and negligible wave activity favor the survival of pressure ridges, probably for several centuries.

The tidal range in the archipelago reaches a maximum on the coasts of the eastern islands,

especially around southeastern Baffin Island (>10 m). Boulder barricades are frequently found in sheltered waters in this sector. The barricades are ridges of boulders, with crests awash at low tide. They may be located from a few meters to 100 m or more offshore.

Permafrost must be anticipated in the ground in the vicinity of all shores in the archipelago above the high tide mark. In the western Arctic (especially the west coast of Banks Island), marine cliffs have developed in fine sand and silt in many areas, and ground ice in the form of massive ice wedges and ice layers is widespread. When the ground ice is exposed, the cliffs retreat by a combination of slumping and sediment flow as the ice melts. In these circumstances annual retreat may be in excess of several meters. Elsewhere in the archipelago, ground ice forms a small part of cliff sediments, but even so, piping at the permafrost table in the cliff and slumping accelerate retreat in cliffs of unconsolidated sediments.

STRANDFLATS

Strandflats, partly submerged arctic lowlands cut across bedrock, are a common element of many fjord coasts and have a circumpolar distribution. Although skerry coasts with a superficial resemblance to strandflats are common in the arctic Canadian Shield, the majority appear to be drowned subpaleozoic shield land surfaces that were stripped of younger sedimentary rocks in recent geological times; they have been affected by the Quaternary processes only to a minor degree. Strandflats of Quaternary origin have been described from the outer coasts of southeastern Baffin Island.

COASTAL CHARACTERISTICS OF THE PHYSIOGRAPHIC REGIONS

The main coastal features of the archipelago may be described on the basis of the major physiographic (and structural) regions (Fig. 36-5). The distribution of the coastal types described in the following pages for the archipelago south of Parry Channel is shown in Bird (1967, Figs. 70-73).

The Canadian Shield

The Shield coastlines of the archipelago are located on either side of the structural arches

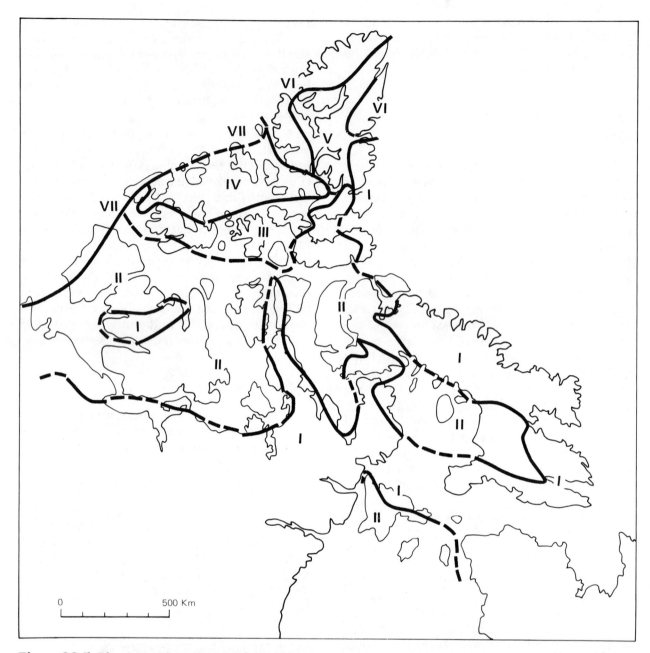

Figure 36-5. Physiographic regions of the Canadian Arctic Archipelago: I-Canadian Shield; II-Plateaus and plains of the Arctic Platform; III-Innuitian Region: Parry Plateau; IV-Innuitian Region: Sverdrup Lowland; V-Innuitian Region: Eureka Upland; VI-Innuitian Region: Ellesmere-Heiberg Mountains; VII-Arctic Coastal Plain.

that project northward from the mainland. In the west, islands in Coronation Gulf and a short length of coastline of southern Victoria Island are formed around partially submerged Precambrian diabase cuestas. The resulting cliffs, which are 300–500 m high, plunge directly into the sea or may be separated from it by extensive cobble beaches.

The Shield coasts of the central Arctic are for the great part upland coasts; hillslopes reach the sea to form headlands separated by shallow bays with shingle beaches at the rear. High cliffs (often over 250 m) are common where the structural arches in the Shield pitch steeply to the sea, as on the east side of Peel Sound, or where faults provide strong structural control, notably along the northeast coasts of Southampton Island.

The Shield coasts of the eastern Arctic are found principally on Baffin Island. The Baffin Bay–Davis Strait coast, with its high cliffs and long, penetrating fjords, gives the impression that eastern Baffin Island rises precipitously out of the sea, but a recent study has shown that nearly 75% of these coasts include a beach (Sempels 1982). Many are pocket beaches, and the majority are formed of boulders, frequently of massive size. Even on the exposed outer coast, beaches of cobbles and finer sediments occur, most conspicuously on the several forelands that separate the Baffin Highlands from the sea between Broughton Island and Clyde. These lowlands, which attain 30 km in width, have developed on Shield rocks that in most localities are covered with glacial and glaciomarine sediments. The coastlines of the forelands are smooth in planform and are mainly cliffs of unconsolidated sediments 15–75 m high, with boulder and sand beaches at their base. The forelands are separated by submerged troughs that extend seaward from fjords across the continental shelf (Gilbert 1982). The origin of the forelands is not known; they have been considered variously as emerged strandflats or the downfaulted outer edge of the Shield from which Paleozoic sediments (which are known to underlie part of Baffin Bay) have been denuded.

Several coastal areas of the Canadian Shield in the archipelago have developed on tilted, crystalline crustal blocks. On the upraised side, the shores are straight and steep (frequently cliffed); on the downtilted side, a rock plain dips gently into the sea to produce an indented, skerry coast. Small-scale examples occur at the west end of Hudson Strait, where Nottingham and Salisbury islands have steep northeast faces that rise precipitously 300 m or more out of the sea except where they are broken by small, partly drowned valleys; rocky coasts dip at a low angle beneath the sea on the southwest side. On a larger scale, Meta Incognita, the peninsula between Frobisher Bay and Hudson Strait, has a similar morphology. The Frobisher Bay side is a prominent wall, 300–500 m high, cliffed in many places and crossed by several short drowned valleys. On the southern side, the peninsula dips beneath Hudson Strait, producing a ria coastline of ice-abraded, rocky islands, small lengths of cliffs, and long, partly drowned river valleys.

Farther west on Baffin Island a less conspicuous block pattern continues to be present, but the relief is measured in a few, rather than hundreds of meters. Much of Foxe Peninsula (excluding the hills around Cape Dorset) is a flat rock plain exhumed from beneath the Paleozoic sedimentaries. Everywhere the coasts are drowned with shallow inlets penetrating far inland. The topography in many places has a pronounced structural grain, where folded metamorphic sediments form the bedrock and long curved strings of islands extend offshore. On the north and northwest side of Foxe Peninsula the exhumed surface slopes at less than 0.5 m/km beneath the sea; around the whole of the southeast and part of the northeast of the Basin, rock flats covered with muds and boulders disappear imperceptibly beneath the water.

Glacier ice, in the form of outlet glaciers, reaches the sea at a few places in eastern Baffin Island; only further north, on east Devon and more particularly on southeastern Ellesmere Island, are more extensive ice sheets in contact with the sea. In these areas, where glaciers have withdrawn from the shore (and especially on Bylot Island on the south side of Lancaster Sound), outwash and glacial sediments mantle the lower ground and coastlines have been constructed with long, smooth, sweeping gravel and sand beaches.

The Coasts of the Sedimentary Plateaus and Plains

This physiographic province is formed of numerous plateaus and lowlands developed on sedimentary rocks, predominantly horizontally bedded Paleozoic limestones. Exceptionally, adjacent to structural features such as the Boothia-Somerset arch, the sedimentaries dip steeply toward the sea.

The sectors where plateaus are the main element frequently terminate abruptly at the coast in high cliffs. Spectacular examples are found along the east coast of Somerset Island, where cliffs up to 400 m high rise directly out of the water. Similar cliffs encircle Akapatok Island in Ungava Bay; much of the Lancaster Sound coast of Devon Island and the south side of Ellesmere Island are of this type. Rock platforms, a little below low water mark, are common in front of the limestone cliffs. The inner edge, where the platforms meet the cliff, is bombarded continuously by weathered limestone fragments from the cliff face, and talus aprons mask the lower parts of many cliffs.

The remaining coasts in the sedimentary province south of Parry Channel have considerable variety depending on the detail of the terrestrial land forms. Where lowlands form the hinterland the shore is normally a flat bedrock surface dipping gently beneath the sea and mantled with limestone fragments and larger erratic boulders. The limestone coasts of much of northern and eastern Foxe Basin and the islands around King William Island are of this type. In other areas where the hinterland rises more steeply, the coast may be formed of low cliffs (often up to 30 m high) and hills covered with elevated strandlines of limestone shingle; in both cases a narrow plain several hundred meters wide covered with raised beaches and lagoons may separate the higher land from the sea. The coasts of Victoria Island and much of Prince of Wales Island are in this category, with several hundred kilometers of boulder-strewn rocky points, long straight limestone shingle beaches, and occasional shorter stretches of low cliffs.

The Arctic Coastal Plain

The Arctic Coastal Plain extends eastward from Point Barrow, Alaska, for over 200 km along the shores of the Beaufort Sea, and northwestward as far as Meighen Island. The coast has developed on a slowly subsiding continental shelf associated with an oscillating sea level; today the surface sediments on the landward side consist largely of sands and gravels of Tertiary age. Northeast of Amundsen Gulf, the Coastal Plain forms a strip of land 30–70 km wide along the western sides of the arctic islands, including Banks, Prince Patrick, Borden, Ellef Ringnes, and Meighen.

The coasts face the Arctic Ocean, but wave action is restricted by the presence throughout the year of heavy polar pack ice a few kilometers offshore. The shore is a succession of sand spits and barrier bars separated by sections of low sandy cliffs containing quantities of ground ice. At its finest development in southwestern Banks Island, lagoons and extended estuaries separate the outer beaches and the inner coast. North of Parry Channel the shores are poorly defined; shoals and low islands lie off mudflats that are the seaward edge of featureless plains of periglacially reworked Beaufort sediments.

The Coasts of the Queen Elizabeth Islands

The characteristics of coasts of the northern half of the archipelago are less easily generalized than are those south of Parry Channel. With the exception of the outer margins, the islands are part of the Innuitian orogen, and the subdivisions of this geological province provide a basis for a physiographic description of the coasts. Immediately north of Parry Channel, occupying much of Melville, Bathurst, northwest Devon, and part of southern Ellesmere islands, are long, parallel and simple Appalachian-type structures of the Parry folded belt (Fig. 36-5, III). Structural control is marked in the drowned coastline (notwithstanding postglacial emergence) with a series of east-west elongated islands and inlets, generally with gentle coastal slopes, rising to hills, ridges, and interior plateaus. Gravel and shingle beaches dominate the coastline. In the highest areas, particularly on Melville Island, the coastline closely resembles the plateau sections of the arctic plateaus and plains province.

The middle of the Queen Elizabeth Islands is occupied by the lowlands of the Sverdrup Basin. The coasts are generally flat, rising across gravel and shingle beaches to the interior. Small sections of cliffs occur on some islands. Morphological evidence of coastal drowning and more recent emergence, which are conspicuous in other parts of the archipelago, is largely absent, although postglacial marine uplift of 25–75 m is known to have occurred.

In the extreme north of the archipelago, mountains occupy the northern and northwestern quadrants of Ellesmere Island, and Axel Heiberg Island is a zone of highly folded sediments (the Eureka and Ellesmere belts) that are broken by two groups of fjords. Several are exceptionally long, including Nansen Sound, which penetrates from the Arctic Ocean to separate Axel Heiberg and Ellesmere islands. In addition there are many smaller fjords, which resemble drowned river valleys that have been modified by the passage of glaciers. The coasts generally rise steeply from the water, but emerged strandlines are common close to beaches. Along the northwest coast of Ellesmere Island for 95 km between Cape Columbia and Yelverton Bay, the Ward Hunt Ice Shelf provides the only major ice coast in the archipelago.

J. BRIAN BIRD

REFERENCES

Andrews, J. T., 1978, Sea level history of arctic coasts during the Upper Quaternary: dating, sedimentary sequences and history, *Prog. Physical Geography* **2:**375–407.

Bird, J. B., 1967, *The Physiography of Arctic Canada*, Johns Hopkins Press, Baltimore.

Bird, J. B., 1977, Coastal morphology and terrain studies, Kivitoo Peninsula, Baffin Island, *Geol. Surv. Canada Paper* 77-1C, pp. 53–55.

Forbes, D. L., 1980, Late Quaternary sea levels in southern Beaufort Sea, *Canada Geol. Surv. Paper* 80-1B, pp. 75–87.

Gilbert, R., 1982, The Broughton trough on the continental shelf of eastern Baffin Island, Northwest Territories, *Canadian Jour. Earth Sci.* **19:**1599–1607.

John, B. S., and D. E. Sugden, 1975, Coastal geomorphology of high latitudes, *Prog. Geography* **7:**52–132.

Kovacs, A., and D. S. Sodhi, 1980, Shore ice pile-up; field observations, models, theoretical analysis, *Cold Regions Science and Technology* **2:**209–288.

Lauriol, B., and J. T. Gray, 1980, Processes responsible for the concentration of boulders in the intertidal zone of Leaf Basin, Ungava, in *The Coastline of Canada,* S. B. McCann, ed., *Canada Geol. Surv. Paper* 80-10, pp. 281–290.

McCann, S. B., J. E. Dale, and P. B. Hale, 1981, Subarctic tidal flats in areas of large tidal range, southern Baffin Island, eastern Canada *Géographie physique et Quaternaire* **35:**183–204.

Sadler, H. E., and H. V. Serson, 1981, Freshwater anchor ice along an arctic beach, *Arctic* **34:**62–63.

Sempels, J. E., 1982, Coastlines of the eastern Arctic, *Arctic* **35:**170–179.

Taylor, R. B., 1978, The occurrence of grounded ice ridges and shore ice piling along the north coast of Somerset Island, N.W.T., *Arctic* **31:**133–149.

Taylor, R. B., 1980, Coastal environments along the northern shore of Somerset Island, District of Franklin, in *The Coastline of Canada,* S. B. McCann, ed., *Canada Geol. Surv. Paper* 80-10: 239–250.

Taylor, R. B., and S. B. McCann, 1976, The effect of sea and nearshore coastal processes in the Canadian Arctic Archipelago, *Rev. Géographie Montréal* **30:**123–132.

37. GREAT LAKES

The Great Lakes consist of six interconnected freshwater lakes: Superior, Michigan, Huron, St. Clair, Erie, and Ontario (Fig. 37-1). The coastline length of these lakes, including islands and connecting rivers, is about 17,000 km. The lakes are underlain, and in places bordered, by rock. Precambrian igneous and metamorphic rocks of the Canadian Shield underlie Lake Superior and the northern shore of Georgian Bay, whereas Paleozoic dolomites, limestones, shales, and sandstones underlie the other lakes. Pleistocene surficial deposits, mostly till and lake-related glacial deposits, mantle the rocks over much of the basin. Major structural features of the basin include the Appalachian Basin to the southeast, which is succeeded to the northwest by the Findlay-Algonquin Arch and then the Michigan Basin; most of the northern part of the Great Lakes Basin is surrounded by the Wisconsin, North Huron, Algonquin Park, and Adirondack structural highs. The shore deposits consist of rock and/or surficial deposits; these deposits are commonly fronted by narrow (< 15 m wide) sand or cobble beaches.

Although the overall physical characteristics of the basin were probably formed before Pleistocene glaciation—Lakes Michigan, Huron, Erie, and Ontario are underlain by shales and carbonates—the Pleistocene epoch left the most visible legacy to the basin in the form of the easily erodible Pleistocene deposits that make up much of the lake bottoms and shores. Isostatic rebound following glacial retreat also has had a profound effect on the basin, notably with respect to lake elevations.

The lakes are a well-regulated natural system because of their small connecting channels; however, the levels of two of the lakes, Superior and Ontario, are regulated by man. Human development along the shores of the lakes is common, particularly near major urban centers such as Toronto, Cleveland, and Chicago.

Because the Great Lakes are located in the interior of the continent, between the source regions of the polar and tropical air masses, the basin has complex, rapidly changing weather patterns. However, the lakes exert a modifying effect on temperature and humidity by acting as heat sources or sinks. Annual precipitation ranges from about 70 cm in the northwest to about 95 cm in the southeast. The prevailing winds come from the west. The winds are the main cause of the surface waves and currents, and can produce short-term fluctuations in lake level during intense storms; these fluctuations can be as great as 5 m on Lake Erie. Because the lakes are small, astronomic tides are limited, usually less than 5 cm in range; however, seasonal fluctuations related largely to variations in precipitation and evaporation cause a winter-to-summer range of about 35 cm. Prolonged periods (several years) of abnormal precipitation/evaporation result in long-term water-level fluctuations of 1–2 m.

INDIVIDUAL LAKES AND SPECIFIC SITES

Lake Superior, the largest and the uppermost (183 m above sea level) of the Great Lakes, has a coastline length of about 4385 km, including 1000 km on islands. The northern shore consists mostly of Precambrian rock; there are cliffs as high as 240 m fronted in places by talus and

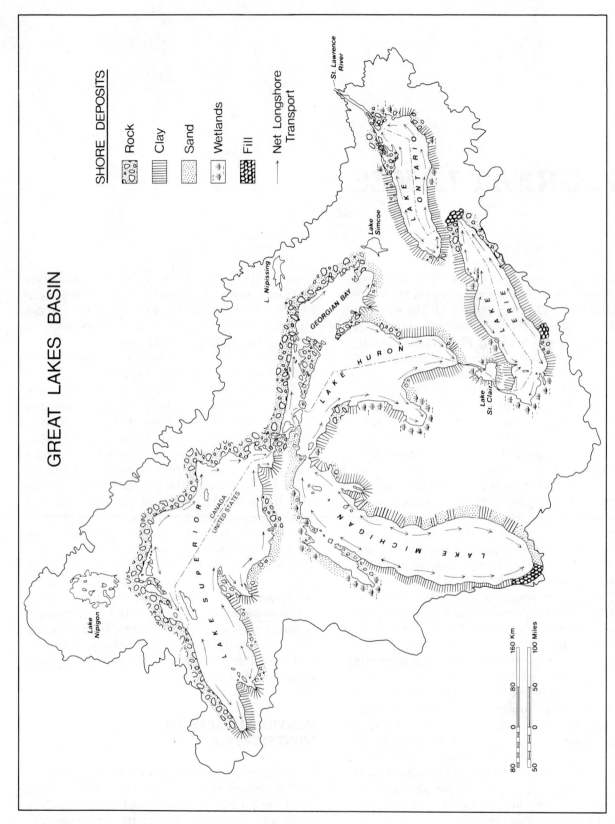

GREAT LAKES BASIN

SHORE DEPOSITS

- Rock
- Clay
- Sand
- Wetlands
- Fill
- → Net Longshore Transport

Lake Nipigon

LAKE SUPERIOR

CANADA
UNITED STATES

L. Nipissing

Lake Simcoe

GEORGIAN BAY

LAKE HURON

LAKE MICHIGAN

Lake St. Clair

LAKE ERIE

LAKE ONTARIO

St. Lawrence River

80   0   80   160 Km

50   0   50   100 Miles

Figure 37-1. The Great Lakes basin, showing the margin of the basin, the lakes, lakeshore deposits, and net longshore transport directions.

cobble pocket beaches and deep bays such as Thunder Bay and Nipigon Bay. The southern shore also consists mostly of Precambrian rock, but the relief is lower (from essentially no relief up to 60 m) and more irregular. In addition to the rock are clay banks, sand and gravel banks and dunes, and marshlands. Sand and cobble beaches separated by rocky stretches without beaches are typical of this shore. Noteworthy stretches along the southern shore include those of Pictured Rocks National Lakeshore (Plate 37-1) and the Grand Sable sand dunes, Quaternary deposits that rise about 60 m above the lake. The Apostle Islands National Lakeshore lies near the west end of the lake. The overflow of regulated Lake Superior drops 7 m in its journey of about 60 km down the St. Marys River before spilling into Lake Huron. Lake Huron is connected to Lake Michigan by the wide Straits of Mackinac, and the two lakes are considered hydrologically as one, both being at 176 m above sea level.

Lake Michigan, the only lake to lie entirely in the United States, has a coastline length of about 2635 km. The northwestern shore, which includes Green Bay, consists of wetlands, limestone banks and bluffs (up to 60 m high), and banks and slopes made up of Pleistocene sediment. Further south, along the western shore, the overall relief increases as till bluffs up to 40 m high begin to make up more of the shore; this setting continues to the Chicago, Illinois/Gary, Indiana reach at the southern end of the lake, which is largely fronted by fill. Northward, along the eastern shore, sand bluffs and dunes up to 135 m high, separated by till bluffs and slopes, dominate the shore until the northeastern reach, which consists in part of marshes and sand and clay banks in addition to till bluffs. Grand Traverse Bay lies along this northeastern reach. In general, narrow sand and gravel beaches characterize the northwestern and northeastern reaches, narrow sand beaches the southwestern shore, and broad sand beaches the southeastern shore. Noteworthy stretches along the southern shore include the Indiana Dunes National Lakeshore and the Sleeping Bear Dunes National Lakeshore (Plate 37-2).

Lake Huron, which has a coastline length of about 6155 km, including 3700 km on islands, has more islands than any of the other Great Lakes. Moreover, a major bay—Georgian Bay, almost a great lake itself, and its northwestern extension, North Channel—and a smaller, yet large bay, Saginaw Bay, lie to the northeast and west respectively of the lake. Along the west side of the lake,

from the northwest into Saginaw Bay, the shore is made up of wetlands and low-relief banks and slopes of sand, clay, or rock. South from the point forming the eastern shore of Saginaw Bay, rock banks pass into till bluffs up to 12 m high. Except for the wetland areas, most of the shore is fronted by narrow sand beaches that increase in width toward the southern end of the lake. Along the east side of the lake the southeastern shore consists mainly of wave-cut, slowly eroding till and glaciolacustrine sediment bluffs 3–25 m in height. These are usually fronted by beaches of varying widths. Separating the main body of Lake Huron from Georgian Bay and North Channel are the Bruce Peninsula and Manitoulin Island, which together form the northeasterly margin of the Michigan Basin. They are characterized by gently sloping limestone shores on the Lake Michigan side and steep limestone cliffs on the Georgian Bay-North Channel side. The northern shore of North Channel and the northeastern shore of Georgian Bay, best known as the 30,000 Islands area (Plate 37-3), are carved in the relatively low-lying bedrock of the Canadian Shield. Sand beaches are atypical for the North Channel-Georgian Bay area with the exception of the southeastern shore of Georgian Bay, which is characterized by a chain of wide and gently sloping beaches, such as Wasaga Beach.

The river/lake system (St. Clair River, Lake St. Clair, and Detroit River) that connects Lakes Huron and Erie flows through a flat low-relief tract of land, with only a 2.5 m fall over a distance of about 120 km. Lake St. Clair, by far the smallest of the Great Lakes, has a shoreline length of about 272 km and is characterized by wetlands, especially around the St. Clair river delta and manmade structures along the western side of the lake.

Lake Erie, the shallowest and southernmost of the Great Lakes, has a coastline length of about 1400 km, including 116 km on islands. Along the south shore of the lake from the western end, the relief is low, and the shore is made up of wetlands, clay and rock banks, and sand barriers. East of the islands to Erie, Pennsylvania, till and shale make up banks and slopes up to 30 m high; east of Erie the shore is made up largely of shale bluffs commonly capped by till. The western end of the north shore is quite complex stratigraphically, with both low (3 m) and high (20 m) glacial drift banks, while the central reach from Pelee Point to Long Point is more uniform, consisting of eroding till bluffs (up to 40 m high) capped by sandy deposits increasing in thickness to the east. From

Long Point easterly, the shore is made up of low limestone bedrock outcrops and up to 15 m high glacial-deposit bluffs. Narrow sand beaches front the Lake Erie shore except the rockbound shore along the eastern end, where pocket beaches are located between headlands. Specific areas of notable interest include the sandy spits at Pelee, Rondeau, Long Point, and Presque Ile and the carbonate islands at the west end of the lake.

The Niagara River joins Lakes Erie and Ontario. It is just over 50 km long and transports an average flow of 57,000 m³/sec over the Niagara dolomite escarpment, falling about 50 m to create the spectacular Niagara Falls. The remaining 50 m difference between the levels of these two lakes is spread over 10 km of a much narrower river channel below the falls, where the thundering current rushes through a deep gorge before it dies out in Lake Ontario.

Lake Ontario, at an elevation of 74 m above sea level, is the last lake of the Great Lakes chain. It has a coastline length of about 1145 km including 125 km on islands. Along the south shore of the lake from the western end are bluffs up to 18 m high composed of till and outwash. Further east, the bluffs decrease in size, and sand barriers and marshes appear. At the eastern end of the south shore there are till bluffs (up to 21 m high), sand barriers, dunes, and marshes. Beaches for the most part are narrow and are composed of sand and/or gravel. Along the north side of the lake the shore from the Niagara River to the Trent River is typically composed of till and glaciolacustrine sediments that make up smoothly curving banks and bluffs from less than 1 m to as much as 100 m high, such as Scarborough Bluffs (Plate 37-4). Beaches of varying widths and lengths front the shore, and Hamilton Harbor at the west end of the lake is fronted by a baymouth bar, the Burlington Bar. East of the Trent River, or where Prince Edward County Peninsula is attached to the mainland by a narrow isthmus, the Lake Ontario shore is irregular. The peninsula, a 1010 km² low limestone plateau, has long bays (Bay of Quinte, Prince Edward Bay) or inlets often closed by barriers (i.e., baymouth bars) (Wellington Bay, Athol Bay). The eastern end of the peninsula adjoins the St. Lawrence River, which transports the outflow of Lake Ontario some 800 km downstream to the Atlantic Ocean.

While there is a great deal of literature concerning the coast of the Great Lakes, the reader is referred to the following publications in particular: Chapman and Putnam (1966), Hough (1958), Limnology Work Group (1976), Sly and Lewis (1972), and U.S. Army Engineer Division, North Central (1971).

C. H. CARTER
W. S. HARAS

REFERENCES

Chapman, L. J., and D. F. Putnam, 1966, *The Physiography of Southern Ontario,* University of Toronto Press, Toronto.

Hough, J. L., 1958, *Geology of the Great Lakes,* University of Illinois Press, Urbana.

Limnology Work Group, 1976, *Limnology of Lakes and Embayments,* Great Lakes Basin Commission, Ann Arbor.

Sly, P. G., and C. F. M. Lewis, 1972, The Great Lakes of Canada-Quaternary geology and limnology, *22nd Internat. Geol. Cong.,* Montreal, Quebec.

U.S. Army Engineer Division, North Central, 1971, *National Shoreline Study,* Great Lakes Region Inventory Report, U.S. 93d Congress, 1st Session, House Document No. 93-121, Vol. V, 1-221.

Plate 37-1. Cambrian sandstone cliff of the Pictured Rocks National Lakeshore, southern shore of Lake Superior (photo by B. Mills).

Plate 37-2. Sandy slope capped by the partially eroded Sleeping Bear dune, eastern shore of Lake Michigan. Sleeping Bear dune, which lies more than 120 m above the lake, was once completely vegetated and formed a prominent landmark when viewed from the lake (photo by U.S. National Park Service).

Plate 37-3. Islands formed on Canadian Shield, 30,000 Islands area, Georgian Bay-Lake Huron (photo by N. Rukavina).

Plate 37-4. Scarborough bluffs and lake fill, northwestern shore of Lake Ontario, Toronto waterfront. The 100 m high bluffs, composed of glacial deposits, reflect both mass wasting and wave erosion processes (photo by K. Weaver).

38. GREENLAND

The Greenland coastal regions owe their present appearance mainly to two basic factors: (1) the variety of rock types, and (2) the activity of glacier ice, during both the Pleistocene and the Holocene. In general, a universal coastal geometry may be recognized, although for most sectors the influence of sea ice is evident.

By far the main part of the Greenland west and southeast coasts consists of bedrock (Fig. 38-1). The coast facing the Polar Sea is primarily built up of Precambrian sedimentary rock types, whereas the northeast coast is dominated by Paleozoic and Mesozoic formations (Fig. 38-1).

Younger geological strata, such as erodible Cretaceous sandstone and plateau basalt of Tertiary age are found both at the east and the west coast, but only between 69° and 72° N latitude (Escher and Watt 1976).

Most of the materials found along the Greenland coasts are thus very resistant to marine erosion, and the coastal outline may well be explained by considering the former extent of the icecap. The appearance of the present coast has been greatly influenced by the inland ice, which covered nearly all of it until about 12,000 years ago. This influence is seen in the enormous fjord systems (Plate 38-1), where the icecap, through selective erosion along the Tertiary valleys, created overdeepened fjord systems in the already existing landscape. This sort of "directed" erosion is in contrast to the development of the archipelagic coasts, the skerries, where glacial erosion has been less controlled (Plate 38-2).

Greenland covers an area of about 2.2×10^6 km², of which only 342,700 km² are ice free. The precise length of the coastline is unknown, but is estimated to be at least 40,000 km. The range of

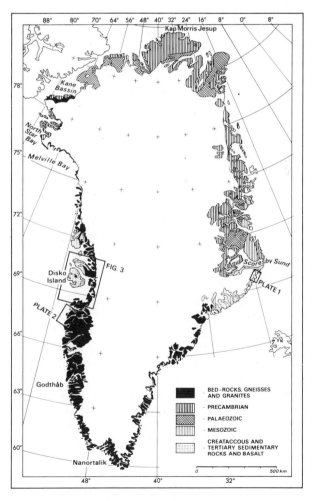

Figure 38-1. The configuration of Greenland and its main geological provinces.

variation in the coastal geomorphology is never-theless relatively limited. About nine-tenths of the coast is rocky, with more than 100 deep, long and heavily branching fjord complexes. A magnif-icent example is the Scoresby Sound fjord sys-tem at the east coast. With its 11 fjords—with lengths as great as 325 km and depths of 1450 m —it is the largest of its kind in the world.

Present marine erosion and accumulation phe-nomena are not conspicuous, but may be found as pocket beaches with shingle-to-boulders as the dominating sediment. In the basalt and lime-stone provinces, however, the coastline does show marine-induced elements (Plate 38-3). On the island of Disko, there are high cliffs along the south and west coast, whereas the east coast has long barriers with lagoons and marshes (Nielsen 1969).

Finally, Greenland has coasts where glacier ice makes up the contact between land and sea. Numerous valley glaciers discharge into the sea, some of them producing icebergs. In northwest Greenland, at Melville Bay, an ice front up to 40 m high forms an impressive coastal stretch for almost 500 km and farther northward, at Kane Basin, about 100 km.

When annual mean wave energy levels are cal-culated for the outer coast on the basis of wind statistics and fetch, far higher values are found than those that actually occur. This effect is partly due to the freezing-up of the sea, and partly to the constant masses of sea ice coming from the Polar Sea. These pass along the east coast, then con-tinue northward again along the west coast up to about 65° N latitude (the Irminger Current). In this connection the many icebergs from the calving glaciers should also be mentioned. All these types of ice hamper the formation of waves. Accretion coasts at exposed locations show great morphological variations as they develop under low-energy conditions because of the sheltering effect of the ice. When occasionally, there is no ice, the full energy of the ocean sea waves gains access to the shore. Nanok (ice bear) hunters on the northeast coast have thus reported that one single gale completely changed the configuration of the shore, which had been stable "as far back as could be remembered." In this case the Storis, the constantly south-moving ice-laden current from the Polar Sea, had been blocked for some time by heavy ice farther north, and thus could not exert its usual subduing effect on the waves. Although the situation is rare, such events must also be considered in a coastal morphol-ogy interpretation.

The tide along the west coast is primarily of the type called mixed tide. Mean spring tide range varies from about 3 m in the southwest at Nanortalik (60°N latitude), 4.5 m at Godthåb (64°N), 2.5 m at Disko Island (70°N), to 3.5 m at North Star Bay (77°N). The coasts facing the Polar Sea have almost no tide; only 0.3 m has been recorded at Kap Morris Jesup (83°40′N). Along the east coast, the mean spring tide is about 3 m in the southernmost part, with decreasing val-ues northward, to below 1 m at Nordostrundingen (the northeastern corner of Greenland, at 81°N).

When the sea freezes in winter, the tide is of great significance because of ice-foot formation (Plate 38-4). The morphological effect on sedi-mentary coasts is partly formation of thermokarst on the backshore, partly accumulation of sedi-ment, or erosion, when parts of the ice foot, with its content of beach material, are pressed up upon the shore or rafted away from it. These processes result in structures characteristic of arctic beaches. Thus it is not uncommon to find sediments alien to the environment, a kind of textural contamination caused by stranded, sediment-loaded fragments from the ice foot (Fig. 38-2 and Plate 38-5) (Nielsen 1978). The ice foot may also influence rocky coasts by breaking off rock fragments in the springtime, when the warmer sea melts the ice foot from below, so that it breaks off and falls into the sea (Fig. 38-2) (Nielsen 1979).

When studying coastal morphology in Green-land, especially as far as sedimentary coasts are concerned, one must also consider the wave effect caused by large capsizing icebergs. Though rare, this type of wave is huge, in both height and length. Thus wave-transported sediment has been found 15 m above sea level in a fjord with a very limited fetch (Nielsen 1969).

Throughout most of the Quaternary period, the icecap covered Greenland, though varying in extent; when the climate improved about 10,000–12,000 years ago, marked displacements of the shoreline took place. The reduction in ice mass resulted in a rapid, isostatic uplift of the coastal region. Though it was only a relative upheaval of land, we can recognize it today because raised marine terraces are frequent along the Greenland coasts (Plate 38-6).

In East and West Greenland the upheaval of land started about 9,000 years ago and apparently ended 4000–5000 years later (Hjort 1979). A similar development seems to have taken place in North Greenland, although somewhat de-layed by the later melting of the icecap in this

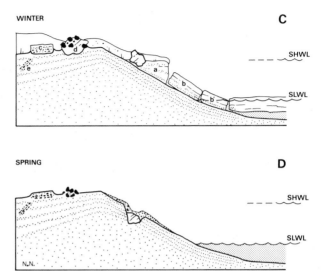

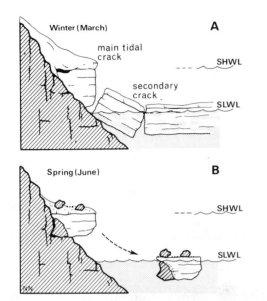

Figure 38-2. Ice-foot erosion on a rocky coast. *A.* Winter situation. During the period from high-water level to low-water level, the sea ice adjoining the ice foot does not move down in a slow, continuous motion, but rather in jerks. This exerts a powerful, mechanical influence on the rocks. *B.* Spring situation. When the sea ice has disappeared from the coast, the ice foot melts primarily from below (snow on the top has an insulating effect). At low water, the ice foot can break loose and tear off pieces of rock. *C.* Ice foot on a beach, winter. The characteristic cracking of the sea ice in front of the ice foot is caused by the low angle of the

foreshore. Under the ice foot (a) the sediments are packed solid during the whole winter, whereas sediments get embedded in the icefloes (b and b'), which flow away in spring or will be pressed or thrown up on the backshore (c). Ice cakes (d) with solid frozen sediment, and (e) icefloe-deposited sediment structure are of an earlier date. *D.* Springtime. Almost all ice has melted away, and the surface of foreshore and backshore is very uneven. Ice lumps buried under sediment above high-water level will not disappear until the summer months.

Figure 38-3. Isolines for the upper marine limit developed during the Holocene deglaciation in the Disko Bay area, central Western Greenland. The numbers indicate meters and refer to present sea level. Black areas indicate the present glaciation.

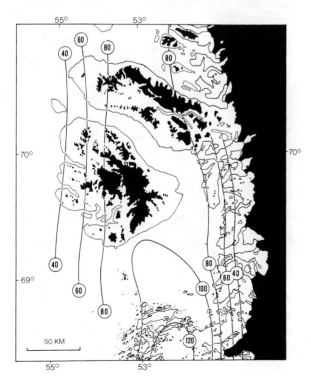

part of the country. Thus the formation of shorelines, today lying 10 m above sea-level, has been dated to 3000–4000 years ago (Weidick 1972, Stäblein 1975).

Shores in the form of marine terraces and beach ridges reach elevations of about 60 m in South Greenland, compared with 100–200 m in the central part of West Greenland, even 216 m above present sea level has been measured in East Greenland (Fig. 38-3).

Only the main trends in coastal development have been outlined. The upheaval of land has varied from one region to the other because of local variations during the melting phase.

Minor, secondary, and relative fluctuations in sea level that can be recorded today must be primarily related to eustatic changes in sea level (Humlum et al. 1980). In connection with "the little ice age," the climatic deterioration that set in during the seventeenth century, a general subsidence of land of about 1 m has been recorded; inundated house ruins have been found. Since the 1940s, a weak upheaval has been taking place.

NIELS NIELSEN

REFERENCES

Escher, A., and W. S. Watt, eds., 1976, *Geology of Greenland,* Geol. Survey of Greenland.

Hjort, C., 1979, Glaciation in northern East Greenland during the late Weichselian and Early Flandrian, *Boreas* **8**(3):281–296.

Humlum, O., *et al.,* 1980, Arktisk Geomorfologi, Enoks havn, Disko, *Geo. Noter No. 5,* pp. 1–142.

Nielsen, N., 1969, Morphological studies on the eastern coast of Disko, West Grenland, *Geog. Tidsskr.* **68**:1–35.

Nielsen, N., 1978, Kystmorfologi i arktiske områder (Arktisk Geomorfologi), *GO. Geografforlaget, Brenderup* pp. 242–247.

Nielsen, N., 1979, Ice-foot processes. Observations of erosion on a rocky coast, Disko, West Greenland, *Zeitschr. Geomorphologie,* N.F., **23**(3):321–331.

Stäblein, G., 1975, Eisrandlagen und Küstenentwicklung in West-Grönland, *Polarforschung* **45**(2).

Weidick, A., 1972, *Holocene Shore-lines and Glacial Stages in Greenland—An Attempt at Correlation,* Geol. Survey of Greenland, Report 41.

Plate 38-1. Satellite photo (Landsat 1) covering the area just south of Scoresby Sound. Fjords with icebergs and glaciers dominate the coastal region (photo by NASA).

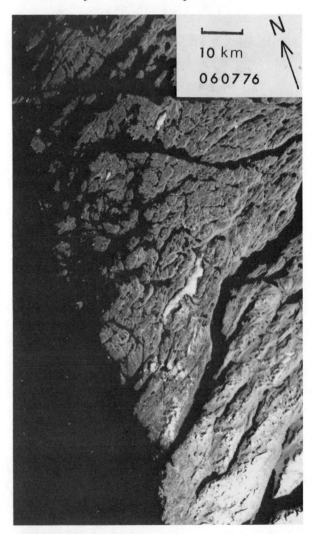

Plate 38-2. Satellite photo (Landsat 1) of the skerries region in the central part of West Greenland (cf. Fig. 38-1). The icecap lies about 60 km E of this section (photo by NASA).

Plate 38-3. Cliffs in a raised marine terrace. Cirques with rock glaciers are common along the west, north, and northeast coasts of Disko Island. In many places the rock glacier front is forming active cliffs. The upper edge of the plateau basalt lies about 900 m above sea level (photo by N. Nielsen).

Plate 38-4. Ice foot in the southern part of Disko Island. The tidal ice-foot platform is difficult to recognize because of the many small and larger ice blocks that have been pressed upward by drifting sea ice or thrown up by waves during formation of the ice foot and later covered with snow (photo by N. Nielsen).

Plate 38-5. "Textural contamination" on a barrier beach, southeast Disko, just after the sea ice has disappeared (1/6/1976). A great part of the ice foot is still left and will not melt away until in July. The barrier is built up of yellowish, well-sorted medium-grained quartz sand, and the stone heap that has been embedded in a big ice lump will appear as a marked, alien element in the former homogeneous beach material (photo by N. Nielsen).

Plate 38-6. Raised marine terraces in Mellemfjord, west Disko. The border between the scree from the basalt rock and the upper terrace edge lies 53 m above sea level and was formed about 9000 years ago (photo by N. Nielsen).

39. ICELAND

Iceland is a volcanic island of 103,100 km². Its coastline is quite irregular in outline, with the exception of the southern coast between the Ölfusá and Djúpivogur, where large volumes of sediment are carried to the sea, especially by powerful glacial streams (Fig. 39-1).

Affected by the numerous arctic- or polar-front cyclones, Iceland is windy. Wind speed and direction are very variable, but the most frequent winds blow from the sector between southeast and northeast, indicating that the main track of the depressions lies close to the southern coast. Gale force winds are common.

Mean spring tidal ranges are generally 1.5–4 m,

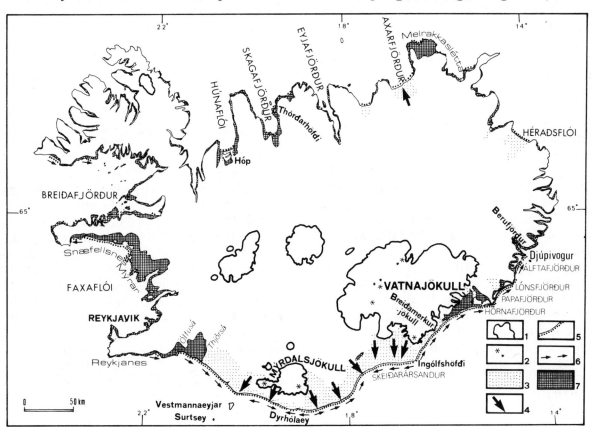

Figure 39-1. Some coastal features of Iceland. 1. Glaciers; 2. Subglacial volcanoes and/or high temperature fields; 3. Outwash plains (sandurs) near the coastline; 4. Track of main glacier bursts (jökulhlaups); 5. Beaches and barrier spits; 6. Predominant longshore drifts; 7. Strandflats.

and a little more along some parts of the western coasts.

The northwestern peninsula presents a typical rocky coastline of deep fjords. Megacliffs (300–600 m) are sometimes affected by landslides. Narrow discontinuous strandflats fringe some inland scarps. The submarine strandflat of Breidafjördur is very broad and presents a swarm of islands, skerries, and shoals. Around the Snaefellsnes, the width of the emerged strandflats ranges from 10 or 20 m up to 30 km in the Mýrar district. Low cliffs in Holocene lava flows are found in the western part of the peninsula, whereas sandy barrier spits, lagoons, and tidal flat areas form its southern coast. Here the barrier spits are unusually yellow because the sand is almost entirely shell.

South of Reykjavik, the Reykjanes peninsula corresponds to the top of the Mid-Atlantic Ridge and, as a consequence, it is a young volcanic area. Low cliffs cut in postglacial lava flows predominate. High-level storm beaches of loose boulders and pebbles are piled up on the top of some cliffs because the winter wave conditions along this coast are very severe. Large beaches are uncommon, but small isolated dune fields can be found.

From Thorlákshöfn to Djúpivogur the southern coastline lies in a storm-wave environment (Hine and Boothroyd 1978). It is a mesotidal and high-sediment discharge coast, built of loose material. Rocky headlands (Dyrhólaey, Ingólfshöfdi) form the major hinge points of flat and broad barrier spits (King 1956).

The western part of this coastline, apart from glaciers, is backed by a raised bedrock plain with marshy areas. Between the Ölfusá and the Thjórsá rivers, a rocky shore platform forms the top of the Thjórsá lavas. An abrupt submarine slope of 50 m high corresponds to the front of this lava flow. Southwest of Vestmannaeyjar, a new island, Surtsey, began to develop in 1963. The postvolcanic period has offered the opportunity to study erosional activity in an environment of strong winds and high wave energy. Rapid recession of the lava cliffs was noticed at the southwest coast, whereas a cuspate foreland was built on the sheltered northern coast by beach drift (Norrman 1980).

Extensive outwash plains (sandurs) spread south of Mýrdalsjökull and Vatnajökull. The bulk of the sediment is supplied by proglacial streams. But sediment discharge has been greatly enhanced by periodic and frequent glacier-burst floods (jökulhlaups), caused by subglacial volcanic erup-

tions or by the sudden draining of ice-dammed lakes. The amount of sediment carried to the coast during an average jökulhlaup of the Skeidarársandur is equivalent to about 70–80 years of sediment discharge under normal flow conditions. The aggradation of sandurs is accordingly accompanied by fast shore progradation. Longshore drift redistributes the sediment very quickly. South of Skeidarársandur, the annual longshore gross sediment flux is about 4–6 million cubic m. The coast of Skeidarársandur has few beach ridges, no tidal inlets with associated ebb deltas, no estuaries, no true lagoons, and no marshes or tidal flats, because of the high rates of fluvial and littoral sedimentation. Maximum wave energy and lowest discharge of glacial streams occur during winter and spring. Therefore, the distributaries are deflected in the direction of net longshore sediment transport. In summer, with low wave energy and high meltwater discharge (Plate 39-1) more direct courses through the barriers are eroded (Ward et al. 1976).

The so-called Hornafjördur, Papafjördur, Lónsfjördur, and Álftafjördur are not true fjords. These shallow lagoons are almost completely surrounded by low-lying land (strandflats and sandurs). Large volumes of material are deposited in the lagoons, and deltas are presently growing. Tidal inlets are open; narrow marshes and tidal flats fringe some parts of the lagoons.

North of Djúpivogur another typical fjord coast is exposed. The lava flows of the deeply dissected Tertiary plateau dip to the west. The greatest altitudes are located relatively close to the coast. The rough strandflats are more continuous in the south, where they cut across the strata. Small parallel asymmetric rocky headlands are to be found, as a consequence of differential marine erosion (Fig. 39-2). The headlands correspond to the strongest and thickest flows. Some dykes have become prominent ridges or walls, others excavated, especially when made of acid and composite rocks. Transverse, oblique, and longitudinal types of structural coastlines may be distinguished.

Héradsflói is a typical sandur fed by Vatnajökull far from the glacier. Dune fields (nebkas) can be found at the back of the barrier beach. The northern coast of Melrakkaslétta is very irregular. It shows a succession of lagoons and lakes separated from the open sea by wide embankments of boulders.

Hrútafjördur and Eyjafjördur are the only true fjords of the northern coast. South of Axarfjördur, a broad sandur is occasionally reached by

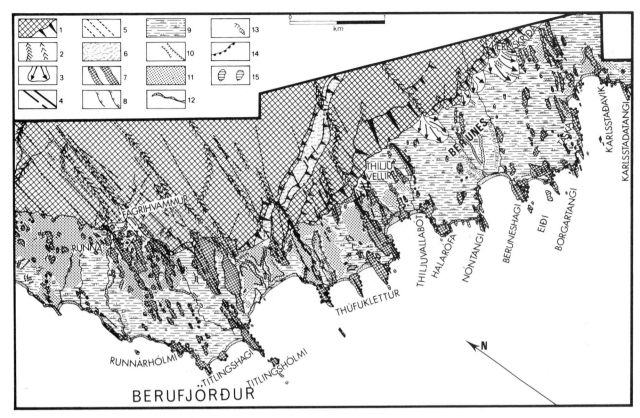

Figure 39-2. The strandflat of Berufjördur, north of Djúpivogur: a rocky coastline with transversal structure. 1. Mountainous slopes and main scarps; 2. Gorges; 3. Talus cone; 4. Prominent dykes; 5. Excavated dykes, faults, fractures; 6. Outcrop of volcanic tuff; 7. Rocky surface of basalt flows; 8. Scarps in basalts; 9. Marshes and swamps; 10. Eroded soils and scarps in unconsolidated material; 11. Raised beaches; 12. Beaches; 13. Marine platform; 14. Cliffs; 15. Lakes and ponds.

jökulhlaups, and some old barrier beaches attest to littoral progradation. Emphasis must also be laid on two morphological sites: the double tombolo of Thórdarhöfdi in Skagafjördur (Bodéré 1973), and the narrow 7 km-long sand bar that divides the lagoon Hóp (Húnaflói).

Raised beaches are known in many parts of Iceland (Jónsson 1957; Einarsson 1961). The height of the marine limit differs from place to place: 130–140 m in the west, only 35–50 m in the north, the east, and the south. The highest shorelines have been dated at 12,300–9,600 B.P. Emergence was rapid. The sea reached approximately the present level by 9,000 B.P. and the isostatic uplift was completed 3,000 years later. In the interim, the marine transgression was in equilibrium with the isostatic recovery. Before 3,000 B.P., the sea level seems to have stood at 2–4 m below the present level. A small further transgression is supposed to have taken place (Thorarinsson 1956).

Roches moutonnées, striations, and some till cover indicate that the Icelandic strandflats (Plate 39-2) must have existed before the last glaciation.

JEAN-CLAUDE BODÉRÉ

REFERENCES

Bodéré, J. C., 1973, Le tombolo double de Thórdarhöfdi, *Norois,* **78:**213–235.

Einarsson, T., 1961, *Pollenanalytische Untersuchungen zur spät- und post-glazialen Klimageschichte Islands,* Sonderveröffentlichungen des Geologischen Instituts der Universität Köln 6.

Hine, A. C., and J. C. Boothroyd, 1978, Morphology, processes, and recent sedimentary history of a glacial-outwash plain shoreline, southern Iceland, *Jour. Sed. Petrology* **48:**901–920.

Jónsson, J., 1957, Notes on changes of sea-level in Iceland, *Geog. Annaler* **39:**143–212.

King, C. A. M., 1956, The coast of south-east Iceland near Ingólfshöfdi, *Geog. Jour.* **122:**241–246.

Norrman, J. O., 1980, Coastal erosion and slope development in Surtsey Island, Iceland, *Zeitschr Geomorphologie* **34:**20–38.

Thorarinsson, S., 1956, *The Thousand Years Struggle against Ice and Fire,* Bókaútgáfa Menningarsjóds.

Ward, L. G., M. F. Stephen, and D. Nummedal, 1976, Hydraulics and morphology of glacial outwash distributaries, Skeidarársandur, Iceland, *Jour. Sed. Petrology* **46:**770–777.

Plate 39-1. The coastline south of Breidamerkurjökull. A. Glacier; B. Proglacial lake Jökulsárlón with icebergs; C. Proglacial stream Jökulsá; D. Old sandurs; E. Frontal moraines (1890–1900); F. Fluted moraines; G. Barrier spit (photo by J.-C. Bodéré).

Plate 39-2. The rocky strandflat south of Álftafjördur with structural headlands. *A.* Scree; *B.* Raised beach (photo by J.-C. Bodéré).

40. NORWAY

Only a few works on the geomorphology of the coast of Norway (Fig. 40-1) have been published, most of them dealing with the fjords and the strandflat. Reusch (1894) introduced the term strandflat and discussed its form and origin. Nansen (1922) made a substantial contribution to the subject. The Hardangerfjord was treated by Holtedahl (1975), who also dealt with the strandflat and the bankflat of the coast of Møre (Holtedahl 1955, 1960). The strandflat had its natural place in a geomorphological study of the Lofoten-Vesterålen area by Møller and Sollid (1973). Strøm (1961) based his short description of the coast on general geomorphological features and landscape types. In addition, shore zone and coastal features are mentioned in different works dealing with Quaternary geology.

The steep western margin and the more gentle eastern slope of the Scandinavian land block strongly influence the type of coast to be found. Further, the zone of the wave attack, the shore, is in Norway composed mainly of bedrock, which makes it necessary to deal with both coastal and shore zone morphology (Klemsdal 1979). A classification of the Norwegian coast has to be built on a combination of the morphology of the shore zone and the land bordering it (Klemsdal 1982). Thus it is natural to consider the shore zone before dealing with coastal types.

THE SHORE ZONE

Along the Norwegian coast the shore zone is mainly a combination of gently and steeply sloping ice-smoothed rocky shores and stony beaches. Next to this comes the abrasion shore, while sandy and clayey beaches are found only at special localties. *Gently sloping ice-smoothed rocky shores* have an enormous variety of forms; from the smallest roches moutonnées (only a few square meters in size and a meter high) to the largest (several tens of meters in both length and height), plus a combination of roches moutonnées, more or less gently sloping ice-smoothed rocky sides with some plastic scouring forms engraved in them. Steep or nearly vertical sides, ice-smoothed or glacially scoured and plucked, plunging into the sea are characteristic of the *steeply sloping rocky shore.*

Abrasion shores are found along small stretches where marine abrasion favored by frost action has been able to transform the glacial heritage. Abrasion forms like notches, stacks, geos, and abrasion platforms in front of cliffs have been produced.

In some places along the coast, Quaternary sediments, mainly till, have been reworked by waves. Winnowing of the finer particles has left the larger ones behind and accumulated the finest material in sheltered areas, producing several types of beaches.

Boulder beach, the lag of boulders little affected by the waves, has been worked out either in till in front of a moraine cliff, or in ground moraine dipping gently into the sea.

Stony beach is either erosional, with large stones, in situ, rounded by the sea, or depositional, with smaller, well-rounded stones often forming a beach ridge. Shingle beaches are almost nonexistent in Norway. A combination of boulder and stony beaches is the most common beach type along the shores of Norway.

Sandy beach is a littoral accumulation of material chiefly washed out of till or fluvioglacial de-

273

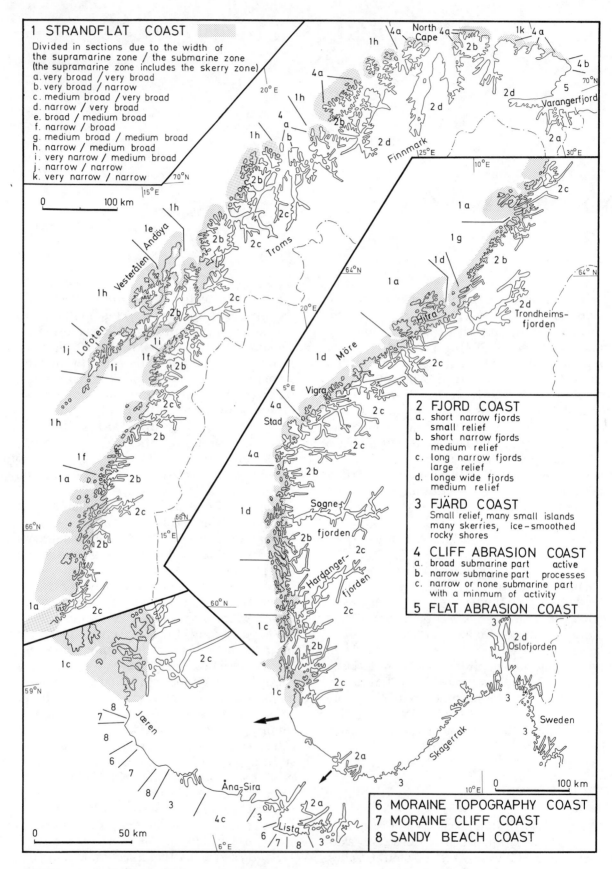

1 STRANDFLAT COAST

Divided in sections due to the width of
the supramarine zone / the submarine zone
(the supramarine zone includes the skerry zone)
a. very broad / very broad
b. very broad / narrow
c. medium broad / very broad
d. narrow / very broad
e. broad / medium broad
f. narrow / broad
g. medium broad / medium broad
h. narrow / medium broad
i. very narrow / medium broad
j. narrow / narrow
k. very narrow / narrow

0   100 km

2 FJORD COAST
a. short narrow fjords
   small relief
b. short narrow fjords
   medium relief
c. long narrow fjords
   large relief
d. longe wide fjords
   medium relief

3 FJÄRD COAST
Small relief, many small islands
many skerries, ice-smoothed
rocky shores

4 CLIFF ABRASION COAST
a. broad submarine part   active
b. narrow submarine part   processes
c. narrow or none submarine part
   with a minmum of activity

5 FLAT ABRASION COAST

0   100 km

6 MORAINE TOPOGRAPHY COAST
7 MORAINE CLIFF COAST
8 SANDY BEACH COAST

0   50 km

Figure 40-1. The coastal types of Norway.

posits and moved by the sea to more sheltered places. The longest continuous sandy beach along the Norwegian coast is only 4 km long, most sandy beaches being only pocket beaches 50–200 m long.

Clayey beach, a gently sloping flat above and below sea level, is found (1) in a sheltered area where a small stream has brought suspended material into the sea, (2) where a plain of clay gently emerges from the sea, or (3) in a tidal area as an accumulation of the finest material washed out of Quaternary deposits.

The mean tide is less than 0.3 m south of Utsira (Fig. 40-2), increases to approximately 1 m on the west coast and 1.5 m farther north, with a maximum of 2 m at Vardø in the northeast. This indicates that clayey beaches resembling salt marshes are present only at small individual places.

COASTAL TYPES

A morphogenetic classification of the Norwegian coast may be based on a combination of the forms of the shore zone and the landforms next to it (Fig. 40-1).

Strandflat Coast

The strandflat is a gently sloping bedrock plain (Plate 40-1) partly sub- and partly supra-marine, only locally covered with deposits of some thickness. It is limited both inland and seaward by steeper slopes. The plain has a rugged terrain with small relief and dips gently into the sea. It produces an uneven coastline with very many bays, coves, inlets, headlands, and promontories, which, together with islands, islets, and skerries are the elements of the skerry zone. The bottom topography is the continuation of the terrain of the skerry zone and the supra-marine part.

The gradient of the supra-marine part varies between 5 m and 25 m per km. As mean values, 40 m above and 40 m below sea level are the upper and lower limits of the strandflat. In places, though, it may extend to 100 m.

The shore zone of the strandflat consists mainly of gently or steeply sloping ice-smoothed rocky shores and stony beaches (Plate 40-1). Sandy or clayey beaches are found only in places with an abundance of loose material.

The strandflat is found from the northern parts of Jæren to the western parts of Finnmark with a narrow flat, more like an abrasion platform,

extending to eastern Finnmark. Figure 40-1 gives a division of the strandflat acording to the width of the supra- and submarine parts. The maximum width of the strandflat is approximately 40 km in the area of Hitra on the Møre coast, but as a mean the strandflat is 16 km wide. The supra-marine part is normally 5–10 km, but can reach 15 km. In Finnmark and Troms, however, it diminishes to a few hundred meters, but even here the strandflat is a very important landform, as a large part of the population lives on it.

The origin of the strandflat is closely associated with the general evolution of the Norwegian landforms. The land was exposed to denudation through the Mesozoic and the first part of the Tertiary. In a warm climate with dry and wet periods, denudation produced a land surface, the *paleic surface* (Gjessing 1967), with well-rounded, mature landforms in the peripheral parts of the land block, a propitious starting point for the development of the strandflat.

In the Tertiary the Scandinavian land block was elevated and tilted, giving a steeper slope toward the west and northwest, and bringing the paleic surface to different heights above sea level. Along the coast it varies from sea level to 500–700 m above sea level.

Probably coincident with the uplift, the climate became temperate and more humid. Fluvial processes produced young forms along a *fluvial pattern* in the paleic surface, most distinct in the west and northwest. Along the coast marine abrasion and denudation, favored by the paleic surface, may have started the development of a peneplain, which can be easily fitted into the development of the strandflat.

Cirque glaciers, descending from higher coastal mountains onto the level surface along the coast, were important in the widening and the splitting up of the strandflat. Valley glaciers from inland, spreading out in the coastal areas (Holtedahl 1929), may also have taken part in the development. In interglacial times and at the beginning of the glacial periods, frost weathering and marine abrasion were momentous, and together with mass movement and littoral transport, most active in the evolution of the strandflat.

Fjord Coast

A fjord is an arm of the sea stretching inland between distinct fjord-sides, which either plunge steeply into the sea or reach it via a more gently sloping valley bench (Plate 40-2). The fjord-sides

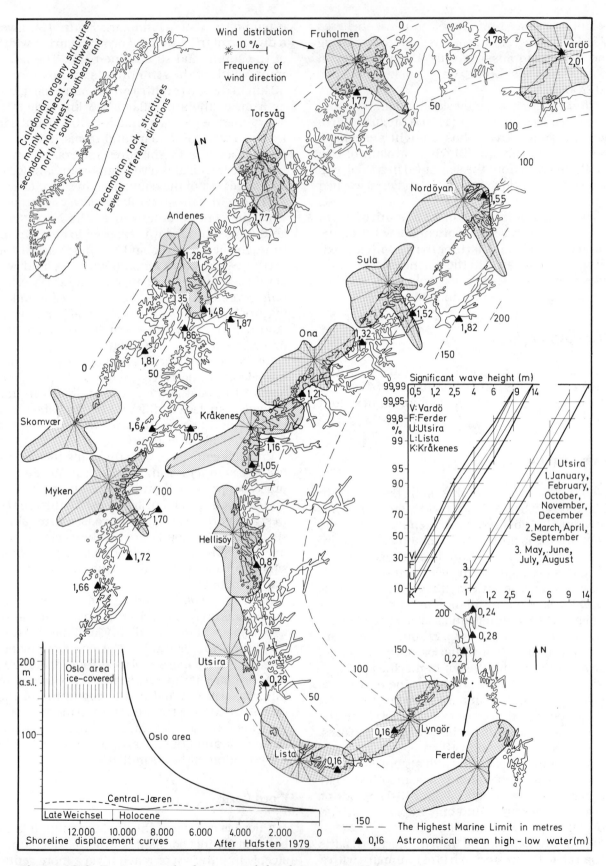

Figure 40-2. Factors involved in coastal development in Norway.

continue down to the floor of the fjord, giving the general U-profile in cross section. The longitudinal profile consists of thresholds and troughs. The fjords are cut into a paleic plateau-like or a mountainous landscape of varying heights above the fjord. The differences in relief and the length of the fjords have given the division shown in Figure 40-1.

The shore zones along the fjords are mainly made up of steeply sloping rocky shores (Plate 40-3), and stony beaches. Where rivers enter a fjord, there are deltas with stony and sandy beaches and sometimes clayey beaches.

Sognefjorden (Plate 40-2) is the longest (200 km) and the deepest (1308 m) fjord in Norway. Its width is 1–8 km, and the surrounding plateaus and mountains rise from 500 m above sea level in the western parts to 1500–1700 m above sea level in the eastern parts. Examples of the smallest fjords are found in eastern Finnmark and in the southernmost part of the country.

The Varangerfjord and the fjords of the middle parts of Finnmark, the Trondheimsfjord and the Oslofjord, are all very wide in relation to the height of the surrounding land, and thus lack some of the typical fjord characteristics.

The fluvial valley system directed the ice movements. Glacial erosion produced large U-shaped valleys and overdeepened troughs, most prominent on the western and northwestern parts of the land block, invaded by the sea, these valleys and troughs became the fjords.

The Caledonian structure, mainly northeast-southwest, secondary northwest-southeast and north-south, is responsible for the pattern of the valley system and the fjords. The imprint of the structure along the same directions is also present at the strandflat. The form of the Oslofjord is due to less resistant down-faulted rocks, Permian faulting zones, and ice convergence.

Fjärd Coast

The fjärd coast is found where an undulating land surface with fissure valleys slopes gently into the sea, making an uneven coastline with numerous islands and islets with headlands and coves (Plates 40-4 and 40-5). The narrow inlet, the fjärd, which is not very deep and is surrounded by a terrain of low relief, is characteristic of the fjärd coast.

As on the strandflat, the skerry zone of the fjärd coast has a shore zone with ice-smoothed rocky shores (Plate 40-4) and stony beaches, with sandy and clayey beaches in smaller bays.

The fjärd coast of southern Oslofjord and the Skagerrak, the continuation of that of the west coast of Sweden, has a rather varied, complicated pattern of fjärds because of the Precambrian crystalline rock structure. This structure was rejuvenated in the Permian and—in part, probably—in Tertiary time. In the inner part of the Oslofjord, the headlands, bays, and islands are due to rock differences and structure produced by Caledonian folding of Cambro-Silurian sedimentary rocks.

On the eastern, gently sloping part of the land block with mature paleic landforms, the ice movement was free, undirected. The glacial erosion smoothed the even surface. Along zones of weakness small depressions and fissure valleys were formed among knolls and hills, which later, when the sea entered, became the fjärd coast.

Cliff Abrasion Coast

The cliff abrasion coast is characterized by a rugged cliff descending from the undulating paleic surface to the sea (Plates 40-6 and 40-7). The cliffed coast may descend straight into the sea, with the abrasion acting directly on the vertical wall; or there may be an abrasion platform with an abrasion shore in front of the cliff. Frost weathering and marine abrasion in zones of weakness and different rocks are responsible for the forms of the rugged cliff. The height of the cliff varies from some tens to a couple of hundred meters.

Single, smaller cliffs may be found at different places along the coast, but the most famous localities of cliff abrasion coast are at Stad and at the North Cape. From eastern Troms to eastern Finnmark, there are also many other localities with a cliffed coast. At the cliffed coast of Åna-Sira, marine abrasion has been of little consequence, and the cliff may be a result of Tertiary faulting, which also is a contributing factor at Stad and along the Finnmark coast.

Waves, causing marine abrasion, have been recorded by lighthouse keepers only through subjective evaluation. Recently, due to the need for better wave data in connection with petroleum installations and research on wave-generated electric energy progress has been made in registration of height and direction of waves. The present data are sufficient to describe a yearly variation of the wave climate, the combined distribution of height, period, and direction of the waves through the seasons, along the coast. There are lower waves in the summer than from October through February, and the data for March, April, and September are close to the mean value for the year. This variation in frequency of the significant wave height is demonstrated by the conditions at Utsira in Figure 40-2, which also shows the variation of significant waves along the coast. The area around Stad and Kråkenes has the largest waves and supply of wave energy, which decrease both north- and southward to nearly the same value at the Oslofjord and Vardø. The variations in wave climate are, however, less important to the effect of marine abrasion than are the properties of the rock, as indicated by the abrasion along the coast of Finnmark.

Flat Abrasion Coast

The flat abrasion coast consists of a bedrock plain concordant with the rock structure of slightly metamorphic sedimentary rocks sloping gently into the sea. Marine abrasion of the rocks favored by frost weathering has produced a rocky abrasion shore with minor stony beaches.

This type of coast is restricted to the north side of the Varangerfjord and as far east as Vardø, partially mapped by Tolgensbakk and Sollid (1980).

Moraine Topography Coast

The moraine topography coast, only found on parts of Lista and Jæren (Figs. 40-1 and 40-3) results from drowning of an uneven ground moraine terrain of low relief, giving a coastline with headlands and bays. This type of coast has a stony beach with some boulders, little affected by the waves, in between well-rounded stones, with finer particles washed away (Plate 40-8).

Moraine Cliff Coast

The moraine cliff coast (Fig. 40-3, Plates 40-8 and 40-10), also found only on parts of Lista and Jæren, is characterized by a slope, 10–15 m high, cut in till. The slope has an inclination of 10–15° and is locally even steeper. The cliff is covered with vegetation and elevated a few meters above the attack of the sea. The moraine cliff is fossil, because of isostatic rebound; it is only a few tens

of meters away from the present shore and acts as an important part of the coastal form. Boulders and stones, the lag of the till, make the stony beach the most important beach type of both moraine coastal types.

Sandy Beach Coast

The sandy beach coast is the only coastal type in Norway whose forms are entirely a result of littoral processes. The main elements are the sandy offshore, foreshore, and backshore, but also some low stony beach ridges inland may be incorporated in this coastal type (Fig. 40-3), as well as dune fields, which have the beach material as their source. Eolian areas of different sizes are connected to sandy beaches (Klemsdal 1969). Only the largest fields are so close to such long beaches that they can be regarded as a part of a coastal form.

The sandy beach coast is found on Jæren (Fig. 40-3) at Skarasanden, Bore, Revesanden at Revtangen (Plates 40-9 and 40-11) Orre, Nærland, Brusand, and on Lista at Kviljo. Long sandy beaches are also found on Vigra, an island on the Møre coast, and on Andøya. The many pocket beaches are only elements of the shore zone of other coastal types.

The wind direction (Fig. 40-2) indicates the direction of wave approach, an important part of the wave climate. This, together with nearly unlimited fetch, the offshore topography, and the sources of material are the most significant conditions for the development of the sandy beach coast.

The moraine and sandy beach coasts are found in the peripheral part of the areas that were covered by inland ice, where glacial and fluvioglacial accumulations became important sources of material. The peripheral location is also reflected in the postglacial isostatic-eustatic movements. The highest marine limit of late glacial time varies from 220 m above sea level to only approximately 10 m at Lista and Jæren (Fig. 40-2). The shoreline displacement curve (Hafsten 1979) is shown in Figure 40-2. The low marine limit on Lista and Jæren, together with the Holocene Littorina transgressions and regressions, has given the sea a long time to attack at a nearly constant level. In the Oslofjord area the relative positions of land and sea in the beginning of postglacial time were not stable long enough to allow littoral forms to develop. In Finnmark, however, some excellent raised beach ridges are found (Plate 40-7).

SUMMARY

The Norwegian coast from Jæren to Finnmark is a combination of the strandflat in the outer parts and the fjords in the inner parts. When the fjärds along the Skagerrak coast are also considered, it is obvious that most of the coastal forms in Norway, with their rocky shores and stony beaches, are a heritage of paleic and glacial forms. The abrasion cliff coast is a result of faulting and marine abrasion: only in the moraine cliff coasts and the sandy beach coasts is the development of the Norwegian coast a result of the action of the sea in postglacial time.

TORMOD KLEMSDAL

REFERENCES

Gjessing, J., 1967, Norway's paleic surface, *Norsk Geog. Tidsskr.* **21:**69–132.

Hafsten, U., 1979, Late and Post-Weichselian shore level changes in South Norway, in *The Quaternary History of the North Sea*, E. Oele, R. T. E. Schüttenhelm, and A. J. Wiggers, eds., Acta Univ. Ups. Symp. Univ. Ups. Annum Quingentesimum Celebrantis, pp. 45–59.

Holtedahl, H., 1955, On the Norwegian continental terrace, primarily outside Møre-Romsdal: Its geomorphology and sediments, *Bergen Univ. Årb. Natur. R.* **14:**1–209.

Holtedahl, H., 1960, The strandflat of the Møre-Romsdal Coast, West-Norway, *Skr. Norges Handels. Geogr. Avh.* **7:**35–43.

Holtedahl, H., 1975, The geology of the Hardangerfjord, West Norway, *Norges Geol. Undersökelse* **323:**1–87.

Holtedahl, O., 1929 *On the Geology and Physiography of Some Antarctic and Subantarctic Islands*, Scient. Res. Norw. Ant. Exp. 1927–28, Vid.-Akad. 3.

Klemsdal, T., 1969, Eolian forms in parts of Norway, *Norsk Geog. Tidsskr.* **23:**49–66.

Klemsdal, T., 1979, Kyst-, strand- og vindgeomorfologi. Forslag til terminologi (Coastal, shore/beach and eolian geomorphology. Proposal for terminology), *Norsk Geog. Tidsskr.* **33:**159–171.

Klemsdal, T., 1982, Coastal classification and the coast of Norway, *Norsk Geog. Tidsskr* **36:**129–152.

Møller, J. T., and J. L. Sollid, 1973, Geomorfologisk kart over Lofoten-Vesterålen (Geomorphological map of Lofoten-Vesterålen), *Norsk Geog. Tidsskr* **27:**195–205.

Nansen, F., 1922, *The Strandflat and Isostasy*, Videnskaps-selskapets Skrifter, I Mathem. naturv. Kl. 1921 v. 11.

Reusch, H., 1894, Strandfladen, et nyt træk i Norges geografi, *Norges Geol. Undersökelse* [*Skr.*], **14:**1–14.

Strøm, K., 1961, The Norwegian coast, *Norsk Geog. Tidsskr.* **17:**132–137.

Tolgensbakk, J., and J. L. Sollid, 1980, *Vardø, Kvartærgeologi og Geomorfologi 1:50,000, 2535 IV*, Geografisk Institutt, Universitetet i Oslo.

Plate 40-1. The strandflat coast at Værøy in Lofoten (photo by Fjellanger Widerøe).

Plate 40-2. The fjord coast illustrated by Sognefjorden (photo by Fjellanger Widerøe).

Plate 40-3. A steep rocky shore along Sognefjorden (photo by T. Klemsdal).

Plate 40-4. A gently sloping ice-smoothed rocky shore along the fjärd coast of Skagerrak (photo by T. Klemsdal).

Plate 40-5. The fjärd coast of Skagerrak (photo by Fjellanger Widerøe).

Plate 40-6. The abrasion cliff coast at Nordkinn-halvøya, east of the North Cape (photo by T. Klemsdal).

Plate 40-7. The abrasion cliff coast northwest of Vårdø, showing abrasion forms, fossil cliff, and beach ridges (photo by J. Tolgensbakk).

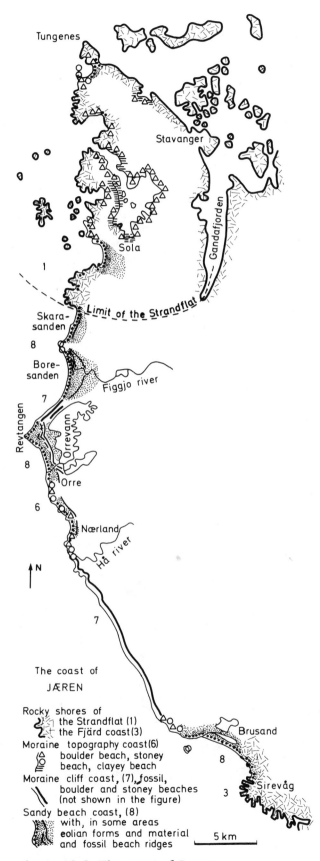

Figure 40-3. The coast of Jæren.

On the map:

Tungenes

Stavanger

Gandafjorden

Sola

1

Limit of the Strandflat

Skara-sanden

8

Bore-sanden

Figgjo river

7

Revtangen

Orrevann

8

Orre

6

Nærland

Hå river

7

↑ N

The coast of
JÆREN

Rocky shores of
  the Strandflat (1)
  the Fjärd coast (3)
Moraine topography coast (6)
  boulder beach, stoney
  beach, clayey beach
Moraine cliff coast, (7), fossil,
  boulder and stoney beaches
  (not shown in the figure)
Sandy beach coast, (8)
  with, in some areas
  eolian forms and material
  and fossil beach ridges

5 km

Brusand

8

3

Sirevåg

Plate 40-8. The morain cliff coast northeast of Revtangen, with stony beach and fossil cliff (photo by T. Klemsdal).

Plate 40-9. The sandy beach coast at Revesanden, Revtangen (photo by T. Klemsdal).

Plate 40-10. The fossil moraine cliff between Brusand and the Hå River, with boulder and stony beach (photo by T. Klemsdal).

Plate 40-11. The passing over from the fjärd coast at Sirevåg to the sandy beach coast on Jæren. Scale approximately 1:16000. (photo by Fjellanger Widerøe).

41. SWEDEN

Sweden (Fig. 41-1, Plate 41-1) forms the Archean marginal basement to the Baltic-Russian sedimentary basin to the east, to the Danish-German basins in the south, and to the Caledonian mountain range in the west. Within the Swedish shield area a rich diversity of gneisses and granites characterizes the bedrock. In the Baltic Sea we find a submerged scarpland of lower Paleozoic rocks (Martinsson 1958, 1979), in which the main features are the northwest margins of Ordovician and Silurian limestone sheets, which make up the islands of Öland and Gotland. The main part of the Bothnian Sea, but not the Bothnian Bay, is also floored by Paleozoic sediments, but there are only a few scattered outcrops on the coast.

During several stages of the Quaternary, Sweden and the surrounding seas were completely glaciated, as well as during the final, Weichselian substage, which culminated only some 30,000 years ago. When the front of the receding ice reached Scania, the southernmost province of Sweden, about 12,000 B.C., a complicated history of shore development started that was dependent on rate of deglaciation, land uplift by isostatic rebound, sea-level variation, and shifting outlets from the Baltic basin.

The altitude of the highest postglacial metachronous shoreline rises from 20 m in southern Scania to about 220 m at the southern end of the Bothnian Sea and to a maximum of 280–285 m in the Höga kusten area at lat. 63°N. From there it falls to 160–220 m within a broad uplifted archipelago zone at the northern end of the Bothnian Bay. Along the west coast the highest shoreline rises from 50 m in the northwestern part of Scania to about 170 m at the Norwegian border.

The inland ice produced a till cover of variable texture and thickness and glaciofluvial sediments of two distinctive types: sandy and coarser sediments that were deposited in ice tunnels and at the mouths of tunnels and meltwater channels to form eskers and deltas, and suspended silt and clay deposited below sea level and in ice-dammed lakes. The suspended load formed density currents that annually distributed varved sediments to the lowest areas.

The average thickness of the till is not more than 3–4 m, which means that on exposed slopes wave action exposed the glacially polished bedrock. Continuous reworking of material already washed down in the swash and breaker zone effectively separated suspended matter that settled on top of the varved sediments. In this way and by man's exploitation, a landscape with forested hills, few bedrock outcrops, and cultivated sediment plains and valleys came into existence (Fig. 41-1, Plate 41-1).

The present rate of uplift varies from 0 in southern Scania to 0.4–0.5 m/century in the Stockholm area and to a maximum of 0.9 m/century on the coast of the Bothnian Bay. The position of the highest coastline and the rate of uplift mean that large areas have, in comparatively recent time, been operated on by coastal processes, but for such a short duration at each level that the coastal influence is often only detectable by a sorting of the top soil. At strongly exposed sites or at levels where the emergence has been slowed down or even reversed by transgression, well-developed relict shores may be found (Plate 41-2). They are especially well preserved where a transgression has been followed by a rapidly falling lake or sea level, as for example in the lowering of the Baltic Ice Lake to sea level (ca. 8300 B.C.).

Bedrock morphology, soil characteristics, and the history of land uplift imply that the present coasts are generally in an early stage of development and could be classified as primary. The inherited bedrock morphology is, in detail, characterized by glacial sculpture, but in the macro scale it is often far older, as more or less modified Precambrian and Mesozoic peneplains dominate large coastal environments.

In recent years a number of important publications have appeared, with important basic data on the coastal geomorphology of various parts of the Baltic Sea. Among these, the reader is referred to Abrahamsson et al. (1977), Davidsson (1963), Gudelis (1967), Gudelis and Emelyanov (1976), Gudelis and Königsson (1979), Finnish-Swedish Committee for the Gulf of Bothnia (1977), Rudberg (1960), Tulkki (1977), Voipio (1981) and Winterhalter (1971).

With regard to the generally primary character of the Swedish coast (Fig. 41-1), a regional division based mainly on the inherited pre-Quaternary macromorphology has been chosen for this review:

A. The Bothnian Bay archipelago coast.
B. The Quark coastal plain.
C. The Bothnian Sea high coast (the High Coast-Höga kusten).
D. The Bothnian Sea coastal plain.
E. The Baltic archipelago coasts.
F. The Baltic cuesta coasts (of Öland and Gotland).
G. The Baltic coastal plain.
H. The Scanian horst and glacial drift coasts.
I. The Kattegat coastal plain (in the province of Halland).
J. The Skagerak archipelago coast.

In the archipelago of the Bothnian Bay, structural elements with a NW-SE orientation dominate the morphological pattern. The same orientation is found in the valleys of the large rivers, which can be traced across the Bay to the Finnish coast (Tulkki 1977). At the margin of the Bay this downbent, presumably Tertiary landscape forms a ria-type archipelago characterized by open basins, enclosed by rather large islands and submarine sills. The same type of archipelago coast is found in the province of Blekinge in the southern Baltic (E2), (Lidmar-Bergström 1982).

In the Bothnian Bay glaciofluvial eskers run along the preglacial valleys; ice frontal meltwater accumulations and series of small end moraines

add oriented elements to the bedrock morphology. The coast is generally low, and slope measurements by Håkanson (1982), together with the present land uplift (0.9–1.0 cm/yr), suggest that a 1.1 m wide strip of land is annually added (Plate 41-3).

The broad archipelago coast (E1) north of Lake Mälaren and the City of Stockholm (S) is largely formed by glacially abraded Archean bedrock structures and fissure valleys etched in an almost horizontal Precambrian peneplain sharply cut off seaward of the Åland deep. South of this region the peneplain is broken up by E-W faults, which cut off N-S and NW-SE fissure valley systems (Rudberg 1970).

The Skagerak archipelago coast in the province of Bohuslän owes its character to a dissected Precambrian peneplain in which glacial excavation has formed fjords. Except for the valleys the bedrock is almost bare, as the thin soil cover has been washed down into the valleys by wave action during the postglacial land uplift.

The coastal plains of the Quark (B), the Bothnian Sea (D), and the Baltic (G) are fringed with isles and skerries, but lack the width of the archipelago coasts (Plate 41-4 and 41-5). These low coasts exhibit Precambrian peneplain surface fragments, which gently dip under Paleozoic sediments in the Bothnian Sea and the Baltic. The present shore morphology is largely dominated by wave-washed till in the more exposed parts and by fine redeposited glaciofluvial sediments and gyttja deposits formed beneath a wide belt of sedges in the shallow sheltered bays. Because of the continuous land uplift, material deposited below the limit of present wave action may be resuspended later on. It has been estimated that most of the annual sediment deposition in the Baltic emanates from resuspension.

The Kattegat coastal plain in the province of Halland (I) is to a high degree characterized by modern shore processes, especially in the southern part, where large open sandy bays are framed by broad dune belts composed of an outer active eolian zone and an inner zone with pine woods, mainly planted during the nineteenth century. The origin of the roughly 20 km broad coastal plain has been compared with the Norwegian strandflat and certainly seems to have had a complex history: "The gross morphology of the bedrock surface was initiated by deep weathering in the Mesozoic. An uneven erosion surface was formed in the Early and early Late Cretaceous, buried in the Late Cretaceous, and exhumed and remodelled in the Neogene" (Lidmar-Bergström 1982).

Inland from the Bothnian coastal plain, we find an undulating, hilly landscape that rises in steps, especially along the rivers, and rapidly reaches relative heights of more than 100 m. This morphology meets the coast in an area named the High Coast (C), where the hills reach heights of more than 300 m and where the maximum depth off the coast is 250 m. On this coast the highest postglacial shore in Sweden has been leveled at 285 m (Hörnsten 1964). Most of the glacial soil has been stripped by wave action from the exposed steep hillsides to form leeward delta-like shore deposits. Only very coarse boulder terraces remain in sea-facing position (Plate 41-2a). During land uplift the glacial deposits in the valleys have been repeatedly reworked at lower levels. This material now forms terraces along the rivers and deltas in present-day estuaries (Plate 41-2c).

The central part of the Baltic is occupied by a submerged scarpland of Lower Paleozoic rocks, in which the main features are the northwestern margins of Ordovician and Silurian limestone sheets (Martinsson 1979). The western coast of the island of Öland is formed by an escarpment cut in Ordovician rocks that can be followed across the Baltic to the northern coast of Estonia. Almost parallel to this runs an escarpment in Silurian rocks that forms a steep submarine slope along the northwestern coast of the island of Gotland. At this coast wave abrasion and frost action have formed a steep cliff and an abrasion platform in conformity with moderate land uplift lowering sea level (Rudberg 1967).

Having been covered by the Late Cretaceous sea, the province of Scania, from a geological point of view, belongs to the European continent rather than to Fennoscandia. The Archean basement was broken up, mainly in the Permian, along NW-SE fracture zones, resulting in horsts and grabens. The former are illustrated by the peninsulas of Kullen and Bjäre, protruding into the Kattegat on the west coast, and the latter by the sandy bay between them and also by the large Hanö bay on the east coast. In the horsts, steep fractured cliffs have formed during an emergence of some 50–60 m in the Holocene (Plate 41-6).

Except for the horst areas, glacial drift deposits are usually thick in Scania—40–50 m is not exceptional—and although low coasts dominate, active cliffs cut in till and glaciofluvial sediments are found along elevated tracts (Plate 41-6). The isoline of present zero-land uplift runs NW-SE through central Scania, which at least partly explains why Scania is the only mainland province with notable coastal erosion (Plate 41-6). Inland the same phenomenon is found at the southern end of Lake Vättern, where the present rate of transgression is 1.7 cm per century and the cliff retreat amounts to 0.3 m per year.

JOHN O. NORRMAN

REFERENCES

Abrahamsson, J., N. K. Jakobsen, E. Dahl, R. Kalliola, L. Wilborg, and L. Påhlson, 1977, *Naturgeografisk regionindelning av Norden*, N.U.B., 34, Helsingfors.

Davidsson, J., 1963, *Littoral processes and morphology on Scanian flatcoasts*, Lund Studies Geogr. Ser. A:23.

Finnish-Swedish Committee for the Gulf of Bothnia, 1977, *Literature on the Gulf of Bothnia*, Havsforskning-institutets Skr., 242.

Gudelis, V., 1967, The morphogentic types of the Baltic Sea coasts (in Russian), *Baltica* **3**:123–143.

Gudelis, V., and E. Emelyanov, eds., 1976, *Geology of the Baltic Sea*, Mokslas Publishers, Vilnius.

Gudelis, V., and L.-K. Königsson, eds., 1979, *The Quaternary History of the Baltic*, Acta Univ. Upsaliensis., Symp. Univ. Ups., Ann. Quingentesimum Celebr.: 1.

Håkanson, L., 1982, Coastal morphometry, the coast of the Gulf of Bothnia, in *Coastal research in the Gulf of Bothnia*, K. Müller, ed., Monogr. Biol. **45**:9–33.

Hörnsten, Å., 1964 Åongermanlands kustland under isavsmältningsskedet, *Geol. Fören. Stockholm Förh.* **86**:181–205.

Lidmar-Bergström, K., 1982, *Pre-Quaternary Geomorphological Evolution in Southern Fennoscandia*, Sveriges Geol. Unders. Ser. C:785.

Martinsson, A., 1958, The submarine morphology of the Baltic Cambro-Silurian area. *Bull. Geol. Inst. Univ. Uppsala* **38**:11–35.

Martinsson, A., 1979, The Pre-Quaternary substratum of the Baltic, in *The Quaternary History of the Baltic*, V. Gudelis and L.-K. Königsson, eds., Acta Univ. Ups., Symp. Univ. Ups. Ann Quin. Celebr.:1, pp. 77–86.

Rudberg, S., 1960, Geology and morphology, in *The Geography of Norden*, A. Sømme, ed., J. W. Cappelens Forlag, Oslo.

Rudberg, S., 1967, The cliff coast of Gotland and the rate of cliff retreat, *Geogr. Annaler*, **49A**:283–298.

Rudberg, S., 1970, Geomorphology, *Atlas över Sverige*, no. 5–6.

Tulkki, P., 1977, *The bottom of the Bothnian Bay, geomorphology and sediments*, Havsforskningsinstitutets Skr., 241.

Voipio, A., ed., 1981, *The Baltic Sea*, Elsevier Oceanography Series, 30.

Winterhalter, B., 1971, *On the Geology of the Bothnian Sea*, Geol. Survey Finland Bull., **258**:1–66.

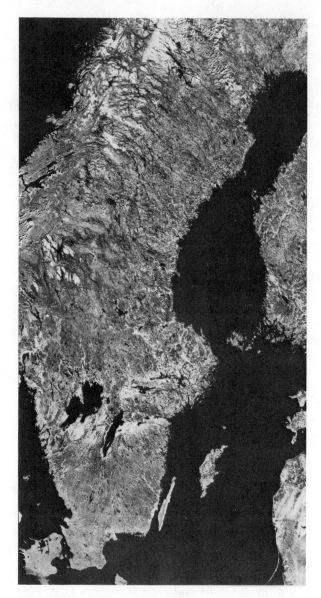

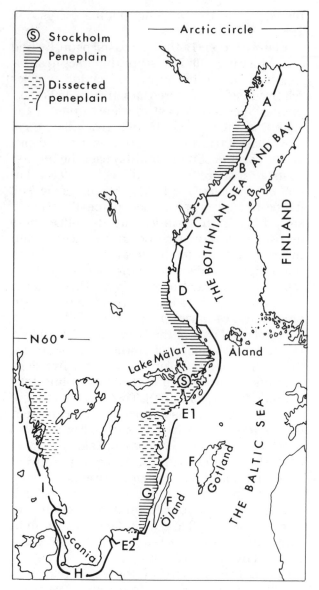

Plate 41-1; Figure 41-1. The coasts of Sweden. Satellite image constructed from Landsat 1 and 2 records by the Land Survey of Sweden (LMV) and map of the distribution of coastal regions. For description, see text.

A

B

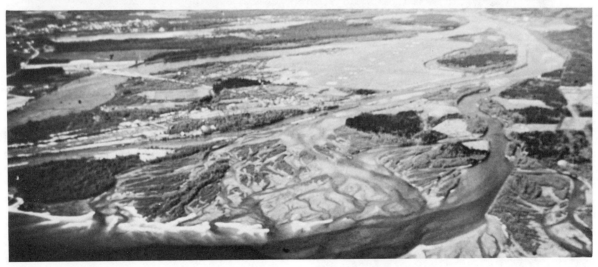

C

Plate 41-2. *A.* Raised, very coarse boulder berms at 250 m above sea level on the exposed eastern slope of Hogklinten in Mjällom, the High Coast. *B.* Even today coarse boulder material is generated by frost shattering and strong swash action. *C.* During the postglacial land uplift, reworked glaciofluvial sediments have been brought down through the deep valleys of the High Coast to form deltas like the delta of the river Indalsälven. Note shore barriers built by wave abrasion at the delta front (photos by J. Norrman).

A

B

C

Plate 41-3. The eastern shore at Sandöklubben is extremely flat. *A.* The oblique air photo shows three strand parallel submarine bars in the foreground and inshore of them a series of perpendicular bars formed by along-shore waves and currents. *B.* This shallow platform is strewn with boulders transported by drift ice, as can be seen at low water. In the foreground is a narrow dune, and inland of that an uplifted platform also strewn with boulders and with an eolian, thin residual pebble cover. *C.* At the inner end of this abrasion surface large dunes, partly stabilized by pine trees have been built up (photos by J. Norrman).

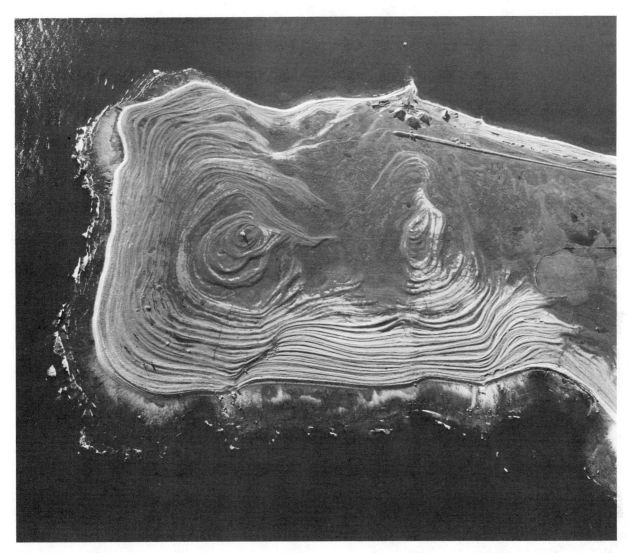

Plate 41-4. The isle of Närsholmen (or Norsholmen). Around the island of Gotland are many small isles with very well-developed raised beaches formed by limestone pebbles and cobbles (photo by Arne Philip).

Plate 41-5. The small fishing village of Hamnskär in the Isles of Kalvhararna. Along the coast of the Bothnian Sea there are large areas with an extremely coarse till and irregular moraines that form narrow archipelagos (photo by LMV).

Plate 41-6. *A.* In the province of Scania, with no present land uplift but a rather a slight transgression, shore erosion is frequent during storms combined with a high sea level. A military bunker built in the fore dunes during the Second World War indicates shore erosion at Löderup on the southern coast of Scania. *B.* Cliffs cut in glacial drift on the west coast of the island of Ven in the Sound. *C.* Slightly uplifted berms on the northern coast of the highly tectonized Bjäre horst at the Kattegat coast (photos by J. Norrman).

42. FINLAND

The coastline of Finland, excluding islands, is some 4650 km in length, comprising 1250 km on the Bothnian Bay, 1970 km on the Bothnian Sea, 950 km on the Baltic Sea, and 1380 km on the Gulf of Finland (Figs. 42-1 and 42-2).

The Finnish peninsula forms part of an Archean bedrock region, the Fennoscandian Shield. The bedrock contains deeply denuded Precambrian orogenic belts of metamorphic and plutonic rocks. Thus the northeastern coast of the Bothnian Bay consists of Prekarelian granite-gneiss some 2700 million years old, while the northern and eastern shores of this same area are reached by schist belts associated with the orogeny of the Karelides and dating back some 1800 million years. A Svecofennian gneiss and schist belt of similar age also runs parallel to the Gulf of Finland coast in the southwest, being broken up by a series of transverse fracture zones (Fig. 42-3). The northwestern Svecofennian migmatitic gneiss belt runs along the Bothnian Sea coast and then turns inland and back to the coast of the Bothnian Bay. The coasts of the eastern Gulf of Finland, the Åland Islands, and the islands of Kustavi have a bedrock formed by ancient rapakivi granites 1600 million years old. Siltstones 1300 million years old are preserved in postgeosynclinal troughs on the Bothnian Bay coast and arkose sandstones 1100 million years old on the coast of the Bothnian Sea (Simonen 1960).

The coast of the Gulf of Finland consists of a Subcambrian peneplain that slopes away into an Early Paleozoic geosyncline, as does the coast of the Gulf of Bothnia, which runs into a depression basin reformed in the Tertiary (Tulkki 1977). These peneplains were open to denudation for a long period in post-Archean time, allowing the exposure of granite domes, ridges of metamorphic rock, and fault zones that are among the oldest bedrock formations in the world, and are responsible for the general irregularity of the coastline.

The Quaternary glaciations removed the soil deposits and exposed the bedrock surface, forming grooves and roches moutonnées, which are to be found chiefly on the coasts of the Baltic Sea and the Gulf of Finland (Fogelberg and Seppälä 1979). The glacial drift then accumulated to form drumlins, which occur mainly on the coast of the Bothnian Bay, while transverse De Geer moraines are found on the coast and islands of the Quark (Fig. 42-4, Plate 42-1; Zilliacus 1981). Major ice margin formations extend to the coast in the area of the southwestern islands, and eskers and glaciofluvial deposits are mostly to be found on the coasts of the Bothnian Bay, the southern Bothnian Sea, and the eastern Gulf of Finland. Silts and clays occur on the shores of bays and inlets.

The whole coastline of Finland is affected by land uplift, which amounts to 9 mm a year at its most rapid, on the coast of the Bothnian Bay, while it is least pronounced in the eastern Gulf of Finland (Kääriäinen 1953). This glacio-isostatic land uplift causes a seaward movement of the shoreline amounting to hundreds of meters a century on the gently sloping shores of the Bothnian Bay, cutting short the development of littoral landforms.

Storms associated with cyclones moving on the polar front are experienced mainly in autumn; the shores of the Gulf of Finland and the south-

All photographs are published with the permission of the Military Division of the Department of Aviation.

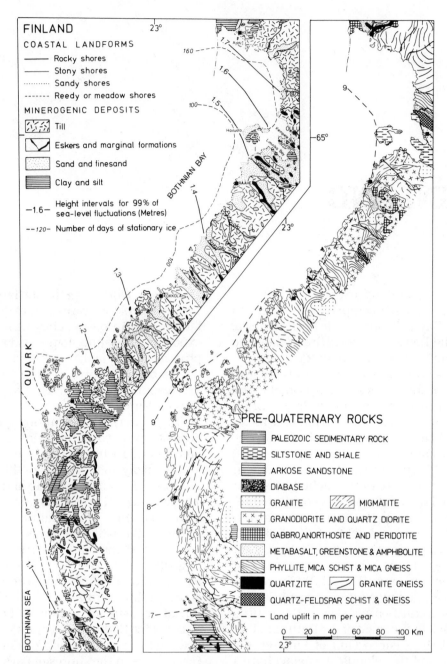

Figure 42-1. Coastal landforms, minerogenic deposits, and Pre-Quaternary rocks on coast of Gulf of Bothnia.

western islands are scoured by waves whipped up by the southerly winds. The wind shifts to the west in the latter part of the cyclone, when the waves wash the shore of the Gulf of Bothnia. Tidal fluctuations in water level are on the order of only a few centimeters, but winds and changes in air pressure can give rise to major variations in water level at the heads of the Gulf of Finland and Gulf of Bothnia, especially in early winter

(Lisitzin 1959). Long-term variations in water level show a periodicity of 11–12 and more obviously 22–23 years (Simojoki 1957). There are weak coastal currents running northward in the Gulf of Bothnia and westward in the Gulf of Finland.

In winter coastal waters and sea areas around the islands are covered by stationary ice for as long as 5.5 months on average at the head of the

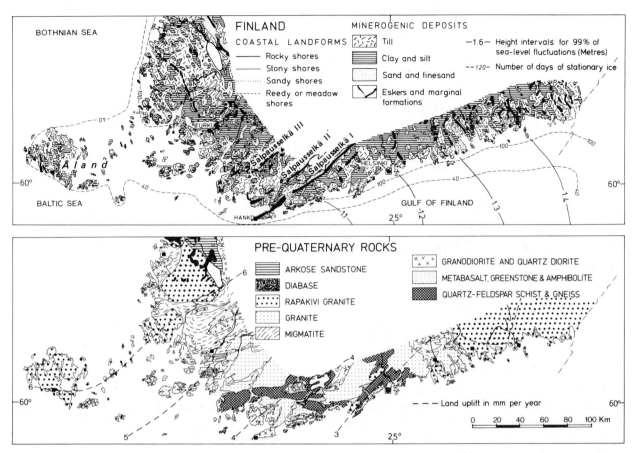

Figure 42-2. Coastal landforms, minerogenic deposits, and Pre-Quaternary rocks on coast of Baltic Sea and Gulf of Finland.

Bothnian Bay and over 3 months on the south-west coast. Low-pressure systems and winds in early winter frequently cause water levels to rise and detach this ice from the shores, leading to rafting, piling up of the ice on the shores, or even ice-push effects extending tens of meters up the shore and involving the transportation and deposition of stones and boulders. The shores of bays and narrow straits are also shaped by thermal ice movement (Alestalo and Häikiö 1976, Mansikkaniemi 1976).

The shores of Finland are controlled by ancient structural and glacial formations, although the littoral landforms are generally poorly developed because of coastline regression. The rocky shores are largely composed of roches moutonnées exposed from beneath a thin soil layer, and there are few signs of abrasion. The stony shores have been formed of till from which the finer material has been washed out, whereupon the ice has smoothed the stones into shore pavements and pushed up the boulders to form a rim at the foot

of the abrasion slope. The material washed out from such shores usually accumulates in pocket beaches. Sandy shores are found extensively in connection with the skirts of sand running along the sides of eskers. The sandy ridges forming on accumulation shores are frequently covered by blown sand bound together by lyme grass (Plate 42-2). Reed and meadow shores are found in bays and river mouths where the bottom is composed of mud or silt.

Capes with a bedrock of diorite and gabbro project from the low-lying northern shores of the Bothnian Bay, and there are many islands formed by emerged NW-SE-oriented drumlins. The islands on the deltas of the Tornio and Kemi rivers have accumulated between the drumlins. The protected shores are generally occupied by meadow, and the open shores by washed-out stone and boulder fields showing the influence of ice thrust. There are some points to the south of Kemi whose tips are occupied by rocky shores of granite-gneiss. The shores of the bays and deltas are of either the

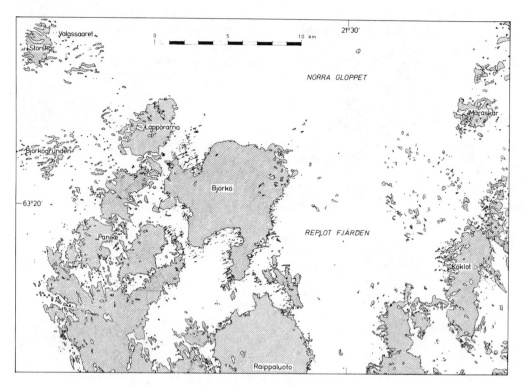

Figure 42-3. Patterns of the distribution of land and water in the southwestern islands, regulated by the orientation of the Svecofennian rocks and their schistosity in the islands of the Rymättylä group—for example, the non-oriented rapakivi bedrock among the islands of Kustavi, the annular dikes of the granite domes in the Åva and Mossala groups, and N-S-oriented fault zones in the straits of Kihti.

sandy or the meadow type. Further south there are NW-SE-oriented phyllite ridges, which stand out to form stony headlands.

South of the town of Oulu the shallow, reedy bays of Kempeleenlahti and Liminganlahti (Plate 42-3) cut into an area of loose siltstone deposits and thick postglacial marine sediments filling a bedrock depression; the two bays are separated by the peninsula of Oulunsalo, with its eskers and sandy shores. The surficial deposits of the island of Hailuoto consist predominantly of glaciofluvial sand, and the western and northwestern shores are of sand with beach and dune ridges and intervening lagoons and marshy swales. The southwestern shore is characterized by parabolic dunes that have advanced toward the northeast, and the sandy northern shore features numerous raised beach ridges accumulated by wave and wind action, which must have formed at intervals of 23 years (estimated from the rate of land uplift) (Alestalo 1979).

The open shores between Siikajoki and Kokkola are composed of sand, with blown sand to be found beside the esker chains at Siikajoki, Kalajoki, and Lohtaja (Plates 42-4 to 42-6). A series of 130 beach ridges have been identified northeast of Siikajoki, which have been deposited in the space of 3000 years—that is, at mean intervals of 23 years (Helle 1965). The mobile dunes of the blown sand fields at Kalajoki and Lohtaja are known to have advanced by 0.5–1 m a year during the eighteenth and nineteenth centuries, but were arrested once grazing and clear-felling were discontinued and forest began to develop on the deflation surface. The drumlins that have emerged from beneath the sea, in the till areas between the esker chains, form peninsulas and islands with stony shores.

The coastline of the Quark from Luoto to south of Vaasa is very irregular because of the lack of orientation in the diorite bedrock, which is broken up by fracture zones running in various directions, and also because of the innumerable WSW-ENE-oriented ridges, or De Geer moraines, which form headlands and chains of islands on the coast off Vaasa (Fig. 42-4, Plate 42-1; Zilliacus

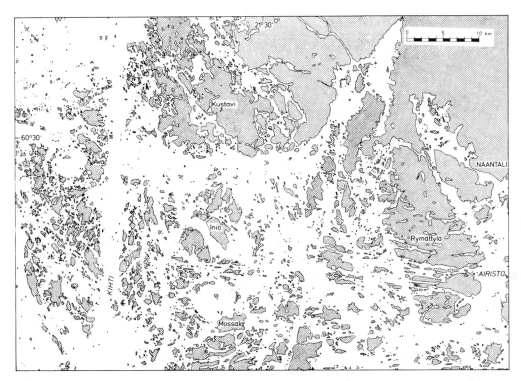

Figure 42-4. The islands in the Quark northwest of Vaasa. Headlands and island chains formed by De Geer moraines are found on the shores of Raippaluoto, Björkö, and Köklot and in the inter-vening sea areas. The shorelines of Björkögrunden, Storskär, and Valassaaret are regulated by Rogen moraines.

1981). The shores feature large numbers of skerries and typically have a high incidence of erratic boulders.

The coast of the Bothnian Sea as far south as Pori has a migmatite bedrock forming curved ridges, which run parallel to the coast in the districts of Kaskinen and Siipyy to give a longitudinal coast with islands and narrow straits. In spite of the openness of the coastline there are few rocky shores, and only the tips of the most salient peninsulas have been exposed beneath the till. This is because of the rapidity of the land uplift. Diabase dikes and sills protrude through the arkose sandstone in the area southwest of Pori to form peninsulas, while Yyteri has sandy shores and blown sand, the material for which is derived from an esker. Further south the coast is broken by bays oriented in a NW-SE direction, regulated by the schistosity of the migmatite gneiss and the presence of fault lines.

The part of the Baltic lying off the southwestern coast of Finland, a veritable labyrinth of land and water, is also known as the Archipelago Sea. The islands of Åland and Kustavi have a rapakivi bedrock, the local surficial landforms are typically steeply sloping and nondirectional, and the bedrock surfaces are fractured and subject to granular disintegration (Plate 42-7). Bare-washed roches moutonnées (Plate 42-8) and boulder fields are common on the shores of the north coast of Åland and the outer islands, while the distribution of land and water in the island area off Turku is governed by the east-west orientation of the petrological zones and their schistosity and the north-south orientation of the fault zones (Plate 42-9). The rings of islands forming the Åva and Mossala groups are evidence of dome formations (Fig. 42-3). The outer skerries have shores of exposed bedrock, while the bays of the inner islands possess reedy shores of clay or silt (Pyökäri 1978). On the coast between the island of Kemiö and the Hanko peninsula the ice margin formations of Salpausselkä I, II, and III reach the coast to form peninsulas and stand out in the form of islands with sandy shores, fields of blown sand, and raised beach ridges (Varjo 1964).

The islands and straits of the Gulf of Finland coast between the peninsulas of Hanko and

Porkkala are oriented in a west-east direction in accordance with the zones of granite and gneiss, the chains of islands typical of a longitudinal coast being interrupted by transverse fractures. The tectonic orientation of the various granites and schists is SW-NE on the Porkkala peninsula, but continues in a variable manner in the area east of Helsinki. The island belt narrows towards the east, and the shores of the outer islands are rocky while those at the heads of the labyrinthine bays are composed of silt or clay supporting a reed vegetation (Plate 42-10).

The bedrock on the Porvoo coast is composed of porphyry granite, which fractures and disintegrates in the manner of rapakivi granite, while further east it is of granite again. The coast contains a number of large N-S oriented peninsulas and islands, but although many eskers extend down to the coast there are very few sandy shores. The shores of the bays are of silt or clay, and the islands of the Pellinki group have shores composed of schistose bedrock.

A continuous area of rapakivi granite extends eastward from Loviisa as far as the border with the Soviet Union, and the relief is flat between Loviisa and Kotka, with few islands. The bedrock in this latter area is overlain by thick surficial deposits, and sandy shores are encountered beside the esker chains. To the east of Kotka the bedrock surface shows a more variable relief and there are extensive bedrock outcrops. Here the shoreline is very irregular, and there is an extensive belt of islands. Rocky shores are predominant on the outer islands and stony shores in the bays (Granö 1960).

The morphology of the coastline is largely dictated by the Precambrian bedrock surface and the glacial formations superimposed on it, with regional variations brought about by littoral processes. Rocky shores are prevalent on the coast and islands of the southwest, where abrasion has been rapid because of the exposed aspect, the long ice-free period each year, and the relatively slow rate of land uplift. Elsewhere stony outwash shores are dominant. A well-developed wave-shaped morphology is found on the coast of the Bothnian Bay, in spite of the rapid rate of land uplift, because the shores are exposed to strong wave action and the surficial deposits are largely of sand.

JOUKO ALESTALO

REFERENCES

Alestalo, J., 1979, Land uplift and development of the littoral and aeolian morphology on Hailuoto, Finland, *Acta Univ. Oul. A. 82. Geol.* **3**:109–120.

Alestalo, J., and J. Häikiö, 1976, Ice features and ice-thrust shore forms at Luodonselkä, Gulf of Bothnia, in winter 1972/73, *Fennia* **144**:5–24.

Fogelberg, P., and M. Seppälä, 1979, General geomorphological map, *Atlas of Finland*, Suomen Maantieteellinen Seura.

Granö, O., 1960, Die Ufer der Südküste Finnlands, *Fennia* **83**:1–49.

Helle, R., 1965, Strandwallbildungen im Gebiet am Unterlauf des Flusses Siikajoki, *Fennia* **95**:1–35.

Kääriäinen, E., 1953, On the recent uplift of the Earth's crust in Finland, *Fennia* **77**:1–106.

Lisitzin, E., 1959, The frequency distribution of the sea-level heights along the Finnish coast, *Merentutkimuslait, Julk.* **190**:1–37.

Mansikkaniemi, H., 1976, Ice action on the sea-shore, southern Finland: observations and experiments, *Fennia* **148**:1–17.

Pyökäri, M., 1978, Airiston alueen rantatyypeistä (Shore types in the Airisto area, SW Finland), *Terra* **90**: 81–91.

Simojoki, H., 1957, On the consideration of the double sunspot cycle in climatic investigations, *Geophysica* **6**:25–29.

Simonen, A., 1960, Pre-Quaternary rocks in Finland, *Finlande Comm. Géol. Bull.* **191**:1–46.

Tulkki, P., 1977, The bottom of the Bothnian Bay, *Merentutkimuslait. Julk.* **241**:5–89.

Varjo, U., 1964, Über finnische Küsten und ihre Entstehung, *Fennia* **91**:1–104.

Zilliacus, H., 1981, De Geer-moränerna på Replot och Björkön i Vaasa skärgard (The De Geer moraines on the islands of Replot and Björkön in the Vaasa archipelago, western Finland), *Terra* **93**:12–24.

Plate 42-1. Emerged De Geer moraines at Björkö. The ridges are oriented WSW-ENE. The area contains large numbers of erratic boulders. The shores experience little abrasion because of their sheltered aspect and the rapid rate of land uplift (photo by J. Alestalo).

Plate 42-2. An emerging esker at Monäs in Munsala. The island in the foreground is the abrasion residue from the stony core of an esker. Opposite it is a sandy shore and blown sand field with a foredune bound by lyme grass, a deflation surface in the process of afforestation and bearing the remains of raised beach ridges, and a ridge of mobile dunes with blowouts on their proximal face (photo by J. Alestalo).

Plate 42-3. An emerging silty meadow shore in the bay of Liminganlahti. The circular patches are spreading stands of glaucus bulrush, *Scirpus tabernaemontani* (photo by J. Alestalo).

Plate 42-4. Raised beach ridges on the south-western side of an esker at Siikajoki. The ridges support pine forest, *Pinus silvestris,* and the swales are occupied by mires and fields (photo by J. Alestalo).

Plate 42-5. The delta of the river Siikajoki has increased in width to over 7 km, as ridges of piled ice close off the flow of water in spring and force the floodwater to run along the shore, where the coastal water is already ice-free (photo by J. Alestalo).

Plate 42-6. Shore ridges and lagoons on the south shore of the bay at the mouth of the river Kalajoki. One ridge, which grew up after a brief blown-sand phase, is now developing a forest vegetation. The material is from an esker running to the south of the site. The shoreline has moved approximately 600 m seaward since 1868 (photo by J. Alestalo).

Plate 42-7. Rocky shores of rapakivi granite on islands of the Kustavi group. The rocks are washed bare of surficial material, fractured, and showing signs of granular disintegration (photo by J. Alestalo).

Plate 42-9. A sheltered transverse shore at Parainen in the inner islands southeast of Turku. The ENE-WSW-oriented ridges are of granite. The bays have silt or clay shores. (photo by J. Alestalo).

Plate 42-8. Bare bedrock islands formed from a granitic annular dike in the Åva island group. The striae on the roche moutonnée show the ice sheet to have moved from the north (top right) (photo by J. Alestalo).

Plate 42-10. The complex island coast at Inkoo, between Hanko and Porkkala. The granite rocks on the shores are steep and washed almost bare (photo by J. Alestalo).

43. BALTIC USSR

The coasts of the eastern Baltic area stretch from the head of the Gulf of Finland to the Bay of Gdansk and include the coastlines of the Leningrad District (Oblast), Estonia, Latvia, Lithuania, and the Kaliningrad District (formerly the northern part of East Prussia) (Fig. 43-1 and 43-2). The total length of the recent shore, without the Estonian Archipelago, is about 3000 km, as follows: Leningrad District—1000 km, Estonia—1350 km, Latvia—500 km, Lithuania—100 km, Kaliningrad District—200 km (Gudelis 1960).

The coastline of Estonia and the Estonian Archipelago is the most curved. The coasts of the eastern Baltic are in general straight and expressed in the form of large, smoothed, shoreline arcs. The coasts are exposed to the prevailing western winds except on the southern coastline of the Gulf of Finland. In the eastern Baltic area there are large gulfs, the Gulf of Finland and the Gulf of Riga, as well as freshwater lagoons, the Kuršių Marios (Kurisches Haff) and Vistula (Frisches Haff). The lagoons are separated from the open sea by long barrier spits. The islands of the Estonian Archipelago are separated from the mainland by Moonsund (Väinemere) Strait.

The Gulf of Finland is a large tectonic depression, formed in the contact zone between the crystalline shield of Fennoscandia and the East European platform. The Gulf of Riga and the lagoon depressions mentioned above were created mainly by glacial erosion during the Pleistocene (Gudelis 1967, 1970, 1973).

The eastern Baltic area belongs to the northwestern outskirts of the East European plain. The coastal zone is represented by a lowland visibly inclined seaward, with some quite limited sectors of cliffy, high coast.

The crystalline basement outcrops only in the Karelian Isthmus. In Estonia it lies at a depth of 150–500 m, in Latvia and Lithuania to 2200 m. On the Sambian Peninsula the crystalline basement was reported at a depth of 2500–2600 m (Gudelis and Jemeljanov, 1976). The topography of the crystalline basement is represented by uplifted and downwarped tectonic features dissected by a complicated fault system. The basement is overlain by a thick cover of sedimentary strata of lower Paleozoic age in the northern part, and of Mesozoic and Cenozoic in the south. In the sedimentary cover there are anticlines and synclines.

The pre-Quaternary in Estonia and Latvia is represented by Paleozoic dolomites, clays, sandstones, and sand. On the Lithuanian coast the bedrock is formed of various Permian-Jurassic sands and clays. Cretaceous rocks (chalk, sands, marls, and clays) are widely spread over a vast area. Tertiary beds form the bedrock surface in the Sambian Peninsula. Among them there are amber-bearing strata. The sub-Quaternary surface consists of elevated and depressed areas. In many places there are deep valley-like incisions (to 200 m below mean sea level), created by glacial and fluvial erosion, and filled up by glacial drift. Relief of the bedrock surface in the coastal zone reaches up to 40–50 m and was created predominately by selective glacial and fluvial erosion (Gudelis 1973).

Quaternary deposits of various thickness cover the bedrock. They are represented by Pleistocene glacial and intermorainal sediment as well as Holocene lagoonal-alluvial deposits, peat, and eolian sand.

Lowland coasts predominate. A cliffy high coast develops only where bedrock outcrops are pres-

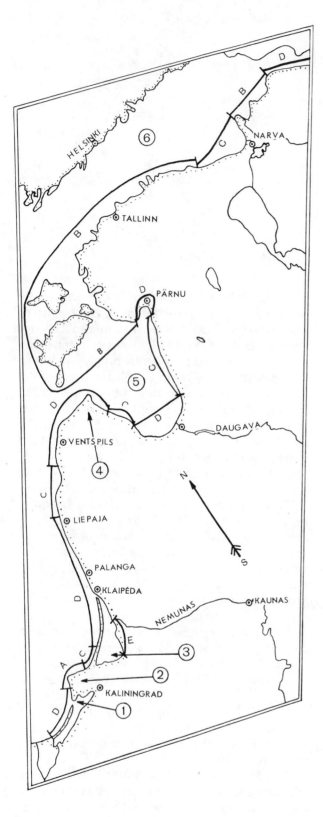

Figure 43-1. Main morphogenetic coastal types of the east Baltic area (USSR): Leningrad District, Estonia, Latvia, Lithuania, Kaliningrad District. *A.* Abrasional (erosional) straightened coast. On the Sambian Peninsula the coastline is slightly curved and represented by high cliffs (up to 60 m) cut in Quaternary and Neogene deposits (tills, sand, and gravel). *B.* Abrasional-accumulative embayed coast. This coast is typical of northwestern Estonia and the Estonian Archipelago. As a rule slight beach aggradation takes place in the heads of bays. There are elevated (cliffed) and lowland coastal sectors. The latter are represented by boulder-cobble, sand-gravel morainic and grass-covered beaches. The high coast is represented by cliffs up to 60–70 m high cut in lower Paleozoic beds (limestones, dolomites, marls). This is the glint or klint coast. *C.* Abrasional-accumulative straightened coast. Sectors of erosion alternate with sectors of slight accumulation. This coastal type is characterized by sand or gravel-pebble beaches. In other places a flat, marshy, or grass-vegetation shore is developed. There are also sectors of sand beaches and foredunes. *D.* Accumulative straightened coast. This coast type is characterized by wide sandy beaches and foredunes exceeding a height of 12–16 m. On the Kuršių Nerija spit there are high mobile coastal dunes, reaching up to 65 m in height. *E.* Deltaic coast, alluvial wetland plain of the Nemunas River.

1. Vistula lagoon (firth). 2. Sambia Peninsula. 3. Kuršių Marios lagoon. 4. Kurzeme Peninsula. 5. Gulf of Riga. 6. Gulf of Finland.

Figure 43-2. *(at right)* Pre-Quaternary rocks, longshore sediment drift, and displacement of shoreline in the east Baltic Area. 1. Cambrian. 2. Ordovician. 3. Silurian. 4. Devonian. 5. Permian. 6. Triassic. 7. Jurassic. 8. Cretaceous. 9. Neogene. 10. Absolute height of elevated synchronous shoreline of the late Glacial Baltic Ice Lake. 11. Isobases of recent shoreline displacement (mm/yr) according to mareographic data. 12. Directions of longshore sediment drift. 13. Capacity (volume) of longshore drift 10^3 m³/yr.

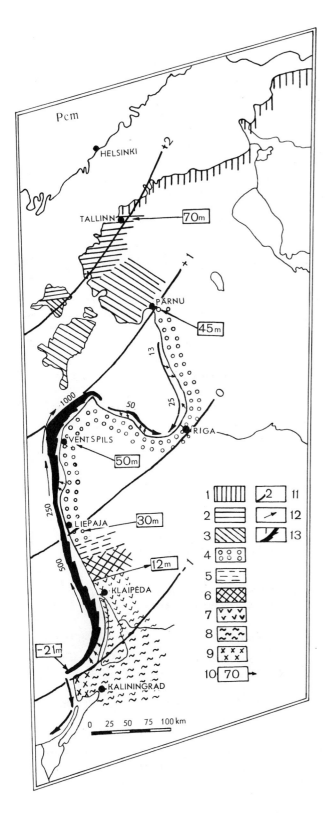

ent or the glacial marginal ridges or morainal plateaus come in touch with the sea (Sambian Peninsula and northwestern Estonia).

The beginning of coastal formation in the eastern Baltic area is connected with the Litorina maximum transgression and the following regression (7000–5000 years ago). During the transgression an energetic erosion of cliffs and offshore platforms set in, producing vast amounts of littoral debris. During the regression, the coastline straightened and spits, marine terraces, deltas, and coastal dunes were formed. In these processes longshore sediment drift and wind action played an important role (Gudelis and Königsson 1979).

The postglacial period was characterized by distinct vertical crustal movements (glacio-isostatic and tectonic). The zero isobase runs through the middle of the Nemunas (Njemen) delta. The Kaliningrad District experienced a slow subsidence, but in the rest of the territory, there was crustal uplift from 5–6 m on the Lithuanian coast to 40–50 m on the northwestern Estonian coast. Recent displacement of the coastline in the East Baltic area varies from -2 mm/yr on the Sambian Peninsula to +3 mm/yr in northwestern Estonia. Nevertheless crustal movements have had limited influence on the recent coastal dynamics.

Waves and currents (especially during heavy storms), longshore drift, eolian processes, and human activity are the main agents of coastline evolution. The role of alluvial deposition is very limited. Among the passive factors are the inherited bathymetry and the landforms of the coastal zone and the lithological composition of rocks and sediments. Swell effects in the Baltic Sea are negligible. The modern shore dynamics become quite intensive during heavy storms, which occur approximately every 20–25 years. Even on open sea beaches, the rise in water level sometimes exceeds 2 m. Such a revolutionary period, when the shore zone experiences major reshaping and redistribution of littoral drift, is followed by a long period of normal, calm development (Gudelis 1960).

THE WEST COAST

This coastal sector includes the whole coast area from the southern end of the Sambian Peninsula to Kolkas Rags Point in the Irbe Strait.

The Sambian Peninsula (Plate 43-1) is a morainic plateau, 40–60 m high, which separates the two above-mentioned lagoons. The base of the peninsula consists of Tertiary sands and clays overlain by a thin cover of Quaternary deposits.

The southern part of the Sambian western coast is represented by accumulative littoral forms, sandy beaches 30–40 m wide bordered by low foredunes. Farther to the north the coast becomes cliffy. Cliffs cut into the moraine and Tertiary beds reach up to 55–60 m (Brüsterort). The coastline is slightly sinuous, beaches narrow and built of sand and gravel, with cobbles and boulders. Landslides, ravine erosion, and groundwater processes play an important role in the destruction of the high cliffs. Off the cliffed coast flat and shallow platforms develop, covered with boulders, pebbles, and gravel. The northern Sambian coast, having a west-east orientation, is also cliffy. The cliff at Svetlogorsk (Rauschen) is 61 m high. From there it becomes gradually lower and the coast is again of a low, accumulative type. Beginning in the twentieth century, intensively eroded sectors of the Sambian coasts underwent shore protection work.

To the north of the Sambian Peninsula is the longest spit in the Baltic, Kuršių Nerija (98 km long, 4 km wide), stretching in a gentle curve (Plate 43-2). The narrow Strait of Klaipeda separates the spit from the mainland. The lagoonal shore of the spit is cuspate. The southern part of the spit is represented by narrow coarse sandy beaches fringed by low cliffs cut into moraines. The middle part of the spit has beaches 30–40 m wide and foredunes 8–12 m high (Plate 43-3). The northern part of the spit has prograded.

On the Kuršių Nerija spit the largest regional coastal dune ridge is developed. Several mobile dunes exceed 60 m in height.

From the Klaipeda seaport to the north (via Palanga, Sventoji, and toward the Liepaja) there is an accumulative coast (Plate 43-4), represented by sandy and sandy-gravel beaches 30–110 m wide, bordered by foredunes. In some places behind the foredunes there are relics of small coastal lakes and swamps (Sventoji-Liepaja). Accumulative littoral landforms are to be seen in Palanga and southward of Liepaja. Where the longshore sediment drift is interrupted by seaport structures or where the morainic plateaus reach the coast, there are local erosional sectors (Olando Kepure, Liepaja-Pavilosta, and to the north of Ventspils town) (Plate 43-4). Northward from Ventspils seaport, the coast is again accumulative. The Kolikas Rags Point is a large sand body that originated as a result of intensive littoral drift accretion in this area. The volume of longshore sediment flow reaches about 1×10^6 m³/yr (Gudelis and Jemeljanov 1976). At Ovisi Point the shore-line turns sharply to the northeast. Irbe Strait separates Kolkas Rags Point from Saaremaa Island.

From Brüsterort Point, which acts as a dividing point for littoral drift along the northern coast of Sambian Peninsula, to the Kuršių Nerija spit and northward to the Kolkas Rags Point, a powerful longshore drift has been in action since the end of the Litorina Sea regression. It consists of some linked local sediment migration systems. Its length, as a whole, is over 450 km. The capacity varies from 200,000–800,000 m³/yr. In the Riga Gulf there are two convergent longshore drifts (capacity 15,000–50,000 m³/yr).

RIGA GULF

From Kolkas Rags Point toward the Daugava River mouth, the coast is of lowland plain type, mainly accumulative, with wetland and relict lagoons in the hinterland. In the vicinity of Roja and Engure, the beaches and foredunes are eroded in some places though sandy beaches prevail. Nevertheless there are so-called meadow beaches too (Ulst 1957). Foredunes are often relatively high especially in the vicinity of Riga (Daugava River mouth area).

The eastern coast of Riga Gulf, between Riga and Ainaži-Pärnu, is represented by accumulative sandy beaches in many places, interrupted by wetlands and coastal meadows. In eroded sectors benches are well developed and the beach material is coarser. In Pärnu Bay, wide beaches of fine sand are present again.

MOONSUND STRAIT AND THE ESTONIAN ARCHIPELAGO

This coastal sector occupies the area between Pärnu Bay and Vormsi Island. The mainland coast here is low, embayed, and formed in Quaternary deposits. The offshore zone is very shallow. There are flat, marshy, silty, and shingle-boulder beaches. In places short scarps, cut in moraine and glaciofluvial deposits, are visible. Eolian landforms are poorly developed or absent (Orviku 1974).

On the large islands (Saaremaa, Hiumaa), the eastern and southern coasts are low and flat, locally marshy, with beaches built up of coarse, clastic material. The northwestern coasts of these islands are, in contrast, represented by 20 m high cliffs, cut in limestones of Ordovician and Silurian age and sometimes in morainic material.

The offshore area here is relatively deep, and

the platform is represented by bare rock. Pebble and boulder beaches are widespread too. In the northern part of Moonsund Strait there are many rocky islets. Because of progressive land uplift, recent cliffs are usually eroded only during heavy storms (Orviku 1974).

SOUTHERN FINNISH GULF

This coastal sector includes northern Estonia, the Prilužskaja lowland, and the coastal zone stretching to the Neva River delta. Here the two types of coasts—cliffed and flat, accretion-erosion—can be distinguished. The highest regional cliffs formed in carbonaceous rocks are to be found in northwestern Estonia (Plate 43-5), between Pakerort Point and Ontika. The average height is 20–30 m, the maximum height about 80 m. This cliff is called glint or klint. At the foot of active cliffs, large rock falls often accumulate.

Narrow beaches are built up of coarse clastic material or bare rock blocks. Platform surfaces are usually covered with numerous pebbles, boulders, and rock blocks. Only in limited sites it is possible to find accumulative sandy beaches and low foredunes (Pirita). In places where cliffs are situated some distance from the sea, low sandy, marshy, or pebble-gravel shores have developed (Narva, Kunda).

Within the Luga and Neva lowlands, coasts are accumulative, marshy, or bordered by peat and wetlands. The head of the Gulf of Finland is represented by the shores of the Neva River delta, occupied by the city of Leningrad. The coastal area here is a low marshy wetland. To the north of Leningrad well-developed sandy beaches and foredunes are to be seen. The northern coast of the Karelian Isthmus belongs to the rock skerry-coast type; it consists of crystalline rocks, sometimes with a thin Quaternary cover.

In the east Baltic area it is possible to distin-guish some morphogenetic coast types and sub-types (Gudelis 1967). In the Lithuania, Latvia, and Kaliningrad districts, and partly in Leningrad District, low, straigthened, accumulative and erosional coastal types dominate. Embayed, mostly erosional, coasts are characteristic of northwest-ern Estonia, and rocky skerries of the northern part of the Karelian Isthmus.

The total amount of clastic material discharged into the Baltic Sea because of erosion of both beaches and platforms, as well as human activity, can be estimated at about 5385×10^3 m³/yr in the east Baltic area (Gudelis and Jemeljanov 1976). The greatest amount is derived from erosion of the nearshore bottom, active cliffs, and beaches. The length of abrasional (eroded) coast in the east Baltic area is about 500 km, or one-sixth of the whole coastline length.

VYTAUTAS GUDELIS

REFERENCES

Gudelis, V., 1960, *The Baltic Sea*, Mintis Publishing House, Vilnius.

Gudelis, V., 1967, Morphogenetic types of the Baltic Sea coasts, *Baltica* **3:**123–145.

Gudelis, V., 1970, Main features of geology and bottom topography of the Mid-Baltic Sea, *Baltica* **4:**103–113.

Gudelis, V., 1973, *Relief and Quaternary of the East Baltic Region*, Mintis Publishing House, Vilnius.

Gudelis, V., and J. Jemeljanov, 1976, *Geology of the Baltic Sea*, Mokslas Publishers, Vilnius.

Gudelis, V., and L.-K. Königsson, eds., 1979, *The Quaternary History of the Baltic*, Almquist and Wiksell, Uppsala.

Orviku, K., 1974, *Estonian Seacoasts*, Academy of Sciences of the Estonian SSR Publishers, Tallinn.

Ulst, V. G., 1957, *Morphology and Development of Marine Accumulation Area in the Gulf of Riga Head*, Academy of Sciences of the Latvian SSR Publishers, Riga.

Plate 43-1. Coast of the Sambian Peninsula. The height of the cliffs exceeds 45–50 m. Their slopes are covered by shrubs and trees. In some places cliffs are dissected by erosional ravines, at the foot of which alluvial fans occur. Cliff-forming agents include landslides, soil creep, and mudflows. With stormy waves, the thin sand cover on the beach is washed away (photo by V. Gudelis).

Plate 43-2. Accumulative (depositional) smoothed sandy coast (Kuršių Nerija spit, Lithuania). Sand beaches are up to 80 m wide and made up of fine-grained sand. Beach-bordering foredunes are 8–12 m high, on average, and covered by dune grass (photo by V. Gudelis).

Plate 43-3. Highest coastal mobile dunes of the Baltic, on the Kuršių Nerija spit (Lithuania). Dunes are migrating toward the Kuršių Mariosa lagoon. Average height of the dune ridge is about 45–50 m (photo by V. Gudelis).

Plate 43-4. Abrasive-accumulative straightened coast sector northward of Klaipeda harbour. Shore scarp is developed in glacial drift. The boulders are derived from till lying just below the thin sand cover (photo by D. Semetulskis).

Plate 43-5. Abrasive (erosional) cliffed coast of northwestern Estonia formed in lower-Paleozoic limestones. In some places the cliff foot is covered with large rockfall blocks, which protect the shore from wave erosion for many years (photo by V. Gudelis).

44. POLAND

The Polish Baltic coast is about 500 km long; including the coastline of the Szczecin and Vistula bays, it approaches 700 km. Sandy coasts constitute about 360 km (52%), swampy about 195 km (28%), and cliffed coasts about 140 km (20%). Sandy and cliffed coasts occur alternately, forming a smooth abrasive-accumulative coastline (Gudelis 1967). The swampy type of coast occurs only within Szczecin, Vistula, and Puck bays (Fig. 44-1).

The cliffed parts of the coast are cut into ground moraine plateaus and end moraine hills consisting primarily of glacial tills and of fluvioglacial sands

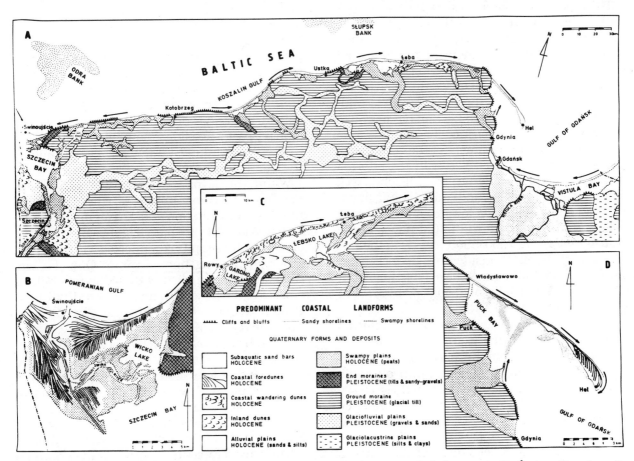

Figure 44-1. The geomorphology of the Polish coastal zone. *A.* Polish coast; *B.* Świna Barrier; *C.* Łeba Barrier; *D.* Hel Spit.

and gravels. In such cases the height of the cliffs is usually 15–40 m, with a maximum height of 80–90 m in the end moraine areas (e.g., east of Świnoujście). The sandy parts of the coast, usually in the form of barriers, enclose depressions and valleys of the late glacial relief to form coastal lakes and swampy plains (Fig. 44-1). The barrier sands are usually underlain by lacustrine deposits and peats, indicating that the barriers have been shifting south following the relative rise of the sea level (Rosa and Wypych 1980). In some places (east of Ustka) coastal dunes connected with the barriers have encroached on ground moraine plateaus, forming cliff-top dunes.

The coastline itself shows a dependence on the geological structure of the bedrock. The Pomeranian, Koszalin, and Gdańsk gulfs, as well as the Szczecin and Vistula bays, relate to tectonic depressions, where even today a clear subsidence is noted, ranging from 7 cm (the Pomeranian Gulf) to 18 cm (the Koszalin Gulf) per century (Kowalik and Wroblewski 1973; Rosa and Wypych 1980).

The Polish coast was formed in the final phases of the late Würm and in the Holocene. Stages in its development were conditioned by the coincidence of isostatic movement of the land and eustatic oscillations of sea level. The different rates of these movements caused the relative lowering of the sea level or the land, thus determining the stages of transgression and regression of the sea during the Holocene. The most decisive influence on the development of the coastline of the southern Baltic was exerted by the Litorina transgression in the Atlantic period. It submerged cliffs and abrasive steps, and caused the aggradation of sediments in the lower sections of river valleys (Rosa 1963). In the initial phase of the transgression (i.e., 7500–5500 years B.P.) the rate of sea level rise was considerable, up to 1 m per century, while in the next phase (starting about 5500 years B.P.) it amounted only to about 0.1 m per century (Wypych 1973).

On the Polish coast, the maximum Litorina transgression occurred from 4000–3500 years B.P. Old coastlines from this period are now situated at different heights because of neotectonic movements. The highest position of these coastlines is in the Łeba region, 3 m above sea level, and the lowest in the region of the Gulf of Gdańsk, 10 m below sea level (Rosa 1963).

The present-day development of the coast is the result of a number of factors, the most important of which are hydrodynamic, such as storm surges and the periodic sea-level oscillations that accompany them, wind waves, and longshore currents. Formation of the coast is also considerably influenced by morphology and geological structure as well as by coastline exposure in relation to the dominant wind direction.

Numerous studies (Czekańska 1948; Czekańska and Dziadziuszko 1964) show that sporadic storm surges have the clearest, frequently even catastrophic, influence on the coastal processes. The strongest of them, connected with westerly winds, occur in the autumn and winter, with a frequency of about 15 surges per century, reaching a height of 2.0–2.5 m. Storm surges often cause destruction of the barriers and the formation of overwash fans, as well as inwashed inlet deltas on the beds of coastal lakes. They also contribute to intensified cliff recession.

The present average rate of cliff recession is 0.6–1.0m/yr (Racinowski 1974; Subotowicz 1980). In some places the coast is being eroded much more quickly—for example, east of Świnoujście, where numerous landslides develop because favorable hydrogeological conditions, cliff crest recession averages 2m/yr.

The prevailing westerly winds and waves cause a periodic appearance of longshore currents transporting considerable amounts of sediment, from both the cliffed coasts and the subaquatic shallows of the Odra and Słupsk banks (Zenkovich 1958). The effect of these currents is to form a smooth coastline and to build spits, today as well as in the past. This effect is particularly well marked in the Pomeranian Gulf (Świna Barrier) and in the Gdańsk Gulf (Hel Spit).

Within the Świna Barrier, separating Szczecin Bay from the Pomeranian Gulf, there has been rapid coastal accretion and development of spits with well-formed foredunes (Fig. 44-1B). The development of those spits is connected with a convergence of two longshore currents. One of them, eastbound, is supplied with sediments by cliff erosion of the East German coast (the Rugia and Uznam islands). The westbound current flows from the region of Kołobrzeg (Fig. 44-1A).

The Łeba Barrier and Hel Spit (Figs. 44-1C and 44-1D) are supplied with sandy material by one of the longest longshore drift sectors along the Baltic coast. It flows east from the region of Kołobrzeg and is supplied with sediments by the erosion of cliffs and submarine banks, especially Słupsk Bank (Marsz 1966; Zenkovich 1958).

The considerable supply of sandy material onto beaches and barriers has led to the formation of wide dune fields, best developed on the Świna and Łeba barriers and on Hel Spit.

On the Świna Barrier, numerous foredune ridges have formed. The oldest, with relative height of 2–8 m and curved form (Fig. 44-1B), developed in the period from 5000 to 1800 years ago (Prusinkiewicz and Noryśkiewicz 1966). Younger dunes, characterized by much greater heights (12–20 m) and parallel courses, have been formed since the fifth century A.D. Analysis of old cartographic sources (Keilhack 1911) shows that from 1694 to 1911 the six youngest foredune ridges developed, and the annual rate of coastal accretion was up to 7.5m/yr. The present rate is much lower, averaging 2–3 m/yr.

Within the Łeba Barrier, a whole group of eolian forms occurs (Fig. 44-1C and Plate 44-1). Besides those dunes developing at present, there are fossil dunes occupying the northern parts of the barrier. They formed in several phases, approximately 5000–1500 years B.P. (Borówka 1975, Borówka and Tobolski 1979; Tobolski 1975, 1979). The modern phase of development of eolian processes started here at the turn of the fifteenth and sixteenth centuries (Tobolski 1975); like the others, it began as the result of human activity. On Łeba Barrier there are at present parabolic dunes and barchans, with average heights of 15–30 m above sea level and a maximum height of 56 m. They move east at a mean rate of 3.5–10 m/yr (Miszalski 1973). Measurements of the rate of dune migration in the annual cycle point up the fact that eolian processes are most intense in autumn and winter, not only because of the wind regime but also because of air temperature and ground moisture (Borówka 1980). On the Łeba Barrier foredune ridges develop and are periodically destroyed by abrasive processes.

Hel Spit (Fig. 44-1D) is 35 km long, and its width varies from 150 m in the western part to 3 km near Hel. As recently as the middle of the seventeenth century, Hel Spit consisted of six elongated islets (Bączyk 1963). In the western part of the spit, where abrasive processes dominate, there is only one foredune ridge 5–10 m high, which is partly destroyed in the autumn and winter, and reconstructed in spring and summer. The eastern part of the spit consists of a few dozen foredune ridges, some of which reach heights of 20 m.

The southwestern coasts of Hel Spit, on Puck Bay and the Gulf of Gdańsk, are marked by a complicated system of longshore subaquatic sand bars formed by currents (Fig. 44-1D).

RYSZARD K. BORÓWKA

REFERENCES

Bączyk, J., 1963, *Geneza Półwyspu Helskiego na tle rozwoju Zatoki Gdańskiej*, Dokumentacja Geograficzna, 6.

Borówka, R. K., 1975, Problem of the morphology of the fossil dune forms on the Łeba Bar, *Quaestiones Geographicae* **2:**39–51.

Borówka, R. K., 1980, Present day dune processes and dune morphology on the Łeba Barrier, Polish coast of the Baltic, *Geog. Annaler* **62A:**75–82.

Borówka, R. K., and K. Tobolski, 1979, New archeological sites on the Łeba Bar and their significance for paleogeography of this area (in Polish), *Badania Fizjogr. nad Polską Zachodnią* **32A:**21–29.

Czekańska, M., 1948, Flood raised by storm on the southern shores of the Baltic Sea (in Polish), *Badania Fizjogr. nad Polską Zachodnią* **1:**58–96

Czekańska, M., and Z. Dziadziuszko, 1964, Raising of waters at the Polish coast of the Baltic during the stormy period in February, 1962 (in Polish), *Badania Fizjogr. nad Polską Zachodnią* **13:**75–104.

Gudelis, V. K., 1967, The morphological types of Baltic Sea coasts (in Russian), *Baltica* **3:**123–144.

Keilhack, K., 1911, Die Verlandung der Swinepforte, *Jahrbuch der Königlich Preussischen Geologischen Landesanstalt* **32:**209–244.

Kowalik, Z., and A. Wróblewski, 1973, Long term oscillations of annual mean sea level in the Baltic on the basis of observations carried out in Świnoujście from 1811 to 1970, *Acta Geophys. Polonica,* **21:**3–10.

Marsz, A., 1966, *Geneza Wydm Lebskich w Świetle Współczesnych Procesów Brzegowych*, PTPN, Prace Komisji Geograficzno-Geologicznej, 4/6.

Miszalski, J., 1973, *Present-day Eolian Processes on the Slovinian Coastline; A Study of Photo-Interpretation* (in Polish), Dokumentacja Geograficzna, 3.

Prusinkiewicz, Z., and B. Noryśkiewicz, 1966, Problems of the podzols age on brown dunes of Świna Barrier in the light of a palynological analysis and dating by radiocarbon C-14 (in Polish), *Zeszyty Naukowe Uniwersytetu im. M. Kopernika, Geografia* **5:**75–88.

Racinowski, R., 1974, Dynamics of the sedimentary environment of West Pomerania coastal zone in the light of heavy minerals and grain size distribution research (in Polish), *Prace Naukowe Politechniki Szczecińskiej* **4:**1–156.

Rosa, B., 1963, *O Rozwoju Morfologicznym Wybrzeza Polski w Świetle Dawnych Form Brzegowych*, Studia Societatis Scientiarum Torunensis, Geographia et Geologia, 5.

Rosa, B., and K. Wypych, 1980, O mierzejach wybrzeża południowoba-ltyckiego, *Peribalticum — Problemy Badawcze Obszaru Bałtyckiego,* **1:**31–44.

Subotowicz, W., 1980, Geodynamika brzegów klifowych regionu gdańskiego, *Peribalticum — Problemy Badawcze Obszaru Bałtyckiego,* **1:**45–58.

Tobolski, K., 1975, *Palynological Study of Fossil Soils*

of the Leba Bay Bar in the Słowiński National Park (in Polish), PTPN, Prace Komisji Biologicznej, 41.

Tobolski, K., 1979, Changes in the local plant cover on the basis of investigations on subfossil biogenic sediments in the beach zone near Łeba (in Polish), *Badania Fizjogr. nad Polską Zachodnią* **32A:**151–168.

Wypych, K., 1973, Genesis of the lagoons of the southern Baltic Sea in the light of recent research (in Polish), *Przegląd Geofiz.* **18:**111–120.

Zenkovich, V. P., 1958, Niekotoryje voprosy dinamiki polskovo bierega Baltijskovo Morija, *Izviestija Vsiehsojuznovo Geograficheskovo Obschestva* **90:** 269–279.

Plate 44-1. Eolian forms on Łeba Barrier. At the top are submarine bars characteristic of almost the entire Polish coast (photo courtesy of the General Staff of the People's Polish Army).

45. EAST GERMANY (GERMAN DEMOCRATIC REPUBLIC)

The German Democratic Republic has a coast-line of 290 km along the Sudeiche Ostsee of the Baltic Sea from the Stettiner Haff in the east to the Lubecker Bucht in the west (Fig. 45-1). To this must be added the 160 km coastline of the island of Rügen (Fig. 45-1). Much of the coast is low-lying and beach-fringed. Sandy sediment, with some gravel and boulders, derived from cliff and sea floor erosion, has accumulated at the foot of cliffs or on flat beaches (Plate 45-1). Intervening sectors are dominated by cliffs up to 10 m high

cut in glacial drift, with recurrent landslides and foreshores strewn with boulders (Plate 45-2). On the northeast coast of Rügen, Cretaceous rocks outcrop, and the cliffs are higher, attaining a maximum of 121 m above sea level in the chalk cliff near Stubbenkammer.

Erosion is extensive along this coastline (Plate 45-3), and there are many artificial structures, including 40 km of sea walls and more than 150 km lined by groins (Plate 45-4) designed to halt erosion and trap beach sediments. Dredging and

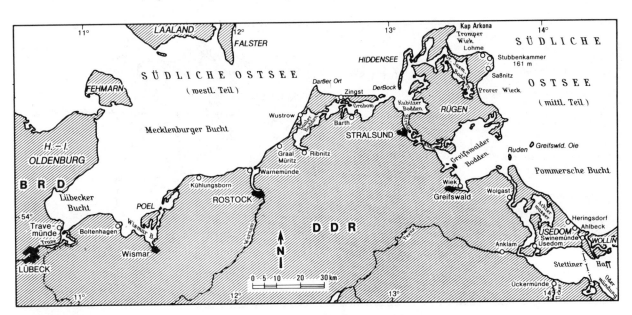

Figure 45-1. Coastline of the German Democratic Republic.

land reclamation have been extensive in and around the major ports of Wismar, Rostock, Stralsund, and Greifswald, and the ferry port of Sassnitz on Rügen.

A predominance of westerly winds in the southern Baltic yields a prevalence of waves from the west and northwest, and a consequent eastward flow of sediment along coastal sectors exposed to these directions; hence the eastward growth of spits from the Darss foreland. However, winds from the northeast, east, and southeast are also frequent, and spit growth on the shores of Rügen is attributable to waves generated from these directions (Fig. 45-2).

The largest depositional feature is the well-known Darss foreland (Plate 45-5), a major cuspate foreland built up in stages commemorated by numerous beach ridges. The pattern of these ridges indicates an eastward migration, for they are truncated on the eroding western shore, but accretion continues in Prerow Bucht, east of the point of Darsser Ort. Bluffs to the south mark an old cliffed coastline, degraded behind the migrating foreland.

Marked changes have also occurred on the island of Hiddensee off the west coast of Rügen, where there has been rapid recession of cliffs cut in glacial drift, which reach a height of 72.4 m and rapid growth of spits, notable Gellen spit, which extended 1130 m between 1695 and 1953 (Gellert 1958).

The adjacent Baltic Sea is shallow. Normal tide ranges are less than 0.25 m, but seiches and storm surges can raise or lower coastal water levels by at least a meter. Major storm surges occurred on this coast in 1864, 1867, and 1954 (Kolp 1955, 1957). The 1954 surge caused coastline recession of up to 11 m on dune coasts, especially between Warnemünde and the Darss foreland.

Along low-lying sectors of the coast there are many lagoons, formed where valley mouths or depressions in the glacial drift topography were submerged by the Holocene marine transgression, then enclosed by the formation of spits or barrier beaches of sand and gravel. The larger lagoons are known as haffs, the smaller as bodden. The bodden are generally of intricate outline, with many small islands; they are shallow (generally 1–2 m) with narrow and deeper traversing channels, and the bottom sediments are mainly silt and clay. Much of the bodden shoreline is fringed by reed swamp, which gradually encroaches on the lagoon waters until they are replaced by swampland, some of which has been reclaimed for agriculture.

The coastal waters and shallow lagoons freeze in winter (Fig. 45-3), and in severe winters shore ice may persist in bays and bodden for up to 100 days (Blüthgen 1954). When the ice breaks up in spring, wave action piles it onto the shore, redistributing beach and nearshore sediments, especially boulders, some of which are rafted by ice and carried along shore or offshore.

H. G. GIERLOFF-EMDEN

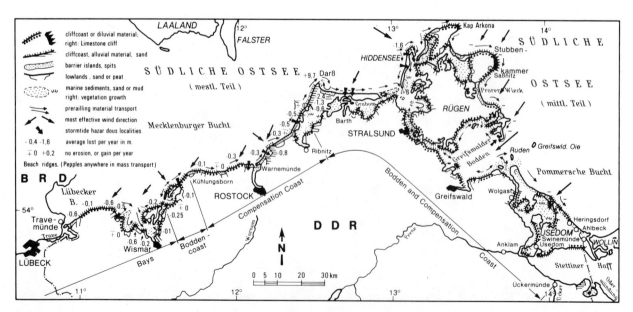

Figure 45-2. Geomorphology and dynamics of the coastline of the German Democratic Republic.

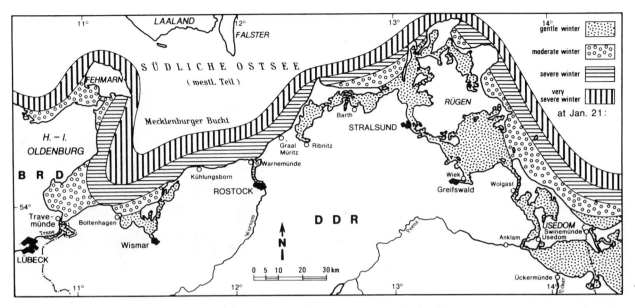

Figure 45-3. Ice distribution on the coast of the German Democratic Republic.

REFERENCES

Blüthgen, J., 1954, Die Eisverhältnisse der Küstenge-
wässer von Mecklenburg-Vorpommern, *Forsch z. Dt.
Landeskunde* **85:**1–142.
Gellert, J. F., 1958, Küstenstudien auf Hiddensee: Der
Strand, *Zeitschr. Pädagogischen Hochschule Pots-
dam* **4:**207–227.
Kolp, O., 1955, *Sturmflutgefährdung der deustchen
Ostsee Küste zwischen Trave und Swine*, Hydro-
Meteorologisches Institut, Stralsund.
Kolp, O., 1957, *Die nordöstliche Heide Mecklenburgs*,
Deutscher Verlag der Wissenschaften, Berlin.

Plate 45-1. Erosion of the dune-fringed coast of
Mecklenburg by the 1954 storm surge (photo by
O. Kolp).

Plate 45-2. Cliff cut in glacial drift fronted by boulder beach at Lobber Ort, Rügen (photo by F. H. W. Dwars).

Plate 45-3. Erosion of sandy coast, Mecklenburg (photo by O. Kolp).

Plate 45-4. Exposure of peat horizon on a receding sandy coast, Mecklenburg. Groins have been built in an effort to retain beach material and halt erosion (photo by O. Kolp).

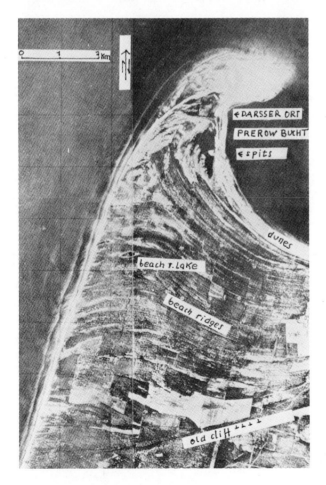

Plate 45-5. Air photograph of the Darss foreland (photo modified from T. Hurtig and K. v. Bulow).

46. BALTIC WEST GERMANY (FEDERAL REPUBLIC OF GERMANY)

The Baltic sector of the Federal Republic of Germany coastline, extending from the East German frontier near Lübeck to the Danish border near Flensburg (Fig. 46-1) is about 530 km long, bordering the sea area traditionally known as the Beltsee (Petersen 1978). Of this length, about 130 km is steep or cliffed coastline, and the remainder low-lying. The adjacent sea area is shallow, the 20 m isobath lying up to 20 km offshore; the water is brackish (approximately 10⁰/₀₀ salinity) at the surface and more saline at depth. Tide ranges are small, generally only 0.1–0.2 m, but larger fluctuations are caused by storm surges that develop when strong winds accompany steep atmospheric pressure gradients as depressions pass across the southern Baltic; these surges may attain 3.5 m above mean tide level. In general, waves are less than 1 m high, but are often steep and erosive during storms.

As a sequel to Late Pleistocene glacial phase lowering of sea level, the Baltic Sea rose during the Litorina transgression (9500–4500 years B.P.), submerging an undulating topography formed by glacial deposition to produce an intricate coastline. Hilly promontories were then cliffed and derived sediment built into extensive beaches, spits, and barriers, enclosing or partly enclosing bays as lagoons (Fig. 46-2), notably on Fehmarn Island (Stremme and Wenk 1969). Submergence of depressions that were previously occupied by ice lobes, and are fringed by moraines, produced

the deep elongated bays known as förden. The Flensburg Förde is 20 km long and up to 25 m deep; the Eckern förde and the Kieler förde are 15 km long and up to 20 m deep. The long, narrow Schlei inlet is a drowned river valley opening to a förde at its mouth. Intervening cliffed sectors expose glacial drift deposits, ranging from boulders and gravel to sand and clay; they are up to 25 m high and are receding as much as 0.5 m per year. At Brodten on the west coast of Lübecker Bucht, cliff recession has resulted in an annual loss of about 1800 m² of land (Kannenberg 1951). Slumping of soft sediments during winter and spring produces fans of shore debris that are consumed and dispersed by wave action in summer, the sand and gravel fraction being distributed to adjacent beaches. Some erosion also results from the pressure of sea ice impacted on the shore by wave action in winter (Gierloff-Emden 1980).

Erosion is predominant along this coastline, but some sectors have prograded as a result of accretion of beaches of white sand and some gravel and boulders. Beach ridges indicating coastal progradation of up to 2 km occur on the western and southern shores of Lübecker Bucht, notably at Timmendorfer Strand (Fig. 46-3) and Pelzerhaken, east of Neustadt, and also on the northern and western shores of Fehmarn (Fig. 46-2). Spits, built and prolonged by drifting beach material, have formed at several localities, the best known being those at Heiligenhafen (Fig.

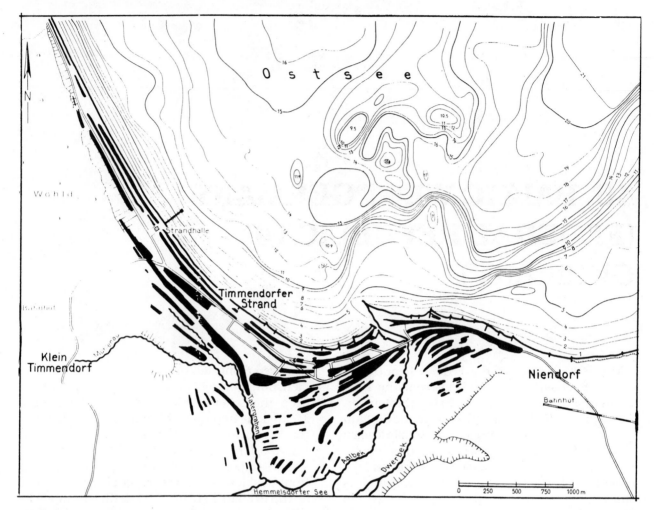

Figure 46-1. The Baltic coast of the Federal Republic of Germany, with cliff and beach ridge and spit development (after Petersen 1978).

46-2), where Graswarder is a detached barrier island that has grown eastward with the addition of successive recurves (Köster 1955). Voss (1967) has traced the evolution of spits at the mouth of the Schlei.

Shallow embayments and lagoons are extensive on this coastline in the lee of spits and barriers, and in some of these sheltered environments salt marshes (total area: 25 km²) have developed. Many recreational centers have been built along this coast.

H. G. GIERLOFF-EMDEN

REFERENCES

Gierloff-Emden, H. G., 1980, *Geographie des Meers, 1 and 2, de Gruyier, Berlin.*

Kannenberg, E. G., 1951, *Die Steilufer der Schleswig Holsteinischen Ostseeküste*, Geograph. Inst., Kiel.

Köster, R., 1955, Die Morphologie der Strandwall-Landschaften und die erdgeschichtliche Entwicklung der Küsten Ostwagrien und Fehmarns, *Meyniana* **4:**52–65.

Petersen, M., 1978, The Baltic coast between Flensburg and the Lübeck Bay, *Die Küste* **32:**109–122.

Stremme, H. G., and H. G. Wenk, 1969, *Die Insel Fehmarn in Schleswig Holstein*, Exkursionsführer, Kiel.

Voss, F., 1967, *Die morphologische Entwicklung der Schleimündung*, Hamburger Geogr. Studien, 20.

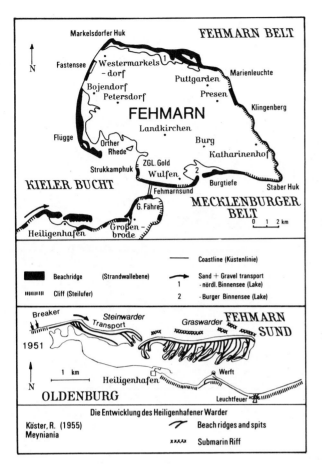

Figure 46-2. The coast of Fehmarn Island and the barrier island and spits of Heiligenhafen (after Köster 1955).

Figure 46-3. Beach ridges of Timmendorfer Strand (thick, black curved lines), southwest Lübecker Bucht. Bathemetry contours are in meters.

47. DENMARK

Most of Denmark is characterized by glacial and glaciofluvial deposits (Fig. 47-1). However, low-lying parts are covered by marine deposits with a surface height from sea level to approximately 55 m above Danish Ordnance Datum (DOD). The tidal range varies from 2 m close to the Danish-German border to 1.5 m at Esbjerg. North of Horns Rev the tide is of less importance. In Kattegat the tidal range is below 0.5 m, but has still some morphological effect in the interior waters of Denmark. Tidal areas with salt marsh formation are found mainly south of Horns Rev. In the interior Danish waters, currents and water-level variations caused by winds are of more importance than tidal movements. Currents up to 9 m/sec have been observed in the Limfjord. In Køge Bugt water-level variations on the order of ± 1 m have been experienced during storms.

Danish coastlines are normally sandy and very easily eroded (Bird 1974). However, some shorelines resistant to erosion make up the entire coastline for a long distance. Horns Rev, a reef covered with erratic blocks, is, as promontories in the shape of cliffs, able to delay the retreat of the Danish North Sea coast. Most of the cliffs consist of boulder clay, but chalk cliffs can be found in northern Jylland, along the coasts east of Aarhus, and in southeastern Sjælland. The west coast of Jylland is a shoreline of adjustment controlled by promontories and with embayments protected by offshore bars. The coasts facing the interior waters of Denmark are to a higher degree characterized by sheltered inlets. Several shallow inlets are reclaimed, but only a few have been successful in all respects.

Five areas illustrating characteristic features of Danish coastal landscapes are discussed below:
a shoreline of adjustment; an embayment with offshore bars; a shoreline under formation; an inlet with features of tidal geomorphology; and an unstable, old outlet.

KLIM STRAND

The typical Danish coast facing the North Sea is a sandy beach, in front of dune ridges, covering a band along the shoreline. Because of wave action, the beach and the dunes at Klim are subject to great variations. The resulting sediment transport is toward the east. The shoreline at Klim has been surveyed at least once every summer since 1968 as a part of a research project on a selected Danish North Sea coast.

During World War II the German forces fortified the dunes, and the blockhouses are now excellent landmarks. To the occasional visitor the general impression would be one of strong erosion, but to the surveyor the development is more uneven. The zero contour (DOD) is moving southward approximately 5 m/yr, but this numerical value includes movements from 2 m over three years to 40 m in one night. The total annual net change in volume from 1968 to 1979 was 144,000 m^3, with 138,000 m^3 eroded and 6,000 m^3 deposited (Christiansen and Møller 1980). In spite of the pronounced southerly retreat, the conditions are very complicated. The blockhouses, originally situated safely on top of the dunes, are now in the North Sea (Plate 47-1) rather far from the shoreline. During two weeks in January 1976, two storms removed the dune ridges completely, and the vegetation limit moved southward. Now the marine foreland is open to the sea. A house

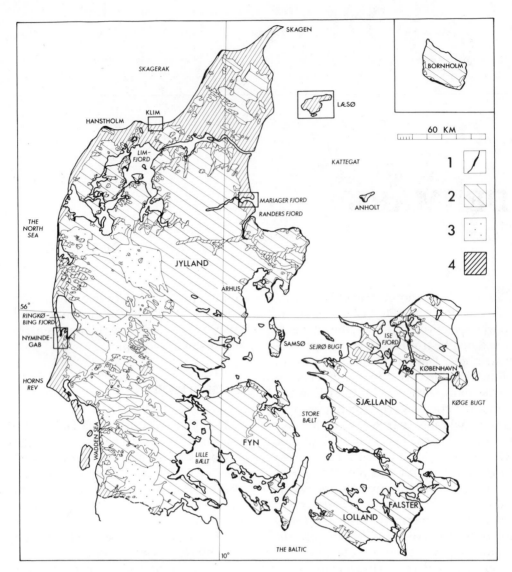

Figure 47-1. Morphology of Denmark: 1, cliffs facing the sea; 2. glacial deposits; 3. fluvial deposits; 4. marine deposits, in the Wadden Sea normally in the shape of salt marsh. The frames indicate the five coastal types described in the text. In Danish the place name *fjord* covers the terms embayment, bay, inlet, and strait.

situated 2.5 m above DOD was destroyed during the last storm. Before the storms of 1976 the sea could not be seen from the marine foreland south of the dunes.

The dunes are well known to re-establish after a period of time. In fact, small approaches to dune formation have been observed. However, the dunes are not stable, because there is little vegetation and tourists are very active in the vegetational period. Equilibrium between erosion and sedimentation can be found approximately 10 km east of Klim. Farther to the east the shoreline is

prograding northward, but until now without any dune formation.

KØGE BUGT

A great part of the Danish coast facing shallow water is characterized by offshore bars and barrier islands in front of lagoons. Shorelines of that type can be found along the eastern coasts of Jylland and in the bays of Sjælland, such as Sejrø Bugt and Køge Bugt.

Køge Bugt has been subject to intensive research for more than 15 years (Nielsen and Nielsen 1978), and the morphology is very well investigated. Situated close to Copenhagen, the shorelines of the bay suffer from a great number of activities. Recreation facilities have been constructed, and the Strandpark (Fig. 47-2, Plate 47-2) in the northern part of the bay is the result of land reclamation works exclusively carried out for recreational purposes. Because the water is shallow and the sea floor faintly sloping, the shore has been subject to pollution from dying seaweed, sewage, and wastewater from industries along the embayment. Residents along the bay are suffering from these foul-smelling deposits.

During the last hundred years a system of barrier islands has developed. They have been welcomed by the authorities because of the fine bathing facilities on the beaches facing east, but they have increased the pollutional effect in the lagoons. The reclamation of the Strandpark was initiated partly as an attempt to solve some of the problems resulting from polluted lagoons. Near the Strandpark the problems were further increased because an older reclamation for industrial purposes formed a corner of the bay area, where seaweed and sewage gathered.

Køge Bugt is a part of the Baltic, and the tide is negligible. Becuase of storms however, the water level can vary ± 1 m according to wind direction. Maps from before 1907 do not show offshore bars or islands. Now a system of barrier islands forms a chain for more than 7 km, broken only by two inlets. Crossing the swamps sheltered by the barrier islands, several dams and small bridges connect the islands with Sjælland. Plate 47-2 shows the inlet between two of the barrier islands. The surf and the offshore bars are clearly seen. The dams connecting the shore with the island facilitate access to the sandy beach, but increase the pollution problems, because they prevent water movement in the lagoon. Houses here can still be flooded during heavy storms.

LAESØ

Læsø (ø = island), situated in the northern Kattegat (gat = gap), has been built up by marine sediments (Hansen 1977, 1979), lifted up since the Litorina Sea. Large parts of the island are covered by blown sand, and dunes are found in the northern parts.

With an average tidal range of 0.5 m, the sea at Læsø is only slightly influenced by tidal movements. However, the water level can vary between 1.0 m above and 0.9 m below DOD during storms. Thus, in spite of the small tidal range, the shorelines of Læsø, except on the north coast, are characterized by salt meadows and sand flats, dry at low water. The wave regime around Læsø, together with the shallow water, have given rise to bars and spits that contribute to the formation of islands and protected lagoons; it is an excellent place for the formation of meadows much like salt marshes. Plate 47-3 shows a very common type of coastal landscape in Denmark, although this example is very well developed. Similar shorelines are found in eastern Jylland, in Sjælland, except on the north coast, and in many places on the other Danish islands. As late as the eighteenth century, the southern salt meadow in Læsø was used for salt production. The sea water was led into natural pools in the meadow and concentrated by natural evaporation. Finally the concentrated solution was refined and dried. Salt production was eventually abandoned because the woods were completely cut down for fuel.

It is difficult to estimate the possible changes of the shoreline. Apparently Knotten is rather stable in its existence if not in its shape. The barrier island can be seen in aerial photographs, but not on an ordnance map corrected in 1928. It is quite likely that the island existed in 1928 but was overlooked by the surveyors.

On the whole Læsø and the surrounding islets are growing in extent and height. Newly created islets are invaded by birds, and after some years their guano gives rise to a very abundant vegetation. Disliking high grasses, the birds then invade another islet with sparser vegetation, if the surface is high enough to prevent flooding during the breeding period. Large parts of the salt meadows and the sand flats are now preserved because of the birds, but the fast growth of the islets makes it necessary to update the regulations frequently.

MARIAGER FJORD

Even if the tidal range in the mouth of Mariager Fjord is only 0.4 m on average, this area has developed much like a typical tidal area, with all the features of a salt marsh (Christiansen 1973). During storms from the west, Kattegat is filled with water from the North Sea, while eastern storms normally cause a low water level in Kattegat.

The water-level variations are so large and so frequent that typical salt marsh stratification has developed. Further, old low-lying marine deposits are now protected by dikes, and pumping stations are draining a large system of canals in the surrounding farming land.

The mouth of Mariager Fjord is a dramatic example of the meeting between the open sea and the sheltered inlet. While the eastern parts are like a tidal area, the interior, western parts form an oblong basin with depths as great as 30 m. Large amounts of water are transported in and out through the mouth according to the wind. In the latter part of the nineteenth century, the sand flats on the east coast were left exposed for several days during a strong easterly gale. The sand dried up and started to move, and in a few days a dune landscape was created. North of the inlet blown sand now covers the old marine deposits, and the area was planted to bind the dunes.

As with the beach at Klim, this part of Mariager Fjord is now a site for research, which started in 1968 with a detailed survey. The diked areas south of the inlet have been reclaimed by the proprietor of a neighboring manor that was extended by approximately 1200 hectares. During the construction of these dikes, the proprietor took advantage of the special local climatic conditions. Easterly storms create rough waves at a low water level, while westerly storms cause high water level but only small waves. Thus, construction of the dike could be done safely over a long period of time and at low costs. This was essential to the proprietor, who was able to reclaim the land without government support.

The land reclamation was started in the traditional manner with silt trenches and the growing of plants suitable for an increase of sedimentation. Seeds and rootstocks of *Spartina sp.*, collected in the tidal areas in southwestern Jylland, were used. Because development was too slow, these efforts were soon given up, but the silt trenches can still be seen south of the inlet. The sediments are silt and fine sand except for the old islets Hesseltørre and Mejlplet. Here the sediments are coarse, because the finer parts were washed out by waves.

The outermost parts of the sand flats, facing Kattegat, are characterized by offshore bars. In Plate 47-4 the border zone between the offshore bars and the sand flats has a dark color because of seaweed vegetation. The dark color in the navigable canal is due to deep water, restricted to a narrow fairway with many bends and outflows from the sand flats. These are covered with small bars created by changing winds. A few bars in the inlet have developed to islets (e.g., Pletten), built up of salt marsh.

NYMINDEGAB

Particularly close to outlets, sandy shorelines facing the North Sea are subject to great variations, especially if large amounts of fresh water from rivers increase the outflow. Nissum Fjord, Ringkøbing Fjord, and the Limfjord immediately west of Thyborøn are embayments separated from the North Sea by offshore bars. The Limfjord stretches from the North Sea to Kattegat, and during storms large amounts of water pass in and out through the gap at Thyborøn. In Ringkøbing Fjord and Nissum Fjord, fresh water from rivers has to find a way to the sea. Now all the outlets are fixed by groins and to some extent by sluices, but earlier the gaps were very unstable.

The outlet from Ringkøbing Fjord has moved southward over time and was finally situated 15 km south of the embayment (Fig. 47-4, Plate 47-5). Owing to the long course through the dunes, the outlet has very often been cut off by sediment transported by waves and wind. Because of the unstable outlet, the water level in Ringkøbing Fjord has varied greatly and the fields around the embayment have been flooded several times a year. To improve the draining, a canal was excavated through the dunes in 1907 at Hvide Sande, very close to the 56°N parallel of latitude (Fig. 47-1). However, this canal was greatly enlarged by currents and grew to a size that was impossible to control. Consequently, the canal was closed in 1915, and a temporary canal was excavated near Nymindegab (Fig. 47-4, #8). Finally the canal at Hvide Sande was opened again, now controlled by sluices and groins.

The development of the channel from Ringkøbing Fjord to the North Sea is shown in Figure 47-4. The southernmost position of the outlet (Fig. 47-4, #1) existed in 1845 after an unsuccessful excavation (#10) in 1844. During 1892 a canal was excavated at #5 and the old outlet cut off by a dam at #3. However, this dam was flooded in the construction period and a new dam had to be established at #2. This dam lasted to 1916 and was replaced by a dam at #4. At #7 a dam was constructed in 1914 in connection with the temporary canal at #9 excavated in 1915 and closed in 1931 with a dam at #9. During World War II the German forces used the dunes for gun testing and constructed a railway dam at #6 and #8.

The position of the outlet has changed considerably. The positions in the years 1700 and 1750 are indicated in the figure. In 1844 (before the excavation at #10), 1875, and 1880 the outlet was situated just north of #1. Since 1931 the area has remained untouched by coastal construction works. The occupation forces, later followed by tourists, have destroyed the surface heavily. However, the traces of many years of activity are still clearly seen.

JENS TYGE MØLLER

REFERENCES

Bird, E. C. F., 1974, Coastal changes in Denmark during the past two centuries, *Skrifter i Fysisk Geografi*, Institute of Geology, University of Åorhus, Åorhus.

Christiansen, C., 1973, Fysisk-geografiske undersøgelser af et østjysk fjordområde med saerligt henblik på hydrografien, *Skrifter i Fysisk Geografi*, Institute of Geology, University of Århus, Århus. (English abstract).

Christiansen, C., and Møller, J. T., 1980, Beach erosion at Klim, Denmark. A ten-year record, *Coastal Engineering* **3:**283–296.

Hansen, J. M., 1977, Sedimentary history of the island Læsø, Denmark, *Geol. Soc. Denmark Bull.* **26:** 217–236.

Hansen, J. M., 1979, Læsø's postglaciale udvikling i relation tel den Fennoskandiske randzone (English summary), *Dansk Geol. Foren. Årsskrift:* 23–30.

Nielsen, N., and Nielsen, J., 1978, Morphology and movements of nearshore sediments in a non-tidal environment, Køge Bugt, *Geol. Soc. Denmark Bull.* **27:**15–45.

Plate 47-1. The beach facing north at Klim, January 1977. The blockhouses are seen in the background in the North Sea. The dunes have disappeared completely. As the shoreline retreated, the dunes grew steeper and higher until they were totally eroded in January 1976. The pole in the foreground is a point on a survey line. Before 1976 the sea could not be seen from this point (photo by J. T. Møller).

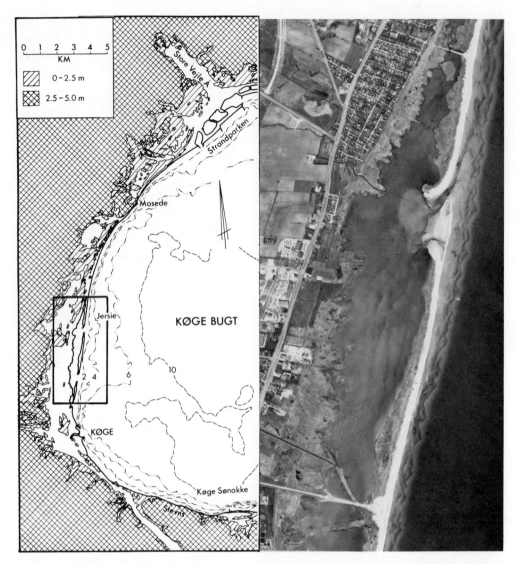

Figure 47-2, Plate 47-2. Køge Bugt. The map (Nielsen and Nielsen 1978) shows the depth conditions and the extent of the marine foreland (up to about 2.5 m DOD). The Strandpark is seen in the upper part of the map. The aerial photograph (May 1980, 1:25,000) shows the offshore bars, the barrier islands, and the inlet to the lagoon. Suburbs of Copenhagen are covering the marine foreland (photo reproduced by permission (A.273/81) of Geodætisk Institut, Denmark).

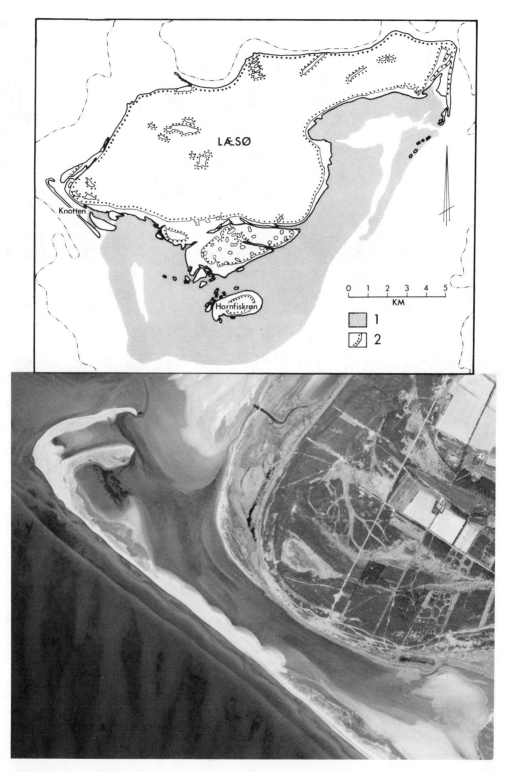

Figure 47-3, Plate 47-3. Map of Læsø showing the extent of sand flats, dry at low water (1), and the limits of the salt meadows (2). The aerial photograph (May 1976, 1:21.000) shows the western part of Læsø with the barrier island Knotten built up as a system of curved spits. Blown sand is covering the entire area above the salt meadows. The height of the salt meadow is 1–2 m DOD. The highest part of the blown sand within the photograph is below 2 m (photo reproduced by permission (A. 273/81) of Geodætisk Institut, Denmark).

Plate 47-4. Aerial photograph (March 1974, 1:25,000) of the eastern parts of Mariager Fjord (east is to the right). The areas reclaimed from the sea are south of the inlet. To the north the dune land is covered with conifers. West of the forest the features of a tidal landscape can still be seen in the old sea floor (the Litorina Sea). The easternmost parts of the sand flats are covered with seaweed alternating with offshore bars (photo reproduced by permission (A. 273/81) of Geodætisk Institut, Denmark).

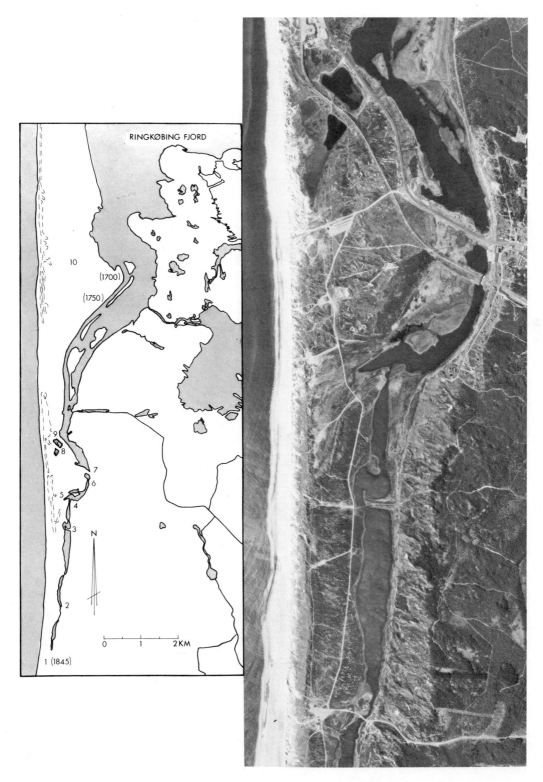

Figure 47-4, Plate 47-5. Nymindegab, the old outlet of Ringkøbing Fjord, illustrated by a sketch map and an aerial photograph (1:21,000, May 1980). Water-covered areas are shaded, dunes indicated by a broken line on the map. For further explanation see the text (photo reproduced by permission (A. 273/81) of Geodætisk Institut, Denmark).

48. NORTH SEA WEST GERMANY (FEDERAL REPUBLIC OF GERMANY)

The Federal Republic of Germany North Sea coast encompasses the sandy barrier islands of the North and East Frisian chains, seaward of the shallow Wadden Sea, into which open the funnel-shaped river-estuaries of the Eider, Ems, Jade, Weser, and Elbe (Fig. 48-1). The southern part of the North Sea is also shallow, the 20 meter isobath being located up to 50 km offshore. Tide ranges are 2–3 m in the Frisian Islands region, increasing to more than 3 m in parts of the Wadden Sea, and over 4 m in the Jade estuary decreasing to 1.5 m in the North Frisian region. The semidiurnal tides are strong enough (up to 1.5 m) to generate currents that form ripples of various dimensions (crest spacing up to 30 m) on the floor of the Wadden Sea; to ensure the persistence of channels (*seegat*) between the sandy barrier islands; and to shape the dynamic morphology of tidal creek systems (*priele*) and their locally deeper scour holes in the Wadden Sea. At low tide, extensive sand flats and mud flats are exposed in the Wadden Sea area, threaded by intricately branching channels shaped by the ebb and flow of tides; these channels vary in form, dimensions, and location as they meander and migrate laterally. The inner, mainland coastline of the Wadden Sea is largely artificial, with dikes built along the seaward margins of low-lying land reclaimed from former salt marshes. The mouths of the estuaries are tidally scoured, with distinct ebb and flow channel systems, and have also been modified by dredging (which removes 30×10^6 m³ of sediment each year) to maintain navigation to the ports of Emden, Bremen, Wilhelmshaven, Bremerhaven, and Hamburg (Fig. 48-1).

Wave action in the southern North Sea is generated by the prevailing westerly winds, and waves reaching the outer shores of the barrier islands are typically up to 1 m in height. Because of the dominance of westerly winds, and consequently westerly waves, longshore drifting is eastward along the beaches of the East Frisian Islands, while in the North Frisian Islands it is alternately northward (southwesterly waves) and southward (northwesterly waves). Sand washed into the gaps between barrier islands is shaped into tidal deltas by ebb and flow currents, with shoals partly emerging at low tide separated by diverging channels, on both the seaward and the landward sides of each inlet. At low tide the sandy beaches are fronted by extensive sand flats with complex and variable bars, shoals, swales, and channels shaped by the interactions of wave action, rip currents, and tidal currents (Gierloff-Emden 1980).

The coastal region is subject to occasional storm surges produced by strong winds accompanying the passage of depressions across the North Sea. These can raise sea level by up to 3 m above normal high spring tides, causing extensive flooding. Storm waves during such periods accomplish substantial erosion of the sandy shores of the barrier island chain, some reshaping of the intertidal morphology, and extensive damage to the dike system that protects farmland (Zitscher

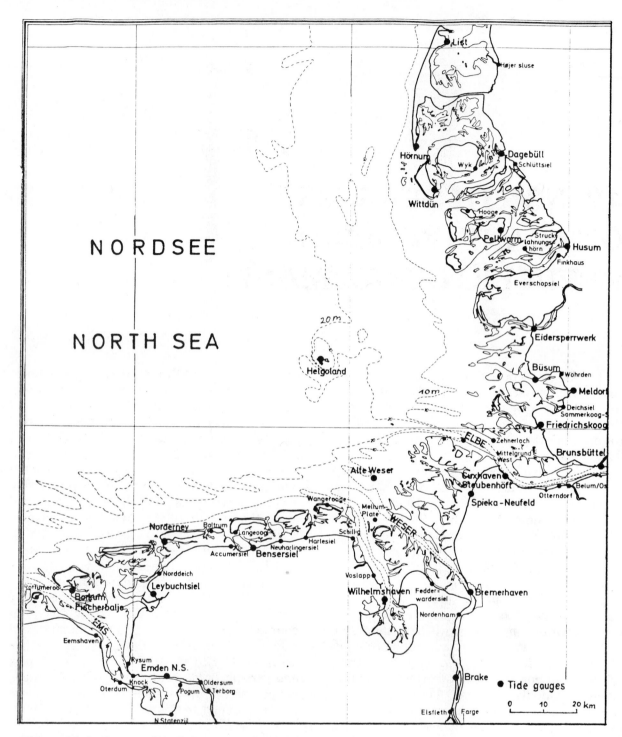

Figure 48-1. German North Sea coast. Coastline shown as a thick line, wadden margin a thin line, isobaths (dashed lines) at 10 and 20 m (after Kübler 1979).

1979). Major storm surges occurred during the years 1164, 1219, 1287, 1362, 1436, 1532, 1570, 1634, 1717, 1756, 1792, 1825, 1904, 1909, 1911, 1953, and 1976. The 1362 surge inundated 1000 km² of land, part of which remained per- manently below high tide level. In recent centuries the building, enlargement, and repair of dikes have maintained the mainland coast and much of the inner shoreline of the barrier islands, but the outer beaches and the channels between barrier islands are subject to continuing changes, especially during stormy periods (Fig. 48-2).

Previously, the Holocene marine transgression had inundated a glacial drift topography in the southern part of the North Sea to produce the submerged outlines of the mainland coast and estuaries, and initiate the accumulation of sandy barrier islands, in some cases built on or around residual foundations of glacial drift. The reworking of glacial drift deposits by waves and tidal currents generated sands, silts, and clays, the sands (predominantly quartz) being deposited mainly on the barrier islands while the finer sediments accumulated on the floor of the Wadden Sea and in the estuaries, relinquished particularly during slack water at high tides.

On the seaward side of the barrier islands, relatively high wave energy has built beaches of well-sorted medium to coarse sand, while finer and muddier sand deposits form the nearshore tidal flats and shoals, and extend along the bottom of tidal channel systems heading back into the Wadden Sea. Within the Wadden Sea the mud flats possess a rich and varied benthic fauna, and the sediments are subject to bioturbation (Reineck 1978). Some areas are dominated by shell accumulations, and a shelly lag gravel occupies the floors of some of the current-scoured channels. The upper intertidal zone carries salt marsh vegetation (*groden*), but large areas of salt marsh have been embanked and reclaimed in recent centuries. In cold winters ice forms on the tidal flats and occasionally on the shores of the barrier islands. Disrupted by wave action, it contributes to erosion of beaches and tidal flats (Gripp 1963, Geirloff-Emden 1980).

South from the Danish border (Fig. 48-3) the first two islands, Sylt and Amrum, consist of beaches and dunes built against a residual core of glacial drift deposits (Plate 48-1). On Sylt these deposits are exposed in cliffs up to 35 m high at Westerland, the island having grown northward and southward by spit prolongation in response to previously mentioned drift alternations. Coastal

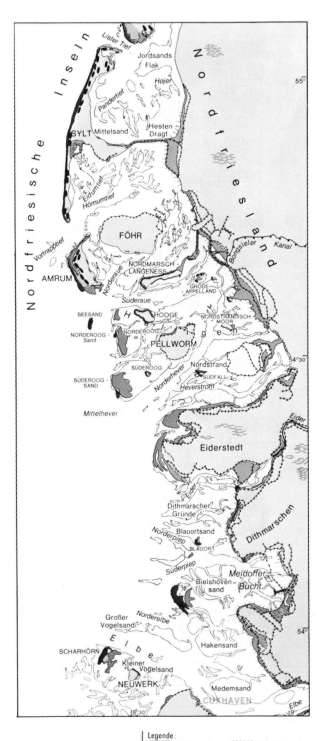

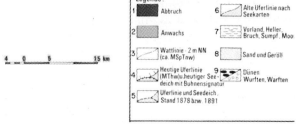

Figure 48-2. Coastline changes 1880 to 1980 (after Mrozek 1980): 1. erosion; 2. accumulation; 3. wadden margin at low spring tide; 4. present coastline at mean high tide; 5. 1880 coastline; 6. older coastline; 7. marine foreland; 8. sand and gravel; 9. dunes (solid) and settlement mounds (circles).

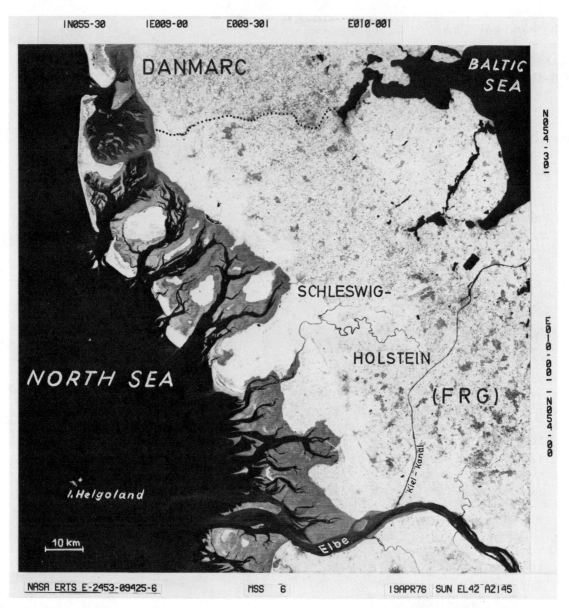

Figure 48-3. Landsat I image (band 6MSS) of part of German North Sea coast. Islands and exposed sand bars are white, tidal flats grey, estuaries and sea areas black. The Landsat scene (185 × 185 km) records quasi-synoptically by scanner, but for this reason the tide-level is somewhat higher in the north than in the south.

erosion has prompted the building of jetties and tetrapod barriers, as well as artificial beach nourishment by sand from the sea floor. In 1928 Sylt was connected to the mainland by the Hindenburg Dam, on either side of which there has since been increased sedimentation and salt marsh formation. Amrum is similar to Sylt on a smaller scale, but in its shelter is the rounded island of Föhr, again with a core of glacial drift bordered by salt marshes, but without major beaches, and completely surrounded by man-made dikes.

South of Amrum are very broad intertidal sand shoals, built up locally to about 1 m above mean high tide level by North Sea waves and sometimes surmounted by incipient grassy dunes and barchans, which persist until they are overwashed and destroyed by storm surges. The broad shallow topography reduces wave action under normal conditions, and thereby protects the islands of Pellworm, and Nordstrand, each of which contains embanked marshlands. The Halligen are a group of small islets on tidal flats, totaling 23 km²

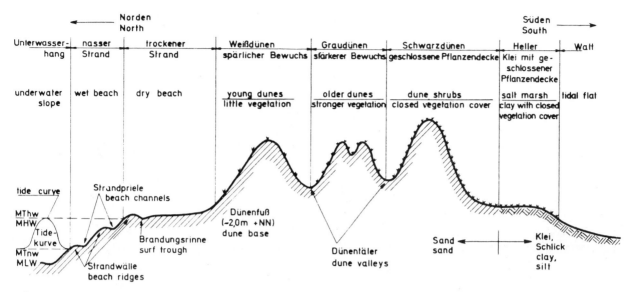

Figure 48-4. Schematic north-south section through an East Frisian island.

in area; they have farms sited on aritifical mounds built up above medium storm surge levels. A broad peninsula of glacial drift then projects to St. Peter Ording, and to the south the estuary of the Eider (restricted in 1973 by dam and weir gate) opens between wide tidal mud flats, which extend south to the Elbe estuary (Göhren 1971). The largest of a number of low sand shoals is the island of Trischen, the history of which has been described by Wohlenberg (1950) and illustrated by Gierloff-Emden (1961).

West of the Elbe estuary are the low islands of Neuwerk and Scharhorn, the latter much reduced by erosion during the past century, on the broad sandy shoal that runs out from Cuxhaven (Fig. 48-2). The small island of Alte Mellum stands in a similar situation on the shoal that extends seaward between the Weser and Jade estuaries.

The East Frisian Islands (Fig. 48-4) are a chain of elongated dune-capped barrier islands (Wangerooge, Spiekeroog, Langeoog, Baltrum, Nordesney, Juist, and Borkum) and three associated low sandy beach islands (Minseneroog, Memmert, and Lütjehörn), extending to the Dutch border. It is thought that this barrier island chain originally formed some distance to the north, and that with a secular rise in the level of the North Sea it was driven southward by a combination of dune migrations and storm surge washovers behind retreating beach alignments (Plate 48-2). Sindowski (1973) has traced the evolution of these islands since the mid-seventeenth century.

Fifty km offshore is the island of Helgoland, consisting of red sandstone uplifted by salt dome development and an elongated sandy island, known as Düne, to the east. Waves have sculptured the margins of the sandstone into cliffs and stacks, fronted by a shore platform exposed at low tides (Plate 48-3). Much reduced in historical times by this erosion, Helgoland has also been modified by its use as a bombing range and by an unsuccessful attempt by the British in 1947 to blow it up and prevent any future use (Wurster 1962).

H. G. GIERLOFF-EMDEN

REFERENCES

Gierloff-Emden, H. G., 1961, *Luftbild und Küsten-geographie am Beispiel der deutschen Nordsee-küste*, BLR, Bad Godesberg.

Gierloff-Emden, H. G., 1980, *Geographie des Meers*, 1 and 2, deGruyier, Berlin.

Göhren, H., 1971, *Untersuchunger über die Sand-bewegung im Elbmündunggebiet*, Hamburger Küs-tenforschung, 19.

Gripp, K., 1963, Winter-phänomene am Meeresstrand, *Zeitschr. Geomorphologie* **7**:326–331.

Kübler, H., 1979, Erfahrungen mit den Hochwasser-schutzanlagen im Hamburg bei den Sturmfluten im Januar 1976, *Die Küste* **33**:102–120.

Mrozek, P., 1980, *Variation of the coastline of the German North Sea coast from 1880 to 1980*, Berliner Geogr. Studien, 7.

Reineck, H. E., ed., 1978, *Das Watt*, Kramer, Frankfurt am Main.

Sindowski, K. H., 1973, *Das ostfriesische Küstengebiet*, Borntraeger, Berlin.

Wohlenberg, E., 1950, *Entsteheung und Untergang der Insel Trischen*, Geog. Gesell. Hamburg Mitt., 49.

Wurster, P., 1962, *Geologisches Porträt Helgolands*, Hamburg.

Zitscher, F. F., 1979, Die Sturmfluten vom. 3 u. 11 Januar 1976 und ihre Wirkung auf die Küste Schleswig Holsteins, *Die Küste* **33:**71–100.

Plate 48-1. Dunes at the north end of Sylt Island on the North Sea coast (photo by H. G. Gierloff-Emden).

Plate 48-2. Dike and artificial sandy beach at Neuharlingersiel, Ostfriesland, on the North Sea coast (photo by H. G. Gierloff-Emden).

Plate 48-3. Cliffs along the coast of the island of Helgoland (photo by H. G. Gierloff-Emden).

49.NETHERLANDS

The coastline of the Netherlands is part of the low sandy shore bordering the southwest part of the North Sea between the French-Belgian border and the north of Denmark. The total length of the Dutch coastline is somewhat more than 400 km, in which three units can be distinguished: the Rhine, Meuse and Scheldt estuary in the southwestern part; the coastal barriers in the central part; and the Wadden Islands bordering a large tidal flat area in the northern part of the country (Fig. 49-1).

Geologically, the Netherlands is a young country. In the major part, Pleistocene surface deposits slope seaward and are covered by Holocene deposits. Today this low portion of the Netherlands, much of it situated below mean sea level, is protected by dunes and dikes against the sea. The present situation is the result of tectonic subsidence, of a eustatic rise of sea level after the last glaciation, and of sand accumulated by rivers or derived from the bottom of the North Sea. Tectonic subsidence is directly related to the subsidence of the North Sea basin.

During the Quaternary, a huge amount of sediment was deposited in this basin; the total thickness of Quaternary sediments in the northwestern part of the country is more than 500 m. The subsidence values, however, are not more than 1.5–2.5 cm per century (Jelgersma 1961). The effect of the eustatic sea-level rise during the melting down of the immense terrestrial icecaps on the coastal plain of the Netherlands can be described as follows.

In the beginning of the Holocene, the western and northern part of the country consisted of a seaward-sloping sandy Pleistocene plain. The southern North Sea was land, and England was still connected with the continent. In late Boreal time the rising sea level reached about 25 m below the present level; the Holocene transgression approached the present coastline of the Netherlands. After that time the low Pleistocene surface was gradually buried and filled up by Holocene sediments as a direct result of the relative rise in sea level (combined effect of eustatic and tectonic movements). The thickness of the overlying Holocene deposits varies considerably. In many places in the coastal area, these deposits are more than 20 m thick and reflect different environments.

In an east-west section through the middle part of the Dutch coastal area, three zones of sedimentation can be distinguished: in the east a zone of peat; then a clayey zone of tidal flats, salt marshes, and brackish lagoons with intercalated peat layers; and near the coast a littoral sandy zone of coastal barriers and dunes (Fig. 49-2). The last environment is only well developed in the central part of the coastline; in the southwest and the northern part, barriers and dunes were destroyed by a landward-moving coast after the Roman period.

The presence of the clayey zone of tidal flats, salt marshes, and brackish lagoons with peat, not only at the surface but also in the subsurface, indicates that during the whole Holocene period the hinterland must have been protected from the open sea by coastal barriers or beach ridges. The present coastal area of the Netherlands is periodically subject to storms from the southwest, west, and northwest. The last direction is the most dangerous one, as the configuration of the southern North Sea causes extremely high tides during northwest storms.

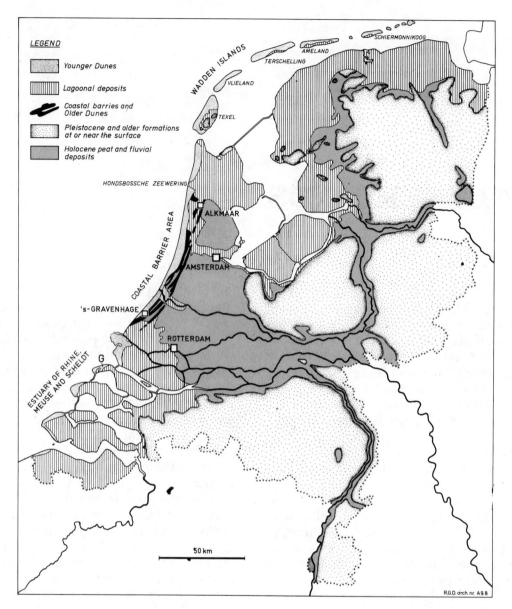

Figure 49-1. Geological map of the Netherlands.

The tidal range on most of the Dutch coast is 1.50–2 m. but in the southwestern part it may be as much as 3–4 m. Sand drift along the coast is of great importance along the Wadden Islands (from west to east), of lesser importance between the Belgian border and the Old Rhine (from southwest to northeast), and is rather ineffective between the Old Rhine and the island of Texel.

The whole littoral area can be classified as a micro-to mesotidal wind-dominated clastic shoreline.

THE CENTRAL PART OF THE DUTCH COAST: THE COASTAL BARRIER AREA

Three coastal units can be distinguished in the central part of the coast: a series of coastal barrier ridges, overlain by dune sands of the Older Dunes, part of which is covered by the Younger Dunes. These coastal sediments have been studied by Van Straaten (1961, 1965), Zagwijn (1965), and Jelgersma et al. (1970).

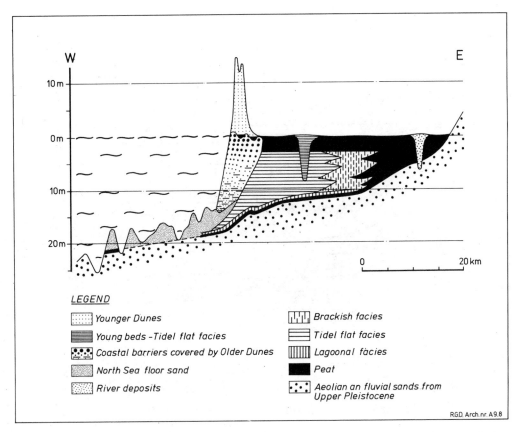

W

E

10 m

0 m

10 m

20 m

0   20 km

LEGEND

Younger Dunes

Young beds –Tidel flat facies

Coastal barriers covered by Older Dunes

North Sea floor sand

River deposits

Brackish facies

Tidel flat facies

Lagoonal facies

Peat

Aeolian an fluvial sands from Upper Pleistocene

R.G.D. Arch.nr. A9.8

Figure 49-2. Section across the Holocene deposits in the central part of the Netherlands.

The coastal barriers consist of sandy ridges separated by depressions filled with peat. The age of the barriers is Early Subboreal, and they are supposed to have developed in two phases. Dune sand accumulated on top of the coastal barriers; on the geological maps these are indicated as "Older Dunes." From excavations in this dune area it is known that eolian deposition was not a continuous process but was interrupted repeatedly by periods of stability when the dunes were covered with vegetation. This is demonstrated by several soil and peat beds intercalated in the sands of the Older Dunes (Fig. 49-3, Plates 49-1 and 49-2). These vegetational phases during the formation of the Older Dunes have been correlated with transgression phases in the back swamp. The latter are not thought to represent fluctuations of sea level, but rather periods of higher precipitation (Jelgersma et al. 1970).

The alternation of soils and windblown sands cannot entirely be attributed to climate and rainfall variations, as widening by accretion and narrowing by erosion of the coast caused fluctua-

tions in the groundwater level (Bakker et al. 1979). The formation of the Older Dunes was completed before the Roman period, and a more or less dense vegetation covered the whole dune area. The western part of the Older Dunes is covered by the Younger Dunes. The major part of these eolian sands must have been deposited between the twelfth and the sixteenth centuries. In contrast to the Older Dunes, the Younger Dunes are rather high, 20–50 m above sea level.

Most of the Younger Dunes consist of a system of parabolic dunes, bordered seaward by a foredune and landward by a precipitation ridge (Plate 49-3). South of Bergen, the Older and the Younger Dunes consist of medium-fine calcareous sand, but north of Bergen the sands are much less calcareous. The mineral content is also different. Both factors cause differences in vegetation, which is denser in the calcareous dunes.

The coastal sands south of Bergen are for a large part fluvial Rhine-Meuse sands deposited in the North Sea area during the Pleistocene. By longshore and transversal transport, this mate-

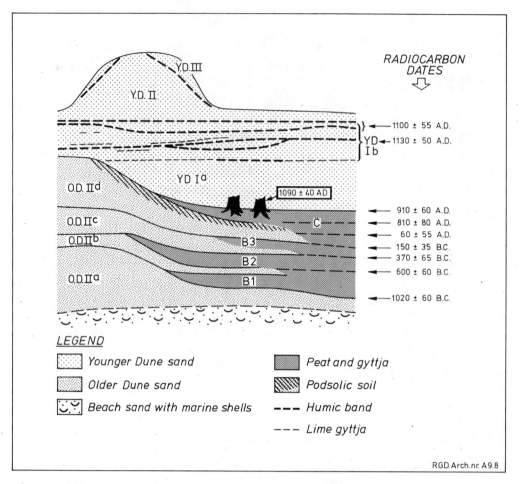

Figure 49-3. Outline of succession of deposits in the coastal barrier area of the Netherlands.

rial was returned to the coast. The sands north of Bergen are derived from erosion by the Holocene transgression of a relatively high Pleistocene area.

During the Atlantic and Early Subboreal time, the topography of the Pleistocene surface caused the development of an estuary near Bergen. On the north side of this estuary, spits were formed from the Pleistocene material in the subsurface. At the end of the Subboreal the inlet near Bergen was closed. Finally, eolian sands covered the area (Older Dunes and Younger Dunes). Figure 49-4A is a map of the Bergen estuary with its typical convex spits. Farther south, two other inlets can be noticed between barriers. These Rhine-Meuse and Old Rhine inlets show the typical concave pattern of spits connected with river mouths. Figure 49-4B shows the former river mouth of the Old Rhine.

THE RHINE AND SCHELDT ESTUARY, LOCATED SOUTH OF HOEK VAN HOLLAND

For centuries this area has fought a battle against storm floods of the North Sea. Only the west side of the islands has dunes; the major part of the coastline on the inlets and outlets is protected by dikes against the sea. After the disastrous inundation in 1953, the so-called Delta Plan was adopted. This plan, now nearly completed, is designed to protect land and inhabitants by shortening the line of defense against floods by closing off the larger inlets and outlets with dams. After completion only the southernmost inlet giving access to the harbor of Antwerp will be left open.

On the island of Schouwen the Younger Dunes overlie Older Dunes and coastal barriers, but in

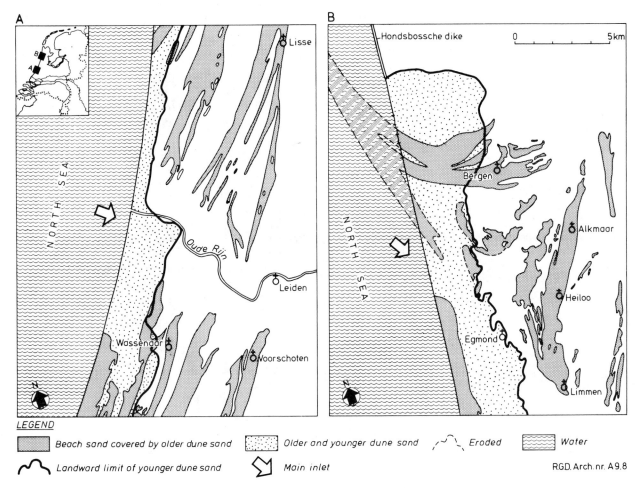

LEGEND

▨ Beach sand covered by older dune sand	⬚ Older and younger dune sand	⌢ Eroded	≋ Water
⌢ Landward limit of younger dune sand	⬡ Main inlet		R.G.D. Arch. nr. A 9.8

Figure 49-4. *A.* River mouth of the Old Rhine with the typical concave pattern of spits. *B.* Estuary of Bergen with curved spits on the north side.

the rest of the area Younger Dunes are found on top of young tidal and lagoonal deposits. The presence of the latter deposits on the surface and in the subsurface of the area suggests that coastal barriers and dunes must have been present throughout the Holocene.

After the Roman period a withdrawal of the coastline caused the destruction of coastal dunes and barriers. The inlets and outlets became larger, and major parts of the peat landscape were either eroded or covered by tidal flat deposits. After the twelfth century, people began to build embankments as protection against the invading sea. At that time, coastal dunes developed on the west side of the islands. Plate 49-4 shows the west point of the island of Goeree, with the dunes and the dam closing the inlet south of the island.

THE WADDEN ISLANDS AND THE COASTLINE NORTH OF BERGEN

The six Wadden Islands border a large tidal flat area. On the North Sea side the islands have a dune coast; on the south side are embanked marshes and tidal flats. There are some indications that the coastal dunes (Younger Dunes) overlie Older Dunes and coastal barriers. The latter, however, are younger (subatlantic) than the barriers in the western part of Holland. The whole area of the Frisian barrier islands is highly dynamic: there is a lateral displacement of the inlets due to strong littoral drift. The tidal flat area, the "Wadden Sea," is rather young. Following the twelfth century the sea invaded a lagoon and swamp area, transforming it into the present tidal flat (Plate 49-5).

The coast north of Bergen was reclaimed from the sea after the fifteenth century. The coastline consists of dikes and young dunes. The latter are part artificial, with a core of man-made sand traps made of screens of twigs and reed (Plate 49-6).

SASKIA JELGERSMA

REFERENCES

Bakker, T. M. W., J. A. Klijn, and J. Van Zadelhof, 1979, *Duinen en duinvalleien; een landschapsecologische studie van het Nederlandse duingebied.* Pudoc Wageningen.

Jelgersma, S., 1961, Holocene sea level changes in The Netherlands, *Geol. Stichting Med.* **7**:101p.

Jelgersma, S., 1979, Sea level changes in the North Sea basin, *The Quaternary History of the North Sea,* E. Dele, ed., Almquist and Wiksell pp. 233–248.

Jelgersma, S., J. de Jong, W. H. Zagwijn, and J. F. van Regteren Altena, 1970, The coastal dunes of the western Netherlands; geology, vegetational history and archeology, *Meded. Rijks Geol. Dienst, N.S.* **21**:93–167.

van Straaten, L. M. J. U., 1961, Directional effects of winds, waves and currents along the Dutch North Sea Coast, *Geol. en Mijnb.* **40**:333–346, 363–391.

van Straaten, L. M. J. U., 1965, Coastal barrier deposits in South- and North-Holland, in particular in the areas around Scheveningen and Ijmuiden, *Geol. Stichting Med.* **17**:41–75.

Zagwijn, W. H., 1965, Pollen-analytical correlations in the coastal-barrier deposits near The Hague (The Netherlands), *Geol. Stichting Med.* **17**:83–88.

Plate 49-1. Excavation in the dune area of the central part of the coast. Older Dune sand with intercalated peaty soils, capped by a peat layer (a) and covered by Younger Dune sand (photo by S. Jelgersma).

Plate 49-2. Section in the dune area of the central part of the coast. Older Dune sand capped by underlying podzolic horizon (a) and covered by Younger Dune sand. In the Younger Dune sand intercalated horizontal peaty bands are present (photo by S. Jelgersma).

Plate 49-3. Coastal dune area south of Bergen: a. foredune; b. several series of parabolic dunes; and c. precipitation ridge (photo by Allied Air Force, 1944).

Plate 49-4. Aerial photograph of the western part of Goeree; Rhine, Meuse, and Scheldt area, seen to the north. In the foreground the enclosure dam of the Delta Works (photo by KLM Aerocarto 80441).

Plate 49-5. Aerial photograph of tidal flats along the Friesland coast seen to the west. In the background the Wadden Islands of Ameland, Terschelling, and Vlieland (photo by KLM Aerocarto 14661).

Plate 49-6. Aerial photograph of Hondsbossche dike seen to the north. In the foreground dune area of Bergen, in the background a narrow strip of dunes. In both dune areas the coast has receded during the past century. Stone jetties were built to lessen shore drift along this part of the coast (photo by KLM Aerocarto K07991).

50. BELGIUM

The coast of Belgium is about 65 km long and forms part of the sandy and rectilinear Southern North Sea coastline that stretches from Cap Blanc Nez (France) in the west to the Schelde estuary (Netherlands) in the east. From the border with France at De Panne to Wenduine the coast's orientation is N 55° E. More to the east it runs east-northeast. The tide is semidiurnal. The mean tidal amplitude reaches 4 m with a slight decrease from west to east.

The coastal zone comprises three main units: a very gently sloping and fine sandy beach; a dune

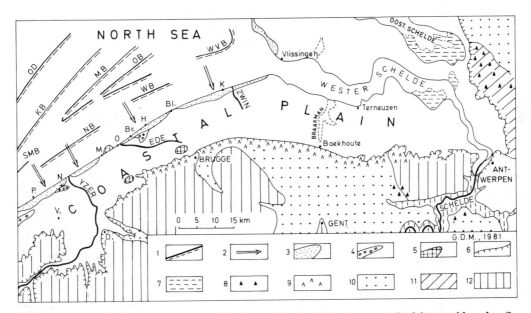

Figure 50-1. The Belgian Coastal Plain and Schelde Estuary. 1. Sublittoral banks; 2. 1960–1980 erosive mega-protuberances; 3. Younger dunes; 4. Older dunes; 5. Outcropping subboreal peat; 6. Limit of the reclaimed Holocene intertidal deposits; 7. Present-day active intertidal flats; 8. Tardiglacial eolian cover sand ridge; 9. Holocene river dunes; 10. Weichselian fluvioperiglacial sands (mainly of the Flemish Valley infillings); 11. Uplands in Lower Pleistocene deposits; 12. Uplands in Tertiary sands and clays. Bl = Blankenberge; Br = Bredene; H = De Haan; M = Middelkerke; O = Oostende; P = De Panne; V = Veurne. KB = Kwinte bank; OD = Oostdyck; WB = Wenduine bank; MB = Middelkerke bank; OB = Oostende bank; WVB = Walvis bank; NB = Nieuwpoort bank; SMB = Smal bank.

ridge generally of less than 20 m height, whose width varies from a few kilometers (at De Panne and east of Knokke) to less than a hundred meters and which is the site of numerous seaside resorts; and more landward, a coastal plain extending over a width of 5–10+ km, backed by a slightly uprising land developed in Pleistocene and Tertiary deposits. This coastal plain lies at a mean level of about 2 m above low-tide sea level, but shows a distinct microrelief of low sandy ridges (inversed sandy creeks) and clayey depressions. It corresponds to reclaimed Holocene intertidal flats, and its landward limit consists of the maximal landward extension of the whole of the Holocene marine transgression. The present-day elevation and micro-relief are mainly due to differential settling induced by the reclamation and draining.

Seaward, the foreshore continues in a broad and shallow sublittoral zone. The −5 m isobath runs at about 1500 m in front of the low water mark.

Farther offshore lies a field of banks and channels forming the Flemish banks. An inner row runs parallel to the coastline; an outer one lies obliquely to the shore.

The geologic substratum of the coastal plain and of the coastline consists of Upper Pleistocene deposits resting on Tertiary formations at a level of 25–35 m below mean sealevel. The Quaternary deposits comprise an alternation of marine and continental sediments: marine Eemian formations, fluviatile and eolian deposits dating from the last glaciation, mid-Holocene (Flandrian maximum) marine deposits covered by surface peat (mainly Subboreal), and finally the sediments of the Dunkerquian transgressions and of the intermediate regressive phases, such as the older dune deposits.

In a few places (Middelkerke), the shore consists of a wave-cut platform in the Subboreal peats, proving a local retreat of the subatlantic coastline over at least a few kilometers. In a few other places (Klemskerke), the subatlantic dune belt is backed by older dunes, proving local accretion.

From a tectonic point of view, the Belgian coast presents a remarkable stability, at least since the last interglacial. The stratigraphic top of the Eemian intertidal flats has been found at about the same elevation as the Subboreal.

The evolution of the coastal plain during the Dunkerquian transgressions can be considered according to the work of R. Tavernier and his various collaborators (1947, 1954, 1970). During

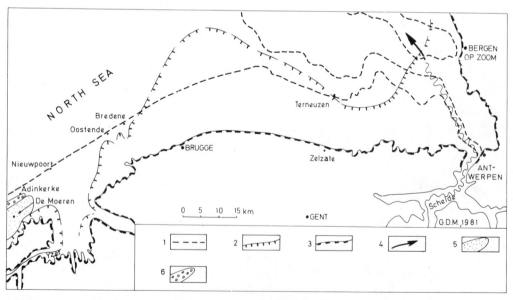

Figure 50-2. The Mid-Holocene Calais Transgression in the Belgian coastal plain and the Schelde estuary. 1. Present-day coastline; 2. Limit of the Calais transgression intertidal deposits (Calais coastline); 3. Limit of the Holocene intertidal deposits; 4. Former course of the Schelde; 5. Present-day outcrop of Calais deposits after post D-II removal of the Subboreal peat; 6. Remnant of the Calais island barrier with older dunes.

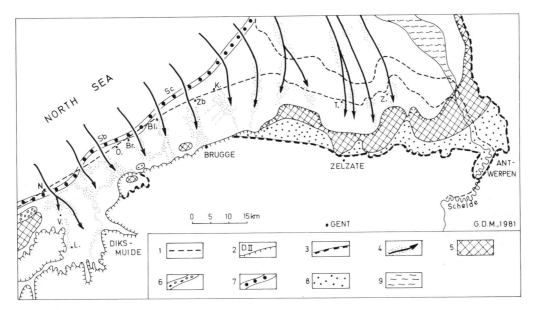

Figure 50-3. The Dunkerque II transgression in the Belgian coastal plain and the Schelde estuary. 1. Present-day coastline; 2. Limit of DII (3–8°C) transgression intertidal deposits (=DII coastline); 3. Limit of Holocene intertidal deposits; 4. Main beach barrier breaching and intertidal channel with sandy levee and channel deposits; 5. Outcropping surface peat (mainly Subboreal); 6. Older dunes (mid-Holocene); 7. Pre-DII beach barrier; 8. Not drowned Weichselian and tardiglacial sands outcropping within the Coastal Plain. Z = Zaamslag; Zb = Zeebrugge; V = Veurne; T = Terneuzen; Sc = Scarphout; Sb = Stroombank; O = Oostende; N = Nieuwpoort; L = Lo; K = Knokke; Br = Bredene; Bl = Blankenberge.

the Dunkerquian II transgressions (3rd to 8th centuries) the whole coastal plain, outside the Schelde estuary, was inundated and became an intertidal flat situated at the back of an important offshore bar. This bar later developed into a barrier island complex, banked against remnants of former Holocene coastlines, and still bears the present-day dune belt.

Soon after the inundation silting enabled man gradually to reclaim the flats. Later on three main dikes were constructed to save the western *oudland* and the central *oudland* from inundation by the eleventh century transgressions. Meanwhile the rest of the coastal plain was inundated again, especially going out from the Yser estuary (north of Diksmuide) and from the Zwin estuary (northeast of Bruges [Brugge]). New dikes were built to reclaim these *middellands*. Because of reclamation and draining, differential settling between the lower-lying sandy creeks, where the peaty subsoil had been cut, and the more elevated clay sedimentation flats, with peat subsoil, provoked inversion of that microrelief.

Since the thirteenth century transgressions (Dunkerquian IIIB) the western Schelde estuary developed very quickly, with an intertidal flat zone extending up to 20 km south of its southern bank and reaching Antwerp (Antwerpen), situated 65 km inland. Meanwhile, however, the important Zwin estuary was greatly silted up, cutting off the medieval harbor of Bruges from its outlet to the sea. These younger intertidal flats were gradually entirely reclaimed by a dense network of dikes during the following centuries.

These Dunkerquian II and III transgressions were, in fact, much more important than the older Dunkerquian I and Flandrian (Calais deposits). Their limits were much more restricted and the present-day extension of the Calais deposits shows that, because of the higher position of the pre-Holocene substratum, part of the coastal plain east of Ostend had only a very restricted Mid-Holocene inundation. To the west the Calais deposits are much more important and Holocene deposits there reach a thickness of 20 m. Nevertheless all marine Holocene sequences show a

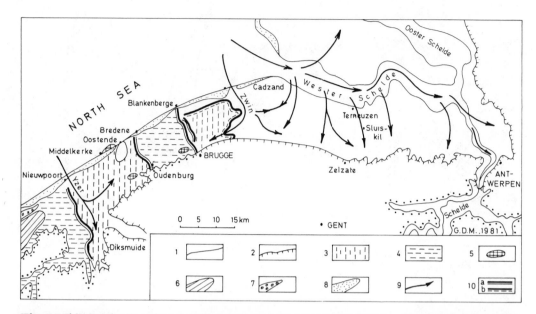

Figure 50-4. The Dunkerque III transgression in the Belgian coastal plain and the Schelde estuary. 1. Present-day coastline; 2. Limit of Dunkerque III transgression intertidal deposits; 3. Outcropping Dunkerque IIIA intertidal deposits (11°C); 4. Outcropping Dunkerque II intertidal deposits; 5. Outcropping Subboreal peat; 6. Outcropping intertidal Calais deposits; 7. Remnant of Calais island barrier; 8. Younger dunes (post Dunkerque II); 9. Main breacher and intertidal channels; 10. Chief dikes (a) post Dunkerque II (b) post Dunkerque IIIA (11–12°C).

juxtaposition and succession of subtidal, intertidal, and supratidal facies. There have also been interruptions by lagoonal deposition, especially during the formation of the surface peat.

Since the eleventh century transgressions the Belgian coastline has mainly been only disturbed by planned inundations provoked by artificial breaking of either the dune belt (Ostend, sixteenth century) or the dikes (Zwin, sixteenth century; Yser, First World War, 1914).

Today large parts of the Belgian coastline are characterized by defense structures such as groins and sea walls. Artificial nourishment has been carried out in several places.

The present-day open, macrotidal, sandy beach foreshore presents a succession of runnels and ridges. It shows lateral variations of slope, width, and sand grain size. The transversal beach slope tends to increase eastward, while its width decreases (Table 50-1), although the tidal amplitude decreases.

In a similar way, grain size distinctly increases from the west to the east, as shown by Table 50-2, which gives results of only three of the many

stations studied by G. De Moor (1980) along the Belgian coast during the period 1977–1979.

This table also illustrates the difference between the lower foreshore, with finer sands, and the upper part of the foreshore. The coarseness of the beach sand increases from west to east on the lower as well as on the upper foreshore. The poor sorting of the easternmost station (Zwin) is partly due to artificial beach nourishment carried out in 1955–1957 and in 1977–1978 at a short distance (1 km) to the west of the sampling station.

During the last few decades several sections have been subject to more or less strong erosion resulting in a lowering of the beach and a retreat of the dune front, while adjacent sections remained nearly unchanged or even had some accretion (De Moor 1979*a, b,* 1980). Such sections extend over several kilometers and their evolution is known to have continued over several decades. Today such erosional sections are situated at Knokke-Heist, Bredene-De Haan, Lombardzijde, and De Panne. These sections are considered to be erosional mega-protruberances characterized by a chronological cyclicity and a spatial repetitivity

Table 50-1. Beach Morphometry along the Belgian Coast

Station (km)	Locality	Date	Overall slope (%)	Width (m)
3	De Panne	8/9/78	1.3	510
12	Oostduinkerke	8/9/78	1.5	480
38	Klemskerke	8/5/78	2.0	340
42	Wenduine	8/28/78	2.1	310
65	Knokke-Zwin	8/24/78	2.4	200

Table 50-2. Variation of the Beach Sand Grain Size along the Belgian Coast

Foreshore section	Grain size grade (mμ)	Percentage at		
		De Panne (west)	Klemskerke	Zwin (east)
High	125–180	30–40	10–20	5–10
	180–250	35–45	50–60	30–35
	250–300	5–30	15–25	30–50
Low	125–180	60–65	15–30	15–30
	180–250	20–30	50–55	30–60
	250–300	0–10	10–20	5–65

that both have been proved. They are mainly attributed to cyclic changes in the bottom morphology and in the current pattern within the sublittoral zone which affects the impact of the tidal currents as well as the energy level of the waves striking the beaches.

The following literature is recommended for further reading in connection with this review: Charlier and Auzel (1961), Codde and De Keyser 1967), Macar (1935), Ozer (1976), and Paepe and Baeteman (1979).

G. DE MOOR
A. OZER

REFERENCES

Charlier, R., and M. Auzel, 1961, Geomorphologie côtière: migration des sables sur la côte belge, *Zeitschr. Geomorphologie* **5:**181-184.

Codde, R., and L. De Keyser, 1967, Mer du Nord. Littoral/Estuaire de l'Escaut, *Atlas de Belgique* 18A-18B, Comité national de Géographie.

De Moor, G., 1979*a*, Recent beach erosion along the Belgian North Sea Coast, *Soc. Géol. Belgique Annales* **88:**143-157.

De Moor, G., 1979*b*, Premiers effets du rehaussement artificiel d'une plage sableuse le long de la côte belge, in *Les côtes atlantiques d'Europe, évolution, aménagement, protection,* vol. 9, A. Guilcher, ed., Centre National pour l'exploration des Océans, Brest, pp. 97-114.

De Moor, G., 1980, Erosie aan de belgische kust, *De Aardrijkskunde,* N.S., **4:**279-294.

Macar, P., 1935, Quelques analyses granulométriques de sables d'origine marine et éolienne de la côte belge, *Soc. Géol. Belgique Annales* **58:**156-164.

Ozer, A., 1976, La morphologie des polders. Les dépôts côtiers holocènes, *Géomorphologie de la Belgique. Hommage au Professeur P. Macar,* Liège, pp. 17-27.

Paepe, R., and Baeteman, C., 1979, The Belgian coastal plain during the Quaternary, *Acta Univ. Ups., Symp. Univ. Ups. Ann. Guing. Cel.* 2, Uppsala, pp. 143-146.

Tavernier, R., 1947, L'evolution de la plaine maritime Belge, *Soc. Geol. Belgique Annales* **56:**332-343.

Tavernier, R., and F. Moorman, 1954, Les changements du niveau de la mer dans la plaine maritime flamance pendant l'holocene, *Geol. en Mijnbouw,* N.S., **16:** 201-206.

Tavernier, R., J. Ameryckx, F. Snacker, and D. Farasijn, 1970, Côte, dunes, polders, *Atlas de Belgique,* Comité national de Géographie.

Plate 50-1. Klemskerke (1978). Runnel and ridge beach morphology. Beach longitudinal wind mega-ripples upon the ridges (photo by G. De Moor).

Plate 50-3. Klemskerke (1978). Effects of erosive megaprotuberance. Concrete dike built in 1910 against past sand waves, afterward completely covered by dune accretion and progression and since 1978 exhumed from underneath the dunes by the present-day retreat of the dune foot due to the repeated erosive action of sand waves (photo by G. De Moor).

Plate 50-2. Klemskerke (1978). Effects of erosive megaprotuberance. Beach pole 38, situated about 45 m in front of the dune foot and spring high-water line. In 1960 it stood about 20 m from the spring high-water line and near the dune foot. The flattened high beach shows typical beach transversal backwash ripples, due to rapid seaward transport of eroded dune sands over the lowered beach (photo by G. De Moor).

Plate 50-4. De Panne (1980). French-Belgian border. World War II blockhouses left on the present-day forebeach after dune retreat due to the local strike of an erosive mega-protruberance (photo by G. De Moor).

51. ENGLAND AND WALES

The combined coastline of England and Wales (Fig. 51-1) measures about 4400 km. Its outlines reflect geological structure, with Paleozoic formations dominating the intricate western peninsulas of Devon and Cornwall, Wales, and Cumbria, and a sequence of Mesozoic sandstone and limestone cuestas with intervening clay vales ending in alternations of cliffs and lowlands on the southern and eastern coasts. Tertiary sediments outcrop only locally in Dorset, Hampshire, and Thanet, but Pleistocene glacial drifts are extensive on the east coast, especially in Holderness and East Anglia (Steers 1964).

The cliffs and depositional features formed during the later stages of the Holocene marine transgression and its aftermath of relative stillstand, but relict Pleistocene raised beaches and periglaciated features persist where erosion has been slow, mainly on the west coast (Plate 51-1). Remains of forests submerged by Holocene transgression are seen at low tide in the Bristol Channel and elsewhere, and continuing subsidence in southeast England is indicated by the foundations of Roman London, now below high-tide level. Tide gauge records show that northern England has been rising and the south and southeast sinking at rates of a few millimeters per year. The rivers of England and Wales flow into estuaries formed by Holocene submergence of their late Pleistocene valleys, and fluvial deposition has formed flood plains (a process hastened by artificial reclamation, especially in Romney Marsh, the Somerset Levels, and the Fenland south of the Wash), but there are no protruding deltas. Marine sand washed into the drowned valley mouths (rias) of southwest England has produced extensive intertidal sandflats, but Milford Haven escaped this accretion and remains as a deep inlet.

Wave energy is strong from the southwest through the Atlantic approaches, diminishing into the English Channel and through St. George's Channel to the Irish Sea; the east coast is sheltered from the prevailing winds, but it receives waves from northerly and easterly directions over the North Sea. Longshore drifting of beach material is eastward along the south coast of England and southward down the east coast, except in north Norfolk, where westward movement of shingle has contributed to the intermittent growth of compound recurved formations at Blakeney Point (Fig. 51-2) and Scolt Head Island (Steers 1960). Beach drifting and cliff recession are most pronounced when onshore winds and low barometric pressure bring large waves in at unusually high levels. Major storm surges have occurred on the east coast several times in the past few centuries, the most recent being in 1953 and 1978 (Steers et al. 1979).

The duration and intensity of wave action on the shore is also influenced by tidal regimes. Mean spring tide ranges (Fig. 51-1) are generally between 3 and 5 m, augmented in the Bristol Channel to more than 12 m at Avonmouth, with tidal bores transmitted up the Severn, Avon, and Parrett rivers, and falling to less than 2 m on the central south coast, where double high tides occur. Strong currents are generated in the Irish Sea and through Menai Strait, and tidal currents have shaped complex shoal and channel topography off the east coast, where wave action is relatively weak. Tidal variations also influence the ecological zonations of plant and animal communities on rocky shores (Lewis 1964).

Cliffs are found on a variety of geological formations where uplands have been truncated by marine erosion. The most characteristic are the

COASTLINE OF ENGLAND & WALES

Selected Features and Mean Spring Tide Ranges

Figure 51-1. Coastline of England and Wales.

vertical white cliffs of thick, gently dipping Cretaceous Chalk on either side of the transected Weald, between Brighton and Eastbourne (Plate 51-2) and between Dover and Deal; however, cliffs in strongly folded chalk occur on the Dorset coast and the Isle of Wight, while at Flamborough Head chalk cliffs are capped by slopes in glacial drift. Cliffs are also well developed on limestones at either end of the Jurassic outcrop that traverses

England from Dorset to Yorkshire, with an outlier in Glamorgan; on the red Permian sediments of St. Bees Head and East Devonshire; and on the Tertiary sands of Bournemouth Bay and the Isle of Wight. Slumping occurs on soft Tertiary clays east of Bournemouth and glacial drift in north Norfolk, and where the Chalk dips seaward over clay beds there have been massive landslides, as between Axmouth and Lyme Regis (Arber

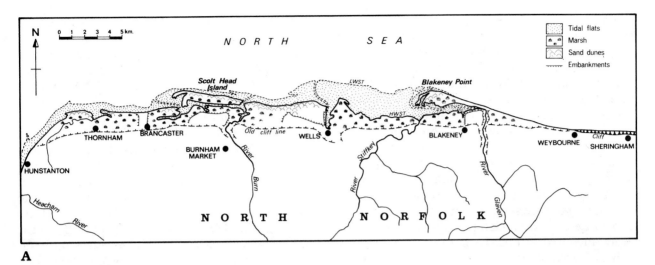

A

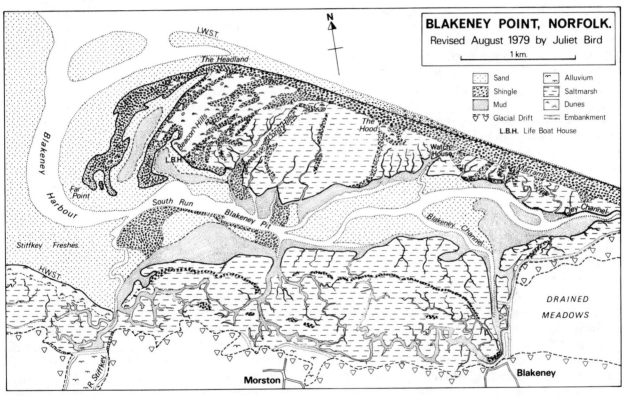

B

Figure 51-2. Depositional formations on the North Norfolk coast (*A*) include Blakeney Point (*B*), a compound recurved shingle spit that has grown intermittently westward, the ridge from The Headland to the present Far Point having developed since 1966. The main shingle ridge east of The Headland is driven landward by successive North Sea storm surges. Extensive salt marshes have developed in the areas between recurves, and on the sheltered southern side of the estuarine area leading out to Blakeney Harbour.

1940), at St. Catherine's Point on the Isle of Wight, and at Folkestone Warren (Plate 51-3). In places, cliff recession has truncated small valleys (chines in the Isle of Wight), and streams emerge in coastal waterfalls.

The older and harder rocks of the southwestern peninsula show cliffs on sectors exposed to strong Atlantic wave action, such as the castellated outcrops of jointed granite at Land's End and the intricate patterns of headland and cove, related to faults, thrust planes, and jointing as local variations on the north Cornish coast (Wilson 1952). More sheltered sectors retain periglaciated slopes formed during the late Pleistocene low sea level and undercut following the Holocene marine transgression to give "slope-over-wall" profiles. Even-crested cliffs and slopes result from Pleistocene marine planation at higher levels, especially the 130-m level. Similar features are seen on the hard rocky Channel Islands to the southeast, but the outlying Scilly Islands are a largely submerged granite upland with bouldery shores and beaches of white quartzose sand. The north Devon coast, also formed of hard rock formations, faces a relatively sheltered sea area where wave action is impeded by large tide ranges; it is a fine example of a steep coast, with only limited basal cliffing (Plate 51-4). Across the Bristol Channel the more exposed south coast of Wales shows cliffs of Carboniferous limestone on the Gower Peninsula and older formations in Pembrokeshire, but in Cardigan Bay exposure to wave attack diminishes northward and sloping coast profiles reappear, becoming prominent on the Lleyn Peninsula and around Anglesey and the Isle of Man. On the coasts of the Irish Sea, where glacial drift deposits frequently border the uplands, coastal plains are extensive. Glacial drift fronts bluffs marking a Pleistocene coastline at Ramsey on the Isle of Man, and Walney Island is a glacial deposit.

On the east coast the soft glacial drift cliffs of Holderness have been cut back up to 200 m in a century (Valentin 1971). In northeast England cliffs in Permian and Carboniferous rock include craggy outcrops of the Whin Sill dolerite intrusion, which also dominates the outlying Farne Islands.

Shore platforms are best developed on Chalk and sandstone outcrops; typically they are abrasion platforms (intertidal sloping ramps) formed where waves move shingle to and fro across the foreshore (Plate 51-2). Solution and bioerosion features occur locally on limestones that have escaped such abrasion. Planation is less advanced on older and harder formations, which often present a rib-and-corridor topography reflecting lithological variations, while on softer sediments (e.g., Holderness) the crumbling cliffs are fronted by beach-mantled abrasion ramps that decline gradually to a smoothed sea floor.

Depositional features include shingle beaches derived from the flint nodules that occur in the Chalk, both directly in the vicinity of eroding cliffs and indirectly by reworking of fluvial, marine, or glacial gravels in post-Cretaceous sediments.

Shingle beach trains dominated by flint extend eastward from Lyme Bay along the Channel coast. They include the major barrier at Chesil Beach, the spits built by longshore drifting on the Solent shore and deflecting the mouth of the Adur River near Brighton, and the cuspate foreland at Dungeness (Fig. 51-3). Shingle is also present on parts of the east coast at Flamborough Head, on the spit that has regrown periodically at Spurn Head (De Boer 1964), on Scolt Head Island and Blakeney Point (where it is partly derived from gravelly moraines deposited at the limits of the last glaciation), at Lowestoft, and in the long fluctuating spit of Orfordness (Carr 1969). The flint shingle that forms barrier beaches enclosing freshwater lagoons at Porthleven in Cornwall (Fig. 51-4) and Slapton in Devon has been washed in from the sea floor during the Holocene marine transgression, as has Chesil Beach, which is backed by The Fleet lagoon and hinterland slopes that escaped marine cliffing.

Beach gravels are also produced by the erosion of Jurassic limestones and Paleozoic sandstones, volcanic rocks, and vein quartz, but away from the flint-dominated shingle beaches there is usually an admixture of sand derived from the weathering mantles of granitic and other quartzose formations. Some beaches are almost entirely sandy, those of Cornish coves reflecting the mineralogy of weathering rocks on the coast and hinterland stream catchments. Atlantic coast beaches include shelly sand washed in from the sea floor by swell, but on the south side of Barnstaple Bay the massive Westward Ho! cobble beach is being driven intermittently landward and lengthened northward by oceanic storm waves. The spit formations of Cardigan Bay (Fig. 51-5) are derived mainly from glacial drift deposits, relics of which persist offshore as partly submerged bouldery *sarns*, but in the Irish Sea, where wave action is weaker, sea-floor shoals and intertidal sand flats remain extensive, particularly in Morecambe Bay, where a current-scoured topography is exposed at low tide. Interacting waves and tides produce variable shoals and ebb-flood channels in the Goodwin Sands off Kent and in the Wash off Gibraltar Point (King 1972). Off the East Anglian coast, the changing pattern of shoals has influenced the location and movement of wave-built coastal formations such as Benacre Ness in Suffolk. Sands derived from glacial drift are also extensive along the Northumbrian coast, especially around Holy Island.

Sandy beaches at St. Ives Bay and Perranporth

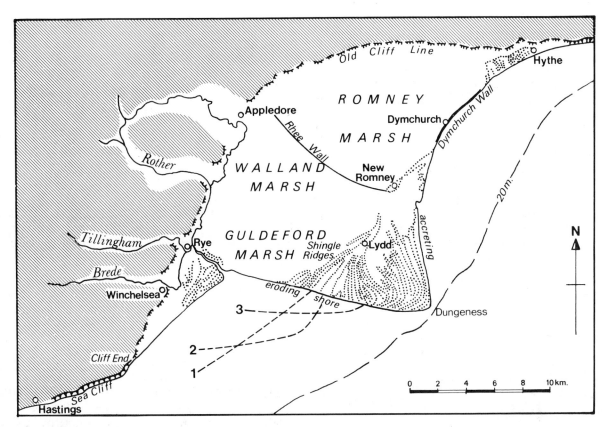

Figure 51-3. The cuspate shingle foreland at Dungeness has grown seaward as it migrated eastward; earlier stages are indicated at 1, 2, and 3. Extensive marshlands to the rear, reclaimed in stages since Roman times, are backed by steep bluffs marking the early Holocene cliff line.

in Cornwall and Barnstaple Bay to the north are backed by derived dune formations that drifted inland and are now largely held in place by grassy vegetation. Elsewhere, successive parallel dune ridges have been built behind sandy beaches at Newborough Warren in Anglesey, Studland Bay in Dorset (where they enclose a lake, Little Sea, on the site of a former marine embayment), Winterton Ness in East Anglia, and on the south Lancashire coast (Gresswell 1953). Deposition of sand and shingle has narrowed and deflected the mouths of several estuaries, notably the Taw-Torridge and Exe in Devon, and the tidal entrances to Poole, Christchurch, and Pagham harbours on the Channel coast (Kidson 1963). The pattern of beach drifting in England and Wales has been much influenced by groin and breakwater construction during the past two centuries. In several localities there is updrift beach accretion alongside breakwaters and downdrift starvation leading to accelerated erosion: the coast at Newhaven, east of Brighton, is an example (Fig. 51-6). Beach gravels are still being extracted from parts of the Dorset coast (West Bay, Seatown) and in Cornwall

(Gunwalloe) despite the risk of accelerating erosion. On the other hand, there have been some artificial beach-nourishment projects (e.g., at Bournemouth), and near Workington on the Cumbrian coast mining waste and industrial slag dumped on the coast are being incorporated in nearby beach sediments.

Muddy sediments extensive in east coast estuaries and around the Wash have come partly from hinterland clay outcrops by way of suspended silt and clay in river loads, and partly from wave-winnowing of fine-grained material from coastal and sea-floor outcrops of clay, especially glacial boulder clay deposits, for eventual deposition in sheltered environments. Salt marshes dominated by halophytic *Salicornia*, *Suaeda*, and *Puccinellia* spp. have grown alongside estuaries and in areas sheltered by spits, as at Blakeney Point (Fig. 51-2) and barrier islands as at Scolt Head (Steers 1960). Salt marsh vegetation occupies the upper intertidal zone and builds a depositional terrace, which is intersected by branching and meandering tidal creeks. There is a contrast between the firm sandy marshlands of west coast estuaries and the softer

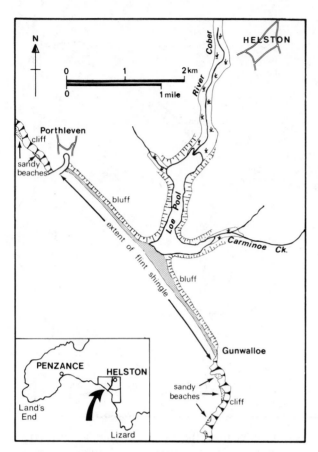

Figure 51-4. A beach of flint shingle washed up from the sea floor (there being no flint sources in adjacent cliffs or hinterland areas) extends as a barrier across the mouth of the drowned valley of the River Cober, impounding a fresh-water lagoon, Loe Pool, into which reedswamp is encroaching around tributary stream inlets.

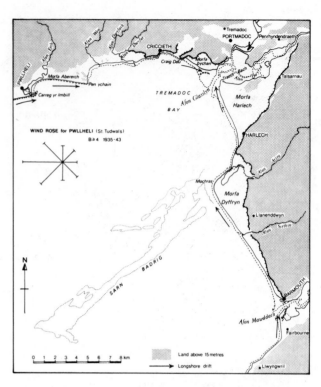

Figure 51-5. The beaches and spits bordering Cardigan Bay have been shaped by longshore drift, produced by the prevailing southwesterly wind-generated wave action, with a convergence toward Tremadoc Bay. Sarn Badrig is a ridge of gravelly glacial drift submerged at high tide but partially exposed at low spring tides.

muddy estuaries of the south and east coasts, where occasional storm waves have emplaced shelly cheniers. In 1870 hybridization took place in Southampton Water between local *Spartina maritima* and American *S. alterniflora*, yielding a vigorous new species, *S. anglica*. This spread rapidly and was introduced to Poole Harbour (Fig. 51-7) and other estuaries in England and Wales, and became established on board intertidal mudflats in Bridgewater Bay. It has accelerated the building of depositional terraces (Plate 51-5), but in some areas it is dying back, and the marshlands are eroding (Bird and Ranwell 1964).

Changes in the outline of England and Wales were reviewed by a Royal Commission in 1911, which concluded that over a period of about 35 years the gains (14,344 ha) largely by reclamation around estuaries substantially exceeded the losses by erosion (1899 ha). Historical evidence shows that on the outer coastline only a few sectors (spits, cuspate forelands, accretion alongside breakwaters) have prograded, while on the Chalk (May 1971) and on the softer formations along the east and south coast rapid cliff recession has consumed much agricultural land, several settlements (e.g., the fourteenth-century port of Dunwich, Suffolk) having been lost, while Selsey Bill receded by 116 m in only 20 years (Bird and May 1976).

Numerous sites of geological and geomorphological interest on the coasts of England and Wales have been designated as nature reserves or otherwise protected for scientific and educational use: they include most of the features mentioned in this article.

ERIC C. F. BIRD

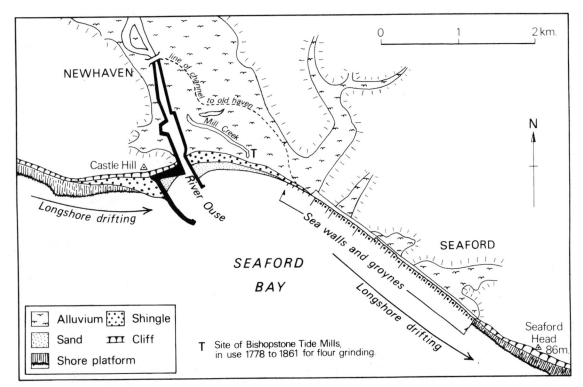

Figure 51-6. Newhaven Harbour has developed at the mouth of the Ouse following its diversion from an older outlet farther to the east. Its entrance is sheltered from southwesterly wave action by a breakwater, alongside which shingle drifting from west to east has accumulated. East of the harbour the beach at Seaford has been depleted because the eastward drift of shingle can no longer replenish it. Sea walls and groins have been built to maintain the Seaford esplanade, and to the east erosion has accelerated on the Chalk cliffs at Seaford Head. Bishopstone tide mills were typical of a number of local installations exploiting tidal energy in estuaries in England and Wales in past centuries.

REFERENCES

Arber, M. A., 1940, The coastal landslips of south-east Devon, *Geol. Assoc. Proc.* **51:**257–271.

Bird, E. C. F., and V. J. May, 1976, *Shoreline Changes in the British Isles during the Past Century,* Bournemouth College of Technology, Bournemouth, England.

Bird, E. C. F., and D. S. Ranwell, 1964, The physiography of Poole Harbour, Dorset, *Jour. Ecology* **52:** 355–356.

Carr, A. P., 1969, The growth of Orford Spit, *Geog. Jour.* **135:**633–653.

De Boer, G., 1964, Spurn Head: its history and evolution, *Inst. British Geographers Trans.* **34:**71–83.

Gresswell, R. D., 1953, *Sandy shores in South Lancashire,* University of Liverpool, Liverpool.

Kidson, C., 1963, The growth of sand and shingle spits across estuaries, *Zeitschr. Geomorphologie* **7:**1–22.

King, C. A. M., 1972, *Beaches and Coasts,* St. Martin's, London.

Lewis, J. R., 1964, *The Ecology of Rocky Shores.* English Universities Press, London.

May, V. J., 1971, The retreat of chalk cliffs, *Geog. Jour.* **137:**203–206.

Steers, J. A., ed., 1960, *Scolt Head Island,* Cambridge University Press, Cambridge.

Steers, J. A., 1964, *The Coastline of England and Wales,* Cambridge University Press, Cambridge.

Steers, J. A., D. R. Stoddart, T. P. Bayliss-Smith, T. Spencer and P. M. Durbridge, 1979, The storm surge of 11 January 1978 on the east coast of England, *Geog. Jour.* **145:**192–205.

Valentin, H., 1971, Land loss at Holderness 1852–1952, in *Applied Coastal Geomorphology,* J. A. Steers, ed., pp. 116–137.

Wilson, G., 1952, The influence of rock structures on coastline and cliff development around Tintagel, North Cornwall, *Geol. Assoc. Proc.* **63:**20–48.

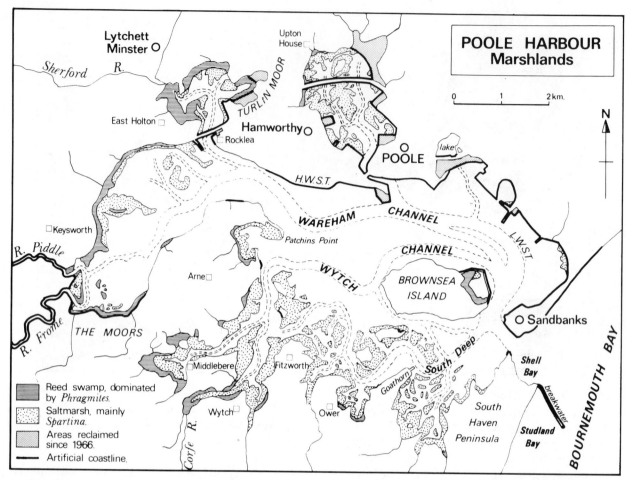

Figure 51-7. Poole Harbour in Dorset is a large estuarine inlet fed by the Frome and Piddle rivers and a number of smaller streams; its mouth is constricted by paired sand spits at South Haven Peninsula and Sandbanks. Although the spring tide range is only 1.5 m, extensive mudflats are exposed at low tide in front of salt marshes, which increased rapidly in area after the introduction of *Spartina anglica* in 1899, but are now being reduced by die-back of this species and by marginal erosion.

Plate 51-1. An emerged Pleistocene shore platform cut in metamorphic rock on the eastern shores of the Dodman in Cornwall is backed by degraded bluffs of relict periglacial rubble, and is being dissected by the sea at its present level (photo by E. C. F. Bird).

Plate 51-2. Chalk cliffs at the Seven Sisters, Sussex, showing truncation of spurs and valleys of the dip-slope of the South Downs in an undulating cliff crest, and a broad, gently sloping shore platform exposed at low tide. The narrow beach at the base of the cliff consists of fallen chalk rubble and flint shingle (photo by E. C. F. Bird).

Plate 51-3. Folkestone Warren, Kent, where massive landslides have occurred in Chalk that dips seaward and rests on soft sandstones and clays. The upper cliff is cut in Chalk, and the hummocky foreground (through which runs the railway line from London to Dover) is a mixture of fallen chalk and sandstone with patches of Gault clay (photo by E. C. F. Bird).

Plate 51-4. The steep coast of North Devon west of Lynmouth, showing slopes mantled by Pleistocene periglacial deposits and only limited basal cliffing (photo by E. C. F. Bird).

Plate 51-5. Depositional marsh terrace on the southern shores of Pool Harbour (Fig. 51-7), built by sedimentation in areas colonized by introduced *Spartina anglica* (photo by E. C. F. Bird).

52. SCOTLAND

It is only about 315 km from the northernmost part of the Scottish mainland to the English border, and about 150 km from west to east; yet the Scottish coastline, including the numerous islands to the north and west, is about 12,000 km long, with approximately 15% classified as estuarine or narrow inlet, and less than 10% being some form of sand beach. These beach and dune areas range from small coves to vast sand plains. Hard coastal forms such as plunging cliffs, pseudo-cliffs, and rock platforms form the greater part of the coastline (Plate 52-1), but there are also good examples of such soft coastal forms as salt marshes and tidal and estuarine mud flats. The immense variety of the long Scottish coastline can be explained as a result of several key factors: rock type, geological structure, patterns of glaciation and deglaciation, sea-level changes, and recent processes, of both the sea and the land. An additional factor, of only local importance, is coastal engineering work.

The bewildering variety of rock type and structure (Fig. 52-1) gives rise both to the general outline of the coast, where one can note a degree of parallelism that is explained by major fault lines (Steers 1973), and to particular small-scale irregularities that relate to structural and lithological differences. It is also possible to discern a broad division between the lower, sedimentary coastlines of the east, and the more rugged, steeper, fjord and island coastlines of the north and west. Major drowned estuaries and firths (Solway, Clyde, Forth, Tay, Inverness, and Dornoch) are deep indentations in the large-scale coastal planimetry, and their existence might be related to preglacial drainage systems and planation surfaces as well as fundamental geological differences.

Such broad divisions break down on the regional scale, especially where volcanic and granitic intrusions produce bold cliffs in an otherwise lowland coastline. There is also the largely unresolved problem of the existence of erosion surfaces that exert a strong control of the absolute elevation of most regional coastlines (Ogilvie 1930; Godard 1965; George 1966).

Glaciation and sea-level changes further reduce the validity of a simple geological explanation for the physiography of the Scottish coastline. Deglaciation is recent, and the evidence of the action of ice and, more significantly, meltwater is fresh on the landscape. To some degree, the coastline is everywhere affected by the several phases of glaciation and subsequent climatic and related environmental changes. This might take many forms, but the clearest indication is derived from the striking dissimilarity between the west and east coasts. The difference is partly explained by the average position of the ice-shed, giving steep gradients and erosion-dominated, deep, fjord-like (sea lochs) coastlines to the west and north. In contrast, lower gradients for ice and meltwater movements to the east produced situations in which coastal plains with more depositional features and fewer indentations could develop. Some writers have also examined preglacial drainage patterns as a means of explaining the patterns of major inlets (Steers 1973; Sissons 1967).

All around the coastline there is clear evidence of abundant deposition by ice and meltwater on the shallow sea platforms—material that a rising Holocene sea level would carry onto the lower parts of the coastline to construct great shingle strand plains, spits and bars, and extensive sand beaches. A widely held opinion is that most

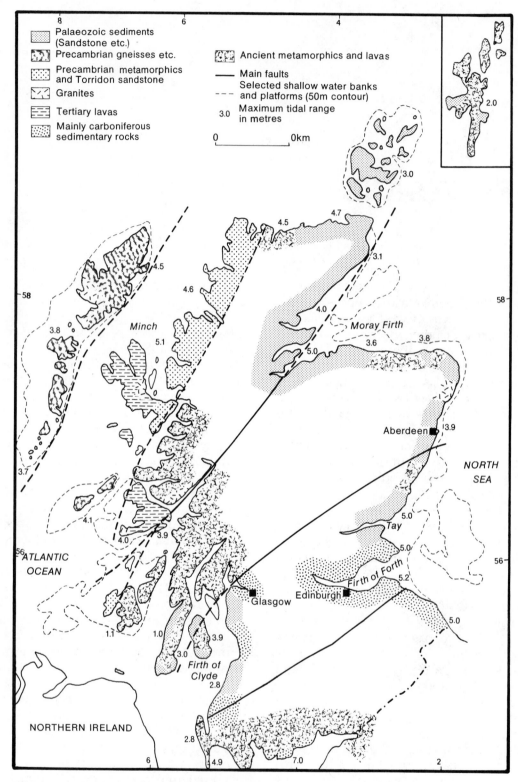

Figure 52-1. Map of Scotland.

Scottish rivers now contribute little to the coastal sediment budget, but torrents of meltwater must have provided vast quantities of sands and gravels in the comparatively recent past. The actual extent of true cliffs, freely exposed to wave action, is less than might be expected for such a mountain- and plateau-dominated country, and the contribution to the coastal sediment budget from cliff sources is largely confined to areas of sandstone and conglomerate rocks. In contrast, along many coastlines the characteristic coastal form is the slope-over-wall profile of a thick till cap on a steeper rock cliff, usually with a basal rock platform, and there are some examples of glacial materials forming low cliffs, especially in peripheral islands; these undoubtedly produce local accumulations of frequently coarse-grained materials.

Salt marsh and intertidal mud and silt banks are restricted to low-energy situations, especially within the firths and estuaries of the east coast (McManus 1976; Smith 1971–1981) and in the inner Solway Firth, but are also found as small features at the head of sea lochs and other indentations where fine sediment is available. Some evidence is available to suggest that the buildup of some estuarine mudbanks might be associated with land use changes, especially deforestation in the historic period.

Another feature of special significance is the remarkable predominance of shell-derived sediment in the beach and dune areas. In the Outer Hebrides there are almost no beaches with less than 10% calcium carbonate content, and more than a quarter have shell sand contents greater than 70%. Thus some of the largest beach and dune systems in Britain are shell based, a fact that has great significance for soils, vegetation, and consequential land use (Mather and Ritchie 1977). High shell sand values are not confined to the outer islands, and there appears to be some correlation with the existence of extensive rock platform areas in the nearshore zone. Associated with shell sand dune systems, 11 sites of eolianite have been recorded (Roberts, Mather, and Ritchie 1973; Mather and Ritchie 1977).

Every visitor to Scotland is impressed by the extent and variety of raised shoreline forms in all but the peripheral areas that lie outside the zero-isobases of the post- and late-glacial raised shoreline zones. These peripheral areas are normally dominated by a drowned appearance, and there is some evidence from dated subtidal organic materials for postglacial submergence. Raised shore-

lines may consist of magnificent suites of shingle ridges 40–50 m above present sea level in exposed locations such as Jura, or they may be subtle breaks of slope in sheltered firths and estuaries. Much research has been devoted to this complex topic (e.g., Sissons 1981). Regional differences are associated with the position of the ice front during the higher relative stands of the sea as well as former coastal configurations and other geomorphological conditions. Isostatic movements also have regional patterns associated with the exact shape and position of ice sheets. Perhaps the most common form, best seen along the Firth of Clyde, the Solway, and most of the North Sea coast, is the low coastal terrace leading to one or more degraded cliff-lines. Depending on lithology and altitude, these old cliff-lines may be gentle slopes, perhaps cut in glacial materials, or stark cliffs with caves and stacks now high and dry above an exhumed abrasion platform. The evidence of higher sea levels may be wholly or partly masked by subsequent deposits associated with mass movements or, more likely, by wind-blown sand. The number of such raised shorelines varies considerably, as does their clarity, but few coastlines, other than the hard rock cliff and pseudo-cliff forms, do not bear some imprint of former higher sea levels. At lower altitudes coastal deposition features formed during higher sea levels provide the basis of contemporary coastal forms whereby ridges have closed embayments—e.g., Rattray (Walton 1956)—or formed platforms upon which later landforms developed (Mather and Ritchie 1977). One of the classic areas showing sequential stages of coastal modification by depositional processes associated with a falling sea level is around the Moray Firth (Ogilvie 1923).

Operating on the varied legacy of inherited coastal landforms, waves and tides give rise to a wide range of contemporary process environments. Broad distinctions can be made on the basis of exposure, which ranges from full exposure to the great fetches of the Atlantic to the moderate exposures of the North Sea coast. There are also sheltered firths and estuaries with progressive changes in energy conditions as well as extremely low-energy environments in the inner sea lochs and in partially enclosed areas among the islands and peninsulas. Exposure is modified by offshore gradient; some of the most exposed coastlines (e.g., the west side of the Outer Hebrides) have extensive shallow rock platforms offshore (Fig. 52-1), which reduce the violence of storm impact on the coastline. Elsewhere glaciation has produced a relatively varied sea-bed topography, but in general the west-east contrast remains valid, with shallower depths and gentler gradients occurring along the North Sea coasts.

To add complexity, tidal ranges vary considerably, from a minimum of about 1 m to over 7 m in the Solway (Fig. 52-1). The east coast is also affected by North Sea surges, which can lead to considerable elevation of water levels and severely destructive effects as the tidal wave progresses southward down the North Sea basin. Even more variable than tides are wave conditions. Atlantic swell is important on all coastlines, even along the North Sea littoral. Most coastlines, however, are dominated by wind waves. Wave climatic statistics are relatively limited, but it is clear that no simple pattern of dominant wave type and direction can be described, except for coastlines that have restricted fetch environments or where refraction and reflection are all-important. Elsewhere, the cyclonic weather patterns can produce strong winds from all directions, which set up highly variable wave inputs. Usually these are short period waves (e.g., 5-7 s) and have heights on the order of 1–2 m (Buchan and Ritchie 1979), but much larger and higher waves can be experienced on most coasts during storms, several times each year. On the more open coastlines, offshore-onshore and longshore movements tend to be highly variable in space and time; some of the best illustrations of this variability are found where rivers reach the sea, and a rapidly changing geometry of spits and shoal banks is a feature of almost all Scottish river outlets (Buchan and Ritchie 1979; Green 1973). Except in bay-head situations rhythmic beach forms tend to be most common, but little research has been done on beach dynamics, and the processes are certainly compounded by variable tidal regimes and high beach water tables.

Most hard rock areas are relatively inert; their characteristics arise from the position of the present interface between the sea and the former coastal slope—a slope that is more likely to have been shaped by terrestrial than marine processes. Perhaps surprisingly in a land of mountains and plateaus, true marine cliffs and active platforms are comparatively rare and are found in distinct separate regional settings. Where they exist, as on the west side of Orkney (Plate 52-2) or Shetland, along the east Caithness coast, or in the spectacular columnar basalt cliffs of the Inner Hebrides, one can see some of the finest examples of plunging cliffs, geos, stacks, caves, and arches in Europe.

In summary, the long Scottish coastline is one of great physiographic and geomorphological variety. It is a complex coastline where present-day processes operate on a great diversity of inherited surfaces and landforms (Plate 52-3). Sediment supply is also variable, but there appears to be a net deficiency (although there are some notable large-scale exceptions), particularly where the inherited supply from glacial sources has been reworked onshore. Contemporary relative changes in sea level are currently a subject of considerable debate, but the meager evidence would suggest an emergence around most of the mainland (Halstead pers. commun.) and submergence of the more peripheral archipelagoes.

Man-made alterations in the form of groins, sea walls, and piers are also comparatively rare except along parts of the coastline of the firths of Clyde and Forth in the central lowland belt. Elsewhere such developments are small in scale and widely separated. Recreational pressures on the beaches and dunes are also relatively moderate in all but a few areas of highly intensive use, usually near population centers, although there are numerous pockets of seasonal pressure associated with caravan sites in all parts of the mainland coastline. The islands tend to have much less recreational and other pressures and have some of the best conservational sites in Western Europe. Industrial and commercial developments tend to occur in the inner estuaries and firths, but there are some large-scale developments such as Sullom Voe in the Shetlands, St. Fergus, and Loch Kishorn, associated with the offshore oil and gas industry. The total effect of these economically vital and much publicized developments is almost negligible in relation to the total length of coastline.

WILLIAM RITCHIE

REFERENCES

Buchan, G. M., and W. Ritchie, 1979, Aberdeen beach and Donmouth spit: an example of short term coastal dynamics, *Scot. Geog. Mag.* **95:**27–44.

George, T. N., 1966, Geomorphic evolution in Hebridean Scotland, *Scottish Jour. Geology* **2:**1–34.

Godard, A., 1965, *Recherches de Géomorphologie en Ecosse du Nord-Ouest*, Université de Strasbourg.

Green, C. D., 1973, *The Sediments of the South Side of the Entrance to the Tay Estuary,* unpublished Ph.D. thesis, University of Dundee.

McManus, J., 1976, Bottom structures of the Tay Estuary and other estuaries, *Scot. Geog. Mag.* **82:**192–197.

Mather, A. S., and W. Ritchie, 1977, *The Beaches of the Highlands and Islands of Scotland,* Countryside Commission for Scotland, Perth.

Ogilvie, A. G., 1923, The physiography of the Moray Firth coast, *Roy. Soc. Edinburgh Trans.* **53:**377–404.

Ogilvie, A. G., 1930, *Great Britain: Essays in Regional Geography,* Cambridge University Press.

Roberts, H. H., A. S. Mather, and W. Ritchie, 1973, Comendation in high-latitude dunes, *Tech. Rep. 31, Coastal Studies Bull.* **7:**95–112.

Sissons, J. B., 1967, *The Evolution of Scotland's Scenery,* Oliver and Boyd, Edinburgh.

Sissons, J. B., 1981, The last Scottish ice-sheet: facts and speculative discussion, *Boreas* **10:**1–17.

Smith, J. S., 1971–1981, *Series of ecological reports on Moray Firth for Highlands and Islands Development Board, Scotland,* Inverness.

Steers, J. A., 1973, *The Coastline of Scotland,* Cambridge University Press, Cambridge.

Walton, K., 1956, Rattray, a study in coastal evolution, *Scot. Geog. Mag.* **72:**85–96.

Plate 52-1. The south coastline of Tiree (Inner Hebrides) exhibits many of the features of the Scottish coastline: offshore reefs and rocks that continue inland, shell sand beaches with coastal dunes, raised beaches of storm-thrown shingle, and considerable diversity in a small area (photo by W. Ritchie).

Plate 52-2. The morphology of steep, active cliffs such as are found on the west side of the Orkney mainland is controlled by rock type (here sandstone) and local structural factors such as the presence of joints or the exact dip and strike of the bedding planes. Such high-energy conditions are comparatively rare, as is full exposure to Atlantic storms (photo by W. Ritchie).

Plate 52-3. The indented, glaciated coastline contains hundreds of bay-head situations where beaches and dunes can develop. Kiloran in Colonsay is a typical beach, and the headlands are equally typical, with the evidence of raised shoreline levels. The rocky coastal margins are usually described as Pseudo-cliffs and have little to do with marine processes either in the past or under present conditions (photo by W. Ritchie).

53. IRELAND

The coastline of Ireland is more than 3200 km long, even when many kilometers of minor inlets and headlands are excluded. The general configuration of the island is controlled by the influence of several major structural units (Fig. 53-1), while many morphological features depend also on Quaternary events (Fig. 53-2 and 53-3).

NORTHWEST ULSTER

In the northwest of the island, the northeast-southwest Caledonian trend exerts a strong geological control on the coastline between Lough Foyle and Donegal Bay. In Inishowen, the beveled cliffs developed on schists and quartzite contrast with the stepped and slumped basalt plateau edge of Binevenagh on the southeast side of the lough, where former sea cliffs are now "dead", or abandoned, because of isostatic adjustment. The mouth of the lough is only 2 km wide because of the growth of the large complex marine foreland of Magilligan, which comprises a series of arcuate sand bars capped in places by extensive sand dunes. The finest and highest cliffs in north-west Ulster are found below Slieve League (598 m), where 30–60° scree-clad slopes terminate in 100–200 m high vertical sea cliffs (Plate 53-1). Quartzite tors 6–12 m high rise above the scree in places and constitute part of the late Pleistocene periglacial modifications to the coastal slope. In contrast, severe scouring and excavation by ice has accounted for the overdeepened and partially drowned and island-obstructed Sheephaven, Mulroy Bay, and Lough Swilly, between Gweebarra Bay and Malin Head. Enormous late-glacial, postglacial, and modern storm beaches of pebbles

and cobbles occur at many places, at elevations exceeding 22 m O.D., such as Bloody Foreland, Rockstown, Fanad Head, and Malin Head. Equally striking are the fine sandy strands, composed mainly of quartz and shell sand, which are particularly well developed at Ballyness, Ballyheiran, and Pollan. Blown sand has proved to be a menace to farmland and settlements at Dunfanaghy and Rosapenna, southeast of Horn Head, where sand blowing has been a serious problem at least since 1784.

At the head of Donegal Bay, drumlins composed of glacial till are linked by marine spits, and there are some fragments of postglacial raised beaches, while low rocky cliffs of Carboniferous Limestone are important features of the coast between Donegal Bay and Sligo Bay.

CONNACHT

In North Mayo cliffs reach heights of 250 m, whereas extensive and still mobile sand dunes containing buried soil horizons mantle the low-lying Mullet Peninsula. The latter encloses Broad Haven and Blacksod Bay, where cliffs 1–2 m high are formed in the widespread blanket peat. Clew Bay is partly occupied by an archipelago of drumlins, some connected by complex shingle spits.

The northern shoreline of Galway Bay is developed on granite with numerous ice-eroded roches moutonnées, and toward Roundstone becomes deeply indented and island-studded, with isolated sand and shell beaches. By contrast the gently tilted Carboniferous Limestone forms 90 m sheer cliffs in the Aran Islands, and the Burren plateau has bold multiple-stepped limestone cliffs.

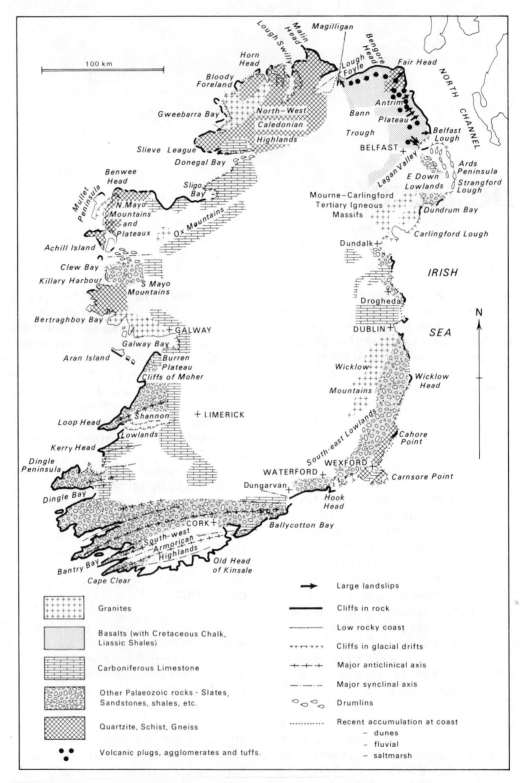

Figure 53-1. Some important geological and geomorphological features of the coastline of Ireland. (Geological outcrops are generalized and shown only for the coastline.)

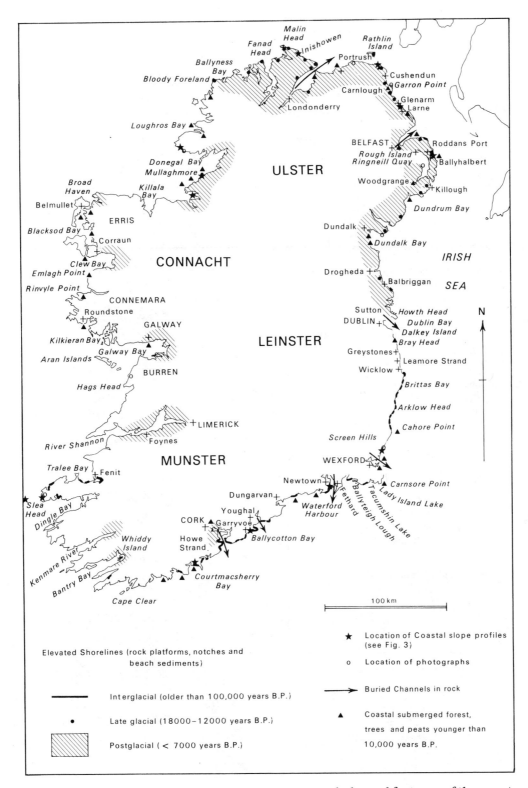

Figure 53-2. Some important Quaternary geomorphological features of the coast-line of Ireland.

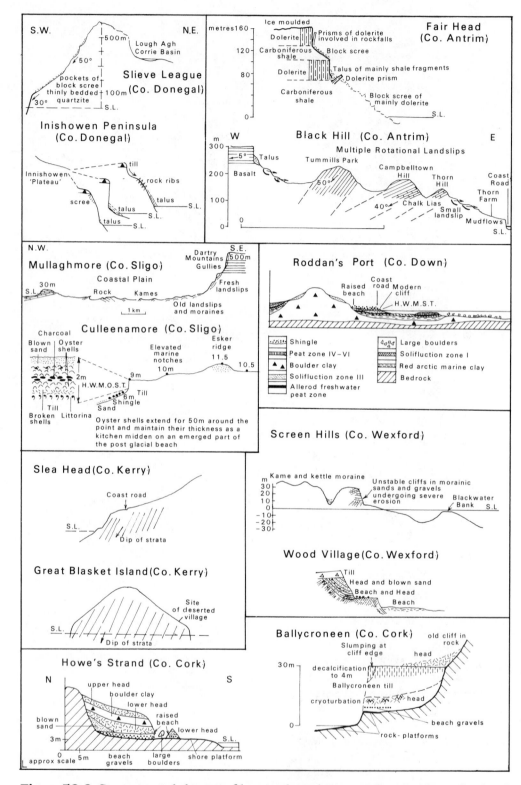

Figure 53-3. Some coastal slope profiles at selected sites on the coastline of Ireland. (The positions of the coast profiles and photographs are indicated on Figure 53-2.)

Carboniferous grits, flagstones, and shales form 8 km of the sheer (122–196 m) Cliffs of Moher (Plate 53-2).

MUNSTER

In southwest Munster, Dingle Bay, Kenmare River, Bantry Bay, Dunmanus Bay, and Roaring Water Bay are the principal rias, with varying amounts of alluvial fill, while the intervening headlands display excellent examples of beveled cliffs (Plate 53-3). Magnificent spits are found at Castlegregory in Tralee Bay, and in Dingle Bay, while drumlins are prominent at the head of Bantry Bay.

Between Cape Clear and Dungarvan, rias cut across the geological and morphological grain, and low plateau remnants (80–120 m) rise gently inland away from the beveled cliffs. There are several prominent headlands, such as Old Head of Kinsale, and also numerous fragments of elevated abrasion platforms in rock, on which rest "fossil" beach deposits (4–8 m O.D.), which have long been accorded an interglacial age.

Between Dungarvan and Carnsore Point there are generally small, low headlands (e.g., Hook Head), and a series of spits is found in Tramore Bay, and enclosing Tacumshin Lake, Lady's Island Lake, and Ballyteigh Lough, some with sand dunes and all showing signs of continuing adjustment to wave activity.

LEINSTER

The Leinster coastline is perhaps the least spectacular coastal segment, with cliffs and low headlands in rock or drift seldom exceeding 30 m in height (Plate 53-4). The general orientation between Carnsore Point and Dundalk Bay cuts across the regional strike of the Silurian and Carboniferous strata. The cliff-line intersects the striking Screen Hills kame-kettle moraine in southeast County Wexford, where the coast has retreated considerably, although abandoned cliffs occur in the glacial deposits because of the temporary accumulation of substantial foredunes (Plate 53-5).

ULSTER

The alignment of the coastline of Ulster is related to intersecting Caledonian, Hercynian, and Tertiary structures.

The eastern edge of the Paleozoic basement in County Down is low-lying and partially drowned by the sea. Wave-planated and ice-scoured rock surfaces are exposed where coast erosion has removed numerous till drumlins. Important late Pleistocene and Holocene sites occur at Roddan's Port, Killough, Ringnaill Quay, Ballyhalbert, Rough Island, and Woodgrange. In Dundrum Bay, sand dunes have accumulated over a series of elevated shingle ridges; buried soil horizons within these dunes reveal Neolithic hearth sites, as well as Bronze Age and medieval monastic remains.

The drowned drumlin country in eastern County Down (Plate 53-6) contrasts markedly with the steep coastal slopes associated with the Mourne-Carlingford Tertiary Igneous massif, with the fault-guided and ice-modified trough of Carlingford Lough, and with the prominent cliffed edges of the Antrim Plateau between Belfast Lough and Lough Foyle. The continuity of the basalt plateau edge is broken by the Lower Bann Valley, a structurally guided trough. Multiple faulting and large rotational landslips frequently bring basalt against chalk, as for example at Garron Point (Plate 53-7) and White Park Bay, west of Bengore Head. The cliffs are consistently lower along the north coast (160–190 m at the Giant's Causeway and Bengore Head) than along the east coast (310 m at Garron Point). Multiple-stepped profiles are common on the basalts (Plate 53-8), but replaced by beveled profiles on the Paleozoic and Precambrian rocks. At the Giant's Causeway huge amphitheaters in the vertical cliffs of basalts are joint- and fault-guided, and contain massive talus slopes. At Fair Head a massive dolerite sill intruded into Carboniferous strata gives rise to cliffs, from which prismatic blocks of dolerite up to 200 m^3 continue to fall, adding to enormous block screes extending below sea level.

Belfast Lough is relatively shallow ($<$ 20 m at its entrance), and is located on Permo-Triassic rocks, exposed between the Paleozoic basement of County Down and the Mesozoic rocks and Tertiary basalts of the Antrim Plateau. Along the County Antrim coast elevated notches, caves, beach deposits, and abandoned cliffs are common at two distinct levels. At 15–24 m O.D. there are late glacial shorelines (14,000–16,000 years old), and postglacial shorelines (4–10 m O.D.) are also well represented. The remains of Mesolithic and Neolithic occupation are found, the most important sites being Larne, Carnlough, Glenarm, and Cushendun.

There is a rich body of literature concerning

the coast of Ireland, only some of which can be referred to here. The reader would be well advised to peruse through the following: Carter (1975, 1982), Davies and Stephens (1978), Charlesworth (1953), Dobson et al (1973), Eden et al (1971), George (1967), Guilcher (1966), Guilcher and King (1961), Kidson and Tooley (1977), King (1965), Mitchell (1976), Nevill (1963), Reffay (1972), Stephens and Glasscock (1970), and Whittow (1974).

NICHOLAS STEPHENS

REFERENCES

Carter, R. W. G., 1975, Recent changes in the coastal geomorphology of the Magilligan Foreland Co. Londonderry, *Royal Irish Acad. Proc.* **75B:**469–497.

Carter, R. W. G. 1982, Sea Level changes in Northern Ireland, *Proc. Geol. Ass.,* **93**(1):7–23.

Charlesworth, J. K., 1953, *The Geology of Ireland: An Introduction,* Oliver and Boyd, Edinbugh and London.

Davies, G. L. H., and N. Stephens, 1978, *The Geomorphology of the British Isles: Ireland,* Methuen, London.

Dobson, M. R., W. E. Evans, and R. Whittington, 1973, *The Geology of the South Irish Sea,* Inst. Geol. Sci., Report 73/11, Her Majesty's Stationery Office, London.

Eden, R. A., J. E. Wright, and W. Bullerwell, 1971, The solid geology of the East Atlantic continental margin adjacent to the British Isles, in *The Geology of the East Atlantic Continental Margin,* F. M. Delany, ed., Inst. Geol. Sci., Report 70/14, pp. 111–128.

George, T. N., 1967, Landform and structure in Ulster, *Scottish Jour. Geology* **3:**413–448.

Guilcher, A., 1966, Les grandes falaises et megafalaises des côtes sudouest et ouest de l'Irelande, *Annales Géographie* **75:**26–38.

Guilcher, A., and C. A. M. King, 1961, Spits, tombolos and tidal marshes in Connemara and West Kerry, Ireland, *Royal Irish Acad. Proc.* **61B:**283–338.

Kidson, C., and M. J. Tooley, eds., 1977, *The Quaternary History of the Irish Sea,* Seel House Press, Liverpool.

King, C. A. M., 1965, Some observations on the beaches of the west coast of Co. Donegal, *Irish Geog.* **5**(2):40–50.

Mitchell, G. F., 1976, *The Irish Landscape,* Collins, London.

Nevill, W. E., 1963, *Geology and Ireland,* Allen and Figgis, Dublin.

Reffay, A., 1972, *Les Montagnes de l'Irelande Septentrionale: contribution à la Géographie Physique de la Montagne Atlantique,* Imprimerie Allier, Grenoble.

Stephens, N., and R. E. Glasscock, eds., 1970, *Irish Geographical Studies in honour of E. Estyn Evans,* Queen's University, Belfast.

Whittow, J. B., 1974, *Geology and Scenery in Ireland,* Penguin Books, Harmondsworth.

Plate 53-1. Slieve League, County Donegal. The cliffs consist of 100–200 m of nearly vertical sea cliffs, above which steep 30–60° scree-clad slopes extend upward to a sharp-crested quartzite ridge some 600 m above sea level (photo by N. Stephens).

Plate 53-2. Cliffs of Moher, County Clare. The 150–200 m cliffs are developed in horizontally bedded Carboniferous sandstones; the cliffs are sheer and in only a few places are there boulder beaches. (photo by N. Stephens).

Plate 53-3. Cliffs near Slea Head, County Kerry. Vertical sea cliffs (30–60 m high) are backed by beveled subaerial slopes carrying a veneer of glacial and solifluction deposits (photo by N. Stephens).

Plate 53-4. Rathcor Lower, Carlingford Peninsula, County Louth. The 20–30 m cliffs are cut in a complex series of glacial tills and fluvioglacial sands and gravels; the foreshore is littered with thousands of granite boulders derived from the drift deposits (photo by N. Stephens).

Plate 53-5. Cliffs near Blackwater, County Wexford. The massive morainic deposits of the Screen Hills, north of Wexford town, are being cliffed and severely eroded, but in places "dead" cliffs are protected by considerable accumulations of blown sand (photo by N. Stephens).

Plate 53-6. Strangford Lough, County Down. Partially drowned drumlin landscape near Killinchy, with the trace of an elevated (postglacial) shoreline shown on the nearest drumlin island (photo by N. Stephens).

Plate 53-7. Garron Point, County Antrim. This part of the Antrim Plateau consists of massive rotational landslips, which involve the chalk and overlying basalts, now tilted at up to 45° from the horizontal. The landslips have been stable for at least 10,000 years and here show cliffs some 100 m high (photo by N. Stephens).

Plate 53-8. Bengore Head, near Giant's Causeway, County Antrim. Multiple layers of basalt lavas and weathering horizons have been etched to produce stepped cliff profiles with a total height of 180 m (photo by N. Stephens).

54. FRANCE

In relation to the size of the country, the oceanic coasts of France are very varied. Rocky coasts of different types are represented, as well as tidal marshes, estuaries, spits, and dunes.

The Mesozoic strata outcropping in the Paris Basin are cut by the coastline from the Straits of Dover to the eastern reaches of the Cotentin Peninsula. Fine chalk cliffs (Prêcheur 1960), up to 120 m high (Plate 54-1), are exposed in Pays de Caux and at Cap Blanc Nez, sometimes capped by Tertiary sands and clays in which the slope is more moderate. The Holocene sea-level rise has destroyed the Pleistocene beaches everywhere except at Sangatte on the Straits of Dover; but at le Tréport recent debris preserves the foot of the cliff. Other cliffs cut the Jurassic strata near Boulogne and, for longer distances, between the Seine estuary and the Armorican Massif (Elhai 1963), with quite varied features related to the nature of the rocks (impressive landslides in the Vaches Noires district where Jurassic clays, capped by Cretaceous chalk, flow after saturation by heavy rains).

The Precambrian, Paleozoic, and granitic formations that frame the Armorican Massif result in a wide set of rocky coasts, when they are not obscured by Holocene beaches or dunes. Very generally, the present coastline was already occupied by the sea during the last Pleistocene high sea level, and probably during other older ones: it has thus been reoccupied by the Holocene transgression. In granitic sectors as at Trégorrois and Pays de Léon, Brittany (Fig. 54-1; Guilcher et al. 1959; Pinot 1963), the Tertiary climate resulted in very irregular weathering in depth; the Pleistocene transgression washed the debris and left stacks of solid rock, which were in turn partly

eroded by frost shattering during the Weichselian glaciation. Since the Holocene, a "contraposed" evolution has been going on: coves are actively cut by waves in the periglacial, soft deposits surrounding the stacks, in which retreat is almost nil. All stages are found, at Lilia for example (Fig. 54-1), between an inland periglacial morphology still intact, and rocks completely washed by waves on the outer marine platform; tails of reworked periglacial material are seen on the leeward side of the stacks, their direction depending on the refraction of the dominant swell. Some of them already existed in the Trégorrois during the last interglacial.

Other interesting cliffs are seen in very hard Ordovician sandstones of the Crozon Peninsula, Brittany. They have not retreated during the Holocene. Their maximum height is 106 m. Very jagged cliffs are found in Precambrian shales along the outer exposed coasts of the isles of Groix and Belle-Ile, southern Brittany (Guilcher 1948). Other fine cliffs lie at Saint Jean de Luz near the Spanish border (Plate 54-2).

Wide tidal flats are exposed on the oceanic coasts of France (Verger 1968), their deposition resulting from shelter in bays, behind spits, or in estuaries, and from the large tidal ranges (at the largest spring tides, up to 15 m at Granville, Mont Saint Michel Bay, and to 10.2 m at the mouth of the Somme River; nowhere less than 4.5 m). The widest flats resemble the *Watten* of the Frisian coasts, especially around the Mont Saint Michel and in the Saint Brieuc Bay, north Brittany, where the sediment is made of *tangue*, a calcareous silt including fine broken shells of local origin. On their inner side is found their usual counterpart, the salt marshes submerged at high spring tides,

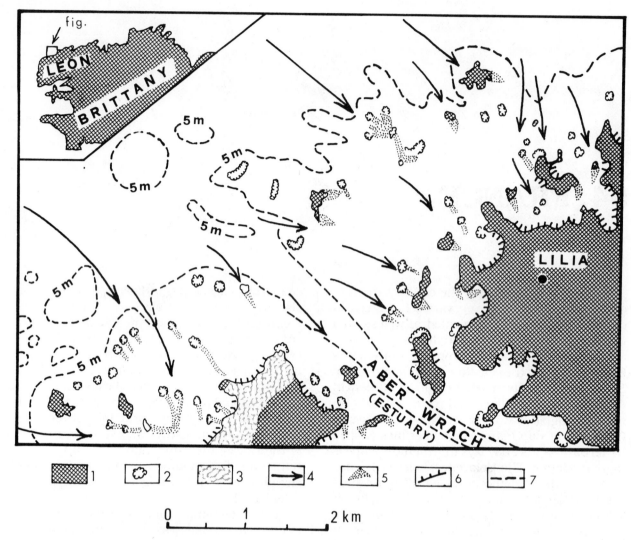

Figure 54-1. Contraposed coast in Léon, northwest Brittany: 1. granite and periglacial deposits; 2. stacks on foreshore; 3. sand dunes; 4. propagation of refracted swell; 5. leeward tails; 6. retreating cliffs in periglacial deposits; 7. 5 m contour below lowest spring tides.

which have been reclaimed as *marais* at Dol, Mont Saint Michel Bay, in Marais Poitevin and Marais Saintongeais, in the French Flanders, and in many other places. The silting-up can be traced from the Middle Ages in such areas as those surrounding the Charente estuary (Fig. 54-2), where the growth of spits tied to former islands and fed in sediment by their cliffs has played an essential part in the sedimentation. Impressive rates of marsh growth have been cited for Anse de l'Aiguillon, in front of Marais Poitevin, with progradation of 150–180 m from 1934 to 1955. Near the isle of Oléron in the same area, progradation of 1100–1700 m took place from 1700 to 1850; and in Picardy, at the mouth of the Somme

River, the salt marshes have grown at 13.5 ha/yr from 1971 to 1975. Near Mont Saint Michel, however, large alternations of growth and retreat have occurred at the outer boundary of the marshes; and, more generally, it seems that in a number of places erosion of mud at micro-cliffs is roughly balanced by sedimentation on the marshes, so that a "cycle of the mud" inside the marsh has been suggested.

These coasts include three large estuaries at the mouths of the Seine, Loire, and Garonne rivers. The latter, called the Gironde (Allen 1973), is the largest in western continental Europe. The dynamics of sediment origin and deposition in these rivers have been amply studied. The Seine estu-

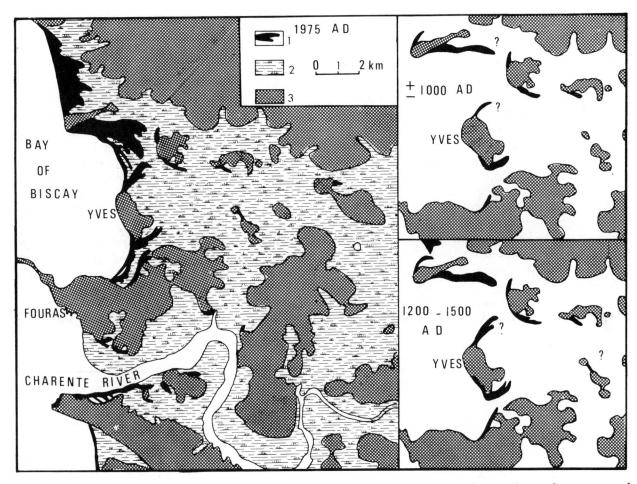

Figure 54-2. Evolution of La Coubre Point from 1825 to 1971. Main data from Volmat, Castaing and Jouanneau.

ary seems to have received the major part of its sediment from the sea, through the tidal current along the bottom, not from the river. In the Loire and the Gironde on the other hand, the supply from upstream amounts to about 500,000 tons and 2,500,000 tons per year, respectively, and is associated with floods. In the course of the last ten years, however, the balance in the Loire estuary has been greatly disturbed by massive dredging for sand utilization just above the tidal area: an example of fatal human action. Mud in suspension is carried to and fro by tidal currents, and plumes are expelled outside the estuaries during floods and, to a lesser extent, at the end of the ebb at spring tides. These plumes contribute to marshes at the edge of the sea. In the Gironde, there are contrasts in salinities and residual currents between the two sides of the estuary, which seem to result from the action of the coriolis force, as has previously been found in Chesapeake

Bay, United States; the residual upstream current along the bottom on the western side brings some sand from the sea.

A number of smaller estuaries skirt the coasts of the Armorican Massif. As the sediment supplied by rivers is almost negligible here, the muds are provided mostly by Pleistocene periglacial deposits, which are in cliffs in the lower parts of the slopes of the estuaries; the coarser particles settle on the upper strand and the finer ones, in suspension, are disturbed on tidal flats and marshes.

Many fine spits have been built in western France. A beautiful compound recurved spit, made of flint pebbles supplied by chalk cliffs, continues to grow at Le Hourdel Point, mouth of the Somme River (Briquet 1930). A remarkable pebble ridge in the Bay of Audierne, western Brittany, is derived from the partial reworking of a much larger Pleistocene ridge (Guilcher 1948); unfortunately, it has been partly destroyed by human activity. Smaller ones, fed by periglacial reworked deposits, have been described around the Rade de Brest and in north Brittany. The spits made of sand are more numerous. The most impressive one, La Coubre Point (Facon 1965), occurs on the north side of the Gironde. Figure 54-3 shows that, from 1825 to 1971, it evolved very quickly by retreat of its inner part and progradation of its distal end, which has now almost closed the Bay of Bonne Anse. Another compound sandy recurved spit, Arçay Point near La Rochelle, encloses the Lay marsh. A special type of spit, which may be called the Darss type after the classic model described on the Baltic shore in eastern Germany, consists of successive ridges initially built by waves, subsequently thickened by eolian sand, and stabilized in situ by vegetation, so that the ridges are dune-like without becoming true dunes. Such a spit has been reported from the northwestern

coast of Brittany (Plate 54-3), and recent studies (Hallégouët 1982) have shown that it has counterparts on the western coast of the Cotentin and in other places around the Armorican Massif.

True coastal dunes, however, were deposited during the Holocene in many places from Flanders to the Armorican Massif. In the latter, the dunes are no longer fed by the beaches, so that they now suffer erosion, especially since the 1950s because of degradation by uncontrolled camping and the driving of cars. They were principally laid down during the Iron Age, some 2500 years B.P., perhaps during a slight regression that provided a large sand supply from the foreshore. But the largest dune belt in France, and even in Europe, is found in Gascony (Quatriéme Centenaire 1979), where extensive inland dunes were first built from fluviatile sediments carried from the Pyrenees, and followed by higher (up to 100 m near Arcachon) coastal dunes, which blocked small estuaries and

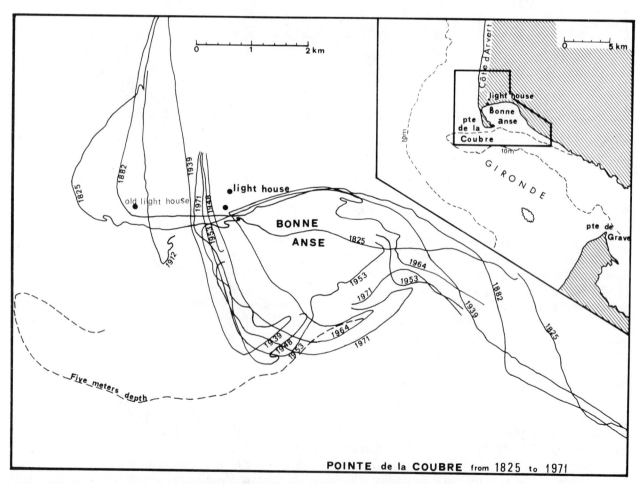

Figure 54-3. Formation of Rochefort marshes, central-west France, from 1000 AD to present. Data from Regrain (1980). 1. spits; 2. marshes; 3. country rock.

created a set of dammed lakes. The present straight, sandy coast, which extends over 230 km from De Grave Point to the mouth of the Adour River, is subject to very severe retreat (700–800 m at Cap Breton from 1881 to 1922; more than 10 m per year at Seignosse). The causes of this retreat are still imperfectly known.

The continental French coast on the Mediterranean is divided into three sectors: a short, mountainous, jagged coast bordering the Pyrenees; a longer coastal plain in Roussillon and Languedoc, ending in the Rhône delta; and another mountainous sector in Provence and Niçois.

The coastal plain of Roussillon and Languedoc is a barrier coast with dammed lagoons (the largest, Etang de Thau, located in a syncline, is the only one still having an outlet). It bears some indentations caused by three isolated volcanic or calcareous hills from which the barriers have grown. In Roussillon at least, the lagoons are former bays that were closed in the late Holocene (Martin 1978). Two barriers were successively built at Etang de Leucate.

The Rhône delta (Kruit 1955) is one of the most interesting in the world in spite of its moderate size, because it clearly shows the results of the shifting course of the distributaries (Fig. 54-4). Two forces are in action: the mistral, a powerful northwest wind with a very short fetch, and the marin, a more moderate onshore southeast wind with a much longer fetch; the chief swell thus comes from the southeast. In 1710, the main distributary was the Bras de Fer, which was then abandoned for the Grand Rhône; at the same time the Petit Rhône discharge decreased more and more. As a result two former headlands related to these distributaries were actively eroded and their sediments transferred to Beauduc and Espiguette points by the southeast swell, while a new spit fed by the Grand Rhône sediments (84% of the solid discharge) grew across Fos Gulf. In most recent times, however, the Rhône catchment area has been harnessed with many large dams, so that the sedimentary discharge to the sea decreased from 40 million tons per year at the end of the nineteenth century to 12 million tons in 1956, and 4 or 5 million in 1970. Erosion largely prevails now except at Gracieuse Point where, as at Beauduc and Espiguette, growth continues locally and moderately with a reworking of the previous sediment supply. It is an example of human interference with coastal evolution.

Between the Rhône delta and the Italian border, rocky coasts prevail, except at such places as the double tombolo of Giens near Toulon. The famous *calanques* near Marseilles (Plate 54-4) are drowned valleys cut into Cretaceous limestones. As around the Armorican Massif, many interglacial beaches and associated eolianites show that recent erosion is generally insignificant. The scenery is impressive (Plate 54-5), but on Côte d'Azur from Cannes to Menton the coast is covered by residential houses and thus completely artificial.

Corsica, one of the most mountainous (Monte Cinto: 2700 m) and splendid Mediterranean islands, has kept many more natural landscapes. The west coast, made of Variscan granites, has a drowned topography in which cliff retreat is again very small (Plate 54-6). As on the continent, Pleistocene (Tyrrhenian) beaches and eolianites, capped by angular debris of the last glacial period, are found in a very large number of coves (Ottmann 1958; Conchon 1980). The east coast is quite different, much flatter, consisting generally of large amounts of Pliocene and Pleistocene marine and continental deposits resting on Alpine metamorphic schists. Lagoons and barriers occur, as in Languedoc. Neotectonics have been active. As usual around the Mediterranean, the coastal Quaternary deposits are better preserved than on the Atlantic side of France because of hardening by calcium carbonate precipitation.

ANDRÉ GUILCHER

REFERENCES

Allen, G. P., 1973, *Etude des processus sédimentaires dans l'estuaire de la Gironde.* Université de Bordeaux, Talence.

Briquet, A., 1930, *Le littoral du Nord de la France et son évolution morphologique,* Librairie A. Colin, Paris.

Castaing, P., and J. M. Jouanneau, 1976, Les mécanismes de formation de la flèche de la Coubre, *Inst. Géol. Bassin d'Aquitaine Bull.* **19:**197–208.

Conchon, O., 1980, Les niveaux quaternaires marins et la tectonique en Corse, in *Niveaux marins et tectonique quaternaires dans l'aire mediterraneenne,* Univ. Paris I, pp. 271–282.

Elhai, H., 1963, *La Normandie occidentale entre la Seine et le Golfe Normand-Breton, étude morphologique,* Imprimerie Bière, Bordeaux.

Facon, R., 1965, La pointe de la Coubre, étude morphologique, *Norois* **12:**165–180.

Guilcher, A., 1948, *Le relief de la Bretagne méridionale,* H. Potier, La Roche sur Yon.

Guilcher, A., B. Adrian, and A. Blanquart, 1959, Les

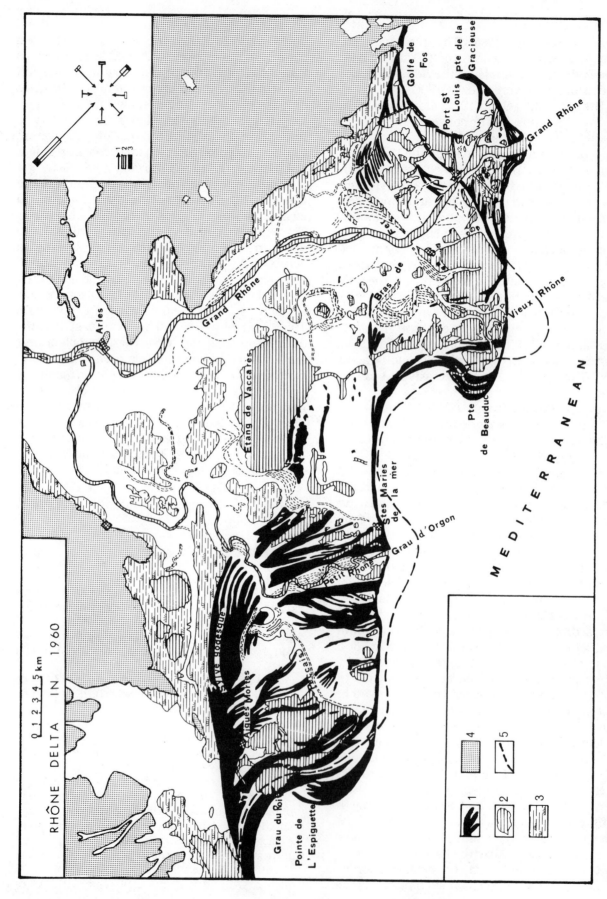

Figure 54-4. Rhône delta in 1960. Mainly from Kruit (1955). 1. successive coastal ridges; 2. lakes; 3. swamps; 4. continental environment; 5. 1710 shoreline (end of Bras de Fer activity). Upper right: annual wind force at Sète city in Beaufort scale; 1. 1–4; 2. 5–6; 3. > 6.

queues de comète de galets et de blocs sur les côtes nord-ouest et ouest de la Bretagne, *Norois* **6:**125–145.

Hallégouët, B., 1982, Les crêtes littorales dunifiées du Massif Armoricain (France), *Géog. Phys. Quat.* **36:**205–218.

Kruit, C., 1955, *Sediments of the Rhône Delta.* Thesis Groningen, S'Gravenhage. Mouton.

Martin, R., 1978, Evolution de deux lagunes du Roussillon depuis le maximum marin holocène, *Assoc. Francaise Étude Quaternaire Bull.* **14:** 108–111.

Ottmann, F., 1958, *Les formations pliocènes et quaternaires sur le littoral corse,* Soc. Géol. France Mém.

Pinot, J. P., 1963, Quelques accumulations de galets de la côte trégoroise, *Annales Géographie,* **72:**12–31.

Prêcheur, C., 1960, *Le littoral de la Manche de Sainte-Adresse à Ault, étude morphologique,* SFIL Poitiers.

Quatrième centenaire du détournement de l'Adour (1578–1978), 1979, Actes du Congrès de Bayonne, 28–29 octobre 1978, *Soc. Sci. Lettres et Arts Bayonne.*

Regrain, R., 1980, *Géographie physique et télédétection des marais charentais,* University, Amiens.

Verger, F., 1968, *Les marais des côtes françaises de l'Atlantique et de la Manche et leurs marges maritimes,* Biscayne Frères, Bordeaux. (2nd ed., 1983, under title Marais et Wadden du littoral français, Minard, Paris.)

Volmat, J., 1952, Evolution de la pointe de la Coubre, *Comité d'Océanographie et d'Etude des Côtes Bull.,* pp. 88–91.

Plate 54-1. Chalk cliffs with hanging valleys showing quick retreat in Pays de Caux, Normandy, between Ault and Le Tréport (photo by A. Guilcher).

Plate 54-2. Cliff and rough abrasion platform in Cretaceous limestones at Saint Jean de Luz near the Pyrenees (photo by A. Guilcher).

Plate 54-3. Penn ar C'Hleuz Spit, Léon, Brittany, with successive dune-like sand ridges of the Darss type. Watt in front (photo by B. Hallégouët).

Plate 54-4. Sormiou *calanque*, drowned valley in Cretaceous limestone, near Marseilles (photo by A. Guilcher).

Plate 54-5. Estérel coast, Provence, in red porphyric rocks. Jagged shoreline (photo by A. Guilcher).

Plate 54-6. Western granitic coast of Corsica between the gulfs of Porto and Sagone. Drowned coastline (photo by A. Guilcher).

55. SPAIN

Spain is made up of a peninsular territory that covers most (85%) of the so-called Iberian Peninsula and insular territories. The Iberian Peninsula has a 4,750 km coastline, 3,904 km of which belongs to Spain. The insular territories consist of the Balearic Islands, and some small islands off north Africa (Chafarinas Islands, Peñon de Alhucemas, and Peñon de Velez de La Gomera) located in the Mediterranean Sea, and the Canary Islands in the Atlantic Ocean off the Saharan coast of Africa. On continental Africa, Spain's territory includes Ceuta and Melilla. The total Spanish coastline is 6,010 km long.

The Iberian Peninsula is situated at the western limit of the Tethys. The following elements give the Spanish coast its specific characteristics: (1) its morphotectonic relation to the prolongation of the active seismic line of the Mesogea; (2) its pronounced elevation, the average height of the country being approximately 700 m; (3) its rectilinear profile, with few re-entrants or forelands, and (4) its geologically very recent coast, with very little low coast and a predominance of rocky, abrupt, cliffy and bluff sections. (Solé and Teran 1969).

The Spanish coasts show an important contrast between the Mediterranean and Atlantic sea environments due to unequal erosion power. The Mediterranean is characterized by weak currents, lack of tides, and rivers with intermittent and poor discharge, with the exception of the River Ebro, the largest Spanish river to discharge into the Mediterranean (85,700 km²). The Atlantic coast, in contrast, has substantial tides (approximately 4.5 m), stronger and more frequent currents and storms, and rivers with a large and constant discharge. Thus the features of the Atlantic and Mediterranean coasts of peninsular Spain are clearly distinguishable: in general, while rocky coasts and erosional shapes predominate on the Atlantic coast (the typical estuaries and rias, for instance), the Mediterranean area is made up of large bay-head beaches between rocky headlands and small deltas (the largest is the Ebro delta, 388 km²).

The Canary Islands require separate treatment since their location (between 27° 47' N and 29° 21' N, and between 13° 20' W and 19° 11' W) and their characteristics are different from those of the rest of Spain. They form an archipelago of volcanic origin with a Miocene substrate.

THE SPANISH MEDITERRANEAN COAST

This part of the peninsular coast stretches from Cape of Creus (42° 20' N), at the eastern end of the Pyrenean Cordillera, to Tarifa Point in the Penibetic Cordillera (Figs. 55-1 and 55-2).

The profile of the coast follows the structural lines of the Neogenic tectonic belts. The most northern area has a north-south direction, and from Cape Begur to Cape Gata northeast-southwest directions dominate. From Cape Gata to Malaga the direction is predominantly east-west and, in general terms, is related to the direction of the Iberian plate at its southern limit. The northeast-southwest direction predominates again from Malaga to Tarifa Point.

This coastline, made up of large sandy bay-head beaches, located mainly in Neogenic tectonic depressions and rocky shorelines, corre-

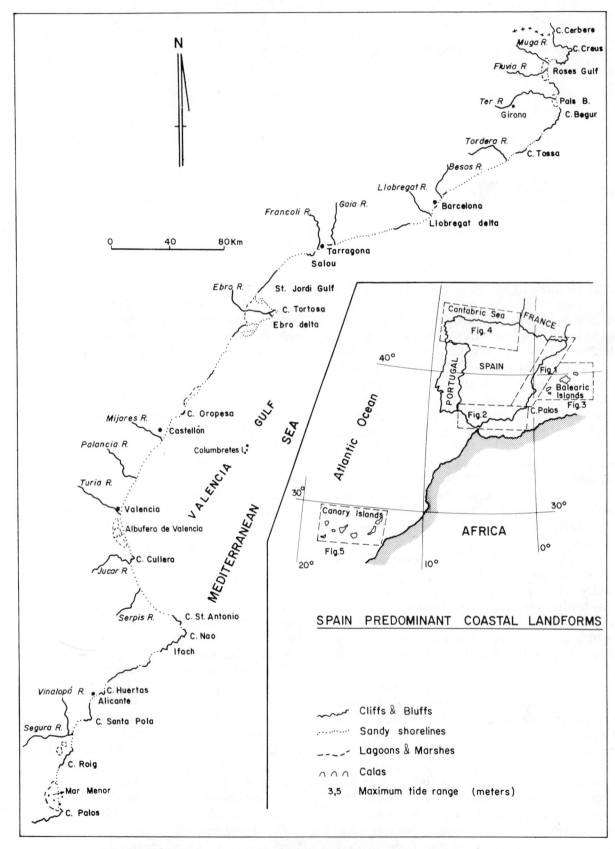

Figure 55-1. Location map for the five coastal sectors of Spain, together with a geomorphic map of the southeast mainland coast.

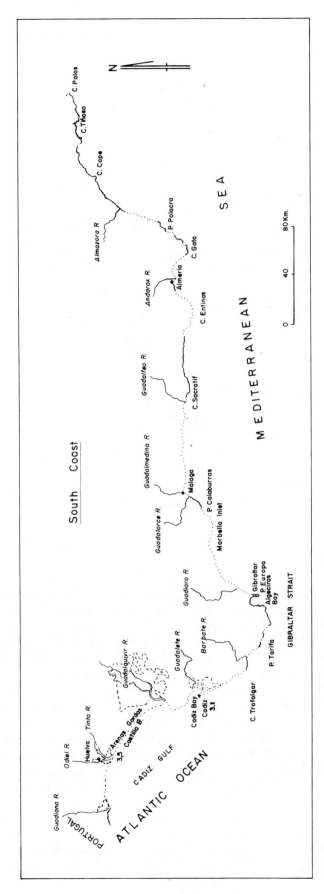

Figure 55-2. Geomorphology of the southern coast of Spain.

399

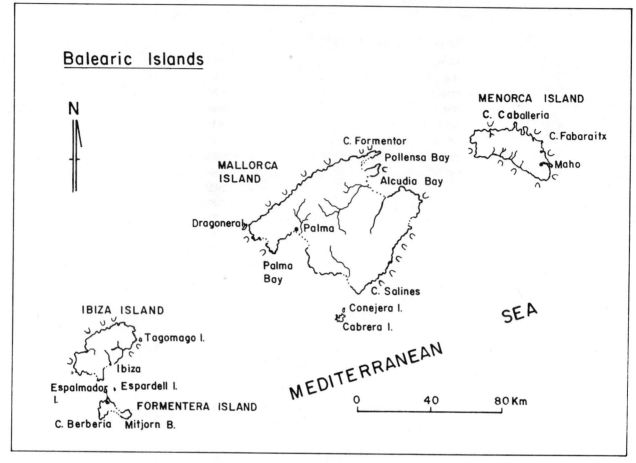

Figure 55-3. Geomorphology of the coast of the Balearic Islands.

sponds to the edges of the alpine orogenic belt mountain chain. It is an active tectonic zone, especially the southern part. The highest peak in the Iberian peninsula is located in this area (Mulhacen: 3,481 m).

The geological history of this coast is governed by the Post-Miocenic evolution of the Mediterranean Basin, considered endoreic (having internal drainage) during the so-called Messinian crisis.

The Neogenic depressions that affect the coast are the southern prolongation of the great central European rift, which has been opening grabens from the Rhine to Africa. These depressions form large sandy bays with coastal lagoons, coastal foredunes, and marshes where the old Pleistocene (Tyrrhenian) beaches and sediments related to the Versilian transgression (dated by Morqués [1975] as 10,900 ± 140 B.P. at 54 m below sea

level in the delta of the River Llobregat) are very clearly represented.

The most important zone of this type corresponds to the Gulf of Valencia, from the Cape San Antonio to the delta of the Ebro, although the sandy beaches stretch northward almost as far as Tarragona. Southward, the sandy shoreline of the southern coast of Alicante includes an important Quaternary (Dumas 1977) platform with coastal lagoons, some of which are used as saltworks. The most important lagoons are La Albufera de Valencia (Plate 55-1) and El Mar Menor.

At present the sandy beaches are being cut back all along the coastline, and in many areas they are protected by groins (Plate 55-2).

The rocky areas are mainly remains of the old Mesozoic crust (Plate 55-3). They have a cliffy morphology, where small re-entrants develop. These contain small blocky gravel or sandy beaches some hundred meters long, locally called *calas;* there are also hanging valleys (Calvet and Gallart 1973). The nature and orientation of these *calas* depend on the local tectonic structure and lithology. This type of coast is particularly developed in the north, where it makes up the Coasta Brava (Barbaza 1971) (Plate 55-4) between Cape Creus and the mouth of the River Tordera, and in the south, between Cape of Palos and Tarifa Point. In the latter area small Quaternary deposits spread out in front of the Penibetic Cordillera relief and cause a mixed type of coast: beaches, at the feet of cliffs whose widths vary according to the structural arrangement of the coast and to the dry, intermittent stream, rambla type, drainage pattern.

The Balearic archipelago (Fig. 55-3) represents the eastern prolongation of the Betic Cordillera, its islands being also placed according to the structural tectonic northeast-southwest orientation, and its features basically corresponding to the scheme described above. The cliffy relief of the northern coasts stands out, with local *calas* and bays open to the southwest and northeast directions in the Island of Mallorca (bays of Palma, Pollensa, and Alcudia).

THE ATLANTIC COAST OF SPAIN

Peninsular Spain's Atlantic coast consists of two well-defined sections: the northern area (Fig. 55-4 and Plate 55-5) and the southern area (Fig. 55-2 and Plate 55-6).

The northern zone (Fig. 55-4) covers the whole coast of the Cantabric Sea, from Cabo Higuer to Cabo Ortegal, the southern part of the Golfo de Vizcaya (Bay of Biscay). The profile has a fairly rectilinear direction in approximately 43° 30′ N latitude. From Cabo Ortegal to Cabo Touriñan the outline, which is very incised, takes a northeast-southwest direction. And finally, from Cabo Touriñan to the estuary of the River Mino (the border between Spain and Portugal), it takes an approximately north-south direction. Here we find the best developed rias (Plate 55-7).

The rectilinear coast of the Cantabric Sea nearly coincides with the northern limit of the Iberian plate, which is located at the edge of the continental shelf a very short distance off the coast. The coastline is rocky and cliffy, with small re-entrants at the mouths of short rivers (about 100 km long), but with constant discharge, forming small rias (Plate 55-5) or bay-head beaches (Plate 55-8).

The structure of the continent governs the micromorphology of this coast, developing vertical cliffs (Plate 55-9) and wave-cut benches, locally called *rasas* (Guilcher 1974). The shapes resulting from marine erosion of dipping flysch-type deposits are remarkable, and give this coast one of its most characteristic features.

From Cape Ortegal, in the crystalline rocks of the Galaico Massif, the coast shows deep re-entrants, which also coincide with the mouths of short rivers. These are the best examples of the so-called rias; (Nonn 1966, Pannekoek 1966), the most important being Vigo, Pontevedra, Arosa (Plate 55-7), Muros, and Noya.

In the southern section the Gulf of Cadiz, from the mouth of the River Guadiana to Cabo de Trafalgar, is the largest low coast of Spain's Atlantic shoreline. It corresponds to the eastern limit of the Neogenic depression of the River Guadalquivir (Plate 55-6), which is situated between Sierra Morena and the Betic Cordillera. Its most remarkable feature is the development of large marshes, which spread inland as far as 50 km behind a coastal dune fringe. These marshes include numerous tidal channels that connect with the drainage outlets (Plate 55-10) of the Guadiana, Tinto-Odiel, Guadalquivir, and Guadalete rivers. Beach ridges are numerous, and they outline different stages of lagoon, marsh, and dune evolution. Some lagoons are used as saltworks, in particular around the Bay of Cadiz. From Cape Trafalgar to Tarifa Point the rocky coast, the eastern limit of the Betic Cordillera, alternates with sandy areas.

The main Canary Islands are, from east to west, Lanzarote, Fuerteventura, Gran Canaria, Tenerife, La Gomera, La Palma, and Hierro (Fig. 55-5). Due to their volcanic origin the coasts are rocky, with cliffs and very few beaches, and have steep slopes (the volcano Teide in the island of Tenerife is 3,718 m high). There is still volcanic activity: for example, the volcano Teneguia, at Fuencaliente Point in the island of La Palma, erupted in 1972. The main morphological features of the coastlines of the Canary Islands are related to volcanicity: semicircular shapes corresponding to calderas, and cliffs to superposition of basaltic sheets.

M. A. MARQUÉS
R. JULIÀ

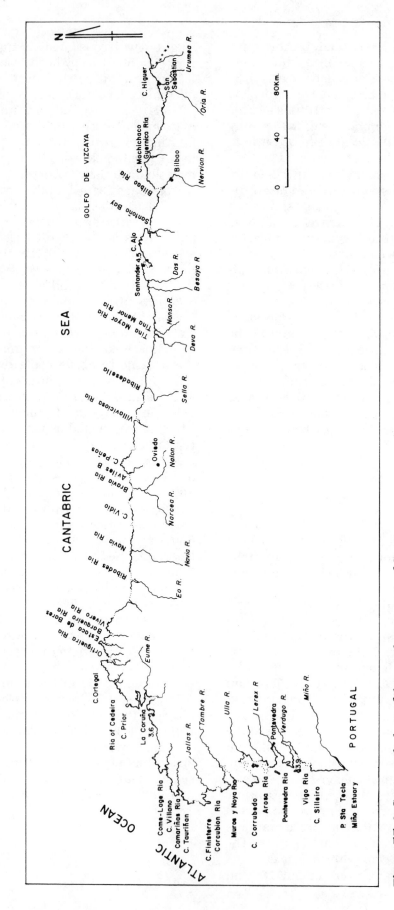

Figure 55-4. Geomorphology of the northern coast of Spain.

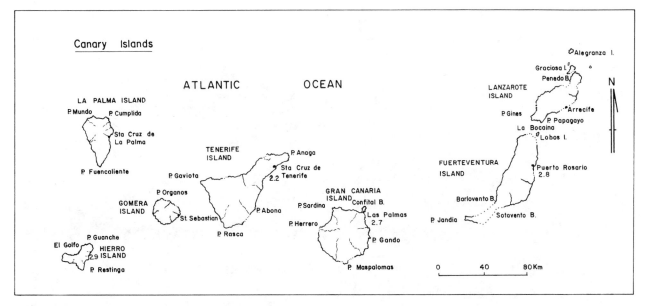

Figure 55-5. Geomorphology of the coast of the Canary Islands.

REFERENCES

Barbaza, Y., 1971, *Morphologie des secteurs rocheux du littoral catalan septentrional*, n.s., **11**:157.

Calvet, J., and F. Gallart, 1973, Esquema morfológico de la Costa Catalana, *Acta Geol. Hispanica* **8**:125-130.

Dumas, B., 1977, *Le levant espagnol. La genèse du relief.* C.N.R.S., Paris.

Guilcher, A., 1974, Les "rasa" un problème de morphologie littorale générale, *Annales Géographie* **83**(4-55):1-33.

Marqués, M. A., 1975, Las formaciones cuaternarias del delta del Llobregat, *Acta Geol. Hispanica* **10**:21-28.

Nonn, H., 1966, *Les regions côtières de la Galice (Espagne) Etude géomorphologique.* Les Belles Lettres, Paris.

Pannekoek, A. J., 1966, The ria problem, *Tidschrift koninck. Neder. Aardrijksk. Genoots.* **83**(3):289-297.

Sole, L., and M. Teran, 1969, *Geografia regional de España.* Ariel, Barcelona.

Plate 55-1. Mediterranean sea coast. Large sandy beach in the Gulf of Valencia. The photo shows the beach of El Saler, near Valencia, which encloses the lagoon of La Albufera de Valencia, appearing in the background. It is an example of a common feature of the Mediterranean coast where the longshore drift has played an important part in building sandy barriers, and in many cases enclosing lagoons (photo by FOAT).

Plate 55-2. Mediterranean coast between Barcelona and the River Tordera (Caldes d'Estrach) in a granitic zone. An example of a sandy coast affected by strong erosion; groins and seawalls have been built to protect the railroad and buildings (photo by FOAT).

Plate 55-3. Oblique air photograph of Peñiscola, one of the few examples of a tombolo on the Spanish Mediterranean coastline. The island is made up of Mesozoic limestones and is connected by a sandy isthmus with a typical piedmont slope. These low slopes develop along nearly all the littoral mountain-border of the Mediterranean Sea (photo by FOAT).

Plate 55-4. The northern part of the granitic Mediterranean coastline corresponding to the area known as the Costa Brava (Calella and Llafranc south of Cabo Begur). It is a rocky coast with typical *calas*, a characteristic example of the morphology of this sector (photo by FOAT).

Plate 55-5. Oblique air photograph showing the sea coast in the northern part of the Spanish Atlantic littoral, the characteristic landscape of this zone. It is a rocky coast, with cliffs and small rias. This photo shows the small Ria de Ondarroa east of Cabo Machichaco, in the Golfo de Viscaya (Bay of Biscay) (photo by FOAT).

Plate 55-7. Partial view of the Ria de Arosa. It is an example of the northwestern coast deeply indented by long branching inlets called rias. The typical ria has an inlet disproportionately large for the size of the small rivers entering it. For example the Ria de Arosa is 27 km long, the River Ulla 126 km, the Ria de Vigo approximately 20 km, and the River Verdugo 39 km (photo by FOAT).

Plate 55-6. Oblique air photograph of the eastern part of the Guadalquivir alluvial plain bordered by sandy beaches. It corresponds with the southern area of Spain's Atlantic Coast. This coast is characterized by low-lying marshes or sand dunes (photo by FOAT).

Plate 55-8. Oblique air photograph of the Cantabric Sea coast (San Sebastian). The sandy beach called La Concha is protected by rocky headlands (Monte Igueldo and Monte Urgull) and Santa Clara island. These promontories have assisted the deposition of sand that has been carried by longshore and tidal currents from the Urumea River. This sort of landscape is fairly common in this zone (photo by FOAT).

Plate 55-9. Rocky coast with cliffs and crenulate forms corresponding with the Spanish Cantabri. The photo shows an erosional surface affecting the thin-bedded rocks of the substrate. The micromorphology of the coast is strongly related to the lithology and dip of the substrate (photo by FOAT).

Plate 55-10. Vertical view of part of the coast bordering the Gulf of Cadiz (Isla Cristina near the mouth of the Guadiana). Note the various channels winding through tidal mud flats and barriers (photo by Spanish Army Geog. Sec.).

56. PORTUGAL

The Portuguese continental coastline (Fig. 56-1) is about 845 km long. Its west-facing sector is exposed to Atlantic swells and waves generated by westerly and northwesterly winds in coastal waters; in winter the southwesterly component is also strong, especially north of Cape Carvoeiro. East from Cape St. Vincent the Algarve coastline receives southerly ocean swell and local wind-generated waves from the southwest (especially in spring and early summer) and southeast (in late summer and autumn). Data from the Instituto Hidrográfico (1978) show higher mean annual wind velocities (about 16 km/hr) on the western coast than in the Algarve (6–9 km/hr). In general, wave energy decreases from north to south (Fig. 56-2).

Tides are semidiurnal, and mean spring tide ranges typically between 3 and 4 m (e.g., 4 m in the ports of Lisbon and Setúbal). Currents in coastal waters flow from north to south.

In response to these processes, predominant longshore drifting is generally from north to south along the western coastline and from west to east in the Algarve. Reversals occur in the lee of major promontories south of Lisbon and in the Bay of Setúbal, where shelter from northwesterly waves permits a local dominance of northward drifting (Fig. 56-3). Castanho et al. (1981) have estimated net annual littoral drift at 150,000 m³ at Leixões, 1 million m³ at Aveiro, 200,000 m³ south of Figueira da Foz, and 40,000 m³ at Quarteira.

Features of coastal geomorphology from north (Minho River) to southeast (Guadiana River) are described in sequence (Fig. 56-4).

From the Minho River to the mouth of the Douro is a low rocky coastline with sandy beaches in a sector where an ancient massif reaches the

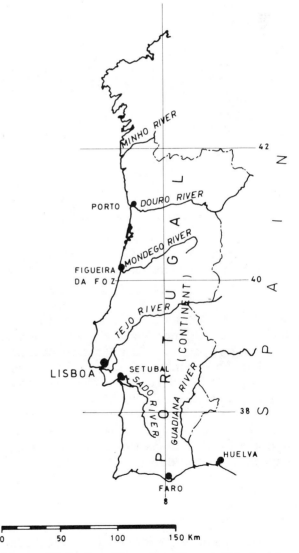

Figure 56-1. Coastline of continental Portugal.

411

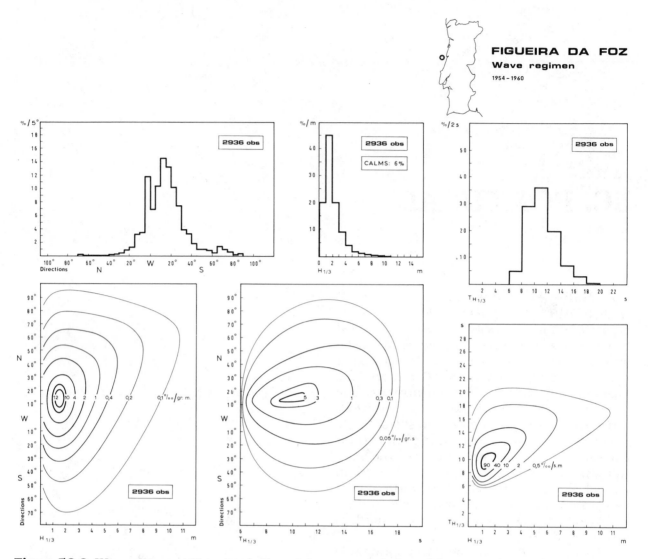

Figure 56-2. Wave regime at Figueira da Foz, giving a general idea of the wave climate on the western coast of Portugal (after Barceló 1975).

sea. Between the mouths of small rivers there are rocky sectors with nearshore reefs. At the Leixões oil terminal, breakwaters intercept southward drifting of beach material, and as a result there has been erosion of beaches to the south at Espinho (Abecasis et al. 1969). The Douro mouth is partly enclosed by a spit, impeding access to the harbor. To the south the coast is low, rectilinear, and sandy, with coalescent spits forming barriers, capped by coastal dunes. Ria de Aveiro is a 60 km² lagoon with an artificial entrance giving access to Aveiro Harbor. Tidal salt marshes are frequent here.

Cape Mondego is a monoclinal Jurassic formation which shelters Buarcos Bay and the harbor of Figueira da Foz at the mouth of Mondego River,

from northwesterly storms. South to Nazaré the coastline is again rectilinear, low, and sandy, and backed by coastal dunes. The submarine canyon of Nazaré heads a short distance offshore, with depths of 200 m close to the coast in front of the bluff of Sitio. Concha de São Martinho do Porto and Lagoa de Óbidos are small tidal lagoons between Nazaré and Peniche, the intervening coastline being rocky and sandy. Groins have been built at Gala, Cova, Costa de Lavos, and Leirosa in an attempt to trap drifting beach material and halt erosion (Castanho et al. 1981). Breakwaters have intercepted the southward drift at Aveiro and Figueira da Foz (Plate 56-1) to cause local progradation and accentuate erosion to the south. Plate 56-2 shows the general outlines of this coast.

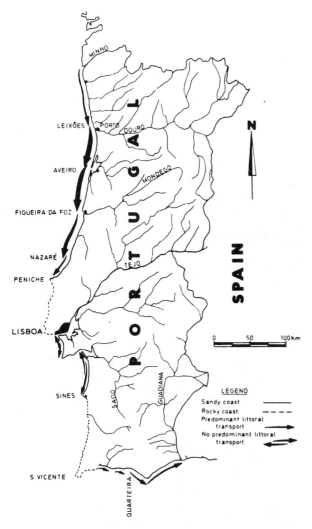

Figure 56-3. General trend of littoral transport (after Castanho et al. 1981).

Cape Carvoeiro (Plate 56-3) is a tombolo, with the fishing harbor of Peniche on its more sheltered southern side. Its line is continued offshore by the rocky islets of Berlengas. To the south are high cliffs with relatively stable pocket beaches and small fishing harbors such as Ericeira. Cabo da Roca, the westernmost point of Europe, is a batholith bordered by towering cliffs, hanging valleys, and boulder-strewn rocky shores. The coast becomes lower to the south, with reentrants cut out by marine erosion along basic dike outcrops. There are shore platforms and pocket beaches extending past Cape Raso along the south-facing sector toward Lisbon.

The Tagus estuary has a narrow mouth with the shoal of Bugio in the channel. It widens inward to the Mar da Palha, with the city and port of Lisbon on the north shore and shipyards at Lisnave to the south; it is essentially lagoonal, with a delta and salt marshes at the inflow of the Tagus River.

South of the Tagus estuary, beach erosion is a problem on the Caparica coast, where numerous groins have been constructed. A long, gently curving coastline, determined by the refraction of northwesterly waves past Cape Raso, has a wide sandy beach backed by degraded cliffs and interrupted by the Albufeira lagoon (Plate 56-4).

Cape Espichel is the western limit of the Serra da Arrabida, the southern flanks of which end in high cliffs. There are small sandy beaches, difficult of access, and fishing harbors such as Sesimbra. The large estuarine lagoon of the Sado has a marine outlet constricted by the northward growth of the Troia sand spit, and is bordered by extensive salt marshes, dominated by *Spartina* grass. The port of Setúbal stands on its northern shore.

A long, gently curving sandy coastline extends south to the Cape of Sines, its outline determined by the refraction of northwesterly waves around Cape Espichel. Behind the beach are the Melides and Santo André lagoons, both with intermittent outlets to the sea through the sandy barrier. The Cape of Sines is a volcanic outcrop, beside which a harbor is under construction. Southward to Cape St. Vincent the coastline is generally cliffed, with rocky shore platforms and intermittent beaches, and some small estuaries, for example the Mila at Vila Nova de Milfontes.

Cape St. Vincent and the nearby Ponta de Sagres are bold headlands on Jurassic outcrops. The south-facing coastline of the Algarve has high cliffs cut in Miocene limestone with some karstic features and nearshore rocky reefs (Plate 56-5). It is interrupted by bay beaches and by small spit-constricted river mouths, for example the Arade estuary at Portimão. Eastward drifting of beach sand is evident at the artificial harbor of Vilamoura, where groins have been inserted to retain beach material on the eroding coastline (Plate 56-6).

East of Quarteira the coast is low and sandy, with dune-capped barriers enclosing lagoons and salt marshes, notably within the cuspate foreland of Santa Maria, where the harbors of Faro and Olhão are sited. (Plate 56-7). The beaches continue to the Spanish border at the mouth of the Guadiana River, the sector east of Faro being subject to occasional *levante* winds blowing from Gibraltar.

CARLOS MORAIS

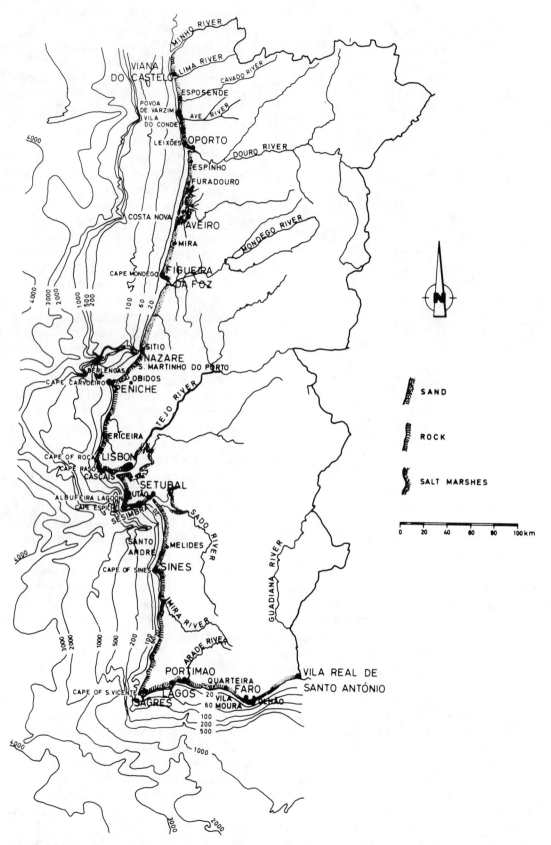

Figure 56-4. Portugal, coastal morphology.

REFERENCES

Abecasis, F., J. Castanho, and M. F. Matias, 1969, Coastal regime. Carriage of material by swell and currents. Model studies and *in situ* observations. Influence of port structures. Coastal defence works. Breakwaters, *22nd Permanent Internat. Assoc. Navigation Congresses Proc.*, Section 2, (4).

Barceló, J. P., 1975, On the Portuguese wave regime, *14th Coastal Engineering Conference Proc.* pp. 112–131.

Castanho, J. P., N. A. Gomes, I. B. Mota Oliveira, and J. P. Simões, 1981, Coastal erosion caused by harbour works on the Portuguese coast and corrective measures, *25th Permanent Internat. Assoc. Navigation Congress Proc.*, Section 2(15) pp. 877–898.

Instituto Hidrogrāfico, 1978, *Roteiro dos portos de Portugal,* Publication 107.

Plate 56-1. Buarcos Bay and Figueira da Foz harbor entrance (after Barceló 1975) (photo by Portuguese Air Force).

Plate 56-2. *(at right).* Coastline from Douro River to Nazaré (Landsat photo by NASA).

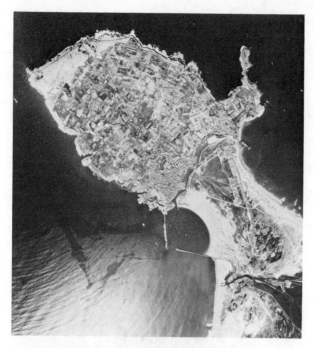

Plate 56-3. Peniche: tombolo and fishing harbour (after Barceló 1975) (photo by Portuguese Air Force).

Plate 56-4. Albufeira lagoon (after Barceló 1975) (photo by Portuguese Air Force).

Plate 56-5. Karstified limestones, western Algarve (photo by Maria Eugénia Lopes).

Plate 56-6. Vilamoura and its field of groins (photo by Portuguese Air Force).

Plate 56-7. Faro-Olhao lagoon (Landsat photo by NASA).

57. ITALY

The Italian coastline, which extends for 7500 km, is influenced by many variables and has shown evolutional tendencies that produce different regional and local characteristics (Plates 57-1, 57-2).

The submergence that has affected the coasts of Sardinia, Liguria, and Carso near Trieste is contrasted with predominant uplift of the middle and low Tyrrhenian, Ionian, and middle and low Adriatic coastlines. This uplift has been discontinuous and unequal, giving rise to various series of marine terraces; repeated eustatic oscillations also took place during these phases. Because these events did not coincide it is difficult to reconstruct and correlate the various cycles. In general, uplift was later along the Adriatic and Ionian coasts than along the Tyrrhenian. It is currently believed that the highest terraces of Quaternary marine abrasion go back to the Lower Pleistocene (Desio 1973).

Along the margin of the coastal plains (that of the Po valley in particular) extensive subsidence is evident. At different depths, submarine geological studies have recognized traces of Pleistocene and Holocene coastal morphology, including shorelines, paleobeaches, paleodunes, and paleoriver beds. Examples may be found in the gulfs of southern Sardinia, La Spezia, Manfredonia, Venice, and the Pontine littoral zone (Segre 1969).

However, even within historical times, Italian beaches have continued to evolve rapidly. They may also present contrasting dynamics, even in adjacent physiographical units (Zunica 1976a).

It is impossible to delve into detail on coastal morphogenesis, but it is useful to trace physiographical features. Figure 57-1 distinguishes high, rocky coasts from low ones. The +100 contour line and the −100 depth contour indicate the width of the plains, coastal articulation, hydrographic trends, and the slope of the sea bed in front of the shore. The maps also show the evolution of beaches over a century (from 1863–1892 to 1953–1972). Retreats and advances are the result of erosion and accretion that took place over stretches of coast during the period considered. Indications should be considered as only general, because of the very small scale of this map. During the last few years almost all Italian beaches have generally receded (Plates 57-3, 57-4, 57-5). Detailed studies of this phenomenon undertaken by the Italian National Council for Research (C.N.R. 1974) are under way, aiming at identifying causes and estimating extent. However, it seems certain that most of the retreat currently taking place is due to human activity (Zunica 1976b).

The most evident characteristic of the Ligurian coast is the vicinity of the Appennine watershed, producing high, steep coasts and short rivers (Plate 57-6). The steep slope of the sea bed hinders the accumulation of detritus brought down by these rivers—another reason for the small, narrow beaches. Exposed to storm waves from the south, they are subject to intense erosion (Bensa et al. 1979).

In both their direction and their morphological aspects, the following beaches are quite different. As far as the Gulf of Naples wide plains open onto the Tyrrhenian coastline; they were built by alluvium from the rivers, which drain large but easily erodible basins. The coast, interrupted by several headlands, is subdivided into large, gently curving beaches, following the prominences of the deltas of the Arno, Ombrone, Tevere, and Volturno rivers.

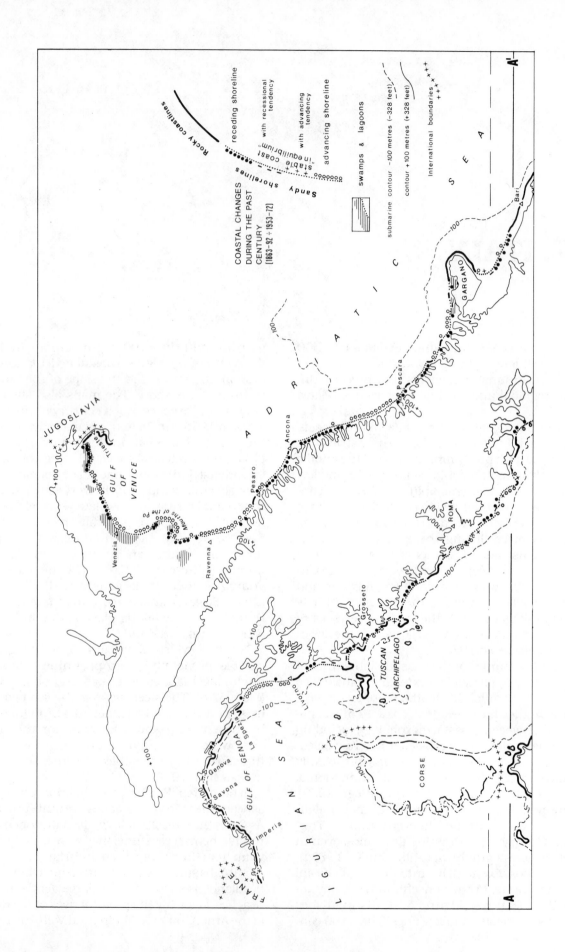

COASTAL CHANGES
DURING THE PAST
CENTURY
(1863–92 ÷ 1953–72)

Rocky coastlines
●●●●●●● receding shoreline
●●●●●●● stable coast "in equilibrium" with recessional tendency
○○○○○○○ advancing shoreline with advancing tendency
○○○○○○○ advancing shoreline
Sandy shorelines
▨▨▨ swamps & lagoons

submarine contour –100 metres (–328 feet)
contour +100 metres (+328 feet)
International boundaries

420

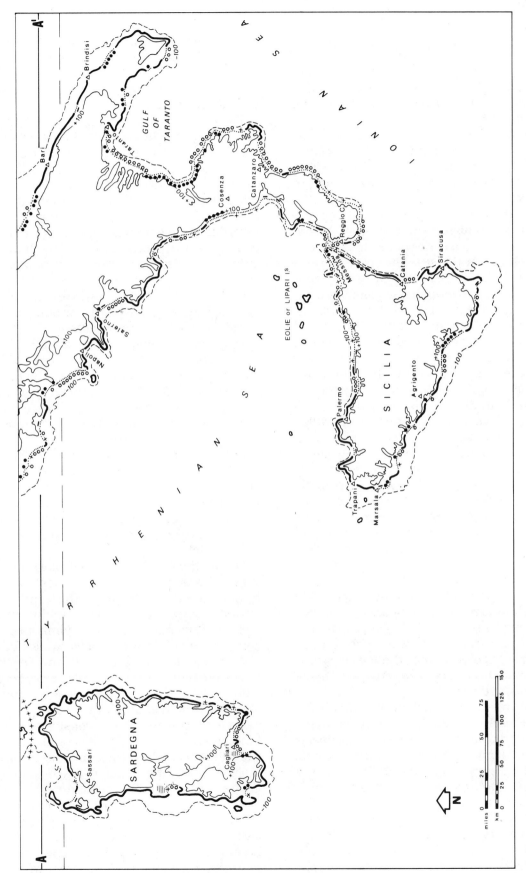

Figure 57-1. Italy: predominant coastal landforms.

421

Inland marshy areas (*maremme*) and parallel dunes (*tomboli* and *tumuleti*) may be traced, indicating that these beaches have advanced in historical times. The dunes are often held in place by vegetation, sometimes including tall trees (Aiello et al. 1975).

Some parts of the Neapolitan coast are of special interest, because of land movements, both positive and negative, sometimes rapid and of considerable extent, connected with the volcanic nature of this area.

South of the gulfs of Naples and Salerno, the coast returns to its high, continuous form. Appennine relief, uplifting a series of marine terraces, rises straight from the sea. The coast shows a discontinuous, narrow, littoral zone that fans out only near the main rivers, characterized by occasional damaging seasonal floods (*fiumare*).

The Calabrian Appennines (Plate 57-7), extend for most of the northern coast of Sicily which thus shows lithology and structure very similar to those of the coasts described above, but with sandy or gravelly, weakly concave beaches of greater width. In the stretch facing the Sicilian Channel, beaches are more uniform, often flat, and rather rectilinear. Pleistocene marine sediments are quite widespread around Sicily. Lastly, the coast facing the Ionian Sea is affected by strong currents that do not favor the accumulation of loose material, but the wide beach of Piana di Catania, restricted northward by the lava flows of Mt. Etna, is worthy of mention. Volcanic landscapes occur on many of the islands surrounding Sicily, where sea action has modeled their coasts in various ways.

Sardinia is quite different, being a Hercynian massif of mainly crystalline composition, the relic of an ancient continent. Lithology and structure have influenced the coast, which shows high, rocky forms. Beaches border the larger coastal plains and are backed by distinctive systems of dunes, lakes, and ponds.

The features of the Sicilian and Calabrian beaches of the Tyrrhenian Sea continue into the Ionian as far as Piana di Sibari. This anticipates the physiognomy characteristic of the whole northwestern side of the Gulf of Taranto. The rivers that flow into the sea in this area from erodible catchments have built the largest beach formations in southern Italy. Sections across it show up to seven series of terraces (Parea et al. 1980).

From the northeast side of the Gulf of Taranto to the headland of the Gargano, the physiography is quite similar. High, rocky coasts prevail, often formed of organogenic calcarenites, with no beaches (Plate 57-8). Only south of the Gargano has sediment from the Ofanto and smaller rivers built a wide beach.

The coast from the Gargano to Pesaro shows special features (Plate 57-9). It begins with the coastal lakes of Varano and Lesina and continues with a sandy or gravelly beach interrupted only by small stretches of high coast defining the different physiographic units (Girardi 1981). This beach is fed by material from numerous waterways descending from the Appennine ridge, with generally short, parallel courses. They have deeply eroded the clays, gravels, and sands, and the coastal slopes show four or five series of terraces.

Lastly, north of the Pesaro headland, the large Po Valley and Venetian plain fans out. Just before Trieste it is terminated by cliffs and bluffs where submergence phenomena predominate (C.N.R. 1979; Zunica 1971). The plain is crossed by the Po, Adige, Brenta, Piave, Livenza, Tagliamento, and Isonzo rivers, and is bounded by low, sandy beaches that enclose bodies of water (*valli*) amphibian areas (*barene* and *velme*), marshes, and lagoons connected to the sea.

Beach continuity is interrupted by the deltaic fans of these rivers. The most conspicuous is the Po delta, whose complicated construction has been recognized as far back as pre-Etruscan times. The Po drains a basin of more than 70,000 km^2 and extends its delta into the sea for about 20 km (Ciabatti 1966).

Among the various Italian coastal sectors, the Venetian beaches have been the most influenced by human activities. From the thirteenth century onward, many river courses were diverted; protection of the barrier islands culminated in the construction of the *murazzi* (seawalls built during the eighteenth century by the Venetians); finally, port entrances were protected by long, protruding stone jetties. The results were that longshore drifting has been drastically interrupted.

Tidal ranges are also of considerable importance along this part of the coast. On the rest of the Italian coast they reach only a few tens of cm, but in the Adriatic, which is practically a closed basin, tides may reach 1 m. Because of the effects of the sirocco winds (from the southeast), low atmospheric pressures, and seiches, sea level may also rise to a height of over 2 m. Such events have become more frequent in recent years, giving rise to exceptionally high tides, known in Venice as *acqua alta* (high water) (Mosetti 1971). These tides may cause serious damage to the barrier islands and the Venetian hinterland, partly because the defenses are not of sufficient dimensions to deal with these anomalous conditions (Istituto Veneto 1972).

An analysis of beach changes over a century shows a variety of situations. The maps (Figs. 57-1a and 57-1b) do not reflect the current state exactly: an almost general retreat of the coastline has been noted in the last few years.

Almost all authors who have worked on this problem agree that the natural processes have been profoundly disturbed by human activities. Along the Italian coastline, human situations have become stratified over the centuries; excavations bring to light not only prehistoric remains but also extensive traces of Greek, Etruscan, Roman, medieval, and modern civilizations. The recent massive occupation of the coasts has added completely new elements that are often totally extraneous to the environment. Residential, tourist, and industrial areas have expanded, port structures have been amplified, defenses of all types and sizes have been inserted, resulting in, among other things, the alteration of longshore drifting (Plates 57-3, 57-4, 57-5, 57-10, 57-11, and 57-12). The use of underground water, the weight of industrial settling, and extensive reclamation works have accentuated natural subsidence.

Events far inland have also sometimes influenced beach dynamics. Forestry and hydraulic operations aimed at protecting mountain areas; the use of rivers for purposes of hydroelectricity, drinking water, and irrigation; and various types of quarrying from river beds have all drastically reduced river transport of sands and gravels, and have also profoundly altered beach regimes.

The combined effect of these factors has been so great that natural conditions are now rarely found along stretches of any length along the Italian coast (Comm. Studio 1970-74).

MARCELLO ZUNICA

REFERENCES

Aiello, E., C. Bartolini, C. Acaputo, L. D'Alessandro, F. Fanucci, G. Fierro, M. Gnaccolini, G. B. La Monica, E. Lupia Palmieri, M. Picazzo and E. Pranzini, 1975, Il trasporto litoraneou lungo la costa'toscana tra la foce del Fiume Magra e i Monti dell'Uccellina, Bollettino della Società Geologica Italiana, **94:**1519–1571.

Bensa, F., E. La Barbera, and F. Toggiasco, 1979, *Particolari aspetti evolutivi delle spiagge liguri*, Sagep, Genoa.

Ciabatti, M., 1966, Ricerche sull'evoluzione del Delta Padano, *Gior. Geologia* **34:**381–406.

Consiglio Nazionale Delle Ricerche, 1974, Ricerche sul regime e la conservazione dei litorali, *La Ricerca Scientifica* **92.**

Consiglio Nazionale Delle Ricerche, 1979, *Le spiagge di Romagna: Uno spazio da proteggere.* Instituto di Geografia, Universitè Bologna, Quaderni 1–2.

Comm. Studio Sistemazione Idraulica e Difesa del Suolo, 1970–1974, *Atti della commissione,* 4 vol., Rome.

Desio, A., 1973, *Geologia dell'Italia.* Unione Tipografico-Editrice Torinese, Turin.

Istituto Veneto Scienze Lettere Arti, 1972, *Rapporti e studi,* **5.** Commissione di studio per la conservazione della Laguna, Venice.

Girardi, A., 1981, *Analisi preliminare dello spazio costiero tra Foce Tronto e Foce Fortore.* Instituto di Geografia, Università, Padua, Quaderno 5.

Mosetti, F., 1971, Considerazioni sulle cause dell'acqua alta a Venezia, *Boll. Geofisica Teor. ed Appl.* **50:** 169–184.

Parea, G. C., D. Fontana, R. Valloni, and A. Vinci, 1980, Dispersione dei sedimenti ed evoluzione della costa fra Capo Spulico e Taranto durante il Quaternario, *Geog. Fis. e Dinamica Quat.* **3:**3–15.

Segre, A. G., 1969, Linee di riva sommerse e morfologia della piattaforma continentale italiana relativa alla trasgressione marina versiliana, *Quaternaria* **11:** 141–154.

Zunica, M., 1971, *Le spiagge del Veneto.* Consiglio Nazionale Delle Ricerche-Ist. Geografia. Padua.

Zunica, M., 1976a, *Human influence on the evolution of the Italian coastal areas,* Italian contributions to the 23rd Int. Geogr. Congr., pp. 87–93.

Zunica, M., 1976b, *Coastal changes in Italy during the past century,* Italian contributions to the 23rd Int. Geogr. Congr., pp. 275–281.

Plate 57-1. Gently curved stretch of beach, mainly composed of gravel and sand, along littoral zone of middle Adriatic. Lacking signs of erosion and human influence, it represents an exception in the context of Italian beaches (photo by M. Zunica).

Plate 57-2. In this stretch of sandy beach in the low Adriatic, not yet used by man, one sees evidence of wave attack on the beach and dune area held in place by vegetation (photo by M. Zunica).

Plate 57-3. Where coastal sectors have been exploited to excess, defense operations have been extensive but not always efficacious. This photograph shows the Lido of Jesolo north of the lagoon of Venice (high Adriatic). After the storm surge of November 4, 1966, the sea penetrated the built-up area. Today the beach has been mostly rebuilt artificially and maintained with the help of many extensive defense systems (photo by M. Zunica).

Plate 57-4. Aspects very similar to those of Plate 57-3 may be found south of the Po along the Emilia-Romagna coast, where defense operations are quite precarious (photo by M. Zunica).

Plate 57-5. Beach at Cesenatico, south of the Po, illustrating the precariousness, variety, and discontinuity of defense systems used along Italian beaches. These are often unsuitable to the local situation and may cause great damage to nearby stretches of coast (photo by M. Zunica).

Plate 57-6. The Ligurian coast (Porto Venere), with vertical walls showing quite resistant subhorizontal rocky strata. Cliffs characterize much of the Italian coastline, with sometimes very different morphological aspects (photo by G. Rotondi).

Plate 57-7. A stretch of the Calabrian coast, incised on strata with notable inclination. Note the rich Mediterranean vegetation, which makes this area ideal for tourist exploitation (photo by M. Zunica).

Plate 57-8. View of calcarenite coastline of Salento peninsula (heel of Italy). Background: paleodunes held in place by vegetation. Later traces of notches are visible; in foreground, surface micromorphology is notable (photo by M. Zunica).

Plate 57-9. Foot of cliff characterizing the Abruzzo coastline (middle Adriatic), made up of recent, easily erodible rocks, continually broken away by storm waves. The material thus removed nourishes nearby beaches (photo by M. Zunica).

Plate 57-10. Effects of transversal defenses may sometimes cause great widening of beaches. In this example from Liguria, man-made structures have a great advantage. However, sometimes these traps may interrupt longshore drifting, with serious damage to nearby beaches (photo by N. Corradi).

Plate 57-12. A situation similar to that shown in Plate 57-11, but along the Ligurian coastline. The damage that may be caused by storms is obvious (photo by N. Corradi).

Plate 57-11. A length of railway line along the middle Adriatic coast; in the background, planes corresponding to marine terraces. The main directions of the large-scale Italian road system were laid down at the end of the nineteenth century. They followed the coast, the easiest route in a country of great morphological irregularity. Nearness to the sea today creates serious problems, partly avoided by moving the most exposed stretches of road into tunnels (photo by M. Zunica).

58. MALTA

The Maltese islands are located between the eastern and western Mediterranean basins, where Europe and Africa come closest together. They are regarded as part of the African plate (Vossmerbäumer 1972).

The archipelago, which covers about 315 km², comprises two main islands, Malta and Gozo, and three little islands, Comino, Cominotto, and Filfla (Fig. 58-1). It is composed almost entirely of Oligo-Miocene limestones and associated marls occurring in a simple succession of the following formations from bottom to top (Felix 1973): Lower Coralline Limestone (over 140 m); *Globigerina* Limestone (20–210 m); Blue Clay (0–65 m); Greensand (0–10 m); and Upper Coralline Limestone (up to 160 m). The rocks, which contain a prolific fauna, are subhorizontal, but normal faulting of varying amplitude is widespread and has a pronounced effect on the coastal morphology.

North of the Victoria Lines Fault, which crosses Malta from east to west and forms a bold scarp, the geological structure is dominated by the development of horst and graben blocks, limited by east-northeast-trending normal faults. Such a structure, perpendicular to the present coastline orientation, is indicated by prominent ridges and low valleys. The latter have been partially (St. Paul's Bay, Mellieha Bay) or entirely (straits separating Malta and Comino, Comino and Gozo) drowned by the sea.

Spectacular cliffs, more than 200 m high near Dingli, characterize the southwestern coast of Malta. They are structurally controlled by a major northwest-trending fault, known as the Maghlak Fault, which downthrows the Upper Coralline Limestone to the south by at least 230 m (Pedley et al. 1976) and probably moved during the Qua-

ternary (Trechmann 1938). Because Malta has been tilted toward the northeast, there is a striking contrast between the precipitous and rectilinear coast of the southwestern part of the island, and the low and indented shoreline of the northeastern side, which gradually plunges under the sea and is locally penetrated by it.

Semicircular coves represent a conspicuous feature of the Maltese coastline. They originate from widely distributed typical karstic landforms inundated by the sea. Post-Miocene solution of carbonates has reached an advanced stage, producing well-developed sinkholes and extensive subterranean cavern and gallery systems in all formations, especially in the coralline limestones.

In the western Gozo, Quawra, there is a large (400 m diameter and 70 m deep) elliptical sinkhole structure of complex origin (Pedley 1974), bounded by vertical walls and developed in the Lower Coralline Limestone. Its bottom has been partially inundated, for a karstic gallery connects the depression with the open sea and allows small boats to pass. In the immediate vicinity, Dwejra Bay is another former closed depression, measuring approximately 340 m in diameter, whose eastern half alone has been preserved; it has been largely invaded by the sea. An islet, Fungus Rock, is the last remnant of its western wall, destroyed by marine erosion.

In subterranean cavernous areas of karstic origin, revealed by cliff retreat, wave action during storms may provoke roof collapse, which forms roughly semicircular coves. Blue Grotto, in southern Malta, is an example of such a form.

Malta and Gozo display inlets that are partially drowned valleys of subaerial erosion. Typical *calanques* are found: Wied iz-Zurrieq in southern

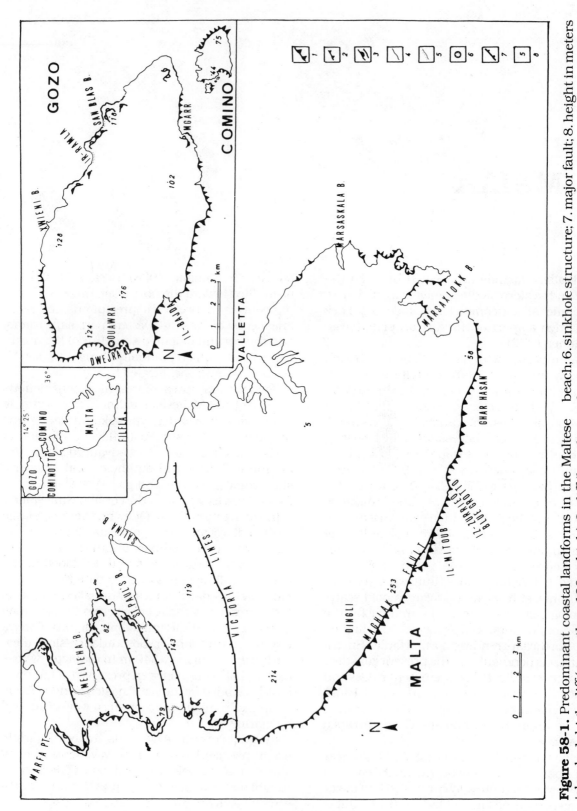

Figure 58-1. Predominant coastal landforms in the Maltese islands. 1. high cliff (more than 100 m high); 2. cliff (less than 100 m high); 3. *r'dum*-type cliff; 4. low rocky coast; 5. sandy beach; 6. sinkhole structure; 7. major fault; 8. height in meters from datum line.

Malta and il-Bajda in southwestern Gozo (Plate 58-1) are narrow, shore inundated valleys with steep sides cut in the Lower Coralline Limestone. Wider and more developed inlets, such as Salina and Marsaskala bays in Malta, correspond to finger-shaped, broader, and more open valleys, subaerially eroded in the soft *Globigerina* Limestone and subsequently submerged. One of the finest anchorages in the world is provided by the amazing finger-like ramifications of creeks and inlets that extend around Valletta (Plate 58-2). These originated as a gently sloping and converging fluvial system that was deeply drowned by the sea.

Steep cliffs, more than 50 m high and in some places more than 200 m, represent half the length of the Maltese coastline (Guilcher and Paskoff 1975; Paskoff and Sanlaville 1978). They characterize southern Malta, eastern Comino, and most of the coast of Gozo (Ellenberg 1983).

Vertical plunging cliffs are generally cut in the Lower Coralline Limestone and lack shore platforms at their feet (Plate 58-3). They probably are of tectonic origin. An undercut notch, about 1 m deep, is visible at mean sea level (average tide range: 0.6 m).

The so-called *r'dums* correspond to a special kind of marine cliff related to a specific geological structure that is prone to mass movements (Plate 58-4). They occur when marls of the Blue Clay formation crop out at sea level and are overlaid with the massive strata of the Upper Coralline Limestone. Unconsolidated marls are easily eroded by wave action. In addition, after heavy winter rains, water percolates through fissures of the limestone into the underlying marls. Moistening and then saturation of previously dry rock layers cause the marls to become plastic, and huge rockslides may occur. *R'dum*-type cliffs are characterized by heaps and confused irregular masses of marl and fragmented limestone rocks that have slid down. In such circumstances, cliff retreat is probably slow, a certain time being necessary for the removal of the large accumulation of boulders that protects the foot of the scarp.

Where bluffs are cut in the marly *Globigerina* Limestone, they are fronted, in most cases, by shore platforms produced by mechanical action of waves, mainly through hydraulic pressure that dislodges and removes blocks from stratified and jointed rocks (Plate 58-5).

In northeastern Malta and northern Gozo cliffs are lacking, and long tracts of low, rocky coastlines of corrosion are found. Pools and lapies give an extremely jagged and hackly topography to such littoral platforms, particularly when they are cut in coralline limestones. Chemical and biological weathering are obviously the prevailing processes of evolution. Evidence of abrasion (polishing, rubbing) is absent. Structural control accounts for the simultaneous development of several platforms at different levels up to more than 10 m above the sea, as can be seen in northern Gozo where the *Globigerina* Limestone crops out. On exposed coasts only, large boulders dislodged by storm waves lie scattered on shore platforms, and corrosion microforms are less developed.

Beaches are uncommon in the Maltese islands. Few limited sandy shorelines exist in northern Malta (St. Paul's Bay, Mellieha Bay) and in Gozo (ir-Ramla). This lack of beaches represents an impediment to the growth of the tourist industry, a goal of the country's development plan.

On the whole, in spite of their reduced extension, the Maltese islands display a surprisingly large array of present-day coastal geomorphic features.

Careful investigations have found unquestionable trace of ancient shorelines higher than the present one in the Maltese islands. Emerged terraces or notches, as well as indisputable marine deposits, are lacking. Formerly reported raised beaches are in fact pediment features (Plate 58-6). Field evidence suggests a late Quaternary crustal subsidence, which is probably still in progress; at St. Paul's Bay, cart tracks of Neolithic age enter the sea at one side and emerge on the opposite side of the inlet (Hyde 1955).

ROLAND P. PASKOFF

REFERENCES

Ellenberg, L., 1983, Die küsten von Gozo, *Essener Geogr. Arb.* **6:**129–160.

Felix, R., 1973, Oligo-Miocene stratigraphy of Malta and Gozo, *Med. Land. Wag.* **20:**1–103.

Guilcher, A., and R. Paskoff, 1975, Remarques sur la géomorphologie littorale de l'archipel maltais, *Assoc. Géographes Français Bull.* **427:**225–231.

Hyde, H. P. T., 1955, *Geology of the Maltese Islands.* Lux Press, Valletta.

Paskoff, R., and P. Sanlaville, 1978, Observations géomorphologiques sur les côtes de l'archipel maltais, *Zeitschr. Geomorphologie* **22:**310–328.

Pedley, H. M., 1974, Miocene sea-floor subsidence and

later subaerial solution subsidence structures in the Maltese Islands, *Proc. Geol. Ass.* **85:**533–547.

Pedley, H. M., M. R. House, and B. Waugh, 1976, The geology of Malta and Gozo, *Geol. Assoc. (London) Proc.* **87:**325–341.

Trechmann, C. T., 1938, Quaternary conditions in Malta, *Geol. Mag.* **75:**1–26.

Vossmerbäumer, H., 1972, Malta, ein Beitrag zur Geologie und Geomorphologie des zentralmediterranen Raumes, *Würzburger Geog. Arb.* **38:**1–213.

Plate 58-1. Il-Bajda, southwestern Gozo. In the foreground is a typical *calanque*, short, partially drowned valley with steep sides cut in the Lower Coralline Limestone; in the distance, cliffs about 150 m high, developed in the *Globigerina* Limestone (photo by R. P. Paskoff).

Plate 58-2. Valletta, Malta. The ramified inlet of Marsamxett Harbor, corresponding to a drowned valley system (photo by R. P. Paskoff).

Plate 58-3. Ghar Hasan, southern Malta. Plunging cliffs, about 50 m high, cut in the Lower Coralline Limestone; the cliff retreat has revealed the karstic gallery of Ghar Hasan, whose visitor access is visible in the foreground (photo R. P. Paskoff).

Plate 58-4. Mistra Rocks, San Blas Bay, northeastern Gozo. *R'dum*-type cliff with talus of marls and fragmented Upper Coralline Limestone rocks that have slid down over the Blue Clay slope (photo by R. P. Paskoff).

Plate 58-5. Qolla i-Bajda, Xwieni bay, northern Gozo. Cliffs cut in the *Globigerina* Limestone; shore platform strewn by large boulders in the background and converted into salt pans in the foreground (photo by R. P. Paskoff).

Plate 58-6. Il-Mitoub, southern Malta. Cliffs related to the major Maghlak fault zone, whose subsidiary fracture is visible; the planated surface that appears in the distance is not a raised wave-cut terrace but an erosional feature of continental origin (pediment) truncating the *Globigerina* Limestone soft strata (photo by R. P. Paskoff).

59. YUGOSLAVIA

Dalmatia is an Adriatic Sea coastal district of Croatia, one of the federative states of the Yugoslav Republic. Separated from inner Croatia by the Dinaric Alps, a defensive rampart against internal dangers, Dalmatians were compelled to look to the sea. The Adriatic Sea not only abounds in valuable marine life, but also forms one possible route to the outside world.

The Yugoslav Dalmatian coast (Fig. 59-1) extends from the Paklenica canyon, near the town of Starigrad, southward along the Adriatic Sea coast to the Neretva River. It comprises the central Adriatic coastal strip and a fringe of islands dotting the eastern littoral of the Adriatic Sea.

Dalmatia runs 271 km in length, including many inlets and bays, and forms one of the most jagged coastlines of Europe. The shape of the Yugoslav coast is so distinctive that geomorphologists recognize a "Dalmatian coast" as a separate type.

The association of land and sea characterizes the Dalmatian coast, and nowhere in the Mediterranean region is there a greater interlocking of the sea, the surrounding islands, a scalloped coast, and mountains. It is here that the crestline hugs the coast, isolated from the interior. Many narrow peninsulas protrude into the Adriatic Sea, and small bays push inland, along a coastline fronted by hundreds of islands. This particular maritime configuration provides a reservoir of warmth during summer and winter; it has been of considerable help to coastal navigation and fishing.

The Phoenicians first established trading posts here; they were succeeded by the Greeks and Romans and later by the Venetians, whose cultural influences are still felt today.

During the Quaternary, the sea invaded a coastal area whose topography of parallel limestone ridges, separated by wide valleys, created a coast with many bays and a number of long islands, stretching parallel and close to the shore.

The ranges of limestone plateaus rise in impressive grandeur and form complex walls above the Adriatic Sea, the Dinaric Alps. They started forming during the Mesozoic era and were then affected by Alpine uplifting and by the sinking of the Adriatic basin. One can still follow the main orientation of the Dinaric Alps along the Dalmatian coast and the Adriatic Sea islands. The subsidence of the area caused the waters of the Mediterranean Sea to invade the sunken region. The littoral plains along the coast were reduced to small patches overlooked by strips of bluffs, beyond which peaks crest at 1900 m.

Dalmatian coasts have been described as abrupt coasts with longitudinal structure (Emmanuel De Martonne 1948). Such coasts show a greater diversity of shapes than do flat coasts. Longitudinal relief is transformed into elongated islands and peninsulas, as the sea covers regions of relatively recent folding; where the shoreline is parallel to the folds, valleys become straits, channels, and long, narrow gulfs. Shepard (1973) associates Dalmatian-type coasts with ria coasts, as was suggested by Baulig (1930) and von Richthofen (1885). The Dalmatian-type coast is thus a drowned mountainous coast consisting of parallel fold ranges; the channels (*canali*) zigzag in directions that are mostly parallel, occasionally normal to the shoreline. This drowned coast, with its channels and radial estuaries, is reminiscent of fjords–the low-relief, irregular inlets of glacial origin of Sweden–but it is of course unglaciated;

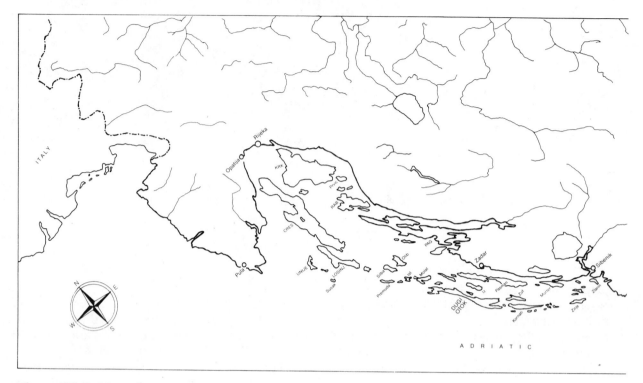

Figure 59-1. Map of Yugoslavian coast.

occasionally, however, the inlets along Yugoslavia's coast are popularly referred to as fjords (e.g., the fjord of Kotor). To von Richthofen (1885) the Dalmatian-type coast is an embayed or ingression coast, to Johnson (1919) it is a type of submergent (or immersion) coast.

The karstic relief is characteristic of the northwest coast; the Dalmatian karst, or olokarst (*dvijic*), is the most typical. Normal development of the karstic cycle involves an impermeable layer below sea level; where one encounters inundated *holje*, they are due to a local uplift of this impermeable layer.

In many places along the Dalmatian coast the limestone peaks abut the dazzling blue waters of the Adriatic Sea, but in some sites, hugging the coast, are pockets of coastal soil with boulders strewn about like the bones of monumental antediluvian beasts. In these pock-marked stone valleys, devoid of fertile soils, peasants struggled for centuries to eke out a barren livelihood in little walled fields, cleared to make way for twisted olive trees.

Water temperatures along the Dalmatian coast range from about 12° C in February to 25° C in August. Warm water flows in from the Mediter-

ranean Sea and northward, so that even during the harshest winters, the Adriatic Sea is never colder than 10° C. In winter, Split averages 11° C. During the summer the water temperature along the entire coast is nearly uniform.

The average depth of the Adriatic Sea along the Dalmatian coast is almost 130 m. The mean salinity of the sea is 3.58%; it decreases near the river mouths and is lowest in May and December, when their discharge is maximal. Conversely the sea water is saltiest in February and September.

The large islands of Brač, Hvar, and Korčula, and many smaller islands, are strung along the Dalmatian coast. Pocket beaches occur locally, and in some places islands have been tied to the mainland by the formation of tombolos (Plate 59-1). In many parts of Brač (e.g., Vidova Gove Mountain), numerous pine woods, vineyards, and olive groves grow. Brač marble is quarried at Pučišca, Selca, and Sumartin.

Numerous bays and beaches may be found on Hvar, and in the Grapceva Cave, Europe's oldest preserved picture of a ship was discovered. Its name is derived from Pharos, the Greek word for lighthouse, and Hvar attracts many tourists.

The island of Korčula, situated south of Hvar,

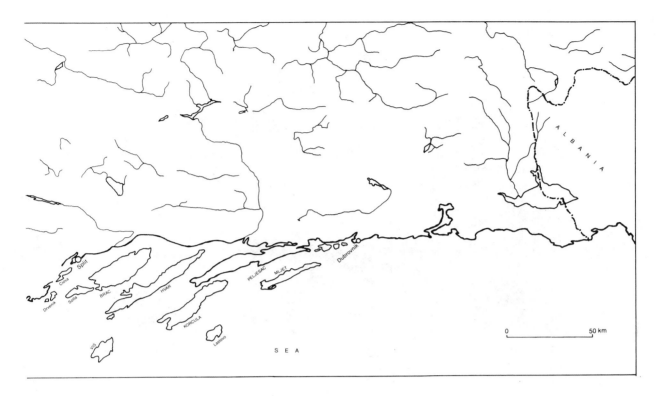

is renowned for its quarries of white marble, mild climate, and beautiful beaches. The town of Korčula, on the eastern side of the island, where Marco Polo is reputed to have been born, is one large museum. Several pebble beaches, with lush vegetation, front the town. Near the mouth of Kvarnes Bay stretch the islands of Krk, Rab, and Cres. Numerous smaller islands line the entire coast. Between Zadar (ex-Pola) and Split, the larger islands include Dugi-Otok and Pašman; among the smaller Iž, Zut, and Murter are best known.

The Dinaric Alps hug the narrow Dalmatian coastal plain. They appear white because of light-colored limestone and the absence of vegetation and soil. Their landscapes include harsh karst, gentle river valleys, and peaks like Velebit, Mosor, and Biokovo. Only a few significant passages cross the rocky heights. These peaks range from 450 m to 1900 m in height. The two main passes are the Krka River canyon and the Neretva Valley leading to the interior. The highly porous and slightly soluble limestone forms a series of parallel ranges, cutting off the coast from its hinterland. There is little surface drainage, and water flows underground to the sea. Locally the limestone has been dissolved, leaving shallow rounded or elongated depressions. The coastal uplands have a karst topography.

ROGER H. CHARLIER
JAMES W. PIETY

REFERENCES

Baulig, H., 1930, Le littoral Dalmate, *Annales Géographie* **219**:305–310.

de Martonne, E., 1948, *Traité de Géographie Physique*, Armand Colin, Paris.

Jokic, G., 1979, *Yugoslavia*, Konora Jugoslavije, Lijubliana.

Johnson, D. W., 1919, *Shore Process and Shoreline Development*, Wiley, New York.

Kotar, V., 1979, *Islands of the Adriatic*, Summerdale Press, Milan.

Shepard, F., 1973, *Submarine Geology*, Harper, New York.

von Richthofen, F., 1885, *Führer für Forschungsreisende*, Jarecke, Hanover.

Vujica, D., 1980, *Facts About Yugoslavia*, Federal Secretariat, Belgrade.

Vujica, D., 1980, *Yugoslavia, Sunny Adriatic*, National Tourist Office, Belgrade.

Plate 59-1. Tombolo on the island of Hvar (photo by Yugoslavia Council Office).

60. ALBANIA

The total length of the Adriatic Sea coastline of Albania is 385 km, from the mouth of the Buna River on the north to Cape Stylos in the Kerkira Strait on the south (Fig. 60-1). Accreting and stable coastlines predominate, their length being 225 km (58% of the total); 110 km (28%) advanced during the last 100 years, and 115 km (30%) are dynamically stable. The length of eroding coastline is 160 km (42%), 65 km (17%) of which are retreating comparatively rapidly. Recession of the remaining 95 km (25%) is relatively slow.

Many factors influence the distribution of coastal types, but it is primarily conditioned by geological composition and structural-geomorphic characteristics of the coastal territory of Albania (Leontiev and Nikiforov 1981). According to the literature (Logachev, Leontiev, and Zvezdov 1964), Albanian coastlines are divided into three geological-morphological regions: northern, central, and southern.

Extending from the mouth of the Buna River to Cape Lagy, the northern region is characterized by repeated alternations of accreting and eroding shores. Eroding sectors are associated with projecting structures composed of allochthonous Cretaceous and Neogene-Paleogene rocks. The marine margins are cut by the sea and form high capes (e.g., Shengini, Rodoni, and Paly). Accreting shores occur within the embayments between these capes, where there are river valleys and plains. Therefore, accreting coastal forms are supplied mostly by river-borne material and are composed predominantly of alluvium from the Buna, Dryn, Maty, and Erzeny rivers. The most extensive coastal features are beach-ridge plains, deltas, and barrier islands.

The central region extends from Cape Lagy to

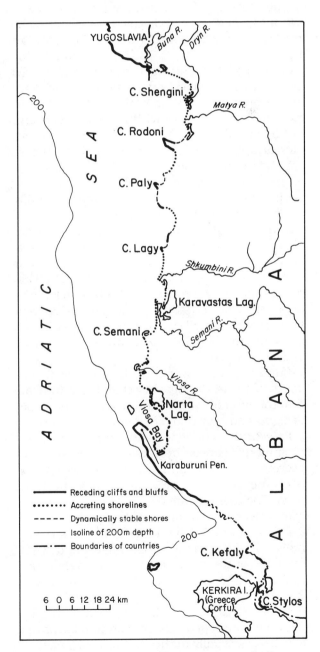

Figure 60-1. Coastal geomorphology of Albania.

443

Viosa (Vlore) Bay. There are many accretion forms composed of sandy-clay deposits along this sector, mostly deltas and spits. Between recent and older river mouth projections (Shkumbini, Semani, and Viosa), broad, arcuate, sandy beaches have formed. During the Holocene this coastline prograded, as a result a wide alluvial plain developed 10–15 m above present sea level. The surface of the plain has been affected by eolian processes, and there are now sectors of eolian sand accumulation; the barriers at Karavastas and Narta lagoons are the largest of these.

The coastline of the southern region, between Viosa Bay and Cape Stylos, is formed mainly by mega-anticlinorium structures of the Albanian Epir (Resa-Kanalit, Chika, Kolasa, and Kefaly ridges). The sea, cutting through high curved slopes, has developed an erosional coast. Erosional processes are especially well exposed on Karaburuni Peninsula, within Palermo Bay, and at Cape Kefaly. Cretaceous limestones and sandstones form vertical cliffs up to 50 m high. Where the cliffs appear to be less actively eroded by wave action, karst topography, similar to that in neighboring Yugoslavia, predominates (Nikiforov 1966).

The Albanian coast is essentially microtidal; the tidal range does not exceed 0.5 m. Tidal current velocities are 0.1–0.4 m/s. Storm waves, accompanying wind velocities over 15 m/s, occur 0.5% of the year, with 2 m wave height and 20–30 m wave length. Waves over 2 m high, with lengths of 60–80 m, occur 3% of the year. Coastal current velocities are usually 0.3–0.5 m/s, but may reach a maximum of 1.5–2.0 m/s. Calm prevails during 1–2% of the year.

Luminescent tracer experiments down to a depth of 12–14 m (Logachev et al. 1964) indicate that the effect of wave action on submarine slopes is significant down to 8 m depth.

Present-day changes in the Adriatic coast of Albania are caused by erosion of the shore or accretion of sediment. The most intense erosion is on the cliffs, which retreat at rates of 0.1–0.3 m/yr. The average rate over a 37-year period, by comparison of 1921 and 1958 maps, is 0.2 m/yr. Cliff height ranges from 15–20 m in the northern region, 10–20 m in the central region, and 20–25 m in the southern region. Calculations show that the actively eroding cliffs in Albania provide 286,000 m^3 of sediment to the coastal system each year (0.2 m/yr $\times$ 22 m $\times$ 65,000 m). This material is supplied to large accretion forms and beaches, especially in the southern region.

In the northern and central regions the coastal accretion features are supplied mainly by river sediment. For example: the sediment yield of the Dryn River is 17×10^6 tons/yr; the Shkumbini River, 3×10^6 tons/yr; the Semani River, 30×10^6 tons/yr; the Voisa River, about 28×10^6 tons/yr. The combined yield of the Albanian rivers is approximately 90×10^6 tons/yr, or 52.9×10^6 m^3/yr. About 25% (13.2×10^6 m^3/yr) of this sediment is bed-load (>0.1 mm), while the remaining 75% (39.7×10^6 m^3/yr) is suspended load. The fine material in suspension very rarely ends up on beaches, since most of it is transported to the open sea.

Assuming that 13.2×10^6 m^3 of sand, and larger fractions, are evenly distributed along the accreting shores of Albania, it may be concluded that 58.8 m^3/yr of sediment is deposited on each linear meter of shore. Map comparisons have shown that 120 m^3/m/yr is being deposited on actively advancing shores. Because of this heavy accumulation of sediment, many parts of the Albanian coast have advanced during the past hundred years.

In the first century A.D. the town of Lesha was situated at the coast, but today it is 8 km inland from the shore near Dryn Bay. Consequently, during the past 2000 years the coastal plain has advanced seaward at an average rate of 4 m/yr. In the central region, the ancient town of Apollonia was founded 2500 years ago, 5 km from the sea. Now it is located 8 km from the shore. During this period therefore, the shore advanced 3 km, or at an average rate of 1.2 m/yr. Many of the lagoonal barrier beaches (Narta, Karavastas, Dukaty, and Patka) were formed during the last 200–400 years.

YURII D. SHUISKY

REFERENCES

Leontiev, O. K., and L. G. Nikiforov, 1981, Geomorphology of the coast and bottom of the Adriatic Sea, *Herald of Moscow University, Geography* **5**:12–18.

Logachev, L. A., O. K. Leontiev, and V. M. Zvezdov, 1964, Main characteristics of morphology and hydrology of the coast and dynamics of the shorelines in Albania, *Sojuzmornii Project Proc.* **4**:70–82.

Nikiforov, L. G., 1966, Morphological distinctions of marine shores in Yugoslavia, *Herald of Moscow University, Geography* **4**:40–48.

61. GREECE

Greece has an extremely long coastline (Fig. 61-1) in comparison with its area (131,944 km²). The entire country has been, and still is, strongly affected by tectonic and volcanic activity. The major Greek peninsula is a part of the Alpine orogeny. It was originally part of the Tethys Sea, but with the beginning of the Alpine orogeny a series of northwest-southeast-trending fault trends of the Hellenides (Kronberg and Günther 1978) led to an extremely rugged topography reflected along the entire coastline. A large number of horsts and grabens extend in a northwest-southeast direction. In addition, major upwarping of the Greek peninsula has led to high spine-like mountain ranges such as the Pindos Mountains in the central north and the Taygetos in the south-central Peloponnese. Further, the Aegean Sea is the locus of the collision of several of the world's continental plates, and is thus a very complex tectonic setting. A large number of islands composed of limestone, metamorphic rocks, and volcanics add to the extremely lengthy coastline of Greece. In addition, a secondary tectonic element is superimposed. East-west faulting has occurred, leading to horsts and grabens oriented in an east-west direction—for example, the gulf of Malia on the east coast of Greece and the Gulf of Corinth, which separates the Peloponnese from the mainland. This east-west trend is also present on the western end of the Anatolian massif in Turkey; however, no one has successfully demonstrated that there is a direct tectonic correlation.

Thus the majority of the coasts of Greece are high and cliff-like. Where the cliffs are of hard limestones or metamorphic rocks, erosion proceeds very slowly. On the other hand, where the cliffs are of soft Neogene sands, silts, and marls,

erosion can be extremely rapid. Tides are not a major factor, the maximum being less than 1 m. Throughout the year the predominant waves that affect the coasts of Greece are produced by north-northeasterly (Meltemia) winds, and storm-generated waves also move north from the Mediterranean Sea. The greater portion of the country is undergoing intensive erosion. Probably the effects of human activity have greatly accelerated this erosion during the Holocene epoch, and in particular the past 5000 years.

A large portion of the coastline is composed of sedimentary embayments with prograding deltas (Fig. 61-1). Sediments tend to flow into the grabens and fill the landward ends of these major tectonic features. Total relief between the horsts and grabens can be up to 2 km vertically. Thus the sediments tend not to fill the grabens completely, as massive hinterland erosion and fluvial delivery of sediment have occurred only in the past 9000 years.

It is, of course, extremely difficult to give a complete short description of the coasts of Greece. We have therefore selected specific areas for discussion and illustration. The coastlines of the Saronic Gulf and Attica are perhaps the most affected by human activity (Fig. 61-2). Marathon Bay to the east is an enigma. Here, a very strong littoral drift has developed a beach accretion plain that forms a barrier between the Aegean Sea and the swamps or marshes of the plain at Marathon, famous as the trap into which the Persian army was maneuvered and defeated in 490 B.C. Although the coastal processes at Marathon are extremely active, the entire plain and shoreline appear as they were described 2500 years ago (Kraft 1972). The shores of the Saronic Gulf are

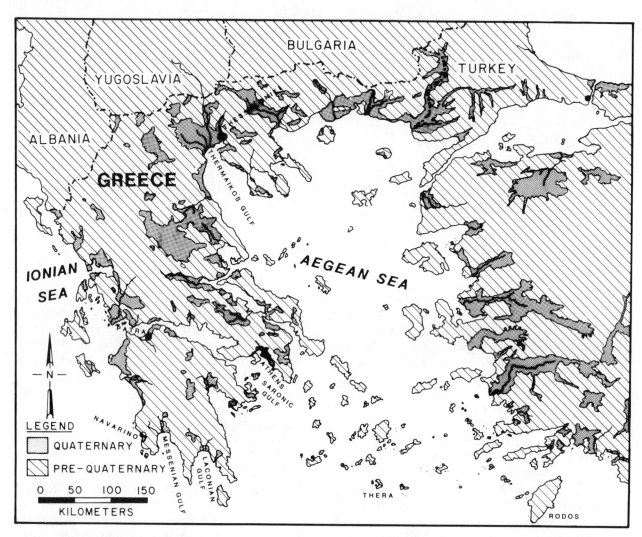

Figure 61-1. The peninsula of Greece and its islands in the Aegean Sea. Shaded areas are areas of Quaternary deposition and active areas of Holocene delta progradation and aggradation.

characterized by a complex of small pocket beaches interrupted by rocky promontories of Mesozoic shales, marbles, and Neogene sediment (Plate 61-1*B*). There is little sand in the coastal littoral transport system along the east coast of the Saronic Gulf; as this is a major resort area, artificial beach nourishment has become necessary. The shoreline east of Athens is one with major formations of beachrock. From Paleo-Phaleron (southeast Athens) west to Megara lies the most heavily industralized and urbanized shoreline of Greece (Plate 61-1*A*). The works of man have almost completely altered the shoreline of this region. West of Megara lie very steep cliffs of Cretaceous and Triassic limestones. Still farther west the landscape becomes more low-lying, and small beaches occur along low cliffs of Pliocene and

Quaternary age. South of the Corinthian Canal the coast again becomes steep, composed of Mesozoic limestones, with very small pocket beaches of sand. There are no major rivers in this area of Greece. The largest rivers are the Kiphisos and the Ilissos, which have formed major alluviation of the plain now completely covered by the city of Athens. Attica is typical of the many types of coasts of Greece. It lies in a semiarid zone but with sufficient rainfall to support a vegetative cover. Unfortunately, human activity has destroyed much of this cover, and massive erosion has occurred over the past 5000 years, as evidenced in Figure 61-1.

A very different situation exists in the plain of Elis in the northwest Peloponnese (Fig. 61-3). The coast is open to wave action from the Ionian

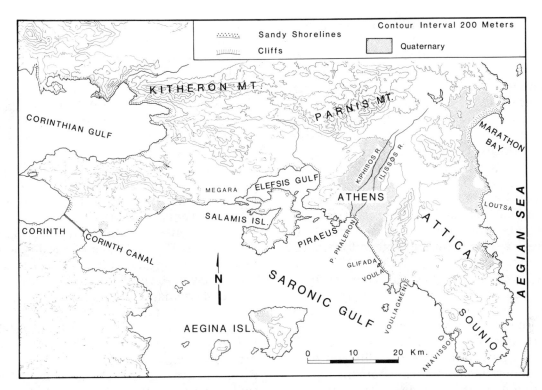

Figure 61-2. The Saronic Gulf and Attica.

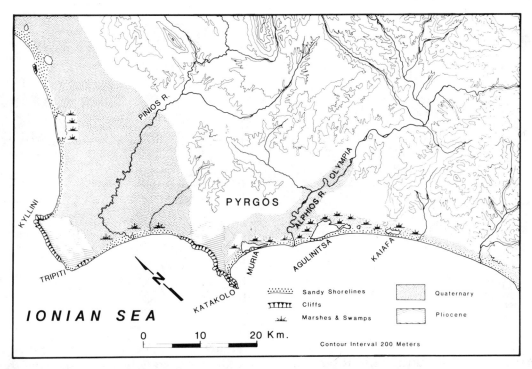

Figure 61-3. The delta-beach accretion plain of Elis and delta lagoon-barrier shoreline of the Alphios River.

Sea. The high lands of Kyllini-Tripiti and Katakolo, composed of Pliocene deposits, are subject to erosion. The very long and steep sandy beaches southeast of Katakolo, with the cuspate delta of the Alphios River and the extensive lagoonal system, are unique on the Greek coasts. Raphael (1969), who presented a detailed map of the coastal area of Elis, showed that most of the accretion ridges indicate a low-lying regressive (prograding) coastal plain.

A different type of coast is that of the Thermaic Gulf, which lies to the north between Thrace and the mainland peninsula of Greece at the important port of Thessaloniki (Figs. 61-1 and 61-4). Here again a deep horst and graben feature occurs. Several large rivers, including the major Axios River, enter the embayment from the north. The large load of sediment carried by these rivers has tended to fill hundreds of square kilometers of the former head of the Thermiac Gulf. For instance, the ancient capital of Macedonian Greece, Pella, was a port in the time of Philip and Alexander, but now lies about 40 km from the rapidly prograding Axios delta. In view of the very large amount of sediment flowing into the Thermaic Gulf, the present head of the gulf is very shallow, approximately 36 m deep in the center with the inner gulf having typical depths of up to 20 m. The rates of sedimentary infilling of the form-er head of the Thermaic Gulf clearly indicate that a great mass of sediment is moving from three major rivers and some minor rivers. Thus it is predicted that the Thermaic Gulf in the vicinity of Thessaloniki will be cut off as a lagoon, and will eventually evolve to a marsh and flood plain. The only question is how long it will take—perhaps 50–200 years, depending on human efforts to prevent it. The east and west coasts of the Thermaic Gulf are formed of low cliffs of Pliocene rocks with small sandy beaches. Fed by littoral transport, extensive sandy beaches lie in the area of Aghia Trias and Peraia (Fig. 61-4).

The Messenian Gulf in southwest Peloponnese presents another example of the filling of the head of a major graben (Fig. 61-5). There is exceptionally high relief between the deep graben of the Messenian Gulf and the high mountain range, the Taygetos, to the east. The shore at the head of the Gulf of Messenia, from Petalidi to Kalamata in the east, is a sand, gravel, and cobble beach receiving sediment from the major Pamisos River and five minor rivers incised into Neogene sediments on the western side at the head of the Gulf. The eastern coast of the Messenian Gulf consists of high cliffs, mainly of hard Cretaceous

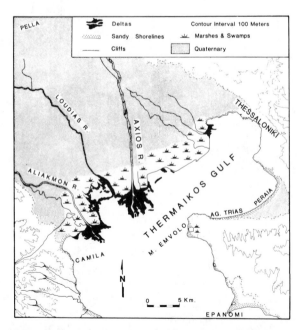

Figure 61-4. The delta of the Axios River and other rivers that are presently filling in the head of the Thermaic Gulf (a graben).

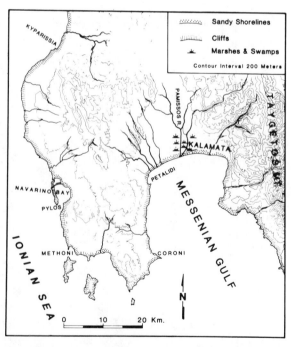

Figure 61-5. The Messenian peninsula and Gulf of Messenia (graben), showing the flood plain–delta of the Pamisos River and the embayment at Navarino.

limestone, with some very small beaches, mostly inaccessible. A similar situation occurs on the western side of the Gulf of Messenia from Petalidi to Coroni to the south. The southern end of the Messenian peninsula, between the Gulf of Messenia and the Ionian Sea, includes a coast consisting of Triassic siliceous shales and Eocene to Miocene shales and conglomerates extending westward to the embayment at Methoni. Northward, from Methoni to the embayment at Navarino and onward to Kyparissia, the coast is formed of hard Eocene limestones. The beaches are narrow, and the deep waters of the Ionian Sea lie close to the shore. Parts of the coastline include Pliocene deposits, particularly north of Navarino Bay, and soft Pliocene sands and silts on the eastern side of the embayment of Navarino, which is probably a small graben. The relationship between low-lying coastal accretion plains and the high Taygetos Mountains is well shown in Plate 61-1*C*. Similarly, in Plate 61-1*D* lower-lying cliffs of soft Neogene sediments are undergoing rapid erosion, with a cobble beach of fragments from hard sandstone layers in the Neogene sands and silts. Softer sediment is winnowed out into the embayment of Methoni and the Mediterranean Sea.

Navarino Bay is of particular interest because of the many types of coast in a small area, and incidentally because of the many historic events that have occurred in this area (Fig. 61-6). Human beings have been active in Navarino Bay for the past 5000 years. The Island of Sphakteria is a high, linear Eocene limestone ridge undergoing extremely slow erosion, with almost no beaches. Navarino Bay itself is deep (about 60 m) and was the site of a major military action between Turks and Egyptians against the combined fleet of the English, French, and Russians during the Greek revolution of the past century.

A number of rivers flow into the embayment at Navarino, providing sediment that is transported by littoral drift set up by waves within the enclosed embayment. A broad sandy spit cuts across the center of the embayment; archaeological sites suggest it existed 2000 years ago. To the north lies a small lagoon, Osmanaga, surrounded by a low-lying swamp. Osmanaga Lagoon is subject to extremes of evaporation, and the muddy sediments are at least 50% calcium carbonates. Still farther to the north, at the head of the embayment that existed 5000–10,000 years ago, lies a flat alluvial plain. Detailed studies in this area (Kraft et al. 1980) show that 8000–9000 years ago the

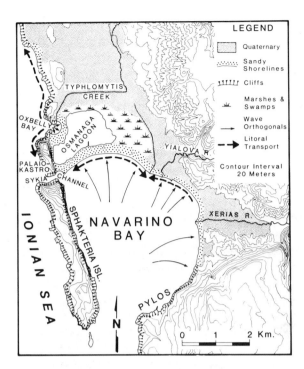

Figure 61-6. Navarino Bay and its environs, showing wave orthogonals, littoral transport, and Holocene sedimentary environments.

Navarino embayment extended at least 4 km farther north than at present. To the northwest of Navarino Bay lies a long curving sandy strandline including large amounts of beachrock and older Quaternary sands of similar derivation, but now tectonically upwarped. A large amount of sand moves inland in the form of coastal dunes.

Although there is almost no sandy strandline along Sphakteria and Paleokastro (probably because of the narrow shelf), a large amount of sand is in transport in the Ionian Sea along this western coast of Greece. For instance, a formerly open channel in the Ionian Sea led into the present Osmanaga Lagoon. It is now sealed off by an arcuate sandy dune from Oxbelly Bay. Similarly, the Sikia channel between two of the large Eocene limestone ridges along the Ionian coast is now very shallow. However, we know it was deep at the time of the Battle of Lepanto, between the Turks and the Venetians. A line of ships was sunk in the channel to stop access into the Bay of Navarino shortly after this battle. This formed a baffle that caused sand to collect and reduced the channel to a shallow depth. The southern entrance to the Navarino Bay is extremely deep and remains so, but waves within Navarino Bay are generated by local winds as there is no large entrance into the embayment. Thus we have a complex situation of local transport and depositional processes and a more regional littoral transport of sand along the Ionian Sea.

Typical photographs of this area are Plate 61-2*A*, showing a series of beach rock in a small embayment; Plate 61-2*B*, an indentation into the high Eocene ridge along the Ionian Sea with a narrow sandy pocket beach; and Plates 61-3*A* and 61-3*B*, which show panoramas of the Eocene limestone ridges known as Coryphasion or Palaeokastro and Sphackteria, which lie between the Ionian Sea to the west and the embayment at Osmanaga and Navarino to the east. In the distant center of Plate 61-3*B* lies the fluvial plain composed mainly of flood-plain silts with narrow stream channels of sands and gravels that have filled the embayment over the past 8000–9000 years.

The Greek islands of the Aegean Sea are highly varied in their geology, their coasts being mainly rocky cliffs with small sandy beaches. The southernmost island of Greece, Crete, lies along the edge of a plate of the earth's crust. It is extremely active tectonically; ancient harbors on the west side of Crete have emerged above sea level while ancient harbors and towns on the east side have been submerged by the sea.

To the north lies the famed Island of Thera (Santorini), considered by many to be ancient Atlantis (Fig. 61-7). This is a volcanic island formed of a composite cone that "blew out" approximately 3200 years ago with a force estimated to have been tens of times as great as that of Krakatoa in Indonesia. Some historians and archaeologists claim that the resultant tsunamis wiped out the Minoan civilization on Crete. In any case, the very heavy fall of pumice and tephra deeply covered the landscape of the island and buried an important city on the southeast of the island. Today, Thera comprises only a portion of the larger, former volcanic cone, but submarine contours show the shape of the cone and the very deep caldera in the center. Other small islands form remnants of the outer edge of the volcanic cone. In the center lies Nea Kamini, a new volcanic cone that has been active within the past 300 years. No one knows whether ancient Thera was Atlantis; however some of the earliest writings of the Greeks suggest that the "Pillars of Hercules" were not at the Straits of Gibraltar, but rather the cape at Sunion to the east of Athens and the high cliffs near Epidarus to the southwest. Thus, from the Athenian point of view, to look "beyond the

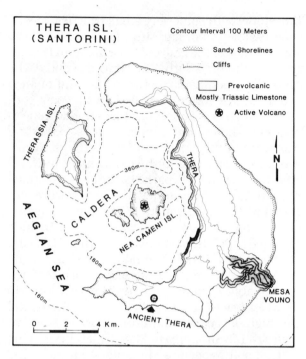

Figure 61-7. The Island of Thera, showing submarine contours that remained after the massive blow-out of the caldera about 3000 years ago and the new volcanic cone developing in the center.

Pillars of Hercules" would have meant facing southeast toward the island of Thera. It is an interesting speculation. As tradition or myth goes, the Athenians were at war with the Atlantians, and as it is unlikely that the pre-Classical Athenians were at war with a nation in the Atlantic Ocean, the hypothesis herein presented is at least within the realm of possibility.

In summary, the coastlines of Greece are almost totally dominated by the tectonism of the Hellenides. The second most important feature of the Greek coasts is that of erosion of soft Neogene rocks and the formation of narrow beaches at the base of the cliffs; in some cases littoral transport of sand has formed significant beaches, as along the west Peloponnese and Ionian coast. Further, the rivers have played a large role in carrying sediment from the eroded highlands into the heads of the graben embayments to form large coastal plains with shores varying from cobble-boulder beaches (Gulf of Messenia) to muddy-marshy shorelines (Thermaic Gulf).

CHRISTOS TZIAVOS
JOHN C. KRAFT

REFERENCES

Kraft, J. C., 1972, *A Reconnaissance of the Geology of the Sandy Coastal Areas of Eastern Greece and the Peloponnese*, Tech. Report No. 9, College of Marine Studies, University of Delaware.

Kraft, J. C., G. R. Rapp, and S. E. Aschenbrenner, 1980, Late Holocene paleogeomorphic reconstructions in the area of the Bay of Navarino: Sandy Pylos, *Jour. Archaeol. Sci.* **7:**187-210.

Kronberg, P., and R. Günther, 1978, Crustal fracture pattern of the Aegean region, in *Alps Apennines Hellenides, Inter-Union Commission on Geodynamics Scientific Report No. 38*, H. Closs, D. Roeder, and K. Schmidt, eds., E. Schweizerbart'sche Verlagsbuchhandlung, Stuttgart, pp. 522-526.

Raphael, C. N., 1969, The Plain of Elis, Greece—An Archaeological Approach, *Michigan Academy of Science* **1**(1-2):73-74.

A

B

C

D

Plate 61-1 A. Athens: the hill of Munychia in the left center, the harbor of Pireaus in the center, with the major portion of the city in the background and to the right along the Phaleron strand (photo by J. C. Kraft). **B.** Typical coastal scenery in the Saronic Gulf, Attica (photo by J. C. Kraft). **C.** The sand and pebble strandline at the head of the Gulf of Messenia (a graben) with the high Taygetos Mountains (a horst) in the background (photo by J. C. Kraft). **D.** The East Coast of the embayment at Methoni in southwest Peloponnese. Soft Neogene silts with a few layers of lithified sandstone are undergoing rapid erosion. The lithified sandstone remains behind on the beach as a cobble or shingle beach. Over the past 3000 years many archaeological sites have disappeared into the sea along this coastline (photo by J. C. Kraft).

A

B

C

D

Plate 61-2 A. A small embayment of the Ionian Sea shoreline near Navarino showing extensive modern beachrock (Roman shards enclosed) surrounded by Quaternary shoreline sands and a modern sand dune in the far distance (photo by J. C. Kraft). **B.** A fracture in the Eocene limestone hills opposite the Bay of Navarino facing the Ionian Sea with a small pocket sandy beach (photo by J. C. Kraft). **C.** The northwestern shoreline of the Gulf of Messenia undergoing present-day erosion by wave attack and relative sea level rise. The tree in the foreground and the building in the background are evidence of continuing erosion (photo by J. C. Kraft). **D.** The southern shoreline of the Gulf of Corinth (a graben) with the hills and alluvial fans to the right, part of a horst or uplifted part of the northern part of Peloponnese (photo by J. C. Kraft).

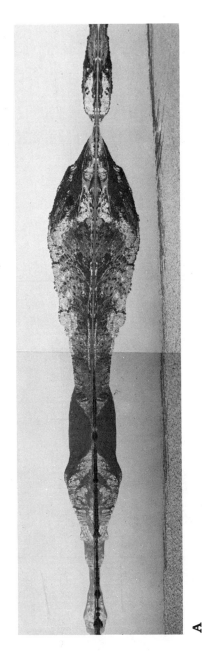

A

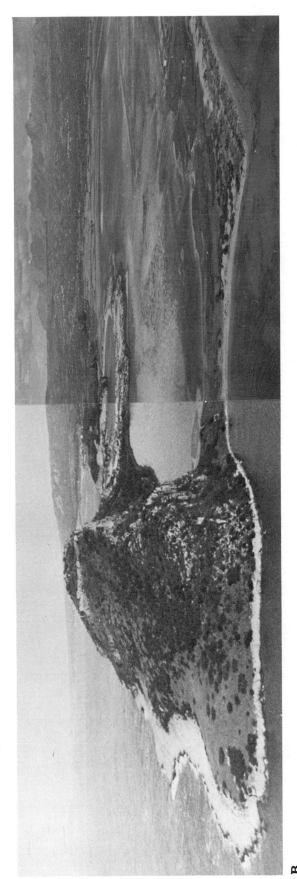

B

Plate 61-3 A. The lagoon at Osmanaga north of the deep water embayment of Navarino facing Eocene limestone ridge Coryphasion (Paleokastro) in the center and the Island of Sphackteria to the left. The lagoon is highly evaporative, with approximately 50% carbonate mud and 50% terrigenous clastic muds (photo by J. C. Kraft). **B.** A panorama taken from the top of Sphackteria, looking north toward the hill Coryphasion and the Venetian-Turkish fortification and its crest, with Oxbelly Bay, a sealed-off former entrance into the ancient embayment of Navarino rimmed by sand dunes, in the center and the shallow Osmanaga lagoon and sandy barrier to the right. The embayment of Navarino drops off sharply to the right and south of the picture to 60 m depth. To the north, or top of the right, lies the Kampos surface upon which was located a major archaeological site, Epano Englianos, the palace of King Nestor of the Iliad (photo by W. K. Pritchett and R. Boslaugh).

453

62. BULGARIA

The Bulgarian sector of the Black Sea coast is 378 km long. It has a complex geological structure, truncating the Balkan mountain ranges (Fig. 62-1). In the north are almost horizontal Miocene and Quaternary strata, including marls, sandstones, clays, limestones, and a loess capping; in the central part highly folded flysch rocks of Upper Cretaceous to early Tertiary age, and to the south igneous formations.

Quaternary marine terraces occur 90–100 m, 55–60 m, 35–40 m, 20–25 m, 12–14 m, 4–5 m, and 1.5–2 m above present sea level, the last two being of Holocene age, the higher ones Pleistocene. There are also submerged Pleistocene marine terraces offshore.

Much of the coastline consists of eroding cliffs, and landslides are extensive. The impact of human activities is evident in port and resort construction, coastal and undersea quarries, and shore protection works (Kamenov et al. 1973; Popov and Mishev 1974; Valkanov and Marinov 1978). Sectors of deposition include deltas, beach ridges, and lagoons. In the south, abrasive-Strandža type coast is to be found (Plate 62-1).

Concave bays are occupied by beaches backed by dunes, especially north from Varna and south of Burgas, the intervening steep coast having only pocket beaches. The dunes are extensive in the north, where they are up to 18.6 m high, the Kamčia-Škorpilov sector being the longest, 11.2 km. At Nessebar engineering works have modified the beach-dune system. South of Burgas sand from the rivers nourishes beach and dune systems behind indented bays.

Sedimentological analyses have shown that beach and dune sands have come mainly from rivers, notably the Batova, Provadiiska, Kamčia,

Dvoiniza, Hadžiiska, Rusokastro, Ropotamo, Djavolska, Karaagač, Oreška, and Veleka (Rojdestvensky 1966). Grain size diminishes offshore, and landslides have acted as breakwaters separating beaches of varying coarseness (Zvetkova and Simeonova 1980, 1984). There has been northward drifting of the Kamčia-Škorpilov beach system (Dačev and Nikolov 1977), but the curving beaches alongside the "tombolo" at Pomorie are rapidly eroding. In general, beach drifting is southward (Malovitsky and Ivanov 1979).

Wind regimes on the Bulgarian coast give a predominance of northeasterly wave action, stronger in the winter months. Severe storms occur from time to time, the period September 1976 to April 1977 having been unusually stormy. Vasilev (1978) has recorded the consequence of these storms in terms of rapid coastline changes: beaches were eroded and landslide lobes cut back as clifflets.

The stability of coastal slopes varies with geology. Near Cape Sabla there are rockfalls on limestone cliffs, which retreat at an average of 0.01 m/yr. North of this cape, erosion is more rapid where underlying clays are exposed, and reaches rates of 8 m/yr locally. The large Tauk-Liman landslide is of block slide type, and shows seasonal variations in mobility, (Koštjak and Avramova 1977) but average cliff retreat is only 0.01 m/yr. The stratified cliffs between Balčik and Varna show the effects of weathering and undercutting, leading to recurrent sliding at rates of up to 1 m/yr (Milev and Cencov 1977). On the more complicated Balkan structures to the south, cliff retreat can be as rapid as 15 m/yr, but the more stable cliffs at Cape Emine are cut back at only a few centimeters a year (Simeonova 1976). It is north of Burgas that the most unstable coastal

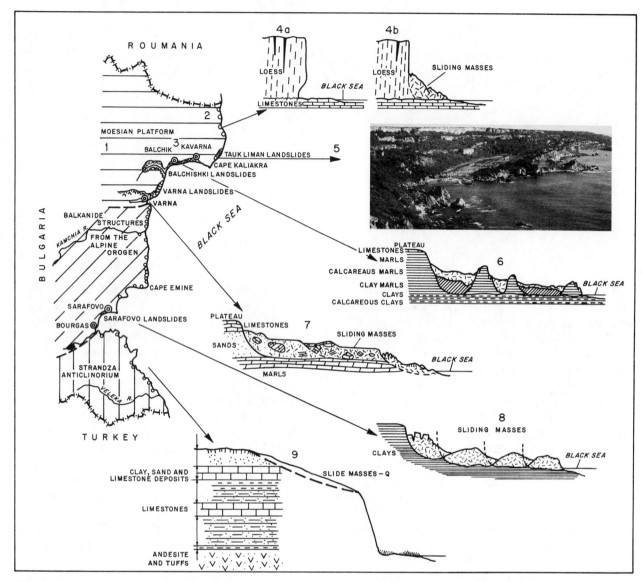

Figure 62-1. Geostructural background for the coastline of Bulgaria. 1. morphotectonic structure; 2. single landslide; 3. complex landslide; 4a. erosion of coast formed in a two-layered structure; 4b. formation of landslides in a coastal slope built of loess; 5. panorama of the block type landslide in the region of Tauk Liman (photo by B. Kamenov); 6. schematic section through the landslide at Balčik; 7. schematic section through a cirque type landslide north of Varna; 8. schematic section through the landslide near Sarafovo-village, formed in a stratified and unstable formation; 9. schematic section through the landslide north of Micurin: a. slide masses—Q; b. limestones—N_1; c. clay, sand, and limestone deposits—N_1; d. andesite and tuffs—8Pg.

Note: Figure 62-1, 1, 4, 6, 7, and 8 from B. Kamenov et al (1973).

slopes are found. Here Mio-Pliocene and Quaternary clays show extensive and rapid slumping. The Sarafovo landslide forms a lobe that is cut back more than 20 m^3/m/yr by marine erosion. An understanding of the hydrogeology, and especially the pattern and critical changes in the level of the underground water, is essential for the application of successful engineering works along this slumping coastline (Stanev and Simeonova 1979). The total volume of material lost by erosion along this coastline is some 1,344,000 m^3 annually (Shuisky and Simeonova 1976, 1982).

The 1976 storms damaged human structures at Balčik, Varna, Nessebar, and Pomorie, and it seems that human interference made the erosion more severe than it would naturally have been. It is hoped that future engineering works needed to protect seaside resorts on this part of the Black Sea coast will be based on a better understanding of coastal processes.

GINKA SIMEONOVA

REFERENCES

Dačev, V., and H. Nikolov, 1977, Modifications intégrales de la ligne côtière près des terrains d'accumulation entre Tcheni Noss et le complexe de villagiature Albena, *Okeanologiya* **2:**57–64.

Kamenov, B., I. Iliev, S. Zvetkov, E. Avramova, and G. Simeonova, 1973, Influence of geological structure on the occurrence of different types of landslides along the Bulgarian coast, *Geol. Applicata e Idrogeologia Estratto* **8**(1):209–220.

Koštjak, B., and E. Avramova, 1977, Present dynamics of block slides, *Čas. Mineralogii a Geologii* **22:** 139–149.

Malovitsky, V., and K. Ivanov, eds., 1979, *Geology and Hydrology of the Western Section of the Black Sea,* Bulgarian Academy of Sciences, Sofia.

Milev, G., and C. Cenkov, 1977, Landslide phenomena investigation in the region of Balčik, *Cartographia Zemeustroistvo* **2:**11–15.

Popov, Vl., and K. Mishev, 1974, *Geomorphology of Bulgarian Black Sea Coast and Shelf,* BAC, Sofia.

Rojdestvensky, A., 1966, Chemischer und Schwedstoffabfluss der Donau im Schwarzen Meer, *Limnolog. Berichte der Donau Forschung* **29:**93–102.

Shuisky, Yu. D., and G. Simeonova, 1976, Effects of geological structure of sea shores on abrasion processes, *Acad. Bulgare Sci. Comptes Rendus* **29:**241–243.

Shuisky, Yu. D., and G. Simeonova, 1982, On the types of abrasion cliffs along the Bulgarian Black Sea coast, *Engineering Geology and Hydrogeology,* **12:**11–21.

Simeonova, G., 1976, Coastal processes along the Bulgarian coast, *Proc. Symp. Dynamics of Shoreline Erosion, Meziereba, Tbilisi,* pp. 235–238.

Stanev, I., and G. Simeonova, 1979, Determination of hydrogeological parameters of the Sarafovo landslide complex, *Eng. Geology and Hydrology* 8–9: 91–106.

Valkanov, G., and A. Marinov, eds., 1978, *The Black Sea,* Bakalov, Varna.

Vasilev, T., 1978, Morphodynamics of the Bulgarian coast in stormy waters, *Problems of Geography* **2:** 51–55.

Zvetkova, V., and G. Simeonova, 1980, Change in the conditions of formation of sediment in the Burgas coastal zone of the Black Sea shelf, *Okeanologiya* **6:**57–68.

Zvetkova, V., and G. Simeonova, 1984, Accumulation of heavy minerals in landslides in the Burgas area of the Black Sea coast, *Marine Geology* **54:**309–318.

Plate 62-1. Strandža tectonic type shore (photo by G. Simeonova).

63. RUMANIA

The Rumanian shore of the Black Sea coast stretches over 245 km. The northernmost point begins at the Chilia arm of the Danube River, which enters the Black Sea at the border of the Soviet Union and extends southward to the city of Vama Veche (which means the old customs point). Slightly inland the Dobrogea plateau provides a modest terrain elevation.

The greatest influence on the character of the Rumanian coast is the Danube River. Together with such altering factors as the wind and waves, the circulation of water, and the geological structure of the Black Sea basin, the Danube discharge creates a varied coast in a relatively short length (Fig. 63-1).

THE RUMANIAN COASTLINE

Two main characteristics strike the observer of the Rumanian coast: the numerous littoral lakes, often hypersaline, and the remarkable separation of the shore into two very different sectors. While the northern areas of the Bulgarian coast are subject to major landslides, the Rumanian littoral is somewhat more stable.

The sea floor adjacent to the Rumanian coast is characterized by a broad continental shelf with a uniform slope of 7–12° to a depth of 200 m. The sediments of the Rumanian littoral are composed of deposits of sand, fluvial mud from the Danube, and deep sedimentary mud well mixed with shells. A sandy bottom extends all along the coast in a relatively narrow band that stays the same from the edge of the shore to a depth of 15–25 m. At the mouth of the St. Gheorghe branch of the Danube, this band of sand extends to the 40 m isobath (Ross 1971; Zenkovitch 1966).

THE NORTHERN SECTOR

The northern sector of the Rumanian coast is usually considered as extending from the Chilia arm of the Danube River at the U.S.S.R. border to Cape Midia south of Gargalic (Fig. 63-1 and 63-2). It represents approximately 63% of the total shoreline. This part of the coast is less stable than that of the southern sector, with sand bars and spits frequently shifting. One such bar has built up to the point of nearly closing the southern arm of the Danube at St. Gheorghe, leaving a depth of only 1.5 m (Ross et al. 1970).

The northern sector can be further subdivided into two parts. The first, from Chilia to another arm of the Danube, St. Gheorghe, constitutes the major contact of the Danube delta with the Black Sea and includes 40 km of maritime shore of the Danube.

At the mouth of the Danube the dynamics of the littoral are characteristic of other seas with weak tides, particularly in the existence of bars that envelop the openings with alluvial deposits. Each deltaic mouth has a regime of waves and currents creating conditions for the formation of bars. The waves contribute greatly to the building of bars, while the currents disperse the deposits of fine sediments.

Of the Danube outlets, only the Chilia arm offers the conditions for the formation of a secondary delta. The branch at Sulina does not have a delta at its mouth because of the permanent dikes built to maintain a channel for navigation. At the St. Gheorghe branch the force of the currents and waves restricts the formation of a delta.

The second subdivision of the northern sector, from St. Gheorghe to Cape Midia, is characterized

459

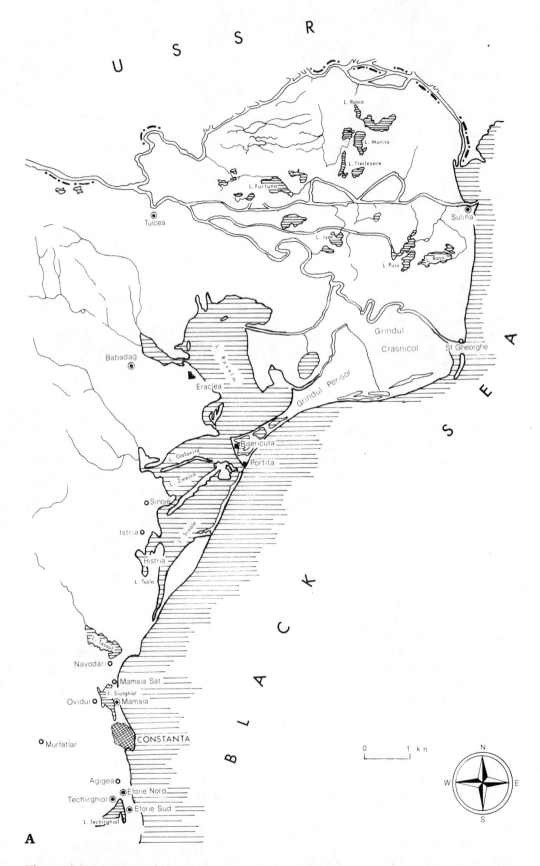

Figure 63-1A. Map of the Rumanian coast; B. Southern portion of the Rumanian coast.

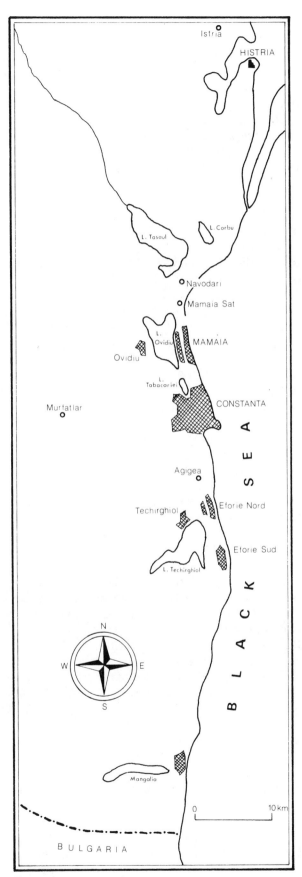

B

by a low sandy zone 1–3 m below sea level. A large complex of lakes is separated from the sea by a coastal cordon approximately 60 km long. In the fifth century B.C. the city of Histria was a coastal settlement situated at the south end of a large gulf, Halmyris, which over the centuries has been cut off from the sea by significant sediment deposition. At present this former port city is approximately 8 km from the sea.

Because of the circulation pattern of Black Sea water, the Rumanian shore is significantly influenced by the Danube discharge. Under the action of oblique waves and currents, the Danube sediments are transported southward to just north of Constanta, where the coastal processes are predominantly depositional (Novitskiy 1964).

THE SOUTHERN SECTOR

The southern sector has far narrower beaches and cliffs that reach the water's edge in several locations (e.g., Eforie) and at some points dominate the beach with 60 m heights. The cliffs are composed of Sarmatic limestones and sandstones commonly underlying a thick cover of loess material. The limestones are frequently rich in fossils (Plate 63-1).

Separated from the sea by a band of lower bluffs and sandy hills, often as high as 35 m, are a number of lakes of ancient origin. Once part of the sea, now severed from it by fluviomarine sedimentation, are lakes or *ghiols*, which include Tasaul, Siut-Ghiol, Tabacarie, Agigea, Tatlageac, Gargalic, Terchirghiol, and Mangalia. Several of these are fresh-water lakes fed by springs and small streams (Chiriac 1966; Dunăreanu 1967).

Situated north of the city of Constanta are three of the larger lakes, Tasaul, Gargalic, and Siut-Ghiol. These lakes are connected by canals and streams, and narrow outlets link them with the sea. Generally shallow, they have a depth of 2–3 m, except Lake Siut-Ghiol, where 4–6 m is average, with trenches reaching a depth of 22 m. Small seasonal variations occur, with the lowest lake level attained in summer.

The salinity of each lake varies, the lowest concentration being found in Siut-Ghiol (0.3‰) and the highest (1–1.5‰) in Tasaul and Gargalic. The chemical balance and oxygen content in each lake are favorable for the development of aquatic life, and each has its own characteristic population providing an important contribution to the area's economy.

Among the littoral lakes of the Rumanian coast

two are completely isolated from the sea and have a limited source of fresh water. Lake Mangalia, near the Bulgarian border, is surrounded by steep banks reaching 20 m in height. Thermal mineral water flows from the banks at some points, and is sought for medicinal purposes.

Lake Techirghiol, the larger of the two, lies in a depression 1.5 m below the Black Sea level. The outlet to the sea for this ancient gulf has been closed by sand deposits, which now form the beach of North Eforie. Sheltered from north winds by the surrounding hills, the surface water temperature ranges from 22–26°C in summer. The salinity of Lake Techirghiol is extremely high (95.5‰), as is the mineral content. Because of the high concentration of minerals and organic material, the black mud from this lake is considered therapeutic for numerous ailments.

WATER ALONG THE RUMANIAN COAST

The Danube has a major effect on the water along the coast; other factors, however, contribute to the varying water levels (Charlier 1971, 1973). Water exchange through the Bosporus, precipitation, evaporation, barometric pressure, and wind, change the sea level. The most significant factor affecting the hydrologic balance is the seasonal variation of river discharge. The lowest runoff is in winter, increasing in spring to a maximum in May, diminishing through autumn, when there is an increase again due to the rainy season, until freezing in winter. Again, the Danube plays a major role, with 38% of the river water entering the Black Sea (Glaskov 1970).

Considering the relatively shallow depth, averaging 30 m, along the broad shelf adjacent to the Rumanian coast, the waves are neither high nor long. Winds come predominantly from the northeast and therefore so do the waves.

The tide of the Black Sea along the Rumanian coast is a semidiurnal type with a period of 12 hours, 25 minutes and a maximum amplitude of 12 cm. Generally, tidal oscillations are in the range of 8–9 cm and are quite unnoticeable when compared with the wind effect of waves, which may reach a height of 3.5 m.

The river currents entering the sea are somewhat weak and thus strongly influenced by the coastal sea currents. As is typical of a large river's contact with the sea, the Danube water forms a large mass of surface water fanning out over the sea with a southward deflection. The mass of river water quickly loses its speed and depth as it moves seaward. At the principal arms of the Danube, the river currents can be detected 1.5–3 km from shore. During times of greatest discharge, the freshwater mass can attain a thickness of 25 m within the first kilometer from shore.

Seasonal variations alter the intensity of the discharge. During the winter, when the volume of water is at its lowest, saline water can penetrate into the river, especially when aided by wind from the sea. This is particularly possible in the deepest channel to the sea at Sulina, where saline water may enter along the river bed for several kilometers (Ross 1971).

Salinity along the Rumanian coast is affected by the influx of fresh water, the circulation pattern of the sea, and the regime of the winds. The salinity varies from 0‰ at the point where the river meets the sea to 22‰ for the bottom water. Surface water near the delta has the lowest salinity, 2.5–12‰, increasing seaward and with depth. The 17‰ isohaline is located at depths from 10–25 m. Below 25 m the salinity increases from 17‰, reaching 21‰ at 100 m and 22‰ at 200 m. Coastal water near Mamaia has an average salinity of 14–17‰.

In addition to the currents, north winds promote a movement of less saline water southward, diminishing the salinity and the marine species of the planktonic population. The water along the southern sector has a more stable gradient (Buachidze 1974).

CONSTANTA-TOMIS

The major city of the Rumanian Black Sea coast, Constanta, developed on the narrow Tomes peninsula, then extended northward toward Lake Tabacarie and southward along the cliff surrounding the harbor. The peninsula, limited by the gulf of Tomes, barely covers 105 km², is about 1500 m long, and has a mean width of 650 m. The shore resort of Mamaia, north of the city, is free of cliffs and submerged rocky formations. Its beach is made of extremely fine sand, and slopes gently seaward: at 100 m from the shoreline, the average depth reaches only 1 m. The width of the beach may be reduced as a result of the development, 5 km to the north of Mamaia, of an industrial petrochemical complex with a long docking jetty.

One of the few islands, Ovidiu, is located in Lake Siut-Ghiol, a former sea gulf where the Carasu River debouches. The lake has been cut off from the sea by the Mamaia spit; it is fed by underground springs. Dunes line the shore north of the resort (Mamaia-Sat).

THE RAZELM LAKE COMPLEX

An ensemble of lagoonal lakes, found between the Dobrogea Plateau and the Black Sea, is known as the Razelm Complex. These lakes developed from the subdivision of the ancient gulf of Halmyris, into which flowed an arm of the Danube currently known as St. Gheorghe. This complex of lakes is the largest group of natural lakes in Rumania and includes Razelm, Sinoe, Babadag, Galovita, and Zmeica.

These shallow lakes, with a total area of 731 km², have a maximum depth of 3 m. There is communication with the sea through four small outlets, the most important of which is Portita, "the little door." Surplus lake water, augmented by Danube water entering the lakes by means of the Dranov and Dunavatu canals, flows through these openings to the sea.

The salinity of the lakes varies, with the normal concentration ranging from 1‰ in Lake Razelm, 2–3‰ in Galovita, and up to 6‰ in Sinoe. During low-water season or occasional breaching of the littoral sand barrier, an influx of seawater augments the salinity. Under these conditions, the salinity may reach 6‰ in Lake Razelm, 10‰ in Galovita and 18‰ in Sinoe. Conversely, the minimum salinity occurring in times of great flow of river water can be 0.2‰ in Lake Razelm to 1‰ in Sinoe.

These lakes are biologically productive and provide a large quantity of fish, contributing significantly to the economy of the area. Macrophytic growth is prevalent on nearly the entire lake bottom, with higher concentrations in the southern portions, where the water is less disturbed.

THE DANUBE DELTA

The newest land of the Dobrogea Plateau is the Danube delta (Fig. 63-2), formed over tens of thousands of years by accumulation of alluvial deposits. The Danube once had an estuary some 100 km long (Shimkus and Tremonis 1974). The delta itself is a vast area extending 4340 km², of which more than half is composed of ponds, islands, lagoons, and floating islands of matted roots and reeds known locally as *plauri*. Numerous sand dunes and wooded areas also exist within the delta. Channels and canals, which facilitate the circulation of river water, traverse the area. Large areas of land are flooded annually, accommodating the further development of the deltaic landforms.

ROGER H. CHARLIER
EMIL W. DE JULIO

REFERENCES

Buachidze, I., 1974, Black Sea shelf and littoral zone, in *The Black Sea — Geology, Chemistry, and Biology,* E. T. Degens and D. A. Ross, eds., Am. Assoc. Petroleum Geologists Mem. 20, pp. 308–316.

Charlier, R. H., 1971, The aquatic sciences in Romania, *Synergist* **3:**5–15.

Charlier, R. H., 1973, *Esquisse Préliminaire d'un Cours d'Océanographie Regional,* Université de Bordeaux I.

Chiriac, V., 1966, *Contributions Roumaines à l'étude de la Mer Noire,* Comité d'Etat des Eaux, Bucharest.

Dunăreanu, I., 1967, Le Côte Roumaine de la Mer Noire, Meridione, Bucharest.

Glaskov, V., 1970, Three-dimensional T-S analysis of the water masses of the Black Sea, *Oceanology* **10:** 771–774.

Novitskiy, V. P., 1964, General features of water circulation in the Black Sea, *Trudy Azcherniro* **23:**3–22.

Ross, D. A., 1971, The Red Sea and the Black Sea, *Am. Scientist* **59:**420–424.

Ross, D. A., E. T. Degens, and J. MacIlvaine, 1970, Black Sea: recent sedimentary history, *Science* **170:**163–165.

Shimkus, K., and E. Tremonis, 1974, Modern sedimentation in the Black Sea, in *The Black Sea-Geology, Chemistry, and Biology,* E. T. Degens and D. A. Ross, eds., Am Assoc. Petroleum Geologist Mem. 20, pp. 249–278.

Zenkovitch, V. P., 1966, The Black Sea, in *The Encyclopaedia of Oceanography,* R. Fairbridge, ed., Reinhold, New York, pp. 145–151.

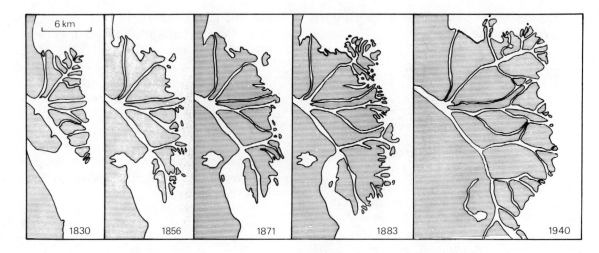

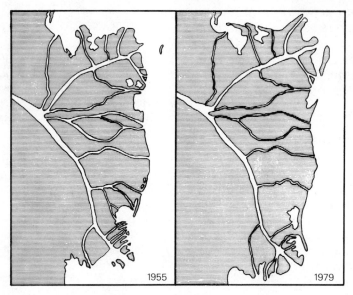

Figure 63-2. Growth of the Danube Delta from 1830 to 1979.

Plate 63-1. Saturn Resort, Rumanian Black Sea coast, created on narrow strip of sand after World War II. Note elevation of land in background (upper center). Originally mostly covered by trees (photo by Rumanian Tourist Office).

64. NORTHERN BLACK SEA AND SEA OF AZOV, USSR

From the Rumanian border on the Kilijski branch of the Danube delta, the Soviet Black Sea coastline extends some 1628 km, past the Crimea to Kerchenski Strait, the entrance to the Sea of Azov. Of this coastline, 486 km (29.9%) are erosional, 553 km (34%) stable, and 589 km (39.1%) prograded, but in recent decades some of the prograded sectors have become subject to erosion.

In this Ukrainian coastal region rock formations have been gently folded, and geomorphological evolution has produced alternations of hilly country, valleys, and wider lowlands (Fig. 64-1). Holocene marine submergence initiated development of a coastline with cliffed sectors bordering hilly country, as in the southern part of the Crimea Peninsula (Fig. 64-2), the Tarkhankut Peninsula, and in Odessa (Plate 64-1 and 64-2) and Feodosia bays. Coastal plains and wide valley mouths have been submerged to form limans, particularly between the Danube and the Dnieper deltas. Narrower valleys incised into hilly country have been submerged to form rias, as in southwestern Crimea (Fig. 64-2). Faulting has influenced the outlines of the northern Tarkhankut Peninsula (Tkachenko 1970).

Where Tertiary limestones, sandstones, shales, and volcanic rocks outcrop at the coast, cliffs (Plate 64-3) up to 100 m high have been cut. These have been retreating at rates of up to 30 cm/yr during the past century. Softer formations, such as clays and loams, have formed steep sectors subject to recurrent landsliding, and on these recession has been up to 9 m/yr. On depositional coastlines, beaches, spits, and beach-ridge plains can gain or lose up to 20 m in a single storm, but over longer periods the rates of change are similar to those on soft cliffs (Shuisky 1970, 1974, 1979). For more detailed reports on these coasts the reader is referred to Shuisky and Schwartz (1979, 1980a, 1980b, 1981, 1983).

The coast north of the Danube delta is low-lying and formed by the deposition of sand, silt, and clay derived from Danube river sediments; it has prograded up to 10 m/yr. The Dniester (Plate 64-4) and Dnieper have built deltaic plains into former limans, rather than protruding deltas.

Where sandy sediments have been deposited, beaches are backed by derived dunes generally 2–2.5 m high, occasionally reaching up to 6 m, in a backshore ridge 30–40 m wide extending intermittently along the coast. Prevailing northerly winds drift sand southward, which on many sectors is seaward, so that large-scale dune development is impeded. Shell sands, mainly mussels, are an important constituent of marine sediments, typically up to 5%, but often more; some beaches consist entirely of molluscan material. Beaches and dunes are dominated by fine sandy material, silt and clay being dispersed seaward. The supply of sandy sediment from rivers, from cliff erosion, and from the sea floor has diminished in recent centuries, and at present only 7.2% of the Ukrainian coastline is actively prograding. Longshore drifting has produced the major barrier spits of Tendra and Jarylgach, the cuspate spit Bakal, and many barrier beaches. Between Odessa Bay and Zhebrianska Bay the longshore sediment flow is over 100,000 m³/yr,

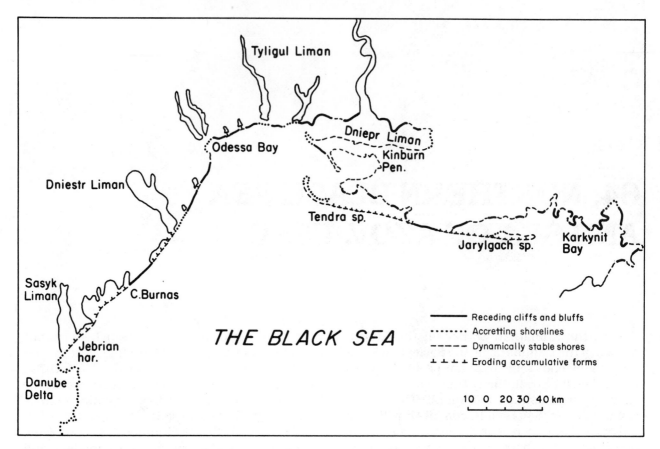

Figure 64-1. Northwestern Black Sea coastline.

between the Dnieper liman and Odessa Gulf about 20,000 m³/yr, and between Khersones Cape and Kalamitski Gulf over 70,000 m³/yr.

SEA OF AZOV

Produced by Holocene marine submergence of an undulating lowland, the Sea of Azov (Fig. 64-3) is bordered by hilly country and tributary valleys. Marine cliffs have developed where the sea inter-

sects uplands, and elongated bays occupy drowned lowlands and valley mouths (Mamykina and Khrustalev 1980). The larger rivers (Don, Kuban) have built deltas, and there has been extensive deposition of both inorganic sediment from rivers and eroded cliffs, and biogenic material, mainly molluscan sand and gravel, washed in from the sea floor, to form beaches, spits, and barriers that enclose lagoons. The largest of these are the Sivash Lagoons, behind the Arabat barrier (Fig. 64-3).

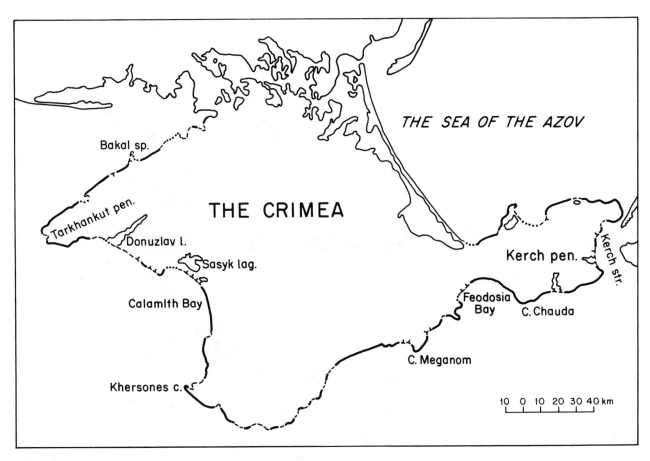

Figure 64-2. Coastline of the Crimea.

The coastline of the Azov Sea measures 1860 km, of which 420 (22.6%) are erosional, and 1440 (77.4%) prograded (Fig. 64-4). Within the latter, only 141 km are actively prograding beaches and 46 km advancing deltas; the remaining 1299 km were formerly prograded and are now undergoing erosion. The Don River discharges 2.8 million tonnes of sediment annually, the Kuban River 4.9 million tonnes, the remaining streams being regulated with almost no sediment yield (Mamykina 1978). Of a total fluvial sediment yield of 4.5

million m³, 70% is retained in limans and on delta shores. The Sea of Azov generates about 25 million tonnes of molluscan shells per year, of which more than 15% (about 1.84 million m³) is added to coastal beaches, spits, and barriers. Cliffs are mainly cut in Tertiary and Quaternary clays, and are receding at rates of up to 6 m/yr. Limestones retreat more slowly, up to 0.4 m/yr (Shuisky 1974). Sediments from eroding cliffs amount to about 6.9 million m³/yr, of which 0.85 million m³ are sands and material coarser than 0.1 mm grain

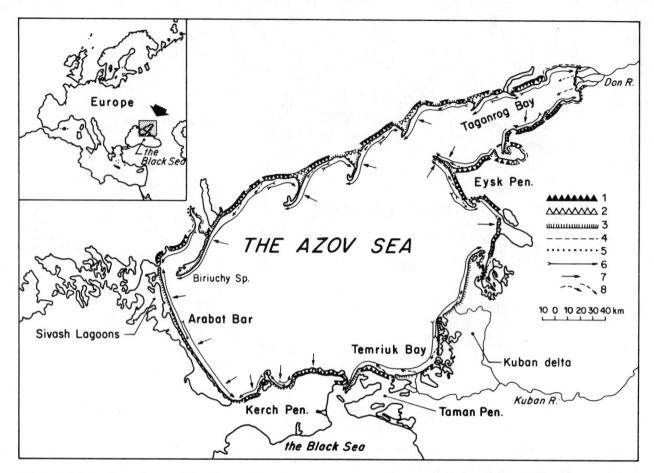

Figure 64-3. Coastline of the Azov Sea: 1. main erosional areas; 2. abandoned cliffs; 3. receding coastlines formerly prograded; 4. stable coastlines; 5. advancing coastlines; 6. direction of longshore drift; 7. delivery of sediments from submarine slope; 8. delivery of sediments from rivers and cliff erosion.

size. A further 4.6 million m³/yr of sediment is generated by sea-floor abrasion, and of this 0.88 million m³ is sand and material coarser than 0.1 mm grain size. Thus only a small proportion of the material produced by cliff and sea-floor erosion is suitable for beach accretion.

The features and dynamics of the coastlines of the Sea of Azov are summarized in Figure 64-3, and rates of advance or retreat of the coastline in recent decades are shown in Figure 64-4.

YURII D. SHUISKY

REFERENCES

Mamykina, V. A., 1978, Recent processes in the coastal zone of the Azov Sea, *Geog. Soc. U.S.S.R. Proc.* **110**(4): 351–359.

Mamykina, V. A., and Y. P. Khrustalev, 1980, *Coastal Zone of the Azov Sea,* Rostov University Press.

Shuisky, Yu. D., 1970, Characteristics of the recent development of the north-west shores of the Black Sea, *Oceanography* **10**:108–117.

Shuisky, Yu. D., 1974, Processes and rate of abrasion of the Ukrainian shoreline of the Azov and Black Seas, *Acad. Sci. U.S.S.R., Proc. Geogr. Ser.* **6**:117–125.

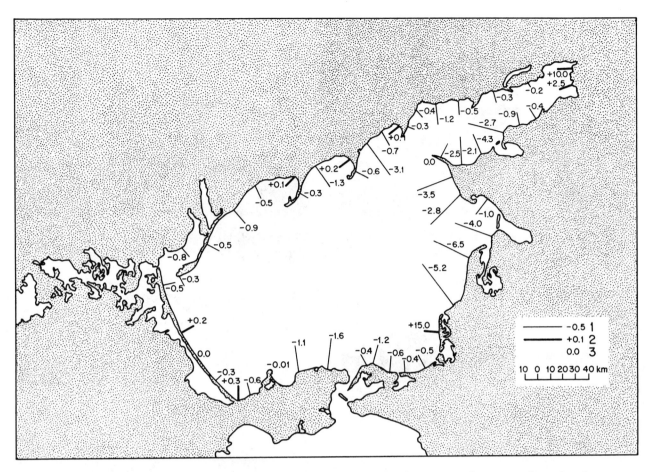

Figure 64-4. Coastline changes in the Azov Sea in recent decades: 1. receding coastline; 2. advancing coastline; 3. mean rate of change in m/yr.

Shuisky, Yu. D., 1979, Sediment balance in coastal zones, *Geomorphology* **4:**89-97.

Shuisky, Yu. D., and M. L. Schwartz, 1979, Natural laws in the development of artificial sandy beaches, *Shore and Beach* **47:**33-36.

Shuisky, Yu. D., and M. L. Schwartz, 1980a, Processes of development of eroding and slumping shores on the Black Sea coast, *Shore and Beach* **48:**36-39.

Shuisky, Yu. D., and M. L. Schwartz, 1980b, Influences of beaches on development of coastal erosion slopes in the northwestern part of the Black Sea, *Shore and Beach* **48:**30-34.

Shuisky, Yu. D., and M. L. Schwartz, 1981, Dynamics and morphology of barrier beaches of the Black Sea coast limans, *Shore and Beach* **49:**45-50.

Shuisky, Yu. D., and M. L. Schwartz, 1983, Basic principles of sediment budget study in the coastal zone, *Shore and Beach* **51:**34-40.

Tkachenko, G. G., 1970, Influence of tectonic movements on coastal morphology, in *Geology of the Coastline and Bottom of the Black and Azov Seas*, vol. 4, G. G. Tkachenko et al., pp. 27-33.

Plate 64-1. North Acadia Bay recreational beach at Odessa (photo by M. L. Schwartz).

Plate 64-3. Large slump block in cliff near Port Yuhzny, east of Odessa (photo by M. L. Schwartz).

Plate 64-2. Oldest existing coastal protection, dating from 1959, along the Odessa city shore (photo by M. L. Schwartz).

Plate 64-4. Dniester Liman on the Black Sea coast, to the west of Odessa (photo by M. L. Schwartz).

65. EASTERN BLACK SEA, USSR

The eastern coast of the Black Sea within the confines of the USSR extends from the Kerch Straits to the Soviet-Turkish frontier, totaling about 600 km in length (Fig. 65-1). East of the Kerch Strait, for about 20 km, loose Neogene deposits predominate along the sea. The coast is being intensively eroded and is subject to landsliding. The clayey composition of the rocks results in beaches composed predominantly of seashell fragments. In front of the cliffs there is a wide submarine platform. Alternation of rocks of different strength accounts for the formation of arcuate coastline irregularities (Plate 65-1).

Farther to the southeast there is a barrier composed of quartz sand, about 50 km long, which separates some large lagoons (limans) from the sea. In the north the barrier is narrow; to the south it spreads out to 1 km in width, with some eolian forms in the shape of small dunes. The sand making up the barrier consists mainly of ancient drift from the Kuban River, which until late in the past century discharged into the heads of the Black Sea limans. Today the northern part of the barrier is slowly retreating, while its southern part is growing because of the effect of a relatively weak sediment drift.

The northern termination of the Caucasian range comes close to the Anapa Cape (Plate 65-2). This is the beginning of an erosional coast composed of sharply dislocated rocks of Cretaceous and Paleogene flysch. The height of cliffs between

Anapa and Novorossiysk reaches 200 m. At the end of the Flandrian transgression vast landslides occurred here, whose outstretched portion has been preserved in the form of small peninsulas. The shelf in the area grows narrow, and the gradient of the offshore sea bed increases. Coquina fragments are no longer thrown onto the coast, and the narrow beaches consist of flysch rock fragments (Plate 65-3).

The cities of Novorossiysk and Gelendzhik lie at the heads of bays of synclinal origin. Southward the flysch complex grows more homogeneous, and the erosional coast as far as Tuapse exhibits only insignificant irregularities. Small bays with beaches composed of alluvial material have formed at the mouths of some rivers. Alluvial clays, which were earlier deposited in small ria-type gulfs, are exposed at the sea bed. They are eroding now because of coastal abrasion, which is taking place at the rate of several centimeters a year. At the open coast, beaches are practically nonexistent. From the foot of the cliffs abrasion platforms begin and extend to depths of more than 15 m. The length of this type of coast, between Anapa and Tuapse, is about 100 km.

Farther southeast the rivers have a significant amount of solid discharge, and their drift protrudes beyond the limits of adjacent coastal embayments. The first of such rivers is the Tuapse. Until the middle of the present century this was the starting point of longshore sediment drift that could be traced as far as the cape of Pitsunda, 150 km away. This flow received additional discharge from other large rivers. At the city of Sochi

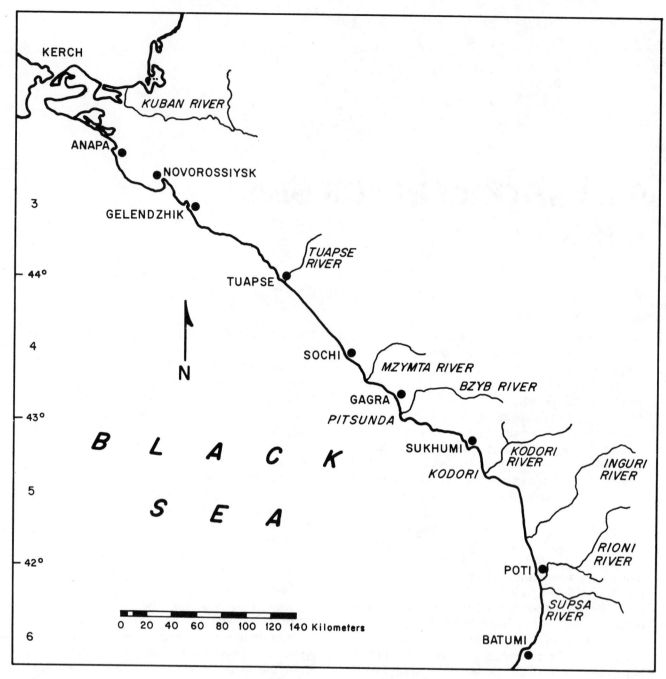

Figure 65-1. Location map of the eastern Black Sea coast.

(about 100 km from Tuapse) the drift volume was 30,000 m³ of pebble and 20,000 m³ of sand annually.

The situation has essentially changed in the middle of the present century as a result of engineering projects. The port of Sochi (Plate 65-4) has been built with long moles extending seaward, and a dam has been set up across the Tuapse River. At the same time about 4 million m³ of

pebble was removed for construction purposes from beaches that were 30–40 m in width (Romashin and Shul'gin 1978).

While formerly the drift material was transported as far as the mouth of the Mzymta River and the Pitsunda Peninsula, today sediments are carried only to Sochi. Beaches to the south have become narrower and at places disappeared altogether. This required the building of groins and submarine breakwaters, and in numerous places sediments have been brought in artificially.

Alluvium from the Mzmyta River, along with that of the Psou River, has formed a wide coastal protrusion. The coastline has moved out to the edge of the shelf, which has become very narrow. The coastline has approached the heads of submarine canyons, and much alluvium is lost into them, going to great depths. However, part of the longshore drift of sediment (20,000–30,000 m³ annually) proceeds further to the south.

At about 12 km downdrift very steep slopes of the Gagra range, composed of resistant Cretaceous and Jurassic limestones, extend to the sea. The sea bottom has a fairly steep gradient, and waves are reflected from the resistant slopes, causing practically no erosion. For this reason the sediment drift moves offshore, being submerged to a depth of 3–6 m. Exposed beaches are practically absent. They do exist, however, at places where groups of groins have been built. Oblique western waves are subject to deformation at the groins, and their reflection from the steep slopes is of little erosional significance.

A wide-open bay is the site of the Gagra resort. The coast here had a wide beach but, erosion has now become evident. It started after the construction of a 150 m long mole in the western part of the resort in 1914. The coast prograded out to the west of the mole, and supply for the Gagra beaches was then resumed. In the middle of this century, because of the removal of beach material in the northern sector for construction purposes, the amount of beach sediment decreased and the entire shore had to be maintained with groins. At present this erosion has affected the western part of the alluvial lowland, which owes its origin to the alluvium of the Bzyb River.

Southeast of the mouth of the Bzyb River lies the well-known Pitsunda Peninsula, whose dynamics have been studied in detail in connection with the construction of large holiday hotels (Plate 65-5). The western shore of the Pitsunda Peninsula has moved out to the shelf edge and is extending along the heads of several canyons. The sediment from the Bzyb River is transported by practically undeformed waves toward the termination of the cape. The annual volume of about 200,000 m³ builds up the shore. At the cape convexity, and along the entire southeastern part of the peninsula, the submarine slope is extremely steep, and from 10–12 m depths it descends at 25–30° to the flat surface of the shelf. This protruding cape has created a "wave shadow" for a large stretch of the shore east of the peninsula. The shore to about 9 km to the south is subject to erosion, and the erosion products are transported along the beach fronting the cliffs of the Myusser upland, some of them opposite to the main sediment drift (i.e., towards Pitsunda), thus building up this part of the peninsula (Zenkovich 1958).

East of Pitsunda the next sediment drift begins, fed by the alluvium of the Belaya River and by transport of fragmentary material from the flat sea bed. (There is a large shallow water protrusion here, presumably an ancient delta.) The capacity of the flow is approximately 15,000–20,000 m³ annually, and it extends 45 km to the mouth of the Gumista River. The solid discharge of this river is much less than that of the Bzyb. Nevertheless, a structure formed here is similar to the structure of Pitsunda, an oblique rounded cape that has moved out to great depths and has approached the heads of submarine canyons. Beyond this cape lies the wide Sukhumi Bay.

East of Sukhumi the mountains gradually retreat from the shore, and the coastal region is formed of Quaternary alluvial terraces. Beaches become broader; their pebbly-sandy material continues to move southeasterly as far as the large alluvial protrusion of the Kodori River. In many features this protrusion resembles Pitsunda, but it has a more rounded outline. In the wave shadow formed by the protrusion, the sediment drift acquires an opposite direction and, along with the Kodori alluvium, is lost at the steep submarine slopes and in the submarine canyons at the Iskuriya Cape.

Therefore south of the Kodori protrusion there is an erosional sector of the shore where, for about 10 km, cliffs undercutting the ancient delta terrace occur. The last form of this type is a large coastal protrusion at the mouth of the Chorokhi River. It lies to the south of the Kolkhida lowland and slopes northward. Western waves, common for this part of the sea, transport the Chorokhi sediment in a northeastern direction, toward the Kolkhida lowland, and the entire protrusion of the Chorokhi delta plain is similar to those features lying north of Kolkhida. Here the sediments are similarly lost in two submarine canyons and there is an erosional section in the wave shadow of the Burun-Tabie Cape (Plate 65-6).

The central concavity of the eastern part of the Black Sea, between the mouths of the Mokva and Natanebi rivers and 90 km in length, adjoins the vast Kolkhida lowland. This is a region of tectonic submergence, which is proceeding at the rate of

6.7 mm/yr in the area of the city of Poti. At the end of the Flandrian transgression it was the site of a vast bay receiving the discharge of the rivers running off from the Main Caucasian range and from the Minor Caucasus. The largest of the rivers is the Rioni, with a discharge now of 13.6 km³/yr. It is these sediments that have filled the former bay. In the western part of the lowland, the Pleistocene deposits attain 500 m in thickness, comprising interlayers and lenses of lagoon peats and sand. The latter are elongated parallel to the present-day shore and represent relict coastal barriers.

The present-day coastal barrier separates vast water-logged areas from the sea. Sand beaches along the Kolkhida shore are not wide, and in most places lagoon and lacustrine clays outcrop beneath them. The erection of dams and the artificial changes in position of the Rioni and Inguri river mouths have transformed the shore, resulting in an abrupt retreat at some places and an advance at others. Generally, the shores of Kolkhida's northern portion are at present retreating; however, the southern shores remain stable. Submarine canyons lie close to the mouths of large rivers (Inguri, Rioni, Supsa), absorbing the alluvial material either completely or in large quantities (Zenkovich 1976).

The Rioni River has given rise to a smooth cuspate delta, which prograded out into the sea until the 1920s. It had gradually come close to the head of a submarine canyon, which now grew deeper, with its head moving toward the shore and the moles in the port as fast as 8 m/yr. In 1939 the river migrated to a new channel 6 km north of the old one. Thereafter the delta started to grow rapidly at the new site, and intensive coastal erosion set in at the old mouth (recently amounting to about 900 m). Simultaneously, the movement of the canyon toward the shore stopped, and at present it is gradually filling with sediment.

The diversity of shore types in the eastern part of the Black Sea and the formation of closed dynamic systems with their proper sediment balance (Kiknadze 1977) are due to the changes of the general geographic conditions in a west-east direction. West of Anapa the shore is totally deprived of an alluvial supply. In the area between Novorossyisk and Tuapse the axial part of the Caucasian range lies only 5–15 km away from the coast, with a height of about 900 m. Climate in this area is dry (annual precipitation is 400–600 mm). Therefore, rivers here are few and shallow. Beaches are found only near their mouths.

In the Tuapse-Sochi area the mountain range is located 40 km from the shore; its height reaches 2000 m. The climate is humid (1200–1500 mm annual precipitation). The long and full-flowing rivers supply significant quantities of shingle and sandy alluvium, which form a longshore sediment drift. The Psezuapse, Sochi, and Shakhe rivers have been unable to produce significant deltaic accumulations.

A large single coastal protrusion has been formed by the Mzmyta and Psou rivers. Farther to the east have arisen the aforementioned cuspate alluvial-marine accretional forms of Pitsunda, Sukhumi, and Kodori. In this area the distance to the axial part of the range increases to 60 km, and the mountains are as high as 3000–4000 m. The precipitation amounts to over 2000 mm a year. Correspondingly, the solid discharge of the rivers sharply increases. Waves are no longer able to move the entire alluvial material along the seacoast. Capes have arisen, dividing it into isolated systems. Thus, the diversity of coastal types in the eastern part of the Black Sea is due to a complex of external geographic factors that have determined the history of coastal development in the Holocene and the present-day dynamics.

V. P. ZENKOVICH

REFERENCES

Kiknadze, A. G., 1977, Dynamic systems and sediment budget at Georgia's Black Sea coasts, in *Man and the Environment*, Alashara Publishers, Sukhumi (in Russian).

Romashin, V. V., and Y. S. Shul'gin, 1978, Changes of the Black Sea coasts under the influence of technical impacts, in *Sea Coast Protection*, All-Union Institute of Transport Construction Publishers, Moscow (in Russian).

Zenkovich, V. P., 1958, *Coasts of the Black and Azov Seas*, State Geographical Literature Publishers, Moscow (in Russian).

Zenkovich, V. P., 1976, Coastal zone dynamics as a basis for designing coastal protection, in *Problems of Investigating Georgia's Coasts*, Metsniereba Publishers, Tbilisi (in Russian).

Plate 65-1. Arcuate coastline east of the Kerch Straits (photo by V. L. Bolayrev).

Plate 65-2. Anapa Cape along the east coast of the Black Sea.

Plate 65-3. Broad submarine beach composed of flysch, viewed from top of cliff, between Anapa and Novorossiysk.

Plate 65-4. Port of Sochi built by extending lengthy moles into the Black Sea (photo by M. L. Schwartz).

Plate 65-5. Large resort complex built on Pitsunda Peninsula (photo by M. L. Schwartz).

Plate 65-6. Protective structures along the erosional section in the wave shadow of the Burun-Tabie Cape (photo by V. V. Kandelaky).

66. CASPIAN USSR

The length of the Caspian Sea coastline within the Soviet Union is about 5950 km, 2400 km of which are in the Northern Caspian, 1350 km in the Middle Caspian, and 2200 km in the Southern Caspian province (Kosarev 1975). The three provinces (Fig. 66-1) differ in their geological setting (Fig. 66-2), shore topography, and hydrometeorology (Leontiev 1964). The morphostructure of the Caspian Sea is also closely related to its geology, with the Derbent depression (780 m deep) and the South Caspian depression (1022 m deep) corresponding with structural troughs.

The major hydrodynamic factors on Caspian Sea coasts are fluctuations of level due to wind and wave action and the effects of swells and currents. Tide ranges are small, only a few centimeters, but strong winds cause changes of level of up to 3 m, especially in the Northern Caspian. Here the prevailing southeasterly winds produce steep waves and occasional storm surges (Kosarev 1975). On the west coast of the Caspian Sea, these winds produce waves and currents that yield northward drifting from the Baku Peninsula, but south of here the northerly winds become more effective, generating a southward drift. On the east coast of the Caspian, onshore westerly winds produce the dominant waves. Storms generate waves up to 6 m high out in the Caspian Sea, where a maximum wave height of 11 m has been recorded.

Long-term fluctuations of sea level have played an important part in the evolution of Caspian coastal morphology. Separated from the oceans in Lower Pliocene times, the Caspian Sea has shown fluctuations related to climatic changes within bordering drainage basins. During the Quaternary there were repeated glaciations of the Russian Plain and the Caucasus Mountains, and intervening deglaciations; the level of the Caspian Sea consequently rose and fell. In the Middle Pleistocene it attained a level 50 m higher than at present, while in late Pleistocene times it fell 50 m below present level. Marine terraces correspond with stillstands during these fluctuations. On the western coasts they have been raised by tectonic movements associated with Caucasian uplift, so that the oldest stand 200–300 m above present sea level, whereas on the relatively stable eastern coasts they extend only up to 50–70 m (Fedorov 1978).

During Holocene times a sea-level rise (Neo-Caspian marine transgression) culminated in the eighteenth century, when it attained 6 m above its present level. Since then there has been a substantial lowering, with a sharp fall of about 2 m between 1929 and 1945 followed by smaller oscillations and further overall reduction (Fig. 66-3). In 1975 the Caspian Sea level was about 28.5 m below the mean level of the Black Sea.

This lowering has reduced the area of the Caspian Sea by more than 40,000 km^2, and resulted in the emergence of extensive shoals and marginal lands (Fig. 66-4). It has also led to the shoreward movement of sea floor material on to beaches. Discharge of fluvial water and sediment has been important to the dynamics and morphology of Caspian coasts. Between 1880 and 1972 the total mean annual discharge of rivers into the Caspian was 294 km^3, 80% of which came from the River Volga and 15% from the Ural, Kura, Terek, and Sulak rivers (Voropaev and Kosarev 1981). Until recently, these rivers transported about 150 million tonnes of sedimentary material to the sea annually, but in the past 30 years major

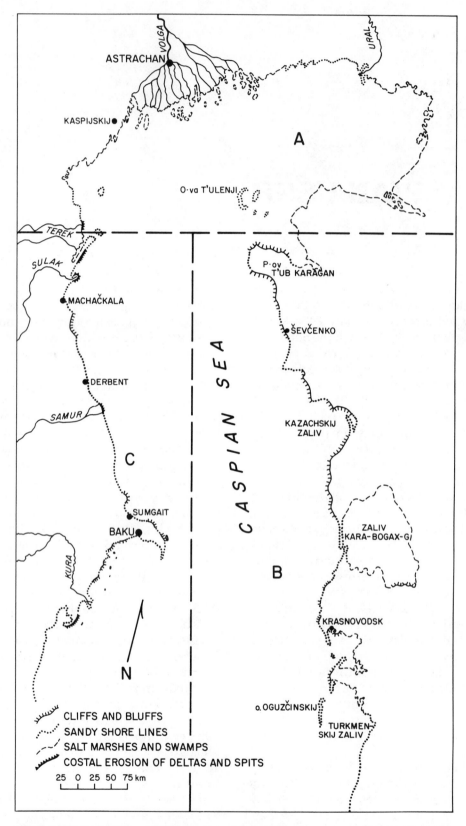

Figure 66-1. Major coastal forms of the Caspian sea: *A.* North Caspian coast; *B.* eastern coast; and *C.* western coast, showing cliffs and crags, beaches, wattens and coastal marshes, and erosion of accumulative coastal forms.

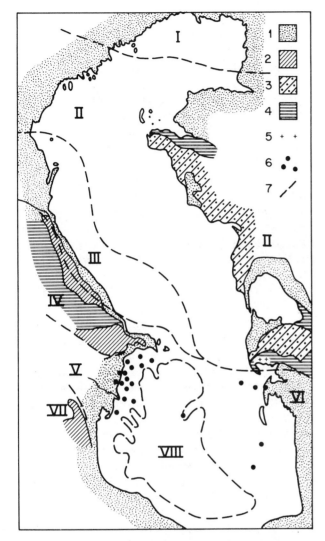

Figure 66-2. Geological sketch map of the Caspian Sea coast: 1. Quaternary deposits; 2. Tertiary sedimentary rocks in folded zones; 3. Tertiary rocks of platform zones; 4. Mesozoic deposits; 5. granites and granodiorites; 6. mud volcanoes; 7. boundaries of structural zones. Structural zones: I. Russian ancient platform; II. Scythian-Turan young platform; III. Terek-Caspian marginal trough; IV. Great Caucasus meganticlinorium; V. Kura-Araks depression; VI. West Turkmen marginal trough; VII. Talysh anticlinorium; VIII. South Caspian basin.

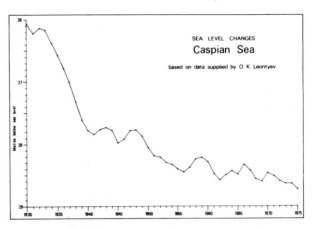

Figure 66-3. Sea-level changes in the Caspian Sea, 1930–1975.

hydroengineering projects have greatly reduced their sediment flow. Moreover, some river mouths (e.g., Terek and Sulak) have been diverted, and deltaic areas previously built up have been eroded, despite the emergence that has been taking place (Mikhailov 1971).

From the Iranian border in the southwest north to Lenkoran the coast is sandy, fed with sediment by streams flowing down from the Talysh Mountains and across a narrow coastal plain. Northward there is a transition to marshy coasts in the lee of the Kura spit. This spit was initiated as a barrier beach formed from sediment brought down by the Kura River, but about 200 years ago the river breached it and began to build its modern delta projecting seaward. Southward drifting of fluvial sediment continued to nourish the barrier beach, prolonging it as a spit, but after the construction of a dam in the Kura River basin this supply diminished, resulting in erosion of the seaward flank of the Kura spit, but continuing accretion at its southern end.

Baku stands on the Apsheron Peninsula, a projection of the Caucasus Ranges into the sea, with bays on synclinal troughs between anticlinal rocky promontories. To the north, Upper Cretaceous rocks outcrop in the eroding margins of the Kilyazinsk promontory.

North Azerbaijan has a sandy coast backed by extensive dune formations (Fig. 66-4). Akzybir was formerly a lagoon behind a sandy barrier, but with falling sea level it has become a marshland (Leontiev et al. 1977). The Samur River, on the Dagestan boundary, has built a blunt delta, now subject to wave erosion. Sandy beaches, known by their mineralogical content to be of sediment from the Samur and smaller Dagestan rivers, continue past Derbent to Izberbash. Emergence and sand deposition have now completely enclosed the Adji lagoon, which used to be open to the sea. Between Izberbash and Makhachkala the sandy beaches are accompanied by bedrock

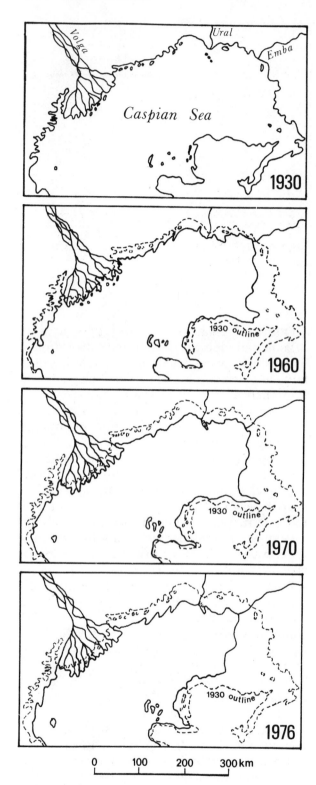

Figure 66-4. Coastline changes in the northern Caspian, 1930–1976.

outcrops of limestone, with some monoclinal ridges occurring just offshore.

At Makhachkala the Caucasian foothills recede inland behind a wide depositional plain. In the south the coast includes the large dune-covered Agrakhan spit, over 50 km long and up to 10 km wide. This originated as a barrier beach formed by wave-working of fluvial shoal deposits off the mouth of the Terek River. About 150 years ago the Sulak River, which formerly flowed into Agra-khan Bay behind this barrier, cut a new outlet and began to build its modern delta at the south-ern end of the Agrakhan spit, thereby supplying sediment to prograde it. However, damming of the Sulak River has been followed by the onset of erosion on the southern part of this spit, and the Sulak delta is also being eroded following the diversion of the river mouth southward about 25 years ago.

The Terek delta has also shown modifications. In recent years the main distributary has been on the southern side, opening into the shallow bay behind the Agrakhan spit, but a decade or so ago a new artificial outflow was cut through this spit, and a new delta is developing vigorously. The northern part of the Terek delta, deprived of sedimentation, now shows rapid erosion despite the Caspian emergence.

North of the Terek delta the coastline of the broad, shallow Kizlyar Bay has advanced several kilometers as the result of the falling sea level. The emerged plain is marshy, with extensive reed growth, and it is subject to occasional marine inundation when easterly storms build up the sea level temporarily.

The vast Volga delta has a seaward fringe of low marshy islets and shoals intersected by complex channel patterns. Klenova (1948) calculated del-taic coastline advance of 0.2 km/yr from 1817 to 1925, but during the phase of rapid lowering of Caspian sea level (1929–1945) it prograded at ten times this rate. However, with a diminution in the rate of sea-level lowering and a reduction in discharge and sediment yield from the Volga, the rate of increase of deltaic land has slowed down since 1945.

Between the Volga delta and the smaller Ural delta, the coast is low and sandy and fronted by wide tidal flats. This sector, together with the fringes of the large bay extending round to the Shevchenko (Tyub-Karagan) Peninsula, has shown substantial gains of coastal land as the result of the lowering of Caspian Sea level, especially since 1929 (Plate 66-1). The use of Ural River water for irrigation has so diminished its discharge and sediment yield that although the river has extended its course across the emerged sea floor, there has been only minor delta development here.

East and south from the Ural River mouth the coast is low and sandy, with wide tidal flats subject to inundation during storm surges. The aridity of the northern Caspian coastal regions is marked by the development of "clay dunes" similar to those found in Mexico; they form distinctive hillocks both east and west of the Volga delta. Emergence has also led to the evolution of *shalygs*, partly submerged offshore sand ridges of barchan-like form, shaped by the interaction of waves and currents in a shallowing sea.

On the Buzuchi Peninsula are barrier beaches formed during the Neo-Caspian marine transgression, while seaward from the present emerged sandy coastline are the Tulen Islands, an archipelago including barrier islands built up during emergence. The Tyub-Karagan Peninsula, to the south, is higher ground in the desert terrain of Mangyshlak. Its margins were formerly cliffed and subject to landslides, but after 1929 the lowering of Caspian Sea level, the cliffs cut in Miocene limestone, clay, and marl were left stranded as bluffs fronted by wide beaches, consisting of molluscan shelly material (*Didacna, Cerastoderma spp.*) and oolites.

The Kazakhstan coast retains some sectors subject to marine erosion, but is notable for its extensive shelly beaches and depositional features, such as the cuspate forelands of Peschany Point (where dunes are extensive) and Rakushechny Point, and the barrier spit of Kendyrli. Some older, lithified calcareous depositional features are also preserved.

Kara-Bogaz-Gol (18,000 km²) is a hypersaline lagoon (salinity exceeding 300‰) bordered by high cliffs, in front of which are vast salt flats more than 3 m thick. These formed after 1930 as a result of the lowering of Caspian Sea level, and are broadest in the northern part of the lagoon. As long as this was a bay, open to the sea, there were losses of water from the Caspian into this area of high evaporation. A dam 6.5 m high has therefore been built to close the gap in the barrier spits and prevent flow of seawater into Kora-Bogaz-Gol. It is calculated that this dam has reduced annual water loss from the Caspian Sea by 5–8 km³ (Voropaev and Kosarev 1981).

Krasnovodsk Bay is another spit-bordered annex to the Caspian Sea, shallow and bordered by wide tidal flats. The Cheleken Peninsula has a cliffed western margin, flanked by spits that run north and south, and there is an outlying shelly barrier beach at Ogurchinsky, which is growing southward as a result of longshore drifting. The south Turkmenian coast is also sandy, with a central eroding sector in which are exposed the Pleistocene deltaic clays of the Atrek River. Behind this sandy coast are old dunes, and vast solonchaks on the sites of former lagoons that have dried out.

This account of the Soviet Caspian coast ends at the mouth of the modern Atrek River, which forms the Iranian frontier.

O. K. LEONTIEV

REFERENCES

Fedorov, P. V., 1978, *Pleistotsen Ponto-Kaspiya*, Nauka, Moscow.

Klenova, M. V., 1948, *Geologiya morya*, Uchpedgiz, Moscow.

Kosarev, A. N., 1975, *Gidrologiya Kaspiiskogo i Aralskogo morei*, Moscow University.

Leontiev, O. K., 1964, Relyef i geologicheskaya struktura dna. Kaspiiskogo morya, *Vestnik Moscow Uniu Geog. Ser.* **5:**27–39.

Leontiev, O. K., E. G. Maev, and G. I. Rychagov, 1977, *Geomorphologiya beregov i dna Kaspiiskogo morya*, Moscow University.

Mikhailov, V. N., 1971, *Dinamika potoka i rusla v neprelivnykh ustyakh rek*, Gidrometeoizdat, Moscow.

Voropaev, G. V., and A. N. Kosarev, 1981, O sovremennykh problemakh Kaspiiskogo morya, *Priroda* **1:** 61–73.

Plate 66-1. A space image of the northwestern and eastern Caspian coasts, showing the Terek River delta, Agrakhan spit, and the Volga delta. Note the linear pattern of the Baer sand hills west of the Volga delta (photo by Soviet Space Agency).

67. CASPIAN IRAN

The Caspian plain of Iran has a length of approximately 600 km. Stretching in the form of a horseshoe around the southern shore of the Caspian Sea, its average elevation varies between 60–80 m above mean sea level near the mountain front to 28 m below mean sea level. The plain varies in width from less than 2 km in some parts of its western and central sections to more than 40 km in the big delta regions and in the Turcoman Steppe. Geologically, it is, in its present form, of late Pleistocene to Holocene age. Because of dramatic fluctuations of the sea level, together with the discharges and sedimentation of approximately 1300 rivers and brooks into the Caspian lowland of Iran, large parts of the plain have been of amphibious nature until recently. (The surface of the Caspian Sea is presently 28 m below the world ocean mean sea level.)

Physiographically, Caspian Iran can be subdivided into three parts: (1) the deltas and delta fans of the larger rivers; (2) the embedded lowlands; and (3) its southern fringe, marked by terraces of Pleistocene sea levels. The deltas and delta fans are generally of steep gradient. Because the Elburz promontories often come very close to the shore of the Caspian and because rainfall is heavy (1834 mm in Bandar Pahlavi/Enzeli, 1265 mm in Ramsar, and 807 mm in Babolsar—i.e., decreasing from west to east), most of them are formed of coarse gravels and sands, and rise above the neighboring stretches of alluvial lowlands. Exceptions to this rule are the deltas of the Sefid River (Plate 67-1) in the west and those of the Haraz, Babol, Talar, and Tejan rivers in the east. The delta of the Sefid River (Plate 67-1), identical with the fertile central plain of Gilan province, is a model of a delta with different branches, cutting

through old beach lines of higher sea levels and forming lagoons, shallow bays, and swampy marshes. Haraz, Babol, Talar, and Tejan rivers, on the other hand, form the Mazanderan plain, with mighty cones of gravel in front of the Elburz mountains and fertile alluvial basins, separated from each other by the levees and banks of the aforementioned rivers (Andriesse 1960).

The lowlands, most of which are situated below mean sea level, are formed mainly by silty and heavy clays with a considerable content of salts. Because of their specific texture and their low location, these areas are affected by an extremely high groundwater table, which is generally not deeper than 0.6 m. The groundwater is fed both by lateral seepage from the river-levees and by aquifers in the gravelly deposits of the river banks and the Elburz foothills. The lowlands of the Caspian plain are separated from the Caspian Sea itself by a distinct barrier, differentiated into two or three distinct levels of 2, 4, and 6 m above the Caspian sea level (Fig. 67-1 and Plate 67-2). While the highest level is partly covered by recently formed dunes, the lower levels are separated from each other by groundwater-affected depressions, partly occupied by offset river mouths. Plate 67-2 and Figure 67-1 demonstrate this situation very well.

The southern fringe of Caspian Iran is characterized by a distinct and mostly very steep border, formed by the promontories and/or foothills of the Elburz ranges. Attachment to the Caspian is proven by the fact that this fringe zone is differentiated by a series of more or less well-developed Pleistocene terraces, marking old shorelines of the Caspian Sea during the last (Würm-Wisconsin) glaciation. The whole series

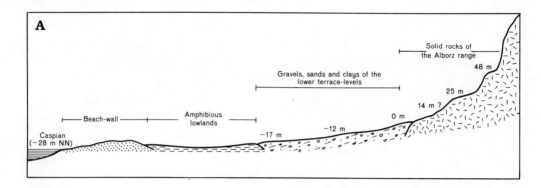

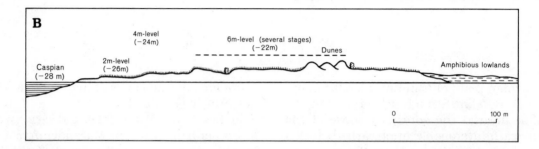

Figure 67-1. *A.* Caspian sea-level terraces (cross-section). *B.* cross-section of the recent beach-wall.

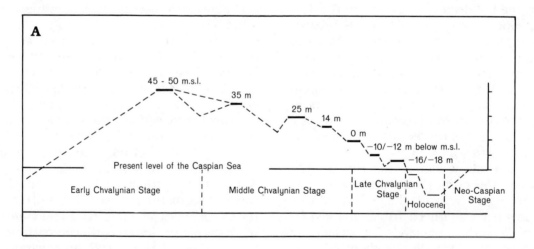

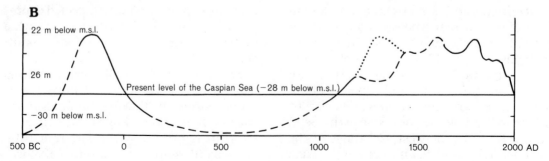

Figure 67-2. *A.* The development of the Caspian Sea during Würm/Wisconsin glaciation (after Fedorov). *B.* The changes in the level of the Caspian Sea since the start of our times (after Fedorov-Skiba).

of terraces, observed also in wide parts of the Caspian coast of the USSR (Federov 1957), is developed only in parts of Caspian Iran (Fig. 67-1); its main levels can, however, be correlated with fluvial terraces of the Elburz north slope. Since these are partly connected with datable moraines of the last glaciation, the whole terrace system of Caspian Iran and the corresponding fluctuations of the sea level seem to be reconstructable.

Fig. 67-2 is an attempt to reconstruct and interpret the geological development and physiographic differentiations of Caspian Iran.

The evolution of the Caspian Sea during the late and post-Pleistocene can be regarded as a reflection of the general climatic fluctuations, in which the cold phases show a rise, the warmer phases a fall of the water level. The most convincing confirmation of this coincidence of the climatic and physical history of the Caspian Sea is the Mangyshlak stage at 50 m below mean sea level. Contemporary with the Holocene climatic optimum and with the appearance of *Cardium edule*, it marks the beginning of the Neo-Caspian transgression. Evidence of Holocene coastlines above and below the present level of the Caspian indicates a sequence of fluctuations of sea level subsequent to the Würm-Wisconsin terraces that mark the higher stages of the Caspian Sea in the Pleistocene. The present coast shows many features (wide beaches, accreting dunes, extended streams) correlative with the lowering of the Caspian Sea that has taken place in the past 50 years.

ECKART EHLERS

REFERENCES

Andriesse, J. P., 1960, The soils of Mazanderan in northern Iran and their suitability for paddy-rice irrigation, *Journal of Soil Science* **11**:227–245.

Fedorov, P. V., 1957, *Stratigraphy of Quaternary Deposits and the Development of the Caspian Sea*, Akad. Nauk SSSR, Trudy Geol. Inst. 10, Moscow (in Russian).

Fedorov, P. V., and L. A. Skiba, 1960, The sea-level fluctuations of the Caspian and the Black Sea during the Holocene, *Izu Akad. Nauk SSSR, Seriya geogr.* **4**:24–34 (in Russian).

Plate 67-1. Section of the eastern fringe of the Sefid River delta, near Rudsar (scale 1:20,000). The picture shows a sequence of 2, 4, and 6 m beach lines, separating the lowland proper from the Caspian Sea, the level of which lies at 28 m below sea level (photo by E. Ehlers).

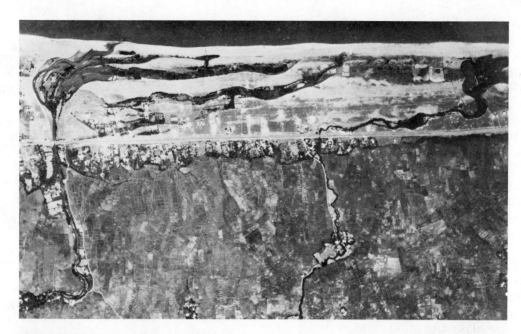

Plate 67-2: A very typical portion of the central part of the Caspian lowland, near Shahsavar (scale 1:20,000). While the higher sections of the rather limited beach line are covered with houses and a highway, the different levels of the beach lines are separated from each other by ancient and recent courses of brooks and riverines. The lowland itself is characterized by intensive rice cultivation (photo by E. Ehlers).

68. TURKEY AND CYPRUS

The coastline of Turkey is 8333 km long. Although shorter in direct distance, the Aegean coastline (3484 km) is longer in comparison with the Black Sea coastline (1701 km) and even the Mediterranean coastline (1707 km) (İnandik 1959). The contradictions of shore types shown in Figures 68-1 to 68-4 are a direct result of the major structural lineaments and geological evolution of the Anatolian peninsula. Thus the coastline of the Black Sea runs directly parallel to the high North Anatolian folded mountain range (Kuzey Anadolu Dağlari), and there are almost no coastal indentations or islands. Three great exceptions are the large prograding deltas of the Kizilirmak and Yesilirmak rivers (Erol 1983) and the Sinop peninsula, which is a Plio-Quaternary extension northward from the mainland. Therefore the Black Sea shore is a highland coast with elevated terrace plains of Plio-Quaternary age. Plateaus are formed only to the east and west of the Bosporus. The continental shelf is extremely narrow, with a greater width at the Sinop peninsula (structural) and at the deltas of the Kizilirmak and Yesilirmak rivers, which protrude into the sea.

Structurally the coastline of the Mediterranean Sea seems very similar to that of the Black Sea. It runs parallel to the Taurus folded mountain chain, and is also a highland coast, partly with elevated terrace plains, but no islands. There are, however, great exceptions dependent upon the general trend of the Taurus Mountains. A great gulf is formed at Antalya in the west, to the north of which is a series of high plateau-like steps of travertine terraces, and in the east the Çukurova delta plain formed by the Seyhan and Ceyhan rivers, which flow from the north forming a large delta–flood plain with significant beach accretion

ridge features (Evans 1971). The northeastern corner of the Mediterranean Sea is strongly structurally controlled, including the plains of the Çukurova and the graben-like Gulf of Iskenderun.

The Aegean coastline, conversely, runs across the structural lines of the Anatolian massif. East-west extending horst and graben systems dominate. Dependent on the rivers flowing into these grabens, broad deltaic plains, such as the Büyük Menderes plain, are prograding and aggrading westward into the Aegean Sea. On the other hand, graben-like structures such as the Gökova Gulf to the south receive very little sediment infill because they lack a major drainage system in the hinterland (Kayan 1975).

The coastlines of the Marmara Sea are of a transitional type from those of the Aegean and Black Sea. The greater Anatolian fault, which runs along the northern part of the Anatolian massif, extends along the axis of the very deep Sea of Marmara (greater than 1300 m). Thus, east-west extending coastlines of the Sea of Marmara are longitudinal to the structural lines, while the north-south coastlines cut across structural lines by means of faults or erosional valleys, as in the Dardanelles and the Bosporus. Flemming (1978) well describes the latest thinking on the extremely complex plate tectonics or collision of continental blocks in the Aegean Sea, which have an extreme effect on the shores of the west coast of the Anatolian peninsula and the offshore islands.

THE BLACK SEA COASTLINE

The eastern coastline of the Black Sea is morphologically dominated by the nearby high

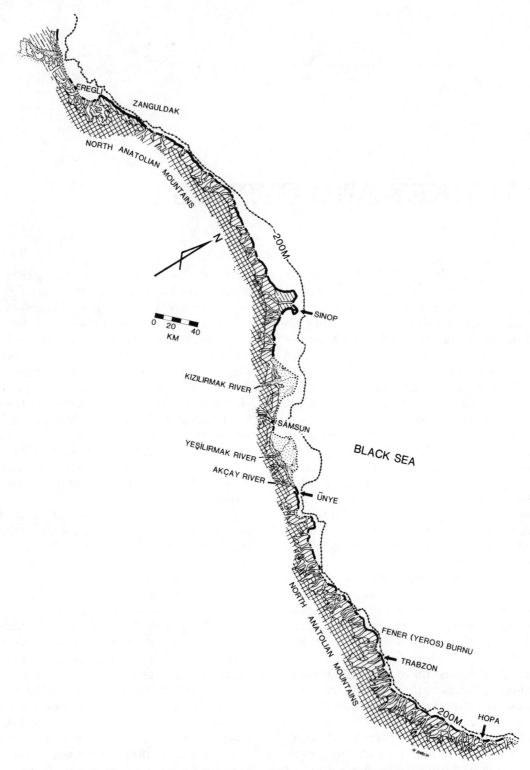

Figure 68-1. Geomorphic and geological features of the Black Sea (Kara deniz) coast, showing the narrow continental shelf of the Anatolian massif. See legend on Figure 68-2.

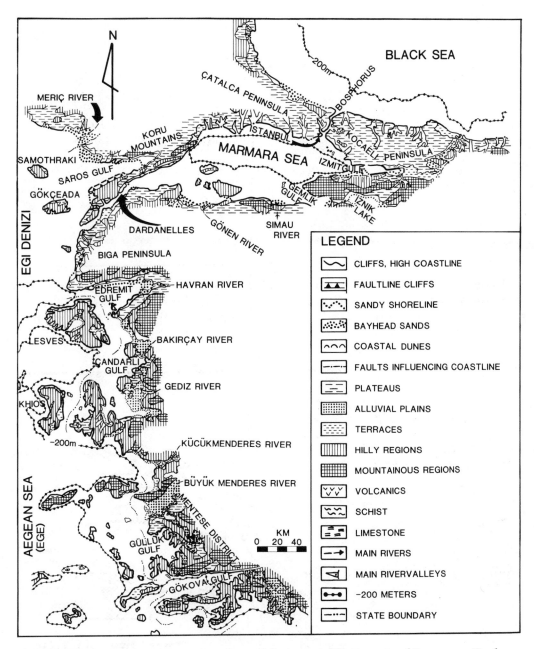

Figure 68-2. Geomorphic and geological features of the coasts of European Turkey and the Aegean Sea (Ege deniz), showing a highly complex tectonically controlled east-west horst and graben structure, in addition to the Sea of Marmara as it relates to the greater Anatolian fault. A submarine contour shows the relationship of the Anatolian massif to the highly variable widths of the continental shelf.

mountains consisting of Mesozoic-Tertiary igneous-sedimentary formations. Sometimes the mountains lie directly along the coast. Thus the coastline includes a series of cliffs or rocky promontories that alternate with bay-head beaches, mainly shingled (Buachidze 1974). The mountainous coast includes high terraces with a fluvial cover at 60–70 m and erosional-depositional surfaces up to 200–250 m of early Pleistocene–late Pliocene age. Middle and upper Pleistocene terraces are well observed at 5, 10–15, and 20–40 m (Erol 1952; Löffer 1970). Heavy mineral concentrations are a common component of the beaches and inner shelf (Evans 1971).

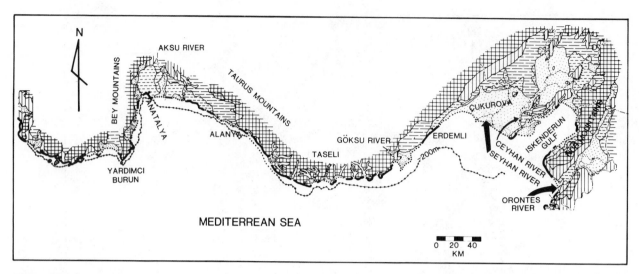

Figure 68-3. A geologic and geomorphologic map of the Mediterranean (Ak deniz) coast of the Anatolian massif from Antalya in the west to the Gulf of Iskenderun in the province of Hatay in the northeastern Mediterranean. The narrow continental shelf is shown as related to the deeper Mediterranean offshore waters. See legend on Figure 68-2.

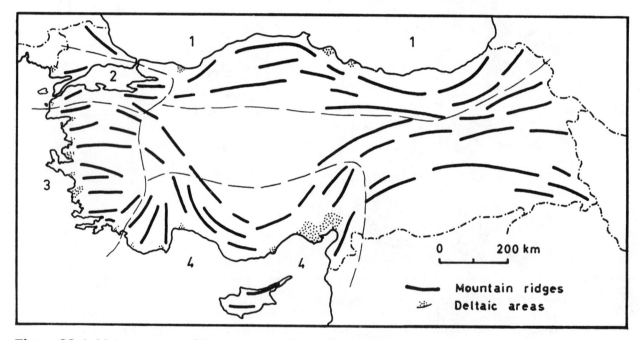

Figure 68-4. Major structural lineaments as they affect the Anatolian coast.

The Middle Black Sea coastline is dominated by the large deltas of Turkey's two largest rivers, the Yeşilirmak and the Kizilirmak. These large deltas cause a widening of the continental shelf to 25–50 km, with corresponding submarine valleys (Erinç 1958; Buachidze 1974; Inandik 1959; Akkan 1970). The deltas (Plate 68-1) are symmetrical, with lagoon, marsh, and barrier features, although the submerged extensions

have an asymmetric easterly trend, probably caused by the dominant easterly surface currents (Akkan 1970).

The coastline westward to the Sinop peninsula is extremely steep with cliffs and the continuation of a fairly wide continental shelf. The Sinop peninsula itself is attached to the North Anatolian Mountains and consists of Upper Pliocene and early Pleistocene sediments surrounded by fairly

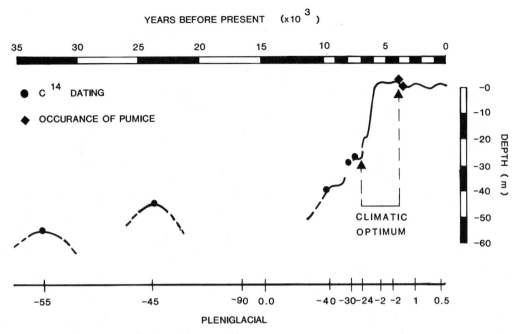

Figure 68-5. A eustatic (with possible local relative elements) Holocene sea-level curve formed from data along the shorelines of the Anatolian massif.

high cliffs. Limited coastal areas include Uzunlarian and Karangat fossils of late Pleistocene age (Erinç and Inandik 1955; Akkan 1975).

The western shoreline of the Black Sea is also bordered by the high North Anatolian Mountains. However, it consists of Paleozoic to Tertiary sediments associated with volcanics. High cliffs with small bay-head shingle beaches dominate this shore (Plate 68-2) (Inandik 1959). To the west, step-like foothills and parts of early Pleistocene plateaus occur. The Sakarya delta is formed in a narrow (3–5 km) but almost 40–50 km long coast-parallel delta. Alluvial material is redistributed by the easterly surface currents and westerly subsurface (20–30 m) deeper countercurrents (Norman 1977). The curious form and age of development of the Sakarya delta is currently a subject of major discussion (Inandik 1963; Russell 1954; Pfannenstiel 1944).

The Black Sea coastline to the east and west of the Bosporus is dominated by the edge of a high plateau (Plate 68-3). Bay-head beaches alternate with cliff promontories and volcanic rocky headlands. The coastal zone is dominated by wide sandy beaches and extensive dune fields, which become extremely high to the west, beyond which the Istranca mountain chain forms a cliff coast. Cliffs are also developed along the edge of the 150–250 m Pliocene plateau (Kurter 1964).

The coastlines of the Sea of Marmara are complex. The north shoreline is bordered by a Neogene plateau with elevations varying from 200–250 m in the north to 100–150 m in the south. Deltas of rivers entering the sea form coastal spits and lagoons. The Sea of Marmara is extremely deep and is part of the greater Anatolian fault system. Its entire shore is structurally controlled with a series of small gulfs or embayments and islands. High cliff-like coastal zones dominate, but small deltas are common (Ardel and Kurter 1957). The straits (the Dardanelles) that connect the Sea of Marmara to the Aegean Sea were originally early Quaternary river valleys established along fault lines. They have been repeatedly invaded by the sea during the Quaternary interglacials. Thus, with their fluvial and marine terraces, the straits and the tributaries such as the Kara-Menderes valley in the vicinity of ancient Troy originated as incised meandering ancient valleys (Darkot 1938a; Erinç 1958; Gunnerson and Özturgut 1974; Erol and Nuttall 1973; Erol 1976, 1983; Kraft et al. 1980; Stanley and Blanpied 1980).

THE AEGEAN COASTLINE

The coastline of the Aegean Sea includes great indentations, structurally controlled with many graben-like features. It is a shore of alternating rocky cliff coasts and deltaic lowland beaches and muddy areas. The submergence of the shore during the Holocene epoch, coupled with progradation of river deltas such as the Gediz at Izmir, the Havran at Edremit, the Küçük Menderes at ancient Ephesus (Efes), and the widely known Büyük Menderes (formerly a major marine embayment with Classical-Hellenistic-Roman cities such as Priene, Miletus, and Heraclea) has now been filled in by the prograding alluvium (Plate 68-4) (Russell 1954; Kraft et al 1977). These may be contrasted with the Gökova Gulf (Kayan 1975) to the south, which has no major drainage system to provide sediment. However, the shelf contours in the offshore Aegean surrounding the promontories and islands suggest an extremely complex tectonic history, which may have included earlier Quaternary or pre-Quaternary (presently submerged) plateaus or sediment-filled valleys. Another interesting feature of the Aegean shoreline is the Saros Gulf to the north of Gelibolu peninsula (Gallipoli). A long linear southern coastline of the Saros graben may be a form of extension of the greater Anatolian fault, which extends eastward to the Sea of Marmara and across northern Anatolia. The northernmost coastline of the Aegean coast is dominated by the Meriç River delta and the plateau surface that extends east of Istanbul to the North Anatolian Mountains.

Overall, the Aegean Sea shore is extremely complex, structurally controlled by horst-graben features or long linear faults such as cliffs west of Edremit. The cliff-type shores to the north are dominated by volcanics and Neogene sediments. Farther to the south, in the extreme southwest corner of Anatolia (Plate 68-5), the cliff-type shore is dominated by the folded Paleozoic-Mesozoic formations of the western Taurus Mountains, with fault lines leading to northwest-southeast or southwest-northeast extending coastal indentations such as the Güllük Gulf. The embayments that are not dominated by river progradation and aggradation are formed of cliffs with alternating bay-head beaches or small deltas. Surfaces and terraces may be identified at 150–200, 90–110, 30–40, and 16–18 m (Darkot 1938b; Erinç 1955; Bilitza 1973; Eisma 1978; Kraft et al 1980, Göney 1973; Kayan 1975).

THE MEDITERRANEAN COASTLINE

The coastline of Mediterranean Turkey is similar to that of the Black Sea in that it is long-itudinally parallel to the Taurus Mountains, consisting of Paleozoic to Tertiary folded formations. The only major exceptions are north-south structural features in the embayment at Antalya, headed by high cliffs and plateaus of travertine, and the northeastern embayment, dominated by the Çukurova deltaic plain and the tectonically downwarped Gulf of Iskenderun. From Antalya east to Alanya there is a generally lower sandy coastline, with the exception of the travertine cliffs at Antalya. Fluviomarine terraces extend along these coastal lowlands. Travertine terraces occur in three steps at 300–260, 190–220, and 60–70 m, all of Pleistocene age (Planhol 1956; Vaumas 1968). Denudation or fluvial terraces occur in this area at 140–120, 100–82, 72–60, 58–72, 24, 18, 10, 6, and 2 m above sea level (Ardos 1969). The area east of Antalya toward Alanya is dominated by extensive beach rock formations (Bener 1974), with extensive coast-parallel dunes extending inland.

The middle Mediterranean coastline narrows east of Alanya, where the Taurus Mountains rise sharply and steeply out of the sea (Plate 68-6). This is an area of extremely high cliff-type coasts formed mainly of Mesozoic limestones and Paleozoic schists. Scattered sandy beaches occur at the mouths of rivers, but the shoreline is dominated by cobble-boulder beaches at the foot of the cliffs. The Göksu delta is a small, lobed delta plain at the eastern end of the cliffs. A southwesterly extending spit indicates northeast-southwest coastal currents (Bener 1967). There are two major physiographic features along the eastern end of the Turkish coast of the Mediterranean (Plate 68-7). The first is the large Çukurova plain, which is an aggradational-progradational plain of the two large rivers, the Seyhan to the west and the Ceyhan to the east. Southeasterly waves have formed broad beach accretion plains here. Much of the plain was formerly swampy or marsh but is now a large well-drained agricultural area. Evans (1971) described three sets of Holocene and pre-Holocene beach-dune-lagoon generations in the delta system of the Seyhan River. The Ceyhan River has frequently altered its course from west to east in a fan-like fashion, presently exiting into the northwesterly flank of the Gulf of Iskenderun. The development of the delta plain is discussed by Erinç (1953) and Göney (1976). A series of terraces occur along the northern side of the Holocene plain at 10-15, 20-35, 50-60 m (Erinç 1953; Vaumas 1968; Göney 1976). The second major physiographic unit lies to the southeast of the Çukurova plain. It is the rectangular-shaped, structurally controlled Gulf of Iskenderun between the Misis Mountains to the north and the Nur Mountains to the south. There are small beaches to the northeast and large ejection cones extending into the gulf along the foot of the Nur Mountains. At the very southern end of the coast of Turkey lies the Orontes River, which flows across the broad inland Amik agricultural plain and lake through a narrow defile at Antakya (Antioch) to the delta. At the delta lies the important Hellenistic-Roman harbor of Seleucia ad Orontes. The harbor works are still extant and above present sea level. A series of marine terraces occurs in the area at 2, 7, 15–20, 35–50, 58–75, 83–100, and 110–140 m. Solutional notches at 2.5, 1.4, and 0.5 m at Cevlik, just to the north of the Orontes delta, are also clear indicators of Holocene sea-level changes (Plate 68-8) (Erol 1969).

It is convenient here to consider the outlying island of Cyprus*, which has a coastline about 450 km long, partly steep and cliffed, partly beach-fringed. There are cliffs of chalk and limestone, especially on the north coast, and of volcanic rocks in the northwest. Segments of low coastal plain occur, particularly on the south coast, where there are brackish lagoons near Limassol and Larnaca. White sandy beaches extend from Famagusta around the southern shores of the long Karpas Peninsula to the east, and there are sandy coves between cliffed and rocky sectors on the north coast. The island shows evidence of differential uplift, with marine terraces at various levels.

OĞUZ EROL

REFERENCES

Akkan, E., 1970, Bafra Burnu Delice kavsagi arasinda Kizilirmak vadisinin jeomorfolojisi (Geomorphology of the Kizilirmak valley between the junction of Delice tributary and Cape Bafra), *Dil ve Tarih Coğrafya Fakultesi Yay* **191**:158 (in Turkish).

Akkan, E., 1975, Sinop yarimadasinin jeomorfolojisi (Geomorphology of the Sinop peninsula), *Dil ve Tarih Coğrafya Fakultesi Yay* **261**:107 (in Turkish).

Ardel, A., and A. Kurter, 1957, Marmaranin denizalti reliefi (Submarine relief of Marmara), *Istanbul Univ. Coğrafya Enst. Dergisi* **8**:83–90 (in Turkish).

Ardos, M., 1969, Problemes geomorphologiques du ver-

sant sud du Taurus Central, Turquie Meridionale, *Méditerranée*, **3**:232–256.

Bener, M., 1967, Göksu Deltasi (The delta of Göksu), *İstanbul Univ Cografya Enst. Dergisi* **16**:86–100 (in Turkish).

Bener, M., 1974, Antalya-Gazipaşa Kiyi Kesiminde yali-taşi oluşumu (Beachrock formations between Antalya and Gazipasa), *Istanbul Univ. Coğrafya Enst. Yay* **75**:95 (in Turkish).

Bilitza, U. V., 1973, *Die agaische Küste Anatoliens. Eine küstenmorphologische Studie unter Berüksichtigung des Problems der eustatischen Terrasen, Dissertation Abteilung Geowissenschaften, Univ. Bochum.*

Buachidze, I. M., 1974, Black Sea shelf and littoral zone, in *The Black Sea*, E. T. Degens and E. A. Ross, (eds.), American Association Petroleum Geologists, pp. 308–316.

Darkot, B., 1938a, Sur l'origine et l'evolution morphologiques des estuaries de la mer Egee, *Istanbul Univ Geog. Inst. Pub.* **4**:93–95.

Darkot, B., 1938b, L'Origine des Détroits, *Istanbul Univ Geog. Inst. Pub.* **4**:84–89.

Eisma, D., 1978, Stream deposition and erosion by the eastern shore of the Aegean, in *Environmental History of the Near and Middle East*, W. C. Brice, ed., Academic Press, New York, pp. 67–79.

Erinç, S., 1953, Çukurovanin aluvial morfolojisi hakkinda (On the alluvial morphology of Cukurova), *Istanbul Univ Coğrafya Enst. Dergisi* **3–4**:149–159 (in Turkish).

Erinç, S., 1955, Gediz ve Küçük Menderes deltalarinin moffolojisi (Geomorphology of the Gediz and Küçük Menderes deltas), *Cografya Meslek Haftasi, Tebligler ve Konferanslar* **9**:33–66 (in Turkish).

Erinç, S., 1958, Karadenizin denizalti morfolojisi (Submarine geomorphology of the Black Sea), *Istanbul Univ Coğrafya Enst. Dergisi* **9**:103–114 (in Turkish).

Erinç, S., and H. İnandik, 1955, Les dépots Pleistocene observés sur la cote Nord de la Turquie, *Istanbul Univ Geog. Inst. Rev* **2**:85–92.

Erol, O., 1952, A note on the terraces of Trabzon, NE of Turkey. *Dil ve Tarih Coğrafya Fakültesi Dergisi* **10**:125–135 (in Turkish with English summary).

Erol, O., 1969, Anadolu Kiyilarinin Holosendeki degismeleri hakkinda gözlemler (Observations on Anatolian coastline changes during the Holocene), *Coğrafya Araştirmalari Dergisi* **2**:89–102.

Erol, O., 1976, Quaternary shoreline changes on the Anatolian coasts of the Aegean Sea and related problems (Changement des lignes de rivage quaternaire sur la côte anatolienne de la mer Egée et problemes lies), *Soc. Géol. France Bull.* **18**(2):459–468.

Erol, O., 1983, Historical changes on the coastline of Turkey, in *Coastal Problems in the Mediterranean Sea*, E. C. F. Bird and P. Fabbri, eds., International Geographical Union, Commission on the Coastal Environment, Bologna, pp. 95–108.

Erol, O., and C. P. Nuttall, 1973, Çanakkale yöresinin

*Paragraph inserted by editors.

bazi denizel Kuaterner depolari (Some marine Quaternary deposits in the Dardanelles area), *Coğrafya Arastirmalari Dergisi* **5–6:**27-91.

Evans, G., 1971, The recent sedimentation of Turkey and the adjacent Mediterranean and Black Seas: A review in *Geology and History of Turkey*, A. S. Campbell, ed., pp. 385-406. International Publications Service, New York.

Flemming, N., 1978, Holocene eustatic changes and coastal tectonics in the northeast Mediterranean: implications for models of crustal consumption, *Royal Soc. London Philos. Trans., A, Math. Phys. Sci.* **289:**405-458.

Göney, S., 1973, Büyük Menderes deltasi (The delta of Büyük Menderes), *İstanbul Uniu Coğrafya Enst. Dergisi* **18–19:**339-354 (in Turkish).

Göney, S., 1976, Adana ovalari (The plains of Adana), *Istanbul Uniu Coğrafya Enst. Yay.* **88:**179 (in Turkish).

Gunnerson, C. G., and E. Özturgut, 1974, The Bosphorus in *The Black Sea*, E. T. Degens, and D. A. Ross, eds., American Association of Petroleum Geologists, pp. 99-114.

İnandik, H., 1959, Etude morphologique de la region cotiere d'Ereğli Akcakoca, Anatolie N., *Instanbul Uniu Geog. Inst. Rev.* **5:**107-122.

İnandik, H., 1963, Sakarya deltasi, *Istanbul Uniu Coğrafya Enst. Dergisi* **13:**83-98 (in Turkish).

Kayan, I., 1975, Didim platosunun Kuaterner Jeomorfolojisi ve gençtektonik hareketler (Quaternary geomorphology and neotectonic movements in the Didim Plateau, southwestern Turkey), *Tubitak Bilim Kongresi* **5:**79-96 (in Turkish).

Kraft, J. C., S. E. Aschenbrenner, and G. Rapp, Jr., 1977, Paleogeographic reconstructions of coastal aegean archaeological sites, *Science* **195:**941-947.

Kraft, J. C., Kayan, I., and Erol, O., 1980, Geomorphic reconstructions in the environs of Ancient Troy, *Science* **209:**776-782.

Kurter, A., 1964, Limanköy platosu ve İğneada Neojen havzasinin morfolojisi (Geomorphology of the Limankoy plateau and the Neogene basin of Igneada), *Istanbul Uniu Coğrafya Enst. Dergisi* **14:**132-148 (in Turkish).

Löffer, E., 1970, Untersuchungen zum eiszeitlichen Formenschatz in den Gebirgen Nordast anatoliens, *Heidelberger Geogr. Arb.,* **27:**162.

Norman, T., 1977, Coastal currents of western Black Sea using Landsat (Erts) imagery, *Bull. of M.T.A.* **20:**55-62. The Mining and Exploration Institute of Turkey.

Pfannenstiel, M., 1944, Die diluvialen Entwicklungsstadien und die Urgeschichte der Dardanellen, Marmameer und Bosporus, *Geol. Rundschau* **34**(7-8): 342-434.

Planhol, X. de, 1956, Contribution a l'Etude Geomorphologique du Taurus occidental et de ses plaines bordieres, *Revue Géographie Alpine.* **44**(4):1-86.

Russell, R. J., 1954, Alluvial morphology of Anatolian rivers, *Assoc. Ann. Amer. Geog.* **44:**363-391.

Stanley, D. J., and C. Blanpied, 1980, Late Quaternary water exchange between the eastern Mediterranean and the Black Sea, *Nature* **285:**537-541.

Vaumas, E. de, 1968, Phenomenes karstiques en Méditerranee Orientale, *Centre Rech. Doc. Cartog. Géog. Paris Mem. et Doc. 1967* **4:**193-281.

Plate 68-1. The deltas of the Kizilimirak and Yesilirimak rivers, north-central Black Sea shore (Landsat photo by NASA).

Plate 68-2. Coastline of north-central Black Sea coast west of Samsun (photo by J. C. Kraft).

Plate 68-3. The plateau surface and shore of Black Sea (north), Bosporus straits (center), and Sea of Marmara (south) (Landsat photo by NASA).

Plate 68-5. The coast of southwestern Anatolia — upper center: river plain filling former graben embayment of the Meander River (Büyük Menderes) (Landsat photo by NASA).

Plate 68-4. Alluvium infill of marine embayment at the Büyük Menderes River (Meander River). View from river of Miletus, foreground to ridge in background, with ancient city of Priene (2000 years old). Entire plain was marine (photo by J. C. Kraft).

Plate 68-6. Coastline of south-central Mediterranean coast along Taurus Mountains (photo by J. C. Kraft).

Plate 68-7. Southeast coast of Turkey showing Cukurova flood plain (Ceyhan River) (to south), Taurus Mountains (to west), and tectonic Gulf of Iskenderun (center) (Landsat photo by NASA).

Plate 68-8. Coastline north of Orontes (Asi) River delta in southeast Turkey showing recent emerged wave-cut notch (photo by J. C. Kraft).

69. SYRIA AND LEBANON

The coastline of Syria is about 170 km long and that of Lebanon about 230 km. The outlines are relatively simple, with only a few tiny islands (Fig. 69-1). Tide ranges are small, rarely exceeding 40 cm. Westerly and especially southwest winds are dominant, particularly in Lebanon; as the fetch is large, the coast receives strong wave action from this direction. In summer, diurnal winds, stronger by day, produce short steep waves unfavorable for swimming. In winter, storms are sometimes severe (in January 1968, with wind speeds of almost 150 km/hr, waves 7 m high were seen in the Beirut area). In April and May, however, and particularly in autumn, winds are weak and the sea calm. Longshore drifting is generally to the north, and sometimes relatively rapid. Sea salinity is high (over 39‰) and the water fairly warm, even in winter, with temperatures ranging from 17.1° C in March to 28.3° C in August at Beirut (Oren and Engel 1965; Sanlaville 1977).

The straight coastline is related to structure: the coast runs parallel to the Jabal Alaouite anticline (north-south) in Syria, and to the Lebanese Mountains (north-northeast–south-southwest), the western slopes of which fall more or less steeply to the coast. Transverse faults, often east-west, are responsible for the main features of the coastline (Lattaquié inlet, Jounié bay, Beirut peninsula). In spite of the proximity of mountains (the culminating peak, Qornet es Saouda, 3083 m, is only 30 km inland), the coast is generally low, though often rocky (Dubertret 1966).

The presence of limestones or marly limestones (mainly Cenomanian-Turonian, but also some Eocene-Miocene) dipping seaward explains the great extent of rocky coasts, but these are also developed on unconsolidated rocks (Bassit) or volcanic formations (Banyas region). The coast is also frequently cut into Pleistocene marine or dune sandstone here called *ramleh* (dune calcarenite), which has been used since ancient times for building stone, so that old coastal quarries are frequent.

In the carbonate rocks—limestones or calcareous cemented sandstones—the generally low cliffs are fronted by shore platforms a little below high tide level, irregular in outline with almost flat surfaces. Built up on their seaward margins by algae and other organisms, these platforms, termed *trottoirs*, are typical of this region, and occur on about two-thirds of the coastline (Plate 69-1). Behind them, for a distance of some tens of meters, the rock is bare and marked by deep lapies (Sanlaville 1977).

Depositional features occur only on one-third of the coastline, and except in the Akkar and the south of Lebanon, are very intermittent, restricted to small bays or inlets. Sometimes there are pebbly shores at the mouths of rivers or wadis, but more often quartzose or biogenic sands (Emery and George 1963; El Kareh 1970). It is common, particularly in Lebanon, to find slabs of beachrock outcropping at the lower edge of the beach. Because of westerly swell, beachrock, *trottoirs*, and severe pollution, this coast is not attractive for swimming, despite the climatic conditions.

Almost all the coastline is receding, even in embayments, because of the meager supply of sand or gravel. Despite the erosional vigor of wadis descending from the mountains, there are only minor deltas, weakly convex in outline. In the lee of islands are sandy tombolos, which have attached the peninsulas of Tripoli (Pleistocene) and Tyre (Holocene, probably historical). Dunes are

501

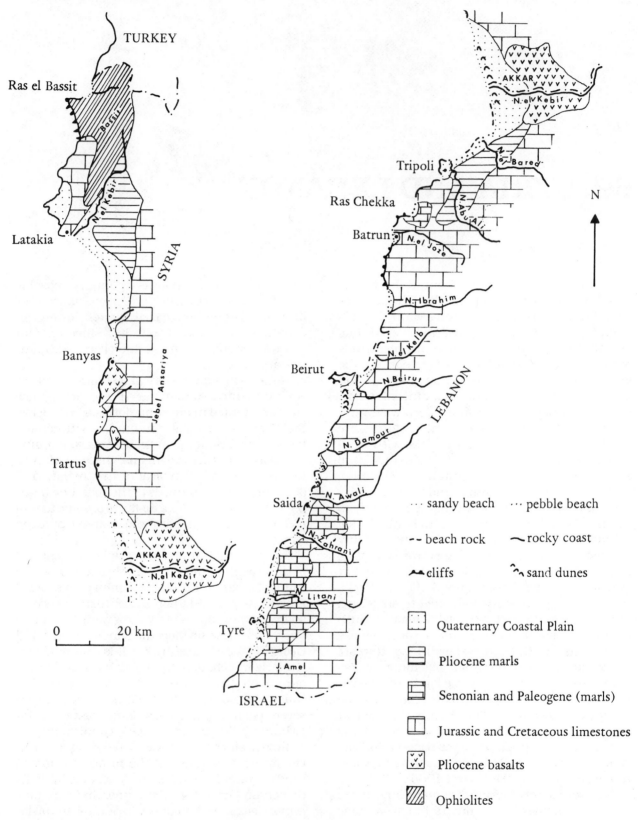

Figure 69-1. Map of the coasts of Syria and Lebanon.

minor and generally fixed by vegetation. They occur in the Syrian Akkar and in the small bays between Beirut and Saida, as well as near Tyre, where they have overrun the site of the Roman hippodrome.

Beaches and emerged platforms indicate recent oscillations of sea level of more than 2 m in the Holocene, up to the historical period. Syria and Lebanon also show fine examples of little deformed, but strongly uplifted, Pleistocene coastlines up to 300 m above present sea level (Sanlaville 1977).

Cut into ophiolites, the Bassit coast is wild and picturesque. High rainfall allows oak and pine forests to extend down to the coast. The Jabal Akra majestically dominates the splendid bay of Bassit with its sandy shores, while an outcrop of Miocene limestone forms the narrow peninsula of Bassit (Plate 69-2), which is followed by a cliffed coast in weak rocks. Beyond that, Mesozoic limestones or Quaternary calcarenites form a series of capes and inlets bordered by corrosion platforms. The little bay of Ramlet el Beida and the Ras Ibn Hani peninsula have sheltered ancient ports (Ugarit), and the town of Lattaquié is built on a raised peninsula that shows remains of Pleistocene coastlines (Syrian Ministry of Industry 1967).

South of Lattaquié the great plain of Jableh begins, limited northward by an important structural feature, the contact of the Arabian and Anatolian plates, which has determined the northern valley of Nahr el Kébir. Except at its sandy extremities, the plain of Jableh has a rocky coast, with platforms developed in Quaternary sandstones of penultimate interglacial age. Between Banyas and Tartous the coastline becomes more irregular, with some cliffs cut in Pliocene volcanic rocks. The tiny island of Rouad, the only inhabited island on the Levant coast, consists of Pleistocene calcarenites much used by early man.

The great bay of Akkar, which separates Syria and Lebanon, corresponds with a trough separating the Jabal Alaouite from the mountains of Lebanon. Developed in soft rocks (dune sands or fluviatile fans, often of historical origin), the coastline is a long, gently curved sandy beach, the rapid recession of which is indicated by active cliffs up to 4 m high and outcrops of beachrock.

The Nahr el Bared and the Nahr Abou Ali, rivers draining from the highest parts of the Lebanese mountains, have each built convex gravelly deltas, which the sea is now trimming back. That of the

Nahr Abou Ali has been partly derived from a sandy tombolo that linked islands of Tyrrhenian marine sandstone to the mainland in a large peninsula occupying the site of the town of Tripoli and its satellite of El Mina. Several kilometers offshore other rocky islets appear, almost denuded of vegetation because of the strong winds. In the Enfé region Cenomanian limestones form an irregular coastline bordered by a shore platform, then open to the plain of Chekka carved in Paleocene marls; pebbly beaches alternate with platform-fringed rocky coasts in Quaternary sandstones.

Ras Chekka presents the highest cliffs of the Syria-Lebanon coast, attaining 160 m, cut in Miocene limestones that lie discordantly on Paleocene marls. From there to Bahr Awali the mountains descend quite steeply to the sea, and the shore is rocky and eroded. The cliffs are low (up to 12 m), however, alternating with inlets backed by pebble beaches. Alongside the bay of Jounié the mountains come close to the coast because of a strong flexure (Plate 69-3).

On either side of the Beirut peninsula, developed on marly Cretaceous limestones, are large sandy beaches, backed southward by large Pleistocene or Holocene dunes on which the airport has been built. The best beaches are farther south, at Damour, Jiyeh, Rmeileh, and beyond the town of Saida. The coastal plain reappears, first narrow, then wider; sandy beaches are often accompanied by extensive outcrops of beachrock. The sandy tombolo of Tyre, of historical age, is surmounted by dunes much exploited by man. On the fringe of Jabal Amel, the final kilometers of the Lebanese coast are scarped and rocky.

PAUL SANLAVILLE

REFERENCES

Dubertret, L., 1966, Liban, Syrie et bordure des pays voisins. Tableau stratigraphique avec carte géologique au millionème, *Notes et Mémoires sur le Moyen-Orient* **8**:251–358.

Emery, K. O., and C. J. George, 1963, The shores of Lebanon, *Am. Univ. Beirut, Misc. Papers in Nat. Sci.* **1**:1–10.

El Kareh, G., 1970, *Some Sedimentological Aspects of St. George's Bay,* Ph.D. thesis, American University of Beirut.

Oren, O. H., and I. Engel, 1965, Etude hydrologique

sommaire du bassin levantin (Méditerranée orientale), *Cahiers Océan.* **17**(7):457–465.

Sanlaville, P., 1977, *Etude géomorphologique de la région littorale du Liban,* Université Libanese, Section des Etudes Géogr., I, Beirut.

Syrian Ministry of Industry, 1967, *The Geology of Syria, Explanatory Notes on the Geological Map of Syria, scale 1:500.000,* Department of Geological and Mineral Research, Ministry of Industry, Syrian Arab Republic, Damascus.

Plate 69-1. *Trottoirs* of Pleistocene calcareous cemented sandstones along the Syrian littoral, cut by lapies and deprived of vegetation (photo by P. Sanlaville).

Plate 69-3. Bay of Jounié, Lebanon. Note the sharp contact between the mountains and the sea, where the beach is composed of pebbles (photo by P. Sanlaville).

Plate 69-2. Calcareous rocky point at Ras el Bassit, northern Syria (photo by P. Sanlaville).

70. ISRAEL

The Israel Mediterranean coast forms the southeastern corner of the Levantine Basin, which itself forms the extreme eastern part of the sea (see the *Red Sea Coasts* entry for further details on the southern coast of Israel). The coastline is about 230 km long from the Lebanese border at Rosh Haniqra Ridge to Rafah at the Sinai border (Fig. 70-1). According to Neev et al. (1973, 1978) it is structurally controlled for the greater part of its length.

The coast has low relief with only two mountains reaching the shore: Mount Carmel in Haifa and the Rosh Haniqra Ridge, both of Cenomanian age. Elsewhere the foothills are separated from the sea by a coastal plain which is fairly wide in the south (up to 40 km) but narrows towards the north, reaching only a few hundred meters in the Carmel Plain. North of Haifa, in Haifa Bay, the coastal plain widens again.

The Zevulun Valley, between the Mount Carmel (Plate 70-1) and Akko (Acre) promontories, is responsible for the only pronounced bay along the relatively smooth and straight shoreline of Israel. North of Akko the shoreline is relatively smooth again (Plate 70-2).

Small bays, usually rocky, a few tens of meters in length, occur in the central and northern parts of the shore, mostly between Dor (Plate 70-3) and Atlit. Some of these bays were used as harbors in historical times (Raban 1980).

Active faulting is responsible for the shape and, to a certain extent, for the morphology of most of the coastline (Neev at al. 1973, 1978). This theory has been objected to by Arad et al. (1978). For most of its length the shoreline is characterized by a cliff composed of kurkar (carbonate-cemented quartz sandstone, red loams, and sands at dif-ferent stages of cementation, all of Pleistocene age). Kurkar ridges are found both on the coastal plain and in the shallow shelf exposed or covered underneath recent Nilotic sediments. These ridges mostly parallel the coastline.

About 13 ephemeral rivers (wadis) drain to the Mediterranean from the mountainous backbone of Israel. As most of the springs are exploited for urban and agricultural use, these wadis are dry much of the year, but they flood during heavy winter rains.

CLIMATE

The climate along the Israel Mediterranean coast is subtropical, with typically Mediterranean hot, humid summers and mild, rainy winters. Summer winds are gentle, but winter storm winds may reach speeds of 80 km/hr and more, creating a very stormy sea. Wind directions are mainly between southwest to northwest.

Average rainfall is 600 mm/yr north of Haifa, 500 mm/yr in the central parts, and about 350 mm/yr and less on the southern shores.

TIDES AND CURRENTS

Data from the Israel Ports Authority (1969) and Uziel (1968) show that the maximum seasonal tide is 80 cm (from −40 to +40 cm), but the amplitude of the daily tides is much smaller, never exceeding 30 cm.

Two main current systems affect the Israeli beaches: (1) the East Mediterranean anticlockwise current, which flows in the near offshore and farther off, distributing the Nile sediments in the

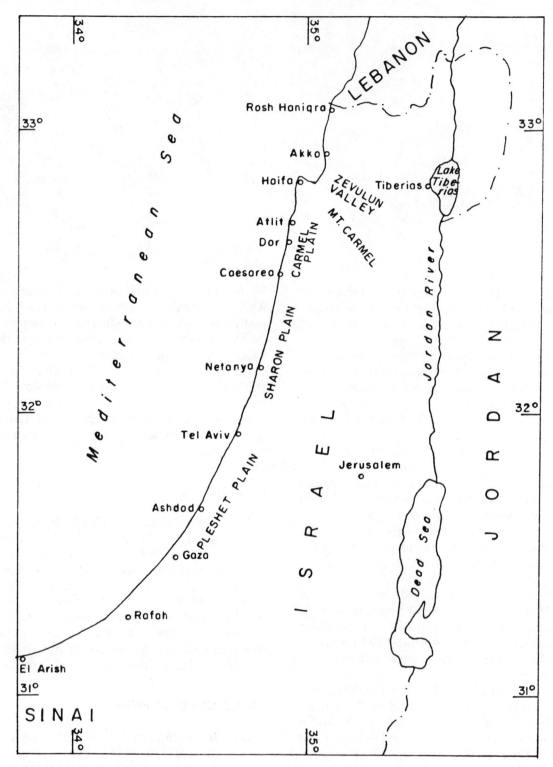

Figure 70-1. Location map.

southeastern part of the Levantine Basin, mostly in the waters 25 m or more deep (Nir, 1973); and (2) longshore currents, responsible for the longshore drift.

HISTORY

Remnants of human inhabitation along the Cana'an coastline date from as early as the Middle Bronze IIa (about 3800 years ago). Various sites represent most of the later historical periods: Cana'anite, Israelite (Philistines, Israelites, and Phoenicians), Persian, Hellenistic, Roman, Byzantine, Moslem, Crusaders, and Turks. This area had its heyday during the Hellenistic-Roman periods. Old land sites (tells) from all these historical periods are found all along the coastline. Many underwater historical remnants have also recently been discovered (Raban 1980).

SEDIMENTS

The Egyptian Nile Delta, the northern Sinai, and the Israeli beaches belong to a very large sedimentary cell, the Nile littoral cell. Its main sources of sediments have been the two Nile mouths of Rosetta and Damietta. Although most of the Nilotic sediments are very fine, the sand fraction is the main sediment forming the beaches.

These coastal sands are mostly composed of quartz grains, a small amount of carbonates (mostly shell fragments), and heavy mineral suites. As the Nile-derived sediment is very poor in carbonate (Nir 1973), it can be assumed that most of the calcium carbonate found in the Israeli beach sediment (Fig. 70-2) is from local sources, principally broken kurkar grains and bivalve shells.

The main longshore drift is from the northern Sinai toward the southern and central Israeli beaches. The Akko promontory, having a zeta-bay shape, stops most, if not all, of the northward sand transport. This barrier to sediment transport is also reflected in the mineralogy of the beach sands: south of Akko the main mineral is quartz, while north of Akko the sediments are mostly coarse-grained carbonates of local marine and terrestrial origin (Emery and Neev 1960; Nir 1973, 1981, 1982).

Figure 70-2 illustrates the variations in grain size, calcium carbonate, and main bivalve components for the beach sands from near Port Said at the northern end of the Suez Canal up to Rosh Haniqra. It shows mainly that there is a very slow

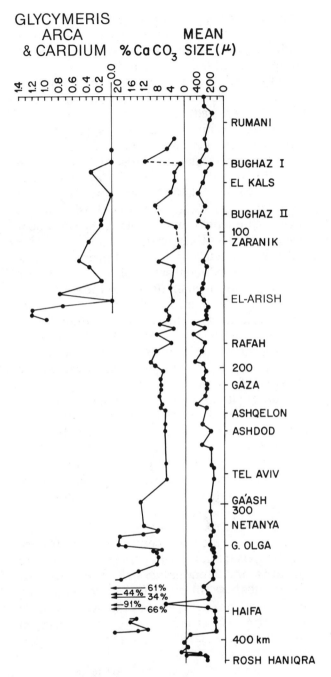

Figure 70-2. Mean sand size, calcium carbonate, and main bivalves along the northern Sinai and Israeli beaches.

decrease in grain size from the source, which is the beaches of the Nile Delta. The calcium carbonate content of the sands is small, with a few exceptions where local carbonate-rich material is introduced (some of the kurkar cliff beaches, the Mount Carmel beaches, and the beaches north of Akko).

Emery and Neev (1960) suggested two sectors for the movement of sand along the beaches: one offshore, with south-to-east direction and a long-shore drift with net northerly direction up to Tel Aviv; the other a southerly transport from Haifa to Tel Aviv. Goldsmith and Golik (1978) suggest three different sediment transport zones, based on theoretical and beach studies: (1) Rafah to Haifa, with the net northern transport decreasing from south to north because of the change in shoreline orientation; (2) Haifa Bay, which acts as a terminus for all Nilotic sediments bypassing the Carmel Head; and (3) Akko to Rosh Haniqra region, where net transport along the sand-poor beaches is essentially zero.

A few artificial barriers found near and south of Haifa have sediment accumulated on the north, showing that the main drift is to the south.

Sand dunes cover most of the northern Sinai "coastal plain," while in Israel their extent diminishes from Tel Aviv to the north. Most of the dune areas occur at river mouths, which provide openings through which the sands can penetrate the kurkar cliffs to the coastal plain.

Beachrock composed of cemented quartz sand with coarse shell fragments is typical of most of the northern Sinai and Israeli beaches (Plate 70-2).

Where beaches are rocky, mainly in the northern parts of the shore, abraded platforms have formed, usually at mean sea level (Plate 70-4 and 70-5).

Underwater rocky exposures are found along most of the northern and central beaches of Israel. These exposures are mostly parallel with the shore and are found in one or two strips a few hundred meters offshore. In many cases they show the outlines of abraded kurkar ridges, wadis, and so forth. The small islets found off the northern shores are associated with these rocky underwater outcrops.

Because of the action of marine and atmospheric agents, the coastal kurkar cliffs are very steep (Plate 70-6) and unstable, retreating landward at a rate of at least 3–4 cm/yr for the last 6000 years (Nir 1973).

Nir (1982) divides the Israeli beaches into five segments, mostly according to their morphological features: (1-2) The Pleshet and Sharon beaches are characterized by a low cliff in the south, which reaches up to 50 m in the north. The beaches of Pleshet are wider than those of the Sharon, which almost disappear during winter storms. The coastline is rather smooth and straight and has no irregularities. (3) In the Carmel (Plate 70-1) the shores are mostly rocky, indented between the kurkar rocks, creating numerous small bays. The beaches here, with a few exceptions, are rocky and narrow. (4) The Haifa Bay beaches are sandy, broad, and smooth, with some dune areas at their eastern side. The coastline itself forms a large smooth arc from Akko to Haifa, and is parallel with an older Pleistocene-age coastline found a few kilometers to the east. (5) The northern beaches from Akko to Rosh Haniqra are isolated from the Nilotic sediments and are formed from local sources only. The shores are sandy and rocky (mostly exposed beachrock—Plate 70-7 and 70-8). In Rosh Haniqra white Cenomanian chalks form quite high cliffs.

Beaches become wider at river mouths, where the kurkar ridge was either not formed or has been removed by the river.

Human activities along the beaches have had mostly destructive results either through quarrying huge amounts of sand ("zifzif") or constructing groins, harbors, and detached breakwaters (Plate 70-9), which accumulated sands, thus removing them from the drifting system. Although these activities have mostly ceased, they have caused beach erosion.

Although the Israeli beaches have received sediments mostly from the Nile and the abraded kurkar cliffs, there is no widening of the beaches, and the cliffs are retreating. The main reasons for this pattern are the sand deficit due to human activities, the dispersal of the newly arriving sands from the Nile Delta and the kurkar over the entire shelf, and the continuing rise in sea level during the last century (Emery and Kuhn 1981).

YAACOV NIR

REFERENCES

Arad, A., Ecker, A., and Olshina, A., 1978, The young (Post Lower Pliocene) geological history of the Caesarea structure: a Discussion, *Isr. Jour. Earth Sci.* **27:**142–146.

Emery, K. O. and D. Neev, 1960, *Mediterranean Beaches of Israel,* Geol. Survey of Israel Bull. 26.

Emery, K. O. and G. G. Kuhn, 1981, *Classification of Seacliffs,* Woods Hole Oceaneographic Inst. Contrib. 4897.

Goldsmith, V. and A. Golik, 1978, *The Israeli Wave Climate and Longshore Sediment Transport Model,* Israel Ocean. and Limnol. Res. Report 78/1.

Israel Ports Authority, 1969, *Annual Report, Ocean-*

ographic Observations, Coastal Study Division, Ashdod.

Neev, D., N. Bakler, S. Moshkovitz, A. Kaufman, and M. Magaritz, 1973, Recent faulting along the Mediterranean Coast of Israel, *Nature* **245:**254–256.

Neev, D., E. Schahnai, J. K. Hall, N. Bakler, and Z. Ben-Avraham, 1978, The young (Post Lower Pliocene) geological history of the Caesarea structure, *Israel Jour. Earth-Sci.* **27:**43–64.

Nir, Y., 1973, *Geological History of the Recent and Subrecent Sediments of the Israel Mediterranean Shelf and Slope*, Geological Survey of Israel, unpublished report.

Nir, Y., 1981, *Recent Sediments of Haifa Bay*, Geo-

logical Survey of Israel, Marine Geology Division, Report 11/80.

Nir, Y., 1982, Asia, Middle East, coastal morphology: Israel and Sinai, in *Encyclopedia of Beaches and Coastal Environments*, M. L. Schwartz, ed., Hutchinson Ross Publishing Co., Stroudsburg, Pa., pp. 86–98.

Raban, A., 1980, The siting and development of Mediterranean harbors in antiquity, in *Oceanography, The Past*, M. Sears and M. Merriman, eds., Springer-Verlag New York. pp. 750–764.

Uziel, J., 1968, Sea level at Ashdod and Eilat: difference between prediction and observations, *Israel Jour. Earth-Sci.* **17:**137–151.

Plate 70-1. A small bay in the rocky shores of the Carmel beaches. The entire beach area is formed of very well-developed beachrock (photo by Y. Nir).

Plate 70-3. A wide sandy bay formed between two small relics of offshore kurkar ridges at Dor (photo by Y. Nir).

Plate 70-2. Beachrock, composed mostly of coarse calcareous sand, forming the shoreline north of Akko (photo by Y. Nir).

Plate 70-4. Typical abraded shore platform (photo by Y. Nir).

Plate 70-5. Abraded kurkar platform found at the beach. Note the cross-bedded "layers" with landward dip (photo by Y. Nir).

Plate 70-7. The rocky coast south of Rosh Haniqra (photo by Y. Nir).

Plate 70-6. The kurkar cliff at Sharon (photo by Y. Nir).

Plate 70-8. Rocky shores and beach pebbles at the outlet of Nakahal Keziv south of Rosh Haniqra (photo by Y. Nir).

Plate 70-9. The Gaza harbor groin with sand accumulation on its southern (right-hand) side, with a small kurkar cliff at the background (photo by R. Erde).

71. EGYPT

Egypt has a Mediterranean coastline 540 km long, and a Red Sea coastline (Gulfs of Suez and Aqaba) of 770 km. The latter is included in the section on *Red Sea Coasts*.

The Nile Delta is the classic example that led Herodotus, nearly 2500 years ago, to apply the Greek letter △ as a geomorphological term. It is a lobate delta (Plate 71-1), built where the supply of fluvial sediment has been abundant and wave and current action have not been excessive. Of the several distributaries of the Nile that once existed, all but two—the Rosetta Branch to the west and the Damietta Branch to the east—are now defunct (Fig. 71-1).

The present delta is the product of sedimentary processes that began in the Upper Miocene, some 10 million years ago. The massive delta cone was deposited mostly in shallow water and subsided nearly 3 km, primarily because of tectonic move-

ments associated with the creation of the present Mediterranean (Nielsen 1977).

The Nile sediments originate from the alumina- and iron-rich soil of Ethiopia and have particular depositional features distinct from those of other soils of the Mediterranean region (Manohar 1981). These sediments, which averaged about 80 million tons per year before closure of the Aswan High Dam in 1964, travel eastward along the Mediterranean coast, reaching the entire Sinai coast and beyond (Shukri and Philip 1960). Only a small proportion of the sediment drifts westward from Rosetta toward Alexandria. The predominant direction of littoral currents is to the east, although with considerable variations in magnitude and direction.

Winds and waves are the major factors influencing shore processes. While the predominant wind and wave directions are northwesterly, the in-

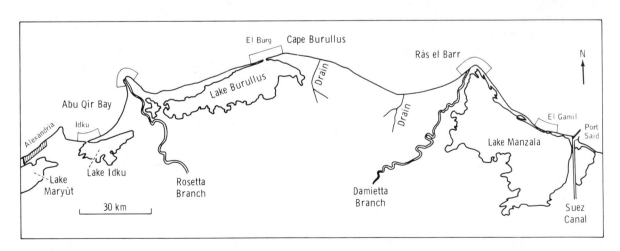

Figure 71-1. Index map showing coastal locations described along the Nile Delta coastline (after El-Ashry 1979).

513

tensity of weather conditions is highly seasonal, with high winds and waves associated with storms and the winter season from November to April (Manohar 1981). Tides along the Egyptian coast are semidiurnal, with the average tidal differences between mean high water level and mean low water level being on the order of 25–30 cm. Thus the tides play a negligible role in coastal processes.

In the moderate wave energy environment of the Mediterranean Sea along the Nile Delta shores, sand contributed by the two branches of the Nile or eroded from the delta shore is built into beaches, spits, offshore bars, or barriers enclosing lagoons as well as forelands (El-Ashry 1979).

Offshore bars exist at various depths. Along the Nile Delta coast, three rows of such bars occur, the nearest one being the summer breakpoint bar, which forms at 2 m depth and migrates shoreward. Another bar then forms at 2 m depth (Manohar 1981). The intermediate and the third (storm) bars are at 3.0–3.5 m and 4.5–5.5 m depths.

To the east of Port Said is El Bardawil lagoon, which occupies most of the Mediterranean coast of Sinai (Plate 71-2). The lagoon is separated from the sea by a long curving barrier island about 0.5 km in width. Exchange of water between the lagoon and the open sea takes place through two principal inlets, each approximately 300 m wide. At the southern reaches of the lagoon, a series of small sand barriers interrupted by very shallow straits separates a shallow-water environment to the south from the rest of the lagoon (Plate 71-2). In this southern area evaporation concentrates lagoon waters to high salinities, with precipitation of gypsum and halite, thus forming extensive salt pans (sabkhas) in which the water depth is only a few centimeters (Levy 1977). Sand dunes extend for a distance of about 4 km to the south of the lagoon beach sabkhas, and small sabkhas occupy depressions between the dunes, particularly in the coastal portion of the dune field.

West of Alexandria is a sequence of Pleistocene ridges representing ancient shorelines. Butzer (1960) identified and mapped eight such ridges, corresponding to at least eight transgressions above present mean sea level during the Pleistocene epoch. At least five of the ridges can be identified on the Apollo-Soyuz photograph (Plate 71-3).

The shoreline of the Nile Delta has undergone severe changes during the last 100 years. Erosion has occurred at several important locations along the coast: (1) El Gamil between Port Said and Ras el Barr, (2) Ras el Barr, (3) Burullus and Baltim, (4) El Burg, (5) Rosetta, (6) Abu Qir, and (7)

Alexandria (Fig. 71-1). At the same time accretion is occurring near the entrance of the Suez Canal, in front of the Port Said breakwater (Plate 71-2), causing navigational problems and requiring dredging at great expense (El-Ashry 1979).

This severe erosion along the shoreline is mainly due to reservoir development on the Nile (for example, the Delta Barrages completed in 1881 and the Aswan Dam completed in 1902), which has gradually decreased the sediment load supplied to the nearshore zone by the two branches of the Nile. In addition, the closure of the Aswan High Dam in 1964 has brought the Nile in Egypt under full control and has reduced the flow and sediment load of the river to insignificant quantities (Kassas 1972).

El Burg, near the Lake Burullus outlet (Fig. 71-1 and Plate 71-2) is one of the most exposed locations on the delta. The shoreline is straight for a long distance and is oriented obliquely to the prevailing wave direction. The slope of the nearshore is also relatively steep (Zenkovich 1964), allowing the waves to reach the shore without being completely transformed or dissipating their energy. As a result, beach erosion has occurred along this section for a long time, and serious property damage has been incurred.

The other areas most affected by beach erosion are the promontories at the mouths of the Rosetta and Damietta branches of the Nile. On the western side of the Rosetta mouth (Plate 71-3), the promontory has lost about 1650 m of its length in 65 years, averaging about 29 m/yr. According to Wassing (1964), the rates are as follows:

	Retreat (meters)			
	1898–1918	1918–1926	1926–1944	1944–1954
Total	300	620	375	350
Average per year	15	81	21	35

In comparison, the foreland at Ras el Barr (Plate 71-2) has retreated by about 1800 m between 1902 and 1960 with an average of 31 m per year.

MOHAMED T. EL-ASHRY

REFERENCES

Butzer, K. W., 1960, On the Pleistocene shore lines of Arabs' Gulf, Egypt, *Jour. Geol.* **68:**626–637.
El-Ashry, M. T., 1979, Use of Apollo-Soyuz photographs in coastal studies, in *Apollo-Soyuz Test Project,*

Summary Science Report, Vol. II, Earth Observations and Photography, F. El-Baz and D. M. Warner, eds., pp. 531–543.

Kassas, M., 1972, Impacts of river control schemes on the shoreline of the Nile Delta, in *The Careless Technology—Ecology and International Development,* M. T. Farvar and J. P. Milton, eds., The Natural History Press, Garden City, N.Y. pp. 179–188.

Levy, Y., 1977, Description and mode of formation of the supratidal evaporite facies in northern Sinai coastal plain, *Jour. Sed. Petrology* **47:**463–474.

Manohar, M., 1981, Coastal processes at the Nile Delta coast, *Shore and Beach* **49:**8–15.

Nielsen, E., 1977, Shore evolution, in *Seminar on Nile Delta Shore Processes Proc.,* Egyptian Academy of Scientific Research and Technology, Cairo, pp. 15–59.

Shukri, N. M., and G. Phillip, 1960, The mineralogy of some recent deposits in the Arish-Ghaza area, *Univ of Cairo Bull. Fac. Sci.,* **35:**73–85.

Wassing, F., 1964, *Coastal Engineering Problems in the Delta Region of U.A.R.,* Report of U.N. Expert to the Dept. of Ports and Lighthouses, Egyptian Dept. of Ports and Lighthouses, Alexandria.

Zenkovich, V. P., 1964, *Report and Some Recommendations on Nearshore Investigations and Protection of the Nile Delta Shores,* UNESCO, Paris.

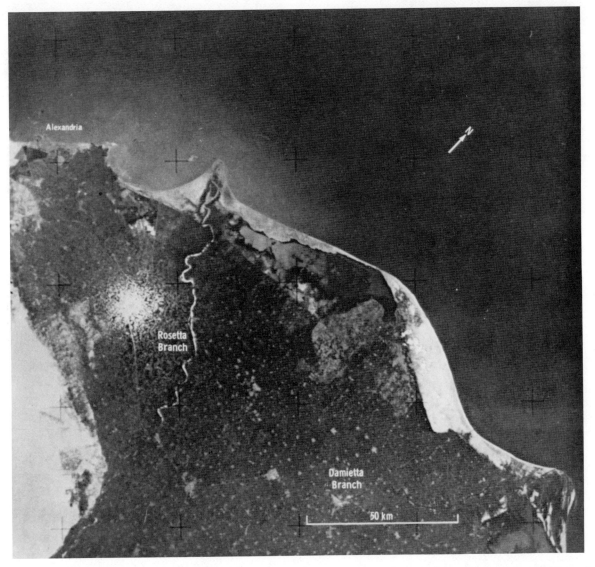

Plate 71-1. Apollo-Soyuz photograph of the Nile Delta. The foreland in the lower right-hand corner, east of the Damietta Branch mouth, consists of a series of recurved spits built by fluvial sediment introduced in the nearshore zone by the Damietta outlet and reworked by wave action. The sand bar or sand spit that separates Lake Burullus from the sea is constantly retreating landward. The features on the western two-thirds of the bar near the Rosetta outlet have been produced by a process of washover (photo by NASA, AST-9-558).

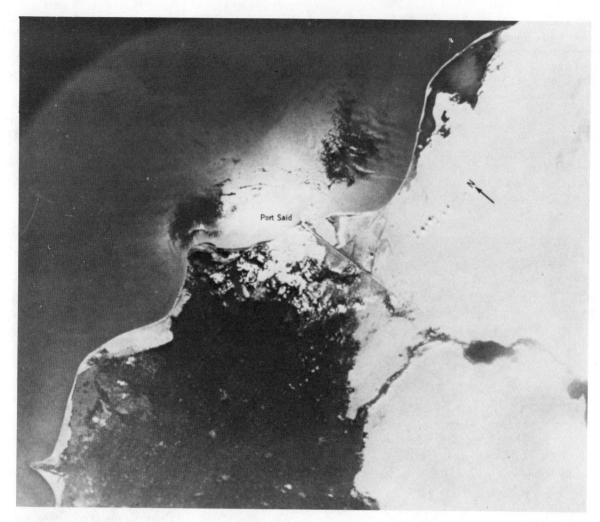

Plate 71-2. Apollo-Soyuz photograph of the eastern half of the Nile Delta, showing the Suez Canal and El Bardawil lagoon. Sediment supplied by the Nile outlets and from erosion along the delta shoreline is carried eastward by longshore currents and deposited near the entrance of the Suez Canal (photo by NASA, AST-9-558).

Plate 71-3. Apollo-Soyuz photograph of the western half of the Nile Delta, showing Abu Qir Bay, Alexandria, and ancient shorelines of Arabs' Gulf. The tonal contrast between the crests of the bars and the floors of the lagoons is due to the accumulation of salts on the former lagoon floors by evaporation. Vegetative cover (darker tones) on crests of the former offshore bars seems to decrease with distance from the shore because of decrease in moisture, making it difficult to distinguish on the photograph the three southerly bars from the surrounding desert sand (photo by NASA, AST-16-1257).

72. LIBYA

The coast of Libya (Fig. 72-1A), along the northern border of the Sahara, extends for 1850 km from Tunisia on the west to Egypt on the east (Van Chi-Bonnardel 1973). A 1900 km coastal highway links Tripoli and Benghazi, the two major ports of the country. Oil trans-shipment ports are located along the coast in near proximity to the interior oil fields. Agriculture is centered in a narrow (10 km wide maximum) coastal plain on the west, where olive, almond, and citrus trees are grown. Offshore, along the whole coastal region, there is a fishing industry based on sponges, sardines, and tuna.

Temperatures in the coastal region range from 12–16° C in January to 24–28° C in July. Rainfall is sparse and variable, with offshore warm tropical continental winds in January and onshore tropical continental winds in July. A Mediterranean climate prevails in the east and west, with a desert climate in the central portion of the coastal sector. Mediterranean steppe vegetation borders the coast inland, and the soil here is the reddish-brown to gray and grayish-brown of a subdesert zone.

The wave environment along the Libyan coast is that of a protected sea (Davies 1973), with less than a 10% frequency of waves of 1.6 m height or more during at least two quarters of the year. Dominant swell is from the northwest (Orme 1982). Tides are semidiurnal in the western half and mixed in the east, and spring range is less than 2 m (Davies 1973). Also according to Davies, average annual runoff in the coastal zone is less than 50 mm.

The geology of the coastal region (Burollet et al. 1971) is briefly as follows: (a) the Precambrian African shield is composed of gneiss, schist, quartzite, and granite; (b) Paleozoic deposits are sedimentary and have undergone tectonic vertical movements and the formation of basins; (c) block faulting and flexures form the present structures (i.e., the Gulf of Sirte) where Cenozoic sediments have accumulated. Tectonically the region is associated with the Ionian Plate in a northwesterly direction of plate motion (Orme 1982).

The present-day surficial geology consists of undifferentiated Quaternary deposits in the west and Neogene continental formations in the east (Van Chi-Bonnardel 1973). Of physiographic note is the Barce Plain plateau in the eastern coastal region of Cyrenacia. With a maximum elevation of 900 m, the plateau reaches 48 km in width and is 240 km in length along the coast (Hance 1975). The major sea cliffs in Libya are developed where the steep slopes face the sea.

The geomorphology of the coastal zone is shown in Figure 72-1B (Defense Mapping Agency Hydrographic Center 1976; McGill 1958; Orme 1982). The eastern end of the coast, near the Libya-Egypt border, is sandy in nature. In the vicinity of Tobruk there are sea cliffs on the mountainous coastal slopes, with white dunes in a low-lying sector. West of Tobruk there are more white dunes, and from here to Rezem the low crenulate coast is sandy. From Rezem past Ras Hilal and almost to Tukrah, the steep frontal slopes of the inland plateau are faced with sea cliffs. From the Tukrah region to Benghazi, the coast is sandy (Plate 72-1). Beyond Benghazi barrier-lagoon systems and sebkhas begin to appear, and these continue along the coast down to Al-Uqaylah. From Al-Uqaylah to Sidra there are dunes behind the beach front. A sandy coast alternates with a similar coast backed by dunes from Sidra west-

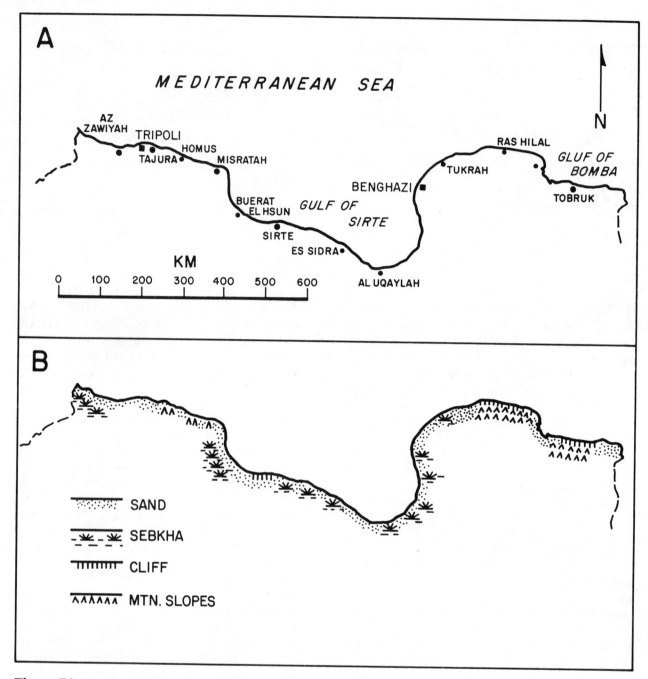

Figure 72-1. Maps of the coast of Libya: *A*. geographic; *B*. geomorphic.

ward to Sirte (Plate 72-2), with some low bluffs cut into the shore in places. Dunes back the shore from Sirte to Hsun. A 100 km long barrier lagoon coast, backed by extensive sebkhas, predominates between Hsun and Misratah. West of Misratah, past Homs, there are intermittent sandy sectors between hilly stretches; and between Tajura and Tripoli there is more sandy coast. From Tripoli to Az Zawiyah the coast is not particularly sandy, with eolianite outcropping in many places (Plate 72-3). From Az Zawiyah to the western border with Tunisia, there is a sandy coast backed in places by sebkhas. Within the context of the coastline described above, short rocky areas are to be found at some ports providing local shelter for boats.

MAURICE L. SCHWARTZ

REFERENCES

Burollet, P. F., P. Magnier, and G. Manderscheid, 1971, La Libye, in *Tectonique de l'Afrique,* UNESCO, Paris, pp. 409–416.

Davies, J. L., 1973, *Geographical Variations in Coastal Development,* New York.

Defense Mapping Agency Hydrographic Center, 1976, *Mediterranean Sea, Libya Bathymetric Charts,* Hafner, Washington, D.C.

Hance, W. A., 1975, *Geography of Modern Africa,* Columbia University Press, New York.

McGill, J. T., 1958, Map of coastal landforms of the world, *Geog. Rev.* **48:**402–405.

Orme, A. T., 1982, Africa, coastal morphology, in *Encyclopedia of Beaches and Coastal Environments,* M. L. Schwartz, ed., Hutchinson Ross Publishing Co., Stroudsburg, Pa., pp. 17–32.

Van Chi-Bonnardel, R., 1973, *Atlas of Africa,* Jeune Afrique, Paris.

Plate 72-1. Sandy coast in vicinity of Cyrenacia, eastern Libya (photo by J. Morelock).

Plate 72-3. Eolianite outcropping along coast 16 km west of Tripoli (photo by J. Morelock).

Plate 72-2. View to the east showing construction of first oil trans-shipment facility at the Gulf of Sirte (photo by J. Morelock).

73. TUNISIA

The coastline of Tunisia (Fig. 73-1) is about 1300 km long, including the shores of the coastal lagoons and the islands. The country's northern and eastern coasts contrast sharply.

The northern coast extends from the Algerian border to the Cap Bon peninsula and relates to the western Mediterranean (Bonniard 1934). The continental shelf is narrow, less than 10 km wide. The coast is rainy (annual average rainfall: 600 mm) and windy. The prevailing winds (in both strength and frequency) blow from the northwest; consequently, the shoreline is exposed to northwesterly swell. Winter storm waves are generally several meters high. Longshore drifting runs from west to east. The tide is semidiurnal, and its average range is small, about 0.2 m. The coastline truncates the highlands of northern Tunisia (Kroumirie and Mogod mountains) and, because of the high-energy littoral environment, rugged cliffs and bluffs cut principally in Oligocene sandstones, represent the main geomorphic features (Plate 73-1). Only short ephemeral streams reach the sea, and west of Tabarka sandy shorelines are few. However, an abundant sand supply derived from eroding cliffs and the regional climatic conditions (strong winds, marked summer dryness) generates extensive mobile dunes (about 300 km²) made of quartzose sand, showing evidence of southeastward movement and transgression over the hinterland topography.

The coastline of the Gulf of Tunis marks a transition between the northern and the eastern seasides of the country. It is relatively protected from the northwesterly swell by its northeastward orientation. Large embayments are controlled by a more open continental topography. Long sandy beaches correspond to deltaic plains built since the end of the Versilian transgression by the only two perennial streams of Tunisia, both prone to heavy floods, the Miliane River and, especially, the Medjerda River.

The eastern coast extends from the Cap Bon peninsula to the Libyan border and relates to the eastern Mediterranean (Burollet 1979). Rain diminishes southward, and semiarid conditions dominate in the Gulf of Gabes, where the mean annual rainfall is under 200 mm. The continental shelf is broad, more than 200 km wide at the latitude of the Kerkennah Islands. Only local winds, blowing from between east and north in spring and summer, from the west in autumn and winter, affect the coastline, which is characterized by a low energy. Waves mainly come from the northeast, also from the southeast in the Gulf of Gabes. They generally die out before reaching the shore because of the shallowness of the wide continental shelf. Submarine meadows of Phanerogams (*Cymodocea nodosa* and *Posidonia oceanica*), which extend between −1 m and −30 m, also help diminish the wave energy; in addition, they increase sand deposition. The Kerkennah Islands add their protection for the segment of the coast situated between Sfax and Gabes. However, during exceptional winter storms, like the one that occurred in January 1981, wave erosion may take place. Generally a weak longshore drifting goes southward. Tide is an important phenomenon in the Gulf of Gabes, with a maximum range reaching 1.8 m. Tidal currents up to 1 and 2 knots are especially noticeable in the narrows surrounding Jerba and Kerkennah Islands; they account for the occurrence of the

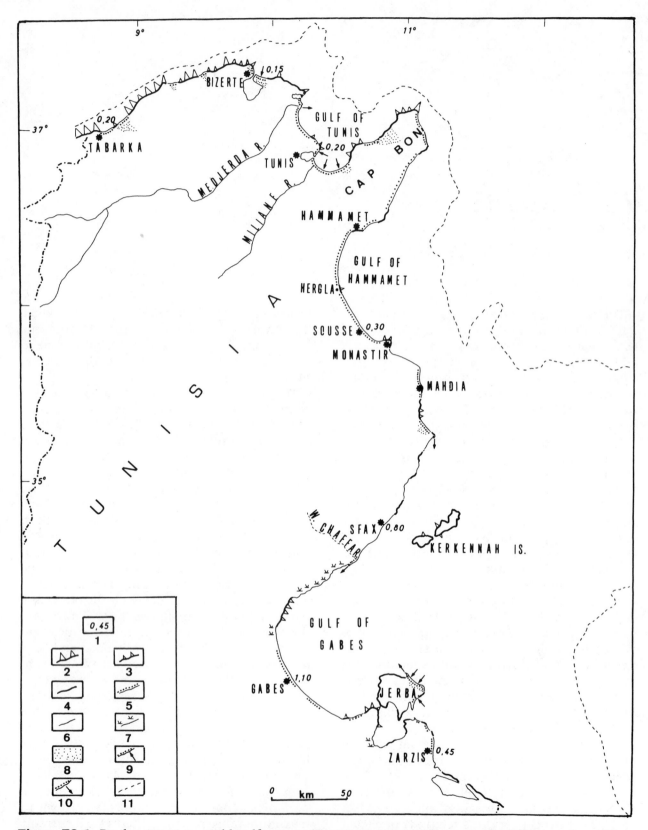

Figure 73-1. Predominant coastal landforms in Tunisia. 1. mean tide range; 2. cliff (more than 15 m high); 3. cliff (less than 15 m high); 4. low rocky shoreline; 5. sandy shoreline; 6. silty shoreline; 7. salt marshes; 8. coastal dunes; 9. retreating beach; 10. prograding beach; 11. −200 m isobath.

so-called submarine wadis (Despois 1955), meandering channels excavated in the shallow continental shelf.

The geomorphic features of the eastern coast of Tunisia are explained by the subdued topography of the hinterland together with the low-energy marine environment. Cliffs are small and infrequent. Sandy beaches predominate, particularly around the Gulf of Hammamet, in the vicinity of Mahdia and Gabes, in eastern Jerba, and near Zarzis. In the last two areas beachrock is occasionally found (Plate 73-2). It appears that sand of the beaches fringing the Gulf of Gabes came from the sea floor during the Versilian transgression; at present there is no significant source of sand supply from wadis or eroding cliffs on this coast. Near Gabes beaches are highly polluted by wastes from industrial plants erected during the last decade. Muddy tidal flats extend south of Sfax. Elsewhere, low rocky platforms cut in Tyrrhenian marine or eolian sandstones (Paskoff and Sanlaville 1979) are found around the Kerkennah Islands (Plate 73-3), in eastern Jerba and south of Zarzis.

Almost the entire Tunisian coastline is currently eroded, and numerous valuable coastal sites of archaeological interest have been destroyed by wave action (Plate 73-4). A slight sea-level rise during the historical period (Plate 73-5) partly accounts for this situation. Beach erosion is a serious problem in Tunisia. The tourist industry, mainly based on sea and sun, has been a major priority of the authorities since 1960 and has become the second source of foreign currency for the country. In fact, if we except a few restricted sectors of progradation (the mouth of the Medjerda River and three spits indicated on Fig. 73-1), sandy shorelines are threatened by erosion. Rapidly retreating beaches are found in the surrounding region of Tunis and particularly at Jerba Island (Fig. 73-2). Here, the accretion taking place at the tip of Ras Rmel is the counterpart of the severe erosion affecting the long beach fringing the northeastern side of the island (Miossec and Paskoff 1979). Erosion probably started after the sixteenth century, since the recurved spit of Ras Rmel did not then exist, according to a reliable map dating back to 1560. Recently shoreline recession has been dramatically increased by unwise human intervention related to the tourist boom that has affected the island during the last two decades. There has been sand mining on the beach for building purposes. In many places the foredune has been completely destroyed to erect

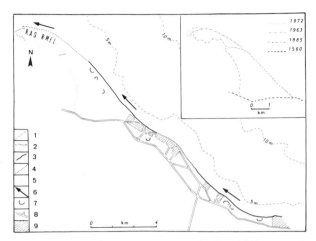

Figure 73-2. Beach erosion and evolution of the recurved spit of Ras Rmel in the tourist area of northeastern Jerba island. 1. isobath; 2. stable sandy shoreline; 3. retreating sandy shoreline; 4. prograding sandy shoreline; 6. prevailing littoral drift; 7. sand pit; 8. road; 9. hotels.

hotels very near the seaside. The removal of dead leaves of *Posidonia*, which accumulate on the shore and inhibit sunbathing, increases wave action, which is also enhanced by the degradation of the infralittoral meadows damaged by sewage.

The delta of the Medjerda river (mean annual discharge: 30 m³/s) is a good example of a delta in a Mediterranean environment; its development is fairly well known from the results of geological and geomorphological studies corroborated by archaeological data (Fig. 73-3). The delta has been formed during the last 5000–6000 years by the filling up, from north to south, of a former bay drowned by the Versilian transgression (Pimienta 1959). Human activity played an important role in its evolution. Deforestation in ancient times considerably increased the solid load carried by the river, and public works (artificial levees, man-made cutoffs, drainage and deviation canals) completed during the present century have interfered with natural phenomena (Jauzein 1971). For instance, during a heavy flood in March 1973, with a water flow reaching 3500 m³/s, a figure higher than the estimated maximum 100-year rate of discharge, the Medjerda River shifted its lowermost course; the natural channel was abandoned and the entire flow is now running through an artificial canal, originally designed to evacuate the excess of water during floods and extending directly to the sea (Paskoff 1978). As a result, the recurved spit (Plate 73-6), which has

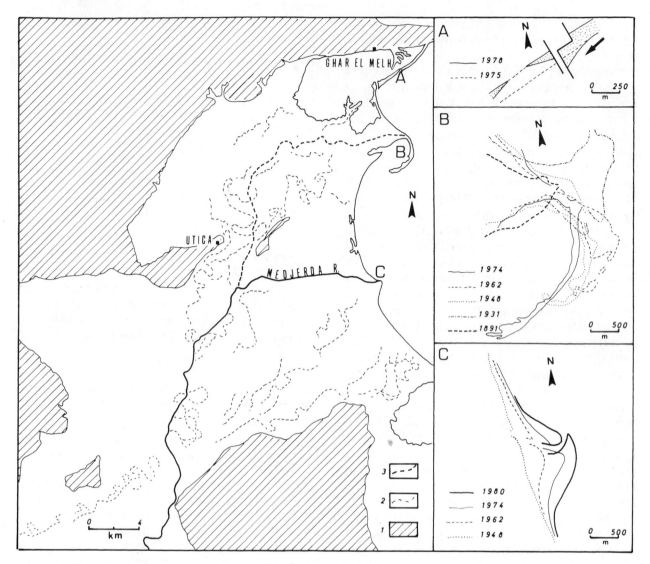

Figure 73-3. The deltaic plain of the Medjerda river. 1. Mesozoic and early Cenozoic bedrock (mainly limestones, soft sandstones, and marls); 2. former channels of the Medjerda river (according to Jauzein 1971); 3. channel abandoned in 1973.

A. Effects of the construction of a new harbour on the barrier isolating the coastal lagoon of Ghar el Melh.

B. Evolution of the recurved spit located at the former mouth of the Medjerda river.

C. Recent evolution of the present mouth of the Medjerda river.

developed at the former mouth since the end of the last century, is presently suffering erosion at its root, extending its tip and migrating westward.

Transformations of the coast on both sides of the new mouth, located about 10 km south of the former one, are also considerable. A cuspate foreland shows rapid extension in spite of sediment trapping behind dams constructed on the Medjerda River and some of its tributaries. Between 1977 and 1980, about 87 acres of new land have been added to the delta.

The building, in 1975, of the outer harbor of Ghar el Melh, on the barrier that isolates a lagoon from the sea, is inducing geomorphic modifications. Accretion on the updrift side of the jetties protecting the entrance of the dock has been followed by erosion in the downdrift sector depleted of traveling beach material, to a such degree that the barrier has been cut off.

The Monastir area (Fig. 73-4) on the eastern coast of Tunisia is a site well known for its Tyrrhenian deposits rich in *Strombus bubonius;*

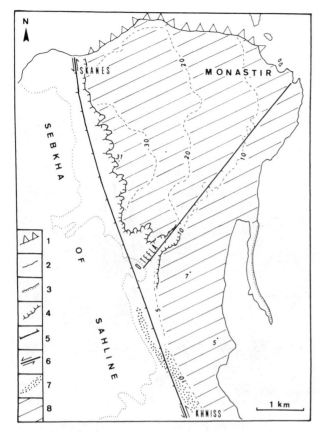

Figure 73-4. Geomorphic sketch of the Monastir area. 1. marine cliff cut in Neogene rocks; 2. low rocky coast; 3. sandy shoreline; 4. erosional scarp of tectonic origin; 5. normal faults; 6. strike-slip movement; 7. coastal barrier of Eutyrrhenian age; 8. wave-cut platform veneered by Eutyrrhenian deposits.

the term *Monastirian*, although no longer in general use, was for some time widely employed to designate a marine Quaternary stage of the Mediterranean standard. The name was first applied to a lower 15 m marine level extending south to Monastir and separated by a cliff, running along the wadi Tefla, from a higher 30 m marine level attributed to the Tyrrhenian. Both levels include *Strombus* in their surficial deposits. It is now firmly established that there is only one wide wave-cut platform at Monastir. This platform, veneered by Eutyrrhenian deposits (Rejiche formation), has been faulted and tilted (Castany et al. 1956). A hinge fault, corresponding to the wadi Tefla thalweg and looking southeastward, was erroneously interpreted as a former sea cliff; it separates two compartments that have been unequally uplifted.

Another major Post-Tyrrhenian fault is the Skanes-Khniss fault, which runs near the foot of

the scarp limiting the platform of Monastir westward and crosses the former coastal barrier of Khniss, which materializes the position of the shoreline at the top of the Eutyrrhenian transgression. Field evidence shows that this fault has both a horizontal and a vertical component (Kamoun et al. 1980; Paskoff and Sanlaville 1981).

Important Post-Tyrrhenian tectonic events are well documented in the surroundings of Monastir. They controlled the present coastal morphology of the area, characterized northward by retreating cliffs cut in soft Neogene rocks and eastward by a low rocky shore developed in Eutyrrhenian sandstones (Paskoff and Sanlaville 1983).

ROLAND P. PASKOFF

REFERENCES

Bonniard, F., 1934, *La Tunisie du Nord*, Geuthner, Paris.

Burollet, P. F., 1979, La Mer Pélagienne, *Géol. Médit.* **6:**13–45.

Castany, G., E. G. Gobert, and L. Harson, 1956, Le Quaternaire marin de Monastir, *Annales Mines et Géol.* **19:**1–58.

Despois, J., 1955, *Sahel et Basse-Steppe*. Presses Universitaires de France, Paris.

Jauzein, A., 1971, Evolution récente du delta de la Medjerda, in *Les agents de la morphogenèse*, A. Jauzein, Ecole Normal Superieure, Paris, pp. 128–151.

Kamoun, Y., D. Sorel, C. Viguier, and N. Ben Ayed, 1980, Un grand accident subméridien d'âge post-tyrrhénien en Tunisie orientale: le décrochement sénestre de Skanès (Monastir), Hammamet, *Acad. Sci. Paris Comptes Rendus* **290:**647–649.

Miossec, J. M., and R. Paskoff, 1979, Evolution des plages et aménagements touristiques à Jerba (Tunisie): le cas du littoral nord-est de l'île, *Méditerranée* **1–2:**99–106.

Paskoff, R., 1978, Evolution de l'embouchure de la Medjerda (Tunisie), *Photo-Interprétation* **5:**1–23.

Paskoff, R., and P. Sanlaville, 1979, *Livret-guide de l'excursion-table ronde sur le Tyrrhénien de Tunisie*, INQUA, Shoreline commission, Mediterranean-Black Sea subcommission, International Union for Quaternary Research.

Paskoff, R., and P. Sanlaville, 1981, Tyrrhenian deposits and neotectonics at Monastir, eastern Tunisia, *Zeitschr. Geomorphologie*, Suppl. Bd. **40:**183–192.

Paskoff, R., and P. Sanlaville, 1983, *Les côtes de la Tunisie, variations du niveau marin depuis le Tyrrhénien*, Collection Maison de l'Orient Méditerrnéen No. 14 Lyon, 192p.

Pimienta, J., 1959, *Le cycle Pliocène-Actual dans les bassins paraliques de Tunis*. Soc. Géol. France Mém. 85.

Plate 73-1. Cliffs near Cap Blanc, west of Bizerte (northern Tunisia). The coast consists of Eocene limestone covered by eolian calcarenite in the foreground (photo by R. P. Paskoff).

Plate 73-2. Beach rock cementing Holocene sand exposed on a retreating beach, Jerba island (southern Tunisia) (photo by R. P. Paskoff).

Plate 73-3. Shore platform cut in Tyrrhenian sandstone on the coast of Gharbi, Kerkennah Islands (eastern Tunisia) (photo by R. P. Paskoff).

Plate 73-4. Roman ruins, mainly warehouses, severely destroyed by wave action at Hergla (eastern Tunisia), suggesting an appreciable recession of the shoreline since ancient times (photo by R. P. Paskoff).

Plate 73-5. Historical submergence indicated by Punic tombs inundated during high tide at Mahdia (eastern Tunisia) (photo by R. P. Paskoff).

Plate 73-6. Recurved sand spit at the former mouth of the Medjerda River, Gulf of Tunis (northeastern Tunisia). On the left, the barrier isolating the lagoon of Ghar el Melh is cut by an artificial entrance. The new harbor of Ghar el Melh is visible in the distance (photo by R. P. Paskoff).

74. ALGERIA

The Algerian coastline is about 1100 km long, from 2°10′ W to 8°30′ E in longitude and from 35° to 37° N in latitude; it is oriented west-southwest–east-northeast from the Moroccan to the Tunisian borders (Fig. 74-1). The coastline is almost completely bordered by chains of mountains plunging abruptly into deep water, with intervening sandy low coasts (Fig. 74-1). In the western zone, the coast is low and sandy, because of the alluvium carried by the Moulouya Wadi

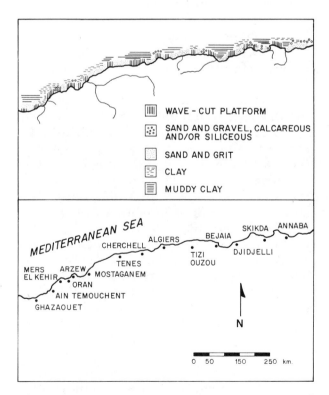

Figure 74-1. Geomorphic and geographic map of the Algerian coastline.

(Morocco). Next to it, the Traras Mountains, constituted of schists, quartzites, and crystalline limestones, are bordered by a steep cliffy coast plunging into deep water, from +200 m down to −50 m. From Beni Saf to Cape Figalo, the shore is cut into Villafranchian and Quaternary continental sediments, whereas from Cape Figalo to Cape Sigale, one finds volcanic rocks (andesites) forming steep cliffs. The calcareous massif of Oran-Region towers more than 400 m above the littoral, except around the tombolo of Cape Falcon and its low sandy coast.

Down to Arzew, the coast is cliffy in Quaternary sediments, with the Carbon Cape and Cape de l'Aiguille cut into the calcareous Djebel Orous. Between the Djebel Orous and the sandstone plateau of Mostaganem, the Bay of Arzew corresponds to the vast low and swampy plain of La Macta, which is an alluvial area deposited by the Wadis Mekerra and El Hammam. From Mostaganem to Tipaza (west of Algiers), the Dahra coastal chain (Tertiary sandstone) and the schistose massif (flysch) of Beni Menacer look down upon the sea from a hundred meters. Between the Jurassic massif of Chenoua and the metamorphic massif (crystalline schists) of La Bouzareah lies a rocky coast, recent (Villafranchian) and slightly elevated (Bay of Bou Ismail).

Eastward, the Bay of Algiers lies between the Bouzareah massif and the Matifou Cape (metamorphic outcrop); this low coast is today widely urbanized by the suburbs of Algiers. Between Cape Matifou and Dellys, we find the same pattern, with large accumulations of sand, especially between Cape Tamentefoust and Cape Djinet, and a narrower sandy area between Cape Djinet and Cape Bengut in front of dead cliffs. From Dellys to

531

the Bay of Bejaia, the Great Kabylia is bordered to the north by a Tertiary (Numidian) and Secondary (sandstone and schistose Cretaceous) mountain that borders the sea until the Bay of Bejaia. This bay corresponds to the tectonic valley of the Wadi Soummam. The calcareous chain of Babors and the volcanic outcrop of Cavallo shape a picturesque cliffy coast called the Corniche Kabyle. The Neogenic basin of Jijel presents a relatively low coast, with dead cliffs cut into Tertiary and Quaternary deposits. East of this basin comes the crystalline massif of the Collo-Kabylia; its altitude is high, and it presents an abrupt marine facade (950 m high a few kilometers from the shore). This massif stretches on until the Djebel Filfilah (east of Skikda).

Next comes the big depression of Lake Fetzara, separating the coastal massif of the Edough from the inland Mounts of Guelma. The coast is low and swampy, with dunes, between the Djebel Filfilah and Cape de Fer. Then, until Chetaibi, the coast becomes abrupt and cliffy in volcanic rocks. The coast form is the same, in Oligocene sandstone from Chetaibi to the beach of Seraidi, and in the metamorphic rocks of Mount Edough to the town of Annaba. From Annaba to the Tunisian border, we distinguish two main features. First, a low coast with ancient dunes, until Cape Rosa, corresponds to a hinterland of plains (continuation of the Fetzara Plain) of Quaternary alluvium filling the Sebouse and El Kebir wadis. Second, a rocky and higher coast corresponds to the Tertiary mountainous hinterland, with north-south oriented folds.

Thus the main features of the Algerian littoral present a certain adaptation to local tectonic and lithologic conditions, generally to the crystalline massifs and to the secondary calcareous or schistic massifs. An abrupt, cliffy shore towers over the sea by a hundred meters, and the same slope extends beneath the sea. Between these resistant massifs, which project many headlands into the sea, we find bays and gulfs corresponding to more horizontal structures and more recent sedimentation, with a low coast, sometimes rocky and indented (in ancient Quaternary lithified deposits), or sandy with recent or fossil dunes.

There is an abundance of literature concerning the coast of Algeria. For further details the reader is referred to Albuisson et al. (1980), Allain and Furnestin (1969), Bourcart and Glangeaud (1954), Caulet (1970), Dagorne (1972), Girardin et al. (1977), Leclaire (1970), and Mahrour and Dagorne (1978, 1980).

DYNAMIC FACTORS SHAPING THE ALGERIAN COASTLINE

Marine Agents: Swells, Waves, Marine Currents, Tides

The swells have two main directions. West-northwesterly (300°) swells represent more than 80% of the winter swells. The period is 8 s on average, reaching 13 s during tempests. The average amplitude is 2 or 3 m, reaching 5 to 6 m during storms. The north-northeasterly swells (20–40°), prevailing in summer, are less strong, with a period of 6 s. Their average amplitude is 0.5–1 m, rarely reaching 3 m.

These swells interfere according to the morphological presentation of the coastline. The redistribution of the sedimentary materials brought into the sea by the wadi depends on the swell regime. The maximum rate of muddy sedimentation is reached in the zones of the winter swell, under the corner of the headlands oriented to the northeast. Drift convergence from opposite directions has resulted in the formation of a tombolo (Sidi Fredj, west of Algiers). The extension of the sands and sandy beach ridges varies according to the dominating swell: in winter, at the mouth of Isser Wadi (Kabylia), the beach erodes 40 m, and marine erosion reaches the ancient dunes. The beach gets rougher and the sea more turbid (influence of the backwash). With summer swells, the beach becomes wider, with huge amounts of fine sand.

The general currents seems to be less important than swells in the littoral and prelittoral, though they are probably responsible, through hydraulic sifting, for the absence of fine sedimentation at the Algerian-Tunisian borders. It is known that the Atlantic current, whose waters are cool and less saline than those of the Mediterranean Sea, gets through the Strait of Gibraltar. This current is balanced, in the deep sea, by an opposing Mediterranean current of more saline waters. The Atlantic current does not flow eastward regularly: the regime of the swells interfere to split it. Locally, the Atlantic current amplifies the role of the swells when the directions are the same because of the wind regime or because of the shaping of the littoral relief (like the countercurrents in the bays of Bajaia and Arzew).

The tides along the Algerian coast do not exceed 0.5 m. This low amplitude has very little geomorphological effect, in contrast with the effects of the swells or littoral currents.

Sub-aerial Agents

The climate of the Algerian coast is Mediterranean with local variations; the western zone is drier than the eastern. Rain-bearing winds come from the northwest (polar front) when the Azores anticyclone is at a lower latitude in winter. These winds play an important part in generating the prevailing northwesterly swells and consequently in the erosion of the Algerian coast; they also bring rainfall and influence the distribution of vegetation, soil erosion, and the flow of water and sediments down wadis.

The alluvial deposits in the sea are all the more important because the winter rainfall in the Mediterranean climate can be violent and can erode considerably. This erosion reaches maximum values in Algeria because the slopes are abrupt and the degraded vegetal cover insufficient to prevent rapid runoff. Erosion on the slopes is intense, and the alluvium taken into the sea is deposited on the continental shelf. The liquid and solid discharges can be considerable (Table 1).

It has been calculated that the average annual silt brought to the sea by all the main wadis of Algeria reaches 22 million tons, and 40–60 million tons if we take into consideration the secondary wadis. Thus the littoral zone is well provided with terrestrial sediment; at the same time, the sea is agitated by the more frequent and stronger swells.

TYPES OF COASTS—
SOME EXAMPLES

Erosional Rocky Coasts

Rocky Cliffy Coasts. The abruptness of the coast comes, in this case, from present erosion or inherited (ancient cliffs shaped during the Quaternary). Very often, this ancient cliff stands back from the coastline (a dead cliff). The cliffs are cut in the local rocks or into older, calcareous or siliceous, lithified dunes.

Structural Rocky, Cliffy Coasts. The abruptness of the coast, in this case, has a structural origin and not an erosive one; the tilting of the sedimentary layers influences the coast. However, there is very often a small emerged platform of abrasion. Sometimes the cliffs consist of long steep slopes plunging into the sea; in this case, the cliffs are false. These rocky coasts, structurally abrupt or erosive, are to be found whenever mountainous massifs border the sea.

Low Rocky Coasts. These coasts appear as littoral platforms at or below present sea level. On this platform, we can find algal terraces (*trottoirs a algues*) and lapies.

Accumulation Coasts

Beaches. Usually situated at the mouths of the wadis, beaches are mainly composed of terrestrial materials brought by the wadis and deposited by the waves on both sides of the mouth. They are also located on the shores cut into recent Quaternary marine deposits where marine erosion has deposited sediment on beaches parallel to the shore. The marine contribution consists of organic fragments.

Littoral Bars. The *fleches litterales* are often found at the mouth of wadis. They are built when the action of the littoral drift is stronger than the action of the outflow current, especially when the wadi flow is irregular and thus has a very weak erosive competence during the dry season. In this case, deposition of sand and gravel forces the current of the wadi to turn left or right according to the direction of the littoral drift. When the current is not strong enough to make its way, a lagoon (*guelta* in Arabic) or a temporary swamp forms until the next overflow frees the way. Because of their type of genesis, the morphology of these littoral bars can vary during the year, according to the seasons; it all depends on the balance between the accumulation actions of the littoral drift and the erosive action of the fluvial current.

Tombolos. This type of marine construction is not frequent on the Algerian coast because of the narrowness of the continental shelf. However, there are two characteristic examples at Sidi Fredj (west of Algiers) and at Cap Falcon near Oran. They are not currently very active and were probably built during the early Holocene.

Littoral Dunes. The littoral dune zones are

Table 1. Wadi Discharges

	Liquid Discharges (million m³/year)	Solid Discharges (million tons/year)
Cheliff	590	2.4
Sebaou	755	—
Isser	420	4.8
Seybouse	429	—
Mazafran	—	3.0
Soummam	—	4.0

found principally near the big wadi mouths where the relief is low and the continental shelf is not deep (i.e., near the Mazafran, Isser, Seybous, and El Kebir wadis). Some dunes are derived from older consolidated dune formations eroded by marine action, the sandy products of which are blown by the wind. Thus we can find active dunes (Isser, Jijel) or inactive dunes presently eroded by swells (Annaba).

Littoral Swamps.   The weak outflow from the mouths of certain wadis produces littoral swamps on the Algerian coast. Upstream the water is very turbid because of the strong gales. Downstream the wadi is less competent because of the abrupt diminution of the slope, and deposits its load, making a vast swampy and muddy zone. This is the case of La Macta swamps near Oran and at the mouth of Seybouse and El Kebir wadis in the eastern part of the country. Active littoral drift has probably contributed to the creation of these swamps by preventing the outflow of water behind spits.

The Algerian coast does not display a wide variety of littoral forms. The compartmentalization of the relief bordering the coast explains the spatial distribution of the littoral forms—the rocky, cliffy coasts alternating with sandy low coasts. The Algerian coastline is picturesque but inhospitable, and so far has been little developed for tourists. The present Algerian coastline attracts those who like natural scenery.

M. MAHROUR
A. DAGORNE

REFERENCES

Albuisson, M., R. Arfi, A. Dagorne, M. Mahrour, and J.-M. Monget, 1980, *De l'aide apportée a l'hydrologie marine par les satellites d'observation de la terre. Applications au domaine maritime algérien.* Report of A.T.P. Teledetection.

Allain, C., and J. Furnestin, 1969, Hydrologie de la Méditerranée occidentale (Secteur meridional et Golfe du Lion) en Automne 1963, *Bull. I.S.T.P.M.* **33**(1):5–78.

Bourcart, J., and L. Glangeaud, 1954, Morpho-tectonique de la marge continentale nordafricaine. *Soc. Géol. France Bull.* **4:**751–772.

Caulet, J.-P., 1970, *Les sediments organogènes du précontinent algérien.* Mus. Natl. Historie Nat. Mém., Paris.

Dagorne, A., 1972, Sedimentologie et bionomie benthiques en baie de Bou Ismail (Ouest d'Alger), Rev. Pelagos **4**(2):40–53.

Girardin, N., D. Hatzfeld, and R. Guirard, 1977, La séismicité du Nord de l'Algérie, *Soc. Geol. France Comte Rende* **2:**95–100.

Leclaire, L., 1970, *La sédimentation holocène sur le versant nord du bassin algérobaleare (precontinent algérien),* Mus. Natl. Hist. Nat. Mém., Paris.

Mahrour, M., and A. Dagorne, 1978, Le projet "Alkalit" (Algerian Kabyle littoral), étude de géomorphologie dynamique, *Centre National d'Etude et de Recherche pour l'Aménagement du Territoire Bull.,* Alger **4:** 102–122.

Mahrour, M., and A. Dagorne, 1980, Le satellite, un nouveau point de vue . . . L'image spatiale, un nouveau document au service du geographe . . . Applications à l'Algérie littorale (Kabylie), *Reu Tunisienne Géographie.*

Plate 74-1. Indented low rocky coast cut into lithified Quaternary dunes (photo by M. Mahrour and A. Dagorne).

Plate 74-2. Rocky coast bordered by a shore platform extending beneath the sea west of Cape Benguit (photo by M. Mahrour and A. Dagorne).

Plate 74-3. Rocky shore giving way to a small beach at the outlet of a secondary wadi near Cape Sigli, west of Sidi Youcef. Note the impeded outflow from the wadi (photo by M. Mahrour and A. Dagorne).

Plate 74-4. The mouth of Wadi Isser (Kabylie). Note sandy sedimentation not yet fixed by vegetation, the form of spits at the river mouth, and the turbid waters with sediment in suspension (photo by M. Mahrour and A. Dagorne).

Plate 75-5. Sandy coast with dunes at Zemmouri, east of Algiers. Note that sand has impeded the fluvial outflow from the small wadi south of the port (photo by M. Mahrour and A. Dagorne).

75. MOROCCO

The Moroccan coast has developed very unequally along the Mediterranean Sea, at the extreme northeast of the country, and along the Atlantic Ocean (Fig. 75-1). The Mediterranean coasts are those of the Rif Mountain and of the Tangiers Peninsula. Lengthened considerably since the annexation of the Western Sahara, the Atlantic coasts have been the subject of many studies between the Rharb and the Anti-Atlas (which is, truly speaking, Atlantic Morocco). The coasts of Saharan Morocco are still very little known.

THE COASTS OF THE RIF AND TANGIERS PENINSULA

For 50 km, from Cape Spartel to Ceuta (Fig. 75-2), the coast of the Strait of Gibraltar cuts across perpendicular to the relief of the Rif; rocky cliffs correspond to the folds, and beaches to the synclines (Maurer 1968; André 1971). This model can be applied to the whole of the Mediterranean coast, with the exception that the littoral, after having been parallel to the relief, cuts it again obliquely. This forms two large sections: (1) a huge structural bay of more than 150 km between Ceuta and Al Hoceima, which is an arc-like form that widens considerably toward the northeast; and (2) the coast, directly overlooked by the mountain and composed nearly everywhere of high cliffs (300 m in the Bokkoya). A more varied eastern section, where prominent forelands (the *Cap des Trois Fourches* just 20 km into the sea) alternate with bays of sand and pebble beaches (Al Hoceima, wadi Kerte); near Nador, a spit of 25 km isolates a large lagoon (Sebkha Bou Areg).

The Rif also influences the extreme north of the Atlantic coast, from Cape Spartel to Larache. The coast, which is very regular, cuts through super-positions of complex thrust sheets where friable rocks, sandstones, and marl sand predominate. Beaches are the dominant feature, therefore, with sections of low cliffs cut into the Cretaceous sandstone and marl or even into the eolian sandstones.

The coasts of the Tangiers Peninsula and of the Rif correspond to a structural area, original to Morocco, which is a geosynclinal alpine chain. Study of the marine Quaternary shorelines (Maurer 1968; Angelier et al. 1976; Barathon 1978) uses their deformation as neotectonic indicators.

THE COASTS OF ATLANTIC MOROCCO

Despite differing structural conditions, resulting from the fact that they cut transversely through the great tectonic units of Morocco, the Atlantic coasts have several features in common (Fig. 75-3). They have a very regular overall outline, which is the result of a lengthy smoothing-out process. Because the continental shelf is not very wide (Summerhayes et al. 1971), the outline, which acquired its main characteristics as early as the Moghrebian (Middle–Upper Pliocene), has since varied little during the Quaternary changes of sea level. The resulting general layout, when seen in profile, appears composed of three main elements (Fig. 75-4):

1. An upper platform 20 km wide on the average and usually above 100 m high. This "Moghre-

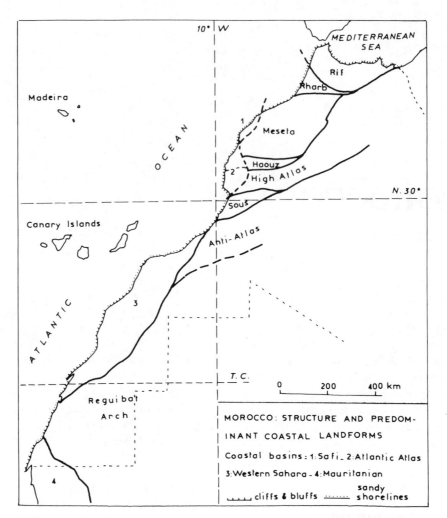

Figure 75-1. Structure and predominant coastal landforms of Morocco.

bian rasa" however, has been folded and culminates in the Atlantic Atlas at a height of more than 600 m (Weisrock 1980).

2. A lower platform (polygenic Quaternary rasa), at the most 1–2 km wide, and close to the present shoreline. The most typical aspect of this lower rasa is the "oulja," when this bench, alone, takes on the shape of a downfold parallel to the littoral, sometimes enclosing a lagoon. This bench can also be made up of several step-like marine terraces.

3. A dead cliff, which marks the farthest extent of the Quaternary Ocean toward the east and separates the upper and lower rasa.

This coastal structure underwent many changes, depending on the height of the dead cliff and its position in respect to the present shoreline. There is also considerable development of the littoral dunes, well supplied with infra-littoral sand, which develop under the favorable dual effect of the long summer drought and the strong prevailing northeast trade wind. These dunes underwent an early calcitic cementation, which assured their preservation; five successive generations can be found in the same place (Weisrock 1980).

The coast also presents variations that depend on each section: low coasts are found along the gulfs corresponding to the subsident plains of the Rharb and the Sous; high coasts, though fairly rare, along the Meseta, the Atlantic Atlas (Plate 75-1), and the Anti-Atlas, which form in all three projections toward the west.

The longest regular beaches correspond, therefore, to the plains of the Rharb (110 km) and of

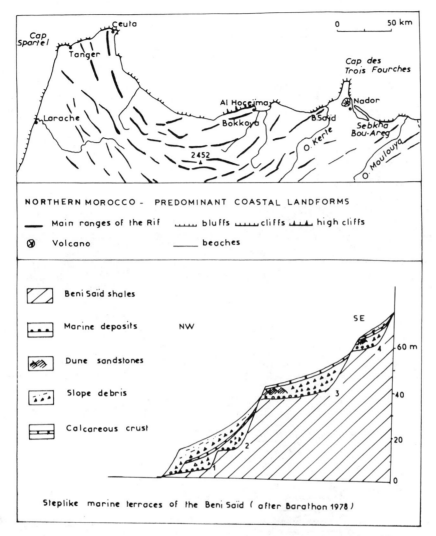

Figure 75-2. Northern Morocco. *A.* predominant coastal landforms; *B.* Step-like marine terraces of the Beni Said (adapted from Barathon 1978).

the Sous (60 km), and secondly to the region of Essaouira (20 km). These beaches supply some very important littoral dune complexes (Plate 75-2) sometimes 80 m high (Rharb), which isolate marshes (*merja*) towards the interior.

Beneath a high Plio-Moghrebian platform (*Sahel*), the Meseta Coast is a typical oulja-coast, where the Paleozoic basement and its covering strata only rarely appear at the shore, producing small, ill-pronounced, monoclinal capes (*skhour*). The oulja is sometimes bordered toward the ocean by a narrow beach, as is often the case between Casablanca and Cape Cantin; or it can come to an end with a low cliff cut into the eolian sandstones. Fine solution-forms are then developed:

visors, solution benches, and littoral clints, as between Rabat and Casablanca (Guilcher and Joly 1954) and from the Tensift wadi to Essaouira (Weisrock 1980). Behind the foredune, the northern marshes make way for lagoons (Oualidia) or for tidal marshes (Sidi Moussa). The coast of high cliffs from Cape Cantin to Jorf el Yhoudi forms an exception; in this area, the oulja has disappeared and the shore has joined the large dead cliff, eroded either at its foot or to its full height.

This erosion of the oulja, or of the lower platform, is constant along the Atlantic Atlas, where low cliffs develop in the calcareous basement, in the eolian sandstones, or in the Quaternary

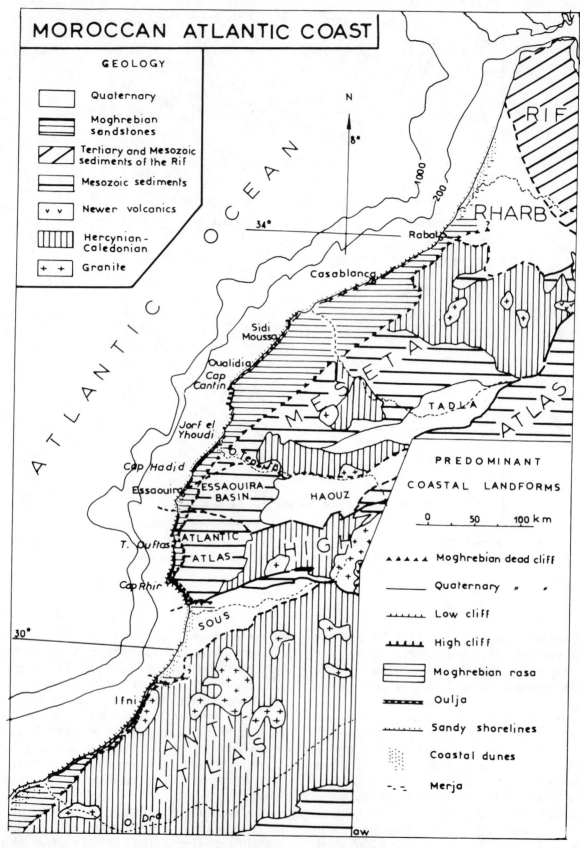

Figure 75-3. Geology and predominant landforms of the Moroccan Atlantic coast.

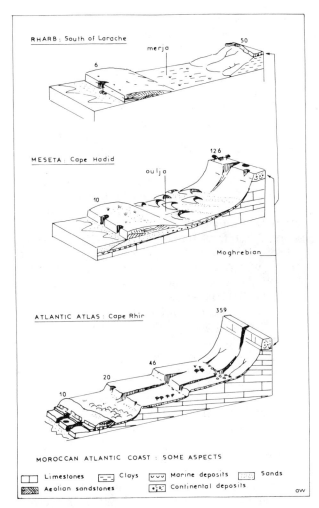

Figure 75-4. Some aspects of the Moroccan Atlantic coast: Rharb, Meseta, and Atlantic Atlas.

THE COASTS OF THE WESTERN SAHARA

Stretching for more than 1200 km (Ortlieb 1975), the western Saharan coasts have a general outline that is clearly "African"—that is, made up of long regular sections (Fig. 75-5). One can recognize both a predominant tectonic influence and a morphodynamic effect that depends on the long northwest swells that give rise to a north-south shore drift, associated with the Canary current (Guilcher 1954). This bearing (north-northeast–south-southwest) is also virtually that of the sand movement caused by the coastal trade wind. The coastal outline, from the Draa wadi to Cape Juby, is almost perpendicular to these bearings and serves as an alimentation area. Large seif dunes lie parallel to the trade wind, often over long distances (65 km from Megriou to the Seguia el Hamra). It seems that these dynamics have had an influence, except for a few variations, since the

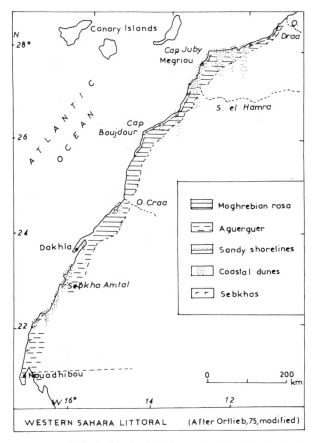

Figure 75-5. Western Sahara littoral (adapted from Ortlieb 1975).

debris. There too in some places, the great dead cliff is partially eroded (Timezguida Ouftas); but the most interesting aspect is the preservation of raised beaches at the extremity of the anticlines, which pitch toward the west (Cape Rhir). Thus it has been possible to reconsider the problem of the chronology of the Quaternary marine shore-lines of Morocco (Weisrock 1980), by a comparison with the Casablanca and Rabat sites (Biberson 1961; Beaudet 1971; Stearns 1978).

Finally, the Anti-Atlas coast (Oliva 1977) presents two main aspects. Along the Sous, the influence of the dunes is still predominant, and low cliffs are cut into thick calcareous sandstones. The coast of the Ifni crystalline stock and its Cambrian outer shell presents ragged cliffs and small beaches beneath wide, stepped rasas.

Moghrebian; the ancient generations of dunes and coastal spits (Dakhla, Nouadhibou) are consolidated and often cut into low cliffs. To the south of the Sebkha Amtal, the eolian landscape of small crusted sand-dunes is cut again by the ocean; this is the "Aguerguer," where the sebkhas multiply at the bottom of the small slacks between the dunes. This is the main morphological difference from the northern area, where, as from the Draa wadi, the coast is always bordered, as with Atlantic Morocco, by the Moghrebian rasa. But the latter only rarely surpasses 40 m in height, which means that the cliff sections (the area of Cape Boujdour, and from the Craa wadi to Dakhla) are never very high. The lower platform is less continuous than in Atlantic Morocco; isolated remains of ouljian beaches are found there (Hoang et al. 1978) and also of the sebkhas which, as in the south, would seem to be remains of the last Nouakchottian shoreline, of about 5,500 B.C. (Ortlieb 1975).

ANDRÉ L. E. WEISROCK

REFERENCES

André, A., 1971, Introduction à la géographie physique de la Péninsule tingitane, *Reu. Géog. Maroc* **19:** 57–77.

Angelier, J., J. P. Cadet, G. Delibrias, J. Fourniquet, M. Gigout, M. Guillemin, M. T. Hogrel, C. Lalou, and G. Pierre, 1976, Les déformations du quaternaire marin, indicateurs néotectoniques. Quelques exemples méditerranéens, *Reu Géographie Phys. et Géologie Dynam.,* **18**(5):427–447.

Barathon, J. J., 1978, Quelques aspects de l'évolution géomorphologique récente Rif du Nord-Est, in *Etude de certains milieux du Maroc,* vol. IV, C.N.R.S., Montpellier, 1–23.

Beaudet, G., 1971, Le Quaternaire marocain, état des études, *Reu Geog. Maroc* **20:**3–57.

Biberson, P., 1961, *Le cadre paléogéographique de la Préhistoire de Maroc Atlantique,* Publicatione du Service des Antiquities Marocaines, Rabat.

Guilcher, A., 1954, Dynamique et morphologie des côtes sableuses de l'Afrique Atlantique, *Inf. Géogr.* **1:**57–68.

Guilcher, A., and F. Joly, 1954, *Récherches sur la morphologie de la côte atlantique du Maroc,* Travaux de l'Institut Scientifique Chérif, "Editions Internationales," Tangier.

Hoang, C. T., L. Ortlieb, and A. Weisrock, 1978, Nouvelles datations ^{230}Th/^{234}U de terrasses marines ouljiennes du S-W du Maroc et leurs significations stratigraphique et tectonique, *Acad. Sci. Comptes Rendus* **286:**1759–1762.

Maurer, G., 1968, *Les montagnes du Rif central, étude géomorphologique,* Editions Marocaines et Internationales, Tangier.

Oliva, P., 1977, La plate-forme moghrébienne: néotectonique et eustatisme sur le littoral de l'Anti-Atlas, *Méditerranée,* **2:**73–91.

Ortlieb, L., 1975, *Recherches sur les formations Plio-Quaternaires du littoral ouest-saharien,* Travaux et Documents, O.R.S.T.O.M., Paris.

Stearns, C. E., 1978, Pliocene-Pleistocene emergence of the Moroccan Meseta, *Geol. Soc. America Bull.* **89:**1630–1644.

Summerhayes, C. P., A. H. Nutter, and J. S. Tooms, 1971, Geological structure and development of the continental margin of northwest Africa, *Marine Geology* **11:**1–25.

Weisrock, A., 1980, *Géomorphologie et Paléo-environnements de l'Atlas atlantique (Maroc).* Notes et Mémoires du Service Géologique du Maroc, mo 332, Rabat.

Plate 75-1. The cape and bay of Tafelney (Atlantic Atlas). A folded area cut by the ocean. The summit of the anticline is flattened by the Moghrebian rasa 200 m above the present shoreline, but the extent of the erosion of the cliffs is limited to a height of about 15 m. In the foreground, low scrub of *Argania spinosa* and *Euphorbia beaumierana* (photo by A. Weisrock).

Plate 75-2. Holocene seif dunes and moving sand dunes of Cape Sim, near Essaouira. The plant cover (forest of *Juniperus phoenicea*) has virtually disappeared, except on the crusted seif dunes. Fixation of the barchan dunes is taking place, but here the sand continues to supply the beach under the effect of the north-northeast trade wind (photo by P. Oliva).

76. SARAOUI

At the western limit of the world's largest desert, the Saraoui coast (previously Spanish Sahara or Rio de Oro) borders the Atlantic Ocean and is about 1400 km long (Figure 76-1). It forms an intermediate environment 100 km wide, between the Sahara desert and the arid archipelago of the Canaries.

GEOLOGY

The Saraoui coast is cut into Tertiary and Quaternary formations. The Tertiary is represented by the continental edge of sandy texture, which, north of 23° N, rests on the Cretaceous that outcrops between Dra Nadd and Tarfaya. South of 23° N the continental margin rests locally on the planed-off Precambrian Shield.

The Quaternary is represented by the old dune ridges of Afrafir and Aguergues, and by fluvial and marine deposits. There is not a single permanent river along this whole coast.

PRESENT CLIMATE

The coastal desert is explained by a climatic regime engendered by the Azores anticyclone, producing trade winds that blow, from the latitude of Mugador, from north to north-northeast through to south to south-southwest, almost parallel with the shoreline (Bourcart 1928).

Driven southward and deflected to the west by the earth's rotation, surface waters are replaced by deeper, colder water (deMartonne and Aufrère 1928). As in many other coastal deserts, the Saraoui coastline is bordered by a cold current, the Canary Current, which is effective between 10° and 40° N. The permanent presence of cold surface water explains the advection fogs and high inversion mists. At night, when solar radiation no longer compensates for the cooling, condensation occurs over the ocean. This generates a fog that rises during the day, just like the stratum of "high fog" in California. The weak uprisings and the stability of the air are responsible for the meager rains. The fogs, more frequent in summer than winter, reduce the duration of insulation and explain the weak thermal amplitudes. At Rio de Oro the dew falls during the night on the shore but diminishes very quickly toward the interior, as far as 30 km from the coastline. In the coastal desert, dew and winter rains, less rare than inland, favor the development of the typical Saharan vegetation associations of chenopods and acacias, especially around closed depressions. At Cape Juby rainfall is 105 mm/yr, and mean temperature 18.3° C; farther south (±100 km), annual rainfall does not exceed 50 mm.

The northern Saraoui coast also receives westerly winds in winter, within the domain of cyclonic depressions of the temperate zone. The Wadi Dra in the north receives orographic rain from the High Atlas; its upper course has a temporary regime, but the lower course (towards 29° N) is waterless. South of Cape Blanc the summer rains are annual, carried by the west- to- southwest monsoon.

Farther south the wadis—the Seheb al Harcha, Wadi Chebeica, Udet Laoguig, and Sahar—are not of coastal "quebradas" type. Still farther south (28°–23° N), external drainage fades out; a large fixed sandy ridge, the Afrafir, is interposed between the coast and the hinterland, causing internal drainage. The Draa Afrafir 4–8 km wide,

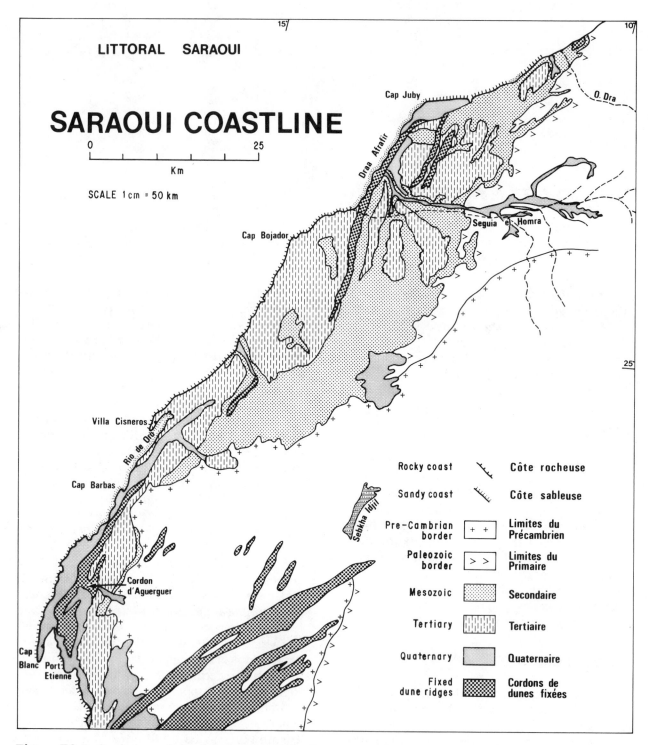

Figure 76-1. Geology and geomorphology of the Saraoui coast.

extends from Cape Juby to 25° 12′ N. There is a coastal sand ridge between Cape Juby and Aaiun, where the Seguiet el Hamra crosses in a gorge to flow into the sea at Fum el Uad. The Seguiet el Hamra is the longest wadi of the Rio de Oro. Its complex braiding and meandering contrast with the aridity of its basin.

In this arid area, some occasional wadis open onto sebkhas, like Wadi Lemnaider, which flows into the sebkha of Aridal around 26° N, in contrast with Wadi Assag, the course of which fades out several kilometers from the ocean.

COASTAL MORPHOLOGY

The Present Coast

The Atlantic coast between Wadi Dra and Cape Blanc includes both rocky sectors and low sandy coasts.

For over 1000 km between Wadi Dra and the Gulf of the Rio de Oro, close to the Tropic of Cancer, the sandstone and limestone cliffs are cut into a plateau interrupted by low areas of coastal sebkhas. This rocky coast is interrupted, between 27° 48'N and south of Cape Juby at the latitude of the Laasailia sebkha, by a sandy coast consisting of the northern part of the fixed Afrafir sand ridge (Lecointre 1962, 1966). The cliff, which forms the coastline, is backed by a plateau of crystalline terrain, shaped as a peneplain called Tiris, from which rise several inselbergs.

Between Cape Barbas and Cape Blanc the cliff is also rocky for 100 km, but this does not extend into Mauritania.

Between the Gulf of Rio de Oro and Cape Barbas, the coast is low and sandy for about 200 km. The coastal zone has many sebkhas, from several square kilometers in area to more than 100 km², separated from the shore by sandy ridges or dunes. *Sebkha* is an Arabic term describing a flat area, generally floodable, often but not always in a depression, where saline soils prohibit all vegetation on most of the surface. Perthuisot (1975) has distinguished three categories: *Paralic sebkhas* are more or less related to the marine environment; they include coastal sebkhas separated from the sea by dune ridges and beaches, with old lagoons isolated from the sea. *Translittoral sebkhas* are old rias or gulfs. *Limnitic sebkhas* are dessicated lake basins in the hinterland.

The Ancient Coastlines

The coastal desert has been subject to the climatic oscillations found throughout the Sahara (Einsele, Herm and Schwarz 1974).

A Plio-Pleistocene marine transgression (the *Moghrebien*) submerged a zone 50–100 km wide all along the coast. It is indicated today by the presence of thick fossiliferous deposits above the cliffs.

Research by Elouard, Faure and Hebrard (1969), Faure and Hebrard (1973), and Hebrard and Faure (1975) has permitted identification of a Holocene marine transgression (called *Mellahien* in Morocco and *Nouakchottien* in Mauritania) 6000–4000 B. P., followed by a lagoonal phase (4000–2500 B. P.) when the modern coastal sebkhas were old gulfs.

The work of Delibrias, Ortlieb and Petit-Maire (1977), using more than 100 radiocarbon dates, has elucidated the evolution of the Saraoui coast in the Holocene. They confirmed the existence of a marine level more than 2 m above present sea level, with shells in situ 4000–6150 B. P. in the old lagoons. From 4000 to 2000 B. P. a lower sea level was accompanied by building of a sandy coastal ridge that separated the lagoons from the sea. Most of the coastal sebkhas date from the Holocene. A large mammalian fauna and numerous human skeletons indicate a biological optimum, with a climatic oscillation towards drier conditions, after 2000 B. P.

MONIQUE MAINGUET

REFERENCES

Bourcart, J., 1928, L'action du vent à la surface de la terre. I: Ablation, *Reu Géographie Phys. et Géologie Dynam.* **1**:26–54.

Delibrias, G., L. Ortlieb, and N. Petit-Maire, 1977, *Le Littoral ouest-saharien: nouvelles dates* ¹⁴C, Recherches francaises sur le Quaternaire, INQUA.

Einsele, G., D. Herm, and H. U. Schwarz, 1974, Sea level fluctuation during the past 6000 yr at the Coast of Mauritania, *Quaternary Res.* **4**:282–289.

Elouard, P., H. Faure, and L. Hebrard, 1969, Quaternaire du littoral mauritanien entre Nouakchott et Port-Etienne, *8th Cong. Int. INQUA* vol. 23.

Faure, H., and L. Hebrard, 1973, Variations des lignes de rivages au Senegal et en Mauritanie au cours de l'Holocene, *9th Cong. Int. INQUA, Quat. Shorelines Commission* vol. 4.

Hebrard, L., and H. Faure, 1975, *Activité de recherche sur les lignes de rivages au Senegal et en Mauritanie (1974-1975), Rap. pour la commission des lignes de rivages,* INQUA.

Lecointre, G., 1962, Sur la géologie de la prequ'ile de Villa-Cisners, Rio de Oro, *Acad. Sci. Comptes Rendus* **254**:1121–1122.

Lecointre, G., 1966, Neogene et Quaternaire du Rio de Oro, *Soc. Geol. France Compte Rendus,* **10**:404.

Martonne, E. de, and L. Aufrère, 1928, *L'extension des regions privées d'ecoulement vers l'Ocean.* U.G.I. (3).

Ortlieb, L., and N. Petit-Maire, 1976, The Atlantic border

humain: le littoral ouest-saharien depuis 10 000 ans, *L'Anthropologie* **83**(1):69–82.

Petit-Maire, N., ed., 1979, *Le Sahara atlantique a l'Holocene: peuplement et ecologie.* Centre Rech. Anthropologiques, Prehist. et Ethnographiques Mém.

Petit-Maire, N., 1979, Cadre ecologique et peuplement of the Sahara in Holocene times, *Palaeoecology of Africa* **9**:4–6.

Perthuisot, J. P., 1975, De la signification du mot "sebkha" en géologie: exemples tunisiens, *Association Senegalaise d'Etude du Quaternaire Africain, Bulletin de Maison de Sênegal.* **44–45:**67–75.

77. MAURITANIA

The Mauritanian coast of West Africa is one of the chief desert coasts of the world. It stretches about 850 km between 16° N and 21° N. Atmospheric subsidence associated with the subtropical high pressure belt accounts for the aridity of those latitudes, but the aridity of coastal Mauritania is intensified by cold-water upwelling and associated temperature inversions induced by the Canary Current setting southward at 0.5 knot. Annual precipitation along the coast ranges from less than 50 mm in the north to little more than 300 mm in the vicinity of the Senegal River delta in the south.

Three promontories, two within Mauritania and the third to the south in Senegal, anchor this coastal zone and create two distinct sections. The northern section between Cape Blanc and Cape Timiris (Fig. 77-1) is most irregular. Rocky headlands often more than 20 m in height reach the sea, and a few large bays, such as Lévrier, Arguin, and St. Jean, intrude the coast. Tidal flats margin nearly the whole of this coastal section, the greatest extent lying north of Cape Timiris and within Lévrier Bay (Plate 77-1). An offshore platform, Arguin Bank, extends seaward 100 km, and small portions reach sea level near the outer limits. Arguin Bank shelters the northern section of the coast, greatly reducing wave energy. The coastal zone between Cape Blanc and Cape Timiris is part of the flyway and stopover areas for migratory birds from Greenland, Europe, and tropical Africa, and in 1976 the area was made a national park (Atlas de la République Islamique de Mauritanie 1977).

The southern section of coastal Mauritania stretches in smooth, nearly unbroken form from Cape Timiris to the Senegal River (Fig. 77-2) and

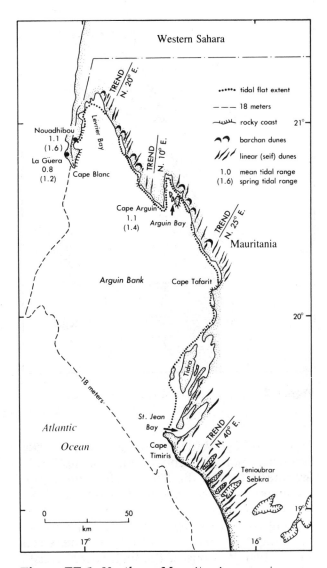

Figure 77-1. Northern Mauritanian coast.

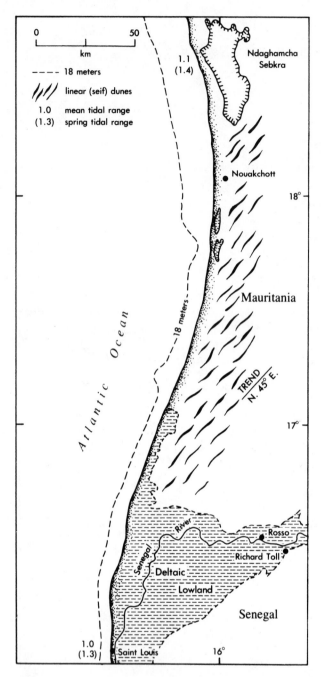

0   50

km

- - - - 18 meters

/// linear (seif) dunes

1.0 mean tidal range

(1.3) spring tidal range

Ndaghamcha Sebkra

1.1
(1.4)

Nouakchott

18°

Atlantic Ocean

18 meters

Mauritania

TREND N. 45° E.

17°

River

Senegal

Rosso

Richard Toll

Deltaic

Lowland

Senegal

1.0
(1.3)

Saint Louis

16°

Figure 77-2. Southern Mauritanian coast.

Western coastal Mauritania lies within the Senegal sedimentary basin that accumulated thousands of meters of terrestrial and marine sediments during the Cretaceous and early Tertiary. Fluvial arkosic sands and gravels ("Continental Terminal") top the sedimentary sequence, after which a long period of tropical weathering developed an extensive, thick iron-bearing crust (*cuirasse ferruginuese*). The crust is regarded as the boundary between Tertiary and Quaternary periods. Pleistocene sea levels during the last interglacial or interstadial reached +4 m–+6 m. Marine regression and extreme aridity followed and resulted in the formation of linear (seif) red dunes. The trend of the seif dunes varies from about N 20° E in the vicinity of Lévrier Bay to about N 45° E near the Senegal River. With the exception of Cape Arguin, the trend of the dunes declines progressively from true north between Lévrier Bay and the Senegal River. Some of the dunes have blocked the lower Senegal River valley and induced alluviation (Elouard 1966).

Evidence of Holocene marine transgression in Mauritania comes from mapping of beach materials and the presence of heavy shells (*Arca senilis*). The Nouakchottian (Flandrian) sea level about +3 m above present datum is based on carbon-dating of the shells and occurred about 5500 B.P. Stromatolithic algae indicate a marine regression to −3.5 m about 4100 B.P. Possibly one or two smaller marine transgressions on this stable coast came between 4000 and 1500 B.P. (Einsele, Herm, and Schwarz 1974). Raised beaches and beige-and-yellow dunes may be associated with these smaller transgressions, and they often cover much of the Nouakchottian evidence. Furthermore, the yellow sands often lie between the red seif dunes and sufficiently dam the interdune areas to create lakes. The white sands fronting the coast form the present dunes and beaches.

Tidal range and variation are not great on the Mauritanian coast. The smallest mean tidal range occurs at La Güera on western Cape Blanc (0.8 m) and the greatest at Nouadhibou (1.1 m) within the partially enclosed, shoaling Lévrier Bay. Minimal and maximal spring tidal ranges occur at La Güera (1.2 m) and Nouadhibou (1.6 m), respectively. Within Lévrier Bay, flood and ebb currents are greatest along the western side. At Nouadhibou, the flood current sets northward with a maximum velocity of 1.5 knots, and the ebb current sets southward with a maximum velocity of 2.5 knots. Shoals within Lévrier Bay are more extensive on its eastern side than on its western side (Plate 77-1).

beyond to Cape Verde in Senegal. Neither rocky headlands nor deep embayments mar its gentle arcuate form, and the Senegal River delta protrudes only slightly to deform the coastal outline. The port at Nouakchott consists of a wharf 350 m long that gives depths of 8 m and permits lighterage. The coast is fronted by a rather steep inner shelf. It is one of the high-energy coasts of the world and is lined by nearly continuous high dunes.

Mauritania is a significant locality in having active eolian dunes that supply sand to an open ocean coast and hence contribute to marine sediments (Sarnthein and Diester-Haass 1977). Barchan dunes reach the coast between northern Lévrier Bay and Cape Tafarit (Fig. 77-1); they seldom exist at the coast south of Cape Tafarit. Northerly and northeasterly trade winds dominate this coastal zone and account for the alignment of the barchan and linear dunes. This belt currently contributes $5-13 \times 10^6 \, m^3$ of quartzitic sand to the continental shelf each year (Sarnthein and Walger 1974). The relatively coarse sand $(180-220 \, \mu)$ is trapped and piled up as sand wedges that laterally prograde from the shore with the upper edge at sea level. The wedge gradually widens the foreshore. During the Pleistocene lowering of sea level, the sand wedges would have formed near the upper part of the continental slope and would have moved to the ocean basins by turbidity currents or sand flows, or both. During Pleistocene peak glacial periods, when the linear (seif) dunes were active and not fixed as they are today, sand discharge to the Atlantic Ocean is estimated to have been at least five to ten times the present rate. The Pleistocene sand contributions were comparable to the present total loads of rivers such as the Nile or Niger.

Sands obtained from active barchan dunes and from erosion of fossil seif dunes provide materials that are reworked and moved progressively southward by longshore drift through the beach and dune systems of the coast. Northwesterly to northerly waves strike the coastal zone more than 65% of the time, and especially stormy conditions prevail during the winter months as the result of cyclonic disturbances that pass to the north (Hogben and Lumb 1967). Sands drifted southward contribute to coastal progradation of southern Mauritania, and they move around the head of steep submarine canyons to reach as far south as Cape Verde in Senegal (Sarnthein and Diester-Haass 1977). The steep inner shelf and exposure to the Atlantic swell permit wave energy of enormous magnitude (112.4×10^7 ergs/s) on the coast; more wave energy hits the southern coastal area in three hours than hits the Mississippi delta in 365 days (Wright and Coleman 1973). The high wave energy and southward longshore drift have flattened the Senegal River delta and turned the river southward (Fig. 77-2). The river flows parallel with the coast behind an elongated sandy spit, on which St. Louis is built, before it discharges its load into the ocean.

Coastal dunes are poorly developed north of Cape Timiris but well developed to the south. Immediately south of Cape Timiris coastal dunes attain heights of 35 m or more, while farther south their heights are generally less than 20 m (Plate 77-2). The width of the coastal dune belt varies from 200-500 m but reaches a maximum of 2 km north of the Senegal River delta. Where coastal dunes truncate seif dunes south of Cape Timiris, salt pans (sebkhas, elsewhere known as sebkras or sabkhas) occupy the interdune areas (Plate 77-3). Farther south the sebkhas parallel the coast and lie immediately behind the dunes. A few are large, such as Ndaghamcha Sebkha, while others north of the Senegal River delta flood during peak river discharge, usually in September or October (Fig. 77-2). They continue south of the delta into Senegal, where they are known as Niayes.

DONALD E. VERMEER

REFERENCES

Atlas de la République Islamique de Mauritanie, 1977, Editions Jeune Afrique, Paris.

Einsele, G., D. Herm, and H. U. Schwarz, 1974, Holocene eustatic (?) sea level fluctuations at the coast of Mauritania, *Meteor Forschungsergebnisse, Reihe C* **18:**43-62.

Elouard, P., 1966, Le quaternaire du bassin du Sénégal, in *Bassins Sédimentairs du Littoral Africain*, D. Reyre, ed., Assoc. des services geologique africains, Paris, pp. 95-97.

Hogben, H., and F. E. Lumb, 1967, *Ocean Wave Statistics*, Her Majesty's Stationery Office, London.

Sarnthein, M., and L. Diester-Haass, 1977, Eolian-sand turbidites, *Jour. Sed. Petrology* **47:**868-890.

Sarnthein, M., and E. Walger, 1974, Der äolische Sandstrom aus der W-Sahara zur Atlantikküste, *Geol. Rundschau* **63:**1065-1087.

Wright, L. D., and J. M. Coleman, 1973, Variations in morphology of major river deltas as functions of ocean wave and river discharge regime, *Amer. Assoc. Petroleum Geologists Bull.* **57:**370-398.

Plate 77-1. Southwestward view of Lévrier Bay and Cape Blanc. Darkened areas represent exposed tidal flats around head of the bay (photo by D. E. Vermeer).

Plate 77-2. Coastal dunes about 20 m in height, approximately 40 km north of Nouakchott. Wreck of wooden vessel embedded in beach materials in foreground (photo by J. R. Illick).

Plate 77-3. Westward view of linear (seif) dunes trending N 40° E and truncated at coast south of Cape Timiris. Interdune sebkhas with salt incrustations lie between darker dunes (photo by D. E. Vermeer).

78. SENEGAL AND GAMBIA

Senegal and Gambia are considered together in this description of their coasts, since Gambia, a small country inserted into Senegal, includes only the immediate surroundings of the lower course of the Gambia River (Fig. 78-1). The part of Senegal situated on the south side of Gambia is called Casamance from the name of the river flowing through it.

The geological structure of these countries consists of a Mesozoic and Cenozoic basin lying on the western edge of the Precambrian and Paleozoic African block. The sedimentary series begins at the Upper Jurassic, and includes mostly Cretaceous sands, sandstones, clays, and marls; Eocene limestones, clays, and phosphates; and Tertiary sandstones belonging to the so-called "Terminal Continental," the precise age of which is not well known. The main coastal outcrops of these rocks (especially the Eocene) are between Dakar and Sangomar Point. At the westernmost tip of the heavily faulted Cap Vert peninsula, volcanic rocks of Tertiary and Quaternary age are found.

During the Upper Pleistocene, the so-called Inchirian transgression (about 35,000 years ago) left coastal deposits lying at 20 m depth beneath the mouth of the Senegal River. Later on, about 18,000 B.P. during the late Wisconsinian regression down to about 120 m below present sea level, the Ogolian red dune belt spread under arid conditions over a large part of western Senegal. The Holocene transgression, which is known there as Nouakchottian and reached its maximum 5500 B.P. widely invaded the Senegal, Sine, Saloum, Gambia, and Casamance valleys. The gulfs thus created were subsequently filled. The modern Senegal delta buried the Nouakchottian marine deposits in the north, where successive coastal spits enclosed lagoons and prograded the general shoreline westward. Some of the highest Nouakchottian beaches, however, are still exposed on rocky coasts of Cap Vert peninsula and in several places of the outer Gambian coast (Faure and Elouard 1967; Michel et al. 1968; Michel 1973).

The climate, which governs the river discharge, belongs to the tropical boreal type, with a long dry season in winter and rains concentrated in summer. The rainfall and the length of the wet season increase from north to south; in the 1931–1960 period rainfall was 370 mm/yr at Saint Louis, 670 mm/yr at Dakar, 800 mm/yr at Kaolack, and 1550 mm/yr at Ziguinchor. In recent years the country has experienced severe droughts, so that the rainfall for 1970–1980 dropped to 208 mm/yr at Saint Louis, 345 mm/yr at Dakar, and 1270 mm/yr at Oussouye near Ziguinchor. The annual curve of the discharge of the Senegal and Gambia rivers shows a prominent peak in September and very low levels from January to July. The Senegal discharge during floods varies from 2500–3700 m³/s according to years, and the mean ratio between the extreme months is 1 to 860. For this reason and because of the very low gradient of this river, the tide is observed as far as 440 km upstream during the low stages and the salt content rises to 29‰ at 60 km. The tidal range at Saint Louis is 1.2 m in spring tides, 0.6 m in neap tides; at Dakar, 1.3 m and 0.5 m; at Banjul, formerly Bathurst, Gambia, 1.6 m and 0.7 m. In the Guier and Rkiz lakes, which receive a part of the annual floods, the level fluctuates accordingly; during the larger floods, the Senegal spreads into coastal lagoons such as Marigot des Maringouins behind the Mauritanian coastline. The data on

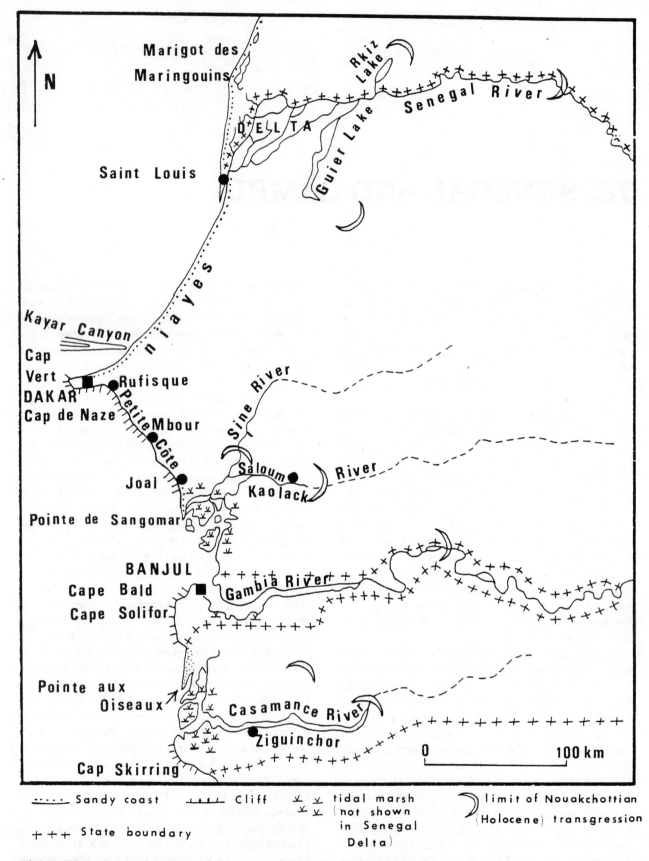

Figure 78-1. General outline of the coast of Senegal and Gambia, from various sources.

the Gambia River are much poorer (Michel 1973; Sall 1982; Guilcher and Nicholas 1954).

On the seaside, the main force in action is the northwesterly swell, generated in the storm belt of temperate latitudes, and acting on the whole coast of Senegal and Gambia as far south as Casamance. The southwesterly swell is extremely rare (less than 2% of the observations). Because of the outline of the coast, this northwesterly swell is, of course, more efficient north of Cap Vert than to the south. The dominant coastal wind, which is moderate, also blows from the north-northwest, in the north at least (Senegal delta), and must be considered in order to understand some coastal and intracoastal features.

SENEGAL DELTA AND LANGUE DE BARBARIE

The distributaries in the Senegal delta are skirted by post-Nouakchottian levees. In smaller creeks, the tidal currents are the only ones in action during the dry season. At this latitude (16° N) on the African west coast, the marshy vegetation (Plate 78-1) consists principally of herbaceous plants, but mangroves (*Avicennia* and *Rhizophora*) also grow in places along the main course of the river upstream to Saint Louis; the trees are rather stunted. The northernmost limit of mangrove is near Cape Timiris in Mauritania (Guilcher and Nicholas 1954).

On the outer beach, sand travels to the south under the impulse of the oblique swell. A pattern of small oblique spits and "bays" is typical of this outer beach, being, as on the coast of the Landes of Gascony in France, an adaptation *par échelons* of the beach to the swell obliquity, with rip currents occurring at the outlets of the bays. The amount of sand in transit in front of Saint Louis has been estimated at 500,000–900,000 tons/yr. The result is that the Senegal mouth is deflected to the south by a long sand spit called the Barbary Tongue (Langue de Barbarie). The length of this spit fluctuates over time, but never exceeding 25 km from Saint Louis. Figure 78-2 shows the relatively long spit that existed in 1954. The northernmost known location of the mouth was 2.5 km north of Saint Louis in 1850. Twenty-four breaches of the Tongue were reported from 1850 to 1980, resulting either from heavy swell on the outer coast or from river encroachment on the inner side during floods. After each episode the Langue grew again to the south (Sall 1982).

The moderate local wind affects the coastal area

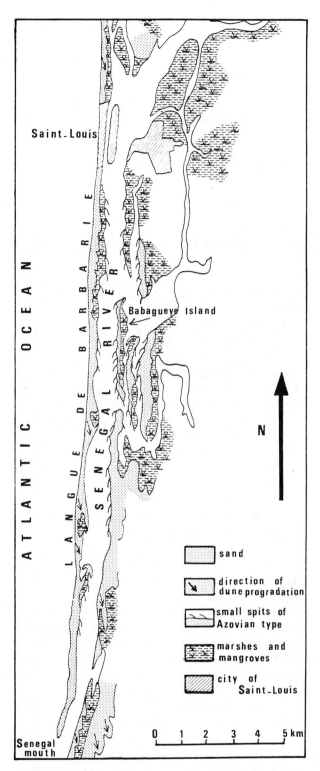

Figure 78-2. Lower course of Senegal River and Langue de Barbarie, from Guilcher and Nicolas (1954).

in two ways. First, it builds low dunes oblique to the coastline, periodically destroyed on the Barbary Tongue, but more stable elsewhere. Second, it generates small waves on the main lower course of the Senegal River and its parallel distributaries. These waves in turn build sets of small recurved spits (Plate 78-2) evenly spaced, belonging to the Azovian type (as defined on the shores of the Sea of Azov), particularly in the vicinity of Babagueye Island. Thus the swell and the wind, acting in the same direction, although of quite different origins, explain respectively the outer and inner coastal landforms.

From the Senegal mouth to Cap Vert occurs the so-called *Niayes coast*. It is a sandy coast with low dunes, behind which is found a set of depressions, the niayes, which are swamps or lakes during the wet season and dry pans in winter. The sand carried to the south by the coastal drift is probably largely engulfed to great depths by the Kayar Canyon, the head of which lies very close to the shore.

The following section is the *Cap Vert Peninsula* and the *Petite Côte* (smaller coast), where cliffs expose dolerites and basalts of Cap Vert itself, west of Dakar City, and clays, limestones, and clayey sandstones from Rufisque to Joal. Comparatively sheltered from the northwesterly swell (sediment drift to the south: only 30,000–70,000 m^3/yr), the Petite Côte cliffs are nevertheless retreating. At Cap de Naze, where the cliff is, exceptionally, 55 m high, the retreat, conditioned by slumping and gullying, is estimated by Sall (1982) at 22 cm/yr at the top. At Ouakam, Cap Vert, in dolerites, corrosion forms with a seaward rampart are observed at the foot of a cliff 25 m high (Guilcher et al. 1962).

The last section is the beginning of the Southern Rivers, *Rivières du Sud*, which continue into Bissau Guinea and the Republic of Guinea. Cliffs and rocky platforms, cut into sandstones of the "Terminal Continental," are found here in Gambia (Cape Bald, Cape Solifor) and south of Casamance River (Cap Skirring), but the most typical aspect is the complex of estuaries and marshes (Fig. 78-3) that extends along the lower courses of Sine-Saloum and Casamance Rivers (Sall 1982; Diop et al. 1978). The lower course of the Gambia River does not spread into so many marshes since this estuary is cut into sandstones capped by a ferruginous crust and hence is generally narrower (Michel 1973). The muddy marshes of the Southern Rivers, fed with seawater by intricate and beautiful sets of creeks, bear many more thriving mangroves than the Senegal delta because of the

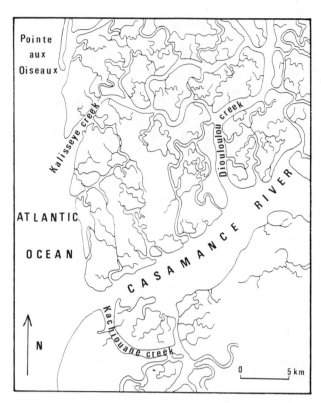

Figure 78-3. Tidal marshes and creeks in Casamance, from Sall (1982).

more southern position and higher rainfall. However, in these green intracoastal landscapes, muddy areas devoid of vegetation, called *tanns*, are found between the mangroves and the inland growth of terrestrial plants. During the dry season the seawater covers all the tidal-flats at spring tides, while at neap tides the inner parts are not submerged for several days; because there is no rain, so that salinity increases in these areas by evaporation and soon becomes too high for mangrove growth. On the other hand, these tidal marshes have been partly reclaimed and transformed in polders for rice cultivation by the Diola population over a very long period, so that the landscape is partly artificial.

The outer coast of Sine-Saloum and Casamance is not so sheltered from the swell as the Petite Côte, so that the sand drift to the south is estimated at some 300,000 m^3/yr at Pointe de Sangomar (Sall 1982). The growth of this sandy headland, which is irregular, amounted to some 3,300 m from 1895 to 1980, with a decrease in accretion since 1930. The Bird Spit (Pointe aux Oiseaux) in Casamance is of the same kind, with a more gradual progradation.

ANDRÉ GUILCHER

REFERENCES

Diop, E. S., M. M. Sall, F. Verger, 1978, Cartographie automatique d'un milieu littoral tropical: îles du Saloum (Sénégal) d'après les données Landsat 1. *Photo-Interprétation* **6-5a, b.**

Faure, H., and P. Elouard, 1967, Schéma des variations du niveau de l'Océan Atlantique sur la côte ouest de l'Afrique depuis 40 000 ans. *Acad. Sci. Comptes Rendus* **265:**784–787.

Guilcher, A., L. Berthois, and R. Battistini, 1962, Formes de corrosion littorale dans les roches volcaniques, particulièrement à Madagascar et au Cap Vert (Sénégal). *Cahiers Océanog.* **14:**208–240.

Guilcher, A., and J. P. Nicolas, 1954, Observations sur la Langue de Barbarie et les bras du Sénégal aux environs de Saint Louis. *Inf. Comité Central Océanogr. Et. Côtes Bull.* (Paris) **6:**227–242.

Michel, P., 1973, *Les bassins des fleuves Sénégal et Gambie, étude géomorphologique.* Off. Rech. Scient. et Techn. Outremer Mém. 63, Paris.

Michel, P., P. Elouard, and H. Faure, 1968, Nouvelles recherches sur le Quaternaire récent de la région de Saint Louis (Sénégal). *Inst. Fondamental Afrique Noire Bull.* (Dakar) **XXX-A:**1–38.

Sall, M. M., 1982, *Dynamique et morphogenèse actuelles au Sénégal occidental,* Thesis, University of Strasbourg.

Plate 78-1. Small *Rhizophora* and herbaceous marine vegetation on the Senegal delta near Saint Louis (photo by A. Guilcher).

Plate 78-2. Series of small sandspits of Azovian type along the Senegal River lower course (photo by A. Guilcher).

79. GUINEA BISSAU AND REPUBLIC OF GUINEA

The coastlines of Guinea Bissau (comprising two parts: one continental, one insular [Bissagos Archipelagoes]) and the Republic of Guinea (Popular and Revolutionary Republic of Guinea) are about 250 and 300 km long respectively (Figs. 79-1 and 79-2). These two sectors are an integral part of the "Southern Rivers"—a series of rias that have dissected this natural environment, where they cross the low coastal plain, with an intricate network of tidal channels and important stands of mangroves (Berthois 1958).

A unique feature of these amphibious, marshy, and uniformly muddy coastal areas (situated 13–18° longitude west and 9–13° latitude north) is the existence of small cliffs, chiefly in the lateritic duricrust on Bissagos Archipelagoes, Verga Cape, and the Kaloum Peninsula (Figs. 79-1 and 79-2). This duricrust at several places plunges some meters in depth onto the inner continental shelf. Some *Rhizophora* or *Avicennia* vegetation is often found on outcrops of duricrust (Plates 79-1 and 79-2).

Geologically, late Quaternary formations outcrop on these ria coasts (Aymé 1965). Indeed, this low plain with its large estuaries and rias, from Casamance to Sierra Leone, was inundated during transgressive periods of the late Quaternary marine transgression. Units dating from this period lie discordantly on those of the early and middle Quaternary, or on older formations (Figs. 79-1 and 79-2). These formations are composed of sand, mud, and other clayey deposits, and continue onto the continental shelf, a present sedimentation and accumulation area. The exis-

tence of submerged deltas, submarine shoals, and former river channels exhibit this clearly. For example the Konkoure River, whose channel direction continues across the continental shelf under the sea (MacMaster and others 1970, 1971). This general presentation of the typical features of the Guinean coastline will center on three themes: analysis of the major geomorphological units chacteristic of these regions, dynamics of their submergence in the late Quaternary, and a study of their littoral evolution.

GEOMORPHOLOGY

The Guinean shorelines can be reviewed as six major geomorphological units:

1. Mangrove swamps and mud flats with salt marshes, sometimes interrupted by cliffs and bluffs (i.e., Kaloum Peninsula, Verga Cape, Ilhei-do-rei).
2. Bare or herbaceous *tannes*, a kind of terrace generally formed by old mud flats.
3. Coastal dunes constructed on old sandy beach ridges.
4. Shallow swale basins between beach ridges.
5. Sandy beaches, very localized, sometimes with recent shore bars.
6. Sandy or muddy shoals, exposed at low tide.

In this coastal area characterized by an intense development of tidal channels, with very frequent cut-off meanders and interconnections between

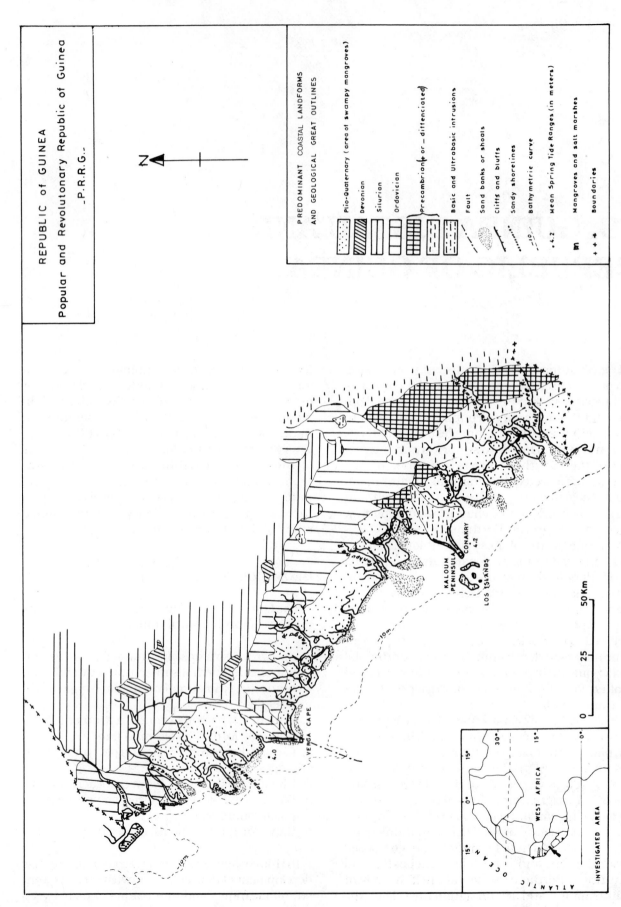

Figure 79-1. Republic of Guinea Bissau: predominant coastal landforms and geological outlines.

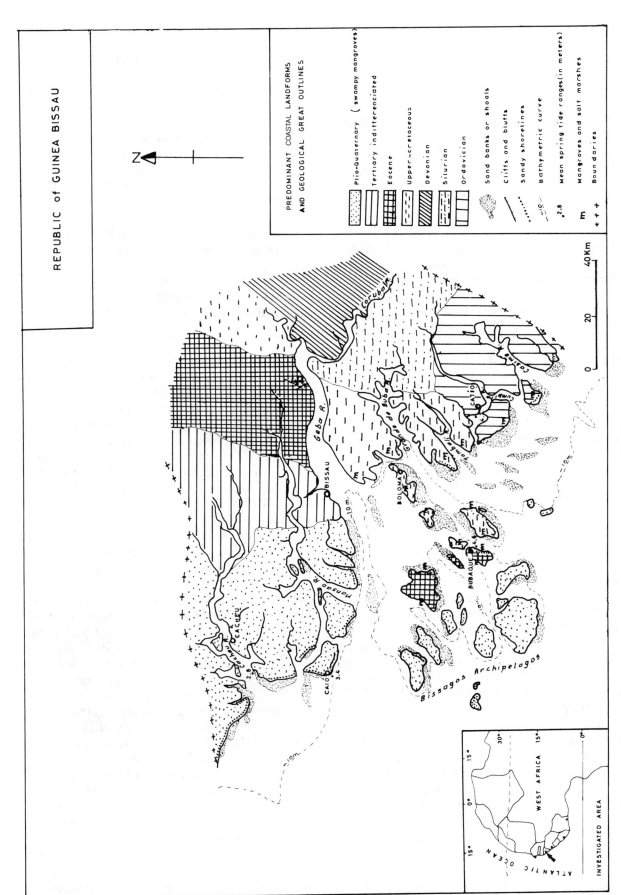

REPUBLIC of GUINEA BISSAU

**PREDOMINANT COASTAL LANDFORMS
AND GEOLOGICAL GREAT OUTLINES**

Plio-Quaternary (swampy mangroves)

Tertiary indifferenciated

Eocene

Upper-cretaceous

Devonian

Silurian

Ordovician

Sand banks or shoals

Cliffs and bluffs

Sandy shorelines

Bathymetric curve

Mean spring tide ranges(in meters)

Mangroves and salt marshes

Boundaries

Figure 79-2. Republic of Guinea: predominant coastal landforms and geological outlines.

563

adjacent channels, the mangrove swamps and mud flats constitute the predominant units (Plates 79-3 and 79-4). Their development is due to multiple processes of sedimentation. The deposits that have built these swampy regions result from a complex combination of fine materials (muddy, clayey or slimy, bluish or grayish colored), often associated with remains of marine organisms. Three species of vegetation prevail because of their adaptation to the salinity and to the permanent tidal submersion: *Rhizophora racemosa* (Plate 79-5), *Rhizophora mangle* (Plate 79-1) and *Avicennia nitida* or *africana* (Plate 79-2); the mangrove vegetation in general is sparse in species.

The mangroves are quite often close to the *tannes*, a kind of sandy terrace. In comparison with the northern coastline, the bare *tannes* (Plate 79-4), without vegetation, occupy little of this region while the herbaceous *tannes*, topographically more elevated, are more important, particularly in the Republic of Guinea. These latter features are covered by a sparse spread of halophytes: *Philoxerus vermicularis*, *Sesuvium portulacastrum*, and *Paspalum vaginatum;* while in the less saline environments *Heleocharis plantiginea* and *Scleria racemosa* are found.

Bluffs and cliffs sometimes interrupt the uniformity of the mangrove sectors and appear in the form of coastal reefs. They are localized on the west and southwest of the large islands of Guinea Bissau, also around Verga Cape and the Kaloum Peninsula (Fig. 79-2). They are exposed to long swells and can be related to the effects of wave abrasion (Plates 79-1 and 79-2).

Sandy beaches are sometimes developed on recent shore bars built by northwest or southwest swells and the resulting longshore drift. These beaches, in general, extend in a straight line and are parallel to the coast. They can be seen to the northwest of the Cacheu River, south of Bolama, and along the Guinean coast (Figs. 79-1 and 79-2), where they indicate the contact between the continent and the ocean. Their materials are sandy, including some heavy minerals like rutile, zircon, and ilmenite, which can be found in the other Quaternary deposits. In general, when these sandy beaches are built on recent shore bars, they may develop mobile sand dunes.

These more recent units should not be confused with the older sandy beach ridges spread in thin and discontinuous sets, generally oriented north-northwest–south-southeast. They are found in the form of dunes behind the mangroves and *tannes*, and have a relatively high altitude (4.2–7.5 m). They often evolve by eolian action. Between the beach ridges are topographically low swales that follow the general direction of the beach-ridge orientation.

Muddy or sandy shoals are very often found in these estuaries and tidal channels in the mouths of the large rivers (Guilcher 1979). At low tide they can be awash and exposed (Plate 79-6), and they frequently obstruct navigation because of their great instability (Figs. 79-1 and 79-2). Thus they testify to the important influence of fluvial sedimentation on these coasts.

SUBMERGENCE IN THE LATE QUATERNARY

All these geomorphological features, built by accumulation of clayey, muddy, and sandy deposits, can be found on West African shores and seem to date from the Holocene, particularly the last 5000 years (Domain 1979).

After the low sea level of the Ogolian period (one of the maximum of Würmian glaciation, around 22,000 years B.P.) (Faure and Elouard 1957), which has been identified everywhere on the West Africa coasts (around 120 m below sea level), a marine transgression occurred. MacMaster et al. (1971) have found different marine levels on the Guinean continental shelf, at −90 m, −80 m, −55 m, −45 m, −35 m, and −25 m. The last one, dated around 8500 years ago, had already been identified by the Geological Institute of Aquitain Basin and the Geological and Mining Research Office on the northern continental shelf. The rise was rapid until 6000 years ago, when sea level reached the present datum, and then it rose 2 m more. This was the Flandrian transgression (known as the Nouakchottian transgression on the West African coasts). At the maximum of this transgression, the sea inundated all the rias and estuaries of the Southern Rivers, and a series of various and mixed deposits, with occasional shell fossils, was laid down in the form of sandy or clayey terraces. *Tannes* and beach ridges date from this old alluviation and mark stages in the sea's retreat after the maximum transgression.

The regularized sandy beaches and the recent shore bars developed during the last 3000 years, while the mangrove swamps and mud flats were built by processes of sedimentation. Most of these features, particularly the more recent (shore bars, mangroves and mud flats, sandy beaches) are still evolving.

EVOLUTION OF THE GUINEAN COASTAL FORMS

The Guinean coast has evolved under the influence of swells (northwest, southwest and perpendicular to the coast), longshore drift, tidal currents, salinity, and dynamic tides.

Guinea Bissau and the Republic of Guinea both have a coastal climate that includes a dry season (between November and May, approximately) when northwest swells predominate and the prevailing winds are north-northwest (tradewinds), and a rainy season (between June and October) when southwest swells prevail and southwest winds (monsoon winds) are dominant. These cycles seem to influence the sedimentary pattern of the littoral and shelf areas. In the dry season, progradation effects seem to dominate over eroding processes. Thus, longshore drifting from the north to the south in conjunction with the northwest swell causes both the development of the recent shore bars, oriented along the coast toward the south, and, a silting up phenomenon, whose northwest origin has been clearly shown. A concrete example can be given at the roadstead (channel) of Conakry where dredging of 750,000 m³ per year is carried out.

Another phenomenon, which complicates the dynamic evolution of this coastal sector, is the amount of "blackish or grayish" mud and other silty or clayey materials (Plate 79-6) deposited in the estuaries and at the mouths of large rivers (Figs. 79-1 and 79-2). Their proportions reaffirm that the continental shelf itself is an accumulation area, with submarine deltas and submerged sand banks as off the mouths of the Kapatchez, Pongo, Geba, and Konkoure rivers. Surface turbidity values recorded in the nearshore and offshore of Conakry are 10–20 mg/l in the dry season, some dg/l in the rainy season; the bottom turbidities are four or five times greater. The salinity value in the dry season is 45 g/l, and in the rainy season it is 20 g/l (data from Marine Office of Conakry).

These turbidity values greatly exceed those registered off the coasts of Senegal and Gambia. At all events, these different results show the discharge coming from upstream, particularly in freshwater, but also in fine suspended materials,

at rainy periods. Because of the silting up and sedimentation phenomena, some fluvial harbors, particularly on the Kapatchez River, have been abandoned.

Tides are also an important factor in the dynamics of this littoral. They take place twice daily on the entire coast, and the tidal range varies between 1 m and 4.3 m. At Conakry (Fig. 79-2) 4.2 m has been recorded at spring tides, with 1.1 m recorded at neap tides. Other readings are: at Cacheu (Fig. 79-1), 2.84 m at mean spring tides, 0.21 m at mean neap tides; at Caío (Fig. 79-1) 3.4 m at mean spring tides, 0.42 m at mean neap tides; at Bubaque (Fig. 79-1) 4.6 m at mean spring tides, 0.53 m at mean neap tides.

All these factors, as well as the current velocities (flood or ebb) and the heights of the waves, play an important role in the evolution of these estuaries, rias, and mangrove areas. Their development, consisting of sand, mud, silt or clay, and ferruginous deposits (Verga Cape, Kaloum Peninsula for this last example), seems to date from the late Quaternary.

To sum up, we can detect two tendencies on the Guinean shores: on the one hand, muddy sedimentation with progradation of the mud flats with mangroves at the mouths of certain large rivers, and a regularization of the sandy beaches and formation of spits; on the other hand, particularly in the Republic of Guinea, the reworking and transportation of the sandy or muddy materials, redeposited by the southwest swells, creating an erosional process of coastline retreat as on Los Islands and in the environs of Conakry (Fig. 79-2).

E. S. DIOP

REFERENCES

Aymé, J. M., 1965, The Senegal salt basin in *Salt Basins around Africa*, Petroleum Institute, London, pp. 83–90.

Berthois, L., 1958, La formation des estuaires et des deltas, *Acad. Sci. Comptes Rendus* **247**:947–950.

Domain, F., 1979, Carte sédimentologique du plateau continental Sénégambien (touchant à une partie de la Mauritanie et de la Guinée Bissau), Centre de Recherches Oceanographiques de Thiaroye.

Faure, H., and P. Elouard, 1967, Schéma des variations du niveau de l'océan Atlantique sur la cote de l'Ouest de l'Afrique depuis 40,000 ans, *Acad. Sci. Comptes Rendus*, **265D**:784–787.

Guilcher, A., 1979, Marshes and estuaries in different latitudes, *Interdisc. Sci. Rev.* **4:**158–168.

MacMaster, R. L., T. P. Lachance, and A. Ashraf, 1970, Continental shelf geomorphic features of Portuguese Guinea, Guinea and Sierra Leone (Afrique de l'Ouest), *Marine Geology* **9:**203–213.

MacMaster, R. L., T. P. Lachance, A. Ashraf, and J. de Boer, 1971, Geomorphology, structure and sediment of the continental shelf and upper slope of Portuguese Guinea, Guinea, and Sierra Leone, in F. M. Delany, ed., Cambridge Institute of Geologic Sciences, Report 70/16, pp. 105–119.

Plate 79-1. Coast formed by cliffs and lateritic duricrust around Conakry, Republic of Guinea, settled by sparse mangroves, *Rhizophora mangle.* One of the exceptional areas of this type (photo by E. S. Diop).

Plate 79-3. Aerial view of the littoral of the Republic of Guinea formed with mangroves, *tannes,* and tidal creek systems. Mangroves here are *Rhizophora racemosa* and *Rhizophora mangle;* they can appear in the form of islands, characteristic of this area, with a drainage system by tidal channels where processes of sedimentation are very notable (photo by E. S. Diop).

Plate 79-2. Mangroves settled on outcropped ferruginous duricrust (uncommon geomorphological unit) on Ilhei-do-Rei, Guinea Bissau. The tree is *Avicennia africana,* with an herbaceous rug of *Philoxerus vermicularis* and *Sesuvium portulacastrum* (photo by E. S. Diop).

Plate 79-4. Organization of geomorphological sequence on the Guinea Bissau shore: *Rhizophora racemosa* (very dark) are along the water (sea and channels); *Rhizophora mangle* (lighter) extend backward; the bare surfaces with no vegetation are the *tannes,* low sandy terraces. The whitish color corresponds to salted efflorescences (photo by E. S. Diop).

Plate 79-5. Characteristic swampy shore with vegetation of mangrove typical not only on the coast of Guinea Republic but also on the littoral of Guinea Bissau. This view is at the falling tide period; *Rhizophora racemosa* (15 m high) edge the external shore and hold the clayey and muddy soils, one of the better areas of sand, mud, and other fine deposits (photo by E. S. Diop).

Plate 79-6. Low water period on the coast of Guinea Bissau, showing an important recess of the sea. The clayey and muddy area can be explained by the accumulation and sedimentation of the suspended fine material transported by the rivers: here, the rio Geba. At high water, all of this zone is completely submerged. The tidal range is between 2–4 m (photo by E. S. Diop).

80. SIERRA LEONE

The coastline of Sierra Leone is 500 km long and oriented northwest-southeast (Fig. 80-1). The southern section between the Liberian border and the Turtle Islands is under the dominating influence of the southwesterly Atlantic swell. To the north the coast trends in a more northerly direction and the influence of strong swell is less. There is a transitional zone on the West African coast that lies between the influence of swells from the South Atlantic and the North Atlantic. In this section (which includes the central and northern coast of Sierra Leone), low waves of no fixed direction are common in the dry season (December to April), and locally generated storm waves are experienced during the wet season (May to November). Mean spring tidal range at Freetown harbor is 2.8 m, but it is slightly higher on the open coast. The tides are semidiurnal.

Four main landform types dominate the coastline (Fig. 80-1): the mountainous section of the Freetown Peninsula, the extensive beach ridges, the low cliffs of unconsolidated Eocene sediment, and mangrove swamps in sheltered areas.

The Freetown Peninsula mountains are unique on the coast of West Africa. They form the easterly edge of a now much eroded and submerged Triassic lopolith and rise to 930 m. The peninsula arc is 45 km long and is continued in the southwest in the Banana Islands, 5 km offshore. The coastline of the peninsula is a succession of headlands and beaches. The gabbro-norite rocks are generally resistant to both mechanical and chemical erosion at the shore. There are sloping headlands (without a recognizable shore platform) and cliffs vegetated down to the spray zone. Many of the longer beaches display longshore movement of sand, some in a northerly direction, as at Tokeh

(Plate 80-1), and others in a southerly direction. Spits divert the mouths of many small mountain streams and enclose mangrove lagoons. The source of the peninsula beaches, quartz sand of medium to fine texture (mean diameter 0.25 mm), is not local. Movement around the headlands is negligible, and an offshore source is suggested, the beaches having formed during the postglacial rise in sea level.

The profiles of the peninsula beaches are distinctly seasonal. During the dry season the beaches build up with a well-developed berm. Seaward of this berm, large cusps form, 25–35 m wide. Cusps are common dry-season features on many beaches in Sierra Leone (Worrell 1969). In the wet season the berm is eroded, the beach flattened, and a low cliff is cut in sand at the high water mark. This is usually buried during the following dry season. The cycle of erosion and construction appears to be balanced, except on those beaches where sand is extracted for building purposes, where erosion rates are high with no dry season buildup.

Behind many of the peninsula beaches and lagoons, and extending up the larger river valleys, is a gently sloping platform (50 m above sea level) abutting the mountains with a marked break of slope. Its seaward edge is usually a low cliff, either at the sea or behind a lagoon. Gregory (1962) calls these platforms raised beaches, and although their surfaces do not bear any beach materials (they are laterized in most cases), they are certainly of marine origin.

In the south, Turners Peninsula and the seaward side of Sherbro Island consist of a series of beach ridges. The ridges are built of quartz sand supplied by the rivers of Liberia and southern

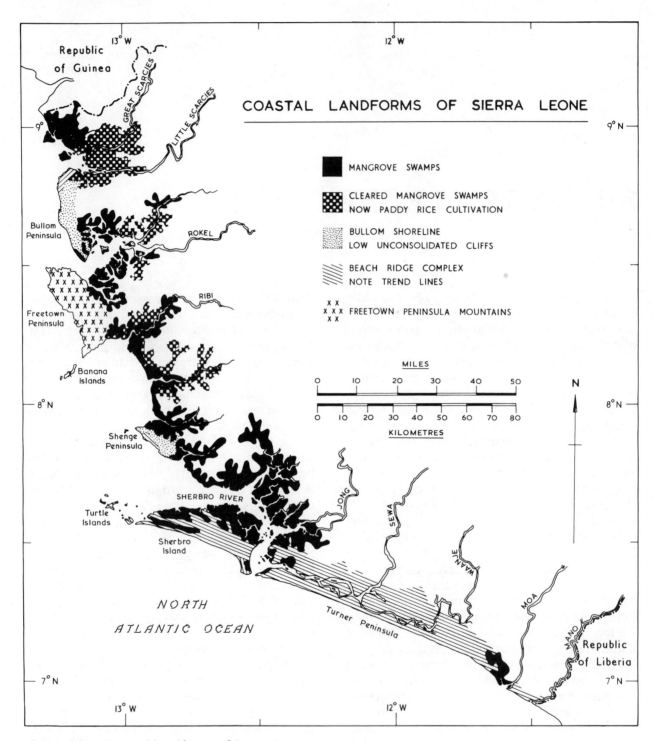

Figure 80-1. Coastal landforms of Sierra Leone.

Sierra Leone, which is carried by a strong north-westerly drifting longshore current. Two sets of ridges occur (Plate 80-2): a narrow series of post-glacial ridges still growing today, and behind them a much wider series thought to be of Pleistocene age, although no dates are available. The Holocene ridges are approximately 70 m wide, with swales between of about the same width, which flood with fresh water in the wet season, preventing tree growth. Palms and low shrubs grow on the ridges. The much wider "ancient" ridges are obviously older, showing signs of dissection by streams and some limited soil development.

Modern beach sand on the Atlantic coast of Sherbro Island (Plate 80-3) is coarse to medium in texture, with a mean diameter of 0.5 mm. The beaches are steeper than those of the Freetown Peninsula. The Sewa and Jong rivers and their tributaries are diverted by the two sets of ridges. The lower course of the Sewa cuts through the older ridges to enter a series of freshwater lakes between the two sets of ridges.

Sherbro Island is low-lying, with no point above 15 m, and is formed of Pleistocene and Holocene beach ridges with mangrove swamp on the Sherbro River side (Worrell 1970). The Turtle Islands are mostly vegetated sand cays, the smaller ones constantly shifting and changing in size and occasionally disappearing altogether.

Small areas of Holocene beach ridges are found in other areas on the coast. The two most noticeable are those south of the Scarcies estuary, where currents have affected their alignment, and a small area south of Shenge.

The third main landform type on the Sierra Leone coast is the area of low cliffs formed of Eocene marine and estuarine deposits (Bullom sediments), which are best developed on the Bullom Peninsula (Fig. 80-1). The cliffs are approximately 20 m high and consist of a series of poorly consolidated, near-horizontal gravels and clays, partly laterized in places. Similar cliffs are found on the small Shenge Peninsula (Plate 80-4). Elsewhere the sediments are not exposed and lie beneath more recent estuarine sediments. Sea cliffs cut in Bullom sediments are almost vertical because erosion has been rapid; falls and slides are common, especially in the wet season, and the debris is removed from the cliff foot by wave action. This fallen material becomes partly indurated on contact with seawater. A narrow beach of sand and scattered shingle is found at the base of these cliffs.

In sheltered lagoons and estuaries, mangrove swamps are extensively developed (Plate 80-5). The largest areas are around the Scarcies and Rokel river estuaries and in the lee of Sherbro Island and the Shenge Peninsula. The four genera of the occidental mangrove province, in which Sierra Leone lies, are all present. The most common, *Rhizophora* (a stilt root mangrove), is represented by three species. All are found in the part of the intertidal zone that is flooded every day, but *R. racemosa* prefers the siltiest substratum near the low water mark and colonizes newly emerged mud flats, while *R. harrisonii* and *R. mangle* are found in stands on slightly higher ground. Nowhere does *Rhizophora* reach its maximum possible height, but *R. racemosa* grows up to 20 m in favorable locations in the Sherbro River. It does not thrive in sandy substratum, which is frequently occupied by *Avicennia nitida*. This species is usually found in stands higher up the intertidal zone, where it is not generally submerged every day; it is more salt tolerant than *Rhizophora*, and rarely grows higher than 5 m. Around the high spring tide mark are found the two other genera, each represented by one species, *Conocarpus erectus* and *Laguncularia racemosa*, usually growing as scattered individuals in a thicket. In some coastal areas of Sierra Leone, especially around the Scarcies, much former mangrove swamp is now poldered and used for rice cultivation (Fig. 80-1).

Of the six main estuaries (Fig. 80-1) the Mano is a simple type with a spit diverting the mouth northward, the Moa has a complex of sand bars at the entrance with a single mangrove island behind. The other four are true estuarine deltas in various stages of development, with mud flats and low mangrove islands diverting the main water courses. Sediments in the estuaries consist of sand bars and mud flats with gravel in the channels (Tucker 1973). Evidence of drowned river channels points to a marine transgression in the Rokel estuary.

P. A. SCOTT

REFERENCES

Gregory, S., 1962, The raised beaches of the peninsular area of Sierra Leone, *Inst. British Georgraphers Trans.* **31**:15–22.

Tucker, M. E., 1973, The sediments of tropical African estuaries, Freetown Peninsular, Sierra Leone, *Geol. Mijnbouw* **52**:203–215.

Worrell, G. A., 1969, Present day and subfossil beach cusps on the West African coast, *Jour. Geol* **77**:484–487.

Worrell, G. A., 1970, Sherbro Island, Sierra Leone, *Inst. France d'Afrique Noire, Bull. Series A* **32**:1–17.

Plate 80-1. Tokeh and Number Two beaches, Freetown Peninsula. Tokeh beach is a northward-trending spit. The lighter shaded treeless area in the middle right is a raised beach surface. The white sand beaches backed by mountains and luxurious vegetation are typical of the Freetown Peninsula (photo by P. A. Scott).

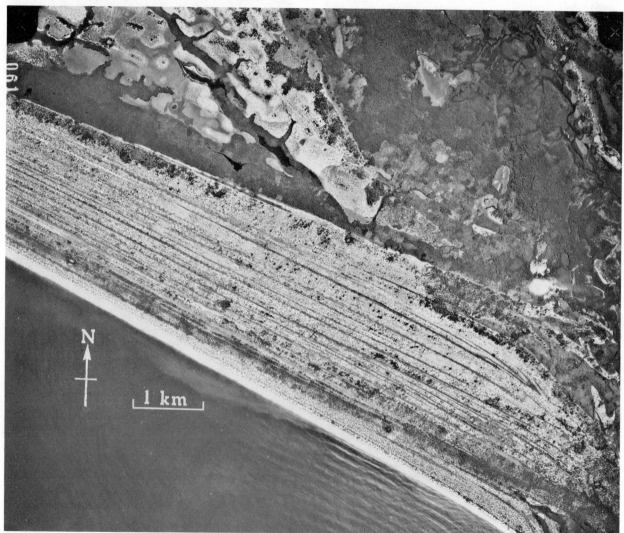

Plate 80-2. A vertical aerial photograph of the southern end of Turners Peninsula. The narrow Holocene beach ridges lie parallel to the present beach. Behind these, much larger ancient ridges lie at an oblique angle to the modern shore. Stream and lake development has caused much denudation and dissection of the ancient ridges. The light areas are ridges, the darker lines between are the swales. Relic beach cusps can just be identified on the seaward edge of some of the Holocene ridges (photo by Fairey Air Surveys Ltd.).

Plate 80-3. The Atlantic coast of Sherbro Island. Steeper beaches and coarser sand than the Freetown Peninsula. The beach is backed by a low sand rise forming the embryo of the newest ridge in the Holocene ridge series (photo by P. A. Scott).

Plate 80-5. *Rhizophora* mangrove swamps east of the Freetown Peninsula at high tide. These swamps extend for many square kilometers (Fig. 80-1). Typical peninsula skyline beyond (photo by J. N. Tristram).

Plate 80-4. Eocene cliffs at Shenge formed of almost horizontally bedded clays. This cliff is lower than the cliffs on the Bullom Peninsula. Note the oil palms on the beach, illustrating a fairly rapid rate of erosion. This photograph was taken at the end of the dry season, and the beach shows no sign of berm buildup (photo by P. A. Scott).

81. LIBERIA

Stretching approximately 560 km in a southeasterly-northwesterly direction, the Liberian coast (long known to mariners as the Grain Coast because of trade in the Malagueta pepper) is a melange of rocky outcrops, some of which are conspicuous landfalls, interspersed with lengthy stretches of spectacular beach formed by wave action and tidal lagoons formed by streams whose outlets to the ocean have been blocked by siltation and beach development. The beauty of its many kilometers of beach masks the relatively few good roadstead anchorages and almost total lack of natural port sites (Gnielinski 1972).

The coastal zone is 16–58 km wide and in several places is covered with unconsolidated sand, clay, and gravel deposits of Quaternary age (Schulze 1973). Often found in proximity to rivers flowing perpendicular to the coast, these deposits also have formed some of the raised beaches found especially in the Monrovia area. These Quaternary deposits partially cover intrusive diabase of Paleozoic age. Scattered sandstone outcrops of Tertiary origin abound between the entrances to the Mesurado and St. John rivers and southeast of the city of Monrovia (White 1972). The more resistant diabase dikes are characterized by conspicuous promontories and cliffs, such as Cape Mount (305 m) in the northwest, near Sierra Leone, and Cape Mesurado (91 m), site of the capital city. Weathered remnants of those dikes and still earlier laccoliths constitute the numerous rocky outcrops and offshore rocks; since weathering appears to occur mainly by solution, their appearance is one of rain-wash flutings or lapies. Details of features produced by weathering processes on rocky shore outcrops of dolerite at Mamba Point have been described by Tricart

(1962). A powerful surf and exceptionally strong rip currents characterize most of the coastline, except where offshore rocks are sufficiently dense to disrupt surf and currents. There are no significant islands although the meandering rivers crossing the coastal plain have led to the development of numerous alluvial islands. Here, as elsewhere in the tropics, substantial surface runoff by way of several main and numerous lesser streams has led to breaks in the beach ridges and lagoons have developed behind many beaches. In brief, Liberia's coast can best be described as a mixture of low rocky outcrops dominated by a few high promontories or cliffs interspersed with some of the most spectacular longshore beach ridges to be found in West Africa, with long, often narrow lagoons and mangrove swamps.

Several outstanding features dominate the coast from the mouth of the Mano River (Sierra Leone border) to Cape Mesurado (Fig. 81-1). Already mentioned is Cape Mount (305 m), the highest point on the entire Liberian coastline. Behind this mountain is Lake Piso, composed of brackish water influenced by tidal action and seldom deeper than 5 m. The peninsular link to the mainland is of depositional origin and has blocked off the coastal indentation that became Lake Piso. This lake was used by Pan American Airways seaplanes in the late 1930s and early 1940s as a major stop on service between the Belgian Congo (Zäire) and North America. Major watercourses entering the sea along this stretch of coast are the Lofa and St. Paul rivers; the latter is navigable to White Plains, some 32 km inland. Shoaling at the entrance to the St. Paul has effectively blocked access to the river, and the better route is to work upstream along the Mesurado River (tidal inlet) and Stock-

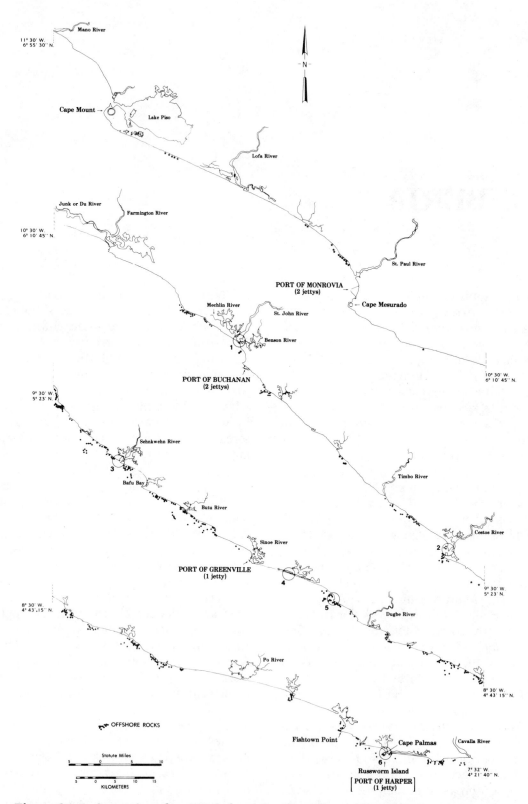

Figure 81-1. Coastal configuration from the Mano River (Sierra Leone border) to the mouth of the Cavalla River (Ivory Coast border). Several promontories dominate a coastline otherwise characterized by beaches, tidal inlets, and lagoons. Three are major settlements: Cape Mount (305 m), Cape Mesurado (91 m), and Cape Palmas (30 m).

ton Creek, north and east of Monrovia, and then to enter the St. Paul in its lower reaches (Stanley 1970). The Lofa is accessible from the sea, but the turmoil caused by an expanding river-mouth sand spit and the discharging of a major river combine to make this passage memorable. The coast along this stretch is fringed with rocks and rocky points interspersed with stretches of light brown sand. The tidal range, however, is small (1.5 m), with bad storms the exception.

Cape Mesurado (91 m) at Monrovia has been quarried to obtain construction material for the two 1.6 km jetties encompassing the port of Monrovia (1944–1947). Thus these cliffs are even more pronounced than would normally be the case. Southeast of Cape Mesurado are two of the country's largest tidal lagoons. First is the backed-up water of the Du and Farmington rivers, due to the river-mouth bar near the now decaying community of Marshall. Before 1947, Marshall was the chief export port for Liberia, because of the nearby Firestone rubber plantation. The eastern portion of this lagoon is navigable for approximately 29 km. To the southeast is the St. John river system shown in Plate 81-1.

The port of Buchanan, several km southeast of the St. John River, is formed by jetties (1920 m and 610 m) constructed of rock from a nearby diabase dike. Indeed, this site was selected for a port (as was the site for Monrovia) because of this nearby construction material. A major world-scale iron ore shipping facility encompassing the washing of iron ore near the port has caused massive discoloration of the ocean in a zone several hundred meters wide along the coast from Grand Bassa Point to the St. John River. The ocean is red because of pollution from surface runoff.

Other prominent features southeast of Cape Mesurado include diabase cliffs at Bassa Point (50 m), 2 km southeast of the entrance to the Du-Farmington river system, and near the entrance to the New Cess River (45 m). The relationship between sand spit, human settlement, and the drainage of a major river is readily discerned at River Cess (Plate 81-2). Probably the most spectacular and surely one of the most beautiful embayments along the coast is Bafu

Bay (Plate 81-3) near the Sehnkwehn River where, just inside the forest and hidden from casual view, are more than 50 rusting pieces of giant earth-moving equipment, all that remain of a development scheme of the early 1950s that collapsed almost at its inception. Baffu Bay is outstanding, but tidal lagoons (Plate 81-4) and embayments (Plate 81-5) characterize the entire Liberian coast and are especially pronounced in the southeast.

Aside from sand for local construction and rock for port jetty construction, little economic use is made of Liberia's coastline materials (Plate 81-6). Fishing is important at several sites, and the four ports (three major and one minor) represent economic activities of a different order. Tourism is a real possibility, but is handicapped by the weak economic infrastructure and the fact that the beaches, while spectacular, are unsafe for swimming. Increased offshore petroleum exploration is under way (1981), and the thickness of the ocean floor sediments even within a relatively narrow continental shelf seems to offer potential for success (Behrendt and Wotorson 1972; Egloff 1972).

WILLIAM R. STANLEY

REFERENCES

Behrendt, J. C., and C. S. Wotorson, 1972, *Aeromagnetic and Gravity Investigations of the Sedimentary Basins on the Continental Shelf and Coastal Area of Liberia,* Geol. Survey Special Paper 2, Monrovia.

Egloff, J., 1972, Morphology of the ocean basin seaward of northwest Africa—Canary Island to Monrovia, Liberia, *Am. Assoc. Petroleum Geologists Bull.* **56:**694–706.

Gnielinski, S., 1972, *Liberia in Maps,* University of London Press, London.

Schulze, W., 1973, *A New Geography of Liberia,* Longman, London.

Stanley, W. R., 1970, Transport expansion in Liberia, *Geog. Rev.* **60:**529–547.

Tricart, J., 1962, Observations de géomorphologie littorale à Mamba Point, *Erdkunde* **16:**49–57.

White, R. W., 1972, *Stratigraphy and Structure of Basins on the Coast of Liberia,* Geol. Survey Special Paper 3, Monrovia.

Plate 81-1. Mouth of the St. John River at its confluence with two large ocean inlets, known locally as the Benson (to the right) and Mechlin rivers, which might better be described as tidal creeks. Housing and road to the right belong to the old Americo-Liberian trading town of Upper Buchanan. The generally low relief of the Liberian coastal plain is readily seen; the fall zone and first rapids on the St. John are approximately 11 km inland. Wave action has resulted in a bar currently blocking much of the entrance to this river; the siltation and wave action here have been accentuated by jetty construction at the new deep-water port (1963) of Lower Buchanan, a short distance to the south. River discharge is sufficient to maintain a gap through this barrier although shoaling has effectively eliminated access to the St. John by ocean carriers, certainly to vessels drawing more than 2.5 m of water. River mouth siltation increases during the dry season when runoff is least (photo by W. Stanley).

Plate 81-2. River Cess, at the mouth of the Cestos River. One sees evidence of constant struggle between wave-built sand spit configurations seeking to block the coastline and the substantial runoff of a major tropical river seeking access to the ocean. All of Liberia's rivers enter the ocean, but those with the greatest runoff do not have lagoons developed immediately inland from the shore. In the case of small rivers, siltation often effectively blocks access to the sea, and considerable inland flooding is the rule. Longshore drift is to the northwest from October to December, and to the southeast for most of the remainder of the year. New channels are cut through the sand, and coastal inhabitants sometimes dig a channel to reduce inland flooding. The sand spit on which the settlement of River Cess developed is one of Liberia's largest, yet so is the river. A navigation channel has been in existence continuously since at least the mid-nineteenth century, and wharf facilities can be seen on the landward side of the spit to the left of the picture (photo by W. Stanley).

Plate 81-3. Offshore rocks near the mouth of the Sehnkwehn River. Intrusive Paleozoic diabase dikes underlie much of the coastal sands and sandstones. In several places, these dikes remain as rocky cliffs high above the generally flat coastal plain. Most often, however, their erosional remnants jut above high tide as offshore rocks and represent a menace to navigation. Lacking coral development and violent storms, the Liberian coast, like much of West Africa, offers few "natural sites" for port development, and its beautiful longshore developed beaches have violent rip currents extremely dangerous to swimmers. Only where offshore rocks break the wave action are the beaches of tourist potential (photo by W. Stanley).

Plate 81-4. Lagoon near Aruan Point to the southeast of Greenville. This is an example of longshore drift building a beach ridge that has blocked a small stream's access to the ocean. Thwarted in one place, the stream flows parallel to the coast for several miles in search of a new channel. Such tidal lagoons are common on the Liberian coast and generally serve to isolate the beach from the hinterland. Water depths in lagoons such as this seldom exceed 5 m (photo by W. Stanley).

Plate 81-5. At Setro there is the worn remnant of a diabase intrusion of Paleozoic age, which has broken the longshore drift, causing a sharp embayment. As with strategic sand spits at the entrance to the major rivers (which formerly served as the principal highways for moving agricultural products from the interior to coastal trading stations), sites such as Setro, with its absence of lagoon activity, were choice locations for settlements. Breaks in the coastal forest represent recently cut farms. Since the shifting cultivation cycle seldom exceeds seven years, the darker-colored patterns would represent farms cut from the forest more than seven years earlier. The airstrip perpendicular to the coast and to the left of the photograph was built to serve a mission station (photo by W. Stanley).

Plate 81-6. Cape Palmas and Russworm Island. Rising 30 m above the surrounding lowland, Cape Palmas is an excellent example of the several diabase dikes whose prominent erosional remnants provided points of reference to early mariners. The important Americo-Liberian settlement of Harper grew on this promontory in the early nineteenth century. It is easy to understand why such promontories were chosen as settlements by the Americo-Liberians. To both the northwest and southeast are large lagoons bordered by low-lying mangrove swamps. If nothing else, the high elevation offered prospects of more solubrious air and healthier living. Cape Palmas also is noteworthy for being the point at which the West African coastline trends sharply east. Russworm Island, a lower remnant of this same diabase dike, is connected to the mainland by a causeway. Here is a port with one short jetty, whose construction rock was taken directly from low-lying cliffs on the island. This so lowered the profile of the island that, in bad weather, the port is frequently inundated by the sea. It is a difficult port to enter, even for the shallow-draft vessels able to use the docking facilities. Logs and sawn timber, the principal export commodities, are usually carried or floated to ships anchored in the roadstead. The beach ridge and lagoon to the left of the photograph are typical of much of the Liberian coastline (photo by W. Stanley).

82. IVORY COAST

Over a distance of some 500 km, from the mouth of the Cavally River to the exit of Aby Lagoon, the Ivorian shoreline displays an ample concavity, of which the deepest point corresponds approximately to the entrance of the Vridi canal, through which the port of Abidjan is reached (Pomel 1980). Off this coast, the continental shelf is very narrow. The 120 m isobath, below which the slope plunges toward the abyssal plains, is only 10 nautical miles from the coast off Abidjan and reaches a maximum of 20 nautical miles off Sassandra. This narrow shelf is only interrupted at one point, off Vridi canal, where the submarine canyon of the *Trou sans fond*, which is probably due to a fault, begins immediately at the shore (Martin 1979).

The narrowness of the continental shelf results in a steep slope; the shelf rises too rapidly to produce any substantial dampening effect on the swell. The great swell of the Gulf of Guinea, originating far offshore in the south Atlantic where it is generated by the "westerlies," unfurls remorselessly on the coast. It is reinforced in the rainy season by the local monsoon winds and is barely subdued during the January dry season, when it encounters the northeast wind, locally called the *harmattan*. The swell gives rise to an incessant surge of tremendous rollers (in French the *barre*, in African dialect the *kalema*), which bathers so legitimately dread (Plate 82-1A). To this can be attributed the steep slope of the beaches, the coarseness of the sands, and the continuous remodeling of these sands into endless garlands of giant "beach cusps."

Because of the curve of the shoreline, the permanent onslaughts of the swell do not produce the same effects everywhere. The dominant swell is south-southwest in origin. From Cape Palmas to Fresco, it is very oblique in relation to the shoreline, reaching the coast at a 45° angle. This results in strong eastward longshore drifting. In this first area (Fig. 82-1) the Precambrian shield comes into direct contact with the sea. The coast is rocky, with moderately high cliffs, and the elevation of the hinterland only occasionally exceeds 100 m.

This western shoreline offsets in steps, because of a series of echelon faults that divide the coast into seven sectors. One of these caused the formation of the Grand Bérébi cove; another shelters the beautiful Monogaga cove, between San Pedro and Sassandra. However, while the main irregularities of the coast thus appear to be tectonic in origin, the lithological influence is directly shown by the detailed outline of the dozens of small bays and the miniscule capes that separate them. The capes correspond to the outcrops of hard rocks, often veins; the bays correspond to less resistant rocks, such as weathered granites (Plates 82-2 and 82-3). Only on the capes does the rock, lashed directly by the sea, become visible at the foot of the cliff. Elsewhere, the cliff is covered by vegetation and protected at the base by a narrow sandy beach, which is continuously migrating eastward (Hinschberger and Pomel 1972, 1979). These are not "abandoned cliffs," however; they evolve by intermittent mass slipping. Tricart (1957) has suggested the term *falaises-versants* (hillside-cliffs) to describe this particular type of tropical cliff.

At Fresco, however, the Precambrian basement disappears under covering strata, consisting mainly of soft sandstones, which are highly subject to erosion by the sea. Here is the only section

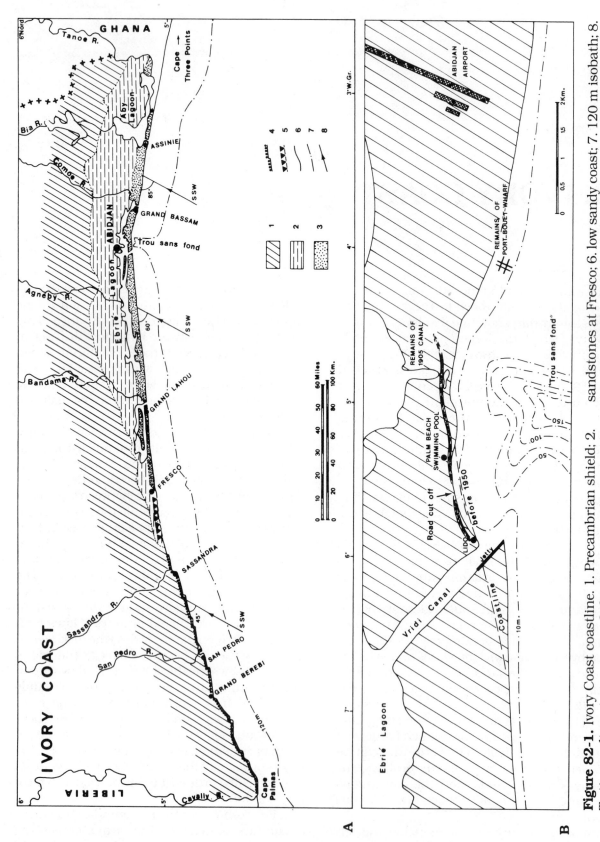

Figure 82-1. Ivory Coast coastline. 1. Precambrian shield; 2. Tertiary sedimentary covering; 3. Quaternary sands; 4. western cliffs, covered by vegetation; 5. bare cliffs, in the Tertiary sandstones at Fresco; 6. low sandy coast; 7. 120 m isobath; 8. direction of dominant swell and angle to shoreline.

of the Ivorian shoreline where bare, vertical cliff walls extend over a distance of several kilometers.

From Fresco to Abidjan, the angle of the swell in relation to the shoreline is less acute than in the west (60°). However, the resultant longshore drifting is still fairly strong and brings about the formation of a sand barrier, which is perfectly straight and almost continuous, but of moderate width.

From Abidjan to the Ghanaian border, the swells are more or less perpendicular to the shoreline, and create very little drifting eastward. On occasion, the less frequent southerly swells create longshore drifting in the opposite direction, westward. It is therefore a sector where sand accumulates. The sand barrier is wide. Behind Grand Bassam, dozens of sand barriers are juxtaposed over a width of several kilometers. North of these barriers there extends a vast system of lagoons (Ebrié Lagoon, Aby Lagoon), which can be accounted for, at least partly, by tectonic subsidence (Tastet 1977).

In this third sector, since drifting can no longer take place, the return to the open sea of the waters brought incessantly by the breakers produces rip currents. These are clearly visible off Assinie beach on certain aerial photographs, where they cause the interruption of the lines of foam.

Longshore drifting due to the swell (not to be confused with the ocean currents, which have no action on the coast) is thus of paramount importance. To understand the varied aspects of the Ivorian shores and predict their evolution, one must constantly bear this phenomenon in mind. Underestimation of this effect led to the failure of the first attempt to build a canal at Port Bouet. The remains of this former canal can still be seen (Plate 82-4). It was dug in 1905 in the narrowest part of the sand barrier and blocked by longshore drifting the very day after its inauguration. The present canal (Plate 82-5), opened at Vridi in 1950, takes the drifting into account, and its oblique course, together with the building of a jetty, has prevented it from sanding up. The sand coming from the west is diverted by the jetty and gives rise to a long submarine bar, which ships must circumnavigate in order to gain access to the canal. This spit disappears near the *Trou sans fond*. The effect of the deviation of sand toward this canyon is to leave the coast unprotected immediately to the east of the canal. For over 1 km, as far as the Palm Beach swimming pool, a marked hollow bears witness to the recent recession of the coast at this point (Fig. 82-1B).

The opening of this permanent artificial channel to the sea has increased the salinity of the Ebrié Lagoon and modified its flora and fauna. The Comoé River now flows toward the Vridi canal. Its natural mouth at Grand Bassam, which was permanently open until 1950 (as is the mouth of the Bandama River at Grand Lahou, Plate 82-6), is now blocked by a sand barrier, which is cleared for only two or three months of the year, at times of flood water.

Other modifications of the coastline are also due to human intervention near San Pedro, the new port built in 1972 to develop the economy of the southwest of the Ivory Coast. This area was virtually uninhabited until thousands of peasants, forced to leave their lands by the rise of the waters at the Kossou dam (on the Bandama), were moved there. At San Pedro, the course of the river was turned eastward to prevent the port's silting up at times of flood water of the San Pedro River. The port was also protected from wave-deposited sand by a jetty positioned as at Vridi, and artificial groins were installed. The latter constitute sand traps that stop the eastward drifting of the sediments, thus permitting the reclamation of several square kilometers for housing development (Plate 82-7).

FÉLIX HINSCHBERGER

REFERENCES

Hinschberger, F., and R. Pomel, 1972, La morphologie des côtes rocheuses entre Monogaga et Sassandra (Côte d'Ivoire), *Annales Univ. Abidjan, G,* **4:**7–37.

Hinschberger, F., and R. Pomel, 1979, Esquisse morphologique du littoral ivoirien, en *Atlas de Côte d'Ivoire,* O.R.S.T.O.M., Paris, et Institut de Géographie Tropicale, Abidjan, Map A1.

Martin, L., 1979, Sédimentologie du plateau continental de la Côte d'Ivoire, en *Atlas de Côte d'Ivoire,* Map A2b.

Pomel, R., 1980, Géographie physique de la basse Côte d'Ivoire, *Norois* **27:**348–350.

Tastet, J. P., 1977, Le Quaternaire littoral ivoirien, *Recherches Françaises sur le Quaternaire,* Assoc. Française Etude Quaternaire Supp. Bull., pp. 172–186.

Tricart, J., 1957, Aspects et problèmes géomorphologiques du littoral occidental de la Côte d'Ivoire, *Inst. Français d'Afrique Noire Bull.* **19:**1–20.

Plate 82-1. Wreck of ship on western coast. The photograph suggests the strength of the swell (photo by F. Hinschberger).

Plate 82-3. Stepped coastline west of Sassandra. In foreground, offset due to a fault. In background, numerous irregularities due to lithological contrasts (photo by F. Hinschberger).

Plate 82-2. Stepped coastline near Grand Bérébi. A fault has split the coastline. The mouth of the Niolia River is blocked by a coarse-sand barrier, which allows the water to percolate toward the sea, however (photo by F. Hinschberger).

Plate 82-4. Remains of former canal of Port Bouet, dug in 1905 in the narrowest part of the sand barrier and sanded up the same year (photo by F. Hinschberger).

Plate 82-5. Vridi canal. In the background, a ship can be seen, which must circumnavigate a sandy submarine bar off the coast before entering the canal (photo by F. Hinschberger).

Plate 82-7. Work in progress on the new San Pedro port (1971). A groin, forming a sand-trap, has stopped the longshore drifting and brought about the formation of a wide beach, already partly covered by vegetation (photo by F. Hinschberger).

Plate 82-6. Mouth of Bandama River at Grand Lahou. Behind the sand barrier, the Bandama winds through a vast marshy area almost inaccessible to man, where many elephants are to be found. On the seaward side, a submarine delta accounts for the semicircular shape of the line of foam brought in by the breakers (photo by F. Hinschberger).

83. GHANA

The total length of the Ghanaian coastline is about 600 km, of which 280 km are entirely sandy. The rest is rocky, with alternating sandy beaches in bays (Fig. 83-1A). The area is underlain by Precambrian and Paleozoic rocks. Isolated outcrops of Devonian sandstones occur around Accra and between Cape Coast and Takoradi (Fig. 83-1B).

SANDY BEACH TERRACES

Three main beach terraces may be easily identified (Dei 1972a). *Terrace I* (between +9 m and +12 m) is presumably the oldest beach terrace. Sieved sand samples characteristically show an asymmetrically sigmoid curve. It is made up of 4.0% coarse sand, 15.5% medium sand, 49.8% fine sand, 12.8% silt, 15.2% clay, and 2.7% organic matter. It is moderately sorted with So values ranging between 1.7 and 2.8. Particle surface characteristics show that most grains are mat, with ferruginization mostly in cavities. Quartz particles are mainly irregular between 200 and 250 microns or below, but subrounded between 400 and 630 microns or above. Materials of this beach were derived mainly from continental deposits that have been partially reworked by wave action.

Terrace II (between +4.5 m and +9 m) is more extensive than Terrace I and separated from it by a well-defined break in slope varying between 10° and 15°. Sieved samples of quartz grains show perfect sigmoid curves. Average So values fall between 1.29 and 1.34. Quartz particles have higher roundness indices than those of Terrace I. Surface texture remains mat, as in Terrace I, but

there is a significant increase in the proportion of grains with polished surfaces, perhaps because of successive reworking of older beach materials.

Terrace III (below +4.5 m) is the most recent terrace along the Ghanaian coastline. Samples show perfect sigmoid curves, and quartz particles are more rounded but less ferruginized than those of Terraces I and II.

LAGOONS AND ASSOCIATED CALCAREOUS NODULES

Seaward terminations of coastal streams are occupied by lagoons of various shapes; some are finger-like, others pear-shaped. A striking feature of the lagoons is the concentration of calcareous nodules about 0.3 m below the surface of former lagoon shores. Their shapes are irregular, resembling the roots and stems of plants that are extinct in the area (Plate 83-1). Fossil shells are found encrusted in these nodules. These indicate the origin of the cementing calcite.

ROCKY COASTLINE

Starting from the west the following characteristic features are encountered (Dei 1975, Fig. 83-1B):

1. Pepre Point (near Axim). Raised beach terraces at 5 m and 12 m above low water margin have been encountered. These contain rounded pebbles of the *Upper Birrimian*. Island "scars" with angular or semirounded boulders mark positions of former islands. Pieces of rounded and angular beachrock occur, and coffee rock

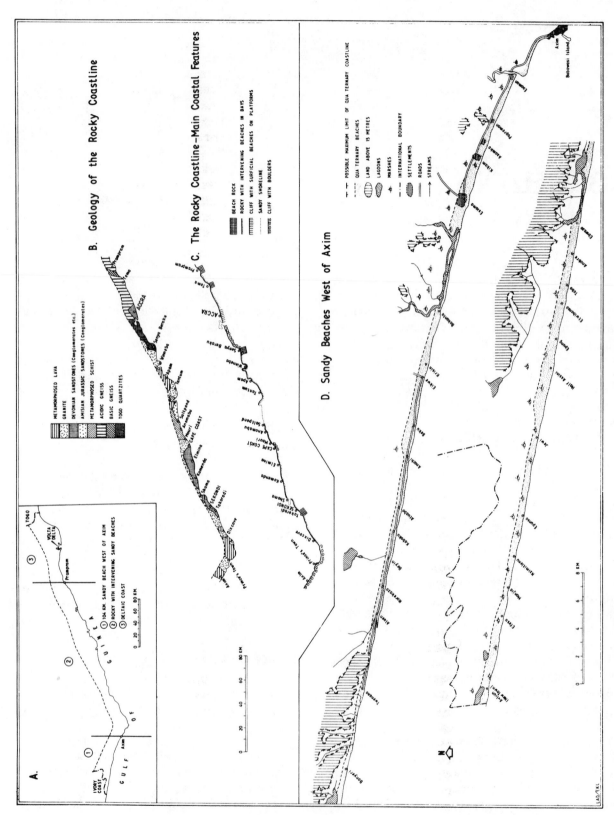

Figure 83-1. Geology and main coastal features of the Ghanaian shoreline.

(iron-cemented beach sand) is seen in various stages of consolidation.

2. Prince's Town. A granite promontory, 30 m above sea level occurs east of the town. There is a wave-cut platform at about 12 m. Recent cliffs rise to about 15 m above sea level.

3. Dixcove. Here there are no platforms, but there are islands and "chaos" of angular granite or granodiorite boulders. Toward the east of the town, a pebbly beach terrace consisting of semiweathered granite pebbles is seen at about 9 m above low water margin. This terrace, which overlies the boulder zone and is ferruginized, indicates a higher sea stand in the past.

4. Takoradi. Terrace heights do not exceed 15 m. Beach erosion is rampant (Plates 83-2 and 83-3). Beachrock occurs alongside coffee rock. Most of the beachrock is fragmented, but it is possible to encounter outcrops of it overlying the feldspathic *Elmina Sandstone* (Plate 83-4). Incipient beachrock is seen in many places (Plate 83-5).

5. Sekondi. Much of the coast of Sekondi is fortified against erosion by the construction of sea defenses. East of Sekondi at Turtle Cove, about 10 km away, beach erosion is very active. Three or more wavecut terraces may be identified in sedimentary formations of varying hardness. There is evidence of a collapsed cave roof; notches and stacks also occur.

6. Gold Hill (Komenda). At Gold Hill, a natural cave about 1 m above high water margin penetrates the hard limonitic face of a cliff and opens into a softer leached zone. There is a gloup, overgrown with plants, about 10 m from the cave entrance (Plate 83-6). To the west of the cave is a raised beach 1 m above high water margin, which has been colonized by herbaceous plants. Behind the beach and to the east of the cave are cliff faces almost completely covered by vegetation. None of these features is related to Holocene marine action.

7. Elmina. The feldspathic Elmina Sandstone outcrops here. Circular holes and polygonal patterns are striking superficial features on rock surfaces (Plates 83-7 and 83-8). Sea erosion takes place easily along joints forming rectilinear channels. Abrasion platforms are found at 0–1 m, 1–2 m, and 3 m.

8. Cape Coast. Much of the coast between Cape Coast and Abandzi, near Saltpond, has rock-cut benches at 12 m above low water margin.

Lower benches at 1–4 m above low water margin are seen at several places.

9. Saltpond. No rock outcrops are seen. The estuary of the Ochi (Amisa), 5 km east of Saltpond, is littered with rounded pebbles, which must have been reworked material from the Amisian formation.

10. Apam. Rounded outcrops of metamorphosed lava are seen. Mini-notches are also common here.

11. Winneba. The beach is rich in calcareous material; there is slight induration of beach sand but no beachrock has yet been formed. Wave-cut terraces exist at 0–1 m, 1–2 m, 3 m, and 10–12 m. Cliffs are generally low except toward the west of the town.

12. Senya Beraku. Three main cliffs may be seen: a high (30 m) cliff, an intermediate cliff (15 m and 10–12 m high) and a low (6 m) cliff. There are also wave-cut benches at 0–1 m, 1–2 m, 3 m, 10–12 m, and 15 m. Caves and notches are seen. Beachrock outcrops at the base of the high cliff.

13. Accra–Tema. Iron-cemented beach sand preserved on a rock bench at +13 m–17 m may be observed (McCallien 1962). Iron-cemented raised beach gravels are also noticed at about the same elevation. The same terrace with a cliff between 14 m and 15 m may be seen at Tema (Davies 1964). Raised beaches between 1.1 m and 8 m above high water margin are also noticed between Accra and Tema (Dei 1975). At the mouth of the Sakumo Lagoon, near Tema, is a beachrock outcrop about 1 m above mean sea level (Dei 1972b).

14. Prampram. Beachrock outcrops here. At low tide it can be traced seaward for a distance of about 40 m or more.

THE VOLTA DELTA

Figure 83-2 shows the Volta delta and its submarine contours. The landward extent of the Quaternary sea is also shown. Field studies indicate that the Quaternary sea level was slightly below the 30 m contour inland—hence the lack of particles of Quaternary marine origin in the area of red Tertiary continental deposits. The seaward margin of the delta is steep, indicating a monoclinal flexure, a phenomenon quite common along many stretches of the Ghanaian shoreline.

The delta sediments are marine, fluviomarine, and fluvial, and occur up to a depth of 170 m

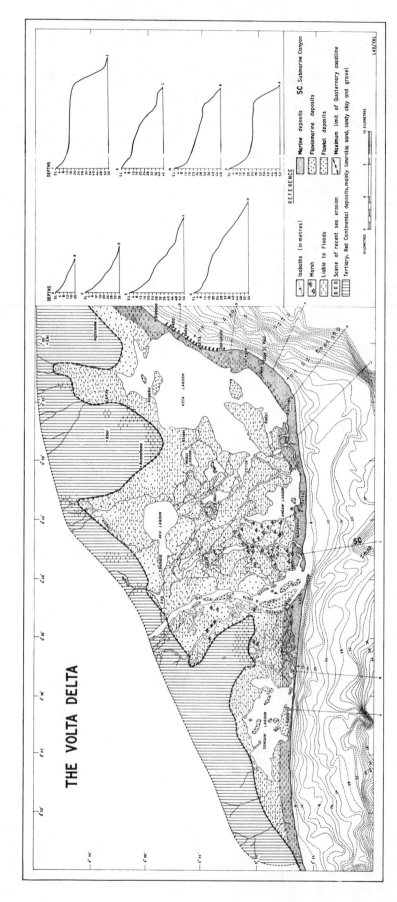

Figure 83-2. The Volta delta.

below sea level. Mudstone and Cretaceous shales have been located at over 200 m depth (Ghana Public Works Department 1960).

The delta frontage has long been the scene of intense marine erosion, which has attracted both national and international attention. Records indicate that the erosion dates back to the beginning of the century or perhaps even earlier. Particle shape analysis (Dei 1975) indicates an increase in wave energy from west to east, which may be responsible for the erosion in the delta zone.

L. A. DEI

REFERENCES

Davies, O., 1964, *The Quaternary in the Coastlands of Guinea*, Jackson Son & Co., Glasgow.

Dei, L. A., 1972a, The central coastal plains of Ghana: a morphological and sedimentological study. *Zeitschr. Geomorphologie* **16**(4):415–431.

Dei, L. A., 1972b, Some observations on Ghanaian beach rocks, *Jour. Tropical Geog.* **35**:26–31.

Dei, L. A., 1975, Morphology of the rocky shoreline of Ghana: Eustatic?, *Ghana Geog. Assoc. Bull.* **17**:1–30.

Ghana Public Works Department, 1960, *Report on Coastal Erosion, Sea Defences and Lagoon Flooding at Keta*, Ghana Public Works Department, Accra.

McCallien, W. J., 1962, *The Rocks of Accra*, Curwen Press, London.

Plate 83-1. Calcareous nodules in former lagoon sediments. Their irregular shapes resemble roots and stems of plants that are extinct in the area. These nodules are associated with gypsum deposits and related to higher sea stands in the past (photo by E. Korsah).

Plate 83-2. Vertical cliff in Takoradi beds. Storm wave action is gradually undermining base of cliff. This phenomenon is common along many stretches of the Ghanaian coastline where outcrops consist of soft unconsolidated materials (photo by E. Korsah).

Plate 83-3. Rapid shoreline retreat at Effia Nkwanta, near Sekondi. Many houses have been lost to the sea as a result of wave erosion (photo by E. Korsah).

Plate 83-4. Beachrock near Hwini estuary, Takoradi. Beachrock also outcrops along the coast of Ghana at the beaches of Senya Beraku, Tema, and Prampram. Rounded or angular particles of beachrock occur in several places along the coast (photo by E. Korsah).

Plate 83-5. Incipient beachrock at Takoradi undermined by wave erosion. Beachrock continues to form along certain sections of the Ghanaian shoreline (photo by E. Korsah).

Plate 83-6. Gloup at Gold Hill, Komenda. At Gold Hill, limonitization has preserved a complex development of cave-gloup-geoformation in an otherwise soft sandstone formation (photo by E. Korsah).

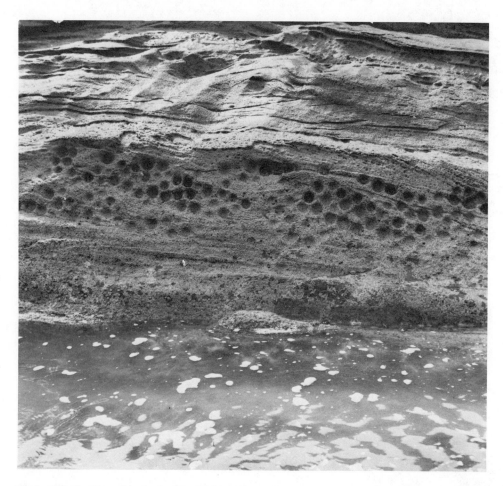

Plate 83-7. Circular holes in feldspathic Elmina Sandstone due to the action of sea urchins. Note surface deposition of calcite in grayish-white color (photo by E. Korsah).

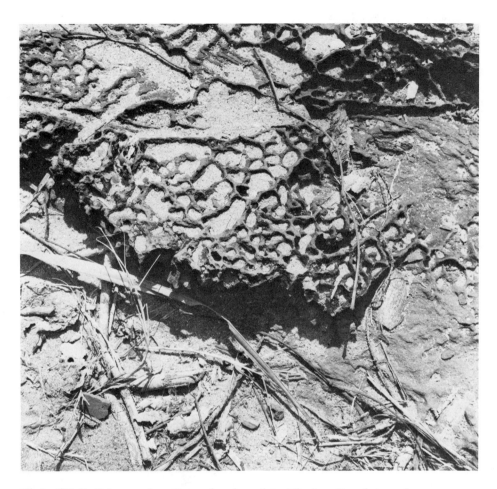

Plate 83-8. Polygonal pattern developed in Elmina Sandstone by sea spray. Coalescence of smaller polygons leads to the creation of larger ones. In this way the Elmina Sandstone is gradually worn away by crystallization of salt (photo by E. Korsah).

84. TOGO AND BENIN

The huge West African Precambrian shield slopes to the south under a belt of Cretaceous, Tertiary, and Quaternary rocks, 35–130 km wide, which frame the coastal area of Togo and Benin. The last Tertiary sediments consist of continental sandy clays, called *terre de barre*, (*barral* meaning clay in Portuguese). These sediments form a plateau 20–70 m high, which has been dissected by rivers during low Pleistocene sea levels; the depressions thus created have been partly filled by sediments that form the coastal complex, bounded along the Atlantic by a long, straight, monotonous sandy beach.

COASTAL DYNAMICS

The coastal dynamics consist essentially of the surf, called *kalema* (Guilcher 1954), which breaks continuously on the shore as a consequence of swell traveling from the south-southwest, that originated in the storm belt of the Southern Ocean. No hurricanes occur in this region, and local cyclones cannot match the westerlies in generating swells. *Kalema* exists even when no wind is locally blowing; sometimes it increases in strength without any local cyclone. The local wind, however, which generally blows from the southwest, has influenced the evolution of the inner lagoonal shores. Another factor in coastal evolution is the river discharge, which differs in the dry and wet seasons, showing a large and long decrease from November to May, and either one prominent peak in September (Mono and Oueme rivers) or two peaks in June and October, with a secondary low in August (Couffo River) (Guilcher 1959).

The sand forming the beach travels to the east because the *kalema* breaks obliquely on the coast. This is true for the entire coast of the Gulf of Guinea from Ivory Coast to the Lagos area in Nigeria. It is a quartzitic sand, which can be supplied by two western sources: the rivers, the largest one being the Volta in Ghana, and the cliffs, which exist in a number of places in Ghana and in Ivory Coast. At present, however, the sand supply has decreased, and the coastline tends to retreat, probably for two reasons: the building of large dams across rivers for purposes of industrialization, which traps the sand, most efficiently in Ghana and in Ivory Coast; and the creation of harbors along the coast, with jetties that prevent normal sand migration by piling it up on their western sides. Every state wants at least one dam and one harbor, sometimes more: that is the problem.

OUTER BEACH, BARRIER ISLAND, AND OUTLETS

The outer beach borders a barrier island built in most recent Holocene times. Where it is wide enough, the barrier island includes several parallel beach ridges (e.g., in the Anecho region, Togo); between the barrier and the coastal plateau, lagoons and marshes are found (Fig. 84-1).

The most interesting point in present coastal evolution concerns the outlets, which tend to be alternately open and closed. This is a result of two antagonistic forces; the surf, which tends to close them, and the river flow, which must escape to the ocean and thus tends to keep them open. The stress of either force depends, of course, on the

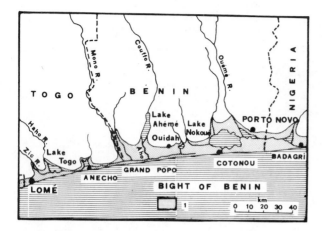

Figure 84-1. General map of the coast: 1. coastal marshes and ridges.

In western Benin, for example (Fig. 84-2), the outlet was situated at Boca del Rio ("mouth of the river" in Portuguese) in 1954–1955. It was closed by the surf during the 1955–1956 dry season; at the beginning of October 1956 (wet season), there was no more outlet in that area, and floods drowned the marshes behind. Then the local authorities ordered a ditch cut across it, and the outlet remained open there, even during the following dry season. Plate 84-1 shows this Grand Popo outlet in October 1957, with a spit normally recurved at the western side of the pass, as a result of the longshore drift directed to the east. When the outlets are closed, the morphology of the barrier island preserves residual features such as recurved spits.

succession of dry and wet seasons; but the opening and closing of the outlets are not regular, not exactly seasonal, because the river discharge varies from year to year, and because some lagoons receive more fresh water than others and are thus better able to remain open throughout the year. The location of outlets may also shift.

COASTAL LAGOONS AND MARSHES, AND ASSOCIATED SEDIMENTS

The coastal lagoons located just behind the barrier islands are only about 1 m deep, except where they include sections of rivers connected

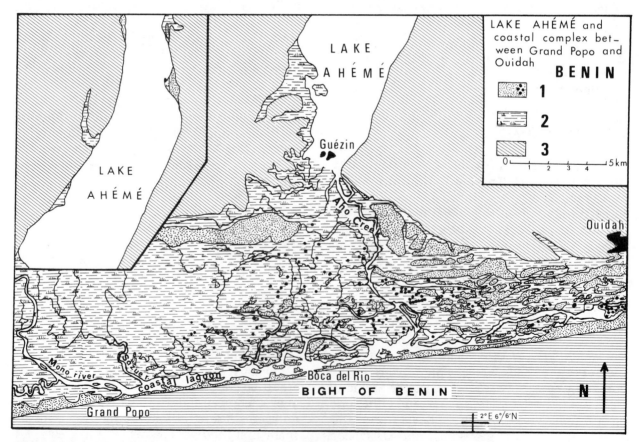

Figure 84-2. Lake Ahémé and coastal complex between Grand Popo and Ouidah, Benin: 1. barriers, ridges and mounds (sand); 2. marshes (mud); 3. coastal plateau (*terre de barre*).

to outlets (Guilcher 1959). The bottom is muddy, but sandy beaches exist on their sides, on which the waves generated by the local southwesterly winds build small hooked spits, evenly spaced, tied to the mainland in the west and recurved at their eastern ends. They belong to the "azovian" type described by Russian authors, and are also found in Angola lagoons and on the Senegal delta.

Behind the coastal lagoons, there are extensive marshes (Plate 84-2), including many sand bodies elongated from west to east and much smaller sandy islands or mounds more or less circular in plan (Plate 84-3). At least a very large proportion of these sand bodies are former spits, which were built along the outer coast when it was not as prograded as it is now. Such is the case in the surroundings of Ouidah, Grand Popo, and Lake Ahémé (Fig. 84-2), and on the Benin-Nigeria border (Guilcher 1978), where the sediment is a well-sorted sand. Some of these spits might date from a former interglacial. The subcircular sandy mounds, which are also found in the Ouidah-Grand Popo area, are made of the same material. They are remnants of former beach ridges that were dissected by the meandering of creeks when isolated inside the marshes. The present shifting courses of rivers work in the same way.

Tastet (1977), followed by Lang and Paradis (1977), thinks that some of the elongated bodies inside the marshes are not old beach ridges or barrier islands, but remnants of an apron of continental deposits carried by rivers during the Ogolian, the end of the last interglacial, 20,000–12,000 B.P. Structures at the western end of the area, between Lake Togo and Lome, have been interpreted in this way. This view can be valid only when an important silty or clayey fraction exists in the sediment, and it remains to be understood how continental aprons sloping to the south can have been dissected, later on, in elongated shapes running from west to east.

In any case, all of these accumulations have straightened the shoreline, which was initially much more indented. It is evident that Lake Ahémé (Fig. 84-2) and other lakes in the lower reaches of the rivers are former rias, drowned valleys that have been isolated from the sea by sedimentation concurrent with the Holocene transgression.

The Benin marshes have been exploited for salt production, which has resulted in curious sets of numerous small ponds in the Grand Popo area. This is an example of human influence on marsh topography (Paradis and Adjanohoun 1974). Another result of this salt extraction has been the extensive cutting of the mangrove trees for firewood. Thus, the mangroves have become scarce and have been replaced by bare marshy zones, even though there is no long dry season, as is generally responsible for such bare zones or *tanns* (in Guinea, Gambia, and so on) (Paradis 1980).

ANDRÉ GUILCHER

REFERENCES

Guilcher, A., 1954, Dynamique et morphologie des côtes sableuses de l'Afrique atlantique, *Cahiers Inf. Géogr.* **1:**57–68.

Guilcher, A., 1959, Coastal sand ridges and marshes and their continental environment near Grand Popo and Ouidah, Dahomey, *2nd Coastal Geog. Conf.* Office of Naval Research, Washington, D.C., pp. 155–167.

Guilcher, A., 1978, Observations comparatives sur un complexe littoral de la côte atlantique africaine, *Norois* **25:**551–556.

Lang, J., and G. Paradis, 1977, Le domaine margino-littoral du Bénin méridional, *Reu Géographie Phys. et Géologie Dynam.* **19:**295–312.

Paradis, G., 1980, Un cas particulier de zones dénudées dans les mangroves d'Afrique de l'Ouest: celles dues à l'extraction du sel, *Mus. Natl. Histoire Nat. Paris Bull.* **4**(2)B:227–261.

Paradis, G., and E. Adjanohoun, 1974, L'impact de le fabrication du sel sur la végétation de mangrove et la géomorphologie dans le Bas-Dahomey, *Annales Uniu Abidjan,* E **7**(1):599–612.

Tastet, J. P., 1977, Les formations sédimentaires Pléistocènes à actuelles du littoral du Togo et de la République Populaire du Bénin, *Rech. Fr. Quat, INQUA,* Assoc. Francaise Étude Quaternaire Suppl. Bull., pp. 155–167.

Plate 84-1. Grand Popo outlet, October 1957. Breakers oblique to the coastline (photo by A. Guilcher).

Plate 84-2. Western Benin coastal area: oblique breakers (*kalema*), barrier island, lagoon, marsh, river (photo by A. Guilcher).

Plate 84-3. Western Benin coastal area. Sandy mounds in marshes, resulting from dissection of former sand ridges by meandering rivers (photo by A. Guilcher).

85: NIGERIA

Lying between Badagry in the west and the estuary of the Cross River in the east, the coastline of Nigeria covers a distance of about 800 km. The entire coastal zone (Fig. 85-1) consists of a low-lying depositional plain characterized by expansive estuarine lagoons and mangrove swamps fronted by beach-ridge barriers. The impressive array of depositional features along the coast represents an interplay between the sediment-laden Niger and its associates and the powerful forces of the Atlantic Ocean, into which these rivers empty. The Niger is the largest of several rivers that transport enormous quantities of

sediment of all grades to the Gulf of Guinea, where waves, tides, and currents sort and redistribute the materials and build them into a series of sedimentary formations (Usoro 1977).

West of the Niger delta, the coast has a remarkable display of a barrier beach–lagoon complex in which parallel sand ridges are spaced between filled depressions and open creeks. The Lagos and Lekki Lagoon, which has provided Nigeria with a magnificent sheltered harbor, is separated from the open sea by a broad sand barrier with a wide surf-bound beach (Plate 85-1). The central portion of the Nigerian coast is dominated by the

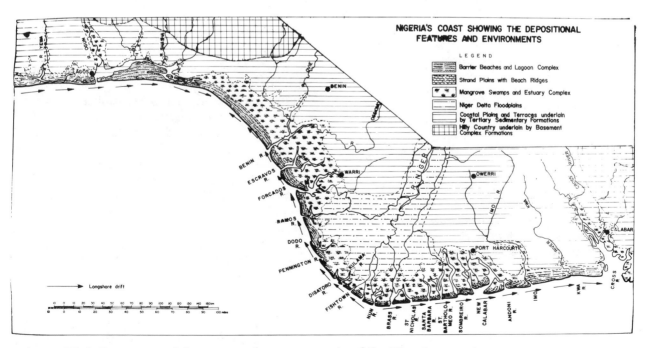

Figure 85-1. Depositional features and environments of the Nigerian coast.

Niger delta, which consists of a thick pile of sediment, much of which accumulated from Cretaceous times onward in a downwarped coastal margin (Allen 1965a). East of the Niger delta, the coastal landscape is typically that of beach ridges spaced between the estuaries of the Imo and Kwa rivers, while much of the Cross River estuary is flanked by mud flats and mangrove swamps. The Nigerian coastal plain indicates a long period of seaward growth and represents an excellent example of a depositional regression of the sea by littoral sedimentation.

PHYSICAL FACTORS OF THE LAND

Geology

The crystalline basement complex and folded Paleozoic strata of West Africa, which are exposed in much of the hinterland areas of Nigeria, pass deeply beneath a thick pile of recent sedimentary accumulations (Fig. 85-1). The Nigerian coastal plain is thus defined by a massive sedimentary basin about 350 km wide and 670 km long (Allen 1965b). The geosyncline is bounded in the east by the volcanic intrusions of the Cameroon and Adamawa mountains. Westward, the geosyncline stretches beyond Nigeria into southern Benin Republic, Togo, and Ghana. Southward, the sedimentary basin protrudes into the Gulf of Guinea oceanic basin.

The structural trend of the basin tilts gently seaward, suggesting that downwarping toward the sea has occurred (Pugh 1953). The Holocene sediments, consisting of fluviolagoonal deposits and littoral sands, extend inland to the apex of the delta near Onitsha and the lower valleys of the Ogun, Shasha, Imo, and Cross rivers. Material from drilling indicates that a marine trangression that deposited an older quartzose sand was followed by a depositional break or regression from late Pleistocene to early Holocene, during which the organic-pitch silts, clays, and sands of the modern delta and the associated barrier island and mangrove swamp environments were deposited (Allen 1965a). The sedimentary history indicates a depositional seaward advance of the coastline.

Climate and Biotic Factors

The Nigerian coast shares the climatic conditions that prevail in the forest zone of southern Nigeria, where the weather is perennially wet, with an annual rainfall of at least 3500 mm. The dominant factor influencing climate is the movement of the Intertropical Front, which gives rise to two seasons, dry and wet. During the long wet season, moisture-laden southwest winds from the Atlantic Ocean produce copious rainfall that make places like Calabar, Bonny, and Port Harcourt among the rainiest in the world. Temperature ranges from 20° C to 35° C, and humidity is persistently high, ranging from 70% at Lagos to over 80% at Calabar.

Although the sand ridges that fringe the lagoons and intertidal flats carry scrub-like bush with stunted palms (Adejuwon 1970), the dominant species of vegetal cover along the coast is the arching stilt-rooted mangrove. The mangroves of the Nigerian coast are of two types. The swamps flanking the lagoons and estuaries are dominated by the halophytic red mangroves (*Rhizophora racemosa*) while *Avicennia* occupy parts of the swamps farther inland. Fresh-water swamp vegetation gradually displaces the mangroves farther inland, and with more elevated land on the flood plains and coastal terraces, rain forest becomes dominant except where clearings for farms give way to secondary forest.

PHYSICAL FACTORS OF THE SEA

Waves and Currents

The Nigerian coastline is characterized by a high intensity of wave action. Along the West African coast, the strong southwest monsoon is the dominant wind and blows persistently onshore all year round. The open Atlantic provides a long fetch, producing powerful waves, generated by these prevailing winds. Two major wave systems have been identified (Clason et al. 1954), the longer waves having greater energy than the short-wave system. Littoral currents set up by the breaking of these waves constitute an important agent distributing sediment along the coast. In the western sector of the Nigerian coast there is a strong west-to-east longshore current; consequently the predominant direction of beach drifting here is eastward. At the Lagos Harbor mouth, the littoral drift has been interrupted for many years by a breakwater, which has trapped sand traveling eastward along the coast (Plate 85-2).

At the tip of the delta, there is an eastward current, which continues to the Cross River estuary, and a westward current on the flank of the delta to the mouth of the Benin River (Fig. 85-1). These currents drive sand brought by the rivers northwestward in the western delta and eastward between Bonny and the Cross River estuary. This littoral drifting is the most important agent molding sandy shoreline features along the Nigerian coast.

Tides

Tidal flows are also important for sediment dispersal, especially in the mangrove belt and nearshore waters. Access to swamps and mud flats is through the mouths of rivers and the major distributaries of the Niger. In the Lagos area, the tide penetrates the lagoon through the harbor entrance. Tidal flows are diurnal and create reversing currents. Tidal currents in the swamp belts of the Niger delta and the lagoon complex west of the Benin River are not consistent because of the intricate geometry and numerous interconnections of the creeks within the mangrove swamps. The maximum tidal velocities in the mangrove swamps vary from 40–180 cm/s (Clason et al. 1954). Such velocities are strong enough to shift coarse sand. The dispersive powers of the tide diminish with increasing depth and distance from the shore. The vertical range of the tide increases eastward from Lagos (1.0 m) to the estuaries of the Imo and Cross rivers (2.6 m and 3.0 m respectively). Brackish water spreads far inland, extending to the apex of the Niger delta near Onitsha, about 220 km from the open ocean.

COASTAL SEDIMENTS AND BEACH MATERIALS

The sediments that have accumulated in the depositional plain of the Nigerian coast are derived mainly from the catchment basins of the Niger, Oshun, Shasha, Oni, Ovie, Imo, Kwa, and Cross rivers. The rivers Volta, Mono, and Oueme have also contributed materials to the Nigerian coast by way of longshore drifting. These rivers are eroded into the basement complex—metamorphic rocks, basic volcanics—and derived Tertiary sandstones, all of which outcrop over extensive areas of the Nigerian hinterland. The rivers transport their sediments from the weathered mantles of these formations and discharge large quantities of material into the Atlantic Ocean to be redistributed by the various marine agents.

The basins of the Niger and Benue yield about 60% of the coastal sands, the remaining contributions coming from the basins of the other Nigerian rivers. The rivers carry mostly medium to coarse sand, their characteristic heavy minerals being green and brown hornblende, epidote, zircon, and staurolite.

Along Victoria Beach in Lagos, coarse quartzose sand is found on the upper parts of the beach while finer sand characterizes the foreshore, which also contains a high proportion of calcareous material. West of the Niger delta, mud pebbles are found on eroding stretches of the beach. The outer barrier beaches consist largely of clean, coarse, angular sand, although medium and very coarse grains occur as well. The inner barriers have predominantly finer and more rounded grains than do the outer barrier beaches. The high degree of roundness of the inner sand ridges may be attributed either to the changes that have affected them between their derivation and deposition or to post depositional physicochemical changes. Silt and some organic debris have been deposited in the swales between the parallel sand ridges.

Apart from sand, these rivers transport vast amounts of silt and clay in suspension during flood discharge to the coast. The deposition of such organic-rich clayey silt and plant debris produces extensive mud flats and swamps. The floors of the large creeks and tidal channels in the delta contain thick sand beds, while many of the smaller channels contain sand unevenly interbedded with dark clayey silt and plant debris. In the estuaries of the Imo, Kwa, and Cross rivers, sediments are mostly interbedded dark gray clayey silt and very fine sand, while the larger shoals consist of interbedded cross-stratified and evenly stratified sand with lenses of clayey silt.

COASTAL FEATURES

Barrier Beaches and Lagoons

Sandy barrier beaches constitute the most striking features along the Nigerian coast, where remarkably long series of barrier beaches occur west of the Niger delta. Along this part of the coast, between Badagry and Mahin, a low degraded cliff about 10 km from the shore rises to the margin of the coastal terrace or plateau.

Between the terrace and the sea, a depositional plain includes a series of long sand ridges trending parallel to the coastline. The sand ridges are separated from one another by elongated muddy depressions, giving a ridge and swale topography, (Plate 85-3). The sand ridges may be classified into a younger outer group, formed during the Holocene, and including active beach ridges, and an older inner group of Pleistocene age. There are two sets of beach ridges on the outer barrier near Badagry: one set runs diagonally across the landward side of the barrier (Plate 85-1), the other set is aligned parallel with the coastline. The beach ridges are no more than 2 m high and vary in width between 40 and 50 m crest to crest. Near Mahin some beach ridges can be traced for distances of several kilometers without breaks in continuity.

The outer barrier is separated from the inner sand ridges by creeks and meandring channels. West of Lagos the lagoon subdivides into several smaller creeks to form an intricate pattern of waterways, but east of the city it broadens into an expansive water body attaining a maximum width of about 7 km in the Lekki Lagoon. Lagos Harbor is located in the lagoon near the only connection with the sea.

The barrier-lagoon complex of western Nigeria constitutes a system in which the parallel sand ridges mark lines of growth, each having been at one time a beach, separated from a previous one by a lagoon. Some of the lagoons eventually silted up as a result of sedimentation to form swampy depressions. Badagry Creek, which continues east of Lagos as the Lekki Lagoon, is the last such enclosed portion of the sea not yet filled with estuarine sediment. The subsequent development of barriers along the full length of the coast in this area led to a marked straightening and shortening of a formerly indented and embayed coast, as indicated by the margin of the coastal terrace (cf. Guilcher 1959).

Strand Plain Barrier

East of the Imo River estuary, the tidal flats and mangrove swamps that characterize much of the Niger delta disappear from the coastal landscape, giving way to a complex strand-plain barrier up to 10 km wide (Fig. 85-2). This barrier consists of numerous subparallel sand ridges formed by successive additions of beach ridges to the coastline. The intervening swamp hollows are reflected

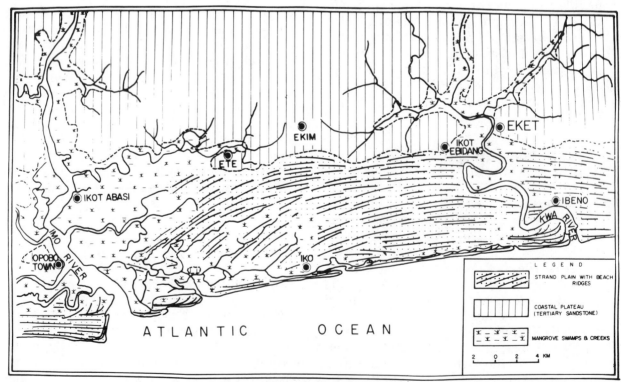

BEACH RIDGE SYSTEMS ALONG THE NIGERIAN COAST EAST OF IMO RIVER ESTUARY

Figure 85-2. Beach ridge systems along the Nigerian coast east of the Imo River estuary.

in the strong lineation of vegetation of dense raffia thicket, which differs markedly from the sparse scrub on the sand ridges. The summit levels of the ridges decrease seaward from 7 m near the margin of the sandstone terrace to 3 m near the coast. Some of the successive sand ridges may have developed from spits growing eastwards with the longshore sand drift (Plates 85-4, 85-5, and 85-6). One such spit can be seen west of the estuary of the Kwa River (Plate 85-5). To the north of this spit, the vegetation pattern reveals the incorporation of former hooked spits. Near the sandstone terrace, the ridges in the strand plain are of greater elevation and may have been longshore bars that emerged above sea level.

Near the Cross River estuary, sets of older beach ridges are truncated by newer ones (Plate 85-7). The lines of discordance between groups of sand ridges indicate that periods of coastal prograda-tion alternated with periods of erosion, presum-ably relating to variations in sediment supply (Allen 1965a).

Mangrove Swamp Environment

Mangrove swamps are extensively developed along the Nigerian coast. Within the Niger delta and its flank areas, the swales between sand barriers are occupied by vast mangrove swamps (Fig. 85-1). East of the delta, the estuaries of the Imo, Kwa, and Cross rivers are flanked by large tracts of mangrove. Mangroves also occupy por-tions of the coastal zone in the lagoonal terrain lying west of the delta. These are found mostly along the northern shores of Lekki Lagoon and extend into the lower valleys of the Yewa, Ogun, Oshun, and Shasha rivers.

The mangrove swamps occupy tidal mud flats laced with tidal channels, a myriad of meander-ing creeks that vary in size and shape, from widths of more than 1 km to small winding waterways about 20 m wide (Plate 85-7). Most of the large channels are the direct extensions of the dis-tributaries of the Niger delta and are arranged radially along the mangrove belt through an arc of about 150° in a coastwise direction (Fig. 85-1). Prominent among these are the Benin, Pennington, Nun, Forcardos, Sombriero, Sagana, and Bonny rivers. At their seaward ends, the channels broaden into large tidal passes more than 2 km wide, and some are studded with complexes of shoals and mud flats called intraswamp deltas.

Small creeks that meander strongly develop as branches of the main channels. Their headward extension through the mud flats sometimes leads to capture of large channels, thereby establishing a connection between all parts of the mangrove swamp. Such a system of intricately intercon-nected creeks can be seen in the vicinity of Port Harcourt, where a complex network of drainage channels has broken the mangrove swamp into a jigsaw of irregularly shaped tidal flats.

The evolution of mangrove swamps is related to the deposition of large quantities of clay and silt transported by rivers from the hinterland. From initial small banks in open water, accretion may continue until a sizable tidal flat is formed. Soon after the banks build above mean tide level, mangrove trees begin to grow. Further accretion is considerably aided by the mangroves, whose spreading roots trap sediment and hinder current scour, thereby inducing rapid deposition of the organic-rich clayey silt. The mangroves are also effective in binding the muddy soil and providing a platform on which further deposition of silt and sand can take place. Gradually, as the inter-tidal flats grade into firmer depositional terrain, the mangroves are replaced by tropical forest.

The mangrove swamp environment along the Nigerian coast forms at an unusually rapid rate. The expansion of mangrove swamp is perceptible on air photographs of Opobo taken at an interval of 20 years. In many parts of the Niger delta, mangrove swamps are expanding rapidly. Strong meandering of tidal creeks enables the mangroves to invade areas formerly occupied by sandy bar-riers. Remnants of the sandy formations can be found widely scattered within the swamp, pro-viding higher ground where settlements and farms are located.

THE DELTA FLOOD PLAINS

The mangrove swamps are succeeded landward by firm alluvial ground, or a depositional terrace constructed by the accretion of sand during flooding. This landform is known as the coastal flood plain (Allen 1965a; Clason et al. 1954). The flood plains occupy a broad space between the mangrove swamp and the sandstone terrace (Fig. 85-1). Large meander scrolls enclosing ridged point bars, low natural levees that descend into heavily forested backswamps, and cutoff channels and oxbows are the prominent features of the landscape on the delta flood plains. The levees vary in height between 4.5 and 8 m above the backswamps; where they are breached by flood-waters, large crevasses have formed. The back-swamps are seasonally flooded, and settlements, farms, and lines of communication are restricted to the levees. The oxbows here vary from permanent lakes to seasonal swamps, depending on the nature of the plugging at their ends.

COASTAL EROSION AND EFFECT OF ARTIFICIAL STRUCTURES

The Nigerian coast is currently in a stage of retrogradation, possibly following a slight rise in sea level (Pugh 1953). Everywhere along the coast sand cliffs characterize the backshore, and beaches are being severely eroded. Between Lagos and the Benin border near Kweme the sandy barrier has been cut back rapidly, at a rate of more than 5 m a year. Severe erosion is also occurring along the shore of barrier islands fringing the Niger delta, especially between Bonny and Andoni.

Victoria Beach near Lagos has been the site of rapid erosion accentuated by the trapping of longshore drift at Lighthouse Beach. The beach has retreated by up to 1300 m, of which 378 m eroded between 1966 and 1975 and 102 m from 1972 to 1975. Beach nourishment with sand pumped in from the sea floor began in February 1976 and built up the beach profile, but renewed erosion in 1980 denuded the entire sea front up to the edge of the first row of houses on Victoria Island.

There have been substantial changes in this area since the coastline was first mapped at the beginning of this century. Lighthouse Beach, for example, has prograded rapidly since the break-water was built in 1912 to maintain a navigable entrance to Lagos Lagoon: between 1924 and 1972 the shore advanced 1200 m seaward, and between 1972 and 1975 it advanced a further 99.7 m alongside the breakwater, thus widening a foreland on which numerous successive beach ridges have formed. By 1985 it is likely that the sand will have built out to the end of the breakwater, and that a bypassing bar system will develop, impeding navigation but allowing longshore drift to reach Victoria Beach for the first time since 1912. An artificial structure has had a similar effect at the mouth of the Escravos River in the Niger delta, where beach sand drifting northwestward is rapidly piling up behind the Escravos breakwaters, while the shore north of the estuary is retreating because of loss of nourishment.

Discordance between sets of beach ridges are indicative of changes in strand lines. At Mahin, for example, there are visible strands whose trend are different by more than 25 degrees from the present one. East of the Kwa River estuary, three distinct episodes of coastal accretion with intervening periods of retreat have been identified (Usoro 1977).

CHANGES OF SEA LEVEL AND EVOLUTION OF THE NIGERIAN COAST

The sedimentary history of the Nigerian coastal plain probably started during the late Wisconsin low stand of sea level, as the rivers entrenched while their mouths and strandlines lay close to the edge of the continental shelf (Allen 1965b). After this low stand of the sea level, a transgressing late Glacial to early Holocene sea advanced inland to deposit littoral sands. This quartzose sand, of late Pleistocene to early Holocene age, was deposited along the strandline of a rising sea and therefore represents the oldest stratigraphic unit in the later Quaternary sedimentary sequence. Once sea level became relatively stable, the strand-line again retreated seaward in a regressive advance of the strand across the transgressive sands, carrying with it the several lithofacies of the younger suite (i.e., sediments that are younger and stratigraphically higher than the transgressive sands of the continental shelf). This younger suite includes the beach-ridge barriers, mangrove swamps, the organic-rich estuarine tidal flats, and the Niger delta flood plain environments—all of which accumulated in the relatively recent past after the sea level had become stable and the shore extended itself seaward by the addition of fresh sediment from a vast source area. The barrier beaches and other depositional features represent progradation, hence a period of regression. These features record a regressive deposition, during which the additional sediment pushed the sea back over a wide front, reclaiming a vast portion of the coastal plain that had been submerged during the Holocene transgression.

The advance of the Nigerian coastline and the progradational processes that have been dominant in the Holocene have now given place to coastal retreat, with widespread truncation of the seaward margins of barrier beaches.

ETOP JAMES USORO

REFERENCES

Adejuwon, J. O., 1970, The ecological status of coastal savanna in Nigeria, *Jour. Tropical Geog.* **30:**1–10.

Allen, J. R. L., 1965*a*, Coastal geomorphology of eastern Nigeria: beach ridge barriers and vegetated tidal flats, *Geol. Mijnbouw* 1–21.

Allen, J. R. L., 1965*b*, Late Quaternary Niger delta and adjacent areas, *Assoc. Petroleum Geologists Bull.* **49:**547–600.

Clason, E. W. H., B. D. H. Tellegen, H. C. Frijlink, J. Th. Thijsse, P. Ph. Jansen, and J. B. Schijf, 1954, *Report on the Western Niger Delta by the Netherlands Engineering Consultants to the Government of Nigeria. Lagos,* NEDECO, The Hague.

Guilcher, A., 1959, Coastal sand ridges and marshes and their environment near Grand Popo and Quidah Dahomey, *2nd Coastal Geog. Conf. Proc.* Washington, D.C., pp. 189–212.

Pugh, J. C., 1953, The Porto Novo–Badagry sand ridge complex, *University College, Ibadan, Dept. Geog. Res. Notes* **3:**3–14.

Usoro, E. J., 1977, *Coastal development in Lagos area,* unpublished Ph.D. Thesis, University of Ibadan, Nigeria.

Plate 85-1. The outer barrier beach separating the Lagos Lagoon from the open ocean. A wide surf beach characterizes the seaward margin of the barrier (photo by E. J. Usoro).

Plate 85-2. The entrance to Lagos Harbor, showing the Lighthouse Beach, where sand accumulation has prograded the coastline toward the seaward end of the groin. The southern limit of the vegetated area marks the position of the original coastline and the extent to which this beach has advanced since the construction of the West Mole, which began in 1901 (photo by E. J. Usoro).

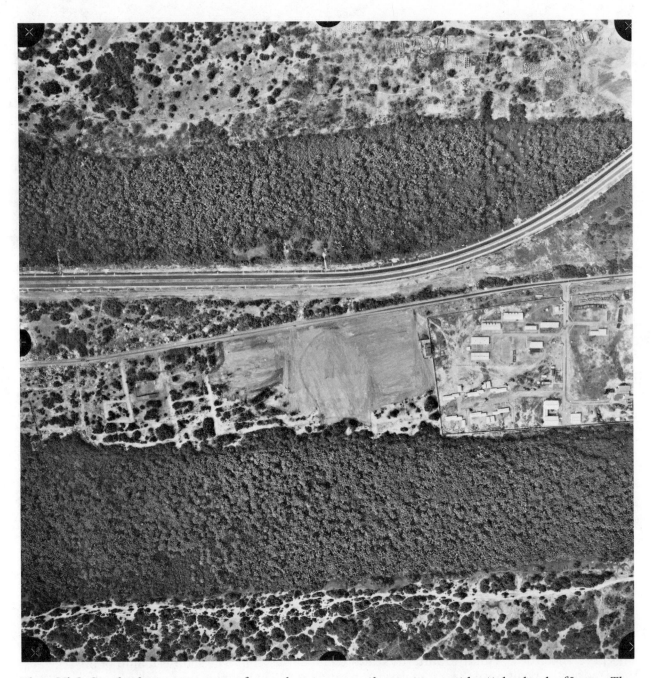

Plate 85-3. Sand ridges representing former barriers near the western residential suburb of Lagos. The successive sand ridges, with light tones alternating with muddy swales, reveal the growth history of this portion of the coast. Buildings and roads are located on the sand ridges, and the swales are carefully avoided (photo by E. J. Usoro).

Plate 85-4. The outer barrier between Andoni River and the Imo estuary, with a remarkable display of successive sets of beach ridges formed as the barrier prograded into the Atlantic Ocean (photo by E. J. Usoro).

Plate 85-5. Development of hooked spits west of the Kwa River estuary. Within the large meander bend, a former hooked spit can be seen incorporated in the vegetation (photo by E. J. Usoro).

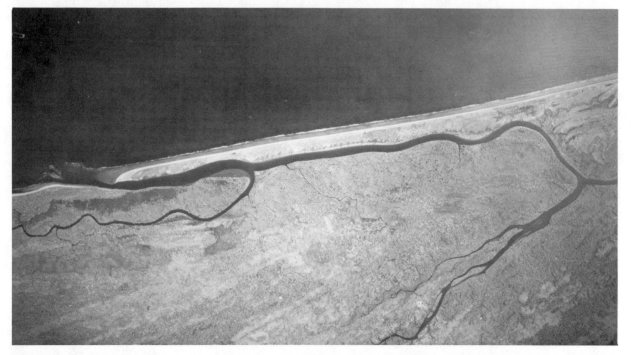

Plate 85-6. A remarkable 5 km long spit built along the coast east of the Imo estuary by littoral drift. This indicates that barrier formation along this part of the coast has been aided by spit formation (photo by E. J. Usoro).

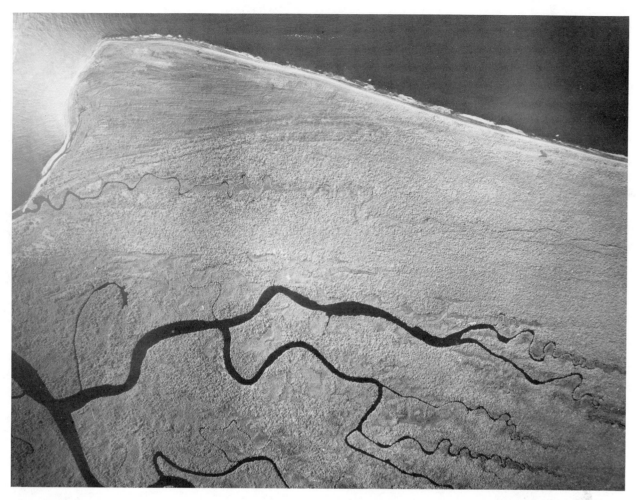

Plate 85-7. The coast near the Cross River estuary. Beach ridges have been formed from sand drifting eastward. The history of the seaward growth and the shifting locations of the former shores are well displayed by the beach ridge patterns. There have been several episodes of truncation followed by formation of new sets of ridges at an angle to the older ones (photo by E. J. Usoro).

86. CAMEROON AND EQUATORIAL GUINEA

The coasts of Cameroon (Fig. 86-1) and Equatorial Guinea (Fig. 86-2) share a very similar physical environment. They lie along the Afro trailing-edge coast where Precambrian basement rocks (gneiss, shist, quartzite, and migmatite) reach the shore, mantled in places by Cenozoic deposits (Orme 1982). The eastern edge of the Niger Basin, a continuation of the Benue graben,

extends into Cameroon. Recent volcanic activity along the Cameroon fault has contributed dramatically, in places, to the evolution of the coastal landscape. Soils in both countries are either latosolic or lateritic (Pritchard 1971), and the two countries lie in a zone of relatively rapid chemical weathering (Davies 1973).

Mainland Equatorial Guinea lies between 1°

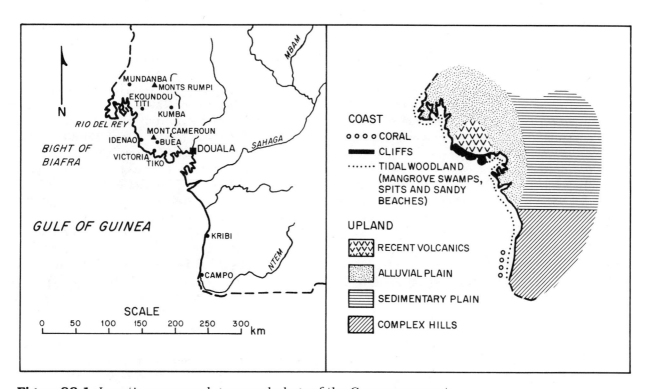

Figure 86-1. Location map and geomorphology of the Cameroon coast.

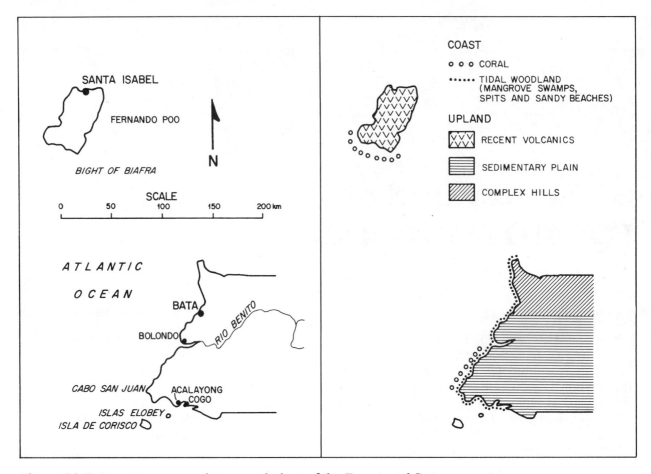

Figure 86-2. Location map and geomorphology of the Equatorial Guinea coast.

and 2° north latitude and Cameroon between 2° and 14° north latitude. Therefore, the climate in Equatorial Guinea, on the continent, and in southern Cameroon is equatorial, while in northern Cameroon it is Sahelian. In the region of Douala annual precipitation is 4–5 m, temperature 24–30° C, and there are four seasons: rainy from March to June and again from September through October, a brief dry spell in August, and a long dry season from November to March (Van Chi-Bonnardel 1973). Average runoff along the whole sector is greater than 1 m/yr.

Offshore, prevailing oceanic currents are the Guinea and Benguela. Waves approach from the southwest, this being a region of Davies' (1973) west-coast swell environment. The highest swell coincides with the strongest and most frequent onshore winds, from June to September. Mean wave heights over 1.5 m occur less than 20% of the year (Orme 1982). Tides are semidiurnal, with a spring range of 2–4 m (Davies 1973).

The coastline of Cameroon (Fig. 86-1), along the Gulf of Guinea, is 200 km in length (Daggs 1970), composed mostly of mangrove forest with occasional sandy beaches. The one section of rocky coast occurs southwest of the active volcano of Mount Cameroon, from Idenao down to the vicinity of Victoria (Ngwa 1967). Here there are rocky islands, cliffs, and capes (Cape Nachtigal). The low-lying coast stretches from Idenao north to the border, and from Victoria south to near Kribi. (The low coastal plain is several kilometers wide in south Cameroon, but widens to 100 km in the Douala area.) Typical of these two regions are mangrove forest, lagoons, low-lying islands, many creeks, sand bars, and spits. Two spits north of Sanje and one at the mouth of the Sanaga River are all developed to the north, indicating the direction of net shore-drift along the main portion of the coast. This fits in well with the picture of southwesterly, west-coast swell and northerly net sediment transport for the area as reported on a gross scale by Davies (1973).

Along the southern part of the coast (Fig. 86-1)

there is some coral of the Atlantic Province (McGill 1958, Davies 1973). Farther north is a large port at Douala and smaller shipping facilities at Kribi, Tiko, and Victoria-Bota (Hance 1975).

The coast of Equatorial Guinea (Fig. 86-2) is divided between two territories: Rio Muni on the mainland and Fernando Poo (2,034 km^2), an island in the Bight of Biafra 50 km west of the Cameroon coast (Van Chi-Bonnardel 1973). There are also three small islands: Corsica and Elobey, near the southwest corner of Rio Muni, and Annobon, at 1° south latitude off Gabon.

Rio Muni has a coastal plain, rising in terraces inland to somewhat less than 1,000 m. The coastline is similar to that of Cameroon in that there are lagoons and mangrove forest, sandy beaches with net sediment transport to the north, and Atlantic Province coral in the south (McGill 1958; Davies 1973).

Fernando Poo (see also *Atlantic Ocean Islands*) is a volcanic island with three basaltic cones, a southwest extension of the volcanic activity along the Cameroon fault (Van Chi-Bonnardel 1973). The highest elevation is 3,000 m at Pic Santa Isabel. The steep slopes of this island are very fertile and have been turned over to intensive farming. Along the southerly end of the island, facing the prevailing swell, there is coral, similar to that at the mainland coast (McGill 1958; Davies 1973).

The only significant ports in Equatorial Guinea are at Santa Isabel on Fernando Poo and at Bata in Rio Muni (Van Chi-Bonnardel 1973).

MAURICE L. SCHWARTZ

REFERENCES

Daggs, E., 1970, *All Africa,* Hastings House, New York.

Davies, J. L., 1973, *Geographical Variations in Coastal Development,* Hafner, New York.

Hance, W. A., 1975, *The Geography of Modern Africa,* Columbia University Press, New York.

McGill, J. T., 1958, Map of coastal landforms of the world, *Geog. Rev.* **48:**402–405.

Ngwa, J. A., 1967, *An Outline Geography of the Republic of Cameroon,* Longmans, London.

Orme, A. T., 1982, Africa, coastal morphology, in *The Encyclopedia of Beaches and Coastal Environments,* M. L. Schwartz, ed., Hutchinson Ross Publishing Co., Stroudsburg, Pa., pp. 17–32.

Pritchard, J. M., 1971, *Africa: The Geography of a Changing Continent,* Africana Publishing Corp., New York.

Van Chi-Bonnardel, R., 1973, *The Atlas of Africa,* Jeune Afrique, Paris.

87. GABON, CONGO, CABINDA, AND ZAÏRE

The coastline of this sector is about 980 km long (1°N to 6°S) and corresponds to the oceanic boundary of two secondary and tertiary sedimentary basins, those of Gabon and the Congo, which are separated toward the ocean by the Mayumba salient of the Precambrian basement (Fig. 87-1 and 87-2).

These basins lie on the Precambrian basement, and their beds are hidden by the piedmont detritic cover of the Série des Cirques, which is generally recognized as of Plio-Pleistocene age. Outcrops are limited to the edge of the Precambrian Mayombe relief, where there are freshwater beds of the Lower Cretaceous, deposited before the opening up of the Atlantic Ocean, and the modern beaches, particularly the Pointes sector, where there are marine deposits of the Upper Cretaceous.

The Upper Cretaceous beds present a general monoclinal structure, but are affected by folding (direction N 110° to N 120°); this folding probably continued until the Miocene with a slightly different direction, N 90° to N 110° (Jansen et al. 1983). After this compressive phase Miocene beds were deposited discordantly and were unaffected by folding.

Faults occurred orthogonally to the Cretaceous and Paleogene fold directions and are the starting point of differential erosion of the coastline and particularly of the outline of the successive Pointes: Pointe Pedras, Pointe Banda, Pointe Kounda, Pointe Indienne, Pointe Noire, and Pointe de Tafe. For example, in the case of Pointe Noire, one of these faults brings sandy Santonian dolomites in the point into contact with uncemented sands of the Cenomanian and clayed marl of the Turonian in the bay (Giresse and Kouyoumontzakis 1971).

No obvious Quaternary marine levels are to be found above the present sea level except to the south (Cabinda, Zaïre), where because of a weak uplift, some Holocene beaches are observed above the present beach. This uplift toward the south is also revealed by the level of the Miocene shoreline, which is at −80 m off the Gabon shoreline and which outcrops on the Cabinda coast (see *Angola*), near Landana.

This coast is generally considered to have been stable, but small earthquakes are occasionally recorded. The sector is notable for its lack of appreciable tilting and emergence due to water loading as a function of distance from the present shoreline, as in Brazil or Australia (Clark and Bloom 1979). This coast, like that of Senegal (Faure et al. 1980), lies on a lithosphere generally assumed to be quite rigid.

The ocean swell has a large period (9 to 15 s) and a mean amplitude of 1 m (with storm maxima of 3 m) and is generally in a southwesterly direction. This swell carries reworked sands from the Série des Cirques and shapes the shoreline (Plate 87-1). The bay concavities are the centers of considerable erosion; the coast is receding and the transported materials are a source of continuing barrier development behind the point serving as relief. The sandy barrier of Pointe Noire tends to obstruct the harbor mouth, where con-

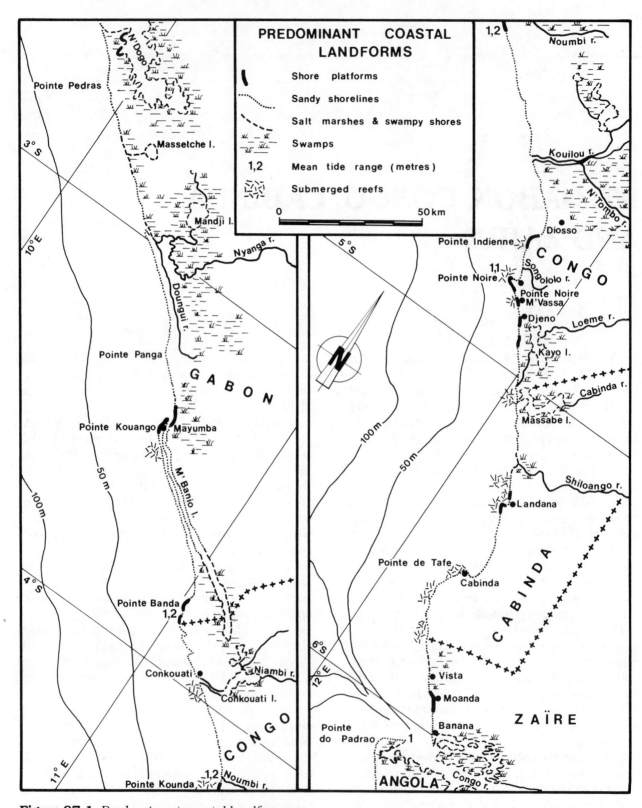

Figure 87-1. Predominant coastal landforms.

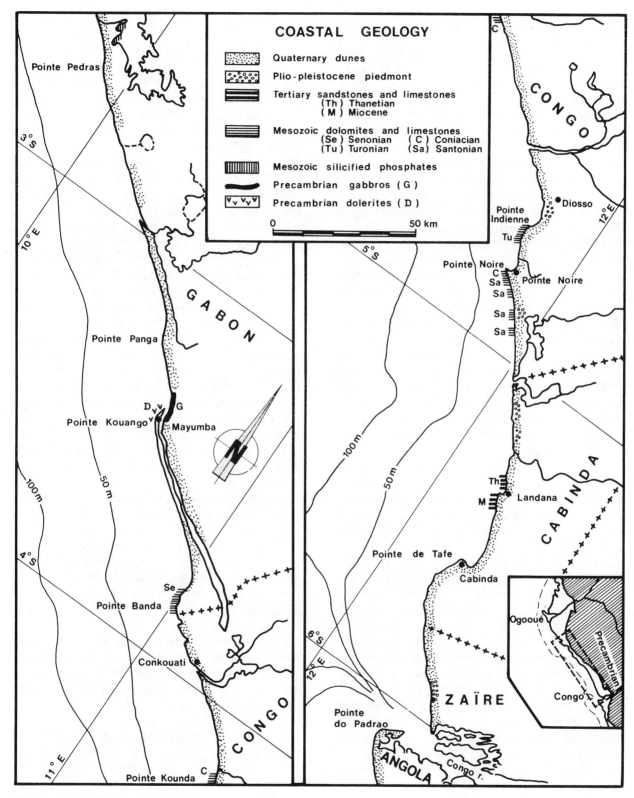

Figure 87-2. Coastal geology.

tinual dredging is necessary. Off Pointe Indienne, small lagoons are temporarily enclosed by sandy barriers. But these lagoons are rapidly isolated from the ocean and turn into small coastal pools. South of Pointe Noire, fishermen periodically open up an artificial entrance by bulldozer and thus allow marine fish to enter, but in a few days the barrier is rebuilt. If the fluvial discharge is great enough (Gabon, North Congo) channels are permanent and real lagoons can be developed; this is particularly the case with the Banio lagoon, where the barrier reaches some 60 km in length. Barrier beaches and lagoons are also well developed along the central and northern coast of Gabon.

On this relatively rectilinear oceanic coastline, mean tidal ranges are always relatively small: 1–1.2 m with slightly higher ranges (up to 1.6 m) during the spring tides. The ranges diminish gradually from north to south. The resulting streams are oriented broadly in a direction parallel to the coast, except in the Congo axis estuary.

The oceanic circulation is quite intricate almost throughout the year, a water body stratification with opposed movements according to the austral seasons. During the austral summer, warm water flows toward the south and overlies cold water, which comes to the surface in winter, when northerly currents are often dominant.

Given geological data (the detritic cover of the Série des Cirques) and oceanic factors (very powerful longshore drifting), it is not surprising that these coasts are predominantly sandy, while cliffs and bluffs or swamps are geographically limited (Fig. 87-1).

Rocky coasts do not form true cliffs or bluffs, but simply a more or less sand-covered platform, sometimes with a weak escarpment that rises above the beach. These platforms produce the shoreline convexities. Proceeding from the north, one can make the following observations: Some decalcified and silicified phosphatic levels of the Senonian outcrop in the N'Dogo lagoon and on the northward beaches (Furon 1932). In Mayumba, the crystalline basement reaches the coast, and gabbro outcrops can be correlated on the right bank of the lagoon channel; the ends of the sandy barriers lie on the dolerite outcrops, which control the Pointe Kouango convexity (Cosson 1955). The Pointe Banda convexity is due to Senonian calcareous outcrops. Pointe Kounda corresponds to sandy dolomites of the Coniacian, generally covered by the beach sand. The rocks of the shore platform of Pointe Indienne belong to

the Turonian (Plate 87-2). The Pointe Noire dolomites date from the Santonian like those of Djéno (Freneix 1966); oyster colonies proliferate on this platform. In Cabinda, near Landana, uncemented Thanetian and Miocene limestones outcrop.

The Série des Cirques overthrust is toward the ocean: at Diosso hills of more than 50 m width extend to some hundreds of meters from the shoreline. This is also the case near Djéno (Côte Matève, Plate 87-3 and 87-4) and in the north of Cabinda. This piedmont comprises the foundation of the present barrier in the Vista-Moanda area (Zaïre). It appears as a regular bluff several meters high, which has generally receded during the past century.

Swampy coasts are extensive, especially on the Gabon coastline, in the Ogooue River region on the north, south of the N'Dogo lagoon, and at the mouth of the Nyanga River. To the south, they are confined to estuaries (Noumbi, Kouilou, Songololo) and to the lagoon channels. In general, according to a colonial scale of observations made over about a century, before offshore petroleum pollution, mangrove vegetation has been dimishing. In several sectors the recent prograding of the shore has induced a little embanking of the channels and as a result a narrowing of the slikkes, areas of mangrove proliferation. A recent regressive tendency of sea level can also be adduced to explain this fact (Moguedet 1980). Exceptions are consituted by several channel mouths where alluvial pelitic deposits allow the mangrove new areas of colonization as in the mouth of the Kouilou (Plate 87-5), and even more so at the great Congo mouth, where a very prolific mangrove forest is developing on the islands and the unstable banks of the estuary. Most of the Congo sediment load (40–50 million m^3/y) is carried offshore in the surface waters; a little is carried toward the north and is deposited on the inner shelf of the Congo (Giresse and Kouyoumontzakis 1971). Thus Congo alluvials do not contribute in any way to the coastal sedimentation of Zaïre, Cabinda, or the Congo.

Sandy beaches consist of a light-beige sand that is reworked from the Série des Cirques. This sand is essentially quartzitic and feldspathic; it contains a weak shelly fraction that is less than 5% carbonate. During storms quartzitic gravels and pebbles are thrown 1–2 m above high water mark.

These sandy beaches are backed by a succession of ridges (2–3 m) that culminate 20 m above the present mean sea level. These ridges were built by winds during regressive pre-Holocene phases when the climate was more markedly arid than today (Plate 87-6). The building of these parallel sand dunes took place in several stages, the last being very recent: ochreous sands, deposited in oblique stratification, were whitened at the top by a podzol process allowing wind reworking, about 2,000 B.P. These white sands overlie various other lithologies (Plate 87-8 and 87-9). R. Lanfranchi (1978) has studied Tshitolian quartzitic implements interstratified in the brackish-water deposits near Pointe Noire (Songololo). Similar artifacts can be observed between the yellow and the white sands, with ^{14}C permitting historic remains to be placed in a stratigraphic context.

The stratigraphy of the end of the Quaternary and particularly of the Holocene is known only through underwater evidence. The Holocene beachrock described in the breaker zone by earlier authors (Rémy 1954) excepted, no significant sedimentary deposits through marine action are apparent on the whole coast. There are shelly accumulations (middens) of very modest size compared with those of Senegal (Descamps and Thilmans 1979) and on the Congo shore. These accumulations were once confused with beach deposits (Plate 87-10). The last eustatic oscillations (probably hydro-isostatic) have left some deposits on the low coast where the ocean can penetrate during minor oscillations (several dm): the Kouilou seaside plain, the Songololo mouth, and so on (Plate 87-11 and 87-12). Some blue and brackish clay beds, freshwater peaty muds and paleoground, uncovered by wave action during the dry season strong swell, were dated by ^{14}C and suggest the following outline of the last sea-level variations: a first transgressive maximum about 5,000 B.P. which does not seem to have extended beyond the present zero; a short regression between 4,000 and 3,000 B.P.; positive oscillation between 3,000 and 500 B.P. which may have exceeded (some dm) the present zero; and a recent regressive tendency.

PIERRE GIRESSE
GEORGES KOUYOUMONTZAKIS

REFERENCES

Clark, J. A., and A. L. Bloom, 1979, Hydro-isostacy and Holocene emergence of South America, *1978 Internat. Symp. on Coastal Evolution in the Quaternary Proc.* Sao Paulo, Brazil, pp. 41–60.

Cosson, J., 1955, Notice explicative sur les feuilles Pointe-Noire et Brazzaville, Carte géologique de reconnaissance au 1/500 000e, Dir. Min. Géol. AEF, Brazzaville.

Descamps, C., and G. Thilmans, 1979, Les tumulus coquilliers des îles du Saloun (Sénégal), *Ass. Sénégal. Et. Quatern. Afr. Bull. Liaison, Sénégal,* **54–55:** 81–91.

Faure, H., J. C. Fontes, L. Hebrard, J. Monteillet, and P. A. Pirazzoli, 1980, Geoïdal change and shore-level tilt along Holocene estuaries: Senegal River Area, West Africa, *Science* **210:**421–423.

Freneix, S., 1966, Faunes de bivalves et corrélations des formations marines du Crétacé des bassins côtiers de l'Ouest africain, *Bassins sédimentaires du littoral africain, 1° partie littoral atlantique,* Paris, pp. 52–78.

Furon, R., 1932, Les roches phosphatées de la côte du Gabon, *Soc. Géol. France Bull.* **5:**501–511.

Giresse, P., and G. Kouyoumontzakis, 1971, Géologie du sous-sol de Pointe-Noire et des fonds sous-marins voisins, *Annales Univ. Brazzaville* **7:**97–114.

Jansen, F., P. Giresse, and G. Moguedet, 1983, Seismic study of the Congolese platform (Air-Gun and Mud-penetrator); intraplate deformation matter of fact, *Netherlands Jour. Sea Research.*

Lanfranchi, R., 1978, *Rapport des missions d'études et de recherches préhistoriques pour l'année universitaire 1976-77,* ronéo Université Marien NGouabi.

Moguedet, G., 1980, La mangrove du Congo, in *Les rivages tropicaux—Mangrove d'Afrique et d'Asie,* CEGET, Talence, pp. 1–21.

Rémy, J. M., 1954, Contribution à l'étude de la terrasse marine de la Pointe Kudevele (Congo), *Rev. Zool. Bota. Afr.* **48**(1,2):24–26.

Plate 87-1. North of the Songololo River mouth. This coast is exposed to southwesterly ocean swell and storm waves and is eroding. Sand is moved to Pointe Indienne, where the beaches are growing. The photograph shows savanna vegetation invaded by the sand; to the left the paleosol savanna outcrops (photo by G. Kouyoumontzakis).

Plate 87-2. Pointe Indienne. Outcrop of calcareous sandstone (Turonian). The coast is fronted by shore platforms with erosion channels (photo by P. Giresse).

Plate 87-3. Karstic erosion at Diosso cirques, an example of dissection in Plio-Pleistocene Série des Cirques formation. This piedmont formation is made of silty clays, gravels, and lateritic layers, and covers all Cretaceous and Tertiary beds of the coastal basin (photo by P. Giresse).

Plate 87-4. Another erosion cirque (doline) at the head of a little stream (near Pointe Kounda); in the background the beach, with parallel sandy ridges (eolian formation) (photo by G. Kouyoumontzakis).

Plate 87-5. Kouilou River mouth. Longshore drifting is to the northwest; it builds various barriers of sand south and north of the mouth. The organic clays of the Kouilou are deposited between these barriers, and the discharge cannot move offshore. Mangrove vegetation (*Rhizophora racemosa, Rhizophora mangle, Avicennia sp*) colonizes the new emerged slikke (photo by G. Kouyoumontzakis).

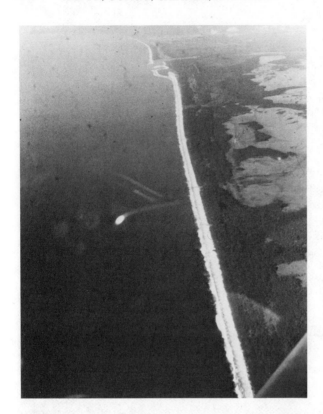

Plate 87-6. South of the Kouilou River mouth, the sandy coast along the eolian ridge covered by arbustive vegetation (*Manilkara lacera* and *Chrysobalanus ellipticus*). In the depressions there is swampy vegetation (*Symphonia globulifera*) or savanna graminaceae (*Schizachyrium thollomii* and *Rhynchelytrum roseum*) (photo by G. Kouyoumontzakis).

Plate 87-7. Artificial cross-section through one eolian ridge (near Djéno). This ridge was built up during the last regression period and raised some 10 m above the actual sea level. At the top is the white A horizon of a typical podsol, above the humiferous B horizon. The white sand was reworked during the end of the Holocene (Plate 87-4) (photo by G. Kouyoumontzakis).

Plate 87-8. Côte Mateve. Eolian white layer (1) directly above sandy gravels (2) of the Série des Cirques. In other *points*, one can see this white sand above Cretaceous limestone or above clayed peat (photo by P. Giresse).

Plate 87-9. Pointe Indienne. Peaty paleosol, dated about 2000 B.P., outcrops on the high beach; this period is connected with a negative pulsation of the Holocene sea level (photo by P. Giresse).

Plate 87-10. Pointe Indienne. *Kjökkenmoddinger* (cooking scraps) of the colonial period, particularly *Arca senilis* and *Tympanotonus fuscatus* (1), which are quite quickly dissolved (photo by G. Kouyoumontzakis).

Plate 87-11. Songololo River mouth. With a weak stream, this channel is a very mobile one, driven by a strong swell. The gap is forced through the fossil eolian barrier (Plate 87-7). The photograph clearly shows eolian cross-stratification (photo by G. Kouyoumontzakis).

Plate 87-12. Conkouati lagoon. Discharge from the river Niambi through the lagoonal delta. The most significant alluvial supply is trapped in lakes and lagoons of the backlands and does not reach the ocean (photo by G. Kouyoumontzakis).

88. ANGOLA

As in the other parts of the southern half of Africa, the Precambrian shield that frames Angola has been warped by a marginal flexure resulting in the Great Escarpment (Jessen 1936; Feio 1964). This event occurred during the opening and the subsequent widening of the South Atlantic and Indian oceans, in the Cretaceous and the Cenozoic. The marine Cretaceous strata have been progressively emerged and warped at the outer edge of the Great Escarpment. Tertiary beds, partly marine, also outcrop nearer the coast. Coastal Angola is thus made of a rand of Mesozoic and Cenozoic sediments, particularly Pliocene red clays and sands near Luanda, and Neogene marls and limestones in the surroundings of Benguela and Moçâmedes. Pliocene and Pleistocene abrasion surfaces, now standing in the coastal area up to 200 m, probably by uplift, have truncated these sediments.

CLIMATIC AND OCEANOGRAPHIC CONDITIONS

Except for the far north near the mouth of the Congo River, or Zaire, the climate of coastal Angola is semiarid or arid (Guilcher et al. 1974). Even at Luanda the annual rainfall amounts to only 337 mm; it decreases to 200 mm at Lobito, 50 mm at Moçâmedes, 20 mm at Porto Alexandre, and 15 mm at Baia dos Tigres and Foz do Cunene. The southerly trade winds, which blow approximately parallel to the coast, create an upwelling that brings cold water to the surface. This cold water, traveling to the north as the Benguela coastal current, stabilizes the air just above it, creates fog (the *cacimbo*), but prevents any rainfall. The process is exactly the same as off Peru and northern Chile, and off southern and Baja California. Inland, the rainfall increases quickly because the influence of the upwelling stops.

The longshore drift is everywhere directed to the north—not because of the trade winds, but under the influence of the powerful southwesterly swell, originated in the big storms of the Southern Ocean and breaking obliquely (the so-called *kalema*) on the shore, as it does also in Namibia and in the Gulf of Guinea (Guilcher 1954).

ROCKY COASTS

The larger part of the coast of Angola is rocky and cut in Cretaceous, Tertiary, and Pleistocene strata. The coastal pattern varies. Around the Bay of Moçâmedes (Soares 1961), the rocks are capped by two sets of Pleistocene beaches, one at 40–50 m, another at 4–5 m. These beaches are hardened by a calcrete (calcareous crust) in the same way as in Mediterranean countries, thus incorporated in the country rock, and cut by low, jagged cliffs. At Serra do Sombreiro, near Benguela, the calcareous marls are cut by cliffs 30–50 m high, in which marine corrosion has carved *taffone*, notches, visors, and pinnacles; pocket beaches occur between headlands. Between Lobito and the Longa River, cliffs some tenths of meters high occur on long distances on either side of Three Points Cape. South of Luanda and behind the Palmeirinhas spit, the Pliocene red clays and sands are cut by a dead cliff finely dissected by dynamic gullies, and now separated from the sea by successive sand ridges and dunes. More studies are required, but it seems certain that the Angola coast displays one of the widest varieties of cliffs in sedimentary rocks found in the dry tropics.

SAND SPITS AND DUNES

Although they cover a shorter length of coastline than the cliffs, the spits deserve more attention because they are better known and relevant to the general evolution; all the spits are shaped by the southwesterly swell (Guilcher et al. 1974).

Before it was severed from the mainland in March 1962, the spit (Fig. 88-1) enclosing *Baia dos Tigres* (Tiger Bay; Great Fish Bay on British charts) was the longest structure of this kind (37 km) on the whole coast of Africa. It reaches 60 m in thickness at its distal end, where it forms a huge pile on the continental shelf. Because of the hyperarid climate it is completely devoid of vege-

tation, as are the high sand dunes that stand on the continental side of Tiger Bay. The gap that truncated the spit in 1962 will apparently not be filled again, since it has been deepened by the tidal current, and an incipient small spit is growing to the north, while Tiger Spit, or Island, now evolves without a supply of fresh sand. On both sides of Tiger Bay, much smaller spits are found. They result from the work of waves generated in the bay by the dominant local south-southwest wind, a combination of the trade winds and the sea breeze, which acts in the same direction as the southwesterly swell does on the outer coast, and is also responsible for the shape and orientation of the high sand dunes on the eastern side. Thus the two forces act in parallel, but in different places, to create this majestic coastal desertic feature. Some 30 km to the north, the dunes take the shape of giant waves divided into barchans (Plate 88-1).

The Palmeirinhas Spit (34 km, Fig. 88-2) is almost as long as Tiger Spit; it should be examined in association with the Luanda Spit. Palmeirinhas Spit has grown normally by formation of successive ridges. It is still fully active. Luanda Spit, which shelters the major seaport of Angola, is, on the contrary, in a stage of decay; it tends to be cut

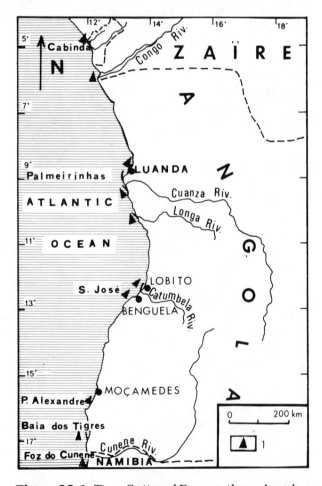

Figure 88-1. Tiger Spit and Bay, southern Angola, in 1970. Dots: dune ridges, with heights in meters in the sea. Dashed line in the south: inner end of the spit tied to the mainland before the 1962 cut.

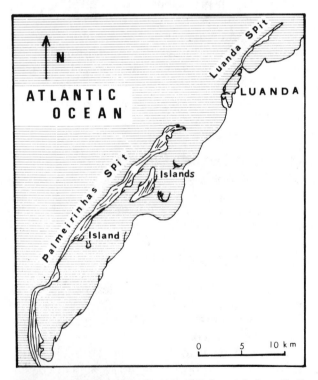

Figure 88-2. Luanda Spit and Palmeirinhas Spit, Angola.

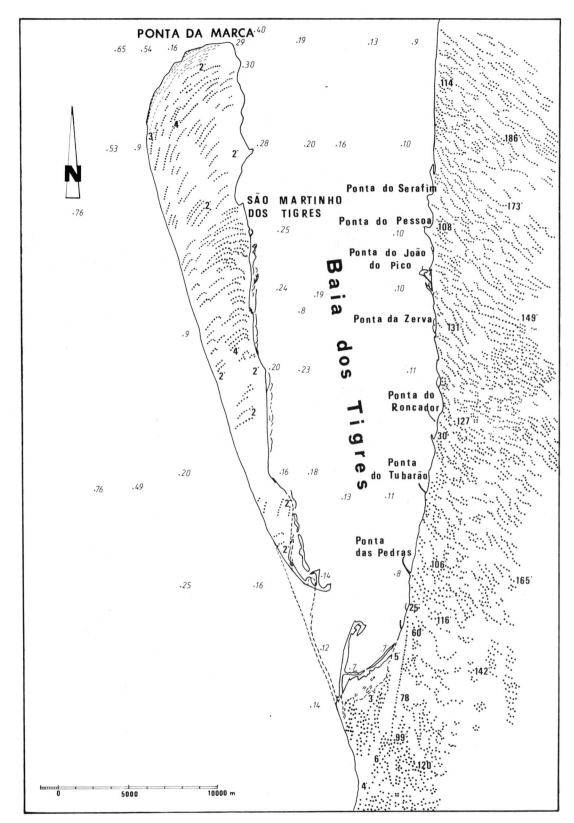

Figure 88-3. Angola coast, general map: 1. spits, location and direction of growth.

from the continent and is no longer fed by sand drift from its inner end, while the sand continues to move to the distal end, as shown by the groin pattern (Plate 88-2). The explanation seems to be that Luanda Spit was built when Palmeirinhas Spit was still much shorter than now. The inner end of Luanda Spit was then São João de Cazango Island, the main island that now lies in Palmeirinhas lagoon, which bears a set of successive ridges impossible to explain in their present lagoonal situation. When Palmeirinhas Spit grew, it came to shelter the previous spit and thus prevented any further substantial supply of sand by the *kalema*, hence a process of disintegration at the base of Luanda Spit. On the other hand, Palmeirinhas lagoon very much resembles Tiger lagoon in that it bears, on its shores and small islands, very short, active spits created by the small waves generated by the local wind. Thus, both Palmeirinhas and Tiger structures bear testimony to a pair of distinct parallel forces.

Another result of the southwesterly *kalema* is the building of Lobito Spit (Fig. 88-3), 8 km long, which shelters the second harbor in Angola. It has received its sediments from the delta of the Catumbela. But this supply is no longer available, since a dam has been built across the Catumbela River. As in many other countries, the equilibrium of the coast is threatened when a river that has built a delta is now harnessed for electric power.

At the mouth of the Cunene River (*Foz do Cunene*), which forms the border between Angola and Namibia, the river is deflected to the north by the *kalema*; parallel former courses of the river can be seen behind the coastline. The Cunene mouth resembles the Senegal mouth in the Northern Hemisphere: both are perennial rivers fed by tropical rains and ending on arid coasts; both have their mouths deflected by the oceanic swell, but in opposite directions, since the counterpart of the *kalema* in Senegal consists of northwesterly swells generated in the North Atlantic.

Other smaller spits in Angola have their distal ends deflected by the *kalema*. From south to north (Fig. 88-3), they are Ponta do Enfião and Ponta Brava near Porto Alexandre (the second one, 5,500 m long, shelters a fishing base); the Rio Longa spit, which deflects the mouth of the river; the Rio Cuanza spit, 3 km long, perhaps temporarily cut by river floods or strong *kalema*; the Congo River spit, very short, probably because the major part of the sand flows into the very deep Congo submarine canyon; and finally the sand bar at the mouth of Rio Lubinda, in the Cabinda *Angolese enclave (see Gabon, Congo, Cabinda and Zaire)*.

The same coastal pattern can be identified all along the southwestern side of Africa, from Cap Lopez in Gabon to Walvis Bay, Swakopmund and other structures in Namibia. Angola is the core of the system.

ANDRÉ GUILCHER

REFERENCES

Feio, M., 1964, A evolução da escadaria de aplanações do sudoeste de Angola, *Garcia de Orta* **12**(2):323–354.

Guilcher, A., 1954, Dynamique et morphologie des côtes sableuses de l'Afrique atlantique, *Cahiers Inf. Géog.* **1**:57–68.

Guilcher, A., C. A. Medeiros, J. E. Matos, and J. T. Oliveira, 1974, Les restingas (flèches littorales) d'Angola, *Finisterra* **9**:171–211.

Jessen, O., 1936, *Reisen und Forschungen in Angola*, Reimer, Andrews and Steiner, Berlin.

Soares de Carvalho, G., 1961, *Geologia do deserto de Moçâmedes*, Junta Investig. Ultramar, Mem. 26.

Plate 88-1. Giant sand waves divided into barchans, 20 km north of Tiger Bay. Foredune and shoreline in foreground (photo by A. Guilcher).

Plate 88-2. Luanda Spit in 1973. Groins show coastal drift directed to north (photo by A. Guilcher).

89. SOUTHWEST AFRICA/ NAMIBIA

The Southwest Africa/Namibia coastline is about 1,400 km long (Fig. 89-1), extending from the Kunene River in the north (17° 16′S) to the Orange River in the south (28° 33′S). Except for a broad (~ 150°) embayment at Walvis Bay, the coastline is roughly linear with a north-northwesterly trend. Two natural harbors capable of handling medium-tonnage vessels exist, one at Walvis Bay and the other at Lüderitz. The former is protected by a large sand spit (Fig. 89-2), and the latter is situated in a northwest-facing rocky inlet.

From the Kunene River to Walvis Bay, the "Skeleton Coast" is backed by salt pans, deflation surfaces, and migrating sand dunes, and the shore consists of sand or gravel interspersed with occasional rocky headlands. In places the coast may be as much as 2 km seaward of the charted position because of shoreline progradation.

Between Walvis Bay and Lüderitz the coast is backed by the Namib Sand Sea which extends inland for about 100 km to the Great Escarpment. The coast varies from low-lying, sparsely vegetated sand flats to dunes 150 m high.

South of Lüderitz to Chamais Bay, the coast is broken by numerous small rocky headlands and intervening sandy bays. Beyond this, it straightens out and becomes sandy with low-lying dunes. Alluvial diamonds are exploited from the backshore between Chamais Bay and the Orange River.

The Southwest Africa/Namibia coast consists predominantly of late Precambrian metasedi-

ments (greenschist to amphibolite facies) of the Damara geosynclinal sequence (650–900 Ma) and associated granitic intrusives. Palaeozoic rocks are restricted to Dwyka glacial beds that infill a basement valley near Cape Fria, and Mesozoic basic lavas occur sporadically over long distances between Cape Fria and the vicinity of Palgrave Point. Mesozoic marine sediments are represented by a single outcrop of sandy limestone near Bogenfels, and several remnants of Tertiary marine sediment occur in the area as well. Large stretches of the coast are blanketed by unconsolidated Quaternary sand, particularly adjacent to the Namib Sand Sea (Martin 1973).

Sediment composing the beaches is predominantly medium- to fine-grained sand consisting of quartz, feldspar, heavy minerals, and minor calcium carbonate. Where a rocky foreshore exists the proportion of heavy minerals (e.g., garnet or ilmenite) increases substantially (up to 80%).

Strong longshore drift is evidenced by numerous spits along the coast and a decreasing occurrence of diamonds northward from the Orange River mouth. Driving this current are two sets of swell that impinge along the coast at a large angle: one originating in the "roaring forties" with a 6–9 s period, and the other, with a period of 4–7 s, developing locally in response to southerly trade winds (Emery et al. 1973). The latter are strongest in the vicinity of Lüderitz, and so too is the intensity of ocean upwelling. Tides are semidiurnal with a maximum range of 1.4 m at Walvis Bay, but since cotidal lines closely parallel the coast, tidal currents are not considered important in terms of sediment transport.

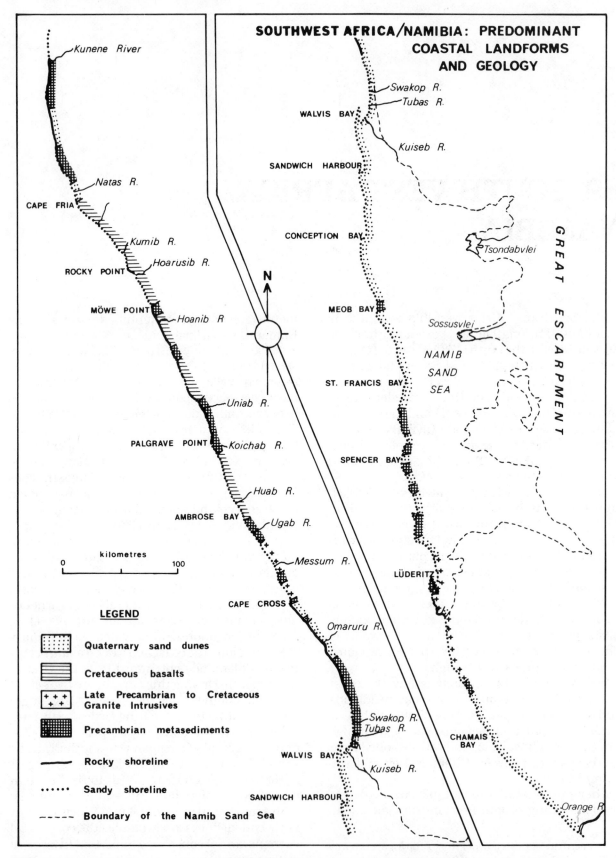

SOUTHWEST AFRICA/NAMIBIA: PREDOMINANT COASTAL LANDFORMS AND GEOLOGY

Kunene River

Swakop R.
Tubas R.
WALVIS BAY
Kuiseb R.

Natas R.
SANDWICH HARBOUR
CAPE FRIA

CONCEPTION BAY

Kumib R.
Hoarusib R.
ROCKY POINT

Tsondabvlei

N

MÖWE POINT
Hoanib R.

MEOB BAY

Sossusvlei

GREAT ESCARPMENT

NAMIB SAND SEA

Uniab R.

ST. FRANCIS BAY

PALGRAVE POINT
Koichab R.

SPENCER BAY

Huab R.

AMBROSE BAY
Ugab R.

kilometres
0   100

Messum R.

LÜDERITZ

CAPE CROSS

LEGEND

Omaruru R.

Quaternary sand dunes

Cretaceous basalts

Late Precambrian to Cretaceous
Granite Intrusives

Precambrian metasediments

Swakop R.
Tubas R.

CHAMAIS BAY

Rocky shoreline

WALVIS BAY

Sandy shoreline

Kuiseb R.

SANDWICH HARBOUR

Boundary of the Namib Sand Sea

Orange R.

Figure 89-1. Predominant coastal landforms and geology of Southwest Africa/Namibia.

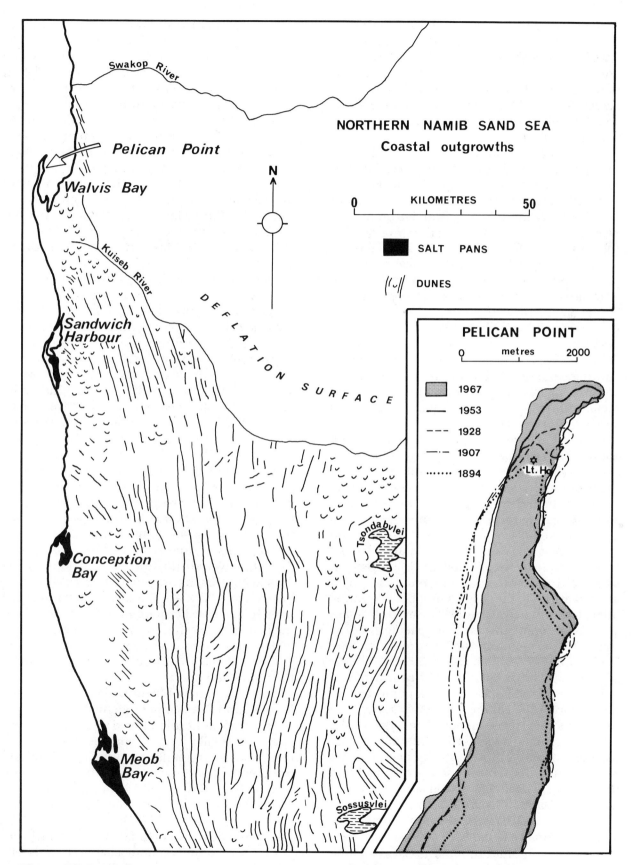

Figure 89-2. Northern Namib Sand Sea coastal outgrowths.

The Kunene River is broad and shallow at the coast, with a sand bar across the mouth in the dry season. Southward from the Kunene River to Cape Fria, the nearshore is strewn with imperfectly charted shoals and rocky reefs of Damara metasediments. The shore itself is mainly sandy and the backshore low-lying, with large, elongate, coast-parallel salt pans.

From Cape Fria to Möwe Point the shore is sandy, with no fringing rocky reefs except at Cape Fria itself, and at Rocky Point. At Cape Fria low-lying hills of Cretaceous basaltic lava crop out behind the beach, and Rocky Point is a prominent headland of the same material that projects into the sea for some 600 m. Behind the headland, the terrain is flat and sandy, with a few small salt pans. From Möwe Point, which is a low-lying foreland composed of Damara metasediments, to Walvis Bay, a heavy unbroken surf prevails along the entire coastline (Tripp 1975).

The next section, from Möwe Point to Palgrave Point, is also low-lying, with a few salt pans, small shifting sand dunes, and scrub vegetation. The shore is rocky, however, consisting of Damara metasediments overlain by, and often faulted against, Cretaceous basalts.

The stretch from Palgrove Point to Cape Cross has low sand cliffs separated by long stretches of open sandy beaches. Numerous salt pans lie on the backshore, particularly at the southern end. In the north, the bedrock geology continues to be alternating Damara metasediments and massive accumulations of Cretaceous basalt. The foliation trend of the metasediments is subparallel to the coast between the Kunene and the Ugab rivers but southward to Meob Bay it swings round and strikes at right angles to the coast. A number of granitic intrusives situated along the core of the Damara geosyncline crop out along the coast (e.g., at the Messum River mouth and at Cape Cross). The foreland at Cape Cross projects some 5 km into the sea and has low rocky cliffs and a nearby reef.

The coast from Cape Cross to a point roughly 50 km north of Walvis Bay is generally rocky, with numerous shoals close inshore. The rocks consist mostly of Damara metasediments alternating with occasional granitic plugs. The lower reaches of the Omaruru River traverse an extensive cover of Quaternary sand that extends northeastward along the Damara foliation trend (McG.-Miller and Schalk 1980). The entire section is low-lying, with a few small salt pans.

The sand spit protecting Walvis Bay is about 8 km long and has advanced northward by about 1,800 m in the last 80 years; it has a maximum elevation of about 13 m, and terminates at Pelican Point (Fig. 89-2). Large "mud islands" occasionally appear in the bay off Pelican Point because of a sediment density-inversion (i.e., an accumulation of terrigenous sand sinks into and displaces low-density diatomaceous mud). Sulfuretted hydrogen is released by the mud, causing periodic mass mortality of fish in the region (Copenhagen 1953).

The Namib Sand Sea backs a desolate, forbidding coast between Walvis Bay and Lüderitz, a distance of about 400 km. The northern half of this section boasts four coastal outgrowths—at Walvis Bay, Sandwich Harbor (Plate 89-1), Conception Bay, and Meob Bay (Fig. 89-2)—all of which were once probably river estuaries (Bremner 1973). Several independent lines of evidence suggest that the Swakop River once entered the sea at Walvis Bay, the Kuiseb River at Sandwich Harbor, and the two vleis, Tsondab and Sossus, breached the intervening dune barrier to reach the sea at Conception and Meob bays respectively. Highly mobile, light brown sand dunes along the coast, which contrast markedly with the semistable reddish dunes of the interior, originate from detritus offloaded at the Orange River mouth (Rogers 1977). In its passage northward by littoral drift and strong southerly winds, the sand has progressively blocked the four river estuaries now represented by coastal outgrowths. The progression is well illustrated by the decrease in salt pans and the increase in water areas from south to north. The coast varies between low-lying sandy bluffs at the coastal outgrowths to high intervening walls of sand adjacent to the shore (e.g., the Lange Wand) (Plate 89-2). Portions of the coastal outgrowths are prograding, as witnessed by the wreck "Eduard Bohlen," which grounded in 1910 and now lies roughly 400 m inland from the beach. Between Conception and Meob bays, metasediments of the Damara Sequence and granitic intrusives crop out sporadically between the dunes and on the shore.

From St. Francis Bay to Lüderitz, the coastal Namib Sand Sea is more indented, with numerous small rocky headlands and intervening sandy bays. Five small islands occur close inshore, and rocky shoals commonly surround them. North of Spencer Bay, the rocks are Damara metasediments with a coast-parallel foliation trend, whereas southward, they are basement gneisses of pre-Damara age (about 1,200 Ma).

Lüderitz lies in a north-facing rocky inlet containing several small guano-plastered islands. The rock types are predominantly basement gneisses and schists of pre-Damara age. The town experienced prosperity with the discovery of diamonds in 1908.

Elizabeth Bay, lying 30 km south of Lüderitz, is flanked on either side by a rocky coast with submerged reefs of pre-Damara acid/basic intrusives. Southward to Chamais Bay, the coast continues to be indented with small rocky headlands and sandy bays, and the nearshore is dotted with seven additional small islands. At Bogenfels, located midway between Lüderitz and Chamais Bay, dolomites of the Gariep Complex (equivalent in age to the Damara Sequence) have been eroded to spectacular cliffs and arches (Plate 89-3). The only marine Cretaceous sediments to be found along the west coast of southern Africa occur in the "Sperrgebiet," at an altitude of 60–70 m (Haughton 1963). In the same area, a few small exposures of Eocene marine sediments lie between 70 m and 140 m above sea level (Siesser and Salmon 1979).

From Chamais Bay to the mouth of the Orange River, the coastline is linear and the backshore covered with low sandy hills. The region is intensively minded for alluvial diamonds, and a sizable town, Oranjemund, located 6 km north of the river, has been established to support the industry. The Orange River is about 1.5 km wide at its mouth (Plate 89-4), but during the dry season it becomes completely blocked by a sand bar. Raised beaches at an elevation of 25 m near the Orange River have yielded warm-water Pleistocene molluscs (Carrington and Kensley 1969).

J. M. BREMNER

REFERENCES

Bremner, J. M., 1973, Report on a desert journey from Walvis Bay to Black Rocks, S.W.A., 6th Jan.–12th Jan., 1973, *Internal Marine Geoscience Unit Report,* 6 p.

Copenhagen, W. J., 1953, The periodic mortality of fish in the Walvis region. A phenomenon within the Benguela Current, *Investigational Report of the South African Division of Sea Fisheries,* 14p.

Carrington, A. J., and B. F. Kensley, 1969, Pleistocene molluscs from the Namaqualand coast, *South African Mus. Annals* **52:**189–223.

Emery, K. O., J. D. Milliman, and E. Uchupi, 1973, Physical properties and suspended matter of surface waters in the southeastern Atlantic Ocean, *Jour. Sed. Petrology* **43:**822–827.

Haughton, S. H., 1963, *Stratigraphic History of Africa South of the Sahara,* Oliver & Boyd Ltd., London.

Martin, H., 1973, The Atlantic margin of southern Africa between latitude 17° south and the Cape of Good Hope, in *The Ocean Basins and Margins,* vol. 1, A. E. M. Nairn and F. G. Stehli, eds., Plenum, New York, pp. 277–300.

McG-Miller, R., and K. E. L. Schalk, 1980, *Geological Map of South West Africa,* Geological Survey of South Africa, Pretoria.

Rogers, J., 1977, *Sediments on the Continental Margin off the Orange River and the Namib Desert,* Ph.D. dissertation, University of Cape Town.

Siesser, W. G., and D. Salmon, 1979, Eocene marine sediments in the Sperrgebiet, South West Africa, *South African Mus. Annals* **79:**9–34.

Tripp, R. T., 1975, *South African Sailing Directions,* South African Navy Directorate of Hydrography, Youngfield, South Africa.

Plate 89-1. Low tide at Sandwich Harbor, located some 35 km south of Walvis Bay. Around the turn of the century this was a good anchorage for vessels, especially cattle freighters, but it is now silting up rapidly. A sand bar sometimes closes the inlet, and at its southern end is a large salt pan. The area is now a proclaimed bird sanctuary and abounds with fish (photo by J. M. Bremner).

Plate 89-2. The southern end "Die Lange Wand" (long wall) between Sandwich Harbor and Conception Bay. A sand escarpment 150 m high abuts directly against the shore and is undermined at high tide by wave action. The dunes are highly mobile, with large flakes of mica tending to accumulate in their lee (photo by J. M. Bremner).

Plate 89-3. The Bogenfels Arch, 51 m high, cut through a recumbent syncline of dolomite belonging to the late Precambrian Gariep Complex (photo by J. Rogers).

Plate 89-4. The mouth of the Orange River in flood (March 1974). A plume of muddy water extending out to sea is clearly evident. The mud forms an acoustical blanketing layer on the inner shelf both north and south of the river mouth, whereas sandy material is transported northward in the surf zone by strong littoral drift. Much of the light brown sand of the coastal Namib Desert is derived from Orange River detritus (photo by J. Rogers).

90. SOUTH AFRICA

The South African coastline, between the Orange River in the west and Ponta do Ouro in the east, covers a distance of about 3,000 km (Fig. 90-1A). This includes the coasts of the two independent states, Transkei, between latitudes 31° 04' S and 32° 40' S (250 km), and Ciskei, between 32° 40' S and 33° 30' S (150 km). To the west of Cape Agulhas the coastline borders on the South Atlantic, and to the east on the Indian Ocean. The east coast waters (Fig. 90-1A and B) are characterized by the warm waters of the southward-flowing Agulhas Current, those of the west coast by sporadic upwelling of cold, nutrient-rich waters typical of the Benguela Current regime. Along the southwest and south coasts extensive mixing of water masses occurs.

These oceanographic conditions determine the coastal climate of southern Africa, with summer rainfall along the east coast, bimodal rainfall along the south coast, winter rainfall along the southwest coast, and semiarid conditions along the west coast (Fig. 90-1A). The variability of these environmental conditions is reflected in the composition of animal and plant communities both on land and in the sea. For example, a wide variety of Indian Ocean corals harboring a diverse Indo-Pacific fish fauna, occur in the subtropical waters of the northern east coast, whereas dense kelp beds provide a habitat for commercially important rock lobster and abalone stocks in the cool upwelling regime of the west and southwest coast. In general the east coast waters are characterized by great biotic diversity, while the main focus of commercial fisheries is centered in the more productive waters of the southwest and south coasts, where fewer species occur in greater profusion.

The wave climate of the South African coast is profoundly influenced by seasonal shifts (southward in summer and northward in winter) of the gale zone of the Antarctic Circumpolar Current region (Fig. 90-1B), and by local winds generated by the regular passage of atmospheric lows over the coast from west to east. The southwest coast appears to be subjected to the greatest amount of wave energy, which decreases somewhat northward along the west coast and eastward along the south coast. These wave patterns strongly influence coastal processes such as longshore sediment transport and hence coastal features such as the orientation of headland bays, sand spits, and the configuration of river mouths.

The landforms of the South African coast can be broadly subdivided into six physiographic regions: Orange River to Olifants River; Olifants River to Berg River; Berg River to Cape Agulhas; Cape Agulhas to Cape Padrone; Cape Padrone to Mtunzini; and Mtunzini to Ponta do Ouro.

ORANGE RIVER TO OLIFANTS RIVER (407 KM)

The shore of this region (Fig. 90-1) is mainly rocky, consisting of Precambrian metasediments. As a result of the semiarid climate, the coastal vegetation is sparse but highly adapted to dry conditions (Plate 90-1). Acocks (1975) classifies it as Strandveld Proper, consisting predominantly of open, semisucculent scrub. Between the Orange and Olifants rivers, nine smaller rivers enter the sea. In the present climate they flow only rarely, but episodic floods are possible. River water tends to be highly mineralized. Some of the rivers have

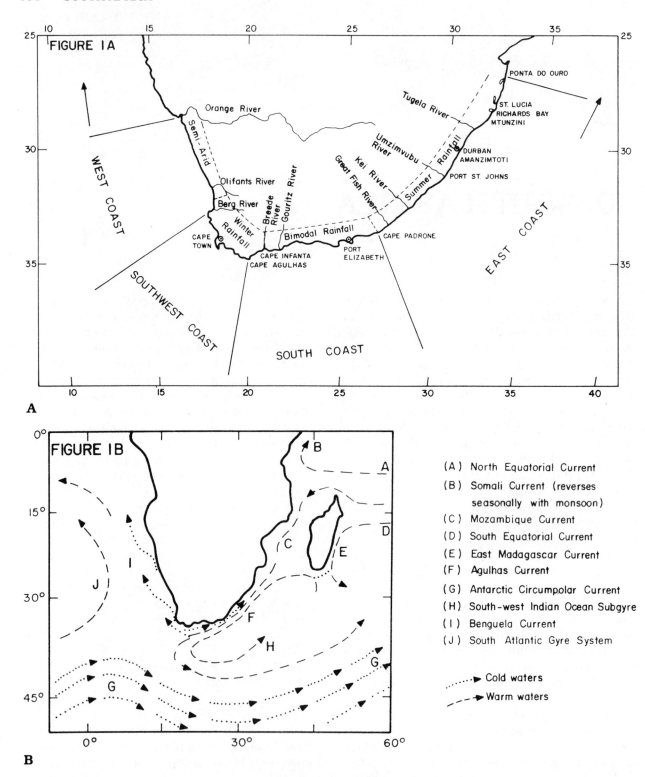

Figure 90-1. Coastline of South Africa. *A.* Sectors of the coastline according to climatic and geomorphological criteria; *B.* Major ocean currents around the South African coastline (after Heydorn et al. 1978).

ephemeral shallow, saline lagoons, separated from the sea by sand bars (except when in flood) and have dune fields fanning out toward the north from their mouths (Plate 90-2).

The shoreline of the west coast is exposed to the continuous pounding of heavy southwesterly swells, which produce a strong northward-directed littoral drift. A typical response is that the bedload of the Orange River (the largest river in South Africa, forming the boundary with Namibia) is fed mainly to the beach systems north of the mouth. To the south the shoreline is lined by rocky and irregular cliffs, which are subject to substantial wave erosion. Some of these cliffs plunge directly into the sea, whereas others have narrow sand or gravel beaches along their bases. These sediments are known for their high heavy-mineral content, especially garnet and ilmenite. The entire coastline between the Orange and Olifants rivers is economically important as a source of alluvial diamonds. Substantial quantities of gem-quality stones are being recovered from old onshore beach deposits, as well as from the present surf zone and shallow offshore. (Submarine recovery of diamonds in the shallow littoral leads to clashing interests with the rock lobster industry of the region). The diamonds are thought to have been supplied to the coast by the headward retreat of local rivers, trapping alluvial deposits concentrated on inland erosion surfaces (Hallam 1964). Considering the semiarid nature of the hinterland, this supply mechanism is unlikely to be active today. However, the wide and deeply incised valleys of the presently ephemeral streams would suggest considerably greater activity in the past.

OLIFANTS RIVER TO BERG RIVER (137 KM)

To the south of the Olifants River, the coastline (Fig. 90-1) gradually changes from steep rocky shores to increasingly wider-spaced rocky headlands separated by sweeping sand beaches (Plate 90-3). At the same time the metamorphic bedrock is progressively replaced by quartzitic sandstones belonging to the Table Mountain Group. The change in bedrock lithology is also recorded in the composition of local beaches, which consist predominantly of shelly quartz sand devoid of heavy minerals. The hinterland is still semiarid, although the influence of winter rains becomes evident toward the south. Most beaches are lined

by low, partially vegetated dunes. According to the Acocks (1975) classification, the coastal "fynbos" or "macchia" makes its appearance near the Berg River under the influence of the winter rains. Gypsum deposits found locally in depressions landward of the dunes indicate former sea-level stands, probably of late Pleistocene age, several meters above the present. Many of the beaches act as source areas for large plumes of eolian sands (see dune fans above), migrating northward in response to strong southerly winds blowing mainly in summer. Many of these dune fields overlie older, carbonate-cemented eolianites formed under similar climatic conditions during the late Quaternary (Tankard and Rogers 1978). The Pleistocene history of this area is discussed in greater detail by Tankard (1976).

BERG RIVER TO CAPE AGULHAS (635 KM)

A dramatic change in coastal morphology (again associated with bedrock lithology), takes place to the south of the Berg River (Fig. 90-1). The entire coastal stretch between the Berg River and the Cape Peninsula (south of Cape Town) is dominated by granite intrusives. The coast tends to be very irregular and its northern half is characterized by numerous pocket bays, headlands, and offshore pinnacles (Plate 90-4). The largest embayment, Saldanha Bay, forms a natural harbor and has the unique feature of a southern appendix known as Langebaan Lagoon (Fig. 90-2A). It is the product of selective marine erosion in the course of the Flandrian transgression and has little fresh-water inflow. There is positive evidence for a high Holocene sea level in and around the lagoon (Flemming 1977). A particularly striking geomorphological expression of this is the former Holocene shoreline, preserved as a continuous scarp cut into calcrete-capped late Pleistocene eolianites situated 1–2 km inland to the west and south of the lagoon (Fig. 90-2A). A summary of the Quaternary evolution of the area can be found in Flemming (1979).

The coastline between Saldanha Bay and Table Bay (Fig. 90-2A) is similar to that between the Olifants and Berg rivers. Again there are widely spaced rocky headlands, separated by long sandy beaches associated with eolian activity. The vegetation cover is somewhat denser because of the higher rainfall of the area, with more coastal fynbos elements making their appearance. Table

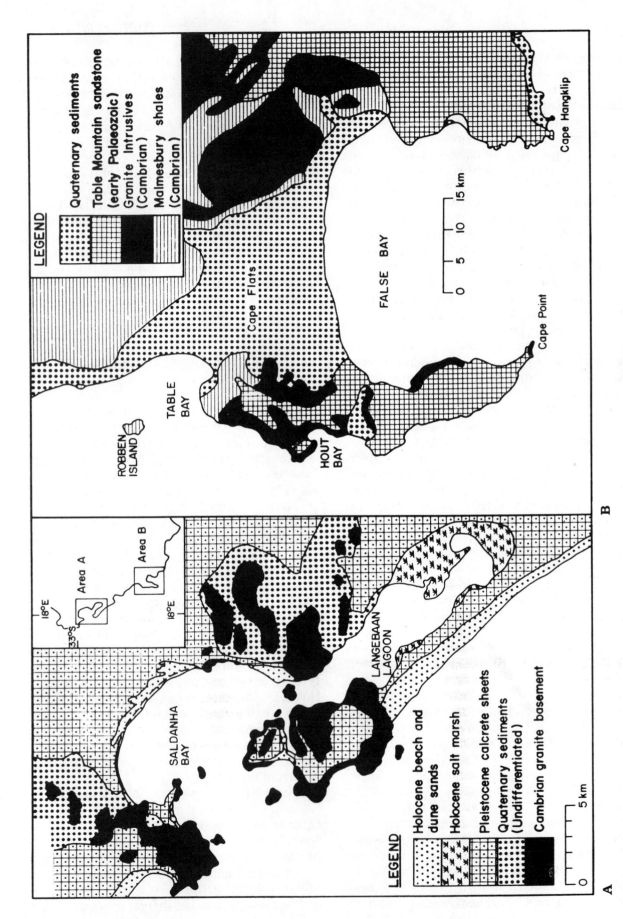

Figure 90-2. Major geological features. *A.* Saldanha Bay/Langebaan area; *B.* Table Bay/False Bay area.

LEGEND

Quaternary sediments

Table Mountain sandstone
(early Palaeozoic)

Granite Intrusives
(Cambrian)

Malmesbury shales
(Cambrian)

CAPE HANGKLIP

FALSE BAY

Cape Flats

TABLE BAY

ROBBEN ISLAND

HOUT BAY

Cape Point

0 5 10 15 km

B

LEGEND

Holocene beach and
dune sands

Holocene salt marsh

Pleistocene calcrete sheets

Quaternary sediments
(Undifferentiated)

Cambrian granite basement

Area A

Area B

18°E

33°S

18°E

SALDANHA BAY

LANGEBAAN LAGOON

0 5 km

A

Bay itself is formed by a pronounced offset in the coastline and marks the northern limit of the Cape Peninsula (Fig. 90-2*B*). The relief is dramatic, and vertical drops of several hundred meters are common (Plate 90-5). Set between granite outcrops and plunging sandstone cliffs are numerous pocket beaches producing a landscape of such scenic beauty that it prompted Sir Frances Drake to call it "the fairest Cape in all the world."

The Cape Peninsula is separated from the high coastal ranges of the hinterland by a low plain known as the Cape Flats. It consists of Tertiary and Quaternary coastal/marine sands, which feed the beaches along the northern shore of False Bay. At Cape Hangklip (Fig. 90-2*B*) the coastline swings to the southeast, initially being flanked by towering sandstone ridges. The irregular rocky shore is interrupted by long curvilinear sand beaches, which in many cases form the seaward margins of barred estuaries (Plate 90-6). The relief gradually diminishes toward Cape Agulhas, although the shore remains predominantly rocky, interspersed with short sandy beaches. The first components of east coast dune forest vegetation make their appearance in this region, mainly in the form of white milkwood (*Sideroxylon inerme*).

CAPE AGULHAS TO CAPE PADRONE (815 KM)

Cape Agulhas marks the southern tip of Africa (Fig. 90-1). To the east the coastal morphology changes markedly. This time the shore is controlled by tectonic factors, rather than lithological ones. The regional strike of the Cape Fold Belt is cut at an oblique angle by the general trend of the coastline. As a result, the alternating sequence of anticlines and synclines has produced a succession of halfheart or crenulated bays opening to the southeast (Plate 90-7). Each morphodynamic unit begins with an anticlinal headland, followed by a halfheart bay occupying the synclinal depression. The crenulated shape of each bay approaches the outline of a logarithmic spiral curve, suggesting that these sections of the coastline are in dynamic equilibrium with the prevailing southwesterly swell regime (Bremner 1979). The valleys extending inland from the bays act as natural drainage channels from inland catchments; usually one or more estuaries are associated with each embayment. Because of their scenic beauty and the availability of fresh water, these areas have become focal points for the development of holiday villages and, in some cases, of towns with associated industries.

The vegetation in this region is still dominated by coastal fynbos (i.e., a vegetation characterized by Ericaeae, Proteaceae and the wiry, tufted plants of the Restionaceae). In this region these plant communities occur typically on the acid soils overlying eolian calcarenites (Plate 90-8). This is a transitional area between the winter and bimodal rainfall regions (Heydorn and Tinley 1980). The intrusion of exotic vegetation, mainly Australian acacias, represents a land management problem of substantial proportions.

To the east of the Gouritz River the character of the coastline changes and becomes dominated by a raised coastal platform beveled at heights of 150-250 m. These elevated shorelines are probably late Cretaceous to early Tertiary in age. The drainage systems along these parts of the coastline are deeply incised as illustrated in Plate 90-9. Again these features have great aesthetic appeal. At Knysna, for example, the erosion of softer inlayers has led to the formation of a large estuary connected to the sea via a narrow rocky channel. The Wilderness Lake System, on the other hand, has developed between successive coastal dune ridges occupying gaps in bedrock ridges. Impressive coastal forests, classified by Acocks (1975) as Knysna Forest and dominated by towering yellowwood trees (*Podocarpus spp.*) give further character to this region, as does the blackwater of the rivers and streams draining the sandstone slopes of the Outeniqua Mountain Range.

The city of Port Elizabeth (Fig. 90-1*A*) is situated on the shoreline of Algoa Bay near the northeastern limit of the Cape Fold Belt. Algoa Bay, which is the last but largest of the south coast headland bay beaches, ends at Cape Padrone. The topography immediately to the west and east of Port Elizabeth is much flatter than that of most of the south coast. The quartzites and shales of the Table Mountain Group are replaced by conglomerates, sandstones, shales, and limestones of the Cretaceous System as well as by unconsolidated sediments of Tertiary/Quaternary origin. Large dune fields are typical of this region, with backshore zones of unvegetated sand ridges orthogonal to the coastline, moving to and fro in response to seasonally alternating westerly and easterly winds. The coastal vegetation is known as Alexandria Forest (Acocks 1975), of which euphorbias and aloes are striking components. The composition of the vegetation is strongly influenced by the fact that this is a transitional region between the bimodal and summer rainfall regimes. From here northeastward, conditions become progressively more subtropical.

CAPE PADRONE TO MTUNZINI (745 KM)

At Cape Padrone (Fig. 90-1), the coastline swings to the northeast, once again accompanied by a significant change in coastal morphology. As along the south coast, there is no coastal plain. Instead the coastline is dominated by more uniform, convex slopes. An exception is the area around Port St. Johns, where complex faulting has produced high cliffs and steep slopes. The rocky coastline is interrupted by short sandy beaches in the vicinity of river mouths. Coastal dunes are mostly of the vegetated hummock type, hugging the slopes of rocky headlands. In the southern sector of the east coast parabolic dunes and blowouts with sand streams running parallel to the coastline until they enter the sea around the next headland are common. Typical of this part of the coast are grasslands that almost reach the sea on the interfluves of rounded headlands and forested valleys in between. Most estuaries in this region have mangroves (Plate 90-10), which are absent on the south and west coasts.

At Amanzimtoti, some 25 km south of the city of Durban, the sporadically occurring coastal dunes merge into a quasi-continuous ridge, which extends northward beyond the Moçambique border. This ridge is not entirely a modern feature, but contains a core of Pleistocene dune sands associated with a different sea level. Its present position on parts of the modern coastline is purely coincidental, as it is preserved along other parts of the coast as a submerged ridge on the adjacent continental shelf (Flemming 1981). Initially the coastal dunes form a single well-defined ridge (Plate 90-11). However, at Mtunzini the convex sloping basement and the coastal dune ridge diverge to form a rapidly widening coastal plain.

MTUNZINI TO PONTA DO OURO (267 KM)

This region (Fig. 90-1) is characterized by the Zululand Coastal Plain, the only true coastal plain found along the entire South African coastline. Hobday (1979) has discussed its geological evo-

lution. Seaward-dipping Cretaceous and Lower Tertiary strata are unconformably overlain by Upper Tertiary to recent sediments. The Quaternary history of the area is particularly complex, and field evidence suggests that there have been several superimposed and reactivated barrier lagoon systems in the wake of successive Pleistocene and Holocene sea-level fluctuations (Hobday and Orme 1974). At present the region is characterized by a number of large estuarine and coastal lake systems, which, according to Orme (1973) and Hill (1975), appear to have developed from more extensive mid-Holocene estuaries by progressive siltation (Fig. 90-3A and 90-4A). It has not been conclusively shown that the retreat of modern estuaries and lakes is associated with a minor late-Holocene regression. However, the evidence quoted earlier from other parts of the subcontinent is strongly in favor of this latter interpretation. Further significant changes to the existing estuarine systems have occurred as a consequence of extensive recent siltation resulting from the intensive use of almost the entire coastal hinterland, including most riverine flood plains, for the production of sugar cane (Begg 1978 and Plate 90-12). Furthermore, the development of a large harbor at Richards Bay (Fig. 90-3B) and the artificial stabilization of the inlet of the St. Lucia lagoon (Fig. 90-4B) has had a profound influence on the character of these major lagoonal systems. In both cases intensive efforts are being made to maintain viable ecological regimes in spite of the modifications brought about by human activity. At Richards Bay, for example, the former bay has been divided by a berm. The northern section is now the harbor and the southern Mhlatuzi lagoon is a "sanctuary" that has been given a separate entrance. Heavy siltation has occurred, however, because the filtering swamps of the flood plain of the Mhlatuzi River were canalized to facilitate the construction of a railway line. It is fortunate that the Zululand Plain to the north of St. Lucia is far less affected by human activity; this part of the coast is a wild, subtropical region of great beauty. Properly managed, it has an enormous tourist potential and may be a substantial source of revenue for the indigenous Zulu people.

CONCLUSION

With the exception of the comments on the Richards Bay and St. Lucia systems, the foregoing

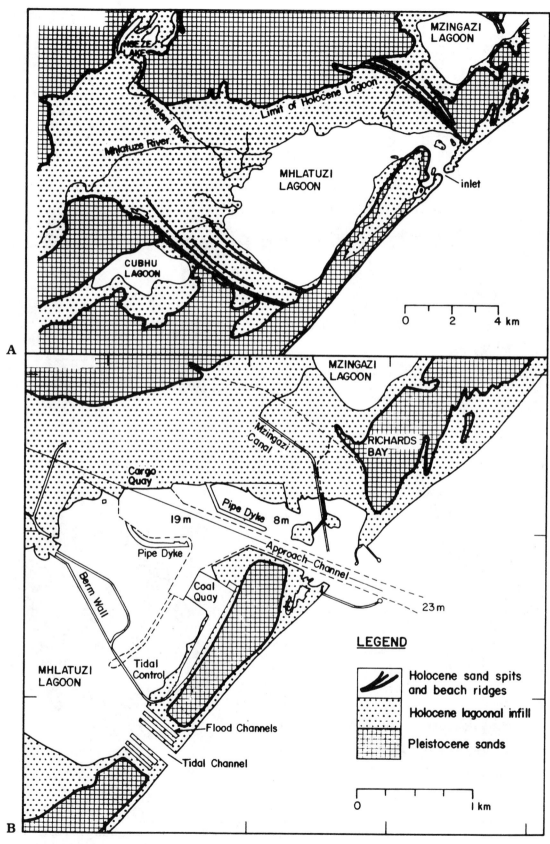

Figure 90-3. Richards Bay. *A.* Geological history of the Mhlatuz lagoon area; *B.* Richards Bay today.

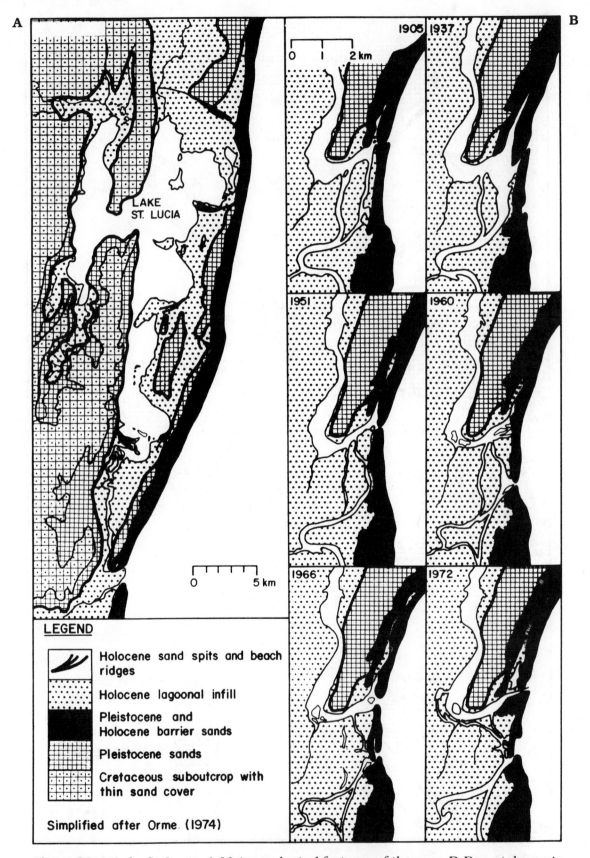

Figure 90-4. Lake St. Lucia. *A.* Major geological features of the area; *B.* Recent dynamic changes in the mouth region.

text has made almost no mention of human activity and its effect on South Africa's coastal environment. Space does not permit detailed comment, but it must be said that human modification (and in many cases degradation) of the coast is taking place at an alarming rate. The modifications relate mainly to disturbance of the equilibrium between unconsolidated sediments and the vegetation binding them, on the one hand, and changes in the hydrological regimes of rivers and estuaries and their interaction with the sea, on the other. As in other countries the ill effects of human activity include open-cast mining (mainly on the west coast); excessive use of water in catchments through artificial impoundments and otherwise; degradation of estuarine flood plains through low-lying agricultural, industrial, and residential developments, road and bridge embankments, and so on; various forms of pollution; and disturbance of dynamic coastal processes through dune fixing. To overcome such problems, governmental agencies are sponsoring a considerable amount of research aimed at the development of a cohesive management policy for the whole coastline. The approach advocated is described in greater detail by Begg (1978 and 1979) and Heydorn and Tinley (1980).

A. E. F. HEYDORN
B. W. FLEMMING

REFERENCES

Acocks, J. P. H., 1975, *Veld Types of South Africa*, Botanical Survey of South Africa Mem. 40, 128p.

Begg, G., 1978, *The Estuaries of Natal*, Natal Town and Regional Planning Commission (Pietermaritzburg) Report 41.

Begg, G., 1979, *Policy Proposals for the Estuaries of Natal*, Natal Town and Regional Planning Commission (Pietermaritzburg) Report 43.

Bremner, J. M., 1979, The planimetric shape of Algoa Bay, in Joint Geological Survey/University of Cape Town, Marine Geoscience Unit, *Technical Report*, no. 11, pp. 107–117.

Flemming, B. W., 1977, Langebaan Lagoon: a mixed carbonate-siliclastic tidal environment in a semi-arid climate, *Sed. Geology* **18:**61–95.

Flemming, B. W., 1979, The late Quaternary evolution of Langebaan Lagoon, *Geokongres 79* (18th Congress of the Geol. Soc. South Africa) Abstracts, Vol. I, pp. 138–141.

Flemming, B. W., 1981, Factors controlling shelf sediment dispersal along the southeast African continental margin, *Marine Geology* **42:**259–277.

Hallam, C. D., 1964, The geology of the coastal diamond deposits of Southern Africa (1959), in *The Geology of Some Ore Deposits in Southern Africa*, S. H. Haughton, ed., Vol. 2, pp. 671–728.

Heydorn, A. E. F., and K. L. Tinley, 1980, *Estuaries of the Cape, Part 1. Synopsis of the Cape Coast; Natural Features, Dynamics & Utilization*, Council for Scientific and Industrial Research, Report 380.

Heydorn, A. E. F., et al., 1978, Ecology of the Agulhas current region: An Assessment of biological responses to environmental parameters in the southwest Indian Ocean, *Royal Soc. South Africa Trans.* **43:**(2):151–190.

Hill, B. J., 1975, The origin of Southern African coastal lakes, *Royal Soc. South Africa Trans.*, **41:**225–240.

Hobday, D. K., 1979, Geological evolution and geomorphology of the Zululand coastal plain, in *Lake Sibaya*, B. R. Allansonn, ed., Monographiae Biologicae, vol. 36, pp. 1–20.

Hobday, D. K., and A. R. Orme, 1974, The Port Durnford Formation: a major Pleistocene barrier—lagoon complex along the Zululand coast, *Geol. Soc. South Africa Trans.* **77:**141–149.

Orme, A. R., 1973, Barrier and lagoon systems along the Zululand coast, South Africa, in *Coastal Geomorphology*, D. R. Coates, ed., State University of New York, Binghamton, pp. 181–217.

Tankard, A. J., 1976, Pleistocene history and coastal morphology of the Ysterfontein-Elands Bay area, Cape Province, *Annals South Africa Mus.* **69:**73–119.

Tankard, A. J., and J. Rogers, 1978, Late Cenozoic palaeoenvironments on the west coast of Southern Africa, *Jour. Biogeog.* **5:**319–337.

Plate 90-1. Typical west coast shoreline, mainly rocky, consisting of Precambrian metasediments and with sparse, drought-resistant vegetation (photo by B. W. Flemming).

Plate 90-2. Typical west coast estuary, barred except when in flood, with saline lagoon and dune field fanning out to the north (photo by A. E. F. Heydorn).

Plate 90-3. Sweeping beach typical of the area between the Olifants and Berg rivers. Note the barred estuary, bisected in the mouth region by a railway embankment (photo by A. E. F. Heydorn).

Plate 90-4. Pocket bays, headlands, and offshore pinnacles typical of the coast to the south of the Berg River (photo by A. E. F. Heydorn).

Plate 90-5. Coastline of the Cape Peninsula with plunging sandstone cliffs overlying a basement of granite (photo by A. E. F. Heydorn).

Plate 90-6. The barred Bot River estuary situated between Cape Hangklip and Cape Agulhas (photo by Department of Natural Conservation, Cape Prov. Administration).

Plate 90-7. Succession of halfheart bays to the east of Cape Agulhas, resulting from the alternating succession of anticlines and synclines (photo by B. W. Flemming).

Plate 90-8. Coast between Cape Agulhas and the Gouritz River mouth, with acid soils overlying eolian calcarenites and coastal fynbos vegetation binding unconsolidated sediments (photo by A. E. F. Heydorn).

Plate 90-9. Raised beveled edge of an anticline with a ravine incised through it and abutting on a wave-cut platform in the mid-region of the south coast (photo by A. E. F. Heydorn).

Plate 90-10. Typical east coast shore to the south of Port St. Johns, with convex grass-covered headlands and the dynamic mouth of a mangrove-lined estuary (photo by A. E. F. Heydorn).

Plate 90-11. Typical straight beach of the Mtunzini area with a high, forest-covered dune ridge separating the hinterland from the sea. The hinterland is largely covered by sugar cane fields (photo by A. E. F. Heydorn).

Plate 90-12. A high forest-covered dune ridge separates the St. Lucia Lake from the sea along the coastal plain of northern Zululand (photo by A. E. F. Heydorn).

91. MOÇAMBIQUE

Moçambique lies on the east coast of Africa between latitudes 10° 20′ to 26° 50′ south, with a coastline more than 2,500 km long, more than 90% of which is a low coastal plain of sand or mud stabilized by plants. Three main natural regions are defined: the northern coast (faulted, embayed coast fringing coral and coral-rock cliffs), the central coast (swamp and estuary barrier coast with simple or arcuate beaches), and the southern coast (parabolic dune coast (Plates 91-1, 91-2, and 91-3) with dune rock at intervals forming north-trending capes, large barrier lakes). The climate is tropical, with single temperature and rain maxima in the summer months. The northern coast has a monsoonal regime and is the main area experiencing hurricanes. The central and southern coasts have easterly anticyclonic regimes with frontal (southerly) and thunderstorm rains.

The country lies due west of Madagascar Island, from which it is separated by the Moçambique Channel, 400 km wide at its narrowest point. Madagascar Island is about 1,600 km long and effectively blocks off the influences of the open ocean except in the extreme south (south of latitude 25° S) and in the extreme north, where Cape Delgado lies open to the direct influence of the Indian Ocean and forms the dividing point of the South Equatorial Current. The warm southward-flowing branch of this current, known as the Moçambique Current, and farther down as the Agulhas, has far-reaching influences on the climate and life of southern Africa.

The coastline (Fig. 91-1) from the extreme south tip of Moçambique to the 16° latitude immediately to the north of Antonio Enes is composed of unconsolidated but compacted Quaternary to Holocene sediments, mostly of sand interspersed with silt and clay at the larger river mouths. Tertiary basalts occur on the coast at the 16° latitude and to the north in Moçambo Bay, Nacala Bay, and Memba Bay. Precambrian metamorphic gneisses, migmatites, and amphibolites meet the shore in small outcrops. From Antonio Enes northward heavily faulted Cretaceous to Tertiary formations line the coast. The cross-faulting is at right angles, the main fractures trending northeast–southwest and northwest–southeast. These appear to have had important influence on the evolution of the deeply embayed northern coastline and the associated submarine canyons.

The extreme north of Moçambique is markedly different from the area south of the fifteenth latitude. In the north the coastline to the Rovuma River mouth is faintly concave but trending due north, and is deeply indented with low coral rock headlands forming rugged cliffs of 3−8 m high, with extensive aprons of fringing coral. Here the continental shelf is extremely narrow, only several hundred meters, and deeply scarred with submarine canyons, it plunges to over 2,500 m deep within 30 km of the beach, as off Nacala. Behind this the land rises fairly rapidly to over 500 m within 20 to 30 km of the coast. Excellent harbors occur along this north coast, such as Nacala, Memba, and Porto Amelia. But at intervals are low swampy shores and arcuate sand beaches similar to those of central Moçambique. These areas are associated with the larger river mouths.

The major rivers in Moçambique are the Zambezi, the Rovuma, and the Lurio in the north, the rivers entering the Bight of Sofala (Pungue, Busi, Gorongose, and Save) and those entering the

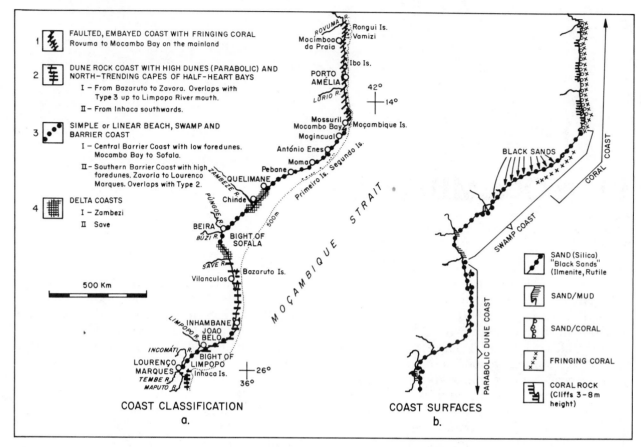

Figure 91-1. Moçambique coastal classification and surface characteristics.

Bight of Limpopo (Limpopo, Incomati, and Maputo). All these rivers carry tremendous volumes of silt; sandbanks occur far out to sea in the Bight of Sofala. This high silt load has important effects on the formation of new land, the maintenance of and accretion of beaches, and the life of the continental shelf; it also affects local or regional changes in level between land and sea.

The major current off the coast is the warm, south-flowing Moçambique Current, which passes close offshore near the bulge of Mossuril and that of Cabo Correntes, attaining its greatest velocity of more than 6 km/h in the period October to February when the northeasterly monsoon is blowing. This current is the southern branch of the South Equatorial Current moving westwards at 3–6km/h, which splits at Delgado into north- and south-blowing streams. These currents reflect closely the seasonal wind changes of the monsoon. South of Moçambique the channels current is joined by a branch of the South Equatorial current that flows southwestward past the

east and southeast shores of Madagascar. Together these currents form the Agulhas Stream.

Large counter-currents occur in the bights of Limpopo and Sofala. But at Beira, for example, there is also a strong and fairly permanent longshore drift (counter-counter-current) from the northeast, due to the prevailing easterly day winds, which is continually shaping the beaches in this area.

Tidal range on the Moçambique coast is shown in Figure 91-2. One of the highest ranges anywhere on the African coast is recorded from Beira, 6.3 m, and is related to the effect of the shallow continental shelf, which is 140 km broad off this point.

Between the Buzi and Save river mouths tremendous areas of bare mud and sand flats are exposed by this high tidal range. When high tide occurs in the afternoons with strong, onshore winds, beaches are eroded to steep profiles.

In Moçambique the major part of the coast has prevailing onshore winds with short fetch; as a

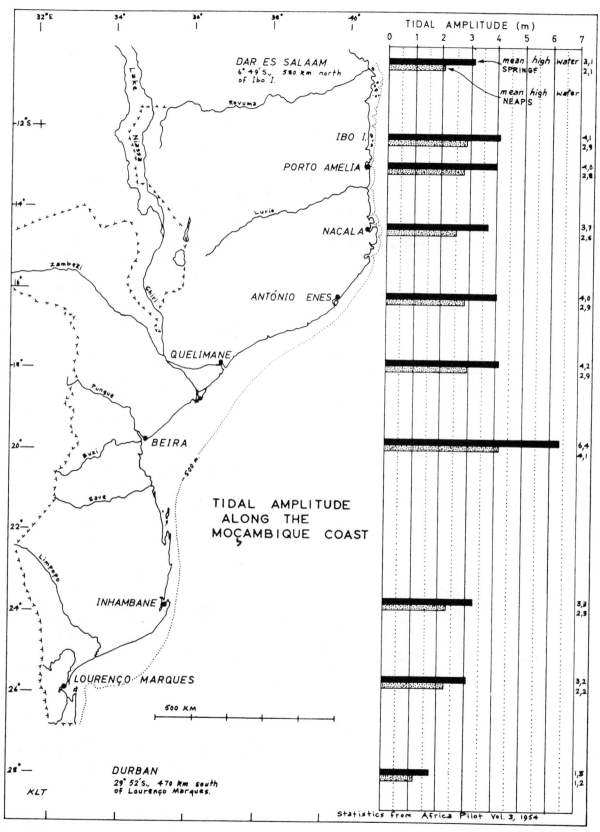

Figure 91-2. Tidal amplitude along the Moçambique coast.

result, destructive "wind" waves prevail, particularly at high tide. Sea swell waves can occur in the southern and northern ends of the Moçambique coast, which face the open ocean. Swell waves may also be generated by southerly gales, but most of these waves are either onshore in the bights or modified by refraction on the north-trending coastlines.

In central Moçambique and parts of the northern and southern coasts, dumping waves occur at high tide, particularly when coincident with onshore winds. At mid and low tide the waves are sliding, and are thus creative in their action, planing the lower beach. The beach profile is then typically flat and gently rising landward, with a steep upward slope at the top of the beach formed by the high-tide dumping waves. Sliding waves occur at high tide only with gale force winds or from large waves generated by storms at sea. But these storm waves can be either creative or destructive according to the local conditions, which govern all other actions of the sea and wind. The largest waves seen by the writer on the southern coast at Pomene attained an estimated 8–10 m in height and were generated by a hurricane in the Moçambique Channel. These waves fell for about 30 hours before losing this height, and for three to four days afterward were 5–6 m high.

Longshore drift is a function of wave refraction, bottom topography, and wind action. The southern two-thirds of the Moçambique coast are subject to southeast trade winds, with the resulting swell approaching parallel to the coast in the region between Beira and Antonia Enes, and between Lourenço Marques and Inhambane. In contrast, the same winds strike the coast obliquely south of Lourenço Marques and between Inhambane and the Save River. Longshore drift generated by these wind patterns is as follows: converging drift, from the south and the northeast, upon Lourenço Marques; drift northwest then north from here, to the northernmost halfheart bay just south of the Save River; drift divergence, to the southwest and northeast, at an eroding sector northeast of Beira; then mainly northeasterly drift, with some local reversal, all along the shore to Antonio Enes.

From Antonio Enes to the northern border at the Revuma River, the coast is dominated by the monsoons. There is no clear net longshore drift, as it appears to be seasonal and both up- and down-coast, because of the monsoon reversals:

from the south in winter and from the northeast in summer.

A recent survey of the Moçambique coast has made it possible to map details of erosion, accretion, and stable shore dynamics. Locally, beach ridges and cheniers are prograding along the outer edge of the Zambezi delta (Plate 91-4 and 91-5). However, erosion predominates along the Bight of Sofala coast from Pebane to the Save River. Overall the record is of fringes of dead mangroves, undercut shores, and slumped dune vegetation or cliffed beaches and some breaching of vegetated barrier islands separating the sea from swampland.

In the north there are prograding beach ridges south of the Luria River mouth. Apart from these two sectors, most of the soft coast sectors of Moçambique are eroding. Locally some accretion occurs at river mouths and estuary spits on the central and northern coast and in Delagoa Bay in the south. The coral cliff and fringing coral north coast is relatively stable, but bays occurring in between them are eroding.

Whether this is an overall transgressive phase, or due to isostatic sinking of the shelf in the bights, or to a temporary rise in the oscillations of sea level is not known. Certainly summer hurricanes cause erosion of the coasts, but erosion over a long term is suggested by the many undercut and slumped trees lying on the beaches and the progressive invasion of the sea as at Beira, aggravated especially by groins along the beach.

The Moçambique coast is a compound shore produced by a succession of emergences and submergences. The coast can be divided into three main natural regions, each with distinct subdivisions (Fig. 91-1).

1. Coral Coast. Faulted, embayed coast with fringing coral, and coral rock cliffs of 3–8 m in high (uplifted, fossil-fringing coral). Submarine canyons and north-trending coastline. Extending on the mainland from the Rovuma River to Moçambo Bay. Fringing coral occurs offshore at intervals southward, forming submarine platforms that make up the Primeira and Segundo archipelago and probably the other islands of the northern Coast. Swamp and arcuate sand beach coasts occur at intervals near river mouths (e.g., Lurio and Messalo).

2. Parabolic Dune Coast. Dune rock coast with high parabolic dunes and north- to northeast-trending capes enclosing halfheart bays, and barrier lakes. Islands formed by separation of

north-trending peninsulas into one or several parts. From Bazaruto (and Bartholomew Dias Point) south to Ouro Point (and thence to the southern end of the Moçambique Plain in Natal at Umlalazi River 28° 57′ S).

3. Swamp Coast. Simple or linear beaches, swamp and estuary barrier coast. Mostly mangrove swamps and estuaries from Moçambo Bay south to the Save River. Black beaches occur between Pebane and the Zambezi River mouth. Islands confined to those formed in river mouths. Barrier coast of a different type occurs in the southern coast, with high coast dunes and barrier lakes, but rightly belongs to type 2 above, despite the presence of small and occasional parabolic dunes on both the central and northern coasts.

4. Delta Coasts. Zambezi and Save River deltas. These intergrade with type 3 on their edges.

This coast classification is a preliminary one, and in many parts there are combinations of features characteristic of each coast type. Types 1 and 2, with crystal clear waters, occur in conjunction with the narrow continental shelf zones with over-steepened slopes. The deltaic, estuarine, swamp, and arcuate coast lines occur where the continental shelf is broad. Turbid waters occur mainly in the bight and off the mouths of rivers carrying muddy waters. The rivers draining the Cheringoma Plateau and the coast of southern Moçambique traverse sand country, hardly discoloring the sea even at the height of the rains.

Configuration of the Moçambique coast shows an alternating, repetitive pattern of embayed rocky coast in the north (coral rock) followed by simple or barrier coast to Bazaruto, and from here to Cape Correntes the reappearance of rocky headlands (dune rock), but with high and steep coast dunes. From Cape Correntes to Lourenço Marques the barrier coast is repeated, this area having large deep lakes behind high barrier dunes. South of Lourenço Marques the high dune and dune rock headland coast again occurs (Plate 91-6 and 91-7). The embayed headland shores all lie on a northerly trend, and the simple or barrier coasts all lie on a northeast to east-northeast trend — a zigzag pattern, which has important relations to the prevailing winds, longshore drift, and wave action.

Fringing coral is confined to the northern coast and extends south along the mainland shore to Moçambo Bay at latitude 15° 09′, where it leaves the mainland and occurs southward to latitude 17° 16′ S as isolated submarine platforms forming the chain of small islands that lie on the shelf edge some 70 km offshore. These reef-forming corals, are classified as hermatypic corals, which require a mean annual sea temperature of about 21° C. Corals occur at intervals offshore from Bazaruto Island southward to South Africa, but these are found in relatively deeper waters than the reef corals and play little or only local part in modifying the direct action of the sea and storms. The southern limit for shallow water fringing coral is reported from Inhaca Island at 26° S latitude. The largest gap in coral distribution appears to be the Bight of Sofala with its broad, shallow continental shelf and turbid waters.

Some of the islands that occur off the northern coast (Plate 91-8) could have originated as erosional remnants of headlands, but the majority appear to be isolated submarine platforms of fringing coral with foundations attached to the top of the higher points of an old submerged coastline that occurred near the break in slope of the continental shelf. Opposite the Primeira– Segundo archipelago, for example, there is wave-planed rock underwater along the mainland shores from south of Pebane to near Moçambo Bay. This rock is dark reddish-black in color and is strongly bedded or jointed (?) parallel to the present coastline (i.e., northeast trend). As seen from the air this rock occurred nowhere above high tide level, but there are cliff headlands immediately south of Pebane, at Pebane (Ponta Matisse), and south of the Sangage Lighthouse that may be outcrops of the same rock. It is possible this rock forms the base of the Primeira archipelago. From the air the Primeira and Segundo Islands look identical to those described by Guilcher (1966) from the northwest of Madagascar. They are isolated submarine platforms of fringing coral, kidney-shaped with the indentation on the leeside opposite to the open sea. A large part of the coral platform is exposed at low tide. The actual islands composed of sand and reef debris are developed by wave refraction across the coral platform. They are thus all perched at the confluence zone of the refracted waves, which is on the farther central edge of the platform next to the indentation. The islands stand at varying heights above the tides and are at varying stages of fixation — from completely bare to dense climax thicket cover. The shallow seas between the island chains and the mainland are important habitats for sea life, especially the sea grass ecosystem.

Estuaries occur at intervals along the entire coast and can be classified according to their substrates and morphology. Some estuaries, for example, abut on the sea directly without any form of protection, with their mangrove fringes forming the foreshore to the open sea, as in the area between the Pungue and Save river mouths and in the Zambezi delta area. These occur mostly on the periphery of shallow seas. The majority of the estuaries occur within the protection of a river mouth or in the lee of some barrier.

The islands of the Bazaruto archipelago and Inhaca Island were once peninsula headlands of the present mainland, which were subsequently severed and isolated along with their continental flora and fauna by sea and/or wind action. The southern islands are dune rock types, and this material is their major protection against marine erosion, although its occurrence is discontinuous.

An earlier version of this report (Tinley 1971) appeared in the Proceedings of the SARCCUS Symposium, *Nature Conservation as a Form of Land Use*, held in the Gorongosa National Park, Moçambique, September, 13–17, 1971.

K. L. TINLEY

REFERENCES

Guilcher, A., 1966 Étude géomorphologique des récifs coralliens du nord-ouest de Madagascar, *Inst. Océanog. Annales* **33:**65–134.

Tinley, K. L., 1971 Determinants of coastal conservation: dynamics and diversity of the environment as exemplified by the Moçambique coast, in *Nature Conservation as a Form of Land Use*, SARCCUS Symposium, Proc. Gorongosa, pp. 126–153.

Plate 91-1. Milibangala Point on the southern coast of Moçambique. The high forested parabolic dunes have been built by opposing winds across the point of a halfheart bay. As the beachrock is eroded away, the point is left as an island in the process of straightening of the coast (photo by K. L. Tinley).

Plate 91-2. High parabolic dunes along the southern shore of Moçambique. Though generally forested, these dunes are bare and eroding on the seaward backshore slopes. Note the low tide exposure of beachrock (photo by T. P. Dutton).

Plate 91-3. Uembje Lake region, south of the Limpopo River mouth. View seaward of dune thicket on stabilized parabolic dunes that have partially filled and segmented the coast-parallel lake system (photo by T. P. Dutton).

Plate 91-4. Mosaic showing the southern section of the Zambezi delta, with chenier ridges and swales. To the left of Baia Nhandaze there are recurved spits with arcuate dune ridges. (photos by K. L. Tinley).

Plate 91-6. Broad, high (up to 183 m) forested parabolic dunes near Cape St. Lucia. Patches of beachrock are exposed along the narrow beach (photo by K. L. Tinley).

Plate 91-5. View seaward on the Zambezi delta, showing parallel dune ridges and swales. The low swale areas are occupied by fresh water marshes, with some patches of swamp forest (*Barringtonia*) in the wetter areas (photo by K. L. Tinley).

Plate 91-7. One of the few uneroded sectors along the Moçambique coast, near Cape St. Lucia. Note the extremely narrow scrub thicket zone (different texture in photo) above the beach (photo by K. L. Tinley).

Plate 91-8. Njevo Island in the northern coast Primeira-Segundo archipelago. Note the thicket-covered island of sand and reef debris, shown at low tide, formed by wave refraction across the isolated coral platform. In the background, 10 km away, are the mainland coast and the Metúle River estuary (photo by K. L. Tinley).

92. MADAGASCAR

Measuring 1,600 km from north to south, with a maximum width of 600 km, Madagascar lies only 300 km off the east coast of Africa, from which it is separated by the Moçambique Channel, more than 4,000 m deep. The island is markedly asymmetrical in both its topography (with gradual slopes toward the Moçambique Channel and a sharper descent toward the Indian Ocean) and its geology (with large sedimentary basins to the west and only a narrow, discontinuous sedimentary fringe on the eastern side). As a result of the topographic asymmetry, the largest rivers drain to the west coast, the eastern side having numerous short streams. There is also a climatic contrast, the eastern slopes being exposed to the southeasterly trade winds and thus very wet (rainfalls of 2–4 m annually), while the western slopes are drier and the southwest semiarid: Tuléar has mean annual rainfall of only 350 mm. The continental shelf is well developed off the west coast and in the far south, but narrow off the east and northeast coasts.

The northwest coast between Cape d'Ambre and Cape Saint André is the boldest (Figs. 92-1 and 92-2). The Flandrian Transgression has invaded a landscape of clayey hills in the Ampasindava peninsula (Battistini 1960a), a basaltic area on the coast of the Montagne d'Ambre (Rossi 1980), and limestone topography on the Narinda peninsula (Battistini 1966). Near Majunga the sea has cut high cliffs in Pliocene sandy clays. There is a ria morphology, the finest example being the ria de la Loza. The three large bays of Narinda (Plate 92-1) and at the mouths of the Mahajamba and Betsiboka (the Bay of Bombetoka) result from the submergence of a cuesta relief, the Flandrian Transgression having led to

penetration of the sea through consequent gaps cut by the rivers, widening in the subsequent depressions behind the cuestas to form broad bays with narrow entrances. Three rivers have deltas: the northern Mahavavy, the Sambirano, and the southern Mahavavy (Fig. 92-1). This sector has the most extensive mangroves in Madagascar (Hervieu 1966; Salomon 1978), within the larger bays and along delta fronts. There are also many offshore islands, of which Nossi-be is the largest.

The west coast, between Cape Saint André (Rossi 1977) and the Mangoky delta, has a simpler outline, with no major indentations. The usual coastal landscape is one of sandy barriers, behind which, protected from ocean swell, are extensive mangroves (Battistini et al. 1970). Similar features border the deltas of the Mangoky, Tsiribihina, Morondava, and Manambolo (Plate 92-2). However, beside these zones of accumulation, certain sectors have been subject to marine erosion; this is the case at Morondava, the site of which has been protected by the building of a series of groins at right angles to the beach.

The south and southwest coast (Battistini 1960b, 1964a), between the delta of the Mangoky and the mouth of the Mandrare, is a semiarid sector, characterized by the development of coastal dunes during the Quaternary. There are thus long sectors of sandy coastline (the Mahafaly and Mikea shores) with active dune fields dominated by parabolic dunes oriented in relation to the prevailing southerly and southwesterly winds (Plate 92-3). Mangroves are absent or poorly developed, as in the Bay of Saint-Augustin and on the Fiherenana delta. The older dunes, including the very reddened dune of Tatsimian (early Qua-

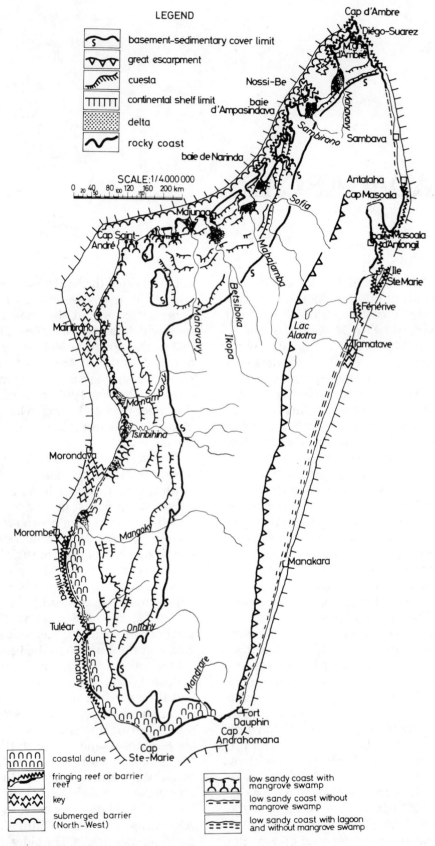

LEGEND

	basement-sedimentary cover limit
	great escarpment
	cuesta
	continental shelf limit
	delta
	rocky coast

SCALE:1/4.000000

0 20 40 80 120 160 200 km

coastal dune

fringing reef or barrier reef

key

submerged barrier (North-West)

low sandy coast with mangrove swamp

low sandy coast without mangrove swamp

low sandy coast with lagoon and without mangrove swamp

Figure 92-1. Madagascar coastal landforms.

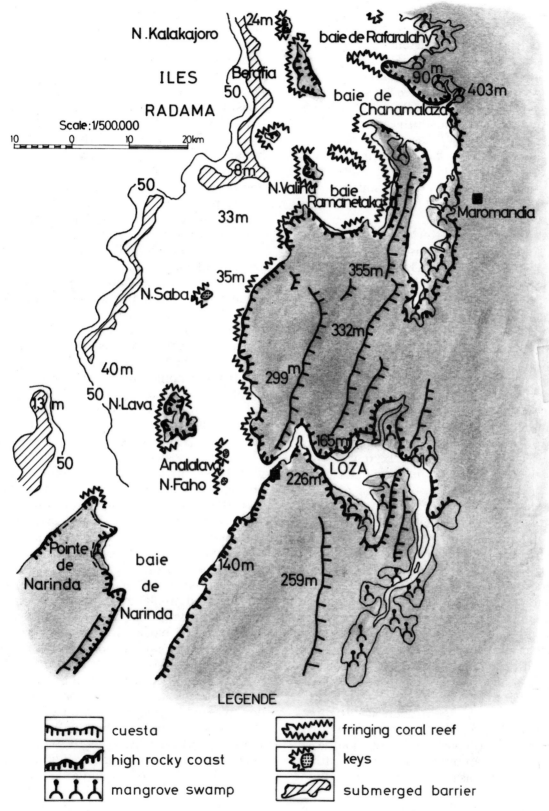

Figure 92-2. Northwestern coast of Madagascar.

ternary) age, the pink or rose-colored dune of Karimbolian age (150,000 to 80,000 years B.P.), have been lithified into sandstones and in places form ridge segments 10–15 km long, parallel to the coastline (Battistini 1973). Marine erosion has attacked these calcareous eolian sandstones, forming cliffs a few meters high, rising to 200 m at Cape Sainte Marie, the southernmost point of Madagascar (Plate 92-4). Associated shore platforms show solution basins (*plateformes à vasques*), as shown in Plate 92-5. Locally in the Bay of Saint-Augustin (at the mouth of the Onilahy), the sea is cutting high cliffs in Eocene marine limestone outcrops.

Between the mouth of the Mandrare and Fort-Dauphin (Fig. 92-3), there is a short sector of indented rocky coastline, locally high, corresponding with the extremities of the granitic chain of L'Anosy (Battistini 1964*a*).

The east coast, between Fort-Dauphin and Fénérive, is low, straight, and sandy for 800 km (Plate 92-6); it is somewhat inhospitable. Its general outline corresponds with one of the major tectonic lineaments of Madagascar, running north-northeast–south-southwest. In detail it has been smoothed by the action of ocean swell, which has built along its length a sandy barrier consisting of numerous beach berms (Battistini 1978). It is a lagoon coast, the chain of lagoons lying between the Flandrian outer barrier and an earlier (Eemian) barrier consisting of white, leached sand. The Canal des Pangalanes has been cut through the low-lying segments between the lagoons to form a waterway that is now practically abandoned. In the Manakara region are fine coral reefs (Battistini 1971). The port of Tamatave is also partly protected by reefs.

The northeast coast, between Fénérive and Diégo-Suarez is further diversified (Battistini 1964*c*), with long sectors of low sandy coast (as to the north of Fénérive and around Sambava) alternating with high rocky coast (in the Masoala peninsula, and here and there in the Bay d'Antongil, shown in Plate 92-7). The outline of the coast is determined, often in detail, by two directions of fracturing: north-northeast–south-southwest and north-northwest–south-southeast. Thus the Bay d'Antongil corresponds with a graben between faults running in the latter direction (Fig. 92-4). In the far north the Bay of Diégo-Suarez is a magnificent fingering ria, the narrow entrance making it one of the best-sheltered naval anchorages in the world.

Madagascar has coral reefs, fringing, barrier, and with cays. In the north (Guilcher 1956) fringing reefs are well developed in the Diégo-Suarez region, at Nossi-Be, on the Ampasindava peninsula, and locally within the Bay of Narinda. Plate 92-8 shows a cay on a patch reef near Nossi-Be. In addition, there is a "submerged barrier" off the northwest coast with generally attentuated coralline life (Battistini 1972), formed by sandy banks beneath several meters of water, located on the outer edge of the continental shelf and bordered by deep sea. Between the delta of the Mangoky and Cape Saint-André there are numerous reef patches bearing cays (Battistini 1964*d*), forming the many small sandy islets south of Morondava and around Maintirano (Iles Barren and Banc Pracel). The best-developed coral reefs are found in the southwest (Battistini 1959), some fringing (on the Mahafaly and Mikea shores), others of barrier type (off the coast north of Tuléar and between the Bay of Assassins and Morombe). On the east coast there are also fringing reefs on the Masoalo peninsula, locally within the Bay d'Antongil, and around the island of Sainte Marie (Lapaire 1979), as well as the reefs with cays in the Tamatave sector. Farther south the reefs disappear along more than 1,000 km of coast between Tamatave and Cape Sainte Marie.

Marine deposits dating from the last interglacial (Eemian or Karimbolien, between 150,000 and 80,000 years B.P.) have been found and dated on various parts of Madagascar (Battistini et al. 1976). Along the whole of the east coast between Fort-Dauphin and Fénérive they form a well-preserved ancient sand barrier on the inner part of the coastal plain, 8–12 m above present sea level (Battistini 1978). In the sector between Fénérive and Antalaha this old barrier has been raised to varying heights by the movement of fault-bounded blocks. In the region of Diégo-Suarez the Eemian is represented by uplifted coral reefs (Battistini 1964*b*; Rossi 1980). In the region of Nossi-Be and around Bas Sambirano in the far northwest, the Eemian coastline has been downwarped below present sea level (Battistini 1960*a*) by negative movements between faults trending north-northeast–south-southwest. This is also the case in the southwest around Tuléar. In the far south, the Eemian coastline is up to 3–4 m above present sea level in the Cape Sainte Marie and Cape Andrahomana areas (Battistini 1957, 1964*a*). Fragments of old sandy barriers attributed to the Eemian have been noted in

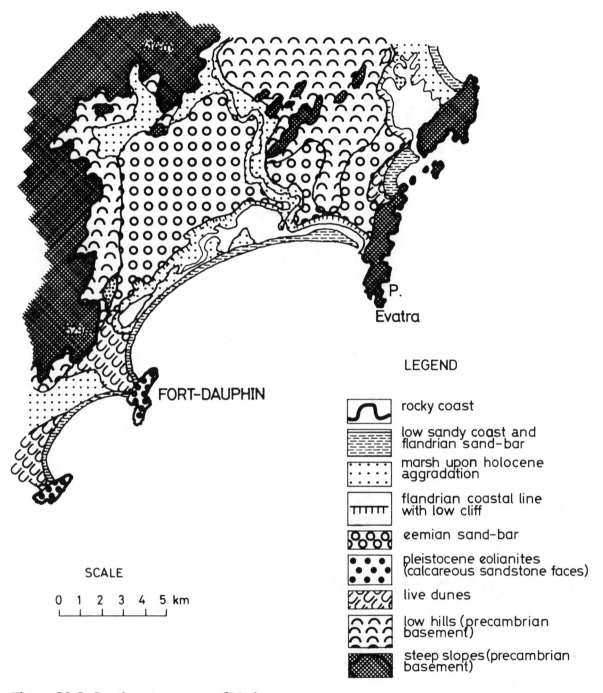

Figure 92-3. Southeastern coast of Madagascar.

LEGEND

- rocky coast
- low sandy coast and flandrian sand-bar
- marsh upon holocene aggradation
- flandrian coastal line with low cliff
- eemian sand-bar
- pleistocene eolianites (calcareous sandstone faces)
- live dunes
- low hills (precambrian basement)
- steep slopes (precambrian basement)

SCALE

0 1 2 3 4 5 km

various places on the west coast, particularly in the lower Tsiribihina and at Tambohorano (Hervieu 1966).

There are also undated Quaternary marine deposits rising to 5–6 m above sea level in the far south (Cape Sainte Marie, Cape Andrahomano) and in the extreme north, where ancient coral reefs at Cape d'Ambre and around Diégo Suarez locally reach altitudes of 25 m.

RENÉ BATTISTINI
PAUL LE BOURDIEC

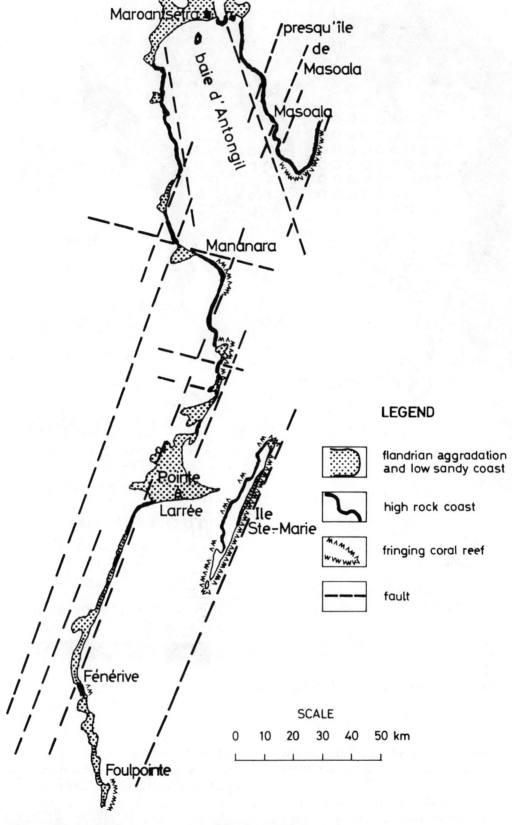

Figure 92-4. Northeastern coast of Madagascar.

REFERENCES

Battistini, R., 1957, Note préliminaire sur le niveau marin de 3 m et les séries dunaires de l'Extrême Sud de Madagascar, *Soc. Géol. France Bull.* **6:**1–3.

Battistini, R., 1959, Observations sur les récifs coralliens du Sud-Ouest de Madagascar, *Soc. Géol. France Bull.* **7:**341–346.

Battistini, R., 1960a, Description géomorphologique de Nosy-Bi, du delta du Sambirano et de la baie d'Ampasindava, *Inst. rech. sci. Madagascar Mém.* ser. F, **3:**121–343.

Battistini, R., 1960b, Quelques aspects de la morphologie du littoral mikea (Côte Sud-Ouest de Madagascar), *Bull. Inform. Com. Océanogr. Etude des Côtes* **12:**548–579.

Battistini, R., 1964a, *L'Extrème sud de Madagascar: étude géomorphologique,* Doctoral thesis, Paris.

Battistini, R., 1964b, Note préliminaire sur le Quaternaire littoral de l'extrême Nord de Madagascar, *C. R. Semaine Géol., Imprimerie Nationale, Tananarive,* pp. 9–12.

Battistini, R., 1964c, Les caractères morphologiques du secteur littoral compris entre Foulpointe et Maroantsetra, *Madagascar Reu Géog.* **4:**5–36.

Battistini, R., 1964d, Une reconnaissance aérienne des Iles Barren, *Madagascar Reu Géog.* **5:**105–115.

Battistini, R., 1966, Le littoral du paléokarst de la presqu'île de Narinda au Nord de Majunga (Madagascar); un exemple de côte contraposée, *Assoc. Géographes Français Bull.* **346–347:**41–49.

Battistini, R., 1971, Sur l'existence d'arrécifes à Madagascar, *Soc. Géol. France Compte Rendu* **2:**73–74.

Battistini, R., 1972, Le problème de l'origine de la barrière immergée du Nord-Ouest de Madagascar, *Bull. Acad. Malgache* **48**(1-2):185–187.

Battistini, R., 1973, Chronologie du Quaternaire littoral de Madagascar, *Assoc. Sénég. Et. Quat. Ouest Afr.* **13:**23–30.

Battistini, R., 1978, Observations sur les cordons littoraux pleistocènes et holocènes de la côte Est de Madagascar, *Madagascar Reu Géog.* **35:**9–37.

Battistini, R., A. Guilcher, and A. M. Marec, 1970, Morphologie et formations quaternaries du littoral occidental de Madagascar entre Maintirano et le Cap Saint André, *Madagascar Reu Géog.* **16:**45–81.

Battistini, R., C. Lalou, and G. Elbez, 1976, Datation par la méthode 230 Th 234 Ur du Pleistocène moyen marin de Madagascar et des îles voisines, *Soc. Géol. France Compte Rendu* **5:**201.

Guilcher, A., 1956, *Etude morphologique des récifs coralliens du Nord-Ouest de Madagascar., Inst. Océanog, Annales* **33**(2):65–136.

Hervieu, J., 1966, *Contribution à l'étude de l'alluvionnement en milieu tropical,* thesis, ORSTOM, Paris.

Lapaire, J. P., 1979, Contribution à l'étude morphologique de l'île Sainte-Marie de Madagascar, *Madagascar Reu Géog.* **34:**83–109.

Rossi, G., 1977, Le Cap Saint-André (Ouest de Madagascar), *Madagascar Reu Géog.* **30:**105–122.

Rossi, G., 1980, *L'Extrème Nord de Madagascar,* thesis, University of Aix.

Salomon, J. N., 1978, Contribution à l'étude écologique et géographique des mangroves, *Reu Géomorphologie Dynam.* **27:**63–80.

Plate 92-1. Bay of Narinda, northwest Madagascar (photo by P. LeBourdiec).

Plate 92-2. West coast of Madagascar between Morondava and the delta of the Tsiribihina. A low coast with extensive mangroves behind a sandy barrier. To the rear of the mangroves a zone of bare clay, covered only at high spring tides, explained by the fact of a long dry season (photo by P. LeBourdiec).

Plate 92-3. The sand spit of Sarodrano, 30 km south of Tuléar. A short section of cliffed coast cut in Eocene marine limestone to the rear, and beyond that the Onilahy estuary. There is a fringing coral reef, with waves breaking on its outer edge, and some mangroves in the lee of the spit (photo by R. Battistini).

Plate 92-4. High cliff of Cape Sainte Marie, cut in early Quaternary calcareous eolian sandstones (photo by R. Battistini).

Plate 92-5. Shore platform with *plateformes à vasques* (solution basins) near Fort-Dauphin. Marine erosion has cut out fissures beneath the platform, so that in places wave pressure forces water up through blowholes. To the rear, the granitic ranges of Anosy (photo by P. LeBourdiec).

Plate 92-6. The sandy east coast north of Tamatave, with plantations of *Casuarina equisetifolia* on beach ridges (photo by P. LeBourdiec).

Plate 92-7. Rocky coast and bay beach between Mananara and Maroantsetra (photo by P. LeBourdiec).

Plate 92-8. Sand cay of Tanikely on a patch reef off Nossi-Be, northwest Madagascar (photo by P. LeBourdiec).

93. TANZANIA

The zigzag shoreline of Tanzania extends from about 4°30′ S to 10°30′ S, a distance of just over 725 km. This general outline of the coast appears to have been established by faulting during the Paleozoic (Kent et al. 1971). However, local movements may have continued into the late Pleistocene and Holocene (Temple 1970a, Kent et al. 1971). The coastal zone where this faulting has occurred consists of a narrow belt of Neogene sedimentary rock extending along the entire coast of Tanzania (Figs. 93-1 and 93-2). The sediments are generally separated from the crystalline basement rock of the interior by faulting and lie in the down-dropped block. Evidence from deep borings at a number of places indicates considerable subsidence of the coastal zone during the Tertiary (Kent et al. 1971). Although faulting has blocked out the basic design of the Tanzanian coast, the geomorphic details have been conditioned by fluvial sediment supply, longshore currents, mangrove growth, coral reefs, and crustal warping.

During the rainy season Tanzanian rivers transport large amounts of sediment to the coast. The rivers flow into two distinct environments. The Pangani, Lukuledi, and Rovuma flow through narrow estuaries and into deep water where most of their sediment is lost. The Wami, Ruvu, and Rufiji rivers discharge into the shallow water in the lee of Zanzibar and Mafia Island, where the Wami and Rufiji have formed deltas. Surplus sediment from the Wami, Ruvu, and Rufiji rivers is carried off by northward-flowing coastal currents, which prevail throughout the year although the rate of flow changes seasonally (Temple 1970a, U.S. Defense Mapping Agency Hydrographic Center 1975, hereafter cited as DMA).

Mangrove forests grow in exposed locations along the coast as well as in sheltered bays and estuaries. Between the Pangani River and Kenya they frequently are found along the open shore, although in places they seem to be under the stress of wave erosion (Alexander 1966). Mangroves are abundant along the margins of the Rufiji, Wami, and Ruvu deltas and occur at places on the open coast between the Rufiji and Rovuma rivers (Figs. 93-1 and 93-2) (DMA 1975).

Coral barrier islands and reefs are best developed in the north between the Pangani River and Kenya, where they form a nearly continuous line (Fig. 93-1). Less well-defined islands and reefs occur between Bagamoyo and Dar es Salaam or in the lee of Mafia Island. To the south of Kilwa Kisiwani they are absent (Fig. 93-2). Fringing reefs, however, are common (DMA 1975).

In general, the Tanzanian shore consists of a sandy beach and a gently sloping intertidal platform. The latter may be composed of sand or coral and may be completely exposed for an hour or so during low tide (Alexander 1966). North of the Rufiji delta is an extensive complex of beach ridges 8–10 km wide (Temple 1970a). Between the Ruvu and Pangani rivers sandy beaches and multiple beach ridges are noticeable shorezone features (Fig. 93-3), but north of the Pangani they are relatively rare (Fig. 93-1) (Alexander 1969).

Between the Ruvu and Pangani rivers the old beach ridges are currently being truncated by the erosion of the shore (Alexander 1966). This episode of erosion may have been going on for some time; erosion was reported at widely separated locations at the turn of the century (Bornhardt 1900). Beach erosion appears most active,

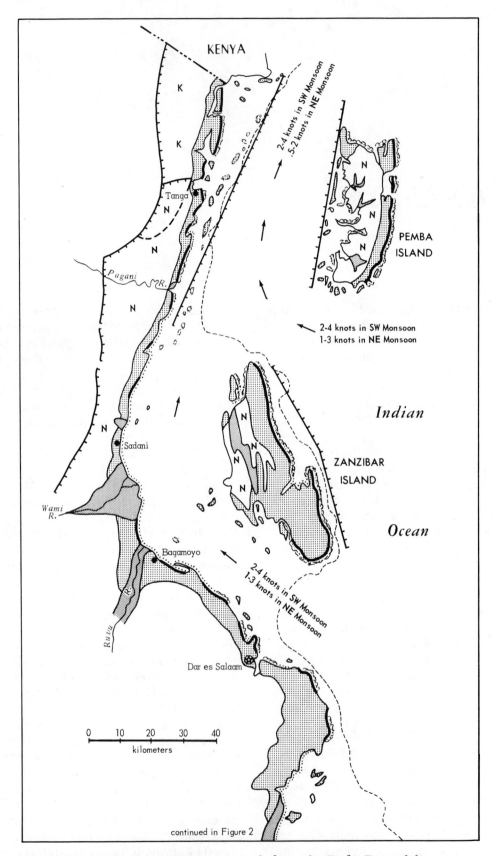

Figure 93-1. The Tanzanian coast north from the Rufiji River delta.

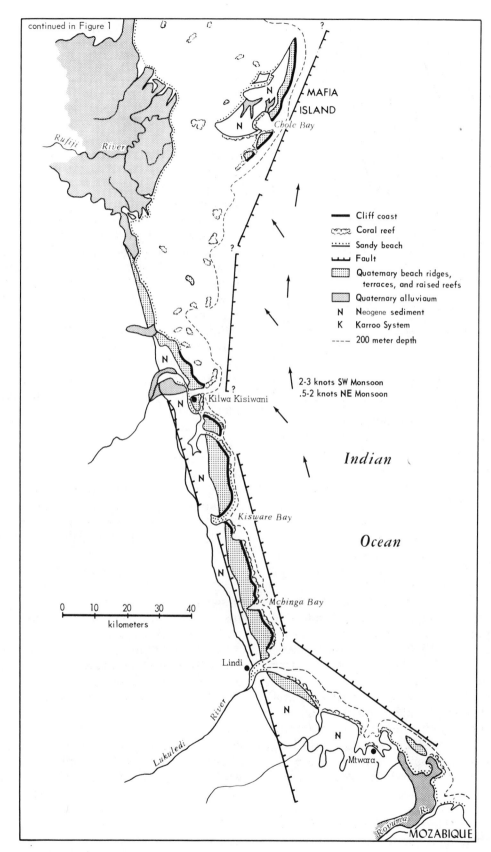

Figure 93-2. The Tanzanian coast south from and including the Rufiji River delta.

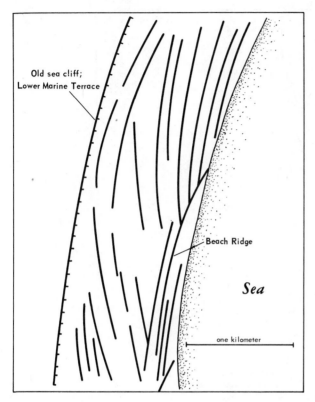

Figure 93-3. The plan of beach ridge crests as they occur north of the Ruvu River (Fig. 93-1). The pattern suggests two, possibly three phases of deposition separated by periods of erosion. The present episode of erosion is truncating the youngest set of ridges.

at least between Dar es Salaam and Bagamoyo, at the onset of the November-January and May-July monsoon season (Duyverman 1981).

Marine terraces occur at many places along the Tanzanian shore, indicating a late Pleistocene uplift superimposed on the general crustal subsidence. Two terraces with local coral veneers, about 20–25 m and 40–50 m high, occur at Dar es Salaam, Lindi, and the Kilwa area (Figs. 93-1 and 93-2) (Bornhardt 1900; Werth 1915). Coastal and fluvial geomorphology evidence suggests there are four former marine levels in the vicinity of Tanga, at 2–3 m, 4.5–6 m, 24–27 m, and 41 m. The latter three are most prominent. All are believed to represent sea-level changes, with the lower two most likely being related to minor Holocene sea-level fluctuations (Cooke 1974). A single coral-covered terrace, 8–10 m in elevation, extends north from Tanga to the Kenya border (Werth 1915; Alexander 1968). In places the terrace platforms have been arched by crustal move-

ment. Von Staff (1914) discusses evidence for tectonic movement along the coast south of Lindi, which has tilted the two marine terrace platforms in that area. Three marine platforms occur between Pangani and Dar es Salaam (Alexander 1969). The two lower terraces show evidence of lateral tilting suggesting coastal uplift, which is disputed by Temple (1970b). Morphologic evidence and radiocarbon dating suggest the middle terrace may have been occupied by two late Pleistocene high stands of sea level. A similar idea was proposed for the terrace at Dar es Salaam (Werth 1901), but evidence for this hypothesis was disputed by Koert and Tornau (1910). Evidence for the highest marine level consists of several small, isolated limestone-covered mesas between Dar es Salaam and Pangani. Some of these, especially in the vicinity north of Dar es Salaam, may be upfaulted remnants of a much older limestone (Temple 1970a). Many of the estuaries along the coast have been eroded 40 m or more below present sea level (Bornhardt 1900; Werth 1915). These drowned valleys suggest a eustatic change of sea level during the late Pleistocene.

The islands of Pemba, Zanzibar, and Mafia show evidence of several terraces, along with indications of a relatively recent subsidence. The islands also have other features in common. They are of comparable size and lie on the continental shelf, although Pemba is separated from the mainland by a 700 m deep channel that is probably the result of graben faulting (Figs. 93-1 and 93-2) (Kent et al. 1971). The three islands are underlain by 3,300–3,400 m or more of marine sediments ranging from Miocene to Cretaceous in age. Their eastern margins, where deep water comes close inshore, are thought to be bounded by faults (Kent et al. 1971).

On the west side of Pemba there are four terraces, three of which, at 23 m, 36 m, and 55–62 m, form relatively prominent features along much of the island's west coast (Stockley 1928). Most of the eastern shore consists of an old, raised coral reef about 5–6 m high. Also there is scattered evidence of a second reef platform at 9 m above sea level. To seaward is a fringing reef 200–500 m wide (Kent et al. 1971). Many of the island's valleys on the western side have flat, swampy alluvial-filled floors. These aggraded valleys may represent a slight recent subsidence of the land (Kent et al. 1971).

On the eastern half of Zanzibar there are a number of reef-covered marine terraces that reflect a Pleistocene uplift of about 50 m. Faulting appears to have occurred in parts of the area, making it difficult to identify the terraces with certainty (Kent et al. 1971). Stockley (1928) identifies five terraces on the west coast at about 10 m, 24 m, 38 m, 55 m, and 70 m. However, Werth (1915) and Bornhardt (1900) describe only two terraces on the island, at 25 m and 55–60 m above sea level.

A low plateau (30–45 m) on the west side of Mafia is separated by flat-bottomed, swampy valleys that may indicate late subsidence of the island. Historical subsidence is indicated by remains of medieval structures on the west coast that now lie between the tidal limits. Nevertheless, inland from the east coast is a belt of raised coral reef about 1.5 km wide that stands about 3–5 m above sea level. The raised reef is covered by poorly bedded eolianite of variable thickness to a maximum of 21 m. Inland a smooth area about 15–18 m in elevation may represent a second marine terrace. A low sea cliff extends all along the eastern side of the island; to seaward is a narrow, modern fringing reef that widens considerably on the south side of the island (Kent et al. 1971).

CHARLES S. ALEXANDER

REFERENCES

Alexander, C. S., 1966, A method of descriptive shore classification and mapping as applied to the northeast coast of Tanganyika, *Assoc. Am. Geographers Annals* **57**:128–140.

Alexander, C. S., 1968, The marine terraces of the northeast coast of Tanganyika, *Zeitschr. Geomorphologie Supp.* **7**:133–154.

Alexander, C. S., 1969, Beach ridges in northeastern Tanzania, *Geog. Rev.* **59**:104–122.

Bornhardt, W., 1900, *Zur Oberflachengestaltun und Geologie Deutsch-Ostafrikas, Deutsche-Ostafrika,* Vol. VII, Dietrich Reimer, Ernst Vohsen, Berlin.

Cooke, H. J., 1974, The coastal geomorphology of Tanga, Tanzania, *Geog. Rev.* **64**:517–535.

Duyverman, H. J., 1981, The occurrence of heavy mineral sands along the Tanzanian coast, *Geol. Soc. India Jour.,* **22**:78–84.

Kent, F. E., M. A. Hunt, and M. A. Johnstone, 1971, *The Geology and Geophysics of Coastal Tanzania,* Geophysical Paper No. 6. Natural Environment Research Council, Institute of Geological Sciences, Her Majesty's Stationery Office.

Koert, W., and F. Tornau, 1910, Zur Geologie und Hydrologie von Dar es Salaam und Tanga (Deutsch-Ostafrika), *Abh. Konig. Preuss. Geol. Landesanstalt,* New Ser. **63**:1–77.

Stockley, G. M., 1928, *Report on the Geology of the Zanzibar Protectorate,* published by the government of Zanzibar.

Temple, P. H., 1970*a*, Aspects of the geomorphology of the Dar es Salaam area, *Tanzania Notes and Records* **71**:21–54.

Temple, P. H., 1970*b*, Discussion of C.S. Alexander's paper on marine terraces of the northeast coast of Tanganyika, *Zeitschr. Geomorphologie* **15**:236–240.

U.S. Defense Mapping Agency Hydrographic Center, *Sailing Directions for the Southeast coast of Africa: Cape of Good Hope to Ras Hafun,* DMA Pub. 60 1975.

von Staff, H., 1914, Beitrage zur geomorpogenie und Tektonik Deutsch Ostafrikas, *Archiv. Biontologie* **3**(3):73–226.

Werth, E., 1901, Zur Kenntinis der jungern Ablagerungen im tropischen Ostafrikas, *Deutsch. Geol. Gesell. Zeitschr.,* **53**:287–304.

Werth, E., 1915, *Das Deutsche-Ostafrikanische Kostenland und die Vorgelagerten Iseln,* Band I, Dietrich Reimer, Ernst Vohsen, Berlin.

94. KENYA

The coastline of Kenya (Figs. 94-1 and 94-2) is about 450 km long. Essentially, the whole length of the coast forms part of Kenya's Lowland Plain (Ojany 1966), which has resulted from earth movements that involved downwarping of the coastal basin (in Palaeozoic times), marine transgression (in Mesozoic times), and a fluctuating sea level (during Quaternary times). A number of small faults have been mapped along the coastal belt (Miller 1952; Caswell 1953, 1956; Thompson 1956). Of these faults, it is probably the inferred continuation of the Ruvu-Mombasa fault (Willis 1936; Williams 1962), thought to be contemporaneous with the Pemba Trough (Stockley 1928), that has had the most significant effect on the relief of the area. The morvan of the Eastern Kenya Half Oval (Pulfrey 1960; Saggerson and Baker 1965) also played an important part.

The tidal range is only accurately measured at Kilindini by the Kenya Ports Authority. The 1981 tables show that the maximum range, at spring tide, is 4.0 m in November, and that the average for most of the months varies from 2.5 m to 3.6 m.

The northern half of the coast (Fig. 94-1), is quite different from the south (Fig. 94-2). The north receives its depositional materials mainly from continental and deltaic (or estuarine) environments while to the south, especially from Vanga to Malindi (and to a less extent up to Fundi Isa), the materials are mainly marine and lagoonal in origin. The geological outcrops also show this basic distinction. The north is dominated by Quaternary sediments, exemplified by such large sand dunes as Mlima Kitanga Tangani (next to Ungwana Bay) and those to the north up to Ras Biongwe. The *Mlima* (literally meaning *hill*)

Kitanga Tangani dune sands have formed high outer (rising to 52 m high) and inner barriers. These barriers have caused a deferred-junction phenomenon at the mouth of the Tana (here called the Ozi) and the other streams in the area. These dunes are responsible for the constant shifting (or migration) of the mouths of these rivers (Williams 1962). In the Lamu archipelago, both the Mongoni and Dodori rivers bring considerable sand and other alluvial material from upstream; they have brought about the rather complex pattern of islands, inlets, channels, and bays in the area. The Ras Ngomeni coral and coquinoid island has now been joined (by a sand bar) with the mainland, thus forming a tombolo.

The coral rock developed on the Kenya Coast is typical of such an equatorial environment. Live coral polyps occur on the present fringing reef. The coral development has been attributed to the growth of polyps up from a marine platform during the Kamasian (Mindel Glaciation) Age, which was at least 61 m below the present datum. Coral is much more continuously developed in the south, as shown by the more or less continuous growth of the fringing reef. Hori (1970) explains this occurrence in terms of thicker coral development in the Mombasa area but Ase (1981) emphasizes the predominance of emergence in the north as opposed to submergence in the Mombasa area. As already stated, terrigenous sedimentation is more important in the north, and this tends to impede coral growth.

The effects of a changing sea level during the Quaternary (Pleistocene to Holocene) have left significant features along the Kenya coast. Raised platforms, beaches, caves, stacks, and nickpoints

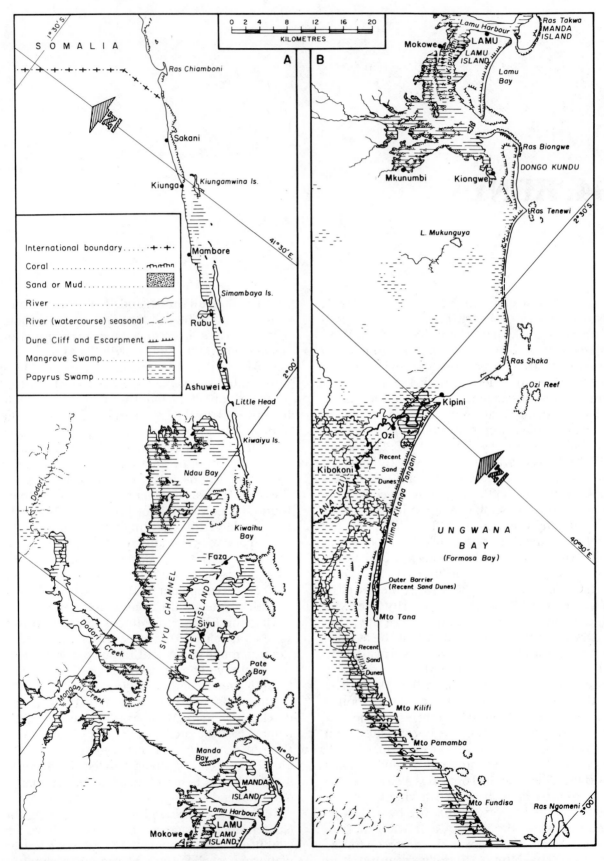

Figure 94-1. Morphology of the north Kenya coast from the Somalia border to Ras Ngomeni.

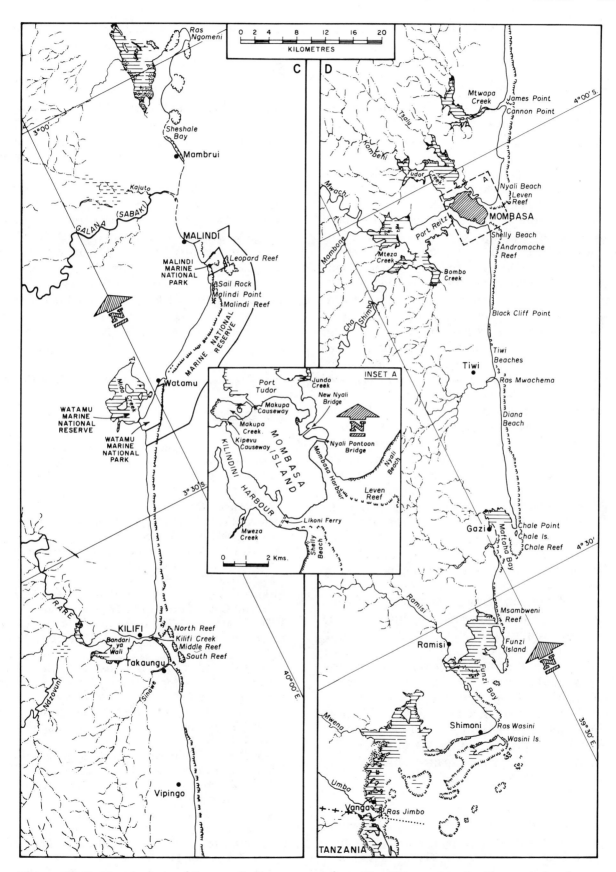

Figure 94-2. Morphology of the south Kenya coast from Ras Ngomeni to the Tanzania border.

are all particularly well preserved along the coastline. Caswell (1953) and Hori (1970) have attempted the most detailed survey of these features. The Changamwe Terrace is at about 45–70 m, Upper Mombasa Terrace about 15–37 m, the Lower Mombasa Terrace at about 10 m, and the Shelly Beach Terrace at about 5 m. All the above features can be seen between Changamwe, Likoni Ferry area, and the Shelly Beach, where some excellent examples of abandoned cliff-lines and former islands can also be seen along the short walk to the Shelly Beach Hotel.

The full sequence of events that brought about these changes clearly started back in Pliocene times when the 107 m nickpoint (the second terrace of Caswell) was formed. The final episode did not come about until the present aggradation and silting had occurred. These most recent events include the drowning of the rivers that flowed through the present Port Reitz and Tudor to form Mombasa Island and the other creeks along the coast. The present mangrove swamps and trees then became established as sea level rose to the present datum. Hori (1970) has given some radiocarbon dates for rock samples from the Nyali, Shelly Beach, and Tiwi areas. The ages of the sample range from 26,500 years B.P. to 2,820 years B.P. These new facts still leave a great deal unexplained about the ages of the features along the Kenya coast. The deepening (incision) of the river valleys to form the present Mombasa and Kilindini harbors obviously created the excellent deep channels that now form the country's most suitable natural harbor. The local geology was also conducive to this development (Ojany 1966, 1973).

The relationships between shore displacement, wave action, fetch, and even the inclination of the shore are important factors in understanding the relative erosion rates and the direction of the general orientation of the coastline. The natural reversal of the monsoon winds has also played a role. In the extreme south, the waves hit the coastline more directly at right angles, and this is responsible for the more extensively developed 36 m marine platform in the Lower Kwale area, which is extensively used to grow sugar cane.

Because of its geographical position, the Kenya coast, like the rest of East Africa's coast, had an early contact with the outside world. The Arabian dhow trade dates back many centuries, while links with southern Europe followed soon after the historic visit of Vasco da Gama. Remains of these early contacts now form part of Kenya's culture. Early Arab settlements at Gedi, Malindi, and Lamu have been recorded by such authors as Kirkman (1966), who has also written the story of Fort Jesus. The general history can be found in Ogot and Kieran (1973). The naturally beautiful coast, warm clear waters, and clean sandy coral beaches have encouraged what is probably the most extensive holiday resort development anywhere along the entire African coast. Here holiday hotels, executive beach bungalows, and beach cottages mingle with tropical coconut and mango trees, just as the small dhows mingle with large ocean liners (Plate 94-1). These developments attract tourists from all over the world. Kenyans have also developed marine national parks and reserves at Watamu and Malindi, and have made Fort Jesus and Gedi into National Monuments. In all, the aim is to develop the natural facilities for economic growth, while clearly maintaining a conservation spirit for posterity.

FRANCIS F. OJANY

REFERENCES

Ase, L. E., 1981, Studies of shores and shoreline displacement on the southern coast of Kenya, *Geog. Annaler* **63:**303–310.

Caswell, P. V., 1953, *Geology of the Mombasa-Kwale Area,* Geological Survey of Kenya, Report 24.

Caswell, P. V., 1956, *Geology of the Kilifi-Mazeras Area,* Geological Survey of Kenya, Report 34.

Hori, N., 1970, Raised coral reefs along the southeastern coast of Kenya, East Africa, *Tokyo Metropolitan Univ. Geog. Repts.* **5:**25–47.

Kirkman, J. S., 1966, *Men and Monuments of the East African Coast,* Lutterworth Press, London.

Miller, J. M., 1952, *The Geology of the Mariakani-Mackinnon Road Area,* Geological Survey of Kenya, Report 20.

Ogot, B. A., and J. E. Kieran, eds., 1973, *Zamani: A Survey of East African History,* East African Publishing House, Longman, London Group.

Ojany, F. F., 1966, The physique of Kenya: a contribution in landscape analysis, *Assoc. Am. Geographers Annals* **56:**183–196.

Ojany, F. F., 1973, *Kenya: a study in physical and human geography,* Longman, London.

Pulfrey, W., 1960, *Shape of the Sub-Miocene Erosion Bevel in Kenya,* Geological Survey of Kenya, Bulletin 3.

Saggerson, E. P., and B. H. Baker, 1965, Post-Jurassic erosion-surfaces in Eastern Kenya and their deformation in relation to rift structures, *Geol. Soc. London Quart. Jour.* **121:**51–72.

Stockley, G. M., 1928, *Report on the Geology of the Zanzibar Protectorate*, published by the government of Zanzibar.

Thompson, A. O., 1956, *The Geology of the Malindi Area*, Geological Survey of Kenya, Report 36.

Williams, L. A. J., 1962, *Geology of the Hadu-Fundi Isa Area, North of Malindi*, Geological Survey of Kenya, Report 52.

Willis, B., 1936, *East African Plateaux and Rift Valleys*, Carnegie Institution of Washington, Washington, D.C.

Plate 94-1. A view of the Shimoni port, extreme south of Kenya, being studied by second-year geography students of the University of Nairobi. Note the typical dhow and the luxuriant mangrove vegetation in the background. Also showing (on the right) are some coconut trees. A typical executive residence (half hidden) is on the right (photo by F. F. Ojany).

95. SOMALIA

The Somali coast is about 3,200 km long, of which 2,100 km face southeast onto the Indian Ocean and 1,100 km face north onto the Gulf of Aden (Fig. 95-1). This is approximately the direct distance from Miami to Boston, thence inland to Detroit. The coast contains few natural harbors, is fronted for much of its length by coral reefs, and is backed throughout by desert or dunes. Coastal access is thus difficult, and our understanding of coastal features remains limited. The coast may be divided into three zones. First, for 1,500 km from Raas Jumbo on the Kenya border (1° 39′ S, 41° 36′ E) to near Gifle (7° 28′ N, 49° 40′E), the generally low coast is backed by massive Quaternary dunes and fronted by coral reefs. Second, from Gifle to Ras Asir (11° 49′ N, 51° 15′ E), the 600 km coast is often steeply cliffed, for example on Ras Hafun (10° 27′ N, 51° 24′ E), Africa's most easterly point. Third, from Ras Asir to the Djibouti border west of Seylac (11° 15′ N, 43°30′ E), the *guban* (sunburnt plain) coast along the Gulf of Aden is partly cliffed, partly backed by alluvial plains, sebkhas, and marine terraces.

The outlines of the Somali coast were defined by Cenozoic tectonism, the details by Quaternary erosion and accretion. In the Lower Tertiary, after prolonged stability extending from Precambrian times, the junction of the present Red Sea, Gulf of Aden, and Ethiopian Rift became the site of intense magmatic and tectonic activity that has continued to the present day (Gass 1970). By the close of Eocene times, vertical uplift had produced the major relief features of the Afro-Arabian dome. Attenuation of the sialic crust across this rising dome caused its trisection by zones of weakness into three crustal segments. Of these, the southeast or Somali segment was bounded to north

and west by crustal flexures and tensional faulting that experienced further movement in the Miocene when the deformation style changed to mainly lateral displacement. Since then, new oceanic crust some 200 km across has formed in the widening Gulf of Aden, while the Somali crustal segment has moved northeast relative to the Nubian segment west of the Ethiopian Rift (Fig. 95-1, left inset). Extensive volcanism accompanied this deformation, including the eruption of peralkali silicic differentiates near the north coast and of low-K tholeiitic basalts in the Gulf of Aden spreading center (whose east-northeast–west-southwest alignment is offset by northeast–southwest transform faults). During Quaternary times, Somalia's north coast experienced variable uplift, as reflected in the *guban*'s marine terraces. Inland, south of the east-northeast–west-southwest fracture zone that extends the Gulf's margins from Ras Khaanziir past Berbera toward the Ethiopian Rift, the north-facing escarpment of the Golis Ranges has been much dissected along fracture zones, exposing Precambrian basement rocks and deformed Mesozoic marine sediments.

Farther south, Somalia is essentially a plateau surface that slopes south and east from the northern mountains and the Ethiopian Rift toward the Indian Ocean. This surface overlies a deep sedimentary basin, the Somali Basin, which originated in late Paleozoic or early Mesozoic times along the rifted margins of Gondwanaland (Beltrandi and Pyre 1973). Marine transgressions followed, and deposition was prevalently carbonate. Late Jurassic uplift and marginal faulting of the Bur basement complex northwest of Mogadishu separated the coastal area from the interior part of this basin (Fig. 95-1, left inset). Carbonate depo-

703

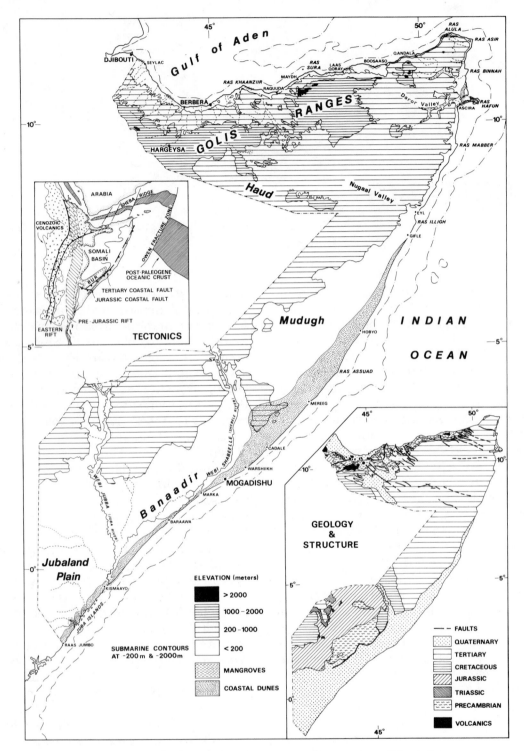

Figure 95-1. Relief, coastal features, geology, and tectonics of Somalia.

sition continued along the coast, accompanied by subsidence governed by northeast–southwest faults bounding the southeast edge of the Bur complex. In early Tertiary times, this coastal fault system was rejuvenated and the coastal basin was segmented into discrete units with differential subsidence and both clastic and carbonate sedimentation. The east coast of Somalia was apparently outlined by these Tertiary faults. The Somali Basin presently descends from above sea level in the Haud and inner Jubaland to more than 7,000 m below sea level at the coast. It is filled with great thicknesses of Mesozoic and Cenozoic sediments that underlie Quaternary sands along the southern and central east coast, and that outcrop in coastal cliffs farther north (Jobstraibizer and Cumarshiire 1977; Perisotto 1978).

The Somali coast is dominated by a reversing monsoon system, which finds expression in surface winds, wave action, ocean currents, and onshore climates. Four seasons are commonly recognized. From late December to March, the *jilaal* season is dominated by the northeast monsoon, and hot dry dusty winds flow parallel with both the north and east coasts at velocities of 15–30 km/hr. From March to May, the transitional *gu* season sees the winds changing direction and bringing rains from the ocean. The long *hagaa* season, beginning in June and continuing through September, is dominated by the southwest monsoon with mean wind speeds often exceeding 40 km/hr (Fig. 95-2). Along the north coast, this is the season of strong, hot, dessicating offshore winds, the so-called *kharif*, which reaches maximum velocity around dawn. The air is filled with blowing sand and dust, and tem-peratures along the Gulf of Aden may reach 50° C. In the south, the cooling winds off the ocean and occasional rains render conditions more pleasant, but northward sand transport is common in the dunes as winds frequently exceed threshold velocities. The *dayr* season in October and November may again bring rains during the lull between the southwest and northeast monsoons.

Although rainy seasons may be recognized in principle, precipitation amounts are everywhere negligible, except in the northern mountains and the extreme southwest. The north coast receives only 50–150 mm/yr of precipitation and is persistently hot and humid, well deserving the name *guban*. The east coast south of Ras Assuad receives as much as 300–500 mm/yr and humidity generally exceeds 70%, but with temperatures ranging from 20° C to 35° C, semiarid conditions prevail. The coast farther north lies between these two climatic extremes but like the *guban* may sometimes be afflicted by flash floods triggered by higher rainfall in the mountains. Generally, however, few streams reach the sea even under flashy ephemeral conditions, and Somalia has only two perennial rivers, the Shebele and Juba

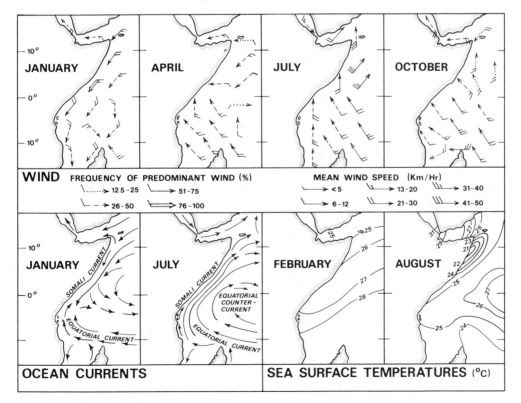

Figure 95-2. Winds, currents, and sea surface temperatures off the Somali coast (based on *Africa Pilot*, 12th ed., 1967).

in the south, which drain from the wetter Ethiopian Highlands. Infrequently, tropical cyclones may penetrate the Gulf of Aden from the Arabian Sea bringing gale-force winds and torrential rains, generally during the changeover seasons between the dominant monsoons. Land and sea breezes are also common when the monsoon flows are weak. Sea breezes add an onshore component to both the northeast and southwest monsoons during the daytime, which tends to explain the orientation of the coastal dunes subparallel with the coast. Mountain/valley winds are found in the north.

Oceanic circulation off Somalia's east coast is dominated by the reversing Somali Current but, because the transitional periods are shorter, these flows do not exactly correspond with the monsoon winds. The southwest Somali Current sets northeast from April to October. It is strongest near the coast, where maximum surface velocities often reach 2–3 m/s and velocities as high as 3.6 m/s (7 knots) have been recorded (*Africa Pilot* 1967). This current weakens away from the coast and becomes indistinct anywhere from 100–225 km offshore. Between latitudes 7° N and 10° N, the main current turns eastward away from the coast to enter the equatorial counter-current or the monsoonal flow across the Arabian Sea (Fig. 95-2). Part of the flow continues north and may round Ras Asir close inshore to enter the Gulf of Aden, which otherwise has a monsoonal flow from west-southwest.

Following a November transition, the northeast Somali Current sets between west-southwest and south-southwest parallel with the coast south of 10° N between December and February. Maximum surface velocities reach 1.5–2.3 m/s. Off the Somali-Kenya border, this current meets the northward extension of the equatorial current, and both turn east into the equatorial counter-current. In March the current again begins to reverse, first in the north, then farther south as the southwest monsoon reasserts itself. The Gulf of Aden circulation sets west–southwest between December and February, consistent with the monsoonal motion up the Gulf.

The combined effects of the southwest monsoon and the southwest Somali Current promote a powerful mass transfer of equatorial waters northward along the east coast for over half the year. Even at other times, the orientation of the coast exposes it to swells generated in the Southern Ocean. Swells and wind-driven seas from the south thus predominate, and such sediment

transport as occurs is mainly toward the northeast. Average wave heights exceed 1.0 m during the southwest monsoon, about 0.5 m at other times. Between Ras Assuad and Ras Hafun, wave heights over 1.5 m occur 20% of the time. Throughout the coast, tides are mixed and spring tides range from 4 m to 6 m. Under present climatic conditions sediment discharge from wadis is minimal, except from the Juba River during occasional floods.

In ecological terms, persistently high air temperatures above 20° C favor mangal vegetation in suitable habitats, while sea surface temperatures over 20° C and low turbidity favor extensive coral growth. Onshore, the coastal vegetation must adapt to intense solar radiation (over 2 Kcal/cm²/yr), high air temperatures, minimal precipitation but high humidities, and average annual potential evapo-transpiration values exceeding 2,500 mm/yr. Of particular note is a zone of cold surface water and low salinity produced by massive upwelling near Ras Hafun during the southwest monsoon in the later *hagaa* season (Fig. 95-2).

For 200 km from Raas Jumbo in the extreme south to the Juba River mouth, the coast is less harsh and more varied than elsewhere in Somalia. Dunes of various ages are covered by modified scrub and open woodland, but their continuity is broken by the valleys of seasonal streams, some of which may reach the sea in long inlets, for example the 20 km long Buur Gaabo. Mangroves are common around such inlets and around the Juba River mouth. *Avicennia marina* is the dominant species but *Rhizophora mucronata, Ceriops tagal,* and *Bruguiera gymnorrhiza* also occur. The once lush mangroves have suffered from centuries of woodcutting, however. Offshore, intermittent coral reefs are found, while the 150 or more Juba Islands and islets appear to represent remnants of raised reef formations.

From the Juba River for 1,300 km to Gifle, the coast is fringed by extensive coral reefs, no rivers reach the coast, natural harbors are lacking, and the principal ports of Baraawa (Brava), Marka (Merca), and Mogadishu (Plate 95-1) have always been difficult to approach. Occasional low headlands are composed of emergent Quaternary reef limestones (a 6–9 m level being locally prominant), eolianites, and beachrock. Otherwise the coast is dominated by paleodunes of various ages, the oldest of which rise to over 200 m above sea level. In places, these dunes can be observed lying on raised coral reefs. Between Warshiikh and

Baraawa, the dunes appear to have deflected the Shebele River away from the coast to flow parallel with the dunes for as much as 400 km toward the Juba River. During the *gu* and *dayr* rains, or following exceptionally heavy rains in the Ethiopian Highlands, the Shebele may actually reach the Juba, but most of the time its waters sink into sands and swamps short of that objective. Fresh foredunes and backshore sands along the immediate coast are colonized by the sprawling beach vine *Ipomoea pes-caprae*, with its 4 m long stolons (Plate 95-2), associated inland with such grasses as *Lepturus repens* and *Sporobolus virginicus*, and occasional *Scaevola taccada* bushes (Pardi 1976). Above the highest tides, thickets of *Canavalia maritima*, *Colubrina asiatica*, and *Cordia somaliensis* occur, with *Cyperus maritimus* in marshy locations. Mangroves occur locally along this coast but are not well developed.

A significant feature of this coast is the extent to which the paleodunes have been destabilized by overgrazing of the covering vegetation by cattle, goats, and camels. Destabilization has been followed by extensive sand movement and by gullying of the more indurated sands on the moister seaward face of the dunes. Around the major settlements, refugees have swelled the local population and tillage has been practiced on the dunes, leading to severe erosion. The reactivation and erosion of the paleodunes over relatively large areas poses the government with an enormous problem (Plates 95-3 and 95-4). Accordingly, since 1973, the Somali government has sought outside assistance, notably from the United Nations, in seeking to arrest erosion and stabilize the dunes (Somali Government, National Range Agency 1977). Much attention has focused on the Marka area, where erosion gullies have been erased by bulldozers and their red sandy sediments sown to vegetation, and where attempts have been made to arrest the migration of the dune front onto the valuable farmlands of the Shebele valley, where some settlements have been buried beneath shifting sand. At the experimental dune reclamation area at Shalaanbood near Marka, both native and introduced plants are being evaluated with respect to their reclamation potential (Plate 95-5). *Opuntia* cactus and *Euphorbia* spp. are being used for initial stabilization, *Commiphora* for shelterbelts, and *Casuarina equisetifolia* for timber. *Prosopis juliflora*, *Acacia ligulata*, *Eucalyptus camolamlusis*, and *Tamarix nilotica* are among other tree species being evaluated for the later stages of dune control (Orme 1982). A promising start to dune reclamation has been made but the root causes of dune destabilization are social and economic rather than physical, and any comprehensive reclamation program must also address these issues.

From Gifle to Ras Asir, the 600 km of coast are much cliffed, as mainly flat-lying or gently deformed Cenozoic carbonate rocks reach the coast (Romagnoli 1966). Ras Illigh is a rocky terraced headland rising 145 m above the sea. From Eyl to Ras Mabber, the bold rocky coast is largely inaccessible, as sea cliffs reach 75–120 m above sea level. On the Hafun peninsula (Plate 95-6), a prominent mass tied to the mainland by a 25 km tombolo, Oligocene marine limestones, including coral limestones, are overlain unconformably by Miocene sandy limestones and compact coral limestones (Furon 1960), forming cliffs up to 203 m high. At Ras Asir, Cenozoic sedimentary rocks form sheer 300 m high cliffs. Between these cliffed sections, the coast exhibits some marine terraces partly blanketed by blown sand and some inlets that favor mangrove development. Two major drainage systems approach the coast from the interior—the Daror and Nugaal valleys—but under present climatic conditions stream flows are localized and erratic, and the valleys have never carried water throughout their lengths in recent times. As in other parts of the Horn of Africa, the size of these valleys and the extensive legacy of fluvial deposits are attributed to past pluvial conditions.

The 1,100 km long *guban*, extending along the north coast from Ras Asir to beyond Seylac, comprises a coastal plain of variable but generally narrow width backed by the dissected Golis escarpment, which reaches 2,408 m on Surud, 60 km south-southwest of Ras Sura. During seasonal rains in these mountains, much sediment may be discharged onto the lowlands in the form of extensive alluvial fans and bajadas. During earlier Quaternary times along this tectonically active coast, successive episodes of alluviation caused fluvial sediments to become interdigitated with marine terrace assemblages. A former coral reef at approximately 8 m is noteworthy along the immediate coast, and the surface of a higher terrace at 18 m is littered with various corals, echinoids, lamellibranchs, and gastropods. Of considerable interest to the Quaternary history of this coast is the occurrence of Pleistocene to Holocene corals in beach deposits 180–280 m above sea level on the Berbera coastal plain (Mason 1962), and of similar materials up to 120 m in the area between Laas Qoray and Boosaaso (Greenwood 1960). Borehole data near Berbera reveal a thick Plio-Pleistocene marine succession, pointing to the relatively late tectonic emergence of this area.

The *guban* is widest in the west, where it is covered by much fluvial debris and veneered by dune sands oriented northeast–southwest with the dominant winds. Farther east, beyond Raguuda, the plain narrows to less than 10 km wide and sometimes disappears as basement rocks and later sedimentary formations reach the coast in bold cliffs. Three specialized ecological habitats characterize the coast: mangrove, coral flat, and sand dune. The mangal vegetation is mostly identical in composition to that noted on the east coast, with *Avicennia marina* dominant, indeed the only species found on Socotra offshore. The low raised reef flats are poorly drained and support sparse perennial herbs such as *Limonium* spp., *Heliotropium* spp., and *Arnebia hispidissima*, together with such ephemeral herbs and grasses as *Tribulus terrestris*, *Zygophyllum simplex*, and *Dipterygium glaucum*. The blown sands near to water sources often support more shrubby vegetation including *Maerua somalensis*, *Maerua sessiliflora*, *Tamarix nilotica*, *Salvadora persica*, and *Indigofera oblongifolius*, together with herbs and grasses such as *Suaeda* spp. and *Durran* spp. (Gilliland 1952). In drier areas, *Panicum turgidum* is a good sand binder.

It is convenient to include here the coastline of Djibouti (formerly French Somaliland), which extends from the Somalia border around the Gulf of Tadjoura to the western shores of the Bab el Mandeb (12° 40′ N) at the southern end of the Red Sea. The nearshore shallows extend westward in the Gulf of Tadjoura, past the port of Djibouti, built partly on a spit formation. This part of the coast is backed by rugged hills of red volcanics. The Gulf then narrows westward between hilly coasts to a strait leading into the almost landlocked Ghoubet Kharab, which occupies a structural depression. North of the Gulf of Tadjoura a hilly coastline with numerous wadi-mouth sand plains declines to a coastal lowland with sandy beaches bordering the Bab el Mandeb, facing across the strait of Aden.

ANTHONY R. ORME

REFERENCES

Beltrandi, M. D., and A. Pyre, 1973, Geological evolution of southwest Somalia, in *Bassins sedimentaires du littoral Africain*, G. Blant, ed., Assoc. des Services Géologiques Africains, Paris.

Furon, R., 1960, *Géologie de l'Afrique*, 2nd ed., Payot, Paris.

Gass, I. G., 1970, Tectonic and magmatic evolution of the Afro-Arabian dome, in *African Magmatism and Tectonics*, T. N. Clifford and I. G. Gass, eds., Oliver & Boyd, Edinburgh.

Gilliland, H. B., 1952, The vegetation of eastern British Somaliland, *Jour. Ecology*, **40:**91–124.

Greenwood, J. E. W., 1960, *The Las Khoreh-Elayu area*, Somaliland Protectorate Geological Survey, Report 3.

African Pilot, 1967, Vol. 3, 12th ed., Hydrographer of the Navy, London.

Jobstraibizer, G., and J. Cumarshiire, 1977, Il Quaternario della Somalia, *Quad. Geologia Somalia* **1:** 51–59.

Mason, J. E., 1962, *The Area North of Hargeisa and Lageruf*, Somali Republic Geological Survey, Report 7.

Orme, A. R., 1982, *Field Observations along the Somali Coast, 1981-82*, Department of Geography, University of California, Los Angeles.

Pardi, L., 1976, Researches on the Somali coast: shore and dune of Sar Uarle, *Monitore Zool. Italiano* **5:** 179–193.

Perissotto, A., 1978, Appunti di geomorfologia della Somalia, *Quad. Geol. Somalia* **2:**45–64.

Somali Government, National Range Agency, 1977, *Experiences of Anti-desertification Campaigns in Somalia*, Mogadishu.

Romagnoli, L., 1966, Appunti de geomorfologia somala: degradazione meteorica della ripa costiera nella Migiurtinia Settentrionale, *Riv. Geografica Italiana* **73:**68–72.

Plate 95-1. Active coral reef and reef flat north of Mogadishu's old harbor breakwater. Use of recreational beach is limited by periodic incursions of man-eating sharks into the lagoon (photo by A. R. Orme).

Plate 95-2. Coastal strand of Marka (Merca), showing pioneer colonization of backshore by *Ipomoea pes-caprae* (photo by A. R. Orme).

Plate 95-3. Destabilized paleodunes with scattered *Acacia* looking southeast toward Baraawa (Brava). Raised reef terraces form flat offshore islets 6–9 m above sea level (photo by government of Somalia).

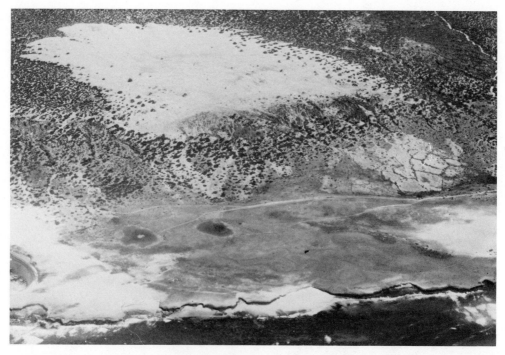

Plate 95-4. Destabilized oxidized paleodunes above raised reef terrace between Mogadishu and Marka. Modern dune sands along the shore contain much white carbonate debris (photo by A. R. Orme).

Plate 95-5. Advanced dune stabilization at Shalaanbood, near Marka, using *Opuntia* cactus in 15 × 15 m plots protected by brushwood fences. The Shebele River valley lies in the right background (photo by A. R. Orme).

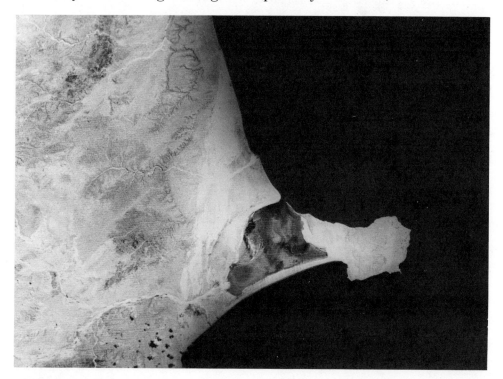

Plate 95-6. Hafun peninsula, northeast Somalia, showing 25 km-long sand tombolo tying the peninsula to the mainland at Ascira. The lagoon north of the tombolo contains mangrove vegetation and productive salt pans. The fluvially dissected peninsula is underlain by gently deformed Oligocene and Miocene marine carbonate formations which reach the sea in cliffs 165–203 m high. Sand dunes, wadi deposits, and marine terraces are observable on the mainland west of the lagoon (photo by NASA).

96. RED SEA COASTS

In the context of plate tectonics, the Red Sea is considered to be an ocean in the making. A mid-oceanic ridge penetrates into the Gulf of Aden, and the rifting is separating Arabia from Africa, so that the two sides of the Red Sea consist of systems of faults running parallel in a southeast–northwest direction. In the north, the Gulf of Aqaba or Elat is the beginning of a second south-southwest–north-northeast rift, which ends near Aleppo, Syria. Ras Muhammad, the southernmost tip of the Sinai Peninsula, thus lies at a triple junction. Lateral displacements have also occurred, especially in the second rift. However, along the coasts of the Red Sea proper and along the Sinai, a coastal plain, the Tehama, is generally present on both sides, between the inner mountains and the shoreline. It consists of alluvial fans, or pediments, not infrequently covered by raised fossil coral reefs. Other large faults, stretching in the same southeast–northwest direction, occur between the coastline and the median, narrow, deepest graben of the sea. Several small depressions at about 2,100 m depth include hot brines, which are thought to come from submarine springs tied to tectonovolcanic activity (Degens and Ross 1969). During the Pleistocene, sea level shifted in the oceans, and its low stages had important consequences in coastal morphology.

The climate is arid and hot. Rainfall amounts to some 50 mm as an average. Rivers are absent, except for occasional wadis. The sea surface temperature in June exceeds 31° C in the south and 27° C in the north; it stands between 24° and 26.5° in January, except in the Gulf of Suez where it can fall to 19°. It is thus warm enough everywhere for coral reefs. Evaporation from the sea surface is 2 m per year, so that a water column of 1.95 m must be supplied yearly from the Indian Ocean through the Bab el Mandeb, in which three currents are superposed in summer and two in winter as a result of water density and seasonal winds. The surface salinity is between 37 %o and more than 40 %o, according to location (Maillard 1972; Neumann and McGill 1961).

CORAL REEFS

Because of its temperature and water transparency (no rivers), the Red Sea is a paradise for coral reefs. Contemporary fringing reefs thrive almost everywhere (Mergner 1971; Loya and Slobodkin 1971). They grow actively in the Gulf of Elat on coarse sedimentary fans forming the Tehama. When wide enough, they are separated from the dry land by a shallow boat channel (e.g., near Jeddah, Saudi Arabia). Sand cays can occur on them in the same area (Guilcher 1955). On their outer side, the percentage of living coral is quite large.

Older fringing reefs point to the same growth during the Pleistocene high sea levels. In Sudan, the fossil corals form an emerged fringe, sometimes several kilometers wide, with colonies in positions of growth and, behind them, detrital material in the former boat channel (Dalongeville and Sanlaville 1981). In the southern part of the Sinai, at Marsa el At, three emerged coral terraces are found, ranging up to 35 m; the oldest one more than 250,000 years old (Guilcher 1979). Because aridity has delayed their destruction by solution, their shape is still fine. On the shores, however, marine corrosion cuts into the limestone overhanging visors (Macfadyen 1931).

Perhaps the most interesting feature of these reefs is their association with tectonism, so typical in this area. The emerged reefs are often extremely faulted. Such is the case at Abulat Island, 200 km south of Jeddah (Fig. 96-1), entirely formed of reefs dissected by numerous very well-preserved fault scarps. Visors, sometimes superposed, exist on shores (Plate 96-1). Entedebir Island (Fig. 96-2) in the Dahlak Archipelago near Massawa, Ethiopia (Nir 1971), also made of subrecent reef limestone, is a part of the Danakil horst, still tectonically active. The parallel scarps dividing the island into stripes, and the adjoining elongated submarine depressions, seem equally to result from recent tectonic movements. The Afar tectonic depression, Ethiopia, emerged but lower than sea level, is surrounded by Pleistocene warped reefs (Lalou et al. 1970).

A type of reef that seems to be almost limited to the Red Sea is the *shab* or ridge reef, well shown on the Farsan Bank off Arabia (Fig. 96-3), and also found off Jeddah and at the southern tip of the Sinai (Guilcher 1979). On the Farsan Bank, the ridge reef consist of narrow submarine north-west–southeast mountains, 600–700 m high, rising very steeply to the surface and bearing living corals. They seem to be horsts running in the Red Sea direction and mantled by corals during a slow subsidence, so that the Farsan Bank is made, over hundreds of kilometers, of alternations of wide stretches of very deep water and of swarms of reefs very dangerous for ships. The same alternations exist off several parts of Eritrea and Sudan and off southeastern Egypt. In southern Sinai, Ras Muhammad consists of emerged coral faulted blocks very similar to the adjoining submerged ridge reef, the former demonstrating the origin of the latter.

Atolls are scarce in the Red Sea, but include, Sanganeb off Port-Sudan (Rathjens and Von Wissman 1933) and Green Reef off Suakin (Guilcher 1955). They are supposed to have grown on subsiding basements. Isolated reefs bearing sand cays as at Marmar (Fig. 96-3) may have the same origin.

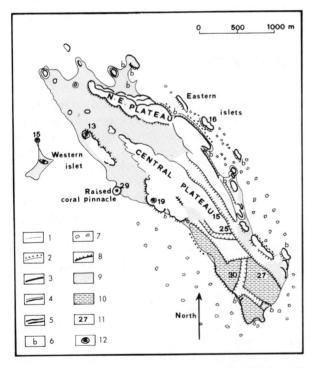

Figure 96-1. Abulat Island, Farsan Bank, Saudi Arabia: a raised coral island: 1. low coast; 2. coast with fallen blocks; 3. overhanging scarp; 4. double overhang; 5. successive overhangs; 6. beachrock; 7. living coral heads; 8. fault scarp; 9. low plain; 10. karstic plateau; 11. altitude in meters; 12. emerged coral knoll.

SHARMS

Sharm (plural: shurum), also known as *marsa*, is a widespread feature (Fig. 96-4 and Plate 96-2). It consists of narrow, deep, long embayments, sometimes meandering, with corals growing on their edges and sediments supplied by wadis at their inner ends. Sharms are valleys cut during the low Pleistocene sea level(s), so that they may be considered as a special kind of rias in a coral arid environment. All stages of filling are found, sometimes with only remnants of the former sharm in the shape of a re-entrant of the fringing reef on the outer coast, as at Shawrat el Manqata, whereas Shab Jubbah is still well open (both on Fig. 96-4). In Sudan (Dalongeville and Sanlaville 1981), where the *marsas* are cut into old fringing reefs, they often display inner widenings behind a narrow entrance, because the Pleistocene valley had been more easily carved into the loose sediments of the former boat channel than into the outer edge of the reef made of coral colonies.

SEBKHAS

Another feature related to the arid climate is the sebkha, or hypersaline pond, which are frequent

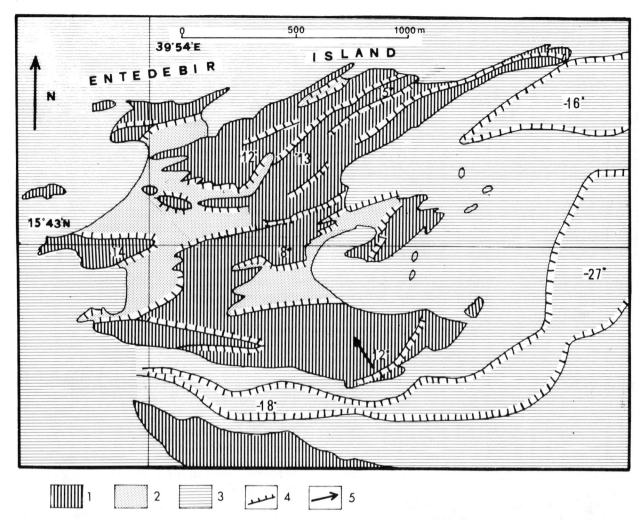

Figure 96-2. Entedebir Island, Dahlak Archipelago, Ethiopia, a raised coral island (from Nir data): 1. plateau; 2. plain; 3. submerged parts; 4. probable fault scarp; 5. plateau slope; altitudes and depths in meters.

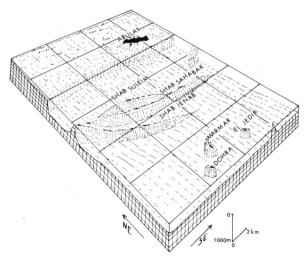

Figure 96-3. Elongated shabs (ride reefs) and coral islands rising abruptly from deep parts of Farsan Bank near Abulat, Saudi Arabia.

just behind the coastline (Fig. 96-4, Shawrat el Manqata). Some are saline because of springs supplying water from the open sea at high tide through fissures in fossil coral, as near Ras Muhammad, Sinai. An even more curious saline pond is the Solar Lake near Elat, 5 m deep, in which the annual cycle results in very high temperatures at the bottom (48–61° C according to month) and in the presence of hydrogen sulphide.

In relation to other coastlines worldwide, the Red Sea shores are among those whose coastal features are most strongly influenced by climate.

ANDRÉ GUILCHER

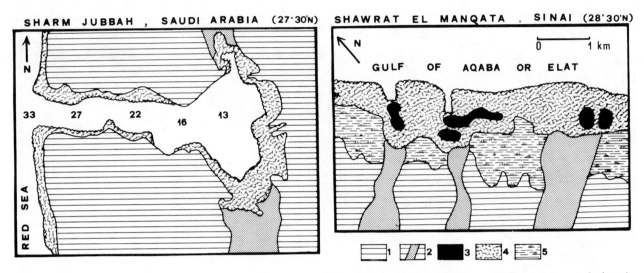

Figure 96-4. Sharms (Shurum) in Saudi Arabia and Sinai Peninsula: 1. Tehama (alluvial coastal plain); 2. wadi; 3. residual pool in drowned valley; 4. Holocene fringing reef; 5. sebkha. Depths in meters. Same scale for both figures.

REFERENCES

Dalongeville, R., and P. Sanlaville, 1981, Les marsas du littoral soudanais de la Mer Rouge, *Soc. Languedoc. Géog. Bull.* **15**(3):39–48.

Degens, E. T., and D. A. Ross, eds., 1969, *Hot Brines and Recent Heavy Metal Deposits in the Red Sea,* Springer, West Berlin.

Guilcher, A., 1955, Géomorphologie de l'extrémité nord du Banc Farsan, Mer Rouge, *Inst. Océanog. Annales* **30**:55–100.

Guilcher, A., 1979, Les rivages coralliens de l'Est et du Sud de la presqu'île du Sinai, *Annales Géographie* **88**:393–418.

Lalou, C., H. V. Nguyen, H. Faure, and L. Moreira, 1970, Datation par la méthode Uranium-Thorium des hauts niveaux de coraux de la dépression de l'Afar (Ethiopie), *Reu Géographie Phys. et Géologie Dynamo* **12**:3–8.

Loya, Y., and L. B. Slobodkin, 1971, The coral reefs of Eilat, *Symp. Zool. Soc. London* **28**:117–139.

Macfadyen, W. A., 1931, The undercutting of coral reef limestone on the coast of some islands in the Red Sea, *Geol. Mag.* **75**:27–34.

Maillard, C., 1972, Etude hydrologique et dynamique de la Mer Rouge en hiver, *Inst. Océanog. Annales* **48**:113–140.

Mergner, H., 1971, Structure, ecology and zonation of Red Sea reefs, *Symp. Zool. Soc. London* **28**:141–161.

Neumann, A. C., and D. A. McGill, 1961, Circulation of the Red Sea in early Summer, *Deep-Sea Res.* **8**:223–235.

Nir, Y., 1971, Geology of Entedebir Island and its recent sediments, Dahlak Archipelago, Southern Red Sea, *Israel Jour. Earth-Sci.* **20**:13–40.

Rathjens, C., and H. Von Wissmann, 1933, Morphologische Problemes im Graben des Roten Meeres, *Pet. Mitt.* **79**:113–117, 183–187.

Plate 96-1. Abulat Island, Farsan Bank. Fossil coral in foreground, jagged by corrosion. In background, raised coral knoll, 29 m high (see Fig. 96-1), with basal visor (photo by A. Guilcher).

Plate 96-2. Sharm Murakh, Sinai Peninsula, in process of filling at its inner end (foreground) (photo by A. Guilcher).

97. SOUTHERN ARABIA

The coastal landforms of southern Arabia have received very little attention from geomorphologists; the following account is based on the author's field work near Aden and Muscat, supplemented by map studies (notably the U.S. Geological Survey map of the Arabian Peninsula, 1-270A, 1963, at 1:2 million) and information from Pilot Handbooks 63 and 64 published by the Hydrographer of the British Navy.

The coastline of southern Arabia, from Cape Bab-al-Mandab near Aden in the west to Ras al Hadd, then northwest past Muscat to the Musandam Peninsula is about 3300 km long (Fig. 97-1). It receives Indian Ocean swell arriving from a southerly direction, accompanied in summer by waves generated by southeasterly trade winds. It is a hot and arid coast (mean annual rainfall at Aden, 38 mm; at Salalah, 112 mm; at Masirah Island, 38 mm; at Muscat, 100 mm) backed by desert landscapes with at best a sparse, shrubby vegetation. However, monsoonal rains in the Yemen uplands produce a number of streams draining wadis and flowing into deltaic fans on sectors of coastal plain in the southwest, and the Samham Hills in southwestern Oman also receive sufficient monsoonal rainfall to sustain a relatively rich vegetation. Tide ranges are moderate, generally between 2 and 4 m. Coral reefs occur intermittently along this coastline.

At the western end of the coastline of the People's Democratic Republic of Yemen are several islands and promontories of denuded volcanic rock (the Aden Volcanics, of Late Cenozoic age), including Perim Island at the entrance to the Red Sea and the tombolos of the Aden district. Aden stands on the rim of a dissected and partly submerged extinct volcano, the coastal cliffs being cut into lavas, agglomerates, and ash, with basalt dykes prominent. Long sandy beaches are backed by dunes on a coastal plain up to 20 km wide, behind which slopes rise to an interior plateau. Raised beaches and emerged coral reefs, horizontal or slightly tilted, occur at intervals along the Gulf of Aden coast (Beydoun 1960). Some wadi fans end in lobate deltas, as at Abyan (Wadi Bana outwash) and Wadi Ahwar, and occasional flooding after heavy rains in the uplands delivers sandy sediment to beaches. Longshore drifting to the west has built the spit that shelters the bay lagoon at Khawr am Umayrah, west of Aden, in which broad tidal mud flats are exposed at low tide.

At Shuqra the coastal plain is narrow in front of the volcanic Khaur Mountains, and it carries a string of small volcanic cones. Ras al Ratl is a high, round volcanic promontory, and Karif Shawrab has a brackish, mangrove-fringed crater lake. To the east, upland spurs reaching the coast end in high cliffs of Tertiary limestone, as at Ras al Mukalla, and there are more coastal lava flows and volcanic cones between Shihr and Sayhut. Locally the black lava has flowed down wadis incised into white limestone to outcrop in cliffs. The largest river valley in southern Arabia, the Wadi Masilah, draining from the Hadhramaut Trough, crosses the coastal plain here, but there is no protruding delta. Mangroves occur in swampy sectors, but surf-washed beaches of white sand and occasional gravel line the coast, which becomes cliffed at Sayhut. Dune sands dominate coastal plains east of here, until the coastline changes orientation at rocky Ras Fartak, where a steep sector with vertical cliffs up to 580 m high

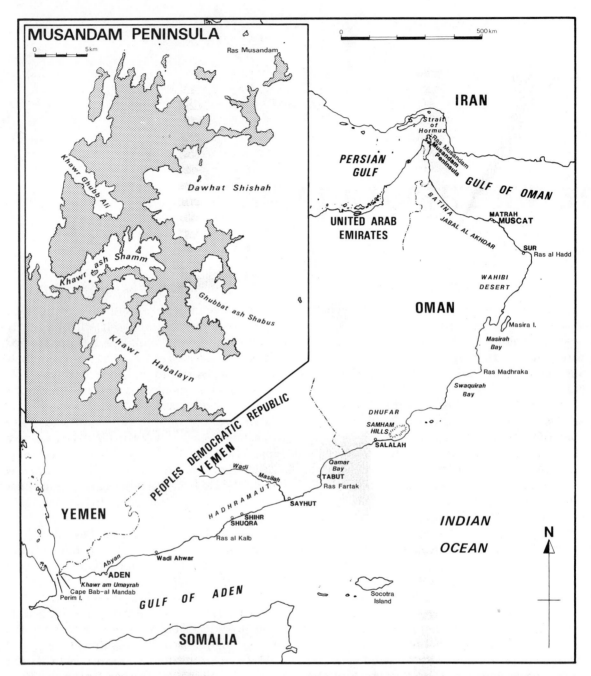

Figure 97-1. The coastline of southern Arabia. Inset: the outline of the Musandam Peninsula, with rias formed by submergence of wadis. Khawr Ash Shamm is also known as Elphinstone Inlet, and Khawr Habalayn as Malcolm Inlet.

truncates the east–west structures of the Mahrah Highlands south of Tabut on the shores of Qamar Bay.

Behind Qamar Bay the coastal plain widens again, consisting of convergent braided wadi outwash fans with dunes along the seaward margin, but it narrows across the Oman border toward the small fishing port of Salalah. About 450 km to the south, Socotra is a barren high island of limestone and granite, 112 km long and 18 km wide, with generally steep coasts and reef-fringed promontories. Valleys in which streams flow during the rainy northeast winter monsoon open to small plains behind sandy beaches on the north coast; on the south coast is the more extensive dune-covered Plain of Naukad. Near the western point, Ras Shoab, is a small tidal lagoon with mangroves behind a sand barrier; mangroves also occupy intertidal shoals in some north coast bays.

The Oman coast (Lees 1928; Tschopp 1967) is very dry, with hilly topography in the Dhufar hinterland. There is a sequence of large bays with sandy beaches washed by ocean swell separated by steep rocky promontories. Precambrian metamorphic rocks form the lowland fronting the Samham Hills, which are bordered by deep sea close inshore, but eastward the continental shelf widens past Swaquirah Bay and Masirah Island toward Ras al Hadd. The rugged Kuria Muria Islands offshore consist of granite and volcanic conglomerate, with occasional gravel beaches interrupting a rocky coastline. Behind Swaquirah Bay the coastal plain widens and coral reefs surround the shore. Ras Madhraka is a promontory of metamorphic rock, and Paleozoic and Precambrian basement outcrops along the western side of Masirah Bay, where again there are coral reefs. The sand ridges of the Wahibi Desert run north–south and reach the coast in the lee of Masirah Island, where shoals and reefs reduce wave action so that the Hikman Peninsula has a broad sabkha fringe, flat sandy terrain inundated occasionally by the sea. Masirah Island, parallel to the coastline, consists of igneous and metamorphic rocks and has generally steep coasts bordering rugged uplands: here, as elsewhere in southern Arabia, these rocks weather to jagged crests and rubbly slopes, in contrast with the more tabular or scarped limestone topography. Northeastward, surf sand beaches line the coast as far as the low sandy promontory of Ras al Hadd, where the coastline swings northwestward alongside the Gulf of Oman.

Just west of Ras al Hadd are low limestone cliffs, interrupted by small tidal inlets, and by a larger sherm (Wadi Falaij) at Sur. Between Sur and Muscat the coastal slopes show terraces marking emerged coastlines at various levels, up to 250 m above sea level at the mouth of Wadi Ali. In the hinterland the ranges of the Oman Mountains (Jabal Al Akhdar) attain more than 3000 m. The coastline runs parallel to the strike of igneous and metamorphic rocks, flanked by

dipping Cretaceous limestones, which form these highlands, their seaward slopes incised by many wadis that open to a narrow coastal plain.

Muscat is sited on a cliffed sector cut in weathered serpentine. Coastal roads, protected by banks of concrete tetrapoda, have been built along the shore (Plate 97-1). To the west, past the oil terminals of Matrah, the Batina coastal plain develops, widening to 16 km. A fertile lowland with acacia trees, date palms, and irrigated plots around spring-fed oases, it is bordered by sandy beaches, locally becoming spits that enclose minor lagoons and salt marshes. Northward, the foothills approach the coast, and there are marine terraces, including emerged coral reefs, about 10 and 28 m above sea level.

Narrowing toward the Strait of Hormuz, the ridges of Jurassic and Cretaceous limestone culminate in the highly indented Musandam Peninsula (Fig. 97-1, inset), an area of gently folded and much-faulted limestone with steep, cliffed coasts bordering branching rias formed by the marine submergence of wadis. There are no raised beaches here, and it is thought that submergence by the Holocene marine transgression was augmented by down-warping of the land (Vita-Finzi 1973). Cliffs are being undercut by the sea, especially where shales outcrop beneath the limestone. Rockfalls and landslides are common. Many of the inlets have sand or pebble beaches at the mouths of wadis, where cemented gravel deposits also form low coastal benches. Locally there are coral reefs. Out beyond Ras Musandam there are towering limestone stacks, the Quoin Islands.

ERIC C. F. BIRD

REFERENCES

Beydoun, Z. R., 1960, Synopsis of the geology of East Aden Protectorate, *21st Internat. Geol. Congress*, vol. 21, T. Sorgenfrei, ed., Berlingske bogtr, Copenhagen, pp. 131–149.

Lees, G. M., 1928, The physical geography of southeastern Arabia, *Geog. Jour.* **71**:441–470.

Tschopp, R. H., 1967, The general geology of Oman, *7th World Petroleum Congress Proc.*, vol. 2, Elsevier, Amsterdam, pp. 231–241.

Vita-Finzi, C., 1973, The Musandam expedition, *Geog. Jour.* **139**:414–421.

Plate 97-1. Artificial coast formed by road construction near Muscat, Oman (photo courtesy of Embassy of the Sultanate of Oman).

98. UNITED ARAB EMIRATES

The coastline of the United Arab Emirates (UAE, Trucial States), on the southeastern shore of the Arabian Gulf, extends from the base of the Qatar Peninsula to Oman, near the Masandum Peninsula. Before the coastal morphology and processes of this coastline are discussed in detail, oceanographic variables and sediment supply will be described.

Water flows into the Persian Gulf through the Strait of Hormuz, along the northern shore, and out along the southern shore, resulting in eastward flow off the Trucial coast. This flow is affected by tidal currents, which flood westward and northwestward and ebb in the opposite direction, and by wind-induced waves. Spring tide ranges are approximately 1.5 m at the Qatar Peninsula, decreasing to 0.9 m at Dubai, and increasing to 1.8 m at the Masandam Peninsula. The most frequent winds (shamal) are from the northwest; during midsummer these blow almost constantly, whereas in winter they are generally more violent but, of shorter duration. Calm or slight seas (<0.9 m) occur more than 75% of the time in the Arabian Gulf, and rough, high seas (>1.5 m) 5–6% of the time, usually in fall and winter. Salinities of the gulf surface waters are very high because of excessive evaporation (Defense Mapping Agency 1975) and virtual lack of rainfall. In Abu Dhabi, for example, evaporation rates average 25 mm/day, with a maximum of 55 mm/day, and rainfall averages <40mm/yr (Schneider 1975). Salinities vary throughout the year, according to evaporation rate and current strength; minimum salinities occur in August, averaging 39.0–39.5 ‰ (Defense Mapping Agency 1975), but in protected bays and lagoons (e.g., the inner lagoon of Abu Dhabi) salinities can be over 60 ‰ (Schneider 1975).

Virtually no terrigenous sediment is supplied to the Trucial Coast from the Arabian land mass (Purser and Evans 1973; Sugden 1963). The principal component of shallow sediments here is calcium carbonate precipitated from seawater; all sediments, especially sands, contain quantities of skeletal detritus. In addition, approximately one-third of Arabian Gulf sediments may have been deposited as windblown sand and dust (Sugden 1963). The distribution and reworking of Trucial coastal sediment is mainly controlled by waves and surface currents, which are modified by (1) shoreline orientation, (2) the Qatar Peninsula, a lateral windward barrier, and (3) the Great Pearl Bank, an offshore barrier (Purser and Evans 1973).

The western and central regions of the UAE coast (Fig. 98-1) are dominated, to a greater or lesser extent, by the presence of sebkha (Plate 98-1). Sebkha extend from just east of the Qatar Peninsula to Ras Ghanada, for a total length of almost 320 km and a maximum width of almost 32 km. Everywhere, they are bordered on the landward side by low bluffs of Tertiary and Quaternary rocks (Evans, Kendall, and Skipwith 1964). Sebkhas are low coastal flats that stand just above normal high tide and are submerged at the highest tides and during surges. They are composed of unconsolidated carbonate sediment with minor amounts of quartz and other minerals, and are the site of deposition of various evaporitic minerals. A series of low linear ridges runs parallel to shore, through the sebkha, especially along the western Trucial coast. These old beach ridges decrease in height inland; like the present seaward ridge, they are comprised of gastropod shell concentrates. In the central region (Fig. 98-1) these well-developed ridges are replaced by old

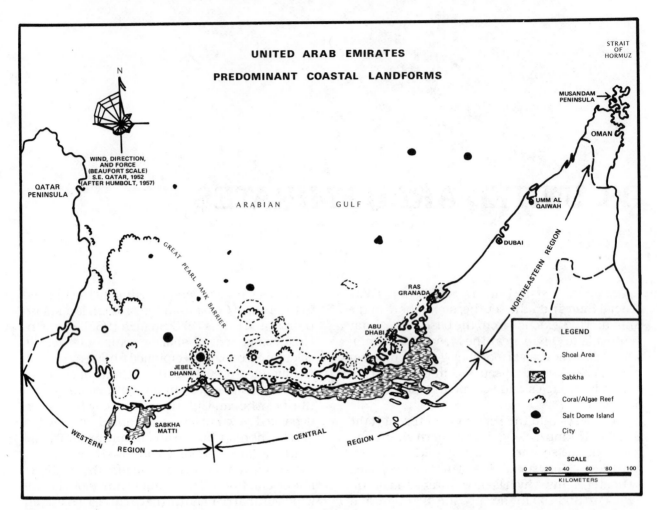

Figure 98-1. Map of the United Arab Emirate coastline, showing predominant coastal and nearshore landforms, city locations, wind direction and force, and the coastal zone subdivisions (western, central, and northeastern) described in the text.

strandlines and drainage channels (Evans, Kendall, and Skipwith 1964).

The internal structure of sebkhas in the vicinity of Abu Dhabi city consists of a basement of Miocene and Pliocene carbonate rocks, overlain by 4–5 m of coastal sediments, typically consisting of eolian, cross-bedded quartzose carbonate sands and fossiliferous carbonate muds, interbedded with sediment lenses, up to 3 m thick, (Gilbert Associates 1980).

Sebkha development in the central region (Fig. 98-1) began more than 7,000 years ago, when late Pleistocene and Holocene sediments along this coastline were dominated by eolian sand deposition; subsequently, a brief transgression by gulf waters led to marine carbonate sedimentation. Approximately 4,000 years ago, gulf waters reached their maximum height, 0.5 m above present sea level (Gilbert Associates 1980). From 4,000 B.P. to 1,000 B.P. a fall in sea level created an intertidal/supratidal environment. This sea-level change may have been mostly apparent, resulting from reduced tidal range and wave heights at the shore due to the growth of offshore islands and reefs (Evans, Schmidt, Bush and Nelson 1969). Finally, during the past 1,000 years, gulf waters have regressed, and seaward deposition of carbonate muds and sands has occurred in lagoons and intertidal/supratidal environments (Gilbert Associates 1980).

The seaward growth of the sebkhas, along the western and central regions of the UAE coast has been intermittent; various growth stages are marked by the beach ridges or old strandlines (Holm 1960) described previously. Outer growth results from material deposited on the intertidal flat from lagoonal sources, the growth of calcareous organisms, and windblown dust from inland and offshore islands. Beach ridges may form as outgrowths from low headlands and knolls of older rocks, with subsequent infilling of landward bays (Plate 98-2) (Evans, Kendall, and Skipwith 1964). If so, in this respect the sebkha plain resembles the chenier plain of Louisiana (Gould and McFarlan 1959) and strandplains in other parts of the world (Price 1955; Curray and Moore 1964). However, sebkhas are composed dominantly of calcareous sediment and are also sites of formation of several evaporitic minerals. Alternatively, beach ridges may develop as a result of storms. According to this theory, in the central region (Fig. 98-1) sebkhas develop without ridges, because of coastal protection by offshore islands (Evans, Kendall, and Skipwith 1964).

Sebkhas can be classified as arenaceous or argillaceous. Those formed today are generally arenaceous, caused by eolian sand filling an embayment and being reworked by waves and currents. Their surfaces are flat and smooth, with gradients less than 0.5 m/km. Because water rises through pore space in the sand, coats the grains, and increases lubrication, these sebkhas develop into soft quicksand with low bearing strength. Argillaceous sebkhas, also numerous along the Trucial coast, were formed from the manufacture of calcareous mud by algae or other organisms in shallow coastal embayments. This wet, soft, and sticky mud has a very low bearing strength, and flows under pressure. Eolian sand blown across the surface sticks to this mud, forming a layer up to 1 m thick; when not covered by sand, the mud dries and hardens in the summer heat (Holm 1960).

Coastal morphology and processes of the UAE coast can be discussed in greater detail by dividing the area into western, central, and northeastern regions (Fig. 98-1). The western Trucial coast (from the base of the Qatar Peninsula to Jebel Dhanna) is a wide northward-facing embayment, protected from the full force of waves and currents by the Qatar Peninsula. The Great Pearl Bank, located to the northeast, exerts little influence in this area. The western subprovince of the western region is made up of a series of north–south oriented rocky peninsulas separated by large embayments; these are probably delimited by fractures related to the "Arabian" tectonic system (Kassler 1973). The peninsulas support many fringing reefs, despite high salinities (45–50 ‰). The embayments are approximately 5 m deep,

and their shores are backed by wide intertidal flats and narrow beaches (Purser and Evans 1973). These beach faces (often well developed on more exposed coasts) are usually covered with thick deposits of wood, and the beach ridges (as well as those of the eastern subprovince of this region) are often capped by dunes and some vegetation (Evans, Kendall, and Skipwith 1964). Landward of these shores are sebkhas, up to 3 km wide. The morphology of this subprovince suggests seaward or oblique longshore transport in this area (Purser and Evans 1973).

The eastern subprovince of the western region is an open embayment, backed to the landward side by the Sebkha Matti. Landward of this is a high (1–3 m) storm beach, extending 55 km west to Jebel Baraka. This ridge is composed of molluscan shell sand and gravel except at the extreme west (where it consists of oolitic sands, formed on adjacent tidal flats) and the extreme east (where it consists of red algal debris derived from adjacent fringing reefs). In this subprovince, the storm beach is prograding mainly seaward to form a sheet of carbonate sands (Purser and Evans 1973).

The central Trucial coast (from Jebel Dhanna to Ras Ghanada) is strongly influenced by the Great Pearl Bank barrier system. This system is oriented obliquely to the coast, parallel to the structural axis of the Arabian Gulf, and is part of the late Tertiary "Iranian" tectonic system (Kassler 1973). It begins approximately 50 km offshore from Jebel Dhanna, at a depth of 5–10 m, angles toward shore and becomes shallower eastward, producing a broad ridge surmounted by a series of carbonate sand shoals and small islands, increasing in size and number. As a result, energy conditions on the barriers increase eastward and those onshore decrease, because of the protection afforded the coast by these islands (Purser and Evans 1973).

The barrier islands of the central region show gradational changes in form and growth mode along the coast. The westward islands develop sediment tails toward shore, perpendicular to the barrier axis, occasionally resulting in tombolos. To the east, this deposition is accompanied by spit accretion at both ends of the islands, parallel to shore (Plate 98-3). Farther east, tail accretion is insignificant and spit accretion is eastward only. This shift reflects the increasing degree of eastward longshore transport due to the increasing fetch across the Gulf (Purser and Evans 1973; Schneider 1975).

The lagoon between these reefs or islands and the coast is 140 km wide and 40 m deep at its western end and becomes narrower, shallower, and increasingly dissected eastward because of the orientation and shallowing eastward of the Great Pearl Bank barrier system. Salinities increase eastward, from 40 ‰ to 60 ‰ (Purser and Evans 1973).

Coastal sediment of the central region is determined mainly by the nature of the adjacent lagoon and barriers. In the west, the lagoon is fairly wide and the barrier offers little protection, creating a shoreline of skeletal sands with fringing reefs. As the lagoon becomes shallower and narrower eastward, protection by the barrier increases and the reefs disappear; shoreline coral debris grades into pelletal and compound-grain carbonate sands. Eastward of this area are wide intertidal flats composed of pelletal sands with abundant gastropods and well-developed blue-green algal mats. The coastline is fringed with small beach ridges of gastropod sand and gravel, or small mangrove swamps. Supratidal sediments landward of these coasts contain dolomite and other evaporite minerals. In the extreme northeast, highly protected lagoons have been completely filled by the accretionary processes previously described, and coastal dunes have migrated landward across the sebkha (Purser and Evans 1973).

Finally, the northeastern region of the Trucial Coast (Ras Ghanada to the Masandam Peninsula) is generally linear, consisting of storm beaches backed by coastal dunes of skeletal carbonate sands. In the extreme northeast, a series of subparallel carbonate sand spits project 5–10 km seaward, curving around to the northeast. These spits enclose lagoons dominated by carbonate muds and are dissected by channels with associated ebb-tidal deltas; the resultant barriers extend laterally near Umm al Qaiwah for more than 15 km (Purser and Evans 1973). The coastline of this region faces obliquely into the west-northwest shamal winds, with associated waves and surface currents. Because of the coastline exposure, long fetch, lack of protective barriers, and steepness of the nearshore slope, this is an area of maximal water agitation and effective longshore transport (Purser and Evans 1973).

KATHLEEN S. DREW

REFERENCES

Curray, J. R., and D. G. Moore, 1964, Holocene regressive littoral sands, Costa de Nayarit, Mexico, in *Developments in Sedimentology*, L. M. J. U. Van Straaten, ed., vol. 1, Elsevier, New York, pp. 76–82.

Defense Mapping Agency, Hydrographic Center, 1975, *Sailing Directions for the Persian Gulf*, rev. ed., Publication 62, Washington, D.C.

Evans, G., C. G. St. C. Kendall, and P. Skipwith, 1964, Origin of the coastal flats, the sabkha, of the Trucial Coast, Persian Gulf, *Nature* **202:**759–761.

Evans, G., V. Schmidt, P. Bush, and H. Nelson, 1969, Stratigraphy and geologic history of the sabkha, Abu Dhabi, Persian Gulf, *Sedimentology* **12:**145–159.

Gilbert Associates, Inc., 1980, *Prefeasibility Study—Freshwater Upwellings, Arabian Gulf: Abu Dhabi, United Arab Emirates*, GAI Report No. 2103, Reading, Pa.

Gould, H. R., and E. McFarlan, 1959, Geologic history of the chenier plain, southwestern Louisiana, *Gulf Coast Assoc. Geol. Soc. Trans.* **9:**261–270.

Holm, D. A., 1960, Desert morphology in the Arabian Peninsula, *Science* **132:**1369.

Kassler, P., 1973, The structural and geomorphic evolution of the Persian Gulf, in *The Persian Gulf*, B. H. Purser, ed., pp. 11–32.

Price, W. A., 1955, *Environment and Formation of the Chenier Plain*, Texas A & M Res. Found. Project 63, Ref. 54-64T.

Purser, B. H., and G. Evans, 1973, Regional sedimentation along the Trucial Coast, SE Persian Gulf, in *The Persian Gulf*, B. H. Purser, ed., pp. 211–231.

Schneider, J. F., 1975, Recent tidal deposits, Abu Dhabi, UAE, Arabian Gulf, in *Tidal Deposits*, R. N. Ginsberg, ed., pp. 209–214.

Sugden, W., 1963, Some aspects of sedimentation in the Persian Gulf, *Jour. Sed. Petrology* **33:**355–364.

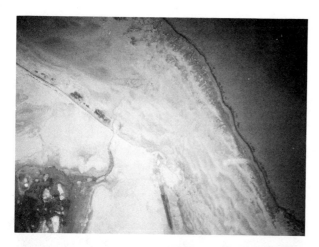

Plate 98-1. Sebkha flat and shoreline, 9.6 km east of Jebel Dhanna (photo by Aero-Marine Surveys, Inc.).

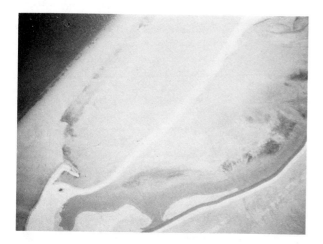

Plate 98-2. Aerial photograph of the Jebel Dhanna region, showing eastward growth of a shore-parallel spit. Growth of these spits, with subsequent filling of lagoons, is one mode of sebkha formation (photo by Aero-Marine Surveys, Inc.).

Plate 98-3. The shore, and southwestern side of an island, 24 km west of Abu Dhabi. The balance between northeastward and southwestward long-shore transport results in spit accretion on both sides of the island along with tombolo formation (photo by Aero-Marine Surveys, Inc.).

[*Author's Note:* I have credited these photos to Aero-Marine Surveys, an aerial photography subcontractor, who did the work for Gilbert Associates, who, in turn, was working for the Water and Electricity Department of Abu Dhabi.]

99. ARABIAN GULF COASTS

The Arabian Gulf shows a remarkable unity despite the contrasts between the Arabian and Iranian coastlines (Fig. 99-1). Extending for almost 1,000 km, with a width of 200–300 km, the gulf is shallow (Seibold and Vollbrecht 1969), with a mean depth of 35 m and local depths rarely more than 80 m. It occupies a zone that is presently dry and hot. Rainfall, coming in winter, is less than 100 mm on the Arabian coast (76 mm at Bahrain) and slightly more on the Iranian coast, with a maximum of 230 mm at Bushire. Minimum temperatures can be quite low in the north (an absolute minimum of $-5°$ C at Abadan), but summers are torrid, with maxima on the order of 50° C, except at Bahrain. The only notable inflow of fresh water is from the Shatt el Arab (Tigris, Euphrates, and Karun). Thus the gulf water is warm and saline; surface water temperature attains 32° C in August (22° to 24° in winter in the south but only 15° to 17° in the north), and salinity is around 40‰, rising to about 70‰ in certain lagoons.

The Arabian Sea has a semidiurnal tide of mean range 2 m, attaining 3 m at the head of the gulf entering the Shatt el Arab toward Basra. Winds are frequent, notably the Shamal from the north to northwest, associated in winter with depressions and in summer with dust- or sandstorms. Extensive intertidal flats are exposed at low tide, while during storms, despite a moderate fetch, seawater is driven far into low-lying coastal areas, where it evaporates to deposit salts. Currents circulate anticlockwise, along the Iranian coast and around down the Arabian coast. Gulf waters support plant and animal life, but species are few. In the southern half of the Gulf the water remains sufficiently warm in winter to permit the growth of coral reefs.

Situated as an extension of Mesopotamia, the gulf is seen as a tectonic basin of Plio-Pleistocene age (Kassler 1973) at the contact of two contrasted structural domains. The Iranian coast is bordered by strongly folded limestones, marls, and evaporites of Jurassic to Miocene age with a northwest–southeast trend produced by Pliocene earth movements. Numerous salt domes are seen (Geological Survey of Iran 1973), producing islands and shoals in the gulf (e.g., Tumb, Abu Musa), and frequent earthquakes indicate that the region is tectonically active. The Arabian coast is low-lying, with only a slight relief corresponding with broad gentle anticlines that trend north–south or northeast–southwest, but the coastline is partially controlled by tectonics (Hasa, Qatar, United Arab Emirates). There is thus a contrast between the steeper east coast of the gulf and the low-lying west coast, but forms produced by sandy clay deposition occur throughout.

Supplies of fluvial sediment are very limited outside the Shatt el Arab and some minor Iranian streams, which are sometimes very active (Purser and Seibold 1973), but the sea is reworking Holocene sediments, especially deposits delivered by eolian action. However, modern sediments are largely more than 50% carbonate, except on the Iranian coast (Seibold et al. 1973). Oolitic sediments are forming, in both exposed and sheltered environments, and are particularly abundant in the southern part of the gulf (Loreau and Purser 1973).

Since the maximum of the Holocene transgression, which may be dated here at about 6,000 years B.P. (Doornkamp et al. 1980), and which may have risen slightly above the present sea level, the coasts of the Arabian Gulf have been

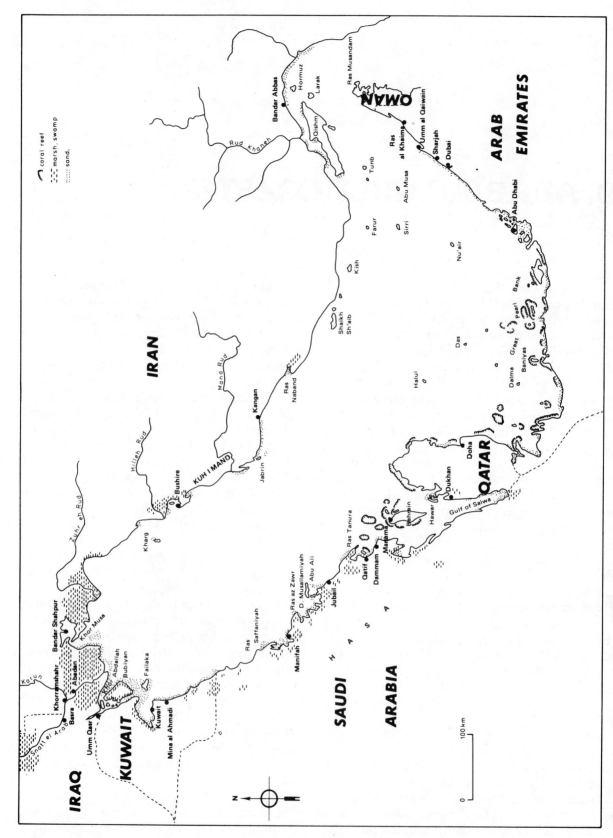

Figure 99-1. Coastal geomorphology of the Arabian Gulf.

subject to deposition and gradual smoothing. Everywhere, but especially between Bahrain and Arabia (Plate 99-1) and on the United Arab Emirates coast, waves and currents have deposited sediments in long barrier spits separated by inlets. Islands or shoals due to salt domes or reef building are trailed by spits gradually built up above sea level (Purser 1973), while along the coast sedimentation has led to the gradual development of sebkhas, at first subject to periodic marine submergence, then progressively drying out (Shinn 1973). Otherwise, Holocene and perhaps even modern deposits can have been partially cemented into beachrock by precipitation of aragonite in the intertidal zone (Evamy 1973; Shinn 1969; Taylor and Illing 1969).

The extreme north of the gulf corresponds with the combined delta of the Euphrates, Tigris, and Karun, of which the Shatt el Arab is the principal channel, invaded by marine tides. Alluvial deposition from these rivers was particularly important in certain phases of the Pleistocene, and has been more or less compensated by subsidence (Lees and Falcon 1952). At present the coast is relatively stable, but consists of an assemblage of marshes, barriers, lagoons, spits, and islands (such as the large island of Bubiyan and also Failaka) due to reworking of fine fluvial sediments by waves and currents, but some large inlets have persisted (Umm Qasr and Bandar Shahpur).

Next comes the large bay of Kuwait, the northern coast of which retains many Pleistocene emerged shorelines (Al-Asfour 1978). Beyond Kuwait the coast is low and rectilinear, with rocky promontories of slightly cemented calcareous oolite, prolonged by sandy spits extending beneath the sea. South of Saffaniyah the bays become deeper, and the coastal configuration reflects Neogene outcrops that form capes, while the embayments (called *dawhat)* have complex outlines, notably Dawhat Musallamiyah, south of the Ras az Zawr, as well as the large arcuate island of Abu Ali. The sandy point of Ras Tanura extends south-southeast for about 10 km.

The Dammam Peninsula is related to an Eocene anticline, as is Bahrain Island, rising to 122 m at Jabal Dukhan. Between Bahrain and Arabia the gulf is shallow, with extensive submerged sandy spits and bars separated by long channels, while the Bahrain archipelago is surrounded by extensive tidal flats, partly coralline, which are almost completely exposed at low tide.

The Qatar peninsula is cut in Tertiary formations dominated by limestones. In the north the coast is rocky and cliffed, with raised shorelines

of last interglacial age, while in the south progradation is dominant, forming extensive lagoons or sebkhas.

The coast of the United Arab Emirates is very complex (see the more detailed account by Kathleen Drew in *United Arab Emirates*). In the western part the Great Pearl Bank is formed by islands and shoals, often coralline, lying obliquely to the shore, behind which there is rapid sedimentation of fine sands, often shelly. In the center, the sector of Abu Dhabi, islands are being attached to the coast (Purser and Evans 1973), with extensive marshes or sebkhas undergoing rapid sedimentation. Beyond, the coast runs southwest–northeast and is much straighter, smoothing having left only complex inlets such as that of Umm al Qaiwain (Plate 99-2) or the large ria on which the town of Dubai is sited. The limestone mountains of Oman extend to the peninsula of Musandam as a rocky coast, eroded into high cliffs.

The Iranian coastline is at first low and flat, and very marshy, with the Khor Musa thrusting into the hinterland to Bandar Shahpur; farther on is the large delta of the Zuhr eh Rud, with extensive areas of soft clay where the tide range is large (up to 4 m). Clay flats and marshy plains are found around Bushire because of the outflow from the river Hilleh, with a large bay that is filling in, but the island of Kharg, rising to 83 m, is bordered by cliffs. A narrow sandy plain borders the Kuh i Mand, a ridge parallel to the coastline but interrupted by the valley of the Mand, which has built a large delta of irregular outline.

South of Kangan the coastal plain becomes narrow, dominated by high scarped mountains, except where bays correspond with subsidence basins or synclinal areas (Naband Bay). The islands are often high: 37 m on Shuaib and Kish, 42 m on the little islet of Tumb, higher still on Larak and Hormuz, because of salt domes, or on the island of Qishm, the largest in the gulf, culminating at almost 400 m. Opposite Ras Musandam, at the entrance to the Gulf of Oman, the Iranian coast includes the large embayment of Bandar Abbas, into which flow numerous wadis, which produce muddy shores, with long discontinuous spits parallel to the coastline, enclosing lagoons.

PAUL SANLAVILLE

REFERENCES

Al-Asfour, T., 1978, The marine terraces of the Bay of Kuwait, in *The Environmental History of the Near and Middle East,* W. C. Brice, ed., Academic Press, London, pp. 245-254.

Doornkamp, J. C., D. Brunsden, and D. K. C. Jones, eds., 1980, *Geology, Geomorphology and Pedology of Bahrain,* Geo Abstract Ltd, Norwich.

Evamy, B. D., 1973, The precipitation of aragonite and its alteration to calcite on the Trucial Coast of the Persian Gulf, in *The Persian Gulf,* B. H. Purser, ed., Springer-Verlag, Berlin, pp. 329-341.

Geological Survey of Iran, 1973, *Tectonic map of Iran,* 1:2,500,000.

Kassler, P., 1973, The structural and geomorphic evolution of the Persian Gulf, in *The Persian Gulf,* B. H. Purser, ed., Springer-Verlag, Berlin, pp. 11-32.

Lees, G. M., and N. L. Falcon, 1952, The geographical history of the Mesopotamian plains, *Geog. Jour.* **116:** 24-39.

Loreau, J. P., and B. H. Purser, 1973, Distribution and ultrastructure of Holocene ooids in the Persian Gulf, in *The Persian Gulf,* B. H. Purser, ed., Springer-Verlag, Berlin, pp. 279-328.

Purser, B. H., 1973, Sedimentation around bathymetric highs in the southern Persian Gulf, in *The Persian Gulf,* B. H. Purser, ed., Springer-Verlag, Berlin, pp. 157-177.

Purser, B. H., and G. Evans, 1973, Reginal sedimenta-tion along the Trucial coast, SE Persian Gulf, in *The Persian Gulf,* B. H. Purser, ed., Springer-Verlag, Berlin, pp. 211-231.

Purser, B. H., and E. Seibold, 1973, The principal environmental factors influencing Holocene sedimentation and diagenesis in the Persian Gulf, in *The Persian Gulf,* B. H. Purser, ed., Springer-Verlag, Berlin, pp. 1-9.

Seibold, E., and K. Vollbrecht, 1969, Die Bodengestalt des Persischen Golfs, *METEOR Forsch. Ergebnisse, C,* pp. 229-256.

Seibold, E., L. Diester, D. Futterer, H. Lange, P. Muller, and F. Werner, 1973, Holocene sediments and sedimentary processes in the Iranian part of the Persian Gulf, in *The Persian Gulf,* B. H. Purser, ed., Springer-Verlag, Berlin, pp. 57-80.

Shinn, E. A., 1969, Submarine lithification of Holocene carbonate sediments in the Persian Gulf, *Sedimentology* **12:**109-144.

Shinn, E. A., 1973, Carbonate coastal accretion in the area of longshore transport, NE Qatar, Persian Gulf, in *The Persian Gulf,* B. H. Purser, ed., Springer-Verlag, Berlin, pp. 179-191.

Taylor, J. C. M., and L. V. Illing, 1969, Holocene intertidal calcium carbonate cementation, Qatar, Persian Gulf, *Sedimentology* **12:**69-107.

Plate 99-1. Ile de Muharraq, Bahrain archipelago, with the city and airport surrounded by a vast shoal 2 km or more in width (photo by P. Sanlaville).

Plate 99-2. Littoral zone spits and lagoons on the United Arab Emirates coast at Umm el Qaiwain (photo by P. Sanlaville).

100. PAKISTAN

The coastline of Pakistan, not including all the lagoons and tidal channels, is about 990 km long from the Iranian border east to the Indian border at the Rann of Cutch (Fig. 100-1). The total length is estimated at 1,365 km, but it is difficult to measure all the tidal estuaries in the Indus delta. Much of the coast has been influenced by uplift of marine platforms and the Makrān mountain ranges. The Las Bela Valley represents a structural trough forming part of the Owens Fracture Zone that extends southward under the Arabian Sea. Both the southeastern part of the Indus delta and the Rann of Cutch appear to be undergoing subsidence. The Pakistan coast is one of the most tectonically active regions of the world, with 20 recorded earthquakes between 1939 and 1960. The November 1945 earthquake was particularly severe; a seismic wave, reported to have been 12–15 m high, moved over the coast, and a section of the shore near Pasni was uplifted 4.6 m (Sondhi 1947).

This coastal region comprises long stretches of sandy shore backed by wide valleys or largely barren coastal plains. The low-lying areas are interrupted in places by uplifted terraces that form hammerhead peninsulas backed by hills and mountains (Ullah 1954). The Makrān ranges, with elevations of 914–1219 m, rise abruptly some 32 km inland from the coast.

A narrow continental shelf borders most of the Pakistan coast except off the Indus delta. Scattered mudbanks and shoals are found along the coast, most of them within 1.6 km of the shore. A concentration of islets, rocks, and shoals clusters around Astola Island some 40 km southeast of Pasni (Sailing Directions 1960).

Most of the Pakistan coast, especially west of Rās Muāri (Cape Monze), is exposed to southwesterly ocean swells that become very choppy during the southwest monsoon months, June through September. An occasional Arabian Sea cyclone (a small but intense hurricane) creates severe erosion and flooding along the coast.

Mean spring tide ranges on the ocean coastline are generally 0.9–1.8 m with slightly higher ranges (up to 2.7 m) around Rās Muāri (Sailing Directions 1960).

Beach sediments are predominantly sandy, and longshore drifting at the ocean coast is generally from west to east; however, in the scalloped-shaped bays the refracted ocean swells direct sand toward the center of the bays, forming long barrier spits and bars. Considerable beach drifting forms large tombolos that connect the Gwādar and Ormāra headlands with the inner coastal plains. West of Manora Point the sands are mainly quartzose, while those east of Karachi harbor and fringing the Indus delta are highly micaceous. Coastal dunes are frequent, mainly on the east side of the Las Bela Valley, east of Karachi harbor at Clifton, and along large sections of the low, very dry, windswept Makrān coastal plain. More stabilized Pleistocene sand deposits are extensive on the east side of the Las Bela Valley (Snead and Frishman 1968).

The Makrān and Las Bela sections of the Pakistan coast have well-developed beach ridges. These accretion ridges, numbering more than 50, occur (1) on the east and west sides of the Las Bela coastal plain, (2) on the tombolos leading to the Ormāra and Gwādar headlands, which close off the Kalmat Khor lagoon from the sea, and (3) southwest of Pasni (Fig. 100-1).

Most of the small intermittent streams sink

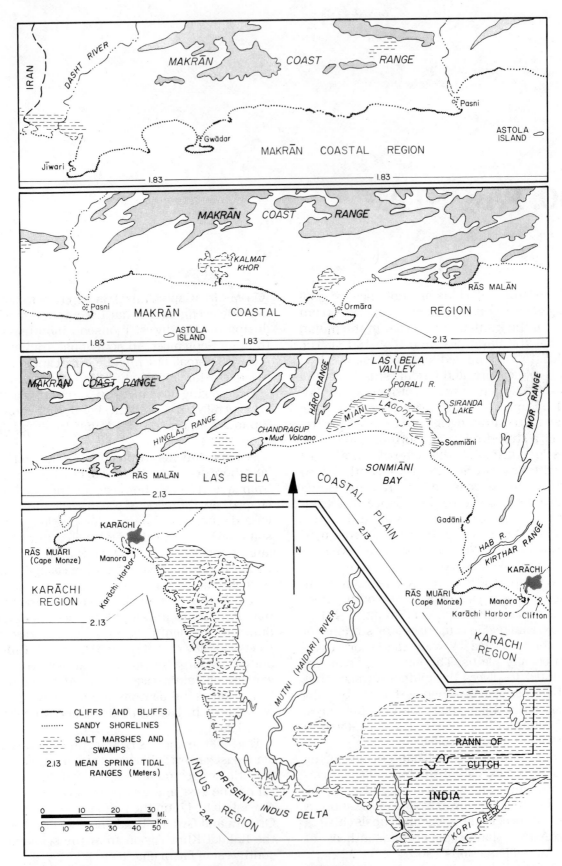

Figure 100-1. Predominant coastal landforms of Pakistan.

into the sands of the coastal plains before they reach the sea. The three larger rivers, the Hab, the Porali, and the Dasht, have very little discharge, except during floods, and drain into estaurine lagoons or shoal-filled river mouths. Except for Karachi harbor, which is dredged, there are no good ports along the entire Pakistan coast. In fact, the coast is largely uninhabited, except for eight or ten small fishing villages (Siddiqi 1956). Ancient seaports, however, have been under investigation by archaeologists. Several of these 3,000-year-old sites lie as much as 32 km inland from the present coast (Field 1959; Dales 1962; Snead 1979).

The Pakistan coast may be divided into four sections: the Makrān coastal region, the Las Bela coastal plain, the Karāchi region, and the Indus region.

THE MAKRĀN COASTAL REGION

Near the Iranian border, west of Jīwani headland, lies a low swampy region that forms the delta of the Dasht River. Here the plain is 48 km long at the coast and extends inland for more than 241 km. The Dasht brings little sediment to the coast. In this arid region (average annual rainfall, 127 mm), it is an intermittent stream that floods only once every two or three years. Most of the water sinks into the sands and gravels of the river bed or is trapped in the shallow lagoons behind the coastal barrier bars and spits.

The Makrān coast between Jīwani headland and Rās Malān consists of long stretches of sand shore backed by valleys or wide coastal plains. These low-lying areas are interrupted, however, in a number of places by uplifted terraces that form hammerhead peninsulas backed by hills and mountains. This section of the littoral makes up the bulk of the Pakistan coastline, approximately 473 km. Inland are segments of the Makrān ranges, which in general lie about 32 km from the coast except at Rās Malān, where the Hinglaj Range comes to the shore as a massive headland. West of the low Mor and Hāro ranges the Makrān hills turn southwest and at Rās Malān begin to trend east–west parallel to the coast. The Hāro, Mor, and Kirthar ranges to the east trend north–south and come to the sea as headlands at Rās Muāri and Gadāni (Fig. 100-1).

The Makrān ranges are composed mainly of Oligocene flysch, poorly indurated sandstones, mudstones, and shales, tightly folded into anticlinal and synclinal ridges. The severe erosion results in a bizarre landscape with large cap-crowned pillars and pedestals that rise abruptly above jagged ridges and ravine-ridden lower hills of clay (Holdrich 1896).

The spectacular marine platforms of Ormāra, Gwādar, and Jīwani are quite different from the inner hills. On the seaward side they are made up predominantly of Plio-Pleistocene marine conglomerates and shelly limestones, while the inner, landward-facing side consists of Miocene-Pleistocene mudstones and sandstones. These platforms represent large fault-blocks, or horsts, that are tilted seaward with a dip of 3–5 degrees. Ormāra, which is higher than Gwādar and Jīwani, has elevations of 183–305 m on the seaward side and 427 m on the inner side (Hunting Survey Corp. 1960).

The Ormāra and Gwādar platforms, formerly islands off the coast, are now connected to the mainland by large tombolos. The Ormāra tombolo is 3.2 km wide and 10 km long (Plate 100-1). From the top its growth, through a series of accretion ridges, can be clearly seen (Snead 1967).

Between the rocky headland control points are found wide scallop-shaped bays or long barrier islands with shallow lagoons (Fig. 100-1). One of the largest of these lagoons is Kalmat Khor, to the west of Ormāra (Snead 1968).

THE LAS BELA COASTAL PLAIN

This section of coast makes up the eastern part of the Makrān coast of Baluchistan (Fig. 100-1). It extends from Rās Malān eastward 260 km to Rās Muāri, and inland to include the southern part of the triangular Las Bela plain and the foothill regions of the low Mor and Hāro mountain ranges. These two ranges, approximately 97 km apart at the coast, merge 113 km to the north to enclose the valley.

Rās Malān bounds the Las Bela coastal plain on the west. It is a spectacular tableland of sandstone and shelly limestone cut into irregular segments by 305 m gorges. The highest point on this tableland is 610 m above sea level, and sheer cliffs, 457–600 m high, drop directly to the sea. The fault scarp itself is 4.8 km long.

On the west side of the Las Bela valley, near the southern end of the Hāro Range, is a group of mud volcanoes. The largest, called Chandragup, is an almost perfect cone less than two miles from the Arabian Sea; it reaches a height of 58 m. About a dozen small, white mud volcanoes, of which the highest is some 32 m, lie 3.2 km east of Chandragup, and a single cone, 20 m high, lies about the same distance to the west. These mud volcanoes represent rapid sedimentation and widespread strike-slip faulting of Tertiary mudstones, sandstones, and shales. The cones occur where plastic clay, overlain by heavier silts and sands, reaches the surface through vents and flows out as viscous mud (Snead 1964).

The main coastal portion of the Las Bela plain comprises a series of beach ridges, shifting sand dunes, two long barrier bars with hooks at their ends, and the tidal flats around Miāni Lagoon (Snead 1963). The largest mangroves along the Pakistan coast grow in this lagoon. Both *Rhizophora conjugata* and *Avicennia alba* can be found, with individual trees reaching to 9 m (Snead and Tasnif 1966).

Several headlands mark the east side of the Las Bela valley. The Kirthar ranges reach the coast at Rās Muāri, where a headland is made up of massive limestones Cretaceous to Oligocene in age, with some intrusion of Deccan lava. Marine terraces occur near Rās Muāri, of which the highest attains an elevation of about 76 m and two lower ones heights of 15–30 m. A small Cretaceous limestone headland at Gadāni reaches a height of 87 m. Wave erosion at the base of this headland has cut sea caves, blowholes, and picturesque rocky promontories (Snead 1966).

Between Rās Muāri and Gadāni is the mouth of the Hab River. This intermittent stream is confined by cliffed coast on the south and by Pleistocene sand deposits on the north. Although the Hab is one of the longest rivers in eastern Baluchistan, with a considerable discharge during floods, it does not have a delta. At its mouth, small compound bars have formed wide, sandy beaches. Shallow lagoons are found behind the bars (Zoha 1952).

THE KARACHI REGION

The 48 km long coastline in the Karachi region, from Clifton Beach to Rās Muāri, consists of about 24 km of sandy barriers and beaches bordering the harbor of Karachi and about 24 km of low, rocky cliffs at the southern end of the Kirthar Hills. The cliffs, which are 12–15 m high on the flanks of the Kirthar Hills, become lower to the east, away from the mountain front. They represent the eroded seaward side of a long pediment surface made up of Tertiary sandstones, conglom-

erates, and shales covered by a thin veneer of gravels and sands. There are several small rocky capes with shallow scallop-shaped bays and a number of sea caves, stacks, and arches. This is a complex coastal region, embracing the deeply dissected pediment surface, uplifted marine terraces, and recent oyster beds that lie 2.4–3 m above present sea level.

A 15 km long sand spit connects the rocky headland of Manora point with the mainland. In places this sand barrier is less than 305 m wide, but nevertheless it is the main resort beach of Karachi. Behind it is a shallow tidal lagoon 8 km long and 4 km wide. Human activity has greatly changed the tidal flats in this lagoon by building a series of salt evaporation ponds and by filling in sections for urban-rural expansion.

Karachi harbor has been made by dredging, widening, and improving the entrance and lower part of the small, intermittent Chinna Creek. Manora Point, a perpendicular cliff, is the southeastern extremity of a narrow hill, 26 m high, which forms the southwestern side of the entrance to the harbor. The lower harbor is nearly 0.8 km wide, but the navigable channel is reduced to 274 m by the banks that extend from either side. The upper harbor stretches northward and northeastward from the southern end of East Wharf for about 3.2 km and has a navigable width of 274–366 m for most of its length. On the incoming tides, during the southwest monsoon, a considerable swell rolls into the outer harbor.

THE INDUS REGION

The Indus delta encompasses about 200 km of the total Pakistan coastline. The landforms are uniform along this entire section. The region consists largely of tidal channels, most of which are remnant courses of the Indus River. Between these channels are extensive mud flats of fine delta silts and clays with a high percentage of micaceous sand. Where the delta meets the Arabian Sea, the fine materials are carried offshore and coarser sands are left to form a series of barrier bars with spits and hooks at the ends. The beaches along the outer bars are some 60–120 m wide, with a gradient of 1–3 degrees. The individual bars number about 15, and they are separated by tidal channels that vary in width from a few hundred meters to more than a kilometer and a half. Most of the sand bars are barren and flat, but in places low dunes reach a height of

3–5 m. The sand bars and delta channels are continually changing as tidal currents, waves, and channel floods move the fine white sands along the beaches. To the south, where the Indus River is now active, mud flats extend to the coast, and there are few barrier bars. The delta merges southward into the mud and salt wastes of the Rann of Cutch (where there is a disputed border with India).

At high tide the coastal region is submerged for as much as 4.8–6.4 km inland because the land is so flat. During the monsoon season, when high tides and Indus floods coincide, the delta is flooded up to 32 km from the coast. Tidal waters, which ascend the Indus River for 97 km to Tatta, at times form a tidal bore that is destructive to small boats. When the tide recedes and the old creeks dry, salt covers the surface or is buried under the muds and silts (Spate 1960).

Changes in the configuration of the Indus delta have been numerous. The seven mouths enumerated by the Roman historian Ptolemy have altered through the centuries as former channels have been choked and new ones opened up. The region is furrowed by these ancient channels, some still intact, others more or less obliterated.

Because the Indus delta shoreline is under constant heavy wave attack, the currents continually redistribute sediments, mainly southeast toward the Rann of Cutch, where winds pick up the fines and carry them inland in the form of large dunes. The Rann of Cutch itself, a rift zone uplifted on the north side and subsiding on the south, is a highly unstable region (Pithawalla 1936).

Although a few small mangrove shrubs, mainly *Avicennia alba*, can be found along the tidal channels, severe flooding and the deposition of delta silts limit their growth.

RODMAN E. SNEAD

REFERENCES

Dales, G. F., 1962, A search for ancient seaports, *Expedition* **4:**2–11.

Field, H., 1959, *An Anthropological Reconnaissance in West Pakistan,* Papers of the Peabody Museum of Archaeology and Ethnology, Harvard University, Cambridge, Massachusetts.

Holdrich, T. H., 1896, Notes on ancient and medieval Makrān, *Royal Geog. Soc. Jour.* **7:**387–405.

Hunting Survey Corporation, Ltd., 1960, *Reconnaissance Geology of Part of West Pakistan: A Colombo Plan Co-operative Project,* Maracle Press, Ltd., Oshawa, Ontario.

Pithawalla, M. B., 1936, *A Geographical Analysis of the Lower Indus Basin (Sind),* Part I, *Indian Acad. Sci. Proc.,* vol. **4:**1–355.

Sailing Directions for the Persian Gulf of Oman and Northern Shore of Arabian Sea Eastward to Ras Muāri, 1960, U.S. Naval Oceanographic Office, Hydrologic Office Publ. 62, Washington, D.C.

Siddiqi, M. I., 1956, *The Fisherman's Settlements on the Coast of West Pakistan,* Schriften des Geographischen Instituts der Universität Kiel.

Snead, R. E., 1963, Disappearing town of Sonmiani, West Pakistan, *Geografia* **1:**26–31.

Snead, R. E., 1964, Active mud volcanoes of Baluchistan, West Pakistan, *Geog. Rev.* **54:**546–560.

Snead, R. E., 1966, *Physical Geography Reconnaissance: Las Bela Coastal Plain, West Pakistan,* Louisiana State University Press, Baton Rouge.

Snead, R. E., 1967, Recent morphological changes along the coast of West Pakistan, *Assoc. Am. Geographers Annals* **57:**550–565.

Snead, R. E., 1968, *Physical Geography Reconnaissance: West Pakistan Coastal Zone,* University of New Mexico Press, Albuquerque.

Snead, R. E., 1979, Morphological changes in the Balakot coastal region of Pakistan, *Field Research Projects,* Coconut Grove, Florida (on microfiche).

Snead, R. E., and S. A. Frishman, 1968, Origin of sands on the east side of the Las Bela Valley, West Pakistan, *Geol. Soc. America Bull.* **79:**1671–1676.

Snead, R. E., and M. Tasnif, 1966, Vegetation types in the Las Bela region of West Pakistan, *Ecology* **47:**494–499.

Sondhi, V. P., 1947, The Makran earthquake, 38th November 1945: the birth of new islands, *Indian Minerals* **1:**147–158.

Spate, O. H. K., 1960, *India, Pakistan, and Ceylon: The Regions,* Methuen & Co., London.

Ullah, A., 1954, Physiography and structure of S.W. Makran, *Pakistan Geog. Rev.* **9:**28–37.

Zoha, S., 1952, The physiographical personality of Baluchistan, *Pakistan Geog. Rev.* **7:**20–29.

Plate 100-1. The tombolo at Ormāra is 3.2 km wide and 10 km long. This view, from the top of the headland looking north, shows the fishing village of Ormāra, the faint pattern of accretion ridges, and a large sand dune complex to the northeast (photo by G. Dales).

101. INDIA

The Indian coastline, including major indentations and the shores of islands, is about 9,000 km long. About 55% has beaches (spits, barriers, or sandy stretches on the shore). The total length of prograding shore, including deltas, is about one-fourth of the Indian coastline. The rest includes rocky overhanging cliffs or combinations of rocky and beachy shore (Plate 101-1).

The Indian coastline has been relatively stable, its outline on maps published three-quarters of a century ago being the same as on current maps. There has been marked progradation near river mouths, however. Coastal erosion by waves can be negated only where the discharge of sediment from land is large. The continental sediment generally moves toward the sea to form deltas, and the larger Indian deltas are therefore sectors of progradation.

Geological mapping of the offshore zone is a matter for the future. The coastal geology (Fig. 101-1) may tentatively be regarded as continuing under the sea, at least for short distances.

The Andaman and Nicobar islands, consisting generally of Eocene to Pliocene conglomerates, sandstones, and limestones, injected by peridotite intrusions, represent the unsunken remnants of the Tertiary folded mountain that once linked the Arakan Yomas of Burma to Sumatra. The indented coastline of these islands is related to this subsidence. These islands as well as the Lakshadweep (formerly Laccadive) and Minicoy islands are located between about 6° and 14° N, and it is possible that corals continued to exist here even during the Pleistocene glaciation, contributing to the formation of the uppermost coralline limestones.

In the deltas of the Ganga, Mahandi, Godavari,

Krishna, and Cauvery, and other smaller deltas between the Cauvery and Cape Comorin, the geological formation is Pleistocene and Holocene alluvium. Coastal dunes occur, in many other sites. Miliolite limestone forms parts of the Kathiawar coast, and desert sand large parts of the Rann of Kutch shore.

Pockets of uplifted Cretaceous to Pliocene marine rocks, with a gentle seaward tilt, occur from Midnapore to Cape Comorin, in Kerala, near Ratnagiri, and in parts of Kathiawar and Kutch. The Kathiawar peninsula is believed to have been an island during the Pleistocene.

A large part of the western coast, from Ratnagiri to Kathiawar and Kutch, is built of Deccan lava. This rock has columnar joints that have probably aided the formation of numerous coves and bays on the coast. The jointed and bedded structure also aids the formation of lava boulders. The Western Ghats, the great scarp overlooking the western shore from near Daman to Cape Comorin, is built, up to Ratnagiri, of Deccan lava, which erupted in the Eocene.

A rough mutual parallelism of the Ghats, the western coastline, and the plain of marine denudation, now supporting low-level laterite extending to the foot of the scarp, suggests that the lava plateau formerly extended much farther west toward the Arabian Sea. Later, faulting led to the subsidence of the western segment, allowing the sea to reach the scarp foot. There is biological evidence (mollusca on the Western Ghats allied to the littoral marine genus *Litorina*) to suggest that the Ghats were once washed by the Arabian Sea. A great sea cliff was a feature of the Tertiary, probably contemporaneous with the Narmada and Tapti rift valleys. After the faulting producing

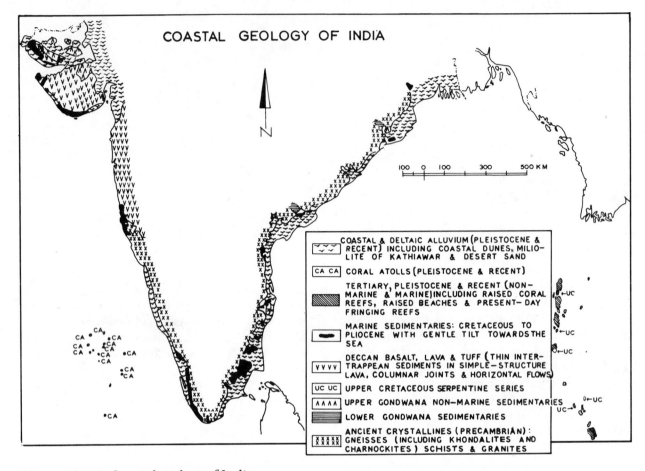

Figure 101-1. Coastal geology of India.

the Western Ghats, there has been more recent uplift to form the low-lying Konkan strip. The faulting of the Western Ghats must be earlier than the marine Upper Tertiary beds of the Ratnagiri region.

Ancient (Precambrian) crystalline gneisses (including khondalites and charnockites), schists, and granites occur on the remaining parts of the coasts. Mostly they are inland, behind the ribbon of alluvium or coastal Tertiary deposits, except near Vishakhapatnam, Cape Comorin, Goa, and adjoining areas, where they form cliffs and rocky shores.

Evidence (Fig. 101-2) regarding recent or historical changes of the levels of sea or land is rather complex. Indications of uplift and subsidence sometimes occur side by side. There are Pliocene marine sediments, particularly on the east coast, giving definite evidence of emergence of about 100 m since their deposition. The various evidences of uplift of land or fall of sea level after the Pliocene are: a raised sea beach in Dalbhum,

90 km inland; raised beaches in North Arcot (contemporaneous with laterites containing paleoliths) about 8 km inland from Madras coast; marine shells at Madras, Pondicherry, near Porto Novo, Cuddalore, Tanjore, and Valimukkam (in the Tirunelveli districts), considerably above sea level; the coral reef north of Rameshwaram peninsula 1–2 m above the present sea level; the recent joining of the islands near Tuticorin to the mainland; fossil species of pectens and oysters 5 m above sea level near Tuticorin; marine, gritty calcareous sandstone above the sea near Cape Comorin; an old sea beach of shelly gravel 4 m above high tide west of Bombay island; the extensive cay sandstone or littoral concrete, a marine shelly grit, from Malvan to Kathiawar, probably an old sea beach, now raised a little above sea level; fossil oysters 8–16 km inland in Kutch; marine shells 6 m above the Rann of Kutch; and coral reefs about 10 m above sea level in the Lakshadweep islands.

The present coastline of India has a dominantly

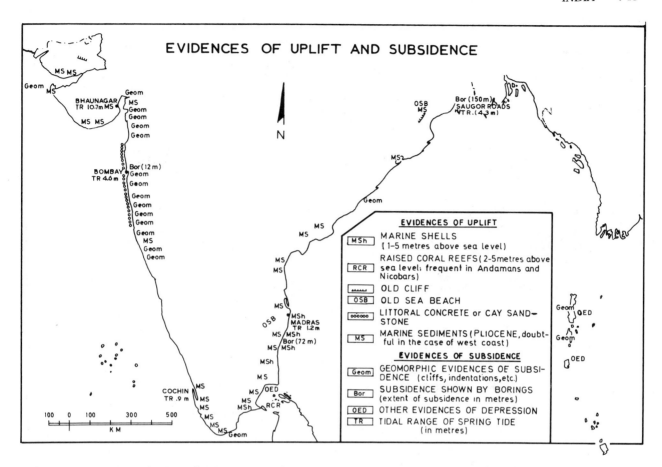

Figure 101-2. Evidences of uplift and subsidence.

emergent aspect. It has rhumbline straightness (Fig. 101-3) over long stretches. The shelf has a gentle uniform gradient. Cliffs and offshore islands are comparatively scarce, while barriers (Fig. 101-3) and spits are common, pointing to recent emergence of the Indian peninsula.

Evidence of historical change is seen at Balasore, once a seaport but now 15 km inland. The escarpment behind Balasore looks like a sea cliff (Fig. 101-2). Isolated hills in this neighborhood are interpreted as former islands; salt marts on the Brahmani River had to be shifted downstream. The Black Pagoda, now 16 km inland, is said to have been built on the shore. Khor village in Kathiawar, on the edge of the Little Rann of Kutch, is said to have been a port in 1765. Virawah, on the Sind side of the Great Rann of Kutch, now about 180 km from the Kori Creek, is also said to have been a port. Much of this evidence is based on hearsay or tradition and may not be correct.

Evidence of subsidence along the Indian shore

is as follows. There is a peat bed, 6–13 m below the surface, at several localities within a radius of about 130 km from Calcutta, always below mean tide level. It contains roots of the Sundri tree, which grows a little above ordinary high water mark. As the peat-bed roots of the Sundri tree always occur below the mean tide level, this evidence points to a relative rise in sea level.

Large gneissic pebbles (5–7 cm across), some 160 m deep, probably point to an earlier lower sea level (Miocene) in the Ganga delta. At Bahuri in Pondicherry, a 10.7 m thick lignite bed was found at a depth of 73 m. A submerged forest of trees, which do not grow on the coast near sea level, occurs below high water mark in Valimukkam Bay near Tirunelveli. The presence of human bones shows that this forest subsided after the advent of man.

Excavations at Princess Dock (Bombay) showed trunks of trees (some of which never grow below highest tide level) in upright position with roots at a depth of 6 m below sea level. At Alexandra

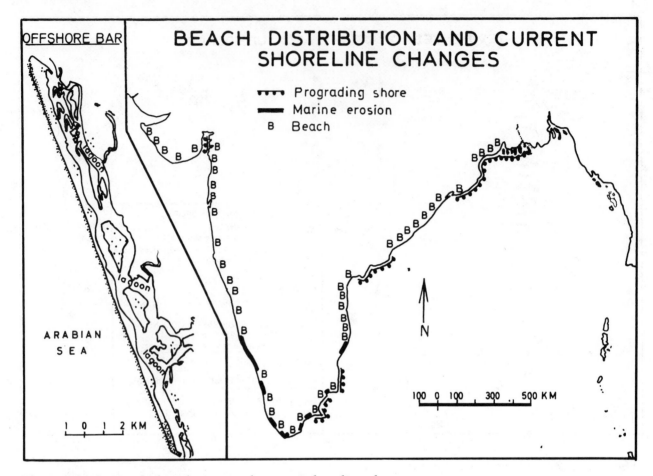

Figure 101-3. Beach distribution and current shoreline changes.

Dock (Bombay) tree stumps were found 12 m below highest tide level.

Local short-lived depression occurred during the earthquake of 1819 in Kutch, with the sea invading an area of about 500 km².

On Havelock and other islands of the Andaman and Nicobar group, a dead forest standing in salt water is also taken as an indication of subsidence.

There is geomorphic evidence (Fig. 101-2) of subsidence on the west coast (e.g., the cliffed and indented coast from Goa [Plate 101-2] to Bulsar, in southeast Kathiawar, and in the Andaman and Nicobar islands). The offshore islands along the west coast, as well as the estuaries and irregular shore of the Cambay region, also indicate subsidence.

Subsidence in the Ganga delta and between Pondicherry and Tirunelveli, or near Bombay, probably occurred before the Dunkirkian transgression 3,000–4,000 years ago, which is believed to have been on the order of 2–6 meters. The subsidence is not uniform. It is 70 m near

Pondicherry and 6–12 m near Bombay. Such subsidence might have been due to local tectonic movements more than to higher, interglacial eustatic level.

The subsidence in the Ganga delta, estimated to be 150 m during the Pleistocene and Holocene, may be due to compaction of particles and removal of water from the loaded sediments and isostatic sinking. The subsidence of the lignite bed (73 m) near Pondicherry is probably local tectonic subsidence.

Dead corals and shells along the Saurashtra coast suggested to Gupta (1977) higher levels of the sea (2–5 m above the present sea level) during the Late Pleistocene. On the basis of his study of the limestone Miliolite (alternatively known as Porbandar stone), composed of casts of foraminifera, compacted into cream-colored freestone, Mehr (1980) noted that the deposits nearer the coast are marine, not windblown. He deduced five levels ranging from 2.3 m (lowest) to 150–200 m (highest). Dune ridges 8–10 m above mean sea level and 200–900 m inland are believed by Mehr to indicate a higher sea level during historical times.

Some believe that the Maharashtra coast from Bombay to Goa underwent submergence and then emergence. Radiocarbon dating of one of the emerged areas gave a date of 4460 B.C., corresponding to Neolithic age.

An air photo of the Kerala coast (Meijerink, 1971) showed fresh-appearing marine cliffs and terraces, 3–5 m above sea level. The laterites below the sediments on the shelf are believed to suggest flexuring of the Kerala lateritized coastal lowland.

Sambasiva Rao and Vaidyanadhan (1979) noted four strandlines in the Godavari delta at successively lower levels from 8 m to 2 m within 35 to 2 km from the shore, and believe them to be Holocene. There are beach ridges in the Krishna delta also, 4–6 m above mean sea level, 20 km inland. Both these deltas show present day progradation.

Near Vishakhapatnam, laterite has been found 20–30 m below the present mean sea level. This indicates a lower sea level probably 7,000–8,000 years old (Prudhvi and Vaidyanadhan 1978).

Sambasiva Rao et al. (1978) have found strandlines 25–30 km inland in the Mahanadi (10 m above sea level) and Baitarani (5 m above sea level) deltas. They probably represent transgression or progradation in the deltas.

Three terraces in the Subarnarekha delta, 6.1, 4.7, and 3.8 m above mean sea level, are believed to be post-Pleistocene. Raised coralline beaches in the Great Nicobar island, up to 15 m above mean sea level and 1–2 km inland, show recent uplift.

Holocene terraces (according to radiocarbon dating) have recently been discovered on the shelf between Bombay and Karwar, at the depths of 92, 85, 75, and 55 m below mean sea level. On the basis of radiocarbon dating of sediments from the submarine floor around India, Shrivastava (1978) concluded that the shoreline of India was 75–330 km seaward during the Holocene.

Thus we have only sketchy information regarding the shoreline changes in India due to transgression or marine withdrawal or local or regional uplift or subsidence of land; there is much yet to be learned about this subject.

Probably more important than the speculations about the Holocene sea levels are the present-day changes of the shoreline. The areas of recession and progradation have been indicated on the map in Figure 101-3.

The Kerala coast is marked by marine erosion. Manohar (1961) noted that this coast is being eroded at the rate of up to 6 m annually. Comparative study of maps of 1850 and 1966 suggested to Earattupuzha and George (1980) that the major part of the Kerala coast has receded during that time.

Over the decade preceding 1966 (*The Statesman*, July 13, 1966) large areas of the Kerala coast were eroded by the sea during the monsoon months. In 1966, a few miles south of Alleppey, the Ernakulam-Trivandrum highway was threatened by the advancing sea, which was less than 50 m away at some places, compared with 300 m in 1957. Here the rate of erosion was about four times the figure of Manohar. About 320 km of Kerala's 565 km coastline was affected; the worst hurt stretches were in the Quilon, Alleppey, and Kozhikode (Calicut) districts.

Granite walls were constructed by 1966 along 64 km of affected coast where the sea threatens to swallow the railway lines, national highways, canals, paddy fields, and the ever-narrowing strips of land separating it from the backwater lakes (Nambiar and Moni, 1970, p. 20).

About 14 years later (*Times of India*, September 9, 1980) 267 km of the Kerala coast was protected by granite walls, but the strong waves of the southwest monsoon period had damaged 70 km of the walls, which had to be repaired.

Erosion also occurs at other vulnerable points of the western coast. For example, there is a real danger that the fishing village of Devbagh, 8 km from Malvan (Maharashtra) may be swallowed up by the sea (*Times of India*, July 26, 1980). A 7 m wide stretch of land was eroded during the monsoon of 1979.

On the other hand, there are cases of progradation. La Fond (1966) noted that the spit called Godavari Point, enclosing Kakinada Bay, had grown northward by longshore drifting during the past century, about 12 km in 100 years or 129 m per year. Because of floods and deforestation, the Godavari delta discharge caused the growth of the spit. La Fond's estimate of sedimentation at Madras, Vishakhapatnam, and Godvari Point was 1 million tons per year, in each case.

Artificial banking of the rivers and enormous sediment discharge accelerate progradation at the deltas. Progradation probably amounts to 60, 10, 15, 15, and 5 m per annum, respectively, in the Ganga, Mahanadi, Krishna, Godavari, and Cauvery deltas. Spate and Learmonth (1967) have noted that the alluvial coast east of the Gulf of Cambay is actively prograding (Fig. 101-3).

The nature of the shore is summarily indicated

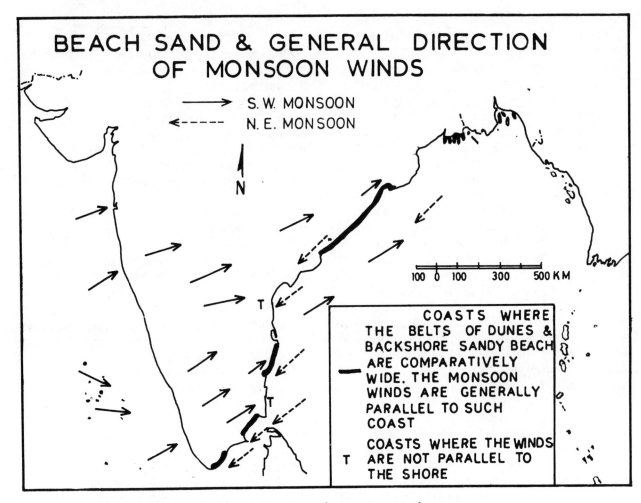

Figure 101-4. Beach sand and general direction of monsoon winds.

on the map (Fig. 101-3). Where the tidal range is high, as at the Hooghly River mouth, there are no barriers, but barriers are frequent on the less tidal Tamilnadu and Kerala coast. Where monsoon winds parallel the coast (Fig. 101-4), beach sand accumulates as a comparatively extensive, continuous dune belt. Where the winds are transverse, sand is blown deeper inland and dispersed. For details on the Indian littoral see Ahmad's *Coastal Geomorphology of India* (1972).

ENAYAT AHMAD

REFERENCES

Ahmad, E., 1972, *Coastal Geomorphology of India*, Orient Longman, New Delhi.

Chatterjee, S. P., 1962, *Fluctuations of Sea Level around the Coasts of India during the Quaternary Period*, Zeitschr. Geomorphologie Suppl., 3.

Earattupuzha, J. J. and V. George, 1980, Shoreline changes on Kerala coast, in *Geology and Geomorphology of Kerala*, G. S. I. Spec. Pub. 5, pp. 83–85.

Gupta, S. K., 1977, Quaternary sea level changes of the Saurashtra coast, in *Ecology and Archaeology of Western India*, D. P. Agrawal and B. M. Pande, eds., Concept Publications, Delhi, pp. 181–193.

La Fond, E. C., 1966, Bay of Bengal, in *The Encyclopedia of Oceanography*, R. W. Fairbridge, ed., Reinhold, New York.

Manohar, M., 1961, Sediment movement at the Indian ports, *7th Conf. Coastal Engineers Proc.*

Mehr, S. S., 1980, The miliolite problem, presidential address to the Section of Geology and Geography (IV), 67th Sess. Indian Sci. Cong., pp. 16–42.

Meijerink, A. M. J., 1971, Reconnaisance survey of the Quaternary geology of the Cauvery delta, *Geol. Soc. India Jour.*, **12**(2):113–124.

Nambiar and Moni, 1970, Coastal erosion in Kerala, *Bhagirath, The Irrigation and Power Quarterly*, vol. 17, Publications Division, New Delhi, pp. 20–24.

Pascoe, E. H., 1964, *A Manual of the Geology of India and Burma*, Manager of Publications, Government of India, Delhi.

Prudhvi, R., and R. Vaidyanadhan, 1978, Geomorphology of Vishakhapatnam, *Geol. Soc. India Jour.* **19**(1): 26–34.

Sambasiva Rao, M. et al., 1978, A morphology and evolution of Mahanadi and Brahmani-Baitarani deltas, *Symp. on Morphology and Evolution of Landforms.*

Sambasiva Rao, M., and R. Vaidyanadhan, 1979, Morphology and evolution of Godavari Delta, India, *Zeitschr. Geomorphologie.* N.F., **23**(3):243–255.

Shrivastava, P. C., 1978, A note on the possible Holocene shoreline of India, *Indian Minerals* **32**(3):44–47.

Spate, O. H. K., and A. T. A. Learmonth, 1967, *India and Pakistan*, Methuen, London.

The Statesman, July 13, 1966.

Times of India, July 26, 1980.

Times of India, September 9, 1980.

Vaidyanadhan, R., 1981, Sea level changes during the Quaternary in India, in *Sea Level*, M. J. Tooley, ed., Information Bulletin of I.G.C.P. Project, vol. 5, pp. 1–5.

Wadia, D. N., 1961, *Geology of India*, Macmillan, London.

Plate 101-1. Bay-head beach on Goa coast. Gentle slope in the distant background on the tip of the promontory is due to greater subaerial weathering than marine erosion (photo by A. Husain).

Plate 101-2. Crystalline (quartzite) promontory on Goa coast (photo by A. Husain).

Plate 101-3. Artificial pile of granite boulders, along with natural rocky outcrops, to protect the Kerala coast (photo by J. Sahdeo).

Plate 101-4. Relatively calm waters in a Kerala lagoon close to the wave action (Plate 101-3) of the open sea (photo by J. Sahdeo).

102. SRI LANKA

The tectonically stable tropical island of Sri Lanka has a coastline about 1,700 km long including that of the Jaffna lagoon and major embayments. The island is subject to the northeast (December to early March) and the southeast (late May to early October) monsoons. Winds rarely attain gale force except in gusts during the height of the monsoons, though cyclones occur once in 10–15 years and affect northern coasts. Waves are generated by the monsoons, local winds, and a southerly swell. Spring tidal range is within 1 m. Rocks are mainly Precambrian, although in the north and northwest Miocene limestone veneered with Quaternary materials occur. The central highlands are surrounded by lowlands; coasts are low-lying and deep indentations rare. Two-thirds of the coastline are open to seasonally strong wave action. Here long sandy shorelines or arcuate beach-lined bays bounded by headlands of Precambrian bedrock (Plates 102-1 and 102-2) are characteristic (Swan 1979a). Along the remainder of the coastline, largely coincident with the sedimentary geological zone in the north and northwest, wave energy is perennially low because of shallow seas and barriers. Shorelines are less regular in plan, the result of differential deposition (Fig. 102-1).

Beach materials are predominantly terrigenous quartzose sands. Coastal dunes are present, mainly along sectors where rainfall is relatively low, a dry season is pronounced, winds are onshore at that time, and sand supply and delivery ashore are efficient (Plates 102-3 and 102-4). Dunes occur especially along shores where wave energy is vigorous, but also where it is low (Swan 1979b). Beachrock commonly lines sandy shores where retrogradation is seasonal. Reefs of it occur offshore, sometimes in a parallel, stepped series: a response to stillstands during the Holocene transgression (Plate 102-5). Traces of higher sea levels occur up to 35 m above present (Swan 1964, 1974).

Mangroves (Arulchelvam 1968) occur in sheltered lagoons and estuaries behind barrier beaches and spits where wave energy is considerable, and also in tidal flats open to the sea in the northwest where energy is low. Corals are widespread and form fringing and even small barrier reefs (Mergner and Scheer 1973) while some reefs are dead. Coral reef remains constitute low capes and headlands in many situations around the island.

The continental shelf extends across to India between the Gulf of Mannar and Palk Strait, but is narrow elsewhere and generally divisible into an inner and an outer zone separated by the 55 m isobath. The continental slope commences around depths of 90 m. There is a net movement of sand northward, especially along the west coast. There is probably an input into Palk Bay and the northeast from southern India (Swan 1979b).

The northern flank of the Jaffna peninsula is low, composed of coralline limestone capped with weathered beach deposits within 3 m of the high water mark (Fig. 102-2A). A coral reef offshore excludes large waves, but slow retreat is evident in low cliffs and small caves (Plate 102-6). Beaches are narrow, intermittent, and composed of coarse calcareous particles. Islands of low level limestone and alluvia lie west of the peninsula; between the peninsula and the mainland is an extensive system of lagoons, collectively known as the Jaffna lagoon. It is affected by tides and wavelets whipped up by monsoon winds. Sedimentation is progres-

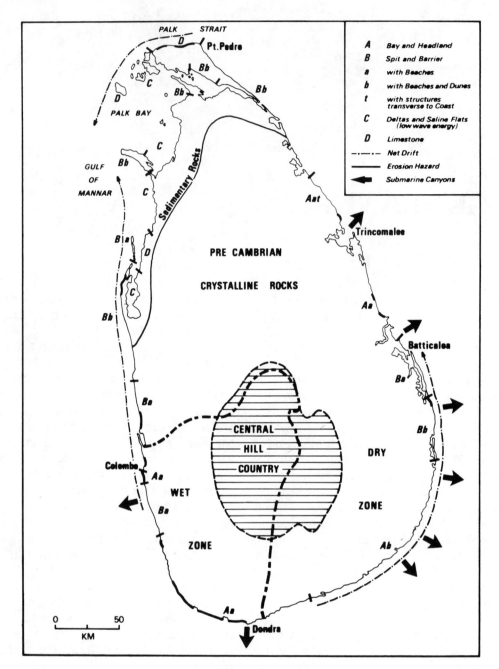

Figure 102-1. Principal shoreline types, Sri Lanka, and relevant aspects of the coastal and interior geomorphic environment.

sive. Mangroves and salt marsh are widespread on tidal flats (Plate 102-7).

Northwest of Pooneryn on the mainland is a stable sand spit, the Pooneryn peninsula, the product of tidal currents, small waves from the southwest, and dune-building winds. From Pooneryn to Mannar Island depositional features dominate the coastal zone in response to low wave energy conditions. An intertidal barrier of fine-textured alluvium, built by wavelets and tidal currents, supports a mangrove forest backed by a lagoon between Vidattaltivu and Illuppaikaddavai. Mantai, now inland, was an important port in early historical times. Mannar Island consists of multiple sand barriers of Holocene age thrown up by southwest monsoon waves. Transgressive dunes extend across most of it. Vegetation is mainly thorny scrub, palmyra palm and baobab.

Adam's Bridge is the submerged shallow ridge (0 to −3 m) of recent conglomerate and sandstone, mantled with islands and shoals of shifting sand, that links Sri Lanka to India. Much sand passes across it during the monsoons.

From Mantai (Fig. 102-2*B*) to the Kalpitiya peninsula, coastal and riverine alluvia, weathered relict beach, and dune deposits overlie limestone. The northern end of this stretch is dominated by the Aruvi delta. From Kudremalai Point, the site of an ancient settlement presumably buried beneath the sand (Seneviratne 1979), to Karuwalakuda, the coastline straightens. It is cliffed and consists of limestone also capped with relict beach and dune deposits, now wooded (de Alwis 1971; Katz 1975). Karativu Island, opposite, is an unstable sand barrier. The mainland coast east of the shallow Kalpitiya lagoon system is similar to the sector north of it. The perched shore sands here were presumably laid down before the peninsula was constructed (Swan 1979*b*). This coastal segment includes the flood plains and deltas of the Kala and Mi Oyas.

The Kalpitiya peninsula (Fig. 102-2*C*) is a compound spit (Cooray 1968), probably Holocene. It appears to have retreated since it was formed. The section south of St. Anne's has stabilized, but that farther north remains unstable (Swan 1979*b*). From this peninsula southward to Colombo (Fig. 102-2*D*) the coast is low-lying and mainly depositional, while the coastline consists of zeta-curved sand barriers, one-time spits built northward, but presently in slow retreat (Swan 1982*a*, 1982*b*). Lagoons and swamps backed by raised beaches are characteristic features.

From Colombo southwards, Precambrian bedrock outcrops intermittently at the shore. These are lateritized above the water table. The older beach deposits common north of Colombo dwindle on account of coast recession. Younger raised beaches occur up to 8 m above sea level. These are 1–3 km wide at Colombo, but narrow southward to a few hundred meters or less. Lagoons and ill-drained terrain, backed by low soil-mantled rises and hills, lie behind these. A sandstone reef offshore, opposite Colombo, excludes large waves and also sand required to nourish beaches (Swan 1974). Between the headlands at Mt. Lavinia and Maggona, the shoreline is smooth and sandy, interrupted by the outfalls of the Panadura and Kalu gangas. South of Maggona, bays and headlands, backed by raised beaches, flood plains, swamps, and lateritic rises, dominate the coastlands. Where headlands have failed or are in-

adequate (Swan 1974), coast erosion is a hazard, because wave energy along the southwest coast is above average. Between Nambimulla and Matara the problem is most severe because sand supply is poor, sand retention on beaches unsatisfactory, and materials at the land-sea interface highly susceptible to cutback. In addition, people have quarried corals at the shoreline and offshore, and extracted beach materials, exacerbating the erosion hazard (Amarasinghe and de Alwis 1980). Galle and Weligama bays (Fig. 102-2*E*) are the only two large, relatively deep embayments of the western half of the island.

Dondra Head (Fig. 102-2*F*), the island's southernmost point, consists of low platforms of resistant granitic rock, capped with beach deposits. From Dondra to Tangalle numerous indentations make the coastline more scenic and varied than elsewhere in the island. Bays, promontories, headlands, cliffs, and barrier beaches backed by swamps and lagoons abound. Foreshores are rocky. Beaches are discontinuous and coarse textured (Plate 102-8). Little sand is supplied by rivers, as none of significance cross this tract. Waves are oblique to the coast in both monsoons, and swell is perennial, resulting in persistent wave attack upon shores of strength.

East of Tangalle, in response to a change in geological structure (Cooray 1967), the coastal morphology alters. Coastlands are low and the coastal plain wide. Headlands are spaced far apart, and behind long barrier beaches are lagoons, estuarine deltas, and ill-drained land. Monsoon winds blow parallel to the coast, and the waves are largely constructive. Sand-rich rivers traverse this sector. From Ambalantota, west of Hambantota, to Sangamakande Point, the easternmost in the island, the coast consists of wide zeta-curved bays contained between well-defined headlands. Beaches are broad and dunes plentiful (Swan 1979*b*) (Plate 102-3). Although beach drift is two-way, predominant movement is anticlockwise, eastward and northward. There is much sand in transit and marked accretion and even oversupply to the downdrift ends of beach compartments. There are signs that supply was even greater in the past (Swan 1979*b*). Behind the shore terrain consists of aluvial tracts, large lagoons, and inselbergs, tors, and other erosional remnants rising above rock plains thinly mantled with soil.

Two linear submarine structures off the southeast coast (Fig. 102-2*G*) are the Great and the Little Basses ridges (Portuguese *Baixos* means reef). Both are steep-sided, rising from a rock and

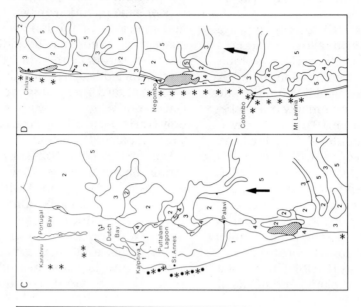

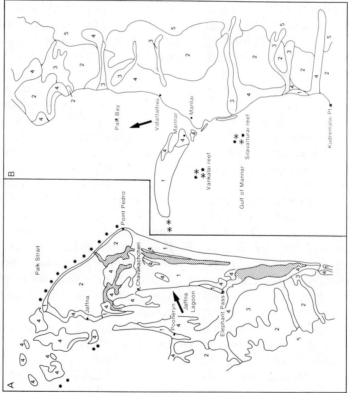

Figure 102-2

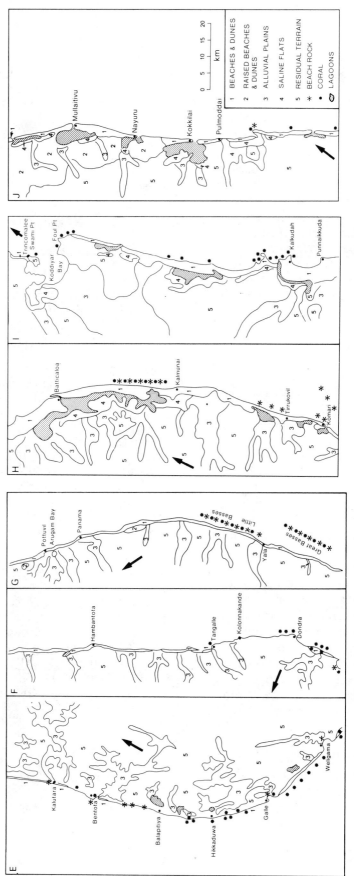

Figure 102-2 (A-J). Geomorphic elements of the coast of Sri Lanka: generalized. 1. beaches and dunes; 2. raised beaches and dunes; 3. alluvial plains; 4. saline flats; 5. residual terrain. ∗ indicates beachrock; • indicates coral; ☞ indicates lagoons.

coral floor that grades to a sandy bottom. These ridges, composed of calcareously cemented sandstone (Throckmorton 1964) probably mark former shorelines (Swan 1982).

From Sangamakande Point to Koddiyar Bay, coastal landforms of bedrock become rare (Plate 102-9). Instead, broad flood plains, with distributary systems that commence at elevations up to 35 m and 25 km inland, river terraces, and lagoons predominate (Fig. 102-2*H*). Sand dunes diminish and disappear, because during the dry season when sand is mobilized, winds blow offshore. Barrier beaches are present, and an inner and outer system are detectable. A series of large interconnecting lagoons, collectively referred to as the Batticaloa Lagoon, constitutes a prominent feature. Between Kalkudah (Fig. 102-2*I*) and Periya Munai Point, the otherwise smooth depositional coast is interrupted by a series of bays and headlands of coral backed by beach ridges, lagoons, and low residual terrain. This tract is intensively mined for coral.

During the Holocene transgression, the valley of the lower Mahaveli Ganga, which empties mainly into Koddiyar Bay, was submerged. It was duly sedimented and modified at its delta by shore processes giving rise to the present patterns of estuaries, deltas, lagoons, and bay-head barrier beaches. The harbor of Trincomalee, with deep coves and inlets, receives no river sediments, and retains much of its earlier highly indented character (Plate 102-10). Koddiyar and Trincomalee bays are associated with a major submarine canyon (Shepard and Dill 1966).

A bay and headland coast, backed by raised beaches, lagoons, ill-drained alluvial flats, and low residual rises with occasional narrow ridges trending northeast, gives the tract between Trincomalee and Nayuru (Fig. 102-2*J*) its character. Some ridges reach the sea as bold headlands. Other headlands are small, or are capes of low coral, which succumb readily to northeast monsoon waves. Old beach deposits topped with relict dunes reappear, reddening the coastal margins. Between the mouths of the Yan Oya and Nayuru there are rich concentrations of ilmenite and rutile. From the mouth of the Nayuru lagoon northward, the coast is extensively prograded. The process has been particularly active at Mullaitivu, where there are large offshore banks of sand.

At Peparaputti, there commences an extensive complex of beaches, dunes, and lagoons, paralleling the coastline. The system is a tombolo that connects the limestone of the Jaffna peninsula to the mainland. It terminates at Point Pedro.

BERNARD SWAN

REFERENCES

Amarasinghe, S. R., and R. de Alwis, 1980, *Coastal Zone Management in Sri Lanka*, 2d Symp. on Coastal and Ocean Management, Florida.

Arulchelvam, K., 1968, Mangroves, *Ceylon Forester* **8**(3&4):1–34.

Cooray, P. G., 1967, *Introduction to the Geology of Ceylon*, Colombo National Museums.

Cooray, P. G., 1968, The geomorphology of the northwestern coastal plain of Ceylon, *Zeitschr. Geomorphologie* **7**:95–113.

de Alwis, K. A., 1971, *The Pedology of the Red Latosols of Ceylon*, Ph.D. thesis, University of Alberta.

Katz, M. B., 1975, Geomorphology and reconnaissance geology of the Wilpattu National Park, *Ceylon Jour. Science (Biol. Sci.)* **11**(2):83–94.

Mergner, H., and G. Scheer, 1973, The physiographic zonation and the ecological conditions of some South Indian and Ceylon coral reefs, *2d Internat. Coral Reef Symp. Proc.* Brisbane, **2**:3–30.

Seneviratne, M., 1979, *Some Mahavamsa Places*, Lake House, Colombo.

Shepard, F. P., and R. S. Dill, 1966, *Submarine Canyons and Other Sea Valleys*, Rand McNally, Chicago.

Swan, S. B. St. C., 1964, *Evidence for Eustatic Changes in Southwest Ceylon*, Master's thesis, University of London.

Swan, S. B. St. C., 1974, *The Coast Erosion Hazard, Southwest Sri Lanka*, New England Research Series in Applied Geography, University of New England, Armidale, Australia.

Swan, B., 1979a, Areal variations in textures of shore sands, Sri Lanka, *Jour. Tropical Geog.* **49**:72–85.

Swan, B., 1979b, Sand dunes in the humid tropics: Sri Lanka, *Zeitschr. Geomorphologie* **23**(2):152–171.

Swan, B., 1982a, *An Introduction to the Coastal and Submarine Geomorphology of Sri Lanka*, National Museums Colombo.

Swan, B., 1982b, *The Coastal Geomorphology of Sri Lanka*, University of New England, Armidale, Australia.

Throckmorton, P., 1964, Appendix A, in A. C. Clarke, *The Treasure of the Great Reef*, Barker, London.

Plate 102-1. Seasonal berm, at Lunawa south of Mt. Lavinia (Fig. 102-2*D*), essential for the beach seine fishing industry, which is suspended during the southwest monsoon when the berm is cut back (photo by B. Swan).

Plate 102-2. Outer edge of sand spit, south of Negombo (Fig. 102-2*D*), stabilized by foundations of beachrock, under assault by swell. Note rip currents and black ilmenite sand at lower end of beach (photo courtesy of Coast Conservation Division).

Plate 102-3. Broad beach and dune system, near Panama (Fig. 102-2G), southeast coast (photo by B. Swan).

Plate 102-4. Mobile dunes and sand sheets, Manalkadu, east coast Jaffna peninsula (Fig. 102-2A). The party stands on the top of a church buried by dunes in the mid 1950s (photo by B. Swan).

Plate 102-5. Microridges built by coralline algae on crest of offshore reef of beachrock exposed at spring tide low water, Barberyn near Bentota (Fig. 102-2*E*) (photo by B. Swan).

Plate 102-6. Miocene limestone shore of the northern flank of the Jaffna peninsula (Fig. 102-2*A*). Large waves are excluded by an extensive shore platform, coral reefs, and offshore shallows. Slow retreat is under way (photo by B. Swan).

Plate 102-7. Salt-tolerant vegetation on coastal flat inundated at high spring tides, Ponneryn (Fig. 102-2*A*) (photo by B. Swan).

Plate 102-8. The multiple bays and headlands of the coast at Tangalle (Fig. 102-2*F*) (photo by B. Swan).

Plate 102-9. Defunct, truncated headland stands as a stack offshore, while the flat coast behind retreats spasmodically. East coast between Kalkudah and Foul Point (Fig. 102-2*I*) (photo courtesy of Coast Conservation Division).

Plate 102-10. Steep rocky coastline, Trincomalee (Fig. 102-2*I*), developed on quartzite (photo by B. Swan).

103. BANGLADESH

The coastline of Bangladesh, ignoring all the tidal channels and delta estuaries, is some 654 km long from the Indian border in the west to the Burmese border in the southeast (Fig. 103-1). The total length of coast, going around all the islands and up the estuaries, is estimated to be nearly 1,320 km. However, the width of the tidal channels, particularly in the Sundarbans, is impossible to measure with any precision, since the Bengal 1:250,000 scale maps are not very accurate. There is also the problem of how far inland the coastline should be considered to extend; tidal estuaries in places reach as far as 130 km inland, and storm surges may drive the Bay of Bengal waters up to 160 km inland.

The Bangladesh coast can be divided into four parts, each with its particular characteristics. In the west, partly in India but mostly in Bangladesh, is the old delta called the Sundarbans. Next, to the east, lies a section where the Sundarbans have been cleared and there is considerable farming. The third division is the delta of the Meghna, the easternmost branch of the Ganges, and the fourth is the Chittagong coast from the Feni River to the Nāf River at the Burma border, a distance of about 274 km.

Except for the Chittagong section, the coastline is low, swampy, and rapidly changing. It comprises a large alluvial basin floored with Quaternary sediments deposited by two vast river systems, the Ganges and the Brahmaputra, with their numerous distributaries (Morgan and McIntire 1956). Discharge and sedimentary load figures are generally unavailable, but it can be said that the maximum flow of the Ganges River is 1.5 million ft^3/s and the Brahmaputra some 2 million ft^3/s (Chatterjee 1947, 1949).

The geomorphic history of this huge deltaic plain is one of rivers that continually shift their courses back and forth as they fill in a large geosynclinal trough (Colebrooke 1803). In more recent times the Ganges has shifted to the east, from a main outlet along the western margins (the Bhagirathi-Hooghly in India) to the present main course, the Padma-Meghna; streams such as the Kobadak, Pursur, Madhumati, and Tetulia represent intermediate, but not necessarily successive, positions of the main channel (Ascoli 1910, 1912). There are several possible reasons for this shift, but the tectonic subsidence theory advanced by Morgan and McIntire (1956) appears to be the most plausible. They suggested deep faulting or structural subsidence along a trough running north-northwest from the active delta to the junction of the Ganges and the Brahmaputra, southeast of Padna. Their ideas are based on the apparent structural trends of the rivers and on the faulting that occurs along the western edge of the Madhupur Jungle.

Whether any parts of the Bangladesh coast are prograding is a matter of debate. Spate and Learmonth (1967) reported that although local erosion exists, accretion apparently predominates. There seems to be little difference, however, between the coastline shown on Rennell's map of 1770 and that of modern surveys, particularly in the western Sundarban region (Rennell 1781). However, the presence of old beach ridges in the western swamps points to earlier Holocene accretion (Fergusson 1863). In the east, where large quantities of silt are brought down by the rivers in flood, all stages in the process of land-building can be clearly seen from the air. But no large delta appears to be extending into the Bay of Bengal,

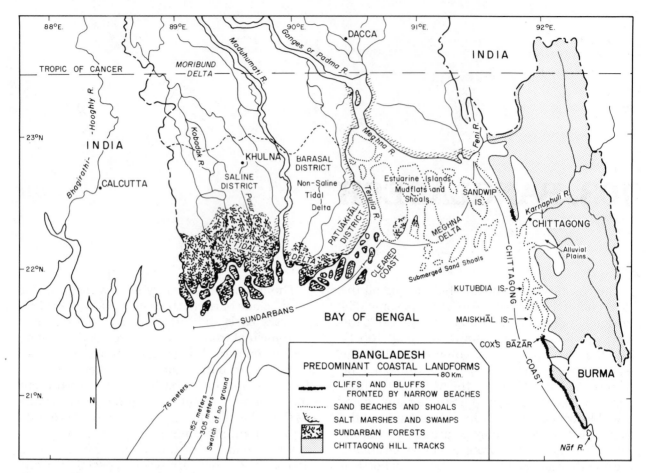

Figure 103-1. Predominant coastal landforms, Bangladesh.

probably because of subsidence and a fairly narrow continental shelf. The rate of subsidence has evidently more than kept pace with the rate of sedimentary deposition (Morgan and McIntire 1956).

Tides along the Bangladesh coast are semidiurnal. Tidal heights vary with the season, being lower in February and March and higher during the monsoon, July through November. The mean range of tide in the Chittagong area is 2.84 m, and the spring range is 3.64 m. For the Sundarbans the tide appears to be higher, reaching 7.0 m during monsoon storms (Sailing Directions 1978).

Surface currents across the head of the Bay of Bengal are developed by the monsoon winds, and can be quite dangerous to small craft venturing into the bay (Heathcote 1862).

SUNDARBANS

The Sundarbans are a heavily wooded mangrove and nipa palm swamp extending from the Hooghly River in India eastward to the Tetulia River, a distance of about 280 km. Nearly 193 km of this distance is in Bangladesh. The area covers about 6,000 km² and represents the older deltaic plain of the Ganges River, with a slope of about 0.076 m per mile (Bhattasali 1941). The largely uninhabited forest formerly extended northward to Khulna and eastward across the Barisal and Patuākhāli districts of Bangladesh. With the encroachment of agricultural land and extensive cutting of the forests, the true mangrove and nipa jungles are now largely confined to the southern part of Khulna district (Johnson 1975).

The region is interlaced with a checkerboard pattern of tidal estuaries and tidal rivers (Plates 103-1 and 103-2). Many of these interconnecting channels are navigable (Rainey 1891). Interstream areas are shallow, saucerlike swamp depressions. Off the immediate coast are a number of flat marshy islands. Navigation in the channels and estuaries is hazardous, especially during the "northeasters" in March, April, and May and the

Bay of Bengal cyclonic storms from June to October.

Tidal mangrove and sundri (*Heritiera littoralis*) forests predominate (Agarkar 1929). The mangrove forest, mainly species of *Rhizophora*, is found along the waterways, the banks of which are composed of soft muds and clays that are under water at every high tide (West 1956). Many of the creeks and channels are fringed by nipa palms (*Phoenix paludosa*) (Ahmad and Khan 1959). Higher up is found the sundri forest, where the land is flooded with moderately brackish water at every high tide. The sundri tree reaches a height of about 16 m, and its red wood is of excellent quality (Chatterjee 1947, 1949). Close to the coast the high forest changes into smaller species, separated in places by low sand dunes (Ahmad and Khan 1959). The Sundarbans are the habitat of cobras, pythons, crocodiles, leopards, small deer, and the famous Bengal tiger, whose numbers are now being threatened by man.

CLEARED SUNDARBAN COAST

In the Barisal and Patuākhāli districts of Bangladesh, over a distance of some 68 km, the Sundarban forest has been cleared, and there is extensive farming (mainly paddy rice) on the drier and less saline interfluves of this part of the deltaic plain. Here population densities reach more than 2,900 per square kilometer. Along the coast lie scattered, partially cut mangrove forests (Johnson 1971).

THE MEGHNA DELTA

The Ganges, Brahmaputra, and Meghna rivers all join into one main trunk stream in central Bangladesh before entering the Bay of Bengal through a single main channel called the Meghna River. Where it meets the Bay of Bengal it divides and spreads out around a series of extensive shoals called the Meghna Flats (Plate 103-3). These largely barren mud and sand shoals, at least ten of them of considerable size, extend from the Tetulia River on the west to the Feni River on the east, a distance of about 100 km. Wide, shallow channels separate these shoals, shifting so often that navigation is dangerous for large boats, especially during monsoon floods and severe cyclones. Only vessels with a draft of 3 m or less can proceed up the channels. The mud and sand shoals, with depths up to 5.5 m, extend southward for some 70 km to the Karnaphuli

River. This is a drowned coastal region with no true delta building out into the Bay of Bengal. During storms waves cover these shoals and, in contrast to the Sundarbans, little vegetation survives on them (*Sailing Directions* 1978).

THE CHITTAGONG COAST

The coast of the Chittagong district extends 274 km from the Feni River in the north to the Naf River on the Burmese boundary. The small Feni River empties into Sandwip Channel about 13 km above the northern end of Sandwip Island. Two other large islands, Kutubodia and Maiskhāl, are found along this stretch of coast, as are several smaller islands and shoals. The coastal plain varies greatly in width here. Near the Karnaphuli River it is from 48–64 km wide, but where the low Tertiary hills and cliffs rise immediately inland it is virtually nonexistent (Fig. 103-1) (Wadia 1949). The Karnaphuli River, with its headwaters in Assam, is short but carries a large volume of water during the monsoon flood season. The entrance to this river is low and flat and would be difficult to find by ship but for the Norman's Point Lighthouse. Sand-covered mud flats, dry at low tide, extend about 1 km seaward of the mouth. Several small beaches and broad sand flats are found along the coast between the headlands, but in the south the coastal plain dwindles away before the uplifted and deeply eroded Chittagong Hills, which inland reach an elevation of 609 m. These hills are of stratified Tertiary marine and freshwater limestone and shale. At Cox's Bāzār (Plate 103-4) there is a beach more than 152 m wide, but south of the town steep cliffs 9–15 m high front directly onto a narrow shore.

RODMAN E. SNEAD

REFERENCES

Agarkar, S. P., 1929, The vegetation of the Ganges Region, *Jour. Madras Geog. Assoc.* **4:**14–16.

Ahmad, N., and F. K. Khan, 1959, The Sundarban forests of east Pakistan—A resource appraisal, *Oriental Geographer* **3:**13–32.

Ascoli, F. D., 1910, The rivers of the delta, *Jour. Proc. Asiatic Society of Bengal* **6:**543–556.

Ascoli, F. D., 1912, Changes in the delta of the Ganges, *Royal Geog. Soc. Jour.* **34:**611–612.

Bhattasali, N. K., 1941, Antiquity of the Lower Ganges and its courses, *Science and Culture* **7:**233–239.

Chatterjee, S. P., 1947, River problems in Bengal, *Punjab Geog. Rev.* **2:**12–20.

Chatterjee, S. P., 1949, *Bengal in Maps,* Orient Longmans Ltd., Calcutta.

Colebrooke, R. H., 1803, On the courses of the Ganges through Bengal, *Trans. Asiatic Society* **7:**1–31.

Dey, N., 1921, The early course of the Ganges, *Indian Antiquity* **50:**8–72.

Fergusson, J., 1863, Delta of the Ganges, *Geol. Soc. London Quart. Jour.* **19:**321–354.

Heathcote, J. A., 1862, Surface current of the Bay of Bengal, *Royal Geog. Soc. Jour.* **32:**234–241.

Johnson, L. B., 1971, *South Asia,* Heinemann Educational Books, London.

Johnson, L. B., 1975, *Bangladesh,* Heinemann Educational Books, London.

Morgan, J. P., and W. G. McIntire, 1956, *Quaternary Geology of the Bengal Basin,* Coastal Studies Institute Technical Report 9, Louisiana State University, Baton Rouge.

Mukerjee, R., 1938, *The Changing Face of Bengal,* University of Calcutta, Calcutta.

Rainey, J. R., 1891, The Sundarban, *Royal Geog. Soc. Proc.* **13:**273–275.

Rennell, J. J., 1781, The Ganges and Brahmaputra Rivers, *Royal Soc. London Philos. Trans.* **71:**91–103.

Sailing Directions for India and the Bay of Bengal, 1978, Defense Mapping Agency, Hydrologic/Topographic Center, Office of Distribution Services, DMA Stock No. SDPUB173, Washington, D.C.

Spate, O. H. K., and A. T. A. Learmonth, 1967, *India, Pakistan, and Ceylon: The Regions,* Methuen and Company, London.

Wadia, D. N., 1949, *Geology of India,* Macmillan, London.

West, R., 1956, Mangrove swamps of the Pacific coast of Colombia, *Assoc. Am. Geographers Annals* **66:**98–121.

Plate 103-1. The Sundarban coast of Bangladesh consists of extensive tidal flats bordering on mangrove and sundri forests. A large crocodile can be seen sunning itself on a mud-flat terrace (photo by R. A. Snead).

Plate 103-2. The low tidal portion of the Sundarbans consists of a dense jungle forest made up of *Rhizophora* mangroves and a large nipa palm (*Phoenix paludosa*). This is the native habitat of the Bengal tiger (photo by R. A. Snead).

Plate 103-3. The Meghna delta of Bangladesh comprises numerous sand shoals and mud flats. At low tide these sand flats are largely uncovered, but during the monsoon season and in severe storms the entire area is flooded, including the low dark mangroves seen in the distance (photo by R. A. Snead).

Plate 103-4. The Chittagong coast of Bangladesh has a sandy beach and coastal plain backed by low hills and mountains. This view of the airport at Cox's Bāzār shows the tidal channels and estuaries separating Maiskhal Island from the mainland. View looking northeast (photo by R. A. Snead).

104. BURMA

The Burmese coastline, about 2,300 km long, consists of three distinct parts. The Arakan coast, from the Bangladesh border south to the Cape Negrais peninsula, runs parallel to mountain ranges of strongly folded Mesozoic and Tertiary rock, dominated by ridges and valleys that follow the geological strike. East of Cape Negrais the deltaic plains of the Irrawaddy border the Gulf of Martaban, and south from Moulmein the coast is again generally steep, bordering the Tenasserim Ranges, mainly Upper Paleozoic rocks, also with a predominant north–south strike.

In a humid tropical setting (monsoonal, with annual rainfall exceeding 5000 mm on many parts of the coast, and only a brief winter dry season) rock formations are deeply weathered and coastal slopes carry evergreen rain forest or bamboo thickets. Ocean waves arriving in coastal waters are weak, but are reinforced by the south-westerly monsoon (late May to early October) to produce moderate wave action on sandy beaches and rocky shores with minor cliffing. Tropical cyclones are rare in this part of the Bay of Bengal. Tide ranges are typically about 2.5 m, increasing to more than 5.5 m in the estuarine distributaries of the Irrawaddy, and to over 6 m at the head of the Gulf of Martaban, where the Sittang River, opening into an estuarine gulf, is invaded by a tidal bore at spring tides.

THE ARAKAN COAST

Near Sittwe (Akyab) the coast is of Dalmatian type, with elongated steep-sided peninsulas and islands separating marine straits, but farther south it becomes more intricate, with intersecting estuarine channels behind Ramree Island. Man-groves are extensive, particularly around river mouths, notably the Kaladan River at Akyab. Coral reefs are patchy, mainly on the outer coastline. Emerged coastal features at various levels indicate a history of tectonic movements, and the 1762 Chittagong earthquake is said to have caused actual emergence around Cheduba Island, which has at least three well-developed raised coastlines. Ramree Island consists of former islands, now hills, rising above emerged alluvial plains. Raised beaches and old sea cliffs are preserved on the west coast, particularly at Minbyin (Pascoe 1962).

Soil erosion in coastal catchments has augmented river loads, and there are extensive tidal mud flats in sheltered areas. Sand spits, as at Cypress Point and the mouth of Sandoway River, have grown to deflect river mouths and protect mangrove areas. Mud volcanoes are a feature of these coastal waters, forming temporary islands up to 4 m high, which are planed off by waves to form shoals. There are good examples in Cheduba Strait, where they are a hazard to navigation (*Bay of Bengal Pilot* 1978). They are evidently associated with submarine volcanic activity where the Indian continental plate is underthrusting the Asian plate. Foul Island, to the south, is a thickly wooded volcanic island that has erupted in recent decades.

IRRAWADDY DELTA

Draining into a major tectonic trough that runs north–south, the Irrawaddy and its tributaries have brought vast quantities of silt, and some sand, to form an extensive delta. The rivers branch into several estuarine distributaries, with shoal

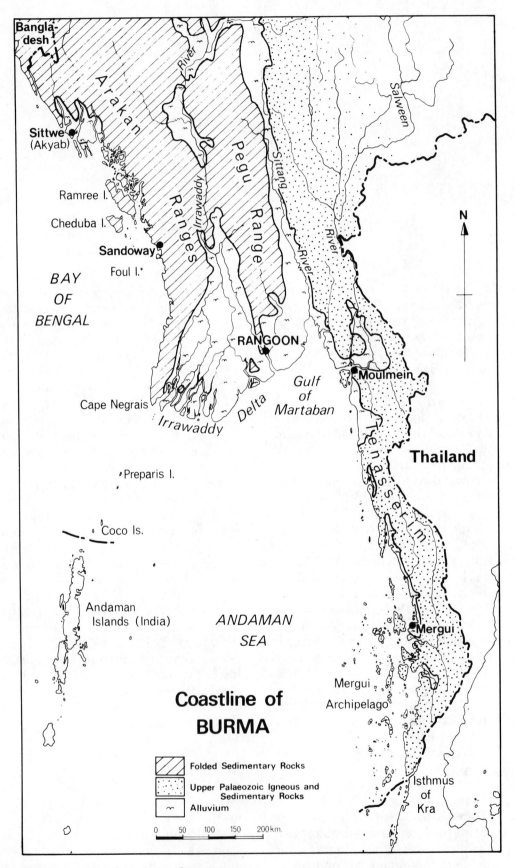

Figure 104-1. Coastline of Burma.

and channel topography shaped by strong ebb and flow currents. Mangroves, forming forests up to 30 m high, and associated dani palms, spread out on to accreting tidal flats, especially on the seaward margin in the lee of wave-built sand bars. Progradation occurs at up to 60 m per year on this deltaic coastline, even though much silty sediment delivered by the rivers is swept eastward into the Gulf of Martaban by southwesterly waves during the monsoon (Volker 1966).

Large mats of water weed are carried downstream by the Irrawaddy during the wet season, and these eventually become incorporated in accreting sediments. Locally the river channels have meandered to undercut and cliff the margins of residual hills of older sandy alluvium. Rangoon, sited where a spur of the Pegu Yoma runs out into the deltaic plains, is a major port on a navigable estuary.

The delta has an area of about 30,000 km^2, of which 5,000 km^2 is intertidal, that is, submerged at high spring tides. In addition, extensive flooding occurs in the wet season, and high natural levees have been built by silt deposition alongside the river channels.

THE TENASSERIM COAST

South of Moulmein the coast borders steeply rising country, but there are a number of sectors of alluvial plain. The Salween River opens into a funnel-shaped estuary bordered by plains from which rise steep karstic hills of limestone. Spurs of the hill country extend to the coast, ending in rocky promontories; the intervening valleys open to mangrove-fringed creeks and estuaries, often with bordering sand spits, and outlets usually at the southern end. Mining has been extensive in the Paleozoic rocks of the steep hinterland, and extraction of minerals and precious stones from valley floors and terrace alluvium has modified runoff and sediment yield from many rivers, but the effects of these activities on the coastal landforms have not been documented. Many estuarine lagoons in bays along the coast have been rapidly silted and converted into mangrove swamps and saline marshes. Coastal sand deposits include heavy minerals, notably ilmenite and monazite. Some beaches are backed by dunes blown inland by the southwesterly winds.

In southern Burma steep coasts predominate, and similar features are seen on the hilly Mergui archipelago, which contains over 800 islands. Coral reefs and reef ledges become more extensive around the outer islands, away from the muddy coastal waters.

ERIC C. F. BIRD

REFERENCES

Bay of Bengal Pilot 1978. Hydrographic Office, Taunton.
Pascoe, E. H., 1962, *A Manual of the Geology of India and Burma*, Vol. 3, Geological Survey of India, Delhi.
Volker, A., 1966, The deltaic area of the Irrawaddy river in Burma, in *Scientific Problems of the Humid Tropical Zone Deltas and Their Implications*, UNESCO, Paris, pp. 373–379.

105. THAILAND

The coastline of Thailand (Fig. 105-1) is about 2,960 km long, of which 750 km is on the west Andaman Sea coast, 1,670 km on the eastern Gulf of Thailand, and the remainder (520 km) on over 258 islands, of which the six largest account for 90% (Table 1 summarizes the distribution of major coastal types given in Fig. 105-1.) It is convenient to deal with both coastlines here, although in a coastwise sequence they are separated by Malaysia and Singapore.

GEOLOGY

The outline of central and peninsular Thailand is controlled by the effect of Upper Paleozoic Hercynian orogeny, modified by Mesozoic orogeny, which produced fold belts that trend north in the south but northwest toward the head of the Gulf of Thailand (Fig. 105-2). These Cambrian to Triassic sediments were intruded by late Cretaceous-early Tertiary granitic masses, which form four major linear ridges: one adjacent to the west coast forms Phuket Island and extends to Ranong and Kanchanaburi; the second, the Satun ridge, gives rise to the islands of the Samui group; while the third and fourth form prominent ridges and headlands at Ko Kra and Narathiwat. Northeast of Phuket Island the peninsula is crossed by a complex of northeast–southwest faults, interpreted as major transcurrent faults that displace the Phuket granites sinistrally 250 km to the southwest along the Khlong Maru fault. The granitic outcrop in southeast Thailand is similarly displaced (Fig. 105-2).

Between these ridges, particularly the Phuket and Samui massifs, major faulting has produced a graben, in which Permian Ratburi limestones occur, giving unique marine karstic landforms in Phang Nga Bay, down to the Malay border and along the gulf coast as far north as Petchaburi. Tertiary sediments are confined to small basins. However, Tertiary orogeny induced the subsidence of the Chao Phraya depression.

The Gulf of Thailand began to form as a result of late Cretaceous to early Tertiary subsidence, which emphasized the north–south tectonic trends, and a series of pronounced depositional basins formed. Quaternary marine sediments form large areas in the south, around Pattani, between Songkhla and Nakhon Si Thammerat, and along the head of the gulf. Tjia et al. (1977)

Table 1. Distribution of Major Coastal Types, Thailand (km)

Area	Andaman Sea	Eastern Peninsula	Head of Gulf	East Coast	Total
Type					
Mangrove/Mud Flat	480.0 (55.7%)	103.8 (12.0%)	168.0 (19.5%)	110.0 (12.8%)	862.0 (33.0%)
Sand Beach	207.5 (16.6%)	795.0 (63.4%)	64.0 (5.10%)	187.5 (14.9%)	1254.0 (49.0%)
Rocky Coast	106.0 (24.1%)	241.2 (54.7%)	7.0 (1.6%)	86.5 (19.6%)	440.7 (17.2%)
Total	793.5	1140.0	239.0	384.0	2556.7 (100)

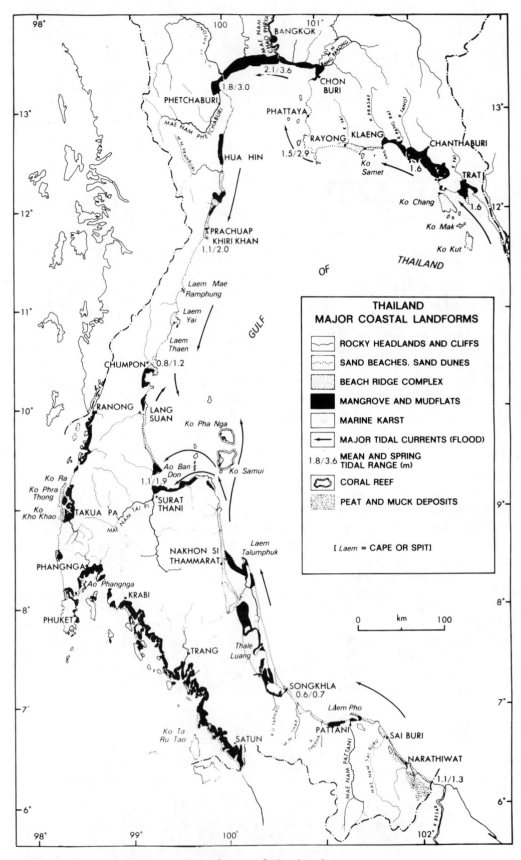

Figure 105-1. Major coastal landforms of Thailand.

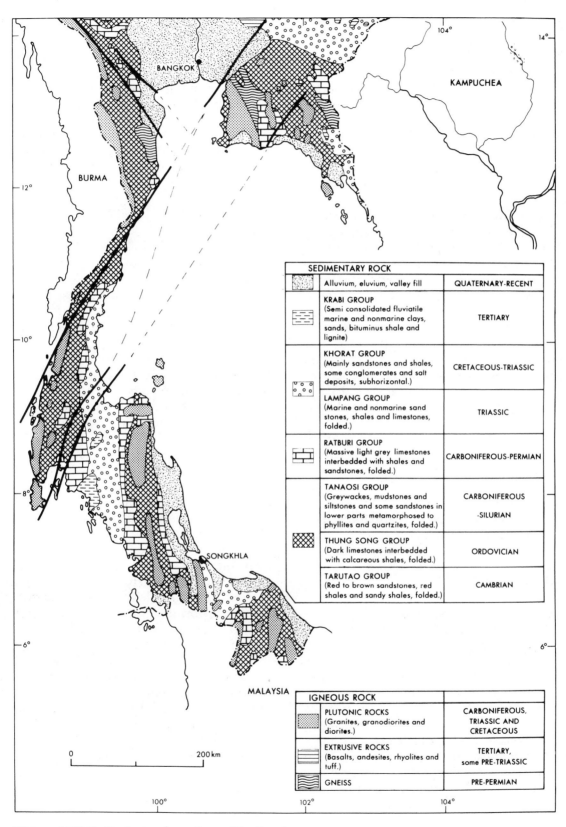

Figure 105-2. Geology of southern Thailand.

have reviewed and described in detail Quaternary sea-level changes in this area, and conclude that there is good evidence for a high Holocene sea level. Soil mapping in the peninsula (Dent 1972) shows evidence of several raised shorelines, marine terraces, and river terraces, indicative of the recent northwest tilting of the peninsula, producing the submergent western coastline and smooth emergent coast of the gulf. This also reflects the shallow offshore gradients characteristic of the gulf (<1: 1,000) compared with the western sublittoral fringe (>1:300).

The major directions of longshore drift reflect the interaction between winds and current. In the south, the northeast monsoon blows from about December to April, giving winds mainly from the east and north. The southwest monsoon blows from May to October, with winds mainly from the west and south. The trends in direction are given in Figure 105-1. Maximum rainfall occurs between September and February on the south peninsula coast, with up to 1,800 mm on the east coast and over 2,200 mm on the west coast. Flooding is common. Occasionally, the peninsula eastern coast is affected by typhoons in October and November.

The tidal range on the west coast is between 1.9 m and 2.7 m, with much lower ranges on the eastern coast, which gradually increase toward the north of the gulf (Fig. 105-1) (Pukasab and Pochanasomburana 1957). Current directions in the gulf have been investigated by Robertson (1974) and Faughn and Taft (1967).

SEDIMENT SOURCES

Along the western coasts, rivers are short because of the proximity of the continental divide; hence sediment influx is low. Along the southeast coast of the gulf, only three significant rivers reach the coast: the Mae Nam Pattani, the Mae Nam Ta Pi, and the numerous streams flowing into the Khlong Taphao. Each of these river systems carries considerable amounts of silt, resulting in wide, flat coastal deposits, and delta formation at Surat Thani and Pattani (Fig. 105-2, Plate 105-1). Between Chumpon and Hua Hin no major rivers occur, while the Mae Nam Phetchaburi gives rise to a wide deltaic plain (Fig. 105-4). However, the Mae Nam Chao Phraya, the Mae Nam Mae Khlong, Mae Nam Tha Chi, and Bang Pakong between them are responsible for the major influx of sediment into the gulf (Fig. 105-4).

The active tidal mud flats, inundated daily by the sea, are 1–1.5 m above mean sea level and cover an area of 990 km^2 (Fig. 105-1). They are composed of fine greyish-green clays and normally occupied by mangrove swamps. South of Bangkok these have been cleared and given over to salt pans and shrimp ponds. Sublittoral mud flats occupy 3,700 km^2 and are most extensive at the head of the gulf, Phang Nga Bay (Sriplung et al. 1978; Sriplung 1978), and south of Chanthaburi.

MAJOR COASTAL TYPES

Mangrove Forest

A major component of the more sheltered river mouths and sea coasts of the Gulf of Thailand, the southeast coast, and the west coast of the peninsula is extensive, luxuriant growth of mangrove forest (Aksornkoae 1976; Banijbatana 1957). In all some 1,620 km^2 occur, 875 km^2 being on the Andaman Sea (Watson 1928) coast. Along this coast extensive tracts occur (Fig. 105-1), particularly between Satun and Phang Nga in association with broad tidal mud flats and north of Takua Pa to Ranong. In the gulf they are found near Narathiwat, Pattani, Songkhla, Nakhon Si Thammarat, and Surat Thani; south of Chumpon; as extensive tracts associated with the deltas of the Mae Nam Phetchaburi, Mae Nam Chao Phraya, and Mae Nam Bang PaKong, and in the east at Rayong, Chanthaburi, and Trat (Figs. 105-1, 105-4, 105-5).

These mangroves reach their maximum development on the Andaman Sea Coast, where individual trees may be 40 m high. These swamps are marked by clearly defined ecological zonation/succession forming five major community types, related to frequency and depth of flooding. Along the seward fringe, *Avicennia alba* and *Sonneratia griffithii*, *S. alba*, occur in association with *Rhizophora mucronata* and *R. apiculata*. The *Avicennia/Rhizophora* association is normally found on more arenaceous soils, the *Sonneratia/ Bruguiera* on more argillaceous sediments. Inland *Bruguiera parvilflora* and *B. gymorrhiza* dominate, in association with *Xylocarpus moluccensis*, *X. obovatus*, *Intsia bijuga*, *Excoecaria agallacha*, *Lumnitzera racemosa*, and *L. coccinea* with *Ceriops roxburghian* and *C. tagel.* Typically the *Rhizophora* forest extends inland along river banks in association with *Nypa fruticans*. Beyond the seaward fringe of the mangroves are extensive mud flats, with gradients

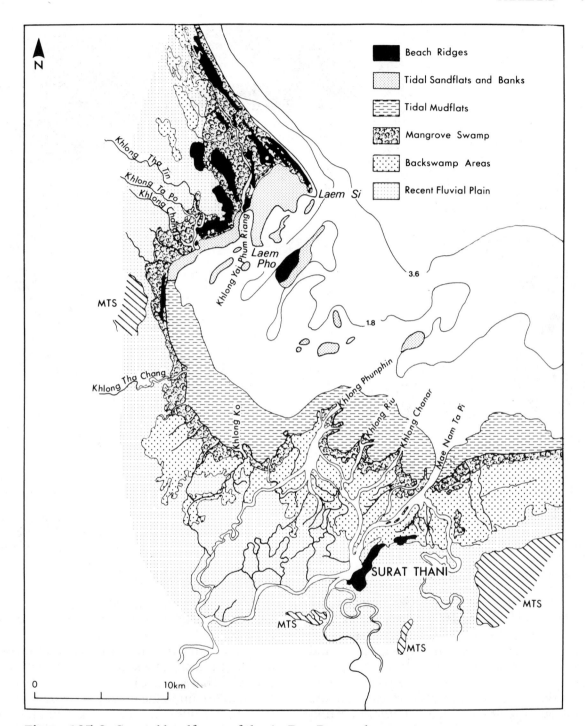

Figure 105-3. Coastal landforms of the Ao Ban Don embayment.

<1%. Inland these estuarine deposits merge into extensive alluvial deposits 5.3 m above sea level.

Sand Beaches

While the western peninsula coast is dominated by mangroves and mud flats, the gulf coast is predominantly composed of alternating sand beach ridges planted with coconut palms and fruit trees, which contrast sharply with the paddy cultivation of the mud-filled depressions between the ridges. Figure 105-1 shows the location of the deposits, and it is particularly noteworthy that the major areas of these ridges are in the peninsula south and in eastern Thailand. Lagoons and beach barriers are common at these locations,

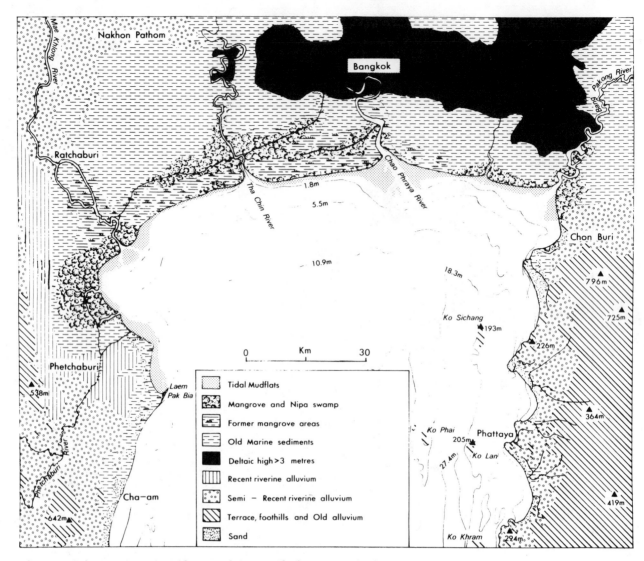

Figure 105-4. Deltaic landforms of the Gulf of Thailand.

and rivers at the coast are deflected by longshore drift (small arrows, Fig. 105-1). This gives rise to a distinctive pattern of drainage parallel to the coast, with major rivers often emerging behind rocky outcrops, as at Narathiwat. The larger depressions are often peat and muck filled, forming convex domes up to 10 m high, covered by *Shorea albida* with *Melaleuca leucadendron* around the fringes (Fig. 105-1).

Rocky headlands are associated with granitic and limestone outcrops, the major area being in eastern Thailand (Fig. 105-2), east of Surat Thani, Phang Nga Bay, and along the coast between Takua Pa and Ranong.

Coral reefs occur on almost all the islands on the west coast, other than those with mangrove or mudbank foreshores, and are being actively exploited for tourism around Phuket Island. Ko Samui and Ko Pangna have extensive reefs, espe-

cially on their southern and eastern coasts, while the smaller islands of this group have surrounding reefs.

Beach sediments are being actively mined for detrital tin along the southwestern coast, especially the Thai Muange Beach (Fig. 105-1) (Garson et al. 1975), and silica sand is being extracted from beach ridges at Songkhla, Chumpon, and Rayong. Mangrove is also being cleared for timber, fuel, and charcoal, while *nipa* is used for roofing. Current estimates are that 75% of the mangrove areas could be converted to shrimp mariculture.

ANDAMAN SEA COAST

As a result of recent submergence, the steep offshore gradient, and the effects of the southwest monsoon, coastal sediments on the western coast between Satun and Ranong are restricted to river

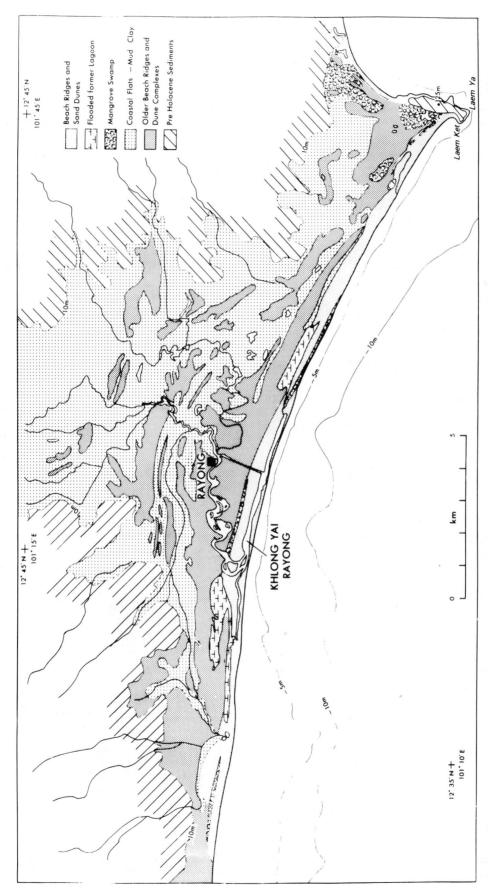

Figure 105-5. Coastal barriers at Rayong.

777

mouth estuaries, behind baymouth barriers, and in sheltered locations eastward of offshore islands. Between Phuket and Satun, mangrove swamps extend up to 10 km inland along tidal creeks and estuaries, gradually giving way to fresh-water vegetation. These swamps are marked by anastomizing channel patterns, flanked by steep mudbanks. Between Phuket and Krabi they reach their maximum extent (Plate 105-2) although here they have been affected by cutting for fuel, and tin dredging. Generally the swamp muds are 3–5 m deep, overlying gravels and alluvium. South of Phang Nga these muds and gravels rest on a limestone bench 10–15 m below present sea level. The occurrence of placer deposits of tin offshore along former river channels attests to the recent marine submergence.

Shores exposed to the southwest monsoon develop marked beach ridges, backed by mangrove swamps and tidal mud flats, as at Ban Chao Yai and south of Kantang. All exposed western shores of islands are rocky, cliffed, and coral fringed. The most dramatic landforms are to be found in Phang Nga Bay, where limestone ridges form marine tower karst (Plates 105-2 and 105-3) that rise to over 300 m. All towers show evidence of a sea-level notch with a second notch 3.0–3.5 m above mean sea level. These higher notches are also to be found inland around Phang Nga. Similar notches found in the Langkawi Islands have been dated as 4,370 ± 110 yrs B.P. (Tjia et al. 1977).

Sand beach deposits are associated with baymouth barriers on the western coast of Phuket Island, separated by rocky headlands. The sand beaches extend 50 km north of the island, as far as Takua Pa, where they are extensively mined for placer tin. Beachrock occurs locally, especially on southern Phuket Island.

Barrier islands with pronounced beach ridges and well-developed cusps are found at Ko Kho Khao and Ko Phra Thong (Plate 105-4); well-developed cusps also occur here. Ko Ra is a rocky headland, part of a ridge extending northward as a chain of rocky islands. A second ridge, parallel to the outer one, forms steep headlands and islands inshore. Sand, mud, and mangrove swamps have accumulated in the lee of the barrier islands and inner ridge (Plate 105-4).

EASTERN PENINSULA COAST

The long, smooth, emergent coast of the southwest of the gulf between the Malay border and Ko Samui is fringed with offshore bars, sand spits, and lagoons (Fig. 105-1). Rocky headlands con-strict the coastal plain east of Pattani, at Chana, and north of Si Chon. Between these outcrops, the coastal plain consists of long stretches of sand beach, broken only by major rivers, and backed by a series of parallel beach ridges. These extend up to 15 km inland south of Narathiwat and form a complex of ridges and depressions. (Dheekaohilok 1980). The height of the beach crests varies from 2–3 m at the coast to over 10 m inland.

Where the coast is protected from the northeast monsoon, as at Pattani, a complex of sand spits and beach ridges has developed (Plate 105-1), with the present sand spit, Laem Pho, extending some 22 km offshore. In the lee of the spit the Pattani River is building a cuspate delta. Mangrove swamps occur between sand ridges east of Pattani. Between Songhla and Tha Sala, 190 km to the north, the coastal plain broadens to over 45 km in width (up to the 10 m contour), and forms one of the two largest areas of Quaternary and Holocene sedimentation in Thailand. The seaward fringe is marked by a major sand barrier, which extends northward for 160 km and terminates at the recurved spit of Laem Talumphuk. Behind this is a series of interconnected brackish-water lagoons, open to the sea at Songkhla: Thale Sap Songkhla, Thule Sup, Thale Luang, and Thale Noi. Thale Noi is fringed on its northern side by mangrove swamps and brackish-water swamps extending for another 20 km north, which in turn link up with the Mae Nam Pak Pahang (see Fig. 105-6). Three features are of interest here; the coastal sand barrier and the spit, the lagoons and swamps, and the complex pattern of beach ridges on the barrier and, inland, remnants of former beach ridges (Fig. 105-6; Plate 105-5).

The latter features are particularly well shown on the ERTS photograph (Plate 105-5). Two major sets of sand beach ridges, arcuate in form, extend from north–south sand ridges at Tha Sala, 30 km to the north. Both were clearly formed in response to a counter-current, similar to that of today, developed behind the sand spit at Thalumpuk; both are also associated at their eastern seaward ends with isolated outcrops of limestone hills, at Kuan Krong and northeastward at Kjao Noi and Khao Klu. The area between these two sets of ridges is fresh-water swamp lying between the outer, later series of ridges and the present shore of Ao Phatang. A continuation of this sedimentary process has further developed an area of alternating ridges and mud-filled depressions, with relief not exceeding 3 m.

The beach barrier, extending from Songkhla

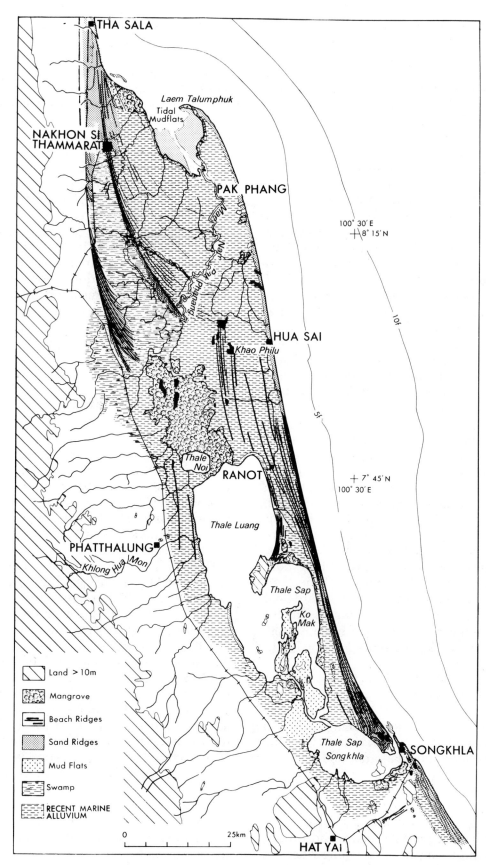

Figure 105-6. Coastal barriers and landforms of the Songkhla-Nakhon Si Thammarat coastal plain.

northward, is slowly prograding seaward as a result of accretion by longshore drift. Where the offshore gradient is shallowest, they are 200–300 m apart. Where it is steepest, toward Songkhla, they become closer together, at 50–100 m, and more complex in form.

Between the beach barriers and the oldest series of beach ridges are three lagoons. They are extremely shallow (< 2m in most places) and clearly undergoing rapid sedimentation.

Mud flats and swamps are found around the islands of Ko Mak and Ko Khop, and between Ko Mak and Thale Songkhla. Sediments are from the numerous short rivers that no longer have direct access to the sea. Mangroves are important in trapping sediment, particularly south of Ko Mak and around Thale Noi.

The coast between Khao Luang and Surat Thani consists of headlands of Permian limestones alternating with bay-head beaches, some complex in formation, as at Ao Thong Nam. These beaches, while sandy when exposed to the monsoonal winds, become mangrove where more sheltered, as at Ao Thong Niam, Ao Tafet Noi, and Ao Bang Nang Kam. An extension of mangrove swamps recurs inland of Khao Chat Soi.

Ao Ban Don, formed between Ko Nok Taphao and the spit Laem Sui, consists of tidal flats of mud and sand banks and bars that dry, forming flats up to 4 km wide (Fig. 105-3). The complete bay is less than 5.5 m deep as far as Kao Phulai, and is rapidly being filled by the sediment brought down by Mae Nam Ta Pi and the counter gyre developed west of the Ko Samui group of islands. The latter gives rise to a southward longshore drift, resulting in the development of the compound spit at Laem Sui, while the westward tidal stream through Chong Thai brings sediment giving rise to the cuspate spits of Laem Khung. Extensive mangrove swamps have developed within the embayment.

The delta of the Mae Nam Ta Pi is a typical high constructive birdsfoot, with marked channel switching, indicative of the high sediment load and low offshore wave energy. Laem Sui spit is still distally prograding, as can be seen from the numerous offshore mud flats and sand bars (Fig. 105-3). A new spit is developing 5 km southeast of the present one.

For 310 km north of Laem Si, the coast continues as long stretches of sand beach, backed by a rapidly narrowing coastal plain, and broken only by the north-northeast trending ridges of Cretaceous and Triassic sandstones and limestones. These form offshore islands between Lang Suan and Prachuap Khiri Khan. The sheltered bays inshore of these islands are commonly filled by beach ridges and lagoons, as at Chumpon, with bay heads being mud flats and mangrove swamp. Where the islands occur in isolation, as at Laem Thaen, Laem Yai, Laem Mae Ramphung, and Prachuap Khiri Khan, tombolos of classic form develop. Typically they have parabolic sand beaches, swamps in the lee of the island, and major streams emerging in the sheltered lee, as at Laem Mae Ramphung. Figure 105-7 illustrates these features at Prachuap Khiri Khan.

The north-northeast trend of the coast is broken at Sam Roi Et, where the Ranong fault crosses the coast. Rocky headlands, beach ridges extending 10 km inland, and swamps are associated with this Permian limestone outcrop (Pitman 1982). At Hua Hin coastal dunes are well developed, and extend 30 km northward to Cha-am, where a large filled lagoon occurs between the dunes and limestone hills.

INNER GULF OF THAILAND

Coastal features at the head of the Gulf of Thailand are dominated by the combined effects of deltaic sedimentation of five major rivers, of which the Mae Nam Chao Phraya is the largest (Coleman and Wright 1976). The eastern side of the gulf is flanked by three smoothly curved sandy bay-head beaches, between rocky headlands of sandstones and granite.

The Chao Phraya River and its tributaries drain an area of 11,329 km^2, producing a flood plain that extends 470 km south from the 100 m contour to the 120 km wide delta front (Fig. 105-4). From Ayutthaya southward the terrain is very flat and averages 2 m above sea level, except for a major area east and north of Bangkok that is 3.5–5 m high; Takaya (1969) considers this to be an old barrier island (Van der Kevie and Yermanas 1972). Peat from the backswamp dated as 3,100 B.P. suggests an advance of the delta front of at least 4 m a year (Kanchanalak 1966; Ohya 1966). Offshore the slope is exceedingly low (< 0.6%) and gives rise to extensive tidal mud flats.

The active and former tidal mud flats are narrow to the east of the Chao Phraya, and fronted by nipa palm, mangroves, and salt flats. To the west these mud flats extend up to 10–15 km inland (Fig. 105-4) and are dominated by mangrove

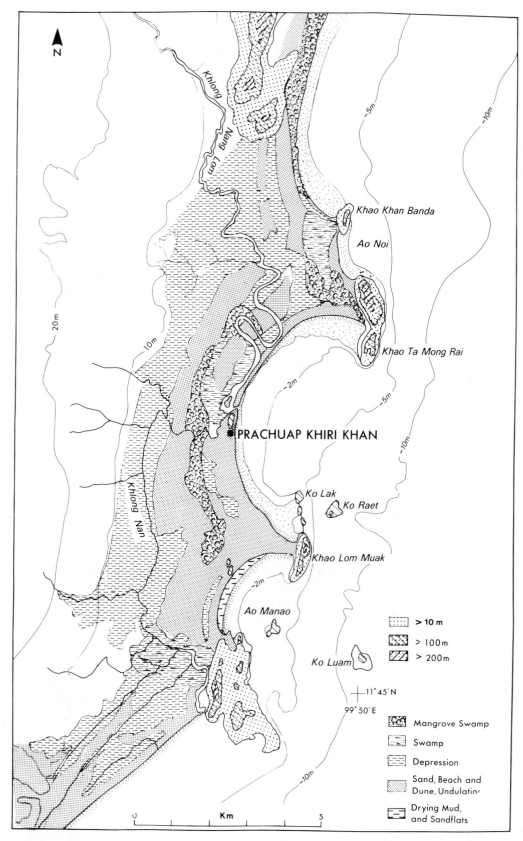

Figure 105-7. Tombolos and beach ridges at Prachuap Khiri Khan.

swamps that give way to brackish-water swamp inland. These are largely under paddy cultivation.

The largest area of mangrove swamp occurs south of Samut Songkhram. The Phetchaburi River has produced a complex delta prograding northward on to the Mae Nam Mae Khlong delta. The former, more southerly mouths of the Phetchaburi River are now marked by three cuspate forelands backed by tidal swamps and old beach barriers. The spit at Laem Pak Bia has extended 2 km between 1961 and 1967.

THE SOUTHEAST COAST

The southeast coast between Satthip and Klaeng is a series of three wide, sandy bays formed between mountainous ridges of igneous rocks and limestones, which here run north–south west of Ko Samet, then northeast–southeast to the

east. These ridges continue offshore as steep, rocky islands (Fig. 105-1). The sandy beaches, of which Rayong is typical (Fig. 105-5), consist of alternating, parallel ridges and depressions, with shallow lagoons in the depressions. Total relief seldom exceeds 5 m, although dunes up to 12 m high occur locally. At Rayong the beach ridges extend up to 7 km inland.

Eastwards of Klaeng broader alluvial plains are formed between the northwest–southeast trending ridges by the sediment influx from the Krasae, Phang Rat, Chanthaburi, and Welu rivers. The more sheltered mouths of the Krasae and Phang Rat rivers are mangrove fringed, with broad tidal marshes inland between inward-curving offshore islands.

The coast south of Chanthaburi is more exposed to the southwest monsoon, so that a complex pattern of beach ridges have evolved (Fig. 105-8). Behind the outer barrier and the former

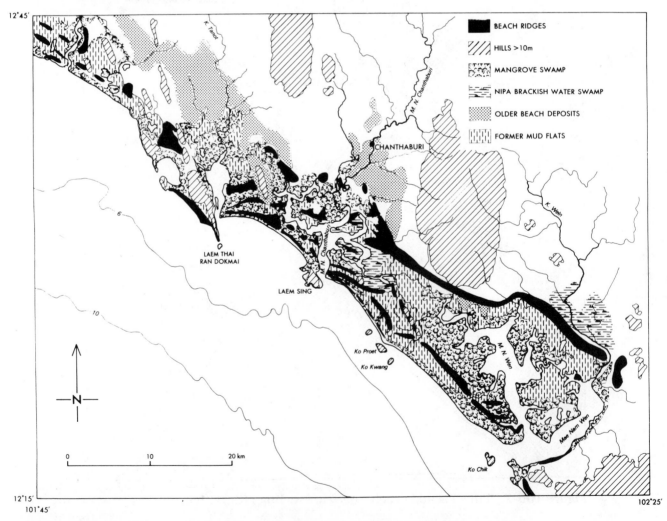

Figure 105-8. Barrier beaches and mangrove swamps at Chanthaburi.

coast extensive (180 km²) mangrove swamps and tidal marshes have developed, broken occasionally by isolated inselbergs, some of which form offshore islands. The mangroves have been comprehensively described by Aksornkoae (1976).

From the Welu River to the mud flat–fronted mangrove swamps of Trat Bay, the coast becomes rocky as shales and sandstones of the Kanchanaburi formation outcrop. Ko Chang forms a rugged island of Tertiary igenous rocks sheltering Trat Bay. South of Trat, to Khlong Yai, the coastal plain rapidly narrows to less than 500 m wide, before rising toward the Banthat Range. Here it is characterized by northward longshore drift, with offshore bars and spits.

JOHN I. PITMAN

REFERENCES

Aksornkoae, S., 1976, *Structure, Regeneration and Productivity of Mangroves in Thailand* Ph.D. thesis, Michigan State University, University Microfilms.

Banijbatana, D., 1957, Mangrove forest in Thailand, *9th Pacific Sci. Geog. Proc.* (Bangkok), pp. 22–34.

Coleman, J. M., and L. D. Wright, 1976, Modern river deltas: variability of processes and sand bodies, in *Deltas: Models for Exploration*, M. L. S. Broussard, ed., Houston Geological Society, pp. 99–149.

Dent, F. J., 1972, *Reconnaissance Soil Survey of Peninsula Thailand*, Rept. SSR-94, Soil Survey Division, Bangkok.

Dheekaohilok, P., 1980, *Relation between the Change of Shoreline along the Gulf of Thailand in Relation to Mineral Resources*, Geol. Sur. Div., Dept. of Min. Res., Bangkok (in Thai).

Faughn, J. L., and B. A. Taft, 1967, Current measurements at the mouth of the Gulf of Thailand, *Jour. Geophy. Research* **72**(6):1691–1695.

Kanchanalak, B., 1966, Significant change of river regions due to delta growth, in *Scientific Problems of the Humid Tropics Deltas and Their Implications*, Dacca Symposium, UNESCO, Paris, pp. 151–156.

van der Kevie, W., and B. Yermanas, 1972, *Detailed Reconnaissance Survey of Southern Central Plain Area*, Rept. SSR-89, Soil Surv. Div., Bangkok.

Ohya, M., 1966, Comparative study of the geomorphology and flooding in the plains of the Cho-Shui-Cha, Chas-Phyn, Irrawaddy and Ganges, *Scientific Problems of the Humid Tropics Deltas and Their Implications*, Dacca Symposium, UNESCO, pp. 23–28.

Pitman, J. I., 1982, *Geomorphology of the Coastline of Thailand*, Occ. Paper, Dept. Geography, King's College, University of London.

Pukasab, P., and P. Pochanasomburana, 1957, *The Types of Tides and Mean Sea Level in the Gulf of Thailand*, Hydrographic Dept., Ragal Thai Navy.

Robertson, M. K., 1974, *The Physical Oceanography of the Gulf of Thailand*, NAGA Rept. 3, (1):1–109.

Sriplung, N., A. Siripong, S. Morai, R. Matsuoka, and R. Tatgishi, 1978, The accretion of mudflats in the Pang Nga Bay from LANSAT MSS Data, *1st Asian Conf. on Remote Sensing Proc.*, Bangkok.

Sriplung, N., 1978, Thailand's littoral mudflats as interpreted from LANDSAT imagery, *12th Internat. Symp. on Remote Sensing of Environment*, Manila.

Takaya, Y., 1969, Topographical analysis of the southern basin of the Central Plain, Thailand, *South East Asia Studies (Kyoto Univ)*, **7**:293–300.

Tjia, H. D., S. Fujii, and K. Kigoshi, 1977, Changes of sea level in the southern South China Sea area during Quaternary times, *Proc. Quat. Geol. of the Malaya-Indonesia Coastal and Offshore Areas Seminar, 13th CCOP Session Tech. 11–49*, Publ. 5.

Watson, J. G., 1928, *Mangrove Forests of the Malayan Peninsula*, Fraser and Neave, Singapore.

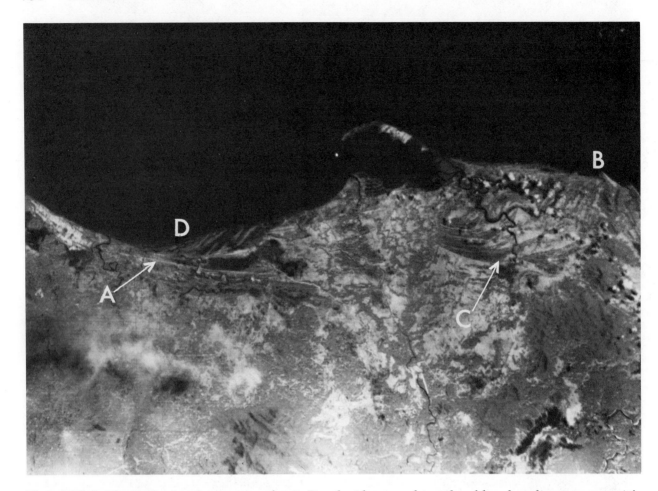

Plate 105-1. The Pattani embayment and spit. Beach ridges marking the older shoreline are seen at A; sand spits originating at B have successively extended westward to the present spit at Laem Pho. Evidence of an eastward extension of counter-current spits is seen at C. Finally, a modern series of beach ridges and intervening mangrove swamps is developing in response to westward longshore drift at D (LANDSAT 2 photo by NASA).

Plate 105-2. Phang Nga Bay and the Andaman Sea coastline, showing the extent of mangrove swamps and mud flats at the head of the bay (dark grey) and typical drainage developed on these swamps. The small islands within the bay are tower karst (Plate 105-3) and are extensions of the inland limestone ridges. The western coastline is marked by linear sand beaches extending from Phuket Island to Leam Kham. The spit-like northern termination is actually an island of Permian/Ordovician conglomerates and sandstones. The white patches mark sites of alluvial tin mining (LANDSAT 1 photo by NASA).

Plate 105-3. Tower karst developed in Phang Nga Bay. The limestone outcrops as faulted linear ridges, rising to over 300 m. All show an older marine-cut notch at approximately +3 m, well cemented with tufa. Mangroves occur around the base of most of the towers (photo by J. I. Pitman).

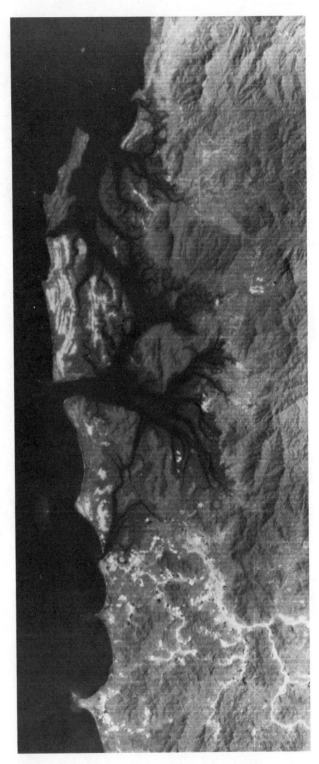

Plate 105-4. Coastline between Laem Kham and Ko Ra. Two barrier islands—Ko Kho Khao and Ko Phra Thong—are marked by well-developed beach ridges rising about 10 m on the seaward side and extensive mangrove swamps and mud flats inshore. On Ko Kho Khao, and to the south cuspate spits have formed (LANDSAT photo by NASA).

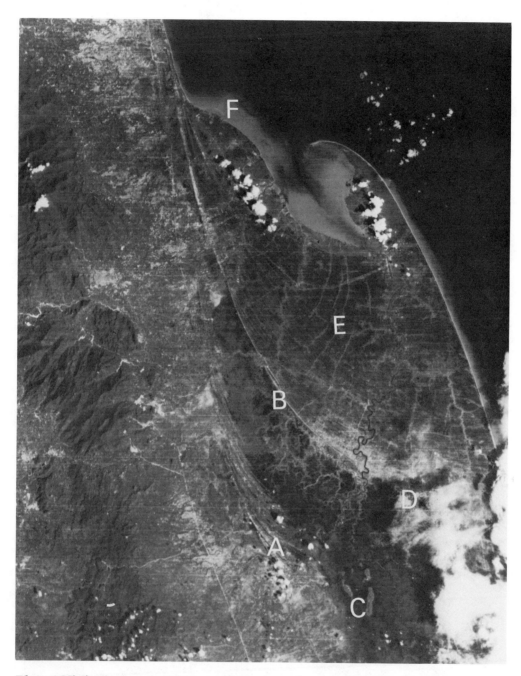

Plate 105-5. The beach-ridge complex east and south of Nakhon Si Thammarat is seen in the LANDSAT 2 picture. The two major sand ridges A and B both terminate on their seaward end at outcrops of Permian Ratburi limestone C and D. The more recent (E) is marked by more subdued ridges and depressions, with the major drainage pattern developed orthogonal to the ridges. The light color offshore is suspended sand and mud. Note the small barrier developing at F (LANDSAT 3 photo by NASA).

106. PENINSULAR MALAYSIA

The 1,926 km long coastline of peninsular Malaysia (Fig. 106-1) is composed of 47% mangroves, 39% sandy beaches, and 14% cliffs, and cut mainly in granite and Devonian sediments on the west coast and Carboniferous and Permian sediments on the east coast. Its configurations are influenced by Late Jurassic orogeny, which formed the mountain ranges that are now the backbone of the peninsula, and by the Holocene marine transgression. Later Holocene fluctuations in sea level initiated barrier formation and extensive coastal progradation along many coastal sectors. The coastline has been stable since Late Tertiary (Gobbett 1973), but there have been some vertical movements along faults and an episode of volcanic activity in Kuantan, Pahang, less than 2 million years ago. Evidences of high sea levels are widespread along the coast in the form of stranded oyster beds (Fig. 106-1), many of which have been dated at less than 5,000 years old (Tjia et al. 1977). The Quaternary sediments, a mixture of marine, swamp and terrestrial deposits, are deep, reaching more than 120 m in Kelantan.

The west coast lies leeward of the island of Sumatra and has an actively prograding mangrove coastline; this contrasts markedly with the sandy beaches on the east coast, which is subjected to northeast monsoon storms and swells from the South China Sea. The mean spring tidal range is generally lower along the east coast, with Tumpat, Kelantan, recording the lowest at 0.8 m. Net littoral drift is weak or negligible along the west coast, without any clear pattern emerging, but can be significant along the east coast, with a southward drift along the southern part of the peninsula. The offshore sediments reflect the different wave regimes on the west and east coasts,

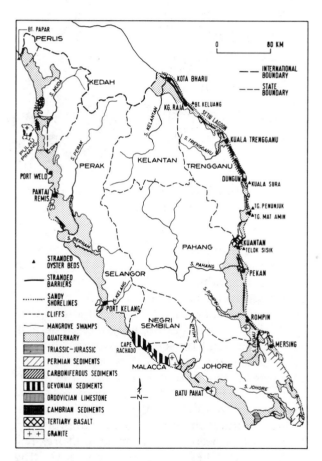

Figure 106-1. Coastal types and geology of Peninsular Malaysia.

but the local geology may influence the type of nearshore sediments (Fig. 106-2).

Mangroves, growing on a variety of substrates and under different coastal conditions, fringe nearly the whole of the west coast, but are confined to sheltered estuaries on the east coast. The

789

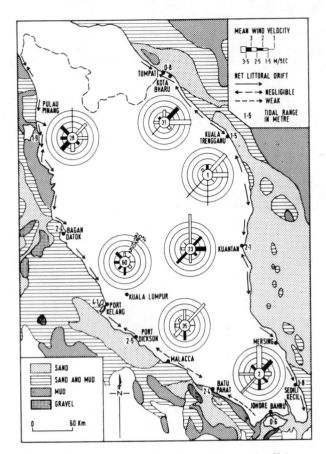

Figure 106-2. Coastal conditions and offshore sediments of peninsular Malaysia.

the beaches are usually backed by a barrier-beach ridge complex locally known as *permatang*.

Cliffs predominate on offshore islands but show restricted development on the mainland. An abandoned cliff fronted by a wave-cut platform can be observed at Mersing.

The Langkawi Island group lying off the Kedah coast has an irregular ria coastline (Tjia 1973) with plunging limestone cliffs often showing notches that are stranded above high tide level. The mangrove-fringed Perlis-Kedah coastline is backed by a wide coastal plain, dotted with former limestone islands, some also showing wave-cut notches and shell remains.

The coastline on Penang Island is composed of steep granite cliffs alternating with sandy beaches on the north and south, and mangroves on the west and east coasts. The prograded western coastal plain has been built up by the formation of a baymouth and mid-bay barrier, now stranded behind the mangroves. On Province Wellesley there are sandy beaches backed by a series of

mangrove formation is usually well developed, extending up to 12 km inland. On an undisturbed actively prograding coastline, *Avicennia marina* is the main pioneer species, succeeded landward by *Bruguiera cylindrica* and *Rhizophora mucronata*. Pure stands of *Ceriops tagal* often develop on cheniers and those of *Avicennia alba* and *Rhizophora apiculata* along estuaries. Recently, mangroves along part of the Selangor and Negeri Sembilan coast have retreated. Such areas have stands of mangroves normally found farther inland. The inner margin of many mangrove formations has been cleared for agriculture. The Matang Forest Reserve in Perak has a working plan to extract mangroves based on a 30-year cycle; elsewhere illegal and uncontrolled felling has initiated or accelerated coastal erosion.

Sandy beaches are rare along the west coast, their presence related to outcrops of weathered granite or sedimentary rocks, but extend nearly the whole length of the east coast. Beach sediments are mainly quartzose and are derived from fluvial or longshore sources. On the east coast

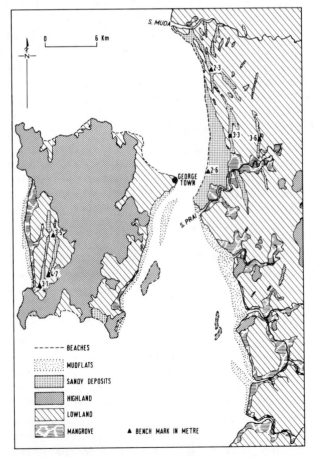

Figure 106-3. Coastal geomorphology of Penang.

cheniers between Sungei Muda and Sungei Prai, and mangroves lie to the south (Fig. 106-3).

The drowned Perak coastline is characterized by an abundance of estuaries and swamps, with extensive mangrove island formation around Port Weld and mangroves backed by a relict barrier at Pantai Remis (Fig. 106-4). The coastal plain has been largely built up by marine sediments; deposition took place initially in a mangrove environment that was later drowned by the rising sea during the Holocene marine transgression, and then recolonized by mangroves in the stillstand (Foo et al. 1977). The changing environment is reflected in the succession from barrier to mangrove formation, the advance estimated at 12.5 m per year between 1881 and 1961 (Koopmans 1964).

Apart from a sandy stretch south of Port Kelang, mangroves, their inner zone reclaimed for agriculture and their landward boundary now marked by bunds, line the Selangor coast (Fig. 106-5). In Negeri Sembilan, Devonian sediments abut the

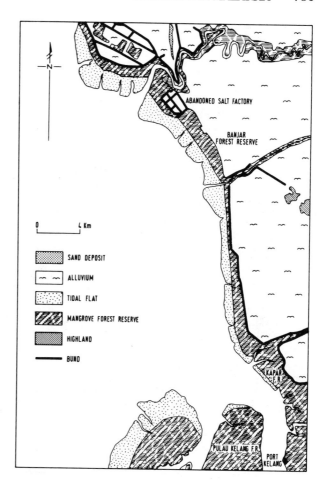

Figure 106-5. Coastal geomorphology of central Selangor.

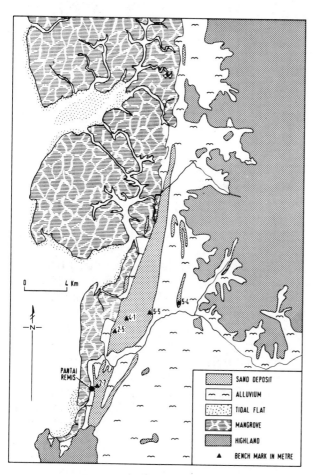

Figure 106-4. Coastal geomorphology of Pantai Remis.

coastline, which is dominated by cliffs and sandy beaches. At Cape Rachado the steep cliffs have an apron of corals offshore, and there is incipient beachrock along the bay to its north.

In Johore the western coast has an uninterrupted belt of mangroves, and the stranded beach ridges at Batu Pahat are relicts of a former high sea level (Swan 1970). The southern coastline has a typically submerged character, while the eastern coastline is composed of small arcuate bays alternating with headlands up to Jason Bay and cliffs, often fronted by a shore platform, farther north.

In the region of Rompin the sandy beaches are succeeded inland by a wide zone of beach ridges. The Sungei Pahang cuspate delta (Fig. 106-6) has a complex pattern of beach ridges, with each beach ridge series related to a particular stage in delta evolution (insert in Fig. 106-6). The sands are derived either from cliffs to the north (Nossin 1964) or from the Sungei Pahang (AUSTEC 1974).

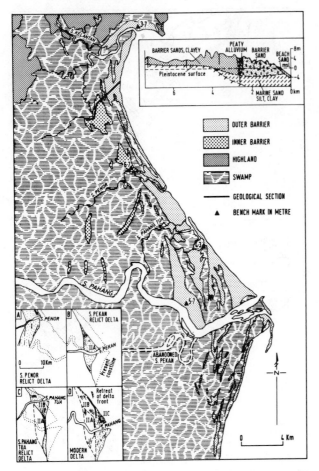

Figure 106-6. Geomorphology of the Sungai Pahang cuspate delta.

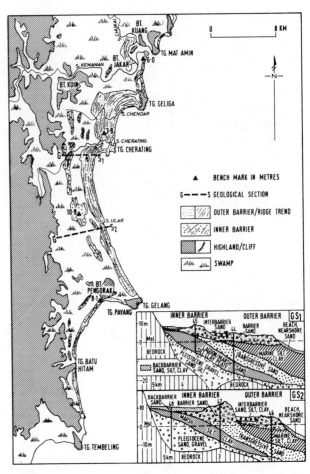

Figure 106-7. Geomorphology of the zeta-form coastline.

Low dunes fringe the Kampung Kepadang coast, and the receded inner barrier here overlies a former Pleistocene terrestrial surface (Fig. 106-6).

The zeta-form coastline between Kuantan and Dungun (Fig. 106-7) is composed of several former deeply indented embayments that have become filled with barrier and lagoonal deposits. Here rivers characteristically discharge into the bay on the downdrift side of headlands. Stranded oyster beds are common on headlands, and there is a well-preserved highly podsolized inner barrier lying at about 11 m above mean sea level north of Kuantan. The height of beach ridges suggests barrier formation when the sea was higher than its present level, and this hypothesis is supported by barrier stratigraphic evidence (Fig. 106-7).

Kuala Trengganu is a former embayment that became filled after it was partially sealed off from the sea by a baymouth barrier. A narrow barrier-lagoon system lies to the south. Setiu lagoon was enclosed when a barrier spit was formed across

the mouth of Sungei Merang and Sungei Setiu, and this stretch of coastline has prograded through a series of barrier-lagoon formations.

The double barrier coast between Kota Bharu and Kampong Raja has a distinct inner barrier composed of broad ridges and an outer barrier of closely spaced narrow ridges (Fig. 106-8). The formation and progradation of these Holocene barriers are related to sea-level fluctuations, and sands for barrier development were derived from the drowned Pleistocene terrace (Teh 1980). The barrier stratigraphy shows that the receded inner barriers were stranded when the sea fell about 3 m after the Holocene marine transgression to reach its present level. The fall in sea level is also reflected in the declining height of beach ridges (Fig. 106-9). The complex beach ridge pattern behind Bukit Keluang is the result of a change in wave-refraction pattern, probably caused by fluctuations in sea level.

The barrier spit coast is dominated by Tumpat

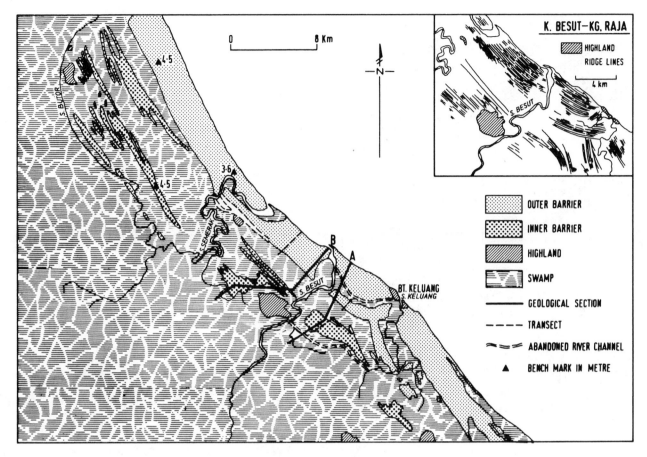

Figure 106-8. Geomorphology of the double barrier coast.

spit at the mouth of Sungei Kelantan, which is a fan-shaped delta (Fig. 106-10). This coastline has undergone a complex evolution as the Sungei Kelantan distributary gradually shifted westward, and the old delta front left behind gradually eroded away. The barrier stratigraphy indicates that the inner barrier is a high-sea-level relict and that the main outer barrier was formed at present sea level (Fig. 106-11). Barrier sands were derived mainly from the delta-front sand and gravel.

TEH TIONG SA

REFERENCES

AUSTEC, 1974, Flood mitigation measures, in *Pahang River Basin Study*, 4, report prepared by an Australian cosortium of consultants for the government of Malaysia under the Colombo Plan.

Foo, K. Y., E. A. van de Meene, and L. H. Teoh, 1977, A systematic investigation of the Quaternary deposits of the Taiping coastal plain, Peninsular Malaysia, in *Symp. Quaternary Geology of the Malay-Indo-nesian Coastal and Offshore Areas Proc.* United Nations ESCAP, CCOP/TP, vol. 5, pp. 54–79.

Gobbett, D. J., 1973, Introduction in *Geology of the Malay Peninsula*, D. J. Gobbett and C. S. Hutchison, eds., Wiley Interscience, New York, pp. 1–12.

Koopmans, B. N., 1964, Geomorphological and historical data of the lower course of the Perak River (Dindings), *Jour. Malaysia Br. Roy. Asiat. Soc.* **37**:175–191.

Nossin, J. J., 1964, Geomorphology of the surroundings of Kuantan (Eastern Malaya), *Geol. en Mijnb.* **43:** 157–182.

Swan, S. B. St. C., 1970, Beach deposits in a low energy environment, west Johore, Southern Malaya, *Jour. Singapore Natl. Acad. Sci.* **2**(2):86–94.

Teh, T. S., 1980, Morphostratigraphy of a double sand barrier system in Peninsular Malaysia, *Malaysia Jour. Trop. Geog.* **2**:45–55.

Tjia, H. D., 1973, Geomorphology in *Geology of the Malay Peninsula*, D. J. Gobbett and C. S. Hutchison, eds., Wiley Interscience, New York, pp. 13–24.

Tjia, H. D., S. Fujii, and K. Kigoshi, 1977, Changes of sea level in the southern south China Sea during Quaternary times, in *Symp. Quaternary Geology of the Malay-Indonesian Coastal and Offshore Areas Proc.*, United Nations ESCAP, CCOP/TP, vol. 5, pp. 11–36.

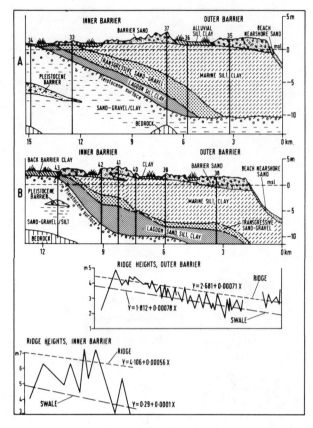

Figure 106-9. Barrier stratigraphy and ridge heights on the double barrier coast.

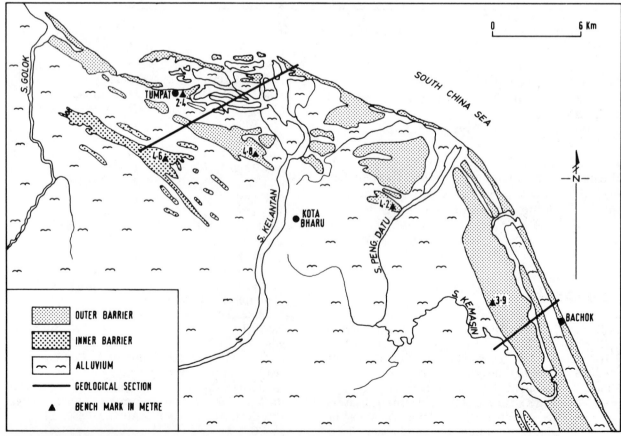

Figure 106-10. Coastal geomorphology of Kelantan.

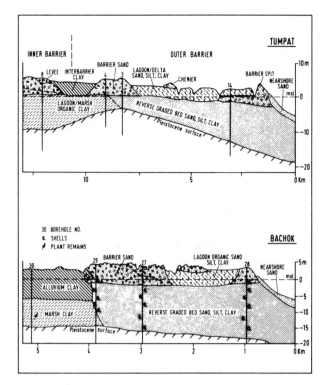

Figure 106-11. Lithostratigraphy of the Tumpat and Bachok barriers.

107. SINGAPORE

The Republic of Singapore, which consists of one main island and fifty-odd smaller islands, has a coastline of approximately 300 km and is in a humid tropical low-energy environment. Its northern shores are separated from Peninsular Malaysia by the narrow Straits of Johore, while the shores of the main island are some 12–15 km away from the Rhio Archipelago of Indonesia. The tides are semidiurnal of a mixed type with large diurnal inequalities in the low-water heights; the tidal range is approximately 2.6 m.

Mangrove swamps were the predominant coastal landforms until recent human activity brought substantial lengths of shoreline behind seawalls, bulkheads, and revetments (Fig. 107-1). Geology influences the character of the cliffs and the availability and composition of material for beach formation. Upper Triassic to Lower Jurassic sedimentary rocks consisting of conglomerates, sandstones, and mudstones are found along the western and southern coasts of the main island and the islands to the south; localized pebbly beaches are limited to these coasts. Lower mid-Triassic granite and its hybrids are along the northwestern coast, including Pulau (Island) Ubin. Palau Tekong and its immediate islets are of variably metamorphosed sedimentary rocks older than those on the west coast. The eastern and southeastern coasts are of Old Alluvium probably of Pleistocene age; this semiconsolidated deposit yields suitable material for beach formation. Coral reefs of Holocene age commonly fringe the southern islands (Public Works Department 1976).

In a humid tropical low-energy environment, the morphology of the coastal cliffs is also influenced by weathering and other subaerial processes. A variety of cut features are found in the intertidal zone. Beaches, except those of the main island, are generally intertidal and narrow. Cemented beach and conglomeratic sand are found in some of the southern islands. Various erosion and residual features found 1.6 m above mean sea level on the surrounding islands have been attributed to recent eustatic changes (Swan 1971).

On the northernmost coast of Singapore Island at Sembawang there is a shipyard and the Sembawang port. The last of the extensive mangrove-fringed coasts are found on the estuaries of Sungei (River) Seletar, Sungei Punggol, and Sungei Serangoon. On the northeastern coast, cliffs are limited to an outcrop of Palaeozoic sedimentary rocks at Punggol and an outcrop of granite at Changi. Sandy shorelines are best developed at Pasir Ris and Changi beaches, and a spit is developing at the western end of Changi beach. Pulau Seletar and Pulau Serangoon were formerly swampy islands but have been reclaimed by quartzose sand dredged off the Punggol peninsula.

Pulau Ubin, Pulau Tekong, and Pulau Tekong Kechil have a variety of coastal landforms; they are largely swampy with intervening cliffs and limited beaches between the headlands (Plate 107-1). Pulau Ketam, a small island south of Pulau Ubin, consists entirely of mangrove swamps. There are plans to reclaim the swamps on the southern coast of Pulau Tekong.

The southeastern coast was formerly sandy, benefiting from a westward littoral drift that has resulted in the growth of a spit across the Kallang estuary. The coastline has been extended seaward by reclamation, and along the East Coast Park it is protected by a series of breakwaters (Fig. 107-2, Plate 107-2), between which beach formation is

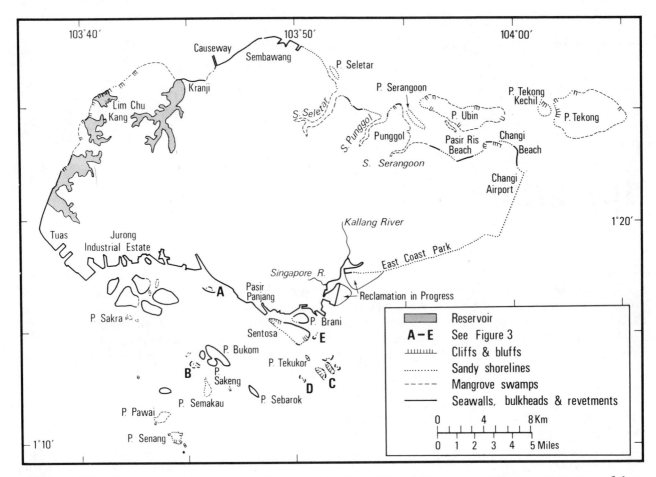

Figure 107-1. Predominant coastal landforms of the Republic of Singapore. A great proportion of this coastline has been modified by human activity, especially in the last 15 years, to meet the needs of the port, industries, recreation, and other uses.

progressing (Wong 1973, 1981; Chew et al. 1975). Reclamation for the Changi Airport has also resulted in the seaward extension of the shoreline, but without any protection by breakwaters.

Modification of the coastline took place first on the southern coast in the 1820s, centering on the Singapore River. Today the configuration of the southern coast is the result of a number of reclamation projects and is dominated by the wharves of the Port of Singapore Authority and the docks of Keppel Shipyard. Pressure for port facilities has resulted in the reclamation of the former sandy Pasir Panjang coast for additional wharves. Toward the west, the former swampy lowlands with intervening ridges were reclaimed for the Jurong Industrial Estate. The Jurong coastline is dominated by the Port of Jurong, a number of shipyards, and other heavy industries. A group of predominantly swampy islands south of the industrial estate were also reclaimed for

industrial purposes, primarily for petrochemical industries. Pulau Sakra, the only major island in this group that has been left in its natural state, is being used as a dumping ground for dredged materials.

What remains of the natural character of the western shoreline is at Lim Chu Kang, where one finds headlands of sedimentary rocks with swamps, estuaries, and limited beaches. Many of the swampy estuaries have been closed by dams to form reservoirs.

On the islands south of Singapore, substantial stretches of cliffs are at the northern tip of Sentosa, the western coasts of Lazarus Island and St. John's Island, and almost the entire coast of Pulau Tekukor. In its development as an oil refinery, Pulau Bukom has been enlarged a number of times to include adjacent Pulau Bukom Kechil in the south and Pulau Ular, which was previously a sandy shoal, in the west. Pulau Sebarok was

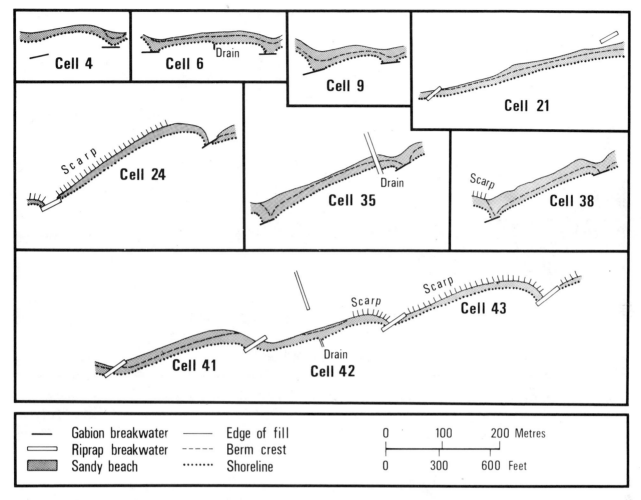

Figure 107-2. Selected beaches (cells) between breakwaters along the East Coast Park. The morphology and planform of each beach is dependent on the formation of the foreshore and the berm from the fill material, in relation to the deployment of gabion and riprap breakwaters and the presence of drains acting as groins.

reclaimed as a slop reception and treatment center. Between 1974 and 1976 the Port of Singapore Authority reclaimed several selected islands and reefs for recreational purposes (Fig. 107-3, Plate 107-3). Sentosa, which has been developed as a resort island, has improved sandy beaches on its western shores and further reclamation on its northeastern shores. Dredged materials are dumped around Pulau Semakau. Of the major southern islands, only Pulau Pawai and Pulau Senang are left in their natural state to be used for military exercises.

P. P. WONG

REFERENCES

Chew, S. Y., et al., 1975, Beach development between headland breakwaters, *14th Coastal Eng. Conf. Proc.* **2:**1399–1418.

Public Works Department, 1976, *Geology of the Republic of Singapore,* Singapore.

Swan, S. B. St.C., 1971, Coastal geomorphology in a humid tropical low energy environment: the islands of Singapore, *Jour. Trop. Geog.* **33:**43–61.

Wong, P. P., 1973, Beach formation between breakwaters, southeast coast, Singapore, *Jour. Trop. Geog.* **37:**68–73.

Wong, P. P., 1981, Beach evolution between headland breakwaters, *Shore and Beach* **49:**3–12.

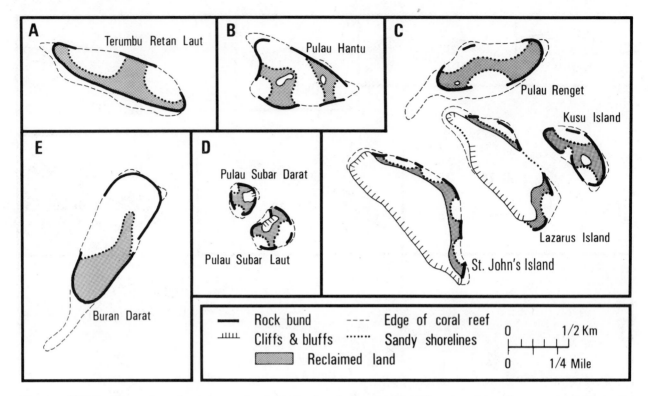

Figure 107-3. Coastal reclamation of selected islands and reefs. This involves the construction of a series of rock bunds on top of the reefs and parallel to their edges, to retain sandy and shelly materials dredged from the navigational approaches to the port. Beaches develop different planforms behind the structures, depending on their orientation to the wave approach.

Plate 107-1. On Pulau Ubin and Pulau Sekudu there are a number of granite boulders fluted by pseudokarren, which often extend below the mean sea level. Such boulders form small rocky headlands between which are small beaches. On Pulau Sekudu they constitute the core around which marine deposition takes place and are almost covered at high tide (photo by P. P. Wong).

Plate 107-2. Reclaimed land protected by a series of breakwaters along the east coast. In the foreground, straight beaches are formed, while in the background beaches take various seaward concave shapes with the breakwaters acting as headlands (photo by P. P. Wong).

Plate 107-3. Pulau Subar Laut is enlarged by sandy and shelly material placed behind an interrupted ring of stone bunds constructed on top of the reef flat. Beaches form readily, with their planforms influenced by wave approach (photo by P. P. Wong).

108. KAMPUCHEA

Kampuchea (formerly Cambodia) has an embayed and island-fringed coastline about 400 km long (Fig. 108-1). The western part is dominated by Mesozoic sandstones, which culminate in the Cardamon Mountains, rising more than 1500 m above sea level. The broad Bay of Kompong Som is a low-lying synclinal region, bordered by the uplifted Réam peninsula to the southeast. The Paleozoic rocks of the Elephant Ranges lie to the east, and beyond these the coast is low-lying toward the Vietnam border and the Mekong Delta.

The coastal climate is tropical, with a wet summer monsoon (May to October) and a dry winter season. Annual rainfall at Kampoh is 1976 mm. River flooding is extensive in the wet season. Wave action in coastal waters is generally slight, but it becomes stronger in the southwest monsoon, especially when it is reinforced by sea breezes. Typhoons from the China Sea occasionally move in through Kampuchean waters, producing temporary storm surges with strong wave action. Tide ranges are generally less than 1 m, the tides being diurnal. Current action is weak, except in narrow straits (e.g., between islands), where tidal scour may be intensified (*China Sea Pilot* 1978).

Just south of the Thailand border, a hilly peninsula borders the wide estuary of the Klong Klun River. The coast hereabouts is penetrated by many branching, mangrove-fringed inlets. Tidal scour is strong north of Koh Kong Island, which shelters a wide, shallow, indented bay from the open sea of the Gulf of Thailand. To the south the coast to Point Samit is steep and hilly, with rocky promontories separating sandy beaches, many of which are backed by dune topography bearing scrub and woodland. Banks of sand and coral are extensive offshore; Condor Reef is the largest of the outlying coral formations.

To the south, Koh Rong is the largest of several steep-sided high islands off the Bay of Kompong Som. Their outer coasts have cliffed promontories, fringing reefs, and sandy beaches; inner embayments have mangroves. The northwestern part of the Bay of Kompong Som is shallow and sheltered, with very extensive mangrove areas passing into the estuaries of the Piphot and Kompong Som rivers. Beach ridges and spits have formed near river mouths. Wharves have been built at Pointe Loune to establish the port of Kompong Som (Sihanoukville).

The Réam peninsula has generally low-lying coasts, bordered by reef-fringed islands and shoals, with wide, funnel-shaped estuaries flanked by mangroves. The nearshore zone is shallow and rocky. To the east the hinterland steepens to the Elephant Range, spurs from which form low promontories; the Kos Sla River on their eastern margin has built a small delta south from the town of Kampoh. From here to Vietnam the coast is low and intricate, with many islands, shoals, reefs, and rocks in the nearshore shallows (the water is sheltered by the large, high Vietnamese island of Quan Phu Quoc).

Carbonnel (1972) found evidence of Quaternary marine terraces 25, 10–15, 4, and 1.5–2 m above present sea level along the higher parts of the Kampuchean coastline. The lowest of these terraces is regarded as Holocene in age.

ERIC C. F. BIRD

REFERENCES

Carbonnel, J. P., 1972, *Le Quaternaire Cambodgien*, Mém. ORSTOM no. 60, Paris.

China Sea Pilot 1978, Hydrographic Office, Taunton.

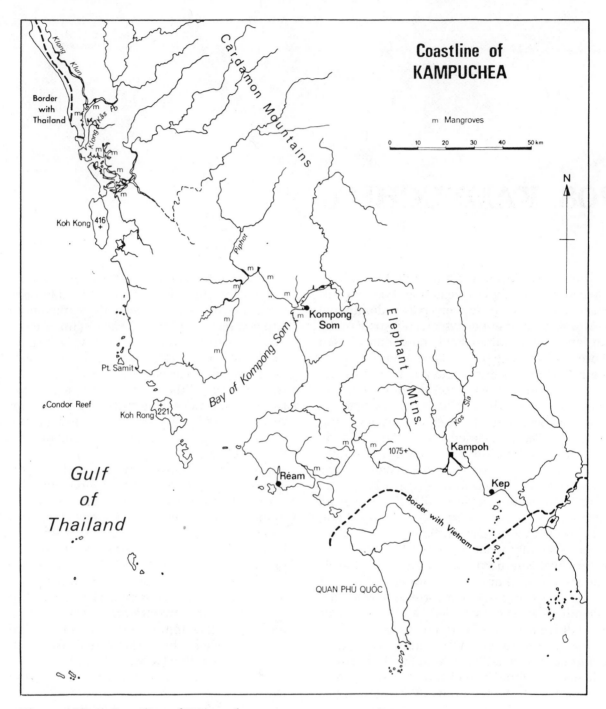

Figure 108-1. Coastline of Kampuchea.

109. VIETNAM

The Vietnamese coast is demarcated by two large river deltas, the Song Hong (Red River) delta in the north and the Mekong delta in the south, with approximately 1,300 km of gently curving coastline between them. The general direction of the coast follows the two main tectonic axes: the more dominant southeast–northwest axis and a subordinate southwest–northeast axis (Hoffet 1933; Fromaget 1941). The main folding and faulting follows the southeast–northwest direction, which is also followed by the general direction of most of the eastern and western coasts along the South China Sea and the Gulf of Thailand, the mountain range in central Vietnam (the Annamite Mountains), and large rivers like the Song Hong and the Mekong. In the north, faulting and folding along this axis dates from the Tertiary, and the Song Hong follows a deep basin with up to 1,000 m of Neogene deposits. In the south the southeast–northwest faulting dates from the Quaternary and has only affected the near-surface; the deeper structures follow mainly the southwest–northeast direction (Ho Manh Trung 1969). This direction is also followed by the coastline from Mui Bai Bung (Cape Ca Mau) to Mui Dinh (Cape Padaran), as well as, in the north, by the coast between Than Hoa and Chin-chou in southeastern China.

The broad river plains of the Song Hong and the Mekong are covered by Holocene (recent or subrecent) alluvial deposits. Basement rocks (Precambrian or early Paleozoic granites, gneiss, rhyolite, porphyrites, and schists) dominate in the southern highlands, partly covered by Mesozoic continental deposits. North from Da Nang to the Song Hong there are a series of southeast–northwest folds and faults. Paleozoic and Mesozoic rocks dominate here, as well as in the Tonkin Highlands northeast of the Song Hong. The main mountain range of Vietnam, the Annamite Mountains, lies near to the east coast, leaving a coastal plain 30–50 km wide. This range forms the watershed between short rivers that flow eastward into the South China Sea and the broad basin of the Mekong to the west. South of Qui-Non down to Mui Vung Tau (Cape St. Jacques) on the northeastern limit of the Mekong delta, the mountains, reaching a height of more than 2,000 m, come near to the shore.

Along the entire coast of Vietnam and along outlying islands like Bach Long Vi (Nightingale Island) in the Gulf of Tonkin, the Paracel Islands, Con Son (Poulo Condor), and the numerous small islands off the west coast in the Gulf of Thailand, there are indications for former sea levels at 1–2 m and 4–5 m above present level (Saurin 1955, 1956, 1957, 1963; Fontaine 1967, 1968; Ta Tran Tan 1967). In some areas, as at Mui Bai Bung (Cape Ca Mau), Mui Vung Tau (Cape St. Jacques) and along Phu Quoc Island, there are indications for a former sea level at +10–15 m, and near Phan Rang at +50 m and +75–80 m. The 1–2 m and 4–5 m levels are indicated by deposits of shells, shell fragments, and coral, by oysters still attached to rocks, by old reefs, beachrock, notches, and sea caves. The deposits associated with these levels are not consolidated or weathered into laterite. The level of 4–5 m has been dated (near Ca Na) as 4,500 yrs B.P. ± 250 yrs (Saurin 1963). The 1–2 m level has not been dated, but archeological evidence indicates an age of about 2,300 yrs B.P. (Fontaine 1968). The 10–15 m level is also characterized by deposits of shells and coral, but this material is consolidated and weathered. It has been dated as 18,500 yrs B.P. ± 250 yrs, but this date is doubtful since sea level never reached that height during the Weichsel glacial period. The (scarce) indications for higher sea levels have not been dated.

Outside the two river deltas the coast consists of rocky promontories, beaches, and small estuaries. Coral grows along most of the mainland coast as well as along the islands (Beach Long Vi, Paracel Islands, Con Son, Tho Chau Islands [Poulo Panjang]), where there is no outflow of river water nearby.

Currents along the Vietnamese coast are from the northeast between November and March during the northeast monsoon. Around Mui Bai Bung (Cape Ca Mau) they turn to the northwest into the Gulf of Thailand during this period, whereas in the Gulf of Tonkin there is a northward counter-current along the coast. In July and August, during the southwest monsoon, currents are predominantly from the southwest. Along the eastern shore of the Gulf of Thailand the current trends southeasterly, then turns around Mui Bai Bung toward the northeast. In the Gulf of Tonkin and farther south along the coast past Mui Varella, the coastal current is southward during that time. Current velocities in January are about 15–85 cm/s; in July, 15–40 cm/s.

The monsoon winds dominate, but along the eastern shore of the more sheltered Gulf of Thailand there is often an alternation of sea breezes by day and land breezes by night, whereas along the eastern Vietnam coast the wind tends to be deflected parallel to the coast. Sea waves and swell follow the same directions as the wind. The strongest waves occur from the northeast in winter, affecting chiefly the northeast–east exposed coast from Vinh to Mui Dinh (Cape Padaran). The Gulf of Tonkin is more protected, the swell entering during the winter from the south, whereas the Gulf of Thailand is fairly sheltered from the southwest as well as from the northeast winds. Typhoons, coming from east–southeast, occur mainly from May to December and are rare from January to May. They occur chiefly north of 10° N and rarely enter the Gulf of Thailand.

The tides are diurnal, with a strong semidiurnal component during the period of equinoxes. The tidal currents are generally weak. Along the central Vietnam coast they are of little influence, increasing to 1–1.5 knots along the north coast in the Gulf of Tonkin. At the Mekong delta the water level and the outgoing current are chiefly determined by the river outflow, which rates up to 2

knots from January to June, when water level in the river is low, and up to 4.5 knots from July to December, when river water level is high.

THE NORTHEAST COAST

In the northeast lies the large Song Hong (Red River) delta with, to the north, a more rocky coast reaching to the border with China (Fig. 109-1). In the latter area the coast consists of Devonian schists, sandstones, and limestones, Permian limestones, and Mesozoic sandstones, claystones, and marls. The former relief was drowned during the postglacial sea-level rise, resulting in numerous small islands and an indented shoreline with inlets that have been partly filled with sediment and mangrove swamps. The Gulf of Tonkin is shallow, reaching little more than 50 m of water depth in its center, with the shelf edge (200 m depth line) situated east of Hainan Island. The depth indications on the sea charts suggest the presence of drowned valleys on the sea floor north of the Song Hong delta.

Where the Song Hong delta, very flat (< 2 m above sea level) and densely inhabited, borders the coast, there are beach ridges, extensive clay flats, and mangrove swamps (Gourou 1936). The outflow of the river water goes predominantly through river channels to the southwest, while the northeasterly part of the delta coast is dominated by brackish tidal channels and mangrove swamps. Complexes of beach ridges and clay flats up to 30 km wide dominate in the center and the southwest. The beach ridges are low (about 1 m above sea level), with low dunes, and are separated by depressions several hundred meters wide. The beach ridges are overgrown with vegetation soon after their formation and subsequently cultivated. They usually offer sufficient protection against the tides, whereas the clay flats are only flooded during very high tides. For further protection dikes have been constructed since the eleventh century. They were primarily built for protection against flooding from the river and its branches, but also extend along most of the coast. The delta progrades seaward about 100 m per year in the south, the rate decreasing toward the northeast. North of the Song Wong river mouth there is hardly any progradation, most parts of the coast being more or less stationary, with local erosion. There are indications that before the nineteenth century the rate of progradation in the south was less, on the order of 30–40 m per year.

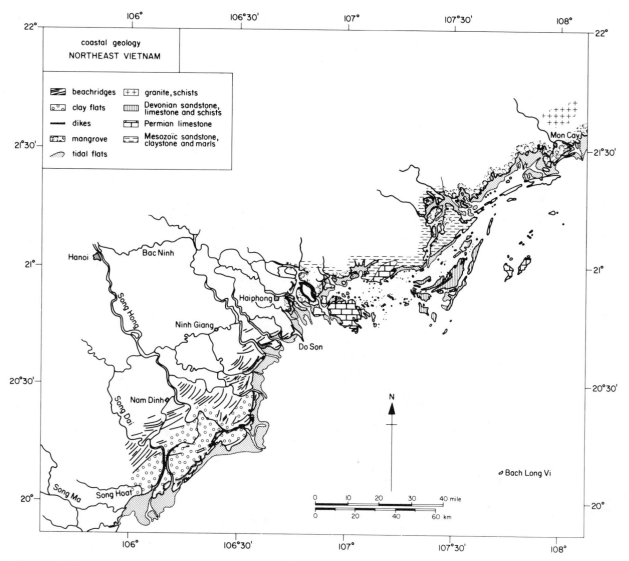

Figure 109-1. Coastal geology of northeast Vietnam.

Southwest of the delta, down to Vinh at 18°44′N, the coast is formed by the alluvial plains of smaller rivers with small estuaries, beach ridges, beach barriers, or spits and promontories of Cretaceous and Tertiary sandstones, siltstones, and conglomerate.

THE EAST COAST

From Vinh southward to Quang Ngai at 15°15′N there is a coastal plain, 30–50 km wide, regularly interrupted by mountain spurs reaching the sea and forming capes (Fig. 109-2). Between the capes, which consist of granite or rhyolite (Mui Ron Ma, Mui Chon May Dong, Tien Shan Peninsula near Da Nang) or basalt (Mui Lay, Mui Batangan), there

are broad beach barriers, cut by small rivers flowing out into South China Sea and covered with low dunes. Behind the beach barriers there are flat alluvial lands, lagoons (as from Hue to Cau Hai) and, landward of the barriers and the lagoons, older beach barrier complexes covered with older dunes (Saurin 1944).

South of Quang Ngai the coast turns south. Here the Annamite Mountains come near to the coast so that rocky spurs, small alluvial plains, and short beach barriers or spits with dunes alternate (Fig. 109-3). The coast is more indented, and there are many smaller and larger bays (as near Qui Nhon, Song Cau, To Bong, Ninh Hoa, Nha Trang, Cam Ranh, and Phan Rang). The spits face east-northeast to northeast, which is the direction of the strongest swell and the strongest

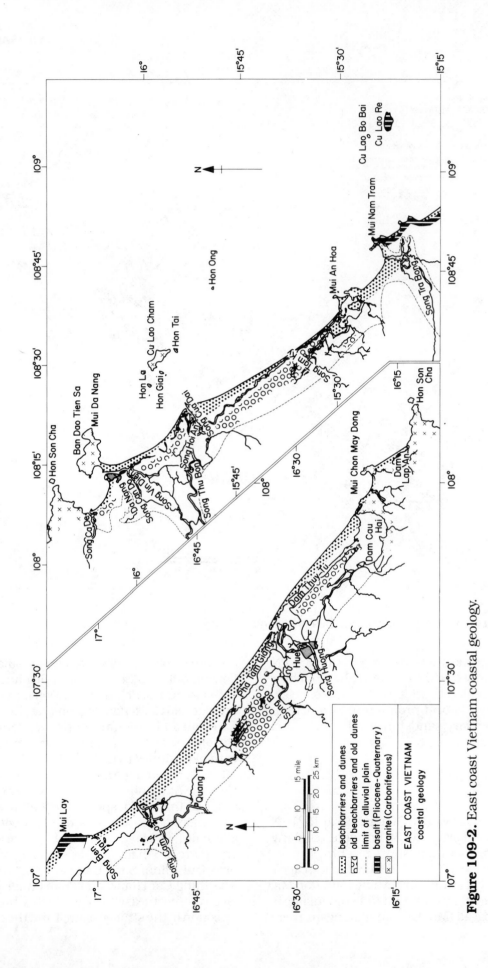

Figure 109-2. East coast Vietnam coastal geology.

beachbarriers and dunes

old beachbarriers and old dunes

limit of alluvial plain

basalt (Pliocene-Quaternary)

granite (Carboniferous)

EAST COAST VIETNAM
coastal geology

Mui Lay

Song Ben

Song Cam

Quang Tri

Pho Tam Giang

Song B

Hue

Song Huong

Dam Thuy Tu

Dam Cau
Hai

Mui Chon May Dong

Dam
Lap An

Hon Son
Cha

Hon Son Cha

Ban Dao Tien Sa

Mui Da Nang

Song Ca De

Song Vin Dien

Song Cau Do

Song Thu Bo

Song Hoi An Cua Dai

Hon La

Hon Giai

Cu Lao Cham

Hon Tai

Hon Ong

Song Tra

Song E

Mui An Hoa

Song Tra Bong

Mui Nam Tram

Cu Lao Bo Bai

Cu Lao Re

N

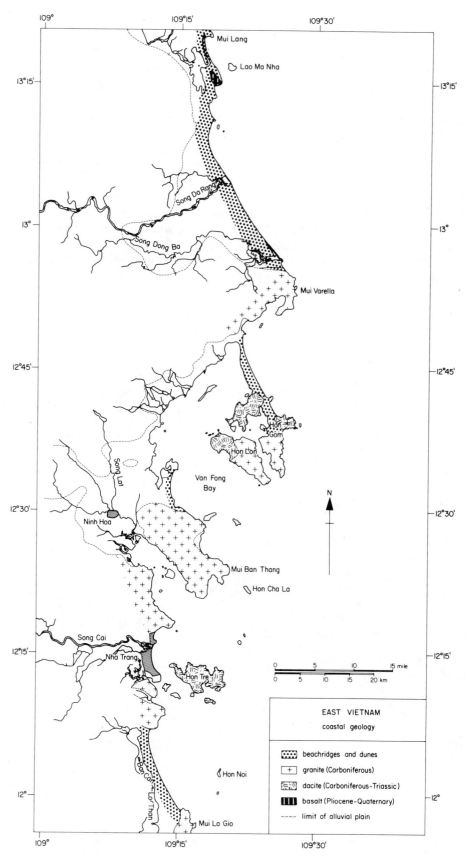

Figure 109-3. East Vietnam coastal geology.

EAST VIETNAM
coastal geology

beachridges and dunes

granite (Carboniferous)

dacite (Carboniferous-Triassic)

basalt (Pliocene-Quaternary)

limit of alluvial plain

monsoon winds. Granites, gneiss, and basalts, with rhyolite, dacite, and micaschists locally, form the capes. Between Quang Ngai and Mui Dinh, where the coast turns to the southwest, the shelf is only 40–70 km wide, much narrower than along the other parts of Vietnam: the Gulf of Tonkin, the Gulf of Thailand, and most of the sea area between southeastern Vietnam and eastern Malaysia (Sarawak) are shelf seas.

THE SOUTH COAST

The south coast consists almost entirely of Quaternary deposits, in part very recent, as at the Mekong River mouth, and some rocky promontories (granite) at Mui Vung Tau (Cape St. Jacques) (Fig. 109-4). Directly northeast of the Mekong

River mouth, which is divided into several large branches, are the estuaries of several smaller rivers (among them Song Vam Ca, Song Saigon, and Song Be). Here a small bay remains, which the rivers have not yet filled. In front of the Mekong River mouth the coast bulges seaward and is formed of mud flats and mangrove swamps. The sediment brought into the coastal sea by the Mekong is largely moved southward under influence of the northeast monsoon and goes around Mui Bai Bung into the Gulf of Thailand. South of the river mouths the coast down to Mui Bai Bung and the west coast from Mui Bai Bung up to Hon Chon consists of mangrove swamps and mud flats, with a short sandy beach west of Ca Mau. The Hon Chon promontory of Paleozoic limestone and the offshore islands up to the Tho Chau archipelago consist of Paleozoic and Mesozoic

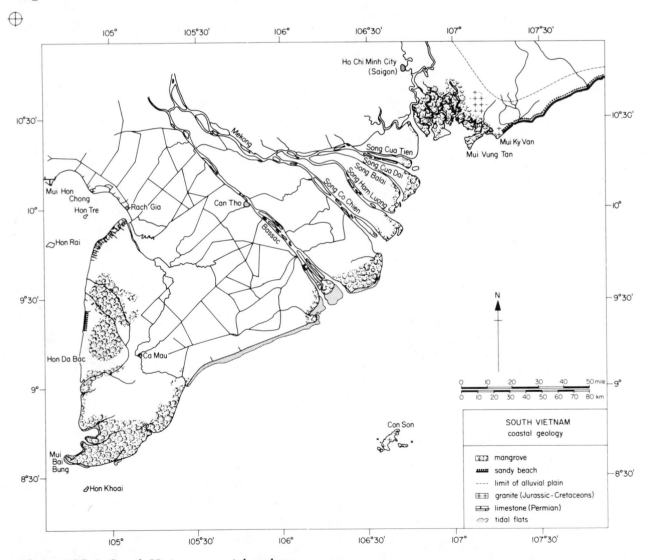

Figure 109-4. South Vietnam coastal geology.

formations, with large blocks and sometimes steep cliffs forming the coast. The large island of Phu Quoc has sandy beaches between promontories with rocky cliffs. Between Mui Bung and Rach Gia the coastline probably follows a north-south fault zone, as is probably also the case along the east coast between Qui Nhon and Mui Dinh.

D. EISMA

REFERENCES

Faure, C., and H. Fontaine, 1969, Géochronologie du Viet-Nam méridional, *Arch. Géol. Vietnam* **12**:213–222.

Fontaine, H., 1967, Note sur l'archipel de Tho-Chau, *Arch. Géol. Vietnam* **10**:17–22.

Fontaine, H., 1968, Notes sur le Golfe de Thailande, *Arch. Géol. Vietnam* **11**:119–147.

Fromaget, J., 1941, L'Indochine française, sa structure géologique, ses roches, ses mines et leurs relations possible avec la tectonique, *Service Géol. de l'Indochine Bull.* **26**(2):1–140.

Gourou, P., 1936, *Les paysans du delta Tonkinois, Publ. de l'Ecole franc. d'Extrême-Orient* Ed. d'Art et d'Histoire, Paris.

Ho Manh Trung, 1969, Esquisse structurale du delta du Mékong, discussion du problème pétrolier, *Arch. Géol. Vietnam* **12**:195–211.

Hoffet, J. H., 1933, Étude géologique sur le centre de l'Indochine entre Tourane et le Mékong (Annam Central et Bas-Laos), *Service Géol. de l'Indochine Bull.* **20**(2):1–154.

Saurin, E., 1944, Études géologiques sur le Centre-Annam Méridional, *Serv. Géol. de l'Indochine Bull.* **27**(1):1–210.

Saurin, E., 1955, Notes sur les Iles Paracels, *Arch. Géol. Vietnam* **3**:9–39.

Saurin, E., 1956, L'ile Bach Long Vi (Golfe du Tonkin), *Soc. Géol. France Bull.*, 6e série, **6**:699–705.

Saurin, E., 1957, Notes sur quelques formations récentes du Viêt-Nam méridional, *Arch. Géol. Vietnam* **4**:25–34.

Saurin, E., 1963, Age, d'après le carbone 14, des terrasses marines de Ca Na (Sud Viet-nam), *Soc. Géol. France Compte Rendu* **1963**:14–16.

Ta Tran Tan, 1967, Contribution à la connaissance pétrographique de l'archipel des Poulo Condore (Province de Con-Son, Sud Viet-Nam), *Arch. Géol. Vietnam* **10**:23–39.

110. CHINA

China has a total coastline of about 32,000 km, including some 5,000 islands of varying size (Fig. 110-1). These border a much indented mainland coastline, which is more than 18,000 km long. The geological structure of the coastal area is complicated. In many cases the relief expresses the underlying tilted fault blocks, as manifested by a wide variety of coastal indentations. The whole coastline may be divided into two portions, north and south of Hangzhou Bay: to the north the coast consists mainly of alternating depositional plains and some hilly regions, and to the south rocky jagged coasts predominate, interspersed with small estuarine plains and local beaches of sand or gravel (Chen Jiyu et al. 1980; Chen Jiyu and Wang Baocan 1981; Wang Ying 1980).

This long Chinese coastline spans several different climatic zones, resulting in a wide variation of natural landscapes. The warm climate and shallow marine environments of southern China have favored the growth of coral reefs and mangroves, so that biogenic coasts dominate in tropical and subtropical China. Farther north, temperate salt marshes are extensive in places, augmented where *Spartina anglica* has been introduced to tidal mud flats (Song Daquan 1983).

Rivers have played an important role in the development of coastal plains. The Yellow (Huanghe) River, remarkable for its high content of silt, and the Changjiang (Yangtze) River deliver a huge amount of suspended sediment into the sea. They have not only built broad deltaic plains and muddy shores around their estuaries, but have dispersed suspended matter to the nearby continental shelf. The silt discharged from the Changjiang River is transported as far as to the coastal region of northern Fujien under the effect of

Jiangsu-Zhejiang longshore current, and has contributed to the formation of the embayed muddy coast of Zhejiang-Fujien. Other major sediment-yielding rivers are the Yalu in the north, the Huai, the Pearl, and the Beilun at the Vietnamese frontier.

Because of the diversity of local landforms along the Chinese coast, tidal variations are complicated (Fig. 110-2). Tides of most coastal areas are regular and semidiurnal, but some sectors have irregular semidiurnal or diurnal tides. The average tidal range varies from place to place, with a minimum of only 0.4 m and a maximum of more than 5 m. A great portion of China's coast is of mesotidal type (tidal range 2-4 m). The coastal section of Zhejiang-Fujien is macrotidal (>4 m). Estuaries where the tide range is large have tidal bores that run upriver. The Guangdong coast, the eastern coast of Taiwan Island, and a portion of Bohai coast are all microtidal (<2 m).

China has a climate dominated typically by monsoonal winds. The northerly wind prevails during winter, the southerly during summer. The prevailing wave direction conforms with wind direction and shows notable seasonal variation, which has a strong impact on the longshore sediment transport. The strong waves produced by northerly winds during the typhoon season have a vigorous influence on the coast.

LIAODONG PENINSULA HILLY COAST

This hilly peninsula coast extends from the Yalu estuary at the Korean frontier westward to Gaiping. The bedrock is Precambrian metamorphic and Lower Paleozoic sedimentary rocks. Salt

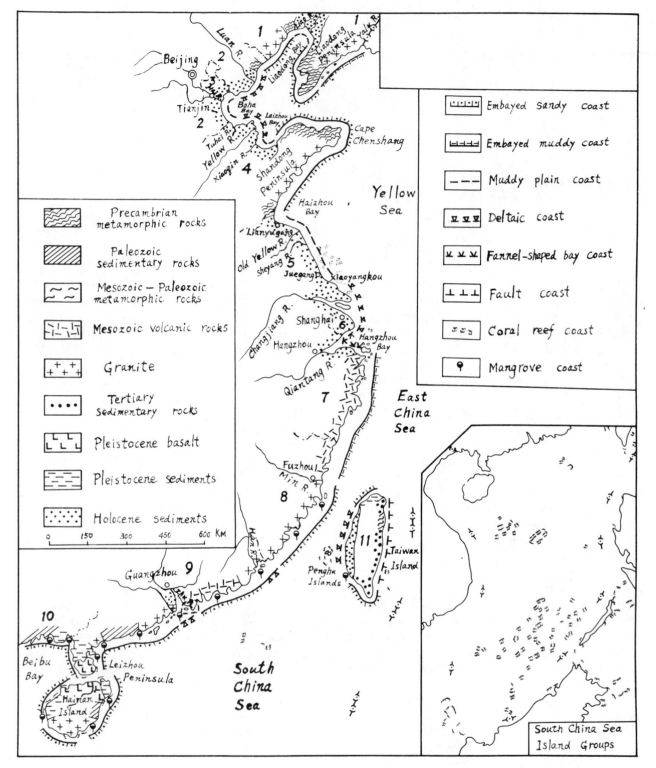

Figure 110-1. Coastal Geology and landforms of China: 1. Liaoning; 2. Hebei; 3. Tianjin; 4. Shandong; 5. Jiangsu; 6. Shanghai; 7. Zhejian; 8. Fujiang; 9. Guangdong; 10. Guangxi; 11. Taiwan.

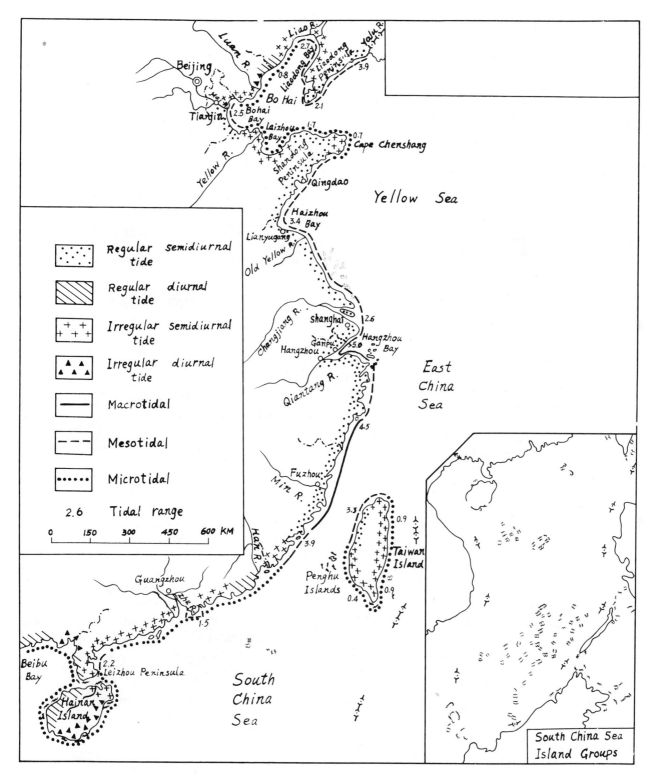

Figure 110-2. Tidal types and tide ranges on the China coast.

marshes and intertidal flats developed on the eastern coast of the peninsula result from sediment dispersion from the Yalu River. The western coast of the peninsula is dominated by a sandy beach. The much indented embayed southern coast is characterized by erosional rocky cliffs as a result of the continuous pounding of waves from the open sea.

LIAODONG BAY PLAIN COAST

This muddy coast is the southern periphery of an immense flat basin developed on either side of the Liao River. Coastal marshes are well developed, with intertidal mud flats 1–2 km wide. The Liao River has been responsible for the sediment supply.

WESTERN LIAONING HILLY COAST

This coastal section consists of an erosional remnant of Precambrian metamorphic rock with granite intrusions. The coastline is less indented. Rivers originating from the Yanshan mountain slopes carry abundant sand to supply beaches, and some of this sand has drifted southwestward under the influence of the northeasterly wind, to form numerous sandy beach ridges along the northern side of the Luan River. Large-scale sand dunes have developed along this coast.

LUANHE DELTAIC COAST

The Luanhe is a river with an abundant sediment discharge. The sediment delivered to the sea consists mainly of medium- to fine–grained sand. Tidal range is small (1–1.5 m), and the northeasterly wind produces maximum wave heights of 4.8 m. The interaction of river runoff and wave action has built a fan-shaped delta. Because distributaries shift frequently, five subdeltaic accumulations have formed. Relics of these form offshore sand bars and barriers formed during different episodes of recorded history, enclosing lagoons and low-lying swamps. The present delta has accumulated over the past hundred years.

BOHAI BAY PLAIN COAST

A vast muddy flat lies along the western coast of Bohai Bay between the Luan River and Yellow River deltas. Changes in sediment supply and deltaic growth rate, caused by the shifting of the main course of the ancient Yellow River, have led to the formation of four shelly ridges, 4700–4000, 3800–3000, 2000–1100, and 600–100 years ago respectively. By the year 1855 the Yellow River had returned to its old outlet, again discharging into the Bohai Sea. Because of suspended sediment dispersed from the Yellow River, the Hai River, and others, this coastal section has prograded seaward, gradually widening its tidal flats, which are now up to 10 km wide (Zeng Xitao 1980). Rapid siltation has been a problem for port maintenance; at Tianjin New Harbor it is necessary to dredge up to 6 million m^3 of silt annually to maintain navigability (Wang Ying 1980).

YELLOW RIVER DELTAIC COAST

This section, which runs from the Tuhai River mouth in the north to the Xiaoqin River mouth in the south, constitutes the deltaic shoreline of the modern Yellow River. It is 186 km long, typically fan-shaped, built out into the Bohai Sea. The Yellow River is notorious for its extremely high silt content; it carries about 1.2 billion tons of silt annually into the sea, 40% of which accumulates on either side of its outlet, forming estuarine silt jetties. These jetties have grown seaward at the rate of 2–3 km per year. Over the last hundred years a lowland with an area of 2,300 km^2 has been built out into the sea. The tidal range in the estuary is less than 1 m, and currents are rather weak. River discharge has been the controlling factor in deltaic development. According to historical records, the lower Yellow River has repeatedly changed its course, shifting between the Hai River and the Huai River. During each shifting cycle, a subaqueous delta was constructed seaward of the outlet. After 1855, when the Yellow River reoccupied its old channel (the Daqin River), it began to form the modern deltaic complex, which is a merging and overlapping of ten subdeltas deposited during different stages (Pang Jiazhen and Si Shuheng 1979).

LAIZHOU BAY PLAIN COAST

This section extends from the mouth of the Xiaoqin River in the west to the Tiger Head rocky cliff coast in the east. It is a silty coast. The marshes and tidal flats are 1–7 km wide. The source of the silty material is mainly suspended sediment dispersed southward from the Yellow River, but local rivers are partly responsible for this sediment supply.

SHANDONG PENINSULA HILLY COAST

The coastal terrain is here composed mainly of Precambrian metamorphic rocks intruded locally by granites. The northern coast is less indented. Tombolos built in a shallow sea connect the islands lying off the coast, such as Zhifu and Qimu. Wave-cut features are well developed at the eastern end of the peninsula, especially at Cape Chenshan and northern Jiangsu (Plate 110-1). The coastline is more indented around the southern side of the peninsula, with alternating promontories and bays (Plate 110-2). Bays of notable size are Jiaozhou Bay and Laoshan Bay. On the northern shore of Haizhou Bay, the southernmost of the peninsula, a straight sandy beach coastline has developed at the edge of a structurally stable erosional plain (Wang Baocan et al. 1980).

THE JIANGSU PLAIN COAST

The coast from the Haizhou Bay to the Changjiang estuary is a low-lying muddy coast, except for the Lianyungang region, where local hilly sectors have developed because of fault block uplifting. Three or four sand ridges on the coastal plain are indicative of south–north shifting of the ancient Yellow River. From 1128 to 1855 the Yellow River flowed out through the lower reach of the Huai River into the sea. A huge amount of silt was supplied to build the delta centered on the now abandoned Yellow River estuary. In 1855 the river migrated northward again, and the coastal section north of the Sheyang River then retreated because of the abrupt loss of river-borne sediment supply and exposure to open sea waves. The recession rate reached 150–200 m/yr. The tidal flat material became coarser and mud scarps (Plate 110-3) and shell ridges were formed at the seaward edge of the marshes. The coastal section south of the Sheyang River, however, still maintained a tendency toward progradation because offshore shoals (both emerged and submerged) protected the coastline. In addition, silt eroded from the previous section was deposited here. A series of offshore sand ridges radiate outward in finger-like patterns produced by the interaction of tidal currents from south and north. In other words, the newly deposited ridges arose from the reworking of surface sediment of the subaqueous delta by tidal currents. In Central Jiangsu, *Spartina anglica* has been planted on mud flats, and in some sectors has developed broad salt marshes (Plates 110-4 and 110-5).

CHANGJIANG DELTAIC COAST

The Changjiang (Yangtze) is well known for its abundant sand and water discharge. It carries about 470 million tons of silt into the sea annually. A huge delta with an area of about 40,000 km² has been built up, and a broad subaqueous delta as well. The Changjiang has also delivered silt to the nearby coast. The silt carried by the Jiangsu-Zhejiang longshore current southward has contributed to building the embayed muddy coast of eastern Zhejiang and northern Fujian. The Changjiang Estuary was originally a funnel-shaped bay 2,000 years ago. At that time, outside the river mouth, there was a series of shoals with intervening channels branching and rejoining. Over the last 2,000 years, as sand bars merged with the northern bank, shoals of the southern bank prograded, and the main river channel narrowed and deepened, the estuary has been migrating seaward. A new sand bar system has been built lying transverse to the mouth of the present Changjiang estuary (Fig. 110-3). Chongming Island is the largest sand bar in the Changjiang estuary (Chen Jiyu et al. 1959, 1979).

HANGZHOU BAY COAST

Hangzhou Bay (Fig. 110-4) is of macrotidal type, with an average tidal range exceeding 5 m. The maximum tidal range at Ganpu reaches 8.93 m. The bay retains its funnel shape because the silt supply from the Qiantang River has not been sufficient to fill it in and build a delta. The average annual sediment yield is only 5.4 million tons. The rapid narrowing of the mouth headward and the abrupt shallowing of the subaqueous topography have produced the sharp deformation of incoming tides to generate tidal bores (Plate 110-6), such as the famous Qiantang bore west of Ganpu. The front of the bore in Hainin may reach as high as 3.7 m, the maximum current velocity of the flood tide being 16–20 knots. The Hangzhou Bay coast, except for a few isolated residual hills standing on the seashore, is a coastal plain. The material of the intertidal flats is mainly silt (Plate

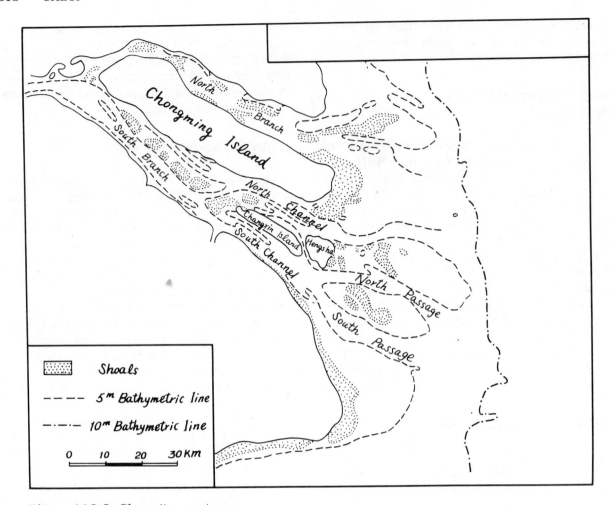

Figure 110-3. Changjiang estuary.

110-7). Over a long historical period, the strong tide and swift currents of Hangzhou Bay, combined with the lateral movement of the deep channel, have resulted in erosion and accretion of parts of the shore. While the coastline on one side was rapidly silted up and hence prograded, the other was strongly scoured and hence cut back. At present the northern bank is subject to slight erosion, while the southern bank in general shows a tendency toward accretion. Sea-walls have been built to protect eroding sections (Plate 110-8).

THE SOUTHEAST HILLY COAST

The whole coastal region from the southern bank of Hangzhou Bay to the Beilun estuary in Guangxi is characterized by undulating hills. The configuration is profoundly controlled by two groups of fracture zones (i.e., the northeast- and northwest-trending faults). The zigzag coastline

has many natural harbors, peninsulas, and islands. Small patches of coastal plain occur near estuaries. The features of coastline have been shaped by the combined effects of many factors, including geological structure, the quantity and quality of sediment supply, and local climatic patterns, which vary from place to place.

Eastern Zhejiang and Northern Fujien Hilly Coast

The bedrock consists of Mesozoic volcanic rocks. Erosional cliffs and terraces are well developed around the promontories (Plate 110-9). Broad hinterlands are found behind the embayed shores, with intersecting networks of channels, which are believed to have been formed under the effect of strong tidal currents. Because of the relatively weak wave action, fine-grained sediments dispersed from the Changjiang estuary

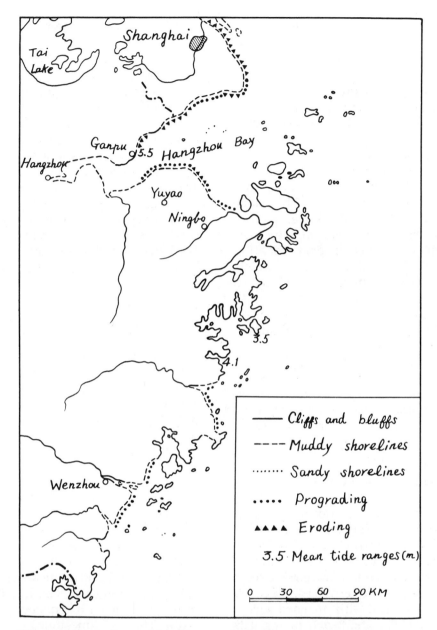

Figure 110-4. Coastal landforms of Zhejiang Province, China.

are carried into the bay by the flood tide, leading to the development of wide muddy marshes and intertidal flats over the littoral zone. The landscape of the embayed muddy coast here is unique.

Southern Fujien and Western Guangdong Hilly Coast

The coastal terrain here consists mainly of granite. Its weathering products have provided abundant source material, reworked by wave action. Geomorphological features of marine ero-

sion and littoral accumulation are remarkable. To the west of the Zhu River estuary, where wave energy is relatively low, the suspended sediment transported from the Zhu River has been deposited to form muddy flats on which a dense mangrove forest grows.

Estuarine Plain Coast

Rivers flowing into the South China Sea are usually formed by the confluence of numerous torrential streams originating in mountainous regions. Though estuarine accumulation has been taking place since the Middle Holocene, the alluvium has grown only slowly because of the slow rate of sediment supply. The Zhujiang estuary and the Han River estuary, the largest in southern China, still maintain the original triangular shape characteristic of an embayed valley-mouth coast formed by the Holocene marine transgression (Zeng Shaoxuan 1957).

The Zhu River delta is formed by the junction of three subdeltas, the Xijiang, the Beijiang, and the Dongjiang (Zhao Huanting 1982). The deltaic plain, dotted with isolated hills, is drained by a network of interwoven channels emptying into the sea through eight outlets. The progradation rate is related to the location of these outlets along the coast, varying from 10 m/yr to 110 m/yr in response to changes in runoff and sediment supply. Broad muddy flats have formed on certain coastal sections where the accretion process is relatively active.

The Han River delta is fan-shaped. It flows into the sea through three distributaries. At present, the delta is growing seaward at the rate of 10–30 m/yr. Numerous sand ridges on the front of the deltaic plain are produced by marine reworking of fluvial sediments.

Leizhou Peninsula Platform Coast

This coast section shows platforms with altitudes of 20–80 m. The platform terrain of the northern coast is composed of Neogene and Early Quaternary clastic rocks, while the southern coast is formed of Pleistocene basaltic lava flows. Except on the relatively straight western coast, the coastline is irregular, indented with drowned valleys and bounded by cliffs. The beach material is mainly sand and pebbles, and mangroves are growing on the tidal flats. Near the southern end of the peninsula, offshore coral reefs emerge 1.5–2.0 m at low tide and have been dated at 7,120±165 years B.P.

Southern Guangxi Hilly Coast

This section runs between the mouths of the Dafeng and Beilun rivers. Coastal ranges are mainly composed of Paleozoic and Mesozoic sedimentary rocks. The coastline is much indented with embayed estuaries penetrating into the hinterland. Mangrove forests grow around the bays.

HAINAN ISLAND COAST

The northern coast of Hainan Island is a platform of lava flows, with extensive pebble and sand beaches. Fringing reefs are well developed. A delta has been built by the Nandu River. Mangrove forests of various species cover the bay area, the taller ones being as high as 10 m.

The southern coast of the island is mountainous, the bedrock consisting mainly of granite. The embayments are often enclosed by spits to form lagoons, beaches and spits have capping sand dunes parallel to the coastline. In addition, coral reefs of both primary and secondary origin are distributed offshore, some of the reefs having been raised above high tide level.

THE SOUTH CHINA SEA ISLAND GROUPS

The South China Sea is dotted with numerous small islands in addition to Hainan. They can be classified into four groups: Dongsha Islands, the Xisha Islands, the Zhongsha Islands, and the Nansha Islands. All are of coralline origin. Since the Miocene Epoch, atolls have gradually evolved from submergence of fringing reefs and barrier reefs. These reefs include skeletal coral and shell growth, the framework being coral in situ, with a large part composed of debris of other littoral species. It is clear that the framework of coral must be firm enough to resist erosion by waves, and its existence depends on the successful growth of coral organisms in the surf. The coral reefs are up to 1,000 m thick, as a result of coastal subsidence. Since the middle Holocene, these reefs have shown a tendency toward uplifting again. The reef limestones of Rock Island, for example, are now 15 m above sea level. Based on carbon 14 dating, samples collected from its terrace (altitude 10 m) are about 4,000 years old.

CHEN JIYU
LIU CANGZI
YU ZHIYING

REFERENCES

Chen Jiyu and Wang Baocan, 1981, The islands of China, in *The Physical Geography of China*, Academia Sinica, ed., Science Press, Beijing, pp. 349–365.

Chen Jiyu, Wang Baocan, and Liu Cangzi, 1980, The coastal geomorphology of China, in *The Physical Geography of China*, Academia Sinica ed., Science Press, Beijing, pp. 313–347.

Chen Jiyu, Yu Zhiying, and Yun Caixing, 1959, Development of the geomorphology of the Changjiang delta, *Acta Geographica*, **25**:201–222.

Chen Jiyu, Yun Caixing, Xu Haigen, and Dong Yongfa, 1979, Evolution of the Changjiang estuary during the past 2,000 years, *Acta Oceanologica Sinica* **1**:103–111.

Pang Jiazhen and Si Shuheng, 1979, The Estuary Changes of Huanghe River. I. Changes in Modern Time, *Oceanol. Limnol. Sinica* **10**:136–141.

Song Daquan, 1983, Salt marsh resources of China, in *Land Resources of the People's Republic of China*, K. Ruddle and Wu Chuanjun, eds., United Nations University, pp. 37–44.

Wang Baocan, Yu Zhiying, Liu Cangzi, and Jin Qingxiang, 1980, Changes on coasts and beaches and longshore movements of sediment in Haizhou Bay, *Acta Oceanol. Sinica* **2**:79–96.

Wang Ying, 1980, The coast of China, *Geoscience Canada* **7**:109–113.

Zhao Huanting, 1982, Evolution of the Zhujiang delta, *Acta Oceanol. Sinica* **4**:595–607.

Zeng Shaoxuan, 1957, Hanjiang delta, *Acta Geographica* **23**:255–273.

Zhao Xidao, 1980, Holocene changes on the west coast of Bohai Bay, in *The Origin and Development of the Fault-Block Region of Northern China*, Academia Sinica, ed., Science Press, Beijing, pp. 302–309.

Plate 110-1. Rocky coast of northern Jiangsu.

Plate 110-3. Eroding tidal mud flats, central Jiangsu.

Plate 110-2. Gravel-strewn sandy beach, northern Jiangsu.

Plate 110-4. *Spartina* plantings on tidal mud flats, central Jiangsu.

Plate 110-5. *Spartina* marshland, central Jiangsu.

Plate 110-8. Sea-wall, Hangzhou Bay.

Plate 110-6. Tidal bore, Hangzhou Bay.

Plate 110-9. Rocky coast with notched cliff base, Zhejiang.

Plate 110-7. Tidal mud flats, north shore, Hangzhou Bay.

111. HONG KONG

Hong Kong's 870 km coastline is long in relation to its area of 1,062 km² (Fig. 111-1). The coastline is highly crenulated, with a large number of bays, projecting headlands, peninsulas, and offshore islands. It owes its ria form to residual submergence related to the Flandrian transgression of a dissected upland terrain that, in predominantly igneous rocks, is over 900 m high.

Opposite changes of the strandline are shown by emerged beaches rising to 5-6 m and 15 m P.D. and erosion surfaces standing at 230, 130, 71, 40, and 22 m P.D. (Principal Datum, i.e. low water level) (Berry 1961).

Situated on the South China coast, Hong Kong is under the influence of the dominant easterlies. Intensified by the northeast monsoon in winter

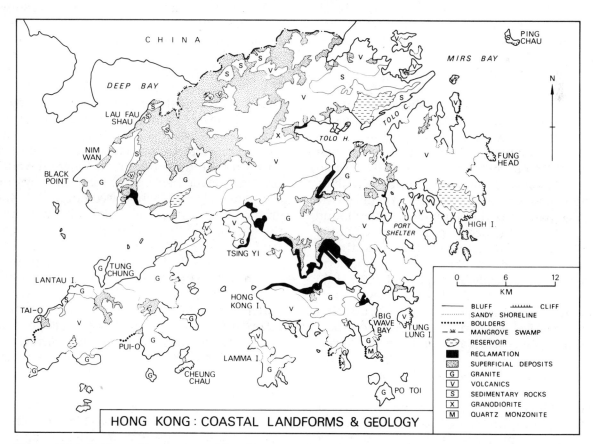

Figure 111-1. Hong Kong: coastal landforms and geology.

and typhoons in summer, together with a greater fetch from the eastern and the southern quadrants, these easterlies direct greater wave attack on east-facing and south-facing coasts. In this, the effect of typhoons, outpacing the impact of monsoon gales (Chen 1979), is seen on beaches (So 1972) and on rocky coasts, within a mesotidal, low-energy coastal environment (Davies 1964). Locally, waves reach up to 6 m in height when the typhoon is some distance away and much higher when the center is near (Cuming 1967). The vertical limit of their effect is determined by the oversplash of storm surges, which, varying in intensity according to coastal configuration (Cheng 1967), have been recorded up to 8 m above the predicted tide (Watts 1959). While local coincidence of onshore winds with flood tides enhances the effect, the limitation of maximum tidal amplitude to 2.5 m with resulting tidal currents of subdued strength, taken together with offshore depth seldom exceeding 15 fathoms except in coastal constrictions, hardly contributes to the action associated with high water.

The coast most affected by the dominant easterlies runs from Fung Head to Tung Lung Island in acid lavas and pyroclastic rocks (Fig. 111-1). The exposed rocky sectors east of Port Shelter, recording substantial coastal recession under marine erosion, are dominated by marked cliff development in which lines of structural weakness (in particular jointing and to some extent fracture zones, shear zones, shatter belts, and minor faults) guide and accentuate marine erosion. Where seaward-dipping joint planes are prominent, ramps develop at the cliff base. Just north and south of the east dam of High Island Reservoir, massive columnar jointing is well developed, and vertical cliffs broken in detail by the stepped pattern of the columns are often found on headlands, the degree of prominence of the vertical faces being determined by any tilting of the columns. The only major constructional form is the bay-head sandy beach west of Fung Head with a backshore partly covered by embryonic foredunes. East of High Island, the Port Shelter area is relatively sheltered. While numerous bays have fringing beaches and mud flats party colonized by mangrove, the area is dominated by the majority of the 230-odd offshore islands found in Hong Kong, some being connected by tombolos (Plate 111-1). An extension of the west arm of Port Shelter to Tung Lung Island, being exposed to the dominant easterlies, displays some large sea caves, geos, hanging valleys, truncated spurs,

and stacks, representing different stages of sequential development of coastal indentations.

Northward from Fung Head to the border with China, the coastal zone becomes increasingly sheltered by the land barrier to the north. North of Tolo Harbor and Tolo Channel there is the largest outcrop of sedimentary rocks in Hong Kong, with beds dipping consistently northward. The dominant northeast–southwest structural trend, to which the bulk of the presubmergence topography is adjusted, finds expression along the coast and also determines the direction of Tolo Channel, which is considered to run along a major fault (Allen and Stephens 1971). On the south side of Tolo Harbor and Tolo Channel, where coarse tuff and pyroclastic rocks with some lava outcrop, because of the relatively subdued wave action coastal slopes have merely been basally trimmed, giving rise to bluffs or notches; minor estuaries related to local stream networks in embayments survive side by side with small deltas. Some coastal sectors have been modified through reclamation and damming-up part of the sea for water supply; by reducing basin capacity, such modifications speed up currents in bottleneck areas and accentuates the impact of storm surges associated with the onset of typhoons, as expressed in coastal floods (So 1981a). Along the northwest bank of Tolo Channel, orthoquartzite, quartz pebble conglomerate, cross-bedded micaceous sandstone, siltstone, and shale outcrop on the coast, which trends with the strike of the beds dipping at 60–80° landward. As a massive bed of conglomerate makes up much of the seaward slope, the overlying sandstone, siltstone, and shale are preferentially stripped from the harder rock. Where the outer resistant layer has been breached, bays are comparatively rapidly hollowed out on the fine-grained members of the series. Westward from the entrance to Tolo Channel, where the coast cuts across the strike of a younger series of sedimentary beds dipping up to 30° northward and including interbedded conglomerate, pebbly sandstone, and cleaved mudstone, an intricate pattern of headlands, bays, and inlets results from differential erosion of sandstone, siltstone, and shale. A thrust bringing these under pyroclastic rocks (Ruxton 1960) and increasing their angle of dip causes pyroclastic rocks to outcrop again farther northwest along the coast. On Ping Chau Island, where a gently folded series of laminated shales and siltstones is interspersed with one or two resistant ash and tuff beds, preferential erosion of siltstones and shales has taken place, especially on the south coast, with marked cliff and platform development.

To the west of Tung Lung Island, the shores of Hong Kong Harbor, a drowned denuded center of a granitic cupola (Berry and Ruxton 1960), have been built up or modified by reclamation (Fig. 111-1). On Hong Kong Island, the northern half of the exposed east coast suffers from substantial recession under marine erosion, with bold cliffs developing side by side with coastal indentations along lines of structural weakness, insignificant changes in structure thus lead to significant changes in coastal morphology. In Big Wave Bay, a pocket beach is backed by a raised sand bank to which migration of foreshore sand induced by wind action makes contribution. To the south, a 22 m erosion surface of marine origin truncates the granite-volcanics divide. Farther south a complex tombolo is found. It consists of a sandy linking spit related to a former higher sea level, providing the site for a village, and an intertidal boulder spit linking up an offshore island. At the southeastern tip of Hong Kong Island, where coarse tuff is intruded by numerous quartz porphyry dikes, an arch and a blowhole have developed. On the south coast of Hong Kong Island, except for minor compartments in quartz monzonite giving rise to boulder streams on coastal slopes and in granodiorite feeding boulder beaches, coastal forms develop either in granite or in pyroclastic rocks with some lava. In the granite areas, including the offshore Po Toi island group and Lamma Island, the dominant coastal form is determined by the preferential exhumation of the pre-existing weathering profiles so that, allowing for overlaps and combinations, clayey sand and sandy clay exposed in Zone I (Ruxton and Berry 1957) form unstable slumping cliffs; Zone II, with kaolinitic silty sand and up to 50% corestones, gives rise to more stable cliffs with some subangular to subrounded boulders and a few pebbles; Zone III, with up to 90% corestones, leads to the development of boulder-strewn coasts with subangular blocks and boulders; and exposure of Zone IV allows a suite of structurally controlled forms and features to be developed on solid rock (Plate 111-2). Where sheet joints are prominent, removal of the regolith by marine agents exposes the sheets themselves, on which inclined, curvilinear surfaces develop and, where the cross joints are marked, may eventually be broken up, giving breaks of slope. In the volcanics area, with close but variable jointing, less mature weathering profiles develop, and coastal forms related to the upper three zones of the weathering profile are not always seen.

On Lantau Island, feldspar porphyry dike swarms intrude into granite on the east coast; being more resistant to chemical weathering because of their fine-grained groundmass and low porosity, and resistant to wave attack because of their widely spaced joints, these dike swarms make distinct coastal promontories on which erosion surfaces of marine origin at 71, 40, and 22 m P.D. may terminate (Berry 1961). The intervening embayments have sandy bay bars banking against the 6 m emerged beaches and enclosing lagoons rapidly being silted up, all related to dominant littoral drifts moving from north to south. The more exposed south coast consists of two large embayments in volcanics, each representing intergrowth of bays as a side effect of dismemberment of drainage following submergence. The headlands at both ends are in granite, with a promontory in quartz monzonite and porphyritic adamellite in the middle. Within the embayments, bay bars related to west–east drift have formed, that in Pui-O being backed by emerged bars rising to 6 m and 10 m P.D., and that in the bay southeast of Pui-O resting against an emerged beach made up of materials representing both higher sea levels. Off the coast, tombolos related to former higher sea levels include Cheung Chau, which reveals a close adjustment between form and structure (Berry and Ruxton 1957). The northwest coast of Lantau Island is dominated by subaerial slopes fringed by residual boulder accumulations in the volcanics sector, and by a mixture of pebbles and boulders in the sedimentaries sector section. At Tai-O, an arch has developed from accentuated marine erosion along a prominent bedding plane in sandstone, while alluvial flats form sites of abandoned salt pans. On the north coast, increasing shelter by land barriers eastward has promoted coastal filling, which at one time has led to silting at Tung Chung, where multiple bay bars, often in hooked form, occur.

Back on the mainland coast opposite Lantau Island, the sector predominantly in granite, between Tsing Yi and Black Point, again shows close adjustment between coastal forms and exposed zones of the weathering profile. Northeastward from Black Point the coast is completely sheltered from the dominant easterlies. Deep Bay, a receptor basin of sediments with additional contribution by the Pearl River and by the Sham Chun River flowing along the border, witnesses active silting and widespread development of mud flats. While in many places headlands alternate with sandy pocket beaches backed by the 6 m emerged beach, a reversal of coastal morphology is seen between Lau Fau Shan and Nim Wan (So 1981b). Displaying a spatial pattern of compartments associated with the development of cuspate spits and cliff recession, the coast departs from the tendency for interfluves to become promontories between valley-mouth embayments. Differential shoreline retrogradation and progradation are held to have given rise to such departures in morphology, and the effective functioning of this coastal process-response system is deemed to depend on the sheltered nature of the coast and the sustained supply of sediments. These low-lying coastal sectors are subjected to flood hazards in storm surges. From the northern tip of the peninsula to the border with China, the low-lying coastland is dominated by mud flats partly colonized and stabilized by mangrove, the main plants being *Avicennia, Kandelia, Bruguiera,* and *Aegicera,* among others. A sequence of stages in the development of mud flats and their colonization by mangrove can be distinguished in this area (Thrower and Cheng 1975).

C. L. SO

REFERENCES

Allen, P. M., and E. A. Stephens, 1971, *Report on the Geological Survey of Hong Kong,* Government Press, Hong Kong.

Berry, L., 1961, Erosion surfaces and emerged beaches in Hong Kong, *Geol. Soc. Amer. Bull.,* **72:**1383–1394.

Berry, L., and B. P. Ruxton, 1957, Structure and form of Cheung Chau Island, Hong Kong, *Geol. Mag.* **94:** 249–260.

Berry, L., and B. P. Ruxton, 1960, The evolution of Hong Kong Harbour basin, *Annals Geomorphology* **4**(2): 97–115.

Chen, T. Y., 1979, *Comparison of Waves Recorded at Wagland Island and at Kwun Mun,* Royal Observatory, Hong Kong.

Cheng, T. T., 1967, *Storm Surges in Hong Kong,* Royal Observatory, Hong Kong.

Cuming, M. J., 1967, *Wave Heights in the Southeast Approaches to Hong Kong Harbour,* Royal Observatory, Hong Kong.

Davies, J. L., 1964, A morphogenic approach to world shorelines, *Zeitschr. Geomorphologie* **8:**127*–142*.

Ruxton, B. P., 1960, The geology of Hong Kong, *Geol. Soc. Lond. Quart. Jour.* **115:**233–260.

Ruxton, B. P., and L. Berry, 1957, Weathering of granite and associated erosional features in Hong Kong, *Geol. Soc. Amer. Bull.* **68:**1263–1292.

So, C. L., 1972, The effect of typhoons on beaches in Hong Kong, in *International Geography 1972,* W. P. Adams and F. M. Helleiner, eds., **2:**1018–1019.

So, C. L., 1981a, Geomorphology and environmental management: the case in Hong Kong, in *Geography and Hong Kong,* Hong Kong Geographical Association, pp. 45–61.

So, C. L., 1981b, Coast changes between Lau Fau Shan and Nim Wan, Hong Kong, *Sains Malaysiana* **10**(1): 51–68.

Thrower, L. B., and D. W. K. Cheng, 1975, Mangroves, in *The Vegetation of Hong Kong* L. B. Thrower, ed., Royal Asiatic Society, Hong Kong Branch, Hong Kong, pp. 64–77.

Watts, I. E. M., 1959, *The Effect of Meteorological Conditions on Tide Height in Hong Kong,* Royal Observatory, Hong Kong.

Plate 111-1. A tombolo linking an offshore island to the mainland north of Tung Lung Island (photo by C. L. So.).

Plate 111-2. Coast in granite south of Big Wave Bay, showing dominance of Zone III material of the weathering profile in the foreground and the headland in Zone IV in the background (photo by C.L. So).

112. TAIWAN

The elliptical-shaped island of Taiwan (Fig. 112-1) is located in the western Pacific, separated from the China mainland by the 100 km wide Taiwan Strait. The eastern half of the island consists of a metamorphic complex of upper Paleozoic age. The Coastal Range, bordering the east coast, is formed of Miocene volcanics and younger sediments. The western foothills of the Central Range are composed of Tertiary sediments that contain coal seams and some oil and natural gas. Coastal tablelands, capped with lateritic soil, are found in the western half of the island of Taiwan.

Since Taiwan is situated in the mobile belt of the western Pacific, some tectonic events are revealed by the coastal features. The present form of the coast also reflects both the marine process operating upon the coastal area and the geological background of the island (Fig. 112-1).

Tremendous amounts of silt, sand, and other erosional products, derived from upstream areas, are brought down to the coast, forming broad tidal flats and chains of offshore barriers. The longshore current, driven by winds during the monsoon period, accelerates the movement of sediment along the western coast, and is favorable to progradation. This phenomenon is common in southwestern Taiwan.

The sea floor in Taiwan Strait is mostly at depths of 50–100 m, but it becomes deeper toward the Pacific, with the greater depths exceeding 3,000 m. Other factors affecting the coastal development are the monsoon climate and typhoon. The winter monsoon from the northeast begins in September and ends in May of the next year. The summer monsoon from the southwest lasts from May to September. The velocity of wind during the monsoons is 5–15 m/s.

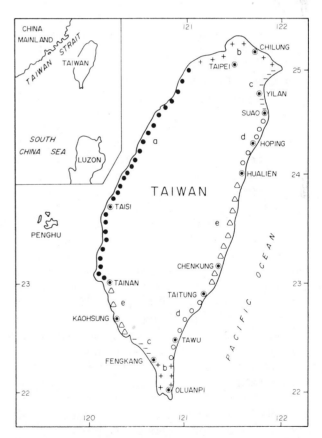

Figure 112-1. Coastal features of Taiwan. ●●●● Advancing coast, resulting from emergence and accretion; ++++ Retreating coast, resulting from emergence and stronger erosion; ——— Retreating coast, resulting from submergence and erosion; ○○○○ Retreating coast, chiefly by erosion; △△△△ Stationary coast, by balance of emergence and erosion.

Typhoons occur several times during the summer, generating high, stormy waves that attack the coast, and usually lasting for 24 hours or so.

The tidal range is up to 3 m on the west coast, whereas the rest of the coast experiences only about 1 m on the average. For this reason there is a broad tidal flat in the west, parts of which have been reclaimed for agricultural uses.

The coast of Taiwan may be classified into five types according to their nature at the present stage of development (Fig. 112-1). This is simply the result of marine action on the coast under various geological controls (Hsu 1962).

Type A. The advancing coast resulting from emergence and accretion. The coast from Taisi to Tainan, in the western part of the island, is apparently an advancing coast. Much sediment brought down from rivers originating in the central mountains provides material for the formation of tidal flats and offshore barriers. Continuous uplift of this area since the Pleistocene has also contributed to the advancement of the coast.

Type B. The retreating coast resulting from emergence and considerable erosion. Both the northern and southern extremities of the island have been continuously uplifted (Plate 112-1) since the Pleistocene. Marine terraces of coral reefs (Plate 112-2) have been well developed in the Oluanpi area in southern Taiwan. The highest one has been elevated over 200 m above sea level. Living corals are also abundant along the coast near Oluanpi.

Though one sees evidence of recent upliftings in the northern Taiwan, there has also been a fluctuation of the coast in the past. The scenic hoodoo rocks in the Yehliu area are remnants of concretionary subaerial sandstone, emerged after undergoing marine erosion (Plate 112-3).

Type C. Retreating coast resulting from submergence and marine erosion. The coast near Yilan in the northeast of Taiwan, and the sector from Fengkang to Kaohsung in the southwest, are retreating coasts resulting from regional subsidence and marine erosion. A ria coast and land-tied islands are seen near Suao. The farmland of the Yilan plain has been protected by coastal dunes and dikes from the invasion of seawater.

The coast from Kaohsung to Fengkang has also been retreating because of erosion from the waves generated by southwest monsoon winds. A drowned valley is located offshore.

Type D. Retreating coast of fault origin. The coasts near Hoping and Tawu, in eastern Taiwan, are both of fault origin, showing a straight and simple coast with continuous sea cliffs.

Type E. The coast of equilibrium, eastern Taiwan. Chengkung is a small fishing port located at the sea side of the Coastal Range, which has been tectonically active since the Pleistocene. The range has been uplifted at different rates in different places (Hsu 1954). Since the coast faces the high seas of the Pacific ocean, erosion offsets the amount of land gained by upheaval, and the coast has almost reached a state of equilibrium. At Taitung, a delta is locally prograding at the present time (Plate 112-4).

Further readings concerning coastal Taiwan include Ho (1975), Hsu (1964, 1965, 1974), Hsu and Chang (1979), and Shih (1980).

T. L. HSU

REFERENCES

Ho, C. S., 1975, *An Introduction to the Geology of Taiwan*, Ministry of Economic Affairs, Republic of China, Taipei.

Hsu, T. L., 1954, On the geomorphic features and the recent uplifting movement of the Coastal Range, eastern Taiwan, *Geol. Survey Taiwan Bull.* **7:**47–57.

Hsu, T. L., 1962, A study on the coastal geomorphology of Taiwan, *Geological Soc. China Proc.* **5:**29–45.

Hsu, T. L., 1964, Hoodoo rocks at the Yehliu area, northern coast of Taiwan, *Geol. Surv. Taiwan Bull.*, **15:** 37–43.

Hsu, T. L., 1965, The tidal flat of the Chiayi area, *Geol. Survey Taiwan Bull.*, **16:**18–54.

Hsu, T. L., 1974, On the coastal landform of northern coast of Taiwan and its significance in neotectonics, *Geol. Soc. China Proc.* **17:**123–130.

Hsu, T. L., and H. C. Chang, 1979, Quaternary faulting in Taiwan, *Geol. Soc. China Mem.* **3:**155–165.

Shih, Tsai-tien, 1980, The evolution of coastlines and the development of tidal flats in western Taiwan (in Chinese), *Geog. Research* **6:**1–36.

Plate 112-1. Sea cliffs, composed of Miocene sedimentary rocks, east of Chilung along the northern coast of Taiwan (photo by T. L. Hsu).

Plate 112-3. Scenic remnants of concretionary sandstone (hoodoos) at Yehliu, west of Chilung, along the northern coast of Taiwan (photo by T. L. Hsu).

Plate 112-2. Marine terrace and beach on raised coral reef near Oluanpi, southern Taiwan (photo by T. L. Hsu).

Plate 112-4. Beach fronting delta near Taitung, eastern Taiwan (photo by T. L. Hsu).

113. NORTH KOREA AND SOUTH KOREA

The Korean coast, from the Tumen River in the east to the Yalu River in the west, with an overall length of 14,819 km, can be divided into four parts: the northeast coast from the Tumen River to the East Korean Bay, the east coast of the Korean peninsula along the Sea of Japan, the south coast along Korea Strait and Cheju Hae-hyŏp, and the west coast of the peninsula along the Yellow Sea and the West Korean Bay. The northeast coast follows a southwest–northeast trend of faulting and folding that dates from the Jurassic and Cretaceous; the general boxlike shape of the peninsula reflects a north–south faulting trend dating from the same period. The north–south fault system, rejuvenated during the Miocene, is supposed to be still active, whereby the Korean landmass is being tilted up in the east and northeast and depressed in the west and southwest. The east coast of the peninsula is therefore a coast of emergence, and the west and southwest are coasts of submergence. The main north–south fault zone lies in the Sea of Japan about 18 km offshore from the east coast along a submarine escarpment.

Because of the tilting the principal mountain range of the peninsula (the Taebaek Mountains) lies near the east coast. Only small rivers flow toward the Sea of Japan, and the coast is relatively steep, with a narrow continental shelf (generally not more than 9 km wide) and a rapid descent to the ocean floor of the Sea of Japan at more than 2,000 m water depth. The west coast is much flatter and gradually merges into the Yellow Sea, which is a shelf sea of not more than 100 m water depth.

It has been an area of subsidence since the late Mesozoic. The south coast has an intermediate position. Like most of the west coast, it abounds with islands, whereas the east coast is almost devoid of them. The total length of the coastline (including the islands) is 5,500 km for the west coast, 5,189 km for the south coast, but only 1,880 km for the east coast (Lautensach 1945).

The tilting is also reflected in the distribution of coastal terraces along the peninsula. A high terrace, mostly abrasive with locally weathered (marine) gravel and pebbles and a cover of red soil and weathering crust, lies along the east coast at 60–100 m, but at 20–30 m along the west coast. A middle terrace, extensively developed as gravel beds without red soil, lies at 30–80 m along the east coast and at 10–20 m along the west coast. Along the east coast there is also a third terrace at 10–20 m that is absent from the west coast (Oh 1980), unless a locally developed rocky platform at +1 m above highest spring tide is correlated with it (Guilcher 1976). The northeast coast is outside the area of tilting and is more stable. Here the southwest–northeast mountain range that follows the coast (the Hamgyong Mountains) lies further inland than along the east coast of the peninsula, and the bays and islands are believed to have been formed primarily as a result of the postglacial sea-level rise.

Precambrian crystalline rocks (granite, gneiss, schists) and Late Cretaceous and Tertiary granites form most of the Korean coast, with Cretaceous fresh-water deposits in the southeast and south. Locally Paleozoic and Mesozoic shallow marine deposits and young basalts are also present. The island of Cheju-Do, south of the peninsula, and the island of Ullung-Do, in the Sea of Japan, are volcanoes. Cheju-Do has been active in historical times.

Currents along the south coast and through Korea Strait are always from west to east. Along the west coast there is an offshore current going north through the Yellow Sea, but nearshore, south of Haeju, there is a south-going counter-current that is strongly developed during the winter. In the West Korean Bay there is a clockwise gyre in summer and a counterclockwise gyre in winter. Along the east coast the current is predominantly north during summer and predominantly south during winter, so that cold water from the north penetrates much farther south during the winter than during the summer. Along the northeast coast the current is from northeast to southwest the whole year round. Sea ice forms during the winter only in the innermost parts of the coastal embayments, on the west coast north of Kunsan and the east and northeast coasts north of Samchok.

The tidal sea-level fluctuations are small along the east and northeast coasts (< 25 cm during spring tide) because of the great depth of the Sea of Japan. The tidal range increases westward along the south coast to more than 3 m at spring tide and increases still more along the west coast to more than 9 m at Inchon and more than 6 m in the innermost parts of the West Korean Bay. The tidal currents are correspondingly low along the east and northeast coasts (less than 1 knot) but increase near Inchon and between the islands of the south and southwest coasts to more than 5 knots. The winds are mostly northerly during the winter and usually variable during the rest of the year, when local winds prevail, including those from nearby mountains and valleys. In many places offshore breezes by night alternate with onshore breezes by day. Gales (above 28 knots) are most frequent in winter, coming from the northwest. Typhoons occur about once a year during the summer, primarily along the southern part of the peninsula coming from west-southwest. Large swell is present mainly along the east coast, coming from north-northeast; to the south and west the shallow shelf and the numerous islands prevent the development of large swell. Sand spits are therefore larger and more prominent along the east and northeast coasts and much smaller along the south and west coasts.

THE NORTHEAST AND EAST COASTS

The northeast coast is characterized by many small and several large bays formed by transgression of the sea over former relief during the postglacial sea-level rise (Fig. 113-1). The rivers in this area, coming from almost barren uplands, carry large amounts of sand and gravel. Where they flow out into a bay, a broad alluvial plain has been formed, filling the inner part of the bay. Because of the swell and the coastal current, both coming from the northeast, spits and bars have been built up; but where the coast is rocky and around islands, cliffs have been formed. This part of the coast is considered to be relatively stable (Lautensach 1945) but toward the southwest it grades into an area of subsidence around the East Korean Bay (the Bay of Wonsan) (Fig. 113-2).

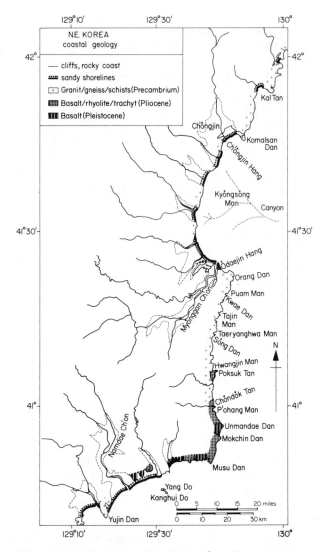

Figure 113-1. Coastal geology of northeast Korea.

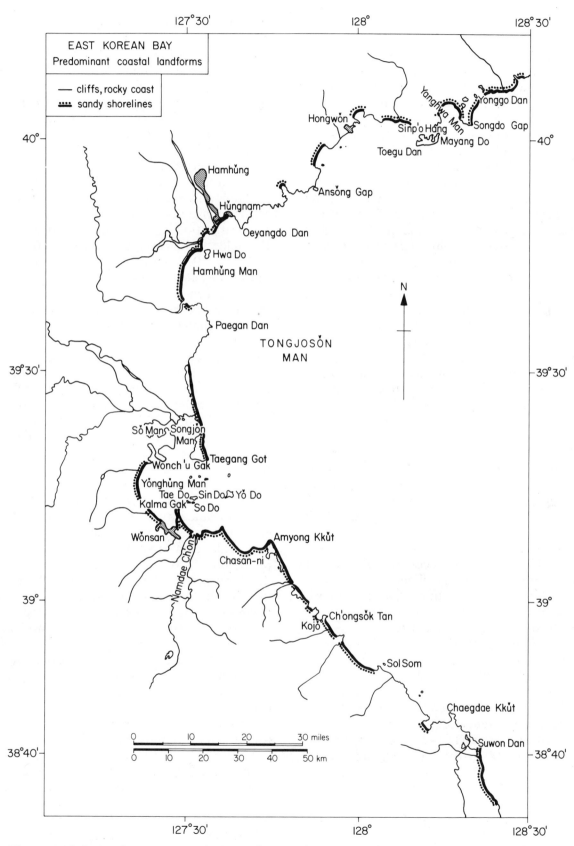

Figure 113-2. Predominant coastal landforms of East Korea Bay.

About half of this basin is filled with alluvial sediment, and the other half is covered by the sea. A 16 km long sandy spit connects a former island of Precambrian gneiss with the mainland, the whole forming the Hodo peninsula. Other small islands have been connected to the mainland in a similar way (like the Galma peninsula) or through the seaward extension of river deltas. Two small sandspits form Cape Amyong Kkŭt.

Farther to the south, the east coast down to Geojin still consists of large alluvial plains and river mouths with beach ridges and spits shutting off lakes or lagoons from the sea. Between the plains there are rocky capes and headlands. Still farther to the south the alluvial parts of the coast become smaller, and the impact of emergence gradually becomes more evident: the coast becomes steeper and coastal terraces, following the coastline, become prominent, up to 150 m above sea level. Where the usually small rivers, coming from the nearby Taebaek Mountains, flow out into the sea, there is a small alluvial plain with spits and beach ridges leaving only a narrow gap for the river water to pass through. At the southern end of the east coast a peninsula points northeastward into the Sea of Japan (Fig. 113-3). This is the northern end of a low mountain range between Pohang and Ulsan, which is separated from the mainland mountain ranges by a broad graben. At the northern end of this graben a large bay has been formed, Yeongil Man, with the Hyungsan River flowing into it, largely closed off with beach ridges (Jo 1978). Near Ulsan lies the drowned valley of the Dong River, forming a large estuary. The rocky coast between Pohang and Ulsan is rather steep, with well-developed terraces up to 130 m (Kim 1973). In total, six levels have been distinguished, the lowest being an only locally-developed and sediment-covered beach at 2–7 m. Peat in sediments at 2 m height has been dated at about 1,700 B.P. (Kim 1973), whereas a terrace at 13 m has been dated from charcoal at about 12,000 B.P. This gives an uplift during the Late Quaternary of 1.1–1.4 mm/yr. Jo (1980) however, concluded, from alluvial deposits along the east coast that sea level reached its present level there around 6,000 years ago, implying that no uplift occurred since that time.

THE SOUTH AND WEST COASTS

The south and west coasts, especially the south-southwestern part, are strongly indented and divided into numerous small bays and islands and small peninsulas (Fig. 113-4). The influence of the tides increases westward, and some islands are isolated only during high tide. The islands decrease in size offshore, where they are mainly grouped in small archipelagoes. Farther offshore there are only small islands scattered along and between the 25 m and 50 m isobaths. The total number of islands of all sizes along the south and west coasts is 2,877 (National Geography Institute 1980).

The drowning of the south and west coasts is probably the combined result of the postglacial sea level rise and subsidence. On the basis of radiocarbon dating of peat, the subsidence during the Holocene has been on the order of 0.4 mm/yr (Y. A. Park 1969). Guilcher (1976) interpreted old marine beaches at +1 m or more along the south and west coasts as Eemian and concluded that the coast had remained virtually stable during the late Quaternary. The same old beaches, together with rocky platforms, old tidal flats, former cliffs with cavities at +3 m, and old spits at 0.5–3 m above spring tide level, have been interpreted as indications for a postglacial high sea level at about 1–2 m above present sea level (Yoon et al. 1977; D. W. Park 1979). The Holocene drowning of the old relief has resulted in a typical ria coast. Southwest–northeast trending hills and low mountain ranges, following one of the main folding and fault directions, have become a series of low peninsulas, large islands, and groups of smaller islands farther offshore. Subaerial weathering has resulted in rather steep conical hills and small isolated mountains, separated by broad plains usually filled with alluvium. This aspect has been preserved because erosion by the sea during and after the transgression has been negligible in most areas. Only along the more exposed islands at the south coast and where loose deposits form the coast, have cliffs been formed. The hardness of the rock is the essential factor, and only locally the exposure to large waves and swell. Below sea level drowned valleys can be traced down to 30–50 m water depth along distances of 50–70 km. At depths below about 40 m they are filled in and covered by Holocene mud.

Along the islands and peninsulas there are numerous small beaches of variable composition ranging from fine sand to coarse gravel, and small spits of various shapes, alternating with rocky promontories. In bays and between the islands, where there is protection against high waves, tidal flats have been formed, increasing in size and occurrence along the south coast with the

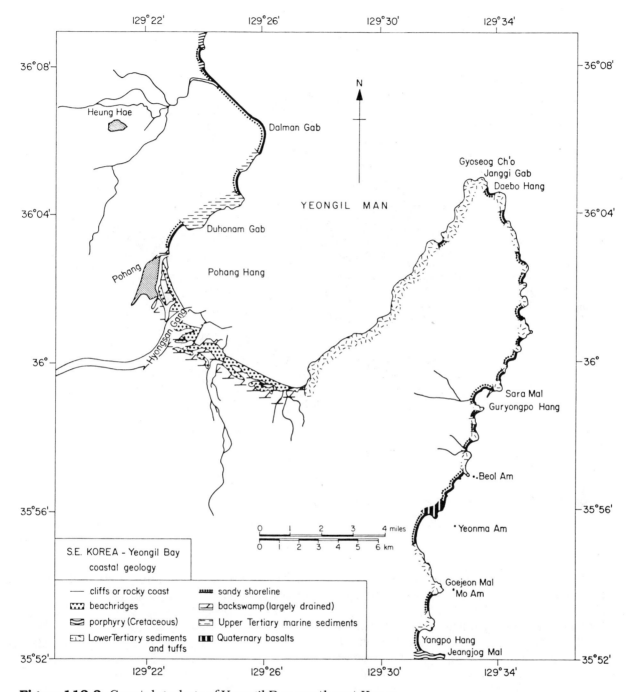

Figure 113-3. Coastal geology of Yeongil Bay, southeast Korea.

increase in tidal range and current velocities. Where large streams flow out, tidal flats have been built up at the river mouth to form a distinct deltaic pattern. Along the west coast, where the tidal range increases still further, there is usually little relation between the aspect or the presence of tidal flats and river outflow (Fig. 113-5). Predominantly intertidal flats are present (Plate 113-1); the former supratidal flats have been largely reclaimed for agriculture since 1900. Sandy flats occur where the coast is eroded or where tidal currents or waves are strong. The upper parts of the flats are often covered by periglacial debris (angular pebbles and a fine matrix), which has moved downward by mass flow from the adjacent slopes. The tidal flats grow upward and

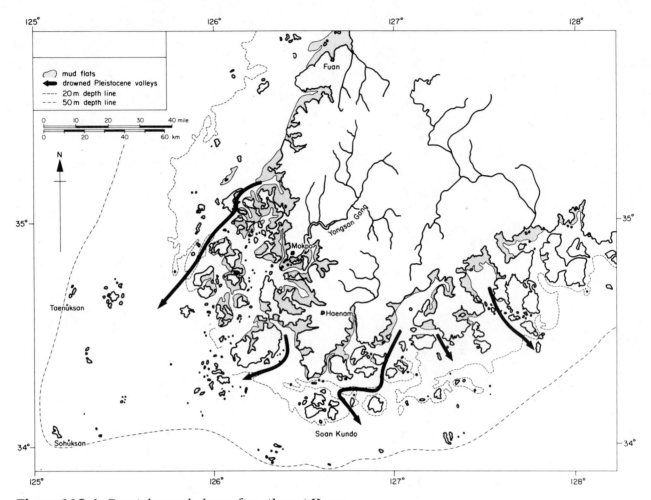

Figure 113-4. Coastal morphology of southwest Korea.

outward in most areas, the total thickness being seldom more than 25 m, usually less than 5 m. They cover a buried older relief.

In the West Korean Bay shallow tidal sand ridges, up to 80 km long, about 2.5 km wide, and with a relative height of up to 30 m, have been formed along approximately the main directions of the tidal currents (Off 1963). The coast is formed by tidal flats and salt marshes with sandy beaches and rocky shores toward the south (Fig. 113-6).

Coastal sand dunes are not large or abundant but are regularly present, the highest being 30–40 m (near Manripo). They are aligned north–south or northwest-southeast, which is the prevailing wind direction. Most dunes are covered by vegetation, but mobile barchans occur locally. Below the recent dunes, which still receive sand from the nearby beaches, there are often older dunes

of yellow-brown sand that probably date from the early Holocene (Park and Yu 1979).

D. EISMA
D. W. PARK

REFERENCES

Bartz, P. M., 1972, *South Korea*, Clarendon Press, Oxford.

Guilcher, A., 1976, Les côtes à rias de Corée et leur évolution morphologique, *Annales Géographie* **85**(472): 641–671.

Jo, W. R., 1978, The geomorphic development of the

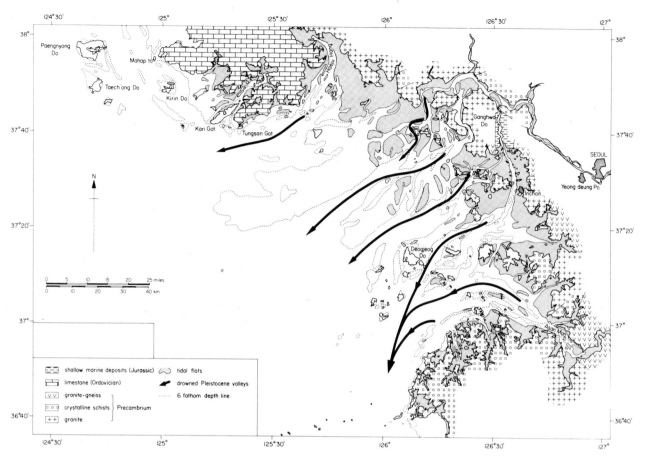

Figure 113-5. Coastal geology of the central part of the west coast of Korea.

Pohang coastal plain, east coast of Korea, *Tohoku Chiri* **30**(3):152–160 (in Japanese with English summary).

Jo, W. R., 1980, Holocene sealevel changes on the east coast of Korea peninsula, *Geog. Reu Japan* **53**(5): 317–328 (in Japanese with English summary).

Kim, S. W., 1973, A study on the terraces along the southeastern coast (Bangeojin–Pohang) of the Korean peninsula, *Geol. Soc. Korea Jour.* **9**(2):89–121.

Kwon, H. J., 1974, The intertidal flat of the west coast of Korea and the origin of its sediments, *Geography* **10**:1–12 (in Korean with English summary).

Lautensach, H., 1945, *Korea.* Koehler Verlag, Leipzig.

National Geography Institute, 1980, *Regional Geography of Korea,* Ministry of Construction, Seoul (in Korean).

Off, T., 1963, Rhythmic linear sand bodies caused by tidal currents, *Am. Assoc. Petroleum Geologists Bull.* **47**(2):324–341.

Oh, G. W., 1978, The charactertistics and the development of the shoreline of the Korean peninsula, *Geography* **18**:22–32 (in Korean with English summary).

Oh, G. W., 1980, *The Quaternary crustal movement viewed from the difference in altitude of the marine terraces in the Korean peninsula,* Paper presented at the 24th IGU meeting, Toyko.

Park, D. W., 1977, A geomorphological study of the tidal flat of Chonsu Bay, western coast of Korea, by means of remote sensing techniques, *Geography* **15**:1–15 (in Korean with English summary).

Park, D. W., 1979, Sea level variations and their impact on coastal geomorphology in the western coast of Korea, *Workshop on Coastal Geomorphology, Singapore and Malaysia,* Singapore, pp. 1–7.

Park, D. W., and K. B. Yu, 1979, A study on the morphology of the coastal dunes of the western coast of Korea, *Seoul Nat. Uniu. Jour. Geog.* **6**:1–10 (in Korean with English summary).

Park, Y. A., 1969, Submergence of the Yellow Sea coast of Korea and stratigraphy of the Sinpyeongcheon marsh, Kimje, Korea, *Geol. Soc. Japan Jour.* **5**(1): 57–66.

Yoon, O. G., B. K. Park, and S. J. Han, 1977, Geomorphological evidence of post-glacial sealevel changes in Korea, *Geol. Soc. Korea Jour.* **13**(1):15–22 (in Korean with English summary).

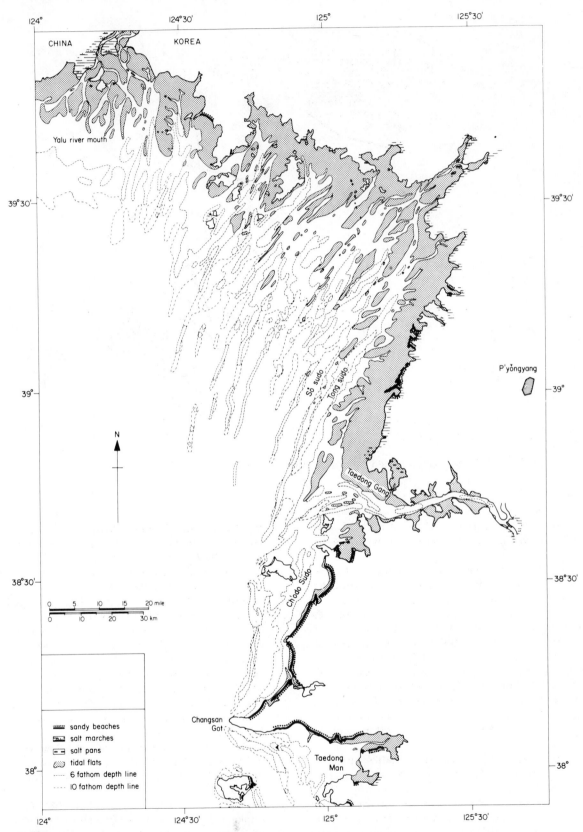

Figure 113-6. Coastal and nearshore submarine morphology of West Korea Bay.

Plate 113-1. Tidal flat and reclamation area along the western coast of Korea near Kunsan at 36°N latitude. The mean tidal range is about 6 m and the mean spring tidal range is about 9 m (photo by D. W. Park).

114. JAPAN

The coastline of Japan (Figs. 114-1 and 114-2) is about 32,000 km long including the coasts fringing the smaller islands. The coastlines of the four major islands total about 18,000 km, one-sixth of which is sandy and/or deltaic, the rest being cliffed, with or without narrow beaches or pocket beaches. Most of the coastal lowlands are now so intensively used that a large proportion of the Japanese coast is man-made. A survey by the Environmental Agency of Japan revealed that only 49% of the major islands' coasts remained natural, 15.6% was seminatural (occupied by roads, shore protection, and other artificial structures, but still natural in the intertidal zone), and 34.1% consisted of artificial coasts, with marked changes caused by port construction, reclamation, and other developments (Table 1).

The Japanese mountains have been so greatly dissected by torrential rivers that the contemporary rate of debris supply from the mountains is very high, reaching a maximum value of 9,817 $m^3/km^2/yr$ in the upper catchment of the Kurobe in central Japan. The debris supply from rivers has been sufficient to maintain accretion of sandy and/or deltaic coastlines in Japan (Koike 1977). Yet human influence has accelerated coastal erosion during the last three decades, especially at the mouths of the rivers. A reduction of debris supply from the rivers has caused coastline retreat on a large scale (Ozasa 1977).

Coastal landforms of Japan are rich in variety. In some parts ria coasts merge into straight sandy shorelines (Plate 114-1). It is common for steep or cliffed coasts to be fringed by a flight of Quaternary marine terraces (Plate 114-2) that have been uplifted, tilted, and faulted in many places. The coasts also include volcanic sectors formed by eruptions close to the sea. The mountainous coasts of Japan have been drowned and deeply embayed by the postglacial (Jomon) marine transgression, which culminated around 6,000 years ago. The embayments have been filled with sediment supplied from rivers and/or nearby sea cliffs to form straight sandy coasts. But some embayments remain unfilled, because they are not fed with sediment from large rivers and so have an insufficient debris supply.

The Japanese islands are located in the north-

Table 1. Present status of the Japanese coastlines (1978-79) (The Environmental Agency, Japan 1980)

	Natural	Seminatural	Artificial	River-mouth	Total
Major islands	9146.3 km 49.0%	2905.0 km 15.6%	6367.5 km 34.1%	239.4 km 1.3%	18,658.2 km
Smaller islands	9820.9 km 72.7%	1435.4 km 10.6%	2231.5 km 16.5%	24.2 km 0.2%	13,512.0 km
Total	18,967.2 km 59.0%	4340.4 km 13.5%	8599.0 km 26.7%	263.6 km 0.8%	32,170.2 km

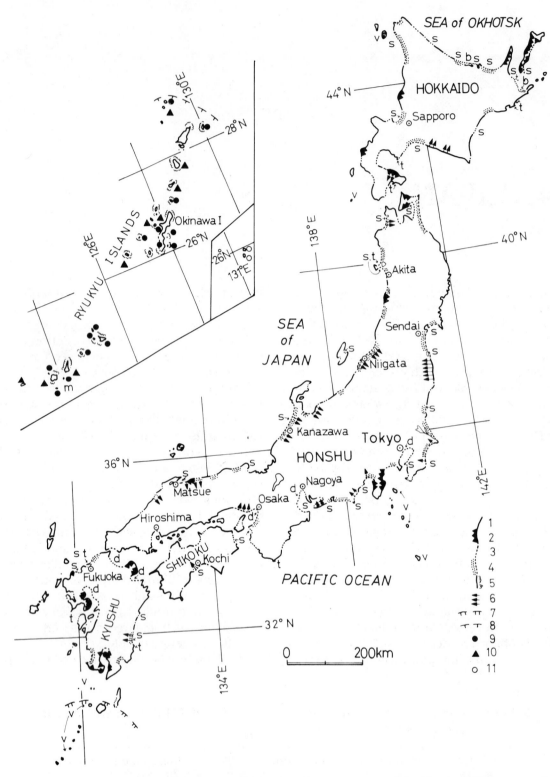

Figure 114-1. Predominant coastal landforms of the Japanese Islands. 1. cliffed coasts; 2. volcanic coasts; 3. sandy coasts; 4. sandy coasts with well-developed coastal dunes; 5. coral reefs; 6. coasts that have suffered severe erosion; 7. northern limits of coral reef growth in Holocene; 8. northern limits of coral reef growth in Pleistocene; 9. emerged coral reefs forming the top of islands; 10. emerged fringing reefs; 11. emerged atolls; b. barrier islands; d. deltaic coasts; m. mangrove swamps; s. spits and bars; t. tombolos; v. volcanic islands (7–11: after Yoshikawa et al. 1981).

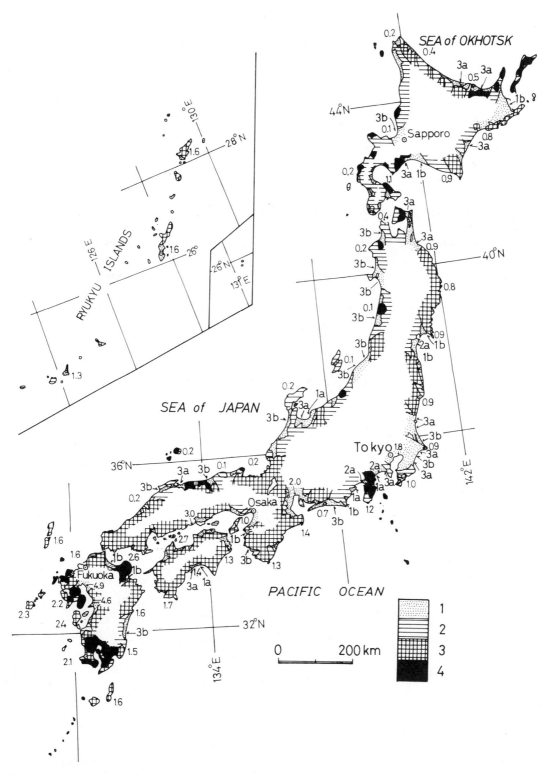

Figure 114-2. Coastal geology of the Japanese Islands. Geology: 1. Quaternary sediments; 2. Neogene sediments; 3. Paleogene and older rocks; 4. Quaternary volcanics. Nearshore topography (after Mogi 1963). 1. beaches with smooth profiles; 1a. steep; 1b. gentle; 2. beaches with stepped profiles; 3. beaches with submarine bars; 3a. single bar; 3b. multiple bars. Mean spring tidal ranges indicated in meters.

western Pacific from 45°30′ N to 24° N. The southernmost small islands are in the subtropical climate zone and are fringed by coral reefs or mangrove swamps (Fig. 114-1). Along the coast of Okhotsk and eastern Hokkaido, however, the sea surface is frozen and the beaches are covered with blocks of drift ice during the winter.

Wave action on the Pacific coastline of Japan includes ocean swell and occasionally larger waves (heights up to 9 m and periods of 14–18 s) generated by typhoons in summer. On the Sea of Japan coastline the strongest waves are those generated by the northwesterly monsoon in winter, with heights of up to 5 m and periods of 8–10 s.

Mean tidal ranges are 0.8–1.6 m on the Pacific coastline, 0.4–0.5 m on the Okhotsk, and only 0.1–0.2 m on the Sea of Japan coast. Higher ranges are recorded around the Seto Inland Sea (up to 2.7 m) and Ariake Bay in Kyushu (up to 4.9 m) (Fig. 114-2).

On Hokkaido, sandy coastlines are well developed, and most of them still remain natural. Summer beaches are covered and eroded by blocks of drift ice in winter along the coasts of Okhotsk and eastern Hokkaido. Several kinds of beach topographies are formed by sands drifting along the coasts (Fig. 114-3). In this area, embayments formed by the postglacial marine transgression have remained as lagoons behind spits or barrier islands built across bay mouths (e.g., Saroma, Tokoro, and Yufutsu). Notsuke-zaki (Fig. 114-3) is the best developed compound recurved spit in Japan.

At some places in Hokkaido, volcanoes have erupted close to the coasts, forming volcanic cliffed coasts (Figs. 114-1, 114-2 and 114-3). But a large part of the Hokkaido coast is composed of Tertiary and older rocks. Cliffs have been cut on the Hidaka coast in poorly consolidated Neogene sediments.

Most of the coast on the Pacific side of north-

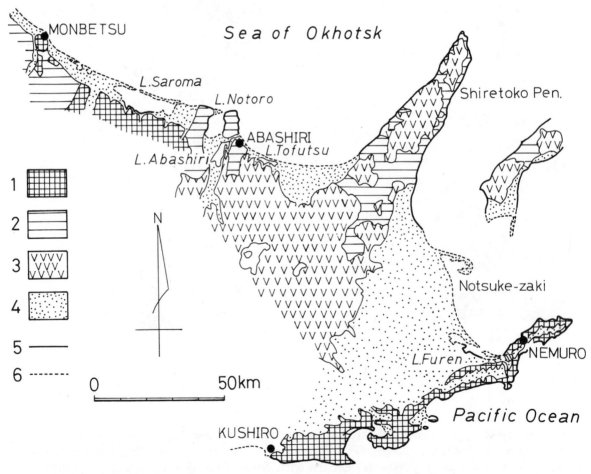

Figure 114-3. Predominant coastal landforms and geology of eastern Hokkaido. 1. Paleogene and older rocks; 2. Neogene sediments; 3. Quaternary volcanics; 4. Quaternary sediments; 5. cliffed coasts; 6. sandy shorelines.

eastern Honshu is cliffed. Sanriku is a typical ria coast, which has frequently suffered violent tsunamis associated with giant earthquakes, mainly centered in the Japan Trench. Maximum inundation was up to 28.7 m in Ryori Bay in 1933 (Plate 114-3). Breakwaters have been constructed across the mouth of Ofunado Bay to protect the industrial and residential areas from such tsunamis.

Matsushima Bay near Sendai is famous for its small islands covered with black pine trees. Some of the small islands have been incorporated into the straight sandy coastline, which has been prograding during the last 60 years (Plate 114-1).

The Iwaki coast, south of Matsushima, faces the Pacific Ocean with cliffs 30–35 m high cut into Pliocene and Pleistocene sediments, which have retreated at a rate of 0.3–0.7 m/yr. Three power plants were recently constructed along this coast, with ports formed by building breakwaters out from the cliffs. Sand drifting northward along this coast is now partially intercepted by these breakwaters so that erosion is due not only to the interception of drifting sand, but also to a decline in sediment yield from a nearby river.

Sandy coastlines are extensive along the coasts of the Kanto Plain, which is composed of Pleistocene uplands and Holocene lowlands (Fig. 114-4). The coastal zone around Tokyo Bay has been so

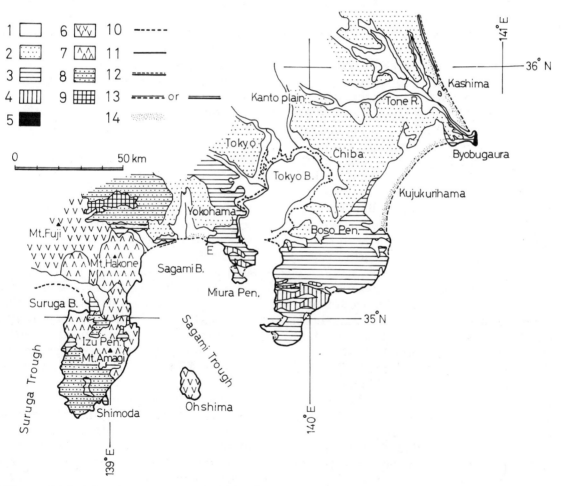

Figure 114-4. Predominant coastal landforms and geology of southern Kanto and the Izu Peninsula. 1. Holocene sediments; 2. Pleistocene sediments; 3. Neogene sediments; 4. Paleogene sediments; 5. Cretaceous rocks; 6. basalts (Quaternary); 7. andesites (Quaternary); 8. green-tuffs (Neogene); 9. granitic and dioritic rocks (Paleogene); 10. sandy shorelines; 11. cliffed coasts; 12. cliffed coasts with narrow beaches; 13. reclaimed coasts; 14. coastal sand dunes; E. Enoshima.

highly developed that almost all the deltaic sectors have been reclaimed and converted to ports and industrial and residential areas.

A significant seaward advance of the sandy coastline is found in the central part of Kujukuri-hama, Chiba Prefecture, where the beach advanced at least 200 m between 1903 and 1967. A comparison of the historical (1735) sketch map with the recent (1967) topographic map shows that beach accretion of approximately 400 m occurred near the mouth of the Sakuta River, central Kujukuri-hama (Moriwaki 1977). There is a fairly good agreement between the area of multiple bar development and that of a coastline accretion exceeding 2 m/yr (Sunamura and Horikawa 1977). The long-term littoral transport directions are here toward the center, as inferred from grain size and heavy mineral distributions.

Raised Holocene marine terraces are well developed on both the Boso and the Miura peninsulas, and at the northern head of Sagami Bay. These are often referred to as the Numa terrace, after the type locality of fossil coral beds at Numa, Tateyama City. Successive uplifts in the Holocene are represented by a flight of raised marine terraces in front of the Oiso Hills and on the southern part of the Boso Peninsula. Near Chikura, Chiba Prefecture, there are four marine terraces, with altitudes of 25, 16, 12, and 5 m above sea level (Yonekura 1975). The first terrace is mainly a depositional surface of marine sediments dated about 6,000 years ago, which is correlated with the fossil coral beds at Numa. The forth terrace emerged at the time of the great earthquake of 1703 (Matsuda et al. 1978).

At Kashima an industrial port was constructed on the sandy coast facing the Pacific Ocean. Long breakwaters were built out into the ocean, then a Y-shaped inner basin with several kinds of port facilities in the coastal lowland (Plate 114-4).

In Tokai District rivers that drain the Kiso and Akaishi ranges (e.g., the Fuji, Abe, Oi, and Tenryu) deliver much debris to their mouths. Their gravelly deltas prograded until the late 1940s, when erosion became prevalent (Plate 114-5). This is presumed to be related to a reduced sediment yield caused by the debris accumulation in man-made reservoirs and the extraction of gravels from the river beds (Koike 1977; Ozasa 1977).

On the Pacific coast of southwestern Honshu, a flight of Pleistocene and Holocene marine terraces is extensive, especially along the coasts of the peninsulas bordering the Nankai Trough, such as Kii, Muroto, and Ashizuri. These terraces have emerged and been tilted northward by local tectonic movements (Ota and Yoshikawa 1978). In contrast, a ria coast is found at the northern part of each peninsula. This is attributed to crustal deformations associated with the giant earthquakes that have occurred along the Nankai Trough.

The Seto Inland Sea is studded with numerous small islands composed mainly of deeply weathered granitic rocks. The beaches, consisting of arkose sands, have been used for salt production, making the most of relatively large tidal range and dry weather in this part of Japan, but they are now being converted to industrial use.

Coastal sand dunes are most extensive on the coasts along the Sea of Japan, where the strong northwesterly winter monsoon blows onshore. In some parts, blown sands now cover Pleistocene uplands, forming dunes up to 80 m high above sea level. Most of the coastal dunes along the Sea of Japan coasts were not covered with vegetation, and were therefore blown inland in the medieval era. Many feudal lords (Daimyo) tried to fix the mobile dunes by planting black pine trees (*Pinus thunbergii*) to protect paddy fields from inundation by blown sands during the Edo era. Today these dunes are covered with beautiful forests, which have fixed the mobile dunes and trapped sand blown from the shores.

Sandy coastlines have retreated markedly on many sectors bordering the Sea of Japan, for various reasons. Near Kanazawa City the coast has tended to retreat in the last 60 years, and rapid erosion would have continued if protection works had not been put in along the coast of Toyama Bay. Rivers draining into Toyama Bay, such as the Kurobe, Joganji, and Jinzu, have steep channels and supply a large amount of debris from the mountains. Nevertheless, the coast has been eroded because each river channel is directly connected to the head of a submarine canyon (Mogi 1978), so that a large proportion of debris supplied from the rivers is carried down to suboceanic abyssal plains.

Coastline erosion around Niigata City has accelerated since the 1930s, mainly because sand supply to the old mouth of the Shinano decreased after the construction of a diversion channel for the purpose of flood control in 1922. Sediment yield from the Shinano is estimated at 12 million tons/yr, three-quarters of which now flows directly into the sea through the new mouth, where wide sandy coasts have been added on both sides of the river mouth since 1922, forming a cuspate delta (Isobe 1978).

Rocky coasts west of Sado Island, facing the Sea of Japan, are fringed by several well-developed marine terraces, which are very useful references for the estimation of tilting and faulting as well as vertical movement in the late Quaternary (Ota 1980) (Plate 114-2).

Volcanic coasts are found around Kyusju and Hokkaido. Sakura-jima volcano in Kagoshima Bay (Plate 114-6), one of the most active in Japan, used to be separated from the mainland, and was tied to the Osumi Peninsula by lava flows in 1914.

Sandy coasts are well preserved along the Pacific side of Kyushu. Typical shore platforms, tombolos, and river-mouth spits around Aoshima, Miyazaki Prefecture, are illustrated in Plate 114-7. Most of the western coasts of Kyushu facing the East China Sea are cliffed, and in some parts volcanoes are directly beside the sea. Deltaic coastlines are prograding around Ariake Bay, which is the place of the highest tidal range (4.9 m) in Japan (Fig. 114-2).

Two islands arcs extend southward into the Pacific Ocean, the Izu-Ogasawara arc from Kanto, and the Ryukyu arc from Kyushu, each reaching as far as 24°N. These are double arcs with non-volcanic islands outside and volcanic ones inside. Coral reefs now fringe most of the Ryukyu Islands (Yoshikawa et al. 1981) (Plate 114-8), and there is a mangrove swamp on Iriomote-jima, southern-most of the Ryukyu Islands.

Nishino-shima Shinto, a new volcanic island located in the southern part of the Izu-Ogasawara arc, began to form soon after a submarine eruption occurred about 800 km south of Honshu in April 1973. Surveys by the Japanese Marine Safety Agency showed that the new island continued to grow by successive eruptions until August 1974. The tendency thereafter has been toward a reduction in the size of the island as volcanic activity subsided and coastal erosion prevailed (Mogi et al. 1980). An abrasion platform more than 100 m wide has formed off the southern coast of the new island, extending to about 15 m below sea level, the depth to which vigorous wave abrasion occurs in this typhoonal environment.

KAZUYUKI KOIKE

REFERENCES

Isobe, I., 1978, A study on modern sedimentation at the Teradomari coast in Niigata Prefecture, *Geol. Surv. Japan Bull.* **29**:773-792 (in Japanese with English abstract).

Koike, K., 1977, The recent change of sandy shorelines in Japan, *Komazawa Geography* **13**:1-16.

Matsuda, T., Y. Ota, M. Ando, and N. Yonekura, 1978, Fault mechanism and recurrence time of major earthquakes in southern Kanto district, Japan, as deduced from coastal terrace data, *Geol. Soc. America Bull.* **89**:1610-1618.

Mogi, A., 1963, On the shore types of the coasts of Japanese Islands, *Geog. Rev. Japan* **36**:245-266 (in Japanese with English abstract).

Mogi, A., 1978, *An Atlas of the Sea Floor around Japan. Aspects of Submarine Geomorphology,* University of Tokyo Press, Tokyo.

Mogi, A., M. Tsuchide, and M. Fukushima, 1980, Coastal erosion of new volcanic island Nishinoshima, *Geog. Rev. Japan* **53**:449-462 (in Japanese with English abstract).

Moriwaki, H., 1977, The formation of sandy ridges on the Kujukuri coastal plain, central Japan, *Tokyo Metropolitan Univ. Geog. Repts.* **12**:105-116.

Nakata, T., T. Takahashi, and M. Koba, 1978, Holocene emerged coral reefs and sea-level changes in the Ryukyu Islands, *Geog. Rev. Japan* **51**:87-108 (in Japanese with English abstract).

Ota, Y., 1980, Tectonic landforms and Quaternary tectonics in Japan, *Geo. Jour.* **4**:111-124.

Ota, Y., and T. Yoshikawa, 1978, Regional characteristics and their geodynamic implications of late Quaternary tectonic movement deduced from deformed former shorelines in Japan, *Jour. Physics. Earth,* 26 Suppl.: S 379-389.

Ozasa, H., 1977, Recent shoreline changes in Japan— An investigation using aerial photographs, *Coastal Engin., Japan* **20**:69-81.

Sunamura, T., and K. Horikawa, 1977, Sediment budget in Kujukuri coastal area, Japan, *Coastal Sediments '77 ASCE/Charleston,* Proc. Univ. of Florida, Tallahassee, pp. 475-487.

Yonekura, N., 1975, Quaternary tectonic movements in the outer arc of Southwest Japan, with special reference to seismic crustal deformation, *Tokyo Univ. Geog. Dept. Bull.* **7**:19-71.

Yoshikawa, T., S. Kaizuka, and Y. Ota, 1981, *The Landforms of Japan,* University of Tokyo Press, Tokyo.

Plate 114-1. Matsushima Bay and its surroundings near Sendai City, looking southward. Drowned bays merge southward into straight sandy shorelines that have prograded during the last 60 years (photo courtesy of Asahi Press).

Plate 114-2. Senkaku Bay, western coast of Sado Island, Niigata Prefecture, looking northward. The western coast of the island is fringed by six steps of marine terraces. The fifth terrace, with an altitude of about 30 m, is well defined in this photo. Present rocky coast is a kind of contraposed shoreline eroding loose terrace deposits (photo courtesy of Asahi Press).

Plate 114-3. Typical ria coast, Sanriku, Iwate Prefecture, looking northward. Small inlets open eastward toward the Japan Trench. The inundation height of 28.7 m by a tsunami was recorded in 1933 at the head of Ryori Bay (fourth one from the top of the photo). The head of Ofunado Bay is seen at the bottom lefthand corner (photo courtesy of Asahi Press).

Plate 114-4. Inubo-zaki Promontory, Chiba Prefecture, and its environs, looking northwestward. Kashima industrial port with Y-shaped inner basin cut into the coastal lowland is seen at right center. The Tone River in the middle has the widest drainage area in Japan (photo courtesy of Asahi Press).

Plate 114-5. Gravelly delta at the mouth of the Tenryu, Shizuoka Prefecture. The Tenryu, like other rivers in Tokai District, delivers a lot of gravel to its mouth, forming a cuspate-type gravelly delta. The coastline of the delta had prograded, but it has been receding at a rate of 8 m/y (maximum) since the end of the 1940s (photo courtesy of Asahi Press).

Plate 114-6. Sakura-jima Volcano in action. Sakura-jima is the active volcanic island located in the northern part of Kagoshima Bay. The island used to be isolated from the main island and was tied to the Osumi Peninsula by lava flows in 1914 (photo courtesy of Asahi Press).

Plate 114-7. Shore platform around Aoshima, Miyazaki Prefecture. Minor relief of shore platform distributed in intertidal zone is controlled by the monoclinal alternation of upper Miocene sandstone and mudstone (Takahashi 1975) (photo courtesy of Geographical Survey Institute of Japan).

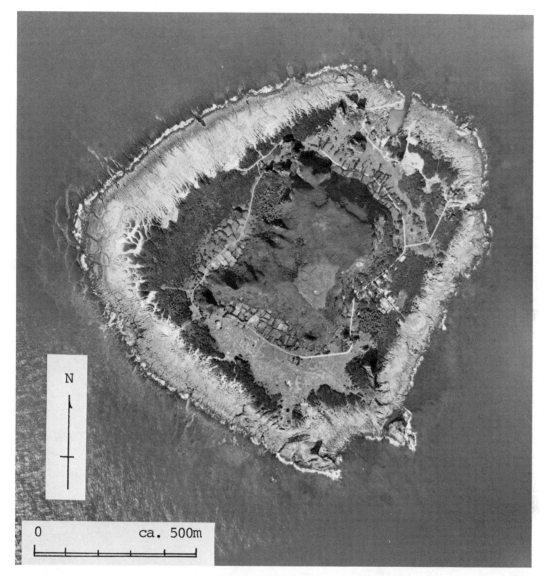

Plate 114-8. Kodakara-jima coral island, northern part of the Ryukyu Islands. The highest part of the island (102 m) is composed of emerged Pleistocene coral reef surrounded by Holocene reefs up to 10 m. Intertidal and subtidal platforms also surround the island (Nakata et al. 1978) (photo courtesy of Geographical Survey Institute of Japan).

115. PACIFIC USSR

The coastline of the Pacific USSR, bordering the seas of Japan and Okhotsk and the Bering Sea, extends for more than 4,500 km from north of the Arctic Circle south nearly to latitude 40°. This great length of coastline spans arctic, subarctic, and temperate climatic zones. Diversity of geological structure and relief is reflected in the varied outlines of the coast and continental shelf in the zone where the largest continent meets the greatest ocean. The main tectonic structures of the Pacific coast region formed during Mesozoic and Cenozoic times: the country is mountainous, with intermontane depressions and a narrow coastal plain (Fig. 115-1).

Mesozoic formations dominate the coastal region and Cenozoic formations dominate Sakhalin Island, the Kamchatka Peninsula, and part of the Chukotsk Peninsula. Block faulting and differential tectonic movement has determined the major outlines of the coast and islands (Fig. 115-2). Pleistocene marine terraces are found only in the Kamchatka Peninsula and the Kuril island arc (Plate 115-1), not on the mainland coast bordering the seas of Japan and Okhotsk (Kulakov 1973). Quaternary volcanic relief occupies large areas of the Kamchatka Peninsula and the Kuril Islands, but on the mainland there are only a few areas of Mesozoic volcanic outcrops. In the Primorie region some embayments (e.g., Rudnaya Bay) have been excavated in ancient volcanic caldera structures.

The Holocene marine submergence produced an intricate coastline by submerging this complex and contrasted land margin: there are fjords, rias, and extensive lagoons behind depositional barriers. Cenozoic block faulting also produced fault

scarps, which form sectors of steep coast on parts of the Chukotsk and Kamchatka peninsulas.

Coastal dynamics are determined by strong wave action from the Pacific and its bordering seas. The Bering Sea and the Sea of Okhotsk are the stormiest seas bordering Soviet coastlines, with prevailing waves 1.5–3 m high and 20–50 m long, and occasional storm waves up to 12 m high in spring and autumn. In the Bering Sea the predominant waves are from the southeast and southwest, and in the Sea of Okhotsk and the Japan Sea from the south. In the northern Bering Sea and northwest Okhotsk Sea, wave action is impeded in winter (and in the north for up to eight months) by the formation of shore ice and drifting ice floes (Zenkovich 1967). The Sea of Japan is less stormy, but has waves up to 2 m high in summer and up to 6 m in winter. Ocean swell up to 7 m high and 130–180 m long passes through the Sea of Japan and the Bering Sea to reach coastlines (Zenkovich 1967).

Tide ranges are varied. On the northwest coast of the Sea of Okhotsk, in some bays bordering the Bering Sea, at the north end of Sakhalin Island, and on the eastern and western sides of the Kamchatka Peninsula, the tide range is mesotidal (2–4 m) and locally macrotidal (as in Penzinskaya Bay, where the tide range attains 12 m). As a result there are extensive intertidal zones, especially in eastern Kamchatka, northern Okhotsk, western Sakhalin Island, and in the Kuril Islands (Plate 115-2) (Zenkovich 1967).

Weathering processes have strongly influenced coastal features. In the arctic zone, nivation, frost weathering, thermal abrasion, and solifluction have shaped coastal landforms and generated

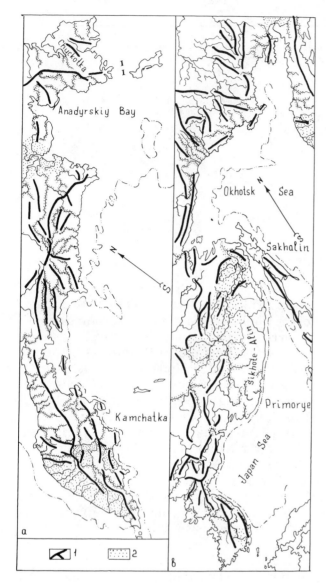

Figure 115-1. Distribution of principal mountain systems and catchment basins of the Far Eastern USSR (northern part, left; southern part, right): 1. mountain ridges; 2. catchment basins.

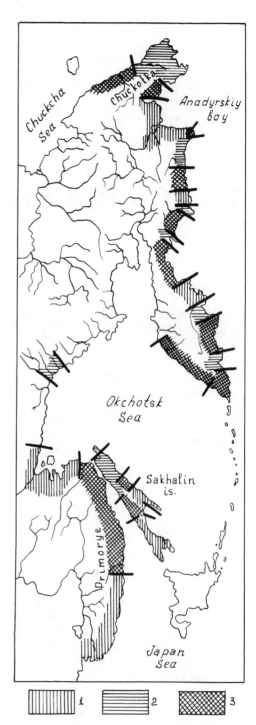

Figure 115-2. Present-day vertical movements on the Far Eastern USSR coasts: 1. areas of emergence; 2. areas of submergence; 3. relatively stable shores.

large quantities of sediment, including gravel and boulders, delivered to rivers and to the coastline. The gravelly beaches of Chukotsk, Kamchatka, and the fringes of the Sea of Okhotsk originated from this predominance of physical weathering in a cold environment. Farther south, on coasts bordering the Sea of Japan, beaches are predominantly sandy. Southward, as the climate becomes warmer, chemical weathering processes have greater effect. In southern Primorie, a warm and moist climate (annual rainfall up to 750 mm) has resulted in intensive surface weathering of

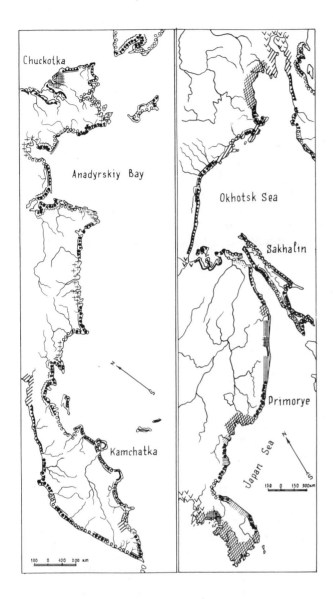

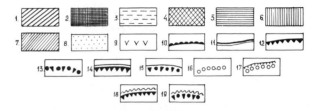

Figure 115-3. Schematic map of morphogenetic types of the Far Eastern USSR coasts (northern part, left; southern part, right): 1. tectonically dissected coasts (fault-inlet coasts); 2. coasts dissected by river erosion (firth, liman coasts); 3. glacially dissected coasts (fjord coasts); 4. coasts dissected by river erosion and tectonics (ria coasts); 5. straight folded coasts; 6. straight faulted coasts; 7. delta coasts; 8. alluvial plain coasts; 9. mud flat and marsh (layda) coasts; 10. thermal erosion coasts; 11. cliffed coasts; 12. erosion inlet coasts; 13. erosion-accretion inlet coasts; 14. graded erosion coasts; 15. graded erosion-accretion coasts; 16. graded accretion coasts; 17. graded accretion coasts with degraded cliffs and recent marine terraces; 18. secondary dissected erosion inlet coasts; 19. secondary dissected erosion-accretion inlet coasts.

volcanic formations; on some abandoned cliffs the weathering mantle is several meters thick.

The range and variety of coastal landforms, reflecting tectonic history, sea-level changes, and climatic contrasts, is summarized in the sketch-map (Fig. 115-3).

The coastline bordering the Bering Sea has been repeatedly glaciated, and its margins submerged by the Holocene marine transgressions have inlets and embayments where glacially formed depressions have been submerged (Aseev and Korzuev 1982). Fjords are well developed in the southeast Chukotsk Peninsula and bordering the Korjaskskoe upland. There has also been extensive deposition of fluvioglacial material, some of which has been built into large gravelly barriers impounding lagoons in former inlets

and embayments. Some of the material in these coastal barriers has been derived from submerged recessional moraines (Plate 115-3). In places, these barriers are tens of kilometers long (Fig. 115-4); one of the best examples is the Meechkin barrier, built along the northwestern shore of the Anadyr Gulf.

The coastline bordering the Okhotsk Sea is simpler in outline than that fringing the Bering Sea. The low-lying coasts of western Kamchatka, eastern Sakhalin, and the country around Okhotsk city are also bordered by barriers and tombolos enclosing coastal lagoons. Locally on the coast of western Kamchatka the lagoon chain is interrupted by promontories of unconsolidated sediment, the seaward margins of which are cliffed, yielding sand and gravel. North of Khairusov, and

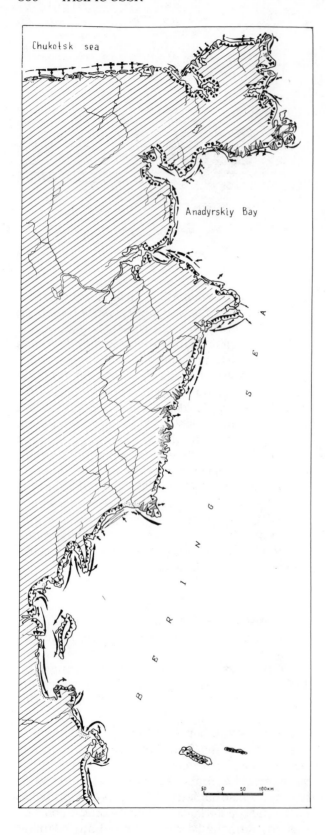

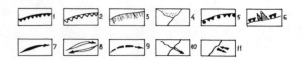

Figure 115-4. A schematic map of the dynamics and morphology of the Soviet Bering Sea coasts: 1. coasts with active cliffs; 2. coasts with abandoned cliffs; 3. steep but inactive coasts; 4. accretion coasts; 5. thermal erosion and erosion-solifluction coasts; 6. rockfall-talus coasts; 7. recent drifts of deposits; 8. migration of deposits; 9. tendency to one-way migration of deposits and ancient drifts of deposits; 10. movement of deposits from rivers; 11. movement of deposits to the bottom and to the shoreline.

on parts of the Kamchatka and Shmidt peninsulas, Sakhalin Island, and Ajansky, the coastal margin has steep sectors of harder pre-Quaternary rocks and is relatively stable.

The coastline bordering the Sea of Japan is embayed between bedrock headlands. In central Primorie the bays are wide and contain depositional features, while in southern Primorie there are rias formed by the submergence of river valleys (Zenkovich 1967; Kaplin 1971; Aseev and Korzuev 1982).

P. KAPLIN

REFERENCES

Aseev, A. A., and S. S. Korzuev, eds., 1982, *The Far East Coast of the U.S.S.R.*, Nauka Press, Moscow.

Kaplin, P., ed., 1971, *Peculiarities of the Relief and Present-Day Sediments of the Far Eastern Coast of U.S.S.R.*, Nauka Press, Moscow.

Kulakov, A. P., 1973, *Quaternary Coastlines of the Okhotsk and Japan Seas*, Nauka Press, Moscow.

Zenkovich, V. P., ed., 1967, *The Coast of the Pacific Ocean*, Nauka Press, Moscow.

Plate 115-1. A marine terrace in the Kuril Islands (photo by P. Kaplin).

Plate 115-2. Tidal bench, Kuril Islands (photo by P. Kaplin).

Plate 115-3. A fjord enclosed by a barrier on the Bering Sea coast (photo by P. Kaplin).

116. ARCTIC USSR

The northern USSR borders on some arctic and polar seas. From west to east, these are the Barents, White, Kara, Laptev, East-Siberian, and Chukchi seas. Their coasts are extremely diversified, and within the limits of a brief article it is possible only to outline their chief or most specific features (Fig. 116-1). These shores have not yet been studied thoroughly.

In the Barents Sea the plateau of the northern Kola Peninsula is composed of Precambrian gneisses and granites. The latter resist erosion, and the relief of the Murmansk coast has retained the forms produced by previous glaciation. Steep gullies with a depth of some dozen meters modify the waves. At relatively flat benches, boulder beaches have been formed, which smooth out the solid coast (Zenkovich 1937). The western part of the coast is dissected by short and deep fjords, which are locally known as *gubas* (lips). At the heads of the fjords, large rivers give rise to sandy deltas of glacial material. Along river valleys, and less vividly at the open coast, there lie terraces recording the different stages of glacier retreat and the phases of tectonic (isostatic) uplifting of the peninsula.

In the west the Rybachii Peninsula and Kil'din Island, composed of metamorphosed Precambrian sedimentary rocks, lie within the USSR boundaries. Their shores are lined with cliffs and are being intensively eroded.

The southern side of the Kola Peninsula lies within the confines of the White Sea. Fjords are rare and not pronounced, since they are filled with glacial deposits incised by rivers. The western

coast of the White Sea has a skerry character and is cut with relatively wide and shallow bays of the fiard type. Morphologically this coast is rather close to the Baltic coasts of Sweden and Finland, as it is composed of the same crystalline rocks and had the same phases of late glacial and postglacial history. Almost no marine erosional or accretional forms are encountered here.

The southern coast of the White Sea is composed exclusively of loose glacial deposits (Medvedev 1977). The mouths of the Onega and North Dvina rivers, constructing typical bay deltas, open up into the heads of two large bays. The outer shores are hardly affected by erosion as they are covered in many places by glacial boulders. Nonetheless, sediments are driven along the shore toward the heads of the *gubas*.

The eastern coast of the White Sea is likewise composed of Quaternary deposits with isolated outcrops of Devonian and Permian rocks. North of the Dvina delta the coast is smooth as far as the Voronov Cape, beyond which the Mezen Gulf begins. Waves enter into the wide straits (the White Sea's "throat") from both the north and the south, and transport sediment along the shore. The two flows converge at the accretional form of Intsy Cape, a wide sandy foreland covered with dunes.

Near the mouth of the Dvina Gulf (at the Kerets Cape) the two other sediment flows diverge. The first moves northward and the second toward the head of the Gulf, where it has built a long spit and Mudyug Island.

The Mezen Gulf is notable for high tides, as high as 10 m at springs. On the eastern side its shores have been smoothed out by erosion, which can be as rapid as 4 m/year (Zenkovich 1937).

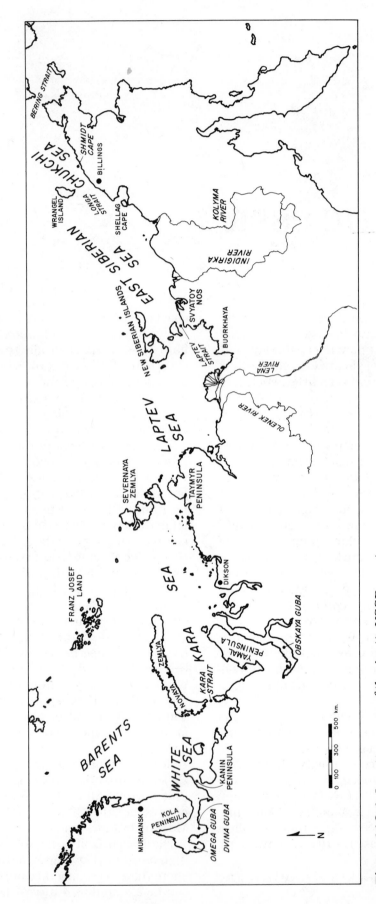

Figure 116-1. Location map of the Arctic USSR coast.

The shores are composed of clays and peat. Melting of the ice-bound peat intensifies the summertime destruction of cliffs. This is the southernmost point where thermal erosion, typical of the rest of the arctic seacoasts, manifests itself. High tides account for the widespread occurrence of waddens and marshes, particularly in river mouths and behind spits and sand barriers. The shores of the Kaninsk Peninsula are similar to those of the Mezen (Kal'yanov and Androsova 1933). They have been leveled off and are being intensively eroded, except for the Kanin-nos Cape, composed of strong sedimentary rocks.

Some large islands and the Franz Josef Land archipelago lie in the Barents Sea. The two-part island of Novaya Zemlya consists of strong Paleozoic rocks and represents a tectonic continuation of the Ural Mountains. Another link in this chain is Vaigach Island. In the southeast of Novaya Zemlya, tectonic structures stretch parallel to the edge of the sea, and this part of the coast resembles the Dalmatian type. The total length of both islands is about 1,000 km. Glacier-smoothed mountains begin at the southern island and extend to the northern island, where their height is 900 m. Glacier cover persists on the northern island. Numerous ice tongues flow down into the heads of the erosion-type fjords. Both shores (eastern and western) are notable for large-scale ice calving. In the middle portion two fjords have joined up at their heads to form the Matochkin Shar Strait.

On the shores of Novaya Zemlya high marine terraces and strand-flat surfaces have been well studied. The protruding parts of the coast are subject to erosion and are lined with cliffs (Panov 1937).

The Franz Josef Land archipelago is composed of loose Jurassic deposits capped by a thick basalt cover. Glaciers ploughed deep trenches along depressions, dividing the once unitary massif into separate islands. The ice-free period on these shores is very short, and coastal processes are not active. Basaltic talus, not subjected to grading or rounding, is usually formed along the water's edge.

A quite different character is exhibited by Kolguev Island in the southern part of the Barents Sea. Its oval outlines are the result of erosion of loose permafrost rocks from the windward side (from west to north) and the formation of sediment barriers on the leeward side.

To complete our survey of the Barents Sea shores, let us consider their southeastern part.

Adjoining the Kanin Peninsula is a large gulf, Cheshskaya Guba. It has rounded outlines, since resistant rocks outcrop only at its entrance, capes Mikulkin and Barmin Nos. The rest of the coast is composed of loose permafrost masses and is retreating under the impact of local waves and high tides. Wide ebb shoals have formed along all the shore.

East of the Cheshskaya Guba the shores are similarly eroding, and open sea waves transport sediments in a northeasterly direction. About 100 km beyond the Svyatoi-nos Cape these sediments have formed a spit and Sengei Island in a coastal concavity. The sediment flow already discussed reappears and moves still farther until, after another 100 km, it forms a large spit known as the Russian band (*zavorot*), which partly separates the Pechora Gulf, with a wide delta of the river bearing the same name, from the sea. A submarine barrier with sand islands, Gulyaevsk *koshki*, extends for another 130 km, as a continuation of the Russian *zavorot*.

Vaygach Island divides the Barents and Kara seas, the straits Kara Vorota and Yugorskii Shar being the entrance to the latter. Thereupon the coast makes a sharp southward turn along the western shore of a vast gulf, Baidaratskaya Guba. This shore extends for 350 km and has been smoothed out by erosion. Presumably, sediment drift is southward along this shore, as suggested by the numerous sandy spits and barriers directed to the head of the gulf.

The next large element to the east is the Yamal Peninsula, which lies between the Baidaratskaya and Ob *gubas*. The latter is the world's largest liman, about 900 km long and averaging 50–60 km in width. Of much smaller dimensions, but of the same origin, are the Tazov, and Yenisey *gubas*. The vast space between the named gubas, and partly beyond their limits, is entirely composed of a low plateau consisting of Quaternary deposits (Gorbatskii 1970). These permafrost-bound masses are subject at the shore to thermal abrasion, which is particularly strong at the sectors exposed to open sea; even though for a short time, the surf is effective. The average annual rate of retreat of the open shores amounts to 5–10 m. The shore is predominantly level, with alternating stretches of erosion and temporary sediment accretion.

East of Dikson Island, for about 200 km, there stretches a smooth shore of erosional character with cliffs composed of bedrock. Beyond the mouth of the Pyasina River the shore makes a sharp turn to the north and its character changes. It follows the outline of the large mountainous Taymyr Peninsula. On the west the Taymyr shore has a fjord-like nature. Locally the vast Nordensheld archipelago begins to resemble skerry areas. The Taymyr shore extends over a 1,000 km and is highly variable. Beyond the northernmost point of the Eurasian continent (Chelyuskin Cape) the shore turns south, already within the limits of the Laptev Sea. All Taymyr shores, like those of the Severnaya Zemlya archipelago, have been mapped and explored by Soviet geographers. However, these researchers did not include coastal specialists, who are expected to make many new discoveries.

In the Kara Sea, northwest of Taymyr, a number of small islands are scattered in the sea. The remnants of a submerged coastal plain lying just below sea level, they are composed of loose sediment. These islands are notable for a fairly intricate configuration, combining erosional and accretional forms (spits). Here the early stages of the leveling process are taking place, which are still very remote from the stage of rounded outlines of Kolguev Island (Barents Sea).

The Taymyr massif in the Laptev Sea is restricted by a large liman, Khatanga Guba. Within its confines and further to the east, the erosional and accretional sectors alternate, so that the shore obtains a lobed character. Even on Taymyr some stretches of the coastal plain composed of loose icebound sediments can be encountered (Plate 116-1). East of the Khatanga and Anabar bays they are predominant. The rate of erosion here varies according to the content of ice in the frozen masses. In the course of erosion there arise significant quantities of sediment, which drift westward.

Farther to the east lies the vast concavity of the Olenek Bay, with a small delta of the similarly named river and with the same character of shore, but without significantly outcropping bedrock (Mitt 1964).

A specific and fairly complex formation is presented by the vast delta of the Lena River. It is a plain 20–30 m high, much dissected by rivers and streams. At the west the delta shore is lined with a sand barrier. At the frontal and eastern side it is dissected into small parts, and in most places is being destroyed by the effects of the thawing of frozen masses, erosion, and ice pressure (Klyuev 1970). The fine-grained alluvium of the Lena River is being transported predominantly into the western part of the delta and

distributed over the sea bed. Accretional forms at the shore are fairly infrequent. Thus, the delta essentially represents a relict formation. Its surface is broken by frost clefts. The loess-like rocks are subject to deflation, and the entire relief of the shore and the delta proper is highly variable. Of interest are the very large dimensions of the delta: about 200 km along solid shores (mountain spurs) and over 100 km in width. The sea around the delta is extremely shallow.

Southeast of the delta lies the large Buor-Khaya Bay, followed by a shore of lobed outline stretching to the mouth of the Kolyma River (about 1,500 km). The only exposed bedrock along its length is the Svyatoi-nos Cape in the Dmitiri Laptev Straits. The rest of the vast coastal stretch is a flat plain bordering on an extremely shallow part of the sea. Beyond the Svyatoi-nos Cape this plain intrudes upon the confines of the East Siberian Sea.

Apart from a major lobe, the shore is diversified by alternating stretches notable for specific dynamic and morphologic features. Quite low areas are predominant; during wind-induced surges, these areas are flooded by the sea up to 30 km inland. During southern offshore winds the muddy sea-bed surface is bared to nearly the same width. Tides are rather insignificant here because of the impact of the wind. The most significant temporary changes of the shore are typical in the area of the Khroma and Omulyakh bays (gubas).

Some stretches of the shore are elevated to several meters. At such places an intensive thermal abrasion occurs (Plate 116-2), since the loose masses consist of lenses and massifs of pure ice and are bound by permafrost.

Over this vast length some large rivers flow into the sea: the Omoloi, Yana, Indigirka, Alazea, and Kolyma. They have filled with sediment their former mouth-adjoining bays, but their deltas are only very insignificantly developed out toward the open sea.

Novosibirsk Ostrova (New Siberian Islands) separate the Laptev and the East Siberian seas. Two of these large islands (Big Lyakhiv and Kotel'-nichyi) have a nucleus of metamorphic bedrock. They outcrop at the sea from the western side of Kotel'nichyi Island, where they form a bay-type shore with cliffs (Sisko 1971). The islands of Little Lyakhov, Novaya Sibir, Faddeev, and Zemlya Bunge are composed of frozen masses of Quaternary deposits and fossil ice. The entire archipelago essentially represents a continuation of the coastal lowland, and thermal erosion processes are extremely intense (Are 1980). The maximum rate of recession is 15 m, and occasionally even up to 50 m, a year. The latter figure refers to the small extinct islands, Semenov and Vasiliev, in the Laptev Sea, which now represent only the sea shoals (Grigor'yev 1966).

East of the Kolyma River mouth the spurs of the Anyuisk and Chukotka mountain ranges come close to the sea. The coastal strip of the plain narrows to a few kilometers, and along the shore there abound stretches composed of stable bedrock (the capes Letyatkin, Baranov, Shelagskii, etc.) as well as the archipelago of the Medvezh'i islands. Some 250 km east of the Kolyma River mouth a large guba, Chaunskaya, cuts into the mainland. Half of it is separated from the sea by Ayon Island, which is composed of loose sediment, its shore has been leveled off in the course of thermal erosion.

About 220 km east of the Chaunskaya Guba, there is a generally straight shore with alternating erosional and accretional sections. Billings Cape, a structure of great interest, extends farther into the sea. This cape is an accumulative barrier about 50 km long, extending into the sea; a wide lagoon is found behind the barrier. Transverse sand bars divide it into a few rounded lakes, whose width, normal to the barrier, exceeds 10 km. There are grounds to believe that Billings Cape formed in the wave shadow of Wrangel Island, although the distance to it from the mainland shore is about 150 km (Long Straits). This strait is usually packed with ice for a long period of time. West and east of it for several months there is open water. Depending on the direction of winds, waves move sediment toward the ice-protected section on which Billings Cape has arisen (Popov and Sovershaer 1979).

Within the confines of the Chukotsk Sea, between Billings Cape and Kolyuchinskaya Guba (about 470 km), lagoon-type shores are predominant. The coast is subdivided into a number of sectors by solid rock capes Yakan, Shmidt, and Vankarem. In the western part of the coast the lagoons are rather short because of the mountain spurs coming close to the sea. However, east of Shmidt Cape a wide, terraced, coastal lowland reappears, and lagoons continue without interruption over many hundreds of kilometers.

Since longshore sediment drifts do not attain high capacity on the coast under consideration (because the iceless period is short), the principal source of material for the barriers fencing off the lagoons from the sea is the sea bed. This process was greatly affected by relative changes in the sea level during the Pleistocene. During low sea level phases, moraine and fluvioglacial masses covered a wide strip of exposed modern sea bed. As these areas were inundated, this glacial material was reworked by waves and thawed out. As a result, large components of former masses of glacial origin (pebble, gravel, sand) were moved toward the shore and formed barriers. Recent investigations have revealed that, apart from recent barriers, there are also ancient barriers lying both above and below present sea level. Thus, this process was of very long duration (Babaev and Zhindarev 1979).

The Chukotsk lagoons are segmented into a great number of lakes of rounded outline. Similar disjunction forms of elongated lagoon areas have been found on many other shores, even in temperate climates. Thus, in the given case we observe a general regularity associated with the fetch of waves and driving of sediments to shape segmented lagoons in dimensions related to wind roses (Zenkovich 1952).

The large Kolyuchinskaya Guba is separated from the sea by two wide spits bent inside the bay area. This is evidence of the existence of a strong longshore movement of sediment. Farther to the east, for another 100 km, there extends the last in the series of long Chukotsk lagoons, and then the mountains come close to the shore. The spurs of the Chukotsk range are cut off by sea and form high, active cliffs. Only in the mouths of wide intermontane depressions have accretional coastal stretches been preserved; the largest of these is the barrier separating the Uellen lagoon from the sea.

In conclusion I would like to offer some general remarks on the dynamics and developmental history of the coasts in the USSR's polar seas (Kaplin 1971). Wherever strong bedrock is exposed to the sea, the most important factor of coastal change proves to be frost weathering. Under its effect strand-flat surfaces are formed, as on the Novaya Zemlya shores, on the shores of the Taymyr Peninsula, and in some areas of the Severnaya Zemlya and Novosibirskyi archipelagoes. At the same time, no strand flat has been produced on the granite-gneiss shores of the Kola Peninsula and the western area of the White Sea.

Indisputably the most characteristic and active factor on the USSR's Arctic shores is thermal erosion (Are 1980). The rate of retreat of the shores is exceptionally high wherever ice wedges and ice massifs are included in the composition of loose permafrost masses. Thawing of permafrost also takes place on the sea bed (down to about 10 m depth), intensifying its overall destruction.

Sea ice plays a much less significant role in coastal development. Ice pressure and piling up of ice account for certain reworking of beaches (Plate 116-3), but any disturbance in their structure will disappear after a couple of months of open water. Far more important is that, wherever stony or sandy material is available at the sea bed, ice floes carry it onto the shore, increasing the volume of the beaches. A reverse process also takes place, however. In spring and summer, when shore ice is moving away from the shore, it may capture and remove sediment frozen into it.

Large ice blocks (*stamukhas*) do not move as far as the shore. However, they plough long trenches into the sea bed (down to about 20 m depth) or wear down the surface of the bench. New quantities of sediment material are then set in motion and brought by waves onto the shore.

Far more important is the indirect effect due to the exposure of the shore to the impact of floating ice and long-term freezing of the offshore sea area. Restricting sea roughness (waves), the ice inhibits the progress of coastal processes. For this reason most of the polar shores are geomorphologically juvenile in age.

Large accumulations of driftwood are found in this area (Plate 116-4). Carried down by rivers or lost during loading of timber-carrying ships, logs are agitated during a storm by the surf and strike repeatedly against the foot of the cliff with great force. The abrasion of loose rocks is greatly intensified.

Starting with the Kara Sea and farther to the east, it is difficult to understand the general structure of the coast and archipelagoes unless we take account of the relative vertical movements of the coast. Recent uplifting is known to be taking place within the limits of the Kola Peninsula, western White Sea area, as well as on the Novaya Zemlya islands. It is a compensational uplifting (postglacial rebound) and began with the thawing of the ice cover. Vertical movements of other regions have not yet been adequately studied, although the predominance of slow relative submergence over vast areas is an established fact.

Under a low stand of the ocean, as was the case several times in the course of the Pleistocene, the sea bed in the western sector of the Soviet Arctic was exposed to a width of several hundred kilometers. No cover glaciation took place here. Ice flowed down only from the large mountain mas-

sifs of Taymyr, from the Verkhoyansk, Cherski, Chukotka, and other ridges. In the area between them, and at other places, a broad flatland composed of loose sediment stretched far to the north. In cold winters the ground would freeze several meters in depth. As the flatland surface built up, the mass of frozen rocks increased and gathered in ice veins (along frost clefts), as well as entire ice blocks and massifs at the place formerly occupied by lakes and river streams. The remnants of this once integral plain are the low-lying parts of the Novaya Zemlya and Novosibirskyi archipelagoes (particularly the surge-flooded Zemlya Bunge), as well as numerous small islands, which are presently being rapidly destroyed. During Holocene times the outer edge of the plain (at the mainland) retreated a few kilometers, and this process is still going on.

V. P. ZENKOVICH

REFERENCES

Are, F. E., 1980, *Thermal Abrasion of Sea Shores*, Nauka Publishers, Moscow (in Russian).

Babaev, Y. M., and L. A. Zhindarev, 1979, Main features of lagoonal relief of the Chukotka Peninsula's coast, in *Investigations of Relief Dynamics of Sea Coasts*, Nauka Publishers, Moscow, pp. 111–119 (in Russian).

Gorbatskii, G. V., 1970, *Physico-geographic Zoning of the Arctic. Part 2. The Position of Marginal Seas with Islands*, Leningrad State University Publishers, Leningrad (in Russian).

Grigor'yev, N. F., 1966, *Perennially-frozen Rocks in Yakutiya's Sea-adjoining Zone*, Nauka Publishers, Moscow (in Russian).

Kal'yanov, V. P., and V. P. Androsova, 1933, Geomorphological observations at Kanin, *Earth Sci.* **3**:6–24 (in Russian).

Kaplin, P. A., 1971, Dynamical and structural specificities of the polar seas' coasts, in *New Studies of Coastal Processes*, Nauka Publishers, Moscow (in Russian).

Klyuev, E. V., 1970, Thermal abrasion of polar seas' coasts, *All-Union Geog. Soc. Repts.* **2**:129–135 (in Russian).

Medvedev, V. S., 1977, Types and character of the White Sea's coasts, in *White Sea, Sedimentogenesis and Developmental History*, Nauka Publishers, Moscow (in Russian).

Mitt, K. L., 1964, On the morphology and dynamics of the Anabar-Olenek shore in the Laptev Sea, *Oceanology* **4**:660–668 (in Russian).

Panov, D. G., 1937, Geomorphological survey of the USSR's polar seas, *Moscow State Univ. Proc.* **11**: 137 (in Russian).

Popov, B. A., and V. A. Sovershaev, 1979, Wind-caused

drying at the coasts of the Arctic seas, in *Studies of Coastal Plains and Shelf in Arctic Seas*, Moscow State University Publishers, Moscow (in Russian).

Sisko, R. K., 1971, Morphology and dynamics of Novaya Sibir island, in *Geomorphology and Lithology of the Coastal Zone of Seas*, Nauka Publishers, Moscow, pp. 63–67 (in Russian).

Zenkovich, V. P., 1937, *Observations of Marine Abrasion and Physical Weathering at the Murmansk Coast*, Moscow State Univ. Proc. No. 16 (in Russian).

Zenkovich, V. P., 1941, *Coasts of the Mezen Bay*, Moscow State Univ. Proc. No. 48 (in Russian).

Zenkovich, V. P., 1952, Evolution of lagoon area, *All-Union Geog. Soc. Repts., Leningrad* 84 (in Russian).

Plate 116-1. Taymyr Peninsula coastal plain composed of ice-bound sediment.

Plate 116-2. Thermal abrasion scarp along the shore in the region of the Khroma and Omulyakh *gubas.*

Plate 116-3. Reworking of the beach by ice pressure and piling up of ice.

Plate 116-4. Large accumulations of driftwood, which become an agent of considerable erosion during storms.

117. PHILIPPINES

The Philippines archipelago consists of about 7,000 islands with an intricate coastline more than 13,000 km long. Extending from latitude 5° N to about 21° N, the islands are generally hilly or mountainous, with steep, locally-cliffed coasts and sectors of alluvial coastal lowland. The climate is tropical, ranging from humid (especially on the eastern side and in Mindanao to the south) to subhumid. In addition to east to northeast trade winds (stronger in the north), there is a northeast monsoon (October to April) and a southwest monsoon (June to September). Wave action is generally light to moderate, produced by these winds in coastal waters, but ocean swell reaches the Pacific coastline, and in summer and autumn typhoons occur, moving in from the Mariana Islands to the east and bringing high winds, strong waves, and storm surges. Tide ranges are generally small, less than 2 m.

From the largest island, Luzon, in the north the archipelago diverges southward on either side of the deep enclosed Sulu Sea (Fig. 117-1). The Pacific coastline is bordered by the Philippine Trench, locally more than 10,000 m deep. Coral formations are extensive, both on the island coasts and as outlying reefs. There are many volcanoes. Some are active (Hibok, on Camiguin Island, north of Mindanao, erupted in 1951; Mayon in southeastern Luzon erupted in 1900, 1928, 1943, 1947, and 1968); others, like Apo in southeastern Mindanao and Maricaban in Verde Island Passage south of Manila, are quiescent. Sands and gravels derived from the products of volcanicity produce dark gray or black beaches, while coral formations yield beaches of white sand and gravel.

Neotectonic activity has been widespread, as evidenced by uplifted and deformed coral terraces (up to 360 m above sea level in Mindanao); landslides triggered on coastal slopes in soft, deeply weathered materials; and tsunamis, which have overwashed beaches and lowlying coastal areas.

Mangroves are extensive in sheltered areas, but they have been reduced to about 106,000 ha by clearance, mainly to establish brackish-water fishponds, which cover 176,000 ha (Juliano et al. 1982). In many areas deforestation has led to erosion on steep slopes and augmented siltation in estuaries and deltas (Plate 117-1).

The study of coastal geomorphology has been neglected in the Philippines. This account is based largely on information from military reports prepared by the Allied Geographical Section, Southwest Pacific area, in 1944 as a prelude to wartime landings; from maps, charts and nautical handbooks; and from field observations.

The north coast of Luzon, facing the Babuyan Channel, consists of a depositional plain narrowing east and west from the mouth of the Cagayan, the longest river in the Philippines (about 330 km). It is backed by hilly country, which runs out to Cape Engano and the steep-sided island of Palaui. To the north the outlying Babuyan and Batan islands are mainly steep-sided volcanic peaks (e.g., Didicas). The wide estuary of the Cagayan at Aparri is fronted by shoals, but in general northeasterly waves (winter monsoon) have built long sandy beaches backed by dunes up to 8 m high, then corridors of swampland, formerly lagoons. Behind these are sectors of an older, inner sandy barrier.

The west coast of northern Luzon is generally steep, with fringing coral reefs and some beaches. Emerged coral sectors have typical notch-and-

Figure 117-1. Philippines location map.

visor profiles. At Luna, a historic coastal watchtower is being undermined by wave scour. San Fernando has a sandy tombolo linking a cliff-surrounded island, and to the south the shore of Lingayen Gulf has small lobate deltas (Bauang, Aringay) with outlines indicating southward longshore drifting that culminates in a large spit at Cabaroan. The southern shores of Lingayen Gulf consist of a long sandy beach interrupted by the mouths of rivers (Calmay, Beud, Dagupan) and backed by numerous low sandy beach ridges, then swamplands largely in use for fishponds or rice cultivation.

South from Cape Bolina the spectacular Zambales coast is steep, rugged, and reef-fringed, with small plains mainly at river mouths. The volcanic Bataan Peninsula has coves at the mouths of radial valleys and intervening cliffy sectors. Manila Bay occupies a sheltered embayment with a large delta built by the Pasag, Pampanga, and Bulacan rivers growing from its northern shores. These have wide bordering mud flats, and the coastal fringe has been intensively used for fishponds. South of Manila the Cavite spit has grown northward, sheltering Bacoor Bay, and a low-lying isthmus separates the muddy lake of Laguna de Bay (which occasionally receives brackish inflow in dry summers) from Manila Bay. Verde Island Passage is a narrow strait bordered by steep coasts, with the island volcano of Maricaban in the middle. To the southeast, Luzon has a more indented coastline, with many sheltered gulfs, some edged with mangroves. The Pacific coast is also steep and indented; the northern part, along the tectonically active Sierra Madre, receives strong ocean swell, which has built and shaped curving bay beaches. Near Legaspi the beaches are black sand of volcanic origin, mainly from the Mayon volcano, but outlying islands are often reef-fringed, with white sandy beaches. In Larap Bay, sedimentation has been augmented by the inflow of silt and clay washed down from iron ore mines in the nearby hills (Rabanal and Datingalang 1973).

Mindoro is a hilly to mountainous island with steep forested coasts in the north, facing the Verde Island Passage, and northwest, from Cape Calavite down to Mambuarao. In the north the hilly peninsula behind Escarceo Point has an irregular outline, sheltering the reef encircled Port Galera. Many short, steep streams flow down forested slopes to rocky shores. Much of the west coast is beach-fringed and consists of swampy plains: a long, gently curved beach runs from Talabasi Point south to the Sablayan tombolo, breached only by the mouths of small rivers. Farther south the Mongpong River has built a substantial lobate delta, and the Lumintau River opens to the sea by way of a wide estuary. Sand washed down the braided Bagsanga River drifts mainly southward as beaches, culminating in the long Caminawit spit in front of mangrove-fringed Mangarin Bay. In the southwest the Caguray River has built a large swampy delta, constricting the strait in the lee of the steep high island of Ilin.

The south coast of Mindoro has several hilly promontories; submergence of a much-dissected volcanic topography produced numerous coves, inlets, and outlying islands east of Bulalacao Bay. Fringing coral reefs and white sandy beaches are present locally here. Much of the east coast is low-lying, a fluviodeltaic plain with fringing beaches of gray sand. In some sectors, multiple beach ridges are separated by swampy swales, and spits flank the mouths of small rivers. Low-lying Duyagan Point is the apex of a large delta built by the Saquisi River and its distributaries. To the north, spiky volcanic hills form the Dumali Peninsula alongside Pola Bay, where a sandy beach is backed by extensive mangrove swamps. The northeast coast is generally beach-fringed, with some coral reef sectors. Marinduque Island, to the east, is a reef-edged volcanic upland with mainly white sandy beaches.

Palawan, an elongated high island southwest of Mindoro, is flanked by submerged barrier reefs (Davis 1928), and has steep coasts with many white sandy beaches. Near El Nido there are high cliffs of dark limestone, but volcanic formations predominate, and fringing reefs border headlands along the embayed coastlines.

Panay Island has many features similar to Mindoro. Its west coast is largely beach-fringed with some surrounding reef sectors fronting the steep cordillera ranges, and deep water close inshore. Several rivers deliver sand to the coast, where prograded beach-ridge plains have been formed. Southward drifting from the Sibalom River has built the foreland of Tubigan Point at San Jose. In the southwest, reefs flank rugged promontories and outlying islands, but the south coast is again sandy, with an eastward drift toward the port of Iloilo in the strait behind the hilly island of Guimaras. Southeastern Panay is essentially a composite deltaic plain built by the Iloilo and Jalauod rivers, but the east coast is hilly and embayed, with many reef-fringed headlands and islands, some of which are uplifted coral reefs. The spring tide range here is slightly higher than in the Philippines generally, attaining 2.4 m in Concepcion Bay. As a result, tidal mud flats are extensive, and fishponds have been built on these, and in the mangrove fringe. In the north the Panay River has built a large delta, the seaward edge of which has sandy beach ridges, backed by broad mangrove and nipa swamps intersected by distributaries and tidal channels. Long sandy beaches and beach-ridge plains extend west from here, forming paired spits at the mouth of the mangrove-fringed Batan Lagoon and curving out to the Aklan Delta.

Negros Island is mountainous and forested, culminating in the Canlaon volcano (2,450 m), with intensively farmed coastal plains in the north and west, where extensive reefs and shoals front mangrove swamps and beach sectors. Low-wave-energy conditions predominate along the shores of Guimaras Strait, where the Malogo and Bago rivers have built substantial deltas, with low sandy ridges and muddy nearshore zones. To the south the coast becomes hilly and more exposed past Sojoton Point, and reefs fringe generally rocky shores: there is a coral lagoon at Tinagong Dugat, near Sipalay. The east coast, bordering Tanon Strait, is also generally steep, with extensive reefs often backed by mangroves, as at Bais. There are many uplifted reef sectors. Outlying Siquijor Island to the southeast is high, hilly, and surrounded by reefs and beaches of coarse coralline sand.

The coastlines of Cebu, an elongated high island with many raised coral reefs, and Bohol, less mountainous, show features similar to those of eastern Negros, with generally low wave energy on the shores of narrow straits. Karstic coastal features occur on emerged coral sectors. Where wave action is stronger, as in northeastern Cebu, there are longer and bolder beaches, and seaside resorts have developed such as at Liloan Beach.

Masbate, to the north, is relatively low-lying and has an embayed coastline, with inlets such as Nin Bay indicative of recent submergence. Samar and Leyte, to the east, continue the forms of southeastern Luzon, their bold and often cliffed eastern coastlines being subject to easterly ocean swell and to recurrent typhoons and surges. The western shores, on the other hand, are more sheltered, with reef-fringed promontories and islands and mangrove-edged muddy bays and inlets. Although segments of curved bay beaches occur on the ocean coasts, there are many cliffed promontories, reef areas, and outlying rocky islands. Emerged reef terraces occur near Guiuan in southeastern Samar. Leyte Gulf is penetrated by ocean swell that breaks on long sandy beaches on the east coast of Leyte (Plate 117-2). Northward drifting here has built a large recurved spit at Cataisan Point, near Tacloban.

Mindanao, southernmost of the large islands, is mountainous. Off its north coast is the active Hibok volcano on Camiguin Island, which has deposited lava and ash on the coast during successive eruptions, notably in 1951. Mambajao, the town on its northern shore, is built on an earlier lava flow. Lava boulders litter the shore, interspersed with beaches of black volcanic and white coralline sand. On Mindanao, beach ridges have been prograded at the mouths of rivers such as the Agusan, entering Butuan Bay, and the streams flowing into Macajalar Bay at Cagayan de Oro. Mangroves back sheltered bays and inlets, and form swamps near river mouths. In the southwest the Zamboangan peninsula has steep, reef-fringed coasts and beaches of shelly and coralline sand, and similar features are seen on Basilan and the chain of high islands running southwest toward Sabah. In the southeast there are beaches of black volcanic sand on the shores of Davao Gulf, beneath the slopes of Mount Apo. Landslides are common on steep coastal slopes here, and there are high cliffs on Cape San Agustin.

ERIC C. F. BIRD

REFERENCES

Davis, W. M., 1928, *The Coral Reef Problem*, Am. Geog. Soc. Spec. Pub. 9.

Juliano, R. O., J. Anderson, and A. R. Librero, 1982, Philippines: perceptions, human settlements and resource use in the coastal zone, in *Man, Land and Sea*, C. Soysa, Lin Sien Chia, and W. L. Collier, eds., Agricultural Development Council, Bangkok, pp. 219-240.

Rabanal, H. R., and B. Y. Datingslang, 1973, Problems of pollution and siltation from mines in some Philippine waters, in *Nature Conservation in the Pacific*, A. B. Costin and R. H. Groves, eds., Australian National University Press, Canberra, pp. 263-270.

Plate 117-1. The delta of the Imus River is growing out into shallow Bacoor Bay, south of Manila, and accretion is proceeding rapidly in the lee of the Cavite spit, seen in the background (photo by E. C. F. Bird).

Plate 117-2. Beach on east coast of Leyte, in vicinity of Tacloban (photo by M. L. Schwartz).

118. INDONESIA

Indonesia consists of about 13,700 islands, with an intricate coastline of just over 60,000 km (Bird and Ongkosongo 1980). In terms of global tectonics, the Indonesian archipelago occupies the collision zone between the Indo-Australian, Pacific and Eurasian plates and is a region of continuing instability marked by frequent earthquakes and volcanic eruptions. It includes mountainous areas of Cenozoic uplift, augmented by large volcanoes, and in coastal regions there is widespread evidence of Quaternary uplift and depression, often accompanied by tilting and faulting. Coralline reef formations are numerous and extensive in Indonesian waters, and in many places they have been raised out of the sea by tectonic movements. Coasts have prograded by the deposition of volcanic lava and ash, and where large quantities of pyroclastic sediment have been brought down by rivers. Many features of coastal topography are related to their development under tropical — generally humid tropical — conditions: deeply weathered rock outcrops, limited cliffing, and extensive deltas built by rivers that bring down an abundance of fine-grained sediment derived from steep hinterlands. At least 50 mangrove species are found in Indonesia, and mangrove bordered shores are extensive, especially on the northeast shores of Sumatra, alongside the estuaries of southern Kalimantan, and on the southwest shores of Irian Jaya. In densely populated areas, as in northern Java, the mangrove fringe has been largely cleared to make way for brackish-water fishpond construction. Coastal features have also been modified by human activities where sediment yields from rivers have increased as the result of accelerated erosion in their deforested and cultivated catchments.

Beaches are extensive, some derived from fluvial sands and gravels, others from cliff erosion, and others from the erosion of calcareous material from fringing coral reefs. Beach sediments derived from volcanic rocks are typically black or gray; those of coralline origin, white or yellow. Coastal dunes are poorly developed in the humid tropics, but on the southern shores of Java and Sumatra prograded beaches are backed by dune topography carrying woodland vegetation.

High sectors of coast are generally steep and forested rather than actively cliffed, but along the southern shores of Sumatra, Java, and the islands to the east, sectors exposed to relatively strong wave action (including swell) from the Indian Ocean have bold cliffs, fronted by shore platforms and coral reefs. Limestone cliffs in particular show the effects of intense physical, chemical, and biological weathering on these tropical shores (Plate 118-1).

Coral reefs are widespread (Molengraaf 1929; Umbgrove 1947), except off the mouths of rivers where the sea is freshened and made turbid by water and sediment discharge, and where active vulcanicity has inhibited coral establishment. There are many reef-fringed islands, reefs that enclose lagoons with central islands, and true atolls, especially in the Flores and Banda seas. The major barrier reefs are the Great Sunda Reef, rising from the submerged shelf margin southeast of Kalimantan, a similar reef south of Sulawesi, and reefs that curve out toward the islands of Batu and Banjak off Sumatra. Algal rims are better developed on reefs surrounding oceanic southern shores than in the inner seas.

Wave action in Indonesian waters is largely generated by local winds, gentle in the equatorial zone but stronger on northern and southern coasts subject respectively to northeast and southeast trade winds. Ocean swells also move in to the southern coast from the Indian Ocean, and in to the northern coast from the southwest Pacific. In general, wave energy is low. Tropical cyclones do not reach Indonesia, but waves generated by such disturbances are occasionally transmitted into Indonesian waters, especially along the southern coasts.

Tidal movements result from impulses that arrive from the Pacific Ocean by way of the South China Sea and the Philippine Sea and from the Indian Ocean through the Straits of Molucca and along the southern coasts to the Timor and Arafura seas. Mean maximum tide ranges, shown in Figure 118-1, are generally less than 2 m, and only exceed 4 m locally on the southwest coast of Irian Jaya. Tides are complicated by wind action, especially in the trade wind zones, and by the effects of tectonic and volcanic disturbances that generate tsunamis. The explosive eruption of Krakatau in Sunda Strait in 1883 generated a tsunami up to 30 m high on adjacent coasts, and lesser surges all around the Indonesian coastline.

The record of changing sea levels in Indonesia has been complicated by Quaternary tectonic movements. There are terraces and former shorelines at various levels, and Tjia (1975) is of the opinion that the higher Holocene stillstand well documented on the east coast of peninsular Malaysia can also be traced through much of Indonesia. During the last glacial low-sea-level phase, Java, Sumatra, and Kalimantan occupied an enlarged Malaysian peninsula, separated by deep straits from Sulawesi and the eastern islands, Australia being linked to New Guinea. The most thorough work on changes of land and sea level has been by Chappell and Veeh (1978) on Timor and Atauro, where stairways of coral terraces have been dated and related to land uplift at rates of up to 0.5 m per thousand years during the late Quaternary sea-level oscillations.

SUMATRA

The southern coasts of Sumatra are partly steep and cliffed, with intervening lowlands dominated by beach-ridge plains, as at Padang (Verstappen 1973). An anticlinal mountain chain with associated volcanoes runs northwest–southeast through the island, and rivers flow northward through a broad depositional lowland with extensive swamps to reach the Straits of Molucca. The Peusangan Delta in the north shows stages in growth and decay related to river capture (Fig. 118-2), but farther south the rivers open into broad tidal estuaries, and ports such as Palembang, which were close to the sea in the fifteenth century, are now far upstream, indicating that there has been rapid coastal progradation. Beach

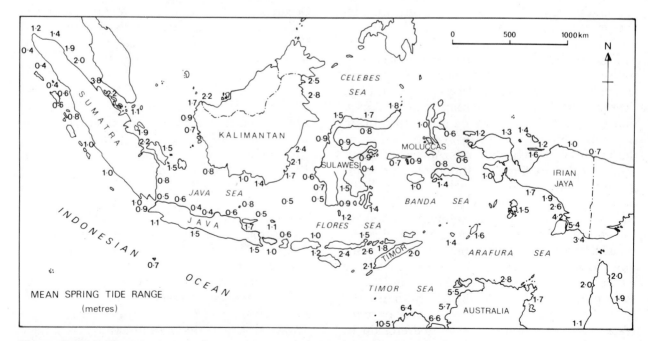

Figure 118-1. Variations in tide range around the Indonesian archipelago.

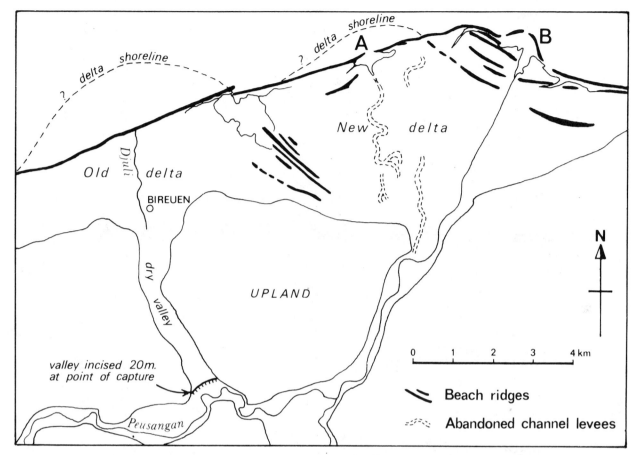

Figure 118-2. After its diversion by river capture, the Djuli River no longer maintained its delta, which has eroded away. The Peusangan then built a new delta at A, which has also eroded away as a younger delta grew at B. Beach ridges enable the sequence of delta growth and decay to be traced.

ridges (probably Holocene) have been found up to 150 km inland, and the shoreline of the Djambi Delta has prograded by up to 7.5 km in the past century.

KRAKATAU

Sunda Strait is bordered by steep volcanic coasts, and the effects of the 1883 eruption of Krakatau (Symons 1888) are still evident. The eruption left a caldera of irregular outline, 7 km in diameter and up to 250 m deep, which has been modified by rapid recession of cliffs cut into soft pumice and by the appearance and subsequent vigorous growth of a new volcanic island, Anak Krakatau, within the caldera (Fig. 118-3). The 1883 tsunami destroyed reefs and mangrove swamps, and the large coral boulders that were thrown up on the shore have since been undercut by up to 35 cm by shore-weathering processes.

JAVA

Long sectors of the north coast of Java consist of deltaic plains built out into the relatively low-wave-energy microtidal environment of the Java Sea by silt-laden rivers. During the past century sectors around the mouths of rivers and canals have prograded, while sectors no longer receiving fluvial sediment have been subject to erosion. In several cases river mouths have been diverted, either naturally or as the result of the cutting of canals, initiating new delta growth; sectors that were formerly prograding are eroding away.

The features of Jakarta Bay were the subject of a classic study by Verstappen (1953), who traced stages in delta progradation, especially on the eastern shores around the mouths of Citarum River distributaries. Earlier shoreline stages are traceable from patterns of beach ridges in the Jakarta region, and also in the deltaic plains to the east. In recent years erosion has become

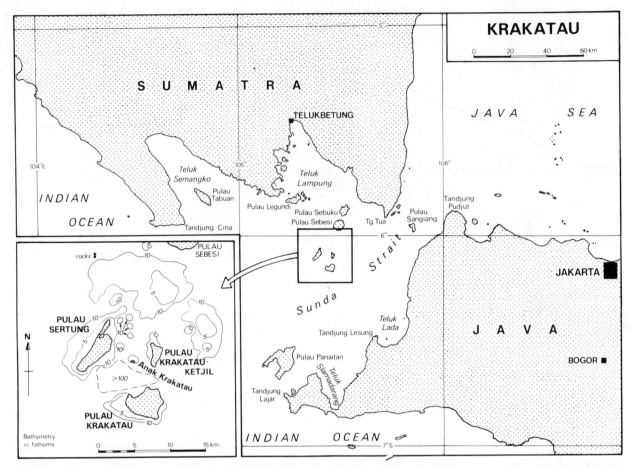

Figure 118-3. Krakatau, an island volcano in Sunda Strait, erupted explosively in 1883, leaving residual steep-sided islands. Subsequently a new volcano, Anak Krakatau, has developed within the caldera.

extensive on the northern flank of the Citarum Delta (Fig. 118-4), partly because river outlets have migrated westward and partly because sediment yield has diminished following the completion of the Jatiluhur Dam upstream in 1970 (Bird and Ongkosongo 1980).

Northwest of Jakarta Bay are the coral reefs and cays of the Thousand Islands, many of which have changed in outline during the past century. Some have enlarged by accretion of sand on cays and shingle on northeastern (windward) ramparts; others show erosion or lateral displacements related to variations in the local wind regime. Some are subsiding, others are rising, and some have been eroded as the result of removal of shingle and coral (Verstappen 1968).

East of Jakarta the Citarum, Cipunegara, and Cimanuk, with smaller intervening rivers, have built up a major confluent deltaic plain. At the eastern end the Cimanuk has shown rapid growth

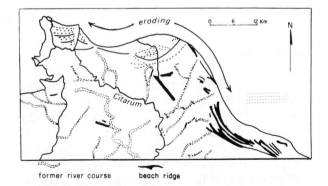

Figure 118-4. The Citarum River formerly built a delta northward, but this is eroding away following a swing to the northwest, where the modern delta is developing. Dam construction upstream has reduced the sediment yield here and slowed delta growth.

following its diversion northeastward during a flood in 1947. Stages in subsequent growth are shown in Figure 118-5, which indicates extension along three distributaries, with further branching developing as the result of median shoal formation in the river mouths. The older delta to the west is eroding away, as is the eastern flank, which curves out to a low-lying promontory, Cape Ujung. This was thought to be a relic of an earlier subdelta, but there are no relics of former channels leading in this direction. Another suggestion has been that it is related to a buried or nearshore reef structure, but no evidence exists for this either. The promontory occurs where an earlier beach-ridge system is truncated by the present shoreline.

On the smaller deltas to the east (Bangkaderas, Bosok, Pemali, Comal, and Bodri), Hollerwöger (1964) traced stages in historical evolution and noted an acceleration of growth after 1920, related to increased sediment yield due to clearance of

forests on steep hinterlands and the introduction of farming to these areas. In detail there have been sectors of advance and retreat related to the changing locations of river mouths. Near Jepara a new delta has formed at the mouth of a canal cut in 1892 to divert the outflow from the Kedung River. Stages in rapid extension of the Solo Delta (Fig. 118-6) have been documented by Verstappen (1977), and there appears to have been substantial progradation of the coastal plains around Surabaya in recent centuries, narrowing Surabaya Strait, which shows tidal scour features indicative of strong current action.

The south coast of Java has cliffed promontories and limestone cliffs, often fronted by shore platforms and fringing reefs, but sand deposition has built extensive beaches, with local cuspate forelands (behind Nusabarung Island) and tombolos (as at Pangandaran). The wide coastal plain near Yogyakarta is related to an abundant fluvial

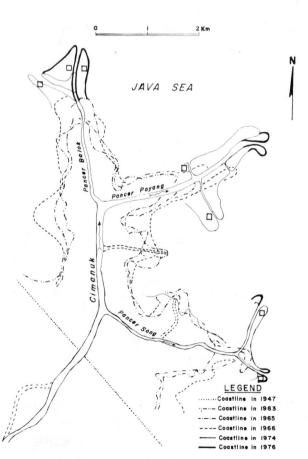

Figure 118-5. Stages in the growth of the modern Cimanuk River, by way of three major distributaries, following its diversion in 1947.

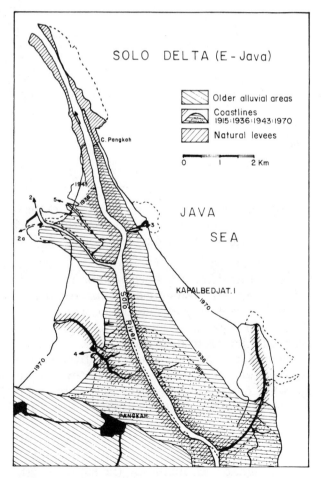

Figure 118-6. Stages in the growth of the Solo River delta, 1915–1970.

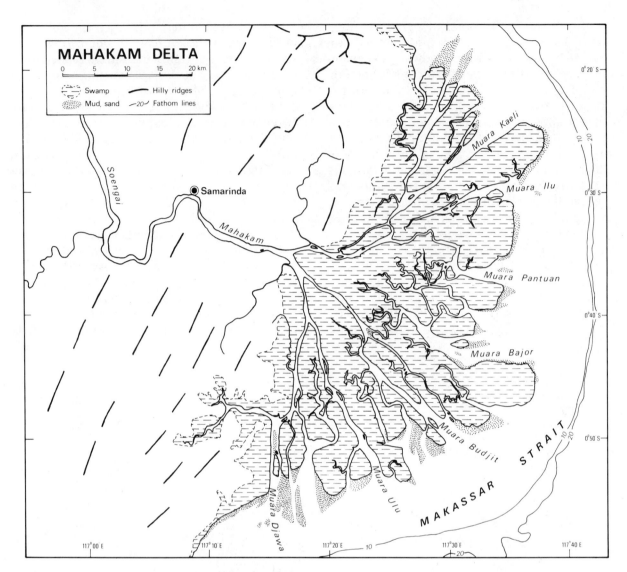

Figure 118-7. Morphological features of the Mahakam delta on the east coast of Kalimantan. The high-tide shoreline is intricate and dynamic, but the delta really extends seaward as a submerged sedimentary lobe with a steep outer slope, here indicated by the 10- and 20-fathom lines.

sediment yield from the steep hinterland, including sand and gravel brought down from the Merapi volcano, particularly after eruptions, when lahars flow down slopes and river discharge is torrential. Formation of protruding deltas of the kind seen in northern Java is prevented by relatively strong wave action, the shoreline being almost straight past the mouths of several rivers, each of which shows westward deflection by longshore drifting produced by waves generated by southeasterly winds. West of Parangtritis the seaward margin consists of beach ridges and active dunes up to 30 m high, driven inland by the southeasterly winds. These dunes were evidently mobilized when their former scrub and woodland cover was

destroyed by sheep and goat grazing and the harvesting of firewood (Verstappen 1957). They are quite anomalous in a humid tropical environment (Plate 118-2).

At Cilacap the coastal plain extends behind a high limestone ridge, and extensive mangrove swamps, intersected by tidal channels and creeks, border the broad shallow estuarine lagoon of Segara Anakan. Inflow of large quantities of silt, especially from the Citanduy River, is reducing the depth and extent of this lagoon system, and promoting mangrove encroachment.

Farther west, sectors of steep coast alternate with beach-ridge plains along to Java Head, at the southern entrance to Sunda Strait.

KALIMANTAN

Geomorphologists have given very little attention to the coasts of Kalimantan. Swampy plains are extensive, but rates of progradation have not been documented. Many river mouths are estuarine, especially on the east coast where the tide range is more than 2 m, but the Mahakam has built a major delta (Fig. 118-7) formed largely of coarse, sandy sediment derived from fluvial erosion of sandstone ridges near Samarinda, with swampy areas between the distributaries (Magnier et al. 1975). On the west coast, only the Pawan and Kapuas rivers have carried sufficient sediment from their extensive catchments to build protruding deltas.

SULAWESI

Sulawesi has generally steep coasts, with terrace features (including emerged, tilted, and warped coral reefs up to 600 m above sea level) indicating tectonic movements. Rivers are short and steep, with waterfalls and incised gorges, and only minor depositional plains at their mouths. Volcanoes are active locally, notably on Menadotua off the north of the island.

BALI

Bali consists partly of volcanic terrain, with active volcanoes such as Agung periodically generating lava and ash deposits that are washed down to the sea by rivers, and partly of coralline limestone formations, which are cliffed on the Bukit Peninsula to the southeast. Beaches border much of the island, with coral sands behind fringing reefs (Plate 118-3). The spit at Gilimanuk shows evidence of alternating growth and truncation, and in the Sanur area spits and barrier islands enclose a broad, mangrove-fringed tidal embayment north of the sandy isthmus of Denpasar.

LESSER SUNDA ISLANDS

Many of the features seen on Bali are repeated on the Lesser Sunda Islands to the east. High cliffs of limestone and volcanic rock fringe the southern coasts of Lombok, Sumbawa, and Sumba, and active volcanoes have deposited material on the coasts of Flores and Halmahera. Uplift is indicated by emerged coral reefs, attaining 700 m on Sumbawa and over 1200 m on Timor, where the sequence dated by Chappell

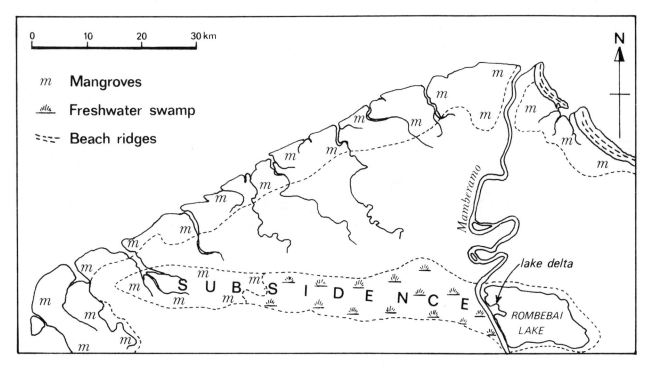

Figure 118-8. Zone of subsidence across the Mamberamo Delta in northern Irian Jaya, showing the Rombebai Lake formed as the land subsided and the spread of mangroves back into the lowered area (after Verstappen 1977).

and Veeh (1978) indicated uplift rates of up to 0.5 m per thousand years. Many of the smaller islands of eastern Indonesia are either high volcanic islands or uplifted coralline structures of various kinds (Davis 1928).

IRIAN JAYA

The north coast of Irian Jaya is generally steep, but rivers have built deltas and beach-ridge plains. Evidence of continuing tectonic activity is common: earthquakes cause landslides on coastal slopes, and the Mamberamo Delta has been modified by subsidence (Fig. 118-8). The south coast borders broad, swampy lowlands, traversed by rivers that open into broad, muddy estuaries with strong tidal currents; tide ranges here are up to 6 m. The rivers have not built protruding deltas, but deposition is locally advancing these swampy shorelines.

ERIC C. F. BIRD

REFERENCES

Bird, E. C. F., and O. S. R. Ongkosongo, 1980, *Environmental Changes on the Coasts of Indonesia*, United Nations University, Tokyo.

Chappell, J., and H. H. Veeh, 1978, Tectonic movements and sea level changes at Timor and Atauro Island, *Geol. Soc. America Bull.* **89:**356-368.

Davis, W. M., 1928, *The Coral Reef Problem*, American Geog. Soc. Spec. Pub. 9.

Hollerwöger, F., 1964, The progress of the river deltas in Java, in *Scientific Problems of Humid Tropical Zone Deltas and Their Implications*, UNESCO, Paris, pp. 347-355.

Magnier, P., T. Oki, and L. W. Kartaadiputra, 1975, The Mahakam delta, Kalimantan, *9th World Petroleum Congress Proc.*, Tokyo, pp. 239-250.

Molengraaf, G. A. F., 1929, The coral reefs of the East Indian archipelago: their distribution and mode of development, *4th Pacific Science Congress, Java* **2B:**57-71.

Symons, G. J., ed., 1888, *The Eruption of Krakatoa, and Subsequent Phenomena*, Royal Society, London.

Tjia, H. D., 1975, Holocene eustatic sea levels and glacio-eustatic rebound, *Zeitschr. Geomorphologie*, Supp. **22:**57-71.

Umbgrove, J. H. F., 1947, Coral reefs in the East Indies, *Geol. Soc. America Bull.* **58:**729-778.

Verstappen, H., 1953, *Djakarta Bay, a Geomorphological Study on Shoreline Development*, Rijkuniversitet, Utrecht.

Verstappen, H., 1957, Short note on the dunes near Parangtritis (Java), *Tijdschr. Kon. Ned. Aardr. Gen.* **74:**1-6.

Verstappen, H., 1968, Coral reefs: wind and current growth control, in *Encyclopedia of Geomorphology*, R. W. Fairbridge, ed., Reinhold, New York, pp. 197-202.

Verstappen, H., 1973, *A Geomorphological Reconnaissance of Sumatra and Adjacent Islands*, Wolters-Noordhoff, Groningen.

Verstappen, H., 1977, *Remote Sensing in Geomorphology*, Elsevier, Amsterdam.

Plate 118-1. Limestone cliffs on the south coast of Java, showing basal solution notch and pitting by shore-weathering processes (photo by E. C. F. Bird).

Plate 118-2. Mobile dunes at Parangtritis, southern Java, where the former stabilizing vegetation has been cleared and dune movement initiated. Unusual in a humid tropical environment, these dunes result from an abundant sand supply brought down by rivers from a volcanic hinterland and the effects of southeasterly trade winds, especially in the winter dry season (photo by E. C. F. Bird).

Plate 118-3. Fringing coral reef and associated calcareous sandy beach on the southeast coast of Bali, Indonesia (photo by E. C. F. Bird).

119. PAPUA NEW GUINEA

The coastal features of Papua New Guinea (Fig. 119-1) are similar to those described for Irian Jaya, with extensive steep sectors backed by uplifted mountain ranges interspersed with low-lying deltas and coastal plains (Löffler 1977). The coastline is about 5,000 km long, and when the coasts of New Britain (1,200 km), New Ireland (800 km), Bougainville (600 km), the associated outlying islands to the north, and the D'Entrecasteaux and Louisiade archipelagoes to the southeast are added, the total is more than 9,000 km.

There is widespread evidence of Holocene tectonic activity, marked by uplifted coral reefs, especially along the north coast of New Guinea, the south coast of New Britain, and the island chain from Manus to Buka. Earthquakes have disrupted coastal features locally, and vulcanicity is active on islands off Madang, and near Rabaul, where deposition of lava or ash has prograded some sectors of coastline. Coral reefs are extensive, most coastal promontories and high islands having a fringing reef while a barrier reef runs off the southeast Papuan coast, looping around Tagula Island and back toward the D'Entrecasteaux Islands, where there are various patch reefs and atolls. Cliffs occur locally on the Papuan coast, but bold coasts are generally steep and forested rather than cliffed. Where Holocene progradation has occurred, it has usually been nourished by sediments brought down by the numerous rivers; the sand fraction has been deposited in successive low beach ridges and the finer silt and clay have formed associated swamps bearing mangrove vegetation. Beach sediments are mainly black or gray sands and gravels brought down by rivers from volcanic and metamorphic rocks in the hinterland, the proportion of white coralline material increasing toward eroding coral reefs. Beach gravels are common on the north coast, fed by short, steep rivers draining uplifted hinterlands, whereas the Papuan coast receives mainly sandy fluvial sediment. Of the larger rivers only the Sepik has built a major protruding delta; the Ramu and the Markham valleys end abruptly seaward, while the Fly, Wawoi, Kikori, and other rivers draining to the Gulf of Papua open into estuarine channels between extensive mangrove-bordered swamps, backed by nipa palms. Coastal dunes are rare, but they occur locally on the south coast, notably at Hood Bay.

The coastal climate is generally humid tropical; a relatively dry winter season becomes more pronounced in Papua. Wave action is low to moderate, especially where reefs break up distantly derived swell. Waves are mainly southeasterly from the Coral and Solomon seas, and northwesterly through the Bismarck Sea. Wave action is generally weak, and tropical cyclones do not occur. Tide ranges are generally less than a meter, except along the southern Papuan coast, increasing westward to 2.8 m at the head of the Gulf of Papua (Fig. 119-1). Tsunamis of up to 3 m have been recorded on the north coast of New Guinea following earthquakes. Evidence of changing sea levels in this region is difficult to interpret because tectonic uplift has been extensive, but some observers have taken raised beach ridges as evidence of a higher Holocene sea level. Human impact has been relatively slight, except where

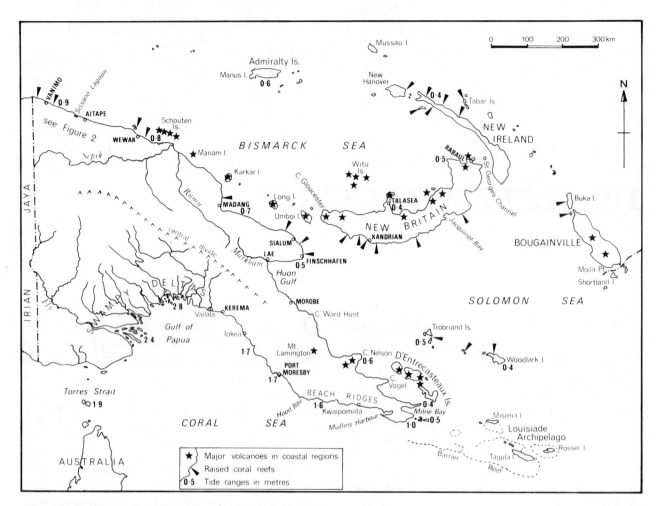

Figure 119-1. Papua New Guinea and the Bismarck Archipelago: location map and distribution of selected coastal features (after Löffler 1974).

artificial structures have locally modified shoreline features, in some cases leading to beach and shoreline erosion.

NEW GUINEA

Near Vanimo, the coast (Fig. 119-2) is dominated by cliffs up to 2 m high cut in emerged coral reefs that form terraces up to 100 m above sea level on the slopes of the Oenake Range. A modern fringing reef is almost continuous here. To the east, a narrow coastal plain with beach ridges is backed by swamps, but the outlet from Leitre Lagoon passes through a gorge between high hills at Ana. The Serra Hills are truncated by 30-m cliffs at Prittwitz Point. Then a broad swampy plain including the Sissano Lagoon (Fig. 119-3)—which formed when the area subsided 2–4 m during a 1907 earthquake—narrows east-

ward past Aitape as the Torricelli Ranges approach the coast. Sand and gravel delivered by swift-flowing rivers is carried eastward along the coast by the prevailing northwest waves from the Philippine Sea (Plate 119-1). In 1935 a major earthquake in the Torricelli Ranges caused landslides and catastrophic flooding, briefly augmenting the yield of sediment to the coast. Muschu Island is one of several uplifted coral reefs, and sand drifting alongshore has accumulated on Cape Pus, a cuspate spit in its lee. At Wewak, emergence has attached several former coralline islands to the mainland as promontories, as at Cape Wom, which intercepts sand drifting from the west. The beaches in the embayments at Wewak, no longer receiving sand, are consequently eroding (Bird 1981). The steep Hansemann Coast, flanking the Alexander Range, consists of vegetated bluffs frequently scarred by landslides and

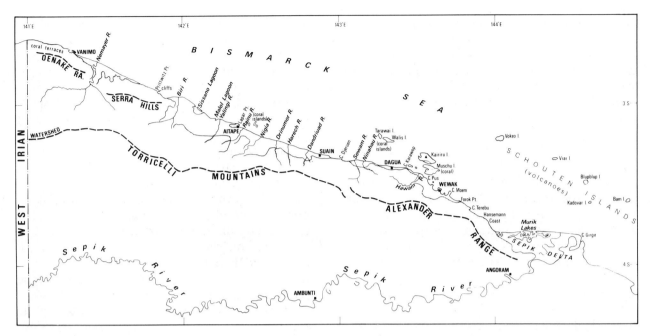

Figure 119-2. Coastal features of northern New Guinea, showing the extent of coastal plains (unshaded) west of the Sepik Delta.

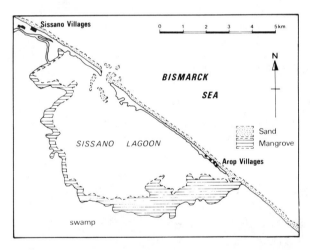

Figure 119-3. Sissano Lagoon, formed by marine invasion of an area of coastal plain that subsided during the 1907 earthquake. A seaward fringe of beach ridges persists as a sandy barrier, on which the Arop villages are situated.

shows only minor basal cliffing. Offshore the Schouten Islands are a chain of volcanoes, some active, part of an arc extending through Manam and Karakar into New Britain.

The swampy Sepik Delta shows evidence of subsidence along its almost straight northern flank, where the Murik Lakes are meanders of a former Sepik distributary enlarged by submerg-

ence. A sandy fringe is migrating landward into mangrove swamps as this shoreline recedes (Plate 119-2). Coastal subsidence may also be responsible for the truncation of the Ramu Delta to the east, where the deep waters of the Bismarck Sea run close inshore.

The Madang coast shows emerged coral reefs, cut back on their seaward margins. Stoddart (1972) described the effects of temporary sea-level changes caused by an earthquake on the ecology of nearshore reefs here. Emerged reefs alternate with truncated alluvial fan deposits eastward to Saidor, and then the terraces of coral and associated deltaic gravels ascend in level and multiply to more than 20 on the Huon Peninsula, where they are deeply incised by fluvial gorges, across a zone of late Quaternary uplift to reach a maximum height of over 600 m above sea level near the Tewai Gorge, east of Sialum. Chappell (1974) has calculated rates of uplift of up to 30 cm per century on reefs up to 250,000 years old here. The emerged reefs fade out and decline below sea level southwest of Finschhafen, and the north coast of Huon Gulf is dominated by features related to river deposition, such as alluvial fans and confluent deltaic plains truncated along a shoreline where the sea floor plunges to deep water. A submarine canyon heads a short distance off the mouth of the Markham, the broad valley of which opens through a swampy area to a shoreline fringed by a beach of sand and gravel. To the north, Lae is built on a gravelly terrace truncated seaward by bluffs.

The southern shores of Huon Gulf show alternations of reef-fringed hilly promontories with low notched cliffs on raised coral between Salamaua and Morobe, and embayments where streams open through mangrove swamps. From Hercules Bay to Holnicote Bay, a sandy beach-ridge plain links hilly areas (such as Cape Ward Hunt) backed by broad swampy terrain traversed by the Tavi, Mambaro, Opi, and Kumusi rivers, flanked southward by the Mount Lamington volcano, the slopes of which descend gently to the Buna coast. There was a major eruption here in 1951, when mudflows and torrential runoff delivered masses of sediment to the nearby shores.

PAPUA

Mt. Trafalgar is another volcanic upland, dissected by a radial pattern of incised valleys, so that the Cape Nelson shoreline is intricate where the sea has risen to submerge numerous valley mouths and form rias (e.g., MacLaren Harbor) between steep interfluvial headlands prolonged by fringing reefs (Fig. 119-4).

Southeastern Papua is mountainous with spurs running out to Cape Vogel (an emerged reef area), East Cape, and the broken Samarai Peninsula and intervening steep-sided embayments, notably Milne Bay. The outlying high D'Entrecasteaux Islands are accompanied by many reefs and atolls, some with cays. The south coast of Misima Island has seven coral terraces up to 460 m indicating episodic uplift, and similar features are seen in the Trobriand Islands (Ollier 1975), whereas Woodlark Island has a tilted coral platform encircling a hilly volcanic core. Reefs are also extensive in the Louisiade Archipelago (Davis 1922).

An intermittent barrier reef extends along the south coast of Papua. Cliffs occur between Samarai and Mullins Harbor, a sector exposed to

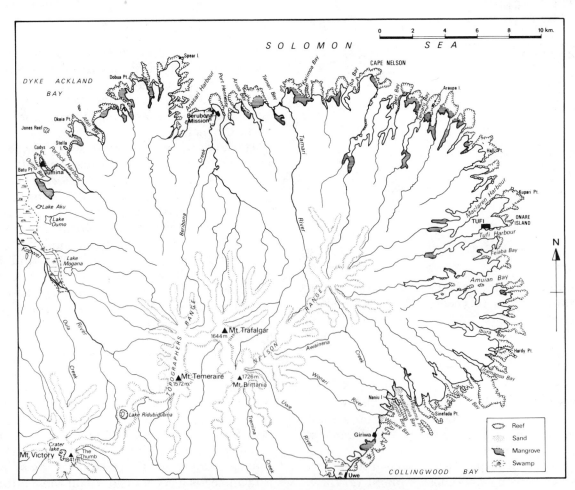

Figure 119-4. Coastal configuration near Cape Nelson, showing the effects of marine submergence of a volcanic slope incised by river valleys.

relatively strong wave action through gaps in the reef, and deep bays have not yet been filled with fluvial sediment because their catchments are small and low-lying. Farther west, larger rivers have carried quantities of sandy sediment, transported rapidly downstream from steep catchments to reach the coast as a partly weathered mixture of lithic fragments and various minerals, with only small proportions of quartz. Sectors exposed to swell from the Coral Sea have long sandy beaches on gently curving alignments, and beach-ridge plains curve out to cuspate forelands at Kwaipomata (Fig. 119-5) and Batumata Point, related to wave refraction around reefs. Progradation continues at Hood Bay, where sand from the Kemp Welch River has been built into parallel dunes, backed by parabolic dunes up to 35 m high, all well vegetated (Löffler 1977). Sheltered inlets and embayments (Mullins Harbor, Cloudy

Bay) are mangrove-fringed, but cliffs reappear between Paira Point and Port Moresby, and on headlands at Cape Suckling and Redscar Cliff. Beyond Port Moresby the coastal waters are more turbid with sediment delivered by large rivers, and coral growth diminishes (Mabbutt 1965; Weber 1973). Beach drifting to the northwest has influenced the pattern of growth of the foreland at Iokea (Fig. 119-6) and river deflection and spit growth at Vailala (Fig. 119-7). Progradation of up to 8 km is indicated by beach ridges at Malalaua, and the coastal plain has had a complex history of fluvial sand supply, beach-ridge building, and subsequent truncation (Ruxton 1969).

West of Kerema the sandy beaches become intermittent between tidal inlets and river mouths along the shoreline of the Purari Delta (Fig. 119-8). Mangrove-edged swamps dominated by *Sonneratia*, *Rhizophora*, and *Bruguiera* spp. occupy

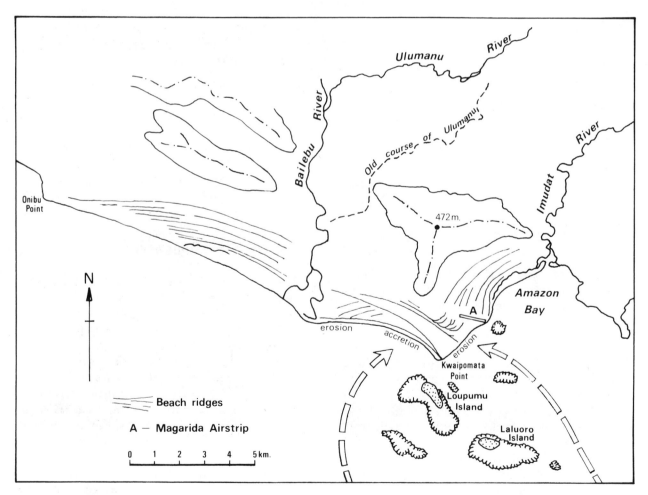

Figure 119-5. Deposition of sand from Bailebu and Imudat rivers in southeastern Papua has formed a beach-ridge plain, including a cuspate foreland at Kwaipomata Point, where converging waves have been refracted around offshore reefs and islands.

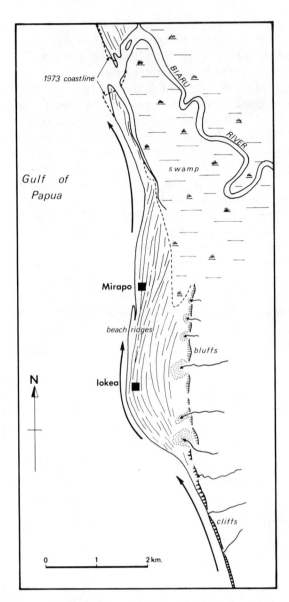

Figure 119-6. Beach-ridge foreland at Iokea, northwest of Port Moresby, supplied by sand drifting along the shore from the south.

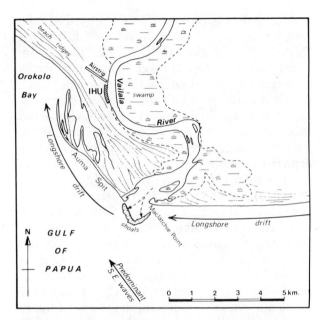

Figure 119-7. Sandy depositional features around the mouth of Vailala River, which replenishes shoals during each flood. The sand is being carried northwestward and added to the growing recurved spit at Auma.

the intertidal zone around the head of the Gulf of Papua. Within the mangrove area the surface is made irregular by mounds 2–5 m wide and up to 1.5 m high built by crabs. Sand brought down during river floods forms nearshore shoals (e.g., in Deception Bay), which are gradually reworked and driven onshore by southeasterly wave action. The swampy deltas are intersected by networks of meandering channels, widening seaward as tidal scour increases. The very wide, funnel-shaped estuary of the Fly, with its elongated deltaic islands and mangrove shoals, has tide ranges of up to 2.5

m associated with strong ebb currents. Extensive progradation is indicated by beach ridges up to 20 km inland. To the south, a broad, gently undulating alluvial plain is fringed by beach ridges and mangrove swamps along the shores of Torres Strait, extending westward to the Irian Jaya frontier.

BISMARCK ARCHIPELAGO

The south coast of New Britain is bordered by emerged coral reefs of varying altitude, with terrace stairways near Kandrian similar to those seen on the Huon Peninsula. In Jaquinot Bay there are up to six terraces, the highest attaining 500 m above sea level. Volcanoes dominate the steep north coast, especially at Cape Gloucester, on the Talasea Peninsula, and around Rabaul, with alluvial fans in intervening areas. Coastal deposition of lava and ash, or of volcanic sediment delivered by rivers, has limited coral reef growth here.

The southern part of New Ireland has mainly steep coasts, but segments of emerged coral reef occur along much of the north coast and the south coast west of St. George's Channel, and on some sectors there are multiple terraces up to

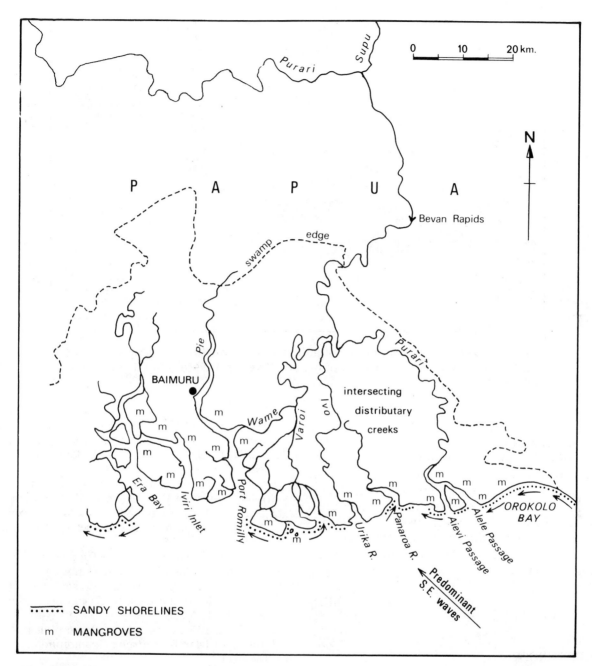

Figure 119-8. Coastal features of the Purari Delta, where sand supplied by rivers is reworked by wave action and deposited as beach ridges on the seaward margin of a prograding swampy shoreline.

400 m above sea level. On the north coast, Christiansen (1963) found paired notches along the shore, one at present level, the other indicating Holocene emergence; the elevation of the upper notch increases to the southeast (Hohnen 1970), indicating tilting. New Hanover is almost encircled by emerged reefs, and they occur also on outlying volcanic islands northeast of New Ireland, and on parts of the coast of the Admiralty Islands.

Bougainville is largely volcanic with steep coasts, but rivers carrying sand and gravel derived from the volcanoes have supplied material for several segments of beach ridge plain, including Moila Point, a major cuspate foreland shaped in the lee

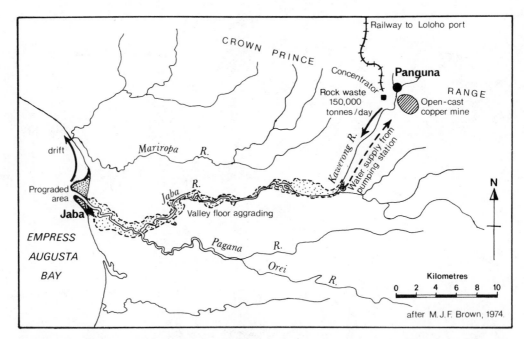

Figure 119-9. On the island of Bougainville, rock waste from open-cast copper mining has aggraded the valley floor of Jaba River and led to rapid delta growth at its mouth.

of Shortland Island to the south. Fallout of ash may have impeded coral reef development on the east coast. In some areas, mining operations have augmented the sediment yield from rivers and accelerated coastal deposition (Fig. 119-9). On the north coast, and especially on Buka Island, a former barrier reef has been raised up to 100 m above sea level, the shore at Cape Putputun consisting of basally notched cliffs behind a modern fringing reef.

ERIC C. F. BIRD

REFERENCES

Bird, E. C. F., 1981, The beach erosion problem at Wewak, Papua, New Guinea, *Singapore Jour. Trop. Geography* **2:**9-14.

Chappell, J., 1974, Geology of coral terraces, Huon Peninsula, New Guinea: a study of Quaternary tectonic movements and sea-level changes, *Geol. Soc. America Bull.* **85:**553-570.

Christiansen, S., 1963, Morphology of some coral cliffs, Bismarck Archipelago, *Geog. Tidsskr.* **62:**1-23.

Davis, W. M., 1922, Coral reefs of the Louisiade Archipelago, *Natl. Acad. Sci. Proc.* **8:**7-13.

Hohnen, P. B., 1970, *Geology of New Ireland,* Australian Bureau of Mineral Resources, Canberra.

Löffler, E., 1974, Explanatory notes to the geomorphological map of Papua New Guinea, *C.S.I.R.O. Land Research Series* **33.**

Löffler, E., 1977, *Geomorphology of Papua New Guinea,* Australian National University, Canberra.

Mabbutt, J. A., 1965, Geomorphology of the Port Moresby–Kairuku area, *C.S.I.R.O. Land Research Series* **14:**106-128.

Ollier, C. D., 1975, Coral island geomorphology—the Trobriand Islands, *Zeitschr. Geomorphologie* **19:** 164-190.

Ruxton, B. P., 1969, Geomorphology of the Kerema-Vailala area, *C.S.I.R.O. Land Research Series* **23:** 65-76.

Stoddart, D. R., 1972, Catastrophic damage to coral reef communities by earthquake, *Nature* **239:**51-52.

Weber, J. N., 1973, Reef corals and coral reefs in the vicinity of Port Moresby, Papua New Guinea, *Pacific Sci.* **27:**377-390.

Plate 119-1. North coast of New Guinea at Dagua, showing a beach with westward drift toward Cape Pus and a deflected outlet of the Dagua River. Note the intersecting northwest and northeast waves and beach cusps on shore (photo by E. C. F. Bird).

Plate 119-2. North shore of the Sepik Delta, showing receding sandy beach with die-back of mangroves to the rear as sand is overwashed. The village also migrates as the sand moves landward (photo by E. C. F. Bird).

120. VICTORIA

The coastline of Victoria (Figs. 120-1 and 120-2) is about 1,600 km long, including the shores of Port Phillip Bay (256 km), Westernport Bay (263 km), and Corner Inlet (300 km) (Bird 1977). Its outlines have been influenced by the uplift of the Otway Ranges, the Mornington Peninsula, and the South Gippsland Highlands, and the subsidence of the Western District, the Port Phillip and Westernport Bay areas, Corner Inlet, and the structural trough that underlies the Latrobe

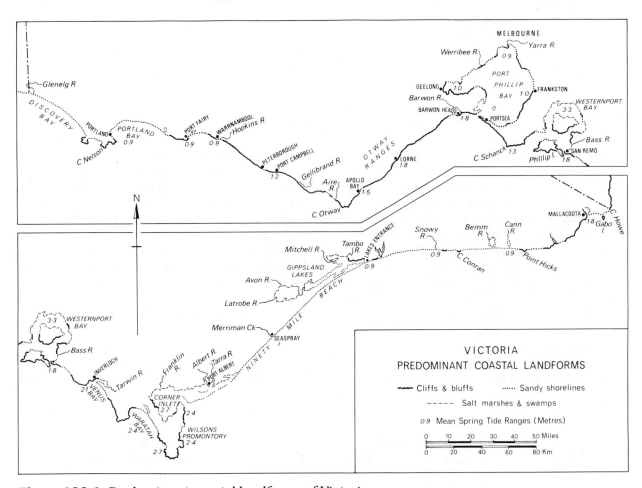

Figure 120-1. Predominant coastal landforms of Victoria.

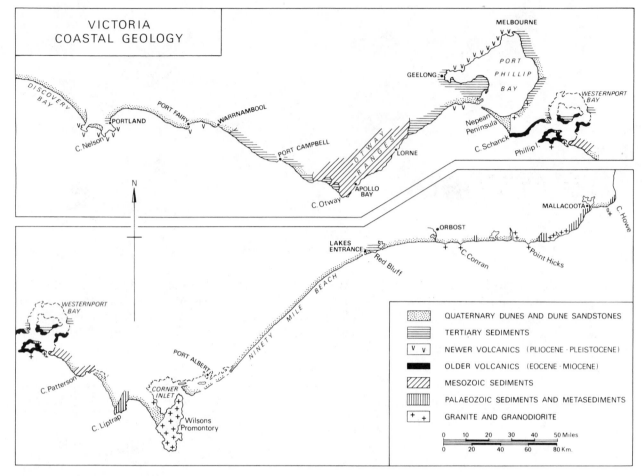

Figure 120-2. Coastal geology of Victoria.

Valley and extends eastward beneath the Gippsland Lakes. In the far east of the state, the coastline truncates the geological formations of the Eastern Highlands of Australia, which here show a north–south trend in the folding and faulting of the rocks and the pattern of granitic intrusions. Wilson's Promontory stands out as a much-dissected granite upland to the south of the Corner Inlet depression, and Tertiary vulcanicity has supplied an Older Basalt (Eocene-Miocene) to south-central Victoria and a Newer Basalt (Plio-Pleistocene) to the Western District (Hills 1975). The coast is considered to have been generally stable in late Quaternary times, and to show evidence of a higher Holocene sea level (Gill and Hopley 1972), but earthquakes are occasionally recorded and the possibility of localized minor warping cannot be ruled out.

West from Wilson's Promontory the coast is exposed to southwesterly ocean swell and storm waves moving into Bass Strait, while the eastern sector, including the Ninety Mile Beach, receives southerly and southeasterly swells, in addition to storm waves mainly from the southwest.

Mean spring tide ranges on the ocean coastline are generally between 0.9 and 1.8 m, with slightly higher ranges (up to 2.7 m) around Wilson's Promontory. In Port Phillip Bay, mean spring tide range diminishes from 1.8 m at the narrow ocean entrance to 0.9 m at Melbourne, while the inner parts of Westernport Bay have augmented ranges (up to 3.3 m).

Cliffs and bluffs are extensive on a variety of geological formations, and in many sectors are fronted by shore platforms produced by erosion and weathering processes, in particular salt-spray effects and recurrent wetting and drying (Hills 1971).

Beach sediments are predominantly sandy, and longshore drifting on the ocean coast is generally from west to east; however, where beaches occupy asymmetrical bays shaped by refracted ocean swell there is little net drifting. West of Wilson's Promontory, beach and dune sands are generally calcareous, whereas to the east they are quartzose (Gell 1978). Coastal dunes also show evidence of eastward movement, and have locally transgressed over headlands to form cliff-top dunes.

Most of Victoria's rivers drain into estuarine lagoons with sea entrances encumbered by in-washed sandy thresholds and flanking spits (Plate 120-1). Swampy shores — typically mangrove-fringed salt marshes — occupy the more sheltered parts of Westernport Bay and Corner Inlet, and the margins of estuaries and coastal lagoons. The only mangrove present in Victoria is *Avicennia marina*, which reaches its southernmost world limit on the shores of Corner Inlet (38°55′ S).

Discovery Bay, in the west of the state, has a gently curved sandy shoreline backed by exten-sive, partly mobile calcareous dunes, and Pleisto-cene dune calcarenites that outcrop locally on the shore (Boutakoff 1963). Dunes were already mobile here when European settlers arrived early in the nineteenth century, but they have become more extensively so as the result of burning and grazing. Among the dunes are fresh-water lakes (notably the Bridgewater Lakes) and associated swamps (Plate 120-2).

The Portland peninsula consists of Plio-Pleist-ocene volcanic formations, dissected by marine erosion into steeply cliffed headlands and em-bayments. The cliffs exhibit the internal struc-tures of extinct volcanoes, while the embayments are enlarged calderas (Boutakoff 1963).

At Portland a large breakwater encloses a mod-ern harbor, and the cliffs to the north show Miocene limestone overlain by Pliocene clay and Pleistocene basalt. Lava flows interrupt the sandy shoreline near Port Fairy, and farther east is Tower Hill, a volcano that last erupted 7,300 years ago, producing tuffs that are exposed on the adjacent shore (Gill 1967).

On either side of Warrnambool are rugged cliffs cut into Pleistocene dune calcarenite, but to the southeast the Port Campbell Limestone (Miocene) emerges at the coast to form spectacular vertical cliffs with slot bays and outlying stacks and arches bounded by joint planes (Plate 120-3): soft, hori-zontally bedded limestone confronts stormy seas that occasionally overtop 60-m cliffs (Baker 1943). Minor sectors that have escaped Holocene cliffing include Two Mile Bay near Port Campbell, where a Pleistocene bluff persists behind an emerged shore platform.

East of the Gellibrand River there are major landslips in the Tertiary formations that rise toward the anticlines of the Otway Ranges. Mes-

ozoic sandstones and mudstones in these ranges outcrop in coastal cliffs and shore platforms between Moonlight Head and Cape Otway, while the same formations exhibit steep forested slopes and only limited basal cliffing behind shore plat-forms along the coast from Cape Otway to Lorne. This sector is notable for the weathering-out of calcareous "cannon-ball" concretions on the shore platforms.

Port Phillip Bay occupies a sunkland between the Bellarine Peninsula to the southwest and the Mornington Peninsula to the east (Bowler 1966). There are low-lying plains of Newer Basalt on the western shore and bordering cliffs in Tertiary formations and granodiorite intrusions on the eastern shore where beaches show seasonal drift-ing, northward in summer and southward in winter. In the southern part of the bay extensive shallows are threaded by tidally scoured channels that diverge from the narrow entrance. Mud Islands (Plate 120-4) consist of salt marshes and lagoons enclosed by shelly beaches that surmount a sand shoal. Along the ocean coast, rugged cliffs and flat platforms have been cut in Pleistocene dune calcarenite between Barwon Heads and Cape Schanck, interrupted by the entrance to Port Phillip Bay. To the east, Selwyn Fault, along which earth tremors are still recorded, marks the begin-ning of the Older Basalt coast that extends from Cape Schanck to the western shores of Western-port Bay and borders much of Phillip Island.

Westernport (Fig. 120-3) is a landlocked marine area enclosing French Island and bordered sea-ward by Phillip Island, which separates a broad western and a narrow eastern entrance. Toward the head of the bay, extensive salt marshes are edged seaward by mangroves and broad intertidal mud flats (Plate 120-5). At low tide the water diverges on either side of a tidal watershed. There have been substantial changes, particularly in the mangrove fringe, since this bay was first mapped in 1842 (Bird and Barson 1975).

Between San Remo and Inverloch the cliffs and shore platforms cut in Mesozoic rocks alternate with sandy beaches backed by dunes. Behind Venus Bay, the Tarwin River opens into the estuary of Anderson's Inlet, an area bordered by man-groves and salt marshes, which has in recent years been modified by the rapid spread of intro-duced European *Spartina* grass. The features are similar to those described when this grass invaded Poole Harbor in England (*q.v.*) early in the present century.

Cape Liptrap has steep cliffs and serrated shore

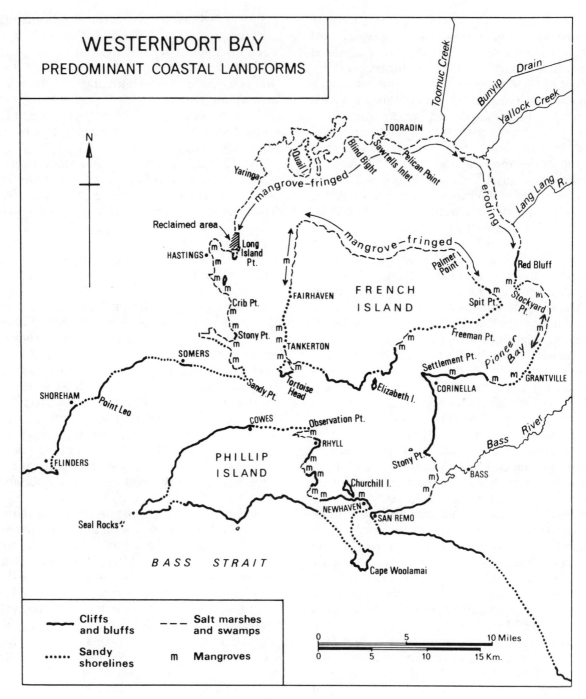

Figure 120-3. Predominant coastal landforms of Westernport Bay, Victoria.

platforms cut in hard Lower Paleozoic mudstones at the seaward limit of the Hoddle Range (Plate 120-6). Derived cobble beaches occupy coves, and relics of emerged shore platforms carry raised beaches, probably of Pleistocene age.

Wilson's Promontory is a granitic upland linked to the mainland by the dune-covered Yanakie Isthmus behind Waratah Bay. Granite ridges end

in steep rocky slopes, which plunge into deep water, rather than eroded cliffs, and intervening valleys open on to sandy coves backed by dunes (Plate 120-7)

Corner Inlet is a broad, shallow marine basin with extensive sandy shoals exposed at low tide and several small granitic islands. The shores are fringed by salt marshes and mangroves except on the western side, where dune sand spills over from Yanakie Isthmus.

East of Corner Inlet the marshy inner shoreline on either side of Port Albert is bordered to seaward by a chain of complex sandy barrier islands with intervening tidal entrances that have varied and migrated historically (Jenkin 1968). Sand shoals offshore are a source of continuing beach progradation here (Plate 120-8) in contrast with the erosion of sandy shorelines that is otherwise prevalent in Victoria (Bird 1979).

The Ninety Mile Beach is the seaward margin of a long dune-capped outer sand barrier developed in front of a Pleistocene coastline marked by bluffs in the Seaspray district and behind the Gippsland Lakes. Lake Reeve is part of the lagoon

and swamp zone behind the outer barrier. It was here shown that the sand deposited from the outer barrier came from the sea floor during and after the Holocene marine transgression, there being no significant sources of sand supply from rivers or eroding cliffs on this coast (Bird 1961).

The Gippsland Lakes (Bird 1978) are a chain of coastal lagoons that occupy a former marine embayment at the eastern end of the Latrobe Valley syncline. Sandy barriers formed here in Pleistocene times and were dissected during the Last Glacial low-sea-level phase, before the Holocene outer barrier was added to enclose the present lakes (Fig. 120-4). In 1889 a permanent artificial entrance (Lakes Entrance) was opened to replace an earlier intermittent natural outlet, and

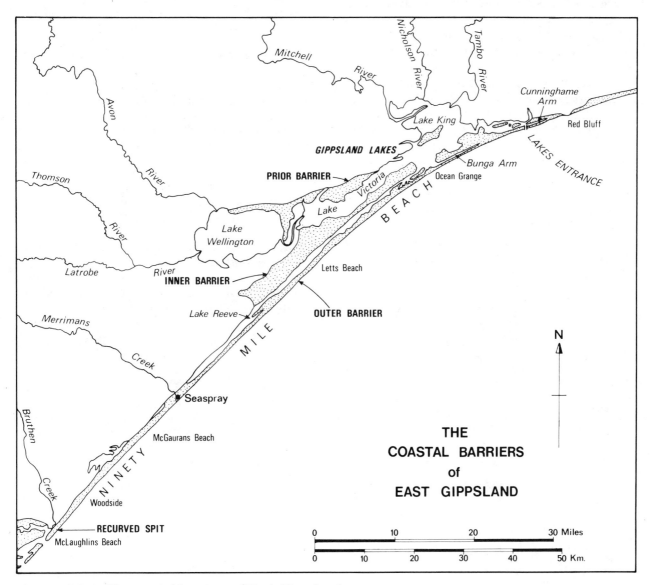

Figure 120-4. The coastal barriers of East Gippsland.

the Gippsland Lakes have subsequently become more estuarine, with salinity diminishing toward the mouths of inflowing rivers, notably in the westernmost lake (Lake Wellington). Reedswamp and swamp scrub persist around the shores of the fresher parts of the Gippsland Lakes, but they have died back and been eroded away in parts that have become more brackish. Deltas built by the inflowing rivers include the long, narrow silt jetties of the Mitchell River, eroding as a sequel to the loss of a former reedswamp fringe (Plate 120-9). Sand has accumulated on either side of the breakwaters bordering the artificial entrance, the navigability of which is impeded by the persistence of a looped sand bar offshore (Plate 120-10).

East of Lakes Entrance the coast consists of long sandy beaches backed by dunes, some of which are mobile, driven by strong westerly winds. At intervals, the beach is interrupted by minor headlands of granite or Lower Paleozoic rock, the cliffs becoming more continuous toward Mallacoota, where they stand at the edge of a coastal plateau. Also interrupting the beach are the mouths of several estuarine lagoons, as well as the Snowy, largest of the rivers draining to this coast, which has developed broad, barrier-fringed deltaic flats south of Orbost. East of Mallacoota are extensive mobile dunes behind a sandy shore that curves out to cuspate points in the lee of offshore islands such as Gabo Island (a breached tombolo); and near Cape Howe, dunes spill across the state border into New South Wales.

ERIC C. F. BIRD

REFERENCES

Baker, G., 1943, Features of a Victorian limestone coastline, *Jour. Geology* **51:**359–386.

Bird, E. C. F., 1961, The coastal barriers of East Gippsland, Australia, *Geog. Jour.* **127:**460–468.

Bird, E. C. F., 1977, *Sites of Special Scientific Interest in the Victorian Coastal Region: Geological and Geomorphological,* Town and Country Planning Board, Melbourne.

Bird, E. C. F., 1978, *The Geomorphology of the Gippsland Lakes Region,* Ministry for Conservation, Victoria.

Bird, E. C. F., 1979, Historical changes on sandy shorelines in Victoria, *Royal Soc. Victoria Proc.* **91:**18–30.

Bird, E. C. F., and M. M. Barson, 1975, Shoreline changes in Westernport Bay, *Royal Soc. Victoria Proc.* **87:** 15–28.

Boutakoff, N., 1963, *The Geology and Geomorphology of the Portland Area,* Geol. Survey Victoria Mem. 22.

Bowler, J., 1966, Geology and geomorphology–Port Phillip Bay, *Natl. Museum Melbourne Mem.* **27:**19–27.

Gell, R., 1978, Shelly beaches on the Victorian coast, *Royal Soc. Victoria Proc.* **90:**257–269.

Gill, E. D., 1967, Evolution of the Warrnambool–Port Fairy coast, in *Landform Studies from Australia and New Guinea,* J. N. Jennings and J. A. Mabbutt, eds., Australian National University, Canberra, pp. 341–364.

Gill, E. D., and D. Hopley, 1972, Holocene sea levels in Eastern Australia, *Marine Geology* **12:**223–242.

Hills, E. S., 1971, A study of cliffy coastal profiles based on examples in Victoria, Australia, *Zeitschr. Geomorphologie* **15:**137–180.

Hills, E. S., 1975, *Physiography of Victoria,* Whitcombe & Tombs, Marrickville.

Jenkin, J. J., 1968, *The Geomorphology and Upper Cainozoic Geology of South-east Gippsland, Victoria,* Geol. Survey Victoria Mem. 27.

Plate 120-1. The mouth of the Snowy River, in eastern Victoria, is almost completely sealed off from the sea by a barrier of sand washed up by wave action. During episodes of flooding a gap is forced through this barrier by the discharge from the river, but when the outflow slackens the sand barrier is rebuilt. Traces of former outlets can be seen (photo by N. Rosengren).

Plate 120-2. Extensive mobile sand dunes, driven inland by strong onshore winds from the surf beach bordering Discovery Bay in western Victoria. Relics of dune scrub that formerly held these dunes in place persist patchily. Fires set by aborigines and burning and grazing in the last century rendered these dunes mobile. In the foreground is Swan Lake, one of several freshwater lagoons and swamp areas found among the dunes, and at their landward margins. The dunes have here ponded back the outflow from Johnstone Creek, entering from the left (photo by N. Rosengren).

Plate 120-3. Joint-guided marine dissection of soft limestone near Port Campbell has produced steep-sided coastal gorges and outlying stacks penetrated by caves and natural arches. Beaches are very limited, confined to the heads of the coastal gorges (photo by N. Rosengren).

Plate 120-4. In the shallow southern part of Port Phillip Bay, wave action has built up an atoll-like formation consisting of shelly sand ridges and low grassy dunes enclosing a lagoon with areas of salt marsh. Known as Mud Islands, this formation shows intricate short-term changes in outline in response to storm wave activity (photo by E. C. F. Bird).

Plate 120-5. In the northwestern corner of Westernport Bay are branching tidal channels flanked by extensive mud flats exposed at low tide, then a dark fringe of mangroves (*Avicennia marina*) in front of salt marshes, with a relict early Holocene sandy shoreline to the rear. A harbor for small boats has been formed by dredging a channel out to the deep water (photo by E. C. F. Bird).

Plate 120-6. Steep bluffs cut in Lower Paleozoic mudstones culminate in a rib of harder rock projecting from Cape Liptrap in eastern Victoria. Shore platforms have been cut across the steeply inclined strata, and to the rear are pocket beaches of coarse gravel derived from the hard mudstones (photo by N. Rosengren).

Plate 120-7. On Wilson's Promontory spurs of granite project seaward between sandy coves shaped by refracted ocean swell and backed by parallel dune ridges held in place by scrub vegetation (photo by N. Rosengren).

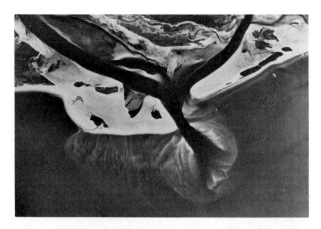

Plate 120-8. A vertical photograph of a tidal inlet between barrier islands on the sandy coast east of Wilson's Promontory. Sand shoals are extensive in coastal waters, and this is one of the few sectors of the Victorian coast where the shoreline continues to prograde as waves move sand onshore for deposition on the beach (photo by E. C. F. Bird).

Plate 120-9. The long, narrow silt jetties built by the Mitchell River into Lake King, one of the Gippsland Lakes, were formerly reed-fringed and growing, but within the past century the reed fringe has largely died away, largely as a consequence of salinity increase following the cutting of an artificial entrance from the sea to these lakes. As a result, the deltaic formations are now eroding away (photo by N. Rosengren).

Plate 120-10. The artificial entrance to the Gippsland Lakes, cut in 1889 and bordered by protruding stone jetties. While the Ninety Mile Beach has generally receded during the past century, sectors on either side of these stone jetties have prograded by accumulation of wave-deposited sand, and new grassy dunes have developed. Longshore drifting takes place in both directions and is roughly balanced at this site (photo by N. Rosengren).

121. SOUTH AUSTRALIA

Although some 3,700 km long, the South Australian coast is in broad view remarkably simple. With the exception of a sector near the West Australian border, where it runs latitudinally, the coast trends northwest–southeast, with only two major indentations (Spencer Gulf and Gulf St. Vincent) and only one large offshore land mass (Kangaroo Island) (Fig. 121-1).

Various factors have determined the shape of the coast. The trend and the major projections and indentations reflect regional structure (Twidale 1971). The northwest–southeast alignment of the west coast of Eyre Peninsula and of the Lower South East appears to be related to fractures in the crust. The east coast of Eyre Peninsula runs parallel to the Lincoln Fault Zone, and the outlines of Yorke Peninsula are also determined by fractures (Crawford 1965). Both Fleurieu Peninsula and Kangaroo Island are developed on folded geosynclinal sequences, but the orogen is also faulted. Fleurieu Peninsula is part of a complex horst, and Kangaroo Island either another horst or a tilted fault block.

The intervening seas, Spencer Gulf, Gulf St. Vincent, and Investigator Strait are also in large measure delineated by faults. Moreover, Backstairs Passage, which separates Kangaroo Island from the mainland, may well be due to the exploitation—by rivers, Permian glacier ice, and the sea—of a fracture zone developed in the acute flexure developed in the orogen in this area.

In detail the nature and disposition of the rocks exposed in the coastal zone are as important as any other factor, and more important than most, in determining local morphology. Crystalline rocks are characteristic of the Gawler Craton, and Precambrian granite and gneiss are exposed in many coastal sectors on Eyre Peninsula and on the west coast of Yorke Peninsula. Blocks and boulders are typically developed, though the deep weathering of the crystallines has also resulted in extensive erosion, and platforms of considerable extent have been formed. Paleozoic granites are exposed in Encounter Bay and give rise to several inselbergs and low hills with rough boulder-strewn flanks. Even in the southeast, near Kingston, there are several large whaleback boulders (Plate 121-1) developed where a small mass of Paleozoic granite of the Padthaway Horst is exposed in the intertidal zone. On Fleurieu Peninsula and Kangaroo Island, on the other hand, folded strata have been differentially eroded into minor ridge and cleft forms, while near the head of Spencer Gulf the flat-lying sediments of the Stuart Shelf give rise to ledged cliffs. The Eucla Basin sediments too are horizontally disposed.

Dune limestone has overwhelmed and largely masked the older structures and forms in many areas. Its distribution is related partly to the orientation of the coast, partly to late Cenozoic climatic events and related sea-level oscillations. During glacial phases sea-level was lowered by at least 100 m. Huge areas of what are now the inner areas of the continental shelves were exposed. The gulfs and Investigator Strait became coastal and riverine plains. Kangaroo Island was then part of the mainland. The present rivers extended far beyond their present outlets; the Murray, for example, ran far to the south beyond its present mouths to reach the sea west or southwest of Kangaroo Island before tumbling over the edge of the continental slope, where its turbid waters eroded a series of enormous submarine canyons (Von der Borch 1968).

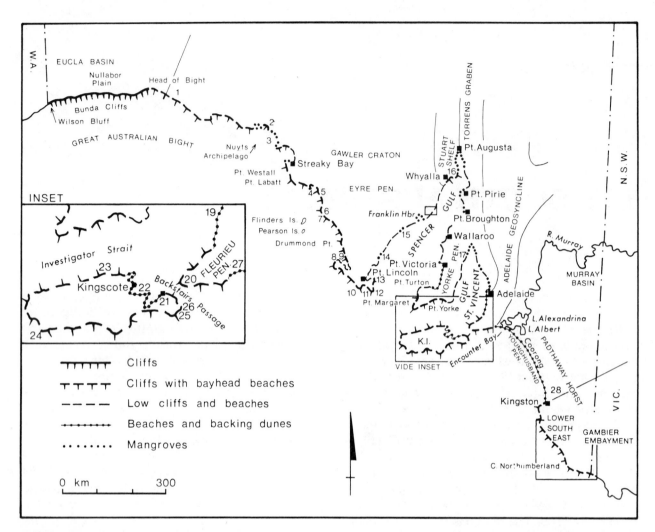

Figure 121-1. The coast of South Australia, showing structural base and major coastal types. Some locations are named, others are indicated by numbers: 1. Yalata; 2. Thevenard; 3. Smoky Bay; 4. Venus Bay; 5. Talia; 6. Elliston; 7. Waterloo Bay; 8. Point Sir Isaac; 9. Coffin Bay; 10. Cape Carnot; 11. West Point; 12. Cape Catastrophe; 13. Cape Donington; 14. Tumby Bay; 15. Arno Bay; 16. Pt. Lowly; 17. Ardrossan, 18. Foul Bay; 19. Hallet Cove; 20. Cape Jervois; 21. Penneshaw; 22. Nepean Bay; 23. Cape Cassini; 24. Cape de Couedic; 25. Windmill Bay; 26. Cape Willoughby; 27. Port Elliot; 28. Taratap.

The broken shells of marine organisms and other debris exposed on the old sea bed were carried onshore by the wind and there deposited in huge coastal dunes (Crocker 1946a). More than 80% lime, these dunes typically display eolian crossbedding; old soils (typically with calcrete prominent) mark stages in the building of the dunes, and now form distinct ledges on the cliff faces. Such dunes developed in many places along the southern Australian coast, but particularly in sections exposed to the dominant westerly and southwesterly winds. The shapes of the old dunes are still clearly discernible on many parts of the coast, for although their seaward faces

have been eroded, the gentle backslopes are commonly preserved (Plate 121-2). The accumulation of dunes on Kangaroo Island caused what had been at least two separate land masses to become linked in the area between Kingscote and Penneshaw to form a single island after the postglacial rise of sea level, just as the toe of Yorke Peninsula became linked to the leg by the formation of, and alluviation behind, such calcareous foredunes.

When the ice sheets waned, water was returned to the ocean basins and sea level rose. Abandoned shoreline features clearly indicate higher stands of the sea on several parts of the South Australian coast. How much higher is as debatable here as it is in other parts of the world, but there are features up to 20 m above present sea level that seem incontrovertibly of marine origin and Pleistocene age (Bauer 1959, 1961; Brock 1964, 1967; Twidale et al. 1967; Twidale et al. 1977; Ward 1965; Ward and Jessup 1965). With the most recent major melting of ice sheets and concomitant rise of sea level, the coast attained its present outline.

The prominent northwest–southeast alignment of the coast brings the edge of the land mass athwart the westerly and southwesterly winds and waves that are typical of the latitudinal zone in which the South Australian coast is situated. Most of the coast is exposed to the westerlies. Only the two major gulfs and to a lesser degree the shores of Investigator Strait are sheltered from them.

These then are the major factors controlling the form of the coast: structure, geological history, particularly the events of the last two million years or so, and location and disposition with respect to prevailing and strong winds, whether the coast is exposed or sheltered.

The Eucla coast, between the West Australian border near Wilson Bluff and the Head of the Bight, consists overwhelmingly of cliffs, 50–60 m high, rising sheer from the sea; these are known as the Bunda Cliffs (Plate 121-3). No coastal plain of any consequence fronts the cliffs in South Australia. Developed in flat-lying Tertiary limestones of the Eucla Basin, the cliffs are distinctly layered, the hard white Miocene Nullarbor Limestone overlying the softer brownish-yellow Wilson Bluff chalk-with-flint of Eocene age. The Nullarbor Limestone in particular is well jointed and finds expression in the otherwise simple zigzag planform of the cliffs. The only variation occurs where wave quarrying of the weaker basal rock has caused undermining and collapse, the fallen debris forming distinct blocky talus cones in places and aprons elsewhere.

The Bunda Cliffs offer no direct evidence of sea-level change, but the horizontal zonation of the deeper caves of the Nullarbor Plain (between 50 and 100 m) suggests that they graded to a base level perhaps 40–50 m higher than present sea level (Jennings 1963).

At the Head of the Bight the character of the coast changes, for though still exposed and dominated by limestone cliffs, the coastline becomes more varied and complex to the southeast. Gawler Craton crystalline rocks are exposed on the west coast of Eyre Peninsula, but are everywhere subordinate to the Pleistocene dune calcarenite,

which blankets the very old rocks. The Mesozoic and early Tertiary strata of the (partly infaulted) Polda Basin–Eliston Trough that extend into the western part of the peninsula are also hidden by the calcarenite, which extends as much as 60 m below sea level and 70 m above it (e.g., at Murphy's Haystacks).

The dunes overwhelmed the pre-existing hilly terrain developed on the crystalline rocks. The old land surface stands well below sea level in many places, but elsewhere it is roughly coincident with the modern tidal range and in other areas the old hills have been partly exhumed from beneath the calcarenite cover. Thus in the Calca area several granite inselbergs have been partly resurrected (Twidale and Campbell 1984).

Where the calcarenite extends below sea level the shoreline is, of course, developed only in it, and the profile is comparatively simple (Plate 121-4). Typically rocky promontories alternate with bay-head beaches, with huge fields of drift sand in the lee of these topographic lows. Thus south of Streaky Bay active dunes cover huge areas of the coastal zone. In addition there are climbing dunes, sand that has accumulated at the back of the beach and against (usually lower than average) cliffs to such an extent that it eventually tops the barrier and begins to migrate inland (Jennings 1967).

Stacks and sea caves are also fairly common. Narrow but remarkably smooth and flat platforms are common, particularly on the flanks of the headlands; they extend beneath the beaches of the embayments and occur at various levels, including some well above high tide level. These high platforms are due to pool weathering and are forming at the present time. At Cape Wellesley, for example, there are platforms with loose shells and salt crystals brought in on the wind up to 20 m above the intertidal platforms.

Waterloo Bay (Plate 121-5), a remarkable feature, may be a huge doline, the western wall of which has been breached by the sea, or it may be a function of attack by waves that penetrate the gap in the dune barrier. Small karst features have been noted in the old dune belt, but none even approaches the size of this circular embayment.

In many places older rocks are exposed at or near the base of the eolianite cliffs. For example, on Cape Westall the unconformity between the granitic rocks and the calcarenite falls within the present tidal range. Wave attack has stripped away the dune rock and the old calcreted regolith, exposing a shore platform of such remarkable width and smoothness, that it is called Smooth Pool. It is strewn with boulders and extends 200 m from the base of the cliffs (Twidale et al. 1977). At Point Drummond also, the base of the regolith stands within the present tidal and spray range. The weathered rock has partly been eroded to expose the weathering front as an etch surface, and most of the shore platforms in this locality are of this type. Elsewhere, as for instance near Mount Greenly, narrow modern platforms have been developed in schists and gneisses. At Talia sandstone of unknown age has been eroded to give platforms, ledges, and a sea cave.

In sheltered embayments, as, for example, south of Port Lincoln, the eolianite cliffs are subdued, and at some sheltered sandy sites (Thevenard, Streaky Bay, Smoky Bay) there are stands of mangrove (Wester 1967).

Several small islands stand off the west coast of Eyre Peninsula. Flinders Island is a low granitic rise capped by calcarenite and the islands of the Nuyts Archipelago are similar. The most spectacular are the Pearson Islands (Plate 121-6), which are literally inselbergs and consist of high domes or bornhardts of granite with an extensive suite of minor forms including sheet structure, tafoni, and flared slopes. There are patches of calcarenite and some coastal terraces suggestive of higher stands of the sea about 10 m above present.

The Gawler Craton (Fig. 121-1) extends eastward under Spencer Gulf to the west coast of Yorke Peninsula; on the exposed toe, between Point Margaret and Point Yorke, similar geological relationships and landform assemblages are found. Calcarenite cliffs with narrow but distinct intertidal platforms alternate with sandy bays, some of the latter (e.g., Maria Bay) backed by low dunes beyond which are low plains with lagoons. Where the underlying crystalline rocks are exposed, they give rise to ridges and clefts as well as platforms. Modern dunes, including climbing dunes, are again prominent. The large offshore islands, such as Althorpe Island, are bounded by vertical cliffs with excellent sections of the dune limestone.

Much of the coast of Kangaroo Island (Daily et al. 1979) is fundamentally similar to the exposed coasts already described (Plate 121-7). The remnants of huge consolidated dunes mask the underlying basement in the western and southern parts of the island, where towering cliffs dominate the scenery. The basement rocks comprise mainly folded Cambrian strata that give rise to ribbed outcrops due to the differential weathering and erosion of the constituent beds. Granite intrusions are exposed at Kirkpatrick Point, at Haslam Point, and near Cape Willoughby, giving rise to characteristic features: huge domes surmounded by large hollowed blocks (Plate 121-8) at the Remarkable Rocks (Kirkpatrick Point) and bouldery cliffs elsewhere. Corestones from the weathered granite are exposed in some of the cliffs at Windmill Bay, and many, released from their grus matrix, have been accumulated by the waves to form a spectacular boulder beach, some components of which are fretted, fitted, or imprisoned (Hills 1970).

The north coast is sheltered and dunes are less prominent (Plate 121-9); indeed the eolian forms fade in significance from west to east so that the northeast coast near Penneshaw, for example, consists of high cliffs and intervening embayments, all developed in sediments and metasediments. Where the coast turns south, at Point Marsden, where Jurassic basalts are exposed, it is sheltered from the westerlies, and the shore of Nepean Bay is low, with low dunes and sandy beaches. The nearshore areas are characterized by sand shoals and banks.

The north coast around Cape Cassini is also unusual in that the Precambrian strata are horizontal; both there and at Stokes Bay honeycomb weathering is very well developed. There are several minor coastal plains, but with the exception of Nepean Bay the north coast is steep and cliffy. There is evidence of stands of the sea some 3–5 m and 6 m above present at several sites, and some suggestion of others at 15–23 m and 30–34 m, but the evidence is equivocal.

Fleurieu Peninsula is similar to the northwest coast of Kangaroo Island. It was far inland during the Pleistocene periods of low sea level; thus no huge coastal dune accumulated. The cliffs and embayments are developed in folded Precambrian strata (Plate 121-10), and here the associated platforms are typically serrated. The south coast of the Peninsula runs almost parallel with the westerly winds and is in addition partly sheltered by Kangaroo Island. As a result, particularly toward Cape Jervis, the cliffs tend to be graded and subdued, in contrast with the rocky forms facing the gulf.

The granitic outcrops of Encounter Bay give rise to low rocky inselbergs (Granite Island, The Pages, Seal Island, Wright Island, etc.), and to rocky promontories like The Bluff (Rosetta Head).

The flat-lying Tertiary sediments of the Willunga and Noarlunga basins give rise to precipitous limestone cliffs and associated smooth platforms. Stacks are prominent, and several of the platforms, like those at Hallett Cove and Cape Jervis, are strewn with Permian glacial erratics. The beaches vary between shingle and sand and mixtures of the two. There is widespread evidence, in the form of raised beaches and perched terraces, of higher sea stands at 8 m and 40–44 m above present (Brock 1964, 1971; Twidale 1976).

The exposed coasts of the southeastern part of the state are of two types, reflecting tectonic contrasts but the preserved sequence of barrier dunes is noteworthy (Cook et al. 1977; Hossfeld 1950; Sprigg 1952).

Southeast of Kingston the land is rising and the shore is rugged. Dormant consolidated calcarenite dunes are dominant in some sectors, but in others the forms are active. Cliffs with platforms and stacks, and bays with sandy beaches are well developed here, dunes with backing lagoons elsewhere. The features are similar in all essential respects to the forms developed on the old dunes of the west coast of Eyre Peninsula, but the cliffs are lower, lagoons larger and more numerous (Plate 121-11), and the whole coast more complex, with frequent changes and variations.

The northwestern region has been subsiding, so that the sector between Port Elliot and Kingston is a low coast despite being open and based on the Padthaway Ridge or Horst. The crystallines are, with the one exception already cited, covered by sediments in the coastal zone.

A long sandy beach backed by high active foredunes separates the Coorong, noted for its modern dolomite formation (Alderman and Skinner 1957), from the open ocean (Plate 121-12). The dunes are encroaching on the lagoon, especially where there has been human interference with the vegetational cover. The only break in the beach and dune complex within this sector occurs at the Murray Mouths (Plate 121-13). These were blocked by the construction of barrages, completed in 1941, which separated the drowned estuary that is Lakes Alexandrina and Albert from the sea.

The Younghusband Peninsula forms a convenient link with the shores developed in the sheltered gulfs region of South Australia, for there too, though dune development is comparatively minor, deposition assumes a greater significance and erosional forms are on the whole subdued.

Between Port Lincoln and Whyalla the east coast of Eyre Peninsula is generally low. There are some high cliffs where especially resistant Precambrian

basement rocks intersect the coast, but most of these rocks have been eroded to form low outcrops. South of Franklin Harbor, especially, the Precambrian basement in the form of gneisses and schists is frequently exposed, but though wave quarrying produces minor shore platforms there is nothing to compare with those at Smooth Pool, for instance. The crystallines are covered by various late Cenozoic strata that have been eroded to give low cliffs, and there are occasional low dunes, as for instance at Lipson Cove. There are mangroves at Arno Bay and Tumby Bay, and they attain considerable development in Franklin Harbor, a virtually enclosed inlet bordered by sandy flats. Here as elsewhere along the South Australian coast the mangroves (*Avicennia marina var. resinifera*) stand on sandy intertidal flats in a zone extending roughly 0.6 m above and below mean sea level.

The shore northeast of Franklin Harbor is noteworthy for the calcareous cores of longitudinal desert dunes that extend beneath sea level. Elsewhere the coast comprises sandy beaches backed by low foredunes until east and northeast of Whyalla the flat-lying sediments (mainly sandstone) of the Stuart Shelf are exposed. They give rise to cliffs, some 10–12 m high, characterized by ledges. There are narrow intertidal platforms. This suite of forms extends as far north as Point Lowly, after which the cliffs are lower (4–5 m), fronted by narrow beaches and by many stands of mangroves (Plate 121-14). Shingle ridges have been traced over long sectors of the coast between Whyalla and Port Augusta (Hails and Gostin 1978). Standing some 3 m above mean sea level, they are undisturbed and of Late Pleistocene age.

Similar forms extend down the eastern side of northern Spencer Gulf though there are no Precambrian sediments exposed. Instead the cliffs are cut in late Cenozoic clay, silt, and coquinite. The mangrove stands are not as numerous or extensive on this slightly more exposed aspect, though they are well developed where the River Broughton reaches the sea near Port Pirie, and has built a considerable delta.

To the south, near Wallaroo, the Precambrian crystallines reappear, and from here to Port Victoria the coast is similar to that developed on southeastern Eyre Peninsula, with crystalline rocks exposed in the intertidal zone and forming crude platforms, but with low cliffs surmounted by dunes developed in Cenozoic materials.

At Point Brown, for instance, there are low vertical cliffs in Pleistocene oölitic limestone and with platforms developed not only in the intertidal zone but also 3–4 m higher in the spray zone (Crocker 1946*b*). The shore between Port Victoria and Point Turton is flat and sandy, with long beaches backed by dunes. In the south especially, the dunes separate lagoons from the open sea, and the same applies to the south coast (e.g., at Foul Bay) between Point Yorke and Point Moorowie. North of Point Moorowie as far north as Ardrossan the shore is marked by low but steep cliffs cut in Tertiary strata. At Black Point a cuspate foreland carries well-developed foredunes. From Ardrossan to the head of the Gulf and then southward on the eastern side of the embayment, the coast is similar to that described from northern Spencer Gulf. There are low cliffs cut in late Cenozoic strata, sandy beaches, and many stands of mangrove (e.g., at Price, Middle Beach, Port Gawler, and Port Adelaide).

South of Port Adelaide to Marino, the shore takes the form of a long continuous sandy beach backed by foredunes. Several sets of such dunes extend back from the beach and relic mangroves beneath the sand at Glenelg, but essentially, this is a simple sandy beach interrupted only by the outflow of the Torrens and Sturt through the artificial cuts near Grange at Patawalonga (Plate 121-15).

C. R. TWIDALE

REFERENCES

Alderman, A. R., and C. W. Skinner, 1957, Dolomite sedimentation in the South-East of South Australia, *Am. Jour. Sci.* **255:**561–567.

Bauer, F. H., 1959, The Regional Geography of Kangaroo Island, *South Australia,* 2 vols., Ph.D. thesis, Australian National University, Canberra.

Bauer, F. H., 1961, Chronic problems of terrace study in southern Australia, *Zeitschr. Geomorphologie Suppl.* **3:**57–72.

Brock, E. J., 1964, The Denudation Chronology of the Fleurieu Peninsula, M.A. thesis, University of Adelaide.

Brock, E. J., 1971, The denudation chronology of the Fleurieu Peninsula, South Australia, *Royal Soc. South Australia Trans.* **95:**85–94.

Cook, P. J., J. B. Colwell, J. B. Firman, J. M. Lindsay, D. A. Schwebel, and C. C. Van der Borch, 1977, The late Cainozoic sequence of southeast South Australia and Pleistocene sea-level changes, *Australia Bureau Min. Resources Jour.* **2:**81–88.

Crawford, A. R., 1965, *The Geology of Yorke Peninsula,* Geol. Surv. South Australia Bull. 39.

Crocker, R. L., 1946*a, Post-Miocene Climatic and Geological History and Its Significance in Relation to the Genesis of the Major Soil Types of South Australia.* CSIRO Bull. 193.

Crocker, R. L., 1946*b,* Notes on a recent raised beach at Point Brown, Yorke Peninsula, South Australia, *Royal Soc. South Australia Trans.* **70:**108–109.

Daily, B., A. R. Milnes, C. R. Twidale, and J. A. Bourne, 1971, Geology and geomorphology, in Natural History of Kangaroo Island, M. J. Tyler, C. R. Twidale and J. K. King, eds., Royal Society, Adelaide, pp. 1–38.

Hails, J. R., and V. A. Gostin, 1978, Stranded beach ridges, Upper Spencer Gulf, South Australia: evidence for high wave energy dissipation during the Late Pleistocene, *Royal Soc. South Australia Trans.* **102:** 169–173.

Hills, E. S., 1970, Fitting, fretting and imprisoned boulders, Nature **226**(5243):345–347.

Hossfeld, P. S., 1950, Late Cainozoic history of the Southeast of South Australia, *Royal Soc. South Australia Trans.* **73:**232–279.

Jennings, J. N., 1963, Some geomorphological problems of the Nullarbor Plain, *Royal Soc. South Australia Trans.* **87:**41–62.

Jennings, J. N., 1967, Cliff top dunes, *Australian Geog. Stud.* **5:**40–49.

Sprigg, R. C., 1952, *The Geology of the South-East Province, South Australia, with Special Reference to Quaternary Coast-line Migrations and Modern Beach Development,* Geol. Surv. South Australia Bull. 29.

Twidale, C. R., 1971, *Structural Landforms,* Australian National University Press, Canberra.

Twidale, C. R., 1976, Geomorphological evolution, in Natural History of the Adelaide Region, C. R. Twidale, M. J. Tyler, and B. P. Webb, eds., Royal Society, Adelaide, pp. 43–59.

Twidale, C. R., and E. M. Campbell, 1984, Murphy's Haystacks, Eyre Peninsula, South Australia, *Royal Soc. South Australia Trans.* in press.

Twidale, C. R., J. A. Bourne, and N. Twidale, 1977, Shore platforms and sealevel changes in the Gulfs region of South Australia, *Royal Soc. South Australia Trans.* **101:**63–74.

Twidale, C. R., B. Daily, and J. B. Firman, 1967, Eustatic and climatic history of the Adelaide area, South Australia: a discussion, *Jour. Geol.* **75:**237–242.

Von der Borch, C. C., 1968, Southern Australia submarine canyons: their distribution and ages, *Marine Geology* **6:**267–279.

Ward, W. T., 1965, Eustatic and climatic history of the Adelaide area, South Australia, *Jour. Geol.* **73:**592–602.

Ward, W. T., and R. W. Jessup, 1965, Changes in sealevel in southern Australia, Nature **205**(4973):791–792.

Wester, L. L., 1967, The Distribution of the Mangrove in South Australia, B.A. thesis, University of Adelaide.

Plate 121-1. From the Victorian border to the Murray Mouths, Quaternary outcrops extend unbroken, save for these low whaleback boulders of Early Paleozoic granite exposed on the beach near Taratap. Behind the modern bank of foredunes is a coastal plain or swale that is delineated on its inland side by an abandoned dune ridge or range (photo courtesy of South Australian government).

Plate 121-2. All of the consolidated Pleistocene coastal dunes have been to a greater or lesser degree eroded by the sea, but at some sites, as here at Pondalowie Bay, on the "toe" of Yorke Peninsula, the gentle backslopes are preserved, though the steeper seaward faces have been replaced by precipitous cliffs (photo by C. R. Twidale).

Plate 121-3. The Bunda Cliffs, seen here near the South Australia–Western Australia border, show the hard white Nullarbor Limestone overlain by the darker Wilson Bluff Limestone, as well as the influence of prominent vertical joints (photo by S. Goode).

Plate 121-4. Steep cliffs developed in Pleistocene calcarenite or eolianite dominate the coastal scenery in many parts of South Australia, but particularly on the west coast of Eyre Peninsula, as for instance near Point Labatt (photo courtesy of South Australian government).

Plate 121-5. Waterloo Bay is a large inlet on the west coast of the Eyre Peninsula where, for reasons that are not known, the barrier of cemented Pleistocene dunes was breached. The headland beyond the Bay is Cape Finniss, with Waldegrave Island beyond (photo by C. R. Twidale).

Plate 121-6. The Pearson Islands are a group of granite outcrops that are, literally, inselbergs. This view, taken from the peak on North Section of Pearson Island, shows Middle and South sections in right and left middle distance, with the Veteran Isles beyond (center) and Dorothée on right horizon (photo by K. P. Phillips).

Plate 121-7. These eolianite cliffs and islands are exposed along the south coast of Kangaroo Island, but are typical of much of the west coast of Eyre Peninsula, the sole of Yorke Peninsula, and to a lesser degree (because there the cliffs are not as high) the Lower South East (photo courtesy of South Australian government).

Plate 121-8. Remarkable Rocks is a granite dome exposed on the south coast of Kangaroo Island. It is partly buried by the eolianite that dominates this and other coasts, and consists of a bare dome with well-developed gutters or *Granitkarren*. A group of large residual blocks with deep and intricate tafoni is preserved on the crest of the larger form, and various boulders and blocks located on the flanks of the feature are characterized by quite well-developed flared slopes (photo by C. R. Twidale).

Plate 121-9. On the north coast of Kangaroo Island the eolianite is thin or absent, and the cliffs eroded in folded Cambrian metasediments are more subdued than on exposed coasts (photo courtesy of South Australian government).

Plate 121-10. Folded Precambrian strata exposed on the eastern side of Gulf St. Vincent just south of Adelaide give rise to steep cliffs and, where worn back by the sea, to beautifully developed serrated shore platforms. The Port Stanvac oil refinery can be seen in the middle distance (photo courtesy of South Australian government).

Plate 121-11. Lake Fellmongery, near Robe in the Upper South East district, is one of several lagoons formed when shallow embayments and valley floors were isolated from the sea by the formation of coastal foredunes in Pleistocene times. The low cliffs are of the cemented eolianite (photo courtesy of South Australian government).

Plate 121-12. The Younghusband Peninsula is a complex coastal foredune fronted by a spectacular beach that extends unbroken for some 200 km. Individual dunes developed on the peninsula are extending inland and encroaching on the Coorong, a saline lagoon noted for its modern dolomite formation, and due to the subsidence of the lower Murray valley. The Coorong is therefore a drowned interdune corridor or swale, and lakes Albert and Alexandrina are inundated portions of the lower Murray valley (photo courtesy of South Australian government).

Plate 121-13. The Murray Mouths have been blocked by various barrages completed in 1941 to prevent the ingress of salt water into the Murray at times when the river level was low (photo courtesy of South Australian government).

Plate 121-14. The shores of northern Spencer Gulf are low and sandy, and commonly support stands of mangrove. The sector seen here is on the western side of the gulf, where the shore is backed by flat-lying Precambrian sediments that have been dissected to give plateau forms (photo courtesy of South Australian government).

Plate 121-15. Patawalonga Lake, in Adelaide's southwestern suburbs, is used as a marina. In an effort to keep clear the channel linking the lake and the sea, a groin has been built. Beach drift is northward, and sand has accumulated on its southern side (right), but the beach to the north, in the lee of the obstacle, has been depleted with serious effects, both for it and for the related dunes (photo courtesy of South Australian government).

122. WESTERN AUSTRALIA

Western Australia covers an area of 2,500,000 km² extending from latitude 13°30′ S to 35°08′ S and from longitude 113°09′ E to 129° E (Australian Bureau of Statistics 1980). The 12,500 km coastline comprises one-third of the total coastline of Australia and includes a vast range of coastal environments. Western Australia has entirely different climates in its northern and southern parts, while in the central region there is a gradual change from the tropical climate of the north to the Mediterranean climate of the south. Weather systems are largely controlled by movement of an anticyclonic wind belt that brings easterly winds to the northern half of the state and westerlies to the south. Prevailing wind patterns in the north are disrupted by late summer tropical cyclones, while in the south, midlatitude depressions occur during winter (Gentilli 1971).

Landforms of the coast reflect the dominant wind, wave, current, and tidal processes and their interaction with the varied basement geology. Western Australia is largely made up of Precambrian igneous, metamorphic, and sedimentary rock. The remainder of the state consists of younger Phanerozoic sedimentary rocks, mainly sandstones and limestones, that flank the older rocks (Geological Survey of Western Australia 1975). In places sedimentary rocks extend offshore as a wide continental shelf. Coastal landforms of the Kimberley and South Coast are strongly controlled by the geological structure of resistant basement rocks. Elsewhere structural control is weaker, and wind, wave, and tidal processes determine gross coastal configuration.

Coastal processes vary with the prevailing and dominant weather conditions, coastal aspect, and changes in the tidal regime. A southwesterly swell generated in the Southern Ocean affects most of the coast. As a result the south coast is subject to a moderate to heavy southwesterly swell; the west coast to a moderate southwesterly swell; and the north coast to a low, refracted westerly swell (Radok 1976). Waves generated by tropical cyclones, inter-anticyclonic fronts and depressions, midlatitude depressions, and sea breezes are superimposed on the prevailing swell so that the wave regime varies markedly for different parts of the coast. In general, littoral currents transport sediment from the southwest corner of the state toward Carnarvon in the north and east toward Esperance. On the northwest coast sediment transport is dominated by tidal currents. Apart from the tidally dominated northern coasts the coastline of Western Australia is characterized by zeta-form embayments of various sizes. North of Cape Leeuwin these face either north or northeast, whereas east of Cape Leeuwin they generally face southeast. In all, eight coastal regions are delineated on the basis of geological structure, dominant processes, and landforms (Fig 122-1). These are described in turn from north to south. The nomenclature applied to each region is consistent with that given to the major tectonic units as identified by the Geological Survey of Western Australia (1975), with the exception of the West and South Coasts.

KIMBERLEY COAST: WESTERN AUSTRALIAN BORDER TO CAPE LEVEQUE

The Kimberley region is largely composed of Proterozoic, crystalline volcanic and sedimentary

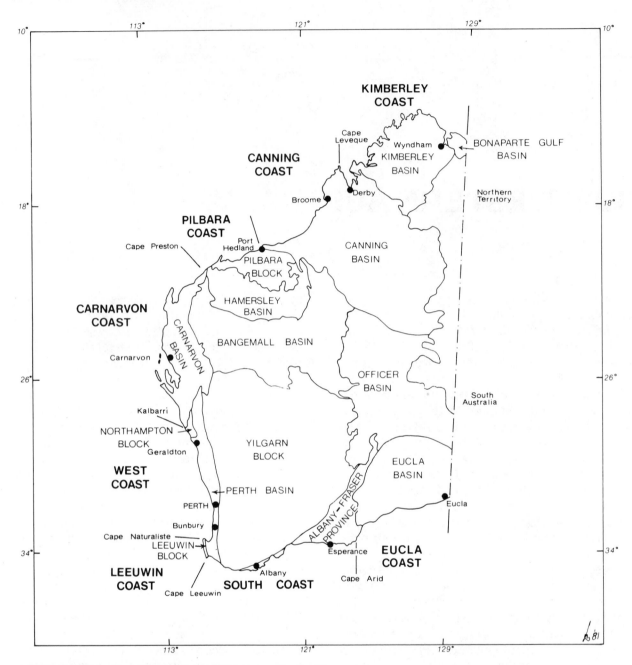

Figure 122-1. Coastal regions of Western Australia.

rocks with strong northwest- and secondary northeast-trending joints and fractures that control the topography (Fig. 122-2). Coastal processes are characterized by a prevailing low westerly swell, offshore winds, and very high tidal range. The semidiurnal spring tide range is over 7 m. Tropical cyclones, which generally move in a southwest direction, parallel to the coast, periodically generate strong onshore winds and high wave conditions.

Coastal configuration is determined by the structural grain of the hinterland. In the west there is an irregular ria coastline with rivers debouching into broad gulfs and narrow inlets. This coast has deeply incised bays, precipitous rocky headlands, and numerous archipelagoes and reefs. The east coast is linear and parallel to the major northwest joint pattern, with comparatively few inshore islands. River-mouth sediment distribution in the region is dominated by

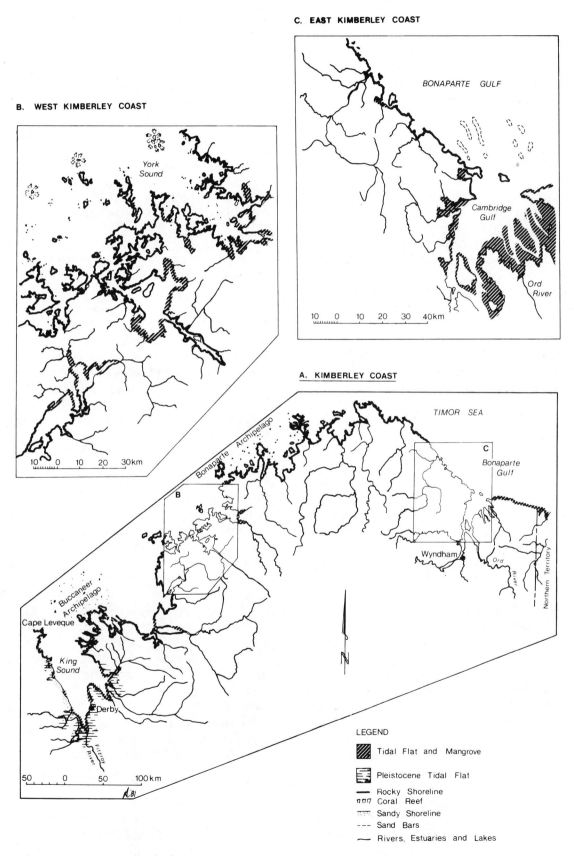

C. EAST KIMBERLEY COAST

BONAPARTE GULF

Cambridge Gulf

Ord River

10 0 10 20 30 40km

B. WEST KIMBERLEY COAST

York Sound

10 0 10 20 30km

A. KIMBERLEY COAST

TIMOR SEA

Bonaparte Archipelago

Bonaparte Gulf

C

B

Wyndham

Ord River

Northern Territory

Buccaneer Archipelago

Cape Leveque

King Sound

Derby

Fitzroy River

50 0 50 100 km

N

LEGEND

Tidal Flat and Mangrove

Pleistocene Tidal Flat

Rocky Shoreline

Coral Reef

Sandy Shoreline

Sand Bars

Rivers, Estuaries and Lakes

Figure 122-2. Kimberly Coast.

onshore-offshore tidal currents and periodic storm wave activity that results in the formation of mangrove swamps (Thom et al. 1975); discontinuous tidal flats (Plate 122-1), cheniers, and deltas. The Ord River forms the largest delta (Coleman and Wright 1975).

CANNING COAST: CAPE LEVEQUE TO PORT HEDLAND

The Canning Basin is occupied by horizontally bedded Phanerozoic sedimentary rocks, mainly sandstones and limestones overlain for the most part by low longitudinal dunes of the Great Sandy Desert (Fig. 122-3). Sediments along the Kimberley contact are uplifted and folded along a northwesterly axis. Although coastal processes are similar to those for the Kimberley Coast, the more open sections are subject to some sediment transfer in weak littoral currents generated by westerly sea breezes. The coastline is dominated by Eighty Mile Beach, a long arcuate, quartzose sandy beach, backed by a Holocene beach ridge sequence that broadens in a northeasterly direction. The modern beach ridges overlie abandoned Pleistocene tidal flats. To the southwest, the beach merges with the De Grey River delta, a major lobate structure extending approximately 20 km beyond the general trend of the coast (Plate 122-2). This is the only instance in Western Australia where fluvial deposition occurs at such a scale on the open coast. To the northeast, Eighty Mile Beach gives way to a less regular coastline where sedimentary bluffs alternate with extensive tidal flats.

PILBARA COAST: PORT HEDLAND TO CAPE PRESTON

The Pilbara Block and Hammersley Basin are composed of Archean and Proterozoic rocks including granites, metasediments, and volcanics. Folded metasediments and volcanics trend northeast on the northern margin of the block. Coastal processes are once again similar to those for the Kimberley region. However, this is the impact zone for the majority of tropical cyclones crossing the Western Australian coast. Strong storm surges, high wave activity, and exceptional heavy rainfall in the inland catchments that feed the De Grey, Fortescue, Ashburton, and Gascoyne rivers are associated with these events. Otherwise, the coast is affected by westerly sea breezes and a weak, refracted northwest swell. Basement rocks outcrop as rocky headlands and islands of the Dampier Archipelago (Fig. 122-4, Plate 122-3). East of Burrup Peninsula the coast is dominated by two large zeta-form embayments separated by Cape Lambert. Broad tidal flats, cheniers, and storm ridges form the shoreline within the embayments. The eastern embayment is characterized by an exceptionally broad band of tidal flats and a chain of elongate islands composed of sandy calcarenite. The islands are remnants of a large zeta-form Pleistocene embayment. Holocene tidal flats overlie extensive relict Pleistocene tidal formations landward of the islands.

CARNARVON COAST: CAPE PRESTON TO KALBARRI

The Carnarvon Basin is the northern of two Phanerozoic sedimentary basins that run parallel to the west coast of Western Australia for 1,600 km. Along the coast, sediments of the Carnarvon Basin are horizontally bedded in the north, folded into large north-northeast trending anticlines in the west, and uplifted on the southern margin where they abut the Precambrian Northampton Block. In conformity with the change of aspect at North West Cape (Fig. 122-5), the dominant coastal processes vary southward as the open coast becomes subject to the prevailing south-southwest Southern Ocean swells and a strong southerly wind wave regime. East of the cape the sheltered coast is subject to a refracted northwest swell and weak offshore winds. The spring tidal range diminishes from 5 m in the north to about 2 m at Carnarvon.

The eastern shore of Exmouth Gulf comprises a broad expanse of tidal flats and fringing mangroves. South of the cape the shoreline is backed by high cliffs cut into folded Tertiary sediment. A Pleistocene coral reef occurs at the base of the cliffs. Offshore a modern fringing barrier reef, Ningaloo Reef, extends over 300 km along the coast, from False Island Point to Pont Quobba. Coral sands accumulate behind the reef and in small embayments where beach ridge and dune complexes have formed (Plate 122-4). Farther north at Carnarvon, the Gascoyne River forms a lobate delta that lies immediately north of an abandoned Pleistocene delta (Johnson 1974). Pleistocene limestones were formed at the extremity of a northerly sediment transport system that operated along the west coast of Western Australia during the Pleistocene. Spectacular cliffs, ranging up to 100 m high, characterize the

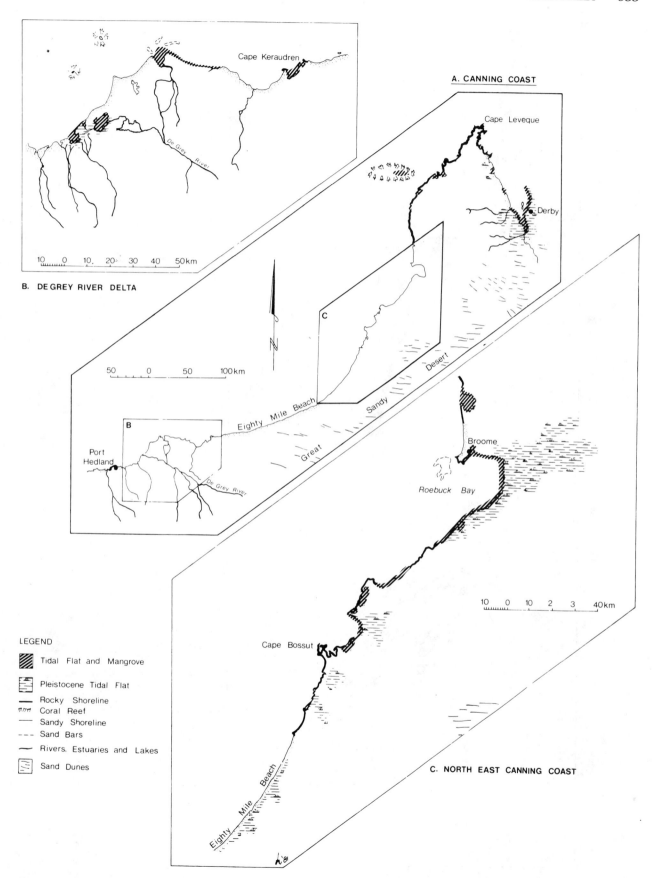

Figure 122-3. Canning Coast.

934

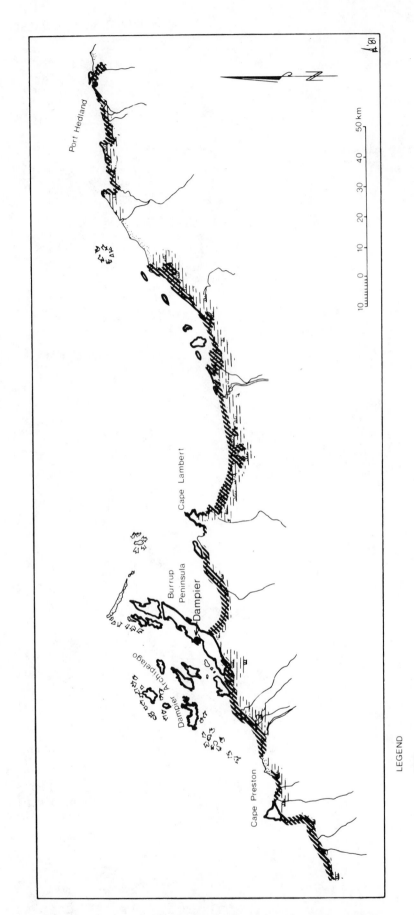

LEGEND

▨   Tidal Flat and Mangrove

    Pleistocene Tidal Flat

—   Rocky Shoreline

    Coral Reef

    Sandy Shoreline

⁓   Rivers, Estuaries and Lakes

Figure 122-4. Pilbara Coast.

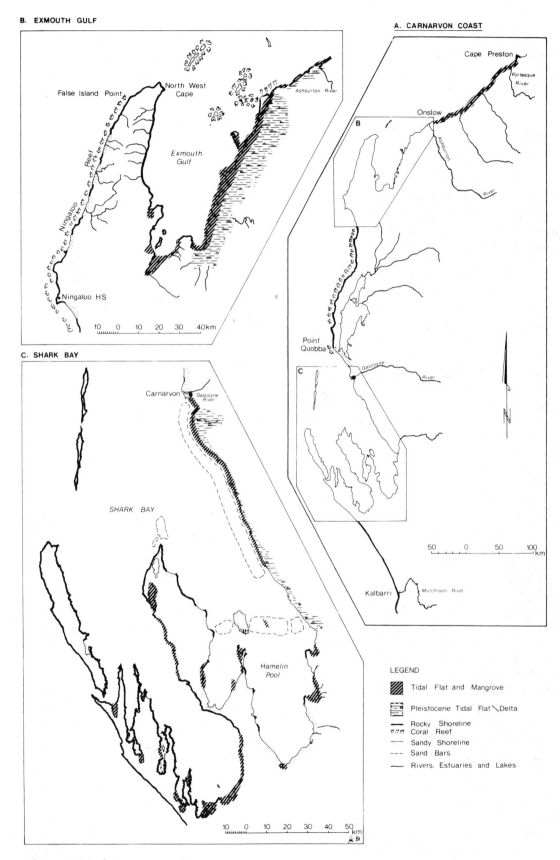

Figure 122-5. Carnarvon Coast.

exposed seaward shoreline. Shark Bay is especially important as a major region of carbonate sedimentation and for the modern occurrence of stromatolites in the hypersaline waters of Hamlin Pool (Logan et al. 1974).

THE WEST COAST: KALBARRI TO CAPE NATURALISTE

Phanerozoic sediments of the Perth Basin provide a basement to Quaternary coastal sand dune sequences that include lithified, Pleistocene calcarenities and unconsolidated Holocene calcareous sands (Semeniuk and Meagher 1981). Onshore and offshore ridges of limestone run subparallel to the present coast, outcropping as dunes, chains of reefs, and offshore islands (Fig. 122-6). By sheltering the mainland beaches from the direct southwesterly swell, these reefs and islands provide structural control for the accumulation of Holocene sediments in complex beach ridge sequences forming cuspate forelands and tombolos—for example, Jurien Bay. Pleistocene and Holocene dune sequences incorporate estuaries and extensive, elongate en echelon coastal lagoons and lakes (Plate 122-5).

Coastal processes strongly reflect the influence of the prevailing winds generated by anticyclonic weather systems and midlatitude depressions. The winds vary from direct southerlies north of Lancelin through southwesterlies in the Perth metropolitan area to westerlies south of Rockingham. The wind pattern varies systematically with north–south seasonal migration of the anticyclones. In the summer months a very strong, locally confined southwesterly sea breeze produces short choppy seas and drives a strong northerly littoral drift. Midlatitude depressions produce strong west to northwesterly seas in early to midwinter. The predominant wave regime, also generated by anticyclonic weather systems and midlatitude depressions, includes southwesterly to northwesterly waves superimposed on a prevailing southwesterly swell. Barometric pressure changes produce sea-level fluctuations of larger amplitude than the local spring tide range, which seldom exceeds 1 m.

North of Fremantle low, cliffed bluffs with extensive rock platforms and reefs alternate with sandy bays and beaches. On more exposed parts of the coast, sporadic outcrops of beach rock occur (Russell and McIntire 1965). Holocene sands frequently form large parabolic dune sequences

and transgressive sand sheets overlying similar massive Pleistocene landforms. South of Fremantle limestone outcrops occasionally interrupt long sandy beaches in zeta-form embayments. The dominant headland is Cape Naturaliste, which shelters Geographe Bay. On a smaller scale a columnar basalt headland at Bunbury and a limestone headland at Manudrah control smaller, shallow embayments. The sandy beaches alternate seasonally between a low-energy, summer condition with cusps to a higher-energy, rhythmic morphology with rip currents in winter (Clarke and Eliot, 1983).

Other features of the coast include the coral reefs and islands of the Abrolhos, a major Holocene sediment accumulation at Rockingham (Woods and Searle 1983), and suites of rock platforms on Point Peron and Rottnest Island (Fairbridge 1950; Playford and Leech 1977). These, and the extensive dune sequences (McArthur and Bettenay 1974) of the Swan Coastal Plain, provide a range of evidence for changes in Quaternary sea level.

LEEUWIN COAST: CAPE NATURALISTE TO CAPE LEEUWIN

The southwest corner of Western Australia is defined by the north–south Leeuwin Block composed of resistant, high-grade metamorphic rocks, which shelter Phanerozoic sediments of the southern Perth Basin. The block is the primary divide for coastal processes in southwestern Australia. It parts the prevailing southwesterly swell so that longshore sediment transport is northward from Cape Naturaliste and eastward from Cape Leeuwin. The Leeuwin Block has acted through geological time as the island front of an immense tombolo separating the massive Geographe and Flinders embayments to north and south. In contrast to the low energy conditions of Geographe Bay, Flinders Bay bears the full impact of both southwesterly swells and wind waves.

The western margin of the Leeuwin Block is exposed to heavy southwesterly swell and dominant westerly winds (Plate 122-6). The coast is rocky, with nearshore reefs and cliffs with small sandy bays where the cliff line is broken (Fig. 122-7). To the north the sandy bays are zeta-form and open to the northwesterlies. To the south, sandy beaches are more common. Transgressive sand sheets and nested parabolic dunes, formed by the prevailing westerly winds, mantle the basement rocks.

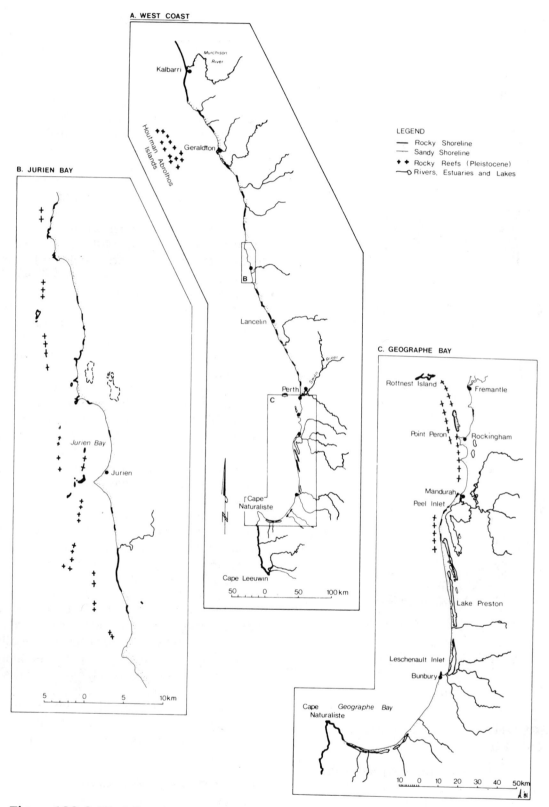

Figure 122-6. West Coast.

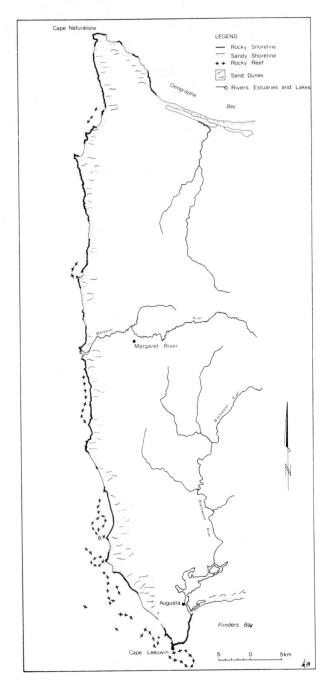

Figure 122-7. Leeuwin Coast.

THE SOUTH COAST: CAPE LEEUWIN TO CAPE ARID

High-grade metamorphic and granite Precambrian rocks of the Albany-Fraser Province form an irregular basement along the South Coast. Basement depressions are partially filled with Tertiary and Quaternary sediments, forming flat coastal plains. Where the basement projects, it forms rugged hills and offshore islands (Fig.

122-8). Structures in the basement rocks trend southeasterly to the west, and southwesterly to the east. Numerous short south-flowing rivers drain the hinterland and debouche into shallow coastal lagoons, estuaries, or rocky inlets (Hodgkin and Lenanton 1980). The estuaries and lagoons are impounded by large Pleistocene dunes and plugged by Holocene sand bars. The lagoons are flushed at irregular intervals, annually in the west and less frequently in the east. Many of the river channels can be traced to submarine canyons on the margin of the continental shelf (von der Borch 1968).

Westerly winds associated with anticyclonic weather systems and midlatitude depressions dominate. The latter are particularly common during the winter months. A variable southwest to southeast onshore wind wave regime is superimposed on a persistent, high-energy southwesterly swell. The coast receives the full impact of swell and wind waves. There is a net easterly littoral drift. The tidal range is less than 1 m.

Flinders Bay is a large southeast-facing, zeta-form embayment, pivoted on Cape Leeuwin and cut in soft sediments of the Perth Basin west of Point D'Entrecasteaux. East of this point the basement is exposed to form the rocky headlands of an unbroken series of east-facing zeta-form bays, which are frequently cut into Pleistocene calcarenite dunes. Extensive cliffs, rock platforms, and nearshore reefs occur along the exposed section of the embayments. In the vicinity of Esperance, basement rocks outcrop as the Archipelago of the Recherche. Here the coast is characterized by arcuate sandy beaches between rocky headlands (Plate 122-7).

Shoreline morphology on the open sandy beaches of the South Coast varies between rhythmic patterns incorporating the rip currents and energy-dissipative, barred beaches: spatially with variation in wave energy distribution along the embayments, and seasonally with changes in the wave regime. Reef gaps frequently fix the position of rip currents. On the updrift ends of the embayments, where beaches are exposed to the southwesterlies, massive parabolic dune sequences are formed.

EUCLA COAST: CAPE ARID TO WESTERN AUSTRALIAN BORDER

The Eucla Basin is occupied by Lower Miocene limestone forming a flat plateau cliffed on its

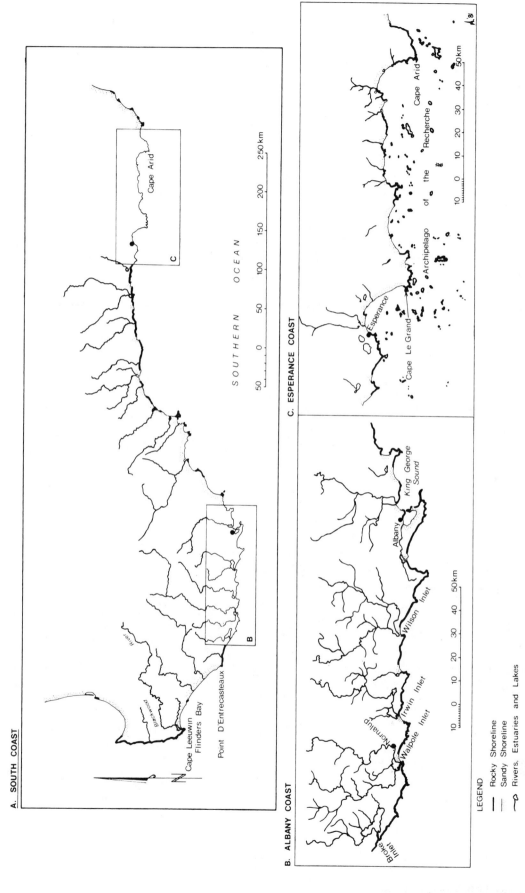

Figure 122-8. South Coast.

A. SOUTH COAST

B. ALBANY COAST

C. ESPERANCE COAST

SOUTHERN OCEAN

Cape Arid

Cape Leeuwin
Flinders Bay
Point D'Entrecasteaux

Esperance
Cape Le Grand
Archipelago of the Recherche
Cape Arid

Broke Inlet
Nornalup
Walpole Inlet
Irwin Inlet
Wilson Inlet
Albany
King George Sound

LEGEND

—— Rocky Shoreline
| Sandy Shoreline
∿ Rivers, Estuaries and Lakes

939

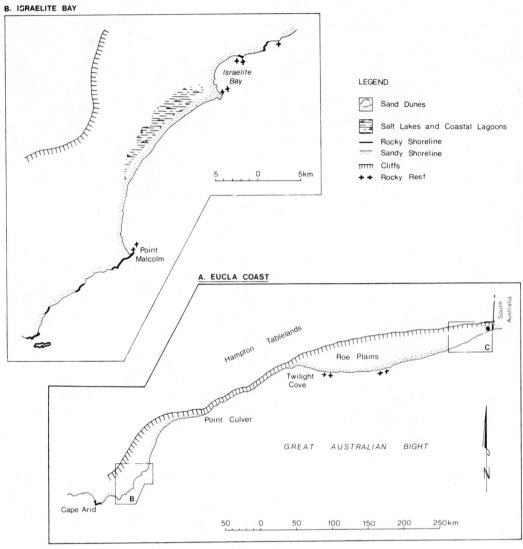

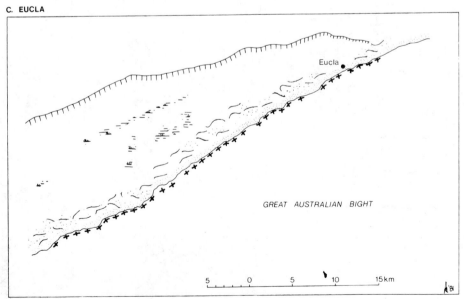

Figure 122-9. Eucla Coast.

southern margin (Lowry 1971). Spectacular sea cliffs occur where the plateau margin forms the coast between Point Culver and Twilight Cove (Plate 122-8). Elsewhere a relict cliff line is fronted by Pleistocene sediments (Fig. 122-9). These form low-lying coastal plains near Israelite Bay and between Twilight Cove and Eucla. The wind, wave, and tidal regimes of this region are similar to those of the South Coast. Winds are dominantly from southern quadrants, and strong southwesterly swell is refracted around Cape Arid. Sediment has accumulated in a Holocene barrier system in the vicinity of Israelite Bay. On the Roe Plains a Pleistocene shoreline sequence is overlain by Holocene sand dunes along its seaward margin. Near Eucla an extensive mobile sand sheet and active barchan dunes are covering much of the plain.

P. J. WOODS
M. J. WEBB
I. G. ELIOT

REFERENCES

Australian Bureau of Statistics, 1980, *Western Australian Year Book* No. 18 — 1980, Government Printer, Western Australia, Wembley.

Coleman, J. M., and L. D. Wright, 1975, Modern river deltas: variability of processes and sand bodies, in M. L. Broussard, ed., *Deltas: Models for Exploration*, Houston Geological Society, pp. 99–150.

Fairbridge, R. W., 1950, The geology and geomorphology of Point Peron, Western Australia, *Royal Soc. Western Australia Jour.* **34**(3):35–72.

Gentilli, J., ed., 1971, *Climates of Australia and New Zealand*, Elsevier, Amsterdam.

Geological Survey of Western Australia, 1975, *The Geology of Western Australia*, Western Australia Geol. Survey Mem. 2, Government Printer, Western Australia, Wembley.

Hodgkin, E. P., and R. C. Lenanton, 1980, Estuaries and coastal lagoons of southwestern Australia, in B. Nielson and A. Cronin, eds., *Nutrient Enrichment in Estuaries*, Humana Press, Clifton, New Jersey.

Johnson, D., 1974, *Sedimentation in the Gascoyne River Delta, Western Australia*, Ph.D. thesis, Department of Geology, University of Western Australia.

Logan, B. W., J. F. Read, G. M. Hagan, P. Hoffman, R. G. Brown, P. J. Woods, and C. D. Gebelein, 1974, *Evolution and Diagenesis of Quaternary Carbonate Sequences, Shark Bay, Western Australia*, Am. Assoc. Petroleum Geologists Mem. 22.

Lowry, D. C., 1971, *Explanatory Notes on the Eucla – Noonaera Geological Sheet, Western Australia*, Australian Bureau of Mineral Resources, Canberra.

McArthur, W. M., and E. Bettenay, 1974, *The Development and Distribution of the Soils of the Swan Coastal Plain, Western Australia*, Soil Publication No. 16, C.S.I.R.O., Melbourne (second printing).

Playford, P. E., and R. E. J. Leech, 1977, *Geology and Hydrology of* Rottnest Island, Western Australia Geol. Survey Rept. 6, Government Printer, Western Australia.

Radok, R., 1976, *Australian Coasts*, Rigby, Perth.

Russell, R. J., and W. G. McIntire, 1965, Southern hemisphere beach rock, *Geog. Rev.* **55:**17–45.

Semeniuk, V., and T. Meagher, 1981, Calcrete in Quaternary Coastal dunes in southwestern Australia: a capillary-rise phenomenon associated with plants, *Jour. Sed. Petrology* **51**(1):47–67.

Thom, B. G., L. D. Wright, and J. M. Coleman, 1975, Mangrove ecology and deltaic-estuarine geomorphology: Cambridge Gulf-Ord River, Western Australia, *Jour. Ecology* **63**(1):203–232.

von der Borch, C. C., 1968, Submarine canyons of southern Australia; their distribution and ages, *Marine Geology* **6:**267–279.

Plate 122-1. Tidal flats and mangroves at Derby on the Kimberley Coast. Despite construction of a 1.5 km causeway the jetty becomes fully exposed at low tide. The scalloped shoreline in the background is formed when continental sand dunes intersect the coast (photo courtesy of Department of Lands and Surveys, Western Australia).

Plate 122-2. LANDSAT image of the De Grey River delta on the Canning Coast. The small, north-trending, linear island west of the delta is man-made. It is a spoil island formed after the channel into Port Hedland harbor was dredged to allow access for bulk iron on ships (photo courtesy of Department of Lands and Surveys, Western Australia).

Plate 122-3. Salt and iron ore loading facilities on islands of the Dampier Archipelago. In the background a third wharf extends seaward from Burrup Peninsula, the major salient of the Pilbara Coast (photo by R. Garwood).

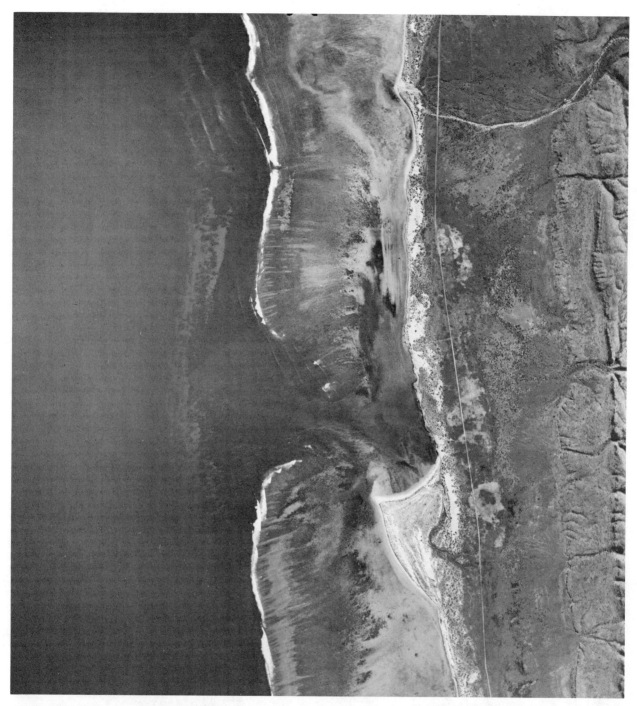

Plate 122-4. Part of the Ningaloo Reef, which extends for 300 km along the central Carnarvon Coast. Here the reef lies 1 km offshore with modern coral sands accumulating in the protected waters behind. Inland is the dissected terrain cut into uplifted Tertiary sediments (photo courtesy of Department of Lands and Surveys, Western Australia).

Plate 122-5. Lake Preston, one of a series of parallel elongate coastal lakes between Pleistocene dune ridges. The seaward ridge is overlain by Holocene dune sands. The sequence is typical of the extensive Quaternary dune landforms of the Swan Coastal Plain on the West Coast (photo by I. Eliot).

Plate 122-6. The Cape Leeuwin lighthouse is located on granite gneiss, which forms Cape Leeuwin, the southwestern extremity of Western Australia (photo courtesy of West Australian Newspapers Ltd.).

Plate 122-7. Cape Le Grande National Park, east of Esperance on the South Coast of Western Australia. On the coast, granitic headlands alternate with quartzose sandy beaches. Islands of the Archipelago of the Recherche are visible in the background. A flat low-lying coastal plain extends inland (photo courtesy of National Parks Authority of Western Australia).

Plate 122-8. Massive limestone cliffs ranging up to 100 m in height extend for over 150 km between Point Culver and Twilight Cove on the Eucla Coast (photo courtesy of West Australian Newspaper Ltd.).

123. NORTHERN TERRITORY

The Northern Territory coast forms a broad peninsula between latitudes 11° S and 16½° S and faces the Gulf of Carpentaria to the east, the Arafura Sea to the north, and the Bonaparte Gulf to the west (Fig. 123-1). A reasonable estimate for the length of the mainland coast is 5,100 km; the

148 offshore islands larger than 1 km² add a further 2,100 km (Galloway and Bahr 1979).

Bedrock in the eastern half is moderately folded, resistant Precambrian sediments. In the center around Darwin more highly folded ancient sediments, metamorphics, and granites occur and

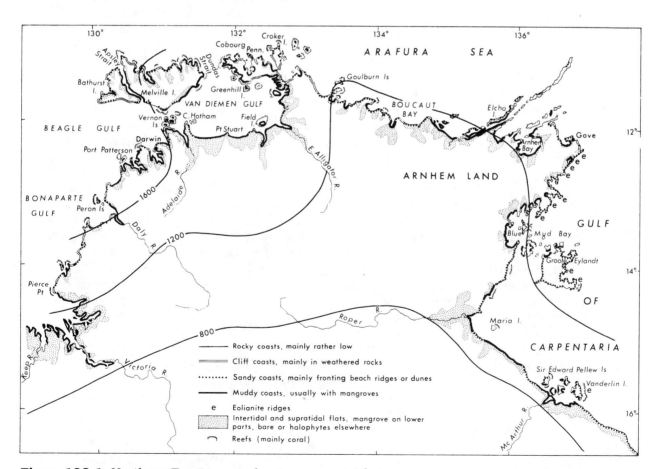

Figure 123-1. Northern Territory: predominant coastal features.

are overlain by weaker Mesozoic and Cenozoic sandstones and claystones on the peninsulas and islands to the north. In the west, Paleozoic sandstones and siltstones dip gently westward under patches of Mesozoic sediments. Much of the area has a cover of Cenozoic terrestrial sediments or deep weathering profiles that pass below sea level at many places. The coast is bordered by wide shelves with low relief of subaerial origin thinly mantled by clayey sands and silts inshore (Van Andel and Veevers 1967). Evidence exists for Pleistocene low sea levels down to −200 m (Jongsma 1974).

The climate is tropical, with a rainy season from November to April in the north and northwest, where mean annual precipitation is 1,400–1,800 mm. In the southeast and southwest rainfall is less (800–1,100 mm) and the rainy season shorter. Winds in the dry season are southeasterly and generally 10–30 km/hr. In the rainy season weaker westerly and northerly winds predominate, but occasional tropical cyclones bring high winds and intense rains. Mean monthly air temperatures at Darwin range from 25° C in July to 30° C in November.

Tidal range (mean spring) is 5.0–5.5 m southwest of Darwin, 2.5–3.5 m in Van Diemen Gulf, and 3.5–4.5 m along the north coast (Easton 1970). In the Gulf of Carpentaria it is 0.2–1.5 m, but the ranges between highest and lowest tides over a lunar month are 0.5–1.5 m greater. Tidal bores up to several meters high occur on the Victoria and Adelaide rivers, while on low coasts storm surges up to 9 m have been reported. Average wave energies are low. Currents flow east to west in the dry season but weaker currents from the west and southwest predominate inshore in the wet season and probably have more significance for sediment transport because rivers are then in flood. Sediment transport in the western Gulf of Carpentaria is from south to north. Water temperatures are around 32° C in the wet season and 27° C in the dry season— amply high for both coral and mangroves.

The low-lying southeastern coast of the Northern Territory, which faces the Gulf of Carpentaria, is a plain on Quaternary sediments, but Proterozoic and Cenozoic rocks crop out in the Sir Edward Pellew Islands and on Maria Island (Fig. 123-1). The shoreline consists of beaches and spits backed by sand ridges and low dunes on exposed sections, and muddy tidal flats with mangrove fringes on sheltered sections. In the southwest of the Gulf, the Roper River contributes sediment that drifts northward to form sand ridge

complexes and mud flats. Despite exposure to the southeasterlies, these mud flats support mangroves, although most have been damaged by waves. Bare or sparsely vegetated supratidal mud flats lie behind the shore. They are subject to flood scouring and are occasionally interrupted by low clay dunes and wind-modified sand ridges (Plate 123-1). Older and more altered sand ridges or cheniers and low dune complexes of last interglacial age lie farther inland, up to 12 km from the coast. Similar features on the east coast of the Gulf of Carpentaria are related to sea level a few meters above the present (Smart 1976). Fragmentary eolianite dunes and sand sheets on Vanderlin Island are also probably last interglacial, but parabolic dunes and beach ridges are Holocene. There are no projecting deltas but the McArthur River is building sediments seaward in the shelter of the Sir Edward Pellew Islands, and similar extensive, bare supratidal flats seamed by winding, mangrove-fringed tidal creeks occur in the Roper River valley. Mangrove fringes river channels, particularly on meander slip-off slopes.

The east coast of Arnhem Land comprises low, rocky peninsulas and islands, wide mud flats in sheltered bays, and extensive sand dunes, behind some of which lie tidal lagoons or lakes. The rocky coasts locally have low cliffs and narrow rock platforms on exposed sites, particularly where soft weathered material occurs. There are minor fringing coral reefs, and older coral has been noted within dunes. Mud flats in sheltered gulfs have zoned mangroves up to several kilometers wide at their seaward edge. Bare supratidal flats behind pass inland into freshwater swamps and are drained by straight channels fringed by mangroves. Extensive parabolic dunes on the mainland south of Gove and on the east and south coasts of Groote Eylandt rise to 70 m above sea level. The oldest may be Pleistocene, and the youngest are modern. An interglacial transverse eolianite ridge up to 88 m high—the sole example in northern Australia—forms the seaward edge of the dune field south of Gove (Plate 123-2). Younger parabolic dunes lie behind this ridge. Beach ridges, spits, and tombolos, often extensively modified by blowouts, are common on the mainland south of Blue Mud Bay and in sheltered bays on the islands. Lagoons behind the sand barriers have only modest tidal deltas and narrow mangrove fringes because of the small tidal flux, sandy sediments, and paucity of riverine input.

The northeast coast of Arnhem Land consists of strike-controlled islands, peninsulas, and inlets. The islands and peninsulas are rocky, with wave-cut platforms and reefs on their southeastern side and small Holocene beach ridges and transverse dunes on the northwest. Sheltered bays are edged by zoned mangroves backed by bare supratidal flats that grade landward into alluvial plains or swamps. Occasional cheniers occur on the flats, which are slightly dissected by straight tidal gutters with broad mangrove fringes. Mangroves also extend far up the rivers and their tributary creeks. Sheltered rocky coasts have narrow mangrove fringes.

On the central Arnhem Land coast, Mesozoic and Cenozoic weathered rocks are exposed in cliffs overlooking platforms armored with ferruginous rock debris, as on Elcho Island. In sheltered situations there are extensive mangroves and supratidal flats with halophytic vegetation slightly dissected by mangrove-fringed tidal creeks. Inland, fresh-water swamps show evidence of former tidal channels. In the more open situation of Boucaut Bay, sand ridges and even low dunes occur at the coast; mangroves are confined to narrow tidal flats in their lee, and supratidal flats have occasional cheniers. The Goulburn Islands have cliffs in soft weathered rocks, beach ridges, and low transverse dunes on the exposed northwest and spits and small parabolic dunes on the southeast related to dry season winds.

The lower Cobourg Peninsula is exposed to winds and waves from the southeast. Steep cliffs in soft weathered rock are retreating rapidly but are soon degraded if the growth of beach ridges at their feet has checked erosion. Patchy Holocene parabolic dunes extend 1–2 km inland, and dunes are also climbing degraded cliffs.

On the northern coast of Cobourg Peninsula, Croker Island, Melville Island, and Bathurst Island, wide, partially drowned valleys contain intertidal flats with some 700 km² of mangrove, an area one-sixth of the Northern Territory total (Galloway 1982; Wells 1982). Bays well exposed to the northwest have extensive sand accumulations including spits, transverse dunes, and beach ridges. Smaller islands on platform reefs have prominent ridges of coral sand. Fringing reefs up to 3 km wide around headlands enclose mangroves or sand accumulations.

The southern coast of Bathurst Island facing Beagle Gulf is exposed to strong southeasterly winds, particularly in its western half, where cliffs up to 20 m high have been cut in weathered rock; they are now vegetated and fronted by a wide beach. Active parabolic dunes overlie lower parts of these cliffs. The eastern half of this coast is protected by spits, sand ridges, and fringing reefs,

behind which lie mangroves, bare supratidal flats, cheniers, and degraded cliffs.

The southern coasts of Melville Island and Cobourg Peninsula are muddy, with extensive mangroves that have been damaged by storms unless protected by fringing coral reefs. To the southeast the mangroves are protected by beaches and sand ridges but are narrow and backed by supratidal flats with occasional cheniers and sedge-covered alluvial plains. Isobaths suggest drowned barriers exist offshore. On Field Island mangroves lie in front of beaches, a common situation in the Northern Territory from this point westward.

The smooth southern coast of Van Diemen Gulf is the seaward edge of extensive flood plains. An almost continuous fringe of mangroves up to 500 m wide is backed by bare flats that grade inland into sedge-covered clay plains and vast swamps on which cheniers lie up to 18 km from the sea. Clarke et al. (1979) have shown that the cheniers at Point Stuart are Holocene and that relative sea level has not been more than 1 m above its present position during the last 6,000–7,000 years. The cheniers contain much shell sand and may be storm-built. Narrow mangroves fringe the main rivers up to 80 km inland, nearly to the tidal limit.

Dundas Strait is the main entrance to Van Diemen Gulf. Its floor has ridges and channels with a local relief up to 30 m; they may be tidal features or drowned reefs. The gulf's western entrance is largely blocked by reefs, notably the oval platforms of the Vernon Islands, which are up to 15 km long and support extensive mangroves (Plate 123-3); partially drowned laterite surfaces may also be present. Fringing reefs around headlands, Greenhill Island, and other islands provide protected sites for mangroves up to 15 m high.

Around Darwin there are five drowned valleys lined with extensive mangroves. The open coasts between the valleys include low cliffs and coastal platforms cut in weathered rocks, beach ridges, or small transverse dunes formed by summer northwesterlies and shores with beach rock (Russell and McIntire 1965).

From Fog Bay to Pearce Point the coast is exposed. Low cliffs and platforms on weathered rocks alternate with broad bays having sand ridges at their more exposed northern ends, mangroves behind sand bars in the center, and mangrove to the water's edge at their more sheltered southern ends. Behind the bays lie extensive swampy alluvial plains, which may once have been tidal flats. More of the supratidal flats are bare as precipitation decreases southward. The Daly River has built up extensive alluvial clay plains mostly above tidal influence but with narrow mangrove fringes at the coast and low cheniers on the western side of the estuary. Isobaths indicate a shallow submarine delta. Daly River sediments are carried northward and contribute sand and mud to the low Peron Islands.

The Victoria River and Keep River estuaries are funnel-shaped, with big tidal ranges and large seasonal sediment supply (Wright et al. 1973). The main channels near the coast are shallow and partially blocked by rapidly changing mud islands readily colonized by mangroves. Extensive intertidal and supratidal flats between the main channels are seamed by tidal creeks (Plate 123-4). Mangroves fringe the channels and creeks, but the supratidal flats are vast bare surfaces occasionally affected by the highest tides. The tidal creeks and mangroves may be extending headward into the bare flats. At the open coast mangroves have suffered storm damage even though the shallow water attenuates the waves. The inner Victoria estuary penetrates 100 km inland through steep ranges. It is bordered by low flood terraces occasionally inundated by the tide and in places supporting stunted mangroves.

ROBERT W. GALLOWAY

REFERENCES

Clarke, M. F., R. J. Wasson, and M. A. J. Williams, 1979, Point Stuart Chenier and Holocene sea levels in northern Australia, *Search* **10**:90–92.

Easton, A. K., 1970, *The Tides of the Continent of Australia*, Flinders Institute for Atmospheric and Marine Sciences Research Paper 37, Flinders University, Adelaide.

Galloway, R. W., 1982, Distribution and physiographic patterns of Australian mangroves, in *Mangrove Ecosystems in Australia*, B. F. Clough, ed., Aust. Inst. Marine Sci., ANU Press, Canberra, pp. 31–54.

Galloway, R. W., and M. E. Bahr, 1979, What is the length of the Australian coast? *Australian Geographer* **14**:244–247.

Jongsma, D., 1974, *Marine Geology of the Arafura Sea*, Bur. Miner. Resour. Aust. Bull. 157.

Russell, R. J., and W. G. McIntire, 1965, Southern hemisphere beach rock, *Geog. Rev.* **55**:17–45.

Smart, J., 1976, The nature and origin of beach ridges, western Cape York Peninsula, Queensland, *Bur. Miner. Resour. Aust. Geol. Geophys.* **1**:211–218.

Van Andel, T. H., and J. J. Veevers, 1967, *Morphology and Sediments of the Timor Sea*, Bur. Miner. Resour. Aust. Bull. 83.

Wells, A. G., 1982, Mangrove vegetation of northern Australia, in *Mangrove Ecosystems in Australia*, B. F. Clough, ed., Aust. Inst. Marine Sci., ANU Press, Canberra, pp. 57–78.

Wright, L. D., J. M. Coleman, and B. G. Thom, 1973, Geomorphic coastal variability, north-western Australia, *Coastal Studies Bulletin*, **7**:35–64.

Plate 123-1. The southeast coast of Arnhem Land is a plain of alluvial and estuarine sediments. Coastal mangroves have suffered severe storm damage. Supratidal flats behind are partly bare and partly carry halophytic vegetation; small shrubby rises may be clay dunes. Wooded sand ridges in the background, modified by wind action, are partly of last interglacial age (photo by R. W. Galloway).

Plate 123-2. On the northeast coast of Arnhem Land south of Gove there are relics of an interglacial eolianite ridge, cliffed and cut by transverse valleys through which sand has moved in the Holocene to form several generations of parabolic dunes (photo by R. W. Galloway).

Plate 123-3. The Vernon Islands are platform reefs up to 15 km long that lie between Melville Island and the mainland. Extensive mangroves grow on the sheltered surface of the reef, whose edge is marked by a line of breakers in foreground (photo by R. W. Galloway).

Plate 123-4. The extensive supratidal flats of the Victoria River Estuary are seamed by tidal creeks with low mangrove fringes, which also occur at the coast. The big tidal range is associated with deep incision of the channels (photo by R. W. Galloway).

124. QUEENSLAND

The coastline of Queensland, 9,880 km long, extends across 19° of latitude from 28°10′ S at the New South Wales border to 9°15′ S in Torres Strait. A marked reduction in wind and wave energy conditions takes place northward. Significant wave height exceeded 50% of the time is 1.15 m at the Gold Coast, 0.8 m near Rockhampton, and 0.5 m at Cairns; similarly, the occurrence of gale force winds declines from 0.7% at Brisbane to 0.1% at Cooktown. Swell waves dominate the wave spectra as far north as the Tropic of Capricorn, but are progressively excluded to the north by the protecting influence of the Great Barrier Reef and are totally excluded from the Gulf of Carpentaria. However, the entire Queensland coastline is prone to tropical cyclones during summer months; on average three cyclones per year occur both in the Gulf of Carpentaria and off the eastern coast. Any part of the coast can experience storms with central pressures of 960 mb and wind speeds in excess of 150 km/hr, but the coastal zone most prone to intense storms stretches from Princess Charlotte Bay to Fraser Island. Cyclonic seas may raise wave heights to 8 m or more, thus producing occasional high-energy events in direct contrast to prevailing conditions (Hopley 1974).

Storm surges, raising water levels by up to 6 m, are also associated with tropical cyclones, which are superimposed on the semidiurnal tidal regime. Tidal ranges reach a maximum of more than 9 m in Broad Sound on the central coast, but decrease rapidly seaward (ranges not exceeding 6 m on the Great Barrier Reef), southward (a 2 m range being characteristic of southern Queensland), and to the north (a 3 m range being experienced from Townsville to Torres Strait). A

2–3 m range is characteristic of most of the Gulf of Carpentaria, but this rises to 4 m in the southeast near Karumba. The tides of the Gulf and of the east coast are frequently not in phase, producing complex and unique tidal conditions in Torres Strait, where strong tidal currents in excess of 3m/s can be experienced.

The eastern coast is overlooked by the escarpment of the Eastern Highlands, which rises in places to over 1,000 m. The north-northwest–south-southeast trend of the coastline is determined by the structure of the Tasman geosyncline and its associated basins, which form the axis of the highlands. Cenozoic uplift and a complex history involving deep weathering and regolith removal ensure a massive yield of sand- and silt-size sediments to the east coast. In contrast the Gulf of Capentaria represents a more recently downwarped area, the surrounding Mezosoic and Cenozoic sediments forming low-lying sandy plains with extensive laterite development (Coventry et al. 1980).

Although the region is relatively stable tectonically, Holocene earth movements, possibly of a hydro-isostatic nature, have occurred around the Queensland coast, affecting the Holocene relative sea-level pattern and influencing many coastal landforms (Hopley 1982). Modern relative sea level appears to have been achieved by 6,000 years ago ubiquitously, with ages as great as 6,500 years being associated with a modern sea level in some areas. Variations in the maximum height of the sea during the Holocene are indications of recent movements. Some areas of the east coast show no level higher than the present, but large areas retain evidence of levels of 1.5 m or higher. Indication of the recent warping seen is in the maximum level found in the Gulf, from 1.5 m in the north to 2.4 m near Karumba (Rhodes 1982) and up to 6 m variations on either side of Broad Sound (Cook and Mayo 1977).

The combination of structural variation, recent history, and variation in energy levels produces a six-fold regional division of the Queensland coastline (Fig. 124-1). Characteristics of the mainland section are given in Table 1.

1. *The Gulf of Carpentaria* (Coventry et al. 1980; Rhodes 1982; Smart 1976). From the Northern Territory border to the Norman River the coastal plain, almost 40 km wide, consists of silty deposits and salt flats with occasional low cheniers. It is drained by numerous meandering tidal creeks and rivers lined with mangroves. Older Pleistocene ridges lie up to 30 km inland and are subparallel to the present coastline. During summer months, the combination of wet season runoff and higher summer tides results in the inundation of wide areas of the outer plain.

The depositional coastline of eastern Gulf of Carpentaria is divided into two parts by the lateritic cliffs of Albatross Bay. To the south the chenier and salt flat environment of farther west is continued, but the plain is narrower (up to 20 km) and series of sandy beach ridges occur close to river mouths (Plate 124-1). These ridge series are larger to the north and form a massive cuspate foreland at Cape Keer Weer. North of Albatross Bay the coastline consists of a series of beach ridges derived jointly from the sands of the Jardine River and from the tidal delta at the western exit of Torres Strait. A broad area of swampland is ponded between the beach ridges and the alluvial fans of the interior.

The Wellesley Islands in the southern gulf consist of a core of laterized Cretaceous and Jurassic sediments extensively overlain by Pleistocene dune calcarenites rising to 40 m, and modern quartzose beach ridges. Shore platforms cut into the sediments and fringing reefs surround the islands.

2. *Torres Strait to Cooktown* (Coventry et al. 1980; Jennings 1972). Reduced wave energy due to the proximity of the Great Barrier Reef makes

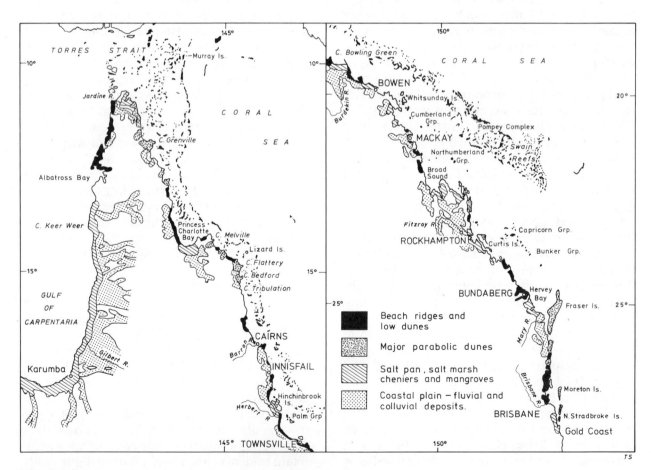

Figure 124-1. Geomorphology of the Queensland coast.

Table 1. Major characteristics of each mainland coastal section

	Gulf of Carpentaria	Torres St. to Cooktown	Cooktown to Hinchinbrook Is	Hinchinbrook to Hervey Bay	Hervey Bay to Border
Bedrock	0 (0)	651 (16.2)	861 (44.4)	1,782 (20.4)	342 (17.8)
Regolith and laterite	720 (6.1)	198 (4.9)	6 (0.3)	267 (3.1)	21 (1.1)
Terraces and fans	144 (1.3)	399 (9.9)	222 (11.5)	1,023 (11.7)	192 (10.0)
Beach ridges	1,809 (15.3)	225 (5.6)	159 (8.2)	612 (7.0)	87 (4.5)
Parabolic dunes	0 (0)	303 (7.5)	18 (0.9)	234 (2.7)	90 (4.7)
Transverse and other dunes	150 (1.3)	684 (17.0)	51 (2.6)	408 (4.7)	378 (19.6)
Mangroves	1,629 (13.8)	531 (13.2)	468 (24.2)	1,602 (18.3)	150 (7.8)
Salt pan and halophytes	3,843 (32.5)	351 (8.7)	36 (1.9)	1,002 (11.5)	57 (3.0)
Saline coastal grassland	2,028 (17.1)	312 (7.7)	6 (0.3)	978 (11.2)	42 (2.2)
Swamps, channels, etc.	1,512 (12.8)	729 (18.1)	111 (5.7)	825 (9.5)	567 (10.0)

Note: Figures are in km². Figures in parentheses show % for each region.
Source: Data from CSIRO Division of Land-Use Research (Galloway 1981).

this a low-energy coastline characterized by sandy beaches with a narrow zone of low beach ridges about 1 km wide separated by rocky headlands. The beach ridges are mainly of Holocene age, but fragmentary remnants of a Pleistocene system may remain separated from the outer series by bare salt pan and saline coastal grasslands. The headlands have convex rocky slopes showing little modification by marine processes except for the removal of regolith developed during low sea level stands. Massive boulders, domes, and tors are typical of granitic headlands such as Cape Melville, and on Lizard Island. More tabular rocky forms are associated with the Jurassic sediments (mainly sandstones), for example, Cape Bedford and the Flinders Islands. On the outer shelf in the far north the high islands of the Murray Group, Darnley, and Stephens, are composed of Pleistocene volcanics. Maer, in the Murrays, retains the morphology of an old crater rim. Extensive fringing reefs are associated with all offshore islands, but are not well developed on the mainland.

The most impressive coastal dunes in tropical Australia occur in this region, notably around Newcastle Bay, Orford Bay, Cape Grenville (400 km²), Cape Flattery (700 km²), and Cape Bedford. They consist of elongate parabolic dunes up to 5 km in length and over 100 m in height, many stabilized beneath heath or rain forest (Plate 124-2). Older sand bodies are ferruginized with thin iron-enriched pisolitic cappings. Their occurrence coincides with the availability of sand-size sediments weathered from the Mesozoic sandstones and an orientation of the coast that allows the higher energy southeasterlies of winter to mobilize the sands. However, much of the dune fields may have formed during glacially lowered

sea level episodes from sand sources on the continental shelf.

Princess Charlotte Bay is completely protected from the southeast, and a chenier plain 25 km wide occurs here. An outer fringe of mangroves is backed by up to 5 km of bare saline mud flats with isolated cheniers. Behind these are extensive clay plains with salt marsh vegetation of short Cyperaceae and salt water couch (*Sporobolus virginicus*).

3. *Cooktown to Hinchinbrook Island* (Bird and Hopley 1969; Bird 1970a, 1970b). This part of the Queensland coast coincides with the highest rainfall region in Australia. Annual totals exceed 2,000 mm throughout the area and reach a maximum of over 4,000 mm near Innisfail. It is predominantly a steep coast but tropical rain forest extends down to the high tide level (Plate 124-3). The intertidal zone is rocky, with massive boulders, washed from the regolith, strewn over the foreshore. Minor forms of chemical weathering are seen on the rocky outcrops. In embayments the piedmont fans of the lower hillslopes may be cliffed, their boulders and gravels forming well-sorted cobble and shingle beaches. Close to the mouths of major rivers, beach ridges have prograded the coastline by up to 1 km. Near Kurrimine a multiple barrier system up to 12 km wide has been formed. At least three phases of progradation are recognized here. Where the sandy barriers are oriented toward the southeast there is sufficient wind energy for dune formation. The largest dunes, rising to 60 m, are found on the northern end of Hinchinbrook Island (Plate 124-4). Although largely stabilized by vegetation, parabolic forms can be recognized and small active blowouts occur. In sheltered locations wide inter-

tidal silt ramps have been deposited and colonized by mangroves. The most extensive mangrove systems are found in the Hinchinbrook Channel and behind Ramsay Bay on Hinchinbrook Island (Plate 124-4), where 31 species have been identified.

The rocky shores of the offshore islands are similar to those of the mainland. Many have small vegetated sand spits on their northern or lee sides. Most have wide fringing reefs although the largest island, Hinchinbrook, has no reefs, probably because of the large fresh water run off from the island. Fringing reefs are rare on the mainland. Small algal reefs are found near Cape Tribulation, and coastal progradation has joined former patch reefs to the mainland at Yule Point and Kurrimine.

4. *Hinchinbrook Island to Hervey Bay* (Coventry et al. 1980; Hopley 1971; Hopley and Murtha 1975). A massive sand-size fluvial sediment yield to the coast and a concentrated summer wet season characterize the wide coastal plains of central Queensland. Much of the coast is sandy, with a series of beach ridges trailing northward from the mouth of almost every stream. Typically the coastline is made of up to ten or more ridges up to 500 m wide, but close to major rivers the sequence may widen to over 5 km. Most of the ridges are Holocene in age, but a fragmentary Pleistocene series is found (Plate 124-5). The ridges are higher in the northern part of each sediment compartment because of the addition of a dune cap where the beach is more exposed to the prevailing southeasterlies, but the dunes are rarely more than 10 m high. The only major dune accumulations on this coast occur on Whitsunday Island, Curtis Island, and north of Rockhampton.

The largest rivers have built up deltas or large estuarine sediment infills. The Fitzroy River, draining 140,000 km², has an estuarine infill 3–18 km wide and at least 45 m thick. It enters the sea in the lee of Curtis Island, and most of the lower estuary (Plate 124-6) consists of bare salt pan and meandering mangrove-lined creeks, a morphology repeated on a smaller scale in most sheltered areas of the coast. The Burdekin, draining 129,000 km², has built Australia's largest cuspate delta with over 150 m of deltaic sediments. Under the southeasterly influence the higher-energy eastern side of the delta has a series of barrier spits extending from the various distributaries. The northernmost, Cape Bowling Green, extending seaward for 18 km, is Australia's largest sand spit (Plate 124-7). The sheltered northern coast of the delta is mainly salt flat, salt marsh, and mangrove.

Only in the south, for example on Curtis Island, do the headlands show any form of shore platform development. Elsewhere their slopes are essentially subaerial weathering forms stripped of their regolith. Boulder beaches or boulder spits are found in some bayhead locations. The most extensive rocky coasts are found opposite the Whitsunday Islands, but similar forms are found on many of the offshore islands. Islands are numerous on this coast, and are drowned extensions of the coastal ranges, continuing the structural trends of the mainland seaward. All but the Northumberland Group have extensive fringing reefs (Plate 124-8). Bay heads are usually occupied by beach ridges. Lee-side sand spits, containing beachrock and older boulder beaches, are very common.

5. *Hervey Bay to the New South Wales* (Hails 1964; Orme and Day 1978). The swell-dominated coast of southern Queensland has massive sand barriers formed by the northward drift of sand from the New South Wales coast. The drift continues as far north as Fraser Island, where it is directed over the continental shelf via Breaksea Spit and into deep water down several submarine canyons. The barriers are of both Holocene and Pleistocene age, but in places Holocene dunes and ridges have been removed, and erosion has exposed extensive areas of Pleistocene humic hard pan on the beach. Part of the system is formed of massive sand barrier islands. On Fraser Island the dunes rise up to 240 m and incorporate some 40 perched lakes, many of them in a rain forest setting. On North and South Stradbroke islands, and on Moreton Island (Plate 124-9) dunes rise to 300 m. Most of these large sand masses are Pleistocene in age and have been weathered into a range of colored sands that form a major tourist attraction. Australia's major tourist resort, the Gold Coast, has been developed on the southernmost section of the barrier coast. Behind the main barriers may be large heathland areas termed *Wallum*, developed in Pleistocene sands of lower relief. Occasional headlands interrupt the long sandy beaches, and many have wide horizontal shore platforms.

Moreton Bay is enclosed by barrier islands. It is 80 km long and up to 35 km wide, reaching depths of 40 m, and is bordered by extensive estuarine flats, beach ridges dominating in exposed sectors, mangroves and salt marsh in more sheltered areas. Small headlands are formed of Tertiary basalt and lateritized clay. A number of the islands of Moreton Bay have small fringing coral reefs that appear to have been more flourishing in Pleistocene and mid-Holocene times.

6. *The Great Barrier Reef* (Hopley 1978, 1982). From 9°15′ S the Great Barrier Reef extends southward along a perimeter of 2,300 km to Lady Elliot Island at 24°07′ S. The outer reef varies greatly in distance from the mainland, approaching within 23 km at 14° S to a maximum of 260 km at 21° S. The whole reef province incorporates an area of approximately 230,000 km², within which lie over 2,500 reefs, varying in size from isolated pinnacles to massive structures up to 25 km long and 125 km² in area. Although the foundations of the Great Barrier reef are Tertiary, the modern reefs form a Holocene veneer up to 20 m in thickness overlying and closely following the morphology of their Pleistocene antecedents.

North of Cairns the outer reefs form a continuous barrier with only narrow passes (Plate 124-10); midshelf reefs are large and oval in shape, while small inner-shelf reefs either have vegetated cays (Plate 124-11) or are capped by complex low wooded islands containing sand cays, shingle ramparts, and mangroves. Between Cairns and the Whitsunday Islands the main reef has experienced some subsidence, reef flats are not as well developed and reefs are often irregular in shape. There are no vegetated cays in this area of the Reef. The largest reefs are those of the Pompey Complex. Separated by narrow passes up to 90 m deep, they form a broad belt up to 23 km wide. To the south the Swains Reefs form a region of smaller oval platform reefs. The Capricorn Channel separates them from the southernmost reefs, the Bunker-Capricorn Group, a series of lagoonal reefs, many with vegetated cays.

DAVID HOPLEY

REFERENCES

Bird, E. C. F., 1970a, The steep coast of the Macalister Range, north Queensland, Australia, *Jour. Tropical Geography* **31**:33–39.

Bird, E. C. F., 1970b, The deltaic shoreline near Cairns, *Australian Geographer* **11**:138–147.

Bird, E. C. F., and D. Hopley, 1969, Geomorphological features on a humid tropical sector of the Queensland coast, *Australian Geog. Stud.* **7**:89–108.

Cook, P. J., and W. Mayo, 1977, Sedimentology and Holocene history of a tropical estuary (Broad Sound, Queensland), *BMR Geol. Geophys. Bull.* **170**:206.

Coventry, R. J., D. Hopley, J. B. Campbell, I. Douglas, N. Harvey, A. P. Kershaw, J. Oliver, C. V. G. Phipps, and K. Pye, 1980, The Quaternary of northeastern Australia, in *The Geology and Geophysics of Northeastern Australia*, R. A. Henderson and P. J. Stephenson, eds., Geological Society of Australia, pp. 365–417.

Galloway, R. W., 1981, An inventory of Australia's coastal lands, *Australian Geog. Stud.* **19**:107–116.

Hails, J. R., 1964, The coastal depositional features of south-eastern Queensland, *Australian Geographer* **9**:207–217.

Hopley, D., 1971, The origin and significance of north Queensland island spits, *Zeitschr. Geomorphologie* **15**:371–389.

Hopley, D., 1974, Coastal changes produced by tropical cyclone Althea in Queensland, December 1971, *Australian Geographer* **12**:445–456.

Hopley, D., 1978, Sea level change on the Great Barrier Reef: an introduction, *Royal Soc. London Philos. Trans. A* **291**:159–166.

Hopley, D., 1982, *The Geomorphology of the Great Barrier Reef: Quaternary Evolution of Coral Reefs*, John Wiley–Interscience, New York.

Hopley, D., and G. G. Murtha, 1975, *The Quaternary Deposits of the Townsville Coastal Plain*, Dept. Geog. James Cook Univ. Monogr. Ser. **8**:30.

Jennings, J. N., 1972, Some attributes of Torres Strait, in *Bridge and Barrier: The Natural and Cultural History of Torres Strait*, D. Walker, ed., Australian National University Press, pp. 29–38.

Orme, G. R., and R. W. Day, eds., 1978, *Handbook of Recent Geological Studies of Moreton Bay, Brisbane River and North Stradbroke Island*, Dept. Geol. Univ. Queensland Papers, 8(2).

Rhodes, E. G., 1982, Depositional model for a chenier plain, Gulf of Carpentaria, Australia, *Sedimentology* **29**:201–221.

Smart, J., 1976, The nature and origin of beach ridges, western Cape York Peninsula Queensland, *BMR Jour. Austr. Geol. Geophys.* **1**:211–218.

Plate 124-1. Beach ridges north of Edward River, Gulf of Carpentaria. Radiocarbon ages range from approximately 5,800 years at the left of the photo to 1,500 years near the modern coast (photo by E. G. Rhodes).

Plate 124-2. Massive parabolic dunes near Cape Bedford, with dense vegetation cover and few active blowouts. The dunes are oriented toward the southeast (photo by D. Hopley).

Plate 124-3. The steep coast near Cape Tribulation, with rain forest growing down to the high water mark. Massive boulders from the regolith occur in the intertidal zone, and a small fringing reef occurs offshore (photo by D. Hopley).

Plate 124-4. Vegetated dunes rising to about 30 m at Ramsay Bay, Hinchinbrook Island. Extensive mangroves grow in the lee of the barrier, covering almost the entire intertidal slope. Compare with Plate 124-6 showing the drier region of the Queensland coast (photo by D. Hopley).

Plate 124-5. Typical central Queensland coastal morphology in Upstart Bay just south of the Burdekin delta. Beach ridges and barrier spits are associated with most rivers. The innermost ridges are Pleistocene in age. Mangroves occur in the estuaries, but large areas of salt pan and saline coastal grassland can be seen (photo by D. Hopley).

Plate 124-6. The Fitzroy River delta consists of an extensive area of bare salt pan where hypersaline conditions build up during the long dry season. Mangroves are limited to tidal creeks flushed by semidiurnal tidal fluctuations (photo by D. Hopley).

Plate 124-7. Cape Bowling Green, Australia's longest sand spit, extending northward from the cuspate Burdekin delta under the influence of the prevailing southeasterlies. Low dunes up to about 5 m high are typical of many beach ridges and spits exposed to the southeasterlies (photo by D. Hopley).

Plate 124-8. Carlisle and Brampton Islands in the Cumberland Group, showing extensive fringing reef flats. Rocky coastlines have massive poorly sorted boulder beaches and convex slopes little altered by marine processes. The lagoon is impounded between a dune barrier to the south and a boulder beach emplaced by cyclonic seas to the north (photo by D. Hopley).

Plate 124-9. Massive blowouts in the vegetated dunes of Moreton Island rising to 300 m. Pleistocene coffee rock can be seen on the beach in the foreground (photo by D. Hopley).

Plate 124-10. Surf pounding the outer edge of Ribbon Reef near Lizard Island. On the northern Great Barrier Reef the near-continuous line of the outer barrier protects the inner shelf and mainland from the swell waves of the Coral Sea (photo by D. Hopley).

Plate 124-11. Green Island near Cairns is typical of many of the vegetated cays of the Great Barrier Reef. It has a vegetation dominated by *Pisonia grandis*, but younger areas of the cay have lower pioneering species, including *Ipomoea* and *Canavalia* sp. This is one of only two cays on the Great Barrier Reef to have a permanent tourist resort (photo by D. A. Kuchler).

125. NEW SOUTH WALES

The continental margin of New South Wales (N.S.W.) is considered to have resulted from tectonic events modified by depositional processes since the formation of the Tasman Sea 60-80 million years ago (Hayes and Ringis 1973; Davies 1975, 1979). Sediment of Cenozoic age covers the initial breakup slope in places by as much as 500 m. However, Cenozoic marine deposits above present-day sea level are limited to the late Quaternary; in fact, south of Newcastle such deposits are only of Holocene age. They occur as sand barriers and associated facies along the present coast within embayments carved into Paleozoic and Mesozoic country rocks. In contrast, shelf sediments extend more or less continuously along the shelf surface, in particular along the outer part (Roy and Thom 1981).

The N.S.W. coast is essentially a drowned embayed coast in which the bays are partially filled by sandy bay barriers, tidal flats, lagoons, and deltaic plains (Langford-Smith and Thom 1969). The sand depositional sequence within embayments appears to increase the age, extent, and morphological as well as stratigraphical complexity from Cape Howe in the far south of N.S.W. into southern Queensland (Roy and Thom 1981). From the limited data available, underlying estuarine mud sequences of late Quaternary age are also more complex in the larger embayments north of Newcastle. The nature and size of individual bays and their distance apart are influenced markedly by bedrock type and orientation, and the direction of approach of predominant waves. Many barriers have the shape of a half-heart or zeta, producing a distinctive offset coastal outline (Chapman 1978).

The N.S.W. coast is oriented north-northeast-south-southwest and is subjected to a dominant south to southeast swell and wind wave regime generated in the south Tasman Sea (Lawson and Abernethy 1975). In northern N.S.W. and southern Queensland the southerly wave climate is overprinted by occasional cyclones generated in the tropics. Because of the narrow and relatively deep continental shelf, frictional loss of wave energy is negligible until close to the surf zone (Wright 1976). As a result the coast is dominated by a high-energy wave climate. At Sydney significant deep-water wave heights exceed 1.5m 50% of the time, 2.5m 10% of the time and 4m 1% of the time (Lawson and Abernethy 1975). Deep-water waves up to 16m high have been recorded. Wright (1976) has shown that incident wave energy on the central N.S.W. coast is 5-10 times greater than on the Atlantic coast of North America and 80 times greater than on the Gulf of Mexico coast near the Mississippi delta. Because of the relationship between dominant wave climate and coastal orientation, there is a tendency toward northward littoral drift. However, in the southern part of the state (south of 32°S) embayments are compartmentalized either by prominent headlands that extend into deep water or by deep estuary mouths. Farther north barriers to littoral drifting are infrequent, and bypassing occurs between most embayments (Roy and Crawford 1977).

Sea-level change on the N.S.W. coast is reasonably well documented. Astronomical tides vary in range from less than 1.0 m at neaps to 2.0 m at springs (average 1.6 m). Historical records over a 100-year period of tidal and sea-level change show oscillations of 5 cm but no discernible trends (Hamon 1965; Thom 1974). Radiocarbon dates have been used to construct an envelope of sea-level change in the Holocene (Thom and Chappell 1975). This curve suggests that along this coast sea level rose rapidly (Postglacial Marine Transgression) at a rate of 10-15 mm per 100 years until about 6,000 years ago. Since that time sea level is unlikely to have oscillated more than ±1 m, and thus the last 6,000 years is referred to as the stillstand period.

As indicated by Langford-Smith and Thom (1969), the embayed coast of N.S.W. can be divided into two general categories: rugged, where the immediate hinterland is hilly or mountainous; and subdued, where relief is lower, embayments broad, and headlands relatively less conspicuous. In general, rugged coasts predominate south of Newcastle, subdued coasts to the north. Within many embayments sand barriers and deltaic plains have been deposited.

In N.S.W. two quite distinct bay-barrier systems can be identified, the so-called Inner Barrier of late Pleistocene age and the Outer Barrier of Holocene age. The general characteristics of these systems are described by Thom (1965) and Langford-Smith and Thom (1969). The Inner Barrier has recently been confirmed by uranium-series dating as being Last Interglacial in age (Marshall and Thom 1976). It has not been observed south of Newscastle in N.S.W. Coastal eolian deposits older than the Inner Barrier are mainly restricted to the far northern region of the state, with isolated occurrences on the central and south coast.

Two main sediment populations are recognized in the N.S.W. coastal zone: marine and fluvial (Roy and Crawford 1977). Marine sediments are generally mature, quartz-rich sands and gravelly sands. Locally they are calcareous, with greater than 60% carbonate (mainly mollusk fragments), but more commonly shell content ranges from 5–25%. Sediment maturity is reflected in a relatively high degree of rounding and the occurrence of a stable heavy-mineral suite (zircon, rutile, and ilmenite; see Hails 1967). These sediments are thought to be the result of marine-eolian reworking during more than one eustatic cycle on the continental shelf (Roy and Thom 1981). They commonly occur in lithofacies associated with the following environments of deposition; near-shore, beach, dune, flood-tidal delta, back-barrier (see Roy et al. 1980, Table 1).

Fluvial sediments are composed of gravels, sands, and muds derived locally by fluvial erosion of country rocks in the hinterland. The sand fraction is of mixed mineralogy and is best described as quartz-lithic. The fluvial sand is mainly trapped

in coastal valley and estuarine sinks (Roy et al. 1980). Only in rare cases does it reach the open coast, where, because of the high wave energy, it is confined to the inshore zone (Roy and Crawford 1977). However, fluvial mud and fine sand may bypass the estuaries during floods, to be dispersed across the inner shelf and either deposited in deep water (>50 m) on the continental shelf (Davies 1975), or entrained by relatively strong eddies of the south-flowing East Australian Coast Current.

Figure 125-1 depicts three general morpho-stratigraphic patterns that have been recognized. Locally, there may occur combinations of and additions to these patterns, such as the development of episodic transgressive dunes on prograded

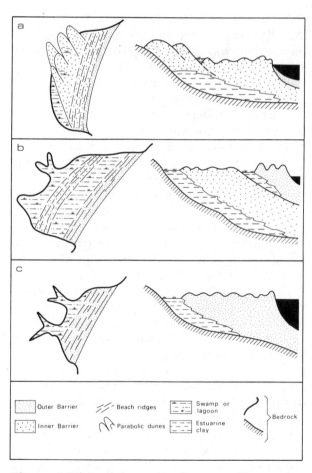

Figure 125-1. Schematic diagram illustrating three basic types of morphostratigraphic patterns of sand barriers occurring on the N.S.W. coast: a) Pleistocene embayment fill with Inner Barrier beach ridges and dunes; b) dual barriers of Pleistocene and Holocene ages separated by an interbarrier depression; c) Holocene sand barrier composed of beach ridges.

outer barriers (e.g., Newcastle Bight; Thom et al. 1981). One pattern occurs within the long, gently curved sandy bays of the north coast of N.S.W. (Fig. 125-1a). Here many bedrock embayments are completely filled with a prograded strand plain of the Inner Barrier type, which has been partly eroded by fluvial processes and marine cliffing. Quartzose sands of the barrier have been impregnated with humic colloids forming a hardpan up to 10 m thick. Beach ridges of the strand plain may lie seaward of a transgressive dune complex (Gardner 1955).

Newcastle Bight embayment is shown in Figure 125-1b in a somewhat simplified form. Here Inner and Outer barriers form a dual barrier system composed of beach ridges. In this area episodic dunes have partially transgressed the Holocene beach ridges, and the Inner Barrier surface has been reworked into longitudinal dunes by westerly winds during the Last Glacial period (Thom 1965; Thom et al. 1981). These dunes are not shown in Figure 125-1b.

The morphology of a prograded Holocene beach-ridge system occupying a bay-head position is depicted in Figure 125-1c (Moruya, 250 km south of Sydney). A more detailed description of this section is provided by Thom (1978). Transgressive dunes of presumed late Pleistocene–early Holocene age (i.e., 6,000 years B.P.) mantle bedrock headlands at a few localities in southern N.S.W. However, sand barrier features of Pleistocene age are absent south of 33° and do not appear until the Gippsland region in Victoria (Bird 1978).

Detailed studies have been conducted in the past decade on the stratigraphy, morphology, and age structure of Holocene marine sand deposits within embayments on the N.S.W. coast. Five basic types of open-ocean sand accumulation have been recognized (Thom 1974; Roy et al. 1980): (1) prograded barriers involving marine transgression to about 6,000 years ago, then beach-ridge accretion to 2,000–3,000 years ago, followed by stable or slightly receding shorelines to the present (e.g., Fig. 125-1c); (2) stationary barriers involving the more or less vertical growth of bay barriers from depths about 20 m below present sea level to the present; (3) receded barriers involving the construction of narrow bay barriers about 5,000–6,000 B.P. followed by recession over paludal sediments to the present; (4) episodic dune development involving phases of dune instability over the last 6,000-8,000 years, with mobile sand sheets migrating downwind over vegetated sand, lagoonal, and bedrock surfaces; and (5) mainland beaches involving the accumulation of sand at the heads of embayments against bedrock slopes.

Besides open-ocean embayments, which are strongly influenced by high energy waves mostly filled by marine sands, Roy et al. (1980) distinguished two other embayment types in central and southern N.S.W.: barrier lagoon and drowned river valley. The first consists of those bays that have been blocked at their mouths by a baymouth sand barrier (usually of Holocene age, but on the north coast may be Pleistocene, e.g., Richmond River). Lagoons or flood plains have formed behind these barriers. The lagoons are generally irregular in shape, following the configuration of drowned bedrock valleys, but some are elongated parallel to the coast. Water depths range from less than 15 m to shallow flat-bottomed surfaces exposed at low tide. There is only a weak relationship between fetch and water depth. These lagoons are dominated by tidal and fluvial processes; shoreline reworking by local wind waves and dispersal of fine sediments by wind and tides also take place. Flood-tide deltas are formed at the seaward mouths of most lagoons with steep threshold slopes facing into the lagoons (Bird 1967). Many lagoon entrances are sealed by sand bars during fair-weather periods. Figure 125-2 illustrates the morphology and stratigraphy of the Shoalhaven Delta and associated baymouth barriers. This is an example of a mid-Holocene lagoon that has been filled by fluvial muds and sands from the west and marine tidal-delta and barrier sands from the east (Roy et al. 1980).

The third embayment type is the drowned river valley. This type occurs only within the massive, vertically jointed Hawkesbury Sandstone of Triassic age north and south of Sydney. Here river erosion has incised very deep (50–100 m) steep-sided valleys that were drowned early during the Postglacial Marine Transgression. The best examples are Broken Bay (lat. 33°S) and Port Jackson (Sydney Harbor). Dendritic valley patterns are clearly evident. In these estuaries open-ocean waves influence morphology and sediment distribution around the entrances to distances of 5 km landward of the mouth. Tidal and fluvial processes dominate upstream, with limited attenuation of the tidal range. Local wind waves are insignificant because of depth and fetch limitations. These embayments are characterized by three main lithofacies: tidal delta, mud basin, and deltaic flood plain. However, barrier sands occur in marginal bays (e.g., Woy Woy to the North of Broken Bay).

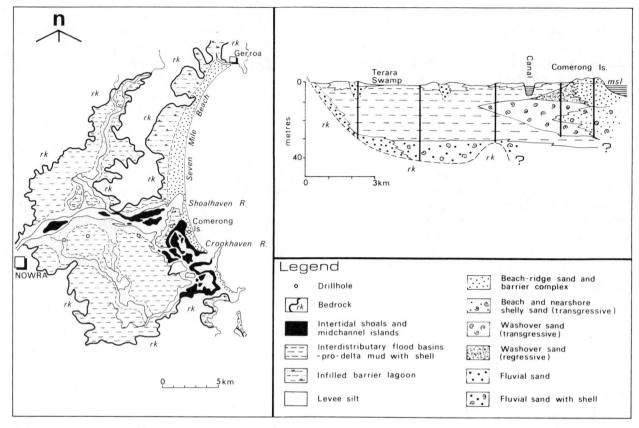

Figure 125-2. Plan and section of Shoalhaven River delta and sand barrier, south coast, N.S.W.

A dramatic feature of the N.S.W. coast (Fig. 125-3) is the rock platforms at the base of cliffs. They are found on almost all coastal headlands, except in massive rocks. Optimum development has occurred in the flat or very gently dipping Permian and Triassic sandstones and shales of the south and central coast (Plate 125-1). Aspects of rock platform and cliff development on this coast are discussed by Bird and Dent (1967) and Langford-Smith and Thom (1969).

BRUCE G. THOM

REFERENCES

Bird, E. C. F., 1967, Depositional features in estuaries and lagoons on the south coast of New South Wales, *Australian Geog. Studies* **5**:113–124.

Bird, E. C. F., 1978, *The Geomorphology of the Gipps-land Lakes Region*, Environmental Studies Ser., Pub. 186, Ministry for Conservation, Victoria.

Bird, E. C. F., and O. F. Dent, 1967 Shore platforms on the south coast of New South Wales, *Australian Geographer* **10**:71–80.

Chapman, D. M., 1978, Zetaform or logarithmic spiral beach. Australian Landform Example No. 32, *Australian Geographer* **14**:44–45.

Davies, P. J., 1975, Shallow seismic structure of the continental shelf, southeast Australia, *Geol. Soc. Australia Jour.* **22**:345–359.

Davies, P. J., 1979, *Marine Geology of the Continental Shelf off Southeast Australia*, Bureau of Mineral Resources Bull. 195.

Gardner, D. E., 1955, *Beach Sand Heavy Mineral Deposits of Eastern Australia*, Bureau of Mineral Resources Bull. 28.

Hails, J. R., 1967, Significance of statistical parameters for distinguishing sedimentary environments in New South Wales, Australia, *Jour Sed. Petrology* **37**:1059–1069.

Hamon, B. V., 1967, The East Australian Current 1960–1964, *Deep Sea Research*, **12**:899–921.

Hayes, D. E., and J. Ringis, 1973, Seafloor spreading in the Tasman Sea, *Nature* **243**:454–458.

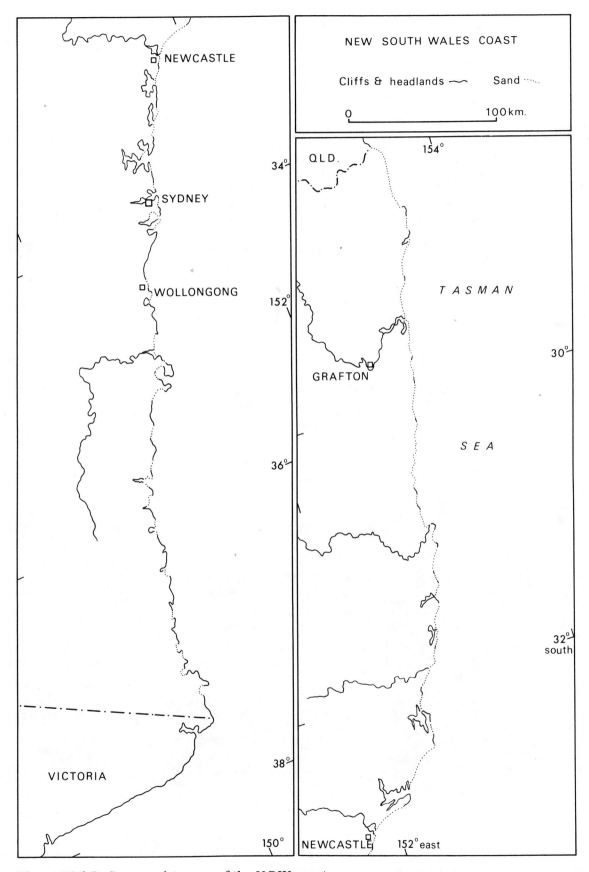

Figure 125-3. Geomorphic map of the N.S.W. coast.

Langford-Smith, T., and B. G. Thom, 1969, Coastal morphology of New South Wales, *Geol. Soc. Australia Jour.* **16:**572–580.

Lawson, N. V., and C. L. Abernethy, 1975, Longterm wave statistics off Botany Bay, in *2nd Australian Conf. on Coastal and Ocean Engineering,* The Institution of Engineers, Australia, pp. 167–176.

Marshall, J. F., and B. G. Thom, 1976, The sea level in the last interglacial, *Nature* **263:**120–121.

Roy, P. S., and E. A. Crawford, 1977, Significance of sediment distribution in major coastal rivers, northern New South Wales, in *3rd Australian Conf. on Coastal and Ocean Engineering,* The Institution of Engineers, Australia, pp. 177–184.

Roy, P. S., and B. G. Thom, 1981, Late Quaternary marine deposition in New South Wales and Southern Queensland—an evolutionary model, *Geol. Soc. Australia Jour.* **28:**471–489.

Roy, P. S., B. G. Thom, and L. D. Wright, 1980, Holocene sequences on an embayed high-energy coast: an evolutionary model, *Sed. Geology* **26:**1–19.

Thom, B. G., 1965, Late Quaternary coastal morphology of the Port Stephens—Myalls Lakes area, N.S.W., *Royal Soc. New South Wales Jour.* **98:**23–36.

Thom, B. G., 1974, Coastal erosion in eastern Australia, *Search* **5:**198–209.

Thom, B. G., 1978, Coastal sand deposition in southeast Australia during the Holocene, in *Landform Evolution in Australasia,* J. L. Davies and M. A. J. Williams, eds., Australian National University Press, pp. 197–214.

Thom, B. G., and J. Chappell, 1975, Holocene sea level relative to Australia, *Search* **6:**90–93.

Thom, B. G., G. M. Bowman, and P. S. Roy, 1981, Late Quaternary evolution of coastal sand barriers, Port Stephens—Myall Lakes area, central New South Wales, Australia *Quaternary Res.* **15:**345–364.

Wright, L. D., 1976, Nearshore wave-power dissipation and the coastal energy regime of the Sydney-Jervis Bay region, New South Wales: a comparison, *Australian Jour. Marine and Freshwater Research* **27:**633–640.

Plate 125-1. An extensive horizontal rock platform developed in tuffaceous sandstone at Boat Harbor, about 150 km south of Sydney (Bird and Dent 1967). The platform surface is approximately 1 m above mean sea level and is covered by most high tides (photo by G. M. Bowman).

126. TASMANIA

Because Tasmania is an island, its coast — more than 2,000 km long even without considering the many smaller islands — displays strong internal contrasts in structure and environment. In the western third of the island and in the northeast, rocks of pre-Carboniferous age are exposed, strongly folded along roughly north–south axes and accompanied by granitic intrusions (Fig. 126-1). In contrast the center and southeast are dominated by nearly horizontal Permian and Triassic sediments, associated with massive dolerite sills and major northeast–southwest, northwest–southeast fault lineaments, which become close to north–south along the east coast. Everywhere here these lineaments tend to control coastal alignment.

The west coast, from Cape Grim to South East Cape, is subject to high wind and wave energy, for it faces the predominant directions of approach of local storm systems and more distantly generated swell. The east coast, from South East Cape to Cape Portland, is more sheltered, with offshore winds much more in evidence and exposure to southern ocean swell significantly reduced. The north coast, facing Bass Strait, is the most sheltered of all. Oceanic swell is considerably attenuated here, and the few local storms have a strong northwesterly component so that onshore energy transmission decreases strikingly from east to west. Everywhere on the open ocean coasts, tides are of mixed type, with strong inequalities between succeeding highs and between succeeding lows, but, even at springs, the range between high, high water and low, low water rarely exceeds 1 m. On the north coast, however, the tides become more markedly semidiurnal and the range at springs rises to 2–3 m.

Figure 126-1 shows an association between the distribution of broad coastal types and prevailing onshore energy levels. Rocky coasts are found especially in the exposed southwest, and the proportion of the shore occupied by beaches increases toward the more sheltered sections of the north. The quartz metamorphic rocks of the southwest have not readily been formed into cliffs and platforms by marine processes, nor have the granite outcrops along the northern part of the east coast. On these sections the sea has drowned, washed, and sharpened up a former subaerial landscape that still owes much to the past. The best-developed cliffs and platforms have been produced in the sandstones, mudstones, and dolerites of the southeast and, to a lesser extent, in the basalts of the Bass Strait coast. The pronounced vertical jointing in these rocks has facilitated the quarrying of free faces by waves and the production at their foot of structural benches, which in sandstones, mudstones, and basalts are often fashioned by weathering processes into horizontal high tide platforms.

Beach sediments are overwhelmingly sandy, but pebbles often form the upper beach in restricted localities. Between Point Sorell and Table Cape on the north coast, pebbles have been supplied by rivers draining areas glaciated in the Pleistocene, and locally elsewhere pebbles are available from suitable lithologies. Beach sands are predominantly siliceous (Davies 1978) but become markedly more calcareous in the northwest corner, where, south of Cape Grim, the only lithified dunes on the main island are to be found. Available evidence indicates that longshore transport of shore sediments is strictly limited and materials are strongly compartmentalized be-

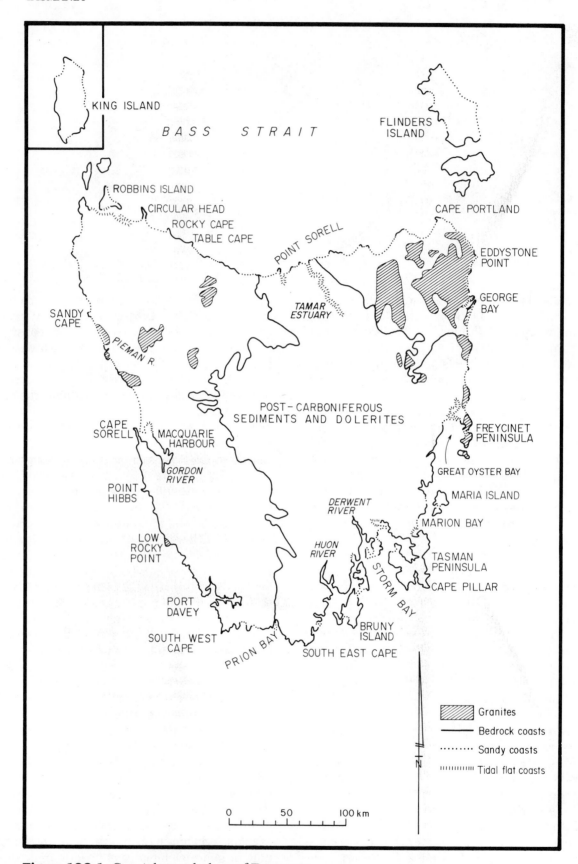

Figure 126-1. Coastal morphology of Tasmania.

tween major headlands (Davies 1973). Large transgressive dunes are found on the northern part of the west coast and on the eastern part of the north coast, the only sections where there is a suitable combination of available sand and strong onshore winds. Elsewhere dune formation is almost entirely limited to minor foredune systems.

Of the ten Australian rivers with the highest discharge to the sea, two are in Tasmania, a reflection of high rainfall and high runoff over most of the island. In comparison with other Australian coasts the number of large, deeply drowned estuaries is considerable. Some, such as the Tamar, Derwent, and Huon, are accumulating muds derived from weathered dolerite and mudstone catchments in the center and southeast. They are largely devoid of salt marsh, although the successful introduction of *Spartina* to the Tamar in the 1940s has changed the situation there (Phillips 1975). Small samphire salt marshes are to be found in sandy estuaries (Curtis and Somerville 1948) and more extensively on the north coast between Cape Grim and Circular Head.

There is much evidence to indicate that, in the last 200,000 years at least, Tasmanian coasts have developed rather differently in relation to sea level than have those elsewhere in southeastern Australia, suggesting differential tectonic and hydro-isostatic deformation of the island (van de Geer et al., 1979). In particular, shore features attributable to the last interglacial high sea level lie at a significantly higher altitude than they do north of Bass Strait, and it is possible that this differential movement has continued, with less visible results, into the Holocene.

On the northern part of the west coast, relatively unmetamorphosed Precambrian rocks form a low and shelving, but rugged, shoreline, covered here and there by dunes transgressing up to 3 km inland. Granite outcrops at Sandy Cape and farther south, notably around the mouth of the deeply drowned Pieman River, but again there is much mantling by sand.

Macquarie Harbour, over 40 m deep in places, occupies a large structural depression into which flows the Gordon River in the south and the King River in the north (Banks et al. 1977). Although the King continues to build a small delta, the shores of the harbor are generally steep, for this reason and because of the small tidal range, salt marsh is very limited. The broad barrier at the entrance incorporates Pleistocene as well as Holocene sediments, and near its northern end there

are mobile dunes reaching 50 m in height and 3 km in length along a wide front. At its southern end in the lee of Cape Sorell, the entrance itself is partially blocked by sandy tidal deltas that very much reduce the value of the harbor to navigation.

South of Macquarie Harbour the low rocky coast resumes, but shore sediment is much less plentiful than farther north, so that beaches and dunes are restricted to relatively small re-entrants. Around the southwestern corner of the island, where Precambrian quartzites outcrop extensively, the coastal morphology is particularly rugged, but cliffs remain few and the ruggedness is due mainly to subaerial erosion. The Port Davey embayment is entered by a large and intricate estuary that consists of a lower, narrow, deep (up to 40 m) section called Bathurst Channel and an upper, broad, shallow (0–10 m) section known as Bathurst Harbor. Bathurst Channel was once thought to be a glacial fjord, but there is no clear evidence for this and it appears to represent the drowned lower reaches of a river system. The contrast between the upper and lower sections of the estuary is probably due to differential sedimentation and tidal scour. Shores are generally steep and rocky, and there is very little development of salt marsh.

Quartzite shores continue east from South West Cape, but past Prion Bay the scenery changes as well-jointed Permo-Triassic sediments and dolerites reach the coast to form nearly vertical cliffs. Between South East Cape and Cape Pillar the coastline is extremely intricate, with numerous estuaries and with former bedrock islands tied by tombolos. The two biggest rivers, the Huon and Derwent, have deep estuaries, whose upper sections are flanked by muddy tidal flats, bare below the *Juncus* zone near high water mark. The smaller, seasonally flowing rivers tend to have sandier estuaries with some samphire marsh. Notable barrier beach features include the isthmus joining the northern and southern parts of Bruny Island, and the isthmuses forming the South Arm Peninsula and the Seven Mile Beach spit behind which Hobart airport is located. By contrast the exposed headlands are formed into spectacular cliffs. Tasman Head and Fluted Cape on Bruny and Cape Raoul, Cape Pillar, and Cape Hauy on the Tasman Peninsula display striking examples of high vertical free faces in the well-jointed dolerite. In more sheltered positions higher in the bays there are similar but smaller-scale cliffs in Permian sandstones. However, some of the best-developed sandstone cliffs are on the exposed eastern side of the Tasman Peninsula, where the Eaglehawk Neck area has a small array of arches, blowholes, stacks, and shore platforms. One horizontal platform, known locally as the Tessellated Pavement, has especially fine features resulting from water layer weathering processes.

Along the east coast, north from the Tasman Peninsula, the proportion of coast taken up by beaches increases steadily. In the south beaches tend to be small and widely separated by low dolerite cliffs. The most notable constructional features are the Marion Bay barrier, behind which there is well-developed salt marsh in the Blackman Bay lagoon, and the Nine Mile Beach barrier at the head of Great Oyster Bay, isolating the large Moulting Lagoon. Another sandy estuary with well-developed salt marsh lies between these two features at Little Swanport. Like Bruny, Maria Island consists of northern and southern sections tied by a narrow tombolo, it too has spectacular cliffs on its exposed eastern side.

The character of the coast changes markedly at the Freycinet Peninsula, where granite makes its appearance. On the peninsula itself, large granite bosses fall 600 m into the sea with little or no evidence of modification by the waves; this sort of landscape is repeated on a smaller scale at headlands farther north. Beaches fringe the coast extensively in wide curving embayments. Rivers are short and estuaries small; the major source of beach sand is weathered granite. An exception occurs at George Bay, where a complex late Pleistocene and Holocene barrier shelters the estuary of the George River. The river has built a small delta at the head of the estuary, while a larger tidal delta creates navigational difficulties at the entrance.

The northern coast, facing the shallow epicontinental sea of Bass Strait, is the sandiest of all. Because the biggest waves, both storm and swell, approach from the west, beaches tend to turn to face this direction, so that in the east they have well-marked zeta forms with sheltered southern ends. Because the strongest winds also come from the west, these beaches are backed by big dune systems. Between Cape Portland and Point Sorell transgressive dunes extend inland in places over a hinterland of low relief. The oldest are thought to be late Pleistocene in age (Bowden 1978), but the most recent phase of activation dates from only about 100 years ago when burning and the introduction of cattle mobilized previously stable dunes.

West of Point Sorell, transgressive dunes become much scarcer and much smaller. The most

characteristic dune form here is low, parallel, sand beach ridges resulting from mid-Holocene progradation. These are a feature of some barriers elsewhere, notably Seven Mile Beach in Storm Bay and Nine Mile Beach in Great Oyster Bay, but they are especially numerous along the low-energy shore from the Tamar estuary west to Cape Grim. In places, notably west to Circular Head, older Pleistocene beach-ridge systems are to be found to landward.

Headlands along this coast are formed in dolerite or basalt, and prominent jointing leads to locally well-developed cliffs. However, because of the relatively low wave energy they are somewhat muted in form. Thus the high cliffs formed at Table Cape in a basaltic volcanic neck are talus fringed and have a considerable cover of vegetation. A similar prominent feature at Circular Head is attached to the present shore by accumulations of sediment. Rather an exception is the quartzite projection of Rocky Cape, a small echo of the topography of the southwest.

Much the biggest estuary on the north coast is that of the Tamar, into which flow a number of large rivers draining central Tasmania. It is largely filled by mud, whereas the smaller estuaries are usually sandy.

To the north of Tasmania are two large contrasting islands that have been relatively intensively studied. King Island is a low plateau of Precambrian rocks much covered by transgressive dunes (Jennings 1959). Flinders Island has high granite peaks fringed by beach barrier systems, which on the east coast impound a chain of shallow lagoons (Kershaw and Sutherland 1972).

J. L. DAVIES

REFERENCES

Banks, M. R., E. A. Colhoun, and N. K. Chick, 1977, A reconnaissance of the geomorphology of central western Tasmania, in *Landscape and Man*, M. R. Banks and J. B. Kirkpatrick, eds., Royal Society of Tasmania, Hobart, pp. 29–54.

Bowden, A., 1978, *Geomorphic Perspective on Shallow Groundwater Potential, Coastal North-eastern Tasmania*, Australia Water Res. Council Tech. Rept. 36.

Curtis, W. M., and J. Somerville, 1948, Boomer Marsh —a preliminary botanical and historical survey, *Royal Soc. Tasmania Pap. Proc.* **1947**:151–157.

Davies, J. L., 1973, Sediment movement on the Tasmanian coast, *1st Australian Conf. Coastal Eng. Proc.*, pp. 43–46.

Davies, J. L., 1978, Beach sand and wave energy in Tasmania, in *Landform Evolution in Australasia*, J. L. Davies and M. A. J. Williams, eds., pp. 158–167.

Jennings, J. N., 1959, The coastal geomorphology of King Island, Bass Strait, *Rec. Queen Victoria Museum, Launceston, N.S.*, **11:**1–39.

Kershaw, R. C., and F. L. Sutherland, 1972, Quaternary geomorphology of Flinders Island, *Rec. Queen Victoria Museum, Launceston*, N.S., **43:**1–28.

Phillips, A. W., 1975, The establishment of *Spartina* in the Tamar estuary, Tasmania, *Royal Soc. Tasmania Pap. Proc.* **109:**65–75.

van de Geer, G., E. A. Colhoun, and A. Bowden, 1979, Evidence and problems of interglacial marine deposits in Tasmania, *Geologie en Mijnbouw* **58:**29–32.

127. NEW ZEALAND

New Zealand consists of two main islands, the sprawling, angular North Island and the more compact, regular South Island (Fig. 127-1). Many smaller islands lie offshore, the largest being Stewart in the far south, Great Barrier in the north, and D'Urville in the center. A number of former islands are now tied to the mainland by tombolos; Banks Peninsula and Mahia Peninsula on the east coast and the Aupouri and Karikari peninsulas in the extreme north are examples.

Open ocean surrounds the country, the nearest continental neighbor, Australia, being nearly 2,000 km to the west across the stormy Tasman Sea. Storm waves and ocean swell emanating from centers in the Southern Ocean result in moderate to high wave energy along the exposed west- and south-facing coasts of both islands (Plate 127-1). Leeward shores include the northern end of South Island and East Cape to North Cape sector, which face to the north and northeast. Both areas are protected from the persistent southern swell and are characterized by lower wave energy, but receive the impact of occasional cyclone-generated waves from the north during summer. Tides around New Zealand are semidiurnal with a mesotidal range (2–4 m); tidal streams and currents reach high velocities between close offshore islands and the mainland, and especially through the narrow Cook Strait (23 km) that separates the two main islands.

For its size (270,000 km²) New Zealand has a long (10,000 km) and richly varied coastline. It includes almost every type of coastal feature found in temperate latitudes throughout the world. It lacks actively glaciated coasts, coral reef, and dry desert shores, though bare sand dunes are found along the west coast and mangroves in the northern estuaries, and recently glaciated coasts are a

feature of the southwest of South Island. This diversity of coastal scenery is matched by the rapidity of change from place to place and reflects New Zealand's diverse rock types, elongated shape, exposed oceanic and midlatitude climate position, and the legacy of an active glacial, volcanic, and tectonic Quaternary, together with its geologic location athwart but boundary between the Indian and Pacific plates.

Lithology has an important role. Figure 127-1 distinguishes coastal rock types of high, medium, and low resistance to erosional forces. To a large extent the broad shape of both islands is controlled by the outcrops of hard rocks at the extremities (Tortell 1981). Hard igneous rocks form resistant bulwarks at North Cape and Matakaoa Point (Plate 127-2) near East Cape. Similar resistant areas are found at Great Barrier Island and along the Wellington coast, where the rock is a durable graywacke. The major promontory on the west coast of the North Island, Cape Egmont, is an exception; it is constructed of volcanic lahar deposits forming the Mt. Egmont volcanic complex. In the South Island hard rock areas also provide the cornerstones of its shape. Resistant conglomerate at Cape Farewell, granite at Separation Point, and the graywacke and schists of the Marlborough Sounds form the three northern promontories of the island, while in the far south, the very hard gneisses and granites of Fjordland and Stewart Island, and the graywackes of southeastern Southland have proved resistant to marine erosion. On the east coast hard volcanic rocks form the two main projecting headlands, Banks Peninsula, which consists of two coalescing volcanoes, and the Otago Peninsula.

On the basis of physiography the New Zealand

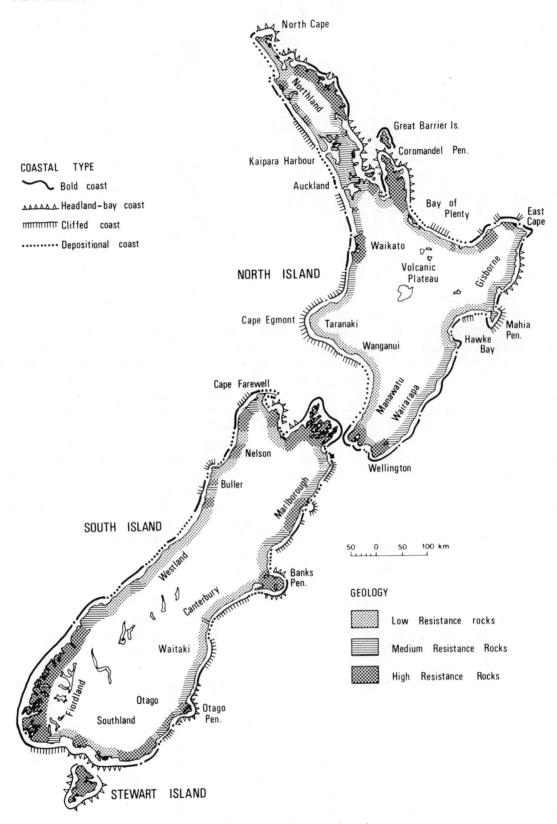

Figure 127-1. New Zealand: coastal types and coastal geology.

coast can be divided into four fundamental types whose distribution is disjunct rather than continuous (Fig. 127-1). *Bold coasts* (Cotton 1974) are those developed in steep hilly or mountainous terrain; they have high relative relief and generally include the corners of the country outlined above as well as some intermediate sectors possessing high- or medium-resistance rocks that are congruent with the main shoreline trends. The most extensive and also the most impressive of these is the Fjordland block of the remote mountainous country in the far southwest of New Zealand. Here the fault-controlled coast includes many hundreds of kilometers of deeply indented fjords whose walls are exceptionally steep and whose basins are exceptionally deep (Plate 127-3). High rocky bluffs separate each of the fjords, which were occupied by large valley glaciers until approximately 10,000 years ago, when the valleys began to be flooded by the sea. Two other areas of bold coast, the Marlborough Sounds at the northern end of South Island and the Bay of Islands on the east coast of Northland, are also deeply indented "loci of submergence" (Cotton 1918), whose flooded V-shaped valleys, separated by sharp hill crests, form an intricate pattern of quiet water, islands, spurs, and hills. Other bold coasts are different; they possess straight steep-to shores rather than dissected ones. Included in this group are the predominantly graywacke areas of eastern Bay of Plenty and eastern Southland and the fault coasts of western Coromandel, Kaikoura, and the Wellington area, the latter continuing northward along the Wairarapa coast in somewhat softer uplifted Tertiary and Cretaceous mudstones and sandstones. High uplift rates are associated with those coasts, especially in central New Zealand and particularly in the Wellington area, where raised beaches and platforms form coastal steps (Plate 127-4). All of the bold coasts are essentially beachless, though river deltas occur in the deeper embayments, and rockfalls, landslips, and slumps along the open coast provide basal debris that is swept away by wave action. Shore platforms are poorly developed mainly because of the high resistance of the rocks.

Headland-bay coasts comprise a succession of rocky headlands separated by narrow shallow bays. Bay-head beaches commonly display regular geometrical outlines resulting from completely refracted waves working on bay-trapped marine and fluvial sediments. Alluvial plains, swamps, lagoons, or a succession of beach ridges and low dunes of late Quaternary and Holocene age com-

monly occur behind the active beach (Plates 127-5, 127-6). Headland-bay coasts are found in eastern Northland, Auckland, Coromandel, the Gisborne and Nelson districts, Banks Peninsula, Otago Peninsula, and southernmost New Zealand, in most places associated with transversely fractured high- to medium-resistance rocks and areas of moderate relief. They are virtually absent from the west coasts of both islands. Because of the close juxtaposition of rocky headlands, shore platforms, and sandy beaches, headland-bay coasts are frequently the sites for summer home and retirement settlements.

Cliffed coasts (Fig. 127-1) have regular, straight or gently curved outlines, often fronted by a narrow gravel or sandy beach. Cliffs are commonly 20–50 m high and are cut into low- to medium-resistance deposits of Cenozoic age, and are backed by low-relief subhorizontal or terraced surfaces. In Westland, Canterbury, Waitaki, and Otago, cliffs are developed in glaciofluvial deposits (Plate 127-7); in Marlborough, Wanganui, Hawkes Bay, and north Taranaki they occur in uplifted marine and fluvial sands and gravels; in Taranaki and parts of Bay of Plenty they are cut into volcanic lahars and ignimbrites; and along the western Auckland and Northland shores partially consolidated old sand dunes form the cliff line (Plate 127-8). In most areas cliff faces are active and are being trimmed back. Three processes are responsible: basal sapping during periods of storm waves when the frontal beach is mobilized; mass movement (rock falls, debris slides, and slumps) on the cliff face itself; and rilling and gullying by runoff from natural creeks and artificial drains from the hinterland. Debris is quickly reworked in the beach environment, and only rarely does enough material accumulate to form a broad backshore and permanently strand the cliff line. Erosion of Pleistocene cliffs has supplied sand and gravel to feed downdrift beaches during the Holocene and provides a continuing sediment source for contemporary progradation in embayments adjacent to cliffed coasts. In some areas of medium-resistance Late Cenozoic sandstones and mudstones, wide shore platforms, rather than beaches, have developed, notably along the Marlborough and north Taranaki coasts, and in the Gisborne district at Mahia Peninsula. In these three areas the present cliff-shore platform complex is backed by one or more uplifted scarps and benches cut during high interglacial sea levels.

Depositional coasts (Fig. 127-1) are low coasts of accumulation that have shown substantial progradation in late Quaternary time. In many parts of the country bays are fringed by broad bands of sand or gravel ridges that separate flood plains, swamps, lakes, or relict bluffs from the sea (Plate 127-9). Coastal barriers, tombolos, spits, and forelands are also found in widely scattered areas. Examples of gravel forms include the long forested barriers of central and southern Westland, the Kaitorete barrier (Armon 1974), which separates Lake Ellesmere from the sea in Canterbury (Plate 127-10), the boulder banks in Nelson and Marlborough (Pickrill 1976), and the graywacke gravel barriers in northern and southern Hawke Bay, the latter being modified by differential uplift and subsidence of 2 m during the 1931 earthquake. Sandy forms include Farewell Spit at the extreme northwestern end of the South Island, the complex spits and forelands at the harbor entrances along the Waikato, Auckland, and Northland west coast, and the barrier islands of Nelson and Matakana (Bay of Plenty), which is located between the westward-trending Mount Maunganui tombolo (Plate 127-11) and eastward-trending Bowentown tombolo. Sand dunes of late Pleistocene and Holocene age (Cowie 1963) fill the broad embayment stretching 150 km from Wanganui to Wellington (Plate 127-12). Other major dune fields are developed along parts of the western seaboard of both islands and in the far north on both sides of the Aupouri Peninsula (Plate 127-1). The distinction between these coastal depositional features and those that occur on headland-bay coasts is simply a matter of scale: they are much more extensive laterally along shore and frequently extend farther inland.

In addition to these four basic coastal types there are some 300 estuaries around the New Zealand coast. Healy and Kirk (1982) recognized five classes of estuary based on physiography: (1) drowned river valleys; (2) barrier-enclosed estuaries and estuarine lagoons; (3) river-mouth estuaries; (4) estuaries resulting from tectonic activity; and (5) glacially excavated valleys or fjords. Clearly most estuaries in New Zealand are to some extent drowned valleys, and are particularly associated with the bold coasts and headland-bay coasts described earlier. Barrier-enclosed estuaries include New Zealand's largest, the many-armed Kaipara Harbor on the west coast of Northland. At the other end of the scale, New Zealand has many rivers that enter the sea in estuaries of relatively small area and width-depth ratios. Within these estuaries fresh-water input is relatively large compared with the tidal prism. In

such circumstances and especially in view of the high sediment yields contributed by rivers, it is surprising that deltas are not a more common feature of New Zealand's coastal scenery. Active deltas are locally found in the Westport, Nelson, Marlborough, and Wellington districts in the shelter of headlands or offshore islands, and at the heads of deep indentations, fjords, sounds, and harbors. They are not common elsewhere mainly because of the efficiency of littoral drift, fluvially contributed sediment being moved rapidly alongshore by wave action.

Extensive tidal flats, usually composed of muddy sand rather than pure mud, are found in many estuaries and also in the lee of some of the most spectacular spits, e.g., Farewell Spit. In the northern estuaries mangroves are common; salt marsh is found throughout the country together with the introduced plant *Spartina.* Banks of shell occur on many tidal flats, and along the western side of the Firth of Thames between Coromandel Peninsula and Auckland a true chenier plain has developed in the last 4,000 years. This prograded coastal plain consists of 13 shell ridges separated by and overlying fine marine muds (Woodroffe et al. 1983).

While shell banks and shores composed of coarse shell are common in quiet water situations throughout the country, on the open coast broken-down molluscan fragments rarely form more than 10% of the beach material. Detrital or terrigenous sediments provide the bulk of beach material. Although there is great local variation in texture and composition three main sediment types can be distinguished (Fig. 127-2). Beaches dominated by light quartzose-feldspathic sands prevail at the extremities of the country, in Southland and Otago, Nelson, Wellington, and Northland (Schofield 1970) as well as around the Bay of Plenty. Source rocks for the sands include the hard metamorphic and plutonic rocks in the South Island and sedimentary and acid volcanic rocks in the North Island. In contrast to these white or golden sands, the central west coasts of both islands have black ironsand beaches dominated by ilmenite in the South and titanomagnetite in the North, the latter being derived from the Egmont volcanic complex. Approximately 60% of New Zealand's beaches are sand, the remainder being dominated by gravel. Numerous small gravel and boulder beaches occur in north and south Westland and in the Nelson and Southland districts, the source rocks being either metamorphic or igneous, but the most extensive gravel and

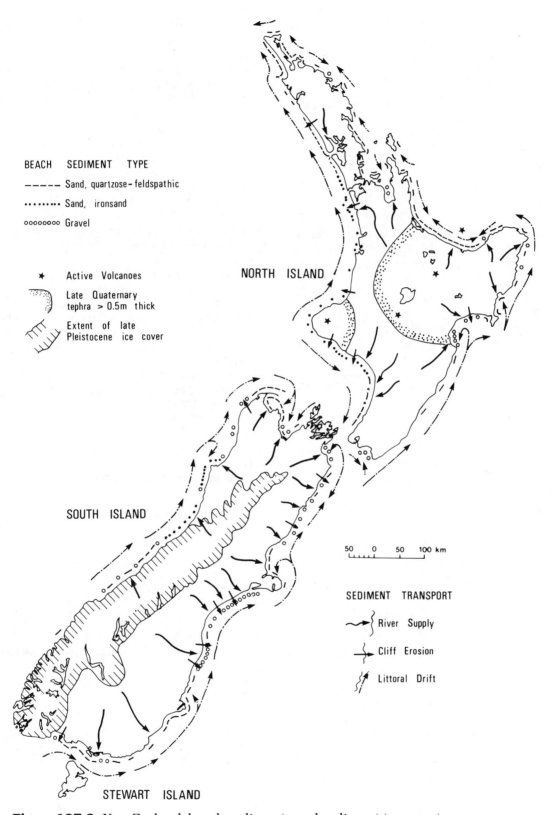

Figure 127-2. New Zealand: beach sediments and sediment transport.

mixed sand and gravel beaches (Kirk 1980) are those on the east coast from Waitaki northward. These graywacke-derived beaches normally occur in one of two situations: either as narrow cliff foot beaches where active erosion is taking place (Plate 127-7), or as single or multiple-ridged barrier beaches (Plate 127-10).

Throughout the Quaternary vast quantities of sand and gravel were shed from the land to the coast. Two important controls on the nature and distribution of coastal sediments were the extent of Pleistocene ice cover in the South Island and volcanic tephra (ash and pumice) in the North Island (Fig. 127-2). In addition, high uplift rates, a rugged terrain, and highly competent streams and rivers have ensured a continual sediment supply, supplemented more recently by cliff erosion. A long history of late Quaternary deposition (McLean 1978) and erosion is revealed at many sites in New Zealand, and even in recent years much of the coastline has undergone substantial change (Gibb 1978).

ROGER F. MCLEAN

REFERENCES

Armon, J. W., 1974, Late Quaternary shorelines near Lake Ellesmere, Canterbury, New Zealand, *New Zealand Jour. Geology and Geophysics* **17:**63–74.

Cotton, C. A., 1918, The outline of New Zealand, *Geog. Rev.* **6:**320–340.

Cotton, C. A., 1974, *Bold Coasts: Annotated Reprints of Selected Papers on Coastal Geomorphology, 1916–69,* B. W. Collins, ed., Reed, Wellington.

Cowie, J. D., 1963, Dune-building phases in the Manawatu district, *New Zealand Jour. Geology and Geophysics* **6:**268–280.

Gibb, J. G., 1978, Rates of coastal erosion and accretion in New Zealand, *New Zealand Jour. Marine and Freshwater Research* **12:**429–456.

Healy, T., and R. M. Kirk, 1982, Coasts, in *Landforms of New Zealand,* J. M. Soons and M. J. Selby, eds., Longman Paul, Auckland, pp. 81–104.

Kirk, R. M., 1980, Mixed sand and gravel beaches: morphology and sediments, *Progress in Physical Geography* **4:**189–210.

McLean, R. F., 1978, Recent coastal progradation in New Zealand, in *Landform Evolution in Australasia,* J. L. Davies and M. A. J. Williams, eds., Australian National University Press, Canberra, pp. 168–196.

Pickrill, R. A., 1976, The evolution of coastal landforms of the Wairau Valley, *New Zealand Geographer* **32:**17–29.

Schofield, J. C., 1970, Coastal sands of Northland and Auckland, *New Zealand Jour. Geology and Geophysics* **13:**767–864.

Tortell, P., ed., 1981, *New Zealand Atlas of Coastal Resources,* Government Printer, Wellington.

Woodroffe, C. D., R. J. Curtis, and R. F. McLean, 1983, Development of a chenier plain, Firth of Thames, New Zealand, *Marine Geology* **53:**1–22.

Plate 127-1. Long period waves from the southern Tasman Sea beat against the west coast of Aupouri Peninsula, Northland, view looking south. The wide beach and wide surf zone are characteristic of exposed west coast beaches. The promontory, The Bluff, is the only break in the otherwise straight and continuous Ninety-Mile Beach. Low bare sand dunes of the coastal deflation zone show the strength of prevailing westerly winds. Such dunes have been the site of extensive exotic forestry (*Pinus radiata*) plantings in recent times (photo by White's Aviation).

Plate 127-2. The northeastern corner of North Island is situated near the southern terminus of the Tonga-Kermadec island arc-trench system. The east coast runs parallel to the trench whereas the trend of Matakaoa Range runs east–west. Marine terraces cut into Matakaoa volcanics are well developed. Volcanic ash from the Taupo volcanic zone is extensively distributed and covers the terraces, subduing the bedrock topography. At Matakaoa Point, near East Cape, the most extensive terrace is of last interglacial age, the surface declining from 60 m in the foreground to 30 m, right background. Matakaoa terrace, 95 m, was formed in the pen-ultimate interglacial. A shore platform of Holocene age is well developed at the base of the present cliffs (photo by D. L. Homer, New Zealand Geological Survey).

Plate 127-3. Sutherland Sound, on the bold coast of the fault-bounded uplifted Fjordland block that covers an area of 10,000 km². Accordant summit levels and surfaces are found at various elevations, the main one being at over 1,000 m. A landscape of glacial erosion features; depositional landforms are rare (photo by D. L. Homer, New Zealand Geological Survey).

Plate 127-4. Spectacular evidence of tectonic processes is displayed at Turakirae Head (foreground) and Baring Head (middle distance) near Wellington Harbor. Raised beaches of Holocene age at Turakirae show as light-colored strips roughly parallel to the coastline. Beaches formed 6,500 (not shown), 4,900, 3,100, and 510 years ago were elevated by intermittent earth movements soon after they formed. The sandy-gravelly beach deposits were left as a ridge, and a zone of rocky shore was exposed below them on which a new beach began to form. The narrow beach line, immediately behind the present shore was elevated by the 1855 A.D. earthquake. At Baring Head two marine (wave-cut) terraces are distinguished, the higher associated with the penultimate interglacial, the lower with the last interglacial (photo by D. L. Homer, New Zealand Geological Survey).

Plate 127-5. Bay-head sand beach, Okains Bay, Banks Peninsula (South Island). The peninsula comprises two late Tertiary–early Quaternary volcanoes dissected by a radial valley pattern. Valley sides are steep, lava flow bedding exposed, truncated spurs terminate at the seaward end as plunging cliffs. Bay-head sand and gravel beaches are found in most bays. The 800 m long Okains Bay beach shown here is backed by a succession of Holocene beach ridges that can be traced 2.4 km inland. Progradation of some 230 m has taken place in the last 100 years. Textural and mineral analyses indicates nourishment from the sea floor and not local fluvial or cliff erosion (photo courtesy of National Publicity Studios).

Plate 127-6. Typical headland-bay coastal type, Mercury Bay, eastern Coromandel Peninsula (North Island). Bedrock-confined embayments filled by estuarine sediments and prograded Holocene beach ridges clearly show at Cooks Beach (foreground) and are marked by lines of trees at Whitianga (background) (photo by Aero Surveys).

Plate 127-7. Cliffed coastline developed in terraced glaciofluvial gravels and sands of Pleistocene age. This cliffline extends 40 km around the Waitaki delta (South Island) and is broken only by the river mouth and narrow gullies such as shown in the middle distance. Cliff-foot gravel beach formed from local cliff erosion (photo by White's Aviation).

Plate 127-8. Cliffed coast developed in partly consolidated sand dunes of Plio-Pleistocene age, north Kaipara barrier looking south, west coast Northland (North Island). Note narrow sandy beach with rhythmic topography, degraded cliff-line and incised gullies, flattish surface of marine terrace dissected by box-shaped valleys, active clifftop dunes (photo courtesy of New Zealand Geological Survey).

Plate 127-9. Northern part of 21 km long curving beach at Cloudy Bay (northeast South Island). Regular lines of gravel beach ridges and swales extend 5 km inland. Extensive progradation in Holocene times has occurred with sediment contributed by littoral drift from the south. Accretion is continuing at approximately 1 m per year. Beach cusps can be seen on the present beach and fossil ridges (photo courtesy of New Zealand Geological Survey).

Plate 127-10. Western end of Kaitorete gravel barrier, Canterbury (South Island). Barrier of graywacke gravel ridges broadens towards Banks Peninsula in background and holds in fresh-water Lake Ellesmere, whose level is artificially controlled by breaching through narrowest point in middle distance. Note swell waves approaching from south. Beach drops steeply offshore, resulting in narrow surf zone and wide swash zone (photo by White's Aviation).

Plate 127-11. Mt. Maunganui tombolo, Bay of Plenty (North Island). Progradation has taken place from left to right in late Pleistocene and Holocene time; linear beach ridges and dunes now obscured by urban development. Matakana, an island barrier, lies across the entrance to Tauranga harbor (photo by Aero Surveys).

Plate 127-12. The broad sweeping curve of the western coast between Wanganui and Wellington, North Island, extends for 120 km. Bare sand, blowouts, and sharp hairpin dunes of the most recent dune phase near Himatangi Beach. These dunes have now been stabilized by marram, lupin, and pine forest plantings. Shell middens on degraded fossil frontal dune show as light-toned patches. A new foredune has been formed in the last 50 years (photo courtesy of New Zealand Geological Survey).

128. NEW CALEDONIA AND THE LOYALTY ISLANDS

New Caledonia (area, 19,800 km^2) has a coastline about 1,000 km long (ORSTOM 1981). It is a mountainous island consisting mainly of crystalline schists with peridotite and serpentine rock. The east coast is generally steep, with only minor plains around river mouths, several of which open into deep rias; the west coast has more extensive plains, backed by a hilly hinterland, with numerous promontories and islands, and intervening embayments into which deltas have been built (Fig. 128-1). Open-cast mining of nickel is extensive in the laterized peridotite highlands of New Caledonia, and has added red clay, sand, gravel and boulders to the natural sediment loads of many of the rivers, eventually acclerating the infilling of estuaries, the progradation of deltas, and the shallowing of nearshore waters. Evidence of such changes is obtained by comparing nineteenth-century maps and charts and air photographs taken in 1954 and 1976.

The coastal climate has a dry winter and a hot wet summer when tropical cyclones occur. Southeasterly trade winds prevail.

The coastal waters of New Caledonia are rich in coral reef formations (Davis 1925; Avias 1959). Encircling barrier reefs include the atoll-like loops of D'Entrecasteaux and Great South reefs, and numerous knolls and patch reefs, some with sandy cays (Guilcher 1965). Fringing reefs are best developed on west-facing shores (Chevalier 1973); some have a shallow boat channel to the rear, and others are attached to the shore, the inner parts bearing algal deposits, sandy flats backed by derived white coralline beaches, or mangroves.

Tide ranges are small, generally less than a meter. Wave action is related to local, mainly southeasterly, winds, except where oceanic waves enter through the passes that interrupt the barrier reef, and strong wave action penetrates to adjacent shores.

Cliffs are found only in a few sectors reached by strong wave action, as at Cape Ndoua and on the southeast of Ile Ouen in the far south of New Caledonia. Bold coasts are more extensive, usually with steep seaward slopes bearing a soil mantle and vegetation cover, and only limited cliffing at the shoreline.

The features of the indented, hilly Nouméa Peninsula and the adjacent Bay of Dumbéa, into which the Dumbéa River has built a large delta with zoned mangrove communities (Baltzer 1969), are typical of the west coast (Fig. 128-2). Farther north, the isleted and reef-protected Bay of St. Vincent receives terrigenous sands and clays from rivers and coralline sediment from the sea floor (Dugas 1974). Dune calcarenites formed during Pleistocene low-sea-level stages on the outer coasts of Puen, Hugen, and Mathieu islands (Avias and Coudray 1965), but these are otherwise rare in New Caledonia. The Tontouta and Ouenghi rivers are building mangrove-fringed deltas into this bay (Plate 128-1), and the clay plain behind the Bay of Déama carries sandy cheniers.

Near Bourail the Néra Delta has a gently curving sandy shoreline behind the Bay of Gouaro (Plate

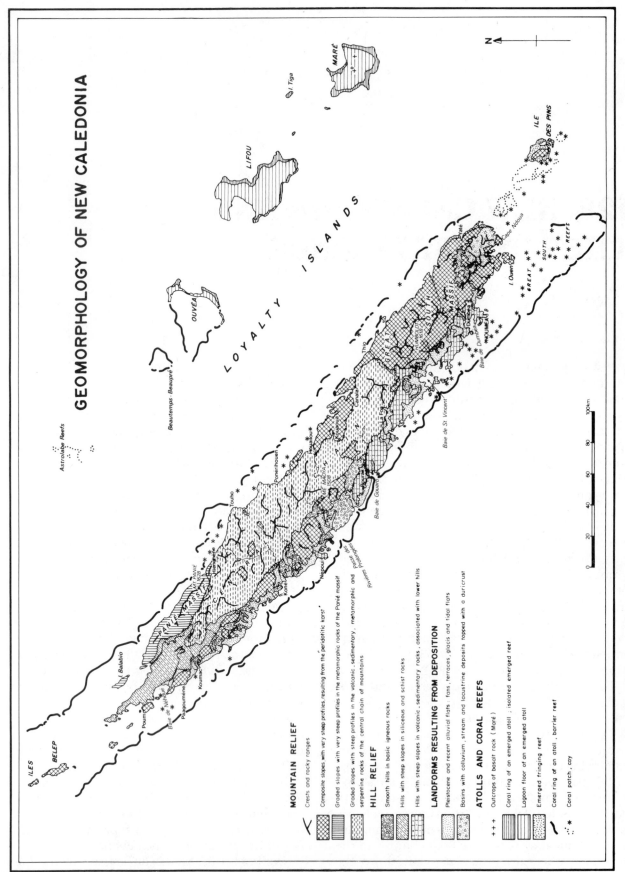

GEOMORPHOLOGY OF NEW CALEDONIA

MOUNTAIN RELIEF

Crests and rocky ranges

Composite slopes with very steep profiles, resulting from the peridotitic karst

Graded slopes with very steep profiles in the metamorphic rocks of the Panié massif

Graded slopes with steep profiles in the volcanic, sedimentary, metamorphic and serpentine rocks of the central chain of mountains

HILL RELIEF

Smooth hills in basic igneous rocks

Hills with steep slopes in siliceous and schist rocks

Hills with steep slopes in volcanic, sedimentary rocks, associated with lower hills

LANDFORMS RESULTING FROM DEPOSITION

Pleistocene and recent alluvial flats : fans, terraces, glacis and tidal flats

Basins with colluvium, stream and lacustrine deposits topped with a duricrust

ATOLLS AND CORAL REEFS

+ + + Outcrops of basalt rock (Maré)

Coral ring of an emerged atoll ; isolated emerged reef

Lagoon floor of an emerged atoll

Emerged fringing reef

Coral ring of an atoll , barrier reef

· ∗ · Coral patch, cay

Figure 128-1. Geomorphology of New Caledonia.

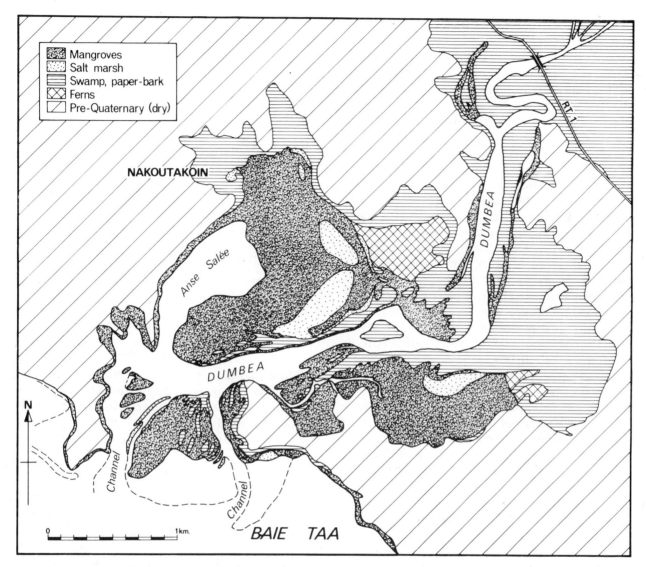

Figure 128-2. The Dumbéa Delta, New Caledonia (after Baltzer 1969).

128-2), which receives oceanic waves through a pass in the outlying barrier reef. This is contrasted with the more intricate delta of the Poya River, to the north, which has mangrove-bordered lobate salients between distributary mouths opening into a bay, sheltered from strong wave action, with numerous shoals threaded by channels in the Passe des Rivières Prolongées. Mangrove-fringed salt marshes and dry saline flats are extensive on these west coast deltas and plains, which are submerged by summer river flooding and cyclone surges, but dessicate in the long dry season. The marshes of Mara, studied by Baltzer (1965), partly overlie a dead coral reef, and have saline flats backed by a clifflet a few centimeters high rising to savanna terrain.

The Iouanga and Koumac rivers carry large amounts of sand and gravel derived from weathering outcrops of phthanite and Pleistocene valley terraces dominated by this material. Their deltas are fringed by beaches and spits that have grown northwestward, that of the Koumac extending past the cuspate foreland of Tangadiou (in the lee of a patch reef) and on toward Paagoumène, to end in a recurved spit. This grew about 100 m between 1954 and 1976, prograding the shoreline by about 250 m as it grew. Behind and beyond this spit the shoreline is mangrove-edged, but north of Paagoumène the coast steepens, and intermittent white beaches of coralline sand lie behind an almost continuous fringing reef.

Mangroves occupy more than 30,000 ha in New

Caledonia. Narrow shore fringes are widespread, but the largest stands are in the Bay of Néhoué, and on either side of the Poum Isthmus in the northwest. In the sheltered situations where sediment is abundant, mangroves advance rapidly: up to 400 m between 1954 and 1976 on the shores of the Népoui Delta, where red mud is accumulating as the result of mining operations upstream.

North of Poum and on Île Balabio, beaches are dominated by reef-derived calcareous sand and gravel, but fluvial deposition is proceeding rapidly in the gulf at the mouth of the Diahot, New Caledonia's longest river, to form a swampy deltaic plain studded with numerous shallow lakes and salt pans.

The east coast is steeper and more exposed to waves generated by the southeasterly trade winds, especially where the barrier reef (which excludes most oceanic wave action) is outlying. At Hienghène the coast is marked by steep-sided crystalline Eocene limestone outcrops, which run out into the sea to from basally notched karstic stacks (Plate 128-3) on either side of a steep ria. South of Ponérihouen several rivers are delivering sand and gravel loads augmented by the effects of mining within their catchments to nourish beaches that are extended northward by longshore drifting. Others are infilling deep rias, as at Kouaoua, where a sandy beach-ridge plain has been built up at the mouths of the Kakenjou and Kouaoua rivers (Fig. 128-3). Considerable changes occur around the mouths of these rivers during floods (e.g., Cyclone Gyan, 1981), and when waves subsequently rebuild spits and bars of sand and gravel washed into the sea by flood waters.

In the southeast of New Caledonia, the coast is bordered by 25 km of emerged Pleistocene fringing reef near Yaté, and similar reefs encircle the peridotite hill of Pic Nga and the ferritic plateau on the Isle of Pines (Fig. 128-4). Their restricted extent and varying altitude indicate that tectonic uplift has taken place here (Launay and Recy 1972). Their seaward margins show typical notch-and-visor profiles with minor shore platforms, developed largely by solution processes (Plate 128-4).

The Loyalty Islands are a chain of uplifted reef formations parallel to, and northeast from, New Caledonia. The southernmost, Walpole Island, is a patch reef raised 75 m above present sea level. Maré has the form of a raised atoll with a rim 60–138 m high, the southwest being higher than the northeast. It is surrounded by a modern fringing reef. Stages in elevation are marked by 15 terraces, the upper ones tilted, those below 12

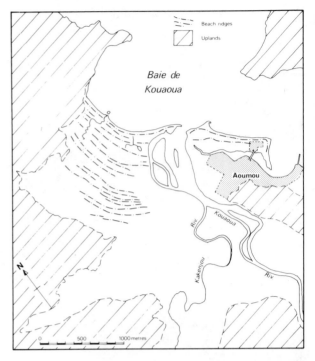

Figure 128-3. Progradation of the coastal plain in the Bay of Kouaoua on the northeast coast of New Caledonia is marked by successively formed sandy beach ridges, the sand being derived largely from sediment brought down by the Kouaoua River.

m horizontal. In the center are three basaltic peaks, all that can be seen of the basement, a volcanic island of early Miocene age around which the reefs developed and were afterward uplifted.

Lifou is similar, but the raised reef rim reaches only 104 m above present sea level. Five terraces mark stages in its uplift.

Ouvéa has the form of a tilted atoll, the eastern rim raised up to 46 m above the present sea level, with four terraces on its seaward flank, the western rim submerged, but with a chain of younger reef segments built up from it to enclose a lagoon with a floor that declines westward. Farther north, Beautemps-Beaupré is similar, the southeastern part raised only 4 m above low-tide level, while the Astrolabe Reefs beyond are not emerged features.

Although it has been generally believed, following Davis (1925), that Maré, Lifou, and Ouvéa were atoll formations raised by tectonic movements and since modified by karstic weathering, it has been alternatively suggested that they originated from reef platforms that suffered differential biochemical erosion after uplift, with excavation of the central areas and persistence

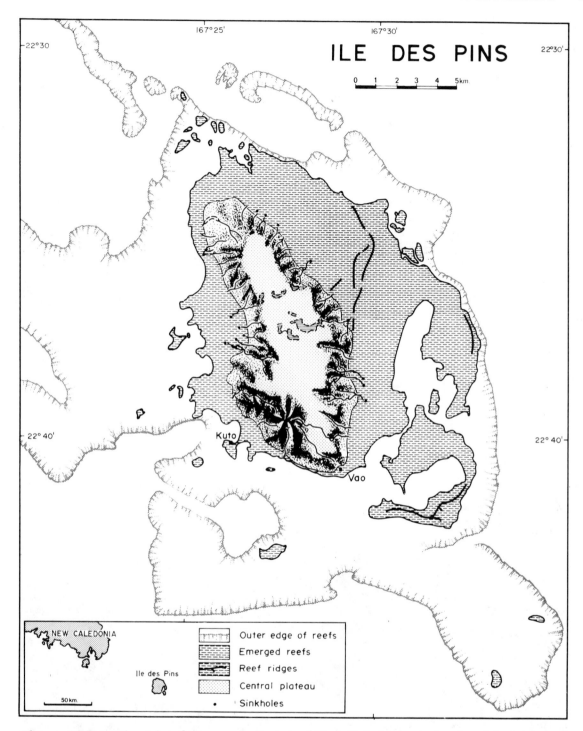

Figure 128-4. The Isle of Pines, southeast of New Caledonia, is bordered by emerged Pleistocene reefs and encircled by extensive Holocene reefs.

only of harder rims of dolomitized rock (Bourrouilh 1977).

ERIC C. F. BIRD
JACQUES ILTIS

REFERENCES

Avias, J., 1959, Les récifs coralliens de Nouvelle-Calédonie et quelques-uns de leurs problemes, *Soc. Géol. France Bull.*, 7th series **4**(1):424–430.

Avias, J., and J. Coudray, 1965, Sur la présence d'éolianites en Nouvelle-Calédonie, *Soc. Géol. France Compte Rendu* **7**:327–329.

Baltzer, F., 1965, Etude sédimentologique du marais de Mara, *Expédition Française sur les récifs coralliens de Nouvelle-Calédonie*, vol. 4, Fondation Singer-Polignac, Paris, pp. 3–146.

Baltzer, F., 1969, Les formations végétales associées au delta de la Dumbéa (Nouvelle-Calédonie) et leurs indications écologiques, géomorphologiques et sédimentologiques, *Cah. ORSTOM, Sér. Géologie*, **1:** 59–84.

Bourrouilh, F., 1977, Géomorphologie de quelques atolls dit "soulevés" du Pacifique W et SW, *B.R.G.M. Mém.* **89:**419–439.

Chevalier, J. P., 1973, Coral Reefs of New Caledonia, in *Biology and Geology of Coral Reefs*, vol. 1, O. A. Jones and R. Endean, eds., Academic Press, New York, pp. 143–167.

Davis, W. M., 1925, Les côtes et les récifs coralliens de la Nouvelle-Calédonie, *Annales Géographie* **34**:244–269, 332–359, 422–441, 521–558.

Dugas, F., 1974, La sédimentation en Baie de Saint-Vincent, *Cah. ORSTOM, Sér. Géologie*, **6**:41–62.

Guilcher, A., 1965, Grand Récif Sud—Récifs et Lagon de Tuo, *Expédition Française sur les récifs coralliens de Nouvelle-Calédonie*, vol. 1, Fondation Singer-Polignac, Paris, pp. 135–240.

Launay, J., and J. Recy, 1972, Variations relatives du niveau de la mer et néotectonique en Nouvelle-Calédonie au Pléistocène supérieur et a l'Holocène, *Reu. Géographie Phys. et Géologie Dynam.* **14**:47–65.

ORSTOM, 1981, *Atlas de la Nouvelle Calédonie.*

Plate 128-1. The mangrove-fringed estuary of the Tontouta River opens into the landlocked, isleted Bay of Saint Vincent, on the west coast of New Caledonia (photo by E. C. F. Bird).

Plate 128-2. Air oblique photograph of the Néra River, opening into the Bay of Gouaro (G) on the west coast of New Caledonia, behind a gap in the fringing reefs (fr) that border this coastline. At Poé (P) a coralline beach has formed to the rear of the fringing reef (photo courtesy of ORSTOM, Nouméa).

Plate 128-3. The limestone stack of Notre Dame on the northeast coast of New Caledonia near Hienghène (photo by E. C. F. Bird).

Plate 128-4. Dissection of emerged coral reefs by marine erosion on the Isle of Pines, New Caledonia, yields cliffs undercut by basal solution notches (right) and beaches of coralline sand (left) (photo by E. C. F. Bird).

129. FIJI

The Fiji archipelago consists of two large mountainous islands, Viti Levu and Vanua Levu, a number of smaller high islands, and numerous low islands and coral reefs (Fig. 129-1). In general, Cenozoic volcanic formations predominate, but there are also marine sediments, extensive emerged coral limestones, alluvial deposits, and modern fringing, nearshore, and barrier reefs. The Great Sea Reef is a major barrier reef running along the northern margin of the shallow sea area west of Vanua Levu. Vulcanicity is no longer active, and the volcanic landforms show various

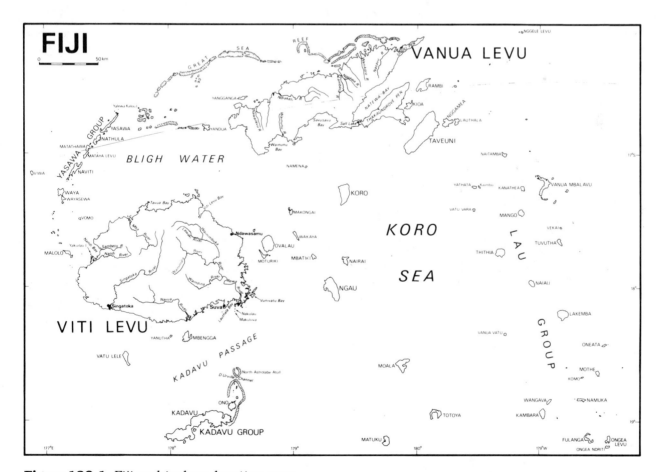

Figure 129-1. Fiji archipelago, location map.

stages in fluvial dissection. Tectonic uplift and tilting are much in evidence, indicated by emerged coral reefs and beach rock outcrops, terracing, and cliff notching. There are still occasional earthquakes. In September 1953 the Suva earthquake caused submarine slumping south of Viti Levu, which generated a tsunami, with large waves breaking across fringing and nearshore reefs. Waves up to 2 m high reached Suva (Houtz 1962).

The archipelago has a tropical oceanic climate, with southeasterly winds dominant and abundant rainfall, especially on windward slopes of high islands. Occasional tropical cyclones bring violent winds, storm surges, and torrential rains, resulting in widespread flooding in river valleys and the delivery of large amounts of water and sediment to the coast. Vegetation is luxuriant, except where it has been modified or cleared for forestry, plantations, or grazing.

Tide ranges in the Fiji archipelago are small, of the order of a few meters: Suva has a mean spring tide range of 1.3 m. Ocean swell approaches mainly from the southwest, breaking heavily on the reefs, but the dominant waves in coastal waters are those generated by southeasterly winds, shores with a northwesterly aspect being exempt from strong wave action. Beaches, consisting either of fluvially supplied sands and gravels, mainly derived from volcanic formations, or of coralline material from the reefs, are best developed on the more exposed shores, particularly behind gaps in the bordering reefs.

In Fiji, interest has centered on the origin of coral reefs (Agassiz 1899; Davis 1928) and the tectonic implications of reef and island structures (Dickinson 1967) rather than the evolution and dynamics of present coastlines. This account is based on reconnaissance field studies, supple-

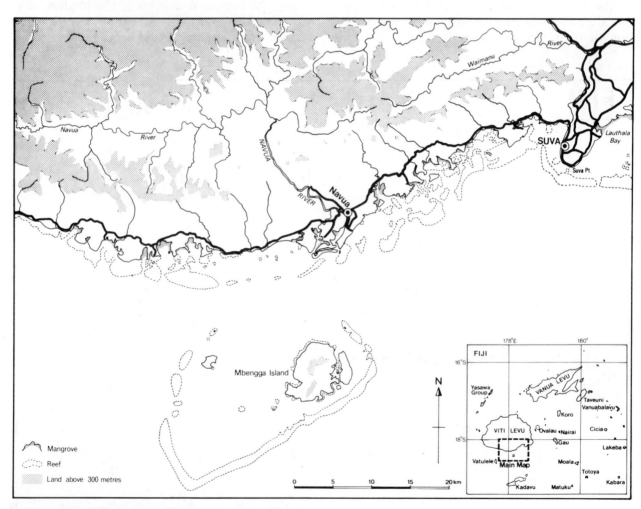

Figure 129-2. The south coast of Viti Levu west of Suva, showing the site of the large Navua Delta, south of which the high island of Mbengga lies in the lee of reefs.

mented by work on maps and air photographs made available by the Mineral Resources Division of the Public Works Department, and by the University of the South Pacific, in Suva.

Viti Levu has a coastline about 500 km long, much of it steep and reef-fringed. From Suva in the southeast the south-facing coast (Plate 129-1) is relatively low-lying and embayed, with many mangrove-encircled bay-head shores, and complicated patterns of fringing and nearshore coral reefs, which are strewn with coralline boulders thrown up by waves during cyclones. The large Navua River has built a substantial delta, with sandy shores washed by waves arriving through gaps in the outlying reefs (Fig. 129-2). During Cyclone Wally at Easter 1980 there was major flooding here, and sediment eroded from slumping hillsides temporarily blanketed coastal reefs and beaches (Howorth et al. 1981). Fringing reefs are backed by narrow beaches of coral sand and gravel. Farther west, at the mouth of the Singatoka River, is an unusual occurrence of black sand beaches and dunes, rich in magnetite, behind a gap in the reefs (Fig. 129-3; Plate 129-2).

South of Viti Levu, Mbennga Island is a high volcanic island with cliffs cut in breccia, and rocky shores, standing within a shallow sea area protected by coral reefs. Vatu Lele to the west is a tilted atoll, its western coast showing cliffs up to 35 m high, with notches at four levels indicating pauses in uplift; its eastern slopes decline to a sandy shoreline facing a reef-enclosed lagoon.

The west coast of Viti Levu is more sheltered, with fringing reefs and sectors of mangrove swamp. Mangroves are extensive on the Nandi Delta (Fig. 129-4), interspersed with beach ridges and earlier islands enclosed as the delta prograded to its present cuspate outline in the lee of Yakuilau Island. Nandi Bay is a wide re-entrant backed by a sandy beach and parallel beach ridges, with the Sambeto River opening into an area of mangroves on its northern side.

Off the north coast coral reefs are extensive and intricate, many with sandy cays (Plate 129-3).

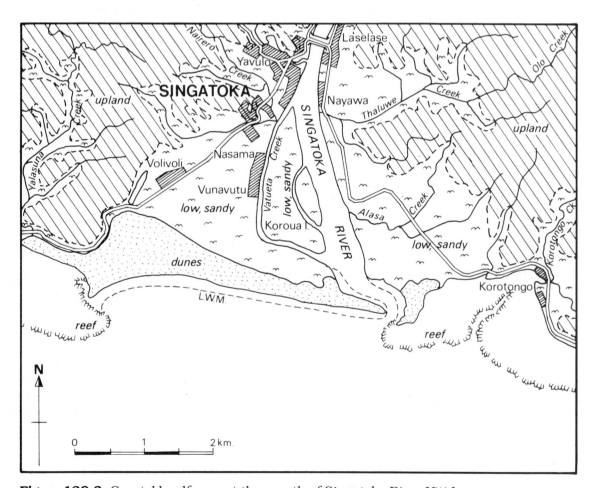

Figure 129-3. Coastal landforms at the mouth of Singatoka River, Viti Levu.

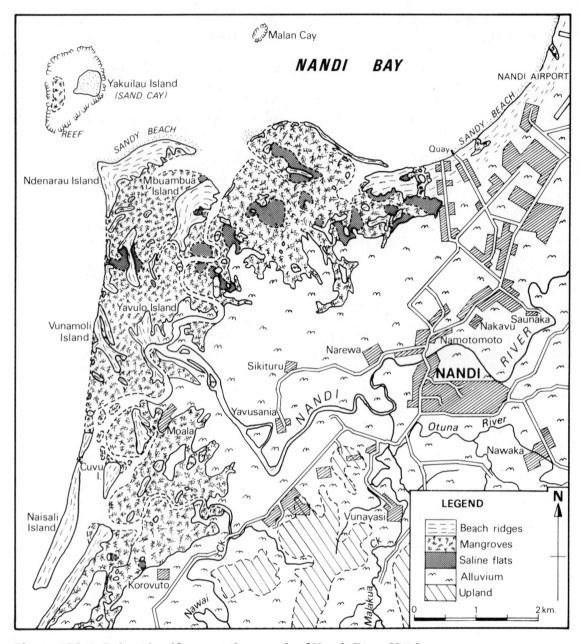

Figure 129-4. Deltaic landforms at the mouth of Nandi River, Viti Levu.

In general this is a steep coast with only minor deltaic plains at valley mouths, apart from the large Mba Delta, with its wide mangrove fringe on tidal mud flats. Reefs line the steep northeastern coast, interrupted only at the swampy head of Viti Levu Bay, and the east coast is similar, with small deltas of the Ndawasamu and Waimbula rivers interrupting the reef fringe. In the southeast the large swampy delta of the Rewa River has prograded into a reef-protected lagoon, with extensive tidal mud flats and mangrove shores alternating with beaches of gray sand of fluvial origin, as in Vanivatu Bay. These contrast with the pale coralline sands and gravels on outlying cays at Nukulau and Makuluva, the latter having migrated westward across the reef in recent decades (Plates 129-4 and 129-5). Lauthala Bay, east of Suva, has extensive tidal flats exposed at low tide, with migrating sand bores and small algal and mussel reefs. Some mangroves persist, but much of the Suva peninsula has an artificial coastline of sea walls and harbor structures.

Vanua Levu, though smaller, has a coastline of similar length to that of Viti Levu, being more indented. Steep coasts of dissected volcanoes dominate the western part, and fringing reefs are almost continuous around the island, with a notable gap off the deep inlet at the mouth of Wainunu River, and smaller ones off the northern deltas, particularly those of the Ndreketi, Waileuvu, Lambasa-Nggawa, and Wainkoro deltas. Intervening sectors are steep, as are both sides of the elongated Undu Peninsula in the northeast and the wider Thakaundrove Peninsula east of Natewa Bay. On the south side of this peninsula a curious reef-surrounded channel leads into a narrow strait that opens into a landlocked lagoon, Salt Lake. The coast behind Savusavu Bay includes a sector of beach-fringed lowland, but it steepens again to the west around reef-circled peninsulas on either side of Wainumu Bay. Evidence of emergence is widespread in Vanua Levu, with uplifted reefs, cliffed and notched along the coastline, as in Natewa Bay.

The Yasawa Group, northwest of Viti Levu, are elongated, mainly volcanic, islands trending southwest to northeast, with steep coasts, fringing reefs, and scattered emerged reef terraces. Outlying Yalewa Kalou Island is notable for its high limestone cliffs. In the south, Waya is tied to Wayasewa by a narrow sandy isthmus at Mbonini Point.

The Kandavu Group, south of Viti Levu, are more high islands of volcanic origin, fringed by reefs that diverge northward to an atoll-like ring, separated by D'Urville Channel from the North Astrolabe Atoll. Only small streams drain the steep island slopes, and beaches occur mainly behind fringing reef sectors. The coastline is intricately embayed, and some of the promontories end in high cliffs.

The high islands in the deep Koro Sea (Ngau, Mbatiki, Nairai, Koro) show similar features, the divergence of surrounding reefs to form outlying loops probably indicating a history of tectonic tilting (Davis 1928).

Taveuni, southeast of Vanua Levu, is a relatively young, little dissected volcanic island, bordered by intermittent and less extensive reefs. Its southern coast is cliffed, and beaches are extensive on the southeastern shore.

The eastern islands of Fiji (Lau Group) are smaller and more scattered (Brookfield 1978). Some are entirely volcanic: Moala, Matuku, and Totoya to the west are dissected volcanoes with embayed coastlines, minor bay-head deltas with mangrove swamps, and some reef-fringed promontories, surrounded by a lagoon and enclosing reefs. On Totoya the volcanic rim has been breached and the crater invaded by the sea to form a deep embayment. Mothe and Komo are also volcanic islands enclosed by modern reefs. Other islands (e.g., Vanua, Mbalavu, Mango, and Thithia) are essentially volcanoes with emerged reef limestone at various levels up to 200 m above present sea level. The south coast of Thithia has high limestone cliffs, the outer flank of an emerged fringing reef. Lakemba, partly volcanic, has been tilted so that emerged reefs rise to 100 m above present sea level on the western coast, declining to the mangrove-edged eastern shores. Oneata and Kambara consist largely of uplifted reef limestone, with central volcanic outcrops, and Tuvutha shows the classic form of an upraised atoll, with the top of the volcanic foundation outcropping in the middle of the enclosed basin, formerly a lagoon (Davis 1928). Fulanga, Namuka, and Ongea Levu are islands entirely of uplifted reef limestone, Fulanga being an atoll that has tilted in the course of uplift.

The coastlines of these small islands are thus partly rocky and cliffed on volcanic or reef limestone outcrops, often with basal notching, partly beach-fringed, the dark volcanic sands and gravels contrasting with the pale coralline beaches, and partly depositional, with minor deltas and alluvial plains, and stands of mangrove on the shore. McLean (1980) observed that beach erosion has recently been prevalent on many of these islands, notably Kambara and Lakemba, and suggested that widening of fringing reefs by seaward growth of coral may have resulted in a diminishing supply of coralline sediment to such beaches.

ERIC C. F. BIRD

REFERENCES

Agassiz, A., 1899, The islands and coral reefs of Fiji, *Harvard Univ. Mus. Comp. Zoology Bull.* **33.**

Brookfield, H. C., ed., 1978, *The Small Islands and the Reefs*, UNESCO/UNFPA Island Reports, No. 4, Australian National University, Canberra.

Davis, W. M., 1928, *The Coral Reef Problem*, Am. Geog. Soc. Spec. Pub. 9.

Dickinson, W. R., 1967, Tectonic development of Fiji, *Tectonophysics* **4:**543–553.

Houtz, R. E., 1962, The 1953 Suva earthquake and tsunami, *Seismol. Soc. America Bull.* **52:**1–12.

Howorth, R., M. J. Crozier, and I. J. Grant, 1981, Effects of Tropical Cyclone Wally in southeast Viti Levu, Easter 1980, *Search* **12:**41–43.

McLean, R. F., 1980, The land-sea interface of small tropical islands: morphodynamics and man, in *Population-Environment Relations in Tropical Islands: The Case of Fiji*, UNESCO MAB Technical Notes, 13, pp. 125–130.

Plate 129-1. View from reef-fringed Suva Point westward along the south coast of Viti Levu, showing the hilly hinterland (photo by E. C. F. Bird).

Plate 129-2. The dune-bordered coastline adjacent to the mouth of the Singatoka River in southwestern Viti Levu. The beach and dune sands, of fluvial origin, are rich in magnetite (photo by E. C. F. Bird).

Plate 129-3. Intricate reefs bordering promontories and islands in northwestern Viti Levu, with small cays on two of the outlying reefs (photo by E. C. F. Bird).

Plate 129-4. Retreat of the west coast of the sand cay of Makuluva, southeast of Suva, Viti Levu, has exposed foundations and former underground water tanks (photo by E. C. F. Bird).

Plate 129-5. The advancing western shore of Makuluva (cf. Plate 129-4) (photo by E. C. F. Bird).

130. HAWAII

The Hawaiian archipelago extends 2,450 km across the central Pacific Ocean, from the large island of Hawaii in the southeast to tiny Kure Atoll at the northwest. The eight main islands of the state of Hawaii at the southeast end of the archipelago (Fig. 130-1)—Hawaii, Maui, Kahoolawe, Lanai, Molokai, Oahu, Kauai, and Niihau—comprise 99 percent of the land area; the remainder is found in the northwestern Hawaiian islands from Nihoa to Kure and as small islands off the shores of the major islands.

Of the 1,650 km of shore on the major islands, about 20% is composed of sandy beaches (U.S. Army Engineer Division 1971). The remainder of the shore, aside from man-made structures, consists mainly of outcrops or boulders of lava but also includes muddy shores, gravel beaches, beachrock, raised reefs, and lithified sand dunes. These rocky shores vary in elevation from raised reefs 1–2 m above sea level to the spectacular sea cliffs 600 m high along the Napali coast of Kauai.

The Hawaiian Islands are the subaerial tops of large volcanic mountains built up from the approximately 5 km deep ocean floor. These volcanoes formed over a hot, localized spot of magma generation now located in the earth's mantle under or just to the south of the island of Hawaii. As the older volcanoes formed great shields and died, the motion of the ocean floor and crust relative to the hot spot moved them to the northwest. This movement is reflected in the age of the islands: Niihau is 5.5 million years, Kauai 5.1 million years, Oahu 3.7 to 2.6 million years, and Maui 1.3 to 0.9 million years old. Three of the

Contribution 1150 of the Hawaii Institute of Geophysics, University of Hawaii, Honolulu, HI 96822

shield volcanoes that make up the island of Hawaii are still active: Hualalai, Mauna Loa, and Kilauea (Macdonald and Abbott 1970). The older islands have higher percentages of sandy shore than the younger ones (Table 1). Since the extinction of the giant shield volcanoes and a period of erosion, several of the islands have had a renewal of volcanism from scattered small vents.

Beaches in Hawaii are smaller than those along continental shores, because of the youth of the islands, the lack of large rivers to supply sediment, beach shape, exposure to the various wave systems that affect the islands, and local topography and bathymetry. The sand on Hawaiian beaches also differs from most continental beach sand in being principally calcareous and of biologic origin. Most of the beach sand originates as shells and tests of animals and algae that live on the fringing reefs or in shallow waters adjacent to the islands. The two major exceptions are (1) some beaches, near stream mouths, with detrital basalt sand, and (2) a few beaches on the island of Hawaii, with black volcanic glass sand resulting from

Table 1. Sandy Shores on the Major Hawaiian Islands

Island	Total Shoreline (km)	Sandy Shoreline (km)	Percent Sandy Shoreline
Kauai	182	80	44
Oahu	319	90	28
Molokai	170	40	24
Lanai	84	29	35
Maui	256	54	21
Hawaii	492	35	7

steam explosions at the chilled glassy margins of hot lava flows that extend to the ocean (Moberly and Chamberlain 1964).

The coastal geology of each island is described in a clockwise sequence, starting at the northwest.

Niihau (Fig. 130-1) is a privately owned island; access is allowed only with permission from the owners. The island consists of the eroded remnants of a shield volcano partially surrounded by rocks from later volcanic eruptions that are partly covered by calcareous dunes. Almost all of the shore around its northern tip is a low marine cliff cut into the most recent volcanic rocks; a few small pocket beaches are found along this coast. South of Kii Landing is a 3 km section of sandy beach backed by actively migrating dunes. The next 14 km of shore is a sea cliff cut into the original basaltic shield; this cliff reaches elevations of 400 m. To the south is a 4 km long stretch of sandy beach. The shore along the southern third of the island is a 3–15 m high sea cliff eroded into lithified calcareous dunes that formed during a lower sea-level stand in Pleistocene time. North of this cliff a beach extends nearly continuously for 20 km along the west coast of the

island, interrupted occasionally by low, rocky headlands.

Kauai is a single large shield volcano that has been deeply eroded and partially covered by lava from several later vents. It has some of the longest and widest stretches of beach in the state. The northwest or Napali coast is a high sea cliff extending 23 km; some small beaches are found at the mouths of large valleys. From the end of the Napali cliffs to the northernmost point of the island at Kilauea, the north coast is 60% large sandy beaches (Plate 130-1), whereas the rest of this section of coast is low to moderate-height cliffs cut into lava bedrock. East and south from Kilauea for 25 km, the coast is predominantly sea cliffs cut into basaltic rock. The 1.5 km beach at Anahola is the only significant sandy shore along this coast. A nearly continuous narrow sandy beach back of a fringing reef extends for 10 km south from Kapaa. The beach widens slightly at Wailua, where a large sand-bottomed channel is cut through the reef. The southern coast of Kauai is predominantly low sea cliffs with some short segments of sandy beaches, as well as some exposures of raised reef and lithified dunes. The

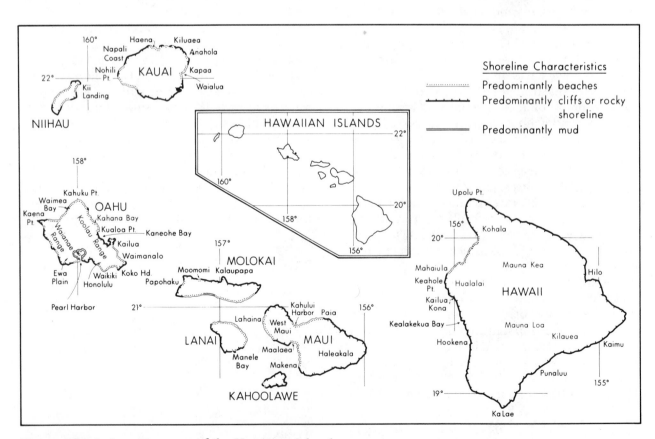

Figure 130-1. Location map of the Hawaiian Islands.

west side of the island is a 28 km long continuous stretch of sandy beach, interrupted only by a section of beachrock outcrops at sea level just south of Nohili Point.

Oahu, although the third largest of the Hawaiian Islands, has the second longest coastline, partly because of the approximately 50 km of shore in the Pearl Harbor embayment. The island is composed of two mountain ranges—Waianae, the older, on the west and Koolau on the east—that are the remnants of two shield volcanoes.

Emerged Pleistocene reef deposits surround large parts of both mountain ranges, forming extensive coastal plains that separate older sea cliffs from the present coastline (Stearns 1978). The only present-day sea cliffs of any extent are found at the north end of the Waianae range, the south end of the Koolau range, and where late-stage volcanic cones formed near the coast, such as the complex of the tuff cones in the Koko Head area (Plate 130-2). Kaena Point at the westernmost end of Oahu is flanked by sections of sea cliff cut into the Waianae volcano and exposed Pleistocene reefs. A few insignificant pocket beaches exist at breaks in the raised reef. The north-facing coast of Oahu is primarily sandy beaches interrupted in places by beachrock, raised reef, and basalt outcrops. Although beautiful, some of these shores are extremely dangerous when large winter swells break along the shore (Clarke 1977). Most of these beaches are stable, but the picturesque beach at Waimea Bay is eroding at about 125 m per century because the last sea-level rise cut off its sources of sand supply (Campbell and Hwang 1982). The windward coast of Oahu, from Kahuku to Kualoa Point, is primarily narrow sandy beaches fringed by a shallow reef (Plate 130-3). Kaneohe Bay is a 15 m deep lagoon behind a barrier reef that absorbs most of the wave energy. As a result, narrow beaches along the bay shore are composed of poorly sorted sediment ranging in size from mud to cobbles. The coast of the bay, especially the southern end where human habitation is concentrated, has been largely modified with sea walls. The southeastern coast of Oahu is composed of two large bays with sandy beaches, Kailua and Waimanalo, separated by a rocky headland.

The Honolulu coastal area from Koko Head to Pearl Harbor is the most densely developed part of the state; as a result, the shore is to a large extent fronted by manmade structures ranging in size from the major harbor facilities at Honolulu to small sea-walls built to protect individual residences. Most of this shore was originally fringed by a shallow reef, making it susceptible to land reclamation projects that have significantly modified its shape. In some areas, artificial beaches have been built in front of these filled areas. Those beaches, such as Waikiki, that exist along this coast are smaller than others on the island. The shores of Pearl Harbor are either artificial structures of the U.S. Naval base or mud flats or exposures of raised reef. Around the Ewa plain, west from the Pearl Harbor entrance, is a 5 km section of narrow beach, then nearly 20 km of rocky outcrops of raised reef or beachrock. Along the west coast of Oahu, rock outcrops of basalt or raised reef limestones alternate with excellent sandy beaches.

The island of Molokai is two shield volcanoes, 1.5 and 1.9 million years old. The center of its straight north coast is interrupted by a low peninsula, Kalaupapa, formed by lava of a small, younger volcano. The East Molokai volcano is deeply eroded, so that its north coast is a spectacular succession of high, marine-cut cliffs separated by deep valleys with alluviated floors (Plate 130-4). In most of the valley mouths beaches are composed of cobbles, but sand may appear during the calmer summer season. The sea cliff extends around the eastern end of the island and gradually disappears as the slope of the island becomes lower along the south coast. The south shore of the island is protected for most of its length by a broad, fringing reef, which absorbs much of the wave energy, allowing only narrow beaches. Much of this southeastern coastline was modified by the ancient Hawaiians who built large fish ponds on the reef that are now filling with silt. An 11 km section in the center of the south coast is fringed by mangroves and mud flats. Farther west are sections of sandy beach separated by low rocky outcrops. Most of the west coast of Molokai is a low sea cliff cut into basalt, interrupted by Papohaku Beach and a few smaller pocket beaches. Papohaku, a 3 km long wide, straight beach, is one of the largest in the state in terms of sand volume; for many years it was harvested as a source of sand for concrete aggregate used on Oahu. With the exception of a small beach at Moomomi, the northwest coast of west Molokai is a marine-cut cliff.

Lanai is a single shield volcano with a shore that can be divided into two segments. The north and northeast coasts are nearly continuous beach fringed for most of its length by a wide, shallow reef. The beach is wide at the western end, where no reef exists, and narrows back of the reef; off stream mouths are small deltas with poorly sorted sediment grading from clay to cobble-size. The south and southwest coast is a continuous sea cliff that is 300 m high in places. Two small beaches are associated with a cinder cone at Manele Bay.

Maui is another island composed of two separate shield volcanoes; West Maui, the older, is extinct, but Haleakala to the east is considered dormant, having erupted in the late 1700s. Most of the shore of the Haleakala area of Maui is sea cliff cut into basaltic bedrock. From Paia on the north coast around the east end of Maui to Makena on the south, beaches are few and are generally found at the mouths of valleys cut into the slope of the island. North from Makena, there is a 10 km section of coast with sandy beaches separated by basaltic promontories, followed by another 10 km of continuous sandy beaches interrupted by minor outcrops of beachrock (Clarke 1980). The southeast end of west Maui from the boat harbor at Maalaea for 9 km is a sea cliff cut into basalt. Northwest of this cliff most of the shore around to Lahaina is beaches comprised of pebbles and cobbles that have washed out of the large valleys cutting the West Maui mountains (Plate 130-5). Kaanapali, west of the old whaling village at Lahaina, is a major tourist destination (Plate 130-6). Most of the western shore is sandy pocket beaches. The north coast of West Maui is a sea cliff cut into basalts from the West Maui volcano. Except for the manmade structures associated with Kahului Harbor, most of the north-central Maui coast is fronted by narrow, sandy beaches with a history of beach erosion that commonly exposes beachrock (Campbell 1972).

Kahoolawe is a single shield volcano almost completely surrounded by sea cliffs cut into volcanic rock. The island is used as a target range by the U.S. Navy, whose special permission is required to visit the island. Small beaches are located along the westernmost shore of the island, which is totally undeveloped.

The "Big Island" of Hawaii is a composite of five volcanoes, whose youth has allowed little time for beach formation. Thus most of the coastline is composed of sea cliffs cut into basaltic bedrock. The northeast coast of Kohala and Mauna Kea have been dissected by stream erosion and some small beaches, many with only boulders and cobbles, are found at the mouths of the valleys. A beach once existed in Hilo Bay but has been almost completely eliminated by the construction of a railroad and later a highway. Aside from a few small pocket beaches of black sand, such as the famous one at Kaimu, there are no beaches around Kilauea. The south and west shores of Mauna Loa are also nearly all sea cliff. Indeed, parts of the Kilauea, Mauna Loa, and Hualalai coasts have grown seaward in historical time from eruptions of those volcanoes. There are occasional small beaches a few tens to hundreds of meters long in embayments in the shoreline (Plate 130-7). The slope of Kealakekua Bay is partly controlled by a fault striking across the trend of the coast. The only beaches of any size on Hawaii are found between Keahole Point and Kawaihae along the northwest shore. Even there, the beaches make up only a small portion of the coastline and not many exceed 100 m in length (Plate 130-8). The west slope of Kohala is a low sea cliff with minor beaches only where the few intermittent streams reach the shoreline.

J. F. CAMPBELL
R. MOBERLY

REFERENCES

Campbell, J. F., 1972, *Erosion and Accretion of Selected Hawaiian Beaches, 1962–1972*, Hawaii Institute of Geophysics Rept. 72-20, University of Hawaii.

Campbell, J. F. and D. J. Hwang, 1982, Beach erosion at Waimea Bay, Oahu, Hawaii, *Pacific Science* **36:** 35–43.

Clarke, J. R. K., 1977, *Beaches of Oahu,* University Press of Hawaii, Honolulu.

Clarke, J. R. K., 1980, *Beaches of Maui County,* University Press of Hawaii, Honolulu.

Macdonald, G. A. and A. T. Abbott, 1970, *Volcanoes in the Sea, The Geology of Hawaii,* University Press of Hawaii, Honolulu.

Moberly, R., and T. Chamberlain, 1964, *Hawaiian Beach Systems,* Hawaii Institute of Geophysics Rept. 64-2, University of Hawaii.

Stearns, H. T., 1978, *Quaternary Shorelines in the Hawaiian Islands,* Bishop Museum Press, Honolulu.

U.S. Army Engineer Division, 1971, *Hawaii Regional Inventory of the National Shoreline Study,* Corps of Engineers, Honolulu.

Plate 130-1. Haena Point, northern Kauai, looking south. Patches of fringing reef are cut by sand-bottomed channels down which sediment is moved into deep water. Patches of offshore sand show through the clear water in the left foreground and left and right middle ground. Narrow beaches of calcareous sand and gravel lie along the shoreline. During the tsunami of April 1, 1946, waves along this shore rose to 13 m and carried ashore automobile-sized blocks of reef rock (photo by A. T. Abbott).

Plate 130-2. Southeastern Oahu, looking northwest. In foreground is a chain of small volcanic vents that were active about 40,000 years ago. The largest include Koko Head (left), Hanauma Bay (breached by the sea), and Koko Crater (right center). The shore is a low sea cliff cut into the tuffs. A sandy beach lies northeast (right) of Koko Crater. Since this photograph was taken, a marina and an extensive residential area have been constructed beyond the craters on a bay barrier and lagoon that had been used as a fish pond by the ancient Hawaiians. Other residential areas on the outskirts of Honolulu lie in valleys between spurs of the Koolau Range, the remains of a large basaltic shield volcano built about 2.3 million years ago. Beyond the range is Oahu's windward coast, with Waimanalo (center) and Kailua (top right) bays, characterized by long beaches and a broad fringing reef (photo by A. T. Abbott).

Plate 130-3. Northeastern (windward) Oahu, looking west. Alluviated valleys that trend into submarine canyons are evidence of the isostatic sinking of the island. The coastal zone has a 500 m wide reef, a discontinuous ribbon of beach, and, to the north (right), a narrow coastal plain supporting sugarcane and other tropical crops. The bay-head beach of Kahana Bay (left foreground) is a mixture of calcareous sand from the reefs and detrital sand from Kahana Stream (photo by A. T. Abbott).

Plate 130-4. North coast of Molokai, looking southwest. The northern half of East Molokai volcano (active about 1.4 million years ago) has been eroded away by streams and the sea. The subaerial canyons are aligned with submarine ones that extend to a depth of 1,995 m, showing a 2 km isostatic subsidence in 1.4 million years. For scale, the two stacks in the right foreground are each about 115 m high, and the sea cliff in the left foreground is 1,084 m high. Cliffs are undercut by tradewind-driven waves and shaped by rock falls, soil avalanches, and downward-drilling waterfalls. Beyond the crest, the dryer leeward slope of the volcano dips away from the observer. Part of Lanai Island shows in the left distance (photo by A. T. Abbott).

Plate 130-5. Southwest coast of West Maui, looking northeast. The right skyline, with small cinder cones, is approximately the original shape of the West Maui volcanic shield, which formed about 1.1 million years ago. Youthful streams radiating from the higher elevation areas of higher rainfall have spread alluvial fans at the valley mouths and small deltas at the coast. Beaches are narrow and gravelly. Lahaina Roadstead (foreground), the waters protected by Maui, Molokai, Lanai, and Kahoolawe, was a favorite rendezvous and anchorage for nineteenth-century whaling ships; today it is again a breeding ground for the humpback whale (photo by A. T. Abbott).

Plate 130-6. Kaanapali, westernmost Maui, looking southeast at a resort area near Lahaina. The slope of West Maui rises to the left. Numerous hotels and condominium buildings line the edge of the coastal plain. In general, the larger beaches such as this one lie on the west coasts of the individual Hawaiian Islands, but few are as crowded with multistory buildings as Kaanapali (photo by J. F. Campbell).

Plate 130-7. Hookena on a calm day, west coast of Hawaii. Cloud-covered slopes of Mauna Loa rise in the background. The youthful surface of the volcano is notched by a 25 m high sea cliff, but stream valleys have yet to form. A lava flow has projected into the ocean (left), allowing a small pocket of sand to accumulate (center). Such beaches were valuable to the ancient Hawaiians as canoe landings. The white band at the edge of vegetation and buildings of the present-day village (left foreground) is a storm beach of sand and gravel; the rocky shore closer to the ocean is swept clean of loose sediment. A similar coastal village 21 km to the south, Hoopuloa, was destroyed by lava of the 1926 eruption of Mauna Loa (photo by A. T. Abbott).

Plate 130-8. The beach at Mahaiula, west coast of Hawaii, is typical of small pocket beaches found along the arid northwestern flank of Hualalai volcano. The beaches are surrounded by very recent lava flows. The flow in the center of the picture is part of the last eruption of Hualalai, in 1801. The small amount of vegetation along this arid and otherwise barren coast and the brackish-water ponds behind the beach owe their existence to ground water seeping into the ocean. The white calcareous sand on the beach and visible in pockets offshore is the skeletal remains of organisms that live in these clear, shallow waters (photo by A. T. Abbott).

131. SOCIETY ISLANDS

As W. M. Davis wrote in 1928 (pg. 283), "no other archipelago in the Pacific coral seas includes so systematic a sequence of island forms as those of the Society group. The sequence begins with a young and reefless volcanic island on the east and ends in several small atolls on the northwest." This pattern is mentioned in *132. Pacific Ocean Islands* and related, after Chubb (1957), to an increasing age of volcanoes from east to west and an associated development of reef growth. According to recent views on deep-sea floor evolution, such a pattern, which is by no means unique in the Central and South Pacific, may result, as in the case of the Galapagos rise (Johnson et al. 1976), from the migration of the oceanic plate over a hot spot, the expression of a narrow plume of mantle material rising and spreading outward. As the plate moves, successive volcanoes come into existence and subsequently collapse, resulting in barrier reefs and finally in atolls. Consequently, the Society group atolls (Tupai, Mopelia, Scilly, and Bellingshausen, but not Tetiaroa) are situated in the west, outside our location map. They will not be described here (Mopelia is reported on in detail in Guilcher et al. 1969); nor will we describe Meetia, an uninhabited, steep rock, 435 m high, bearing only discontinuous fringing reefs, or Maiao, 154 m high, around which the expected lagoon is replaced by lakes and fringing reefs. Attention will focus on the larger "high" islands.

TAHITI

This famous island consists of twin volcanoes, 2,241 m and 1,332 m high, connected by the low Taravao isthmus. These mountains are deeply dissected by valleys, two of which widen in their upper reaches inside the larger volcano in incipient erosion calderas and carry appreciable amounts of volcanic pebbles and sands to the sea. Davis paid much attention to the fact that the ridges sloping from the summits to the coasts have been truncated at their outer ends by "circumferential cliffs" still visible in the topography. This feature is particularly represented in the southeast. It dates from a time when reefs had not yet been built by the corals around the twin volcanoes.

Today these reefs are generally barrier reefs separated from the island by a narrow lagoon, 500–2,000 m in width; along some parts of the west coast, the lagoon is absent and the reef becomes fringing. However, where the lagoon exists, it commonly reaches 30–50 m in depth. In addition, the barrier reef is drowned in some places, especially in the north, the east, and the southeast (Fig. 131-1), under several meters of water, possibly because of a recent, local subsidence. In these areas, the swell generated by the trade winds penetrates into the lagoon and breaks on the inner shore, so that the pebbles supplied by the rivers become well rounded by the waves, while elsewhere the beaches are sandy and quiet. Numerous passages break the barrier and allow large ships to enter.

As in other lagoons behind barriers, it is interesting to know if the sediments are supplied by local marine organisms or by rivers flowing from the central island. This question has been answered (Guilcher et al. 1969) by titration of the calcium carbonate content in 82 samples, which showed that the influence of the central island is generally large. The lime content sometimes fell

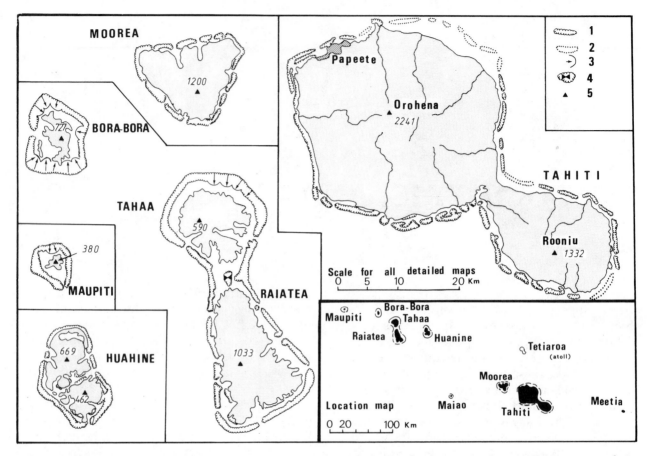

Figure 131-1. The Society Islands. 1. barrier reef (sometimes fringing); 2. drowned barrier reef; 3. sedimentary apron protruded in the lagoon by overwash; 4. reef growing in juxtaposed alveoles between Tahaa and Raiatea; 5. tops of volcanoes, with altitudes in meters.

below 5% close to land, and exceeded 90% in six samples only. The mean lime content was found to be much smaller around the main volcano (21%) than around the smaller one (66%), because the larger one has larger rivers, supplying more sediments to the lagoon. The conclusion is that the terrigenous or organogenic nature of the lagoon sediments depends on the ratio between the area covered by the central island and the area of the lagoon.

MOOREA

Moorea, which is more dissected inland than Tahiti and has one of the finest skylines of the archipelago, is surrounded by a lagoon even narrower and more discontinuous than at Tahiti: the barrier reef, which is wide, merges into a fringing reef in a number of places (Plate 131-1).

This island provides, on its north coast, excellent examples of the relationship of passages across the reef with drowned valleys, now forming Cook and Papetoai bays, thus showing the course of events that created the marine landscape.

HUAHINE

Huahine (Plate 131-2), which is also considerably dissected, is divided into two parts by a central channel in which the mean depths reach 30–40 m. It seems that, as in the Banks Peninsula, New Zealand, this feature results from the drowning of an erosion caldera. As around Tahiti and Moorea, the barrier reef lies close to the mainland. The lagoon, 20–45 m deep, is discontinuous, and becomes a lake in the north; it is connected with the ocean by five passages, four of them more than 20 m deep. As with many other high islands

(Bora-Bora, Moorea, and others), fringing reefs commonly grow on the inner side of the lagoon.

RAIATEA AND TAHAA

(Plates 131-3 and 131-4) Unlike Tahiti, these twin volcanoes are separated by a shallow drowned area, but both are surrounded by a single barrier reef in the shape of a figure eight. The lagoon is somewhat wider than in the preceding cases. In its expansion between the two islands, coral reefs have grown in the form of large juxtaposed alveoles, a rare but not unique pattern also found on a larger scale at Mataiva Atoll, Tuamotus, at Canton Atoll, Phoenix group, and at Christmas Atoll, Line Islands (structure described for Canton in Smith et al. 1978). In many instances, the passages connecting the lagoon with the open sea bear sand cays (islets) on both sides, a feature by no means unique to Raiatea and Tahaa but well exemplified here, which results from swell refraction and diffraction at the passage. The relation of passages to inner valleys is as evident as at Moorea.

BORA-BORA

Many scientists consider that this island displays the most beautiful marine landscape in the world, and Darwin (1842) cited it as one of the best examples of a barrier reef island (Plates 131-5 and 131-6). Because of its western position, the volcano is smaller and the lagoon wider. The result is that the influence of runoff on lagoon sedimentation becomes almost negligible; practically all particles are calcareous, coming from marine organisms (Guilcher et al. 1969). There is only one passage, Teavanui, more than 20 m deep, situated on the leeward side of the barrier; but the lagoon receives oceanic water by overwash of the trade wind swell in the north and east between the low islands of the barrier, and in the south when storms passing over the Southern Ocean generate heavy swells traveling as far as the tropics. The overwash has built aprons of sediments, gradually filling the lagoon. So far, however, it is still fairly deep, often more than 30 m, and devoid of pinnacles, a feature that led to wide use of the lagoon by the U.S. Navy during World War II.

MAUPITI

The last volcano of the group that has not yet been completely engulfed by subsidence resembles a smaller Bora-Bora. One difference, difficult to explain, is that the lagoon is full of pinnacles. A large apron, fed in sediments by overwash, is found in the north; the same feature appears also on the north side of Tahaa barrier, and is typical in several Society Islands.

ANDRÉ GUILCHER

REFERENCES

Chubb, L. J., 1957, The pattern of some Pacific island chains, *Geol. Mag.* **94:**221–228.

Darwin, C., 1842, *The Structure and Distribution of Coral Reefs,* Smith Elder and Co., London.

Davis, W. M., 1928, *The Coral Reef Problem,* Am. Geog. Soc. Spec. Pub. **9** (Society Islands, pp. 254–270, 283–307).

Guilcher, A., L. Berthois, F. Doumenge, A. Michel, A. Saint-Requier, and R. Arnold, 1969, Les récifs et lagons coralliens de Mopelia et Bora-Bora (îles de la Société), et quelques autres récifs et lagons de comparaison (Tahiti, Scilly, Tuamotus occidentales), ORSTOM Mem. 38, Paris (English summary).

Johnson, G. L., P. R. Vogt, R. Ney, J. Campsie, and A. Lowrie, 1976, Morphology and structure of the Galapagos Rise, *Marine Geology* **21:**81–120.

Smith, S. V. and R. S. Henderson, eds., 1978, An environmental survey of Canton Atoll lagoon, *Atoll Research Bull.* **221:**183.

Plate 131-1. Moorea, north coast seen from the east. Note wide reef, narrow and discontinuous lagoon, and relation of passages across the reef with drowned valleys (Cook Bay in foreground, Papetoai Bay behind) (photo by A. Guilcher).

Plate 131-4. Tahaa-Raiatea lagoon. Reef growth in large juxtaposed alveoles (photo by A. Guilcher).

Plate 131-2. Huahine. Central channel cutting through the island. Fringing reefs on inner sides of lagoon, barrier reef in the distance (photo by A. Guilcher).

Plate 131-5. Bora-Bora, western side: reef, Teavanui passage, lagoon, central mountain. Tahaa in the far distance (photo by A. Guilcher).

Plate 131-3. Tahaa-Raiatea barrier reef seen from north to south, with sand cays on either side of passage (photo by A. Guilcher).

Plate 131-6. Bora-Bora. Overwash channel across barrier (open during exceptionally heavy swells) closed by sand spit on lagoon side when the picture was taken (photo by A. Guilcher).

132. PACIFIC OCEAN ISLANDS

Although individual treatment has been given to some Pacific Island groups—*Fiji, Hawaii, New Caledonia, Papua New Guinea*, and *Tahiti* (q.v.)—it is not possible to describe the shorelines of the remaining several hundred Pacific Islands separately. Nor will those islands, close to the continents, that Kaplin (1981) grouped into "continental" and "transition-zone" types, be considered. This article is restricted to Kaplin's third group of islands, the "oceanic;" several main classes— purely volcanic, coral-fringed volcanic, atolls, and "raised" reefs—will be discussed. The localities in which the islands of these classes are found are shown in Fig. 132-1. For further details see, for example, Dana (1872), Darwin (1842), Davis (1928), and Fairbridge (1975).

VOLCANOES

Most of the active volcanoes are confined to the active volcanic arcs along the western margin of the Pacific Ocean, for example, the island arcs of the Solomons and Vanuatu (formerly New Hebrides) (Fig. 132-1). East of these volcanic arcs, active volcanoes are confined to four isolated regions: the islands of Hawaii and Maui at the southeast end of the Hawaiian chain of islands (see *Hawaii*); Revilla Gigedo, west of Mexico; the Galapagos Islands near the equator on the eastern margin of the Pacific Basin, where Darwin considered there could be 2,000 craters; and at the northwest end of the Samoan chain, where again there are a remarkable number of craters. Other volcanoes, probably dormant, are Uvea in the Wallis Islands northeast of Fiji and Mehetia at the southeast end of the chain of Society Islands.

The most youthful or shoal-stage coast of an active volcano is typified by Falcon Island in the Tongan Volcanic Arc, an island that is sometimes there and sometimes not! More commonly volcanic coasts reflect long histories of development and are steep and rocky. Some of the older coasts, particularly those exposed to the prevailing winds, have been cut back to form high cliffs, commonly more than 300 m high, for example, the active volcano of Raoul Island in the Kermadecs (Plate 132-1). Where coastal retreat has been faster than stream downcutting, the cliffs feature hanging valleys and waterfalls, as on Norfolk Island (Kaplin 1981). Some steep, straight or curvilinear coasts may be due to faulting or slumping, as along the southeast coast of Upolu in Samoa (Kear and Wood 1959). Where relatively young lava flows project beyond the older parts of the coast, they form protective headlands.

The newness of the coast around an active volcano and the easily eroded sediments inhibit coral reef growth. However, coral, foraminiferal, and molluscan fragments are important constituents in some beaches, such as those on the leeward side of Hawaii (q.v.). Other beaches, where coastal erosion is active or where streams export large quantities of sediment, are dark with volcanic fragments. The steep offshore slope carries eroded material out of the coastal system, and thus prograded coasts are absent.

CORAL FRINGED VOLCANOES

Dependent on suitable conditions of light, food supply, oxygen supply, and temperature, coral reefs occur mainly in a zone between the Tropics

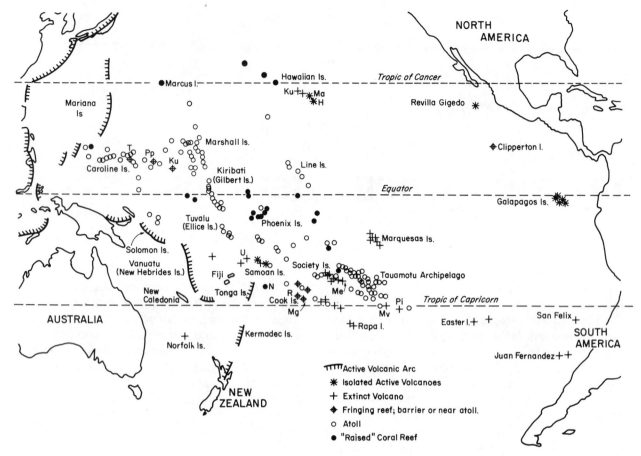

Figure 132-1. Map of the Pacific Ocean. Individual islands mentioned in text are Hawaii (H), Kuraie (Ku), Maui (Ma), Mehetia (Me), Mangaia (Mg), Mangareva (Mv), Niue (N), Pitcairn (Pi), Ponape (Po), Rarotonga (R), Truk (T), and Uvea (U).

of Cancer and Capricorn. The absence of coral reefs around the Marquesan Islands, despite their low latitudes, could be due to an occasional influx of the cold Humboldt Current, but may reflect the eastward dwindling in the number of coral species (Vaughan and Wells 1943). Nevertheless, the near-atoll of Clipperton lies still farther east and is much more isolated than the Marquesas but not reached by the Humboldt Current.

Living coral reefs that encircle volcanic islands have two forms: a barrier reef separated from the island by a lagoon and a fringing reef attached to the island except at the mouths of rivers. A fringing reef forms an extension of a low-tide, shore platform, whereas an island with a barrier reef has, in effect, a triple coastline; an outer reef coast exposed to the full force of the ocean, particularly boisterous on the windward side; an

inner, lagoonal reef coast (Plate 132-2); and an innermost, lagoonal volcanic coastline. Both barrier and fringing reefs provide a living and hence renewable bulwark against coastal erosion, softening the effects of even tsunamis and hurricane force seas.

The reef coasts are described more fully in the following section on atolls. The usually tranquil volcanic coast on the inside of a barrier lagoon is of particular interest. As early as 1849 Dana recognized that its commonly irregular embayed outline is due to drowning of stream valleys—such embayment could not be produced by sea action but must ultimately be destroyed by it. Davis (1928) made full use of this principle to support Darwin's subsidence theory for the origin of barrier reefs and atolls and to argue against that part of Daly's glacial-control theory that considered reefs were killed during a glacio-eustatic low sea level, allowing part planation of the unprotected island.

"Like Daly he supposed that wave abrasion could only have been effective in producing cliffed headlands if the protective influence of a surrounding reef were completely removed . . . . In fact Davis found that cliffed headlands were singularly absent within the barrier reef lagoons of the central coral sea but become increasingly apparent toward the northern and southern limits of present day coral growth. He therefore concluded that the limits of reef growth were merely narrowed by colder water temperatures during the glacial low stand of sea level and that consequently Daly's hypothesis was only applicable to this marginal belt" (Purdy 1974, p. 11).

Fringing coral reefs and barrier lagoons are an important and usually almost exclusive source of coastal sand. For example, not only are the beaches around the high volcanic island of Rarotonga formed of carbonate sands but these continue inland as a continuous vegetated strip of carbonate sand up to a height of 8 m and commonly 200–500 m wide (Wood and Hay 1970). Similar relationships are shown on the geological maps for Samoa (Kear and Wood 1959), while on Lord Howe Island in the Tasman Sea the world's southernmost coral reefs are a source of calcareous beach sands and eolianites (Guilcher 1973).

ATOLLS

An atoll, that "most extraordinary of natural structures" (Davis 1928), consists of a coral reef surrounding and protecting a usually tranquil lagoon from a usually restless ocean, and supporting small vegetated islets 3–4 m high. The opalescent light greens and blues of the lagoon are in marked contrast to the startling-white beaches, deep palm-green islands, algal-red outer reef, and deep clear blue ocean. "Yet these low, insignificant coral islets stand and are victorious . . . . Let the hurricane tear up its thousand huge fragments . . . what will this tell against the accumulative labour of myriads of architects at work night and day" (Darwin 1840, p. 553).

Boulder Ramparts, Beach Rock, and Negro Heads

In addition to Darwin's "myriads of architects," rapid chemical solution and redeposition of cal-

cite and aragonite cement are an important agency in beach protection. Cementing of beach sand to form beachrock (Plate 132-3) and of storm-built boulder banks (Plate 132-4) to form boulder ramparts is particularly active within the intertidal zone, and can be very rapid, as is shown by the inclusion of recent artifacts such as flotsam from the Second World War.

Negro heads are isolated reef blocks that project above the general level of the reef platform. They may represent remnants of a higher reef, particularly if present on the leeward side of an atoll, or they may be large boulders torn from the reef front during a hurricane. In the latter case they are probably the remains of a much more extensive storm ridge (Plate 132-4), the smaller blocks having been removed before the ridge could be cemented to the reef flat.

Passes

Passes into the lagoon, if any, may be as deep as the maximum depth of the lagoon. Where present they are thought to be due to the rapid rise in postglacial sea level. Rapid rates of sea-level rise, relative to the average coral growth (Weins 1962), meant that reef growth could not be maintained up to low-tide level in some regions. Conditions on the leeward side of an atoll are less conducive to coral growth, and it is here that passes have most often developed. A change to less than ideal conditions would account for some drowned atolls and for the incomplete development along the leeward sides of many Kiribati (Gilbert Islands) atolls.

Islets

Islets owe their preservation from all but the greatest storms to the presence of cemented boulder ramparts on their windward sides, partly aided by beachrock. In some islets, multiple parallel ramparts may form much of their width. In others, their greater width consists of unconsolidated sand on the leeward side of the rampart. The predominance of islets on the windward reefs is probably due to a more common construction of boulder ramparts there.

Skeletal soils and radiocarbon dates (Schofield 1977) suggest the islets are late Holocene in age. If, as the CARMARSEL Expedition (Shepard et al 1967), suggested, there has been no postglacial sea level above the present in the West Pacific, then there could be no relationship between sea-level fall and islet formation. However, the well-dated, second-order Gilbert transgressions for the same West Pacific region (Schofield 1980) demonstrate that the Flandrian transgression reached a maximum of +2.4 m for Kiribati (Gilbert Islands) almost 1,000 years B.C. The six post-glacial Gilbert transgressions are supported by uncommon high-level remnants of biohermal reef rock but are mainly based on subtidal, backreef breccias (Plate 132-5) that were not differentiated from reef-rubble by the CARMARSEL Expedition. Quantitative and mineralogical studies of pro-graded coasts in New Zealand show that 95% or more of the coastal sand has been derived from the sea floor as a result of the 2 m fall in late Holocene time. This is also probably true for atoll islets. Even those on the windward reef are built from distinctive lagoonal sand (Schofield 1977), but this is to be expected, as the wide, shallow, marginal lagoonal floors are the only suitable source from which sand could be derived as a result of sea-level fall. The preservation of more or less permanent islets has almost certainly been favored by the net fall in sea level since the maximum of the Flandrian transgression, which locally took place about 1,000 B.C. It may be no coincidence that this is also about the earliest known Polynesian settlement date within the Pacific Ocean.

Low-Tide Platform

The outermost zone (zone A, Plate 132-6) is a 0.5–1 m high algal ridge, alive in constant spray at the breaker line. Deep grooves running across it give a saw-toothed appearance to the edge of the reef. Inside the ridge in some places there is the so-called boat channel or string of deep pools that persist even at low tide, interconnected with the ocean, they support live corals (Zones C and B, Plate 132-6, poorly developed). Inland, the platform proper may consist of an older reef and its outer algal ridge which have been abraded flat, but in which the saw-toothed nature can still be recognized from the air (Zones E and D, Plate 132-6); presumably as the algal ridge was abraded the cross grooves have been infilled. In Kiribati (Gilbert Islands) this abraded part of the platform lies about 0.3 m above low spring tide and forms a barrier to another more inland set of shallow pools supporting *Heliopora* and *Porites,* which probably are remnants of an older, incompletely filled boat channel (Plate 132-7). The older reef

probably lived during some slightly higher sea level and died when sea level fell. At the same time a new breaker line was developed farther offshore, where a new algal ridge grew and continued to grow upward to its present position with the present rise in sea level.

RAISED REEFS AND PACIFIC-BASIN STABILITY

"Raised" reefs and their coastal terracings are dotted throughout the Pacific Basin and provide some of the most interesting and least investigated coastlines. Their origin is inextricably intertwined with the stability or instability of the Pacific Basin. "The assertion is commonly made that the island areas of the South Pacific represent . . . parallel folds of the ocean floor," noted Williams (1933), but he concluded that despite local tilting such as in the Hawaiian Islands (which is "only proper to volcanic regions") "the islands of the South-central Pacific as a whole seem to indicate a vast region of comparative stability." More recently, drilling in the Marshall Islands (Emery et al. 1954) has shown that the average rate of oceanic sinking for that part of the Pacific has been about 25 m per million years during the Cenozoic and perhaps twice that rate for the last 5 million years. If this is the order of crustal movement within the Pacific Basin, there could be areas rising at 25–50 m per million years, which could explain much of the raised reefs (see, for example, Dubois et al. 1975). Nevertheless, unless there has been epeirogenic uplift over a distance of 1,300 km, it does not explain the very close correlation of nontilted, raised reefs and coastal terrace sequences of 70 m, 55 m, 34–39 m, 23 m, 12–15 m, and 4–6 m at Niue and Mangaia and at other islands in the Cook Group (Wood and Hay 1970; Schofield 1959). Other raised reefs within the Pacific Basin have not received the same detailed study, but it may be significant that the few levels recorded (Fairbridge 1975, Davis 1928) lie closely within this framework. Where they are not tilted, these raised levels could be truly eustatic, but there are also examples of emerged reefs that have been dislocated by tectonic movements, for example in the Solomon Islands and Vanuatu, island arcs subject to frequent earthquake activity.

Whatever their origin, raised reefs (Plates 132-8 and 132-9) usually present a steep coastline, in some places with plunging cliffs and in others fringed with a living reef, but everywhere rugged with karrenfeld solution features. A wave-cut or solution notch is common at the base of the cliff and in some cliffs is preserved at levels of higher oceanic stillstands. Solution has lowered the 23 m and 70 m strandlines at Niue by 3 m and perhaps 15 m respectively (Schofield 1959) but is unlikely to have constructed the interior basin of this raised atoll. This basin contains uncemented carbonate sand with Plio-Pleistocene lagoonal faunas that probably lived well below tide mark. The theory that such basins have been formed solely through solution (Purdy 1974) depends on the comparison with solution effects on blocks of nonpervious limestone. In fact raised reefs are extremely permeable, and there is no differential runoff of regional significance so necessary for such a theory. The rain soaks straight into the ground, and any lowering of the surface is likely to be fairly general, with some more cemented parts such as beachrock and cemented boulder ramparts possibly being preferentially preserved as relict or "shadow" structures (Schofield 1959). However, solution at the contact between a fringing reef and less impermeable weathered volcanic rock, from which there is runoff, results in the development of swampy hollows that are much favored for growing taro. Such might even be the origin of the so-called raised barrier reef at Mangaia, 70 m high, which may, before taro-swamp solution, have been a fringing reef (Wood and Hay 1970).

Notwithstanding the possibility that some Quaternary raised reefs had their origin in high eustatic sea levels, crustal movement, particularly subsidence within the Pacific Basin, seems to have been important in the long term. This overall tendency for subsidence has been illustrated by Chubb (1957) for a number of island chains in which "vulcanicity began at one end and moved progressively along the chain, erecting a series of volcanoes, each of which passed through a succession of stages, ending as an atoll." (p. 221). He cited a number of atolls in the northwest end of the Society Islands. Southeastward from these there are Maupiti, a near-atoll; then Bora-Bora, a deeply dissected and embayed volcano with a barrier reef and broad lagoon; thence progressively less dissected and less embayed volcanoes, Tahaa, Raiatea, Huahine, Moorea and Tahiti, the last consisting of two volcanoes, both still showing their original volcanic form and having an almost unindented shoreline. All these islands have barrier-reefs which on Tahaa extend to nearly two miles from shore, on the succeeding islands generally to about a mile, and around parts of Tahiti to only half a mile, becoming a fringing reef in places. Finally, at the eastern end of the chain, lies Mehetia, a bold volcanic cone, hardly dissected and unembayed, with a narrow fringing-reef and a well preserved crater from which many recent lava-flows have issued, though there is no record of activity within human memory. p. 222.

Other examples given by Chubb include the Hawaiian chain (q.v.), the Samoan chain, which becomes older southeastward, and the older Tuamotu (Mangareva to younger Pitcairn) and eastern Caroline chains (Truk, Ponape, to youngest Kuraie).

J. C. SCHOFIELD

REFERENCES

Chubb, L. J., 1957, The pattern of some Pacific island chains, *Geol. Mag.* **94:**221–228.

Dana, J. D., 1872, *Corals and Coral Islands*, Sampson Low, London.

Darwin, C. R., 1840, Journal of researches into the geology and natural history of the various countries visited by H.M.S. Beagle . . . from 1832 to 1836, H. Colburn, London.

Davis, M. D., 1928, *The Coral Reef Problem, Am. Geog. Soc., Spec. Pub.* 9.

Dubois, J., J. Launay, and J. Recy, 1975, Some new evidence on lithospheric bulges close to island arcs, *Tectonophysics* **26:**189–196.

Emery, K. O., J. I. Tracey, Jr., and H. S. Ladd, 1954, *Geology of Bikini and Nearby Atolls, Part 1, Geology,* U.S. Geol. Survey Prof. Paper 260-A.

Fairbridge, R. W., ed., 1975, *The Encyclopedia of World Regional Geology, Part 1: Western Hemisphere,* Dowden, Hutchinson & Ross, Stroudsburg.

Guilcher, A., 1973, Lord Howe, l'île à récifs coralliens la plus méridionale du monde, *Assoc. Géographes Français Bull.* **404:**427–437.

Kaplin, P. A., 1981, Relief, age and types of oceanic islands, *New Zealand Geographer* **37:**3–12.

Kear, D., and B. L. Wood, 1959, *The Geology and Hydrology of Western Samoa,* New Zealand Geol. Survey Bull. 63.

Purdy, E. G., 1974, Reef configurations, cause and effect in *Reefs in Time and Space,* L. F. Laporte, ed., Soc. Econ. Paleontologists and Mineralogists Spec. Publ. 18, pp. 9–76.

Schofield, J. C., 1959, *The Geology and Hydrology of Niue Island, South Pacific,* New Zealand Geol. Survey Bull. 62.

Schofield, J. C., 1977, Effect of Late Holocene sea-level fall on atoll development, *New Zealand Jour. Geology and Geophysics* **20**(3):531–536.

Schofield, J. C., 1980, Postglacial transgressive maxima and second-order transgressions of the south-west Pacific Ocean, in N. Morner, ed., *Earth Rheology, Isostasy and Eustasy,* John Wiley and Sons, Chichester, pp. 517–521.

Shepard, F. P., J. R. Curray, W. A. Newman, A. L. Bloom, N. D. Newell, J. I. Tracey, Jr., and H. H. Veeh, 1967, Holocene changes in sea level, Evidence in Micronesia, *Science* **157**(3788):542–544.

Vaughan, T. W., and J. W. Wells, 1943, *Revision of the Suborders, Families, and Genera of the Scleractinia,* Geol. Soc. America Spec. Paper 44.

Weins, H. J., 1962, *Atoll Environment and Ecology,* Yale University Press, New Haven.

Williams, H., 1933, *Geology of Tahiti, Moorea and Maiao,* Bernice P. Bishop Museum Bull. 105.

Wood, B. L., and R. F. Hay, 1970, *Geology of the Cook Islands,* New Zealand Geol. Survey Bull. 82.

Plate 132-1. North coast of active volcano Raoul Island, Kermadec Group, view westward from meteorological station. The rapidly eroding, apparent high-level coastal plain is the head of a late Holocene fan not a "raised" marine-formed platform (photo by J. C. Schofield).

Plate 132-3. Beachrock, Lefaga Bay, south coast of Opolu Island, western Samoa. Almost certainly very late Holocene to modern in age, uncemented beach sand having been recently eroded from immediately behind the ridge of beachrock (photo by J. C. Schofield).

Plate 132-2. Barrier lagoon between an islet-bearing reef in the background and the inner lagoonal beach, east coast of Rarotonga, Cook Group (photo by J. C. Schofield).

Plate 132-4. Hurricane boulder bank on windward coast, east of airport, Funafuti Atoll, Tuvalu Islands. Built during Hurricane Bebe, 1972, this bank is slowly moving inland (R. F. McLean, pers. comm.), where it may eventually unite with the older boulder rampart that formed the previous coast topped by coconut palms in right background (photo by J. C. Schofield).

Plate 132-5. Remnant of reef platform underlain by subtidal backreef breccia and formed during transgression Gilbert 5, 1,570±50 yrs B.P. 1.65 m above local low-tide reef platform, windward reef, Abemama Atoll, Kiribati (Gilbert Islands), 2 km south of Government Resthouse (photo by J. C. Schofield).

Plate 132-6. Reef zonation, windward reef, Tabiteuea Atoll, Kiribati (Gilbert Islands). For discussion of zones, see text (photo by J. C. Schofield).

Plate 132-7. *Porite* colonies living in remnants of an incompletely filled boat channel formed when sea level was slightly above the present. The modern boat channel lies close to the reef's edge marked by breakers in left background. North Tabiteuea (Karibati), windward coast, 0.8 km south of Government Resthouse (photo by J. C. Schofield).

Plate 132-8. "Raised" atoll, west coast of Niue Island from Alofi to Tepa Point, where the two main marine-formed coastal platforms at +23 m and +67–71 m can be seen in profile (photo by J. C. Schofield).

Plate 132-9. Marine-formed platform 13 m above sea level on seaward side of raised barrier reef, Oneroa, Mangaia, Cook Islands. Note caves in cliff in background. These caves have floors at about +23 m and extend for a considerable distance along the cliff face, probably representing the same sea-level stillstand recorded by the +23 m platform at Niue (photo by J. C. Schofield).

133. ATLANTIC OCEAN ISLANDS

The Atlantic Ocean islands (Fig. 133-1) fall into three groups: those on the Mid-Atlantic Ridge, from Iceland south to Bouvet Island; those on the American shelves to the west, such as Bermuda and the Falkland Islands; and those on rises and the Eurafrican Shelf to the east, from the Faeroes south to the islands in the Gulf of Guinea. The Caribbean Islands, Bahamas, Iceland, and the British Isles have been discussed separately.

In contrast with the Indian and Pacific oceans, which have many low coral islands and cays, the Atlantic has mainly "high islands," many of them of volcanic origin. Coral reefs are poorly developed in the Atlantic Ocean, although extensive in Caribbean waters; even the Atol das Rocas off Brazil is not a true coral atoll.

The Atlantic islands show variations in size and shape, and features that reflect contrasts in lithology, in the nature of vulcanicity (active, dormant, extinct), and in climate and vegetation (from the lush Azores to the dessicated Cape Verde Islands and the iciness of Bouvet). Details of the geology and physiography of Atlantic islands are given by Mitchell-Thomé (1970, 1976) and by Nairn and Stehli (1973, 1974).

ISLANDS OF THE MID-ATLANTIC RIDGE

The islands of the Mid-Atlantic Ridge are of volcanic origin. The Azores consist of 10 islands (total area, 2,344 km^2) having a hilly volcanic topography with many peaks and hollows, the mild climate and abundant rainfall (c. 950 mm/yr,

winter maximum) permitting a good vegetation cover. The slopes are dissected by deep and narrow gulleys, but relics of raised beaches and marine platforms occur at various levels up to 60 m. The coasts are generally steep, with cliffs up to 500 m high cut into lavas, tuffs, and scoria (Plate 133-1). There are a few low-lying areas where gravel and sand derived from volcanic formations have been piled up by wave action in beach-ridge plains, and tombolos that attach small volcanic islands, such as Porta Pim on Faial, whence a sand spit has grown northward. Wave action can be strong, for there is deep water close inshore, the 100-m isobath being usually within 3 km of the coastline. Some craters (e.g., Franca do Campo on Ilha Terceira) have been breached by the sea to form circular embayments. There is still occasional volcanic activity (Capelhinos, off the west of Faial Island, is a cone built in the 1957–1958 eruption), and neotectonics have influenced the coast, as at Praia da Victoria on Terceira, where beaches and swamps occupy a graben. The highest peak, Ponta do Pico (2,351 m), has a smoking crater.

St. Paul Rocks (including St. Peter Rocks) consist of 12 islets of dunite, an olivine-rich periodotitic rock, possibly the oldest outcrops on the earth's surface, dated isotopically at 3,500–4,500 million years and thought to be unaltered mantle material. They are unvegetated but bear extensive deposits of white guano, calcium photsphate derived from seabird droppings. The highest point is only 23 m above sea level, and there is an emerged marine platform at 5 m. The coasts are cliffed and rocky, with wave-scoured potholes.

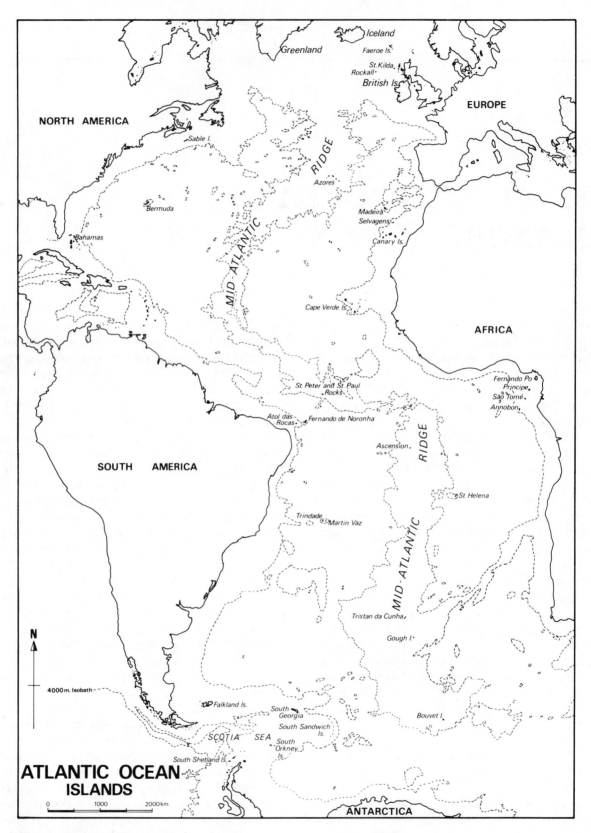

Figure 133-1. Atlantic Ocean islands.

Ascension Island is the peak of a dormant volcano rising 3,000 m from the sea floor and a further 859 m to the Green Mountain summit. In its 98-km^2 area are more than 100 vents, and eruptions continued into Quaternary times. Vegetation is sparse, and guano deposits are scattered. Imposing sea cliffs line the more exposed eastern coast, where Boatswain Bird islet, a monolithic stack of trachyte 98 m high, has a natural arch.

St. Helena, slightly east of the Mid-Atlantic Ridge, is an isolated volcanic peak rising 4,400 m from the sea floor to culminate 823 m above sea level in Diana Peak. With an area of 115 km^2, it is a composite volcanic cone, deeply eroded with radiating valleys intersected by cliffs up to 670 m high, where valley mouths terminate in coastal waterfalls of up to 200 m. There are good examples of plunging cliffs, which have emerged platforms standing 4–6 m above present sea level. Sandy Bay on the south coast has a beach backed by calcareous dunes, which have been driven far inland by the southeast trade winds.

Tristan da Cunha is another circular volcanic island (95 km^2) rising to Queen Mary's Peak (2,062 m), with a main crater, about 30 parasitic scoria cones, and bordering cliffs up to 900 m high. The township of Edinburgh is located in a low-lying area, Settlement Plain, on the northwest side. Radial dykes and lava flows are prominent. In 1961 earthquakes and an eruption on Settlement Plain led to temporary evacuation of the 300 inhabitants. Lava cliffs formed on the flanks of the new volcanic dome but were rapidly cut back (10 m recession in two months in early 1962), producing gravelly material that was deposited as a longshore spit enclosing a small lagoon. The island is bleak and barren, but zoned vegetation occurs above 1,350 m. Four small islands are associated with Tristan: Inaccessible (10 km^2; peak, 548 m), Nightingale (2.6 km^2; peak, 396 m), Stoltenhoff (0.25 km^2; peak, 105 m), and Middle (0.26 km^2; peak, 65 m), all bordered by towering cliffs cut into lavas and tuffs. Emerged beaches, platforms, and caves occur at 5 m on Tristan, but at 12 m on Nightingale and Middle islands, suggesting local differential uplift.

Gough Island (Diego Alvarez) is another deeply dissected volcano (area, 65 km^2; Edinburgh Peak, 910 m) surrounded by high cliffs with hanging valleys and waterfalls and a narrow bouldery strand, with outlying stacks such as Tristania Rock (165 m). Luxuriant evergreen scrub forest thins out above the 300-m contour. The island is notable for dyke swarms and wind-dissected tuff deposits.

Bouvet Island (60 km^2; peak, 935 m) has rugged ice-mantled Quaternary volcanic terrain, with five glaciers ending seaward in ice cliffs. It is extremely remote: there is no land in any direction for more than 1,500 km. The adjacent seas have pack ice in winter but are disturbed by frequent gales. Cliffs cut back by stormy seas attain 500 m on the more exposed west coast, where in 1955–1957 an eruption added new lava from which a gravelly beach has been derived.

ISLANDS OF THE WESTERN ATLANTIC

The islands of the Scotia Arc, a tectonically disrupted link between the South American cordillera and the mountainous Antarctic peninsula, include Late Paleozoic–Mesozoic sedimentary formations with granitic intrusions and associated volcanics. Their combined area is about 10,000 km^2, with peaks exceeding 2,000 m. The South Georgia, South Orkney, and South Shetland islands contain metamorphic gneisses, schists, and marble, but the South Sandwich islands are composed entirely of Cenozoic volcanics, and a submarine eruption north of Zavodovski in 1962 generated pumice deposits, which are extensive on the beaches. The islands are barren and rugged, with snow and ice caps, angular periglaciated peaks, and torrential streams in summer. Their coastlines are generally cliffed and rocky, with many inlets and some bay beaches. Deception Island has a lagoon where a volcanic crater has been invaded by the sea.

The Falkland Islands (Islas Malvinas) number several hundred, with a total area of 11,718 km^2. There are two main islands, West Falkland (Gran Malvina) and East Falkland (Isla Soledad), which are separated by steep-sided, fjord-like Falkland Sound (San Carlos Strait). Mt. Adam on West Falkland reaches 698 m. The coastline is lengthy and highly indented with numerous rias at the mouths of winding valleys; the landscape is treeless, with tussocky grasses and extensive peat bog mantles, and Pleistocene periglacial "stone rivers" (solifluxion deposits) are prominent. Apart from a Precambrian basement outcrop at Cape Meredith, the islands consist of Devonian to Triassic sedimentary rocks and metamorphic rocks with granitic and doleritic intrusions. Folding and faulting have influenced coastal outlines. In general, coasts are subdued, but sectors exposed to the frequent westerly gales show rapid cliff recession, consuming the rubble-mantled slopes produced by periglaciation.

Trindade (8 km²; peak, c.600 m) and the nearby Martin Vaz rocks are a complex of successively built volcanoes, the last (Paredo) a Holocene cone 217 m high on the southeast coast. The margins show high receding cliffs and truncated ravines, and a wave-cut tunnel 130 m long has been excavated in a volcanic headland. The exposed northeast coast has a coral reef, and there are beaches and dunes of calcareous sand as well as older dune calcarenites. Principe, on the south coast, has a sandy beach in front of a degraded cliff, and there is widespread evidence of emergence (raised platforms, beach rocks) of about 3.5 m.

Atol das Rocas, 250 km off the Brazilian coast, is not a coral atoll but a circular algal bank capping a seamount and enclosing a small lagoon. Two low sandy islands, Farol (106,000 m²) and Cemeteria (53,200 m²), rise above the intertidal platform of algae, and have a capping of dune calcarenite (Ottmann 1962).

Farther out, the Fernando de Noronha archipelago is again volcanic, with a main island (16.9 km²) and about 20 associated islets, the emergent parts of a large cone that rises 4,000 m from the sea floor. The relief is gentle, but the coastline is rocky and cliffed, with headlands in phonolite and bays carved in tuff. Wave action is strongest on the southeast coast, where *Lithothamnion* reefs have developed, while on the rugged north coast are beaches of sand, gravel and boulders, and some tombolos. Dune calcarenites and marine limestones occur above present sea level on the east coast. The tide range, generally small on oceanic islands, here attains 3.2 m at springs.

Bermuda consists of numerous islands (54 km²) of dune calcarenite and associated marine deposits, forming an emergent northern rim of the Bermuda Platform. The coasts are low-lying, with minor cliffs, notched behind platforms that locally carry corals and algae, and associated calcareous sandy beaches (Emery and Uchupi 1972).

Sable Island, rising from shallow banks 150 km southeast of Nova Scotia, is a long, narrow island of variable configuration with a central lagoon that is sometimes open to the sea. Erosion during storms has necessitated relocation of the lighthouse, but deposition also occurs, and the land area has remained at about 30 km² over the past two centuries.

ISLANDS OF THE EASTERN ATLANTIC

The Faeroes (1,398 km²) are rugged mountainous islands of Tertiary basalt that have been glaciated and periglaciated. The coastline is indented, with fjord-like inlets, and the more exposed westerly sectors have cliffs up to 350 m high (e.g., Fuglabjørg), but there are some beaches of gray basaltic sand, backed by dunes at Sandur, and other sectors of gravelly and bouldery debris. The tide range is small but tidal currents are nevertheless strong through the narrow straits of Nordskala.

St. Kilda is the largest of a group of outlying Hebridean islets and stacks, a complex of Tertiary volcanic rocks with steep slopes mantled with Pleistocene periglacial rubble undercut by cliffs. Hirta, the largest, 630 ha, rises to 419 m. Rockall, 300 km to the west, is an isolated stack of bare granitic rock 21 m high, standing on a submerged bank from which blocks of basalt, trachyte, and sandstone have been dredged. Leonidas Rock and Helens Reef are awash at low tide nearby.

Madeira consists of one large and several small islands (810 km²) composed of extinct (mainly Miocene) volcanoes much dissected by deep ravines. Terraces mark stages in successive (Quaternary) uplift. The slopes are steep, but well vegetated (annual rainfall, c.600 mm, dry summer) and terminate in high coastal cliffs (Cabo Girao, 580 m), especially on the sectors facing waves produced by the prevailing northeast trade winds. Beaches are mainly gravelly, derived from cliff talus, but a long sandy beach borders the southeast coast of Porto Santo.

The Selvagens archipelago consists of one island and eight smaller islets, as well as scattered rocks, totalling 4 km² in area with a summit of 153 m at Pico da Atalaia. They are rugged, sparsely vegetated, and not permanently settled. Lava and ash surmount Oligo-Miocene marine limestones, and there are cliffs up to 100 m high on the northwest coast, with gentler slopes to the more sheltered, beach-fringed southeast coast. There are raised beaches, and dune calcarenites occur on Pleistocene marine terraces 3 and 7 m above present sea level, behind sectors that are now cliffed.

The Canary Islands, much drier, number seven (total area, 7,500 km²) and are steep and high:

Pico de Teide on Tenerife (3,718 m) is the highest peak on any Atlantic island. The slopes show radiating ravines, short, steep, and gravelly. The north and west coasts are bold, with cliffs up to 300 m high in massive lavas, surrounded by fallen boulders. There are no biological reefs, but the north coasts have sectors of shelly beach and calcareous dune sands, some of the dunes having drifted inland to form the desert landscape of Lanzarote on the island of Arrecife. On the southeast coasts, valley-mouth inlets are partly blocked by pebbly beaches, and there are incipient deltas; beaches of black volcanic sand occur locally.

The Cape Verde Islands are drier still because of the northeast trades and the dessicating Harmattan winds from the Sahara. Barren dissected volcanoes partly overlie Mesozoic marine limestones, as observed by Darwin in 1832. There are 15 islands (total area, 4,033 km²), in two arcuate groups. Some are low and undulating (Boa Vista); others are higher, steeper, and surrounded by cliffs. Some bays contain narrow fringing algal reefs. Stormy seas have hurled boulders up to 200 m inland and undermined cliffs to produce massive rock falls. Emerged features have been noted at six levels up to 100 m. Volcanic activity occurred in the cone of Pico (2,829 m), on Fogo, in 1951.

The group of islands in the Gulf of Guinea include the large Fernando Po (20,254 km²), a high, forested volcanic island, rising to a peak of 2,850 m at Santa Isabel, with steep rocky coasts interspersed with sheltered sandy bays and mangrove swamps (see also *Cameroon and Equatorial Guinea*).

Principe, to the south (110 km²; peak, 948 m) has a low, embayed north coast and a higher cliffed south coast. It consists of Tertiary volcanic deposits, emergent since the Miocene with shelly limestone deposits at 130 m in the Forca Valley. It is dissected by streams that deliver muddy waters to mangrove-fringed inlets behind barrier beaches, notably at Burras and Lapa.

Sao Tomé is large (854 km²; peak, 2,023 m), densely vegetated, with a generally subdued volcanic relief with occasional cones and plugs (Cao Grande, 663 m). Beaches of white calcareous sand interrupt high cliffs cut in basalt and phonolite, with columnar jointing well exposed in the Baio do Iologologo. To the south, Ilheu das Rolas is a smaller volcanic island, as is outlying Annobon, last of the group.

ERIC C. F. BIRD

REFERENCES

Emery, K. O., and E. Uchupi, 1972, *Western Atlantic Ocean,* Am. Assoc. Petroleum Geologists Mem. 17.

Mitchell-Thomé, R. C., 1970, *Geology of the South Atlantic Islands,* Beitrage zur Regionalen Geologie der Erde, vol. 10, Gerbrüder Borntraeger, Berlin.

Mitchell-Thomé, R. C., 1976, *Geology of the Middle Atlantic Islands,* Beitrage zur Regionalen Geologie der Erde, vol. 12, Gerbrüder Borntraeger, Berlin.

Nairn, A. E. M., and F. G. Stehli, eds., 1973, *The Ocean Basins and Margins, vol. 1, The South Atlantic,* Plenum Press, New York.

Nairn, A. E. M., and F. G. Stehli, eds., 1974, *The Ocean Basins and Margins, vol. 2, The North Atlantic,* Plenum Press, New York.

Ottmann, F., 1962, L'atol das Rocas dans l'Atlantique sub-tropical, *Reu. Géographie Phys. et Géologie Dynam.* **5**(2):101–106.

Plate 133-1. High cliff on the northeast coast of San Miguel Island (Azores). Note the basaltic boulders at the cliff foot (photo by Maria Eugénia Lopes, courtesy of Carlos Morais).

134. INDIAN OCEAN ISLANDS

The eastern part of the Indian Ocean has only a few islands (e.g., Cocos, Christmas), but the western part has very many, arranged in discrete archipelagoes (Figs. 134-1 and 134-2). There are three kinds of islands: high islands, either volcanic or granitic; islands of raised coral bordered by low cliffs; and low cays of coral sand, usually with beachrock of recent origin.

HIGH VOLCANIC OR GRANITIC ISLANDS

The Comores archipelago, in the north of the Moçambique Channel, includes four high islands, Grand Comore, Moheli, Anjouan, and Mayotte. Grand Comore (Fig. 134-2) consists of a large active volcano, Kartala (2,361 m) to the north of which is attached a chain of strombolian cones of Upper Quaternary age, forming the Grille peninsula. The coastline comprises low cliffs (Plate 134-1) cut into recent basaltic lava flows, with occasional sandy beaches generally associated with fringing reefs in the north (Mitsamiouli), facing Moroni in the extreme south. Anjouan (1,595 m) and Moheli (790 m) are older (Pliocene) volcanic islands, much dissected by erosion. The coastline is more eroded, with sectors of cliff, sometimes high, cut in lavas, alternating with sandy bays that include small mangrove areas. Fringing reefs are extensively developed. Mayotte (660 m) (Fig. 134-2) is a much dissected volcano, partly of Miocene age, with deep embayments such as Boueni, and a surrounding barrier reef, which in the south becomes a double barrier. None of these islands shows Pleistocene raised beaches.

The Mascareignes archipelago is formed by three high volcanic islands, Réunion, Mauritius, and Rodriguez. Réunion (Fig. 134-2) is a large Hawaiian-type volcano that includes an older part, the massif of Piton des Neiges (3,069 m), incised by three large cirques, and an active volcano to the southeast, the massif of Fournaise. The coast is generally rocky, with low cliffs cut in lavas, the cliffs becoming higher between Saint Denis and the Plaine des Galets. Sectors of low coast correspond with the three large depositional cones built below the three cirques and show pebbly beaches, while the rare sandy beaches are related to embryonic fringing reefs (Saint Gilles, Etang Salé, and Saint Pierre).

180 km northeast of Réunion, Mauritius is a less elevated island (826 m at Piton de la Rivière Noire) with more varied relief. It consists of a much-dissected Pliocene volcano with residual escarpments (mornes) from which has emerged a newer, flatter Quaternary volcano consisting of basaltic flows of faint relief. The coast is generally low, cut in the basalts, with many sandy beaches related to fringing reefs, especially on the eastern, southeastern, and northern flanks. There are also the remains of old emerged coral reefs, some slightly recalcified at 3 m, other strongly recalcified at 10 m, indicating recent uplift, at least in the southern part of the island.

Rodriguez is also a volcanic island, bordered on the south, west, and north by fringing reefs 3–8 km wide, enclosing a shallow lagoon (less than 2 m deep at low tide).

Among high islands in the Indian Ocean those of the Mahé group in the northern Seychelles are granitic. The most important, Mahé, is 30 km long and 700 m high, with a steep eroded coastline

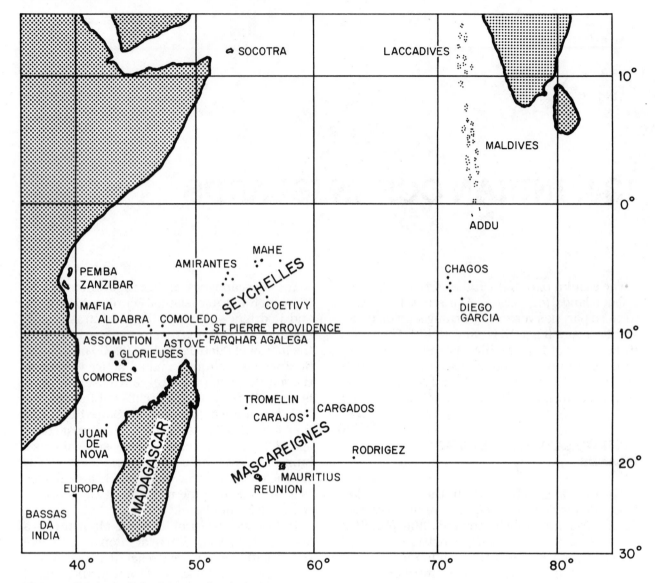

Figure 134-1. Indian Ocean islands location map.

where rocky sectors alternate with small sandy beaches. A fine fringing reef has developed, particularly on the eastern seaboard, exposed to the monsoonal swell.

In the eastern Indian Ocean the Andaman and Nicobar Islands are a chain of high islands, essentially the unsubmerged peaks of a southward continuation of the Arakan Yoma Range in western Burma. Deep valley-mouth inlets, submerged during the Holocene marine transgression, remain unfilled because of meager sediment yields from small river catchments. Steep coasts are typical, cliffed on the more exposed westerly shores, with beaches, spits, and mangrove-fringed bays and inlets on more sheltered sectors. Fring-

ing reefs are extensive. Raised beaches, emerged shore platforms, and uplifted reefs have been noted at various elevations up to 5 m, with evidence of tectonic deformation, while to the east Narcondam (710 m) and Barren Island (353 m) are of volcanic origin.

UPLIFTED CORAL REEF ISLANDS

Christmas Island is a strongly uplifted coral reef, culminating at 350 m, and bordered by high limestone cliffs. The four islands of the Aldabra group in the southern Seychelles are slightly elevated reefs, at Aldabra of Eemian age. At Aldabra

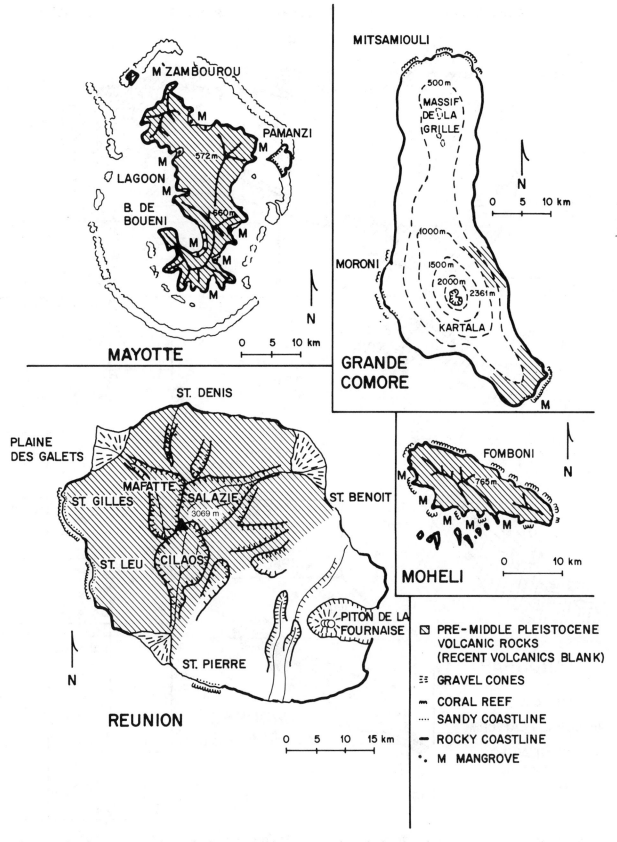

Figure 134-2. Mayotte, Grande Comore, Réunion, and Moheli islands.

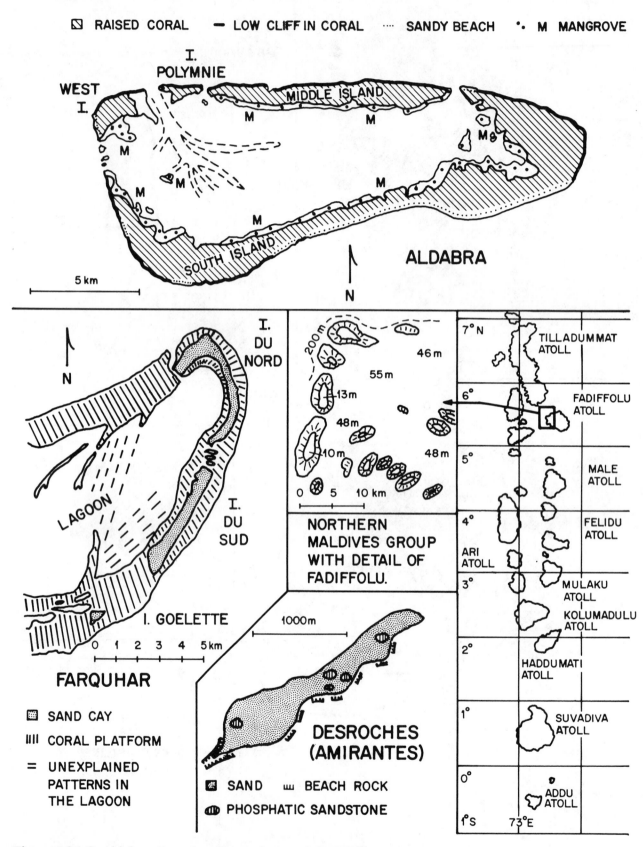

Figure 134-3. Aldabra, Farquhar, Desroches, and the Maldives.

(Fig. 134-3) the Eemian atoll is well preserved, the Holocene marine transgression having merely reoccupied the older lagoon; the surrounding coastline is cliffed in older coral limestone. Cosmoledo is an old raised reef in the form of scarped rocky islets. Astove is a small raised annular reef, and Assumption an old cay-capped platform, uplifted and fringed by rocky cliffs. In the southern Seychelles, Saint-Pierre shows the same morphology, as does the island of Lys (Glorieuses) in the Mozambique Channel. Europa and Bassas da India are here small Eemian atolls, whose shallow lagoons are occupied by mangroves.

LOW SANDY ISLANDS

Holocene deposition of coral sand and gravel on a coralline platform may be sufficient to form an emergent island, which can be colonized by vegetation. The littoral landscape is that of vast beaches, sometimes with storm-placed coral blocks and outcrops of recent beachrock. In the Maldives (Fig. 134-3) and the Laccadives there are hundreds of small islets of this type on faros arranged in chains and atolls of large dimensions. The Amirantes (Seychelles) (Fig. 134-3) are small Holocene sandy islets, as are Providence, the islands forming the atoll crown of Farquhar (Fig. 134-3), Grande Glorieuse (Plate 134-2), and Juan de Nova in the Mozambique Channel, and Cococs in the eastern Indian Ocean. Agalega, Cargados, Carajos, Tromelin, and the low islets of the Chagos Bank are of the same origin, although here some of the lithified sands may be of pre-Holocene origin.

Relevant literature for the interested reader includes the following fine selection: Battistini (1966), Battistini and Cremers (1972), Battistini and Jouannic (1979), Defos du Rau (1959), Guilcher et al. (1955), Lewis (1968), Pichon (1967), Stoddart (1967, 1970), and Stoddart and Yonge (1971).

RENE BATTISTINI

REFERENCES

Battistini, R., 1966, La morphologie de l'île Europa, *Mus. Natl. Histoire Nat. Mém. A* **41:**7–18.

Battistini, R., and G. Cremers, 1972, Geomorphology and vegetation of Iles Glorieuses, *Atoll Research Bull.* **159:**1–10.

Battistini, R., and C. Jouannic, 1979, Recherches sur la géomorphologie de l'atoll Farquhar (Archipel des Seychelles) *Atoll Research Bull.* **230:**1–20.

Defos Du Rau, J., 1959, *Le relief de la Réunion*, Public. Univers, Bordeaux.

Guilcher, A., L. Berthois, Y. Le Calvez, R. Battistini, and A. Crosnier, 1955, *Les récifs coralliens et le lagon de l'île Mayotte (Archipel des Comores, Océan Indien)*, ORSTOM, Paris.

Lewis, M. S., 1968, The morphology of the fringing coral reefs along the east coast of Mahe, Seychelles, *Jour. Geol.* **76:**140–153.

Pichon, M. M., 1967, Caractères généraux des peuplements benthiques des récifs et lagons de l'île Maurice, *ORSTOM série Océanogr.* **5:**31–45.

Stoddart, D. R., 1967, Ecology of Aldabra Atoll, Indian Ocean, *Atoll Research Bull.* **118:**1–141.

Stoddart, D. R., 1970, Coral Islands of the Western Indian Ocean, *Atoll Research Bull.* **136:**1–224.

Stoddart, D. R., and M. Yonge, 1971, Regional Variation in Indian Ocean Coral Reefs, Academic Press, London.

Plate 134-1. The west coast of Grand Comore, north of Moroni. The coast is rocky, with small cliffs in recent basalt lava flows. Fringing coral reefs and sandy beaches are rare (photo by R. Battistini).

Plate 134-2. The south coast of Grande Glorieuse. Example of a Holocene sand cay formed by the crest of a recently formed beach of coralline sand. In the foreground the sand cay rests on coralline limestone rocks, the only indications of an earlier (Eemian) reef. The present reef shows an external slope with spurs and grooves, an outer rampart, and a mainly sandy reef flat (photo by R. Battistini).

135. ANTARCTICA

The Antarctic region comprising the great southern continent, its surrounding cold, ice-strewn ocean, and the islands it contains, is customarily thought of as lying beyond latitude 66° 30′ S, but it can be defined in several other ways. However, it is clear that it covers a vast area and that there are distinct latitudinal variations within the region. These affect such things as the extent and thickness of ice cover on both land and sea, the duration of open water in summer, and the rate and type of rock weathering and erosion, thus Antarctic coastal landforms present a wide array of forms and origins.

There has been little previous study of the formative processes of Antarctic coastal landforms, and work has understandably clustered around the locations of scientific bases in the Antarctic Peninsula and the Ross Sea. There has also been a preoccupation with the relationship between ancient shorelines and the glacial history of the continent.

The Antarctic continent has an area of 13.1 million km² and a coastline of just over 30,000 km. Of this, 44% is ice shelf margin, 38% ice walls, 13% glacier snouts, and only 5% rocky or beach-fringed (Drewry et al. 1982). Figure 135-1 shows the shape of the continent comprising the broadly circular, little indented coastline of East Antarc-

Note: The editors acknowledge advice from Dr. G. de Q.Robin of the Scott Polar Research Institute, Cambridge, England, for references to Robin (1979), Drewry et al. (1982), and the Institute's 1982 outline map of Antarctica. The Australian Division of National Mapping has produced maps at various scales showing parts of the Antarctic coastline, as have other mapping agencies concerned with Antarctica, but geomorphological information on the relatively limited sectors of rocky and beach-fringed coastline is still very sparse.

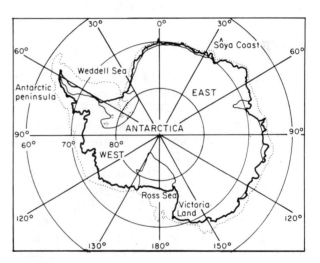

Figure 135-1. Antarctica, showing the coast and the outer edge of the continental shelf.

tica, the two large, ice-shelf-covered indentations of the Weddell Sea and the Ross Sea, and the long projection of the Antarctic Peninsula. Conventionally East Antarctica is divided from West Antarctica along a line joining the southern extremities of the Ross and Weddell seas. East Antarctica occupies three-quarters of the area of the continent and comprises a vast, domed ice sheet rising to an elevation of more than 4,000 m and having only small ice-free areas at the coast, many of which occur along the western Ross Sea where the Victoria Land mountains form the shore. By contrast, the much smaller area of West Antarctica can be thought of as a large archipelago submerged in ice. Much of its ice-free coastal area is also mountainous and occurs in the Antarctic Peninsula. According to Robin (1979) the

Antarctic ice shelves have formed largely by the seaward movement of ice that formed over the land rather than by continued thickening of sea ice bordering the shore.

Because of the past and present extent of ice cover the continental crust is considerably depressed. Most of the coast and much of the continental shelf have been extensively glaciated. Ice-free areas form only 1.5% of the area of the continent. Consequently, the coastline represents the contact between oceanic water and continental ice over very large stretches (Plate 135-1), particularly in East Antarctica. This fact probably accounts in part for the smoothly curved outline of the coast, since it is known from seismic and other survey work that fjords and rocky archipelagoes occur beneath the ice.

CONTINENTAL SHELF

According to Zivago and Evteev (1969) the Antarctic continental shelf has an area of about 4 million km², some 60% (2.4 million km²) of which is ice-free. The shelf has a mean depth of 350 m (almost twice that of other shelves), a mean width of 128 km, and a minimum width of 48 km. Maximum widths occur in the Weddell Sea (611 km) and the Ross Sea (1,127 km).

These characteristics, together with the problems posed by stormy seas, drifting pack-ice, and icebergs, pose important constraints on the presently intensifying search for exploitable Antarctic resources, particularly offshore oil and gas reserves.

ISLANDS OF THE SOUTHERN OCEAN

Antarctica is separated from the other continents by a vast ocean belt having an area of 37.8 million km² and a mean depth of 4,000 m. Dotted through this ocean and lying for the most part nearer the continent are a series of mainly small islands having a total area of about 38,000 km². Though separated by very large distances, these islands present distinctly cliffed coasts with small associated beaches (Fig. 135-2, Plate 135-2). They have many other features in common, since most are of volcanic origin and they rise steeply from deep water to high elevations. Many support icecaps or permanent snow fields, and their precipitous shores are commonly subjected to very heavy surf action together with the erosional effects of ice.

ANTARCTIC BEACHES

Antarctic beaches differ from those of temperate latitudes chiefly in the seasonal effects of ice on land and sea. There is little difference (apart from the relative levels of the land and sea and the extent of ice cover) between today's conditions and those that have obtained throughout the Quaternary (Kirk 1972).

Polar beaches are interesting to the geomorphologist concerned with process studies because they are landforms where, in a sense, conditions at opposite ends of the erosion/sedimentation spectrum are combined. The unselective action of ice in eroding and transporting sediments of a wide variety of sizes and shapes is juxtaposed with the highly selective action of waves and currents. Further, this combination is somewhat unique to very cold climates because the action of the waves is seasonally excluded from beaches by the formation of sea ice. Ice action and wave action follow each other in seasonal rhythm, and permafrost consolidates the resulting deposits.

According to Nichols (1961) the characteristic features of polar beaches are:

1. They rest on ice.
2. They are pitted by melt features.
3. They have ridges and mounds because of ice-push and/or deposition from stranded ice. Ridges formed by ice-push from wind or current-drifted pack ice are commonly associated with beach scars.
4. They have beach ridges that terminate abruptly because ice was present when they were formed.
5. Ice-rafted rock fragments and erratics are found on them.
6. They commonly have poorly rounded pebbles.
7. Frost cracks and mounds, stone circles and polygons, and solifluction deposits are found on them.
8. They are associated with striations formed by grounding sea ice and icebergs.
9. Beaches may have short erosional gaps that were formed by meltwater streams.
10. Beaches are associated with ice-contact features (proglacial deltas, proglacial ramparts, and esker-like features) and glaciomarine deposits.
11. Ventifacts are commonly present.
12. They contain cold-water fossils.
13. They may contain the soft parts of marine organisms.

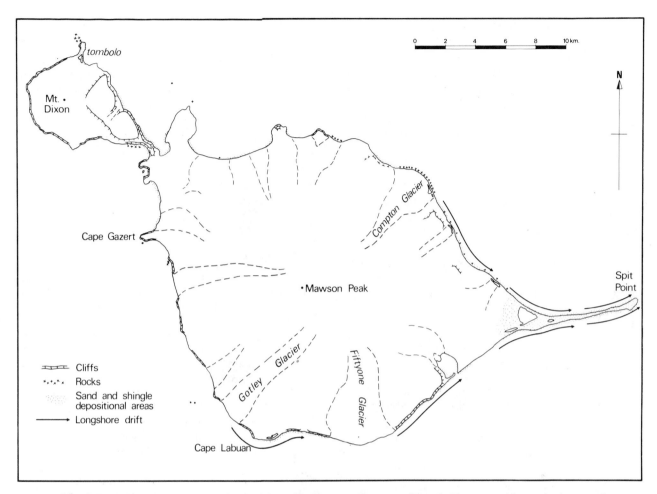

Figure 135-2. Subantarctic Heard Island, 3,700 km southwest of Perth (Western Australia) is a volcanic island on the Kerguelen-Gaussberg Ridge. Mawson Peak is a volcanic cone, and recurrent volcanicity supplies abundant sand and gravel, which is carried down to the coast in glaciers. Very strong westerly winds produce waves that sweep beach material along the northern and southern coastlines to accumulate in a large trailing spit at the eastern end of the island.

Because Antarctic beaches are commonly the nesting sites of large numbers of penguins, ridges are often cemented by appreciable thicknesses of guano, and the swales are devoid of pebbles because they have been gathered for nesting materials.

Extensive beach-ridge complexes occur at several sites around the Ross Sea, in the Antarctic Peninsula, and on several of the offshore islands. Foreland complexes such as that shown in Plate 135-3 have commonly accumulated from longshore drift at sites that lie to leeward of steep, eroding peninsulas or the cliffed coasts of islands.

According to Nichols (1969) raised beaches, wave-cut platforms, sea caves and sea stacks are common on the Antarctic Peninsula and its islands. There ground moraine is thought to be the most important source of beach materials.

In contrast, studies now being conducted in the Ross Sea area by the writer and a co-worker show that talus, eolian action, and the products of cliff abrasion are by far the predominant sources of beach materials, though ground moraine is locally important at higher latitudes.

RAISED BEACHES

By far the greatest attention given to the study of Antarctic coastal landforms has concerned raised beaches and platforms, because of their readily perceived significance in unraveling the

Quaternary glacial history of the continent and its relationship with changing world climates and sea levels. Calkin and Nichols (1972) noted that raised beaches have been found on all sides of the Antarctic continent and that some predate the most recent glacial episode, although most are younger. They commonly occur at elevations of less than 60 m above sea level, though higher areas exist.

Omoto (1977) examined the geomorphic development of the Soya coast in East Antarctica and concluded there has been up to 16 m of emergence over the last 6,000 years. Beaches under 6 m in elevation were thought to be younger than 500 years.

In the western Ross Sea raised beach ridges dating to 5,000 years B.P. occur at elevations up to 20 m above sea level. Nichols (1969) notes that more than 20 well-developed ridges occur up to 34 m above sea level at Marguerite Bay on the southwest coast of the Antarctic Peninsula and concludes that the oldest known raised ridges in Antarctica are probably of Late Pliocene Age, whereas the youngest are Late Holocene.

Little is known of the spatial patterns of ridge heights even in the McMurdo Sound region of the Ross Sea, where the glacial history of the later Quaternary is now well known. Raised beaches therefore present interesting problems concerning glacio-isostacy and glacio-eustacy and their existence in large numbers at appreciable altitudes on most sectors of the Antarctic coast argues that in the recent past the rate of isostatic uplift has exceeded the rate of sea-level rise that resulted from retreat of the ice sheets.

CONCLUSION

Much of the long Antarctic coastline is submerged in ice, but the limited stretches of ice-free shore present a great variety of landforms. Little is known about the characteristic processes that create and modify these forms, though their typical morphologies and sediments have been documented. Numerous sites present a record of past events in the form of raised beaches and rocky platforms. Regional studies of both processes and Quaternary histories are hampered by remoteness and the difficult logistic and working conditions of the Antarctic. However, these studies are proceeding, particularly along the western shores of the Ross Sea.

R. M. KIRK

REFERENCES

Calkin, P. E., and R. L. Nichols, 1972, Quaternary studies in Antarctica, *Antarctic Geology and Geophysics. Symposium on Antarctic and Solid Earth Physics,* R. J. Adie, ed., *Oslo,* Universitetsforlaget.

Drewry, D. J., S. R. Jordan, and E. Jankowski, 1982, Measured properties of the Antarctic ice sheet, *Annals Glaciology* **3:**15–26.

Kirk, R. M., 1972, Antarctic beaches as natural hydraulic models, *7th Geography Conf. Proc.* New Zealand Geographical Society, pp. 227–234.

Nichols, R. L., 1961, Characteristics of beaches formed in polar climates, *Am. Jour. Sci.* **259:**694–708.

Nichols, R. L., 1969, Geomorphic features of Antarctica, in *Antarctic Map Folio Series. Folio 12 Geologic Map of Antarctica,* V. C. Bushnell, ed., American Geographical Society, New York.

Omoto, K., 1977, Geomorphic development of the Soya Coast, East Antarctica—chronological interpretation of raised beaches based on levellings and radiocarbon datings, *Sci. Repts. Tohoku Univ., 7th Ser. (Geography)* **27**(2):95–148.

Robin, G. de Q., 1979, Formation, flow and disintegration of ice shelves, *Jour. Glaciology* **24:**259–271.

Zivago, A. V., and S. A. Evteev, 1969, Shelf and marine terraces of Antarctica, in *Symposium on the Evolution of Shorelines and Continental Shelves,* INQUA/UNESCO, Paris.

Plate 135-1. Ice margin and rocky shore at Ivanoff Head, Vincennes Bay, Wilkes Land, Antarctica (Australian Antarctic Division photograph by P. G. Law).

Plate 135-2. The steep periglaciated coastline of Macquarie Island, looking south from Rockhopper Point to South West Point (Australian Antarctic Division photograph by S. Brown).

Plate 135-3. A large depositional foreland and beach-ridge complex at Cape Adare, North Victoria Land. The ridges are colonized by Adelie penguins and separated by melt pools. The complex extends for 2 km left to right and has accumulated from longshore-drifted abrasion products in the lee of the peninsula behind (photo by R. M. Kirk).

AUTHOR CITATION INDEX

SUBJECT INDEX

50, 57, 129, 163, 203, 207,
236, 278, 296, 321, 335, 374,
411, 444, 462, 481, 501, 519,
523, 532, 551, 622, 625, 645,
672, 706, 723, 824, 846, 857,
889, 957, 969
Weathering, 57, 62, 106, 879,
881, 887, 900, 901, 913, 915,
916, 950, 959, 975, 977, 978,
997, 998, 1047
Weir Gate, 339
Wind tidal flats, 132, 136, 137,
142

Xylocarpus moluccensis, 774
Xylocarpus obovatus, 774

Zeta-bay, 507, 751, 792, 929, 932,
936, 938, 969, 978
Zifzif, 508
Zygophyllum simplex, 708

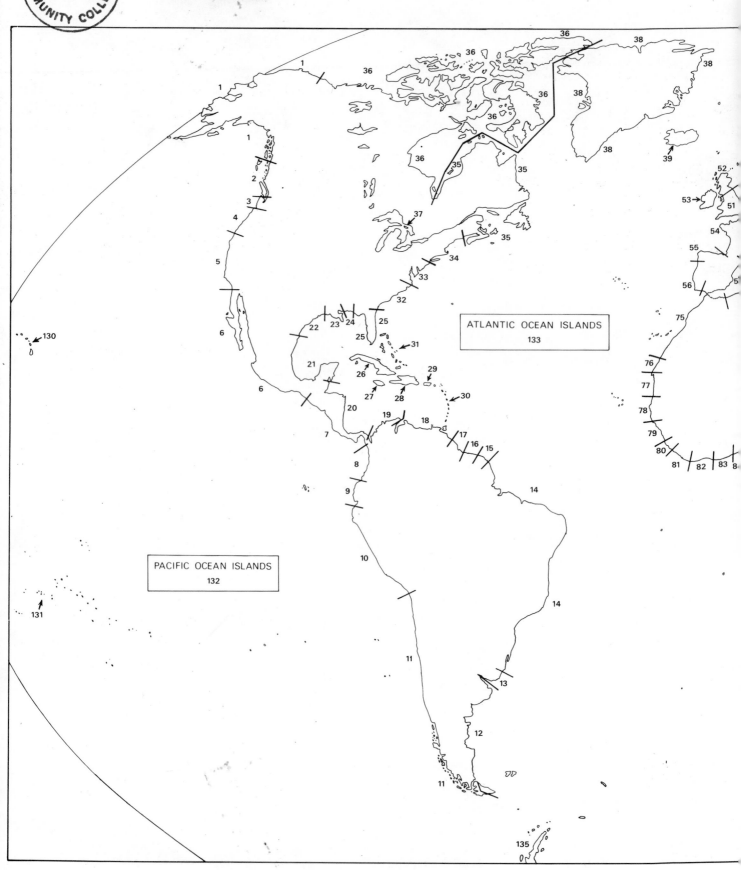

ATLANTIC OCEAN ISLANDS
133

PACIFIC OCEAN ISLANDS
132